Property

of

CHARLES B. HOEVEN
Alton, Iowa

PUBLIC PAPERS OF THE PRESIDENTS

OF THE UNITED STATES

PUBLIC PAPERS OF THE PRESIDENTS

OF THE UNITED STATES

Lyndon B. Johnson

*Containing the Public Messages, Speeches, and
Statements of the President*

1966

(IN TWO BOOKS)

BOOK I—JANUARY 1 TO JUNE 30, 1966

UNITED STATES GOVERNMENT PRINTING OFFICE

WASHINGTON : 1967

PUBLISHED BY THE
OFFICE OF THE FEDERAL REGISTER
NATIONAL ARCHIVES AND RECORDS SERVICE
GENERAL SERVICES ADMINISTRATION

For sale by the Superintendent of Documents, U.S. Government Printing Office
Washington, D.C. 20402 - Price $6.50

FOREWORD

THESE PAPERS, addressed to the major issues that confront our people, record the progress of a nation meeting its responsibilities at home and abroad.

1966 was the sixth year of unbroken prosperity in the Nation. That is a proud fact for any volume to document.

But these pages speak also of an urgent, continuing effort on behalf of those who do not share in our abundance—the poor and the disadvantaged. In education, in health, in programs designed to rebuild America's cities and train her people for tomorrow's tasks, 1966 was a year of promise and achievement. Helped by a progressive Congress, we strengthened the Government's capacity to meet the complex challenges of urban life.

A new Department of Transportation was established. The Department of Housing and Urban Development experienced its first full year's operation. Through these new agencies, programs to rebuild America's cities and strengthen her transportation system began to move from blueprint to action.

The beginning of Medicare realized a dream of decades. The burden of medical costs began to be lifted from the backs of elderly Americans and their families.

The citizen as a consumer gained greater protection in the market place.

A study of the causes and correction of crime—by the President's Commission on Law Enforcement and Administration of Justice—continued throughout the year. It would lead to the submission of the most comprehensive Federal program ever devised to help local authorities improve their law enforcement systems—and make American streets safe for law-abiding citizens.

In space, we moved closer to the day when man will land on the moon.

The shadow of Vietnam falls across this volume, as it extended over the consciousness of the Nation itself. These pages tell of our constant search for an honorable settlement to that conflict. Twice during the year I traveled beyond the shores of this continent to talk with the leaders of Asia, and with those who conduct America's military and diplomatic efforts in Vietnam.

During one of those visits I traveled to Vietnam itself, and met first-hand the courageous men who carry the fight for us there. Those men—the best trained and equipped soldiers who have ever gone into battle under American colors—are bringing the day closer when Vietnam will be at peace, able to repair the destruction of a long and savage war.

I believe those who read these pages in the years to come will conclude that in 1966 the United States served the cause of peace in the world—and of social justice here at home. That was, and is, our mission and purpose.

Lyndon B. Johnson

PREFACE

IN THIS VOLUME are gathered most of the public messages and statements of the 36th President of the United States that were released by the White House in 1966. Similar volumes are available covering the period November 22, 1963–December 31, 1965, and the administrations of Presidents Truman, Eisenhower, and Kennedy. A volume covering the year 1967 is under preparation.

The series was begun in 1957 in response to a recommendation of the National Historical Publications Commission. An extensive compilation of the messages and papers of the Presidents, covering the period 1789 to 1897, was assembled by James D. Richardson and published under congressional authority between 1896 and 1899. Since that time various private compilations were issued, but there was no uniform, systematic publication comparable to the *Congressional Record* or the *United States Supreme Court Reports*. Many Presidential papers could be found only in mimeographed White House releases or as reported in the press. The National Historical Publications Commission therefore recommended the establishment of an official series in which Presidential writings and utterances of a public nature could be made promptly available.

The Commission's recommendation was incorporated in regulations of the Administrative Committee of the Federal Register issued under section 6 of the Federal Register Act (44 U.S.C. 306). The Committee's regulations, establishing the series and providing for the coverage of prior years, are reprinted at page 1496 as "Appendix D."

Preface

The text of this book is based on Presidential materials issued during the period as White House releases and on transcripts of news conferences. Original source materials, where available, have been used to protect against errors in transcription. A list of White House releases from which final selections were made is published at page 1467 as "Appendix A."

Proclamations, Executive orders, and similar documents required by law to be published in the *Federal Register* and *Code of Federal Regulations* are not repeated. Instead, they are listed by number and subject under the heading "Appendix B" at page 1489.

The President is required by statute to transmit numerous reports to Congress. Those transmitted during the period covered by this volume are listed at page 1494 as "Appendix C."

The items published in this volume are presented in chronological order, rather than being grouped in classes. Most needs for a classified arrangement are met by the subject index. For example, a reader interested in veto messages sent to Congress during 1966 will find them listed in the index under the heading "veto messages."

The dates shown at the end of item headings are White House release dates. In instances where the date of the document differs from the release date that fact is shown in brackets immediately following the heading. Other editorial devices, such as text notes, footnotes, and cross references, have been supplied where needed for purposes of clarity.

Remarks or addresses were delivered in Washington, D.C., unless otherwise indicated. Similarly, statements, messages, and letters were issued from the White House in Washington unless otherwise indicated.

The planning and publication of this series is under the direction of David C. Eberhart of the Office of the Federal Register. The editor of the present volume was Warren R. Reid, assisted by Mildred B. Berry.

Preface

Dorothy P. Territo, Staff Assistant to the President, and William J. Hopkins, Executive Assistant to the President, provided aid and counsel in the selection and annotation of the materials. Frank H. Mortimer of the Government Printing Office developed the typography and design.

ROBERT H. BAHMER
Archivist of the United States

LAWSON B. KNOTT, Jr.
Administrator of General Services
November 1967

CONTENTS

Book I

Book II

LIST OF ITEMS, Book I

Page

List of Items, Book I

List of Items, Book I

Page

LIST OF ITEMS, Book II

List of Items, Book II

List of Items, Book II

Lyndon B. Johnson

January 1–June 30, 1966

1 The President's Telegram to Admiral Nimitz on Hearing of His Illness. *January 6, 1966*

LADY BIRD and I were greatly saddened to hear of your illness. We pray for the full recovery of a great American and an old neighbor. The indomitable spirit that gave us hope twenty years ago will surely overcome again.

LYNDON B. JOHNSON

[Admiral Chester Nimitz, Oakland Naval Hospital, Oakland, Calif.]

NOTE: The text of the telegram was posted on the bulletin board in the Press Room at the White House. It was not made public in the form of a White House press release.

See also Item 80.

2 The President's Telegram Greeting Carl Sandburg on His 88th Birthday. *January 6, 1966*

[Released January 6, 1966. Dated January 5, 1966]

YOU ONCE WROTE that, "The people will live on." Thanks to you, the people live on with a deeper insight into their nation, their fellow citizens, and their own inherent dignity. You spoke to them in verse. You sang to them of their traditions. You wrote to them of Lincoln's greatness and of the greatness of the land that produced him.

And now, in return, we say "Happy 88th Birthday" to you. It does not ring with poetry, but it comes from deep within a nation's heart.

LYNDON B. JOHNSON

[Carl Sandburg, Flat Rock, N.C.]

NOTE: The text of the telegram was posted on the bulletin board in the Press Room at the White House. It was not made public in the form of a White House press release.

3 Statement by the President Upon Announcing the Appointment of Members of the Advisory Council on Insured Loans to Students. *January 7, 1966*

IN EVERY community and on every level of American life, we seek a better education for our citizens. We want that education to fit the needs and meet the challenges of the 20th century. And we are coming closer to that goal. The program of insured loans to students now makes it possible for the middle-income family to spread the heavy costs of a college education over a longer, less burdensome period of time. It thus lends new strength to our national commitment of offering every child the fullest educational opportunity.

NOTE: The President's statement was made public as part of a White House release announcing the appointment of the Council, created by the Higher Education Act of 1965 (Public Law 89–329, 79 Stat. 1219), to advise the Commissioner of Education on all matters pertaining to the administration of Federal, State, and private programs of low-interest insured loans to students.

The release noted that the President had cited the following as evidence of the importance of the Council's task:

1. Existing loan programs were under strong and

growing pressures. More than 600,000 students had already borrowed some $453 million from National Defense Student Loan funds.

2. The costs of higher education were mounting. To cover average annual expenses for college students, middle-income families must spend about $10,000 during a 4-year period.

3. A relatively small Federal investment now would make a very large amount of credit available to such families. Fourteen million dollars, for example, would pay the interest at 2 percent on a principal of $700 million. Such a sum could provide an average loan of $700 to a million students.

The release included a list of members of the Council, appointed by the Secretary of Health, Education, and Welfare with the approval of the President (2 Weekly Comp. Pres. Docs., p. 11).

4 Statement by the President Upon Announcing the Appointment of Dr. James L. Goddard as Commissioner of Food and Drugs. *January* 10, 1966

THE CONGRESS has significantly enlarged both the authority and the responsibility of the Food and Drug Administration in recent years. The magnitude and the complexity of its responsibilities are of concern to every American.

Shortly after taking office last fall, Secretary Gardner initiated a thorough reappraisal of the Food and Drug Administration's organizational problems and a far-reaching search for a new Commissioner. Dr. Goddard has earned wide recognition for his administrative skill and his scientific competence. I share Secretary Gardner's confidence that Dr. Goddard will bring to his new assignment the quality of leadership that will enable the Food and Drug Administration to fully meet its vast and varied responsibilities for consumer protection.

NOTE: The President's statement was made public as part of a White House release announcing the appointment of Dr. James L. Goddard to succeed George P. Larrick as Commissioner of the Food and Drug Administration, Department of Health, Education, and Welfare. The release stated that Dr. Goddard, a graduate of the George Washington School of Medicine, had spent 14 years in clinical, research, and administrative assignments in the field of public health, and was then serving as Assistant Surgeon General of the U.S. Public Health Service and Chief of the Communicable Disease Center in Atlanta, Ga. (2 Weekly Comp. Pres. Docs., p. 26).

5 Statement by the President on the Death of Prime Minister Shastri of India. *January* 10, 1966

OUR NATION mourns the death of Prime Minister Lal Bahadur Shastri of India. As the leader of the world's largest democracy, he had already gained a special place in American hearts. His tragic loss, after fruitful discussions at Tashkent, is a grievous blow to the hopes of mankind for peace and progress.

Lal Bahadur Shastri, in only 19 months in office, proved a fitting successor to Pandit Nehru by holding aloft the highest ideals of Indian democracy. His modesty in high office did not conceal his strength and wisdom as the recognized leader of his people. The world is a smaller place without him, and our hearts go out to his family and to the people of India.

NOTE: The statement was read to members of the press by Bill D. Moyers, Special Assistant to the President, in his office at the White House at 5:45 p.m., on Monday, January 10, 1966. It was not made public in the form of a White House press release.

6 Annual Message to the Congress on the State of the Union. *January* 12, 1966

[Delivered in person before a joint session at 9:04 p.m.]

Mr. Speaker, Mr. President, Members of the House and the Senate, my fellow Americans:

I come before you tonight to report on the State of the Union for the third time.

I come here to thank you and to add my tribute, once more, to the Nation's gratitude for this, the 89th Congress. This Congress has already reserved for itself an honored chapter in the history of America.

Our Nation tonight is engaged in a brutal and bitter conflict in Vietnam. Later on I want to discuss that struggle in some detail with you. It just must be the center of our concerns.

But we will not permit those who fire upon us in Vietnam to win a victory over the desires and the intentions of all the American people. This Nation is mighty enough, its society is healthy enough, its people are strong enough, to pursue our goals in the rest of the world while still building a Great Society here at home.

And that is what I have come here to ask of you tonight.

I recommend that you provide the resources to carry forward, with full vigor, the great health and education programs that you enacted into law last year.

I recommend that we prosecute with vigor and determination our war on poverty.

I recommend that you give a new and daring direction to our foreign aid program, designed to make a maximum attack on hunger and disease and ignorance in those countries that are determined to help themselves, and to help those nations that are trying to control population growth.

I recommend that you make it possible to expand trade between the United States and Eastern Europe and the Soviet Union.

I recommend to you a program to rebuild completely, on a scale never before attempted, entire central and slum areas of several of our cities in America.

I recommend that you attack the wasteful and degrading poisoning of our rivers, and, as the cornerstone of this effort, clean completely entire large river basins.

I recommend that you meet the growing menace of crime in the streets by building up law enforcement and by revitalizing the entire Federal system from prevention to probation.

I recommend that you take additional steps to insure equal justice to all of our people by effectively enforcing nondiscrimination in Federal and State jury selection, by making it a serious Federal crime to obstruct public and private efforts to secure civil rights, and by outlawing discrimination in the sale and rental of housing.

I recommend that you help me modernize and streamline the Federal Government by creating a new Cabinet level Department of Transportation and reorganizing several existing agencies. In turn, I will restructure our civil service in the top grades so that men and women can easily be assigned to jobs where they are most needed, and ability will be both required as well as rewarded.

I will ask you to make it possible for Members of the House of Representatives to work more effectively in the service of the

Nation through a constitutional amendment extending the term of a Congressman to 4 years, concurrent with that of the President.

II.

Because of Vietnam we cannot do all that we should, or all that we would like to do.

We will ruthlessly attack waste and inefficiency. We will make sure that every dollar is spent with the thrift and with the commonsense which recognizes how hard the taxpayer worked in order to earn it.

We will continue to meet the needs of our people by continuing to develop the Great Society.

Last year alone the wealth that we produced increased $47 billion, and it will soar again this year to a total over $720 billion.

Because our economic policies have produced rising revenues, if you approve every program that I recommend tonight, our total budget deficit will be one of the lowest in many years. It will be only $1.8 billion next year. Total spending in the administrative budget will be $112.8 billion. Revenues next year will be $111 billion.

On a cash basis—which is the way that you and I keep our family budget—the Federal budget next year will actually show a surplus. That is to say, if we include all the money that your Government will take in and all the money that your Government will spend, your Government next year will collect one-half billion dollars more than it will spend in the year 1967.

I have not come here tonight to ask for pleasant luxuries or for idle pleasures. I have come here to recommend that you, the representatives of the richest Nation on earth, you, the elected servants of a people who live in abundance unmatched on this globe, you bring the most urgent decencies of life to all of your fellow Americans.

There are men who cry out: We must sacrifice. Well, let us rather ask them: Who will they sacrifice? Are they going to sacrifice the children who seek the learning, or the sick who need medical care, or the families who dwell in squalor now brightened by the hope of home? Will they sacrifice opportunity for the distressed, the beauty of our land, the hope of our poor?

Time may require further sacrifices. And if it does, then we will make them.

But we will not heed those who wring it from the hopes of the unfortunate here in a land of plenty.

I believe that we can continue the Great Society while we fight in Vietnam. But if there are some who do not believe this, then, in the name of justice, let them call for the contribution of those who live in the fullness of our blessing, rather than try to strip it from the hands of those that are most in need.

And let no one think that the unfortunate and the oppressed of this land sit stifled and alone in their hope tonight. Hundreds of their servants and their protectors sit before me tonight here in this great Chamber.

III.

The Great Society leads us along three roads—growth and justice and liberation.

[1.] First is growth—the national prosperity which supports the well-being of our people and which provides the tools of our progress.

I can report to you tonight what you have seen for yourselves already—in every city and countryside. This Nation is flourishing.

Workers are making more money than ever—with after-tax income in the past 5 years up 33 percent; in the last year alone, up 8 percent.

More people are working than ever before

in our history—an increase last year of 2½ million jobs.

Corporations have greater after-tax earnings than ever in history. For the past 5 years those earnings have been up over 65 percent, and last year alone they had a rise of 20 percent.

Average farm income is higher than ever. Over the past 5 years it is up 40 percent, and over the past year it is up 22 percent alone.

I was informed this afternoon by the distinguished Secretary of the Treasury that his preliminary estimates indicate that our balance of payments deficit has been reduced from $2.8 billion in 1964 to $1.3 billion, or less, in 1965. This achievement has been made possible by the patriotic voluntary cooperation of businessmen and bankers working with your Government.

We must now work together with increased urgency to wipe out this balance of payments deficit altogether in the next year.

And as our economy surges toward new heights we must increase our vigilance against the inflation which raises the cost of living and which lowers the savings of every family in this land. It is essential, to prevent inflation, that we ask both labor and business to exercise price and wage restraint, and I do so again tonight.

I believe it desirable, because of increased military expenditures, that you temporarily restore the automobile and certain telephone excise tax reductions made effective only 12 days ago. Without raising taxes—or even increasing the total tax bill paid—we should move to improve our withholding system so that Americans can more realistically pay as they go, speed up the collection of corporate taxes, and make other necessary simplifications of the tax structure at an early date.

I hope these measures will be adequate. But if the necessities of Vietnam require it, I will not hesitate to return to the Congress for additional appropriations, or additional revenues if they are needed.

[2.] The second road is justice. Justice means a man's hope should not be limited by the color of his skin.

I propose legislation to establish unavoidable requirements for nondiscriminatory jury selection in Federal and State courts—and to give the Attorney General the power necessary to enforce those requirements.

I propose legislation to strengthen authority of Federal courts to try those who murder, attack, or intimidate either civil rights workers or others exercising their constitutional rights—and to increase penalties to a level equal to the nature of the crime.

Legislation, resting on the fullest constitutional authority of the Federal Government, to prohibit racial discrimination in the sale or rental of housing.

For that other nation within a Nation—the poor—whose distress has now captured the conscience of America, I will ask the Congress not only to continue, but to speed up the war on poverty. And in so doing, we will provide the added energy of achievement with the increased efficiency of experience.

To improve the life of our rural Americans and our farm population, we will plan for the future through the establishment of several new Community Development Districts, improved education through the use of Teacher Corps teams, better health measures, physical examinations, and adequate and available medical resources.

For those who labor, I propose to improve unemployment insurance, to expand minimum wage benefits, and by the repeal of section 14(b) of the Taft-Hartley Act to make the labor laws in all our States equal to the laws of the 31 States which do not have tonight right-to-work measures.

And I also intend to ask the Congress to consider measures which, without improperly invading State and local authority, will enable us effectively to deal with strikes which threaten irreparable damage to the national interest.

[3.] The third path is the path of liberation. It is to use our success for the fulfillment of our lives. A great nation is one which breeds a great people. A great people flower not from wealth and power, but from a society which spurs them to the fullness of their genius. That alone is a Great Society.

Yet, slowly, painfully, on the edge of victory, has come the knowledge that shared prosperity is not enough. In the midst of abundance modern man walks oppressed by forces which menace and confine the quality of his life, and which individual abundance alone will not overcome.

We can subdue and we can master these forces—bring increased meaning to our lives—if all of us, Government and citizens, are bold enough to change old ways, daring enough to assault new dangers, and if the dream is dear enough to call forth the limitless capacities of this great people.

This year we must continue to improve the quality of American life.

Let us fulfill and improve the great health and education programs of last year, extending special opportunities to those who risk their lives in our Armed Forces.

I urge the House of Representatives to complete action on three programs already passed by the Senate—the Teacher Corps, rent assistance, and home rule for the District of Columbia.

In some of our urban areas we must help rebuild entire sections and neighborhoods containing, in some cases, as many as 100,000 people. Working together, private enterprise and government must press forward with the task of providing homes and shops, parks and hospitals, and all the other necessary parts of a flourishing community where our people can come to live the good life.

I will offer other proposals to stimulate and to reward planning for the growth of entire metropolitan areas.

Of all the reckless devastations of our national heritage, none is really more shameful than the continued poisoning of our rivers and our air.

We must undertake a cooperative effort to end pollution in several river basins, making additional funds available to help draw the plans and construct the plants that are necessary to make the waters of our entire river systems clean, and make them a source of pleasure and beauty for all of our people.

To attack and to overcome growing crime and lawlessness, I think we must have a stepped-up program to help modernize and strengthen our local police forces.

Our people have a right to feel secure in their homes and on their streets—and that right just must be secured.

Nor can we fail to arrest the destruction of life and property on our highways.

I will propose a Highway Safety Act of 1966 to seek an end to this mounting tragedy.

We must also act to prevent the deception of the American consumer—requiring all packages to state clearly and truthfully their contents—all interest and credit charges to be fully revealed—and keeping harmful drugs and cosmetics away from our stores.

It is the genius of our Constitution that under its shelter of enduring institutions and rooted principles there is ample room for the rich fertility of American political invention.

We must change to master change.

I propose to take steps to modernize and streamline the executive branch, to modernize the relations between city and State and Nation.

A new Department of Transportation is needed to bring together our transportation activities. The present structure—35 Government agencies, spending $5 billion yearly—makes it almost impossible to serve either the growing demands of this great Nation or the needs of the industry, or the right of the taxpayer to full efficiency and real frugality.

I will propose in addition a program to construct and to flight-test a new supersonic transport airplane that will fly three times the speed of sound—in excess of 2,000 miles per hour.

I propose to examine our Federal system—the relation between city, State, Nation, and the citizens themselves. We need a commission of the most distinguished scholars and men of public affairs to do this job. I will ask them to move on to develop a creative federalism to best use the wonderful diversity of our institutions and our people to solve the problems and to fulfill the dreams of the American people.

As the process of election becomes more complex and more costly, we must make it possible for those without personal wealth to enter public life without being obligated to a few large contributors.

Therefore, I will submit legislation to revise the present unrealistic restriction on contributions—to prohibit the endless proliferation of committees, bringing local and State committees under the act—to attach strong teeth and severe penalties to the requirement of full disclosure of contributions—and to broaden the participation of the people, through added tax incentives, to stimulate small contributions to the party and to the candidate of their choice.

To strengthen the work of Congress I strongly urge an amendment to provide a 4-year term for Members of the House of Representatives—which should not begin before 1972.

The present 2-year term requires most Members of Congress to divert enormous energies to an almost constant process of campaigning—depriving this Nation of the fullest measure of both their skill and their wisdom. Today, too, the work of government is far more complex than in our early years, requiring more time to learn and more time to master the technical tasks of legislating. And a longer term will serve to attract more men of the highest quality to political life. The Nation, the principle of democracy, and, I think, each congressional district, will all be better served by a 4-year term for Members of the House. And I urge your swift action.

IV.

Tonight the cup of peril is full in Vietnam.

That conflict is not an isolated episode, but another great event in the policy that we have followed with strong consistency since World War II.

The touchstone of that policy is the interest of the United States—the welfare and the freedom of the people of the United States. But nations sink when they see that interest only through a narrow glass.

In a world that has grown small and dangerous, pursuit of narrow aims could bring decay and even disaster.

An America that is mighty beyond description—yet living in a hostile or despairing world—would be neither safe nor free to build a civilization to liberate the spirit of man.

In this pursuit we helped rebuild Western Europe. We gave our aid to Greece and Turkey, and we defended the freedom of Berlin.

In this pursuit we have helped new nations toward independence. We have extended the helping hand of the Peace Corps and carried forward the largest program of economic assistance in the world.

And in this pursuit we work to build a hemisphere of democracy and of social justice.

In this pursuit we have defended against Communist aggression—in Korea under President Truman—in the Formosa Straits under President Eisenhower—in Cuba under President Kennedy—and again in Vietnam.

Tonight Vietnam must hold the center of our attention, but across the world problems and opportunities crowd in on the American Nation. I will discuss them fully in the months to come, and I will follow the five continuing lines of policy that America has followed under its last four Presidents.

[1.] The first principle is strength.

Tonight I can tell you that we are strong enough to keep all of our commitments. We will need expenditures of $58.3 billion for the next fiscal year to maintain this necessary defense might.

While special Vietnam expenditures for the next fiscal year are estimated to increase by $5.8 billion, I can tell you that all the other expenditures put together in the entire Federal budget will rise this coming year by only $.6 billion. This is true because of the stringent cost-conscious economy program inaugurated in the Defense Department, and followed by the other departments of Government.

[2.] A second principle of policy is the effort to control, and to reduce, and to ultimately eliminate the modern engines of destruction.

We will vigorously pursue existing proposals—and seek new ones—to control arms and to stop the spread of nuclear weapons.

[3.] A third major principle of our foreign policy is to help build those associations of nations which reflect the opportunities and the necessities of the modern world.

By strengthening the common defense, by stimulating world commerce, by meeting new hopes, these associations serve the cause of a flourishing world.

We will take new steps this year to help strengthen the Alliance for Progress, the unity of Europe, the community of the Atlantic, the regional organizations of developing continents, and that supreme association—the United Nations.

We will work to strengthen economic cooperation, to reduce barriers to trade, and to improve international finance.

[4.] A fourth enduring strand of policy has been to help improve the life of man.

From the Marshall plan to this very moment tonight, that policy has rested on the claims of compassion, and the certain knowledge that only a people advancing in expectation will build secure and peaceful lands.

This year I propose major new directions in our program of foreign assistance to help those countries who will help themselves.

We will conduct a worldwide attack on the problems of hunger and disease and ignorance.

We will place the matchless skill and the resources of our own great America, in farming and in fertilizers, at the service of those countries committed to develop a modern agriculture.

We will aid those who educate the young in other lands, and we will give children in other continents the same head start that we are trying to give our own children. To advance these ends I will propose the International Education Act of 1966.

I will also propose the International Health Act of 1966 to strike at disease by a new effort to bring modern skills and knowledge to the uncared-for, those suffering in the world, and by trying to wipe out smallpox and malaria and control yellow fever over most of the world during this next decade; to help countries trying to control population growth, by increasing our research—and we will earmark funds to help their efforts.

In the next year, from our foreign aid sources, we propose to dedicate $1 billion to these efforts, and we call on all who have the means to join us in this work in the world.

[5.] The fifth and most important principle of our foreign policy is support of national independence—the right of each people to govern themselves—and to shape their own institutions.

For a peaceful world order will be possible only when each country walks the way that it has chosen to walk for itself.

We follow this principle by encouraging the end of colonial rule.

We follow this principle, abroad as well as at home, by continued hostility to the rule of the many by the few—or the oppression of one race by another.

We follow this principle by building bridges to Eastern Europe. And I will ask the Congress for authority to remove the special tariff restrictions which are a barrier to increasing trade between the East and the West.

The insistent urge toward national independence is the strongest force of today's world in which we live.

In Africa and Asia and Latin America it is shattering the designs of those who would subdue others to their ideas or their will.

It is eroding the unity of what was once a Stalinist empire.

In recent months a number of nations have cast out those who would subject them to the ambitions of mainland China.

History is on the side of freedom and is on the side of societies shaped from the genius of each people. History does not favor a single system or belief—unless force is used to make it so.

That is why it has been necessary for us to defend this basic principle of our policy, to defend it in Berlin, in Korea, in Cuba— and tonight in Vietnam.

For tonight, as so many nights before, young Americans struggle and young Americans die in a distant land.

Tonight, as so many nights before, the American Nation is asked to sacrifice the blood of its children and the fruits of its labor for the love of its freedom.

How many times—in my lifetime and in yours—have the American people gathered, as they do now, to hear their President tell them of conflict and tell them of danger?

Each time they have answered. They have answered with all the effort that the security and the freedom of this Nation required.

And they do again tonight in Vietnam.

Not too many years ago Vietnam was a peaceful, if troubled, land. In the North was an independent Communist government. In the South a people struggled to build a nation, with the friendly help of the United States.

There were some in South Vietnam who wished to force Communist rule on their own people. But their progress was slight. Their hope of success was dim. Then, little more than 6 years ago, North Vietnam decided on conquest. And from that day to this, soldiers and supplies have moved from North to South in a swelling stream that is swallowing the remnants of revolution in aggression.

As the assault mounted, our choice gradually became clear. We could leave, abandoning South Vietnam to its attackers and to certain conquest, or we could stay and fight beside the people of South Vietnam.

We stayed.

And we will stay until aggression has stopped.

We will stay because a just nation cannot

9

leave to the cruelties of its enemies a people who have staked their lives and independence on America's solemn pledge—a pledge which has grown through the commitments of three American Presidents.

We will stay because in Asia and around the world are countries whose independence rests, in large measure, on confidence in America's word and in America's protection. To yield to force in Vietnam would weaken that confidence, would undermine the independence of many lands, and would whet the appetite of aggression. We would have to fight in one land, and then we would have to fight in another—or abandon much of Asia to the domination of Communists.

And we do not intend to abandon Asia to conquest.

Last year the nature of the war in Vietnam changed again. Swiftly increasing numbers of armed men from the North crossed the borders to join forces that were already in the South. Attack and terror increased, spurred and encouraged by the belief that the United States lacked the will to continue and that their victory was near.

Despite our desire to limit conflict, it was necessary to act: to hold back the mounting aggression, to give courage to the people of the South, and to make our firmness clear to the North. Thus we began limited air action against military targets in North Vietnam. We increased our fighting force to its present strength tonight of 190,000 men.

These moves have not ended the aggression but they have prevented its success. The aims of the enemy have been put out of reach by the skill and the bravery of Americans and their allies—and by the enduring courage of the South Vietnamese who, I can tell you, have lost eight men last year for every one of ours.

The enemy is no longer close to victory. Time is no longer on his side. There is no

cause to doubt the American commitment.

Our decision to stand firm has been matched by our desire for peace.

In 1965 alone we had 300 private talks for peace in Vietnam, with friends and adversaries throughout the world.

Since Christmas your Government has labored again, with imagination and endurance, to remove any barrier to peaceful settlement. For 20 days now we and our Vietnamese allies have dropped no bombs in North Vietnam.

Able and experienced spokesmen have visited, in behalf of America, more than 40 countries. We have talked to more than a hundred governments, all 113 that we have relations with, and some that we don't. We have talked to the United Nations and we have called upon all of its members to make any contribution that they can toward helping obtain peace.

In public statements and in private communications, to adversaries and to friends, in Rome and Warsaw, in Paris and Tokyo, in Africa and throughout this hemisphere, America has made her position abundantly clear.

We seek neither territory nor bases, economic domination or military alliance in Vietnam. We fight for the principle of self-determination—that the people of South Vietnam should be able to choose their own course, choose it in free elections without violence, without terror, and without fear.

The people of all Vietnam should make a free decision on the great question of reunification.

This is all we want for South Vietnam. It is all the people of South Vietnam want. And if there is a single nation on this earth that desires less than this for its own people, then let its voice be heard.

We have also made it clear—from Hanoi to New York—that there are no arbitrary limits to our search for peace. We stand by the Geneva Agreements of 1954 and 1962. We will meet at any conference table, we will discuss any proposals—four points or fourteen or forty—and we will consider the views of any group. We will work for a cease-fire now or once discussions have begun. We will respond if others reduce their use of force, and we will withdraw our soldiers once South Vietnam is securely guaranteed the right to shape its own future.

We have said all this, and we have asked—and hoped—and we have waited for a response.

So far we have received no response to prove either success or failure.

We have carried our quest for peace to many nations and peoples because we share this planet with others whose future, in large measure, is tied to our own action, and whose counsel is necessary to our own hopes.

We have found understanding and support. And we know they wait with us tonight for some response that could lead to peace.

I wish tonight that I could give you a blueprint for the course of this conflict over the coming months, but we just cannot know what the future may require. We may have to face long, hard combat or a long, hard conference, or even both at once.

Until peace comes, or if it does not come, our course is clear. We will act as we must to help protect the independence of the valiant people of South Vietnam. We will strive to limit the conflict, for we wish neither increased destruction nor do we want to invite increased danger.

But we will give our fighting men what they must have: every gun, and every dollar, and every decision—whatever the cost or whatever the challenge.

And we will continue to help the people of South Vietnam care for those that are ravaged by battle, create progress in the villages, and carry forward the healing hopes of peace as best they can amidst the uncertain terrors of war.

And let me be absolutely clear: The days may become months, and the months may become years, but we will stay as long as aggression commands us to battle.

There may be some who do not want peace, whose ambitions stretch so far that war in Vietnam is but a welcome and convenient episode in an immense design to subdue history to their will. But for others it must now be clear—the choice is not between peace and victory, it lies between peace and the ravages of a conflict from which they can only lose.

The people of Vietnam, North and South, seek the same things: the shared needs of man, the needs for food and shelter and education—the chance to build and work and till the soil, free from the arbitrary horrors of battle—the desire to walk in the dignity of those who master their own destiny. For many painful years, in war and revolution and infrequent peace, they have struggled to fulfill those needs.

It is a crime against mankind that so much courage, and so much will, and so many dreams, must be flung on the fires of war and death.

To all of those caught up in this conflict we therefore say again tonight: Let us choose peace, and with it the wondrous works of peace, and beyond that, the time when hope reaches toward consummation, and life is the servant of life.

In this work, we plan to discharge our duty to the people whom we serve.

v.

This is the State of the Union.
But over it all—wealth, and promise, and

expectation—lies our troubling awareness of American men at war tonight.

How many men who listen to me tonight have served their Nation in other wars? How very many are not here to listen?

The war in Vietnam is not like these other wars. Yet, finally, war is always the same. It is young men dying in the fullness of their promise. It is trying to kill a man that you do not even know well enough to hate.

Therefore, to know war is to know that there is still madness in this world.

Many of you share the burden of this knowledge tonight with me. But there is a difference. For finally I must be the one to order our guns to fire, against all the most inward pulls of my desire. For we have children to teach, and we have sick to be cured, and we have men to be freed. There are poor to be lifted up, and there are cities to be built, and there is a world to be helped.

Yet we do what we must.

I am hopeful, and I will try as best I can, with everything I have got, to end this battle and to return our sons to their desires.

Yet as long as others will challenge America's security and test the dearness of our beliefs with fire and steel, then we must stand or see the promise of two centuries tremble. I believe tonight that you do not want me to try that risk. And from that belief your President summons his strength for the trials that lie ahead in the days to come.

The work must be our work now. Scarred by the weaknesses of man, with whatever guidance God may offer us, we must nevertheless and alone with our mortality, strive to ennoble the life of man on earth.

Thank you, and goodnight.

7 Remarks Upon Accepting an Award From the American Football Coaches Association. *January 13, 1966*

Gentlemen:

I want to welcome you this morning to the Cabinet Room in the White House, and to thank each of you for coming here, and thank you especially for this great honor that you do me and the Office I hold.

This award is a very special honor. It means more to me than a presentation of this kind ordinarily would, because it comes from a group of men who are real authorities on the subject of leadership and public service.

As I walked down the line this morning greeting each of you, I wondered if you really knew the contributions that your dedication has made to your country over the years. There is not a day passes that I do not see the results of the training that you have given

our young people: first, on the battlefield; second, in our services throughout our installations in the continental United States; third, in the farflung corridors of the various Government offices that I attempt to direct and whose personnel I attempt to lead.

You men are the natural leaders of our youth. But I think you do more than just lead. You are building, developing, and creating not only the leaders of today out on the athletic field, but the leaders of tomorrow in the world in many fields.

In the nearly 100 years that Americans have been enjoying this great sport, Presidents and Cabinet officers and Justices and leaders in every walk of life have first learned the lessons of discipline, of dedication, out on the athletic fields of the United States.

Your award makes specific reference to our efforts for peace. I think if all the nations of the world would conduct their affairs with the same dedication, and with the same fair play, and with the same friendly competition that the game of football stands for, peace would have been secured a long time ago.

Football is really and truly an American institution. It embodies our highest ideals of character and courage.

So, as President of your country, it is a very great pleasure to me to accept this award from a group which contributes so much to our national life and which sets the finest example to our youth.

I think that there is a greater casualty rate among football coaches than we have in combat. My heart started beating a little faster when I heard over the television that Oklahoma had even communicated with Darrell Royal a short time ago.

But I do want to say this to you, without regard to institution, party affiliation, if you have any, or political influence. If any of you are available away from the athletic field, I want to put a "See Me" sign on my door, like I have with Bud Wilkinson and others in the past, because in my judgment the men who are the great leaders in college athletics throughout our university system, will make great leaders for the Government of the United States. And I am looking for men of that type.

The greatest administrator I have ever known, I hired after he got fired as a football coach. He just couldn't win the Thanksgiving game—he lost it 3 years in succession. That took place in the early thirties and he still works for some of our family interests.

So I not only have a very healthy respect for the game and the institution, but I have respect for the men who have developed it and who have built it. And this award is particularly appreciated because of that.

And, if I may, I have asked that they send me the "con" wires that I got on my State of the Union last night, and I want to take this award and put it right beside me. While I go through these wires that tell me that I ought to be banned from the country and I ought to leave it, I'll glance down and read the words on the plaque, if you will.

Thank you very much.

NOTE: The President spoke at 11:15 a.m. in the Cabinet Room at the White House. During his remarks he referred to Darrell Royal, football coach at the University of Texas, and Charles B. (Bud) Wilkinson, former football coach at the University of Oklahoma and former president of the American Football Coaches Association, who served as Chairman of the President's Council on Physical Fitness, February 1961–February 1964.

The Tuss McLaughry Award is presented annually by the American Football Coaches Association to the person recognized as having made the highest contribution in the field of public service.

The text of the plaque presented to the President reads as follows:

"Tuss"
McLaughry Award
The highest of distinctions is service to others.

Presented to Lyndon Baines Johnson, President of the United States, January 13, 1966

". . . As long as I am President, I will spare neither my office nor myself in the quest for peace."

American Football Coaches Association

8 The President's News Conference of January 13, 1966

ANNOUNCEMENT OF APPOINTMENT OF SEC-
RETARY AND UNDER SECRETARY OF HOUSING
AND URBAN DEVELOPMENT

THE PRESIDENT. Good afternoon, ladies and gentlemen.

[1.] I think that all of you are aware of the effort that we have been making in the past months since the Congress adjourned, to make a thorough study of the new Department of Housing and Urban Development, its problems, its situation, its approach, the general nature of the programs they will be carrying out, the criteria, the costs, the benefits, the administration, the financing, the advances, the new application of technology as well as the formulating of a proposed plan of organization for that Department.

Without criticizing what may have taken place in the organization of other departments in the Government in times past, we tried to make sure that those mistakes were not repeated this time. I have reached a decision today that I am now delighted to announce to you and to the country. We have conducted a very thorough search to find the best man in the United States to head this new Department of Housing and Urban Development.

No man is going to have a more difficult or a more challenging job. No man is going to be better able to leave a mark on the generations of Americans to come than the man who takes on this very vital undertaking. The Chairman of the Civil Service Commission and members of my own staff have reviewed biographical data and studied experts in this field from a substantial number of the States in the Union, from a substantial number of the universities and business organizations of the country—it numbers a little over 300 men that have had their names presented and some consideration given to them.

After looking over these potential candidates, after carefully reviewing the proposed operations of the Department, its functions as well as its organization, I came to the conclusion that the man for this job is Mr. Robert Weaver.

I talked to Dr. Weaver this morning before I arose, in my bedroom, and I informed him then that I planned to send his nomination to the Senate, announcing it today.

He and I have decided on the man that I expect to nominate as Under Secretary of the Department, and he is here with us this afternoon, together with his charming wife. His name is Mr. Robert Wood, head of the Political Science Department of MIT—one of America's most imaginative students of the urban scene. Dr. Wood is the author of "Suburbia, Its People and Their Politics," "1400 Governments, the Political Economy of the New York Region," "Metropolis Against Itself," "School Men and Politics," and "Government and Politics of the United States."

I am very proud of this team. We have reviewed a number of men whom we expect to attempt to draft for the Assistant Secretaryship and for the General Counsel of this Department. In due time their names will be announced.

Mr. Weaver is here with his charming wife this afternoon. I think his performance as Administrator of the Housing and Home Finance Agency has been marked by the highest level of integrity and ability, and I think he has been able to stimulate a very genuine team spirit in that Department.

I just presented him to the Cabinet, and his colleagues there welcomed him with open arms.

I have worked with Bob Weaver for a good many years, and I believe him to be a deep thinker and a quiet but articulate man of action. As you know, he has had an outstanding administration in the Housing and Home Finance Agency. He is the author of "Negro Labor, A National Problem," "The Negro Ghetto," "The Urban Complex" (1964), and "Dilemmas of Urban America" in 1965.

He is as well versed, I think, in the urban needs of America as any person that we could find. So it adds up to saying this, that I believe him to be exactly the right man in the right place to pursue the right goals of bringing a full measure of the Great Society to our urban areas and carrying forward the major new urban programs that I will propose to the Congress in the days ahead.

Professor Wood is currently the chairman of the Political Science Department of MIT. He has chaired two Presidential task forces on urban affairs, this year and last year, and has worked very closely with the President, with members of the Cabinet, with members of Government—formerly employed in the Budget Bureau—and with my special assistants. Working with Bob Weaver, Professor Wood has been a major architect of the urban programs of this administration. He is a well known author, he is an outstanding manager, he is a perceptive analyst of the urban scene.

So the talent and the ability and the experience of these two men sets them apart from the hundreds of candidates that have been proposed and have been considered.

I am sending to the Senate, and presenting to the American people, the best men that I can to fulfill the pledge of this administration to bring the Great Society to the American people.

And now, it gives me great pleasure to sign the nominations for Mr. Robert C. Weaver of New York to be Secretary of Housing and Urban Development, and Mr. Robert C. Wood of Massachusetts to be Under Secretary of Housing and Urban Development. They will be sent forward to the Senate at the appropriate time.

Dr. Weaver will now take the proposed plan of organization, which he is familiar with, the proposed programs for the Housing Department—and may the Good Lord have mercy upon you!

QUESTIONS

THE PRESIDENT. I will be glad to answer any questions that any of you may have about this, or about any other matters that may be of interest to the press at this time.

VIETNAM: U.S. PEACE EFFORTS

[2.] Q. Mr. President, sir, have you heard anything from the Vice President since his talks with the Soviet Prime Minister? [1]

THE PRESIDENT. Yes, we have had detailed reports on the conversations through State Department channels.

Q. Mr. President, can you give us the benefit of your thinking on the hopes you expressed last night in your speech for limiting the Vietnam war? [2]

THE PRESIDENT. I think that I covered about everything that I could say, that I thought was appropriate to say last night. There have been no new developments this

---

[1] Vice President Hubert H. Humphrey and Soviet Premier Aleksei Kosygin met in New Delhi following the funeral of Indian Prime Minister Lal Bahadur Shastri in early January.

[2] See Item 6.

morning.

Q. Mr. President, could you evaluate for us your recent peace drive? Do you think that there have been other benefits perhaps than what you may or may not have heard from Hanoi, for example?

THE PRESIDENT. I reviewed pretty well what we have done last night, and I think the Secretary of State, Mr. Goldberg, and Mr. Williams [3] have brought you up to date. I don't know anything that I could add to it, other than the Secretary and Ambassador Harriman [4] will be reviewing our objectives and our hopes in this field with other governments in the days ahead.

DEPARTMENT OF HOUSING AND URBAN DEVELOPMENT

[3.] Q. Mr. President, in connection with the appointments in the Housing and Urban Development Department, there have been reports that a task force headed by Dr. Wood recommended——

THE PRESIDENT. What reports? I want to know who reports what so I can see if it is——

Q. There have been published reports in the newspapers.

THE PRESIDENT. Whose?

Q. There have been published reports in the newspapers.

THE PRESIDENT. Who published it? That's what I want to know. I don't want to comment on something that——

Q. Well, I saw something in the Washington Post.

THE PRESIDENT. All right, go ahead.

---

[3] Secretary of State Dean Rusk, Arthur J. Goldberg, U.S. Representative to the United Nations, and G. Mennen Williams, Assistant Secretary of State for African Affairs.

[4] W. Averell Harriman, Ambassador at Large.

The Washington Post. Now, what did the Washington Post say?

Q. That a task force headed by Professor Wood had recommended the transfer of the Community Action Program from the Office of Economic Opportunity to the new Department, and there have been subsequent reports that you have decided against this. Can you make any comment on that?

THE PRESIDENT. I would say that so far as the report that I have made a decision on the matter, I would say it is more propaganda than accurate. I have made no decision. I have not been called upon to make any decision. We will, in the days ahead, consider a good many reorganization proposals, but the best authority for a Presidential decision is the President or the President's Press Secretary, and you can always get guidance on that, if you have the time or the disposition to obtain it.

Q. That's why I asked you.

THE PRESIDENT. Well, you got it. [*Laughter*] That's why I told you!

DISTRICT OF COLUMBIA HOME RULE

[4.] Q. Mr. President, last night in your message you urged the House to act on a number of Senate-passed bills; one was home rule for the District of Columbia. I wonder if you are supporting the Senate version of this home rule bill, or if you would be for a compromise?

THE PRESIDENT. I am supporting the Senate version, as I did when I recommended it to the Congress. It's a matter for the Congress to work out, but my position is abundantly clear. I favor the Senate bill. I did when it was before the Senate. I did when it was defeated in the House.[5]

---

[5] See 1965 volume, this series, Items 39, 402, 481, 486.

PLANS FOR SPECIAL MESSAGES

[5.] Q. Mr. President, do you plan a special message with regard to consumer problems, such as truth in packaging, truth in lending, etc., that you referred to briefly in your speech?

THE PRESIDENT. There will be a good many special messages—on what particular subjects will have to be announced later. That will depend on our conferences with the members of the committee and with the authors of the legislation. Just what subjects they will be on, and the timing, have yet to be developed.

INTENSITY OF FIGHTING IN VIETNAM

[6.] Q. Mr. President, do we have any indication that the other side in Vietnam is reducing the number of incidents, reducing the intensity of the war at all?

THE PRESIDENT. The number of incidents has dropped off some. I don't say that there is any connection with that and our peace moves, but that is a fact.

THE PRESIDENT'S HEALTH

[7.] Q. Mr. President, it's been a little over 3 months now since your operation. How do you feel?

THE PRESIDENT. Fine.

Q. No more soreness in the side or the back?

THE PRESIDENT. Oh yes, I have a little soreness.

DATE OF ADJOURNMENT OF CONGRESS

[8.] Q. Mr. President, in light of the proposals you made last night, do you still think Congress can adjourn in June?

THE PRESIDENT. Well, I don't know if I have ever thought it could adjourn in June. That's the answer.

Q. Do you have any prediction?

THE PRESIDENT. No, I don't. I never have done that. I came here 35 years ago, and the first thing I learned was never to predict when they would adjourn during the day, or during the week, or during the year. And I have never done so. I have read reports about my predictions, but the wish was father to the thought by the person announcing it. I have never made any prediction when Congress could get out. I don't know. I would like for them to go home as early as they can, consistent with discharging of their duties and consistent with their own desires.

Congress is an independent branch of the Government and I want to cooperate with them and suit their pleasure as much as possible, consistent with the performing of my duties. In an election year I realize the importance, not only from the standpoint of the individual Member of Congress, the people concerned, but from the standpoint of the administration, to have the Congressmen at home—60-odd Democratic Senators and 290-odd Democratic Congressmen—discussing what we have done and why we have done it. So I would like to see them go as soon as they can. But whether they can go in June or January, I don't know. And I have never known; I have never made any such prediction.

THE PRESIDENT AND THE PRESS

[9.] I do get a little bit sensitive sometimes when I see Presidential decisions being made, and predictions being made, and recommendations being made that I never heard of. I saw in a UP item this morning how I had eliminated the redwood forest from my State of the Union Message at the last minute. And while I was handling that ticker, I was reading the recommendations on the redwood forest in the Budget Message that's to go up on the 24th, and had never been submitted to the State of the Union. That could have been ascertained.

So, those things get out and then when I change them, some of you reporters think I changed them because of something that you may have said. [*Laughter*]

REACTION TO STATE OF THE UNION MESSAGE

[10.] Q. Mr. President, can you characterize the reaction to your speech last night? You talked about some "con" telegrams, which we understand you said were in the minority. How do you feel the reaction was?

THE PRESIDENT. I think it was very good. I was very pleased with it. Any time that you receive the welcome we received and the some 50-odd applauses you receive—it makes you feel good. We got some messages favoring what we had said and some messages violently opposing some of the recommendations we made. That is generally true of almost every Presidential recommendation, and certainly one as inclusive as the State of the Union. But, on balance, I expect that the percentage of wires was perhaps heavier than we would get if we polled the country, because maybe your friends are disposed to wire you and encourage you and stimulate you.

Q. Mr. President, can you tell us which of your proposals drew the biggest opposition?

THE PRESIDENT. I didn't observe any concentrated, leveled opposition to any particular one. One fellow amused me by saying he thought he would leave the country, and I asked Bill Moyers to check up and see if that was the same fellow that was going to leave

last year. [*Laughter*]

PLANS FOR FOREIGN TRAVEL

[11.] Q. Mr. President, we have been given to understand that you would like to do some foreign travel this year. Is there anything you can tell us now about these plans?

THE PRESIDENT. Not a thing, Sid.[6] I have no such plans now. I always enjoy exchanging views with leaders of other countries and meeting other peoples. But right at the moment I have no plans.

THE MANSFIELD REPORT ON VIETNAM

[12.] Q. Mr. President, do you think that your report to the Nation coincides with Mansfield's report on Vietnam?[7]

THE PRESIDENT. No—it was somewhat later. [*Laughter*]

Q. Other than that, I mean?

THE PRESIDENT. I thought it was somewhat different. I think the Mansfield report that he made to me and that he wrote to me and that he subsequently published in another form, gave his impressions of the situation in Vietnam. What I attempted to do last night was to give the President's impressions.

DEPARTMENT OF HOUSING AND URBAN DEVELOPMENT

[13.] Q. Mr. President, could you say

---

[6] Sid Davis of the Westinghouse Broadcasting Co., Inc.

[7] The report of Senator Mike Mansfield of Montana and four other members of the Senate Committee on Foreign Relations, based on their tour of the region in December 1965, is entitled "The Vietnam Conflict: The Substance and the Shadow" (Congressional Record, Jan. 13, 1966, p. 140).

what you consider the first priority for Mr. Weaver and Mr. Wood in their new Department?

THE PRESIDENT. To bring together a staff of experts, assemble the outstanding men in this country without regard to politics or party, but only with regard to serving the needs of this Department of Housing and Urban Development. And after he assembles the tools, the manpower, then he can get on with the proposals that we have, and the reorganizations that will come about, and the legislation that we will formulate and present.

THE PROPOSED DELAY IN EXCISE TAX REDUCTION

[14.] Q. Mr. President, the proposal of yours last night that seemed to invoke the most resistance on the Hill——

THE PRESIDENT. The most what?

Q. Resistance on the Hill——

THE PRESIDENT. Well, I don't think you can really tell this early——

Q. —— well, backtalk then—was the proposal to delay the excise cuts—suggestions were made by some people that it would be better to get that billion dollars by a further cut in domestic spending. What is your comment on that?

THE PRESIDENT. I would think that is a very inaccurate poll of the sentiments of the Congress. I expect that we spent a reasonable amount of probing with the various Members as to the alternatives that face us—larger deficits, different forms of taxes, no taxes at all—and I detected minimum opposition. Everyone would like to have all the tax reductions we could have, but conditions have changed a good deal within the last few months, and I did not detect overwhelming resistance to it.

I think most of the people are patriotic,

including the industries affected. And I would expect in the light of our economy that if we are going to have substantially increased expenditures in Vietnam, as we are going to have—running several billion dollars this year—that the Congress and the people would be willing to forgo the repeal of the excise tax on long-distance telephone and on new automobiles, particularly in view of the fact that we have already had some reduction in those excise taxes, particularly on automobiles, particularly in view of the fact that some automobiles you have to wait to get delivered now because there is adequate demand, and sales are at an alltime high. I think most of the legislators would prefer receiving revenue in this form than levying a new tax on reporters or corporations or individuals.

THE NEW YORK TRANSIT STRIKE SETTLEMENT

[15.] Q. Mr. President, could you comment, sir, on the New York transit strike settlement,[8] particularly in reference to the administration's guideposts for noninflationary wage and price behavior?

THE PRESIDENT. I know that the people of New York must be relieved that the subway strike has been settled and that normal life in one of the Nation's largest cities has been restored. I share the feeling and I want to express my pride in the admirable way that these people met the demands and the inconveniences that they have been subjected to during the last 2 weeks.

Candor requires me to say that I am quite

---

[8] The transit strike in New York City began on January 1, 1966, and was settled on January 13 when the New York Transit Authority and the Transport Workers Union agreed on a 2-year contract which granted workers $60 million to $70 million in increased benefits.

disturbed that essential services could be paralyzed for so long and I am equally concerned by the cost of the settlement. Although this settlement involves municipal employees, the settlement, I am informed by the Chairman of the Council of Economic Advisers, violates our national guideposts for noninflationary wage increases. And I do not believe that any settlement that violates the guideposts to this extent is in the national interest.

Q. Could I follow up on that, sir? Is there anything further than denunciation that the Government can do or perhaps plans to do about situations of this sort?

THE PRESIDENT. I will say that the Chairman will probably have a statement for you, if it has not already been issued, giving the viewpoint of the Council of Economic Advisers. If you are asking about what weapons we may have or what controls we may have, the answer is that we have no controls. These are voluntary matters.

Most of the labor organizations in the country, most of the business organizations in the country, have been willing to consider the guideposts and to take them into account in connection with their agreements, and I am glad to have—and I am always sorry when there are exceptions that may contribute to inflation. It is not a personal matter with me, this is your inflation and our inflation, and anything that contributes to it is a matter of concern, as I observed last night.

WOMEN IN THE MILITARY SERVICES

[16.] Q. Mr. President, I understand that the women in the military services—the WAC's, the Waves, the women Marines, and so forth—are distressed because they are not being called upon to serve in Vietnam. Is

there any chance that this might take place—of course not in a combat area, but to relieve men who could be in the combat areas?

THE PRESIDENT. Well, there is always a chance of anything taking place when our women are sufficiently distressed. [*Laughter*] I will explore your inquiry and if you will check with Bill Moyers a little later, maybe he can make a more adequate response.

CONTINUATION OF U.S. PEACE EFFORTS

[17.] Q. Mr. President, will you continue your diplomatic peace offensive by sending special envoys to foreign capitals?

THE PRESIDENT. Yes, there will be envoys going to other capitals all the time. As I observed, we have had more than 300 diplomatic discussions and visits this year between the President, the Secretary of State, and leading Ambassadors, with representatives of other nations in the search to promote peace in the world. And as long as I am President, that will continue.

OTHER TAX RECOMMENDATIONS

[18.] Q. Mr. President, you mentioned last night in your tax recommendations other simplifications of taxes. Can you elaborate on what other tax recommendations you might have in this area?

THE PRESIDENT. The Secretary of the Treasury, I think, will elaborate to the extent that my recommendations cover the tax proposals in a letter, I think, that will be made public probably tomorrow.[9]

---

[9] Treasury Department proposals for an improved system of withholding income taxes, one which would eliminate or reduce large year-end tax payments, were submitted to Congress on January 13.

Reporter: Thank you, Mr. President.

NOTE: President Johnson's fifty-third news conference was held in the Fish Room at the White House at 4:15 p.m. on Thursday, January 13, 1966. The unscheduled conference followed the President's meeting with his Cabinet and was attended by Cabinet members.

9   Message to the Congress Transmitting First Annual Report on the Operation of the International Coffee Agreement. *January 14, 1966*

To the Congress of the United States:

This is the first annual report on the operation of the International Coffee Agreement required by Section 5 of the International Coffee Agreement Act of 1965 (P.L. 89-23).

The International Coffee Agreement represents an important element of our foreign economic policy, especially as that policy is directed towards the problems of the less developed countries. Our participation in the Agreement should help make it possible to avoid the sharp rises and falls in coffee prices that have adversely affected United States consumers and growers of coffee in foreign countries alike. Stability of prices will help those countries heavily dependent on coffee exports to plan for and carry out their economic development and diversification programs. The steady economic progress of these countries is, in turn, an important stimulus to a healthier and more stable political climate in each.

I believe that during 1965 the dual aims of the Agreement—adequate supplies of coffee to consumers and markets for coffee to producers at equitable prices—have been met. I am also confident that the Congress will view with satisfaction the spirit of international cooperation that has increasingly come to characterize the operation of this Agreement. The passage of the International Coffee Agreement Act permitted its implementation for the year that began October 1, 1965. The results to date justify our confidence that the Agreement will further advance the national interest of the United States.

LYNDON B. JOHNSON

The White House
January 14, 1965

NOTE: The report, entitled "First Annual Report of the President of the United States on the International Coffee Agreement" (26 pp., processed), was released with the President's message.

For a statement by the President upon signing the International Coffee Agreement Act of 1965, see 1965 volume, this series, Book I, Item 272.

10   Letter to the Postmaster General Approving Recommendations for Improving Postal Services. *January 15, 1966*
[Released January 15, 1966. Dated January 14, 1966]

Dear Mr. Postmaster General:

I approve your recommendations to improve postal service by increasing post office window hours and by restoring six-day parcel post delivery service.

I have said in the past, and I repeat now, that I want you to provide this country with the finest mail service it has ever known, while managing the Post Office Department efficiently and prudently. I want you to explore all the techniques available to modernize our postal service and make certain that they are being used to provide the American people with the best postal system in the world at the lowest possible cost to the taxpayer.

A good, stable, dependable postal system is vital to the well-being of the nation's economy.

I therefore intend to seek the necessary funds from the Congress to restore the postal services that were curtailed in 1964.

Sincerely,

LYNDON B. JOHNSON

[The Honorable, The Postmaster General, Washington, D.C. 20260]

NOTE: On the same day the White House announced that, under the Postmaster General's proposal, 6-day parcel post delivery would be restored in 6,091 cities, and post office window service on Saturdays and Sundays would be authorized on an as-needed basis in nearly 15,000 post offices. Late hour window service would also be resumed on weeknights, where needed, and postmasters would be authorized to resume selling money orders on Saturdays as part of the window service restoration in those cities where money order sales had been curtailed.

The release stated that the proposed improvements would be made "as soon as the Congress provides the funds, hopefully within the next 6 months" (2 Weekly Comp. Pres. Docs., p. 50).

11 Message to the Congress Transmitting Annual Report on the Foreign Assistance Program, Fiscal Year 1965. *January 17, 1966*

To the Congress of the United States:

The Annual Report on the Foreign Assistance Program of the United States for fiscal year 1965, which I here transmit, shows what Americans have done during the past twelve months to help other people help themselves.

The record of these months offers new testimony to our continuing conviction that our own peace and prosperity here at home depends on continued progress toward a better life for people everywhere.

In pursuit of that goal, we have, during this past year, placed new emphasis on the basic problem of securing more food for the world's population.

We have agreed to extend technical assistance to countries asking for help on population programs. At the same time, our overseas missions have been directed to give priority to projects for achieving better agriculture. Additional resources of our great universities have been applied to rural development efforts abroad, and we have moved

to increase the nutritional value of food shipped overseas for children.

During these past twelve months we have also:

—Begun to make education a more vital part of our assistance to other nations. Today, 70 American universities are engaged in the development of 39 Asian, African and Latin American countries through this program.

—Given our full support to development of a new life for the people of Southeast Asia through a regional development program—a true and hopeful alternative to profitless aggression. We have made progress toward the establishment of an Asian Development Bank, and accelerated plans for development of the critical Mekong River Basin.

The twelve months covered by this report also reflect our progress toward making our aid programs both more realistic, and more efficient. For example:

—Foreign assistance has become a smaller

factor in our balance of payments. In fiscal year 1965, more than 80 cents of every AID dollar was spent for the purchase of American goods and services. American products and skills went overseas as aid; most of the dollars which paid for them stayed in this country.

—Foreign aid has become a smaller burden on our resources. The $3.5 billion committed for military and economic assistance in fiscal year 1965 represented 3.5 percent of the Federal budget and one-half of one percent of the U.S. gross national product.

At the height of the Marshall Plan, in comparison, foreign aid accounted for more than 11 percent of the Federal budget and nearly 2 percent of our gross national product.

Perhaps the most important single change in our AID programs has been the shift from simply helping other countries stay afloat to helping them become self-supporting, so that our assistance will no longer be needed.

Three-fourths of our AID program in fiscal year 1965 was devoted to development assistance: programs of technical and capital assistance in agriculture, industry, health and education that strengthen the ability of other nations to use their own resources.

Finally, private participation in AID programs is at an all-time high. Through contracts with American universities, business firms, labor unions, cooperatives, and other private groups, AID has sharply increased the involvement of non-governmental resources in international development.

Two of every five AID-financed technicians in the field today are not Federal employees, but experts from private American institutions.

There is much in the less-developed world that causes us deep concern today: enmity between neighbor nations that threatens the hard-won gains of years of development effort; reluctance to move rapidly on needed internal reforms; political unrest that delays constructive programs to help the people; an uncertain race between food supplies and population.

We are right to be concerned for the present. But we are also right to be hopeful for the future. In this report are recorded some of the solid, human achievements on which our future hopes are based.

Whether it provides strength for threatened peoples like those in Southeast Asia, or support for the self-help of millions on the move in Latin America, in Africa, in the Near East and South Asia, our foreign assistance program remains an investment of critical and promising importance to our own national future.

LYNDON B. JOHNSON

January 17, 1966

NOTE: The report is entitled "The Foreign Assistance Program, Annual Report to the Congress, Fiscal Year 1965" (Government Printing Office, 77 pp.).

The President's message was made public as part of a White House release summarizing the report. The release stated that two-thirds of the $3.5 billion total, the lowest foreign aid commitment since fiscal year 1961, was for economic assistance programs administered by the Agency for International Development and the balance was for military assistance administered by the Department of Defense.

The release noted that 90 percent of the economic assistance went to just 25 countries, although 77 countries had received some kind of assistance during the year. It pointed out that four countries (Vietnam, Laos, Korea, and Jordan) accounted for 80 percent of AID supporting assistance during the year, and that seven countries (Brazil, Chile, India, Nigeria, Pakistan, Tunisia, and Turkey) accounted for 80 percent of AID development loans. The report noted that AID programs had been brought to a close in five additional countries during the year.

The release pointed out that greater amounts of military assistance were allocated to Southeast Asia because of increased Communist pressure on South Vietnam and other countries in the area (2 Weekly Comp. Pres. Docs., p. 51).

12 Remarks Upon Announcing Appointments in the Peace Corps and in the Department of Housing and Urban Development. *January 17, 1966*

Ladies and gentlemen:

At my request, Mr. Sargent Shriver has directed the Peace Corps while heading the war on poverty. Few men in the life of our Nation have ever held such broad responsibilities at the same time, and few have discharged them as well.

Mr. Shriver has waged peace abroad and waged war on poverty at home, and he has done both with rare energy and with rare ability.

The Peace Corps has grown from 8,000 to 14,000, and the war on poverty has touched the lives of more than 2 million of our fellow Americans.

Now today, I am asking Mr. Shriver to give full time to the war on poverty. We are going to enlarge that war, as you will observe in the Budget that will go to the Congress in a few days, and we are going to prosecute it with all the vigor and determination at our command.

Mr. Shriver will be working double time now as he has been for 2 years, but it will be on one rather than on two different jobs. To direct the Peace Corps, I have selected one of my most trusted advisers and one of our most talented young men, the Assistant Secretary of State, Mr. Jack Vaughn.

Mr. Vaughn served as Associate Director of the Peace Corps, before I drafted him to be our Ambassador to Panama. He has been for almost the last year in one of our most distinguished and most difficult jobs, Assistant Secretary for Latin America. I have personally asked him to take over the Peace Corps, to return, in fact, to his first love, after talking about it at length with Mr. Shriver.

Secretary Vaughn will bring to the Peace Corps a compassion and understanding for the world that will serve him and this fine organization well.

Last Thursday, you will recall, I nominated Mr. Robert Weaver and Mr. Robert Wood to be the Secretary and the Under Secretary of the Department of Housing and Urban Development. I deeply appreciate the swift action by the Senate in confirming these outstanding Americans unanimously this afternoon.

Today I wish to announce my intention to nominate very shortly Professor Charles Haar of the Harvard Law School as Assistant Secretary for Metropolitan Planning and Development, and Mr. Philip Brownstein, presently Commissioner of the Federal Housing Administration, to be the Assistant Secretary for Mortgage Finance.

I am also approving the appointment of Mr. William B. Ross, one of the outstanding management experts in the Bureau of the Budget, as Deputy Under Secretary for Planning, Programs, and Evaluation.

Each of these men working with Mr. Weaver and Mr. Wood will, I believe, form a first-rate team that will take on the great challenges that lie ahead to build and to reinvigorate our urban areas. These men are equal to the task.

Mr. Brownstein is no stranger either to the housing field or to Mr. Weaver. He is a distinguished lawyer and administrator, and he has been serving as Federal Housing Commissioner since 1963.

Professor Haar is generally regarded as the Nation's leading expert in land-use planning. He has been one of the architects of our natural beauty and urban development program, and has written a number of important books, including "Land Planning Law in a Free Society," "Federal Credit and Private Housing," and "Law and Land."

Finally, Mr. William Ross, a graduate of Indiana University and Princeton University, is a career Government employee who brings his years of experience as a management expert in the Bureau of the Budget to the important management job of Deputy Under Secretary.

Mr. Moyers will, while I am conferring with the leadership, make available to you biographical sketches of each of these men.

NOTE: The President spoke at 4:14 p.m. in the Fish Room at the White House during a news briefing conducted by Bill D. Moyers, Special Assistant to the President.

For the President's remarks at the swearing in of Robert C. Weaver and Robert C. Wood as Secretary and Under Secretary of Housing and Urban Development, see Item 13.

13 Remarks at the Swearing In of Robert C. Weaver and Robert C. Wood as Secretary and Under Secretary of Housing and Urban Development. *January* 18, 1966

Dr. and Mrs. Weaver, Dr. and Mrs. Wood, Mr. Vice President, distinguished Members of the Cabinet, Members of the Congress, my friends who are guests here at this memorable moment in American history:

I am sure this is a very proud moment for all of us and for all of America.

It is the beginning of a very exciting adventure. We are setting out to make our cities places where the good life is possible.

There are voices saying the problems of this age have so outstripped our common resources that the city can no longer effectively serve its citizens.

Some say that the city has become unmanageable, unworkable, and unliveable. Some point to our crowded schools and to our shortage of decent houses, to our growing welfare burden, to our diminishing tax base, to our shapeless growth, the tension between its peoples, the crime in its streets, the breakdown in its services, and the pollution of its air and its water.

I do not deny the existence or the gravity of these problems, nor do I pretend that they are going to yield to easy solutions.

But I do not believe for a moment that the cause of the American city is yet lost. A powerful and a prosperous Nation, blessed with the human and natural resources at our command, just must not fail in its most vital quest: to improve the quality of life for 135 million people who presently inhabit these cities.

Yet I know we are going to fail if we are timid for a moment.

We will fail, if we pursue the old paths merely because they have been venerated by custom.

To make our cities liveable will require the commitment of our best minds, our selfless determination, our willingness to explore new ways of building, and new dimensions of planning, and new methods of coordinating what we know about man and what we know about man's environment.

The great new Department that must meet this challenge was built upon the foundation of the Housing and Home Finance Agency. That Agency provided shelter for millions of American citizens.

But it will no longer be enough merely to provide housing for people. For the challenge of the city is so complex and so intricate a fabric of interwoven problems—social and psychological, physical and financial, and racial, that any arm of public policy charged with responding to this challenge must be competent to deal with its human needs, as well as with its brick and its mortar.

And because I believe this so deeply, and because the Congress shares this belief, I have selected, as the first principal officers of the Department of Housing and Urban Development, two men who have spent lifetimes in the service of the city. They are scholars of the city—of its practical affairs as well as its human needs.

As Secretary, I have selected—I am so proud to say that the Senate yesterday unanimously approved the man that I believe best fitted by experience and skill to take control of his Department from the start, and to provide it with the leadership, and the understanding, and the commonsense, and the drive, and the determination that it must have to serve urban America—Robert Weaver.

Bob Weaver now has his charge. It is to build our cities anew. Maybe that is too much to put on the shoulders of one single man. But we shall never know, Bob, until we try it.

I thought that he should have some help, and the Congress agreed. I thought he should have as his principal deputy someone who knows almost as much about cities as Bob does. And lastly, I thought that we should prove that Harvard is not the only institution of higher learning in the Boston area, so I went to MIT for the Under Secretary. I may say that I had a hard time locating my man because he seemed to be in Washington more often than he was in

Boston. But I finally found him, and he is here by Bob Weaver's side this morning. His name is Robert Wood.

And in the presence of these witnesses, let me repeat the charge that I give you as you accept this public trust:

Take the authorities vested in you, and so manage the responsibility that is yours, that years from now those four Americans out of five who will live in cities will honor your names.

No one has ever borne such a charge before. No one could receive it more endowed with the confidence of his President and his fellow Americans.

Thank you.

[*At this point, the oaths of office were administered to Dr. Weaver and Dr. Wood by Judge E. Barrett Prettyman, Senior Circuit Judge of the U.S. Court of Appeals for the District of Columbia. The President then resumed speaking.*]

The problems of our cities and the problems of people are not confined to our country alone. We have many in the world and many particularly in this hemisphere. For the last hour and a half the Vice President and I, along with the distinguished Acting Secretary of State, have been discussing the problems of this hemisphere, and I am proud to announce this morning that I have succeeded in prevailing upon the distinguished Ambassador to Brazil, the Honorable Lincoln Gordon, to accept the assignment to succeed Mr. Jack Vaughn, who has moved to the Peace Corps, as Assistant Secretary of State.

I'd like to present Mr. Gordon, the present Ambassador to Brazil.

NOTE: The President spoke at 10:05 a.m. in the East Room at the White House. In his opening words he referred to Dr. and Mrs. Robert C. Weaver, Dr. and Mrs. Robert C. Wood, and the Vice President, Hubert H. Humphrey.

14 Special Message to the Congress Recommending Approval of U.S.
Participation as a Member Nation in the Asian Development
Bank. *January* 18, 1966

To the Congress of the United States:

I recommend that the Congress promptly approve United States participation in the Asian Development Bank.

This new institution expresses the will of Asia to develop her manifold human and natural resources, and thereby to lift the burden of poverty that has been the lot of her people since ancient times.

Conceived and sponsored by Asians, the Bank is open to all countries in that region, regardless of ideology, who are members of the United Nations or its specialized agencies. Of its $1 billion authorized capital, 65% is to be subscribed by nations in the Asian area.

United States representatives—led by Mr. Eugene Black and a distinguished Congressional delegation—signed the Charter of the Asian Development Bank at Manila last December 4. But only the Congress itself can authorize the final acceptance of U.S. membership.

That is the action I request today.

I.

I take this step because of my urgent belief that the works of peace in Asia—the building of roads, dams, harbors, power plants, and all the other public and private facilities essential to a modern economy—are vital to peace in the entire world.

An Asia torn by conflict, depressed by hunger, disease and illiteracy, deprived of the means and the institutions that alone can offer hope to her people, must ever be a source of turmoil and anxiety for nations beyond her borders, as well as those within. Because this is so—and because we have recognized our moral obligation to our brothers on this earth—the United States has committed itself over a decade and a half to major assistance programs in Asia, making food, development loans, and technical assistance available to those who required our aid.

We have sought no American empire. Our purpose has never been to exploit, but to encourage; not to master, but to magnify the works of those who truly served the Asian people.

Now the Asians themselves have formed an institution by whose hand new works of peace may be accomplished. They have committed precious resources to that institution. They are determined to join in a cooperative endeavor, uniting the talents and resources of diverse cultures in pursuit of a common vision of progress.

They have asked us to join with them— to subscribe 20% of the institution's total capital—and thus to help make that vision a reality.

I recommend that we respond quickly and affirmatively.

II.

This proposal is neither utopian nor vague. It is the product of careful deliberation by the foremost experts in international finance. It rests solidly on the lessons learned in building the World Bank, and other organs of international finance, into the powerful forces for good they are today. It will take its place among regional financial institutions alongside the Inter-American Development Bank and the newly-formed African Development Bank.

Loan terms will be similar to those offered by the World Bank. Project justifications will be as rigorous as prudent management requires. Special efforts will be made to develop and finance projects involving more than one country, so that the Bank may be an agent of unity as well as development.

The Bank will reinforce existing aid programs in Asia, and thereby multiply their effectiveness. It will link its resources—financial and human—to such institutions as the Mekong Coordinating Committee, already joining the countries of the Mekong River Basin in major water resource projects.

Its Charter permits it to administer special development funds, contributed by either member or non-member countries. Thus it will serve as a channel for funds beyond its own resources.

These advantages are developed further in the Special Report of the Secretary of the Treasury on the Asian Development Bank which accompanies this message.

III.

The largest share of the Bank's subscriptions will be provided by Asians themselves.

The United States has been asked to pledge $200 million, equally divided between paid-in and callable shares. The paid-in shares are payable in five equal annual installments of $20 million each, half of which will be in cash, half in the form of a letter of credit.

The callable shares will constitute a guarantee for borrowings by the Bank in private capital markets. They would be drawn on only in the unlikely event that the Bank were unable to meet its commitments.

Our pledge is equalled by that of Japan. India has pledged $93 million; Australia another $85 million. More than $100 million has already been pledged by European countries and Canada, and further pledges

may be made.

Joint action with these major subscribers provides another instrument of cooperation between the donors of aid. That is a long-sought goal of the United States, for it offers the most efficient use of all the free world's aid resources.

Finally, our commitment to the Asian Bank should have little negative effect on our balance of payments. Procurement financed through the Bank's regular capital will normally be limited to member countries. Purchases of U.S. goods and services will approximately offset the dollar outflow occasioned by our $10 million annual cash subscription.

IV.

The Asian Development Bank is a necessity—not a luxury.

It was needed yesterday. It is needed even more today. Tomorrow, when the demands of Asia's millions on her struggling economies are more pressing still, it can mean the difference between opportunity and chaos.

It is practical and imaginative. It is the product of Asian initiative, and it offers the nucleus around which Asians can make a cooperative response to the most critical economic problems—national and regional.

Because it is all these things, it is also an avenue of good will and sound policy for the United States. For our destination is a world where the instinct for oppression has been vanquished in the heart of man. Given the means to work, to build, to teach, to heal, to nourish his family, man may yet achieve such a world—if not in our time, then in the generations that will succeed us on this planet. I believe the Asian Development Bank is an essential tool in providing the means of life for hundreds of millions of human beings who live between the Caspian Sea and the South Pacific.

It will become a reality when fifteen signatories, ten of them Asian, have ratified the Charter. It appears now that this will be achieved by early Spring. Our own constructive influence in the organization and management of the Bank will be increased if we can become active at its very beginning.

Last April in Baltimore I spoke of our dream of a world "where all are fed and charged with hope." I promised that "we will help to make it so." Our partnership in the Asian Bank is a step in keeping that pledge. It brings us nearer that day when our resources—and the world's—can be devoted to the constructive works of peace, not the destructive forces of war.

I urge the Congress to adopt the Asian Development Bank Act. Asia's future—and the world's—requires it.

LYNDON B. JOHNSON

The White House
January 18, 1966

NOTE: For the President's remarks at the signing of the Asian Development Bank Act of 1966, see Item 133.

The "U.S. Treasury Department Special Report on the Proposed Asian Development Bank, January 1966" (32 pp., processed), transmitted to the Congress as an attachment to the foregoing message, was also made public, together with the text of a draft bill providing for U.S. participation in the Bank. They are printed in House Document 361 (89th Cong., 2d sess.).

For the President's Baltimore address, delivered at Johns Hopkins University on April 7, 1965, see 1965 volume, this series, Book I, Item 172.

---

15   Letter to the Secretary of the Treasury on the Need for Higher Interest Rates on U.S. Savings Bonds. *January 18, 1966*

Dear Mr. Secretary:

Over the years, one of the strongest links between this Government and its citizenry has been the United States Savings Bond program. Born in the critical days before our entry into the Second World War, this program has been, for the Government, a vital source of noninflationary financing for needed Government programs. For the public, it has provided a matchless means for accumulating savings with absolute safety, and with an attractive rate of return.

A successful Savings Bond program is of particular urgency at this time—facing as we do a firm commitment to the defense of freedom in Vietnam and a strongly rising economy at home. We must not, and will not, at this juncture, permit our strength to be sapped by inflation.

Today, above all, is a time for all Americans to rededicate themselves to the spirit that animated the Minutemen of Concord—who serve as the symbol of the Savings Bond program. For today, as at the founding of our nation, it is freedom which is again at stake. Not all of us are called upon to fight in the jungles of Vietnam, but while our men are there, in the frontlines of a distant land, none of us can remain aloof on the sidelines. We must all do our share—in every way we can—to support our men in Vietnam. One sure way is open to all Americans through the Savings Bond program.

On several occasions during the postwar period it has been necessary to improve the rate of return on Savings Bonds in view of the higher rates available to many savers in various private savings accounts. The last change was made in 1959. To have failed to make those adjustments would have been a disservice both to the Government and to the public at large—risking inflationary dangers, complicating the task of managing our Government finances, and depriving millions of small savers of a reasonable rate of return on their funds entrusted to the Government.

We are again at a point where rates available on a variety of alternative forms of savings have moved above the rate now paid on U.S. Savings Bonds. At the same time, we are at a point where maximum savings are vital to our national welfare—indeed, to our national future. Another increase in rate on those bonds is now timely.

In order to sustain and enlarge the vital role of the Savings Bond program, I therefore direct you to set in motion the necessary machinery for raising the interest rate on these bonds as of the earliest feasible date.

Please submit to me as soon as possible your specific recommendations.

As in past rate changes, I would like you to make appropriate rate adjustments on outstanding savings bonds as well, so that no current bondholder need cash in his current holdings in order to gain the advantage of the attractive new rate, and no prospective buyer need feel that he should delay his purchase to await the higher rate.

Sincerely,

LYNDON B. JOHNSON

[Honorable Henry H. Fowler, Secretary of the Treasury, Washington, D.C.]

NOTE: On February 16 the White House made public a letter from the Secretary of the Treasury to the President in response to the President's directive, together with the President's reply (Item 73; see also Item 72).

16 Message to the Delegates to the Fourth Meeting of the Inter-American Cultural Council. *January* 18, 1966

I HAVE a special pleasure in welcoming to Washington the delegates to the fourth meeting of the Inter-American Cultural Council.

Your Council—as the agency through which the Organization of American States directs its efforts in educational, scientific, and cultural fields—symbolizes the patient and painstaking pursuit of the conditions of durable peace which we all seek. This search for peace is no less significant by being relatively unseen and unheard in a world in which men talk more loudly of issues that seem to divide them than they do of common interests that can unite them.

I am confident your meeting can have a significance beyond the days of your deliberations. Though you build quietly, you build no less firmly the sure foundations of societies in which free men can truly know and enjoy the possibilities of cultural interchange in this hemisphere.

We in our country stand in need of greater knowledge and understanding of the old and honored cultures to the south of us; and we likewise stand in readiness to help those in the other American Republics who wish to understand us better by learning more about our cultural growth and aspirations. In efforts our governments are making to realize the goals of the Alliance for Progress, the United States seeks to encourage greater emphasis on bringing about better social and educational opportunities for all our growing populations.

I wish for your deliberations the full success they deserve in planning ways to closer intercultural understanding among the Americas.

NOTE: The President's message was read by Daniel Arango, former Minister of Education of Colombia, who served as the presiding chairman at the first session of the Council.

17 Letter to the Chairman, House Committee on Ways and Means, Urging Prompt Action on Pending Tax Proposals. *January* 19, 1966

Dear Mr. Chairman:

In my State of the Union Message, I recommended a number of tax changes to help pay for the increased costs associated with the war in Vietnam. I deeply appreciate your swift action in beginning hearings on those measures just one week later.

When I began preparing my budget several weeks ago, Departments and Agencies of this Government initially requested more than $130 billion for fiscal year 1967. I established three principles in my review of those requests:

—Hold all expenditures to a minimum consistent with our defense commitments and other essential programs.

—Eliminate all unnecessary and obsolete activities.

—Conduct essential activities at the lowest possible cost.

As a result, apart from the special cost of Vietnam, I reduced budget expenditures to a level only $600 million above fiscal year 1966.

My proposed expenditures for fiscal year 1967 are $112.8 billion. More than half—$58.3 billion—will be for defense purposes.

Our present estimates for Vietnam will add $10.5 billion to the amount originally estimated for this purpose last January—$4.7 billion to fiscal year 1966 and $5.8 billion to fiscal year 1967.

These expenditures come at a time of unparalleled prosperity.

We have virtually reached our long sought initial goal of 4 percent unemployment. And unemployment will be reduced below 4 percent during the coming year.

In the past five years, consumer income after taxes is up $129 billion; corporate profits have risen an unprecedented 67 percent.

Your Administration's fiscal policy has been the main stimulus for this 59 months of unparalleled prosperity. A further stimulus to keep the economy on its rising path is no longer necessary. The basic economic policy that justified tax cuts in recent years must be set aside until the uncertain but increasingly high demands of hostilities in Vietnam are no longer with us.

The monies that will flow into the Federal Treasury under present tax laws will not be sufficient to maintain the right fiscal balance during the coming year. Without any changes in the tax laws, budget receipts will rise sharply in response to the sustained economic expansion. But they still would be too low to maintain our economic growth and prosperity without running the risk of inflation.

Under these circumstances, I was faced with three choices:

—A deficit in excess of $6.5 billion, which would require the Government to borrow the additional money.

—An increase in corporate and personal income tax rates, or other new taxes.

—Temporary restoration of certain excise taxes, and adoption of graduated withholding of individual income taxes and current payment of corporate income taxes—to put the American people on a pay-as-you-go basis without increasing the total tax bill due.

Over the past several weeks I discussed

these alternatives and countless variations of them with my advisers. I made two decisions.

First, we could raise revenue or borrow it. I chose to raise the money.

Second, I chose to raise that money without any increases in personal and corporate income tax liabilities, but through changes that affect only the timing of tax payments and the temporary restoration of certain excise taxes on telephones and automobiles.

I realize that two of these measures—the graduated withholding proposal and accelerated corporate income tax payments—are measures that will provide increased revenues for the Government on a one-time basis only. But this is precisely why I recommended them.

I believe these measures are preferable to increasing personal or corporate income tax rates or other tax measures, which are not clearly required at this time. For my advisers and I cannot predict how long the Vietnam conflict will last and what the financial needs of your Government will be for Vietnam beyond the next year.

If our needs in Vietnam require additional revenues, I will not hesitate to request them. On the other hand, if our efforts for a peaceful resolution of the Vietnam situation are successful—and those efforts will continue day and night—then your Government's need for revenues will be sharply reduced, thus permitting downward tax revisions as we had following Korea.

These tax changes will:
—Balance the cash budget.
—Reduce the deficit in the Administrative budget to the lowest level in seven years.
—Help to maintain economic growth without the risks of inflation.

I believe that the changes are moderate, equitable, responsible and essential. I hope that your Committee and the Congress will act promptly, if at all possible, so they can reach my desk for signature before March 15 in order that all our taxpayers will have adequate notice and we can thus secure full compliance.

Sincerely,

LYNDON B. JOHNSON

[Honorable Wilbur D. Mills, Chairman, Committee on Ways and Means, House of Representatives, Washington, D.C.]

NOTE: Legislation to carry out the President's tax proposals was enacted by the Tax Adjustment Act of 1966, approved March 15, 1966 (see Item 132).

18 Letter to the Speaker Transmitting Proposed Supplemental Appropriations in Support of Operations in Southeast Asia. *January* 19, 1966

Sir:

I have the honor to transmit herewith for the consideration of the Congress proposed supplemental appropriations for the fiscal year 1966. These appropriations, amounting to $12,760,719,000, are for the Department of Defense and for military and economic assistance primarily in support of our operations in Southeast Asia. They are required to support our growing national activities in helping the people and Government of Vietnam as they face continuing aggression. I also transmit the necessary authorizing legislation.

I urge that Congress act promptly to provide these needed funds.

We are currently engaged in a major effort to open a road to a peaceful settlement.

Whether the present effort is successful or not, our purpose of peace will be constant; we will continue to press on every door.

But until there is a response—and until the aggression ends—we must do all that is necessary to support our allies and our own fighting forces in Vietnam. That is the purpose of the present request.

The bulk of this request—$12.3 billion— is for a military appropriation. These funds will provide for the operations of our men in Vietnam and the weapons, ammunition, ports and airfields which should be available to support them if the aggression continues.

We need about $4 billion of this amount for military expenditures such as ammunition and about $8 billion for items with a "long lead time." Items with long lead time (the time it takes the contractor to make the item once he receives the order) range from about a year for helicopters, to fourteen to eighteen months for jet aircraft like the A-4E "Sky Hawk" and the A-6A "Intruder," and up to three to five years for ships.

We hope the aggression will end; we must be prepared if it does not. This military appropriation request also includes about $200 million which will be applied to military assistance for the forces of South Vietnam and other allies fighting there. This method of appropriation will permit our commanders in Vietnam to simplify and expedite supply operations for all fighting forces there.

An additional sum of $415 million is requested for the Agency for International Development, again primarily for Vietnam. These economic appropriations are for import financing, for rural construction, for port expansion, for refugee relief and for development. They have an equal basic importance with our military effort itself.

On the military side we do what aggression requires. On the economic and social side we work also for the true future of South Vietnam.

In the last two years, in repeated acts of authorization and appropriation, the Congress has provided continuing support for our national decision "to prevent further aggression" in Southeast Asia. The quoted words come from the Joint Resolution of the Congress—Public Law 88-408—approved on August 10, 1964. It is in the letter and the spirit of the Resolution that I request this supplementary appropriation. While that Resolution remains in force, and until its obligations are discharged, we must persevere. I believe the Resolution is right, and I believe the course we follow is necessary. I intend that those who must face danger and death as we follow that course shall be supported. I am confident that the Congress will agree.

This is an opportunity for us to demonstrate once again—to friend and foe alike— that there is no difference between one party and another or between the Congress and the Executive Branch when it comes to effective and sustained support of our fighting men and their allies. Whatever differences there are on other issues, we are as one in support of our men in Vietnam. As I said just one week ago, "Until peace comes, or if it does not come . . . we will give our fighting men what they must have: every gun, every dollar, and every decision—whatever the cost or whatever the challenge." And we will continue to help the people of South Vietnam and our allies in resisting aggression and in protecting the independence of that beleaguered country.

Sincerely,

Lyndon B. Johnson

[The Speaker of the House of Representatives]

NOTE: The following items were made public with the press release containing the text of the President's letter:

1. A bill "To authorize appropriations during the fiscal year 1966 for procurement of aircraft, missiles, naval vessels, and tracked combat vehicles and research, development, test, and evaluation for the Armed Forces and for other purposes."

2. A bill "To authorize certain construction in support of military activities in Southeast Asia, and for other purposes."

3. A bill "To amend further the Foreign Assistance Act of 1961, as amended, and for other purposes" together with a section by section analysis of the bill's provisions.

4. A letter to the President from the Director, Bureau of the Budget, submitting for his consideration and recommending transmittal to the Congress of the proposed supplemental appropriations.

On March 15 the President approved the supplemental military authorization bill (see Item 128) and on March 25 the Supplemental Defense Appropriation Act, 1966 (Public Laws 89–367, 89–374; 80 Stat. 36, 79).

The recommended amendments to the Foreign Assistance Act of 1961 were approved March 18 (Public Law 89–371, 80 Stat. 74).

In his letter the President referred to the joint resolution of Congress of August 10, 1964, "to promote the maintenance of international peace and security in Southeast Asia" (Public Law 88–408, 78 Stat. 384).

19   Remarks at a Ceremony Marking 1966 as the "Year of the Bible." January 19, 1966

Senator Pell, Mr. Nettinga, ladies and gentlemen:

I am deeply grateful to you for coming here to the White House this morning and presenting me with this beautiful Book. It represents the 750 millionth volume of the Scriptures distributed by the American Bible Society in the past 150 years. I accept it on behalf of the millions of Americans who support your great work and who believe in its goals.

The spirit and the purpose which your Society represents are older than America itself. For we can truly be said to have founded our country on the principles of this Book. The Holy Bible was the most important possession that our forebears placed aboard their ships as they embarked for the New World.

So many of our pioneer ancestors often ventured into the wilderness with only three possessions—their rifle, their axe, and their Bible. And of the three, the Bible was by far their greatest personal treasure. For it contained the hope, and the promise, and the inspiration which gave them the necessary courage to keep going.

One hundred years ago, a group of your predecessors presented a Book such as this to Abraham Lincoln. President Lincoln said at that time, and I quote: "In regard to this great Book, I have but to say, it is the best gift that God has given to men. All the good Saviour gave to the world was communicated through this Book. But for it we could not know right from wrong. All things most desirable for man's welfare, here and hereafter, are to be found portrayed in it."

No human accountant can calculate the immense good that your Society has done over the years.

You have been the main source of supply for the Holy Scriptures for the men and women throughout our Armed Forces.

Thanks to you, millions of the underprivileged people in countries throughout the world have had the Word of God placed in their hands. More often than not, it is the first written word that they ever learn to read.

So you have been a source of solace in time

of war—and a force for enlightenment and progress in time of peace.

The time is not far off when some future President will be standing here to receive the one billionth copy of this Book. Let us pray that, by then, the world will be genuinely at peace, and will be peopled by men of good will.

Thank you very much.

NOTE: The President spoke at 11:45 a.m. in the Cabinet Room at the White House. In his opening words he referred to Senator Claiborne Pell of Rhode Island, a vice president of the American Bible Society, who made the presentation, and to the Reverend James Z. Nettinga, secretary of the Society, who was in charge of the 150th anniversary celebration.

The American Bible Society aids in the translation, publication, and distribution of the Bible in some 500 languages in 150 countries.

20   Remarks Upon Presenting the Presidential Unit Citation to the 38th Air Rescue Squadron, USAF. *January* 19, 1966

I TAKE particular pleasure in welcoming to the Cabinet Room the Secretary of the Air Force, Secretary Brown, the Chief of Staff of the Air Force, General McConnell, and the most distinguished representatives of the 38th Air Rescue Squadron.

The 38th Air Rescue Squadron of the United States Air Force has inscribed its name on the honor scroll of American heroes because the men of the 38th have risked their lives so their comrades might live. They join that company of the valiant to whom we all owe our freedom and our national honor.

Time and time again they have reached into the jungle, the mountains, the sea, to rescue other brave men who have been downed in combat. In the face of enemy fire, in almost prohibitive weather, in every terrain, at every hour, they have carried out their missions of mercy. So men live today, carry on freedom's struggle today, and will return to their families tomorrow because the 38th Air Rescue Squadron has lived by its motto—"that others may live."

With this citation we pay a grateful Nation's tribute to that selfless gallantry. The 38th Air Rescue Squadron stands in the finest tradition of service to our great country. Its members have added lustre to that tradition, brightening it with the courage of a new generation of Americans.

Gentlemen, I am very pleased to have you here, and we honor and salute you all.

[*At this point, Secretary of the Air Force Harold Brown read the citation, the text of which follows:*]

PRESIDENTIAL UNIT CITATION

By virtue of the authority vested in me as President of the United States and as Commander in Chief of the Armed Forces of the United States I have today awarded

THE PRESIDENTIAL UNIT CITATION

TO THE 38TH AIR RESCUE SQUADRON

FOR EXTRAORDINARY GALLANTRY

The personnel of the 38th Air Rescue Squadron distinguished themselves by extraordinary gallantry in connection with military operations against an opposing armed force in Southeast Asia from 1 August 1964 to 31 July 1965. They repeatedly jeopardized their own lives by exposing themselves to hostile air and ground fire while flying unarmed aircraft in order to rescue survivors downed in hostile territory.

Their actions have directly resulted in saving the lives of 74 persons during the period reported. The extraordinary heroism displayed by this unit in effecting rescues under the most perilous of circumstances has had a most beneficial effect upon the morale of all who fly over hostile territory in Southeast Asia. By their gallantry and untiring devotion to duty, the personnel of the 38th Air Rescue Squadron have reflected great credit upon themselves and the United States Air Force.

LYNDON B. JOHNSON

The White House
January 19, 1966

NOTE: The President spoke at 1:30 p.m. in the Cabinet Room at the White House.

The Press Secretary to the President stated that four members of the squadron were in the Washington area and that the President was taking advantage of that fact to present to them personally, for the whole squadron, the citation honoring their work in Vietnam.

---

21 Special Message to the Congress Proposing Constitutional Amendments Relating to Terms for House Members and the Electoral College System. *January* 20, 1966

To the Congress of the United States:

In 1816 Thomas Jefferson wrote:

"Some men ascribe to the men of a preceding age a wisdom more than human, and suppose what they did to be beyond amendment. . . . I am certainly not an advocate for frequent and untried changes in laws and constitutions. . . . But I know also, that laws and institutions must go hand in hand with the progress of the human mind."

I believe that in the interest of progress and sound modern government—and to nourish and strengthen our creative Federal system—we must amend our Constitution, to provide a four-year term of office for Members of the House of Representatives.

I believe that for the same reasons we must also eliminate those defects in the Electoral College system which make possible the frustration of the people's will in the election of their President and Vice President.

FOUR-YEAR TERM FOR HOUSE MEMBERS

I.

Debate over the length of the House term is not new. It began in the Constitutional Convention, where those who thought annual elections were essential to freedom clashed with others, such as Madison, who held that three years were required "in a government so extensive, for members to form any knowledge of the various interests of the States to which they did not belong," and that without such knowledge "their trust could not be usefully discharged." Madison's thoughts are ruefully familiar to Members of the House today: he was certain that a one-year term would be "almost consumed in preparing for and traveling to and from the seat of national business," and that even with a two-year term none of the Representatives "who wished to be re-elected would remain at the seat of government."

Between the advocates of a one-year term—those who, bearing in mind recent English experience, feared the despotism of a government unchecked by the popular will—and those who saw a tenure of three years as necessary for wise administration, a compromise of two years was reached.

Thus there was little magic in the number two, even in the year of its adoption. I am convinced there is even less magic today, and that the question of tenure should be re-examined in the light of our needs in the twentieth century.

II.

The authors of the Federalist Papers said about the House of Representatives:

"As it is essential to liberty that the government in general should have a common interest with the people; so it is particularly essential that the branch of it under consideration should have an immediate dependence on, and an intimate sympathy with the people. Frequent elections are unquestionably the only policy by which this dependency and sympathy can be effectually secured. *But what particular degree of frequency may be absolutely necessary for the purpose, does not appear to be susceptible of any precise calculation; and must depend on a variety of circumstances with which it may be connected.*"

The circumstances with which the two-year term is presently connected are—

—*the accelerating volume of legislation* on which Members are required to pass. In the first Congress, 142 bills were introduced, resulting in 108 public laws. In the 88th Congress, 15,299 bills were introduced, of which 666 were enacted into public law.

—*the increasingly complex problems that generate this flood of legislation,* requiring Members to be familiar with an immense range of fact and opinion. It is no longer sufficient to develop solutions for an agricultural nation with few foreign responsibilities; now a man or woman chosen to represent his people in the House of Representatives must understand the consequences of our spiralling population growth, of urbanization, of the new scientific revolution, of our welfare and education requirements, and of our responsibilities as the world's most powerful democracy.

—*longer sessions of Congress,* made necessary by the burden of legislation and outstanding public issues. In less turbulent times, Members of Congress might conduct the public business with dispatch during election years, and spend the summer and autumn campaigning in their districts. Congress adjourned in April of 1904, June of 1906, May of 1908, and June of 1910. But increasing work loads have substantially extended the sessions. Thus it was in August of 1958 that Congress concluded its work, in September of 1960, October of 1962, and again in October of 1964. The competitive pressures imposed by the two-year term, when the incumbent must remain in Washington into the Fall to attend the public business, reduce his capacity to do either task—campaigning or legislating—with the complete attention his conscience and the public interest demand.

—*the increasing costs of campaigning* that biennially impose heavy burdens on those who represent vigorously contested districts, and that magnify the influence of large contributors, pressure groups, and special interest lobbyists.

It may be said that every elected official confronts similar circumstances in the 1960's. Yet it can be said of none that his power for the public good or ill is both so great as the Congressman's, and so sharply pressed in time.

For this public servant—part judge and author of laws, part leader of his people, part mediator between the executive branch and those he represents—is scarcely permitted to take his seat in the historic Hall of the House, when he must begin once more to make his case to his constituency.

The Congressman's effectiveness as a legislator is reduced by this.

His district's right to be fully represented in Congress is diminished by this.

The nation's need to be led by its best qualified men, giving their full attention to issues on which our security and progress depend, is ignored by this.

In the States, in private business, and indeed, in the Federal government itself, the wisdom of longer terms for senior officials has come steadily to be recognized. State after state has adopted a four-year gubernatorial term.

This Administration has made every effort to extend Ambassadorial tours of duty, to promote career civil servants to posts of higher responsibilities, and to retain Cabinet and sub-Cabinet officers on the job for longer periods than before. For we have learned that brief and uncertain periods in office contribute—not to the best interests of democracy—but to harassed inefficiency and the loss of invaluable experience.

III.

Thus I recommend that the Congress adopt this Amendment to the Constitution in the belief that it will—

—*provide for each Member a sufficient period in which he can bring his best judgment to bear on the great questions of national survival, economic growth, and social welfare.*

—*free him from the inexorable pressures of biennial campaigning for re-election.*

—*reduce the cost—financial and political—of holding Congressional office.*

—*attract the best men in private and public life into competition for this high public office.*

I am mindful of the principal reason advanced for maintaining the two-year term—that it is necessary if the voice of the people is to be heard, and changes in public opinion are to be registered on the conduct of public policy. My own experience in almost three decades in public office—and, I believe, the experience of Members of Congress today—is otherwise.

For we do not live in a day when news of Congressional action requires weeks to reach our constituents, nor when public opinion is obscured by time and distance. Communications media rush the news to every home and shop within minutes of its occurrence. Public opinion polls, and mountains of mail, leave little doubt about what our people think of the issues most vital to them. I do not fear deafness on the part of those who will take their seats in Congress for a four-year term.

It is also vital to recognize the effect of a longer term on the authority of the House in making known the will of the people. Established in office for four years, the weight of the House in the councils of government is certain to increase. For the sake of democracy, that is a development devoutly to be welcomed.

IV.

I recommend that the amendment become effective no earlier than 1972.

It is imperative that each Member of the House have the opportunity of campaigning during a Presidential election year. To divide the House into two classes, as some have proposed—one elected during the "off-year," one with the President—would create an unnecessary and wholly unfair division in that Body. It would also create severe problems in every state: as reapportionment is ordered and redistricting takes place.

"Off-year" elections are notorious for attracting far fewer voters—perhaps as much as 15% fewer—than Presidential elections.

If our purpose is to serve the democratic ideal by making the people's House more effective in its performance of the people's business, then we must require that its Members be chosen by the largest electorate our democracy can produce. That, assuredly, is the electorate called into being during a Presidential year.

I do not believe the Congress will wish to make the House the least representative of our three elective elements; by perpetually condemning half its membership to a shrunken electorate. Such a body could not long sustain its claim to be an equal partner in the work of representative government.

V.

If this Amendment is to serve the public interest—if Members are to be free of campaigning for a period sufficiently long to enable them to master the work of the House—it is right that they should remain at that work during the entire term to which they are elected.

It would defeat the purpose of the Amendment, if a Member were free to campaign

for the Senate without resigning his seat in the House. Because we seek to strengthen the House, and through it, representative government—not to provide a sanctuary and platform for further electoral contests—I recommend that no Member of either House be eligible for election as a Member of the other House until his own term has expired, unless, at least 30 days prior to that election, he submits his resignation from the office he holds.

VI.

Our democracy cannot remain static, a prisoner to the past, if it is to enrich the lives of coming generations. Laws and institutions—to paraphrase Jefferson—must go hand in hand with the progress of the human mind, and must respond to the changing conditions of life itself.

One law that should be changed limits the term of office for one of the great arms of our government to a period too brief for the public good.

Let us no longer bind ourselves to it. Let us reform it. We shall better serve our people when we do.

Because I profoundly agree with former President Eisenhower, when he said, "Congressmen ought to be elected for four years, at the same time with the President," I urge the Congress promptly to consider a Constitutional amendment extending the term of office for the House of Representatives to four years.

REFORM OF THE ELECTORAL COLLEGE
SYSTEM

In my special message to the Congress last January, I urged an amendment to the Constitution to reform the Electoral College system. I renew this recommendation and strongly reaffirm the need to reform the Electoral College system.

There are several major defects in the existing system. They should be eliminated in order to assure that the people's will shall not be frustrated in the choice of their President and Vice President.

First, there presently exists the possibility that the constitutional independence of unpledged electors will be exploited, and that their votes will be manipulated in a close presidential race to block the election of a major candidate in order to throw the election into the House of Representatives. This grave risk should be removed.

Second, if the election is thrown into the House of Representatives, the existing system suffers from other fundamental defects. In such an election, the House of Representatives would be empowered to elect a President from the three highest candidates. However, each State casts only one vote, with the result that the least populous States have the same vote in the election of the President as the most populous States.

As early as 1823, Madison reached the conclusion that "the present rule of voting for President by the House of Representatives is so great a departure from the republican principle of numerical equality, and even from the Federal rule, which qualifies the numerical by a State equality, and is so pregnant also, with a mischievous tendency in practice, that an amendment to the Constitution on this point is justly called for by all its considerate and best friends."

I firmly believe that we should put an end to this undemocratic procedure.

Third, if the electoral vote is indecisive under the existing system, the President is elected by the House of Representatives, but the Vice President is elected by the Senate. This creates the possibility of the election of

a President and a Vice President from different parties. That possibility should not exist. To prevent its realization, the President and the Vice President should both be elected by the same body.

Fourth, the Twenty-third Amendment makes no provision for participation by the District of Columbia in an election of the President by the House of Representatives, or of the Vice President by the Senate.

I firmly believe that we should extend to the District of Columbia all the rights of participation in the election of a President and Vice President which the 50 States may exercise.

Fifth, existing law fails to provide for the death of the President-elect or Vice President-elect between election day and the counting of the electoral votes in December. There is also no provision in the Constitution to cover the contingency presented by the death of a candidate for President or Vice President shortly before the popular election in November. These gaps should now be filled.

Elimination of these defects in our Constitution are long overdue. Our concepts of self-government and sound government require it.

Congress can now, in the words of Daniel Webster, "perform something worthy to be remembered," by uprooting the more objectionable features in the system of electing a President and Vice President, and thereby helping to preserve representative government and the two-party system.

LYNDON B. JOHNSON

The White House
January 20, 1966

NOTE: The text of a joint resolution "Proposing an amendment to the Constitution of the United States providing that the term of office of Members of the House of Representatives shall be four years" was made public with the President's message and is printed in House Document 364 (89th Cong., 2d sess.).

For the President's special message to Congress on January 28, 1965, urging a reform of the electoral college system, see 1965 volume, this series, Book I, Item 34.

22 Remarks in Independence, Mo., at a Ceremony in Connection With the Establishment of the Harry S. Truman Center for the Advancement of Peace. *January 20, 1966*

President Truman, Mrs. Truman, Mr. Chief Justice, Senator Symington, Senator Long, Members of the Missouri delegation in the Congress of the United States, Senator Anderson, Congressman Boggs, ladies and gentlemen:

I come back to Independence to be with one of the world's most persistent searchers for peace in the world. It is quite fitting that this day is set aside for the announcement of the Harry S. Truman Center for the Advancement of Peace in the world.

I first want to congratulate the men here today whose generous public spirit is making this Center possible.

I take my text from the words which President Truman spoke just 17 years ago in his inaugural address of January 20, 1949.

"We must embark," he said, "on a bold new program for making the benefits of our scientific advances and industrial progress available for the improvement and the growth of underdeveloped areas in the world."

This was, as we know now, point 4. It was a bold and vital idea then, and it is just as bold and just as much alive as we meet here this afternoon.

The initial point 4 program of technical assistance was enacted in 1949 and has continued from that day to this. Congress after Congress has continued to appropriate to that program—with growing confidence—sums which now, I believe, add up to more than $3 billion. American experts have traveled the globe to every continent, bringing their skills to the worldwide war against ignorance, and against hunger, and against disease.

And to measure the success of this effort we have only to ask: What would the world be like today if President Truman had not launched this program?

In this year 1966, I am proposing, on behalf of our Nation, a major new effort in this same field that he began so long ago, and I am proud to add to the point 4 of President Truman, the fourth principle of this year's State of the Union speech: "to help improve the life of man."

How will we help improve the life of man?

First, we propose a radical increase in our response to the needs of international education. There can be no decent life for any man or any people without education.

The International Education Act of 1966 will help build partnerships between American and foreign schools.

It will recruit teachers for overseas work.

It will make possible long-term commitments by American universities toward solving the problems of international education.

It will launch a series of projects to attack illiteracy and to find new ways to teach basic skills. It will begin to provide for an Exchange Peace Corps to bring able young people from other countries to live and work here with us.

41

Second, we are going to enlarge our work for world health. And the twin of the International Education Act will be the International Health Act of 1966.

And with that act we will strike at disease by establishing an international medical mission in our Public Health Service.

We plan to triple our effort to train medical manpower in the developing countries.

We plan to double the size of our nutrition program for mothers and for children. We plan to increase by 80 million those who will receive adequate diets.

We plan to set targets and to develop programs so in the next decade we can completely wipe out smallpox in the entire world. We can eliminate malaria in this hemisphere and large parts of Africa and Asia. We can end yellow fever in this hemisphere, and we can find new controls for cholera, rabies, and other epidemic diseases.

Third, we will launch a major new attack on worldwide hunger. We will present this year a new food aid program, designed around the principle of intense cooperation with those in all hungry countries who are ready to help themselves. We will direct our assistance program toward a cooperative effort to increase agricultural production. We will ask the countries which we help to make the necessary land reforms—to modernize marketing and distribution—to invest greater energy and resources in their own food production.

And in return, we will triple our assistance to investments in the powerful weapons of modern agriculture—from fertilizer to machinery we will direct the efforts of our agricultural scientists to the special problems of the developing countries—to the development of new foods and concentrates. We will call for an international effort, including institutions like the World Bank, to expand the world's supply of fertilizer.

Fourth, we will increase our efforts in the great field of human population. The hungry world cannot be fed until and unless the growth in its resources and the growth in its population come into balance. Each man and woman—and each nation—must make decisions of conscience and policy in the face of this great problem. But the position of the United States of America is clear. We will give our help and our support to nations which make their own decision to insure an effective balance between the numbers of their people and the food they have to eat. And we will push forward the frontiers of research in this important field.

Fifth, the underlying principle of all of our work with other nations will always be the principle of cooperation. We will work with those who are willing to work with us for their own progress, in the spirit of peace and in the spirit of understanding.

And while we work for peaceful progress, we will maintain our strength against aggression. Nothing is more false than the timid complaint that we cannot defend ourselves against the aggressor and at the same time make progress in the works of peace. A celebration which unites the United States is a fit time to reaffirm that energy in the defense of freedom and that energy and progress in the building of a free society and it should be the common objective of any free people, large or small.

Now this is the central necessity today of the brave people with whom we are associated in South Vietnam. Just this week, the Prime Minister of Vietnam has pledged his country to this necessity. He has spoken for progress in rural education, in housing, in land reform, and above all, of the need for progress in social revolution and in the building of democracy—by constitutional process and by free elections. All this he has said in the shadow of continuing aggression from the North. In all this he will have the full support of the United States of America.

And so, President Truman, as we dedicate today in your honor the Harry S. Truman Center for the Advancement of Peace, we recall the vision that you gave us to follow when you gave your farewell address, and I quote:

"I have a deep and abiding faith in the destiny of free men. With patience and courage we shall some day move on to a new era—a wonderful golden age—an age when we can use the peaceful tools that science has forged for us to do away with poverty and human misery everywhere on earth."

That is still our goal, President Truman. And now we are today redoubling our efforts to achieve it.

Today I informed President Truman of our worldwide efforts to move the violence of Southeast Asia to the table of peaceful discussions. I received a report this morning before I left Washington from Secretary Rusk and Ambassador Harriman on their recent travels. I shall be meeting with the Secretary and the Ambassador again later this afternoon. Both the Secretary and the Ambassador told me that in all the capitals they visited—and Ambassador Harriman went to almost a dozen—government leaders recognized the United States' genuine desire for peace in the world.

And of this one thing I am sure, the door of peace must be kept wide open for all who wish to avoid the scourge of war. But the door of aggression must be closed and bolted if man himself is to survive.

It is tragic that in the 1960's there are still those who would engulf their neighbors by force, still those who require that vast resources be used to guard the peace rather than to bring all the people in the world the wonders that are really within their grasp.

The central purpose of the American people is a peace which permits all men to remain free. But we must do more. We must work, and we must build upon the solid foundations, as the Chief Justice said, of law among nations. And this is America's determination, and this is America's commitment.

Now let me leave this one last thought with you. I think every schoolboy knows that peace is not unilateral—it takes more than one to sign an agreement. And it seems clear to all that what is holding up peace in the world today is not the United States of America. What is holding back the peace is the mistaken view on the part of the aggressors that we are going to give up our principles, that we may yield to pressure, or abandon our allies, or finally get tired and get out. On the day that others decide to substitute reason for terror, when they will use the pen instead of the hand grenade, when they will replace rational logic for inflammatory invective, then on that very day, the journey toward peace can really begin.

If the aggressors are ready for peace, if they are ready for a return to a decent respect for their neighbors, ready to understand where their hopeful future really lies, let them come to the meeting place and we will meet them there.

Here in the presence today of the great man who was the 33d President of the United States, who labored so long and so valiantly to bring serenity to a troubled world, the 36th President of the United States speaks with the voice of 190 million Americans: We want a peace with honor and with justice that will endure!

Now, President Truman, there is one more bit of business that I would like to take care of so long as I have come out here to Independence. I was here not long ago in connection with a little project that you inaugurated two decades ago, but when the fellows last night in the Social Security office learned that I was coming out here again to see you and Mrs. Truman today, they asked me to bring along your new Medicare card.

And it is now my great pleasure to present here, in the presence of these distinguished friends of yours, and many of the young men of yesteryear who fought these battles with you, to bring Card No. 1 for you, and Card No. 2 for Mrs. Truman.

They told me, President Truman, that if you wished to get the voluntary medical insurance that you will have to sign this application form, and they asked me to sign as your witness. So you are getting special treatment since cards won't go out to the other folks until the end of this month. But we wanted you to know, and we wanted the entire world to know that we haven't forgotten who is the real daddy of Medicare. And because of the fight that you started many years ago, 19 million Americans will

be eligible to receive new hope and new security when the program begins on July 1, and 19 million Americans have another reason, another cause to bless Harry S. Truman.

Again, I want to thank all of you who made this great day possible.

NOTE: The President spoke at 11:15 a.m. at the Harry S. Truman Library in Independence, Mo., at a ceremony in connection with the establishment of the Harry S. Truman Center for the Advancement of Peace at the Hebrew University in Jerusalem. In his opening words he referred to former President and Mrs. Truman, Chief Justice of the United States Earl Warren, Senator Stuart Symington of Missouri, Senator Edward V. Long of Missouri, Senator Clinton P. Anderson of New Mexico, and Representative Hale Boggs of Louisiana. During his remarks the President referred to Secretary of State Dean Rusk and Ambassador at Large W. Averell Harriman.

The International Education Act of 1966 was approved by the President on October 29, 1966 (see Item 557). The proposed International Health Act of 1966 was not adopted by the 89th Congress.

For President Truman's inaugural address of January 20, 1949, see "Public Papers of the Presidents, Harry S. Truman, 1949," Item 19.

For the remarks of the President and Mr. Truman on July 30, 1965, at the signing in Independence of the Medicare bill, see 1965 volume, this series, Book II, Item 394.

23 Reply to a Letter From a Group of House Members Relating to the Situation in Vietnam. *January 22, 1966*

Dear Mr. Congressman:

I am responding to you as the first in alphabetical order of those Members of the House who have written to me under date of January 21 on the search for peace in Vietnam. I hope you will share this answer with your co-signers.

I am grateful for your strong support of our effort to move the war in Vietnam to the conference table. This support is a real encouragement, coupled as it is with the equally strong support of our determination to meet our commitments in Vietnam.

I share your interest in effective action

through the United Nations, and I want you to know that there is no part of this whole problem to which we give closer attention. I have reviewed this matter many times with Ambassador Goldberg, and we have repeatedly considered the suggestion you offer. You can be assured that he and I are firmly determined to make every possible use of the United Nations in moving toward peace, and toward an effective ceasefire as part of that purpose.

Unfortunately, you are correct in your statement that the response from the other side has not been encouraging. The evidence available to this government indicates only continuing hostility and aggressiveness in Hanoi and an insistence on the abandonment of South Vietnam to Communist takeover. We are making no hasty assumptions of any sort, but it is quite another matter to close our eyes to the heavy weight of evidence which has accumulated during the last month.

I can give you categorical assurance that there will be no abandonment of our peace efforts. Even though it is increasingly clear that we have had only a hostile response to the present pause in bombing North Vietnam, you can be sure that our unflagging pursuit of peace will continue. As I said this week in a letter to Speaker McCormack, "Whether the present effort is successful or not, our purpose of peace will be constant; we will continue to press on every door."

And at the same time, I am confident that as elected representatives of the American people, you will share my determination that our fighting forces in Vietnam shall be sustained and supported "by every dollar and every gun and every decision" that they must have—"whatever the cost and whatever the challenge." For a month we have held our hand in an important area of military action. But the infiltration of the aggressor's forces has continued, and so have his attacks on our allies and on our own men. I am sure you will agree that we have a heavy obligation not to add lightly to the dangers our troops must face. We must give them the support they need in fulfillment of the commitment so accurately stated in your letter—"the determination of our Government to resist the terror and aggression which deny the people of South Vietnam the right freely to determine their own future."

Sincerely,

LYNDON B. JOHNSON

[Honorable Brock Adams, House of Representatives, Washington, D.C.]

NOTE: The letter to which the President replied, signed by 77 Members of the House of Representatives, is printed in the Congressional Record of January 24, 1966 (p. 844).

For the President's reply to a similar letter signed by 15 Senators, see Item 36

24 Message to Prime Minister Menzies of Australia Upon Learning of His Decision To Retire. *January 24, 1966*

[Released January 24, 1966. Dated January 19, 1966]

IT IS with mixed feelings of regret and understanding that I have learned of your decision to retire from active public life. I say regret because I have deeply valued your friendship, your understanding, and your support on a range of world issues and, in particular, in connection with the struggle to defend the Republic of Vietnam against Communist aggression and subversion. I say understanding because after 19 years of distinguished service as Prime Minister of Australia and a lifetime spent in vigorously supporting and defending democratic ideals in your own country, in the British Commonwealth, and in the world, you have fully established your right to a period of rest and contemplation. I will miss your wisdom and sturdy good sense. With cordial best wishes,

LYNDON B. JOHNSON

25 Remarks Upon Signing the Budget Message for Fiscal Year 1967. *January 24, 1966*

Director Schultze, Deputy Elmer Staats, dedicated members of the Budget Bureau, my friends:

We are pleased to come here this morning to sign and submit to the Congress the budget that we are sending up today. We have worked, with your help and advice, for many weeks and months now in an attempt to make this a responsible budget, and a prudent budget, and a reasonable budget that is in keeping with the times in which we live.

I think the budget is responsible because it reflects the needs and aspirations of our people. I think it launches and reinforces some of the most exciting and beneficial American programs that we have known, particularly in the field of human development—health and education.

I think it is a prudent budget because it was conceived within the framework of commonsense economy and as much efficiency as we could obtain in the Federal Government—under at least our management.

We have tried since the beginning of this fiscal year to get the managers of our Government to reduce expenditures wherever they possibly could, to eliminate what we thought could be termed "fat" programs that were obsolete or outmoded. And we have done that to a point where, with the exception of Vietnam, our budget this next year will be increased by 600 million over the budget last year.

Now in order to do that we had to—by eliminating programs, by reducing expenditures, by sale of assets and other means—cut 4 billion 700 million out of the budget.

And I said to most of my Cabinet officers several times that you people over here wanted me to say to them—before we passed

on how many new dollars they could get for new programs—to be able to tell us how many old dollars they were saving from the elimination of old programs.

So in short, it came up that they eliminated 4 billion 700 million. But when we started passing it out we had to go further than that; we passed out 5 billion 3—600 million more than last year. Unfortunately, 700 million of that is in interest payments, or we would be actually under last year.

So that is what we are hoping at the end of the year our figures will reflect. We think they will be judged by our fellow man and our fellow citizen as reasonable. We think that they will meet the test of fiscal responsibility. We think that they reflect that we realize that these are somber and uncertain times.

And we know that if our problems in Vietnam can be solved, that we can take some of the funds that we necessarily must spend there in defending our freedom and stopping aggression and put on programs for human advancement.

Now as I sign this budget today, it reflects what the Budget Director, the Deputy Director, and members of what I consider one of the most outstanding and dedicated staffs in all the Government—it reflects what we believe is a realistic and honest assessment of our needs.

When I sent the budget to the Congress last year, I estimated we would have a deficit of something over 5 billion. Actually, it looks like now, with 5 months yet to go, that we will have a deficit of over 6 billion. So it will be up a little over a billion dollars. I hope that I'm wrong. I hope it comes down between now and June and maybe we will hit it close to right on the nose.

But what we are putting in this budget here is what we think is realistic, and we are going to try to do everything we can to stay within our estimates and make our dreams come true. If we do, we think that they will be approved by the American people and be rewarded.

In any event, I wanted you to know that this is the third budget I have presented. Each time, I marvel at the energy, the dedication, the imagination, and the uncomplaining hard work that the employees of the Budget Bureau give to their country and give to their Government.

You people have a passion for anonymity. The spotlight rarely shines on you. But today, I want it to shine on you, and I came here to tell you that on behalf of the American people, the Congress, the other branches of the Government, that we respect you and we recognize the many sacrifices you have made to bring about this final result.

Also, I want to perform a little act, as requested by Mr. Schultze, this morning. I want to recognize one man in the Budget Bureau who for 34 years has made a very tremendous individual contribution to the budget. His name is William F. McCandless. He has added to the quality of his Government by giving all of his adult life to public service. As Assistant Director of the Budget his achievements in budgeting have left a very enduring mark on the executive branch of the Federal Government. He has served now five Presidents. He has

served with eleven Budget Directors, and he has served all of them with great energy and with great fidelity. He has served them without regard to political party or to political power.

So today, Mr. McCandless, in the presence of your wife, Irene, and your daughter, Susan, I want to bring you the President's Award for Distinguished Federal Civilian Service to your country. And, through you, I especially want to thank the other men and women who have worked with you and helped to enlarge the strength and knowledge of their Nation, and thank those whose skills and spirit have produced a responsible and, as I said, a prudent, and what I believe will be judged as a reasonable budget for all the citizens of the United States and the Government of the United States.

Thank you.

NOTE: The President spoke at 11:34 a.m. in the Indian Treaty Room at the Executive Office Building. In his opening words he referred to Charles L. Schultze, Director of the Bureau of the Budget, and Elmer B. Staats, Deputy Director. During his remarks he referred to William F. McCandless, Assistant Director for Budget Review.

The citation accompanying Mr. McCandless' award follows:

"With extraordinary effectiveness he has served five Presidents in the annual development of the Federal Budget—its formulation, its interpretation to Congress and the public, and its administration. He has made the Budget a constructive force in Government management.

"His achievements, his authoritative knowledge, his wisdom, and his integrity have been of utmost benefit to the Government and the people."

For the budget message, see Item 26.

26   Annual Budget Message to the Congress, Fiscal Year 1967. *January 24, 1966*

To the Congress of the United States:

With this message I transmit to you today the budget of the United States of America for the fiscal year 1967.

A budget is not simply a schedule of financial accounts.

It is a program for action.

The program of the Federal Government

which this budget recommends is grounded on these fundamental premises:

- In international affairs we are determined to seek peace with every means at our command
    —but we are fully prepared to meet the costs of opposing aggression.
- In domestic affairs we are determined to press confidently forward toward the Great Society
    —but we shall do so in an orderly and responsible way, and at a pace which reflects the claims of our commitments in Southeast Asia upon the Nation's resources.

The budget for 1967 bears the strong imprint of the troubled world we live in.

It provides the funds we now foresee as necessary to meet our commitments in Southeast Asia. If our efforts to secure an honorable peace bear fruit, these funds need not be spent. Yet it would be folly to present a budget which inadequately provided for the military and economic costs of sustaining our forces in Vietnam. And those costs are substantial.

In this setting I have sought to frame a balanced program.

- We are a rich nation and can afford to make progress at home while meeting obligations abroad—in fact, we can afford no other course if we are to remain strong. For this reason, I have not halted progress in the new and vital Great Society programs in order to finance the costs of our efforts in Southeast Asia.
- But even a prosperous nation cannot meet all its goals all at once. For this reason, the rate of advance in the new programs has been held below what might have been proposed in less troubled times, many older and lower priority activities have been reduced or eliminated, and economies have

been sought in every operation of the Government.

- At the same time, I want to insure that the necessary increase in budget expenditures is so financed as to promote economic stability. For this reason, I am proposing several tax measures designed to increase Federal revenues.

With this balanced program we can:

- Meet our international responsibilities with firmness.
- Maintain continued prosperity and economic stability at home.
- Raise the productivity, earnings, and living standards of our poorer citizens.
- Improve the quality of life for all citizens.
- Preserve and protect our national resources for the generations to come.

And we can achieve these ends without unduly straining our economic resources or impairing our steady economic expansion.

THE BUDGET AND ECONOMIC GROWTH

The unprecedented and uninterrupted economic growth of the past 5 years has clearly demonstrated the contribution that appropriate fiscal action can make to national prosperity. Aided by the judicious use of tax and expenditure policy, the Nation continues to benefit from the longest period of sustained economic growth since the end of World War II.

With proper policies, this growth will extend through the current calendar year and beyond. In calendar year 1966, the Nation's output of goods and services—the gross national product—is expected to grow by $46 billion over 1965, reaching $722 billion, plus or minus $5 billion. This increase will follow on the heels of last year's healthy growth, when the real gross national product advanced by 5½%.

During that year:

- Nearly 2½ million additional jobs were created.
- Countless new and previously idle plants and machines were drawn into productive use.
- Consumer and business incomes reached record levels.
- The unemployment rate fell to 4.1%, the lowest in more than 8 years.

A growing economy provides rising Federal revenues and expanding economic resources both for meeting our military and international commitments and for moving closer to our Great Society goals. But this does not relieve us of the obligation to weigh expenditure decisions carefully and carry them out efficiently. Inflation need not be the price of social progress; nor should it be a cost of defending freedom.

Our fiscal and monetary policies must also be designed to help reduce further the balance of payments deficit. During the past calendar year, the deficit declined by more than half from the preceding year. Private banks and other businesses contributed significantly in a variety of ways through voluntary programs announced last February. In addition, the Federal Government has been eliminating or reducing payments abroad wherever possible and consistent with essential program requirements. We will continue these efforts.

FISCAL PROGRAM

This budget presents a responsible fiscal program. It accommodates our foreign and domestic responsibilities in an environment of strong but noninflationary economic growth.

The 1967 fiscal program consists of the following elements:

First, apart from the special costs of operations in Southeast Asia, increases in Federal *expenditures* for high priority Great Society programs and for unavoidable workload growth have been largely offset by reductions in lower priority programs, management improvements, and other measures. As a consequence, total *regular* administrative budget expenditures—i.e., outside of special Vietnam costs—rise by only $0.6 billion between 1966 and 1967—and this increase is virtually the same amount as the congressional additions to my 1965 pay proposals for military and civilian employees.

Second, I propose to supplement the expansion of Federal *revenues* which is a consequence of economic growth by a series of tax measures which will yield $1.2 billion in fiscal year 1966 and $4.8 billion in 1967:

- A plan for improving the pay-as-you-go effectiveness of the withholding system on personal income taxes.
- A corresponding plan to accelerate the transition of corporate income tax payments to a full pay-as-you-go basis.
- A temporary reinstatement of the excise taxes on passenger automobiles and telephone service which were reduced at the beginning of this calendar year and deferral of the further reductions scheduled in the future.

Third, the combined increase in revenues from economic growth and from my tax proposals will amount to $11.0 billion in 1967. This is substantially larger than the growth in administrative budget expenditures. In fact, it virtually covers the total special costs of operations in Vietnam as well as the small increase in regular budget expenditures from 1966 to 1967.

Fourth, as a consequence, the overall 1967 deficit in the administrative budget is $1.8 billion, sharply lower than in 1966 and the smallest deficit in 7 years, despite the added

49

costs we are incurring in Southeast Asia.

Fifth, on a consolidated cash basis—which is the most comprehensive measure of budget totals—the 1967 budget will show a surplus of $0.5 billion.

No one can firmly predict the course of events in Southeast Asia. They depend not only upon our own actions but upon those of our adversaries. As a consequence, ultimate budgetary requirements could be either higher or lower than amounts I am now requesting. Prior experience shows that such estimates are extremely difficult to make. During the Korean war, for example, actual military expenditures fell substantially below the original budget estimate. The amounts which I am presenting here reflect the best judgment which can be made at this point in time.

Because of the uncertainties inherent in this situation, the 1967 budget is designed to provide flexibility of response to changing conditions. In the new programs authorized by Congress in the last several years, we have an effective array of weapons to attack the major domestic problems confronting the American people—in the fields of health, education, poverty, housing, community development, and beautification. The 1967 budget provides funds to press forward vigorously with these new programs. But because of the costs of maintaining our commitment in Vietnam, those funds are, in many cases, less than the maximum authorized in the enabling legislation. Should our efforts to find peace in Vietnam prevail, we can rapidly adjust the budget to make even faster progress in the use of these new programs for the solution of our domestic problems.

If, on the other hand, events in Southeast Asia so develop that additional funds are required, I will not hesitate to request the necessary sums. And should that contingency arise, or should unforeseen inflationary pressures develop, I will propose such fiscal actions as are appropriate to maintain economic stability.

BUDGET SUMMARY

Administrative budget.—Administrative budget expenditures in the fiscal year 1967 are estimated at $112.8 billion, an increase of $6.4 billion over 1966. Apart from the special military and economic assistance costs in Vietnam, expenditures for the *regular* programs of the Federal Government in 1967 are estimated at $102.3 billion, a rise of $0.6 billion from 1966, only six-tenths of one percent.

Administrative budget receipts are also expected to increase in 1967, to $111.0 billion. Of the $11.0 billion increase over 1966, $3.6 billion results from the tax measures I am proposing. Most of the remainder results from the sound and orderly economic growth expected for calendar year 1966.

Excluding both special Vietnam costs and the recommended tax measures, the 1967 administrative budget could have been in surplus. When I urged the Congress to enact the Revenue Act of 1964, I stated that the growth in economic activity yielded by the tax reduction, in combination with economy and efficiency in Government expenditures, would lead to a balanced budget in a prosperous economy. Barring the then unforeseen costs we are incurring in Southeast Asia, that forecast remains a correct one.

Consolidated cash statement.—The administrative budget does not include a number of important Federal activities which are financed through trust funds, such as social security, medical care for the aged, and aid for highway construction. A more complete measure of the Government's finances is the consolidated cash budget which covers all of the Government's programs and transactions with the public.

Total payments to the public on the consolidated cash basis are estimated at $145.0 billion in fiscal year 1967, an increase of $10.0 billion over 1966. Excluding special Vietnam costs, cash payments are estimated to rise by $4.2 billion in 1967, primarily because of the recently enacted hospital and medical insurance programs for the aged which begin in 1967 and are being financed in large part by special taxes.

Total receipts from the public are estimated to be $145.5 billion in 1967, an increase of $17.4 billion over 1966. Of the total in 1967, $6.5 billion represents the yield from special trust fund taxes that were recently enacted or are proposed in this budget.

Federal sector, national income accounts.—A third measure of Federal finance is based on the national income accounts. This concept is designed to indicate the direct impact of Federal fiscal activity on the economy. In this set of accounts, Federal

SUMMARY OF FEDERAL RECEIPTS AND PAYMENTS

[Fiscal years. In billions]

Description	1965 actual	1966 estimate	1967 estimate
FEDERAL RECEIPTS			
Administrative budget receipts......................................	$93.1	$100.0	$111.0
Trust fund receipts..	31.0	33.5	41.6
Deduct: Intragovernmental transactions and other adjustments..........	4.4	5.4	7.1
Total cash receipts from the public.............................	119.7	128.2	145.5
Deduct: Loans, differences in coverage, and other adjustments...........	1.0	.6	.7
Add: Cash to accrual basis and other adjustments......................	.9	1.2	—2.6
National income account receipts—Federal sector.................	119.6	128.8	142.2
FEDERAL PAYMENTS			
Administrative budget expenditures..............................	96.5	106.4	112.8
Excluding special Vietnam costs....................................	*(96.4)*	*(101.7)*	*(102.3)*
Trust fund expenditures (including Government-sponsored enterprises)....	29.6	33.8	37.9
Deduct: Intragovernmental transactions and other adjustments..........	3.7	5.2	5.7
Total cash payments to the public.............................	122.4	135.0	145.0
Excluding special Vietnam costs...................................	*(122.3)*	*(130.3)*	*(134.5)*
Deduct: Loans, differences in coverage, and other adjustments...........	5.8	4.0	1.6
Add: Cash to accrual basis and other adjustments......................	1.7	....	—.7
National income account expenditures—Federal sector............	118.3	131.0	142.7
Excluding special Vietnam costs.................................	*(118.2)*	*(126.3)*	*(132.2)*

EXCESS OF RECEIPTS (+) OR PAYMENTS (−)

	1965 actual	1966 estimate	1967 estimate
Including special Vietnam costs:			
Administrative budget..	—3.4	—6.4	—1.8
Receipts from and payments to the public..........................	—2.7	—6.9	+.5
National income accounts—Federal sector.........................	+1.2	—2.2	—.5

receipts and expenditures, including trust fund transactions, are generally estimated on an accrual rather than a cash basis. In addition, purely financial transactions are excluded because they do not directly result in current output and income. Total Federal sector receipts and expenditures are estimated to show a deficit of $2.2 billion in 1966 and $0.5 billion in 1967.

FEDERAL REVENUES

Since 1962, private demands for investment and consumption have been stimulated by several major tax revisions. The stimulus resulting from these tax changes has been the single strongest contributor to 5 full years of sustained economic growth. In the current year, private wage earners and investors are benefiting from tax reductions totaling $20 billion as a result of:

- The Revenue Act of 1962, highlighting an investment tax credit for business.
- Liberalized depreciation allowances.
- The Revenue Act of 1964, providing a record cut in personal and corporate income tax rates.
- The Excise Tax Act of 1965, authorizing a broad program to abolish most Federal excise taxes and reduce others.

Despite this massive tax reduction, administrative budget receipts under existing legislation are estimated to be about $21 billion greater in 1966 than they were 5 years earlier in 1961. This increase is more than double the increase during the previous 5 years, when there were no significant tax cuts. Thus, we have a clear illustration of the direct relationship between tax policies, economic growth, and Federal revenues.

Tax policy, however, must be used flexibly. We must be equally prepared to employ it in restraint of an overly rapid economic expansion as we were to use it as a stimulus to a lagging economy.

The current situation calls for a modest measure of fiscal restraint. As a consequence, I am recommending a tax program which consists primarily of desirable reforms in tax collection procedures, having the effect of increasing revenues in the current and coming year. In addition, I am proposing the deferral of certain scheduled excise tax reductions.

Larger corporations are beginning the third step of a seven-stage transition to a full pay-as-you-go system for corporate income taxes by 1970. I propose that this transition be accelerated this year and completed in 1967 to produce increased corporate tax collections of $1.0 billion and $3.2 billion, respectively.

Similarly, higher income individuals now find that withheld taxes under the existing flat-rate system fail to cover the full tax liability at the end of the year. Establishment of a graduated withholding system will increase tax collections by $0.1 billion in fiscal 1966 and $0.4 billion in 1967, without a change in total personal tax liabilities.

In the case of the self-employment social security tax, individuals may now elect to make payments annually instead of quarterly. By requiring these payments to be made quarterly, trust fund receipts will be increased by $0.1 billion in both fiscal 1966 and fiscal 1967.

Together, these three changes in collection procedure will put higher income individuals and corporations closer to the full pay-as-you-go schedules which now apply to moderate and lower income wage earners.

However, it is desirable that the economic impact of these three collection speedup reforms should be supplemented by temporarily rescinding reductions in excise tax rates on automobiles and telephone service which took effect in January of this year and

RECEIPTS FROM THE PUBLIC

[Fiscal years. In billions]

Source	1965 actual	1966 estimate	1967 estimate
Administrative budget receipts:			
Individual income taxes...	$48.8	$51.4	$56.2
Corporation income taxes......................................	25.5	29.7	34.4
Excise taxes...	10.9	9.2	8.9
Other...	7.9	9.7	11.5
Total administrative budget receipts..........................	93.1	100.0	111.0
Trust fund receipts:			
Employment taxes......	16.9	18.8	24.3
Deposits by States, unemployment insurance........................	3.1	2.9	2.9
Excise taxes...	3.7	3.9	4.4
Federal employees retirement system..............................	2.2	2.2	2.2
Interest on trust fund investments................................	1.8	1.8	2.0
Veterans life insurance premiums.................................	.5	.5	.5
Other...	3.0	3.4	5.3
Total trust fund receipts.....................................	31.0	33.5	41.6
Intragovernmental transactions and other adjustments (deduct)..........	4.4	5.4	7.1
Total receipts from the public.................................	119.7	128.2	145.5

by postponing the reductions in rates on these items now scheduled to take place in the future. Together these temporary tax measures will yield $0.1 billion in 1966 and $1.2 billion in 1967.

An increase in the payroll tax rate and wage base to finance higher social security benefits and the new hospital insurance programs took effect on January 1, 1966. A further increase in the rate will occur on January 1, 1967, under existing law. These increases are expected to provide additional trust fund receipts of $1.5 billion in fiscal year 1966 and $6.2 billion in 1967.

The nature of many government services is such that they should be provided without any charge or with only a nominal charge. However, in certain cases when a Government program provides special benefits or privileges to specific, identifiable individuals or businesses, appropriate user charges should be initiated. To this end, legislation will be proposed when necessary, and equitable user charges will be instituted administratively where authority exists to do so.

This budget proposes a number of new or increased charges, the largest of which are in the transportation field. I again urge the Congress to enact legislation so that the primary beneficiaries will defray a larger part of the costs incurred by the Federal Government in providing transportation facilities and services to these beneficiaries.

Increased highway user charges are essential for completing the Interstate Highway System on a pay-as-you-go basis and for financing certain additional activities of importance to highway travelers, such as safety programs.

The users of the airways bear substantially less than the full cost of the Government investments and services upon which they rely.

53

Accordingly, I am recommending an increase in the passenger ticket tax, increased taxes on fuels used by general aviation, and a new tax on air freight. Receipts from the fuel tax on general aviation which now go into the highway trust fund should be retained in the general fund.

The facilities of the inland waterways system, which have been improved steadily by the Federal Government, presently are available to general and commercial users free of charge. I propose that they meet a portion of the cost of the system through a fuel tax.

NEW OBLIGATIONAL AUTHORITY

The recommendations in this budget will require $121.9 billion in new obligational authority for fiscal year 1967 in the administrative budget. The special costs of Vietnam represent $9.1 billion of this amount.

Of total new obligational authority:
- $106.3 billion requires action by the Congress this year.
- $15.6 billion represents permanent authorizations not requiring further congressional action; the largest of these is for interest on the public debt.

In addition to the new obligational authority required for the administrative budget, $42.6 billion will be available for the trust funds in 1967, an increase of $7.5 billion from the estimate for 1966. Most of this is in the form of automatically appropriated revenues from special taxes.

The total recommended for 1967 in the administrative budget is $4.1 billion below the estimate for 1966. Most of this decrease—$3.5 billion—is in the Department of Defense (including military assistance), reflecting the large supplemental appropriations requested for 1966 for financing special Southeast Asia costs.

New obligational authority in 1967 for all other agencies has been held at or below the 1966 levels wherever possible. The total estimated decline of $0.6 billion includes a number of significant changes in the authority requested for individual agencies and programs.

Major decreases other than for the Department of Defense are:
- $1.8 billion for the Department of Agriculture.
- $163 million for the National Aeronautics and Space Administration.
- $110 million for the Federal Aviation Agency.
- $103 million for the Atomic Energy Commission.

Major increases are:
- $1.4 billion for the Department of Health, Education, and Welfare.
- $750 million for interest on the public

NEW OBLIGATIONAL AUTHORITY

[Fiscal years. In billions]

Description	1965 actual	1966 estimate	1967 estimate
Total authorizations requiring current action by Congress:			
Administrative budget funds	$93.6	$111.6	$106.3
Trust funds	1.6	.6	1.7
Total authorizations not requiring current action by Congress:			
Administrative budget funds	13.1	14.4	15.6
Trust funds	30.4	34.4	40.9
Total new obligational authority:			
Administrative budget funds	106.6	126.0	121.9
Trust funds	32.0	35.0	42.6

debt.

- $316 million for the Office of Economic Opportunity.

The administrative budget estimate for fiscal year 1966 includes a recommended $15.8 billion in new obligational authority not enacted to date. The special Vietnam supplemental represents $12.8 billion of this total. Other supplemental funds will be required to finance legislation enacted last year for which no funds have yet been provided, such as higher military and civilian pay and a Teacher Corps to help in the education of underprivileged children. Additional funds will also be needed for the Asian Development Bank and for the new activities authorized by the Elementary and Secondary Education Act of 1965 and the new hospital and medical insurance programs for the aged. Finally, relatively uncontrollable veterans benefits, public assistance grants, and disaster relief will require more funds than provided by the Congress last year.

FEDERAL PROGRAMS AND EXPENDITURES

The programs proposed in this budget are designed to serve the national interest to the full extent possible within an expenditure level appropriate to the time.

Our military needs are heavy. But they have not led us to a short-sighted policy of abandoning the war on poverty, ignorance, blight, and disease. We will continue to advance toward our goals for a Great Society. This budget provides for a significant increase in programs which attack urgent domestic problems.

To achieve better returns for the taxpayer's dollar, every Government activity has been subjected to exacting standards of necessity and priority. Some have been redirected to increase the benefits they produce, some have been reduced, and others have been elimi-

nated. Savings from these actions are permitting greater expansions in programs of more immediate urgency.

Over the 3 years—from fiscal 1964 to 1967—the structure of the Federal budget will change substantially. Excluding special Vietnam costs, total administrative budget expenditures for *regular* Federal programs will rise by $4.6 billion, an increase of only 1½% per year.

Within the total, however, expenditure trends among various programs are sharply different. Between 1964 and 1967, combined expenditures on major programs directed toward the aims of the Great Society—

- in health
- in education
- in the war on poverty
- in manpower training
- in housing and community development

will rise by $6.2 billion. Unavoidable interest costs will rise by $2.1 billion. But expenditures on all other activities will decline by $3.7 billion.

As we have moved forward with new programs to improve the quality of life for all Americans, we have sought to reduce or eliminate activities of lower priority, and to pursue every technique of modern management which reduces governmental costs. The expenditure trends since 1964 demonstrate anew what I have stated on many occasions in the past:

- a compassionate Government need not be a profligate Government.
- concern for the needs and aspirations of people can go hand in hand with responsibility and efficiency in the management of the public's business.

The 1967 budget continues this approach. Net expenditures for Great Society programs rise by $2.1 billion—reflecting a gross increase of over $3 billion, partly offset by the substitution of private for public credit in

THE CHANGING FEDERAL BUDGET

[Fiscal years.   In billions]

| Description | Administrative budget expenditures, excluding special Vietnam costs | | | | |
	1964 actual	*1965 actual*	*1966 estimate*	*1967 estimate*	*Change, 1964 to 1967*
Interest..	$10.8	$11.4	$12.1	$12.9	+$2.1
Health, labor, education, housing and community development, economic opportunity program, and aid to the needy......................................	6.7	7.3	10.8	12.9	+6.2
All other..	80.2	77.6	78.8	76.5	—3.7
Total......................................	97.7	96.4	101.7	102.3	+4.6

several of these programs; interest costs rise by $0.8 billion; while all other regular expenditures decrease by $2.3 billion.

During the course of the year, unforeseeable events may call for prompt action by the Government. We will also want to act on matters—such as developing a civil supersonic transport—for which the amounts required cannot now be precisely estimated.

In addition, there are other matters—such as the pay and retirement benefits of Federal civilian employees—which are under study and on which decisions have not yet been reached. To make it clear that the budget totals provide adequately for such situations, I have included $500 million in new obligational authority and $350 million of expenditures as an allowance for contingencies.

The following are my major expenditure recommendations:

NATIONAL DEFENSE.—Aggressive forces are now testing our will and commitment to help a brave ally under attack. This Nation will continue to seek a just settlement in Vietnam. At the same time, we must provide the funds and forces required to sustain us until that goal is reached. The 1967 budget meets those requirements as we now see them.

The costs will not be light. Defense expenditures necessary to meet the special requirements in Southeast Asia will amount to $4.6 billion in 1966 and $10.3 billion in 1967. If early settlement is secured, many of these expenditures need never be made. But prudence requires that we budget for them at this time.

We must also continue to maintain defense forces equal to possible challenges elsewhere. The funds recommended in this budget provide for maintaining and improving the broad range of forces we need to meet all our defense requirements.

In 1967, we will:

• Improve our strategic missile forces with additional Minuteman II and Polaris A–3 missiles, with further development of the Poseidon submarine-launched missile, and with initial procurement of the Minuteman III missile to be delivered in future years.

• Initiate procurement of the new, high performance FB–111 to replace older, less effective bombers.

• Begin to purchase giant C–5A transport aircraft to increase greatly our airlift capability.

• Begin to build a new nuclear-powered aircraft carrier—our second—to augment the Navy's general purpose forces.

• Add to the readiness, mobility, and staying power of our conventional war forces.

- Continue the vigorous research and development programs vital to our continued ability to field the most modern and potent forces in the world.

While meeting our requirements in Vietnam and bolstering our forces, we must maintain our unrelenting efforts to operate our defense establishment efficiently and economically. In 1967, we will continue to weed out those forces and installations which have served their purpose and which are no longer essential. The successful Defense Cost Reduction Program will seek further savings. Moreover, because of the rising costs in Vietnam, we will defer certain programs where this can be done without harm to our defense capabilities.

PAYMENTS TO THE PUBLIC

[Fiscal years. In billions]

Function	1965 actual	1966 estimate	1967 estimate
Administrative budget expenditures:			
National defense	$50.2	$56.6	$60.5
Excluding special Vietnam costs	*(50.1)*	*(51.9)*	*(50.2)*
International affairs and finance	4.3	3.9	4.2
Excluding special Vietnam costs	*(4.3)*	*(3.8)*	*(4.0)*
Space research and technology	5.1	5.6	5.3
Agriculture and agricultural resources	4.9	4.3	3.4
Natural resources	2.8	2.9	3.1
Commerce and transportation	3.5	3.2	2.7
Housing and community development	—.1	.1	.1
Health, labor, and welfare	5.9	8.4	10.0
Education	1.5	2.3	2.8
Veterans benefits and services	5.5	5.1	5.7
Interest	11.4	12.1	12.9
General government	2.4	2.5	2.6
Allowance for contingencies	....	.1	.4
Interfund transactions (deduct)	.9	.6	.7
Total, administrative budget expenditures	96.5	106.4	112.8
Total, administrative budget, excluding special Vietnam costs	*(96.4)*	*(101.7)*	*(102.3)*
Trust fund expenditures:			
Health, labor, and welfare	23.2	26.6	31.1
Commerce and transportation	3.9	3.8	3.9
Housing and community development	1.1	2.0	1.2
National defense	.8	.9	.9
Veterans benefits and services	.6	.6	.7
All other	.7	.8	.9
Interfund transactions (deduct)	.6	.8	.8
Total trust fund expenditures	29.6	33.8	37.9
Intragovernmental transactions and other adjustments (deduct)	3.7	5.2	5.7
Total payments to the public	122.4	135.0	145.0
Total payments to the public, excluding special Vietnam costs	*(122.3)*	*(130.3)*	*(134.5)*

These twin goals—insuring that we have the forces we need and operating them at the lowest reasonable cost—will require an increase of $4.0 billion in national defense outlays in 1967. In the absence of the special costs of supporting our operations in South Vietnam, however, defense expenditures would decline in 1967.

INTERNATIONAL AFFAIRS AND FINANCE.—As we meet the direct military threat to freedom and security, we must also continue our pursuit of a world at peace, in which:

• Freedom can thrive.
• Hunger and disease are no longer a common condition of life.
• Education is available to everyone.
• All people and nations prosper together.

The long-run security and the innate compassion of the American people both call for policies which bring such a world closer.

The Congress and the public rightly demand that our assistance programs be effective in achieving their objectives. In the past several months I have carefully reviewed these programs. As a result of that review I am proposing the following steps:

First, I shall send to the Congress a special message proposing major initiatives in international health and education. Healthy and educated people are the most important resource a nation can possess. Therefore, the 1967 budget provides for expanded activities in education and health as next steps toward a better world.

Second, I am proposing to expand and reorient our food and agricultural assistance to the hungry peoples of the developing countries. We will emphasize assistance to the recipient countries in raising their own agricultural production so that they may eventually lessen their dependence on food aid from the United States. In this effort, increased economic aid for agricultural development will be closely coordinated with a new Food for Peace program.

Increased expenditures of the Agency for International Development for activities in health, education, and agriculture are provided within an economic assistance budget which, apart from special Vietnam costs, is no higher than in 1966.

Third, we will step up our efforts to encourage recipient nations to take vigorous measures of self-help. Our economic assistance will be provided to countries which are taking determined steps to help themselves.

Fourth, we will further concentrate our economic assistance efforts. In 1967 almost two-thirds of expenditures by the Agency for International Development outside of South Vietnam will be in nine key developing countries.

Fifth, to increase the effectiveness of our assistance, I am proposing that the program be authorized for a 5-year period.

My recommendations will be set forth in greater detail in other messages.

We will carry forward our long-term commitment to the Alliance for Progress. To this end, funds are included in this budget for continued expansion of the resources of the Inter-American Development Bank's Fund for Special Operations. Our own Alliance activities are also being increased.

As part of a cooperative effort to promote economic development in Asia, I will propose legislation to authorize the United States to become a charter member of the Asian Development Bank. The budget also includes funds to pay our share of the current replenishment of the resources of the International Development Association. As soon as future needs and an appropriate sharing formula are determined, I will seek legislation to authorize additional contributions to this highly successful affiliate of the World Bank.

This budget will also enable us to expand

the Peace Corps, of which we can be justly proud; to continue our overseas information activities; and to maintain our firm support of the United Nations.

SPACE RESEARCH AND TECHNOLOGY.—Just over 60 years ago, man entered the age of controlled flight. Today, men orbit the earth at speeds measured in thousands of miles an hour. In 1967, less than 6 years after this Nation set the goal of a manned landing on the moon within the present decade, we will begin unmanned test flights of the giant Saturn V rocket and the Apollo spacecraft—the complete space vehicle required for achieving that goal. Later on in the 1960's, we will undertake the manned lunar mission itself.

Our many space achievements—both manned and unmanned—have dramatically advanced our scientific understanding and technological capabilities. They have also clearly demonstrated our remarkable progress in the peaceful exploration of space. In 1967, our large space projects will be progressing from the more expensive development phase into operational status, and new projects of equivalent cost will not be started. Accordingly, expenditures of the National Aeronautics and Space Administration are estimated to decline by $300 million in 1967. This level will sustain our progress in space exploration and continue the advancement of science and technology.

AGRICULTURE AND AGRICULTURAL RE-SOURCES.—Our increasingly efficient agricultural production is a bulwark of strength for the Nation. It provides us with an ample supply of high quality food at home and a large volume of commercial exports. It also allows us to assist the economic development of other countries.

Our increasing productive efficiency, however, has not been fully matched by new employment opportunities for rural people who are no longer needed in farming and farm-related occupations. Consequently, large numbers of farmers and other rural people do not share fully in the benefits of this increased efficiency.

To help eligible rural people and communities participate more fully in all available Federal programs, the Department of Agriculture is expanding its services to advise and inform them about these programs and to furnish information to other Federal agencies about rural problems. The Department will also participate with other agencies and local representatives in establishing pilot multi-county development districts to coordinate the planning of programs to improve rural life.

The Food and Agriculture Act of 1965 represents a milestone in modernizing our farm commodity programs. Under this act, greater emphasis will be given to direct payments to farmers. Moreover, the Secretary of Agriculture will have more discretion in adapting farm programs to new conditions. Nevertheless, we must explore new approaches to the problems of commercial farming and seek new ways to adapt our programs for low-income people to rural conditions.

In November 1965, I appointed a National Advisory Commission on Food and Fiber and directed it to make a penetrating appraisal of all aspects of agricultural policy and to report in 18 months. The Commission's recommendations, along with valuable experience under the 1965 farm legislation and our general programs to help low-income people, should provide a firm basis for further improvements in programs for agriculture and rural people.

NATURAL RESOURCES.—In developing and conserving our natural resources, we must always look ahead to the Nation's changing needs.

We must act now to meet the outdoor recreation needs of our growing population and to preserve our historic and scenic sites. I again urge the Congress to authorize the national park, seashore, and lakeshore areas recommended in my message last year on Natural Beauty. I also recommend legislation to establish a Redwoods National Park in northern California. With some of California's magnificent State park lands as a nucleus and Federal acquisition of key adjoining lands, a substantial area of the redwoods will be preserved for future generations.

Water is a worldwide concern. It is often not available in the proper amount and quality, or at the time it is needed. Lack of water or poor use of it can be a major deterrent to the growth of developing nations. At my request, the Secretaries of the Interior and State, together with other concerned agencies, are preparing a program to cooperate with other nations in finding solutions to the world's water problems.

Future water supplies both at home and abroad can be greatly expanded by the economical conversion of sea and brackish water. The Office of Saline Water, in conjunction with the Atomic Energy Commission and other agencies, is intensifying its research efforts on this problem. The 1967 budget includes funds for the Office of Saline Water to complete construction of an advanced distillation unit at the west coast test center. This project will accelerate development of large-scale economical processes for converting sea water to fresh water.

The 1967 budget provides for starting construction on a number of new water resources projects. These projects represent a national investment in land, water, and power resources which will yield dividends for years to come.

Improved use of nuclear energy will assure a major source of economical power for the future. In working toward this objective, the Atomic Energy Commission is intensifying its long-term program to develop "fast breeder" nuclear power reactors which, by producing more fuel than they consume, would greatly e x p a n d usable energy resources.

COMMERCE AND TRANSPORTATION.—In the year ahead, strong overall economic growth will contribute importantly to the improvement of conditions in the Nation's depressed areas. In addition, the 1967 budget provides for an orderly expansion in Federal assistance for those areas.

The Public Works and Economic Development Act of 1965 has given us new means for helping develop depressed areas throughout the Nation. Loans, grants, and technical assistance will be provided. The Federal Government will also offer special incentives in 1967 for consolidating such areas into development districts better able to plan and achieve economic expansion.

The special development program for the Appalachian region will continue at a rapid pace. This unique Federal-State effort provides new opportunities for the 17½ million people of the region through highway construction, natural resource development, and construction of needed public facilities.

The new Office of State Technical Services in the Department of Commerce will be in its first full year of operation in 1967. This Office will make grants to State and regional centers to provide the latest scientific and technical findings to American business.

An efficient and safe transportation system is essential to a nation whose economy is growing, whose population is increasing, and whose urban areas are expanding at a very rapid rate. Nearly one-fifth of our annual gross national product is spent on transportation of people and goods.

60

The Federal Government is not now organized to deal effectively with this major segment of the American economy. Public programs for research, promotion, and investment in transportation are scattered among a host of Federal agencies. Where we need consolidation we find fragmentation. I shall propose, in a later message to the Congress, the creation of a new Department of Transportation to provide a realistic and consistent approach to the Nation's transportation problems.

There is no single statistic of American life more shocking than the toll of dead and injured on our highways. Each day we kill 135 of our fellow citizens—each year we injure 3 million more. I will shortly recommend to the Congress a major new highway safety program providing for the reorganization and centralization of the Federal Government's highway safety activities and a sharp expansion of their scope. The program will give particular attention to comprehensive research into the causes and prevention of highway accidents and to cooperative efforts with State and local governments in strengthening accident-prevention programs.

We will continue to give special attention to the transportation problems facing our growing cities and metropolitan areas. Research and demonstrations to improve intercity high speed ground transportation and urban mass transit will be actively pursued next year.

During the past year progress made by industry on the development of a civil supersonic transport aircraft has been promising. I will therefore propose to the Congress a joint Government-industry program to build the prototype of a safe and commercially profitable supersonic airplane.

HOUSING AND COMMUNITY DEVELOPMENT.— During its last session, the Congress passed two far-reaching acts that greatly improve our ability to solve the problems of:
- Providing good housing for those who cannot now afford it.
- Restoring the central cores of the cities.
- Achieving a rational pattern of growth in metropolitan areas.

The Housing and Urban Development Act of 1965 is the most important piece of substantive legislation for the American city since the Housing Act of 1949. The act creating the Department of Housing and Urban Development will enable the Government to launch a coordinated attack on the problems of housing and the city.

The new programs authorized by the 1965 legislation must be effectively carried out. Accordingly, this budget provides funds for:
- Maximum use of existing housing in the low-rent public housing program.
- Well-planned water and sewer systems.
- Beautification of our cities.
- Facilities to house social services and recreation in lower income neighborhoods.

The 1967 budget also provides for full use of the rent supplement program. I ask that the Congress immediately take the action needed to start this necessary program.

Federal aid will be approved in 1967 for over 160,000 additional housing units for low- and moderate-income families and elderly individuals. Progress will continue on restoring older areas of cities, and greater emphasis will be given to rehabilitation and provision of land for housing that most people can afford.

Public actions to improve poor housing conditions, to upgrade deteriorating neighborhoods, and to tackle the social blight associated with slums too often have not worked to support each other's objectives. The leadership resources of private business, civic, and labor organizations have not been.

61

fully utilized in formulating and carrying out the actions needed to preserve for all citizens the human dimensions of city life. I am requesting legislation authorizing assistance to qualifying cities across the Nation to show how complex and intertwined urban problems can be effectively attacked on a large scale through the coordinated use of local, State, and Federal programs.

I again urge the Congress to grant home rule to the District of Columbia so that its citizens may exercise the right of self-government enjoyed by other Americans.

HEALTH, LABOR, AND WELFARE.—Outside of defense, the Federal Government's largest outlays are devoted to improving the Nation's health, protecting workers and their families against loss of income, and assisting the disadvantaged to overcome poverty and unemployment.

Last year, the Congress enacted more than a score of major bills which will advance us toward the goal of a better and more secure life for our citizens. This was an unsurpassed achievement. However, there are still a number of important gaps which we should begin now to fill.

Health.—Last year, the enactment of Medicare marked a milestone in the social history of the United States. To make that legislation effective and to assure that the American people have access to high quality medical care at reasonable costs, we need to concentrate our efforts on the provision of adequate medical facilities and manpower. The 1967 budget is designed to that end. Increased funds are made available under legislation enacted last year to help educate more doctors, dentists, nurses, and graduate public health personnel. Funds are also provided for newly enacted programs to increase the number of community mental health centers and help support their staff. I shall propose legislation to assist our com-

munities in modernizing and replacing older hospitals. Similarly, legislation should be enacted to extend training assistance to medical assistants and other health personnel not now eligible.

Apart from Medicare and other programs I have already mentioned, the impressive listing of health measures passed last year and financed in this budget includes:

- Regional medical programs to provide up-to-date diagnosis and treatment for heart disease, cancer, stroke, and related diseases.
- Comprehensive medical treatment and care for preschool and school age needy children in selected areas of low income.
- Increased efforts to safeguard and purify the air we breathe.
- Improvements in vocational rehabilitation so that over 200,000 disabled or handicapped people can return to productive work.

Pollution control.—Clean and sparkling rivers ought to be a part of every American's environment. I intend to propose a new and expanded program to combat the problem of polluted water. This program will call for the improved enforcement authority needed to conquer pollution. It will also provide for large-scale cooperative efforts of Federal, State, and local governments to show how pollution can be eliminated throughout entire river basins.

Labor.—I urge enactment of legislation to:

- Provide long-needed improvements in our unemployment compensation system.
- Repeal Section 14(b) of the Taft-Hartley Act.
- Increase the minimum wage and extend protection of the Fair Labor Standards Act to over 5 million more workers.

Activities under the Manpower Development and Training Act of 1962 will be reoriented in 1967 to place more emphasis on the training of persons who now have little or no skill. Special attention will also be given to training for skills in particularly short supply. Not only will this raise the earnings of the poor, but it will increase the availability of productive labor to meet the demands of our expanding economy.

Economic opportunity programs.—The war on poverty launched in 1965 will continue to help low-income people develop the skills and abilities needed for them to break out of the cycle of poverty handed down from one generation to the next. The budget will increase this program to reach individuals whom even full prosperity does not touch.

In 1967, community action programs will be in effect in 900 communities, making a concerted attack on the poverty in their midst. The Head Start preschool program, the Neighborhood Youth Corps, and the Job Corps will again help at least 1 million children and youths. Work experience, adult literacy, small business loans, and special employment projects will help over 250,000 adults.

Other aids to the needy.—I intend to propose legislation to:

- Strengthen programs giving assistance to unemployed parents of needy children by providing work experience, services, and training to equip them for regular employment.
- Improve the nutrition of needy children.

Older programs will be redirected, shifting more of their resources to helping the disadvantaged:

- The school lunch and special milk programs will focus more on needy children, helping to provide them with adequate and well-balanced meals.
- The public assistance program will provide more financial aid and better medi-

cal care to families with dependent children.

- The Federal-State vocational rehabilitation program will enroll more handicapped persons who are receiving public assistance.

EDUCATION.—There is no greater challenge than that of providing our children and youth with the opportunity to develop fully their talents and interests. Education is vital to the achievement of a Great Society and is our major weapon in the war on poverty.

The 89th Congress has made education history. It has truly opened the doors of opportunity to preschool, elementary, secondary, and college education for millions of our young people. The Elementary and Secondary Education Act of 1965 and the Higher Education Act of 1965 will benefit this generation and clear the way to greater opportunity for future generations.

This budget reflects the added Federal responsibility for improving our Nation's educational system. The expenditures proposed for 1967 are more than 85% above the 1965 level. In 1967 this will make possible:

- An increase of $905 million in expenditures for school aid under the Elementary and Secondary Education Act of 1965, mostly for grants to improve the education of more than 7.5 million disadvantaged children.
- A Teacher Corps of more than 3,700 members to serve in schools with large numbers of children from low-income families.
- Scholarships, loans, and part-time work for well over one million college students, 3 times the number in 1965.
- Commitments exceeding $1 billion for loans and grants to help more than 1,300 colleges build needed academic and college housing facilities.

We should continue to build upon the programs to enlarge educational opportunity and improve the quality of teaching. The Elementary and Secondary Education Act of 1965 should be extended beyond June 30, 1966, and improved. To increase its effectiveness, the income criterion for allocating funds for fiscal year 1968 should be raised from $2,000 to $3,000 and the incentive grant provision should be dropped.

VETERANS BENEFITS AND SERVICES.—The Nation properly provides special help to those who suffer disabilites while in the service of our country; this help is extended through programs of income maintenance, vocational rehabilitation, and medical care. We also have a continuing obligation to the widows and children of those who have died in performing military service.

The first session of the 89th Congress recognized both of these basic trusts by:
* Increasing disability compensation payments.
* Liberalizing vocational rehabilitation benefits.
* Affording more generous allowances for children receiving educational aid under the War Orphans Act.
* Providing a new program of insurance coverage for men in our uniformed services.

We are currently engaged in armed conflict and have called upon the youth of our Nation to serve in that conflict. We should develop and expand programs to ease their readjustment to civilian life by providing education and training assistance.

The 1967 budget also provides for further improvements in the high quality of medical care administered in VA hospitals. New services will continue to be added to bring to veterans the latest advances of medical science.

Veterans programs should continue to emphasize the needs of the service-disabled. All veterans and their families are, of course, eligible to participate in the steadily improving general health, education, and welfare programs provided by the Government for all citizens.

GENERAL GOVERNMENT.—Action by the Congress is urgently needed in several different areas of governmental responsibility.

In recent years, we have made giant strides toward the goal of *equal rights* for all citizens. We still have far to go. To guarantee equal protection to individuals and to minorities under the law, there are clear and positive additional legislative actions which must be taken. I will shortly recommend such actions to the Congress.

A Great Society cannot be marked by rising *crime* rates. Americans, rich and poor, are as one on this. In 1965, I proposed and the Congress enacted the Law Enforcement Assistance Act. Under that program Federal, State, local, and private institutions can work together to:
* Improve training of law enforcement personnel.
* Promote research and spread information on law enforcement and correctional techniques.
* Strengthen the administration of justice.

The 1967 budget provides for an 89% increase in the funds allotted to this program.

I am determined to take whatever further steps are necessary to combat crime. I will propose to the Congress additional legislation to meet that objective.

The *stockpile* of strategic and critical materials will be reduced further in 1967 as we continue to dispose of materials excess to our long-term needs. To permit management improvements and reduce costs, legislation should be enacted to consolidate inventories and facilitate disposals from the stockpile.

PUBLIC DEBT AT END OF YEAR

[Fiscal years. In billions]

Description	1964 actual	1965 actual	1966 estimate	1967 estimate
Owned by Federal agencies and trust funds.................	$60.7	$63.0	$64.9	$69.8
Owned privately and by Federal Reserve banks..............	251.8	254.8	255.1	251.9
Total...	312.5	317.9	320.0	321.7

PUBLIC DEBT

The size of the public debt varies from year to year primarily as a result of the Government's surplus or deficit. Based on the estimates of receipts and expenditures in this budget, the debt on June 30, 1966, will be $320.0 billion. On June 30, 1967, it will have risen to $321.7 billion.

Present law provides a temporary debt limit of $328 billion until June 30, 1966. After that date—if no action is taken—the limit will revert to the permanent ceiling of $285 billion. It is necessary, therefore, that the ceiling for the period after June 30, 1966, be raised.

A workable debt limit should allow for two factors in addition to the estimated size of the debt at the end of fiscal year 1967:

* Seasonal fluctuations in the size of the debt.
* The need for flexibility in managing the debt.

The first is necessary to allow for periods when the debt will exceed the end-of-year total. This results from the seasonal pattern of receipts, which are lower in the first half of the fiscal year.

Adequate provision for flexibility will permit the Treasury to take full advantage of favorable market conditions and thus avoid unnecessary interest costs.

IMPROVING GOVERNMENT MANAGEMENT

As a Nation we have much to do. We have the will. We have the resources. But we must conserve these resources, investing them wisely. We dare not waste them.

This calls for improved Government organization, better programing, cost reduction, and effective employment policies. I intend shortly to present the Congress with a number of proposals designed to accomplish these objectives.

GOVERNMENT ORGANIZATION.—In moving toward the goals of the Great Society, the enactment of substantive legislation is only the first step. The 89th Congress has, through its accomplishments to date, provided the basis for advancing in such critical areas as civil rights, economic opportunity, medical care for our older citizens, improvement of our cities, and regional development.

However, if these laws are to produce the desired results—effectively and at minimum cost to the taxpayer—we cannot afford to cling to organizational and administrative arrangements which have not kept pace with our changing needs.

Government organization must provide for fast and flexible response to new problems and conditions. We must be as bold and imaginative in reshaping and modernizing the executive branch as we have been in de-

65

vising new programs. A structure designed in major part to carry out programs and policies of the 1950's and earlier years will not give us the organization we need as we move toward the 1970's. I will propose shortly to the Congress a series of reorganization measures which will enable the Government to manage its business more effectively.

FEDERAL, STATE, AND LOCAL COORDINATION.—Many of our critical new programs involve the Federal Government in joint ventures with State and local governments in thousands of communities throughout the Nation. The success or failure of those programs depends largely on timely and effective communications and on readiness for action on the part of both Federal agencies in the field and State and local governmental units. We must strengthen the coordination of Federal programs in the field. We must open channels of responsibility. We must give more freedom of action and judgment to the people on the firing line. We must help State and local governments to deal more effectively with Federal agencies. We must see that information gets to the field and to cooperating State and local governments, promptly and accurately.

I intend to see to it that this dimension of the new public management receives major attention and action in the coming year.

PLANNING-PROGRAMING-BUDGETING SYSTEM.—I have directed the executive branch to develop and introduce a new planning-programing-budgeting system which will incorporate the most modern management techniques now used in government and industry. This system will enable us to:

• Be more concrete and precise about the objectives of our programs.
• Examine longer term problems and consequences more systematically.
• Consider more alternatives before reaching decisions.
• Link our planning efforts more directly to budget decisions.
• Get more effectiveness for the dollars we spend.
• Provide more benefits to the American people in more economical ways.

During the next year, I expect to see much progress made in this system with results that will be reflected in the budget for fiscal year 1968.

SUBSTITUTION OF PRIVATE FOR PUBLIC CREDIT.—In recent budgets, I have pressed for the encouragement of private financing in the major Federal credit programs wherever I have felt it to be consistent with the public interest. I will need the cooperation of the Congress to carry this effort still farther in the coming year.

This is an important and sensible way to manage our Federal credit programs. I, therefore, urge prompt action on legislation being proposed to authorize a considerable expansion in the sale of participations in Government loans. The budget assumes its enactment. With the authority provided by such legislation, my budget proposals for encouraging the substitution of private for public credit will reduce 1967 expenditures by $4.7 billion from what they would have been otherwise.

AUTOMATIC DATA PROCESSING.—The Federal Government has obtained great benefits from the use of electronic computers. With the direct annual cost of acquiring and operating this equipment now in the range of $2 billion, I intend to make sure that this huge investment is managed efficiently—through such means as research, equipment sharing, careful purchasing, and coordinated Government-wide utilization policies.

COST REDUCTION.—During the past 2 years, I have not ceased to demand an exacting standard of cost-consciousness in every department and bureau of the executive branch. I believe neither in padded budgets nor in lax habits of organization and management. Every dollar of expenditures must produce results. I expect each Government employee to spend the public dollar with the same care and concern he would exercise if it came out of his own paycheck.

In preparing this budget, all existing programs have been re-examined closely. Wherever a program could be cut back on grounds of less priority, I have cut it. Despite the appeal of many of these programs to affected groups, I urge the Congress not to restore them to their previous levels.

There are many ways to reduce costs and eliminate unnecessary spending:

- By curtailing or eliminating activities of declining importance.
- By closing marginal branch offices or installations.
- By pooling common services.
- By simplifying organization.
- By increasing productivity.
- By installing up-to-date systems and equipment.
- By interagency coordination of plans and operations.
- By stringent budgetary reviews.

Last March, I set in operation a Government-wide, formal program for systematic cost reduction in which each agency must identify savings goals for the year ahead and report to me on actual results. This program is working.

Agencies have identified specific savings in 1965 and 1966. Additional savings will be made in 1967. Altogether, the civilian cost reduction program will reduce the costs of operating the Government by some $1 billion in each of the fiscal years 1966 and 1967.

The Department of Defense accomplished $4.8 billion of savings in fiscal year 1965, and the annual rate of savings in that Department is expected to exceed $6 billion in 1969.

No agency, regardless of size or importance, is exempted from the duty to save the taxpayer's money by better management and alert business methods.

One of the most gratifying developments to come to my attention is the remarkable progress of Government agencies in *improving productivity*. With workloads increasing in nearly every category of Government activity, the only way to restrain mounting Federal employment is by persistent management improvement and higher productivity. These are just a few of the changes in productivity which are reflected in this budget:

- The Social Security Administration is achieving a productivity gain of 2½% by automating the recomputation of benefits, with a saving of 1,742 man-years and $12.4 million.
- The Post Office Department's budget reflects an increase in mail processing productivity of 1.4%, resulting in a saving of 3,900 man-years and $23 million.
- The Federal Aviation Agency is increasing productivity by 5% in airways facilities operation and maintenance, thus absorbing nearly all the workload increase resulting from the growth in aviation activity, with a budget saving of almost $4 million.
- By using advanced medical techniques, the Veterans Administration has been able to reduce the duration of patient stay in its hospitals. In 1967, about 1% more patients can be accommodated than in 1966. This means that the same number of beds operated in 1966 will take care of 7,000 more patients in 1967.

These actions are the result of tireless effort by many officials and employees of the

Federal Government. It is often harder work to save money than to find productive ways to spend it. But it is equally important to the public interest.

I believe we are making good progress in reducing costs and improving efficiency, but I will never be satisfied that we have done all we should. I expect the top officials of every department and agency to press hard in the coming year to do still better—and not only in headquarters operations. Only 10% of all Federal employees are in Washington—most of our employees and operations are spread throughout the 50 States and overseas. I intend to stress particularly this year the urgency of management improvement and better public service in the field establishment of the Federal Government.

CONCLUSION

This Nation has committed itself to help defend South Vietnam against aggression. We are determined to fulfill that commitment.

This Nation has also committed itself to a major effort to provide better economic, social, and cultural opportunities for all Americans. We are also determined to ful-

fill this commitment.

Both of these commitments involve great costs. They are costs we can and will meet.

The objectives we are seeking are interdependent.

We cannot fight for peace and freedom in Vietnam, while sacrificing individual dignity and opportunity at home. For it would be a hollow victory if our pursuit of world peace were carried out at the expense of domestic progress.

Yet we must also recognize that a truly Great Society looks beyond its own borders. The freedom, health, and prosperity of all mankind are its proper concern.

The struggle in Vietnam must be supported. The advance toward a Great Society at home must continue unabated.

This budget provides the means for both these goals.

I urge the support of Congress and all Americans for its principles and its programs.

LYNDON B. JOHNSON

January 24, 1966

NOTE: As printed above, illustrative diagrams and references to the budget document have been deleted.

For the President's remarks upon signing the message, see Item 25.

27 Annual Message to the Congress on the District of Columbia Budget. *January 25, 1966*

To the Congress of the United States:

I present the budget for the District of Columbia for the fiscal year beginning July 1, 1966.

The great domestic challenge of our time lies in our cities. Significant efforts are being undertaken to meet this challenge, and to make it possible for every citizen to lead a productive and satisfying life.

The Federal Government has a special re-

sponsibility for the Nation's Capital. We have long resolved that the District can and should be an example of the best among our urban communities, but in many ways the District continues to fall short of that goal.

Programs for the future must recognize that there is much room for improvement. Yet, even to avoid regression is both difficult and expensive. The District, as the central portion of a major metropolitan area, must cope with unusual demands.

The past decade, for example, has seen a substantial increase in the need for services to meet the requirements of a changing population. During that short span, while total population of the District remained virtually unchanged—

- School-age population (5–19) increased by 23,700 (15%).
- Actual school enrollments increased more than 37,000 (35%), due primarily to expanded kindergarten programs and a modestly successful program to reduce school dropouts.
- Working-age population (20–64) decreased 21,100 (4%).
- The over-65 age group increased 14,000 (24%).

The student group certainly, and the older age group in many cases, require greater public services and public facilities. These needs cannot be ignored.

The District must also replace and modernize a physical plant that is aged and rapidly becoming obsolete. Of the public schools, for example—

- Over 38% were built totally or in part before 1920.
- Over 60% have some substandard classrooms.

Yet, the demands of the rapidly increasing school population, combined with limited appropriations for school construction, have made it impossible even to house new students, much less to modernize the existing school plant. Indeed, there is no fact of which we should be less proud than that in the Capital City of this great Nation there are some 2,100 children compelled by lack of classroom space to accept part-time education.

These and other program demands mean, therefore, that an increased level of appropriations will be required. To some extent

that increase has been held in check by the cost reduction and management improvement program developed by the Commissioners. This program, similar to that required in each Federal department and agency, will continue to help in holding down the need for additional personnel and other resources despite the rapidly increasing program requirements. Moreover, to increase even further the productivity of District agencies, I have directed the Bureau of the Budget to work closely with the Commissioners in the development of—

- A planning, programing, and budgeting system.
- New management techniques.
- Improved methods and procedures.
- Intensified use of data processing equipment.

In addition, I have insisted that the increases in expenditures reflected in this budget be held to the minimum needed to—

- Assure continuation of essential services.
- Provide an adequate level of staffing to carry out essential services.
- Permit only such improvement in services as is required to assure an acceptable rate of progress toward our ultimate goals.

Revenues.—Increases in District resources must, as always, come largely from local taxes. Commensurate increases in support by the Federal Government are necessary. The Federal payment, which is now authorized at $50 million, should be authorized at a substantially higher level by approval of the formula contained in H.R. 6889, and appropriations should be increased accordingly. That formula provides a fair, equitable, and flexible measure of the amount of Federal support that should be provided the District government. The need for this type of flexible authorization and the inadequacy of the present laws are apparent. In 1965, the formula would have authorized only $4.8 million more than the present authorization of $50 million. In 1967, the formula indicates $61.9 million as the appropriate level of support—$11.9 million more than is now authorized. The propriety of thus measuring the appropriate level of Federal support to the District has twice had the approval of the Senate. I urgently commend it.

Increases in District taxes to accompany the larger Federal payment should be substantially greater than the $4 million provided for the general fund in H.R. 11487, the revenue bill which has been passed by the House of Representatives. While it is true that the contribution made by District taxpayers has substantially increased in the past year, both through larger receipts from existing taxes and from the increase of 20 cents per $100 of assessed valuation in the real estate tax, these increases fall far short of meeting the District's needs. I support, therefore, the recommendation of the Commissioners to the Congress of a tax package which will increase tax revenues in the general fund by $8.4 million annually beyond those provided in H.R. 11487.

Borrowing.—The authority of the District to borrow for general fund purposes is now fixed at $225 million, of which $50 million is specifically allocated for the purposes of the National Capital Transportation Act of 1965. When this amount has been borrowed the authority will be exhausted, irrespective of repayments. This form of lump-sum authorization should be replaced by the provisions of H.R. 6889, which relate the maximum amount which the District may borrow from the Treasury to a percentage of the assessed value of real and personal property in the District. This would—

- Conform to debt limits generally used throughout the United States for local governments.

- Relate the debt limit more closely to ability to repay.
- Enable the District to incur new debt as repayments are made.

Since at current levels of annual borrowing the District will soon exhaust its present borrowing authorization for general public works purposes, this matter deserves prompt consideration by the Congress.

With the additional revenues now being proposed, the District will measurably advance toward the goals outlined in my message to the Congress of February 15, 1965. Some of the more significant recommendations are—

EDUCATION

Operation of the school system in 1967 will require $82.6 million, an increase of $6.9 million over 1966. These increased funds will provide—

- Additional classroom teachers needed to maintain the pupil-teacher ratios now in effect.
- Additional positions in special subject areas such as science, mathematics, and reading needed to enrich and strengthen the District's educational program.
- Addition of 24 librarians to provide one in every school in which physical facilities exist to house a library.
- Additional counselors to achieve the Board of Education pupil-counselor ratios of 750:1 in elementary schools and 400:1 in secondary schools.
- Four pupil personnel service teams. Each team will be composed of psychiatrists, clinical and school psychologists, social workers and attendance officers. They will be able to meet acute needs of literally thousands of pupils whose opportunities to achieve the

REQUIREMENTS AND FINANCING OF THE GENERAL FUND, 1966–72

[In millions of dollars]

	Estimates		Projections				
Funds required:	1966	1967	1968	1969	1970	1971	1972
Under existing legislation:							
Operating expenses..........................	280.1	307.3	322.6	338.7	355.6	373.4	392.1
Capital outlay:							
Public works, including Federal obligations (cash required)........................	37.1	48.3	54.6	53.7	53.9	52.6	50.0
Rail rapid transit system....................	2.0	8.5	39.5	.....	.....	.....	......
Repayment of loans and interest:							
Loans for public works.....................	1.9	2.0	3.3	4.8	6.2	7.7	9.2
Loans for rail rapid transit.................	.....	.....	.1	.2	1.4	3.0	3.0
Repayable advances.........................	20.0	.....	.....	.....	.....	.....	.....
Total under existing legislation..............	341.1	366.1	420.1	397.4	417.1	436.7	454.3
Under proposed legislation:							
Operating expenses—Pay increases for teachers, policemen, and firemen.....................	2.9	4.3	4.3	4.3	4.3	4.3	4.3
Reserves for indefinite appropriation and contingencies...................................	3.6	.6	7.0	7.0	7.0	7.0	7.0
Total estimated funds required..............	347.6	371.0	431.4	408.7	428.4	448.0	465.6
Revenues and balances:							
From existing legislative sources:							
Taxes, fees, etc.[1]...........................	256.0	266.9	281.2	299.3	318.2	334.5	351.3
Balances....................................	−1.4	4.1	2.0	2.0	2.0	2.0	2.0
Federal payment............................	48.7	50.0	50.0	50.0	50.0	50.0	50.0
Repayable advances.........................	20.0	.....	.....	.....	.....	.....	.....
Loan authorization:							
Public works.............................	22.4	17.2	20.3	9.0	.....	.....	.....
Rail rapid transit.........................	2.0	8.5	39.5	.....	.....	.....	.....
Total estimated availability from existing legislative sources......................	347.7	346.7	393.0	360.3	370.2	386.5	403.3
From proposed legislative sources:							
Taxes......................................	1.0	12.4	12.7	13.0	13.4	13.7	14.2
Federal payment............................	.....	11.9	14.4	16.9	20.9	25.1	28.0
Loan authorization—public works.............	.....	.....	.....	20.0	20.0	20.0	20.0
Total from proposed legislative sources.......	1.0	24.3	27.1	49.9	54.3	58.8	62.2
Total estimated revenues and balances........	348.7	371.0	420.1	410.2	424.5	445.3	465.5
Additional financing required to meet total estimated requirements...................................	.....	.....	11.3	.....	3.9	2.7	.1

[1] Includes recent increase in real estate tax rate from $2.50 to $2.70 per $100 assessed valuation in fiscal year 1966. Also, rate increase from $2.70 to $2.80 in fiscal year 1969 and from $2.80 to $2.90 in fiscal year 1970.

NEW OBLIGATIONAL AUTHORITY, ALL FUNDS

[In thousands of dollars]

CURRENT AUTHORIZATIONS	1965 actual	1966 estimate	1967 recom- mended
Education:			
Operating expenses..............................	72,038	75,727	82,609
Capital outlay................................	14,405	17,569	32,935
Welfare and health:			
Operating expenses..............................	76,154	80,957	90,549
Capital outlay................................	487	6,014	4,888
Highways and traffic:			
Operating expenses..............................	13,714	14,197	14,982
Capital outlay................................	13,769	9,852	15,455
Public safety:			
Operating expenses..............................	73,724	80,024	85,752
Capital outlay................................	336	1,687	2,715
Parks and recreation:			
Operating expenses..............................	10,150	10,972	12,256
Capital outlay................................	680	1,035	1,896
General operating expenses:			
Operating expenses..............................	19,444	20,550	22,708
Capital outlay................................	5,030	2,111	1,298
Sanitary engineering:			
Operating expenses..............................	22,385	23,097	24,248
Capital outlay................................	23,066	12,546	14,107
Repayment of loans and interest......................	5,363	5,690	6,078
Payment of District of Columbia share of Federal capital outlays.........	1,860	987	1,350
Contribution to rapid transit system.....................	....	2,000	8,525
Additional municipal services—inaugural ceremonies....................	283	....	....
Additional municipal services—Shrine and American Legion conventions..	....	221	233
Judgments, claims, and refunds...........................	885	33	....
Personal services, wage board employees............................	....	660	1,320
Total current authorizations.....................	353,773	365,929	423,904
Permanent authorizations.............................	1,626	1,593	1,637
Operations of D.C. trust funds.......................	58,178	58,961	63,480
Repayment (—) of advances from Federal funds.......................	9,000	−26,000	....
Proposed for separate transmittal (under proposed legislation)............	....	3,000	4,510
Total authorizations........................	422,577	403,483	493,531
Recapitulation of current authorizations:			
General fund........................	298,100	322,863	371,297
Highway fund................................	28,876	25,314	31,719
Water fund..................................	11,049	10,397	11,884
Sanitary sewage works fund..........................	15,668	7,270	8,930
Metropolitan area sanitary sewage works fund.......................	80	85	74
Total, all funds.................................	353,773	365,929	423,904

maximum of their potentialities are now impaired because the schools do not have adequate information on their abilities, achievements, and emotional stability.

In addition, an increase in the salaries of teachers will be proposed to the Congress.

There has already been a substantial increase in funds available to the District school system through the several national programs for aid to education. In 1967, these funds will approximate $14.5 million. This Federal assistance has properly been concentrated in low-income areas of the city, where the needs are the most severe and potential for accomplishment is the greatest. While these funds make possible many improvements, they cannot and should not be used as a substitute for the basic educational program financed directly by the community. Together, however, the two sources of funds make the opportunities for major educational progress in the District brighter than ever.

The budget also includes $32.9 million for various stages of construction of 35 school construction projects, including 7 new schools, 18 additions to existing schools, and 10 school replacements, including the critically needed Shaw Junior High School. When they are all completed, they will provide 19,550 additional pupil spaces. This will, at long last, eliminate foreseeable part-time classes; and permit in 1968 the beginning of a concerted program to replace obsolete school buildings.

PUBLIC SAFETY

The budget provides $85.8 million for operating expenses for the District agencies concerned with public safety—an increase of $5.7 million over fiscal 1966.

Budget proposals for District agencies con-cerned with crime are necessarily made without benefit of the recommendations by the Commission on Crime in the District of Columbia which I appointed last July. That Commission, I hope and expect, will point the way toward further improvement of the District's efforts to achieve effective and fair law enforcement. Budget amendments appropriate in the light of its recommendations will be transmitted to the Congress promptly. I am determined that both citizens and visitors in our National Capital shall be secure in their persons and their property.

Pending receipt of the Commission's recommendations, however, we can proceed with confidence on several items. The pistol registration bill, S. 1632 and H.R. 6745, should be promptly enacted. The Police Department has been encountering great difficulties in recruiting qualified candidates. An increase in the salaries of policemen is necessary to bring the police force to its currently authorized strength. Legislation to accomplish this will be proposed to the Congress. A decision on increasing the authorized strength can await the Commission's report.

Funds are also appropriate, and are included in the budget, for several improvements that will enable the force to operate more effectively—

- Civilian employees will be used to fill 31 administrative positions now filled by uniformed personnel who will be freed to utilize their training to greater advantage.
- Closed-circuit, departmentwide television will be installed to increase the effectiveness of lineups and the efficiency of training programs.
- A planning and development unit will be established to improve the utilization of computers and other technological advances in the field of crime prevention

and control.

I am also recommending that the roving tactical force be continued in 1967. That force, the one-man scout cars, and the additional two-way radios for foot patrolmen, all provided last year, have contributed in a major way to the hopeful change in the trend of serious offenses reported in recent months.

Finally, there are funds for the more active recruitment that is needed to bring the police force to its authorized strength and for an increase from 25 to 60 trainees in the highly successful police cadet program.

Also, salary increases for firemen are proposed for later transmittal.

PARKS AND RECREATION

The budget provides those agencies concerned with parks and recreation with an increase of $1.3 million over the 1966 level of $11 million. Recreation facilities in the District remain well below needs and accepted standards. This is particularly unfortunate in areas where low incomes make it difficult for the residents to take advantage of facilities not in their immediate neighborhoods. Until these deficiencies can be remedied, maximum utilization must be made of existing facilities. This can be done only through the extension of hours during which facilities are open, and expansion of programs to enlarge the opportunity for participation by various age groups. The budget provides funds for these purposes, as well as $1.9 million for new facilities and expansion and improvement of those already in existence.

Funds are provided for an expansion of the Roving Leader program which has had a record of success with hard-to-reach delinquent and potentially delinquent youth. The budget also provides funds to enable the Recreation Department and the National

Park Service to continue, in cooperation with the many nongovernmental efforts, to beautify the city, particularly through improved landscaping and planting. The needs of the Park Police for a larger force, and the National Zoological Park for increases in operating and maintenance staff, are likewise met.

HEALTH AND WELFARE

For health, welfare, and vocational rehabilitation programs for 1967, the budget proposes funds of $90.5 million, an increase of $9.6 million over 1966. These funds, together with the expanding levels of grants to the District for participation in Federal programs in these fields, will maintain the momentum already achieved in the District's public health and vocational rehabilitation efforts, substantially reduce the present deficiencies in the welfare program, and permit the District's full participation in the programs made possible by recent amendments in the Social Security Act.

In the field of public health the District is moving forward rapidly in the prevention and treatment of mental illness. Funds are provided to complete the staffing of the first of four Community Mental Health Centers, begun two years ago at D.C. General Hospital and operated during the past year with the aid of a grant from the National Institute of Mental Health. The second center, to be located in the northwest section of the District, will be a part of the Northwest Community Health Center for which site funds are requested. Funds are also requested for a demonstration project for the treatment of alcoholics on a volunteer basis. It is hoped that this program will reduce the burden now imposed on the police, the courts, and the correctional system by the chronic alcoholic.

Two demonstration projects heretofore operated with funds granted by the Department of Health, Education, and Welfare—the Nursing Home Improvement program and the Rheumatic Fever Prophylaxis program—have fully proven their usefulness, and are now proposed for partial financing by the District itself.

The welfare program must continue to meet the basic needs of the poor, the aged, and the disabled. This program has increasingly emphasized rehabilitation services which encourage and assist families in achievement of independence and self-sufficiency. This budget continues that emphasis.

Funds contained in this budget will permit the District to participate more fully in Federal programs. Maximum attention is paid to the needs of children. This is as it should be. Under this budget—

- Additional staff will be provided to bring the number of social workers closer to the national standard of 60 cases per worker, particularly for families with dependent children, and to expedite the current welfare eligibility review.
- Special programs will be continued and expanded to provide immediate help for families not eligible for regular welfare services but who face crises which might result in family breakup.
- Needy children of the unemployed will be assisted through an improved program, which will provide training and job placement assistance for their parents. This program will be closely related to Title V of the Economic Opportunity Act and will be designed to reduce relief rolls by equipping parents for productive employment.
- An enlarged child welfare staff will be provided.
- Higher rates of payment will be made to

foster parents and group foster homes.
- Homemaker and day care services will be expanded.

The favorable results of special efforts which have contributed to a marked reduction in the population of Junior Village during 1965—from over 900 in February to 630 at the end of the year—make it the more imperative that these efforts be further intensified.

TRANSPORTATION

The Congress, at its last session, took a major step toward resolving one of the significant transportation problems of the National Capital Region by authorizing construction within the District of the rail rapid transit system. The budget provides for the appropriation of a loan in the amount of $8.5 million to the District to enable it to meet its share of the cost of this project during 1967.

Problems remain, however, in connection with the highway portion of the District's transportation system. One is the urgent need for additional resources for the Highway Fund if any highway program at all is to continue. The Commissioner's requests for a 1-cent increase in the gasoline tax and for an increase in the Highway Fund's borrowing authority are included in H.R. 11487, which has been approved by the House of Representatives. I commend these proposals to the Senate as well.

Another problem which should be promptly resolved concerns the dimensions and locations of the interstate freeway system within the District. The report of the District of Columbia Committee of the House of Representatives on H.R. 11487 requests a further review and appraisal of some of the present plans. The Highway Department has already taken some steps in this direction, and a possible relocation of a portion of the inner loop is now under active consideration by the Policy Advisory Committee.

The magnitude of these projects, however, makes it important that both the Federal Government and the Washington community have full assurance that there will be no needless expenditures of moneys or dislocations of persons and businesses. Accordingly, I am requesting the Policy Advisory Committee to consider whether it should secure, in conjunction with the National Capital Planning Commission's work on the 1985 comprehensive plan, a review of present highway plans. This review would examine not only methodology but also the basic assumptions regarding dislocation of families and businesses, real costs, Federal needs, and other community values on the basis of the most recent data available.

In order that the highway program not be delayed, and in order also that the Congress may have as much information as possible before completing its consideration of the District's 1967 highway budget, I am requesting the Committee to complete both its current studies and any further reviews it may consider appropriate by April 1, 1966. The Commissioners have advised me that the status of the most controversial items—the north leg of the inner loop and the north-central freeway—is such that in the next few months there would be no major expenditures on these projects in any event except for planning.

I am encouraged by the close cooperation which has been evident among the Federal and District agencies with responsibilities for developing the District's transportation system. Continued cooperation will insure a coordinated and efficient transportation network—one which will best serve the needs of the Nation's Capital.

MUNICIPAL CENTER

During the past few years the District government has not been provided with additional government-owned office space for new or expanding programs. Rental space, at high cost in both dollars and efficiency, has been required. I am recommending an increase of $1 million for additional rental space as a temporary relief of overcrowding.

In this budget, a small but critical item of $75,000 is sought to finance the first step toward a permanent solution. These funds will enable the District to prepare floor plan layouts and budget estimates for two buildings in the Municipal Center area to house education, recreation and technical services. These buildings, which help to fulfill the long-range plans for Pennsylvania Avenue, not only will permit consolidation of scattered fragments of several departments and relief from outmoded, inadequate and overcrowded space, but will also be of definite economic advantage to the District.

CONCLUSION

In addition to this expenditure program, and the revenue measures which I am recommending, there are a number of other measures of importance to the District of Columbia that are already before the Congress.

Of preeminent importance is the passage of a Home Rule bill. I urge the House of Representatives to complete action on the bill already approved by the Senate. My views on the need for this legislation are well known to the Congress. There is no reason to repeat them here.

Among the other important District measures pending in both houses are—

• A bill to authorize in the District of Columbia a community college and a college of arts and sciences under a Board of Higher Education.

• A bill to create a Pennsylvania Avenue Commission.

• A bill to establish an international center.

The House has already passed H.R. 8126, which would extend the coverage of the District of Columbia minimum wage law to men.

Enactment of these measures would make the 89th Congress as memorable for the District as it is already for the Nation.

LYNDON B. JOHNSON

January 25, 1966

NOTE: The District of Columbia Revenue Act of 1966 (H.R. 11487) was approved by the President on September 30, 1966 (Public Law 89–610, 80 Stat. 855).

For statements upon signing related legislation, see Items 527, 586.

28   Special Message to the Congress Proposing a Program for Rural America. *January 25, 1966*

To the Congress of the United States:

Last year in my message on Agriculture I described poverty's grip on rural America:

—nearly half of the poor in the United States live in rural areas.

—almost one in every two rural families has a cash income under $3,000.

—one-fourth of rural non-farm homes are without running water.

—rural people lag almost two years behind urban residents in educational attainment.

—health facilities in rural areas are so inadequate that rural children receive one-third less medical attention than urban children.

These deficiencies persist in 1966. Their effect is grievous on urban America—the recipient of millions of unskilled migrants from rural areas in the past two decades. It is tragic on the run-down farms and impoverished communities that still house 4.4 million poor rural families.

ADMINISTRATIVE ACTIONS

Last year I directed

—each Department and agency adminis-

tering a program that could benefit rural people, to assure that its benefits were distributed equitably between urban and rural areas.

—the Secretary of Agriculture and the Director of the Budget to review the administrative obstacles that might stand in the way of such a distribution.

—the Secretary of Agriculture to put his field offices to the task of assisting other Federal agencies in making their programs effective in rural areas.

As a result, the Rural Community Development Service was created and charged with assuring that the Department made that assistance available.

This mission of the Department is now firmly established in practice. Its field personnel are active in informing rural people of their eligibility for medicare, and of its requirements. They work with the Economic Development Administration in planning and encouraging new rural industrial developments. In several pilot counties, concerted projects are underway. The Departments of Labor, HEW, and Agriculture are joined in a common effort to bring social services to poor rural communities. The

77

water and sewer facilities program has been simplified. They have been made more responsive to the needs of small towns and communities.

The Office of Economic Opportunity has increased its efforts in rural areas. Community Action Programs are underway in a number of rural counties

—supporting community action planning,

—providing remedial reading courses, vocational instruction, and adult education,

—and assisting small cooperatives to acquire farm machinery. These programs have inspired a new sense of hope among the rural Americans who have experienced them.

More—much more—needs to be done if their effects are to reach the dispersed but very real pockets of rural poverty throughout America.

THE NEED FOR PLANNING

Legislation enacted by the first Session of this Congress, and in prior years, provides the means for a massive attack on poverty in America.

But—even with the help of these great new programs—too few rural communities are able to marshal sufficient physical, human, and financial resources to achieve a satisfactory level of social and economic development.

The central advantage of the city has been a large and concentrated population to provide the leadership and technical capability. This leadership can achieve economies of scale in operations, to provide adequate public services and facilities for its people.

On the other hand, it is difficult, if not impossible for every small hamlet to offer its own complete set of public services. Nor

is it economic for the small city to try to achieve metropolitan standards of service, opportunity, and culture, without relation to its rural environs.

The related interests of each need to be taken into account in planning for the public services and economic development of the wider community. In this way the benefits of creative Federalism can be brought to our rural citizens—in small cities as well as its rural neighbors.

WHAT MIGHT BE DONE

The base exists for such coordinated planning.

New communities are coming into being—stimulated by advanced means of travel and communications. Because of these it is possible to extend to people in the outlying rural areas a richer variety of public services, and of economic and cultural opportunities.

Resources must be combined—in larger areas, as well as rural and small urban communities. In a population base large enough to support a full range of efficient and high-quality public services and facilities, we can achieve the conditions necessary for economic and social advance.

THE DIMENSIONS OF THE COMMUNITIES

The dimensions of an area within which residents should join to carry out integrated planning are likely to be already marked by the trading or commuting patterns.

In most such communities, the total population will be large enough, with enough potential users of each essential service, to justify employing competent full-time resident specialists in medical services, schools, and the like. In some such communities, where towns of even 10,000 are scarce, it may be more practical to provide major services to people at the outer limits through mobile facilities.

BENEFITS OF PLANNING

Coordinated planning can stimulate economic growth.

It can provide the economies of efficient public services—which attract business and industry.

It can make possible adequate vocational training. Rural workers who lack present job opportunities can become qualified for work in new and expanding industries within reach of their homes or farms.

It can provide the schools to spare young children the fate of their fathers. Seventy-two percent of all poor rural families today are headed by persons who have finished only eight years of schooling or less.

It can greatly enlarge the effectiveness of public and private resources.

It can ensure that programs will comprise a logical and comprehensive effort to solve the community's interrelated problems at minimum cost.

It can bring us closer to achieve *a more beautiful, more livable* rural America. An increasing combination of local, State, and Federal resources is already beginning to transform the countryside. This cooperation is making multiple uses possible—for production, for outdoor recreation, and for the restoration of natural beauty. Planning can help make this beneficence a part of the lives of millions of urban Americans.

Above all, planning is an affirmative act. It signifies the willingness of rural men and women to make their part of America a place of hope. Rural America need not be a wasteland from which the young, however ill-prepared, flee to the cities. It does not have to be a place where live only those too old, too poor, too defeated to seek other horizons.

COMMUNITY DEVELOPMENT DISTRICTS

I propose that we show how broad-based planning can inspire the people of rural America to unite the resources of their rural governments and small cities.

I propose this union to improve the quality of life for the citizens of both.

I propose that we assist in the establishment of a number of Community Development Districts to carry out, under local initiative, such comprehensive planning.

The boundaries of Community Development Districts will correspond to the normal commuting or trading patterns of the rural and city residents.

Planning activities for the District will be performed under the direction of representatives selected by each of the participating county or municipal governments. They will be responsible for planning the coordination of all governmental development and service functions within the District.

Federal grants would be provided:

1. For District-wide planning of public services and governmental functions where other Federal planning assistance is not available; and

2. For District-wide coordination of local planning activities with Federal programs and private initiatives, in a comprehensive attack on rural community problems.

The Secretary of Agriculture will certify that the area has met the requirements for designation as a Community Development District. Selection of the pilot districts will be made to afford experience in a representative variety of geographic, economic, and social conditions. Funds will be requested to augment those presently available for planning grants.

Federal assistance would help to support:
—*coordinated and comprehensive planning for all public services, development programs, and governmental functions within the District,*
—*a continuing liaison with Federal and State agencies,*
—*a comprehensive survey of resources and needs within the District, such as labor skills, industrial sites, land and water resources, health care, education, cultural opportunities, and public services.*

Thus the scope of planning to be supported would extend beyond physical development. It would encompass as well the social and economic needs of the area, and its potential for growth.

Each agency of the government charged with administering a program relevant to these needs will be requested to cooperate with the Community Development Districts. For example, a comprehensive survey of medical conditions in the area would be undertaken by the Department of Health, Education, and Welfare. The Teacher Corps—which I again urge the Congress to support at a level commensurate with its promise—would be asked to make teams available for the Districts. The Department of Agriculture will offer a concerted emphasis in its resource development programs within the pilot Districts.

The purpose of the planning effort I recommend is to assist these Districts to achieve significant economies of scale and rational use of resources. This achievement can lift them, and their peoples, above their present level of development.

Our purpose is to demonstrate how a common effort can provide the needed district vocational school in one county, the hospital in another, the police training in a third, industry or an adequate library in a fourth. This effort can avoid the waste of duplica-tion—or worse still, the total lack of such facilities or services because of a failure to pool common resources.

Our purpose is not to supplant present efforts of local, State or Federal governments. Our purpose is to supplement them. Then we do not forsake the small community, but help to avoid under-representation in decisions that affect its life.

MEDICAL NEEDS

Rural families share with the urban poor a greater need for modern medical services. Infant mortality and infectious disease rates are higher, life expectancy is lower, and the need for chronic illness care is just as prevalent. Yet rural families have had less access to physicians, with rural States averaging only a third the number of physicians per person as the heavily populated urban States. The continuing decline in the per capita number of physicians, therefore, strikes harder at rural families.

The beneficial effects of recent legislation, providing for more extensive professional relationships between rural hospitals and urban medical centers; the improved schooling that will soon be available in rural areas; improved roads and transportation—all will reduce the difficulty in recruiting physicians for rural areas by increasing the professional and educational opportunities available to them.

Nevertheless, we are not recruiting sufficient numbers of medical students from the families of the urban poor and rural areas. We need a financial incentive that will make it possible for children of these families to undertake a medical career. At the same time we need to draw upon medical students from other areas to settle in rural medical practice.

I shall soon propose, therefore, that a loan

forgiveness program modeled upon the National Defense Education Act Amendments of 1965 be applied to medical students who choose to practice in poor rural areas.

RURAL POVERTY

The efforts of five Administrations have provided some relief for hundreds of thousands of poor families who remain on small farms and in rural communities. Yet the old task remains undone: to end the travail of unemployed and under-employed men; to teach their children the skills they must have to prosper in a competitive society; to provide enough food, adequate shelter, and decent medical care for their families, and to help them achieve freedom from want and fear in their later years.

I do not believe we should stand idly by and permit our rural citizens to be ground into poverty—exposing them, unassisted and unencouraged, to the neglect of a changing society. Few other elements of our population are so treated by our humane and progressive people.

Yet I believe we need the counsel of those best qualified by experience and understanding of rural America's problems, to help us chart our course of assistance to her poor.

Consequently I shall soon appoint a Commission on Rural Poverty, whose task it will be to make recommendations to me, within one year of its appointment, on the most efficient and promising means of sharing America's abundance with those who have too often been her forgotten people.

Rural poverty has proved an almost intractable problem in past decades. Its abolition may require a journey of a thousand miles.

But the first step in that journey is the pooling of the common resources of rural Americans—joining them in a common planning effort that will magnify the resources of each.

In the program I propose, I ask the Congress to take that step with me today.

LYNDON B. JOHNSON

The White House
January 25, 1966

NOTE: The text of a draft bill, transmitted with the President's message and entitled "Community Development District Act of 1966," was also made public. It is printed in House Document 367 (89th Cong., 2d sess.). The bill passed the Senate and was reported out favorably by the House Agriculture Committee. No final action was taken by the House (2 Weekly Comp. Pres. Docs., p. 1547).

On September 27, 1966, the President approved Executive Order 11306 "Establishing the President's Committee on Rural Poverty and the National Advisory Commission on Rural Poverty" (2 Weekly Comp. Pres. Docs., p. 1373; 31 F.R. 12769; 3 CFR, 1966 Comp., p. 153).

For the President's special message to the Congress on agriculture of February 4, 1965, see 1965 volume, this series, Book I, Item 47.

See also Item 29.

---

29 Statement by the President on the Message Proposing a Program for Rural America. *January 25, 1966*

THERE IS one purpose in the message that I sent to Congress today. We must improve the lives of those who live in rural America.

The need for improvement is clear and is here, and the time is now.

Here are the facts:

Nearly half of the poor of this country now live in rural areas.

Almost one in every two rural families has a cash income under $3,000.

One-fourth of rural nonfarm homes are today without running water.

Rural people lag almost 2 years behind city people in educational attainment.

Health facilities in rural areas are very inadequate. Rural children receive one-third less medical attention than urban children.

All of these voids existed last year and despite the efforts of both the Executive and the Congress, they exist this year. They just must not be allowed to extend into the years ahead.

To do so would mock the abundance of this great land of ours. We must do all that it is possible to do to improve conditions now. Whole communities in our Nation are now denied the benefits of the strongest, the wealthiest country on earth. And that is why today I ask for the help of the Congress.

We already have the means for a massive attack on poverty. The legislation that we need was passed by the first session of this 89th Congress.

Today, however, many rural communities are not able to combine their available physical, human, and financial resources. They just must be able to do this if we are to achieve a satisfactory level of social and economic development.

I believe that the key to the rural future in America is planning for rural people. My recommendation, therefore, today is that the measures that I have requested for tomorrow be built on planning that will lead to action tomorrow.

Our purpose is to supplement and not supplant the present efforts of local and State and Federal Governments—but we must make it crystal clear that we do not, repeat, do not intend to forsake the small community in this land. We are going to do what it is needed to do in order to make the rural future brighter for the rural people who live in our rural areas.

NOTE: The President also recorded the statement for radio and television broadcast.

For the text of the President's message, see Item 28.

30 Special Message to the Congress Recommending a Program for Cities and Metropolitan Areas. *January 26, 1966*

To the Congress of the United States:

Nineteen-sixty-six can be the year of rebirth for American cities.

This Congress, and this people, can set in motion forces of change in great urban areas that will make them the masterpieces of our civilization.

Fifty years from now our population will reach that of today's India. Our grandchildren will inhabit a world as different from ours, as ours is from the world of Jefferson.

None can predict the shape of their life with any certainty. Yet one thing is sure. It will be lived in cities. By the year 2000, four out of five Americans will live and work in a metropolitan area.

We are not strangers to an urban world.

We began our national life gathered in towns along the Atlantic seaboard. We built new commercial centers around the Great Lakes and in the Midwest, to serve our Westward expansion.

Forty millions came from Europe to fuel our economy and enrich our community life. This century has seen the steady and rapid migration of farm families—seeking jobs and the promise of the city.

From this rich experience we have learned much.

We know that cities can stimulate the best in man, and aggravate the worst.

We know the convenience of city life,

and its paralysis.

We know its promise, and its dark foreboding.

What we may only dimly perceive is the gravity of the choice before us.

Shall we make our cities livable for ourselves and our posterity? Or shall we by timidity and neglect damn them to fester and decay?

If we permit our cities to grow without rational design—

If we stand passively by, while the center of each city becomes a hive of deprivation, crime, and hopelessness—

If we devour the countryside as though it were limitless, while our ruins—millions of tenement apartments and dilapidated houses—go unredeemed—

If we become two people—the suburban affluent and the urban poor, each filled with mistrust and fear one for the other—

If this is our desire and policy as a people, then we shall effectively cripple each generation to come.

We shall as well condemn our own generation to a bitter paradox: an educated, wealthy, progressive people, who would not give their thoughts, their resources, or their wills to provide for their common well-being.

I do not believe such a fate is either necessary or inevitable. But I believe this will come to pass—unless we commit ourselves now to the planning, the building, the teaching and the caring that alone can forestall it.

That is why I am recommending today a massive Demonstration Cities Program. I recommend that both the public and private sectors of our economy join to build in our cities and towns an environment for man equal to the dignity of his aspirations.

I recommend an effort larger in scope, more comprehensive, more concentrated—than any that has gone before.

THE WORK OF THE PAST

I know the work of the past three decades. I have shared in the forging of our Federal housing and renewal programs. I know what they have done for millions of urban Americans:

Eight million single family dwellings assisted by the Federal Housing Administration.

An additional 6.7 million assisted by the Veterans Administration.

1.1 million multiple units created.

605,000 families moved out of decayed and unsanitary dwellings into decent public housing.

300,000 dwelling units supported under urban renewal.

Without these programs, the goal I recommend today would be impossible to achieve. Because Federal sponsorship is so effective a part of our system of home-building, we can conceive a far larger purpose than it has yet fulfilled. We must make use of every established housing program—and of social, educational, and economic instruments as well—if the Demonstration Cities Program is to succeed.

THE PROBLEM TODAY

Our housing programs have built a platform, from which we may see how far away is the re-born city we desire. For there still remains:

—some 4 million urban families living in homes of such disrepair as to violate decent housing standards.

—the need to provide over 30% more housing annually than we are currently building.

—our chronic inability to provide sufficient low and moderate income housing, of adequate quality, at a reasonable price.

—the special problem of the poor and the Negro, unable to move freely from their ghettoes, exploited in the quest for the necessities of life.

—increasing pressures on municipal budgets, with large city per capita expenditures rising 36% in the three years after 1960.

—the high human costs: crime, delinquency, welfare loads, disease and health hazards. This is man's fate in those broken neighborhoods where he can "feel the enclosure of the flaking walls and see through the window the blackened reflection of the tenement across the street that blocks out the world beyond."

—the tragic waste and, indeed, the chaos that threatens where children are born into the stifling air of overcrowded rooms, destined for a poor diet, inadequate schools, streets of fear and sordid temptation, joblessness, and the gray anxiety of the ill-prepared.

—and the flight to the suburbs of more fortunate men and women, who might have provided the leadership and the means for reversing this human decline.

THE INADEQUATE RESPONSE

Since 1949, the urban renewal program has been our chief instrument in the struggle for a decent urban environment.

Over 800 cities are participating in urban renewal programs. Undertaken and designed by the cities themselves, these efforts have had an increasing influence on the use of urban land. Last year the Congress

wisely extended the authorization for urban renewal, at a higher level than before.

Years of experience with urban renewal have taught us much about its strengths and weaknesses.

Since 1961 we have made major alterations in its administration. We have made it more responsive to human needs. We have more vigorously enforced the requirement of a workable program for the entire community. Within the limits of current law, we have achieved considerable progress toward these goals.

Nevertheless the social and psychological effects of relocating the poor have not always been treated as what they are. They are the unavoidable consequences of slum clearance, demanding as much concern as physical redevelopment.

The size and scale of urban assistance has been too small, and too widely dispersed.

Present programs are often prisoners of archaic and wasteful building practices. They have inhibited the use of modern technology. They have inflated the cost of rebuilding.

The benefits and efficiencies that can come from metropolitan planning are still unrealized in most urban regions.

Insufficient resources cause extensive delays in many projects. The result is growing blight and over-crowding that thwart our best efforts to resist them.

The goals of major federal programs have often lacked cohesiveness. Some work for the revitalization of the central city. Some accelerate suburban growth. Some unite urban communities. Some disrupt them.

URBAN DILEMMAS

Virtually every forward step we have taken has had its severe limitations. Each of those steps has involved a public choice, and created a public dilemma:

—major clearance and reconstruction, with its attendant hardships of relocation.

—relieving traffic congestion, thereby widening the gulf between the affluence of suburbia and the poverty of the city.

—involving urban residents in redeveloping their own areas, hence lengthening the time and increasing the cost of the job.

—preserving the autonomy of local agencies, thus crippling our efforts to attack regional problems on a regional basis.

These dilemmas cannot be completely resolved by any single program, no matter how well designed. The prize—cities of spacious beauty and lively promise, where men are truly free to determine how they will live—is too rich to be lost because the problems are complex.

Let there be debate over means and priorities.

Let there be experiment with a dozen approaches, or a hundred.

But let there be commitment to that goal.

WHAT IS REQUIRED

From the experience of three decades, it is clear to me that American cities require a program that will:

—concentrate our available resources—in planning tools, in housing construction, in job training, in health facilities, in recreation, in welfare programs, in education—to improve the conditions of life in urban areas.

—join together all available talent and skills in a coordinated effort.

—mobilize local leadership and private initiative, so that local citizens will determine the shape of their new city— freed from the constraints that have

handicapped their past efforts and inflated their costs.

A DEMONSTRATION CITIES PROGRAM

I propose a Demonstration Cities Program that will offer qualifying cities of all sizes the promise of a new life for their people.

I propose that we make massive additions to the supply of low and moderate-cost housing.

I propose that we combine physical reconstruction and rehabilitation with effective social programs throughout the rebuilding process.

I propose that we achieve new flexibility in administrative procedures.

I propose that we focus all the techniques and talents within our society on the crisis of the American City.

It will not be simple to qualify for such a program. We have neither the means nor the desire to invest public funds in an expensive program whose net effects will be marginal, wasteful, or visible only after protracted delay.

We intend to help only those cities who help themselves.

I propose these guidelines for determining a city's qualifications for the benefits—and achievements—of this program.

1. The demonstration should be of sufficient magnitude both in its physical and social dimensions to arrest blight and decay in entire neighborhoods. It must make a substantial impact within the coming few years on the development of the entire city.

2. The demonstration should bring about a change in the total environment of the area affected. It must provide schools, parks, playgrounds, community centers, and access to all necessary community facilities.

3. The demonstration—from its beginning—should make use of every available

social program. The human cost of reconstruction and relocation must be reduced. New opportunities for work and training must be offered.

4. The demonstration should contribute to narrowing the housing gap between the deprived and the rest of the community. Major additions must be made to the supply of sound dwellings. Equal opportunity in the choice of housing must be assured to every race.

5. The demonstration should offer maximum occasions for employing residents of the demonstration area in all phases of the program.

6. The demonstration should foster the development of local and private initiative and widespread citizen participation—especially from the demonstration area—in the planning and execution of the program.

7. The demonstration should take advantage of modern cost-reducing technologies without reducing the quality of the work. Neither the structure of real estate taxation, cumbersome building codes, nor inefficient building practices should deter rehabilitation or inflate project costs.

8. The demonstration should make major improvements in the quality of the environment. There must be a high quality of design in new buildings, and attention to man's need for open spaces and attractive landscaping.

9. The demonstration should make relocation housing available at costs commensurate with the incomes of those displaced by the project. Counseling services, moving expenses, and small business loans should be provided, together with assistance in job placement and retraining.

10. The demonstration should be managed in each demonstration city by a single authority with adequate powers to carry out and coordinate all phases of the program.

There must be a serious commitment to the project on the part of local, and where appropriate, state authorities. Where required to carry out the plan, agreements should be reached with neighboring communities.

11. The demonstration proposal should offer proof that adequate municipal appropriations and services are available and will be sustained throughout the demonstration period.

12. The demonstration should maintain or establish a residential character in the area.

13. The demonstration should be consistent with existing development plans for the metropolitan areas involved. Transportation plans should coordinate every appropriate mode of city and regional transportation.

14. The demonstration should extend for an initial six-year period. It should maintain a schedule for the expeditious completion of the project.

These guidelines will demand the full cooperation of Government at every level and of private citizens in each area. I believe our Federal system is creative enough to inspire that cooperative effort. I know it must be so creative if it is to prosper and flourish.

SIZE OF THE PROGRAM

The program I recommend is intended to eliminate blight in the entire demonstration area. Through efficient rebuilding it must replace that blight with attractive and economic housing, social services, and community facilities.

There are many ways by which this can be done, once the commitment has been made to do it. Total clearance and reconstruction; partial clearance and rehabilitation; rehabilitation alone—any of these methods may be chosen by local citizens.

Whatever approach is selected, however, must be comprehensive enough to be effective and economic.

There are few cities or towns in America which could not participate in the Demonstration Cities Program. We shall take special care to see that urban communities of all sizes are included. For each such community, the impact of the program will be significant, involving as much as 15 to 20 percent of the existing substandard structures.

For the largest qualifying cities a relatively modest program could provide decent housing for approximately 5,000 families now living in substandard dwelling units. It could rehabilitate other marginal housing sufficient to affect 50,000 people. A typical program could well involve a total of 35,000 units or 100,000 people.

For cities of approximately 100,000 people, 1,000 families could be rehoused, and 3,000 units rehabilitated, affecting a total of 10,000 people.

BENEFITS OF THE PROGRAM

I recommend that participating cities receive two types of Federal assistance:

First, *the complete array of all available grants and urban aids* in the fields of housing, renewal, transportation, education, welfare, economic opportunity and related programs.

Second, *special grants amounting to 80% of the non-Federal cost of our grant-in-aid programs included in the demonstration.* These grants are to supplement the efforts of local communities. They are not to be substituted for those efforts.

In every qualifying city, a Federal coordinator would be assigned to assist local officials in bringing together all the relevant Federal resources.

Once authorized, the supplemental funds would be made available in a common account. They would be drawn at the discretion of the community to support the program. They would be certified by the Federal coordinator.

It is vital that incentives be granted for cost reductions achieved during the performance of the program.

At least as vital as the dollar commitment for rebuilding and rehabilitation is the social program commitment. We must link our concern for the total welfare of the person, with our desire to improve the physical city in which he lives. For the first time, social and construction agencies would be joined in a massive common effort, responsive to a common local authority.

There is another benefit—not measurable in dollars, or even in the extended range of social services—that qualifying cities would secure by participating in this program.

It is a sense of hope:

—that the city is not beyond reach of redemption by men of good will

—that through wise planning, cooperation, hard work, and the sacrifice of those outmoded codes and practices that make widespread renewal impossibly expensive today, it *is* possible to reverse the city's decline.

That knowledge, that confidence, that hope can make all the difference in the decade ahead.

FEDERAL COST

Funds are required in the first year to assist our cities in the preparation of demonstration plans. We should not underestimate the problems involved in achieving such a plan. The very scale of the demonstration, its widespread and profound effects on the social and physical structure of the city, calls for marshaling the city's planning and administrative resources on an unprecedented scale.

I estimate the appropriate Federal contribution to this planning effort at $12 million.

For the supplemental demonstration grants I will recommend appropriations, over a six-year period, totalling over $2.3 billion, or an average of some $400 million per year.

It is impossible to estimate exactly—but it is necessary to consider—the rising cost of welfare services, crime prevention, unemployment and declining property values that will plague all governments, local, state, and Federal, if we do not move quickly to heal and revitalize our cities.

METROPOLITAN PLANNING

The success of each demonstration will depend on the quality of its planning, and the degree of cooperation it elicits from the various governmental bodies concerned, as well as from private interests.

Most metropolitan areas conduct some degree of metropolitan planning now. The Federal Government has made funds available throughout the country so that state and local planning agencies might devise—many for the first time—comprehensive plans for metropolitan areas.

I recommend improvements and extensions of this program. The Congress enacted them recognizing that the problems of growth, transportation, housing, and public services cannot be considered by one entity of government alone.

The absence of cooperation between contiguous areas is wasteful. It is also blind to the reality of urban life. What happens in the central city, or the suburb, is certain to affect the quality of life in the other.

The widespread demand for these funds has resulted in their being spread thinly across the fifty states. Thus, the benefits of a truly coordinated attack on metropolitan problems have not generally been realized.

INCENTIVES TO ORDERLY METROPOLITAN DEVELOPMENT

Over the past five years, the Congress has authorized Federal grants for urban mass transportation, open space, and sewer and water facilities. The Congress has required that such projects be consistent with comprehensive planning for an entire urban or metropolitan area. The Federal Government has thus not only helped our localities to provide the facilities they need. It has also stimulated cooperation and joint planning among neighboring jurisdictions.

But more remains to be done. The powerful forces of urban growth threaten to overwhelm efforts to achieve orderly development. A metropolitan plan should be an instrument for shaping sound urban growth—not a neglected document.

I now propose a new incentive to help assure that metropolitan plans achieve their potential.

The Federal Government should bear a larger share of the total cost of related Federal aid programs. This share would be borne where local jurisdictions show that they are ready to be guided by their own plans in working out the patterns of their own development and where they establish the joint institutional arrangements necessary to carry out those plans.

DEMONSTRATIONS OF EFFECTIVE PLANNING

I propose that a series of demonstrations in effective metropolitan planning be undertaken promptly.

Metropolitan areas would be selected to return the broadest possible data and experience to Federal, state and local governments. They should therefore be of varying size and environment, in widely separated locations. They would be selected to assure that their benefits reach small communities surrounding the large cities.

Advanced techniques and approaches should be employed. There must be

—balanced consideration of physical and human development programs.

—coordinated treatment of the regional transportation network.

—technical innovations, such as metropolitan data banks and systems analysis.

—new educational and training programs.

—new arrangements for coordinating decisions of the various local governments involved.

I estimate the cost of the demonstrations at $6,500,000.

I shall impose on the new Department of Housing and Urban Development the continuing responsibility to stimulate effective planning. If local governments do not plan cooperatively and sufficiently in advance of inevitable urban growth, even adequate funds and an aggressive determination to improve our cities cannot succeed.

HOUSING FOR ALL

The programs I have proposed—in rebuilding large areas of our cities, and in metropolitan planning—are essential for the rebirth of urban America.

Yet at the center of the cities' housing problem lies racial discrimination. Crowded miles of inadequate dwellings—poorly maintained and frequently over-priced—is the lot of most Negro Americans in many of our cities. Their avenue of escape to a more attractive neighborhood is often closed, because of their color.

The Negro suffers from this, as do his children. So does the community at large. Where housing is poor, schools are generally poor. Unemployment is widespread. Family life is threatened. The community's welfare burden is steadily magnified. These are the links in the chain of racial discrimination.

This Administration is working to break that chain—through aid to education, medical care, community action programs, job retraining, and the maintenance of a vigorous economy.

The time has come when we should break one of its strongest links—the often subtle, but always effective force of housing discrimination. The impacted racial ghetto will become a thing of the past only when the Negro American can move his family wherever he can afford to do so.

I shall, therefore, present to the Congress at an early date legislation to bar racial discrimination in the sale or rental of housing.

NEW COMMUNITIES

Our existing urban centers, however revitalized, cannot accommodate all the urban Americans of the next generation.

Three million new residents are added each year to our present urban population. The growth of new communities is inevitable. Unless they are to be casual parts of a general urban sprawl, a new approach to their design is required.

We must:

—enlarge the entire scale of the building process;

—make possible new efficiencies in construction, land development, and municipal services;

—relieve population densities;

—offer a variety of homes to a wide

range of incomes.

These communities must also provide an environment harmonious to man's needs.

They must offer adequate transportation systems, attractive community buildings, and open spaces free from pollution. They must retain much of the natural beauty of the landscape.

The private sector must continue its prominent role in new community development. As I recommended to the Congress last year, mortgage insurance should be made available for sites and community facilities for entire new communities.

It is apparent that new communities will spring into being near an increasing number of major metropolitan areas. Some, already in existence, promise dramatic efficiencies through size and new construction techniques, without sacrificing beauty. Obviously such a development should be encouraged. I recommend that the Congress provide the means of doing so.

RENT SUPPLEMENT PROGRAM

Rarely has a new housing program evoked such a dramatic and positive response as the rent supplement program.

The Department of Housing and Urban Development has already received preliminary proposals from sponsors to construct nearly 70,000 low-income units under this program as soon as funds become available.

The proposals involve 424 projects in 265 localities in 43 States, the District of Columbia, and Puerto Rico. The sponsors have already selected sites for some 40,000 of these units. The interested groups are about equally divided between non-profit organizations and private limited dividend developers.

The need for this program is obvious. It is the need of the poor and the disadvan-

taged. The demand for the means to meet this need by private enterprise is demonstrated by the figures I have just cited.

I strongly urge the Congress to pass a supplementary appropriation to fund the rent supplement program at the $30 million level it has authorized in the Housing and Urban Development Act of 1965.

MASS TRANSPORTATION PROGRAM

We must continue to help our communities meet their increasing needs for mass transportation facilities. For this purpose, I propose an additional one-year authorization for the urban mass transportation program.

THE NEW DEPARTMENT

No Federal program can be effective unless the agency that administers it is efficient. This is even more crucial for programs that call for comprehensive approaches at both the Federal and local level.

Progress was made after 1961 toward unifying the Housing and Home Finance Agency. But the very nature of that agency limited the extent to which its several parts could be welded into a truly unified whole. Its Administrator lacked the statutory basis for gaining full control over partially independent agencies.

With this in mind, I requested—and you enacted—legislation to create a Department of Housing and Urban Development.

As a result, the Secretary of the new Department now has the authority and the machinery for implementing the new programs I have asked for.

I see five ways by which he can do this:

1. He can organize the Department so that its emphasis will be upon meeting modern urban needs—rather than fitting new

programs into old and outworn patterns.

2. He can strengthen the regional structure so that more decisions can be made in the field.

3. He can assert effective leadership throughout the Department.

4. He can mesh together all our social and physical efforts to improve urban living.

5. He can assume leadership among intergovernmental agencies dealing with urban problems.

Such a Department, and such leadership, will be worthy of the program I recommend you adopt.

A YEAR OF REBIRTH

The evidence is all about us that to be complacent about the American city is to invite, at best, inconvenience; at worst, a divided nation.

The programs I have proposed in this message will require a determined commitment of our energy and a substantial commitment of our funds.

Yet these programs are well within our resources. Nor do they compare in cost with the ugliness, hostility, and hopelessness of unlivable cities.

What would it mean to begin now, and to bring about the rebirth of our cities?

It would mean:

—a more tolerable and a more hopeful life for millions of Americans.

—the possibility of retaining middle-income families in the city, and even attracting some to return.

—improving the cities' tax base, at a time of heavy strain on city budgets.

—ultimately reducing welfare costs.

—avoiding the unnecessary waste of human resources.

—giving to both urban and suburban families the freedom to choose where they will live.

—a clean room and a patch of sky for every person, a chance to live near an open space, and to reach it on a safe street.

As Thomas Wolfe wrote, "to every man his chance—to every man, regardless of his birth, his shining, golden opportunity—to every man the right to live, to work, to be himself, and to become whatever thing his manhood and his vision can combine to make him—this . . . is the promise of America."

I believe these are among the most profound aspirations of our people. I want to make them part of our destiny.

I urge the Congress promptly to adopt the Demonstration Cities Act of 1966. If we began now the planning from which action will flow, the hopes of the twentieth century will become the realities of the twenty-first.

LYNDON B. JOHNSON

The White House
January 26, 1966

NOTE: The Demonstration Cities and Metropolitan Development Act of 1966 was approved by the President on November 3, 1966 (see Item 574).

Supplementary appropriations to fund the rent supplement program were approved by the President on May 13, 1966 (see Item 223).

See also Item 31.

31 Statement by the President on the Message Recommending a Program for Cities and Metropolitan Areas. *January 26, 1966*

TODAY, I have placed before the Congress and before you, the people of America, a new way of answering an ancient dream. That dream is of cities of promise, cities of hope, where it could truly be said, to every man his chance, to every man, regardless of his birth, his shining golden opportunity, to every man the right to live and to work and to be himself and to become whatever thing his manhood and his vision can combine to make him.

The new way of answering that ancient dream is this:

—to rebuild where there is hopeless blight;

—to renew where there is decay and ugliness;

—to refresh the spirit of men and women that are growing weary with jobless anxiety;

—to restore old communities and to bring forth new ones where children will be proud to say, "This is my home."

What I have offered is a massive program, involving everything that we know about building homes and schools and parks and streets that are safe from fear.

This is a program of cooperation. The cities, private enterprise, the Federal Government, all together will commit this Nation to the planning and the building and the teaching and the caring that alone will bring about a rebirth in our cities.

For 2 years now the best minds that we could enlist in this effort have worked together with Secretary Weaver to bring forth this program. I believe that our people, in great cities and in small towns, are now ready to dedicate themselves to this effort. I believe this great Congress will make this possible.

So let us begin—begin now, this year—so that a decade from now our cities may be what we have dreamed them to be—the masterpiece of our civilization.

NOTE: The President also recorded the statement for radio and television broadcast.

For the text of the President's message, see Item 30.

32 Message to the Eighteen-Nation Disarmament Committee on Its Reconvening in Geneva. *January 27, 1966*

THE AVOIDANCE of war and particularly nuclear war is the central, common concern of all mankind.

My country is dedicated to this end. The effort to control, and reduce—and ultimately eliminate—modern engines of nuclear destruction is fundamental to our policy. We have, with all mankind, a common interest in acting now to prevent nuclear spread, to halt the nuclear arms race, and to reduce nuclear stocks.

For this reason, we must press on with our work in Geneva. It is true that our meeting is shadowed by continuing aggression against the people and Government of South Vietnam. There are differences among the members of the Conference on Vietnam, but these differences make our common interest in preventing nuclear spread and curbing the nuclear arms race all the more important to pursue. Even while our own Nation is engaged in necessary resistance to aggression in Southeast Asia, it must continue to pursue every avenue for stable peace, both in Vietnam and throughout the world. That great general effort has no more important set of goals than those of disarmament, which are the business of this conference.

I have instructed the United States delegation to urge upon your meeting the following 7-point program:

1. First, let us seek a nonproliferation treaty which, in the words of the United Nations General Assembly, is "void of any loopholes which might permit nuclear or nonnuclear powers to proliferate, directly or indirectly, nuclear weapons in any form." We are prepared to sign such a treaty, making it applicable to nuclear and nonnuclear countries alike. We are prepared to work with other countries to assure that no nonnuclear country acquires its own nuclear weapons, gains national control over nuclear weapons, achieves the power itself to fire nuclear weapons, or receives assistance in manufacturing or testing nuclear weapons. We are prepared to agree that these things should not be done directly or indirectly, through third countries or groups of countries, or through units of the armed forces or military personnel under any military alliance.

2. Second, through a nonproliferation treaty and through efforts outside such a treaty, we must continue to secure application of International Atomic Energy Agency or equivalent international safeguards over peaceful nuclear activities. To this end, I urge agreement that all transfers of nuclear materials or equipment for peaceful purposes to countries which do not have nuclear weapons be under IAEA or equivalent international safeguards. At the same time, the major nuclear powers should accept in increasing measure the same international safeguards they recommend for other states.

Recently, many responsible Members of both Houses of the Congress of the United States introduced resolutions dealing with measures to prevent the spread of nuclear weapons. These resolutions are an indication of the importance that the people of the United States attribute to such measures, and to the role that international safeguards should play in them. I fully share these views.

3. Third, so that those who forswear nuclear weapons may forever refrain without fear from entering the nuclear arms race, let us strive to strengthen United Nations and other international security arrangements. Meanwhile, the nations that do not seek the nuclear path can be sure that they will have our strong support against threats of nuclear blackmail.

4. Fourth, my country persists in its belief that the perils of proliferation would be materially reduced by an extension of the limited test ban treaty to cover underground nuclear tests. For such an extension, the United States will require only that number and kind of inspections which modern science shows to be necessary to assure that the treaty is being faithfully observed. We call upon those nations truly interested in such a ban to provide to this Committee any improvements in means for the detection and identification of seismic events which their research efforts may have developed.

5. Fifth, let us seek agreement not to increase, and indeed to reduce, nuclear materials in weapons stockpiles. The United States continues to urge a verified halt in the production of fissionable materials for use in weapons. We continue to urge that such a halt be accompanied by the transfer of large quantities of fissionable material to peaceful purposes, under international safeguards. We continue to urge the demonstrated destruction of thousands of nuclear weapons by the United States and the

U.S.S.R. to produce this fissionable material. We have also stated our willingness, if others cannot now agree to halting all production of fissionable material for use in weapons, to accept step-by-step reductions of such production by the shutting down of equivalent facilities on a plant-by-plant basis, with the same type of effective inspection applicable to all.

6. Sixth, as another step to reduce the dangers and burdens of nuclear arms, let us direct our attention to modern, long-range, high-speed carriers of nuclear destruction. I urge continued exploration of the terms and conditions which could make acceptable to all the proposals I put before you in 1964 for a freeze on offensive and defensive strategic bombers and missiles designed to carry nuclear weapons. If progress can be made here, the United States will be prepared to explore the possibility of significant reductions in the number of these delivery vehicles. To facilitate agreement, let us begin now to seek common understanding of some of the issues involved in both these proposals.

7. Seventh, as we focus on nuclear arms, let us not forget that resources are being devoted to nonnuclear arms races all around the world. These resources might better be spent on feeding the hungry, healing the sick, and teaching the uneducated. The cost of acquiring and maintaining one squadron of supersonic aircraft diverts resources that would build and maintain a university. We suggest therefore that countries, on a regional basis, explore ways to limit competition among themselves for costly weapons often sought for reasons of illusory prestige. The initiative for arrangements of this kind should, of course, come from the regions concerned. The interested countries should undertake not to acquire from any source, including production of their own as well as importation from others, military equipment which they proscribe. If such arrangements can be worked out and assurance can be given that they will be observed, the United States stands ready to respect them.

Each of these steps would contribute toward reducing the danger and destruction of war. Each of them would take us further down the path toward our ultimate goal of general and complete disarmament. Yet each of them is possible of achievement today if only all nations have the will.

The limited test ban treaty lit a candle of hope in the darkness. The gleam of that candle shows the way to a brighter tomorrow if we will but follow. We must move toward it quickly while there is yet time.

NOTE: The President's message was read by William C. Foster, U.S. Representative to the 18-Nation Disarmament Committee. The committee resumed its discussions in Geneva on January 27.

33 Remarks at the Signing of the Economic Report for 1966. *January 27, 1966*

Chairman Ackley, Mr. Eckstein, Mr. Okun, members of the very valued staff of the Council of Economic Advisers:

I have come here today to sign the President's Economic Report for 1966. I submit it with both pride and confidence. For I believe it reflects a productive past and, I think, a promising future. It reflects a strong and a growing and a vibrant America.

This report chronicles achievement that is unprecedented in America's peacetime history—5 years of uninterrupted prosperity that have brought to this Nation record employment, record wages, record buying power, record production, record sales, and record profits.

This achievement was not only the work of the President or the Congress or the Government alone. It was the work of all of the American people, of their industry, their faith, and their cooperation. And so now, today, we turn and look at the future, and I think we can do so with confidence and with determination.

Our gross national product for 1966 is expected to rise by 5 percent in real output, to a total of $722 billion. Our price stability is expected to remain the best of any industrial nation in the world. Our unemployment rate is expected to fall well below 4 percent, to the lowest rate since 1953.

But none of this can or will come about by pure accident. We can sustain and we can enlarge our prosperity, but we can do so only if we are willing to work for it and if we are willing to sacrifice for it.

This year we must sacrifice the luxury of tax reduction. We must hold the expansion of our civilian Great Society programs below what would have been possible without Vietnam. We must all exercise wage and price restraint—in Government, in business, and in labor.

We must work to eliminate the remaining balance of payments deficit. We have made a good start and we are very proud of it, but we must realize that there is much work ahead.

We must retrain our jobless, we must educate our young, we must care for our sick, and we must house our poor. We must protect the public against strike emergencies. We must extend and raise the minimum wage. We must strengthen unemployment insurance.

We must be prepared, if necessary, to move quickly on tax changes. We must improve regulation of our financial institutions. We must protect consumers through fair packaging and labeling and through truth in lending.

Yes, the United States is closer today than any nation in history to man's ancient goal of abundance for all. If we are wise, if we are daring, if we are prudent, we can achieve that goal, I believe, in our lifetime.

This Economic Report charts the course for all of us. I believe that all America is ready to follow. There will be some who disagree. We do have diverse opinions in this country, but I hope and believe that there will not be opposition just for opposition's sake. Just as I do not want or expect every member of my own party to support every administration program or every administration policy, so do I hope and so do I pray that the members of the opposition will not necessarily or automatically criticize or nit-pick or point out weaknesses in every single move we make.

We are at a point in world history in our time when this Nation is called upon to exercise leadership, to lead the way, not only in international policies but to lead the way here at home in our domestic policies. And the unity and the coordination and the cooperation of diverse groups of all peoples from all regions is extremely important, and I don't know of any time in our history when this Nation has had better understanding and better cooperation, certainly in questions of economic policy.

Just as the three branches of Government are working closely together and understand the true American philosophy, so are the various elements of our society—Government and business and labor.

And so I not only commend those elements of our society who have made it possible for us to reach this high state of prosperity in this country, but I commend this very exceptional nonpartisan, highly trained staff who have provided the leadership and the thought and the judgment and the plans that have resulted in bringing such good times to all the American people, and at least to improving the lot of men everywhere in the world.

NOTE: The President spoke at 11:39 a.m. on January 26 in the Cabinet Room at the White House. In

his opening words he referred to Gardner Ackley, Chairman of the Council of Economic Advisers, and Otto Eckstein and Arthur M. Okun, members of the Council.

After signing the report the President personally greeted members of the Council's staff, a number of whom were present at the ceremony.

For the text of the Economic Report, see Item 34.

34 Annual Message to the Congress: The Economic Report of the President. *January 27, 1966*

To the Congress of the United States:

A year ago I reported that we were "in the midst of the greatest upsurge of economic well-being in the history of any nation." That upsurge, now about to enter its sixth year, continues without let-up.

- The value of our Nation's annual output of goods and services rose more than one-third from 1960 to 1965. Last year alone, our gross national product (GNP) made a record advance of $47 billion.

- This swelling production has generated an unprecedented rise in the incomes of the American people. Total personal income in December was at an annual rate of $550 billion, up 37 percent in the past 5 years and 7½ percent in the latest 12 months.

- In the past 5 years, the number of Americans at work increased by nearly 7 million; in 1965 alone, by about 2½ million. The rate of unemployment dropped from 6.6 percent in December 1960 (and a high of 7.1 percent in May 1961) to 4.1 percent in December 1965.

- And American jobs are better than ever before. The weekly take-home pay of the average manufacturing worker with three dependents has risen 26 percent in the past 5 years. In the last 12 months alone his gain was 4 percent.

- The profits of our corporations, after taxes, last year were 67 percent ahead of their earnings 5 years earlier—up 20 percent over 1964.

- And average farm income last year rose 23 percent, breaking all records.

Our Nation's industries, shops, and farms—our workers, owners of businesses, professional men and women—prosper today far beyond the dreams of any people, anytime, anywhere.

NEW ECONOMIC ENVIRONMENT

In the light of these unprecedented and continuing gains, some observers are posing questions not heard in almost a decade.

- Will there be enough plant capacity to produce all the goods and services buyers will seek?

- Can our employers find the labor they will require to man their production lines?

- Can we avoid bottlenecks in major industries or key skills that would hamper our expansion?

- Can we keep a destructive price-wage spiral from getting underway?

- Can we move ahead with the Great Society programs and at the same time meet our needs for defense?

My confident answer to each of these questions is YES.

But the fact these questions are seriously asked and require serious answers is proof enough that we are in a new economic environment. We are approaching full use of our resources, and this brings new problems.

To those who fear these new problems, I say this:

- These are the problems we have been waiting to encounter for nearly 10 years.
- These problems are the price of our success.
- These are the welcome problems of prosperity.

Over the past 5 years we have faced very different economic problems. In meeting these problems we have learned that

—recessions are not inevitable;

—high production does not necessarily mean overproduction;

—expansion need not generate inflation or imbalances that make further expansion unsustainable;

—affluence has not sapped the inherent strength and dynamism of the American economy;

—automation need not create mass unemployment;

—millions who were unemployed are not unemployable;

—prudently expansionary fiscal policies can restore high employment; and

—domestic expansion can go hand in hand with strengthened external payments and a sound dollar.

We have learned how to achieve prosperity. Now we must sustain it, deal with its problems, and make the most of the opportunities it presents.

VIETNAM AND OUR ECONOMY

We face the challenges of prosperity while some 200,000 of our fellow citizens and bil-lions of dollars of our resources are engaged in a bitter defense of freedom in Vietnam. The true costs of this conflict are death, pain, and grief; interrupted careers and separation from loved ones. They are incalculable. But the *economic* cost of Vietnam imposes no unbearable burden on our resources.

Vietnam does, however, add to the usual problems of maintaining balanced prosperity. It imposes special burdens on some industries, and raises, as well, uncertainties both for the fiscal planning of Government and the private planning of business. These uncertainties underscore the need for flexibility in Government policies and responsibility in private decisions.

Production for Vietnam accounts for less than 1½ percent of our GNP. These expenditures are a part of the total demand that provides a full market for our manpower and our production. But the private demands of consumers and businesses, and high-priority civilian programs of Government, could and would provide a far more welcome market for that output if there were no war in Vietnam. Our prosperity does not depend on our military effort.

THE PRINCIPLES OF ECONOMIC POLICY

In a time of high prosperity, economic policy faces new problems. But it is still guided by the basic principles that have served us so well.

Twenty years ago next month, the Employment Act of 1946—which prescribes this Report—became law. The principles of our policy emerge from that Act and from our two decades of experience under it.

The essential and revolutionary declaration of the Employment Act was that the Federal Government must accept a share of responsibility for the performance of the American economy. The nature of that share has been more and more clearly defined over the years, by the recommendations of four Presidents and the enactments of ten Congresses.

I see these as the main tasks of Federal economic policy today:

1. To attain full employment without inflation; to use fiscal and monetary policies to help to match total demand to our growing productive potential, while helping to speed the growth of that potential through education, research and development, manpower policies, and enlarged private and public investment;

2. To help to open the doors of opportunity to all, through developing human resources and removing barriers of discrimination, ignorance, and ill-health;

3. To help to solve social and economic problems that neither private action nor State and local governments can solve alone—an efficient transportation system, the protection of our environment, the health of our agriculture, the reconstruction of our cities;

4. To achieve and maintain equilibrium in the Nation's external payments, and to press for improvements in the international economic order;

5. To maintain and enhance healthy competition;

6. To achieve national purposes as far as possible by enlisting the voluntary cooperation of business, labor, and other groups.

Recognition of these responsibilities of the Federal Government neither lessens the responsibilities nor impairs the freedoms of individuals and private groups; nor does it challenge the authority of State and local governments.

The tasks involve new and growing problems of an increasingly complex and interdependent economy and society. Only the Federal Government can assume these tasks. But the Federal Government by itself cannot create prosperity, reduce unemployment, avoid inflation, balance our external accounts, restore our cities, strengthen agriculture, eliminate poverty, or make people healthy.

Only through a creative and cooperative partnership of all private interests and all levels of government—a creative Federalism—can our economic and social objectives be attained. This partnership has written the story of American success. And a new vitalization of this partnership and a new confidence in its effectiveness have produced the extraordinary economic and social gains of recent years.

OUR ECONOMIC GAINS

Our economy is so vast, and our progress has been so rapid, that it is difficult to keep our gains in proper perspective. Here are a few examples:

• In only seven other countries of the world is *total* output in a year as large as the *increase* in our output last year.

• Our stock of private plant and equipment, valued in constant prices, *increased* as much in 1965 alone as it did in the 4 years 1957 through 1960.

• The *increase* in Federal cash receipts between fiscal years 1961 and 1967—in spite of $20 billion of tax cuts—will exceed the entire cash receipts of the Federal Government in any peacetime fiscal year prior to 1951.

JOBS, INCOMES, AND PRODUCTION.—The register of our economic gains during 1965 starts with jobs:

—2.4 million more, over-all;

—1.0 million more for teenagers;

—350,000 more for Negroes;

—900,000 more for women;

—1.2 million more for blue-collar workers;

—900,000 more on manufacturing payrolls;

—450,000 more on State and local government payrolls;

—1.0 million more in trade and services.

It continues with pay:

—average hourly earnings up 3 percent in manufacturing, 4½ percent in retail trade;

—average weekly earnings up 3½ percent in manufacturing, 3⅓ percent in trade.

Other forms of income rose, too:

—farm proprietors' average income up 22 percent;

—average income of owners of unincorporated businesses and professional workers up 7½ percent;

—total dividends paid up 12 percent.

And corporations prospered, with

—profits before taxes up 15 percent;

—profits after taxes up 20 percent;

—corporate retained earnings up 29 percent.

With more people earning, and earning more,

—total personal incomes rose $39 billion, or 7½ percent;

—aggregate consumers' incomes after taxes rose $34 billion, also 7½ percent.

Governmental units benefited from the surge of incomes.

• Federal cash receipts rose $8½ billion.

• State and local governments took in $4⅓ billion more, reducing the need for tax rate increases to meet their expanding burdens.

The higher incomes of individuals, businesses, and governments came from expanding production (year 1965 over year 1964):

Production of goods and services for consumers........ Up $29½ billion.
Production of new plants and machinery .... Up $9½ billion.
Production for use of the Federal Government........ Up $1½ billion.
Production for use of State and local governments........ Up $5 billion.
Production for additions to inventories .... Up $2½ billion.
Residential construction...... No change.
Production for export (less imports) .... Down $1½ billion.
　Total production (GNP). Up $47 billion.

We could produce $47 billion of additional output last year because:

• We had a large net addition of 1.4 million to our labor force;

• We put to work this entire net increment plus about 400,000 who were previously unemployed;

• On the average, each employed person worked a few more hours during the year; and

• Each man-hour worked in the private economy produced on the average 2.8 percent more output than in 1964.

Increased employment and higher productivity were possible because business investment had provided a substantial expansion of plant capacity; because the new and the previously existing capacity were used more fully than in the year before; and because our labor force was better educated and more skilled than ever before. Our efforts to equip the unskilled and inexperienced to take advantage of rapidly expanding job opportunities have been—and will continue to be—an investment in our productive capacity.

The enlarged market demands which called forth this higher output came from every sector. The two dominant forces, however, were the growing boom in business spending for new plant and equipment and the continued dependability of consumer spending, following close on consumer income. Excise tax cuts and larger social security benefits in 1965 helped to swell the income and buying of households. The tax cuts provided by the Revenue Act of 1964 were sustaining private demand all year. By

99

year's end they had added $30 billion to GNP.

GAINS FOR THE DISADVANTAGED.—The disadvantaged and less fortunate members of our society also shared in our 1965 economic gains.

* For the poor who were able to earn, there were lower unemployment, fuller work schedules, and higher pay.
* For the poor who were capable of earning more, there were job training and help in finding jobs, improvements in education, and the breaking down of barriers of discrimination.
* For the poor who could not earn, there were more adequate social security benefits, new medical programs, and better social services.
* For the poor too young to earn, there were more effective education, assistance to enable them to stay in school, and better health services.

Between 1964 and 1965, an estimated 2.2 million persons moved above the poverty line. Millions of others, mostly children and young people, will have a better chance to break out of poverty in the years ahead as a result of the help they will receive from new Federal education, health, and antipoverty programs enacted in 1964 and 1965.

But 32 million Americans remain in poverty, and millions more are unable to realize their full economic potential. America's abundance leaves behind too many who are aged, who are stranded in declining rural areas, who are in broken families, who are uneducated or handicapped or victims of discrimination. Unemployment among Negroes remains twice that of whites. And an unemployment rate of 13 percent among teenagers means that too many youths find disappointment in moving from school into jobs.

The war on poverty, ignorance, ill-health,

discrimination, and inadequate opportunity must go forward.

STRENGTHENED PAYMENTS BALANCE.—In 1965 we reduced our balance of payments deficit to less than half that in 1964 and 1963. We have shown a skeptical world that a voluntary program—relying on the patriotic cooperation of businesses and banks—could work.

We made substantial progress in 1965

—despite the fact that our new program did not start until late in the first quarter of the year;

—despite increased responsibilities in Vietnam;

—despite a temporary decline in our trade surplus;

—despite conversion by the U.K. Government of more than $½ billion of U.S. securities and other assets.

Last year we moved forward toward payments balance without sacrificing our vital domestic or international objectives. And we intend to complete the job this year.

THE RECORD OF COSTS AND PRICES.—Until a year ago, American costs and prices had been essentially unchanged since 1958. Last year, largely through a surge in agricultural and food prices, the record was blemished. Even so, we have not lost ground to our major competitors overseas, whose prices and costs have generally risen more than ours.

Some internationally traded raw materials—particularly metals and hides—are costing us more. And higher prices for petroleum products and some machinery have also nudged up our price indexes.

But labor costs—the most basic element in the structure of our costs—have barely moved, as gains in productivity have largely offset moderate increases in hourly labor costs.

In many major sectors of our economy,

price stability is still the rule, and some important prices are still going down, in line with lower costs. In December, some of the wholesale prices that were lower than a year earlier were:

fresh and dried fruits and vegetables	millwork
plant and animal fibers	building paper and board
coal	motor vehicles
electric power	heating equipment
packaged beverage materials	household appliances
manmade fibers	televisions, radios, phonographs
inedible fats and oils	floor coverings
paint materials	flat glass
crude rubber	gypsum products.

Many industries and markets have demonstrated that the gains of lower costs and rapidly rising productivity can be shared with consumers. Wholesale prices of the following categories of products in December averaged at least 5 percent lower than in 1957–59:

fresh and dried fruits and vegetables	crude rubber
grains	tires and tubes
plant and animal fibers	plywood
packaged beverage materials	building paper and board
manmade fibers	heating equipment
paint materials	household appliances
drugs and pharmaceuticals	televisions, radios, and phonographs
	asphalt roofing.

Those who proclaim inflation is already here have not turned over all the price tags.

ECONOMIC OUTLOOK FOR 1966

Demand will continue to grow rapidly in 1966 and production will respond. The vigor of *investment spending* demonstrates strong business confidence in the growing sales, rising profits, and firm operating rates which spur expansion and modernization. The rising *defense needs* of the Federal Government are an important new force in the economy. With growing support from Federal grant programs, *State and local purchases* will keep moving ahead. Rising consumer incomes from wages, dividends, interest, professional work, and farming will again largely be devoted to *expenditures for better living*.

These forces should add very nearly as much to our GNP in 1966 as the record gain of $47 billion last year. As the midpoint of a $10 billion range, $722 billion is the projected level of GNP in 1966. With that output, we foresee

—an extra $40 billion of spending and production for civilian needs, both private and public;

—unemployment shrinking below 4 percent, and below any yearly average rate since 1953;

—great advances in the productive capacity of our industries;

—further good gains in productivity; and

—full use, without overuse or strain, of our productive capacity.

FISCAL AND MONETARY POLICY.—The fiscal program I recommend for 1966 aims at full employment without inflation. It is a responsible program. It recognizes that vigorous private demand and required defense spending could upset the balance of supply and demand so diligently pursued by fiscal and monetary policies in recent years, and now so effectively achieved.

Until this year, pursuit of this balance has pointed fiscal policies toward the stimulation of demand. Now a stimulus is no longer appropriate.

I have reviewed every program of Government to make room for the necessities of defense. I have sharply reduced or eliminated those civilian programs of lowest priority.

But, as I indicated in my State of the Union Message, I am unwilling to declare a moratorium on our progress toward the Great Society. My budget will add $3.2

billion to our war against poverty, ignorance, and disease. Yet savings elsewhere will hold the rise in the Administrative Budget—apart from the added costs of Vietnam—to only $600 million.

Moreover, I am asking the Congress to enact promptly a combination of proposals affecting tax payments in the year ahead:

—a rescheduling of the January 1, 1966 and later excise tax reduction enacted last June for automobiles and telephone service;

—a graduated withholding system that will improve the pay-as-you-go basis of our personal income taxes without increasing tax rates or tax liabilities;

—a corresponding speed-up in payments of corporate income taxes this year and next, also without increasing tax rates or tax liabilities; and

—a method of paying self-employment Social Security taxes on a current basis.

These measures will let us stay close to a high-level balance between the revenues that the Federal Government draws out of the economy and the expenditures that it puts back into the spending stream, and to a high-level balance between total demand and the economy's capacity to produce. It is my judgment that this budget provides the appropriate fiscal environment for the maintenance of basic price stability with continued growth.

I will also look to the Federal Reserve System to provide assistance in promoting the objectives we all share:

—meeting the credit needs of a vigorous and growing economy, while

—preventing excessive credit flows that could carry the pace of expansion beyond prudent speed limits.

THE UNCERTAINTIES.—We have made the best economic judgments we can. This year, they were unusually difficult. If the tax measures I am now proposing, in conjunction with the moderating influence of monetary policy, do not hold total demand within bounds of the Nation's productive capacity, I will not hesitate to ask for further fiscal restraints on private spending. Nor will I hesitate to ask for such further fiscal action if additional defense requirements demand it during the year. And I will welcome the opportunity to alter my budget in the event that a relaxation of international tensions permits lower defense outlays than are now foreseen.

Our defense needs are great; but our growth is far greater. The demands on our economy are strong; but its productive capabilities are enormous. Surprises surely lie ahead; but our ability to cope with change is strong and improving.

MAINTAINING COST-PRICE STABILITY
IN 1966

One of the problems of prosperity we face in 1966 is that of achieving stability of prices and costs at full employment.

The basic precondition for price stability is a fiscal-monetary policy that deters total demand for goods and services from outrunning potential supply. But history proclaims that something more is needed: a sense of responsibility to the public interest by labor and business in setting wages and prices.

The vigorous economy we foresee in 1966 will tempt labor unions to demand wage increases that would raise costs, and businesses to raise prices when profit margins are already fully adequate. Labor must remember that growing employment and productivity are the foundation of higher wages, and business that an expanding economy is the basic source of profit gains. These foundations must not be jeopardized.

The Federal Government does not have authority to impose ceilings on wages and prices.

But when 200,000 of our fellow citizens are risking their lives in the defense of freedom overseas, the Government's duty is to ask those who enjoy a comfortable prosperity at home to exercise responsibly their freedom to set prices and wages.

Foregoing the freedom to act irresponsibly is no real sacrifice. For irresponsible action can only bring on an inflation that would damage all—labor, business, and the national interest.

The attached Report of the Council of Economic Advisers contains a thorough discussion of its guideposts for noninflationary wage and price behavior. To maintain price stability in the expanding economy of 1966, it is vitally important that labor and industry follow these guideposts.

The public can expect that the responsible actions of labor and management will be strengthened and supplemented by all the policies of the Federal Government:

• Manpower, education, and rehabilitation programs will continue to train the unemployed and to prepare our youth, increasing the supply of qualified workers and their productivity.

• Where available, surplus Federal stockpiles will be used to prevent unnecessary shortages of materials and commodities.

• Defense procurement, agricultural, and other policies will be adjusted where necessary to avoid contributing to instability of prices.

• Fair Labor Standards legislation and Government pay increases should be consistent with the guideposts.

There are no general labor shortages in our economy now, and none should develop in the year ahead. But in some industries,

occupations, and areas, limited stringencies are appearing.

Prompt and effective action will be taken to meet any problem of specific labor shortage. I have instructed the Secretary of Labor to take all possible and necessary steps. And I have asked all other Departments to cooperate in this effort.

It will not be easy to reconcile price stability and full employment. Some price movements reflect worldwide changes in supply and demand. But over-all stability of costs and prices will be preserved in the year ahead, provided that during 1966

—public policies maintain a balance between overall supply and demand and address themselves vigorously to any emerging sectoral imbalances, and

—business and labor accept the principles of the guideposts for noninflationary behavior.

We will have demonstrated that a free economy can both maintain full employment and avoid inflation—and do so without arbitrary controls.

INTERNATIONAL ECONOMIC POLICIES
FOR 1966

These are the objectives of our international economic policies in 1966:

—to correct our remaining balance of payments deficit, so that the dollar will remain strong;

—to work toward reduction of trade barriers, so that all nations may reap the benefits of freer trade;

—to improve the international monetary system, so that it will continue to facilitate sound and orderly growth of the world economy;

—to press forward with the other fortunate nations in the great international task of our age: helping those countries now economically less advanced which are prepared to help themselves make rapid progress toward a better life in freedom.

BALANCE OF PAYMENTS.—Decisive progress was made in 1965 toward reducing our balance of payments deficit. Though the results for 1965 are gratifying, we cannot afford to relax. We have not yet balanced our external accounts.

For 1966, external balance is our goal. It requires that

- Business continue to cooperate wholeheartedly in following the strengthened guidelines governing capital flows announced in December;
- Banks and financial institutions maintain their excellent performance of last year;
- Businesses sell even more abroad this year, in spite of full domestic order books;
- Business and labor keep costs and prices stable in order to maintain the competitiveness of our goods and services in international markets;
- Government work vigorously to minimize the dollar drain abroad of its aid and defense programs as well as all other activities;
- The Congress pass the tax legislation I recommended last year to enhance opportunities for foreigners to invest in the United States;
- We intensify our efforts to encourage our own citizens and foreigners to travel in the United States. I am directing that high priority be given to these efforts.

TRADE.—The year 1966 is the year when the world can take a giant step forward in liberalizing international trade by successfully concluding the Kennedy Round of negotiations to reduce trade barriers on all classes of products. The resulting growth of world trade and world income will benefit all countries, developing as well as industrial. The United States will bend every effort to get meaningful negotiations back on the track. This great venture in international cooperation must not fail.

We shall continue our efforts to improve the trade prospects of the developing countries by helping to stabilize commodity trade, by supporting regional integration among them where practicable, by providing access to markets, and by giving positive assistance to export promotion.

INTERNATIONAL MONETARY REFORM.—As we achieve and maintain balance in our external accounts, dollars will no longer add to international monetary reserves as they have in the past. We learned long ago that we cannot rely on gold alone. The free world must look to new sources of liquidity—rather than to deficits in the U.S. balance of payments—to support growing international trade and payments.

We are, therefore, pressing forward with other nations

—to assure the adequate and orderly growth of world monetary reserves;
—to improve the adjustment of imbalances by both surplus and deficit countries;
—to strengthen the monetary system that has served the world so well.

I hope that the major industrial nations—and then the entire community of free nations—will reach an agreement that will make creation of new reserve assets a deliberate decision of the community of nations to serve the economic welfare of all.

ECONOMIC ASSISTANCE.—We have molded our foreign assistance policies into more efficient tools with which to confront one of history's gravest challenges—the development of the impoverished but awakening and turbulent two-thirds of the world.

The United States stands ready to continue to assist those countries which have demonstrated their commitment to the task of moving their economies forward toward self-sustaining growth under freedom.

In recent years, I have consciously held back further increases in our foreign assistance request while we designed a lean but effective program to give maximum impact to each dollar we spend.

Today, we are ready to move forward with special emphasis on three areas in which the United States is particularly well qualified to help:

—*agriculture,* to stimulate food production where it fails to keep pace with spiraling populations;

—*health,* to strengthen millions who could contribute more fully to their own economic progress;

—*education and training,* to provide the modern skills needed for development.

URBAN PROBLEMS AND POLICIES

We are an urban society. In 1900, America's urban areas contained 30 million people, 40 percent of our population. By the year 2000, 250 million, 80 percent of our population, are likely to be urban. The quality of American life increasingly depends on the physical, economic, aesthetic, and social qualities of our urban centers.

American cities possess some of the rarest treasures of art, the finest music and theater, the greatest universities, the loveliest parks, the most splendid vistas, the most elegant and luxurious living, in the entire world. Yet they also contain degrading poverty, revolting slums, incredible traffic congestion, bitter racial tensions, physical decay and ugliness, political disorganization, and rising crime and delinquency.

The Congress created last year a Department of Housing and Urban Development, giving it responsibilities for coordinating Federal programs affecting housing, urban areas, and urban people, and for administering many such programs. I have no intention of letting it become merely a housekeeping agency to supervise miscellaneous programs.

With the help of the finest minds in the Nation, we have been developing a program to rebuild—in cooperation with State and local governments, private agencies, business enterprises, and local citizens—the physical, institutional, and social environment of our urban areas. Each city should plan on an integrated basis for its own physical, economic, and social development. And where those plans are imaginative, farsighted, and efficient, the Federal Government should help to make them realities.

I am asking the Congress to consider proposed legislation to carry out these objectives. I am also preparing proposals for legislation to bar discrimination in the sale or rental of housing—a condition which has contributed to many urban problems.

TRANSPORTATION

The revolutionary changes in transportation technology of the past half century have not been matched by equal progress in our public policies or our Federal organization.

I am recommending the creation of a Department of Transportation

—to manage the vast Federal promotional programs in highways, waterways, air travel, and maritime affairs, and

—to take leadership in the development of new transportation policies in accord with current realities.

I am proposing again this year increased user charges on highways and aviation and the introduction of nominal user charges on inland waterways. Such charges will improve efficiency in the use of resources, and reimburse the Federal Government for a part of its expenditures which directly benefit the users of these facilities.

We spend billions of dollars in medical research each year to conquer disease and prolong life. Yet we still put up with the senseless slaughter of thousands of Americans on our highways.

Fifty thousand Americans met their death in traffic accidents during 1965. About 3½ million were injured. The economic cost of accidents is estimated at around $8 billion a year.

We can no longer ignore the problem of automobile safety. We can no longer procrastinate and hope that the situation will improve. I will propose new programs to protect the safety of our citizens and the efficient flow of our commerce.

CONTROLLING POLLUTION

Our means for attacking the shameful pollution of our environment were strengthened in the first session of this Congress by important new standard-setting authority over water quality and automotive exhausts.

Federal agencies have begun cleaning up the numerous and extensive sources of water pollution from their own facilities, in response to my Executive Order. Despite budgetary stringency, expenditures for this purpose will be given high priority. I shall issue an Executive Order covering air pollution from Federal installations.

I propose that, in cooperation with appropriate State and local authorities and private interests, we carry out projects to clean up several entire river basins, following the example of our efforts to clean up the Potomac.

Special Federal financial assistance will be necessary; this should be conditioned on new financial and organizational arrangements by State and local authorities.

LABOR AND MANAGEMENT

UNION SECURITY AGREEMENTS.—Strong and responsible collective bargaining is an important instrument of a free and healthy economy.

To improve its functioning and to make the national labor policy uniform throughout the country, I again urge the Congress to repeal Section 14(b) of the Taft-Hartley Act.

STRIKE EMERGENCIES.—The recent transit strike in New York City illustrates our helplessness in preventing extreme disruption to the lives and livelihoods of a city of 8 million people. I intend to ask the Congress to consider measures that, without improperly invading State and local authority, will enable us to deal effectively with strikes that may cause irreparable damage to the national interest.

UNEMPLOYMENT INSURANCE.—Our system of Unemployment Insurance has not kept pace with our advancing economy. The time to modernize it is now, when unemployment is low and the cost of improved protection can be readily absorbed. We need a program that will provide more realistic benefits, including benefits for more workers and for longer periods of joblessness; that will correct abuses and assure efficient and responsible administration; and that will broaden the system's tax base and strengthen its financing. I urge the Congress to enact such a program.

FAIR LABOR STANDARDS.—Millions of workers at the bottom of our wage scale still lack the protection of Federal minimum standards. At the same time, we need to reinforce this protection by raising the minimum wage.

I recommend the extension of the Fair Labor Standards Act to large numbers of additional workers. In enacting higher minimum wage levels, the Congress should consider carefully their effects on substandard incomes, on cost and price stability, and on the availability of job opportunities for marginal workers.

TAX REFORM AND SIMPLIFICATION

Against a background calling for fiscal restraint, I cannot this year endorse any specific legislative measure, however meritorious, involving significant net tax reduction. The danger of inflation from increased demand would be too great, and any special tax reduction now would postpone the time when we can achieve a meaningful general tax reduction.

Although tax reduction is not feasible this year, improvement of our tax system is a continuing need which will concern this Administration and which deserves the support of all Americans.

One major goal must be simplification of the tax law. Another aim must be a more equitable distribution of the tax load. The great variation of tax liability among persons with equivalent income or wealth must be reduced. Further, when tax reduction once again becomes feasible, particular attention must be given to relief of those at or near poverty levels of income.

Finally, we must review special tax preferences. In a fully employed economy, special tax benefits to stimulate some activities or investments mean that we will have less of other activities. Benefits that the Government extends through direct expenditures are periodically reviewed and often altered in the budget-appropriation process, but too little attention is given to reviewing particular tax benefits. These benefits, like all other activities of Government, must stand up to the tests of efficiency and fairness.

We must constantly seek improvements in the tax code in the interests of equity and of sound economic policy.

I welcome the concern over these problems shown by the Chairmen of the tax committees of the Congress.

As a specific tax reform which can be accomplished this year, I call upon the Congress to deal with abuses of tax-exempt private foundations.

We must always be prepared to meet quickly any problems that arise in the path of continued, stable economic growth, whether the problems call for fiscal stimulus or fiscal restraint. Background tax studies by both the Congress and Executive Branch should therefore be adequate to permit quick decisions and prompt action to accommodate short-run cyclical changes. If quick action is ever needed, we should not have to begin a long debate on what the changes in taxes should be.

FINANCIAL INSTITUTIONS IN OUR CHANGING
ECONOMIC ENVIRONMENT

The vigor and soundness of our financial institutions are vital to the vigor and soundness of our economic expansion. Actions to ease unnecessarily restrictive regulations have been taken in the past; they have borne fruit in stronger competition and a more efficient flow of funds from savers to borrowers with the most urgent needs.

But appropriate regulations are clearly required to protect the safety of savings of American families, to assure the most efficient and equitable regulation of financial institutions, and to create still better channels for the flow of funds to borrowers.

For these reasons, I recommend congressional action on financial legislation to
—arm regulatory agencies with a wider range of effective enforcement remedies;
—strengthen statutory provisions dealing with savings and loan holding companies;
—increase the maximum amount of insurance coverage for bank deposits and savings and loan accounts; provide safeguards against conflict of interests in the management of these institutions; and make regulations applying to various types of institutions as parallel as possible;
—provide for Federal chartering of mutual savings banks.

CONSUMER PROTECTION

I have already asked for the cooperation of business and labor in preserving the stability of costs and prices. But the consumer also has a responsibility for holding the price line.

To fulfill his responsibility, the consumer must have access to clear, unambiguous information about products and services available for sale. This will enable him to reward with his patronage the most efficient producers and distributors, who offer the best value or the lowest price.

We should wait no longer to eliminate misleading and deceptive packaging and labeling practices which cause consumer confusion. The fair packaging and labeling bill should be enacted.

While the growth of consumer credit has contributed to our rising standard of living, confusing practices in disclosing credit rates and the cost of financing have made it diffi-cult for consumers to shop for the best buy in credit.

Truth-in-lending legislation would provide consumers the necessary information, by requiring a clear statement of the cost of credit and the annual rate of interest.

Our legislation protecting the public from harmful drugs and cosmetics should be strengthened. I shall propose legislation for this purpose.

CONCLUSION

A few years ago, much was heard of the "European economic miracle." Today, across the Atlantic and around the world one hears once again of the "American economic miracle."

For the American economy, in the past 5 years, has demonstrated anew the confident vitality, the internal dynamism, and the enormous productivity which had long been its hallmark. We had settled for a while on what seemed a plateau of affluence; now, once again, there has been the strong thrust of progress—but a newly steady and balanced progress.

We have again shown the world what free men and a free economy can achieve. The peoples struggling toward economic development see with renewed interest that free markets and free economic choices can be a mighty engine of progress.

Moreover, there is new respect in the world for an America concerned with using its abundance to enhance the quality of human life: for a people
—who undertake a war on poverty along with the defense of freedom;
—who seek to restore their cities to greatness and to conserve the beauties of their landscape;
—who are determined to break down a centuries-old barrier of prejudice and injustice;

—who are resolved to lift the quality of education at every level;

—who are determined to promote and reward excellence in every endeavor;

—who have provided new health services and better social security for their older citizens;

—who offer to share their abundance and technical skills with a needy world.

The new vigor and progress of America can be a source of satisfaction. Yet we cannot rest on past accomplishments. Continuing problems challenge our determination and our resourcefulness.

Perhaps our most serious economic challenge in 1966 will be to preserve the essential stability of costs and prices which has contributed so significantly to our balanced progress.

I do not know what additional burdens of defense the American economy will be asked to assume in 1966. Whatever they are, they will be met, and they will be small relative to the growth of our abundance. But in an economy approaching full use of its resources, the new requirements of Vietnam make our task of maintaining price stability more difficult.

To insure against the risk of inflationary pressures, I have asked Americans to pay their taxes on a more nearly current basis, and to postpone a scheduled tax cut. If it should turn out that additional insurance is needed, then I am convinced that we should levy higher taxes rather than accept infla-

tion—which is the most unjust and capricious form of taxation.

We know that we do not need to put our growing economy into a straightjacket, or to throw it into reverse. But the extent of the fiscal or monetary restraint that will be needed to avoid inflationary pressures will depend directly on the restraint and moderation exercised by those who have power over wages and prices.

I again ask every leader of labor and every businessman who has price or wage decisions to make in 1966 to remember that his decisions affect not alone the wages of his members or the returns of his stockholders. Shortsighted pursuit of short-run interests fails in the longer run to advance the interests of either labor or management. And it surely does not advance the interests of the Nation.

I am confident that the overwhelming majority of private decisions in 1966 will be sound and responsible—just as I am determined that public decisions will be fully responsible.

If they are, the American economic miracle will remain in 1966 the single most important force in the economic progress of mankind.

LYNDON B. JOHNSON

January 27, 1966

NOTE: The President's message together with the Annual Report of the Council of Economic Advisers is printed in "Economic Report of the President, Transmitted to the Congress January 1966" (Government Printing Office, 1966, 306 pp.).

35　Remarks to Students Participating in the U.S. Senate Youth Program. *January 28, 1966*

MY YOUNG FRIENDS, I am delighted to welcome you here to the East Room this morning.

Nothing that I do during the year gives

me greater pleasure than welcoming you young folks to the White House.

As some of you doubtless will remember, I began my life as a schoolteacher. For more than 35 years now, I have been in some branch of the Federal Government. So all of my adult life has been mainly concerned with two things: youth and public service.

You are here today because you are young people with a very special interest in government. Seeing you here is a very rewarding and very stimulating experience for me because, first, it renews my hope and my faith in the future of my country to know that we have young people like you that have an interest in that future.

The philosopher Rousseau said: "As soon as the public service ceases to be the chief business of the citizens, and they would rather serve with their money than with their person, the State is not far from its fall."

Your own presence here today—the interest that you have already demonstrated in government—reassures me that our country is in no danger.

As I said to the student delegates who visited me here last year, the thing that I have wanted most to do when I left public office would be to try to inspire and to promote young people's interest in government. So I am very pleased and I am grateful to the fine organization—the William Randolph Hearst Foundation—which makes it possible each year for us to get together.

Seldom, if ever, in our country's interest has, I think, public service been of greater importance. For never have any people of any nation ever faced such awesome, but challenging, opportunities.

Thirty years ago, when I was not much older than some of you are now, President Franklin Delano Roosevelt said that his generation of Americans had "a rendezvous with destiny."

Well, I say to you today, that your generation has a rendezvous with tomorrow. You are the first generation which has grown up in the atomic age. The atomic age is a very dangerous age, and I think we know the dangers. It has taken all of our efforts, and all of the Lord's help, to hold mankind back from the brink of disaster. But so far we have succeeded. And I have abiding faith that we will not only continue to hold back—but that we will return someday to the bright uplands of peace.

But while there is great danger, there is also great promise—greater than man has ever known. The world of the seventies—and beyond—can be the beginning of the golden age of civilization.

It can be a world where every child has enough to eat, a world where every man can hold up his head with dignity.

It can be a world where every mother watches her children grow into strong, healthy men and women, free from disease and pain.

It can be a world where every family has a decent home and enjoys a decent way of life.

It can be a world where a man and his family can enjoy beautiful paintings and beautiful music, and read what he chooses, and fill his own library with the books that he loves.

And most of all, it can be—and it just must be—a world where wars are abandoned forever.

At this very moment many of your brave young brothers, not much older than yourselves, are locked in bitter combat in the rice paddies of Vietnam. They are there because a few fanatical leaders still belong to the cult of force. Those leaders talk much about building a rich and peaceful Vietnam, but it seems to me that they practice the opposite. They are pursuing the old cynical strategy of rule or ruin. We cannot, and we must not, let that strategy succeed.

Peace can be restored in Vietnam, restored whenever the Vietcong, and their mentors to the north, are finally convinced that violence is of no avail. We have told them, we have told them time and time again, that we prefer words to bullets, that we would much rather negotiate and talk than fight. We believe that the days when men's problems can be solved on a battlefield are really gone forever, and it is the deepest wish of this Nation that others will some day join us in the only goal which, to us, really makes any sense— the goal of making this planet a safe and a fit place for the human race to live.

In a world of peace there will be challenge enough and work enough in the fight to raise the quality of human life all over this earth. Many of the critical decisions which must create the world of tomorrow are going to be made right here in Washington, and some of them made right here in this room. And I hope that some of you will be here to help as we try to make this the kind of a world that I have described, and the kind of world that I believe all of our young people want it to be.

I believe there is no greater calling and no greater challenge to any young person today than public service, serving the public of your country. The hours are long. The work is hard. The pay is often small. But there are other rewards and other satisfactions. And the greatest reward is the knowledge that you are personally contributing something to shaping the destiny of your fellow human beings throughout the world.

Your generation is especially challenged, and especially blessed. You live in a rare period of human history. The effects of what you do now in your lifetime will be looked back upon by future ages as events which changed the course of history and which remade the world.

My generation is doing its best. We have made progress. We have moved down the road. We have achieved results. We are going ahead. Our life today, I think it is reasonable to say, is better than it was yesterday, and by the end of this century I think it is going to be still better. But how much better the world will be and how soon we achieve the victory we seek, will someday depend entirely upon you.

It is a source of profound confidence to see that so many of you are already preparing yourselves to take up the torch.

I thank you so much for coming this morning, and I hope that nothing I may have said will discourage you from the undertaking in which you have indicated such an interest.

Thank you very much.

NOTE: The President spoke at 12:05 p.m. in the East Room at the White House. The students, two from each State and from the District of Columbia, were in Washington in connection with the United States Senate Youth Program. The program, established in 1962 by Senate Resolution 324, provides selected officers of public and private school student bodies with a week's internship in the U.S. Senate and in the Federal Government generally. It operates under a grant approved each year by the trustees of the William Randolph Hearst Foundation.

36 Reply to a Letter From a Group of Senators Relating to the Situation in Vietnam. *January 28, 1966*

Dear Senator Hartke:

I write to acknowledge your letter of January 27, in which a group of Senators join you. I am glad to have this expression of opinion.

I continue to be guided in these matters by the resolution of the Congress approved on August 10, 1964—Public Law 88–408— by a vote of 504 to 2. My views of the present situation remain as stated in my recent reply to a group of Members of the House, of which I enclose a copy.

Sincerely,

LYNDON B. JOHNSON

[Honorable Vance Hartke, United States Senate]

NOTE: The text of the President's letter was read by Bill Moyers, Special Assistant to the President, at his news conference at 4:15 p.m. on Friday, January 28, 1966, in his office at the White House. It was not made public in the form of a White House press release.

The President referred to a joint resolution of the Congress "to promote the maintenance of international peace and security in Southeast Asia" (Public Law 88–408, 78 Stat. 384).

The letter to which the President replied was signed by 15 Members of the Senate. For the President's reply to a letter signed by 77 Members of the House of Representatives, see Item 23.

37 Letter to the Postmaster General on Accelerated Mail Delivery for Servicemen in Vietnam and the Pacific Area. *January 29, 1966*

Dear Mr. Postmaster General:

I approve your recommendation to accelerate delivery of first-class mail to and from our servicemen in Vietnam and the Pacific.

I request that you make the new program effective immediately.

This faster mail service—speeding delivery time from one to four days—will be welcomed by the thousands of our countrymen halfway across the world and by their families and friends at home. Mail is the vital link that bridges vast distances, bringing warmth and news and, most important, easing the pain of separation. To have mail delivered sooner is to bring home that much closer.

As I have said many times before, I am determined that our troops in Vietnam shall have all the guns, planes and equipment they

need. And I am determined to do all we can to support their high morale. That is why we have been unremitting in our search to bring to our men the very best in mail and other services. The new program I approved today is another key step forward and I ask you to continue your efforts to take every possible action to improve mail delivery to and from Vietnam.

Sincerely,

LYNDON B. JOHNSON

[The Honorable Lawrence F. O'Brien, The Postmaster General, Washington, D.C.]

NOTE: The President's letter was made public as part of a White House release announcing that all first-class mail to and from members of the Armed Forces serving in the Pacific area would be domestically transported by air or the fastest possible means. The release noted that under the new program a mother in New York who wished to send a letter to her son in Vietnam would have the letter carried by air within the United States to a west coast terminal point even though she paid only the first-class (5 cents) rate. From the west coast point the letter would be sent by air to Vietnam.

The Postmaster General's letter making the recommendation, also released by the White House on January 29, is printed in the Weekly Compilation of Presidential Documents (vol. 2, p. 146).

38 Message to the Congress Transmitting 15th Annual Report of the National Science Foundation. *January 29, 1966*

To the Congress of the United States:

I said in my State of the Union Message this year that, "We must change to master change."

Failing that, this nation will surely become a casualty to the relentless tide of history. For in assessing our prospects, we must remember that mankind faces not one but many possible futures. Which future our children's children enjoy—or endure—depends in large measure on our ability to adjust to the needs of the times.

But change comes not of itself. Neither the requirement for change nor the desire for change will see us through. In a complex world—growing more complex every year—only knowledge can keep us apace.

We must achieve a better understanding of our environment and our place in that environment.

We must continue to unlock the secrets of the earth below us, the sea around us, and the heavens above us.

And we must intensify our search into the very meaning of life itself.

It is not too much to say that every aspect of our lives will be affected by the success of this effort. The military and economic strength of our nation, and the health, the happiness, and the welfare of our citizens all are profoundly influenced by the limits—and potentialities—of our scientific program.

In the furtherance of this program, no organization, agency or institution has had a more profound or lasting influence than the National Science Foundation. The establishment of this Foundation by the Congress, fifteen years ago, was one of the soundest investments this nation ever made.

In the field of basic research, many of the major scientific breakthroughs of our time would have been impossible—or at the very least, much longer in coming—had it not been for National Science Foundation grants in the basic sciences.

In the field of education, it is enough to say that more than half of all our high school teachers have now received vital refresher training through the Foundation's education program.

In the classrooms, the Foundation has played a major role in modernizing scientific curricula to make them responsive to our age.

And in a more recent activity, the Foundation has launched a *program to strengthen the science departments* of many of our smaller universities throughout the nation by providing new laboratories, modern equipment, and fellowships to promising graduate students.

It should be emphasized that the role of the National Science Foundation is to aid, not to arbitrate. But through its aid—skillfully administered and intelligently applied—it has brought American science to a new level of excellence.

This, the 15th annual report of the National Science Foundation, reflects another year of scientific growth and progress, and I am pleased to commend it to the attention of the Congress. It mirrors the past and illuminates the future.

It is the story of change—to master change.

LYNDON B. JOHNSON

The White House
January 29, 1966

NOTE: The report, transmitted to the President on January 10, 1966, is entitled "15th Annual Report, 1965, National Science Foundation" (Government Printing Office, 203 pp.).

On January 29 the White House made public the following highlights of the report:

Science education

NSF has provided 300,000 teacher-training opportunities since initiating institutes for science teachers.

It has granted a total of $166 million in support of graduate students and advanced scholars.

A total of 38,463 fellowship awards have been granted from 136,173 applicants.

In fiscal 1965, NSF's support for graduate students reached an alltime high—5,942, with 1,934 graduate fellowships, 1,224 cooperative graduate fellowships, and 2,784 graduate traineeships offered.

Research support

Foundation support of basic research reached a new high in 1965, with 3,228 grants, totaling $122,238,141, made for the direct support of basic research projects.

Grants were to a total of 387 institutions of which 288 were colleges and universities located in every State in the Union and the District of Columbia. The NSF sponsored work at the University of Wisconsin, California Institute of Technology, and the University of California; advances in genetic biology—at Yale, Cornell, Columbia, and Illinois; anthropological studies at Tulane and the Florida State Museum; scientific projects in Antarctica; progress in Project Mohole; progress made by NSF's national research centers.

Other Foundation activities

Progress of the science development program, initiated by President Johnson in 1965, is traced. Selected institutions received grants in support of long-range plans to develop into top quality centers of science and engineering.

NSF's efforts in science information exchange and international cooperation are also reviewed.

During the fiscal year, more than 600 travel grants were awarded to U.S. scientists, primarily to permit them to attend international scientific meetings.

39 Statement by the President Announcing Resumption of Air Strikes on North Vietnam. *January 31, 1966*

[Broadcast from the White House Theater at 10 a.m.]

Good morning, ladies and gentlemen:

For 37 days, no bombs fell on North Vietnam. During that time, we have made a most intensive and determined effort to enlist the help and the support of all the world in order to persuade the Government in Hanoi that peace is better than war, that talking is better than fighting, and that the road to peace is open.

Our effort has met with understanding and support throughout most of the world, but not in Hanoi and Peking. From those two capitals have come only denunciation and rejection.

In these 37 days, the efforts of our allies have been rebuffed. The efforts of neutral nations have come to nothing. We have sought, without success, to learn of any response to efforts made by the governments of Eastern Europe. There has been no answer to the enlightened efforts of the Vatican. Our own direct private approaches have all been in vain.

The answer of Hanoi to all is the answer that was published 3 days ago. They persist in aggression. They insist on the surrender of South Vietnam to communism. It is, therefore, very plain that there is no readiness or willingness to talk, no readiness for peace in that regime today.

And what is plain in words is also plain in acts. Throughout these 37 days, even at moments of truce, there has been continued violence against the people of South Vietnam, against their Government, against their soldiers, and against our own American forces.

We do not regret the pause in the bombing. We yield to none in our determination to seek peace. We have given a full and decent respect to the opinions of those who thought that such a pause might give new hope for peace in the world.

Some said that 10 days might do it. Others said 20. Now, we have paused for twice the time suggested by some of those who urged it. And now the world knows more clearly than it has ever known before who it is that insists on aggression and who it is that works for peace.

The Vietnamese, American, and allied troops that are engaged in South Vietnam, with increasing strength and increasing success, want peace, I am sure, as much as any of us here at home. But while there is no peace, those men are entitled to the full support of American strength and American determination—and we will give them both.

As constitutional Commander in Chief, I have, as I must, given proper weight to the judgment of those, all of those, who have any responsibility for counseling with me or sharing with me the burdensome decisions that I am called upon to make: the distinguished Secretary of State, the Secretary of Defense, my National Security Adviser, and America's professional military men, represented by the Joint Chiefs of Staff.

These advisers tell me that if continued immunity is given to all that support North Vietnam aggression, the cost in lives—Vietnamese lives and American lives and allied lives—will only be greatly increased.

In the light of the words and actions of the Government in Hanoi for more than 37 days now, it is our clear duty to do what we can to limit these costs.

So on this Monday morning in Vietnam, at my direction, after complete and thorough consultation and agreement with the Government of South Vietnam, United States aircraft have resumed action in North Vietnam.

They struck the lines of supply which support the continuing movement of men and arms against the people and the Government of South Vietnam.

Our air strikes on North Vietnam from the beginning have been aimed at military targets and have been controlled with the greatest of care. Those who direct and supply the aggression really have no claim to immunity from military reply.

The end of the pause does not mean the end of our own pursuit of peace. That pursuit will be as determined and as unremitting as the pressure of our military strength on the field of battle.

In our continuing pursuit of peace, I have instructed Ambassador Goldberg at the United Nations to ask for an immediate meeting of the United Nations Security Council. He will present a full report on the situation in Vietnam, and a resolution which can open the way to the conference table.

This report and this resolution will be responsive to the spirit of the renewed appeal of Pope Paul, and that appeal has our full sympathy.

I have asked Secretary Rusk to meet with the representatives of the press later this morning to give to the country and to the entire world a thorough and a comprehensive account of all of the diplomatic efforts conducted in these last 5 weeks in our continuing policy of peace and freedom for South Vietnam.

NOTE: For Secretary of State Dean Rusk's statement on Vietnam at his press conference on January 31, see the Department of State Bulletin (vol. 54, p. 223).

The text of Ambassador Goldberg's letters and statements on the subject, dated January 31 and February 1, is printed in the Department of State Bulletin along with the text of a draft resolution submitted by the United States to the United Nations Security Council (vol. 54, p. 229).

On February 2, 1966, the Security Council agreed to place the question of Vietnam on its agenda.

Pope Paul VI's message to the President, delivered in person by Ambassador Goldberg on January 4, 1966, together with a letter of the same date from Ambassador Goldberg to the Secretary General of the United Nations, is printed in the Weekly Compilation of Presidential Documents (vol. 2, pp. 8–10).

40   Message to the Congress Transmitting Annual Report on U.S. Aeronautics and Space Activities. *January 31, 1966*

To the Congress of the United States:

The record of American accomplishments in aeronautics and space during 1965 shows it to have been the most successful year in our history.

More spacecraft were orbited than in any previous year. Five manned GEMINI flights were successfully launched.

Our astronauts spent more hours in space than were flown by all of our manned spacecraft until 1965. Ten astronauts logged a total of 1,297 hours 42 minutes in space.

The five manned flights successfully achieved included a walk in space, and the first rendezvous between two manned spacecrafts.

A scientific spacecraft completed a 325-million-mile, 228-day trip to Mars. MARINER 4 thereby gave mankind its first close-up view of another planet.

The RANGER series, begun in 1961, reached its zenith with two trips to the moon that yielded 13,000 close-up pictures of that planet. The entire RANGER series produced 17,000 photographs of the moon's surface which are being studied now by experts throughout the world.

Equally important were the contributions of our space program to life here on earth. Launching of EARLY BIRD, the first commercial communication satellite brought us measurably closer to the goal of instantaneous communication between all points on the globe. Research and development in

our space program continued to speed progress in medicine, in weather prediction, in electronics—and, indeed, in virtually every aspect of American science and technology.

As our space program continues, the impact of its developments on everyday life becomes daily more evident. It continues to stimulate our education, improve our material well-being, and broaden the horizons of knowledge. It is also a powerful force for peace.

The space program of the United States today is the largest effort ever undertaken by any nation to advance the frontiers of human knowledge. What we are discovering and building today will help solve many of the great problems which an increasingly complex and heavily-populated world will face tomorrow.

The year 1965—the year of GEMINI, RANGER, and MARINER—is a brilliant preface to the coming years of APOLLO, stations in space, and voyages to the planets. I have great pride and pleasure in transmitting this remarkable record to the Congress that, through its enthusiastic support, has made possible.

LYNDON B. JOHNSON

The White House
January 31, 1966

NOTE: The report is entitled "Report to the Congress From the President of the United States, United States Aeronautics and Space Activities, 1965" (172 pp.).

41   Special Message to the Congress on the Foreign Aid Program.
February 1, 1966

To the Congress of the United States:

I recommend a Foreign Aid program to help those nations who are determined to help themselves.

I recommend a program to help give the people of the less-developed world the food, the health, the skills and education—and the strength—to lead their nations to self-sufficient lives of plenty and freedom.

I propose to carry forward the best of what we are now doing in the less-developed world, and cut out the worst. I also propose to make the basic changes the times demand.

My recommendations are grounded in the deep conviction that we must use foreign assistance to attack the root causes of poverty. We must concentrate on countries not hostile to us that give solid evidence that they are determined to help themselves.

This is the lesson of the past. It is the hope for the future. It is the guiding principle for a nation ready and willing to cooperate with the industrious, but unwilling to subsidize those who do not assume responsibility for their own fate.

During the past year I have given our foreign assistance program the most sober and searching review. I have questioned the merit of each program. Special groups have concentrated on the particular areas of food, education and health. A Cabinet committee has examined the details of our general economic and military assistance.

Thus, the steps I recommend today have been developed in the light of advice from senior officials in the Executive Branch, Congressional leaders, and experienced advisors from outside government. They also have been developed with full recognition of our balance of payments situation.

They emerge from a rigorous examination of our past experience.

They are informed by compassion and shaped by the history of two decades.

They are the proof of our devotion to the works of peace.

They reflect our vision of a world free from fear and ripe with opportunity.

They will shape the legacy we leave our children.

I.

The quest for peace is as old as mankind.

For countless centuries man struggled to secure first his home, then his village, then his city. It is the unique heritage of our century that men must strive for a secure world.

Peace, plenty, freedom—our fathers aspired to these as we do now. But the fateful truth of our age is that all our personal and national hopes hang in a balance affected by events and attitudes half a world away.

We have paid a fearful price to learn the folly of isolation. We have learned that the human misery which infects whole nations with a thirst for violent change does not give way to mere slogans. We have learned that the works of peace require courage and foresight. The need knows neither national boundary nor narrow ideology.

We have demonstrated this understanding in many ways over the past two decades. Our military strength has protected many countries threatened by invasion from without or subversion from within. Our economic assistance programs have rebuilt Europe. We have helped untold millions to gain confidence in peaceful progress, where there has been neither peace nor progress for centuries.

We will never know how many crises have

117

been averted, how much violence avoided, or how many minds have been won to the cause of freedom in these years. But I believe we have many such achievements to our credit.

Yet today the citizens of many developing nations walk in the shadow of misery:

—half the adults have never been to school;
—over half the people are hungry or malnourished;
—food production per person is falling;
—at present rates of growth, population will double before the year 2000.

These are the dominant facts of our age.

They challenge our own security.

They threaten the future of the world.

Our response must be bold and daring. It must go to the root causes of misery and unrest. It must build a firm foundation for progress, security and peace.

II.

Although we recognize the shortsightedness of isolation, we do not embrace the equally futile prospect of total and endless dependence. The United States can never do more than supplement the efforts of the developing countries themselves. They must supply most of the capital, the know-how—and the will to progress. If they do we can and will help. If they do not, nothing we can supply will substitute. Nothing can replace resources wasted in political or military adventures.

For the essence of economic development is work—hard, unremitting, often thankless work. Most of it must be done by the people whose futures and whose children's futures are directly at stake.

Only these people and their leaders can:

—invest every possible resource in improved farming techniques, in school and hospital construction and in critical industry;

—make the land reforms, tax changes, and other basic adjustments necessary to transform their societies;
—face the population problem squarely and realistically;
—create the climate which will attract foreign investment, and keep local money at home.

These are just a few of the steps on the road to modernization. They are far from easy. We would do well to remember how difficult many of them were for us. But they are absolutely necessary. Without them, outside help is wasted. Neither we nor they can afford waste, and we will not continue any partnership in which only we recognize that fact.

As I said last October, "Action, not promises, will be the standard of assistance." It must be clear that the principle of our assistance is cooperation. Those who do not fulfill their commitments to help themselves cannot expect help from us.

III.

In this spirit of cooperation, I propose that the United States offer to join in new attacks upon the root causes of world poverty.

The incessant cycle of hunger, ignorance, and disease is the common blight of the developing world. This vicious pattern can be broken. It must be broken if democracy is to survive.

The problem of hunger is a continuing crisis. In many parts of the world we witness both the ravages of famine born of natural disaster and the failure of food production to keep pace with rising needs.

This is a catastrophe for all of us. It must be dealt with by all who can help. In many other countries food output is also falling behind population growth. We cannot meet the world food needs of the future, however willing we are to share our abundance. Nor would it serve the common interest if we could.

The solution is clear: an all-out effort to enable the developing countries to supply their own food needs, through their own production or through improved capacity to buy in the world market.

I will shortly send to the Congress a special message which will recommend new legislation to redirect and strengthen our food aid programs to:

—induce greater agricultural self-help abroad;

—make food aid a more integrated element of general programs of economic cooperation;

—move as quickly as our mutual interests permit toward harder financial terms, thereby adding to our commercial markets and a favorable balance of payments result.

In addition, I propose that the Agency for International Development increase its efforts in the field of agriculture by more than one-third, to a total of nearly $500 million. One-third of this total will finance imports of fertilizer from the United States. The remainder will finance:

—transfer of American farming techniques, the most advanced in the world;

—improvement of roads, marketing and irrigation facilities;

—establishment of extension services, co-operatives and credit facilities;

—purchases of American farm equipment and pesticides;

—research on soil and seed improvements.

These programs will also have long-range benefits for our own farmers. Higher incomes abroad mean greater exports for our highly efficient food producers.

To combat *ignorance*, I am proposing a major new effort in international education.

I propose a 50% increase in AID education activities to a total of more than $200 million. Shortly I will transmit to the Congress a special message proposing an International Education Act which will commit the United States to a campaign to spread the benefits of education to every corner of the earth. Nothing is more critical to the future of liberty and the fate of mankind.

To fight *disease*, I will shortly propose an International Health Act which will provide for extensive new programs at home and abroad.

We now have the capacity to eliminate smallpox from the list of man's natural enemies; to eradicate malaria in the Western Hemisphere and in large areas of Africa and Asia; and to relieve much of the suffering now caused by measles, cholera, rabies, and other epidemic diseases.

I will propose a two-thirds increase in FY 1967 in AID support of health programs, to a total of more than $150 million. In addition to financing disease eradication, we will step up our program to combat malnutrition. We will expand help to community water supply projects. We will finance the training of more doctors and nurses, needed for new health centers and mobile health units.

I also propose to provide nearly $150 million in Food for Work programs, and more than $100 million in contributions to international organizations to further support the war on hunger, ignorance and disease.

IV.

We stand ready to help developing countries deal with the population problem.

The United States cannot and should not force any country to adopt any particular approach to this problem. It is first a matter of individual and national conscience, in which we will not interfere.

But population growth now consumes about two-thirds of economic growth in the less-developed world. As death rates are steadily driven down, the individual miracle of birth becomes a collective tragedy of want.

In all cases, our help will be given only upon request, and only to finance advisors, training, transportation, educational equipment, and local currency needs.

Population policy remains a question for each family and each nation to decide. But we must be prepared to help when decisions are made.

v.

In many areas, the keys to economic and social development lie largely in the settling of old quarrels and the building of regional solidarity. Regional cooperation is often the best means of economic progress as well as the best guarantor of political independence.

I propose that we continue and enlarge our support of the institutions and organizations which create and preserve this unity.

Last April I pledged full United States support for regional programs to accelerate peaceful development in Southeast Asia. We have already begun to implement this pledge by support to the Nam Ngum Dam in the Mekong Basin and to other projects.

In my legislative proposals, I am requesting new and specific authority to carry forward this support for regional progress.

We must make it clear to friend and foe alike that we are as determined to support the peaceful growth of Southeast Asia as we are to resist those who would conquer and subjugate it.

These efforts in Asia will be further enhanced by the formation of the Asian Development Bank, which was the subject of my message to the Congress of January 18. I am confident that this Bank will be a ma-jor unifying force in the region, and a source of vital development capital invaluable to our mutual interests.

In Africa, we look forward to working closely with the new African Development Bank as its programs materialize.

We also look forward to progress toward an East African economic community and other sub-regional common markets on that massive continent. As these institutions and arrangements develop, the United States intends to make greater use of them as channels for our assistance. We will move in the direction of more regional administration of our bilateral programs.

We have recently extended our on-going commitment to the Alliance for Progress, which includes strong support for the successful economic integration of Central America. The movement toward greater cooperation among all Latin American economies will gain momentum in the years ahead. It has our strong support.

The United States will support the proposal of the Inter-American Committee of the Alliance for Progress and the Inter-American Development Bank to establish a new fund for feasibility studies of multinational projects. These projects can be of enormous value to countries which share a river valley or another natural resource. They are sound combinations of good economics and good politics.

vi.

I propose that the United States—in ways consistent with its balance of payments policy—increase its contributions to multilateral lending institutions, particularly the International Development Association. These increases will be conditional upon appropriate rises in contributions from other members. We are prepared immediately to support negotiations leading to agreements of this nature for submission to the Congress. We urge other advanced nations to join us in supporting this work.

The United States is a charter member and the largest single contributor to such institutions as the World Bank, the International Development Association, and the Inter-American Development Bank. This record reflects our confidence in the multilateral method of development finance and in the soundness of these institutions themselves. They are expert financiers, and healthy influences on the volume and terms of aid from other donors.

I propose that we increase our contributions to the United Nations Development Program, again subject to proportionate increases in other contributions. This Program merges United Nations technical assistance and pre-investment activities. It promises to be among the world's most valuable development instruments.

VII.

We will expand our efforts to encourage private initiative and enterprise in developing countries. We have received very useful advice and guidance from the report of the distinguished Advisory Committee on Private Enterprise in Foreign Aid. Many of the recommendations of that report are now being put into effect.

We will review frankly and constructively with cooperating countries the obstacles to domestic and foreign private investment. We will continue to support:

—elimination of inefficient controls;
—formation of cooperatives;
—training of labor and business leaders;
—credit facilities and advisory services for small and medium-sized farms and businesses.

The United States Government can do only a small part of the job of helping and encouraging businessmen abroad. We must rely more and more on the great reservoirs of knowledge and experience in our business and professional communities. These groups have already provided invaluable service and advice. We in government must find ways to make even greater use of these priceless assets.

I propose to:

—continue our support for the International Executive Service Corps;
—increase the AID authority to guarantee U.S. private investments in developing countries.

VIII.

To signify the depth of our commitment to help those who help themselves, I am requesting five-year authorizations for our military and economic aid programs.

For development loans and loans under the Alliance for Progress, this is merely a reaffirmation of the principle adopted by the Congress in 1961 and 1962. It will not impair the ability or the duty of the Congress to review these programs. Indeed, it will free the Congress from the burden of an annual renewal of basic legislation, and provide greater opportunity for concentration on policy and program issues.

Annual Congressional consideration of both economic and military programs will be maintained through full annual presentations before the substantive committees, if they so desire, as well as through the annual appropriation process.

The military and economic authorization requests are contained in two separate bills. I believe this is a forward step in clarifying the goals and functions of these programs in the minds of the public and the Congress.

IX.

I am requesting a total appropriation of $2.469 million in FY 1967 to finance programs of economic cooperation. As in the last two years, I am requesting the absolute minimum to meet presently foreseeable needs, with the understanding that I will not hesitate to request a supplemental appropriation if a clear need develops.

Aid to Vietnam: The largest single portion of my request—$550 million in Supporting Assistance—is to support our effort in Vietnam. Our help to the government of Vietnam in carrying forward programs of village economic and social improvement is of crucial significance in maintaining public morale in the face of the horror of war. With the help of AID advisers, who often serve at great personal risk, the Vietnamese government is patiently building the foundations of progress in the rural areas.

Other Supporting Assistance: The remainder of my request—$197 million—is for aid to countries whose security is directly threatened. This is concentrated in programs for Laos, Korea, and Thailand. Each country is a key link in our defense system. Each lives in the shadow of great and hostile powers. Each is well worth the investment.

Alliance for Progress: I am requesting a total of $543 million in FY 1967 appropriations for the countries cooperating in the Alliance for Progress. Of this total $88 million will be used to finance technical cooperation.

At the Rio Conference, the United States announced its intention to support this great hemispheric effort beyond 1971. Our ultimate goal is a hemisphere of free nations, stable and just—prosperous in their economics and democratic in their politics.

We can cite many indications of heartening progress
—in 1965 alone, Chile settled about 4,000 families on their own land, about as many as had acquired land during the preceding 35 years;
—Brazil, as a result of courageous economic policy decisions, has reduced its rate of inflation, restored its credit, encouraged private investment, and modernized many of its economic institutions;
—in only two years, the five members of the Central American Common Market have increased intramarket trade by 123%.

These are not isolated or exceptional examples. The keynote of the Alliance for Progress has always been self-help. The pattern of our assistance—65% of which is concentrated in Brazil, Chile and Colombia—demonstrates our determination to help those who help themselves.

Most heartening of all, a new generation has risen to leadership in Latin America as the Alliance for Progress has taken hold. These young men and women combine a belief in democratic ideals with a commitment to peaceful change and social justice. We are happy to welcome them as leaders of great nations in the community of freedom.

Development Loans: Nine-tenths of the $665 million requested for this account is for five countries—India, Pakistan, Turkey, Korea and Nigeria.

We have long recognized the importance to all the world of progress in the giant nations of South Asia. But in the past year we witnessed a tragic confrontation between India and Pakistan which forced us to withhold all new assistance other than food. We will not allow our aid to subsidize an arms race between these two countries. Nor can we resume aid until we are reasonably certain that hostilities will not recur. The progress of reconciliation—first at the United Nations and then at Tashkent—holds promise that these two great countries have resolved on a course of peace. My request for development loan funds is made in the hope and belief that this promise will be fulfilled.

Turkey has continued her steady progress toward self-sustaining growth, and has remained a staunch NATO ally. She deserves our continued support.

Korea has made similar economic progress and has shown her dedication to the cause of freedom by supplying a full military division for service in Viet Nam.

Nigeria has recently suffered a painful upheaval, but we are hopeful that she too will maintain her responsible and progressive course.

The uncertainties of world affairs permit no guarantees that these hopes will be fulfilled. But I do guarantee the Congress and the American people that no funds will be used in these or other countries without a clear case that such expenditures are in the interest of the United States.

Technical Cooperation: This request—$231 million—will finance American advisors and teachers who are the crucial forces in the attack on hunger, ignorance, disease, and the population problem. The dollar total is relatively small. But no appropriation is more critical. No purpose is more central.

Contributions to International Organizations: I am requesting $140 million for these contributions in FY 1967. The majority of these funds will support such efforts as the United Nations Development Program and the U.N. Children's Fund. The remainder

represents our share of the cost of maintaining essential United Nations peace-keeping and relief activities in areas of tension and conflict.

Other: The remaining $142 million of my request is distributed among the Contingency Fund, AID administrative expenses, and support of American schools and hospitals abroad.

X.

In making these requests, I assure the Congress that every effort will be extended to minimize the adverse impact on our balance of payments. I think the record is proof of the sincerity of these commitments.

AID procurement policies have been tightened to the point that, with minor and essential exceptions, all funds appropriated to AID must be spent in the U.S. for American goods and services. As a result, offshore expenditures of AID funds declined from $1 billion in 1960 to $533 million in 1964.

Further steps have been taken. I now expect that the figure will drop to about $400 million in FY 1967. Receipts are expected to rise to $186 million in FY 1967, yielding a net outflow of only $214 million.

XI.

I am transmitting the Military Assistance and Sales Act of 1966 as separate legislation. This new Act will provide a five-year authorization for the program which strengthens U.S. security by building the strength of others to deter and resist aggression.

The new Act will provide:

—*Effective coordination between our economic and military programs.* I request the Congress to retain in the new Act those provisions which place responsibility for continuous supervision and general direction of all military as- sistance programs in the Secretary of State.

—*Greater emphasis on self-help*. As with economic aid, we must condition our military aid upon commitments from recipients to make maximum contribu- tions to the common defense.

—*Greater emphasis on civic action pro- grams*. We shall give new stress to civic action programs through which local troops build schools and roads, and provide literacy training and health services. Through these programs, military personnel are able to play a more constructive role in their society, and to establish better relations with the civilian population.

—*Emphasis on training*. One of our most effective methods of building free world security is through the training provided foreign military personnel. Today, 8,500 foreign trainees come to this country each year and a similar number are trained at our service schools over- seas. They return to their home coun- tries with new professional skills and a new understanding of the role of the armed forces in a democratic society.

—*Continued shift from grant aid to mili- tary sales*. We will shift our military aid programs from grant to sales when- ever possible—and without jeopardiz- ing our security interests or progress of economic development. Military sales now exceed the dollar volume of the normal grant aid program. This not only makes a substantial favorable im- pact on the balance of payments, but it also demonstrates the willingness of our allies to carry an increasing share of their own defense costs.

I am requesting new obligational author- ity of $917 million for military assistance in fiscal year 1967. This is the bare mini- mum required if we are to keep our com- mitments to our allies and friendly armed forces to provide the equipment and training essential to free world defense.

The military assistance request for FY 1967 does not include funds for support of South Vietnamese and other allied forces who are engaged in the crucial struggle for freedom in that country. Financing for this effort will come directly from Depart- ment of Defense appropriations.

Almost three-fourths of the total program will go to countries adjacent to the borders of Soviet Russia and Communist China. The armed forces of such countries as Greece, Turkey, Iran and the Republics of China and Korea are effective deterrents to aggression. The balance of the funds will strengthen the capacity to maintain internal security in countries where instability and weakness can pave the way for subversion.

XII.

Americans have always built for the future.

That is why we established land grant colleges and passed the Homestead Act to open our Western lands more than 100 years ago.

That is why we adopted the progressive programs proposed by Woodrow Wilson and Franklin Roosevelt.

That is why we are building the Great Society.

And that is why we have a foreign assist- ance program.

We extend assistance to nations because it is in the highest traditions of our heritage and our humanity. But even more, because we are concerned with the kind of world our children will live in.

It can be a world where nations raise armies, where famine and disease and ignorance are the common lot of men, where the poor nations look on the rich with envy, bitterness and frustration; where the air is filled with tension and hatred.

Or it can be a world where each nation lives in independence, seeking new ways to provide a better life for its citizens:

—a world where the energies of its restless peoples are directed toward the works of peace;

—a world where people are free to build a civilization to liberate the spirit of man.

We cannot make such a world in one message, in one appropriation or in one year. But we can work to do this with this appropriation in this year. And we must continue to build on the work of past years and begin to erase disease and hunger and ignorance from the face of the earth.

But the basic choice is up to the countries themselves. If that choice is for progress, we can and we must help. Our help can spell the difference between success and stagnation. We must stand ready to provide it when it is needed and when we have confidence that it will be well used.

This is the price and the privilege of world leadership.

LYNDON B. JOHNSON

The White House
February 1, 1966

NOTE: The Foreign Assistance Act of 1966 was approved by the President on September 19, 1966 (see Item 469).

See also Item 42.

42 Statement by the President on the Message on the Foreign Aid Program. *February* 1, 1966

THE foreign assistance program that I have sent to the Congress has a new look and a new purpose. We serve notice here and now from this day on that our foreign assistance will go to those nations and only those nations who are willing and ready to help themselves.

Unless nations and peoples are determined to do all that must be done in their own country and by their own work to lift the quality of their own lives, then we cannot really effectively help them. We want to see other countries achieve for their people a life of freedom and security.

We must pursue that goal with all the talent that we have. Today the majority of the people in this world are living in desperate need. Americans, I think, are not going to just sit complacently and idly by, wringing their hands and doing nothing while this suffering goes on. But compassion is not enough.

While our wealth is great, our wealth is not unlimited. Our wealth must be used to root out the causes of dangerous disorder so that the lasting values can survive and prosper, and that is why we are not going to allow American aid to become an international dole.

Our assistance must be concentrated on those particular nations which will put it to the best use. It must be based on merit as well as need, on action as well as aspiration, on responsibility as well as despair. We are eager to cooperate with the industrious and the willing and the responsible, and I believe that this is the kind of program that our Congress advocates and the kind of program that our Congress desires.

NOTE: The President also recorded the statement for radio and television broadcast.

For the text of the President's message, see Item 41.

43 Special Message to the Congress Transmitting Report Relating to Classification in the Tariff Schedules of Textured Yarns. *February 1, 1966*

To the Congress of the United States:

I am transmitting herewith, in accordance with section 2 of Public Law 89–229, a report concerning the feasibility and desirability of separate classification in the Tariff Schedules of the United States for those articles of man-made fibers commonly referred to as textured or texturized yarns.

The report concludes that such separate tariff classification for textured yarns is feasible but not desirable in view of the current situation.

Textured yarn production in the United States has been rising steadily in recent years, from 74 million pounds in 1960 to over 250 million pounds in 1965. During this period, the independent throwster industry, which processes a major portion of textured yarn, has had rising employment. At the same time, imports have been declining. The Tariff Commission has estimated that the annual imports of textured yarns declined from more than two million pounds in 1962 to less than one million pounds in 1965, representing less than one-half of one percent of the domestic market.

However, the representatives of the domestic industry have argued that a serious threat of injury looms in the future. In part because of this concern, the report recommends that more accurate import data for textured yarns be provided in the future, so that Congress, the Executive Branch, and the industry can keep close watch on import levels and consider additional measures should they be warranted. I am therefore directing that steps be taken to obtain more accurate data on imports of textured yarns.

I am also transmitting for the information of the Congress the report of the Tariff Commission on textured yarns which I requested.

LYNDON B. JOHNSON

The White House
February 1, 1966

NOTE: The report of the United States Tariff Commission, dated December 1965, is entitled "Textured Yarns, Report to the President on Investigation No. 332–46 Under Section 332 of the Tariff Act of 1930 Pursuant to the President's Request of October 1, 1965" (TC Publication 166, 52 pp.).

A "Presidential Report on Textured Yarns of Man-Made Fibers" (5 pp., processed) was also made public by the White House.

44 Remarks at the Swearing In of Dr. James Duesenberry as a Member, Council of Economic Advisers. *February 2, 1966*

Dr. and Mrs. Duesenberry and family, Chairman Ackley, Members of the Cabinet, distinguished Members of the Congress, my friends:

We are here this morning to engage in a bit of barter with Harvard University. Harvard made us give them back Otto Eckstein. We wouldn't do it until they gave us Jim Duesenberry.

Dr. Duesenberry is, as we all know, one

of this Nation's leading economists. When I was growing up, that didn't seem to mean very much, but since I grew up we have learned the error of our ways.

In fact, it occurs to me that the legal profession had itself better be on guard. I haven't had any head count, but it wouldn't surprise me a bit to find today that the economists in Government already outnumber the lawyers.

Someone once defined an economist as a person who says that we move in cycles instead of running around in circles. The new breed of economists that we have on our Council of Economic Advisers are busy proving that we don't even have to put up with the cycles any more. For the fact is that for 5 years now, if the press will accept my apology, this country has been moving straight ahead and we think in the right direction.

We are now in the 60th month of record-breaking prosperity, I read this morning, and the Council of Economic Advisers has a lot to do with that amazing achievement.

Abraham Lincoln once described the problem of government in these words: "If we could first know where we are and whither we are tending, we could better judge what to do and how to do it." That is what we think Gardner Ackley and his brilliant associates are trying to do for this economy of ours.

We believe that they have taken some of the guesswork out of the job of trying to steer this Ship of State. With their help, with the close relationship and constant contact with American business, and American labor, and American Government, we have tried to chart a common course that has kept us in the mainstream of prosperity in this country.

It has taken more than their advice. It has taken industrial statesmanship. It has taken labor responsibility. It has taken a Government which is looking out every minute of the day for the best interests of all the people. And we are going to continue to encourage this great partnership.

Prosperity, I think, then will take care of itself. But prosperity by itself is not just enough. We have already proved that recessions are not a necessary fact of life. Now we must prove that inflation is not necessarily a result of prosperity.

I, for one, do not believe that it is. I believe that with the continued cooperation of all Americans, if we can get that cooperation, we can hold inflation in check. At least this is our goal. And this is our objective and this is our determination.

So this morning I again appeal to all my fellow Americans to help their country in this hour of need. I appeal to business not to raise prices. I appeal alike to labor to observe the guideposts.

I believe that the fiscal 1967 budget is designed to hold our economy in balance. I would remind you that in this budget cash receipts exceed cash outlay. Your Government will, we think, the next fiscal year, take in $500 million more than your Government will spend in that fiscal year.

So I appeal to the Congress to enact the revenue measures that I have proposed. I urge the Congress to keep the recommended appropriations within the limits that we have requested.

It gives me a very great pleasure this morning to welcome Dr. Duesenberry to the Government and to my administration.

I think we should observe that he comes here at no small personal sacrifice. He has come to Washington because he loves his country and he wants to serve it, and he loves his Government and his Government needs him.

He and his lovely wife and their four

wonderful children are most welcome additions to our official family. I think that they will write a record here, as his colleagues on the Council have written, that will excite the admiration of not only all their fellow Americans, but will excite the admiration of leaders in other governments throughout the world who frequently comment to me about the wisdom, the foresight, the stability of the United States of America and its policies.

There is no group that is more responsible for that stability or that leadership than the Council of Economic Advisers.

Dr. Duesenberry, we are delighted to have you. Welcome aboard.

NOTE: The President spoke at 12:05 p.m. in the Cabinet Room at the White House. In his opening words he referred to Dr. and Mrs. James Duesenberry and Gardner Ackley, Chairman of the Council of Economic Advisers. During his remarks he referred to Otto Eckstein, former member of the Council of Economic Advisers.

45 Special Message to the Congress Proposing International Education and Health Programs. *February 2, 1966*

To the Congress of the United States:

Last year the Congress by its action declared: the nation's number one task is to improve the education and health of our people.

Today I call upon Congress to add a world dimension to this task.

I urge the passage of the International Education and Health Acts of 1966.

We would be shortsighted to confine our vision to this nation's shorelines. The same rewards we count at home will flow from sharing in a worldwide effort to rid mankind of the slavery of ignorance and the scourge of disease.

We bear a special role in this liberating mission. Our resources will be wasted in defending freedom's frontiers if we neglect the spirit that makes men want to be free.

Half a century ago, the philosopher William James declared that mankind must seek "a moral equivalent of war."

The search continues—more urgent today than ever before in man's history.

Ours is the great opportunity to challenge all nations, friend and foe alike, to join this battle.

We have made hopeful beginnings.

Many of the programs described in this message have been tested in practice. I have directed our agencies of government to improve and enlarge the programs already authorized by Congress.

Now I am requesting Congress to give new purpose and new power to our efforts by declaring that:

—programs to advance education and health are basic building blocks to lasting peace.

—they represent a long-term commitment in the national interest.

—the Department of Health, Education, and Welfare is charged with a broad authority to help strengthen our country's capacity to carry on this noble adventure.

EDUCATION

Education lies at the heart of every nation's hopes and purposes. It must be at the heart of our international relations.

We have long supported UNESCO and other multilateral and international agencies. We propose to continue these efforts with renewed vigor.

Schooled in the grief of war, we know certain truths are self-evident in every nation on this earth:

—Ideas, not armaments, will shape our lasting prospects for peace.

—The conduct of our foreign policy will advance no faster than the curriculum of our classrooms.

—The knowledge of our citizens is one treasure which grows only when it is shared.

International education cannot be the work of one country. It is the responsibility and promise of all nations. It calls for free exchange and full collaboration. We expect to receive as much as we give, to learn as well as to teach.

Let this nation play its part. To this end, I propose:

—to strengthen our capacity for international educational cooperation.

—to stimulate exchange with students and teachers of other lands.

—to assist the progress of education in developing nations.

—to build new bridges of international understanding.

I. TO STRENGTHEN OUR CAPACITY FOR INTERNATIONAL EDUCATIONAL COOPERATION

Our education base in this country is strong. Our desire to work with other nations is great. But we must review and renew the purpose of our programs for international education. I propose to:

1. *Direct the Secretary of Health, Education, and Welfare to establish within his Department a Center for Educational Cooperation.*

This Center will be a focal point for leadership in international education. While it will not supplant other governmental agencies already conducting programs in this field, it will:

—Act as a channel for communication between our missions abroad and the U.S. educational community;

—Direct programs assigned to the Department of Health, Education, and Welfare;

—Assist public and private agencies conducting international education programs.

2. *Appoint a Council on International Education.*

Our commitment to international education must draw on the wisdom, experience, and energy of many people. This Council, to be composed of outstanding leaders of American education, business, labor, the professions, and philanthropy, will advise the Center for Educational Cooperation.

3. *Create a Corps of Education Officers to serve in the United States Foreign Service.*

As education's representatives abroad, they will give sharper direction to our programs. Recruited from the ranks of outstanding educators, they will report directly to the Ambassador when serving in foreign missions.

4. *Stimulate New Programs in International Studies for Elementary and Secondary Schools.*

No child should grow to manhood in America without realizing the promise and the peril of the world beyond our borders. Progress in teaching about world affairs must not lag behind progress made in other areas of American education.

I am directing the Secretary of Health, Education, and Welfare to earmark funds from Title IV of the Elementary and Secondary Education Act of 1965, so that our regional education laboratories can enrich the international curricula of our elementary and secondary schools.

5. *Support Programs of International Scope in Smaller and Developing Colleges.*

Many of our nation's institutions have been unable to share fully in international projects. By a new program of incentive grants administered through HEW these institutions will be encouraged to play a more active role.

6. *Strengthen Centers of Special Competence in International Research and Training.*

Over the past two decades, our universities have been a major resource in carrying on development programs around the world. We have made heavy demands upon them. But we have not supported them adequately.

I recommend to the Congress a program of incentive grants administered by HEW for universities and groups of universities—

(a) to promote centers of excellence in dealing with particular problems and particular regions of the world,

(b) to develop administrative staff and faculties adequate to maintain long-term commitments to overseas educational enterprises.

In addition, I propose that AID be given authority to provide support to American research and educational institutions, for increasing their capacity to deal with programs of economic and social development abroad.

II. TO STIMULATE EXCHANGE WITH THE STUDENTS AND TEACHERS OF OTHER LANDS

Only when people know about—and care about—each other will nations learn to live together in harmony. I therefore propose that we:

1. *Encourage the Growth of School-to-School Partnerships.*

Through such partnerships, already pioneered on a small scale, a U.S. school may assist the brick-and-mortar construction of a sister school in less developed nations. The exchange can grow to include books and equipment, teacher and student visits.

To children, it can bring deep understanding and lasting friendships.

I recommend a goal of 1,000 school-to-school partnerships.

This program will be administered by the Peace Corps, in cooperation with AID, particularly its Partners of the Alliance Program. The chief cost will be borne by the voluntary contributions of the participating schools.

2. *Establish an Exchange Peace Corps.*

Our nation has no better ambassadors than the young volunteers who serve in 46 countries in the Peace Corps. I propose that we welcome similar ambassadors to our shores. We need their special skills and understanding, just as they need ours.

These "Volunteers to America" will teach their own language and culture in our schools and colleges. They will serve in community programs alongside VISTA Volunteers. As our Peace Corps Volunteers learn while they serve, those coming to the United States will be helped to gain training to prepare them for further service when they return home.

I propose an initial goal of 5,000 volunteers.

3. *Establish an American Education Placement Service.*

We have in the United States a reservoir of talent and good will not yet fully tapped:

—school and college teachers eager to serve abroad;

—professors and administrators who are retired or on sabbatical leave;

—Peace Corps volunteers who desire further foreign service.

To encourage these men and women to assist in the developing nations and elsewhere, I recommend that we establish an

American Education Placement Service in HEW.

It will act as an international recruitment bureau for American teachers, and will provide supplemental assistance for those going to areas of special hardship.

In time, I hope this Service will lead to the development of a World Teacher Exchange—in which all nations may join to bring their classrooms into closer relationship with one another.

III. TO ASSIST THE PROGRESS OF EDUCATION
IN DEVELOPING NATIONS

To provide direct support for those countries struggling to improve their education standards, I propose that we:

1. *Enlarge AID programs of education assistance.*

In my message on Foreign Assistance, I directed AID to make a major effort in programs of direct educational benefit. These will emphasize teacher training—vocational and scientific education—construction of education facilities—specialized training in the U.S. for foreign students—and help in publishing badly needed textbooks.

2. *Develop new Techniques for Teaching Basic Education and Fighting Illiteracy.*

Our own research and development in the learning process can be adapted to fit the needs of other countries. Modern technology and new communications techniques have the power to multiply the resources available to a school system.

I am calling on HEW to support basic education research of value to the developing nations.

I am requesting AID to conduct studies and assist pilot projects for applying technology to meet critical education shortages.

3. *Expand U.S. Summer Teaching Corps.*

The Agency for International Develop-

ment now administers programs for American teachers and professors who participate in summer workshops in less developed countries. They serve effectively to support teacher-training in these countries. They also enrich their own teaching experience.

I propose this year that AID double the number of U.S. participants in the Summer Teaching Corps.

4. *Assist the Teaching of English Abroad.*

Many of the newer nations have a vital need to maintain English as the language of international communication and national development. We must help meet this demand even as we extend the teaching of foreign languages in our own schools.

I have directed AID, supported by other agencies, to intensify its efforts for those countries which seek our help.

5. *Establish Bi-National Educational Foundations.*

We have at our disposal excess foreign currencies in a number of developing nations. Where conditions are favorable, I propose that significant amounts of these currencies be used to support Bi-National Educational Foundations. Governed by leading citizens from the two nations, they would have opportunities much like those afforded major foundations in the United States to invest in basic educational development.

To the extent further currencies are created by our sales of agricultural commodities abroad, I propose that a portion be earmarked for educational uses, particularly to assist technical training in food production.

IV. TO BUILD NEW BRIDGES OF INTERNATIONAL
UNDERSTANDING

The job of international education must extend beyond the classroom. Conferences of experts from many nations, the free flow of books and ideas, the exchange of works of science and imagination can enrich every citizen. I propose steps to:

1. *Stimulate Conferences of Leaders and Experts.*

I have directed every department and agency to support a series of seminars for representatives from every discipline and every culture to seek answers to the common problems of mankind.

We are ready to serve as host to international gatherings. I have therefore called on the Secretary of State and the Attorney General to explore ways to remove unnecessary hindrances in granting visas to guests invited from abroad.

2. *Increase the Flow of Books and Other Educational Material.*

I recommend prompt passage of legislation to implement the Florence Agreement and thus stimulate the movement of books and other educational material between nations. This Agreement was signed by representatives of the U.S. Government in 1959 and ratified by the Senate in 1960. This necessary Congressional action is long overdue to eliminate duties and remove barriers for the importation of educational materials.

I also recommend that Congress implement the Beirut Agreement to permit duty-free entry of visual and auditory materials of an educational, scientific or cultural nature.

Finally, we must encourage American private enterprise to participate actively in educational exchange. I urge the Congress to amend the United States Information and Educational Exchange Act of 1948 to permit improvements in the Informational Media Guarantee Program.

3. *Improve the Quality of U.S. Schools and Colleges Abroad.*

We have a potentially rich resource in the American elementary and secondary schools and colleges overseas assisted by the Department of State and AID.

They should be showcases for excellence in education.

They should help make overseas service attractive to our own citizens.

They should provide close contact with students and teachers of the host country.

I request additional support to assist those institutions which meet these standards.

4. *Create Special Programs for Future Leaders Studying in the United States.*

There are some 90,000 foreign students now enrolled in U.S. institutions. Many of them will someday play leading roles in their own countries. We must identify and assist these potential leaders.

I recommend that HEW and AID provide grants to enrich their educational experience through special courses and summer institutes.

HEALTH

The well-being of any nation rests fundamentally upon the health of its people.

If they are cursed by disease, their hopes grow dim.

If they are plagued by hunger, even the blessings of liberty give little comfort.

We have committed ourselves for many years to relieving human suffering. Today our effort must keep pace with a growing world and with growing problems.

Therefore, I propose a program to:
—create an International Career Service in Health;
—help meet health manpower needs in developing nations;
—combat malnutrition;

—control and eradicate disease;

—cooperate in worldwide efforts to deal with population problems.

I. CREATE AN INTERNATIONAL CAREER SERVICE IN HEALTH

The first requirement of an International Health Program is trained manpower.

I propose to:

1. *Increase the supply of trained Americans.*

I recommend a program of Public Health Service grants to our universities and professional schools. Our first year goal will be to increase by at least 500 the number of graduate students preparing to participate in international health activities.

2. *Establish a select corps of International Health Associates.*

The Public Health Service will recruit young professionals in the health disciplines to be available for assignments at home and overseas. Through service with AID, the Peace Corps, and international organizations, they will gain experience as the first step in building careers in international health.

I recommend recruitment of 100 outstanding young Americans to be the freshman class of International Health Associates.

3. *Establish a program of Fellows in International Health.*

I propose that 50 special fellowships be awarded to the best qualified young Americans with previous experience overseas and demonstrated capacity for leadership. With the help of advanced training, they will prepare for ever more rewarding service in this challenging career.

4. *Create an International Corps in the Public Health Service.*

I have directed the Secretary of Health, Education, and Welfare to build a career service corps competent to sustain the international health programs in which this country participates.

II. TO HELP MEET THE HEALTH MANPOWER NEEDS OF DEVELOPING NATIONS

In many countries, the struggle for better health is crippled by severe shortages not only of physicians but of all health workers— nurses, sanitarians, laboratory technicians, public health workers, health educators, hospital administrators, and others.

We must work for the day when each country will be able to train, in its own institutions, the health workers it needs. Meanwhile, we must assist in relieving critical manpower needs. Toward these ends I propose to:

1. *More than double the present AID program to strengthen medical and health training institutions in the developing nations.*

This program supports construction of teaching and laboratory facilities, modernization of teaching materials and methods, and assignments of American faculty abroad.

2. *Enable the Peace Corps to recruit and provide more volunteers for service in the health manpower programs of the developing nations.*

This will require an expanded recruitment effort, new programs of training and an increased emphasis on health.

III. TO COMBAT MALNUTRITION

Last year, in a special message to Congress, I emphasized the cost of malnutrition to the developing nations. This cost is counted in stunted human and national growth.

Since then, we have done much to combat hunger. Today, our Food for Peace programs reach about 100 million people.

With our help, a number of countries have

133

begun to establish self-sustaining programs to conquer malnutrition. Through international organizations—the Food and Agriculture Organization, UNICEF, the World Health Organization—we have added further resources to this struggle.

But food production has not kept pace with the increasing demands of expanding population.

Where food is scarce, babies, young children, and mothers are the first affected. By 1967, nearly 270 million of the world's children will suffer from malnutrition. The legions of the hungry will grow unless mankind acts to meet this peril.

This nation must play a larger role in combatting malnutrition, especially among the young. I propose to:

1. *Establish a Head Start Nutritional Program* to increase the number of infants, children, and mothers receiving adequate diets under the Food for Peace Program.

Our assistance currently reaches about 70 million children, 10 million of whom are under 5 years of age. Our goal must be to help the developing nations start or expand programs that will reach 150 million children within the next five years.

To overcome the most serious nutritional diseases, I have directed AID to enlarge its program for enriching milk and other Food for Peace commodities with vitamins and minerals.

2. *Provide Training in Nutrition.*

The developing nations need trained manpower—professional, technical and administrative—to carry out effective nutrition programs.

I am requesting that Congress appropriate funds for AID to support training in the United States for nutrition specialists from the developing countries and to support training institutions that have been established in 27 nations.

3. *Expand Research on Malnutrition.*

We need to know much more about the effects of nutritional deficiency; the cheapest and best ways to apply technological advances; and how to develop new, rich sources of protein. I am requesting funds for AID to expand basic and applied research in these areas.

IV. TO CONTROL AND ERADICATE DISEASES

In the rich nations, a healthy childhood is the birthright of most children.

But in the poor nations, children die daily of diarrheal diseases and cholera. Smallpox, malaria and yellow fever—all preventable diseases—drain the health of the people and the economy of the nation. Animal diseases destroy desperately needed food.

To launch a simultaneous and concerted attack upon these major infectious diseases, I propose that we initiate or enlarge programs to:

1. *Eradicate malaria—within ten years— from the Western Hemisphere, Ethiopia, Nepal, Jordan, the Philippines, Thailand, India, Pakistan and Iran.*

The United States assists 15 malaria eradication programs now in progress. I am requesting additional funds to expand these programs, and thus bring freedom from this disease to more than 800 million people in the coming decade.

We will strengthen the Pan American Health Organization as coordinator of the hemispheric attack on malaria. We will support the efforts of the World Health Organization.

2. *Eradicate smallpox throughout the world by 1975.*

Toward this goal, we will continue our support for the World Health Organization and provide special AID support for 19 West African countries which have requested our assistance.

3. *Reduce the hazard of measles.*

Measles, a relatively mild disease in our country, is virulent in others. It kills many children. It leaves others blind, deaf, or mentally retarded. AID and the Public Health Service have conducted a successful pilot project in measles immunization in Upper Volta. Since then, nearly all the neighboring West African countries have requested similar assistance. AID will expand its vaccination program to help those countries control measles within the next five years.

4. *Develop the means to control cholera and diarrheal diseases in developing nations.*

Because cholera cannot yet be prevented, we must develop more effective means of control. Through our own research, through cooperative programs with Japan, and through continued assistance to the SEATO Cholera Research Center in East Pakistan, we will move actively to curb the outbreak of this dread disease.

Diarrheal disease, a major cause of infant death in the poor nations, is transmitted largely through contaminated water. Working directly with these nations and with international organizations, AID will expand worldwide programs to ensure safe water supplies.

5. *Control animal diseases.*

Control or eradication of animal diseases could increase the meat supply by more than 25 percent in a number of developing nations. As many as three-fourths of the rural population suffer from debilitating diseases that originate in animals.

I am requesting funds to support the Pan American Health Organization in developing and testing vaccines against rabies and foot and mouth disease. In addition, we will support PAHO as it initiates and expands control measures against foot and

mouth disease in several Latin American countries.

6. *Expand U.S.-Japan Science Cooperation.*

In 1965 we joined Japan in a cooperative science program to combat some of the major diseases of Asia—leprosy, parasitic diseases, tuberculosis, cholera and malnutrition. I am requesting funds to expand this important venture administered through the Department of Health, Education, and Welfare.

V. TO COOPERATE IN WORLDWIDE EFFORTS TO DEAL WITH POPULATION PROBLEMS

By 1970, there will be 300 million more people on this earth. A reliable estimate shows, that at present rates of growth, the world population could double by the end of the century. The growing gap—between food to eat and mouths to feed—poses one of mankind's greatest challenges. It threatens the dignity of the individual and the sanctity of the family.

We must meet these problems in ways that will strengthen free societies—and protect the individual right to freedom of choice.

To mobilize our resources more effectively, I propose programs to:

1. *Expand Research in Human Reproduction and Population Dynamics.*

We are supporting research efforts through the Department of Health, Education, and Welfare, AID and the World Health Organization. I am requesting funds to increase the pace and scope of this effort. The effort to be successful will require a full response by our scientific community.

2. *Enlarge the training of American and foreign specialists in the population field.*

We are supporting training programs and the development of training programs through the Department of Health, Education, and Welfare and AID. We will expand these programs at home and abroad.

3. *Assist family planning programs in nations which request such help.*

Here at home, we are gaining valuable experience through new programs of maternal and infant care as well as expansion of private and public medical care programs.

Early last year we made clear our readiness to share our knowledge, skill and financial resources with the developing nations requesting assistance. We will expand this effort in response to the increasing number of requests from other countries.

THE CHOICE WE MUST MAKE

We call on rich nations and poor nations to join with us—to help each other and to help themselves. This must be the first work of the world for generations to come.

For our part, the programs in International Education and Health I am recommending this year will total $524 million:

—$354 million in the foreign assistance program.

—$103 million in the Health, Education, and Welfare Department program.

—$11 million in the Peace Corps program.

—$56 million in the State Department cultural and education program.

As I indicated in my message on Foreign Assistance yesterday, these programs will be conducted in a manner consistent with our balance of payments policy.

Last Fall, speaking to a gathering of the world's scholars at the Smithsonian Institution, I said: ". . . We can generate growing light in our universe—or we can allow the darkness to gather."

In the few months since then, forty-four million more children have come into the world. With them come more hunger—and more hope.

Since that time the gross national product of our nation has passed the $700 billion mark.

The choice between light and darkness, between health and sickness, between knowledge and ignorance, is not one that we can ignore.

The light we generate can be the brightest hope of history. It can illuminate the way toward a better life for all. But the darkness—if we let it gather—can become the final, terrible midnight of mankind.

The International Education and Health Acts of 1966 present an opportunity to begin a great shared adventure with other nations.

I urge the Congress to act swiftly for passage of both measures.

Our national interest warrants it.

The work of peace demands it.

LYNDON B. JOHNSON

The White House
February 2, 1966

NOTE: The International Education Act of 1966 was approved by the President on October 29, 1966 (see Item 557). The proposed International Health Act was not adopted by the 89th Congress.

See also Item 46.

46 Statement by the President on the Message on International Education and Health. *February 2, 1966*

LAST YEAR Congress, by its acts, declared this Nation's number one task is to now improve the education and health of our people.

Today I call upon Congress to add a world

dimension to this task. The International Education Act of 1966 marks our commitment to help others to rid themselves of the slavery of illiteracy and ignorance.

The International Health Act of 1966 pledges us to join in banishing the curse of disease.

I have bold yet prudent goals for all of us to meet: To create 1,000 school-to-school partnerships with the young of other nations; to bring 5,000 exchange Peace Corps volunteers from abroad to live and work in our country; to conquer or control some of the world's killer diseases—cholera, smallpox, malaria; to enrich diets of 150 million infants and mothers in less developed nations.

Half a century ago the philosopher William James declared that mankind must seek a moral equivalent of war. That search has become more desperate today than ever before. So we call on all rich nations and all poor nations, friend and foe alike, to join us in this combat. It can be the first work of the world for generations yet to come.

NOTE: The President also recorded the statement for radio and television broadcast.

For the text of the President's message, see Item 45.

47 Message to the American Trial Lawyers Association Meeting in New York City. *February 2, 1966*

MY MESSAGE to the American Trial Lawyers Association is simple and urgent—

We must stop the slaughter on our highways.

I applaud your dedication to this vital task. I share your sense of sharp anxiety and deepening concern. You and I know that the gravest problem before this nation—next to war in Vietnam—is the death and destruction, the shocking and senseless carnage, that strikes daily on our highways and that takes a higher and more terrible toll each year.

It must stop. There is cause for sacrifice in Vietnam. There is no excuse for suicide at home.

There is no excuse for 49,000 Americans killed—3½ million maimed and injured—billions lost in property damage and man hours—all in the one frightening and tragic year of 1965.

There can be no excuse for a nation that tolerates such anarchy on wheels. It is anarchy when each week nearly 1,000 of us die in auto accidents and when 70,000 more are crippled or hurt.

Since 1960, 1,675 Americans have been killed in Vietnam fighting Communist aggression. But the number of Americans killed on the highways in 1965 *alone* was more than 30 times greater. It is time we started doing our homework.

There is no excuse for a country—and no future for a people—that continues to ignore the mounting weight of evidence.

—It is a fact that 605,000 Americans have died in all wars from the Revolution to Vietnam—190 years—while 1½ million Americans have died on our highways in only 25 years.

—It is a fact that if we continue at our present suicidal rate, half of all Americans will one day suffer death or serious injury on our highways.

—It is a prediction, an official government estimate, that our death toll may exceed 70,000 each year within the next decade.

I accept the facts. I refuse to accept the prediction. This Administration has moved and will move to stop the slaughter—to replace suicide with sanity, and anarchy with safety.

The existing Federal-Aid Highway Program gave new and high priority to the elimination of dangerous highway locations. Some 39 states have already spent $55 million on such projects, of which $26 million was provided by the Federal Government.

But more—much more—remains to be done.

I will shortly propose a comprehensive Highway Safety Act of 1966 to arrest the destruction of life and property on our highways.

I want to encourage your organization to carry the crusade for highway safety to every state, community and individual. Your constant and constructive efforts have already achieved much. Now, together with every American of sense and conscience, we can and must achieve more.

LYNDON B. JOHNSON

NOTE: The Highway Safety Act of 1966 was approved by the President on September 9, 1966 (see Item 449).

48 Statement by the President Announcing an Increase in Enriched Uranium To Be Made Available for Peaceful Uses. *February* 2, 1966

IN ACCORDANCE with the Atomic Energy Act of 1954, the President determines the quantities of special nuclear material to be made available for distribution at home and abroad. Such a Presidential determination of quantities of enriched uranium for peaceful uses was announced on July 3, 1963. Since that time, there has been considerable progress in plans for the increased utilization of enriched uranium in nuclear powerplants. In order to give assurances that enriched uranium can be supplied to meet these needs, I am announcing today a further increase in the quantities of material to be made available.

I have determined, pursuant to section 41b of the Atomic Energy Act of 1954, as amended, that the quantities of uranium–235 in enriched uranium to be made available are raised from 200,000 to 300,000 kilograms for domestic distribution under section 53, and from 150,000 to 250,000 kilograms for foreign distribution under section 54. These amounts have been recommended by the Atomic Energy Commission with the concurrence of the Secretaries of State and Defense. The new total of 550,000 kilo-

grams is more than 50 percent higher than the previous total.

The material will be distributed as required over a period of years and will be subject to prudent safeguards against unauthorized use. Charges for this material will result in substantial revenues to the United States Government. As nuclear programs develop in the future, it will undoubtedly be necessary to make further determinations increasing the amounts of material to be available. The large capacity of U.S. diffusion plants for the production of enriched uranium permits them to meet both civilian and military requirements.

A discussion of the new determination is contained in the attached statement by the Chairman of the Atomic Energy Commission.

NOTE: The statement by Glenn T. Seaborg, Chairman, Atomic Energy Commission, pointed out that the material, most of it of low enrichments, would be used in research and development and as fuel in nuclear reactors, with the bulk of it being utilized in generating electricity.

The statement noted that "Allocation of enriched uranium to a reactor project includes material for the fuel loading, for fuel consumption over the period of the domestic license or foreign agreement for cooperation, and for the inventory outside of the reactor associated with the manufacture and storage of fuel elements, cooling and shipment of irradiated fuel, and chemical processing of irradiated fuel to recover the remaining uranium and plutonium. The amount of U–235 contained in enriched uranium returned to the AEC is deducted from the amount supplied by the AEC in computing how much is available for further distribution. The material allocated to a reactor project may not be completely distributed for several decades.

"As of December 31, 1965, there were in effect in the United States construction permits or operating licenses for 18 power reactors, 5 test reactors, 75 research reactors, and 17 critical-experiment facilities, and 583 licenses for other uses of special nuclear material, not including the AEC's own reactors,

facilities, and uses. Agreements for cooperation in the civil uses of atomic energy are in effect between the United States and a large part of the free world, including 34 countries and West Berlin; 16 of these agreements provide for cooperation on power reactors. In addition, agreements are in effect with the International Atomic Energy Agency and the European Atomic Energy Community (Euratom).

"Enriched uranium for peaceful uses is distributed abroad only under civil agreements for cooperation. All such agreements contain a guaranty by the cooperating country that the material supplied will be used exclusively for peaceful purposes. Safeguard provisions allowing inspection of materials, facilities, and records by United States or international inspectors are also included, as appropriate." (2 Weekly Comp. Pres. Docs., p. 164)

---

49 Remarks Upon Presenting the Heart-of-the-Year Award to Representative John E. Fogarty. *February 3, 1966*

Congressman Fogarty and Dr. Taussig, ladies and gentlemen:

When we read that a fully functioning artificial heart is possible within 5 years, we pay tribute to congressional leadership, and particularly to Congressman John Fogarty of Rhode Island.

And when we finally call a halt to the wholesale murder of heart disease, all of us will bless the day that Congress took effective action. John Fogarty represents the little State of Rhode Island in the United States Congress, but his crusade for better health has led him often to the first house of the land.

He came here last August 4th for the signing of the Community Facilities Act. He was back again the next day at the signing of the Community Health Services Extension Act—community mental health centers one week, Community Health Services Extension Act the next week.

Four days later he came back to see us as a sponsor of the National Institutes of Health for the signing of the Health Research Facilities Act. In October he was back at the

White House again for the signing of the Heart, Cancer, and Stroke Amendments, to establish regional medical centers to help us in fighting these killer diseases.

Now he is back with us again this morning. He doesn't have a bill in his pocket— a congressional bill, I mean—but this, I think, I can tell you: When he comes to this house, he is always welcome.

For John Fogarty knows what we all must learn, and that is that no society can be great which is not first of all healthy. The healing miracles that we achieve must not be gifts for Americans only, and that is why we have suggested another health measure for this Nation to discuss, debate, consider, and, I hope, ultimately act upon. That is the International Health Act of 1966 that is to launch a cooperative effort by all of the world's people to make a determined and organized attempt to conquer disease wherever it exists in human beings.

I don't let you in on any secret when I say I am hopeful that after this International Health Act of 1966 is considered in the House and the Senate that it will not be long before John Fogarty is back here, and Dr. Taussig, paying us another visit, and waiting for his pen.

The world cannot wait. The clock is ticking.

I know that as we work on these messages and outline our hopes and our purposes and our ambitions in the world, that some people may think that we have too many "goodies," that we are pretty visionary, and that we have something for everyone.

The cynical sometimes are critical. But I know of no more worthy motive or purpose that a human being can have than to try to lay out as his or her goal a program that will educate the mind, and that will conquer disease in the body, and that will permit your children and your people to live in an atmosphere and an environment of beauty and culture and enjoy the better things of life.

Now, we cannot conquer disease, and we cannot educate all humanity, and we cannot have a symphony in every town, and we cannot have a Mellon Art Gallery in every capital, but we can hope for them and we can work for them and we can give what we have to them, and we can urge them and provide leadership and ideas and try to move along.

I was reading a speech late last night that the Postmaster General under President Roosevelt had made, and he talked about his first 100 days and his first 100 bills, and how most of them lived on today and none of them had ever really been repealed.

What I hope the sixties will be remembered for are the steps that we have taken in education and in health and in under-

standing of our fellow man, not just in the 50 States of this Union, but in all the continents of the world.

It may just be a few thousand or a few million that start the program. The poverty program was really started with the NYA and the CCC back in the thirties, and it has developed from there. The whole great conservation movement in water resources in this country started with something we proudly call the TVA that Senator Norris did.

The health program that this man picked up when he was a lone wolf—when he got lonely he'd go over and see Lister Hill in the Senate, but outside of the two of them there weren't many around that really believed that you could do something about it. Yet there are people in this room today that are living testimonials to the fruits of his research.

It gives me such great satisfaction to attempt in the best way I can to pay tribute to Congressman Fogarty from the great State of Rhode Island.

Thank you.

NOTE: The President spoke at 11:40 a.m. in the Theater at the White House. In his opening words he referred to Representative John E. Fogarty of Rhode Island and Dr. Helen B. Taussig, President of the American Heart Association. During his remarks he referred to James A. Farley, Postmaster General 1933–1940, George W. Norris, Representative from Nebraska 1903–1913 and Senator from Nebraska 1913–1943, and Senator Lister Hill of Alabama.

The President presented the award on behalf of the American Heart Association at the request of Dr. Taussig, codeveloper of the "blue baby" surgical procedure. In 1959 President Johnson, then majority leader of the Senate, received the first Heart-of-the-Year Award.

50   Message of Congratulations Following the Landing on the Moon
of the U.S.S.R.'s Luna 9. *February 3, 1966*

Dear Mr. Chairman:

You and the people of the Union of Soviet Socialist Republics are to be congratulated for the great success of Luna 9. Your accomplishment is one that can benefit all mankind. And all mankind applauds it. Your scientists have made a major contribution to man's knowledge of the moon and of space.

Sincerely,

LYNDON B. JOHNSON

[His Excellency Nikolai Viktorovich Podgorny, Chairman, Presidium of the Supreme Soviet, U.S.S.R.]

NOTE: The text of the telegram was read by Bill D. Moyers, Special Assistant to the President, at his news conference at 4:40 p.m. on Thursday, February 3, 1966, in his office at the White House. It was not made public in the form of a White House press release.

The unmanned Soviet spaceship had made a successful soft landing on the moon, the first of its kind. Following the landing telemetric signals were transmitted back to earth.

51   Remarks at the Swearing In of Roger Wilkins as Director,
Community Relations Service. *February 4, 1966*

Good morning, ladies and gentlemen:

Seven years ago I had the privilege of introducing the first Community Relations Service measure in the Congress of the United States. I did so out of a lifelong belief that conciliation is always stronger than confrontation.

At that time I observed that such an organization would place heavy responsibilities upon the conciliator. He would have to be a very imaginative man. He would have to be a very understanding man. He would have to be a man of absolute integrity.

Such men, I told the Congress, are very difficult to find, but they are not impossible to find. We did find such a man in Governor LeRoy Collins, who I am proud to welcome here this morning.

And now I think we have found another such man in Roger Wilkins, who I am glad to have here to take the oath. Although he, as you can observe, is very young in years, Roger Wilkins has the experience and, I believe, the poise and the calm judgment which is demanded of a conciliator.

He has had extensive experience in social welfare. He has had experience in dealing with the problems of developing nations. The very able and beloved Attorney General Katzenbach tells me that he has experience that will be very valuable to him as a practicing lawyer.[1] He has had now nearly 4 years' experience as a public servant. And above all, I believe that he has understanding.

Not long after I announced my intention of nominating Roger Wilkins to be the Director of the new Community Relations Service, he was asked whether the fact that Roy Wilkins was his uncle had anything to do with this appointment. Now I want it known that to be related to Roy Wilkins is no small honor.

There are few Americans that I believe have worked longer, harder, more intelligently, or more effectively for racial and social justice in our country, and I consider him not only one of my close counselors, but one of the great citizens of this generation.

But today we have met here in this White

---

[1] The President would shortly thereafter recommend transfer of the Community Relations Service to the Department of Justice (see Item 59).

House Theater not so much to honor Roger Wilkins because he has a distinguished uncle; I think it is better that we should congratulate Roy Wilkins because he has such a distinguished nephew.

We place high priority on the task that we have given you, Roger. We have secured the services of a very wise and able man, Brooks Hays, to work with you. We have proposed a very sharp increase in the budget of the Community Relations Service, from $1.3 million to $2 million. We have proposed an increase in the manpower of the Service from 67 to 100.

We are shifting the focus of the Service away from business groups and enlarging its mission by having it report directly to the Attorney General of the United States.

With the approval of the Congress, Mr. Wilkins, as Director, will have the rank of Assistant Attorney General of the United States.

So, Roger, you have been given a very critical task, at a very critical hour, a critical period in your Nation's history.

More than a century ago, Abraham Lincoln said, "I believe this Government cannot endure permanently half slave and half free." Today, I believe that this Nation cannot endure torn by hatred, and bigotry, and racial strife. I believe that we are, at this very moment, at a crossroads in America.

And I believe that the destiny of our children and our grandchildren await its decision. That decision will not be made by a powerful, strong Federal Government here in Washington. Of course, that Government can and will help. That Government can and will right injustices. That Government can fill empty plates and it can try to help nourish eager minds.

But after all is said and done, as I just related to Mr. Heineman in the library, it is with the people in the communities of this Nation that really the ultimate decision rests and where the ultimate responsibility lies. It rests in their hearts. It rests in their sense of decency and fair play. Above all, it rests in their commonsense.

So it is to these people and their communities that you must direct the efforts of the Community Relations Service. There are high responsibilities here. You can carry them with our high hopes and with our warm confidence. Our prayers will be with you and our efforts will support you every step of the way.

[*At this point the oath of office was administered by Secretary of Commerce John T. Connor. The President then resumed speaking.*]

I have just finished a preliminary meeting with the chairman of the civil rights conference to be held this spring here at the White House. He is one of our most gifted businessmen, one of our most dedicated patriots. He is going to give every weekend and as much nighttime as necessary from now until late in the spring to organize the conference and bring the best people in the Nation here to the White House to discuss the civil rights problems that face us, to try to work out an agenda of not only problems, but solutions and programs.

I would like all of you who are interested in this field to know him, and I would like to publicly thank him for the great sacrifices he is making, trying to serve his country in this critical field in this critical period—Mr. Ben Heineman.

NOTE: The President spoke at 11:38 a.m. in the Theater at the White House. During his remarks he referred to LeRoy Collins, Under Secretary of Commerce and former Governor of Florida, Attorney General Nicholas deB. Katzenbach, Roy Wilkins, Secretary of the National Association for the Advancement of Colored People, Brooks Hays, Representative from Arkansas 1943–1959 and Special Assistant to the President 1961–1963, and Ben W. Heineman, chairman of the forthcoming White House conference on civil rights.

52   The President's News Conference of *February* 4, 1966

THE PRESIDENT. I have two or three items of interest, I think, to give you.

FOOD SITUATION IN INDIA

[1.] First of all, I spent some time this week working on the food situation for India. I think I need not dwell at length on the very serious situation that confronts the Government of India and the people as a result of the drought and the famine that exists there.

I have counseled with the appropriate Members of the House and Senate, in agriculture and foreign affairs and foreign relations and appropriations fields, and I am today making an allotment of 2 million tons of wheat and 1 million tons of maize to be immediately available, and to be shipped as quickly as is possible.

The wheat will be worth in the neighborhood of $160 million, and the maize will be between $45 million and $50 million.

I plan to see the Prime Minister[1] at her convenience, and we will at that meeting go further into the problems, the mutual problems, to try to arrive at a further course of action and additional measures that we can take and our people can take to be helpful to our friends and to the people of India, and also to talk about things that the people of India can do to help their friends, the people of America.

I have reviewed this at some length with the Ambassador, at great length with the Secretary of State and the Secretary of Agriculture. We have had a number of our best technical personnel there. Some are still

---

[1] Mrs. Indira Gandhi, Prime Minister of India.

there. Others will be going in the next few days.

If there are questions on that, I will take them now, and then I will go into some other things.

QUESTIONS CONCERNING INDIA

Q. Mr. President, I would gather, then, that the resumption of economic aid will await the visit of Mrs. Gandhi.

THE PRESIDENT. I wouldn't want to foreclose or preclude any allotments in between, but none have been made as of now. I would anticipate that she would be here in the reasonably near future. I am just passing on the most urgent at the moment. That is food. We have allotted 3½ million tons already this fiscal year, and this will be an additional 3 million—2 million of wheat and 1 million of maize.

You can say that we are formulating legislation that we will discuss with the Indian Government, but we are formulating legislation that will be discussed and debated and sent to the Congress unless we change our mind. That is our present plan—to ask for a commitment of the Congress and the American people and to also use whatever influence we have, what leadership in the world, to ask other countries to come in and contribute.

Now, in just what form we will do that is still in the detail state. I went into it last night and I spent some time today with the Secretary of Agriculture on it, but he is going to be working on it today.

Q. Can you say how this might affect the American farm situation?

THE PRESIDENT. I wouldn't think it

would affect it a great deal one way or the other. We have adequate supplies.

Q. It will cut down surpluses, though, will it not?

THE PRESIDENT. Yes.

Q. Mr. President, would you expect Mrs. Gandhi to come here within the next few weeks? [2]

THE PRESIDENT. I think that is a matter for her to announce. She is welcome any time she can come. We have been very receptive to visits of the Prime Minister of India since we got our foreign aid legislation last year and we were in a position to know what we were authorized to do.

Q. Mr. President, this shipment you just announced is in addition to the emergency grain shipments you authorized late last year?

THE PRESIDENT. Yes. This will be a total of 6½ million tons. We have authorized 3½ million and we will authorize another 3 million today. I haven't even told the Secretary the amount. I have been studying this since he left here.

But, as a matter of fact, I am announcing a little more than I thought. I want to be sure that we announce what we can, and then I am going to ask Congress to join me in authorizing me to make a rather substantial increase in allotments and ask the world to help us every way it can. [3]

Q. Mr. President, is the aim to try to get it up to approximately a million tons?

THE PRESIDENT. I would say that is pure speculation. We don't have any aim, goal, or objective. We want to do whatever we can to try not to have more than we need or less than we need, but we are surveying that now. We don't know what other nations will do. You can be sure America will do more than her part.

I think we do a great disservice when we speculate that America is going to contribute x or y amounts before we have even decided that, because you then wed us to a position in the public mind which is not justified, and which I am not authorized to make.

Q. Mr. President, would this be a part of your Food for Peace message, or will you put in a special bill that would apply to India?

THE PRESIDENT. This will be India, a special emergency situation for India.

Q. Mr. President, can you tell us what India's needs are at this point on a monthly basis or a yearly basis?

THE PRESIDENT. They have a shortage of roughly 19 million tons, and they are taking steps to ration and pull that down to several million tons—6, 7, 8, maybe down to 11 or 12 million. They can speak better about that than I can, although I had a detailed report from the Ambassador last night that I reviewed with the Congress.

Is there anything else?

Q. Will you take questions on other subjects, sir?

CONFERENCE ON VIETNAM IN HAWAII

THE PRESIDENT. [2.] Yes. I am going to make another little announcement and you will probably want to ask me something on that.

For some time I have been wanting to visit with Ambassador Lodge and General Westmoreland. [4] Last week we explored the possibility of General Westmoreland coming here and addressing a group, and that did not work out. So I ascertained he would be in Pearl Harbor and Honolulu

---

[2] See Items 148, 149, 152.

[3] See Item 153.

[4] Henry Cabot Lodge, U.S. Ambassador to the Republic of Vietnam, and Gen. William C. Westmoreland, Commander, United States Military Assistance Command, Vietnam.

this weekend. I have tentative plans to have Ambassador Lodge come——

Q. What was that, sir?

THE PRESIDENT. I have plans to ask Ambassador Lodge to come into Honolulu and join General Westmoreland there. I will ask the Secretary of State, the Secretary of Defense, the Secretary of Agriculture, and the Secretary of Health, Education, and Welfare, with appropriate education and health officials, to join me and a very limited White House working group. We will leave here sometime late tomorrow and go to Honolulu.

We will ask the Chief of State, General Thieu, and the Prime Minister, Mr. Ky, to also come there for a visit and to exchange views with us. We will have both military and nonmilitary briefings.[5]

Following those meetings on Tuesday I will return to Washington with some of the Cabinet, and perhaps Mr. Bundy,[6] the Secretary of Agriculture, and other technical people may go on to explore and inaugurate certain pacification programs in the fields of health, education, and agriculture in Vietnam.

As I said, I have been wanting to have a chance to review with Ambassador Lodge and General Westmoreland our complete program there. Since General Westmoreland is going to be there anyway, I thought it would be good for us this weekend to meet him there instead of trying to have them all come over here. It is a little trip for each one of us, but neither one of us has to go too far. We will do that. I expect to come back Tuesday. I don't know what General Westmoreland plans to do. Sometimes he stays there for as long as a week. I am not sure, and they are not sure, just

what his plans are. I believe his wife is in Honolulu.

QUESTIONS REGARDING THE CONFERENCE

Q. Mr. President, do you have any assurance that the Vietnamese officials you mentioned will be meeting you there?

THE PRESIDENT. Yes.

Q. Sir, have you met Prime Minister Ky before?

THE PRESIDENT. No.

Q. Have any political or military developments prompted this?

THE PRESIDENT. No. Just as I stated, for some time I have been wanting to see them and talk to them, and this seems to be a good time to do it.

Q. Are you asking any Member of Congress to go with you?

THE PRESIDENT. No.

Q. Will you use the Navy base for your headquarters?

THE PRESIDENT. We have our security people working on that, and that will be a matter that will be handled by the State Department and Admiral Sharp's[7] group out there.

Q. Mr. President, just to review your timetable, you are going to leave here tomorrow afternoon or tomorrow night?

THE PRESIDENT. Tomorrow afternoon. It will be as soon in the afternoon as I can. I plan to return Tuesday night.

Q. You will be back in here Tuesday night?

THE PRESIDENT. I will probably leave out there Tuesday night.

Q. Mr. President, is there any possibility of other allies who are associated there with us in combat to participate in this?

THE PRESIDENT. No.

---

[5] See Items 53–56.

[6] McGeorge Bundy, Special Assistant to the President.

[7] Adm. U. S. Grant Sharp, Jr., Commander in Chief of U.S. Forces in the Pacific.

Q. Will the discussions be mainly on military matters or political?

THE PRESIDENT. Just as I said, it will be on nonmilitary and military matters. We will have a good deal on the pacification matters, particularly on agriculture. Secretary Freeman [8] has been working on this for some time. I asked him about 10 days ago to go out, and then I asked him to have his technical people wait until this thing jelled a little bit.

I had planned to ask Mr. Bundy to go out, but I asked him to hold back until we could try to put this all together. I have asked Mr. Gardner [9] to try to make arrangements to get excused from hearings that he will have so that he can have the health and education people, too.

We are going to emphasize in every way we can, in line with the very fine pronouncements that the Prime Minister has made concerning his desires in the field of education and health and agriculture. We want to be sure that we have our best planning and our maximum effort put into it. That will occupy a substantial part of the conference.

But we will, of course, very thoroughly go into the military briefing and have Admiral Sharp and General Westmoreland bring to my attention anything and everything that they feel will be worthy. I would like to know them a little better and I would like them to know me a little better.

Q. Perhaps you mentioned this before, Mr. President, but will the conferences run the full 3 days—Sunday, Monday, and Tuesday?

THE PRESIDENT. I would expect I would be coming back late Tuesday night. I would expect that I would leave here some-time after noon tomorrow. Now, the precise moment, I just frankly do not know.

Q. Sir, is Mr. Bell going to go?

THE PRESIDENT. Yes. I haven't talked to him, but I would hope that either Mr. Bell or Mr. Gaud [10] could go. Mr. Bell, I believe, is testifying, and I don't know whether he has concluded or not. I wouldn't want to interrupt it. It is a matter for him to work out. We have had detailed conferences with him in this field and he is prepared for the action we have discussed.

Q. Will some of Mr. Lodge's staff, like General Lansdale,[11] be included in this?

THE PRESIDENT. There will be appropriate officials from some of the staffs.

THE FOREIGN RELATIONS COMMITTEE HEARINGS

[3.] Q. Mr. President, in Senator Fulbright's [12] committee, Mr. Bell has been testifying in public hearings, and Mr. Rusk and Mr. McNamara [13] both have declined to do so.

THE PRESIDENT. Mr. Rusk testified——

Q. I mean today.

THE PRESIDENT. ——in a public hearing before television.

Q. Today, it was Mr. McNamara and General Wheeler,[14] I'm sorry. Can you tell us what prompted this decision, please? Is there any comment on it you would like to make?

THE PRESIDENT. No, I think all of you

---

[8] Orville L. Freeman, Secretary of Agriculture.

[9] John W. Gardner, Secretary of Health, Education, and Welfare.

[10] David E. Bell, Administrator, Agency for International Development, and William S. Gaud, Deputy Administrator.

[11] Maj. Gen. Edward G. Lansdale, senior liaison officer with the Saigon government.

[12] Senator J. W. Fulbright of Arkansas, Chairman of the Senate Foreign Relations Committee.

[13] Dean Rusk, Secretary of State, and Robert S. McNamara, Secretary of Defense.

[14] Gen. Earle G. Wheeler, Chairman of the Joint Chiefs of Staff.

who have been around here through the years—particularly when we have had testimony on military matters and times when we are engaged with the enemy or when we are fighting Communists—know that we have tried to work out a procedure, at least in the years I was on Armed Services in the House and Senate, to make available all the information we could make available without aiding the Communists and aiding the enemy.

I guess the most notable case was the MacArthur case where the committee in its wisdom—and the administration agreed—decided they would take full testimony and the witnesses could make complete and detailed answers, and then appropriate judicious officials would review that testimony and not furnish damaging testimony to the enemy.[15]

I am sure that that procedure has been satisfactory and it is the general practice in Appropriations Committees now. And the Armed Services Committees, who really have some experience in this field, and who have practices, I would think could work out something along that line without any difficulty. Of course, you are always faced with this problem.

I think the Preparedness Committee that I headed for years, I think still follows this rule though I could be wrong. I haven't looked into it but it is just my impression that they take full and complete testimony and release everything that can be released.

If not, the witness is confronted with this problem: He cannot be fully responsive, or if he is fully responsive he endangers and places in jeopardy the lives of a good many of our men.

I saw the other day on television one of our witnesses testifying and he was asked the question about bombing a certain country, some Senator having made a statement about it. Just the connotation of the question, just the question itself created a problem that when you fellows get through writing about it and putting a headline on it, could really become a problem for the Nation, and particularly for our men.

He was attempting to form an answer before television that would try to satisfy the Senators, and at the same time protect the men. The Senator said, "Well, if you don't want to be responsive, that is all right, if you are not going to be responsive." So he points up the problem.

The problem is that if you are fully responsive in some military matters, the Chief of Staff can very quickly get your men involved.

If you are not fully responsive, then you don't satisfy the Senators. So how do you serve the national interest?

Well, through the years, I think Senator Russell,[16] when he was chairman of the MacArthur committee—and we had the Republicans, a number of them, on the committee—they all agreed to these procedures and I think they use them pretty well now. I am sure they will work out.

I don't know what General Wheeler's position is. He has not discussed it with me, and Secretary McNamara hasn't. But I don't think that is any great problem for informing Senators. It is not a matter that is spectacular, or it is not a matter that you want to have a show about.

---

[15] In June 1951 Senate committee hearings were held to look into the dismissal of Gen. Douglas MacArthur from his command in the Far East. The testimony is printed in "Hearings Before the Committee on Armed Services and the Committee on Foreign Relations, United States Senate, on the Military Situation in the Far East" (Government Printing Office, 1951, Parts 1–5, 3691 pp.).

[16] Senator Richard B. Russell of Georgia, Chairman of the Senate Armed Services Committee.

When you are talking about military matters and men out there dying, you want to be very careful that you don't involve them or endanger them.

FURTHER QUESTIONS ON VIETNAM

[4.] Q. In regard to the Honolulu meeting, do you think it is possible that a shift in policy on Vietnam might result from these consultations?

THE PRESIDENT. That is not anticipated at all.

Q. Is it a policy review?

THE PRESIDENT. We are there to get military and nonmilitary briefings and to exchange viewpoints. I wouldn't want to anticipate getting off and making any changes one way or the other. I wouldn't say that we wouldn't learn some things from the meeting that would cause us to either improve the situation or strengthen it, but I would not want you to anticipate that the purpose of the meeting was to formulate any different policy at all, because that is not the purpose.

Q. Mr. President, are you thinking about a report to the American people when you return from Honolulu?

THE PRESIDENT. No. I am reporting to them every day. I am reporting to them now.

Q. I was thinking of a speech on television or something like that.

THE PRESIDENT. I just finished one on television.[17] I know of no President that has been given the opportunity to report more or who has taken advantage of it more.

As a matter of fact, last year I got some criticism for using the television 58 times, almost twice as much as my predecessor, in reporting to the people.

I had a rather detailed report on Vietnam in the State of the Union.[18] I have gone into some of the decisions involved in the statement when I resumed activities out there a few days ago.

We will report to you, following these discussions and these meetings, everything that we can and, through you, to the American people.

[5.] Q. Mr. President, is there anything you can tell us about the response you have had to your decision to resume the bombings of North Vietnam?

THE PRESIDENT. I don't think there is anything that you don't know about. I reviewed last night here the responses from all of the countries of the world. I pretty well know the measure of public sentiment that we have had.

Substantially large groups, some 70-odd percent, felt that the pause was advised and they approved of it, and I think a very substantial percent approved of ending it. It went somewhat longer than anyone had anticipated, even the proponents of it, and even the nonaligned countries or neutral countries, some of whom felt that it was indicated.

But that was a series of circumstances. We would hear something here, and we wanted to be sure that we didn't get Mr. Sevareid[19] confused, and so we would follow it right out to the last inch.

But by the time we traveled down that road, we would hear some rumor over here, and we would go and follow that one out. By the time you did that with 115 countries and you get them all wrapped up, it takes time.

Finally, the last 2 or 3 days we received a note that there was going to be a very

---

[17] See Item 39.

[18] See Item 6.

[19] Eric Sevareid of the Columbia Broadcasting System.

urgent message delivered to one of the large powers in a very critical capital, and so we had to wait a couple of days for that.

The substance of that was the Ho Chi Minh [20] letter that had been printed here 2 or 3 days before. So by that time we had used 38 days, and we felt that we had exhausted all of the possibilities there.

Therefore, we had no real hope of accomplishing anything in these capitals and we were free to pursue other efforts, which we are now pursuing at the United Nations and any other places that may offer possibilities from time to time.

Q. Mr. President, on that subject, the United Nations, could you give us your evaluation of what has happened so far? Is there any movement, in your opinion, toward the peace table, through the U.N. or anywhere else?

THE PRESIDENT. I am glad that we took the action that we did, after we had thoroughly exhausted all of the possibilities with other countries. I am happy that the Security Council took the action that it did. I am not as accurate in my predictions as Drew Pearson.[21] I do not have any batting average like that, and I would rather let developments up there emerge and not try to predict what course they will take.

We will do everything that we can to thoroughly search for a course that will lead to peace. Ambassador Goldberg,[22] with the help of his staff, and the friends of peace in the United Nations, are going to be working around the clock until peace is achieved.

[20] Ho Chi Minh, President of North Vietnam.
[21] Author of the syndicated column "Washington Merry-Go-Round."
[22] Arthur J. Goldberg, U.S. Representative to the United Nations.

[6.] Q. Mr. President, to clarify an earlier question or answer, it would be wrong in your view, would it not, to interpret your trip as coming at a crucial point in the war in Vietnam?

THE PRESIDENT. I do not see any reason why I ought to interpret it one way or the other. I just say that I am going. I am going in a 707, and as to what phase of the war, I don't think that that has much to do with it.

[7.] Q. Mr. President, could I ask if the overseas polls on opinion were made by USIA and what use we are making of that polling technique now in directing foreign policy?

THE PRESIDENT. I do not know what you are talking about, but if it is USIA, I would talk to USIA.

Q. I was merely asking if the polls you have were made by USIA.

THE PRESIDENT. What polls are you talking about?

Q. On overseas opinion.

THE PRESIDENT. I don't know what you are talking about. You will have to get it clear. I haven't discussed any polls with you, have I?

Q. I was referring to the polls that you mentioned, the 70 percent.

THE PRESIDENT. They are here, in this country.

Q. They are domestic polls?

THE PRESIDENT. I believe your Washington Post publishes Lou Harris. I am talking about the feeling here on Lou Harris' poll, where 73 favored the pause—that is, 73 percent of the people of this country.

Reporter: Thank you.

NOTE: President Johnson's fifty-fourth news conference was held in his office at the White House at 2:45 p.m. on Friday, February 4, 1966.

53 Remarks of Welcome to Vietnamese Leaders Upon Arriving at Honolulu International Airport. *February 6, 1966*

Mr. Chairman, ladies and gentlemen:

I welcome these two brave leaders of the Vietnamese Republic and their colleagues to American soil. We meet here in a time of testing and trial, but we will talk also of hope and harvest.

Our friends in Korea and Australia and New Zealand have sent their own men to join with Vietnamese and Americans in a conflict to decide if aggression and terror are the way of the future or whether free men are to decide their own course.

It is a question of the gravest importance to all other nations, large or small, whose peoples seek to walk in independence and peace. For were the Communist aggressors to win in Vietnam, they would know that they can accomplish through so-called "wars of national liberation" what they could not accomplish through naked aggression in Korea, or insurgency in the Philippines, in Greece and Malaya, or the threat of aggression in Turkey, or in a free election booth anywhere in the world.

During the past year more than 1,300 Americans have lost their lives from Communist action in Vietnam. But more than 11,000 of our Vietnamese brothers-in-arms died last year protecting their homeland.

Why do these Vietnamese fight on? Because they are not going to let others enslave them or rule their future. And with their soldiers are the administrators and civil officials, and the villagers themselves—to many of whom each darkness of the evening is filled with fear, and to many of whom each noise in the night may be a terrorist's bomb or an assassin's grenade.

And yet they fight on.

They fight for dreams beyond the din of battle—the dream of security in their village, a teacher for their children, food for their bodies, medicine for their sick, the right to worship in the way they choose. They fight for the essential rights of human existence, and only the callous or the timid can ignore their cause.

There are special pleaders who counsel retreat in Vietnam. They belong to a group that has always been blind to experience and has been deaf to hope. We cannot accept their logic that tyranny 10,000 miles away is not tyranny to concern us, or that subjugation by an armed minority in Asia is different from subjugation by an armed minority in Europe. Were we to follow their course, how many nations might fall before the aggressor? Where would our treaties be respected, our word honored, and our commitments believed?

In the forties and the fifties we took our stand in Europe to protect the freedom of those threatened by aggression. If we had not then acted, what kind of Europe might there be today?

Now the center of attention has shifted to another part of the world where aggression is on the march and enslavement of free men is its goal.

Our stand must be as firm as ever.

If we allow the Communists to win in Vietnam, it will become easier and more appetizing for them to take over other countries in other parts of the world. We will have to fight again someplace else—at what cost no one knows. And that is why it is vitally important to every American that we stop the Communists in South Vietnam.

To these beautiful islands and the newest

of our States have come the leaders of South Vietnam and the United States—come here to talk of our resolution to defend the peace and to build a decent society for the people of South Vietnam. Because we are here to talk especially of the works of peace, we will leave here determined not only to achieve victory over aggression, but to win victory over hunger, disease, and despair.

We are making reality out of the hopes of the common people—hope for a better life. We will talk here of health and education, of agriculture and economics—and we will talk of those other important aspects of a vital future for the people of Vietnam. In all of these endeavors, we will give all the support possible to the energetic efforts of our Vietnamese allies.

As leaders of our two nations, engaged in this struggle, it is appropriate that we should meet together in order that we may best move forward together. So this afternoon I extend to these two friends and these allies of ours a most warm welcome to our country.

NOTE: The President spoke at 5:25 p.m. at Honolulu International Airport where Lt. Gen. Nguyen Van Thieu, Chairman of the National Leadership Committee (Chief of State), Republic of Vietnam, was given a formal welcome with full military honors. In his opening remarks the President referred to General Thieu and Prime Minister Nguyen Cao Ky.

General Thieu responded as follows:
"Mr. President:

"Today as we set foot on American territory, on behalf of the people and the Government of the Republic of Vietnam, we extend to the people of the United States our friendly greeting.

"We also express our gratitude for the warm support and the precious assistance of the American people and Government.

"Your words have gone beyond the usual welcoming address, for they have told Vietnam and the world of a renewed and much stronger determination on the part of the United States to draw a line and stop Communist aggression in Vietnam, and now.

"Your review of the past Communist aggressions the world over leaves no doubt whatsoever as to the logical conclusion that has been drawn. Once again the Americans have confirmed themselves as the champions of liberty, the worthy descendants of the Minuteman. By adopting the Vietnamese cause, you have not only carried on the American tradition of coming to the assistance of a friend in need, but you have also shown enlightenment, vision, and realism in the best American tradition.

"We welcome your initiative, Mr. President, in inviting us to this conference. This is a precious occasion for the leaders of our countries to personally meet. This also serves to further strengthen the friendship and the close cooperation already existing between our Governments in the common struggle against Communist aggression so as to maintain world peace and protect the freedom of mankind.

"This is also a meeting between friends who already are in agreement for the purpose of showing the Communists our unwavering determination to call a stop to their efforts at enslaving the people of the world, notwithstanding the force they may adopt in going about this task.

"Our determination is also to go one step further toward the complete eradication of the Communist wish, for whereas the Communists only promise a better society, we will wage every effort to make a reality of this dream for a better society that is in the mind of every Vietnamese.

"We Vietnamese have a great admiration for the remarkable fighting spirit of the Americans, and are grateful to those who have sacrificed their lives for a just cause and for the sake of our people. We send to the families of those valiant fighters our most sincere admiration for their loved ones and our condolence.

"Mr. President, we firmly believe that the efforts of our two nations in the service of the ideals of liberty and peace in the world will lead to final victory.

"In closing, we sincerely thank you, Mr. President, for the warm and heartening welcome which you have extended to us, and we take this opportunity to reiterate the solemn pledge of the Vietnamese people to continue to fight this war for as long as is necessary, and to be willing and ready to make sacrifices so as not to betray all those brave Americans and Vietnamese who have given their lives so that we may be free."

See also Items 54–56.

54   Joint Statement Following Discussions in Honolulu With the Chief of State and the Prime Minister of Vietnam. *February 8, 1966*

1. THE PRESIDENT of the United States and the Chief of State and Prime Minister of the Republic of Vietnam have concluded 3 days of the most intense and friendly discussion, and their fundamental concord of purpose and policy is stated in the Declaration of Honolulu which they are issuing together today. In addition there has been opportunity for extended review of many urgent specific questions, both at the level of the Chiefs of Government and at the level of Cabinet Ministers. The results of this immediate discussion are reported in the remaining paragraphs of this communique.

2. The leaders of the two Governments, with their advisers, reviewed the intense efforts for peace undertaken by the Government of the United States between Christmas and the end of January. Both Governments noted with regret the total absence of a present interest in peace on the part of the Government of North Vietnam. They reviewed the present diplomatic situation in the United Nations and elsewhere, and they agreed upon continued diplomatic efforts for peace.

3. The economic advisers of the two Governments had a thorough discussion of their cooperative programs for maintaining economic stability and controlling the cost of living in a war-torn country. On the basis of their reports, the President and the Chief of State and Prime Minister have agreed that their two Governments will take further concrete steps to combat inflation in Vietnam.

4. The leaders of the two Governments received comprehensive reports on the intensified program of rural construction.

The Government of Vietnam set forth a plan for efforts of particular strength and intensity in areas of high priority, and the President gave directions to ensure full and prompt support by all agencies of the United States Government.

5. In the construction program three particular points were agreed on as essential for rapid progress:

(1) Continued emphasis by both Vietnamese and Allied forces on the effort to build democracy in the rural areas—an effort as important as the military battle itself.

(2) Continued emphasis on the design of rural construction work to meet the people's needs for larger output, more efficient production, improved credit, handicrafts and light industry, and rural electrification.

(3) Concentration of resources—both Vietnamese and American—in selected priority areas which are properly related to military plans so that the work of rural construction can be protected against disruption by the enemy.

6. Cabinet members of both Governments had thorough discussions of special needs of the people of South Vietnam in the fields of agriculture, health, and education. In agriculture it was agreed that special effort would be made to move agricultural know-how—particularly new species of highly productive rice and corn and vegetable seed—from the experimental station to the farmer in the fields. Steps for more rapid land reform were carefully reviewed. It was agreed that Secretary of Agriculture Freeman and a team of agricultural experts would proceed at once to Vietnam for the purpose of developing enlarged programs of

agricultural cooperation.

7. It was also agreed that programs in health and education would be intensified. The President pledged that he would soon dispatch teams of experts in those fields to Vietnam under the direction of Secretary Gardner. Both Governments agreed to make increased efforts in the training of health personnel, in providing teams for medical care, and creating a stronger medical logistics system. They also agreed to strengthen their cooperation in building elementary schools, in training teachers, in reinforcing vocational and technical education, and in supplying textbooks.

8. It was agreed that the refugees who have of their own free will come over from the enemy side must be adequately cared for and prepared to resume a useful role in society. The Government of Vietnam described its plans to meet this problem and the President assured them of full American support. It was agreed that a special effort will be made to provide good schools for refugee children.

9. There was a full discussion of the military situation and of military plans and programs. The leaders of the two Governments reached full agreement upon a policy of growing military effectiveness and of still closer cooperation between the military forces of Vietnam and those of the United States. They reaffirmed their determination to act with all possible regard for the rights of innocent civilians, to adhere to the Geneva Convention of 1949 on the treatment of prisoners of war, and to act with full respect for the independence and territorial integrity of neighboring countries which wish to live in peace.

10. Finally, it was agreed that the leaders of the two Governments will have further meetings like this one in the future for the continued execution of the policies and purposes of the Declaration of Honolulu.

NOTE: The joint statement was released at Honolulu, Hawaii.

See also Items 53, 55, 56.

55   The Declaration of Honolulu. *February* 8, 1966

PART I

The Republic of Vietnam and the United States of America jointly declare:
—their determination in defense against aggression,
—their dedication to the hopes of all the people of South Vietnam, and
—their commitment to the search for just and stable peace.

In pursuit of these objectives the leaders of their Governments have agreed upon this Declaration, which sets forth:
—the purposes of the Government of Vietnam,
—the purposes of the Government of the United States, and
—the common commitment of both Governments.

PART II. THE PURPOSES OF THE GOVERNMENT OF VIETNAM

Here in the mid-Pacific, halfway between Asia and North America, we take the opportunity to state again the aims of our Government.

We are a Government—indeed a generation—of revolutionary transformation. Our people are caught up in a mortal struggle.

This struggle has four sides.

1. *We must defeat the Vietcong and those illegally fighting with them on our soil.* We are the victims of an aggression directed and supported from Hanoi. That aggression—that so-called "war of national liberation"—is part of the Communist plan for the conquest of all of southeast Asia. The defeat of that aggression is vital for the future of our people of South Vietnam.

2. *We are dedicated to the eradication of social injustice among our people.* We must bring about a true social revolution and construct a modern society in which every man can know that he has a future; that he has respect and dignity; that he has the opportunity for himself and for his children to live in an environment where all is not disappointment, despair, and dejection; that the opportunities exist for the full expression of his talents and his hopes.

3. *We must establish and maintain a stable, viable economy and build a better material life for our people.* In spite of the war, which creates many unusual and unpredictable economic situations, we are determined to continue with a policy of austerity; to make the best possible use of the assistance granted us from abroad; and to help our people achieve regular economic growth and improved material welfare.

4. *We must build true democracy for our land and for our people.* In this effort we shall continue to imbue the people with a sense of national unity, a stronger commitment to civic responsibility. We shall encourage a widened and more active participation in and contribution to the building of a free, independent, strong, and peaceful Vietnam. In particular, we pledge again:

—to formulate a democratic constitution in the months ahead, including an electoral law;

—to take that constitution to our people for discussion and modification;

—to seek its ratification by secret ballot;

—to create, on the basis of elections rooted in that constitution, an elected government.

These things shall be accomplished mainly with the blood, intelligence, and dedication of the Vietnamese people themselves. But in this interdependent world we shall need the help of others: to win the war of independence; to build while we fight; to reconstruct and develop our nation when terror ceases.

To those future citizens of a free, democratic South Vietnam now fighting with the Vietcong, we take this occasion to say come and join in this national revolutionary adventure:

—come safely to join us through the Open Arms Program

—stop killing your brothers, sisters, their elders, and their children

—come and work through constitutional democracy to build together that life of dignity, freedom, and peace those in the North would deny the people of Vietnam.

Thus, we are fighting this war. It is a military war, a war for the hearts of our people. We cannot win one without winning the other. But the war for the hearts of the people is more than a military tactic. It is a moral principle. For this we shall strive as we fight to bring about a true social revolution.

PART III. THE PURPOSES OF THE GOVERNMENT OF THE UNITED STATES

(1) The United States of America is joined with the people and Government of Vietnam to prevent aggression. This is the purpose of the determined effort of the

American armed forces now engaged in Vietnam. The United States seeks no bases. It seeks no colonial presence. It seeks to impose no alliance or alignment. It seeks only to prevent aggression, and its pledge to that purpose is firm. It aims simply to help a people and Government who are determined to help themselves.

(2) The United States is pledged to the principles of the self-determination of peoples, and of government by the consent of the governed. It therefore gives its full support to the purpose of free elections proclaimed by the Government of South Vietnam and to the principle of open arms and amnesty for all who turn from terror toward peace and rural construction. The United States will give its full support to measures of social revolution including land reform based upon the principle of building upward from the hopes and purposes of all the people of Vietnam.

(3) Just as the United States is pledged to play its full part in the worldwide attack upon hunger, ignorance, and disease, so in Vietnam it will give special support to the work of the people of that country to build even while they fight. We have helped and we will help them—to stabilize the economy—to increase the production of food—to spread the light of education—to stamp out disease.

(4) The purpose of the United States remains a purpose of peace. The United States Government and the Government of Vietnam will continue in the future, as they have in the past, to press the quest for a peaceful settlement in every forum. The world knows the harsh and negative response these efforts have thus far received. But the world should know, too, that the United States Government and the Government of Vietnam remain determined that no path to peace shall be unexplored. Within the framework of their international commitments, the United States and Vietnam aim to create with others a stable peace in southeast Asia which will permit the governments and peoples of the region to devote themselves to lifting the condition of man. With the understanding and support of the Government of Vietnam, the peace offensive of the United States Government and the Government of South Vietnam will continue until peace is secured.

PART IV. THE COMMON COMMITMENT

The President of the United States and the Chief of State and Prime Minister of the Republic of Vietnam are thus pledged again:
—to defense against aggression,
—to the work of social revolution,
—to the goal of free self-government,
—to the attack on hunger, ignorance, and disease, and
—to the unending quest for peace.

NOTE: The text of the Declaration was released at Honolulu, Hawaii.

See also Items 53, 54, 56.

---

56 Remarks at the Los Angeles International Airport Following the President's Return From Honolulu. *February 8, 1966*

Governor Brown, Mayor Yorty, ladies and gentlemen:

We went to Honolulu to meet the leaders of the Government of South Vietnam. They and their people understand, and we understand, that the war we are helping them fight must be a war that will be won on two fronts.

One front is the military. The other front is the struggle against social injustice, against hunger and disease and ignorance, against political apathy and indifference.

The meeting in Honolulu could take place, and take place successfully, because, as our friends from Saigon said in their part of the Declaration of Honolulu, "We are a Government, indeed a generation, of revolutionary transformation." And as I looked across the table at these brave and determined young men, I thought also of the young Vietnamese soldiers and province chiefs, and teachers and student leaders, who are really a part of this new generation.

They know and we know that this revolutionary transformation cannot wait until the guns grow silent and until the terrorism stops.

With that common understanding, we took these last 3 days together to take stock of where we are and where we must go in the days and the weeks and the months that are ahead of all of us.

We talked of many very special and specific things. We talked of rural construction, of agricultural credits, of rural electrification, of new seeds and fertilizers for their crops, of schools and teachers and textbooks for their children, of medical schools and clinics and equipment to give them better health, of how to give training and education to the refugees, of how to deal with inflation in a war-torn country, of how to build the bases for a democratic constitution and for free elections, of how to seek the peace, and of how to effectively conduct the war.

In all of these fields we set targets, and we set concrete targets. Progress is not going to be easy. And I think I should tell you in many fields it is not going to be even

quick. But the leaders of both of the Governments are determined that we are going to move forward and we are going to make progress.

We shall meet again in the next few months, and we will measure the progress that we have made. On our part, Secretary of Agriculture Orville Freeman, with an expert staff, with the Vice President, Hubert Humphrey, will be going to Saigon tomorrow morning to see how we can help with the food and rural developments.

Missions will follow that have been organized by Secretary Gardner in the field of education, in the field of health, and in other fields where our people can help with the work of social construction in South Vietnam.

The distinguished Vice President, standing with me here tonight, has followed our work over the cable lines, and I have been in frequent contact with him the last 3 days. He is leaving Los Angeles immediately to carry forward the mission that we outlined and we agreed upon, and we defined at this very unusual conference in Honolulu.

He will go first to Saigon, to assure that our representatives there get to work rapidly and effectively on the tasks that we laid out at Honolulu. He will fly to Saigon with the leaders of the Government of South Vietnam, and on the way he will learn how they intend to carry forward their part of the plan in these fields.

The Vice President will go from Saigon to other capitals in Asia, to explain what was done at Honolulu and the real meaning of our work there. He will also, on behalf of our Government, ask for the understanding and the support of other nations.

With him will be some of those who were at the Honolulu conference, like our revered Ambassador, Averell Harriman, and my Special Assistant for National Security,

McGeorge Bundy.

So I have come back here tonight to the mainland refreshed and confident. The road ahead may be long and may be difficult. It will require the unfailing unity of our people in support of the courageous young Americans who, with their comrades from South Vietnam and Australia, and Korea and New Zealand, are tonight fighting and suffering for us. They are out there dying in order to save freedom. We shall give them that support, and we shall fight the battle against aggression in Vietnam to a successful conclusion.

We shall fight the battle for social construction and throughout the world we shall fight the battle for peace. And to the American people who have given us their strength in every hour of trial, I say to you that we shall fight all of these battles successfully, and we shall prevail.

NOTE: The President spoke at 9:40 p.m. at the Los Angeles International Airport. His opening words referred to Governor Edmund G. (Pat) Brown of California and Mayor Samuel W. Yorty of Los Angeles. During his remarks he referred to Lt. Gen. Nguyen Van Thieu, Chairman of the National Leadership Committee, and Prime Minister Nguyen Cao Ky, both of the Republic of Vietnam, Secretary of Agriculture Orville L. Freeman, Vice President Hubert H. Humphrey, Secretary of Health, Education, and Welfare John W. Gardner, Ambassador at Large W. Averell Harriman, and Special Assistant to the President McGeorge Bundy.

Following the President's remarks the Vice President spoke briefly. His remarks are printed in the Weekly Compilation of Presidential Documents (vol. 2, p. 189).

With respect to the missions to Vietnam of Vice President Humphrey, Secretary Freeman, and Secretary Gardner, see Items 85 and 106.

See also Items 53–55.

57 Remarks Upon Receiving the "Report to the Nation" From the Boy Scouts of America. *February 9, 1966*

IT IS always a pleasure, Mr. Watson, to receive you at any time and especially so when you are engaged in such a worthwhile endeavor as the Boy Scouts. It is always a pleasure to hear about scouting. It is a fine example that a man of your stature and leadership would find time in your busy life to give leadership to such a worthwhile movement as this.

It is thrilling to have these fine examples of young manhood here. They are fine figures and we are glad to see you.

NOTE: The President spoke at 11:45 a.m. in his office at the White House. In his opening words he referred to Thomas J. Watson, Jr., President of the National Council, Boy Scouts of America, and Chairman of the Board of International Business Machines Corp. A group of 14 outstanding Scouts and Explorers, representing the 5,732,708 members of the Boy Scouts of America, had been selected to present to the President their annual "Report to the Nation."

58 Telegram to the Director, Office of Cost Reduction, National Aeronautics and Space Administration. *February 9, 1966*

I WANT to take this opportunity to congratulate NASA and its participating contractors on the accomplishments of the NASA–Contractor Cost Reduction Program and to wish you a successful Seminar.

The continued strength of this country depends upon our ability to provide for national security, to meet our international obligations, and to pursue important endeavors here at home within budget limitations that will enable us to maintain a sound and healthy economy. This means that we must continue to look for better and less costly ways to do the job. I intend to continue to emphasize the necessity for efficiency and economy throughout the government and in concerns that are doing business or seeking to do business with the government.

NASA and its contractors have started a fine Cost Reduction Program. This program has already saved NASA $200 million. I am confident that your participation in this Seminar will stimulate further progress in this very important effort.

LYNDON B. JOHNSON

[Mr. Brooks C. Preacher, Director, Office of Cost Reduction, National Aeronautics and Space Administration, c/o NASA-Industry Cost Reduction Seminar, Ling-Temco-Vought Tower, Dallas, Tex. 75222]

NOTE: In a cost reduction report made public by the White House on February 15, Lawson B. Knott, Jr., Administrator of General Services, stated that the Federal Government had avoided $11.1 million in costs as a result of the President's directive of January 9, 1965, which placed a moratorium on purchases of new file cabinets and required a reduction in the purchase of office furniture and typewriters. The report pointed out that cost reduction had been achieved through use of rehabilitated and used equipment and by retiring records to low-cost storage space in Federal Records Centers (2 Weekly Comp. Pres. Docs., p. 221).

59 Special Message to the Congress Transmitting Reorganization Plan 1 of 1966 Relating to the Community Relations Service. *February 10, 1966*

To the Congress of the United States:

I transmit herewith Reorganization Plan No. 1 of 1966, prepared in accordance with the Reorganization Act of 1949, as amended, and providing for reorganization of community relations functions in the area of civil rights.

After a careful review of the activities of the Federal agencies involved in the field of civil rights, it became clear that the elimination of duplication and undesirable overlap required the consolidation of certain functions.

As a first step, I issued Executive Orders 11246 and 11247 on September 24, 1965.

Executive Order 11246 simplified and clarified executive branch assignments of responsibility for enforcing civil rights policies and placed responsibility for the Government-wide coordination of the enforcement activities of executive agencies in the Secretary of Labor with respect to employment by

Federal contractors and in the Civil Service Commission with respect to employment by Federal agencies.

Executive Order 11247 directed the Attorney General to assist Federal agencies in coordinating their enforcement activities with respect to Title VI of the Civil Rights Act of 1964, which prohibits discrimination in federally assisted programs.

As a further step for strengthening the operation and coordination of our civil rights programs, I now recommend transfer of the functions of the Community Relations Service, established in the Department of Commerce under Title X of the Civil Rights Act of 1964, to the Attorney General and transfer of the Service, including the office of Director, to the Department of Justice.

The Community Relations Service was located in the Department of Commerce by the Congress on the assumption that a primary need would be the conciliation of disputes arising out of the public accommodations title of the act. That decision was appropriate on the basis of information available at that time. The need for conciliation in this area has not been as great as anticipated because of the voluntary progress that has been made by businessmen and business organizations.

To be effective, assistance to communities in the identification and conciliation of disputes should be closely and tightly coordinated. Thus, in any particular situation that arises within a community, representatives of Federal agencies whose programs are involved should coordinate their efforts through a single agency. In recent years, the Civil Rights Division of the Justice Department has played such a coordinating role in many situations, and has done so with great effectiveness.

Placing the Community Relations Service within the Justice Department will enhance the ability of the Justice Department to mediate and conciliate and will insure that the Federal Government speaks with a unified voice in those tense situations where the good offices of the Federal Government are called upon to assist.

In this, as in other areas of Federal operations, we will move more surely and rapidly toward our objectives if we improve Federal organization and the arrangements for interagency coordination. The accompanying reorganization plan has that purpose.

The present distribution of Federal civil rights responsibilities clearly indicates that the activities of the Community Relations Service will fit most appropriately in the Department of Justice.

The Department of Justice has primary program responsibilities in civil rights matters and deep and broad experience in the conciliation of civil rights disputes. Congress has assigned it a major role in the implementation of the Civil Rights Acts of 1957, 1960, and 1964, and the Voting Rights Act of 1965. The Department of Justice performs related functions under other acts of Congress. Most of these responsibilities require not only litigation, but also efforts at persuasion, negotiation, and explanation, especially with local governments and law enforcement authorities. In addition, under the Law Enforcement Assistance Act the Department will be supporting local programs in the area of police-community relations.

The test of the effectiveness of an enforcement agency is not how many legal actions are initiated and won, but whether there is compliance with the law. Thus, every such agency necessarily engages in extensive efforts to obtain compliance with the law and the avoidance of disputes. In fact, Title VI of the Civil Rights Act of 1964 requires each agency concerned to attempt to obtain compliance by voluntary means before taking further action.

Among the heads of Cabinet departments the President looks principally to the Attorney General for advice and judgment on civil rights issues. The latter is expected to be familiar with civil rights problems in all parts of the Nation and to make recommendations for executive and legislative action.

The Attorney General already has responsibility with respect to a major portion of federal conciliation efforts in the civil rights field. Under Executive Order 11247, he coordinates the Government-wide enforcement of Title VI of the Civil Rights Act of 1964, which relies heavily on the achievement of compliance through persuasion and and negotiation.

In the light of these facts, the accompanying reorganization plan would transfer the functions of the Community Relations

Service and of its Director to the Attorney General. In so providing, the Plan, of course, follows the established pattern of Federal organization by vesting all the transferred powers in the head of the department. The Attorney General will provide for the organization of the Community Relations Service as a separate unit within the Department of Justice.

The functions transferred by the Reorganization Plan would be carried out with full regard for the provisions of section 1003 of Title X of the Civil Rights Act of 1964 relating to (1) cooperation with appropriate State or local, public, or private agencies; (2) the confidentiality of information acquired with the understanding that it would be so held; and (3) the limitation on the performance of investigative or prosecutive functions by personnel of the Service.

This transfer will benefit both the Department of Justice and the Community Relations Service in the fulfillment of their existing functions.

The Attorney General will benefit in his role as the President's advisor by obtaining an opportunity to anticipate and meet problems before the need for legal action arises. The Community Relations Service, brought into closer relationship with the Attorney General and the Civil Rights Division of the Department of Justice, will gain by becoming a primary resource in a coordinated effort in civil rights under the leadership of the Attorney General. The Community Relations Service will have direct access to the extensive information, experience, staff, and facilities within the Department and in other Federal agencies.

Finally, the responsibility for coordinating major government activities under the Civil Rights Act aimed at voluntary and peaceful resolution of discriminatory practices will be centered in one Department. Thus, the reorganization will permit the most efficient and effective utilization of resources in this field. Together the Service and the Department will have a larger capacity for accomplishment than they do apart.

Although the reorganizations provided for in the reorganization plan will not of themselves result in immediate savings, the improvement achieved in administration will permit a fuller and more effective utilization of manpower and will in the future allow the performance of the affected functions at lower costs than would otherwise be possible.

After investigation I have found and hereby declare that each reorganization included in Reorganization Plan No. 1 of 1966 is necessary to accomplish one or more of the purposes set forth in section 2(a) of the Reorganization Act of 1949, as amended.

I recommend that the Congress allow the reorganization plan to become effective.

Lyndon B. Johnson

The White House
February 10, 1966

NOTE: Reorganization Plan 1 of 1966 is printed in the Weekly Compilation of Presidential Documents (2 Weekly Comp. Pres. Docs., p. 192) and in the Federal Register (31 F.R. 6187). It became effective on April 22, 1966.

The President referred to Executive Orders 11246 and 11247 of September 24, 1965 (1 Weekly Comp Pres. Docs., pp. 305, 310; 30 F.R. 12319, 12327 3 CFR, 1965 Supp., pp. 167, 177), and to the Civil Rights Act of 1964 (Public Law 88-352, 78 Stat 241).

See also Item 60.

60 Statement by the President Upon Submitting to the Congress Reorganization Plan 1 of 1966. *February 10, 1966*

THE APPROACH of Lincoln's birthday reminds us that the final vestiges of intolerance and hatred must be eliminated from our land. This is a challenge to all of us—in our States, in our communities, in our homes, and most of all in the depths of our hearts. The Community Relations Service will help to meet that challenge in its quiet but determined way, through conciliation and cooperation, by reason and by understanding. Its aim is to achieve peaceful progress in civil rights.

NOTE: The President's statement was made public as part of a White House release on the proposed transfer of the Community Relations Service from the Commerce Department to the Department of Justice under Reorganization Plan 1 of 1966 (see Item 59). The release pointed out that one of the principal reasons for locating the service in the Commerce Department was no longer compelling because of the progress made by merchants and business organizations under the public accommodations section of the 1964 Civil Rights Act. The release also stated that the Justice Department had deep and broad experience in racial matters and had "long settled, mediated, and negotiated disputes 'out of court' in the civil rights area."

The release noted that the proposed transfer was recommended in September 1965 by Vice President Humphrey as part of a program to strengthen the operation and effectiveness of the Government's civil rights activities (see 1965 volume, this series, Book II, Item 530 and note).

See also Item 51 above.

61 Remarks at the National Medal of Science Presentation Ceremony. *February 10, 1966*

Members of the Cabinet, Members of Congress, Dr. Hornig, distinguished guests, my friends:

I have heard it said that "everyone wishes to have the truth on his side, but it is not everyone that sincerely wants to be on the side of truth."

We are very pleased today to welcome men who have chosen to be on the side of truth, and to pursue truth as a way of life. They honor us by their presence—and by their accomplishments they honor the entire Nation.

We recognize those accomplishments today by conferring on these men the National Medal of Science, the highest tribute their Government can pay them.

One of these medals is being awarded posthumously to Dr. Hugh Dryden, who died last December after nearly 50 years of exceptional service to his Government. His work lives on. His contributions will enrich the lives of generations of Americans.

The National Medal of Science honors individual achievement. It reminds us that in a Nation of millions, and in a world of billions, the individual is still the first and basic agent of change. Without the unfettered curiosity of individual men probing and reaching for new truth, our planet would be a dry and dreary place.

It is a truism, almost, to say that the individual matters most. The very simplicity of the statement lends itself to misunderstanding. Certainly the welfare and happiness of all our people must be the continuing quest of science and government. As neglected needs mount, a nation indifferent to the interests of the larger community of citizens only invites disorder and, ultimately, ruin.

But that pursuit must never tolerate apathy

to the right of one man to be different. We are a Nation of differences, and the values and principles that protect those differences are the source of a unity far more lasting and strong than any contrived harmony could ever be.

One man alone with his conscience—whether in the laboratory, or the study, or the classroom, or on the street corner—is to be jealously guarded from the thousand who, believing him wrong, would deny his right to search and his right to speak the truth. On that fact we have built a free and great and diverse society.

The National Medal of Science symbolizes that from one individual's freedom to be different comes achievement to bless all of us.

The work of these men has been for all mankind. They have extended the frontier of our minds and the comfort of our bodies, and we are all the better for their efforts.

This is the 20th year of the atomic age. The power of the sun is in our hands. From this day forward there will be no excuses. There can be food, and shelter, and clothing, and health, and education, and meaningful leisure for every single human being on this earth.

Our children and our grandchildren are going to judge us. They are going to judge us by a standard more demanding than we have ever known before. For they will truly know if we fail at the moment of man's greatest opportunity, the fault will lay not in the stars, but the fault will lay in ourselves.

Now we will read the citations for the 1965 award of the National Medal of Science, and to each of you here this morning Mrs. Johnson and I extend a most cordial welcome.

NOTE: The President spoke at 11:30 a.m. in the East Room at the White House. In his opening words he referred to Dr. Donald F. Hornig, Special Assistant to the President and Director of the Office of Science and Technology, who introduced the recipients and read the citations, as follows:

Dr. John Bardeen, Professor of Physics and Electrical Engineering, University of Illinois. Cited "For his brilliant contributions to the theory of electrical conductivity in solid materials, and especially those which led to the development of a successful theory of superconductivity."

Dr. Peter J. W. Debye, Professor Emeritus, Department of Chemistry, Cornell University. Cited "For sustained contributions of major concepts of modern chemistry and especially for the application of physical methods to the understanding of large molecules and their interaction in solution."

Dr. Hugh Latimer Dryden, former Deputy Administrator of the National Aeronautics and Space Administration. Cited posthumously "For contributions as an engineer, administrator, and civil servant for one-half century to aeronautics and astronautics which have immeasurably supported the Nation's preeminence in space."

Dr. Clarence Leonard Johnson, Vice President for Advanced Development Projects, Lockheed Aircraft Corporation. Cited "For bold innovations in the use of materials and in the design of aircraft of unusual configurations that pioneered new vistas for the possibility of flight."

Dr. Leon Max Lederman, Professor of Physics, Columbia University. Cited "For systematic studies of mesons, for his participation in the discovery of two kinds of neutrinos and of parity violation in the decay of mu-mesons."

Dr. Warren Kendall Lewis, Professor Emeritus of Chemical Engineering, Massachusetts Institute of Technology. Cited "For contributions as a scientist, teacher, and inventor who as the leader of modern chemical engineering has made the American chemical industry preeminent in the world."

Dr. Francis Peyton Rous, associated with the Rockefeller Institute. Cited "For the original discovery and continued elaboration of the relationship between viruses and tumors, which has come to form the biologic base for so much of our present research effort on cancer."

Dr. William Walden Rubey, Professor of Geology and Geophysics, University of California at Los Angeles. Cited "For showing by profoundly original observations and clear physical reasoning how sand grains and mountains move and from whence the oceans come."

Dr. George Gaylord Simpson, Agassiz Professor of Vertebrate Paleontology, Harvard University. Cited "For penetrating studies of vertebrate evolution through geologic time, and for scholarly synthesis of a new understanding of organic evolution based upon genetics and paleontology."

Dr. Donald Dexter Van Slyke, research chemist, Brookhaven National Laboratory. Cited "For classic studies of the chemistry of blood and of amino acid metabolism, and for the quantitative biochemical methodology underlying much of clinical medicine."

Dr. Oscar Zariski, Professor of Mathematics, Harvard University. Cited "For his creation of a rigorous abstract theory of algebraic geometry, and his profound influence—especially through many brilliant students—on the algebraic structure of contemporary pure mathematics."

The awards were made by the President on the basis of recommendations received from the President's Committee on the National Medal of Science, chaired by Dr. H. E. Carter of the University of Illinois.

The medal for the posthumous award to Dr. Hugh Dryden was presented to Mrs. Dryden.

62 Special Message to the Congress: Food for Freedom. *February* 10, 1966

To the Congress of the United States:

Men first joined together for the necessities of life—food for their families, clothing to protect them, housing to give them shelter.

These are the essentials of peace and progress.

But in the world today, these needs are still largely unfulfilled.

When men and their families are hungry, poorly clad and ill-housed, the world is restless—and civilization exists at best in troubled peace.

A WAR ON HUNGER

Hunger poisons the mind. It saps the body. It destroys hope. It is the natural enemy of every man on earth.

I propose that the United States lead the world in a war against hunger.

There can only be victors in this war. Since every nation will share in that victory, every nation should share in its costs. I urge all who can help to join us.

A PROGRAM FOR MANKIND

The program I am submitting to Congress today, together with the proposals set forth in my message on foreign assistance, look to a world in which no man, woman or child need suffer want of food or clothing.

The key to victory is self-help.

Aid must be accompanied by a major effort on the part of those who receive it. Unless it is, more harm than good can be the end result.

I propose:

1. *Expanded food shipments to countries where food needs are growing and self-help efforts are under way.*

Even with their maximum efforts abroad, our food aid will be needed for many years to come.

2. *Increased capital and technical assistance.*

Thus, self-help will bear fruit through increased farm production.

3. *Elimination of the "surplus" concept in food aid.*

Current farm programs are eliminating the surpluses in our warehouses. Fortunately the same programs are flexible enough to gear farm production to amounts that can be used constructively.

4. *Continued expansion of markets for American agricultural commodities.*

Increased purchasing power, among the hundreds of millions of consumers in developing countries, will help them become good customers of the American farmer.

5. *Increasing emphasis on nutrition, especially for the young.*

We will continue to encourage private industry, in cooperation with the government, to produce and distribute foods to combat malnutrition.

6. *Provision for adequate reserves of essential food commodities.*

Our reserves must be large enough to serve as a stabilizing influence and to meet any emergency.

AMERICA'S PAST EFFORTS

This program keeps faith with policies this nation has followed since President Franklin D. Roosevelt proclaimed the Four Freedoms of mankind.

After World War II, we helped to make Europe free from want. We carried out on that continent massive programs of relief, reconstruction and development.

This great effort—the Marshall Plan—was followed by President Truman's Point Four, President Eisenhower's Act of Bogota and its successor, President Kennedy's Alliance for Progress. Under these programs we have provided technical and capital assistance to the developing nations.

Our food aid programs have brought over 140 million tons of food to hungry people during the past decade.

Hunger, malnutrition and famine have been averted.

Schools and hospitals have been built.

Seventy million children now receive American food in school lunch and family and child feeding programs.

Nevertheless the problem of world hunger is more serious today than ever before.

A BALANCE IS REQUIRED

One new element in today's world is the threat of mass hunger and starvation. Populations are exploding under the impact of sharp cuts in the death rate. Successful public health measures have saved millions of lives. But these lives are now threatened by hunger because food production has not kept pace.

A balance between agricultural productivity and population is necessary to prevent the shadow of hunger from becoming a nightmare of famine. In my message on International Health and Education, I described our increased efforts to help deal with the population problem.

IMPROVING LOCAL AGRICULTURE

Many of the developing countries urgently need to give a higher priority to improving and modernizing their own production and distribution of food. The overwhelming majority of those who till the soil still use the primitive methods of their ancestors. They produce little more than enough to meet their own needs, and remain outside of the market economy.

History has taught us that lack of agricultural development can cripple economic growth.

The developing countries must make basic improvements in their own agriculture.

They must bring the great majority of their people—now living in rural areas—into the market economy.

They must make the farmer a better customer of urban industry and thus accelerate the pace of economic development.

They must begin to provide all of their people with the food they need.

They must increase their exports, and earn the foreign exchange to purchase the foods and other goods which they themselves cannot produce efficiently.

In some developing countries, marked improvement is already taking place. Taiwan and Greece are raising their food output and becoming better cash customers for our food exports every year. Others have made a good beginning in improving agricultural production.

THE NEED FOR SELF-HELP

There is one characteristic common to all those who have increased the productivity of their farms: *a national will and determination to help themselves.*

We know what would happen if increased aid were dispensed without regard to measures of self-help. Economic incentives for higher production would disappear. Local agriculture would decline as dependence upon United States food increased.

Such a course would lead to disaster.

Disaster could be postponed for a decade or even two—but it could not be avoided. It could be postponed if the United States were to produce at full capacity and if we financed the massive shipments needed to fill an ever-growing deficit in the hungry nations.

But ultimately those nations would pay an exorbitant cost. They would pay it not only in money, but in years and lives wasted. If our food aid programs serve only as a crutch, they will encourage the developing nations to neglect improvements they must make in their own production of food.

For the sake of those we would aid, we must not take that course.

We shall not take that course.

But candor requires that I warn you *the time is not far off when all the combined production, on all of the acres, of all of the agriculturally productive nations, will not meet the food needs of the developing na-*

tions—unless present trends are changed.

Dependence on American aid will not bring about such a change.

The program I present today is designed to bring about that change.

BETTER NUTRITION

Beyond simple hunger, there lies the problem of malnutrition.

We know that nutritional deficiencies are a major contributing cause to a death rate among infants and young children that is *thirty times higher in developing countries* than in advanced areas.

Protein and vitamin deficiencies during pre-school years leave indelible scars.

Millions have died. Millions have been handicapped for life—physically or mentally.

Malnutrition saps a child's ability to learn. It weakens a nation's ability to progress. It can—and must—be attacked vigorously.

We are already increasing the nutritional content of our food aid contributions. We are working with private industry to produce and market nutritionally rich foods. We must encourage and assist the developing countries themselves to expand their production and use of such foods.

The wonders of modern science must also be directed to the fight against malnutrition. I have today directed the President's Science Advisory Committee to work with the very best talent in this nation to search out new ways to:

—develop inexpensive, high-quality synthetic foods as dietary supplements. A promising start has already been made in isolating protein sources from fish, which are in plentiful supply throughout the world.

—improve the quality and the nutritional

content of food crops.

—apply all of the resources of technology to increasing food production.

NEW DIRECTIONS FOR OUR ABUNDANCE

Our farm programs must reflect changing conditions in the United States and the world. Congress has provided—
—For American farmers, a continuing prospect of rising incomes.
—For American consumers, assurance of an abundance of high quality food at fair prices.
—For American taxpayers, less dollars spent to stockpile commodities in quantities greater than those needed for essential reserves.

Today—because of the world's needs, and because of the changing picture of U.S. agriculture—our food aid programs can no longer be governed by surpluses. The productive capacity of American agriculture can and should produce enough food and fiber to provide for:
1. domestic needs,
2. commercial exports,
3. food aid to those developing countries that are determined to help themselves,
4. reserves adequate to meet any emergency, and to stabilize prices.

To meet these needs, I am today directing the Secretary of Agriculture to:
1. *Increase the 1966 acreage allotment for rice by ten percent.*

   Unprecedented demands arising out of drought and war in Asia require us to increase our rice crop this year. I know that our farmers will respond to this need, and that the Congress will understand the emergency that requires this temporary response.

2. *Buy limited amounts of dairy products under the authority of the 1965 Act.*

   We must have adequate supplies of dairy products for commercial markets, and to meet high priority domestic and foreign program needs. Milk from U.S. farms is the only milk available to millions of poor children abroad. The Secretary will use authority in the 1965 Act whenever necessary to meet our needs for dairy products.

3. *Take actions that will increase soybean production in 1966.*

   The demand for soybeans has climbed each year since 1960. Despite record crops, we have virtually no reserve stocks. To assure adequate supplies at prices fair to farmers and consumers, the Secretary of Agriculture will use authority under the 1965 Act to encourage production of soybeans on acreage formerly planted to feed grains. Feed grain stocks are more than sufficient.

These actions supplement earlier decisions to increase this year's production of wheat and barley. Although our present reserves of wheat are adequate to meet all likely shipments, the Secretary of Agriculture has suspended programs for voluntary diversion of additional spring wheat plantings.

Our 60 million acres now diverted to conservation uses represent the major emergency reserve that could readily be called forth in the critical race between food and population. We will bring these acres back into production as needed—but not to produce unwanted surplus, and not to supplant the efforts of other countries to develop their own agricultural economies.

These actions illustrate how our domestic

farm program will place the American farmer in the front ranks in the world-wide war on hunger.

FOOD FOR FREEDOM

I recommend a new Food for Freedom Act that retains the best provisions of Public Law 480, and that will:
—make self-help an integral part of our food aid program.
—eliminate the "surplus" requirement for food aid.
—emphasize the development of markets for American farm products.
—authorize greater food aid shipments than the current rate.
—emphasize the building of cash markets and the shift toward financing food aid through long-term dollar credits rather than sales for foreign currencies. Except for U.S. requirements, we look to the completion of that shift by the end of five years.
—continue to finance the food aid program under the Commodity Credit Corporation.
—increase emphasis on combating malnutrition. The Act will authorize the CCC to finance the enrichment of foods.
—continue to work with voluntary agencies in people-to-people assistance programs.
—provide for better coordination of food aid with other economic assistance.

FOOD AND FIBER RESERVES

I recommend a program to establish the principle of the ever-normal granary by providing for food and fiber reserves.

This program supplements Food for Freedom.

It establishes a reserve policy that will protect the American people from unstable supplies of food and fiber, and from high prices in times of emergency.

The legislation I recommend to the Congress will enable us to draw strength from two great related assets:
—the productive genius of our farmers.
—the potential that lies in the 60 million acres now withdrawn from production.

In case of need, most of those acres could be brought back into productive farming within twelve to eighteen months. But because of the seasonal nature of farming time would be needed to expand production even under the flexible provisions of the Agriculture Act of 1965. Therefore we need a reserve to bridge this gap.

We have been able to operate without a specific commodity reserve policy in recent years, because the surpluses built up in the 1950's exceeded our reserve needs. This condition has almost run its course.

Under present law, the Secretary of Agriculture must dispose of all stocks of agricultural commodities as rapidly as possible, consistent with orderly marketing procedures. As we continue to reduce our surpluses we need to amend the law to authorize the maintenance of reserve stocks.

The Act I recommend will do that.

It will authorize the Secretary of Agriculture to establish minimum reserve levels. Under the Act, he must take into account normal trade stocks, consumer and farm prices, domestic and export requirements, crop yield variations and commitments under our domestic and foreign food programs.

The reserve would be used to meet priority needs, under prices and conditions to be determined within the broad guidelines established by existing law.

The Act could be implemented in the year ahead without any additional cost to the

Government. We are still reducing our surpluses of most agricultural commodities. During the first year of the new program, it is not likely that we will have to purchase any commodity to build up a reserve.

* * * * * * *

Under the two Acts I recommend today, with the farm legislation now on the statute books—and with the foreign assistance program I have recommended—we will be able to make maximum use of the productivity of our farms.

We can make our technology and skills powerful instruments for agricultural progress throughout the world—wherever men commit themselves to the task of feeding the hungry.

A UNIFIED EFFORT

To strengthen these programs our food aid and economic assistance must be closely linked. Together they must relate to efforts in developing countries to improve their own agriculture. The Departments of State and Agriculture and the Agency for International Development will work together, even more closely than they have in the past in the planning and implementing of coordinated programs.

In the past few years AID has called upon the Department of Agriculture to assume increasing responsibilities through its International Agricultural Development Service. That policy will become even more important as we increase our emphasis on assisting developing nations to help themselves.

Under the Food for Freedom Act, the Secretary of Agriculture will continue to have authority to determine the commodities available. He will act only after consulting with

the Secretary of State on the foreign policy aspects of food aid and with other interested agencies.

We must extend to world problems in food and agriculture the kind of cooperative relationships we have developed with the states, universities, farm organizations, and private industry.

AN INTERNATIONAL EFFORT

It is not enough that we unify our own efforts. We cannot meet this problem alone.

Hunger is a world problem. It must be dealt with by the world.

We must encourage a truly international effort to combat hunger and modernize agriculture.

We shall work to strengthen the Food and Agriculture Organization of the United Nations. The efforts of the multilateral lending organizations, and of the United Nations Development Program should be expanded—particularly in food and agriculture.

We are prepared to increase our participation in regional as well as world-wide multilateral efforts, wherever they provide efficient technical assistance and make real contributions to increasing the food-growing capacities of the developing nations. For example, we will undertake a greatly increased effort to assist improvements in rice yields in the rice-eating less developed countries, as part of our cooperation with FAO during this International Rice Year.

FOR A WORLD AT PEACE

The program I recommend today will raise a new standard of aid for the hungry, and for world agriculture.

It proclaims our commitment to a better

world society—where every person can hope for life's essentials—and be able to find them in peace.

It proclaims the inter-dependence of mankind in its quest for food and clothing and shelter.

It is built on three universal truths:

—that agriculture is an essential pursuit of every nation,

—that an abundant harvest is not only a gift of God, but also the product of man's skill and determination and commitment,

—that hunger and want—anywhere—are the eternal enemies of all mankind.

I urge Congress to consider and debate these suggestions thoroughly and wisely in the hope and belief we can from them fashion a program that will keep free men free, and at the same time share our leadership and agricultural resources with our less blessed brothers throughout the world.

LYNDON B. JOHNSON

The White House
February 10, 1966

NOTE: The Food for Peace Act of 1966 was approved by the President on November 11, 1966 (see Item 608).

See also Item 63.

63 Statement by the President on the Food for Freedom Message to the Congress. *February* 10, 1966

THE Food for Peace Act of 1966 charts a new course for world agriculture. It faces up to the inescapable fact that man is losing the race between the size of population and the supply of food. Before the peace of the world can be secure, this problem must be solved. For—as was said long ago—

"A hungry people listens not to reason, nor cares for justice, nor is bent by any prayers."

During the past 10 years, America has sent over 140 million tons of food to feed hungry people in other countries. We will continue that effort—but it alone is not enough. Compassion itself does not strike at the root causes of hunger. And the time is coming when even the fabulous abundance of America will not be enough to feed the world's hungry millions.

The answer is for these nations to develop their own capacity to produce the food that their people must have. They must learn to depend less on us and more on themselves. And that is the purpose of the program I have sent to Congress. The Food for Freedom program will encourage and assist those who try to help themselves. In the long run, that is the gateway to abundance.

NOTE: The President also recorded the statement in the Theater at the White House for radio and television broadcast.

For the text of the message, see Item 62.

64 Letter to the Chairman, Civil Aeronautics Board, on Transoceanic Air Routes. *February* 11, 1966

Dear Mr. Chairman:

Upon consideration of the Transatlantic Route Renewal Case (Docket 13577 et al.) I have decided to approve the Board's rec-

ommendations, with the following exceptions:

1. For reasons of foreign relations, I have determined that only one United States Flag

carrier should be authorized to serve Dublin. Therefore, I am returning this phase of the case to the Board for its recommendation, on the basis of the present record, as to the carrier to be selected.

2. I am returning to the Board for further hearing Pan American's request to convert its East and West Coast terminals into coterminals. The reopened hearing should enable the Board to assess the impact of coterminal status on our balance of payments. In addition, it will afford the Board the opportunity to consider the desirability of placing Pan American on a comparable basis with foreign flag carriers such as Qantas and BOAC (and any Japanese Flag carrier which may hereafter be authorized to serve New York and beyond to Europe) carrying international traffic between points in the Pacific and points in Europe via California and New York. It is requested that this matter be processed on an expedited basis and that your decision be transmitted to me at the earliest practicable date.

Please submit for my approval a revised order in the Transatlantic Route Renewal Case, consistent with the comments expressed above.

With regard to air service in the Pacific, I believe the Board should proceed expeditiously to re-examine the route pattern of United States carriers in foreign and overseas air transportation in the Pacific. In view of the present operating rights of BOAC and Qantas, and the recently negotiated Bilateral Air Transport Agreement with the Government of Japan, embracing a route to New York and beyond to Europe, it is important that we proceed quickly to determine whether our transpacific route pattern should be altered so as to place our carriers in a satisfactory competitive position in the Pacific with foreign flag carriers operating into the East Coast.

Sincerely,

LYNDON B. JOHNSON

[Honorable Charles S. Murphy, Chairman, Civil Aeronautics Board, Washington, D.C. 20428]

NOTE: The recommendations of the Civil Aeronautics Board in the Transatlantic Route Renewal Case are contained in Docket 13577 et al. (208 pp., processed).

65 The President's News Conference of *February 11, 1966*

THE PRESIDENT. I had some announcements I thought maybe you would want before the weekend is over.

ANNOUNCEMENT OF APPOINTMENTS

[1.] I am appointing as Assistant Secretary of State for Public Affairs, Mr. Dixon Donnelley, who is presently serving as Special Assistant to the Secretary of the Treasury for Public Affairs.

He is a Foreign Service officer. You can get the details on his background. He is succeeding Mr. Greenfield, who is leaving shortly.

I am appointing Mr. Lee White, who is presently Special Counsel to the President, as Chairman of the Federal Power Commission. You can get the details from Mr. Moyers.

I am appointing Mr. Staats, Deputy Director of the Bureau of the Budget, as Comptroller General. Mr. Staats joined the Bureau in 1939, and was born in Kansas in 1914. He married a daughter of former Congressman Rich of Pennsylvania. I think you all know him well.

I am appointing Mr. Harry McPherson to succeed Mr. White as Counsel to the President. There is a good deal of information on Harry here. I didn't know that much about him myself.

I am appointing Cliff Alexander as Deputy Special Counsel.

PRESS SECRETARY

[2.] I am appointing Bob Fleming as Deputy Press Secretary, but he will be my Press Secretary from time to time as well, and help out generally. Robert Fleming is formerly of the Capital Times, Milwaukee Journal, Newsweek, and present Washington Bureau Chief of the ABC.

I think that is all I have. I will answer any questions.

Q. Mr. President, what happens to Bill Moyers after that? Where does he go?

THE PRESIDENT. Bill will continue to go wherever the ball is and work wherever we need him. There are a good many different places. As his title implies, he will be Special Assistant to the President.

Q. Mr. President, do you mean, sir, that Bob Fleming is now the White House Press Secretary?

THE PRESIDENT. No. I think the press prefers that we have one man who does more of the briefing than anybody else called the Press Secretary. I have talked to some of them about it. We are going to call for your convenience and pleasure—Bob will be Deputy Press Secretary for the moment, but he will be doing a good deal of the Press Secretary's work.

As far as I am concerned, I will want to call him my Press Secretary and try to satisfy both of you.

Q. Mr. President, if he is yours, he can be ours, too.

THE PRESIDENT. Smitty [1] didn't think so. I talked to him about it.

Q. Pull together.

Q. Mr. President, will Bill Moyers be working on national security affairs primarily?

THE PRESIDENT. No, he will be doing just what I said. I couldn't give him one answer and you another. He will be working on anything I want him to from time to time. It may be a personnel matter. This afternoon it was, for an hour. Tomorrow it may be a legislative matter. The next day it may be an appointment matter, as it was yesterday. A good deal of the time it will be nursing the press.

Q. Mr. President, will Mr. Laitin [2] remain, sir?

THE PRESIDENT. Yes.

Q. Mr. President, Mr. Moyers' title will be that of Press Secretary?

THE PRESIDENT. Special Assistant to the President. It has always been that. You can call him Press Secretary, though, if it gives you any thrill.

Q. Mr. President, I would like to know your preference.

THE PRESIDENT. I would say Special Assistant to the President. That is his title. But I talked to some of the boys in the press about it, and they say that since Bill does a good deal of the briefing, they want one man to be responsible. They would like to call Bill the Press Secretary. I don't object to what you call him. I am ultimately responsible and I will take it all. If you can't get to me, you can get to Bill. If you can't get to him, you can get to Fleming. If you can't get to him, you can get to whoever else is around.

I have no objection to your getting to anyone you want to if they know what I am

---

[1] Merriman Smith of United Press International.

[2] Joseph Laitin, an assistant press secretary.

thinking. My special problem here with 11 Cabinet officers and 10 Special Assistants is for them to be all on the same course at the same time and all know what the policy is, without one having one idea and another one another. Sometimes I can't get them all briefed, but I can brief whoever is briefing that day, and Bill Moyers.

I do hope Fleming will take over some of the heavy briefing because I think it is too much for Bill with what else he is doing, too.

QUESTIONS ON APPOINTMENTS

[3.] Q. Is Mr. Fleming here, Mr. President?

THE PRESIDENT. Welcome aboard.

MR. MOYERS. And so is Dixon Donnelley, Mr. President.

THE PRESIDENT. And here is Dixon Donnelley, who will be over with Mr. Rusk.[3]

Q. What becomes of the present Assistant Secretary of State for Public Affairs, Mr. Greenfield?

THE PRESIDENT. Ma'am?

Q. What becomes of the present Assistant Secretary of State, Jim Greenfield? Does Mr. Donnelley replace him?

THE PRESIDENT. Yes.

Q. Is he resigning, Mr. President?

THE PRESIDENT. That is right.

THE DOMINICAN REPUBLIC

[4.] Q. Mr. President, are you open for other questions?

THE PRESIDENT. Yes. I have been waiting on them, Smitty.

Q. I wonder, sir, if you could appraise this situation in the Dominican Republic, the resumption of fighting down there seeming to be increasing a little each day. Are you at all concerned about this?

THE PRESIDENT. Yes. I am concerned. I deeply regret what is taking place there. I am very hopeful that the President will be able to bring peace to the island as early as possible. It is a very difficult situation.

CONGRESSIONAL VIEWPOINTS ON FOREIGN POLICY

[5.] Q. Mr. President, Senator Gore[4] said, in effect, what he and some Senators have done is go over your head to the American people and reach you that way. Do you think that is a legitimate approach?

THE PRESIDENT. I think it is always legitimate to go to the American people with a program or any problem you have. They are the bosses in this country, and they are the ones that make the decision, and they are the ones to whom we are all responsible.

Any Congressman, any Senator, has a right and a duty to submit his program to the people and get their support.

FOREIGN RELATIONS COMMITTEE HEARINGS ON VIETNAM

[6.] Q. Do you think that the hearings before the Foreign Relations Committee are helpful, Mr. President?

THE PRESIDENT. I don't see that I would be the proper one to judge, because I haven't had the intimacy with them that the members of the Committee have. But that is a matter for the Senate to determine. I wouldn't find any fault with any committee having any hearings at any time, as long as they are conducted in an atmosphere of objectivity, fairness, judiciousness.

I have not observed that these have been conducted in any other manner, so far as I can see. They had Secretary Rusk for

[3] Dean Rusk, Secretary of State.

[4] Senator Albert Gore of Tennessee, member of the Senate Foreign Relations Committee.

awhile and he is going to be appearing again, and General Taylor.[5] They have had General Gavin.[6] From what I read about him, his program or his testimony, and what I have seen about Mr. Kennan's,[7] I don't see that they have done any harm to anybody.

I think it is a question for everyone fully exploring the problems that face our country coming up with the best recommendations and best programs they can. I have tried to take every recommendation submitted to me and carefully consider it and pursue it to the extent I thought justified. I will continue to do that. I welcome any suggestions any of you have.

Have you some, Pete? [8]

Q. No, but I would like to ask you about the fact that you used to have some official concern here about how Hanoi might misread this kind of debate in the Senate as well as the demonstration. Do you think they might misread the present Senate hearings and think there are differences in the country which are not really legitimate?

THE PRESIDENT. I haven't read the transcript of the hearing, but I gather from what General Gavin said in summary there is not a great deal of difference between what he and Kennan are saying and what the Government is doing. No one wants to escalate the war and no one wants to lose any more men than is necessary. No one wants to surrender and get out. At least no one admits they do. So I don't see that there is any great difference of opinion. If there is, I guess in their report they will recommend

the program. Whatever it is, we will be glad to consider what any Senator says.

I had a letter from Congressmen giving me their views, and I thanked them and considered them and tried to tell them what the Government was thinking here. I had a letter from some Senators and they gave me their views, and I thanked them and told them I appreciated it and said to them substantially what I said to the Congressmen.[9]

This was our feeling. But as, if, and when the circumstances justify other decisions, why, we will make them, but we are always glad to have their suggestions and recommendations if they have any. Some of them recommended the pause, and some recommended resuming the bombing, and some recommended not resuming the bombing. We carefully considered it.

I was just looking at one Senator's record this morning who was making some recommendations. I asked to see his card and I had seen him 21 times last year. I think it is very important that we give careful and thorough consideration to every suggestion made by every Senator of either party, and every Congressman and every citizen that we can.

I get almost a hundred letters a week from the boys in Vietnam and I try to read them and get help from them. I do get strength from them.

QUESTIONS ON VIETNAM POLICY

[7.] Q. Mr. President, earlier this week in Honolulu, General Ky, the Prime Minister of South Vietnam, said that they would not negotiate with the Vietcong. Do you think this position would present any difficulties should negotiations develop at some future date?

THE PRESIDENT. When you get Hanoi

---

[5] Gen. Maxwell D. Taylor, Special Consultant to the President, former U.S. Ambassador to the Republic of Vietnam, and former Chairman of the Joint Chiefs of Staff.

[6] Lt. Gen. James M. Gavin, former Chief of Research and Development, Army General Staff.

[7] George F. Kennan, former U.S. Ambassador to the Soviet Union and to Yugoslavia.

[8] Raymond P. Brandt of the St. Louis Post-Dispatch.

[9] See Items 23, 36.

ready to negotiate, I think that the viewpoint of all the people interested in negotiations can be considered and no one will have any trouble hearing them. If you are prepared to produce Hanoi, I am prepared to negotiate.

Q. Mr. President, how is your mail in the country running on this issue?

THE PRESIDENT. I think that there are a good many people in the country that are troubled about Vietnam and wish we could find some way to negotiate, but I think the country overwhelmingly supports the position that we have taken. I believe that the Members of the House and the Senate do likewise.

All these days and weeks, all that has been said and done, I don't see any real program that anyone has presented that offers a clear alternative to recommend itself in preference to what we are doing. General Gavin didn't, or Mr. Kennan. They both are ex-public servants. General Gavin—I remember hearing him when he resigned from the Army because he felt that he wanted to leave. I remember his testimony then and I saw it in the papers the other day. I didn't see anything that I could really catch onto as any great difference between us.

He said he had been misunderstood on the enclave thing. He said he didn't want to get out. He said he didn't want to escalate. That is the way we feel about it.

Mr. Kennan said he hadn't ever been to Southeast Asia. He started off by saying that he didn't want to escalate, but that he didn't want to pick up and run out.

So those are the only two experts that I have seen put on, and I have been given that feeling.

Q. Mr. President, Mr. Kennan apparently believes that withdrawal, if we left South Vietnam, would have a bad effect on other countries—or rather he does *not* believe it would have a bad effect on other nations. How do you feel about that?

THE PRESIDENT. I didn't see that in his testimony. When I get the testimony I will read it and give careful consideration to any recommendations that he makes.

HONOLULU CONFERENCE ON VIETNAM

[8.] Q. Mr. President, when you were in Los Angeles reporting on the Honolulu conference,[10] you listed 11 items which you said were discussed, and you said that in all these fields you set targets, concrete targets.

Would it be possible to get a list of these concrete targets?

THE PRESIDENT. I don't have any. I think what I had in mind there was saying that we hoped to make certain progress in certain fields. And we expect to have another conference after a reasonable length of time, in which we will take the hits, runs, and errors and see what we have achieved, and everybody would be answerable, so to speak, as to the progress they have made and whether or not they are nearing their goals.

We distributed 8 million textbooks and hope to distribute 16 million. The next time we meet we will probably have 12 million distributed.

We have doubled the rice production and we hope to substantially increase that after these technicians we have selected from all over the country get through with their study and their recommendations.

Then we will get General Westmoreland, Prime Minister Ky, and Ambassador Lodge,[11] the civilian counterparts to Mr. Westmoreland, and we will keep score and come back.

---

[10] See Items 53–56.

[11] Gen. William C. Westmoreland, Commander, United States Military Assistance Command, Vietnam, Nguyen Cao Ky, Prime Minister of the Republic of Vietnam, and Henry Cabot Lodge, U.S. Ambassador to the Republic of Vietnam.

I hope to be in Honolulu in the next few months, maybe in the middle of the year, and see what has been done. I thought it was good that we could go there and have the Government, and the military leader, General Westmoreland, and the Ambassador, and the Deputy Ambassador,[12] meet with the Vice President, the Secretary of Agriculture, and technicians, and try to expose to the world for 3 days what this country is trying to do to feed the hungry, and to educate the people, and to improve the life span for people who just live to be 35 now; to show that we really had goals, we had targets, and we were going to put the very best that we had into it.

A lot of our folks have felt that it is just a military effort. We don't think it should be that, and we don't want it to be that. We have social objectives. One of our main goals is to defeat social misery. We were very glad to see the leader of their Government state what he did in the January 15th speech.

We want to follow up and try to contribute everything we could to realizing that objective. A good many Senators and a good many Congressmen have felt that we ought to place more emphasis in this field. That is what I was trying to do, and that is what I think we did do.

The tendency is for all of us to talk about casualties and military operations, bombs, ammunition, and things of that kind. I was trying to talk about some of these other things that I thought were quite important.

VISIT OF MRS. GANDHI

[9.] Q. Mr. President, have any definite arrangements been made for Mrs. Gandhi[13]

to come and visit you?

THE PRESIDENT. Yes. We have told her she would be very welcome. She has told us that she wants to come as early as possible. I had a letter from her last night. She doesn't say when she is coming, but she wants to come at as early a date as possible.

I would say you can say that it is believed that she will try to be here in the latter part of March or April. But the Vice President is discussing with her, in response to her letter of February 9th, some of the matters that she mentioned, such as food, economic aid, and things of that type.

FUTURE HONOLULU CONFERENCE

[10.] Q. Mr. President, will the leaders of Vietnam with whom you met in Honolulu be invited to Washington?

THE PRESIDENT. No, we have no plans to.

Q. Mr. President, but the next meeting would be, again, in Honolulu?

THE PRESIDENT. We haven't definitely set a meeting, but we are going to review the hits and runs and errors down the road in the next few months, and follow through on these various missions after they have had a chance to get their recommendations put in practice.

Agriculture will come back in the next few days and then the education people will go and work for a while. They will come back and then the health people will go and work for a while. Then the AID people.

I spent some time this morning talking to Mr. David Bell[14] and his group, and they are working on price problems, inflation problems, import problems—things of that kind.

Then we will probably, after those three or four groups come in, have a meeting. I

---

[12] William Porter, Deputy U.S. Ambassador to the Republic of Vietnam.

[13] Mrs. Indira Gandhi, Prime Minister of India. See Items 148, 149, 152.

[14] David E. Bell, Administrator, Agency for International Development.

am guessing now, but I would guess in June or July we would have an accounting, so to speak, kind of an examination—like Luci's [15] finals that she takes.

We would say what we have done in these fields and kind of check up. We are very anxious to make a maximum effort in these fields because we want to show the people what I tried to bring out in my Baltimore speech,[16] and what we are trying to do in a good many parts of this country.

We have increased the number of children in school from some 300,000 to 1 million 300 thousand—multiplied several times.

We have doubled the rice production.

Each one of these things—we built 6,500 classrooms—all of those things we were talking about the other day.

We are saying: "Let's get going" and "Let's move into high gear." We are spending more economic money in that country than any place in the world and we desire doing it expeditiously, efficiently, and getting results. "We are going to call you back in here," and I am going to look at them and see what they have done.

PRESIDENTIAL RATINGS IN POLLS

[11.] Q. Mr. President, a recent Gallup Poll showed that while high, your rating is about the lowest it has been since you have been in office, and I wonder how you interpret this?

THE PRESIDENT. I haven't noticed much change. It is about the same thing every

---

[15] Luci Baines Johnson, the President's daughter.

[16] For the President's address in Baltimore at Johns Hopkins University on April 7, 1965, see 1965 volume, this series, Book I, Item 172.

day for me. I am very happy with it. I just hope it stays that way.

FURTHER QUESTIONS ON VIETNAM

[12.] Q. Mr. President, did the Vietnamese leaders indicate to you that they think they can find the personnel to carry out the rural reconstruction programs?

THE PRESIDENT. The Vietnamese leaders were very hopeful and appeared to be very earnest. And both Ambassador Lodge and General Westmoreland were quite encouraged, when they left, about the results of our 3 days of discussion.

I don't know how to predict the outcome of 3 days with people that you don't know and that you haven't known before personally.

I had just met General Westmoreland once. That was one reason I wanted to spend some time with him. I saw him at West Point and liked him, and admired him. I read his cables every day and I just wanted to see the fellow who was writing them.

I would say the conference was, I thought, productive and addressed itself to constructive subjects. I think the reaction I have had from the country was that they were glad that their Government was putting the spotlight on education and health and production, and higher living standards, trying to get other people to put proper emphasis on it, too.

Q. Mr. President, do you have any plans, sir, to ask Congress for a resolution or some other formal expression of approval of the administration's policy in Vietnam?

THE PRESIDENT. I have a resolution saying

that. I have one passed in August, I think, 1964. You read that one. I think if you get familiar with it, it pretty well explains my view.[17]

Q. Mr. President, could you say what you feel are the drawbacks, if any, to the enclave theory that Mr. Kennan set forth yesterday?

THE PRESIDENT. No, I don't want to debate with Mr. Kennan. I don't think Mr. Kennan follows the enclave theory as I read it. I would be glad to have you give me a memo on what Mr. Gavin and Mr. Kennan advocate and let me look at it, and then I will talk to you and give you my views. From what I have seen, I don't see any diversions.

Most people wish we weren't out there, most people wish we didn't have a war, most people don't want to escalate it, and most people don't want to get out.

U.N. CONSIDERATION

[13.] Q. Mr. President, has there been any change in the war or peace picture since you resumed the bombing and went to the U.N.?

THE PRESIDENT. I don't know how to answer that. I just don't know.

Q. Mr. President, Ambassador Goldberg[18] gave us the impression we were not pressing the Vietnam situation through the U.N. but hoping the U.N. would get it to Geneva. Is that a correct assessment of that?

THE PRESIDENT. The Ambassador is the best source for the Ambassador's impressions. I think we made our position clear to the U.N. We made it clear to the world.

What the U.N. does about it is a matter for them. I don't want to interfere in their matters.

We have asked the Security Council. As you know, we agreed with the Secretary General[19] when he wanted to go out as Secretary General and go to Hanoi and they didn't receive him. We agreed with him when he wanted them to come to the United Nations after the Gulf of Tonkin. They didn't want to come.

We felt, after we had explored with all the other 115 nations, that we ought to ask the Security Council to give its consideration and attention to it and we have done that. I have tried, really, to take every position that someone suggested and analyze it, and in good faith explore it and try to run it out to its end, whether it was a pause or whether it was an economic venture or whether it was a United Nations question, or whether it was a nonaligned proposal, or whether it was a reconvening of the Geneva Conference, or whether it was the ICC,[20] or whether it was a 20- or 30-day pause. I think I have taken every single suggestion that anyone has made that seemed to offer any possibility and carried it out. I welcome any other suggestions that any of you may have.

STRENGTH OF MILITARY FORCES

[14.] Q. Mr. President, do you think that it will require substantially greater numbers of men to pursue this conflict and, if so, how will they be gotten? Are there any plans to call up Reserve units, or anything like that?

---

[17] A joint resolution to promote the maintenance of international peace and security in Southeast Asia was approved by the President on August 10, 1964 (Public Law 88–408, 78 Stat. 384).

[18] Arthur J. Goldberg, U.S. Representative to the United Nations.

[19] U Thant, Secretary General of the United Nations.

[20] International Control Commission, established by the Geneva Accords of 1954 which terminated the war in Indochina between the French and Communist forces.

THE PRESIDENT. We have no present plans to do that. There will be additional men needed and they will be supplied as General Westmoreland is able to use them and as he may require them. His requests will always be carefully considered and promptly acted upon here. That is what we have done and that is what we are doing.

As you know, he has a problem of fitting them in and providing for necessary installations to take care of them, things of that nature. If your hopes were all realized and we had peace in the area, he wouldn't need any additional troops. But I don't see that at the moment. There will be additional ones. As he requests them, they will be supplied, as I have stated on several occasions.

Q. Sir, are you in a position to give any figures?

THE PRESIDENT. No.

Q. Are you able to judge, tell us, Mr. President, whether that will involve Reserves or any approval by Congress?

THE PRESIDENT. I wouldn't want to predict because you all are very critical of Mr. McNamara [21] when he makes predictions. I see at this moment no requirement for the Reserves, but I wouldn't want to say that firmly. I don't want to guess. At the moment we don't have any plans for that.

Reporter: Thank you, Mr. President.

NOTE: President Johnson's fifty-fifth news conference was held in his office at the White House at 5 p.m. on Friday, February 11, 1966.

---

[21] Robert S. McNamara, Secretary of Defense.

66 Statement by the President on the Anniversary of the Birth of Abraham Lincoln. *February* 12, 1966

ON THIS DAY each year, we pause to honor the memory and the wisdom of a great American. It is especially appropriate that we do so on this occasion, for in the past year America has made unprecedented progress in fulfilling the ideal for which Abraham Lincoln stands.

Six months ago, I signed into law the Voting Rights Act of 1965.

Since that time, Federal examiners in 37 counties in 5 Southern States have enrolled 100,000 formerly disenfranchised Negro citizens.

Even more encouraging, however, is the widespread, voluntary compliance by local voting officials, who have registered nearly 200,000 Negro citizens in those same Southern States in the same period of time.

The Nation can be assured and encour-

aged by this progress. But these same figures also illustrate not only how far we have come but also how far we have to go.

More than half the adult Negroes of the South are still not participating in this most basic right of citizenship, the right to vote. Until every American, whatever his color or wherever his home, enjoys and uses his franchise, the work which Lincoln began will remain unfinished.

For, as Abraham Lincoln himself declared: "Allow all the governed an equal voice in the government, and that, and that only, is self-government."

That ideal must be—and can be—and will be fulfilled in our time.

NOTE: For the President's remarks upon signing the Voting Rights Act of 1965, see 1965 volume, this series, Book II, Item 409.

67   Letter to the Speaker Requesting Supplemental Appropriations for the National Teacher Corps, the Rent Supplement Program, and the Selective Service System.   *February* 14, 1966

Dear Mr. Speaker:

I have the honor to transmit, for the consideration of the Congress, a supplemental appropriations request for three urgently needed and essential programs of government:

—for the National Teacher Corps, $13,200,000.

—for the Rent Supplement Program, $30,000,000.

—for the Selective Service System, $12,681,000.

Two of these programs are vital to our efforts to improve the quality of life in America. The third is a direct effect of our commitment to freedom in Southeast Asia.

Together they testify to a progressive, compassionate and resolute people. They are not the frills of luxury. They are the necessities of a nation devoted to the improvement of man's estate.

NATIONAL TEACHER CORPS

The National Teacher Corps was authorized by the landmark Higher Education Act of 1965. Funds are needed now—so that the first teams to be chosen for the Teacher Corps may begin training this summer. This fall, in poor rural and urban areas, they will be sharing their skills and understanding with the children and teachers who need them most of all.

Parents know how much good teaching means to their children's future. School administrators know how a few teachers, trained in today's advanced methods of instruction, can raise the entire level of education in their schools. Most poignantly, children themselves know what it is to be taught with enthusiasm and skill.

Our country is blessed with young men and women who desire to serve those less fortunate than themselves. In the ranks of experienced teachers there are others who would devote part of their lives to children in most critical need. The Teacher Corps offers a practical means of uniting the idealism and wisdom of each—young graduates and accomplished teachers—and thus enriching the lives of coming generations.

RENT SUPPLEMENT PROGRAM

The Rent Supplement Program responds to the critical shortage of decent low-income housing in many of our cities.

It makes possible the construction and management of such housing by private enterprise. Rental assistance would be provided, to make up the difference between the market rent for modestly designed dwellings and 25 percent of the occupant's income.

Since it was authorized last year, the Department of Housing and Urban Development has received preliminary proposals to construct nearly 70,000 low-income units under this program—as soon as funds become available.

These proposals involve 424 projects in 43 States, the District of Columbia, and Puerto Rico. Sponsors have already selected sites for some 40,000 units. Non-profit organizations and private limited-dividend developers are actively interested in the program and its promise for our poor.

Since the last session of Congress adjourned, responsible officials in the Department have reviewed all aspects of the program. They have paid particular attention to the views of the Congress on a family's eligibility for rent supplements. They have confirmed the following guidelines:

Income limits: A family must have an income below the income limits established for entrance to public housing in the various communities.

Asset limitations: Asset limitations are well within the limits usually imposed in the public housing programs.

Changes in income: All tenants receiving rent supplements (except the elderly) must re-certify their current incomes each year. FHA will examine any income changes revealed by this review and will make appropriate adjustments in rent supplement payments—including elimination of payments where incomes have risen above those imposed for eligibility.

Quality of housing: Mortgage limitations and other FHA restrictions will require that new construction under this program must provide housing of modest design and cost. Luxury items, such as swimming pools and two bathrooms, will not be permitted.

We have now prepared sound policy guidelines and administrative procedures for the rent supplement program.

Sponsors in 43 States have responded with extensive proposals for new low-income housing.

Yet the Congress alone can convert procedures and proposals into decent shelter for our people.

This is the action I recommend today.

SELECTIVE SERVICE SYSTEM

The Selective Service System requires additional funds because accelerated inductions into the Armed Forces have substantially increased the workload of the System.

We now estimate that inductions in fiscal year 1966 will total approximately 360,000, as compared to the estimate of 125,000 upon which the original 1966 appropriation was based.

In addition, funds are needed to meet the costs of the recently enacted civilian and military pay acts.

The attached letter from the Director of the Bureau of the Budget examines these proposed appropriations in greater detail.

I urge the Congress to act promptly and favorably on each of the requests. The hopes aroused by the Teacher Corps and Rent Supplement programs—and the world responsibility to which the Selective Service System responds—require our full and vigorous support.

Sincerely,

LYNDON B. JOHNSON

[Honorable John W. McCormack, Speaker of the House of Representatives, Washington, D.C.]

NOTE: The Second Supplemental Appropriation Act, 1966, providing additional funds for the National Teacher Corps, the rent supplement program, and the Selective Service System, was approved by the President on May 13 (see Item 223).

The letter from the Director of the Bureau of the Budget, to which the President referred, is printed in House Document 380 (89th Cong., 2d sess.).

68   Message to the Congress Transmitting First Annual Report of the
     National Capital Transportation Agency.   *February* 14, 1966

To the Congress of the United States:

This is the first annual report required of the National Capital Transportation Agency by section 6 of the National Capital Transportation Act of 1965 (P.L. 89–173).

1965 was marked by significant advances toward solving the transportation problems of the Washington area.

Congress approved plans for a rapid transit system, authorized its construction, and authorized grants from the Federal and District Governments as a first stage in financing its development. As soon as funds were made available, the Transportation Agency began the necessary work still remaining before actual construction can begin.

There is, nonetheless, much left to do. The rapid transit system will achieve maximum usefulness only when it is extended into Maryland and Virginia suburbs. The interstate compact among Maryland, Virginia and the District of Columbia will be promptly presented to Congress for its consent, in order that the interstate authority may develop plans for a full regional system and a financial plan for its construction. Arrangements must be perfected to transfer the responsibility for the system in an orderly and proper way from the Agency to the interstate authority. These tasks are not easy, and it will require diligent effort on the part of many people and agencies to master the problems that remain.

The Congress can be assured, however, that all of these problems are being given the fullest and most diligent consideration, and that none of them will be allowed to stand in the way of an uninterrupted schedule of construction.

LYNDON B. JOHNSON

The White House
    February 14, 1966

NOTE: The first annual report of the National Capital Transportation Agency (7 pp., plus exhibits) is dated January 1, 1966. Copies were made available by the Agency.

69   Message to the Congress Transmitting Second Annual Report on
     the Status of the National Wilderness Preservation System.
     February 14, 1966

To the Congress of the United States:

The period of expansion and exploration, the great era of successive western frontiers, has now become a part of our American past. To the pioneer of history the wilderness was a foe to be conquered, so that he might make farms and pastures out of the endless forests.

Today's pioneer has a new purpose—to preserve some remnants of that wilderness from the onrush of modern civilization.

The axe and the plow will not serve us in this struggle. Today's instruments are more subtle. They are progressive law and informed public opinion—demanding that we maintain our wilderness birthright.

The Wilderness Act is one in the long list of creative conservation measures that Congress has passed and I have signed into law.

Legislation is one thing; administration is another. The Executive Branch must fulfill its responsibility with common sense and imagination. Our people must be given the opportunity to know, even for short periods of time, the wonders of God's creation expressed in earth's wilderness areas.

The maintenance of our existing Wilderness System is a priority program of the Federal government. We are constantly reviewing Primitive and Roadless Areas to determine whether they should be recommended for preservation as part of our Wilderness System.

The Congress has wisely provided for public participation as reviews of the Primitive and Roadless Areas proceed. I am determined to assure that both the Department of Agriculture and the Department of the Interior will provide full opportunity for the expression of public views before final recommendations are prepared for transmittal to the Congress.

I am pleased to send to Congress today the second annual report of our progress in implementing the Wilderness Act. We are well under way toward protecting God's gift of mystery and wonder that is the American Wilderness.

LYNDON B. JOHNSON

The White House
    February 14, 1966

NOTE: The President transmitted the Second Joint Annual Report of the Secretary of Agriculture and the Secretary of the Interior on the Status of the Wilderness Preservation System (17 pp., processed). The report is printed in House Document 381 (89th Cong., 2d sess.).

70 Message to the Congress Transmitting Annual Report of U.S. Arms Control and Disarmament Agency. *February 15, 1966*

To the Congress of the United States:

I am transmitting the Fifth Annual Report of the United States Arms Control and Disarmament Agency.

This report describes a year of intense negotiation and research. It reveals an increased seriousness on the part of many nations toward the problems of arms control and disarmament.

In 1965, under the increasing pressure of the nuclear threat, arms control and disarmament was taken up at the first meeting of the United Nations Disarmament Commission in five years; at the Eighteen Nation Disarmament Committee in Geneva; in the fall session of the 20th General Assembly; and in private diplomatic exchanges.

In all of these activities the United States' position benefited from the thorough research and careful preparations of the Arms Control and Disarmament Agency, carried out under the authority granted it by the Congress.

This research and preparation has been carried out on a wide variety of problems— from weapons inspection to the economic consequences of reductions or shifts in military spending. In all this work our guiding principle has been the long-range security of the United States, which inevitably involves the long-range peace and stability of the world.

HALTING THE SPREAD OF NUCLEAR WEAPONS

During 1965 the concern of the world turned increasingly to the vital question of preventing nuclear weapons from becoming standard equipment in the world's arsenals. We are approaching a critical period in efforts to prevent the spread of nuclear weapons. Many countries now have the resources, the technical ability and the scientific manpower needed to build nuclear weapons systems. We hear voices saying that these countries can afford such costly weapons, even though they would have to be bought at the expense of the basic needs of their people.

I have committed my administration to the task of persuading the non-nuclear countries that it is neither in the interests of their security, nor of world peace, to develop nuclear weapons. This has been the main thrust behind the efforts of the Arms Control and Disarmament Agency during the past year, and it will continue to be in the year we are now entering.

On January 27, 1966, I presented to the Eighteen Nation Committee on Disarmament at Geneva a seven-point program designed to prevent the spread of nuclear weapons, to halt the nuclear arms race, and to reduce nuclear stocks. I have instructed our negotiators to walk the extra mile necessary to insure that the weapons of war submit to man's need for peace.

In giving these instructions, and in transmitting this report, I reaffirm my belief that it is possible through reason and through patient effort to translate the world's common interest in survival into concrete acts of restraint and accommodation between the nations.

LYNDON B. JOHNSON

The White House
    February 15, 1966

NOTE: The 65-page report, entitled "Fifth Annual Report to Congress, January 1, 1965–December 31, 1965," was released with the President's message.

For the January 27, 1966, message to the 18-Nation Committee on Disarmament, see Item 32.

---

71 Statement by the President on the Death of Representative Albert Thomas of Texas. *February 15, 1966*

OF THE QUALITIES that made Albert Thomas a remarkable man, devotion to the people he served and loyalty to his friends stand higher than all. I knew him—and knew him well—for a long time. He loved Houston and the Congress of the United States. He worked hard. He served well.

His death leaves a lonely place in the lives of those who knew him best.

NOTE: Mr. Thomas served as U.S. Representative from the eighth congressional district of Texas from January 3, 1937, until the time of his death.

The text of the statement was posted on the bulletin board in the Press Room at the White House. It was not made public in the form of a White House press release.

---

72 Statement by the President Announcing an Increase in the Interest Rate on U.S. Savings Bonds. *February 16, 1966*

I AM TODAY announcing an increase in the interest on U.S. savings bonds from 3.75 percent to 4.15 percent.

This means that the bonds that you have, and the bonds you buy in the future, will earn you more money. It means a fairer return for those millions of Americans that are already enrolled in the savings bond program. And I hope that it will encourage millions more of you to join.

The savings bond program is both prudent and patriotic. It is prudent because it strengthens the security of your own family. It is patriotic because it strengthens the economy of our country, it supports our fighting men in Vietnam who need to be supported at this very hour, and it supports the cause of our freedom everywhere in the world. It helps to preserve the buying power of our American dollars.

And for all of these reasons, I believe that savings bonds are the most important investment that any American can make. I urge you to invest regularly through the payroll savings plan at your office, your factory, or your bank.

Your President, your Vice President, and the members of the Cabinet are themselves enrolling in such a plan. I am purchasing bonds today for myself and Mrs. Johnson, for Luci and Lynda, and I am instructing my department and agency heads to immediately begin a campaign so that every employee of the Federal Government can set an example for the rest of the Nation to follow.

Not all of us are called upon to fight for freedom in Vietnam, but we can help in that cause by strengthening our country and by strengthening its economy here at home.

NOTE: The President read the statement at 12 noon in the Theater at the White House.

See also Items 15, 73.

73 Letter to the Secretary of the Treasury Approving an Increase in the Interest Rate on Series E and H Savings Bonds. *February 16, 1966*

Dear Mr. Secretary:

I am returning with my approval your proposal to increase the interest rate on all United States Series E and H Savings Bonds.

I believe that this increase will insure a fair rate to all those patriotic Americans who buy U.S. Savings Bonds.

It has been vital in quiet and stormy times alike—as a source of non-inflationary financing for government—as a matchless means of personal savings.

I want those great benefits to continue. I want them strengthened so that we can continue to carry our burden in Vietnam and sustain our economic boom without danger of inflation.

We can do no less to bar inflation, improve fiscal management, and keep faith with millions of investors.

It is my earnest hope that purchases and holdings of U.S. Savings Bonds will rise substantially—both through signing up new buyers and through increased support from those who already are buying bonds. I am sure that the higher rate of return on Savings Bonds—together with the patriotic spirit of all Americans—will make this hope a reality.

Sincerely,

LYNDON B. JOHNSON

[The Honorable Henry H. Fowler, Secretary of the Treasury, Washington, D.C.]

NOTE: Secretary Fowler's proposal, in the form of a letter to the President dated February 15, was also made public by the White House. Referring to the President's letter of January 18 on the need for higher interest rates on U.S. savings bonds (see Item 15) the Secretary recommended an increase from 3.75 percent to 4.15 percent on Series E and H bonds sold after December 1, 1965. He also recommended increasing the yield on outstanding bonds sold before that date (2 Weekly Comp. Pres. Docs., p. 224).

See also Item 72.

74 Letter to the President of the Senate and to the Speaker of the House Transmitting Report on Earthquake Recovery Assistance to Alaska. *February 16, 1966*

Dear Mr. President: (Dear Mr. Speaker:)

I have the honor to transmit a report of activity under authority of Public Law 88–451, describing the efforts of five Federal departments and agencies to assist in the recovery of Alaska following the earthquake of March 27, 1964.

The Act, entitled "1964 Amendments to the Alaska Omnibus Act" was designed to speed reconstruction of the areas devastated by the earthquake.

This report covers the period from July 1, 1965, through December 31, 1965. It clearly indicates that most of the actions authorized by Public Law 88–451 had been completed prior to this six-month period. Only about $8 million was furnished through the grant and loan programs authorized by the Act, while the *total cumulative amount during the eighteen months* the amendments have been in effect approximates $60 million. Even this latter figure represents only a small part of the total recovery programs provided by the Federal Government under the various disaster relief authorities.

As of this date, more than $344 million in total Federal aid has been provided for the State, its communities and its people. Of this amount, nearly $169 million has been in the form of direct grants. More than $93 million was provided in the form of loans to individuals, business concerns, and other organizations. The balance represents the cost of repairs to damaged Federal facilities.

It is a tribute to the Congress, to the individual citizens of the State, and to the thousands of State and Federal personnel who worked so diligently following the disaster that Alaska has today substantially recovered from the earthquake that devastated her cities less than two years ago.

Sincerely,

LYNDON B. JOHNSON

NOTE: This is the text of identical letters addressed to the Honorable Hubert H. Humphrey, President of the Senate, and to the Honorable John W. McCormack, Speaker of the House of Representatives.

The text of the report was not made public by the White House.

The 1964 Amendments to the Alaska Omnibus Act was approved by the President on August 19, 1964 (Public Law 88–451; 78 Stat. 505).

75 Statement by the President on the Government's Employee Safety Program. *February 16, 1966*

ONE YEAR AGO today I called upon this administration's department and agency heads to reduce the number and cost of injuries to Federal employees 30 percent by 1970.

Since then more than 50 agencies have surveyed their safety problems and developed plans for resolving them.

The first year of Mission SAFETY–70 brought widespread and increased attention to safeguarding those who serve their country in the civilian service of the United States. This is as it should be—there must be constant and vigilant concern for the welfare of the men and women who serve their Nation in the Federal service.

But there can be no letup. I have today requested the heads of all agencies to continue and intensify their efforts and to send to me, by May 1, a summary report of their safety actions and their plans.

Secretary of Labor Wirtz has given me an interim report of some 1965 highlights:

—We have reduced from 5 to over 20 percent the injury frequency rates in a number of larger Federal agencies including the General Services Administration, National Aeronautics and Space Administration, Tennessee Valley Authority, Agriculture, Health, Education, and Welfare, Justice, Interior, Veterans Administration, and D.C. Government. These improvements took place in the 9 months immediately following the launching of Mission SAFETY-70.

—We have reduced disabling injuries in 13 of the 19 largest agencies and preliminary figures indicate a 2.4 percent reduction in the overall Federal injury rate.

—In the Atomic Energy Commission we reduced its already low frequency by 30 percent and its private contractors reported a 22 percent reduction last year.

—Sharpe Army Depot near San Francisco, a growing supply link to our fighting forces in Vietnam, reduced its injury frequency over 50 percent in the last 6 months of 1965. As its 3,000 civilian employees entered their February work schedules, they had completed 158 days without a disabling injury.

—The Air Force reports a 19 percent reduction in motor vehicle fatalities last year, reaching its best accident prevention record since 1950.

—Three Department of Treasury units reduced their injury frequency from 20 to over 30 percent. When injuries rose following round-the-clock production of new coins, the U.S. Mint reevaluated and upgraded its safety program.

These examples demonstrate that waste in manpower and resources can be reduced and must be attacked relentlessly. Agency efforts separately, and jointly with the Federal Safety Council have given strength and meaning to Mission SAFETY-70.

I congratulate and commend all agencies on their achievements during the first year of Mission SAFETY-70, but, as we enter the second year of this long-range program to cut the number and costs of accidents, our course is clear.

We must see that our Federal programs bear fruit and stimulate greater safety efforts throughout our Nation and in every community.

On this, the first anniversary of Mission SAFETY-70, I again call upon Federal administrators and employees to provide the necessary leadership and that full measure of support so essential to success.

NOTE: For a statement by the President upon inaugurating the new employee safety program on February 16, 1965, see 1965 volume, this series, Book I, Item 73.

See also Item 76 below.

76 Memorandum to Agency Heads Requesting Reports on Their Employee Safety Programs. *February 16, 1966*

Memorandum for the Heads of Executive Departments and Agencies:

A year ago today I wrote you of my desire to improve the Federal Government's employee safety programs.

At that time I issued a Safety Policy for the Federal Service and initiated Mission SAFETY-70 to achieve a 30 percent reduction in each agency's work injuries and costs by 1970.

Your reports to me last spring set forth your plans to meet our long-range objective to reduce the waste in manpower and materials arising from accidents.

I should now like to receive by May 1, 1966, from the head of each executive department and agency a summary report of developments in 1965.

This Mission SAFETY-70 report should include:

(a) actions taken;

(b) specific accomplishments;

(c) areas of weakness which still need

strengthening;

(d) agency plans for 1966.

I appreciate that steps have been taken in the past year to strengthen the government's safety programs but much more must be undertaken to emphasize our continuing concern and to assure effective implementation.

LYNDON B. JOHNSON

NOTE: In the opening paragraph the President referred to a memorandum to heads of executive departments and agencies dated February 16, 1965. The memorandum and a related statement of policy are printed in the Federal Register (30 F.R. 2517, 2519) and in the Code of Federal Regulations (3 CFR, 1965 Supp., pp. 198, 199).

See also Item 75.

---

77   Remarks in Atlantic City at the Convention of the American Association of School Administrators. *February 16, 1966*

Mr. Chairman, Governor Hughes, distinguished Members of the most distinguished New Jersey congressional delegation, Mr. Brain, Mr. Platt, Dr. Carr, my dear friends:

As I was observing the presentation of these awards, before you reached the last one, I was almost tempted to say, "California, here I come."

I want to thank Governor Hughes for permitting me to come back to this great city. This is my favorite convention city. And the New Jersey congressional delegation, here on the platform with me tonight, are my favorite congressional delegation. And I don't think that we'll need any help, but if we do, it will be prayers, and I brought Dr. Billy Graham along with me to do the praying.

I am very honored to accept your award and I'm very happy to be here tonight with the big brass of American education. I might have been with you tonight under other auspices—except that 30 years ago I left teaching for a different pursuit.

Tonight, our professions differ, but actually we have the same task: to build a society that is worthy of free men. Two hundred years ago our fathers laid the foundation. Two years ago I challenged my fellow citizens to get on with the job. I said that we must build the Great Society in our cities, and in our countryside, and in our classrooms.

Tonight our work is underway. Much of the needed legislation has already been enacted: more than a score of landmark measures in the field of education alone.

So it is a real thrill to me to read the rollcall of these historic acts of the last few months in the Congress:

—the Economic Opportunity Act of 1964,

—the civil rights laws of 1964 and 1965,

—Medicare,

—the Natural Beauty Act,

—the Higher Education Act of 1965.

And—not last and not least—the Elementary and Secondary Education Act of 1965.

Laws are only designs for achievement.

The barriers that we must overcome do not yield merely because Congress takes a vote or because the President signs a bill.

Two barriers are the most unyielding, each reinforcing the other in blocking our progress.

The first is poverty. Those of us who have worked in schools know what it means for someone who starts life as a victim of poverty. It is hard to teach a hungry child. Poverty breeds handicaps of mind and body which cripple him before he ever has a chance to get ahead. And we have learned all too well that poverty passes on its curse generation to generation.

The second barrier is racial discrimination. Because of it, children grow up aliens in their native land. For a ghetto—whether white or black or brown—is less than half a world. No child can be fully educated unless his life is opened to the wonderful variety that this world affords.

Two weeks ago, I called for the International Educational Act of 1966 to promote the worldwide commerce of knowledge—to declare that learning is not a commodity which can be confined at the water's edge.

Yet within our own country there are still, tonight, racial walls against hope and opportunity. Between the slums of the inner cities and their spreading suburbs, there are gulfs as deep and as wide as any ocean.

And if education is to be worthy of its good name, we must find the ways to span these gulfs.

I pledge to you tonight that the Federal Government will not be a silent partner in this enterprise.

Therefore I am sending Congress five top priority requests:

—to enlarge each one of the programs in the Elementary and Secondary Education Act—and to make them run through 1970;

—to double funds for our imaginative and our precedent-breaking Operation Head Start, which will next year help more than 700,000 youngsters from poor homes get ready for the rigors of learning;

—to fund the new National Teacher Corps so that our best college graduates can be recruited to work in our worst schools;

—to pass the Child Nutrition Act of 1966 to help pay for school lunches for those children who really need them, without subsidizing those who can afford to buy their own. We also want school breakfasts for children who would otherwise start their day with empty stomachs.

Finally—and this summarizes, really, the reams of recommendations in one single sentence—my budget this year proposes a $10 billion investment in education and training. In 1960 your Government was spending only a third this much. The Office of Education alone will spend on programs *six* times as much as it spent only 6 years ago.

And I came up here to Atlantic City tonight to tell you that this is only the beginning of what we're going to do in the field of education.

It was almost 200 years ago that James Madison declared that Federal and State Governments "are in fact but different agents and trustees of the people, constituted with different powers, and designed for different purposes." They are not "mutual rivals and enemies." They are partners.

Madison's definition, Governor Hughes, has not changed, though the partnership has grown closer and more creative.

If education is to achieve its promise in America, it cannot and must not be done in Washington alone. Each State and each community must fashion its own design and shape its own institutions.

But we will need a common vision to build schools to match our common hopes for the future.

Every school will be different, but the differences will not range as they do today between satisfactory and shocking. We will have instead a diversity of excellence.

Tomorrow's school will be a school without walls—a school that's built of doors which open to the entire community.

Tomorrow's school will reach out to the places that enrich the human spirit: to the museums, to the theaters, to the art galleries, to the parks, to the rivers, and to the mountains.

It will ally itself with the city, with the city's busy streets and its factories and its assembly lines and its laboratories—so that the work does not seem an alien place for the student.

Tomorrow's school will be the center of community life, for the grownups as well as the children: "a shopping center of human services." It might have a community health clinic, a public library, a theater, and recreation facilities.

It will provide formal education for all citizens—and it will not close its doors any more at 3 o'clock. It will employ its buildings round the clock and its teachers round the year. We just cannot afford to have an $85 billion plant in this country open less than 30 percent of the time.

In every past age, leisure has been a privilege enjoyed by the few at the expense of the many. But in the age that's waiting to be born, leisure will belong to the many at the expense of none. Our people must learn to use this gift of time, and that means another challenge for tomorrow's schools.

I am not describing a distant Utopia, but

l am describing the kind of education which must be the great and the urgent work of our time. By the end of this decade, unless the work is well along, our opportunity will have slipped away from us.

Many people, as William James once said, shed tears for justice, generosity, and beauty, but never really recognize those virtues when they meet them out on the street.

Some people are this way about rebuilding our society. They love the idea. But in the heat and grime, somehow they just lose their zeal. They discover that progress is a battle and not a parade—and they fall away from the line of march.

You know that the job of building a better school and a better Nation is hard and often thankless work. Someone must take on the perilous task of leadership. Someone in shirtsleeves must turn ideas into actions, dollars into programs. Someone must fight the lonely battles in each community—make the accommodations, win the supporters, get the results, and finally get the job done.

Many of you have endured this hard and long journey from hope to reality—when the applause died, and the crowd thinned out, and you were alone with the dull administrative details still to be done.

But this is how a Great Society is really built: brick by brick, and in the toil and the noise of each day.

We have so little reason to be discouraged. Others face tasks so much more difficult than ours. Only last week out in Honolulu I sat across the table from the very young leader of South Vietnam and I heard him say of his country: "We were deluding ourselves with the idea that our weaknesses could not be remedied while we were fighting a war. . . . We will not completely drive out the aggressor until we make a start at eliminating these political and social defects." In other words, while we are winning a war, we must get at the defects that caused it.

The work of his government will not be easy. But these are not timid tasks for timid men. They have learned that government must meet the outreach of its people's hopes.

And there at Honolulu, I pledged support and the support of the American people to their plans for education in their country where men die at 35, and where the per capita income is less than $100 a year. This year alone we will help them build 2,800 classrooms, three times the average for the last 10 years.

We will help them train 13,400 teachers, eight times the yearly average of the last decade.

We will help them distribute 6 million textbooks. We've already distributed more than 8 million.

And we will help them educate almost a fourth as many doctors as the total number of doctors they now have in their entire country.

This little country maintains 700,000 men in its armed forces tonight, over 2½ times as many for its size as the United States of America.

Yet, these leaders voiced no weariness before the task of getting on with reforms in education and health and agriculture. And if they keep their commitments, they will be the real revolutionaries of Asia. For the real revolution is to build schools, and through building these schools, build a nation.

What they are committed to do, with America's help, must be done under the most brutal conditions that you can imagine. Their civilian population lives in constant danger of terror and death at the hands of the Vietcong.

Last year over 12,000 civilians were kidnapped or killed by the Communist terror-ists. There were more than 36,000 incidents of terror last year—an increase of 10,000 over the year before. Two days ago the Vietcong killed 39 civilians and wounded 7 others as they rode on buses.

Terrorism—deliberately planned and coldly carried out—continues to be the chief instrument of the Vietcong aggression in South Vietnam. It is not just a byproduct of their military action; it is the way that they actually hope to win the war.

Who—and what—are their targets? School teachers and school administrators, health officials, village leaders, schools, hospitals, research stations, and medical clinics—all of those people and places that are essential to the growth of a healthy and a free society.

This is the terrible scarred face of the war that's too seldom seen and too little understood. Often it is not even reported by our journals that are most concerned about the war in Vietnam. The war on the other front is not heard from nearly enough. These incidents usually happen in the rural areas that are rather remote from either the reporter's or the camera's eye. Observers are not invited when the Vietcong murder the mother of an officer in the Army of Vietnam as reprisal against her son—or torture and dismember the master of a local school.

But people who hate war ought not ignore this strategy of terror.

What is its purpose? *It is through fear and death to force the people of South Vietnam into submission.* It is just as simple and as grim as that.

And it just must not and will not succeed.

If these tactics prevail in Vietnam, they can and they will prevail elsewhere.

And if the takeover of Vietnam can be achieved by a highly organized Communist force employing violence against a civilian population, then it can be achieved in another country, at another time, with an even greater cost to freedom.

If this "war of liberation" triumphs, who will be "liberated" next?

There *is* a job of liberation in South Vietnam. It is liberation from terror, liberation from disease, liberation from hunger, and liberation from ignorance.

Unless this job is done, a military victory in South Vietnam would not be victory at all. It would only be a brief delay until the aggressor returns to feed on the continuing misery of the people.

We have the military strength tonight to convince the Communists that they cannot achieve the conquest of South Vietnam by force. They may delay us, but I warn them and I pledge you they will never deter or or defeat us.

But the building of a better society is the main test of our strength—our basic purpose. Until the people of the villages and the farms of that little unhappy country know that they personally count, that they are cared about, that their future is their own—only then will we know that real victory and success is possible.

I came away from Honolulu filled with new hope and new energy. I came away convinced that we cannot raise a double standard to the world. We cannot hold freedom less dear in Asia than in Europe or be less willing to sacrifice for men whose skin just happens to be a different color!

If this little young nation that's ridden with dangers can show such determination, we—we, with all of our wealth and promise—must be no less determined.

Our time is filled with peril. So it has been every time that freedom has really ever been tested.

Our tasks are enormous ones. But so are our resources.

Our burdens are heavy and will grow heavier. But the Bible counsels that we "be not weary in well-doing."

The house of freedom may never be completed, but it will never fall—so long as you and I and those who share our commitment keep this vision of what we in America stand for, and for what we Americans are determined to build throughout the world.

Thank you, and good night.

NOTE: The President spoke at 8:45 p.m. at Convention Hall in Atlantic City, N.J., following the presentation to him of the National Education Award of 1966. In his opening words he referred to Frank K. Platt, President of Associated Exhibitors of the National Education Association and chairman of the convention, Richard J. Hughes, Governor of New Jersey, George B. Brain, Dean of the College of Education, Washington State University, and William G. Carr, Executive Secretary of the National Education Association.

More than 5,000 delegates attended the annual convention of the American Association of School Administrators.

78 Remarks at the 14th Annual Presidential Prayer Breakfast. *February* 17, 1966

Dr. Graham, my beloved friend Senator Carlson, distinguished guests at the head table, my dear friends:

I am pleased to return again to our annual prayer breakfast and to be among so many of my old friends. In this room this morning we have been privileged to hear one of the great speakers and leaders of our time. He has been heard by some of the great leaders of the most powerful Nation in all the world. Yet not a single one of us is ashamed to say, "I will lift up mine eyes unto the hills, from whence cometh my help."

Just a few blocks from here, on the front

of the National Archives, is an inscription, "The past is prologue." As your President, I have had many occasions to realize the truth of that statement. Throughout our long history our Presidents have struggled with recurring problems. The way they handled those problems and their successes or failures can guide us in the actions that we are called upon to take today.

But there are some things that history cannot teach us and among them is how to bear, without pain, the sending of our young Americans into battle, and how to fill the aching void as we wait for the news of their fate, and how to console the wife or the mother or the little children when that news is bad.

These are the times when I recall the wisdom of Abraham Lincoln when he said, "I have been driven to my knees many times by the overwhelming conviction that I had nowhere else to go. My own wisdom and that of all about me seem insufficient for the day." In private prayer at unusual moments, I have found courage to meet another day in a world where peace on earth is still only an empty dream.

The Prophet Isaiah tells us, "They that wait upon the Lord shall renew their strength; they shall mount up with wings as eagles; they shall run, and not be weary; and they shall walk, and not faint."

I believe that with all my heart, but in these troubled times I am sustained by much more than my own prayers. I am sustained by the prayers of hundreds of Americans who daily take the time to look up from their own problems in order to try to give me a little encouragement in mine. Not long ago I received a letter one morning from a mother whose son had been killed in Vietnam. She spoke of the pain and the loss, and the tears that are ever ready to flow, but through all of this were words of encouragement for me from this dear little lady.

In her letter she concluded: "Mr. President, I wish I could tell you all that I feel in my heart. But there just aren't words, so we ask God to bless you and your little family, that He will guide you in all the terrible decisions that you must make. As long as we believe, our strength is in our faith in God and He will never fail us."

So, my countrymen, in those words from that dear mother are to be found the greatness of this Nation and also the strength of its President.

NOTE: The prayer breakfast of International Christian Leadership, Inc., a nondenominational group of laymen, was held at the Shoreham Hotel in Washington. The President spoke at 9:18 a.m. In his opening words he referred to Rev. William F. (Billy) Graham, who gave the principal address, and Senator Frank Carlson of Kansas, chairman of the board, International Council for Christian Leadership.

79   Message to the Congress Transmitting the National Science Foundation's Annual Report on Weather Modification. *February* 18, 1966

To the Congress of the United States:

I am transmitting, for the consideration of the Congress, the Seventh Annual Report on Weather Modification (for Fiscal Year 1965) submitted to me by the Director of the National Science Foundation.

Highly encouraging steps are being taken toward establishing safe and effective programs for modifying the weather. We can now begin to see the day when such programs may become operationally feasible. This is an exciting and encouraging development—not only for Americans, but for men everywhere.

Last year, in transmitting to the Congress the Sixth Annual Report, I indicated the need for a larger effort in basic research and in the development of means to put the knowledge we have to work.

That increased effort is noted in this report. It describes not only the vigorous pursuit of weather modification programs by agencies of the Executive Branch—but also the valuable stimulus afforded by Committees of the Congress, and the significant activities of nongovernmental groups.

RECENT STUDIES

The list of recent activities in this field is heartening. For example, on January 1, 1966, the first Federal regulation on weather modification became effective. The National Science Foundation issued rules providing that advance notice of intention to modify the weather must be given to the Foundation.

More recently, two significant reports by advisory groups have been issued. A two-volume study by a National Academy of Sciences Panel, released January 14, reviewed in detail the physical science aspects of weather and climate modification. Five days later the National Science Foundation's Special Commission on Weather Modification issued a broad report covering the biological and social aspects, statistical problems, problems of law and organization, and international implications, as well as physical science aspects. Additional reports by the Special Commission will soon be forthcoming.

Congress, too, has indicated its interest in scheduling additional hearings on weather and climate modification during this session. It is striking that separate groups dealing

seriously with this problem have, after long study, arrived at similar and significant conclusions.

The National Academy of Sciences report, for example, says: "In a sense, weather modification today is a reality. Man can and does interfere with the atmosphere in a number of ways. His ability to produce deliberate beneficial changes is still very limited and uncertain, but it is no longer economically or politically trivial."

The report of the Special Commission, in a markedly similar passage, says, "Weather and climate modification is becoming a reality. The daily activities of man influence the atmosphere in a number of ways and his ability to induce deliberate changes in measurable magnitude by artificial means is progressing."

The report I submit today says it another way: "In 1965, key words are no longer 'whether' and 'when.' They are 'what' and 'how' and 'who'."

PROBLEMS—AND PROGRESS

Two sets of problems face us and both are difficult. One consists of finding out how to modify the weather and climate. The second consists of determining how best to utilize this knowledge for the benefit of mankind once it is achieved.

The scientists and engineers inside and outside the Government must address themselves particularly to the first set of problems. All of us, as concerned citizens, must seriously consider the second.

At present it appears feasible, under appropriate conditions, to seed some kinds of clouds and achieve increased precipitation. It is also possible, under certain conditions, to dissipate some types of fog. Partial success has been reported from abroad in reducing hail damage.

As our understanding of atmospheric processes increases, our ability to do more will also increase. Even now, men are dreaming and planning of projects that will some day enable us to mitigate the awesome and terrible forces of hurricanes and tornadoes. Such a time is still far off, but perhaps not so far off as we thought only a few years ago.

That so much is being done now is a credit not only to the men of science working in the field, but also to the understanding and support of the Congress which has expressed its interest in and support of this field of great national interest. I commend to your

continuing interest this report and the important efforts that it describes.

LYNDON B. JOHNSON

The White House
  February 18, 1966

NOTE: The report, transmitted to the President on January 12, is entitled "Weather Modification; Seventh Annual Report, 1965" (Government Printing Office, 109 pp.).

The President also referred to a report published by the National Academy of Sciences, dated January 1966 and entitled "Weather and Climate Modification—Problems and Prospects" (2 vols., 28 pp. and 198 pp.), and to a report of the Special Commission on Weather Modification, National Science Foundation, entitled "Weather and Climate Modification" (149 pp.).

80 Statement by the President on the Death of Admiral of the Fleet Chester W. Nimitz. *February* 20, 1966

ADMIRAL NIMITZ loved his country and the sea. His devotion to one inspired his mastery of the other, earning for his quiet courage and resolute leadership the undying gratitude of his countrymen and an enduring chapter in the annals of naval history.

NOTE: In addition to the statement, the President issued Executive Order 11271 (2 Weekly Comp.

Pres. Docs., p. 244; 31 F.R. 2991; 3 CFR, 1966 Comp., p. 104) which provided that as a mark of respect to the memory of Admiral Nimitz, the flag of the United States should be flown at half-staff on all Government buildings, grounds, and naval vessels until interment.

The text of the statement was posted on the bulletin board in the Press Room at the White House. It was not made public in the form of a White House press release.

See also Item 1.

81 Memorandum on Brotherhood Week. *February* 21, 1966

[Released February 21, 1966. Dated February 19, 1966]

Memorandum for the Heads of Executive Departments and Agencies:

It is my privilege again this year to serve as Honorary Chairman of Brotherhood Week.

We observe it during the week of George Washington's birthday, February 20–27, because his voice still stirs and guides us: "To bigotry no sanction, to persecution no assistance."

It is a week for remembrance: social and economic injustice remain the unfinished tasks of the Great Society, the personal and moral responsibility of every citizen.

It is a week for rededication: our traditional ideals of tolerance, compassion and respect for individual dignity can only survive as they are replenished by personal commitment.

It is a week for thankfulness and expectation: we can be grateful for blessings granted and victories won, as we resolve to extend them and expand them.

Americans of all races, creeds and walks of life must join hearts and hands to stay the poisons which threaten our nation's life. Starting with the family and community, we must together extend to every American those rights of freedom and opportunity that are the wellspring of America's strength.

I hope the men and women of each Department and Agency will, in their own way, pursue this vital purpose during Brotherhood Week—and throughout the year.

LYNDON B. JOHNSON

82   Special Message to the Congress Proposing Measures To Preserve America's Natural Heritage.   *February 23, 1966*

To the Congress of the United States:

Albert Schweitzer said:

"Man has lost the capacity to foresee and to forestall. He will end by destroying the earth."

The most affluent nation on earth may feel that it is immune from this indictment. A nation that offered its people—a century ago—uncharted forests, broad sparkling rivers, and prairies ripe for planting, may have expected that bounty to endure forever.

But we do not live alone with wishful expectations.

We live with history. It tells us of a hundred proud civilizations that have decayed through careless neglect of the nature that fed them.

We live with the certain future of multiplying populations, whose demands on the resources of nature will equal their numbers.

We are not immune. We are not endowed—any more than were those perished nations of the past—with a limitless natural bounty.

Yet we are endowed with their experience. We are able to see the magnitude of the choice before us, and its consequences for every child born on our continent from this day forward.

Economists estimate that this generation has already suffered losses from pollution that run into billions of dollars each year. But the ultimate cost of pollution is incalculable.

We see that we can corrupt and destroy our lands, our rivers, our forests and the atmosphere itself—all in the name of progress and necessity. Such a course leads to a barren America, bereft of its beauty, and shorn of its sustenance.

We see that there is another course—more expensive today, more demanding. Down this course lies a natural America restored to her people. The promise is clear rivers, tall forests and clean air—a sane environment for man.

I shall propose in this message one means to achieve that promise. It requires, first, an understanding of what has already happened to our waters.

THE POLLUTION OF OUR WATERS

"Pollution touches us all. We are at the same time polluters and sufferers from pollution. Today, we are certain that pollution adversely affects the quality of our lives. In the future, it may affect their duration."

These are the words of the Environmental Pollution Panel of the President's Science Advisory Committee. They were written in November, 1965.

At that time, every river system in America suffered some degree of pollution.

At that time, discharges into our rivers and streams—both treated and untreated—equalled the raw sewage from almost 50 million people. Animal wastes and waste from our cities and towns were making water unfit for any use.

At that time, rivers, lakes and estuaries were receiving great quantities of industrial chemicals—acids from mine runoff—detergents and minerals that would not "break down" in the ordinary life of the water. These pollutants were re-entering domestic and industrial water supplies. They were killing fish. They posed hazards to both human and animal life.

By that time, on Lake Erie six of thirty-two public recreation and swimming areas had been closed down because the water was unsafe for human beings. The blue pike catch in the lake had fallen from 20 million pounds in 1937 to 7,000 pounds in 1960. The oxygen that fish need for life was being rapidly devoured by blooms of algae fed by pollutants.

At that time, in the lower Arkansas Red River Basin, oil field development and irrigation were dumping salt into rivers. The result was an additional annual expense of $13 million to bring in fresh water.

I have placed these comments in the past tense not because they are no longer true. *They are more tragically true today than they were four months ago.*

I seek instead to make them a bench-mark in restoring America's precious heritage to her people.

I seek to make them that point in time when Americans determined to resist the flow of poison in their rivers and streams.

I seek to make them ancient history for the next generation.

And I believe the conditions they describe can become just that—if we begin now, together, to cleanse our rivers of the blight that burdens them.

A START HAS BEEN MADE

The first session of the 89th Congress launched a major effort to save America's water resources.

It authorized quality standards for all interstate waters.

It provided—in the Water Pollution Control Act of 1965—new resources for treating the wastes from our cities.

It created the Water Resources Council to coordinate all aspects of river basin planning. This unified effort promises to make the work of pollution control more effective.

We mean to make full use of these new instruments. They will require increased expenditures, in a year of few increases for urgent domestic programs. We shall make them.

Yet at this point the development of new knowledge, and new organizations to carry on this work, is as crucial as our dollars.

We must combine all the means at our disposal—Federal, State, local and private—progressively to reduce the pollution of our rivers.

A CLEAN RIVERS DEMONSTRATION PROGRAM

I propose that we begin now to clean and preserve entire river basins from their sources to their mouths.

I propose a new kind of partnership—built upon our creative federal system—that will unite all the pollution control activities in a single river basin. Its task is to achieve high standards of water quality throughout the basin.

The Clean Rivers Demonstration Program I recommend has four requirements:

1. Appropriate water quality standards—authorized by the Water Quality Act of 1965—must be adopted for every part of the basin.

2. The States and local communities must develop long-range plans to achieve those standards and to preserve them. The plans must be comprehensive, and they must be practical.

3. Where it does not already exist, a permanent river basin organization must be created to carry out the plan. It must represent the communities and the States. It must work closely with the Federal Government. The organization must be prepared to revise the plan as conditions require, so that new threats to the quality of the river may be turned back.

4. Communities must be willing and able to contribute funds necessary for constructing facilities. They must be prepared to levy charges for their use—charges adequate to maintain, extend, and replace them when needed.

THE FEDERAL ROLE

Federal financial assistance will be necessary if the Clean Rivers Demonstration Program is to succeed.

In most watersheds there are communities wholly without treatment facilities. There are some with only the most basic means for removing solid wastes.

Substantial funds will be necessary to construct the initial facilities. I therefore propose to:

—*eliminate the dollar-ceiling limitation* on grants for sewage treatment facilities in these Clean River Demonstra-

tions—but only in the Demonstrations.

—*provide special funds* to finance both planning and project costs in Clean River Demonstrations.

In the first year, I am asking $50 million to begin this program.

To administer the program most effectively, we must reorganize the Federal effort. In the past, the Federal anti-pollution effort has been organizationally separate from water conservation and use programs.

One agency should assume leadership in our clean water effort.

That agency should be the Department of the Interior.

Today the Department's water management programs range from saline water research to irrigation. It is responsible for wildlife preservation, and for administering the National Park system. Its Secretary serves as chairman of the Water Resources Council. Thus its present task, and the logic of good government, require that it be entrusted with an important new effort to clean and preserve entire river systems.

I shall shortly submit to the Congress a reorganization plan to transfer to the Department of the Interior the Water Pollution Control Administration now housed in the Department of Health, Education, and Welfare.

BENEFITS OF THE PROGRAM

The program has one ultimate goal: to clean all of America's rivers. This year we shall start with those few basins whose States and communities are prepared to begin. As additional organizations are formed and their plans drafted, more basins will qualify.

The projects will be self-sustaining. Federal assistance is planned for the initial construction of local treatment works. Thereafter, local communities will collect revenues from users sufficient for the operation, expansion, and replacement of the facilities. Continuing responsibility will reside where the benefits accrue—with local authorities.

The projects will allow experiment with new forms of organization. State and local participation may be based on an interstate compact, a river basin commission, or even a conservancy district. The central requirement is for sufficient jurisdiction and authority to develop and carry out the long-range plan.

These projects will enable us to curtail and control pollution in entire river basins. Broad-scale planning of water standards in broad stretches of a river can achieve substantial economies. More efficient plants can be built to treat the wastes of several communities and nearby industries. Integrating the control of steam flow and treatment plant operation can reduce costs—for example, by fitting the type and amount of day-to-day treatment to varying stream conditions.

OUR ESTABLISHED PROGRAMS

The Clean Rivers Program now holds great promise for restoring and preserving water quality. But in the beginning it can affect only a few areas.

Our existing programs must continue. They must be improved—not only to help rescue other rivers from pollution, but because they provide the foundation for the river basin demonstration projects.

Federal grants for waste treatment plants now total more than $725 million. More than 6,000 projects are under construction or already completed. For Fiscal 1967 I have requested the Congress to appropriate $150 million, the full authorized amount, to continue this vital effort.

Under last year's act, the initiative for water quality standards rests, until July 1967, with the States. State governments now have an obligation to demonstrate their willingness and ability to control pollution. Some have already done so. The Federal Government must extend all possible help to enable the States to meet this responsibility.

I am therefore recommending that support for State water pollution control agencies be doubled. The added amount should be used at the Secretary's discretion to assist States in devising effective water quality standards. It should be used to prepare plans for abating pollution.

ENFORCEMENT AUTHORITY

Standards, however, mean little without the power to enforce them. Existing Federal authority to abate water pollution is unnecessarily time-consuming, complex in procedure, and limited in jurisdiction. Steps must be taken to simplify and strengthen these procedures.

I recommend that:

1. The Water Pollution Control Act be amended to eliminate the two mandatory six-month delays that unnecessarily burden its procedures;

2. The Federal Government have authority immediately to bring suit to stop pollution, when that pollution constitutes an imminent danger to public health or welfare;

3. More weight be given by the courts to the evidence produced in administrative enforcement hearings;

4. The Federal Government have the right to subpoena witnesses to appear at administrative hearings;

5. The Secretary be given the right to initiate enforcement proceedings when pollution occurs in navigable waters, intra-state or interstate;

6. Registration be required of all existing or potential sources of major pollution, and U.S. officials be given the right to inspect such sources; and

7. Private citizens be allowed to bring suit in Federal court to seek relief from pollution.

These are strong measures.

But the menace of pollution requires them.

It poses a major threat to the quality of life in our country.

RESEARCH FOR COMPREHENSIVE POLLUTION CONTROL

The river basin proposals I am submitting take advantage of the best techniques available today. They apply new concepts of efficient organization. But if pollution control is to cope with increasing volumes of waste from our growing industry and population, new knowledge and technology are required. It is a challenge to research organizations, both private and public, to develop these technologies.

1. *There must be new integrated systems of disposal.* Many liquid wastes can be transformed to solids or gases—or vice versa. Research can show which form is least harmful and least costly. Research can reduce costs through combined solid-liquid disposal systems.

2. *The technology of water treatment must be improved.* We must find ways to allow more "re-use" of waste water at reasonable costs. We must remove or control nutrients that cause excessive growth of plant life in streams, lakes and estuaries. We must take steps to control the damage caused by waters that "heat-up" after cooling generators and industrial engines.

3. *More must be learned about the effects of pollutants and the present level of pollu-*
tion. Better equipment must be developed to measure pollution load and movement. We must assess the results of particular pollutants on plant, animal, and human populations. We should continually monitor the quality of our environment, to provide a yardstick against which our progress in pollution abatement can be measured. We must apply the most modern techniques of systems analysis.

Such research will lead to pollution standards suited for each location and type of pollutant. It will permit us to direct our control efforts more efficiently. I am proposing that we spend over $20 million next year on this research.

CONTROL OF AIR POLLUTION

The Clean Air Act of 1963 and its 1965 amendments have given us new tools to help attack the pollution that fouls the air we breathe.

We have begun to counter air pollution by increasing the tempo of effort at all levels of government.

In less than two years Federal financial assistance has stimulated a 50 percent increase in the air pollution budgets of States and local governments. Federal standards for the control of automobile exhausts will apply to the 1968 models. The Federal interstate abatement program will significantly supplement State and local efforts to deal with air pollution.

I am heartened by the progress we are making. But I am mindful that we have only begun our work. *I am forwarding to the Congress proposals to improve and increase Federal research, financing, and technical assistance to help States and local governments take the measures needed to control air pollution.*

POLLUTION FROM FEDERAL ACTIVITIES

The Federal Government is rightly expected to provide an example to the nation in pollution control. We cannot make new demands on State and local governments or on private industry without putting the Federal house in order. We will take the necessary steps this year to ensure that Federal activities do not contribute to the deterioration of our water and air.

Last November I signed an Executive Order requiring that all new Federal installations include adequate water pollution control systems. Agencies are required to submit long-range plans to bring existing installations up to the high level of pollution control required of new facilities. These plans are to be submitted by July 1 of this year. We are providing the funds necessary to implement them.

I also intend to issue an Executive Order dealing with air pollution from Federal activities. The potential dangers of air pollution have only recently been realized. The technical and economic difficulties in conserving the purity of our air are, if anything, greater than in protecting our water resources. Nevertheless, I intend to see that the necessary steps are taken to curtail emissions from Federal installations.

HUMAN RESOURCES FOR POLLUTION CONTROL

New projects and new technology are of little value without skilled people dedicated to putting them to effective use.

I propose to enlist the services of those in industry and the universities.

I propose to attract skilled administrators and scientists to the challenges of full-time occupations in pollution control.

Critical skills are in short supply in all public pollution control operations. We

need to train scientists and social scientists in these activities, and to demonstrate the advantages of government service as a life time occupation. I propose to establish traineeships, fellowships, and an internship program in Federal pollution control activities. The participants will be in residence in Federal pollution control programs throughout the country.

IMPACT ON OUR CITIES

The Pollution Control programs I have recommended will benefit all Americans.

But nowhere will the impact be greater than on our cities.

These steps can clean the air that is today blighted by smoke and chemicals.

These steps can bring to growing urban centers abundant supplies of pure water to sustain today's prosperity and to satisfy tomorrow's needs.

These steps can enrich the daily life of the city dweller and his children by restoring surrounding waterways to their unspoiled natural beauty. For we know that ugliness is degrading and costly, but that beauty can revive the human spirit and enlarge the imagination.

NATIONAL WATER COMMISSION

In no area of resource management are the problems more complex—or more important—than those involving our nation's water supplies. The water shortage in the Northeastern United States is a dramatic reminder that we must take every possible step to improve the management of our precious water resources.

I propose the establishment of a National Water Commission to review and advise on the entire range of water resource problems—from methods to conserve and augment existing water supplies to the application of modern technology, such as desalting, to provide more usable water for our cities, our industries, and our farms.

This Commission will be composed of the very best minds in the country. It will judge the quality of our present efforts. It will recommend long-range plans for the future. It will point the way to increased and more effective water resource measures by the Federal Government, working in close cooperation with states, local communities, and private industry.

SAVING OUR FORESTS

Since the century's beginning the national government has labored to preserve the sublime legacy that is the American forest.

Time after time public intervention has prevented the destruction of irreplaceable forest lands.

Our National Park and Forest Systems are America's principal trustee in the vital task of conservation. That task cannot be accomplished in a single stroke. It requires patient determination and careful planning to secure for our people the beauty that is justly theirs. It merits careful planning.

I propose that we plan now to complete our National Park System by 1972—the 100th anniversary of Yellowstone, the world's first national park.

Substantial progress has been made during the last four years. Yet many scenic masterpieces remain unprotected and deserve early inclusion in the National Park system.

A REDWOOD NATIONAL PARK

I propose the creation of a Redwood National Park in northern California.

It is possible to reclaim a river like the Potomac from the carelessness of man. But we cannot restore—once it is lost—the majesty of a forest whose trees soared upward 2,000 years ago. The Secretary of Interior—after exhaustive consultations with preservationists, officials of the State of California, lumbermen and others—has completed a study of the desirability of establishing a park of international significance.

I have reviewed his recommendations, and am submitting to the Congress legislation to establish such a park. This will be costly. But it is my recommendation that we move swiftly to save an area of immense significance before it is too late.

OTHER OUTDOOR RECREATION PROPOSALS

Other major outdoor recreation proposals which should be approved in 1966 are:

1. Cape Lookout National Seashore, North Carolina

2. Sleeping Bear Dunes National Lakeshore, Michigan

3. Indiana Dunes National Lakeshore, Indiana

4. Oregon Dunes National Seashore, Oregon

5. Great Basin National Park, Nevada

6. Guadalupe Mountains National Park, Texas

7. Bighorn Canyon National Recreation Area, Montana-Wyoming

8. Flaming Gorge National Recreation Area, Utah-Wyoming

For a region which now has no national park, I recommend the study of a Connecticut River National Recreation Area along New England's largest river, in the States of New Hampshire, Vermont, Massachusetts, and Connecticut.

I propose the early completion of studies

and planning for two new parks—the Apostle Isles Seashore along Lake Superior and North Cascades in Washington State.

NATIONWIDE TRAIL SYSTEM

In my Budget, I recommended legislation to extend federal support to the Appalachian Trail, and to encourage the development of hiking trails accessible to the people throughout the country.

I am submitting legislation to foster the development by Federal, State and local agencies of a nationwide system of trails and give special emphasis to the location of trails near metropolitan areas.

PRESERVATION OF HISTORIC SITES

Historic preservation is the goal of citizen groups in every part of the country. To help preserve buildings and sites of historic significance, I will recommend a program of matching grants to States and to the National Trust for Historic Preservation.

WILD RIVER SYSTEM

I am encouraged by the response to my proposal for a National Wild Rivers System, and I urge the Congress to complete this pioneering conservation legislation this year.

COSTS OF LAND ACQUISITION

The spiraling cost of land acquisitions by the Federal Government, particularly for water resource and recreational purposes, is a matter of increasing concern.

Land owners whose property is acquired by the Federal Government are, of course, entitled to just compensation as provided by the Constitution. At the same time, land for the use of the general public should not be burdened with the increased price resulting from speculative activities.

I have requested the Director of the Bureau of the Budget, together with the Attorney General, the Secretary of the Interior, and the heads of the other agencies principally concerned, to investigate procedures for protecting the Government against such artificial price spirals.

A CREED TO PRESERVE OUR NATURAL HERITAGE

To sustain an environment suitable for man, we must fight on a thousand battlegrounds. Despite all of our wealth and knowledge, we cannot create a Redwood Forest, a wild river, or a gleaming seashore.

But we can keep those we have.

The science that has increased our abundance can find ways to restore and renew an environment equal to our needs.

The time is ripe to set forth a creed to preserve our natural heritage—principles which men and women of good will will support in order to assure the beauty and bounty of their land. Conservation is ethically sound. It is rooted in our love of the land, our respect for the rights of others, our devotion to the rule of law.

Let us proclaim a creed to preserve our natural heritage with rights and the duties to respect those rights:

—The right to clean water—and the duty not to pollute it.

—The right to clean air—and the duty not to befoul it.

—The right to surroundings reasonably free from man-made ugliness—and the duty not to blight.

—The right of easy access to places of beauty and tranquility where every family can find recreation and refreshment—and the duty to preserve such places clean and unspoiled.

—The right to enjoy plants and animals in their natural habitats—and the duty not to eliminate them from the face of this earth.

These rights assert that no person, or company or government has a right in this day and age to pollute, to abuse resources, or to waste our common heritage.

The work to achieve these rights will not be easy. It cannot be completed in a year or five years. But there will never be a better time to begin.

Let us from this moment begin our work in earnest—so that future generations of Americans will look back and say:

1966 was the year of the new conservation, when farsighted men took farsighted steps to preserve the beauty that is the heritage of our Republic.

I urge the Congress to give favorable consideration to the proposals I have recommended in this message.

LYNDON B. JOHNSON

The White House

February 23, 1966

NOTE: For remarks upon signing related legislation, see Items 119, 522, 574.

In the section entitled "Pollution From Federal Activities," the President referred to Executive Order 11258 of November 17, 1965, "Prevention, Control, and Abatement of Water Pollution by Federal Activities" (1 Weekly Comp. Pres. Docs., p. 506; 30 F.R. 14483; 3 CFR, 1965 Supp., p. 188), and to Executive Order 11282 of May 26, 1966, "Prevention, Control, and Abatement of Air Pollution by Federal Activities" (2 Weekly Comp. Pres. Docs., p. 696; 31 F.R. 7663; 3 CFR, 1966 Comp., p. 117).

83   Message to the Economic Symposium Commemorating the 20th Anniversary of the Employment Act of 1946.   *February* 23, 1966

YOUR SYMPOSIUM today celebrates one of the great turning points in the economic and political history of this Nation.

Twenty years ago, the Nation's economy had just emerged from almost 4 years of test by fire, immediately following a decade of test by ice. Men of vision and goodwill in both political parties, in labor as in business, in the universities and professions as in Government, were resolved that we should learn from these experiences; that depression and mass unemployment equally with unbridled inflation must be and could be mastered; and that only the Federal Government's leadership could accomplish it.

Their resolution was reflected in the Employment Act of 1946.

To be sure, some regarded the declaration that the Federal Government must accept a share of responsibility for the performance of the American economy as a revolutionary threat to our system of free enterprise. Others regarded the commitment to maximum employment as a pious gesture toward a visionary objective.

The last 20 years have demonstrated that the Employment Act was neither dangerous nor visionary. Instead, the act, and the machinery it created, have allowed us to develop an increasingly fruitful partnership between business, labor, and Government in the great task of building a better society for all Americans.

The success of that partnership is demonstrated by the present state of our economy. Our prosperity is unequaled; and our growth rate and price stability are the envy of the world.

Our recent gains prove the dynamism of our prevailingly private economy. They also show the contribution of sound and positive Government policies.

In developing an awareness of problems, in improving our knowledge and understanding, and in designing appropriate policies, the machinery created by the Employment Act has proved its value many times over. Hearings and reports of the Joint Economic Committee have educated the Congress and the Nation on all aspects of our economy. The advice of the Council of Economic Advisers has helped four Presidents and their administrations to propose and to carry out policies that have preserved and advanced our economic strength. And the requirement of an Annual Economic Report of the President has spurred coherence and consistency in the far-flung activities of the many agencies of Government, and, at the same time, made a major contribution to public understanding of economic policy.

But most important of all was the spirit of the act: the recognition that all plans and policies of Government should be bent toward protecting and promoting the health of our economy.

The knowledge we have gained and the policies we have designed to achieve and maintain full employment, to avoid inflation, to speed our economic growth, and to eliminate poverty, demonstrate man's ability to master his social as well as his physical environment. They are achievements worthy of celebration.

After 5 years of record expansion, we now face the new task of sustaining full employment without inflation. I have recommended a budget and fiscal policy which, in the best judgment of my advisers and myself, will allow us to sustain solid expansion without overheating the economy. But this is an area where, in spite of all we have

learned over 20 years, we still have little experience. We have no choice but to advance with courage tempered by caution. We will need to watch unfolding events closely, and to remain flexible in our tax and other policies so that we can change quickly if the need should arise.

The task of managing economic policy so as to achieve high employment without overheating will always be difficult.

It is made more difficult at the moment by the fact that we are in a transitional period. The rapid growth of output which has enabled us to reduce unemployment has placed special—and temporary—strains on some of our raw material resources. And the problems of matching men and jobs during the transition to an era of high employment are more difficult now than they will be after we have maintained high employment for some time.

To make the transition to sustained high employment without inflation will test our energy and ingenuity. And it requires us to seek new ways in which business, labor, and Government can cooperate to avoid inflationary wage and price movements.

These are grave challenges, but I am confident that we shall meet them.

The years ahead can bring economic and social achievements which will far outpace the gains of the past. It is our task so to set the goals and to lay the plans that 20 years from tonight men looking back can honor our vision and our resolution as we tonight celebrate the events of 20 years ago.

NOTE: The President's message was read to the members of the Symposium, meeting at the Washington Hilton Hotel, by Henry H. Fowler, Secretary of the Treasury.

For President Truman's statement upon signing the Employment Act on February 20, 1946, see "Public Papers of the Presidents, Harry S. Truman, 1946," Item 39.

84   Letter to the Administrator, National Capital Transportation Agency.   *February* 23, 1966

[Released February 23, 1966.   Dated February 22, 1966]

Dear Mr. McCarter:

The Congress, in enacting the National Capital Transportation Act of 1965, authorized construction of a rail rapid transit system that eventually will be expanded to serve the entire National Capital Region. Transportation is a critical problem for all major urban centers, and what is done here will have significance far beyond this region.

While we seek to resolve problems of moving people and goods within the congested National Capital area, our concerns must not be confined to the utilitarian requirements of transportation alone. We must take this opportunity to make our Capital a more attractive and inspiring place in which to live and work. The Congress has already enacted legislation to assure that beautification is a major consideration in the development of our highway system. The same concern must guide development of plans for mass transit.

In designing the system for the Nation's Capital, I want you to search worldwide for concepts and ideas that can be used to make this system attractive as well as useful. It

should be designed so as to set an example for the Nation, and to take its place among the most attractive in the world. In selecting the architects for this system, you must seek those who can best combine utility with good urban design. As you search for the new and innovative, you must also take advantage of the experience of other cities.

I know that your efforts to accomplish these objectives will be of great interest to this community and to other cities faced with the task of coordinating mass transportation facilities with other urban needs. I ask that you report to me periodically on your accomplishments so that we can join in encouraging public discussion of your plans and in taking steps that others may benefit from your experience.

Sincerely,

Lyndon B. Johnson

[Hon. Walter J. McCarter, Administrator, National Capital Transportation Agency, Washington, D.C. 20432]

note: For the President's remarks on signing the National Capital Transportation Act of 1965, see 1965 volume, this series, Book II, Item 499.

85   Remarks of Welcome to the Vice President Following His Mission to Asia.   *February* 23, 1966

Mr. Vice President and Mrs. Humphrey, Secretary Rusk, ladies and gentlemen:

We are very happy this afternoon to welcome the Vice President and Mrs. Humphrey back to Washington and to the White House. The Vice President has visited eight or nine countries in areas of the world that

are very important. He has carried the message of all Americans to the people of free Asia, and today I think there is much better understanding among the people of the United States and the people of Asia than was true before he left.

I have read your reports, Mr. Vice President, daily. I have been encouraged by the manner in which you presented the viewpoint of this country. I have been heartened by your understanding of the viewpoint of the countries you visited. Tomorrow morning at 8 o'clock we will ask you to meet with the bipartisan leadership in the Cabinet Room. At 9 o'clock you will meet with the leaders of the Armed Services, Appropriations, and Foreign Affairs, and Foreign Relations Committees of the House and Senate in the East Room of the White House to hear your report.

We are delighted you are back. We think you performed a most useful and constructive service. The years of experience that you have devoted to public life in Minnesota, and in the United States Senate in a position of leadership and as a member of the Foreign Relations Committee, have certainly served you in good stead in your mission of peace that you have just completed.

I know the people are eager and anxious to hear from you. I hope that you say what is in your head and your heart, and then, if you will, I would like to go over to the office with Secretary Rusk and Mr. Bundy and others, and to stay with you as long as we can this evening before I have to go to New York.

The Vice President. Thank you very much, Mr. President. Thank you for your expression of faith and confidence.

Mr. President, on this journey of some 43,000 miles, I have been very fortunate to have as a counselor, adviser, and as one of your most trusted advisers and diplomats, the distinguished Ambassador, Averell Harriman, and also of course Ambassador Hand, Mr. Valenti, and other members of our Government that have given us encouragement, guidance, and strength wherever we have been in the presentation of our views and policies.

At your request, we have traveled long and we have traveled far—as I have said, in fact, some 43,000 miles. And it is great to be home to our own beloved America.

Everywhere we were received with warm friendship and cordial hospitality. We have had the privilege of visiting with the people and the leaders of nine countries in Asia and the Pacific—in South Vietnam, Thailand, Laos, Pakistan, India, New Zealand, Australia, the Philippines, and Korea. In each country, Mr. President, we reviewed with the leaders of government the decisions of that historic Honolulu Conference. We came to these countries to learn and to observe. We came to discuss matters of mutual concern and interest, and we did so with frankness and with candor.

Of course, I shall be reporting, as you have indicated, to you, sir, in detail and to the Members of Congress whom you have mentioned here today.

Mr. President, we return from this journey with renewed confidence and with determination and renewed encouragement. I am encouraged because the tide of battle in Vietnam has turned in our favor. The spirit of our fighting men and those of our great allies is good. Their courage and their performance in battle is superb. Their humanitarian assistance to a wartorn country is an inspiration. They bring honor to themselves and to our country. They deserve, and thank goodness, Mr. President, from you and the Nation they are receiving support and justified praise.

Then, too, there are other Americans of equal courage and skill and determination fighting the battle against man's ancient enemies of disease and hunger, and of poverty and ignorance. Yes, as you have stated it yourself, we wage two battles. One is to prevent the success of aggression, and we are succeeding in that battle. The other is to help rebuild a new society of new promise and new hope based on justice and opportunity. We shall succeed in this, too. This is the meaning of the Declaration of Honolulu.

I am encouraged by the determination of the Asian people and their leaders to help themselves to build a better life. I return with a profound sense of appreciation—appreciation of our comradeship with the peoples of Asia and the Pacific in their struggle against aggression and subversion and tyranny, and an appreciation of our partnership with the nations of this troubled region in the creation of their own far-reaching social revolution, and, Mr. President, an appreciation of our leadership, your leadership, and of our unity in the pursuit of a just and honorable peace.

It should warm the heart of every American to know that we have staunch friends in all of the countries that we visited. Rightfully proud of their own history and culture and with a deep sense of self-respect and self-determination, they look to America for understanding, for help, and for assistance in their fight against the wrongs of the past, and the threat of subversion and aggression.

The challenge that we face is widely understood as a test of free men everywhere, and the leaders of free Asia and the Pacific are confident of success, just as we are confident of success. They are increasingly eager to give of their resources to the wider battle for a better life for their people. They, too, Mr. President, want their "Great Society."

In short, I return with a deep sense of confidence in our cause, and in its ultimate triumph. I have been singularly honored, Mr. President, to be your emissary and to observe what I hope can be and will be the cause of peace, the peace that you relentlessly pursue in your leadership and your statesmanship.

Thank you.

THE PRESIDENT. The success of the Vice President's visit was contributed to a great deal by the presence of a man who is always there when the decisions are being made and wherever the problems exist. He has been a distinguished public servant for decades in this Government. I want to publicly thank Ambassador Averell Harriman for being available and making the contribution he did in connection with this mission.

I also want to thank Jack Valenti and Ambassador Hand, Mr. Connell, and Mr. Rielly, and others who contributed so much.

Secretary Rusk, would you like to say something?

SECRETARY RUSK. Mr. President, I have had many echoes from the Vice President's trip. I think you and this country are both fortunate in having this spokesman to go to Asia and take the message of determination—both in resisting aggression and in building a peace—and also the message of hope in building a better life, just as soon as our resources can be fully committed to that great task of building a decent society with the peoples of that part of the world.

It is a great privilege for me to be here to help receive the Vice President.

THE PRESIDENT. Ambassador Harriman, would you say a word?

AMBASSADOR HARRIMAN. Mr. President, I appreciate the opportunity you have given me to be with the Vice President. I can say that he is a very fast operator. He moves very rapidly, and it takes quite a little energy to keep up with him.

But in all seriousness, he was extraordinarily well received everywhere, not only because of his own warmth of personality and the message that he brought, but it was in respect for you, sir, the President of the United States, for whom he was the emissary, and for the American people.

This trip was important and useful, and I think will contribute to an understanding in Asia of your objectives, Mr. President, and those of the American people.

THE PRESIDENT. Thank you very much, ladies and gentlemen. We will go into the office of the White House now.

Thank you.

NOTE: The President spoke at 5:40 p.m. on the South Lawn at the White House. In his opening words he referred to Vice President Hubert H. Humphrey and his wife and to Secretary of State Dean Rusk. During his remarks he referred to McGeorge Bundy, Special Assistant to the President, W. Averell Harriman,

Ambassador at Large, Jack Valenti, Special Assistant to the President, Lloyd N. Hand, Chief of Protocol, Department of State, William Connell, Administrative Assistant to the Vice President, and John E. Rielly, Assistant to the Vice President.

The Vice President departed on his mission following the President's return from the Honolulu Conference on February 8 (see Item 56). He returned to Washington on February 23.

On March 6, 1966, the White House released a report, dated March 3, to the President from Vice President Humphrey summarizing his conclusions and recommendations. The text is printed in the Weekly Compilation of Presidential Documents (vol. 2, p. 332).

See also Item 106.

86 Remarks in New York City Upon Receiving the National Freedom Award. *February 23, 1966*

Mr. Chief Justice, Mr. Secretary, Senator Kennedy, Members of the fine delegation from New York, ladies and gentlemen at the head table, my fellow Americans:

To be honored with this award by this organization is a very proud moment for me. I accept it with the gratitude of my heart and with renewed commitment to the cause that it represents, the cause of freedom at home and the cause of freedom abroad.

Twenty-five years ago, to a world that was darkened by war, President Franklin Roosevelt described the four freedoms of mankind:

—Freedom of speech and expression.

—Freedom of every person to worship God in his own way.

—Freedom from want.

—Freedom from fear.

Franklin Roosevelt knew that these freedoms could not be the province of one people alone. He called on all his countrymen to assist those who endured the tyrant's

bombs and suffered his opposition and oppression.

He called for courage and for generosity, and for resolution in the face of terror. And then he said,

"Freedom means the supremacy of human rights everywhere. Our support goes to those who struggle to gain those rights— or keep them."

Wendell Willkie, Franklin Roosevelt's opponent in the campaign of 1940, shared his belief that freedom could not be founded only on American shores or only for those whose skin is white. "Freedom is an indivisible word," Wendell Willkie said. "If we want to enjoy it and fight for it we must be prepared to extend it to everyone, whether they are rich or poor, whether they agree with us or not, no matter what their race or the color of their skin."

That was Republican policy 25 years ago. It was Democratic policy 25 years ago. It is American policy here tonight.

Then how well have we done in our time

in making the four freedoms real for our people and for the other people of the world?

Here in America we accord every man the right to worship as he wills. I believe we are more tolerant of sectional and religious and racial differences than we were a quarter of a century ago. The majority of our people believe that a qualified man or woman, of any race, of any religion, of any section, could hold any office in our land. This was not so—not very clear at all in 1940.

We are committed now, however great the trial and tension, to protecting the right of free expression and peaceful dissent. We have learned to despise the witch hunt, the unprincipled harassment of a man's integrity and his right to be different. We have gained in tolerance, and I am determined to use the high office I hold to protect and to encourage that tolerance.

I do not mean to say that I will remain altogether silent on the critical issues of our day. For just as strongly as I believe in other men's freedom to disagree, so do I also believe in the President's freedom to attempt to persuade.

So let me assure you and my fellow Americans tonight that I will do everything in my power to defend both.

Twenty-five years ago freedom from want had the ring of urgency for our people. The unemployment rate stood at 14.5 percent. Millions of Americans had spent the last decade in the breadlines or on farms where the winds howled away any chance for a decent life.

Tonight there are still millions whose poverty haunts our conscience. There are still fathers without jobs, and there are still children without hope.

Yet for the vast majority of Americans these are times when the hand of plenty has replaced the grip of want. And for the first time in almost 9 years tonight the unemployment rate has fallen to 4 percent.

This liberation from want—for which we thank God—is a testimony to the enduring vitality of the American competitive system, the American free enterprise economy.

It is a testimony also to an enlightened public policy, established by Franklin Roosevelt and strengthened by every administration since his death.

That policy has freed Americans for more hopeful and more productive lives.

It has relieved their fears of growing old by social security and by medical care.

It has inspired them with hope for their children by aid to elementary and higher education.

It has helped to create economic opportunity by enlightened fiscal policies.

It has granted to millions, born into hopelessness, the chance of a new start in life by public works, by private incentive, by poverty programs.

For the Negro American, it has opened the door after centuries of enslavement and discrimination—opened the doors to the blessings that America offers to those that are willing and able to earn them.

Thus we address the spirit of Franklin Roosevelt, 25 years after his message to America and the world, with confidence and with an unflagging determination. We have served his vision of the four freedoms essential to mankind—here in America.

Yet we know that he did not speak only for America. We know that the four freedoms are not secure in America when they are violently denied elsewhere in the world.

We know, too, that it requires more than

speeches to resist the international enemies of freedom. We know that men respond to deeds when they are deaf to words. Even the precious word "freedom" may become empty to those without the means to use it.

For what does freedom mean
—when famine chokes the land,
—when new millions crowd upon already strained resources,
—when narrow privilege is entrenched behind law and custom,
—when all conspires to teach men that they cannot change the condition of their lives?

I do not need to tell you how five administrations have labored to give real meaning to "freedom," in a world where it is often merely a phrase that conceals oppression and neglect.

Men in this room, men throughout America, have given their skills and their treasure to that work. You have warned our people how insatiable is aggression, and how it thrives on human misery.

You have carried the word that without the sense that they can change the conditions of their lives, nothing can avail the oppressed of this earth—neither good will, nor national sovereignty, nor massive grants of aid from their more fortunate brothers.

You have known, too, that men who believe they can change their destinies will change their destinies.

Armed with that belief, they will be willing—yes, they will be eager—to make the sacrifices that freedom demands. They will be anxious to shoulder the responsibilities that are inseparably bound to freedom.

They will be able to look beyond the four essential freedoms
—beyond to the freedom to learn, to master new skills, to acquaint themselves with the lore of man and nature;
—to the freedom to grow, to become the best that is within them to become, to cast off the yoke of discrimination and disease;
—to the freedom to hope, and to build on that hope, lives of integrity and well-being.

This is what our struggle in Vietnam is all about tonight. This is what our struggle for equal rights in this country is all about tonight.

We seek to create that climate, at home and abroad, where unlettered men can learn, where deprived children can grow, where hopeless millions can be inspired to change the terms of their existence for the better.

That climate cannot be created where terror fills the air.

Children cannot learn, and men cannot earn their bread, and women cannot heal the sick where the night of violence has blotted out the sun.

Whether in the cities and hamlets of Vietnam, or in the ghettos of our own cities, the struggle is the same. That struggle is to end the violence against the human mind and body—so that the work of peace may be done, and the fruits of freedom may be won.

We are pitting the resources of the law, of education and training, of our vision and our compassion, against that violence here in America. And we shall end it in our time.

On the other side of the earth we are no less committed to ending violence against men who are struggling tonight to be free.

And it is about that commitment that I have come here to speak now.

Tonight in Vietnam more than 200,000 of your young Americans stand there fighting for your freedom. Tonight our people are determined that these men shall have whatever help they need, and that their cause, which is our cause, shall be sustained.

But in these last days there have been

questions about what we are doing in Vietnam, and these questions have been answered loudly and clearly for every citizen to see and to hear. The strength of America can never be sapped by discussion, and we have no better nor stronger tradition than open debate, free debate, in hours of danger. We believe, with Macaulay, that men are never so likely to settle a question rightly as when they discuss it freely.

We are united in our commitment to free discussion. So also we are united in our determination that no foe anywhere should ever mistake our arguments for indecision, nor our debates for weakness.

So what are the questions that are still being asked?

First, some ask if this is a war for unlimited objectives. The answer is plain. The answer is "no." Our purpose in Vietnam is to prevent the success of aggression. It is not conquest; it is not empire; it is not foreign bases; it is not domination.

It is, simply put, just to prevent the forceful conquest of South Vietnam by North Vietnam.

Second, some people ask if we are caught in a blind escalation of force that is pulling us headlong toward a wider war that no one wants. The answer, again, is a simple "no." We are using that force and only that force that is necessary to stop this aggression. Our fighting men are in Vietnam because tens of thousands of invaders came south before them. Our numbers have increased in Vietnam because the aggression of others has increased in Vietnam. The high hopes of the aggressor have been dimmed and the tide of the battle has been turned, and our measured use of force will and must be continued. But this is prudent firmness under what I believe is careful control. There is not, and there will not be, a mindless escalation.

Third, others ask if our fighting men are to be denied the help they need. The answer again is, and will be, a resounding "no." Our great Military Establishment has moved 200,000 men across 10,000 miles since last spring.

These men have, and will have, all they need to fight the aggressor. They have already performed miracles in combat. And the men behind them have worked miracles of supply, building new ports, transporting new equipment, opening new roads.

The American forces of freedom are strong tonight in South Vietnam, and we plan to keep them so. As you know, they are led there by a brilliant and a resourceful commander, Gen. William C. Westmoreland. He knows the needs of war and he supports the works of peace. And when he asks for more Americans to help the men that he has, his requests will be immediately studied, and, as I promised the Nation last July, his needs will be immediately met.

Fourth, some ask if our men go alone to Vietnam, if we alone respect our great commitment in the Southeast Asia Treaty. Still again the answer is a simple "no." We have seven allies in SEATO, and we have seen five of them give us vital support, each with his own strength and in his own way, to the cause of freedom in Southeast Asia.

Fifth, some ask about the risks of a wider war, perhaps against the vast land armies of Red China. And again the answer is "no," never by any act of ours—and not if there is any reason left behind the wild words from Peking.

We have threatened no one, and we will not.

We seek the end of no regime, and we will not.

Our purpose is solely to defend against aggression. To any armed attack, we will reply. We have measured the strength and the weakness of others, and we think we know our own. We observe in ourselves, and we applaud in others, a careful restraint in action. We can live with anger in word as long as it is matched by caution in deed.

Sixth, men ask if we rely on guns alone. Still again the answer is "no." From our Honolulu meeting, from the clear pledge which joins us with our allies in Saigon, there has emerged a common dedication to the peaceful progress of the people of Vietnam—to schools for their children, to care for their health, to hope and bounty for their land.

The Vice President returned tonight from his constructive and very highly successful visit to Saigon and to other capitals, and he tells me that he and Ambassador Lodge have found a new conviction and purpose in South Vietnam—for the battle against want and injustice as well as the battle against aggression.

So the pledge of Honolulu will be kept, and the pledge of Baltimore stands open—to help the men of the North when they have the wisdom to be ready.

We Americans must understand how fundamental is the meaning of this second war—the war on want. I talked on my ranch last fall with Secretary Freeman, Secretary of Agriculture, and in my office last week with Secretary Gardner, Secretary of Health, Education, and Welfare, making over and over again the same central point: The breeding ground of war is human misery. If we are not to fight forever in faraway places—in Europe, or the far Pacific, or the jungles of Africa, or the suburbs of Santo Domingo—then we just must learn to get at the roots of violence. As a Nation we must magnify our struggle against world hunger and illiteracy and disease. We must bring hope to men whose lives now end at

two score or less. Because without that hope, without progress in this war on want, we will be called on again to fight again and again, as we are fighting tonight.

Seventh, men ask who has a right to rule in South Vietnam. Our answer there is what it has been here for 200 years. The people must have this right—the South Vietnamese people—and no one else. Washington will not impose upon the people of South Vietnam a government not of their choice. Hanoi shall not impose upon the people of South Vietnam a government not of their choice. So we will insist for ourselves on what we require from Hanoi: respect for the principle of government by the consent of the governed. We stand for self-determination—for free elections—and we will honor their result.

Eighth, men ask if we are neglecting any hopeful chance of peace. And the answer is "no." A great servant of peace, Secretary Dean Rusk, has sent the message of peace on every wire and by every hand to every continent. A great pleader for peace here with us tonight, Ambassador Arthur Goldberg, has worked at home and abroad in this same cause. Their undiscouraged efforts will continue. How much wiser it would have been, how much more compassionate towards its own people, if Hanoi had only come to the bargaining table at the close of the year. Then the 7,000 Communist troops who have died in battle since January 1, and the many thousands who have been wounded in that same period, would have lived at peace with their fellow men.

Today, as then, Hanoi has the opportunity to end the increasing toll the war is taking on those under its command.

Ninth, some ask how long we must bear this burden. To that question, in all honesty, I can give you no answer tonight.

During the Battle of Britain, when that nation stood alone in 1940, Winston Churchill gave no anwer to that question. When the forces of freedom were driven from the Philippines, President Roosevelt could not and did not name the date that we would return. If the aggressor persists in Vietnam, the struggle may well be long. Our men in battle know and they accept this hard fact. We who are at home can do as much, because there is no computer that can tell the hour and the day of peace, but we do know that it will come only to the steadfast and never to the weak in heart.

Tenth, and finally, men ask if it is worth it. I think you know that answer. It is the answer that Americans have given for a quarter of a century, wherever American strength has been pledged to prevent aggression. The contest in Vietnam is confused and hard, and many of its forms are new. Yet our American purpose and policy are unchanged.

Our men in Vietnam are there. They are there, as Secretary Dillon told you, to keep a promise that was made 12 years ago. The Southeast Asia Treaty promised, as Secretary John Foster Dulles said for the United States—"that an attack upon the treaty area would occasion a reaction so united, and so strong, and so well placed that the aggressor would lose more than it could hope to gain." But we keep more than a specific treaty promise in Vietnam tonight. We keep the faith for freedom.

Four Presidents have pledged to keep that faith.

The first was Franklin D. Roosevelt, in his State of the Union Message 25 years ago. He said:

". . . we are committed to the proposition that principles of morality and considerations for our own security will never permit us to acquiesce in a peace dictated by aggressors and sponsored by appeasers. We know that enduring peace cannot be bought at the cost of other people's freedom."

The second was Harry S. Truman, in 1947, at a historic turning point in the history of guerrilla warfare—and of Greece, Turkey, and the United States. These were his words then:

"I believe that it must be the policy of the United States to support free peoples who are resisting attempted subjugation by armed minorities or by outside pressures.

"I believe that we must assist free peoples to work out their own destinies in their own way."

The third was Dwight D. Eisenhower, in his first Inaugural Address. He promised this:

"Realizing that common sense and common decency alike dictate the futility of appeasement, we shall never try to placate an aggressor by the false and wicked bargain of trading honor for security. Americans, indeed, all free men, remember that in the final choice a soldier's pack is not so heavy a burden as a prisoner's chains."

And then 5 years ago, John F. Kennedy, on the cold bright noon of his first day in Office, proclaimed:

"Let the word go forth from this time and place, to friend and foe alike, that the torch has been passed to a new generation of Americans—born in this century, tempered by war, disciplined by a hard and bitter peace, proud of our ancient heritage—and unwilling to witness or permit the slow undoing of those human rights to which this Nation has always been committed, and to which we are committed today at home and around the world.

"Let every nation know, whether it wishes us well or ill, that we shall pay any price, bear any burden, meet any hardship, support any friend, oppose any foe to assure the survival and the success of liberty."

This is the American tradition. Built in free discussion, proven on a hundred battlefields, rewarded by a progress at home that has no match in history, it beckons us forward tonight to the work of peace in Vietnam.

We will build freedom while we fight, and we will seek peace every day by every honorable means. But we will persevere along the high hard road of freedom. We are too old to be foolhardy and we are too young to be tired. We are too strong for fear and too determined for retreat.

Each evening when I retire, I take up—from a bedside table—reports from the battlefront and reports from the capitals around the world. They tell me how our men have fared that day in the hills and the valleys of Vietnam. They tell me what hope there seems to be that the message of peace will be heard, and that this tragic war may be ended.

I read of individual acts of heroism—of dedicated men and women whose valor matches that of any generation that has ever gone before. I read of men risking their lives to save others—of men giving their lives to save freedom.

Always among these reports are a few letters from the men out there themselves.

If there is any doubt among some here at home about our purpose in Vietnam, I never find it reflected in those letters from Vietnam. Our soldiers, our Marines, our airmen, and our sailors know why they are in Vietnam. They know, as five Presidents have known, how inseparably bound together are America's freedom and the freedom of her friends around the world.

So tonight let me read you from a letter that I received from an American father, a warm friend of mine of many years, about his son, a young Army captain.

He said, "I have never known a man at

war who showed less bravado in his communications with home. When he was not flying missions in his helicopter or working out of the battalion headquarters he and some of his buddies on their own visited the orphanages as individuals and played with the kids. He was deeply interested in the Vietnamese people, particularly the peasants, and he told me how sorely they wanted, more than anything else, to just be left alone in some semblance of freedom to grow their rice and to raise their families.

"This good young American, as thousands like him, was not on the other side of the world fighting specifically for you or for me, Mr. President. He was fighting in perhaps our oldest American tradition, taking up for people who are being pushed around."

The young captain described in this letter is dead tonight, but his spirit lives in the 200,000 young Americans who stand out there on freedom's frontier in Vietnam. It lives in their mothers and in their fathers here in America who have proudly watched them leave their homes for their distant struggle.

So tonight I ask each citizen to join me, to join me—in the homes and the meeting places our men are fighting to keep free—in a prayer for their safety.

I ask you to join me in a pledge to the cause for which they fight—the cause of human freedom to which this great organization is dedicated.

Is ask you for your help, for your understanding, and for your commitment, so that this united people may show forth to all the world that America has not ended the only struggle that is worthy of man's unceasing sacrifice—the struggle to be free.

NOTE: The President spoke at 9:35 p.m. at the Waldorf-Astoria Hotel in New York City upon receiving the National Freedom Award of Freedom House, a nonprofit, nonpartisan organization. In his opening words he referred to Earl Warren, Chief Justice of the United States, C. Douglas Dillon, former Secretary of the Treasury, and Robert F. Kennedy, Senator from New York.

During his remarks the President referred to, among others, Hubert H. Humphrey, Vice President of the United States, Henry Cabot Lodge, U.S. Ambassador to South Vietnam, Orville L. Freeman, Secretary of Agriculture, John W. Gardner, Secretary of Health, Education, and Welfare, Dean Rusk, Secretary of State, Arthur J. Goldberg, U.S. Representative to the United Nations, and John Foster Dulles, Secretary of State during the Eisenhower administration.

The award consisted of a bronze sculptured head of the President done by Leo Cherne, economist and chairman of the executive committee of Freedom House. A plaque on the base of the sculpture was inscribed with the President's name and the words, "Freedom at home was never more widely shared nor aggression abroad more wisely resisted than under his leadership of the Nation."

The National Freedom Award has been given annually since 1943 by the Board of Trustees of Freedom House to the person deemed to have done the most in the cause of freedom during the year. President Johnson is, to date, the only President to receive the award while still in office. It was given to General Eisenhower in 1945 and to Harry S. Truman in 1965.

---

87   Statement by the President at the Presentation of the Medal of Honor (Posthumous) to Staff Sgt. Larry S. Pierce.
February 24, 1966

THIS IS a special moment for me. There is in it pride and heartache—tragedy and majesty.

We have gathered here in the first house of our land to honor one who has been first among the brave. We have come to salute extraordinary courage—to mark extraordinary dedication. We bestow this Nation's highest honor on an heroic young American who can be with us in spirit only.

Sergeant Larry Pierce was only 24 years old. But he was wise and skilled beyond his years in his profession. His uniform was his badge. He wore it with pride.

Sergeant Pierce died young in a distant land, far from the land he loved and the family he cherished. He made the ultimate sacrifice for the ultimate cause.

Why was this brave American called upon to give up the promise of his youth? Why are his comrades still called upon to fight on after him? Why are we in Vietnam?

The answers to these questions are to be found in Hanoi and Peking where greed and ambition reach out to strangle peaceful nations.

They are to be found throughout South Vietnam where brave men are fighting to live as they choose.

And they are to be found woven in the very fabric of American tradition where freedom—any man's freedom—is prized above life itself. And Sergeant Pierce has added another chapter to that tradition.

From Saratoga to the Marne to Okinawa and now Vietnam—the Sergeant Pierces have come in legions to light the darkness and drive out tyranny and war. They do so today. They shall do so tomorrow. They will defend the ideal and pursue the dream forever.

We at home must be worthy of their sacrifice. We must be united in our purpose to create a world where terror will not go unchallenged—where aggression and violence will shatter on the rock of our courage and our conviction.

We must be committed as individuals to a common pledge: Free men shall not stand alone against the enemy that menaces all free men.

To you, Mrs. Pierce—and to you, Theresa—and to you, Kelley—and to you, Gregory—your bravery is no less heroic than

215

your soldier husband and father. We are equally uplifted by it and grateful for it.

I promise each of you that none of us shall falter in our purpose until we have secured the kind of world for which Sergeant Pierce gave his young and gallant life.

The Secretary of the Army will now read the citation.

[The text of the citation read by Stanley R. Resor, Secretary of the Army]

The President of the United States of America, authorized by Act of Congress, March 3, 1863, has awarded in the name of The Congress the Medal of Honor, posthumously, to

STAFF SERGEANT LARRY S. PIERCE

UNITED STATES ARMY

for conspicuous gallantry and intrepidity in action at the risk of his life above and beyond the call of duty:

Staff Sergeant Larry S. Pierce distinguished himself by conspicuous gallantry and intrepidity at the risk of his own life above and beyond the call of duty while leading a Squad against hostile forces near Ben Cat, Republic of Vietnam, on September 20, 1965.

Sergeant Pierce was serving as squad leader in a reconnaissance platoon when his patrol was ambushed by hostile forces. Through his inspiring leadership and personal courage, the squad succeeded in eliminating an enemy machine gun and routing the opposing force. While pursuing the fleeing enemy, the squad came upon a dirt road and, as the main body of his men entered the road, Sergeant Pierce discovered an anti-personnel mine emplaced in the road bed. Realizing that the mine could destroy the majority of his squad Sergeant Pierce saved the lives of his men at the sacrifice of his own by throwing himself directly onto the mine as it exploded. Through his indomitable courage, complete disregard for his own safety, and profound concern for his fellow soldiers, he averted loss of life and injury to the members of his squad.

Sergeant Pierce's conspicuous gallantry, extraordinary heroism, and intrepidity at the cost of his own life, above and beyond the call of duty, are in the highest traditions of the United States Army and reflect great credit upon himself and the Armed Forces of his country.

NOTE: The ceremony took place at noon in the President's office at the White House. Mrs. Larry S. Pierce of Wasco, Calif., accepted the Medal of Honor posthumously awarded to her husband. She was accompanied by her three small children. Sergeant Pierce's mother, Mrs. Lillie Pierce of Crayana Valley, Calif., also attended the ceremony with other members of the family.

88   The President's News Conference of *February 26, 1966*

ECONOMIC AND SOCIAL DEVELOPMENTS
IN ASIA

THE PRESIDENT. [1.] I have met this morning with Mr. Eugene Black, the great American who has done so much in company with Asian leaders to make the Asian Development Bank a reality.

Mr. Black has told me of the strong support which he has found for the Bank in his discussion with congressional leaders and congressional committees. As you know, it has passed the House and been reported unanimously by the Senate Foreign Relations Committee and will be taken up shortly.[1]

I have asked Mr. Black to continue as my personal adviser on the great issues of economic and social development in Asia, and I am glad to say that after discussing it at some length this morning he has agreed.

In particular, I have asked him to visit major Asian capitals early in the spring as my personal representative to discuss the prospects for increased cooperative effort with Asian leaders. I hope that Mr. Black will be able to go to Tokyo and to Manila, to Bangkok and to other major capitals.

Mr. Black has told me of his own belief in the special importance of cooperative efforts in the field of education, and I have asked him to consult with Secretary Gardner[2] and to give very special emphasis to this subject during his trip. He will be provided with a Presidential 707 and he will assemble his own staff. In the next few days they will begin to work with him and assemble material and briefings in connection with his trip. Some of them are going to Florida to meet with him there.

ANNOUNCEMENT OF APPOINTMENTS

[2.] After long thought and much consultation, I have selected Andrew F. Brimmer to join the Board of Governors of the Federal Reserve Board. Mr. Brimmer is presently Assistant Secretary of Commerce for Economic Affairs. I named him to that post last year, after he had served with distinction in banking (Federal Reserve, New York), in education, and in Government. His record at Commerce has been excellent. He has inspired not only his colleagues in the Government, but the wide array of businessmen with whom he has worked. And Secretary Connor[3] has strongly recommended him.

He is a young man, 39 years old. He brings to the Federal Reserve Board a unique combination of qualifications. He worked with the Federal Reserve Bank of New York. He has been a member of the economics faculty at Harvard, Massachusetts Institute of Technology, Michigan State University, and the University of Pennsylvania.

He has worked closely and effectively with the business community. He has studied and taught in the field of economics with which the Federal Reserve is concerned. He has been an active participant in the development and the administration of the economic policies of this Nation.

I have given this appointment exhaustive concern for some months now. Of the many men considered, Mr. Brimmer emerged as the choice of so many with whom I discussed this question.

He is a man of wide professional experience and great personal integrity, a man of moderation, whose brilliance is combined with a sense of fair play that I believe will enable him to serve with distinction in this new and important assignment.

[3.] I am today announcing my intention to appoint Mr. William W. Sherrill to the Board of the Federal Deposit Insurance Corporation. Mr. Sherrill is 39 years old. He is an honor graduate of Harvard Business School with a distinction in finance and a master's degree in business administration.

For the past 4 years he has been a bank president, a savings and loan association officer, and a corporation executive. For the previous 4 years he was treasurer and chief

---

[1] The Asian Development Bank Act of 1966 was approved by the President on March 16, 1966 (see Item 133).

[2] John W. Gardner, Secretary of Health, Education, and Welfare.

[3] John T. Connor, Secretary of Commerce.

administrative officer of the city of Houston.

He had an unusual military career. At the age of 15 he enlisted in the Marine Corps, serving overseas on two separate occasions, participating in the campaigns of Bougainville, Guam, and Iwo Jima. He was wounded by rifle fire on Iwo Jima; he spent 14 months in the Oakland Naval Hospital before he was 20 years old. He will bring to the FDIC a youthful, keen, logical mind, as well as an energetic and imaginative spirit.

[4]. I am pleased to appoint Mr. James M. Quigley to the post of Commissioner, Federal Water Pollution Control Administration.

Mr. Quigley, who has played a major role in shaping Federal water resource policies, has been Assistant Secretary of Health, Education, and Welfare since 1961. We are making an all-out attack on water pollution in our rivers, lakes, and streams—and Mr. Quigley is going to be one of the most important generals in that attack.

[5.] I am naming three men as Assistant Attorneys General in the Department of Justice today:

Mr. Mitchell Rogovin, now the Chief Counsel for the Internal Revenue Service, to take charge of the Tax Division upon the recommendation of Attorney General Katzenbach.

Also Mr. Ernest C. Friesen, presently Assistant Deputy Attorney General, to become Assistant Attorney General for Administration.

I am also naming Mr. Frank M. Wozencraft, former editor of the Yale Law Journal and now a private attorney, to direct the Office of Legal Counsel. He is with Baker, Botts in Houston, Texas.

To succeed Mr. Rogovin as Chief Counsel of the Internal Revenue Service, I am appointing Mr. Lester R. Uretz. He is now the Deputy Chief Counsel of IRS.

[6.] Several days ago I announced the appointment of Mr. Elmer Staats to be Comptroller General. To succeed Mr. Staats in the crucial job of Deputy Director of the Bureau of the Budget, I am naming Phillip S. Hughes. Mr. Hughes has been the Assistant Director for Legislative Reference during the past 8 years.

More than any other man not immediately on the President's staff, Sam Hughes has been responsible for the drafting of the President's Great Society legislative program. Not a single bill has escaped his personal attention, and all the important legislation bears his personal mark.

He is one of those quiet but highly effective civil servants whose influence reaches into every corner of this Government, and I am delighted to be able to give him this recognition on the basis of merit and to promote him to be the Deputy Director of the Budget Bureau.

[7.] Mr. Milton P. Semer is joining the White House staff as Counsel to the President. He will work on legal and legislative matters. Mr. Semer was General Counsel and Deputy Administrator of the Housing and Home Finance Agency before coming to the White House. He has served at the University of Chicago, the Brookings Institution, and as counsel for the Senate Banking and Currency Committee.

[8.] I will have a swearing in this week for Mr. Lee White, who is Counsel—maybe this week or the next week; he has been confirmed—as Chairman of the Federal Power Commission, in the Cabinet Room, and you will be invited to that.

GERMANY'S ANTIPOLLUTION PROGRAM

[9.] I am sending a factfinding mission to the Federal Republic of Germany next week to study natural resource management, with a very special emphasis on environmental pollution.

Secretary of the Interior Stewart Udall will head the mission. High-ranking officials from State and HEW will accompany him. This trip marks the first round of what Chancellor Erhard and I envision as a continuing consultation between the two Governments of our countries on common matters.

The antipollution programs of Germany are said to be among the most effective in the world, and I am sure this beginning trip will provide us with valuable insights and information.

White House Conference "To Fulfill These Rights"

[10.] I am today naming a council of distinguished Americans to prepare for the conference on "To Fulfill These Rights" which will be held in Washington June 1 and 2.[4]

These men and women, under the chairmanship of Ben W. Heineman, of the Chicago & Northwestern Railroad, will develop a substantive agenda for the concepts, proposals, and programs outlined in the 1965 planning session. The council will also consult with experts across the country.

To make equal opportunity a reality in America is one of the most vital tasks that we face in this generation. This conference and this council can help us meet undertaking of that task more successfully than ever.

U.S. Circuit Judge, Third Circuit

[11.] I am nominating Honorable Collins J. Seitz, chancellor of the State of Dela-

ware, to be the new United States Circuit Judge for the Third Circuit. He succeeds John Biggs, Jr., retired.

Government Services to the Public

[12.] I have a very interesting and exciting report[5] from John Macy, Chairman of the Civil Service Commission, and adviser to the President. Last November, I told him I wanted to improve the services to our citizens from every Federal agency and department, and this is his first report on that program. This report shows vigorous action to improve the quality of Federal service to the public. All units of the Federal Government, from the smallest to the largest, have acted, here at home and overseas.

—More and more agencies have extended their office hours to serve the public.

—We are speeding up replies to mail from the public.

—There are now information desks to serve the public who visit Federal buildings.

—24-hour, 7-day-a-week telephone emergency service by many departments and agencies.

—In many large cities, we now provide a one-stop service for people doing business with the Federal Government, so instead of someone having to make seven or eight calls at different Government agencies and traveling from one building to another, all a person has to do now is to make a single stop in some places.

John Macy tells me the prospects for additional improvement are excellent. I have had his detailed memorandum mimeographed for you.

---

[4] See Item 248. A list of the council members is printed in the Weekly Compilation of Presidential Documents (vol. 2, p. 282).

[5] Mr. Macy's report is printed in the Weekly Compilation of Presidential Documents (vol. 2, p. 283).

QUESTIONS

[13.] Any additional information on biographies or personal questions you want to ask, I will have Bob Fleming and Bill Moyers [6] available to you.

I will try to talk loud enough in response to questions for those of you in the back to hear me. I will be glad to take your questions now.

VIETNAM

[14.] Q. Mr. President, the other night, sir, in New York,[7] you said that the tide of the battle has turned in Vietnam. Yesterday, General Walt [8] told us that he had said to you that we are winning there. Was that roughly what you meant by saying the tide was turning?

THE PRESIDENT. I think I will just stand on what I said in New York. I am not familiar with what General Walt said. I wasn't there. I had a long talk with him, though, and he reviewed the situation with me. And I was very glad to hear what he had to say.

REPLACEMENT FOR MC GEORGE BUNDY

[15.] Q. Mr. President, can you tell us what you intend to do to replace Mr. Bundy [9] when he leaves next week?

THE PRESIDENT. No. I have no announcements to make now. We have a very efficient staff operating in that field, and I

will work very closely with the Secretary of State, the Secretary of Defense, the Security Council, the Vice President, and others.

I have no appointee to recommend now. I may do some shifting, changing, promoting, and transferring, but we will do that after Mr. Bundy leaves.

PUBLIC AND CONGRESSIONAL VIEWS ON
VIETNAM POLICY

[16.] Q. Mr. President, do you see any evidence that the so-called "hawk" sentiment is on the rise in this country?

THE PRESIDENT. Oh, I don't brand sentiment one way or the other. I think many people are interested in the developments that are taking place and opinion-molding in this country. And I think that basically all of us want to do what is best for our country and what is best for the world, and attempt to avoid war, and to bring about successful peace negotiations. Some of us feel differently at times. That is the strength of this democracy. We express ourselves pretty strongly upon occasions.

The Vice President gave four excellent briefings on his trip to eight countries in 9 days. Mr. Bundy and the Secretary of State, and the Secretary of Defense reviewed in some detail the progressive developments and the decisions that were made at Honolulu. I think pretty generally they were accepted by those who heard these briefings. We invited every Member of the House and Senate to these unusual four meetings in 2 days.

We started by asking the chairman of the Foreign Relations Committee and every member of that Committee from both parties, the Foreign Affairs Committee, both Armed Services Committees, both Appropri-

---

[6] Robert H. Fleming, Deputy Press Secretary to the President, and Bill D. Moyers, Special Assistant to the President.

[7] See Item 86.

[8] Lt. Gen. Lewis W. Walt, Commanding General of the III Marine Amphibious Force in Vietnam.

[9] McGeorge Bundy, Special Assistant to the President.

ations Committees—they have 50 members on them. Then we asked all of those who were not on the committees. And then the Vice President went to the Hill and briefed 100 others.

From time to time we will be sitting in informally with other groups. We have briefed all the leadership. Certainly there are different approaches. There always are on almost any problem that troubles us. There is much more that unites us than divides us.

I think the fact that the House passed the foreign aid authorization supplemental with less than 40 votes against it, less than 10 percent against it, I think the fact that the military authorization was reported unanimously (will be considered Tuesday by the House), I think the fact that the Asian Bank was reported unanimously by the Foreign Relations Committee (that could have been a very controversial matter, establishing a new bank out in that area involving over $1 billion with some 14 or 15 nations)—all these are good signs.

I expect the military affairs authorization bill in due time to be passed with a minimum of opposition. Of course, with as many people as we have, and as many different approaches, there will be differences of opinion. But I am rather pleased that the differences are as minimal as they are.

I am very grateful for the support of the leaders of both parties where I have received that support. And I think it will continue. I believe that out of these discussions, the New York speech, the hearings of these committees, and other things, it will bring about a unity that will serve us in good stead in the days ahead.

[17.] Q. Mr. President, some Members of Congress are quite puzzled. They wonder if you think that this Gulf of Tonkin resolution[10] is more important than operating under the Constitution, and letting Congress declare war.

THE PRESIDENT. I think it is very clear to the Members of Congress that the President has authority to take the action he has taken, first as Commander in Chief, and second, under the treaty that the Congress has ratified 82 to 1, and third, under the resolution that said that the Congress believes it should be our national policy to support our treaty commitments in Southeast Asia, and that the Congress supports and approves the Commander in Chief preventing aggression and responding to armed attack and supporting the treaty.

I think the Members understood that resolution. It went to the House for a hearing; it had a hearing in a committee. It received a rule and it was discussed thoroughly on the floor. It went to the Senate and it was considered by the Foreign Relations Committee. It was reported 31 to 1 in the Foreign Relations Committee and the Armed Services Committee. It went to the floor; it was debated.

Many, many questions were asked and raised, very penetrating questions. One of those questions, by the Senator from Kentucky,[11] was about the President's authority to pledge ground forces. The chairman of the committee pointed out that this resolution clearly gave him that authority; that he hoped it would not be necessary, but it authorized him.

I did not feel that it was essential that the President have a resolution in order to take the action that was taken. As a matter of

---

[10] A joint resolution to promote the maintenance of international peace and security in Southeast Asia was approved by the President on August 10, 1964 (Public Law 88–408, 78 Stat. 384).

[11] Senator Thruston B. Morton of Kentucky.

fact, in the Tonkin Gulf, I took the action before the resolution.

But in the light of what Senator Vandenberg [12] had said about people being in on the takeoff as well as on the landing, in view of what Senator Taft [13] had said about President Truman, that he was justified in going to Korea, but he should have asked the Congress for a resolution; and in view of the advice I had given President Eisenhower in connection with the Formosa and Lebanon resolutions, I said to the Secretary of State and the Secretary of Defense:

"Before we go in there to a more advanced state or involve ourselves more substantially, I want the Congress to go in with me. Let us ask them to act upon this resolution and discuss it and debate it, and give us their views: first, to declare the policy; second, to support the treaty; third, to approve and support whatever actions we might take to prevent aggression; and fourth, to approve and support whatever actions we might take to respond to armed attack."

Now, they did that after discussion. That has been passed. I understand that Senator Morse [14] is going to make a motion to rescind it. We anticipated that when they passed it.

I have no desire to operate without authority, although if the resolution is repealed I think I could still carry out our commitments there. But they provided in the last paragraph, upon recommendation of one of the chairmen of the Senate committees, that they could repeal this resolution any time by a majority vote, without Presidential signature. It would have required a two-thirds vote, if it had the President's signature. So upon the recommendation of Senator Russell [15] we put that amendment in.

The Congress is free to act, and I am not going to try to direct or force one course of action over another. I think they will act wisely. I am a product of the Congress and I have great confidence in it. I am not worried about it.

[18.] Q. Mr. President, Governor Harriman [16] said that he found the recent debate had given encouragement to the enemy. Can you give us your view of the impact of the recent debate abroad?

THE PRESIDENT. I think that I would not want to try to evaluate public opinion abroad on this. I have not been abroad. I think the Members of the Congress are going to follow the course that they think is best for this country. And I don't want to be critical of that course unless I feel it is much more damaging.

MILITARY EVALUATION OF VIETNAM CONFLICT

[19.] Q. Mr. President, the military news out of Vietnam seems to be somewhat more encouraging. Indeed, a number of people around town are talking with considerable enthusiasm about the possibility of cracking the enemy, or at least cracking the hard core. Do you share this kind of optimism or do you think it is premature?

THE PRESIDENT. I talked to General Westmoreland [17] about his plans and his evaluations and his hopes. I was pleased with what he had to say. I don't think that public predictions on battle strategies and possible or likely results in the days ahead would serve the national interest. I have no desire

---

[12] Arthur H. Vandenberg, Senator from Michigan 1928–1951.

[13] Robert A. Taft, Senator from Ohio 1939–1953.

[14] Senator Wayne Morse of Oregon.

[15] Senator Richard B. Russell of Georgia, Chairman of the Senate Armed Services Committee.

[16] W. Averell Harriman, Ambassador at Large and former Governor of New York.

[17] Gen. William C. Westmoreland, Commander, United States Military Assistance Command, Vietnam.

to put any deadline on what might happen when.

I think General Westmoreland better understands that position than anyone here in Washington. I was very pleased at what he observed was ahead and how he felt about it.

Now, we will have a long and hard road. I don't want to try to repeat Mr. Churchill's phrase of "blood, sweat, and tears," but it is not going to be easy and it is not going to be short. It is going to be difficult and it is going to require sacrifices. We want everyone to know that. But we are determined to do what we think ought to be done there.

We have told you over and over that our objectives are limited; that the Prime Minister of South Vietnam very well stated them at the Honolulu Conference:[18] We want to defeat aggression.

We are not trying to seize power and overturn other governments and try to dominate other peoples. We are trying to defeat aggression in South Vietnam. We are trying to defeat social misery. We are trying to establish a stable democratic government, and we are searching for an honorable and just peace.

I think that we have the forces in motion that are calculated to attempt to get good results in each of those fields. It will take time, but I don't want to put a limit on it.

MAINTENANCE OF FINANCIAL STABILITY

[20.] Q. Mr. President, with respect to the AFL–CIO rejection of your wage guideposts, should organized labor generally disregard them, what steps might the administration take or ask Congress to authorize to curb them?

THE PRESIDENT. I think very generally that organized labor is going to follow a course that is in the national interest. I never have been, as a candidate, willing to predict my own defeat, and I am not going to predict any defeats on the basis of some newspaper stories out of Florida.

I think that this country has the most stable financial policy of any nation in the world. We have been able to maintain stability better than any nation in the world. We have, because we have had the cooperation and the wise leadership of labor as well as business.

Now there will be individual situations. It may be temporarily in the aluminum industry, when the industrial leaders read that their President "is sputtering mad," and it may take a week to clean up a situation like that. But the situation is very generally good in that field now.

The same thing will be true in the labor field where the President reads that someone feels very deeply about the guidelines.

I have seen Mr. Meany[19] and the other leaders of labor several times since the first of the year. I think they understand my problem, and I have an understanding of theirs.

I am hopeful that we can keep our wages in line with our increased productivity and maintain stability, because I know that the first persons to suffer from inflation and high costs of living are the working people that they represent.

I hope that employers and business people will forgo any price increases, just as I have asked labor to forgo any increases above their productivity gains. Now there will be exceptions when neither can do that. Sometimes there may be a justification. Other times the President will not think so. But we are going to hope for the best, and we think we can work it out. And if we can't,

---

[18] See Items 53–56.

[19] George Meany, President of the AFL–CIO.

we will recommend whatever legislation we may think is desirable after consulting with both groups.

FUTHER QUESTIONS ON VIETNAM

[21.] Q. Mr. President, to clear up some confusion, Mr. President——

THE PRESIDENT. Oh, I always want to do that. The first 20 years I was here I did that every time I met with the press. They were always confused and I found out that after I got through explaining it, I was confused.

Q. All right, sir. To clear up some confusion that seems to have arisen the past week or so about the role of the American military in Vietnam, could you, for the record, set the record straight on whether the American troops in Vietnam are fighting to stabilize and maintain a democratic, non-Communist government, or whether their goal is to get some free elections in which the Communists might emerge as part of a coalition government?

THE PRESIDENT. Well, I would refer you to the detailed statements of Secretary Rusk on that, which I think are very clear. If they are not satisfactory, I would refer you to the statements of the Prime Minister [20] at Honolulu. Then if that doesn't satisfy you and doesn't clear it up, I just refer you to the four objectives that we have out there now, which I just stated.

I think that in due time we will prevent aggression, establish a stable government by democratic methods, defeat social misery, and obtain a just and honorable peace. And I think those are objectives that any person in this country can embrace.

Q. Mr. President, while you are in the department of clearing up details, as to the

objectives that you stated we have in Vietnam, do they not preclude both the necessity and the desirability of a declaration of war against anybody?

THE PRESIDENT. I think I explained in the beginning of my press conference today how I felt about a declaration of war, and I think it is very clear how I felt, by my own action.

TAX POLICIES

[22.] Q. What is your reaction to Senator Dirksen's [21] statement earlier this week that a 5 percent tax increase is in the offing?

THE PRESIDENT. I have no information about it. I have said all along that when and if we felt additional taxes were necessary, we would confer with the business and labor communities, the legislative leadership of both parties, and particularly the Chairman of the Ways and Means Committee and Mr. Byrnes, and Senator Long and Senator Williams,[22] and make such proposals.

We have not made any studies or made any recommendations as of this time. I would not want to preclude them. We are very happy at the action the House took on our tax bill. We are very hopeful that with Senator Dirksen's assistance—and he has been very helpful and patriotic and cooperative—we will get action on the tax bill by the deadline I set. Once we get that, then we will have to watch developments.

We don't want to put the brakes on too fast. There are some encouraging signs and some discouraging signs every day. I saw an encouraging one this morning on the

---

[20] Prime Minister Nguyen Cao Ky of South Vietnam.

[21] Senator Everett McKinley Dirksen of Illinois, minority leader of the Senate.

[22] Representative Wilbur D. Mills of Arkansas, Chairman of the House Ways and Means Committee, Representative John W. Byrnes of Wisconsin, member of the committee, and Senator Russell B. Long of Louisiana and Senator John J. Williams of Delaware, members of the Senate Finance Committee.

Consumer Price Index. I see some increases in some prices and some downturns in some prices.

The housing situation fluctuates up and down. We just can't speak with complete, cool authority at this moment on the necessity of tax increases, but we are watching it closely, it will be high on our priority agenda.

SECRETARY OF STATE DEAN RUSK

[23.] Q. Mr. President, there have been reports that there may be a change——

THE PRESIDENT. What reports? I don't want to deny just rumors.

Q. There have been newspaper reports.

THE PRESIDENT. What newspaper?

Q. Several newspapers, including the Washington Post, including the New York Herald Tribune, and others, that Ambassador Goldberg [23] may be replacing Secretary of State Rusk sometime this summer. Would you care to comment on it?

THE PRESIDENT. No. I have not seen those reports. I would not believe that the Washington Post and the New York Herald Tribune would be in the business of either predicting or nominating my Secretary of State. They are usually more constructive than that.

I have said a number of times how I feel about the Secretary of State. When we get in these difficult periods there are always campaigns against individuals that participate in these developments. I remember the campaign that was waged on President Diem [24] for many, many months, and then on the military leadership in Saigon, and then on the CIA and the economic leader-

ship, and then on some of the Cabinet leadership—"Secretary McNamara's War." And Secretary Rusk gets his share of it.

But I think if your friends on the Washington Post and New York Herald Tribune could have observed what happened over there yesterday with almost 300 Members of Congress, when one Congressman said, "Mr. President, I want to tell you that the American Nation is proud of the Secretary of State," there was a spontaneous outburst and every Member in the room stood and applauded, and applauded, and applauded. And we had to stop them so we could go on with our business.

So I have told you how I feel. And I think that is how the country feels about Secretary Rusk.

I would say to any individuals who may have some particular motive in writing these stories or spreading them around that the best way they have to find out about how I feel about the Secretary of State is to ask me, and I will tell them every time what I have already told them and what I repeat to you now: that he sits first in the Cabinet and first with me. I don't think the Post or the Herald Tribune will have much to do with replacing him.

FURTHER QUESTIONS ON VIETNAM

[24.] Q. Mr. President, would you be willing to speculate on the months ahead and the possible need for troop buildup in Vietnam on our part?

THE PRESIDENT. I have said to the American people, last July, that we had substantially over 100,000 troops in Vietnam, and we would be sending others as requested.

Secretary McNamara and the Defense Department have done the greatest job in the history of the Armed Forces in my judgment by moving almost 200,000 men from last

---

[23] Arthur J. Goldberg, U.S. Representative to the United Nations.

[24] Ngo Dinh Diem, former President of South Vietnam.

spring to the end of the year to Vietnam—
and providing housing and food, hospitalization, equipment, and everything for those
men.   Never has an army moved so fast, so
efficiently, so economically.

I have said that as General Westmoreland
made requests, they would be carefully evaluated by our Joint Chiefs and the Secretary
of Defense and the Secretary of State, and be
acted upon promptly.

We do not have on my desk at the moment
any unfilled requests from General Westmoreland.   We have something in excess of
200,000 men in South Vietnam.   A considerable number of those men are support forces.

General Westmoreland will make additional requests, as he told me in Honolulu,
and as the Marine general told me yesterday,
but the numbers of those requests have not
been made known to me.

I have a general impression perhaps between now and summer what will be asked
for, but no one has told me, and I don't want
to predict.   But I would think we would be
able to fulfill those orders without any great
strain on our forces.

And so far as I am concerned, I repeat now

what I said last July, and what I said in New
York the other night: As he makes his requests, they will be considered and they will
be met.

[25.]   Q. Mr. President, did the British
Prime Minister or any of his colleagues carry
the diplomatic game any farther with either
the Soviets or the North Vietnamese in
Moscow?

THE PRESIDENT. The British Prime Minister had a visit of some duration in which
he covered a wide field of subjects.[25]   I have
no doubt but what any Prime Minister in this
day and age would discuss Vietnam at some
length with the people that he visited with.

We have received reports from him, and
we are now in the process of reading them.
I just finished one before I got up this morning, and I want to study it further during
the day.

Reporter: Thank you, Mr. President.

NOTE: President Johnson's fifty-sixth news conference
was held in his office at the White House at 12 noon
on Saturday, February 26, 1966.

---

[25] Harold Wilson, British Prime Minister, visited
the United States in December 1965.

89   Remarks at the Sixth Annual Federal Woman's Award Ceremony.   *February* 28, 1966

WE ARE very pleased to welcome you to the
White House today.   We are proud of you
and we congratulate you.   Your coming
here today serves as a dual reminder to all
of us: first, that American women can hold
their own in every segment of our national
life and, second, less happily, that all too
often we withhold the opportunity for them
to do so.

Today millions of bright, young women
would like to train for professional careers
and we discourage them.   Today millions of

mothers seek gainful employment to provide
a better life for their children and yet we discriminate against them.   Today millions of
women with grown children seek new meaning in their lives through a second career and
then we ignore them.

The Federal Government has sought to
correct this situation, particularly within its
own ranks.   Our policy, since I became President, has been to hire and to promote on
the basis of ability alone.   In that period, the
number of women in jobs paying $10,000 or

more has already increased by 26 percent. Yet despite such advances and similar advances in the private sector of our country, this problem remains largely unsolved.

The underutilization of American women continues to be the most tragic and the most senseless waste of this century. It is a waste that we can no longer afford. Our economy is crying out for their services. In the next decade alone we will need 900,000 additional school teachers and college instructors; 1 million additional specialists in the health services; 800,000 additional science and engineering technicians; 700,000 additional scientists and engineers; and 4½ million additional State and local employees, exclusive of our teachers.

The requirements in these fields alone will be 110,000 additional trained specialists every month for the next 10 years. That requirement cannot be met by men alone. And unless we begin now to open more and more professions to our women and unless we begin now to train our women to enter those professions, then the needs of our Nation just are not going to be met.

Already we are suffering an acute shortage of nurses. This very moment 60,000 additional nurses in our hospitals and clinics and another 5,000 additional nurses are needed in our Armed Forces. To make sure that these needs are met, to help open the doors of opportunity to every American woman, I am today announcing the establishment of a new group on careers for women.

This study group will be made up of women whose qualifications, I think, are very amply established—the recipients of the Federal Woman's Award since its establishment 6 years ago. I expect the members of this study group to probe deeply into the problems of the working woman. I want them to tell us which career fields appear to offer

the greatest promise for our women.

I want them to tell us what our colleges and universities can do to help young women to prepare and to train for these fields. I want them to tell us what we can do to change the attitudes of employers toward hiring women. I want them to seek new ways of making government service attractive to women who have demonstrated ability.

The time has come for the American woman to take her rightful place in American society. We are about to take a major step toward that goal.

I want to apologize to you for being late on account of conditions that I could not control.

I want to congratulate each of you and all of you, particularly you six women who are the forerunners of what I think is a new era: Miss Fannie M. Boyls of the National Labor Relations Board, Miss Stella Davis of the United States Information Agency, Dr. Jocelyn Gill of the National Aeronautics and Space Administration, Dr. Ida C. Merriam of the Social Security Administration, Miss Irene Parsons of the Veterans Administration, and Dr. Ruth Van Cleve of the Department of Interior.

You ladies honor your sex and your Government and your professions by your accomplishments. You have risen to the top of your chosen fields in law, in the sciences, in economics, in the foreign service, and in administration. I am confident that you will put your experience and your leadership to good use on behalf of all the women of America and I believe that all the women of America will be encouraged by the example that you have set and by the ability that you have demonstrated.

Thank you very much.

NOTE: The President spoke at 12:30 p.m. in the Theater at the White House.

The recipients of the Federal Woman's Award were Fannie M. Boyls, Hearing Examiner (Violations-Labor), National Labor Relations Board, cited "for her outstanding competence in conducting hearings for the National Labor Relations Board involving difficult and complex questions of law and the resolution of disputed factual issues"; Stella E. Davis, Desk Officer for East and South Africa, United States Information Agency, cited "for her exceptional achievements in promoting United States relations in East and South Africa"; Dr. Jocelyn R. Gill, Program Chief, In-Flight Sciences, Manned Space Science Programs, National Aeronautics and Space Administration, cited "for her outstanding leadership in planning and coordinating activities of NASA engineers, scientists, and astronauts, to prove man's ability as a scientific investigator in outer space"; Dr. Ida C. Merriam, Assistant Commissioner for Research and Statistics, Social Security Administration, Department of Health, Education, and Welfare, cited "for her distinguished contributions to the evolution and development of social security in the United States"; Irene Parsons, Assistant Administrator for Personnel, Veterans Administration, cited "for her unique record of achievement in directing personnel management for the Government's third largest agency—the Veterans Administration, with 170,000 employees"; and Dr. Ruth G. Van Cleve, Director, Office of Territories, Department of the Interior, cited "for her distinguished career as an attorney and administrator devoted to the problems and welfare of United States territories."

90   Letter to the President of the Senate and to the Speaker of the House Proposing Establishment of a National Visitor Center in the Nation's Capital. *February 28, 1966*

Dear Mr. President: (Dear Mr. Speaker:)

Visitors to the Nation's Capital are increasing every year. In 1960, their number was estimated to be 15.4 million, and this number is expected to rise to 24 million in 1970 and to 35 million in 1980. They come from every State in the Union, and increasingly from foreign countries as well. They come to learn as well as to see.

While not all of these millions come to Washington as tourists, the need for better facilities for visitors has long been a matter of concern. Student visitors in particular are coming in constantly greater numbers and should be helped to make their visits more rewarding—more instructive in our history, in the manner our government operates, in the development of our democratic institutions. The unique educational opportunity which Washington should afford to American and foreign visitors alike is largely lost without perspective on the historic, political and symbolic significance of the places and institutions to be visited.

This is particularly a Federal concern. The prime attraction of Washington is the presence here of the Federal Government. Here one can observe its immediate, day-to-day workings, can visit its buildings and shrines, and can examine the records of its past. As a nation we are properly interested in fostering, through visitors to our National Capital, a better appreciation of our democracy. We can be justly proud of what Washington offers to those who come here, and we should see to it that our visitors are not disappointed or disillusioned by inadequate facilities for their help.

To meet this need I am transmitting, for the consideration of the Congress, the attached bill to authorize the Secretary of the Interior to establish a National Visitor Center in the District of Columbia.

Under this proposed bill, the Secretary is authorized to establish a Center which will provide through exhibits, films, lectures and displays an orientation in the history and operation of the Federal Government, as well as information on the Nation and its Capital. The bill also authorizes him to make arrangements with the individual States to have their own exhibits, and to provide help and encouragement for foreign visitors in particular in visiting other parts of the United States.

The Secretary will also be authorized to arrange at the Center, through concessions and otherwise, for the kinds of assistance to visitors which should add to their comfort and convenience and make their visit more enjoyable and rewarding. He can give special assistance to student groups and foreign visitors. He can provide necessary auxiliary services, such as parking, shuttle buses, and subsidiary information centers.

An Advisory Committee would be established to assist the Secretary in designing and administering the program. The Secretary of the Smithsonian Institution is included on the Advisory Committee in furtherance of the objective of taking full advantage of the resources of the Smithsonian Institution, which will be of great value in carrying out the activities of the Center.

It may not be necessary to construct a new building to house a Visitor Center if a suitable existing facility can be obtained. The bill is flexible in permitting the Secretary to explore a wide range of alternatives, including the feasibility of adapting the Pension Building to this use, or acquiring Union Station and preserving it as a landmark, with appropriate improvements. The bill does not foreclose any specific course of action, but will make it possible to move ahead toward accomplishing our basic objective.

I hope that the Congress will give early and favorable consideration to this legislation.

Sincerely,

Lyndon B. Johnson

NOTE: This is the text of identical letters addressed to the Honorable Hubert H. Humphrey, President of the Senate, and to the Honorable John W. McCormack, Speaker of the House of Representatives.

The text of the draft bill transmitted by the President is printed in House Document 389 (89th Cong., 2d sess.).

Legislation to establish a Visitor Center in Washington was not enacted by the 89th Congress.

91   Special Message to the Congress Transmitting Reorganization Plan 2 of 1966: Water Pollution Control. *February 28, 1966*

To the Congress of the United States:

I transmit herewith Reorganization Plan No. 2 of 1966, prepared in accordance with the provisions of the Reorganization Act of 1949, as amended, and providing for reorganization of certain water pollution control functions.

Thirty-five years ago Justice Oliver Wendell Holmes said: "a river is more than an amenity, it is a treasure."

Only recently has the truth of this observation entered the public conscience. For we now recognize that the Nation's rivers, far from being treasured, have been carelessly neglected for too long.

Today we face a harsh reality. Our waters are burdened with blight. We know that every river system in America suffers from some degree of pollution. This menace is growing more serious with every passing day.

We have just begun to take the steps to clean and restore our waters.

The task is immense. The journey will be long.

If our new programs are to succeed we must combine our efforts—Federal, state, local and private—in new and creative partnerships.

The attack against water pollution should

be unified and coordinated.

It should be carried forward as an integral part of comprehensive planning for the development of river basins.

But most importantly, the Government's management structure must be strengthened and reshaped to meet the challenges that lie ahead.

In my February 23 Message on the Quality of Our Environment I stated:

". . . we must reorganize the Federal effort. In the past, the Federal anti-pollution effort has been organizationally separate from water conservation and use programs.

"One agency should assume leadership in our clean water effort.

"That agency should be the Department of the Interior."

The Department of the Interior, for many years, has been concerned with the comprehensive management and development of the Nation's water resources.

It plans, constructs, and operates multiple-purpose water and related land resources projects.

It carries on research and development on the removal of minerals from water.

It administers the Water Resources Research Act.

The Secretary of the Interior also serves as Chairman of the Water Resources Council responsible for coordinating river basin planning. Under the Clean Rivers Restoration Act of 1966 and other legislation which I have recently proposed, the Secretary will become the focal point for Federal efforts in this area.

It is wise management to place under his control the related resources and authority now in the Department of Health, Education, and Welfare.

The reorganization plan maintains a proper and effective role for the Department of Health, Education, and Welfare with re-

spect to the health aspects of pollution. At the same time it places in the Department of the Interior all of the necessary tools to move forward the drive to clean America's waters.

The reorganization plan herewith transmitted will transfer to the Secretary of the Interior the functions of the Department of Health, Education, and Welfare under the Federal Water Pollution Control Act except for responsibilities relating to public health for which the Department of Health, Education, and Welfare has special competence. That Department will retain responsibility under section 3(b) of the Act for advising on public health questions involved in determinations by Federal agencies of the need for and value of the inclusion of storage for water quality control in Federal reservoirs. The Federal Water Pollution Control Administration would be transferred to the Department of the Interior.

The Secretary of the Interior in administering the Act will also be required to consult with the Secretary of Health, Education, and Welfare on public health aspects relating to water pollution. This consultative responsibility is now vested in the Surgeon General by section 2(k) of the Water Quality Act of 1965. The plan transfers that responsibility to the Secretary of Health, Education, and Welfare.

The Water Pollution Control Advisory Board and the hearing boards provided for in the Act would be transferred to the Department of the Interior, together with their respective functions. The reorganization plan also makes the Secretary of Health, Education, and Welfare a member of the Advisory Board and gives him the opportunity to select a member of each hearing board.

The reorganization plan would in no way impair the rights and benefits of commissioned officers of the Public Health Service who may transfer to the Water Pollution Control Administration.

The reorganization to be accomplished by the plan transmitted herewith will enable the Federal Government to organize for action against pollution on a river basin basis under the unified leadership of the Secretary of the Interior.

After investigation, I have found and hereby declare that each reorganization included in the accompanying reorganization plan is necessary to accomplish one or more of the purposes set forth in section 2(a) of the Reorganization Act of 1949, as amended. I have also found and hereby declare that it is necessary to include in the accompanying reorganization plan, by reason of the reorganizations made thereby, provision for the membership of the Secretary of Health, Education, and Welfare on the Water Pollution Control Advisory Board and for the appointment and compensation of an additional Assistant Secretary of the Interior. The rate of compensation fixed for that officer is that which I have found to prevail in respect of comparable officers in the executive branch of the Government.

The reorganizations provided for in the reorganization plan transmitted herewith will produce significant long-range savings and economies by reason of the efficiencies in organization and in the elimination of duplication of effort it will bring about. It is, however, impracticable to specify or itemize at this time the reductions of expenditures which it is probable will be brought about by the taking effect of the reorganizations included in the reorganization plan.

I recommend that the Congress allow the accompanying plan to become effective.

LYNDON B. JOHNSON

The White House
February 28, 1966

NOTE: Reorganization Plan 2 of 1966 is printed in the Weekly Compilation of Presidential Documents (vol. 2, p. 289), the Federal Register (31 F.R. 6857), and Title 3 of the Code of Federal Regulations (3 CFR, 1966 Comp., p. 188). It became effective on May 10, 1966.

92   Remarks Recorded for the Opening of the 1966 Red Cross Campaign. *February* 28, 1966

AT THIS very minute, somewhere in Vietnam, the American Red Cross is saving a soldier's life—feeding a starving child—sheltering a refugee family.

At this very minute, somewhere in America, our Red Cross is helping with a personal tragedy—easing a community crisis—tackling and solving the problems and emergencies of life.

At this minute, in these difficult hours, I am deeply grateful for the Red Cross. We should all be grateful—and very proud.

We should all remember Hurricane Betsy —and how the Red Cross rescued thousands from the brink of that disaster. We should all remember the nurses, doctors, and countless volunteers who stand watch around the clock in hospitals, tents, shelters—wherever there is human need or suffering—here and in Vietnam this very minute.

We should remember and give thanks—by giving our personal support to Red Cross Month. The Red Cross needs volunteers and funds. No dollar sign can measure the priceless service they provide. I ask every American to give—and generously—to the Red Cross.

The Red Cross has never failed us. We cannot fail it now. We owe it the goodness of our hearts and the labors of our hands.

I know we shall offer a full measure of both volunteers and funds.

NOTE: On February 24 the President signed Proclamation 3705 designating the month of March as Red Cross Month, 1966 (2 Weekly Comp. Pres. Docs., p. 262; 31 F.R. 3221; 3 CFR, 1966 Comp., p. 28).

On the same day the White House made public a memorandum from the President to the heads of executive departments and agencies urging support of the 1966 campaign by civilian employees of the Government and by members of the Armed Forces (2 Weekly Comp. Pres. Docs., p. 263).

93 Remarks on the Fifth Anniversary of the Peace Corps at the Swearing In of Jack Hood Vaughn as Director. *March 1, 1966*

Mr. Vice President, Mr. Secretary of State, Your Excellencies, the Ambassadors and representatives of the 46 countries where the Peace Corps is today operating, returned Peace Corps volunteers, members of the Peace Corps National Advisory Council, the first Peace Corps Director and the new Director, Members of Congress, all other members of our Government, all other members of the Peace Corps, ladies and gentlemen:

Happy birthday.

All of you have earned that greeting. Every person here, and many more who could not be here, helped to turn the Peace Corps from an intriguing idea into an inspired operation. You acted on faith—

—faith in the power of men and women to always translate their convictions into action;

—faith in the ability of our society to trust its citizens when they choose to be different;

—faith in the desire of other nations to welcome with patience and good will those who come to them offering not money or goods, but only themselves.

It was an act of faith on the part of that great President who established the Peace Corps by Executive order 5 years ago today. And it was faith on the part of the Congress of the United States that voted by increasingly overwhelming majorities to support this wonderful activity.

All of that faith, I think, has been vindicated. The constructive work of more than 20,000 people over 5 long years—the collaboration of the peoples with whom they have lived—is a real testament to the trust upon which the Peace Corps was founded.

In a world of violence, these volunteers have shown that there is really another way—the way of private dedication, the way of quiet courage working unheralded for ends that each has accepted as valuable and as vital.

In this way those of you in the Peace Corps have carried forward the real revolution of our day and time, the revolution of peaceful change. In this way you are really waging the only war that we in America want to wage—the war against the inhumanity of man to his neighbor and the injustice of nature to her children.

In Vietnam today there is another war. It is fueled by those who believe that they somehow might be able to accomplish their ends by means of terror and violence.

America's purpose there is to give peaceful change a real chance to succeed. In that struggle, soldiers are necessary not only to prevent but to halt aggression, and to provide security for those who are determined to protect themselves and to raise their families. So, too, are the other workers of peace necessary who must lay the foundation for economic and social progress in that land. Political freedom, no matter how dearly bought, can flourish only when men and women are free from want and free from despair.

We have already begun that important work in Vietnam. The day, I hope, will soon come when the Peace Corps will be there, too. It must somehow find the day and the time that it can go and make its contribution when peace is assured. The same spirit that the Peace Corps volunteers brought to thousands of villages and cities in 46 countries should be carried to the hamlets of Vietnam.

Yesterday, at the University of Michigan, your new Director, Mr. Vaughn, said, "All of the energy, the faith, the devotion which we in the Peace Corps bring to our service serves a single cause." I can only say, then, that no group, no organization, contributes more to the cause of peace, in my judgment, than the Peace Corps which we honor here today. You are fortunate. You are equipped with an idea whose time has really come.

It has come in Vietnam. We are there in order to restore peace and in order to let the works of peace serve the life of man.

So to the people of that land—North and South—we acknowledge that there are great differences between our people and our nations. But these gulfs of culture and tradition are spanned by a common humanity and shared needs of man—of food and shelter and education, a decent life for each family, the chance to build and to work and to till the soil free from fear and the arbitrary horrors of battle—and to walk in the dignity of those who have chosen their own destiny.

It is more than a shame; it is a crime—perhaps the greatest crime of man—that so much courage, and so much will, and so many dreams must be carelessly flung on the fires of death and war.

The long history of this conflict is filled with misunderstandings and invectives and passions. I think the time has come to strike off the chains of the past so that we may be free to shape anew the future. We should not permit endless and unrewarding argument over what has already happened to bar us from accomplishing what should happen.

Peace is within our grasp, if we will both reach for it together, and beyond peace are the wondrous gifts of peace, and beyond that a time when hope can reach unbounded for consummation.

There may be those who do not want peace, those whose ambitions stretch so far that war in Vietnam is but a welcome and a convenient episode in an immense and doomed design to subdue history to their will. But let them not suppose that our desire for peace springs either from weakness or from hesitation. Our desire for peace springs, rather, from a further recognition of our knowledge that the search for peace also always requires great skill and great courage.

If there are others, however, who do want peace, and if it is equally true that total victory is beyond expectation for them, as they must now know that it really is, then we think there is only one answer: Negotiate peace and let war stand aside while the people of Vietnam make their choice. For our part, here in America, we are eagerly willing to abide by the outcome.

We sincerely desire neither territory nor bases in Vietnam, neither economic domination nor military alliance. We fight for the principle that the people of South Vietnam should be able to choose their own course, free from the coercions of violence and terror and fear. We believe that the people of South Vietnam, through the process of elections, can select their own leaders and their own way of life.

That is the example we have set. That is the procedure we follow in our own land, and all the people of Vietnam can then freely express their will on the great questions of unification and national destiny.

Now, ladies and gentlemen, that is what your country wants for the people of South Vietnam. That is what the people of South Vietnam, we think, want. So together we seek the day when we can be as generous in peace as we must be determined in battle. We are ready when that day comes, ready to join in a massive effort of reconstruction and development that is open to all, including North Vietnam.

The Asian Bank, which we suggested in our speech in Baltimore, is only a beginning of what can be done when aggression ends and when men decide that peace and not war should be the testing ground of human experience. That measure has already passed the House and been reported in the Senate Foreign Relations Committee unanimously, and we hope it can be acted upon this week. It will be a great step forward.

The Peace Corps has already shown us what it can do. For the Peace Corps is a movement; it is a movement to place the vessel of peace in the hands of individual men and women who are driven by their own conscience to do something about healing this wounded world in which we live.

The man who, more than any other man, gave fire and gave purpose to your movement is stepping aside today on the fifth anniversary of the day that that movement began.

Is there any doubt of the enormous bequest that he is leaving?

For generations to come, as the harvests of his efforts are reaped time and time again, men will marvel at his contributions.

Of Sargent Shriver, it can be said that he is a man to whom excellence and public service are synonymous, one of those rare men of whom Virgil spoke when he said, "They can because they think they can."

Five years ago only a few thought he could.

There were moments, I am sure, at least from some of the cables I received from him when he was out in other parts of the world, when he, himself, doubted that he could. But he did.

He was, of course, inspired, so inspired that he ran off rather rudely, I thought, with one of my assistants back in 1961. In the last few months I have tried to pay him back. I have run off with several of his.

One of them is here today to succeed him. Jack Vaughn I first met out in a little fishing village in Africa, but he, like Sargent Shriver, I observed on that first meeting, is a disciple of peace. His life has been spent in the service of the cause of peace. This is the third job that I have asked Jack Vaughn to take since I met him in that fishing village in 1961. Each of these jobs he has served with great distinction.

This is going to be the last time, though, that I make a request for him to take another job, because, frankly, I am tired of attending his swearing-in ceremonies!

Jack, I think you know that you are stepping into the shoes of a man who has done more for his country than his country really knows. His hands are going to be full with poverty and yours are going to be full with peace, and I hope that all of us will be the better for the work that both of you do.

In you two men I have the greatest confidence, and I have no doubt but what you will prove worthy of it.

Thank you very much.

NOTE: The President spoke at 11:20 a.m. in the East Room at the White House. In his opening words he referred to Vice President Hubert H. Humphrey who administered the oath of office, Secretary of State Dean Rusk, and R. Sargent Shriver, Director of the Office of Economic Opportunity and outgoing Director of the Peace Corps.

During his remarks the President referred to Executive Order 10924, entitled "Establishment and Administration of the Peace Corps in the Department of State," which was signed by President John F. Kennedy on March 1, 1961 (3 CFR, 1959–1963 Comp., p. 447).

The Asian Development Bank Act was approved by the President on March 16, 1966 (see Item 133).

For the President's address at Johns Hopkins University in Baltimore on April 7, 1965, see 1965 volume, this series, Book I, Item 172.

94 Message to the Congress Transmitting Annual Report on U.S. Participation in the United Nations. *March 1, 1966*

To the Congress of the United States:

Pursuant to the provisions of the United Nations Participation Act, I submit herewith the nineteenth annual report covering United States participation in the United Nations during 1964.

This report, like its predecessors, describes the activities of the United Nations agencies and programs that together carry out the aims of the Charter: to maintain peace and security, to adjust and settle international disputes, to cooperate in economic and social development, and to promote the self-determination of peoples and worldwide respect for human rights. It also covers legal, administrative, and financial matters at the United Nations.

The activities covered in this report document the commitment of this Nation to the purposes and programs of the United Nations—a commitment demonstrated by the extent and character of our participation in and financial support for a broad range of United Nations activities over the past twenty years.

During 1964 the constitutional-financial crisis in the General Assembly tended to overshadow in the public mind all other affairs at the United Nations. The Assembly was limited to those minor actions which

could be taken by unanimous consent without a vote. It is regrettable that a major organ of the United Nations could not function normally. However, the other elements of the United Nations system carried forward.

The Security Council in 1964 had one of its busiest years; it held over 100 meetings and dealt with some of the most intractable problems of peace and security.

—It successfully organized the difficult peacekeeping operation in Cyprus, averting the threat of a direct military confrontation between two of our NATO allies, Greece and Turkey.

—It aired the Kashmir dispute, the Malaysian charges against Indonesia, and the question of *apartheid* in South Africa.

—It sent a factfinding group to report on the border situation between Cambodia and South Viet-Nam.

—It requested the Secretary-General to help the United Kingdom and Yemen resolve their differences over the Yemen-Aden border.

—It provided a forum for the United States to explain the action it had taken to counter the attacks by Hanoi against United States naval vessels in the international waters of the Gulf of Tonkin. In this connection, regrettably, Hanoi was unwilling to admit that the United Nations had any competence in the conflict in Viet-Nam. Despite the fact that Hanoi and Peking rejected United Nations involvement, given its responsibility for international peace and security, the United Nations should clearly be concerned about the conflict in Viet-Nam. It was with this thought in mind that in San Francisco on June 25, 1965, at the celebration of the twentieth anniversary of the United Nations, I urged United Nations members, individually and collectively, to use their influence to bring to the negotiating table all governments involved in an attempt to halt all aggression and evolve a peaceful solution. I also wrote the Secretary-General the following month saying how much I appreciated his efforts to remove the Viet-Nam dispute from the battlefield to the negotiating table and expressed the hope they would be continued. The Secretary-General replied by expressing his determination to pursue such efforts by all means at his disposal.

Elsewhere in the world during 1964 the United Nations continued to maintain several active peacekeeping operations. United Nations peacekeepers continued to police the Sinai and Gaza lines. The United Nations also supervised the borders between Israel and its Arab neighbors, and the truce line in Kashmir between India and Pakistan.

During 1964 the United Nations ended its military (but not its civilian) operation in the Congo and its observer mission in Yemen.

On the economic front, the United Nations Conference on Trade and Development (UNCTAD) during the summer of 1964 was unquestionably the most significant development of the year. It opened a search by the developing nations for trading and financial arrangements designed to accelerate their development. Machinery was established to carry on the dialogue within the United Nations among developed and less developed countries concering international trade and related questions of development. A hopeful sign was the adoption by UNCTAD of a system of mutual adjustment and conciliation designed to achieve a meeting of minds before arriving at decisions on important matters.

The record of operations of United Nations Specialized Agencies in the economic and social fields was impressive.

—The World Bank and its affiliates—the International Development Association and the International Finance Corporation—made loans, credits, and investments totaling over $1 billion.

—The World Health Organization spurred important advances in the worldwide campaigns to eradicate malaria and smallpox and in the field of epidemiology.

—The World Meteorological Organization moved ahead toward a projected World Weather Watch—a worldwide cooperative venture to improve man's ability to predict the course of the weather.

—The Food and Agriculture Organization dispatched about 1,000 technical experts to member countries to assist in agricultural productivity, pest control, animal health, and rural community development.

As science and technology develop, there will be new opportunities for international cooperation and common undertakings to serve mankind. On October 2, 1964, I proclaimed 1965 International Cooperation Year

(ICY) in the United States. To implement our national program for ICY, on November 24, 1964, I named a Cabinet Committee for International Cooperation Year (1965) and called on our national citizens' organizations to help find new areas for common endeavor against the ancient enemies of mankind—ignorance, poverty, and disease. Every such enterprise helps in some small way to strengthen the fabric of peace. As I said at that time—the quest for peace through cooperation is the "assignment of the century."

In transmitting this report, I should like to add a more general observation about our policy toward the United Nations. Every President since the founding of the United Nations has expressed the deep commitment of this Nation to the purposes of the Organization. This commitment has been expressed in our dedication to the purposes of the Charter and in our participation in the entire range of United Nations operations described in this report.

I reaffirmed our dedication on the occasion of the twentieth anniversary of the United Nations at San Francisco on June 25, 1965, when I said:

". . . I come to this anniversary not to speak of futility or failure nor of doubt and despair. I come to raise a voice of confidence in both the future of these United Nations and the fate of the human race.

  •   •   •   •   •

"And let all remember—and none forget—

that now more than 50 times in these 20 years the United Nations has acted to keep the peace.

"By persuading nations to justify their own conduct before all countries, it has helped, at many times and in many places, to soften the harshness of man to his fellow man.

"By confronting the rich with the misery of the poor and the privileged with the despair of the oppressed, it has removed the excuse of ignorance, unmasked the evil of indifference, and has placed an insistent, even though still unfulfilled, responsibility upon the more fortunate of the earth.

"By insisting upon the political dignity of man, it has welcomed 63 nations to take their places alongside the 51 original members—a historical development of dramatic import, achieved mainly through peaceful means.

"And by binding countries together in the great declarations of the Charter, it has given those principles a strengthened vitality in the conduct of the affairs of man."

The record of our participation in the United Nations for 1964—set forth in this report—documents the deeds that support these words.

LYNDON B. JOHNSON

The White House
March 1, 1966

NOTE: The 19th annual report is entitled "U.S. Participation in the UN, Report by the President to the Congress for the Year 1964" (Government Printing Office, 1966, 353 pp.).

95   Special Message to the Congress on Domestic Health and Education. *March 1, 1966*

To the Congress of the United States:

A nation's greatness is measured by its concern for the health and welfare of its people. Throughout the history of our democracy, this commitment has grown and deepened.

The education of our people is a national investment. The health of our people is essential to the pursuit of happiness.

Today we can set ambitious goals for the future:

—full education for every citizen to the limits of his capacity to absorb it;

—good health for every citizen to the limits of our country's capacity to provide it.

The 88th and 89th Congresses have moved toward these goals. During the past three sessions, Congress has:

—enacted 20 landmark measures in health and 19 in education;

—doubled the appropriations for health programs and increased the budget for our Office of Education more than fivefold.

The achievements of the past three years promise a dramatic enrichment of American life. They already include in the field of health:

1. The Medicare program which, on July 1, will make benefits available to more than 19 million older Americans.

2. Health services for more than 200,000 migrant workers in 34 states.

3. Maternal and infant care for mothers and children previously receiving inadequate services.

4. Expanded services for crippled children.

5. Thirty-two new clinics for retarded children.

6. Construction assistance for 1300 hospital and health facilities to add more than 56,000 new hospital beds.

7. Financial support for more than 16,000 medical research projects and advanced training for 25,000 scientists.

8. Construction starts for 62 institutions to enroll more than 2400 additional students each year for training in the health professions.

Our achievements in education are equally impressive. Among them are:

1. Funds to improve educational opportunities for nearly 7.5 million underprivileged children in 20,000 school districts.

2. Summer head start programs for 560,000 preschool children in 13,350 community education projects and year-round programs for 120,000 children.

3. Textbooks and other learning materials for more than 40 million children in every state.

4. College work study programs for more than 110,000 needy college students.

5. Construction aid for 1300 institutions of higher learning—including new classrooms, laboratories and libraries.

6. 12 million books to improve public libraries and training programs for more than 400 librarians.

Health

With these programs and those I am recommending today, we can move closer to attainment of our goals:

—to bring every child the care he needs to develop his capacity to the fullest.

—to reduce infant mortality, concentrating particularly on those minority groups whose death rate is highest.

—to eradicate major communicable diseases as a threat to life and health in the United States.

—to reduce the burden of mental illness, and mental retardation.

—to cut the toll of the three great killers—heart disease, cancer and stroke.

The health budget which I have proposed for fiscal year 1967 is $4.67 billion—an increase of almost one billion dollars. In addition more than $3 billion in social security trust funds will be spent under Medicare to assist our older citizens.

Funds for health manpower, facilities and services are up $707 million. Funds for environmental activities and consumer protection are up $158 million. Funds for health research activities are up $78 million.

To insure continuing progress, we must:
—improve the administration of federal health activities.
—develop comprehensive health planning and services on the state and community level.
—strengthen our system of health care.
—train needed health workers.
—increase our research efforts.
—take additional steps to meet special health problems.

I. TO IMPROVE ADMINISTRATION OF FEDERAL HEALTH SERVICES

Our first concern must be the efficient and effective administration of the federal health programs.

Over the last 12 years the budget of the Public Health Service for research, training and services has grown almost tenfold—from $250 million to $2.4 billion. Yet major elements of the basic structure of the Public Health Service remain set by a law that is more than 20 years old.

The Secretary of Health, Education, and Welfare and the Surgeon General of the United States have consulted leading experts—physicians, administrators, scientists and public health specialists—in a thorough search for the best means to improve the administration of federal health programs. They all agree that the need to modernize the administration of the Public Health Service is urgent.

To fulfill that need, I will shortly submit to Congress a proposed reorganization of the health functions of the Department of Health, Education, and Welfare.

The ultimate success of federal health programs depends on the men and women who direct them. At present, the personnel system of the Public Health Service is inadequate to recruit and retain the talent needed for its rapidly changing and expanding role.

I will recommend legislation to improve the personnel system of the Public Health Service.

This legislation will:
—promote career development,
—encourage more flexible use of health workers,
—provide them with broader opportunities,
—stimulate higher standards of performance.

II. TO DEVELOP COMPREHENSIVE HEALTH PLANNING AND SERVICES ON THE STATE AND COMMUNITY LEVEL

The focus of our efforts is the individual and his family, living in their own community. To meet their health needs requires the cooperation of many agencies, institutions and experts—of state and local governments, of doctors, nurses and paramedical personnel.

These are the front line fighters in our battle against disease, disability and death. As in military battle, a winning strategy demands wise and well planned use of manpower. It demands coordinated use of all the resources available.

I recommend to Congress a program of grants to enable states and communities to plan the better use of manpower, facilities, and financial resources for comprehensive health services.

At present, the federal government offers the states formula grants for categorical programs dealing with specific diseases. This leads to an unnecessarily rigid and compartmentalized approach to health problems.

Our purpose must be to help redirect and reform fragmented programs which encourage inefficiency and confusion and fail to meet the total health needs of our citizens.

I recommend a program to initiate new state formula grants for comprehensive public health services. This program would begin in fiscal 1968.

At the same time, we must recognize that special health problems occur in some parts of our nation and not in others. Certain diseases, such as tuberculosis and venereal disease, are concentrated in metropolitan communities. Others, such as rabies and parasitic diseases, are prevalent in certain geographic areas.

Resources to serve health needs are not evenly distributed throughout the nation. Special problems arise in remote rural areas and in the city slums. We need greater flexibility to pinpoint our attack.

To make certain we have that flexibility, I recommend a program, to commence in fiscal 1968, of grants to states, communities, medical schools and hospitals to meet special health problems.

III. TO STRENGTHEN OUR SYSTEM OF HEALTH CARE

The Hill-Burton program for hospital construction is an outstanding example of creative federalism in action. Now in its nineteenth year, this federal-state-local partnership has added more than 300,000 hospital and nursing home beds to our nation and more than 2,000 other health facilities in areas of great need.

My budget requests the full authorization of $270 million for facilities construction under the Hill-Burton Act.

Medical advances demand new equipment and up-to-date laboratories. Intensive care units, as well as ambulatory and extended care facilities, require changes in the structure and function of aging hospitals, particularly in urban areas.

General hospitals containing 260,000 beds—one third of our nation's—are now in obsolete condition.

When Medicare becomes operative this July, the pressure on many hospitals will grow even more intense.

To begin to meet this urgent need, I recommend legislation to mobilize public and private resources to revitalize our obsolete hospitals. This will require a loan and grant program to assist in the long-term financing of hospital renewal projects.

The need for modernization goes beyond the bricks and mortar of construction. We must find new ways to lower the cost and raise the quality of health care, to organize health services more efficiently, to develop information systems. It will take the combined efforts of university, hospital, industry, group practice clinics and many other organizations.

I am directing the Secretary of Health, Education, and Welfare to conduct systems analyses and other studies to determine the most effective means of bringing high quality medical services to all the people at the lowest cost.

I also propose a five-year program of grants for research and demonstration projects in the organization, financing, utilization and delivery of health services.

As medical practice becomes more complex, specialization becomes more common. The number of general practitioners is declining—66,000 today compared to 95,000 fifteen years ago. In 1950, there was one family physician for every 1600 Americans. Today 2900 Americans must depend on one family doctor.

Group practice benefits both physicians and patients. It makes expert health care more accessible for the patient. It enables the physician to draw on the combined talents of his colleagues.

High initial capital requirements and a shortage of long-term financing have restricted the development of this form of medical and dental practice.

I recommend that the Congress consider legislation now pending making mortgage insurance available for group practice facilities.

The first session of this Congress has liberated our citizens from the haunting fear of an inability to meet the cost of medical care in their later years. This landmark legislation assures that community hospitals, physicians and others who provide for their health will be paid the reasonable cost and customary charges for such services. I propose that this same principle be extended to the care of patients in our own Federal hospitals and I recommend legislation to permit the reimbursement of these hospitals in the same manner.

IV. TO TRAIN NEEDED HEALTH WORKERS

Trained men and women continue to be in critically short supply in the field of health. Congress has already acted to help meet that need by enacting:
—The Health Professions Educational Assistance Act to provide assistance to both schools and students.
—The Nurse Training Act to provide federal aid to increase the supply of professional nurses.
—The Vocational Education Act to provide for training of practical nurses and other health workers.

But critical specialties remain dangerously under-staffed—medical technologists, biomedical engineers, dental hygienists and other college-trained health workers.

These personnel, allied with doctors, dentists, and nurses, constitute the modern health care team.

They extend the reach and the scope of the physician.

I recommend a three-year program to provide grants for training in allied health professions:
—to construct and to improve needed educational facilities.
—to offer fellowships for students in advanced training.
—to stimulate institutions to develop new types of health personnel.

Last year, in the Higher Education Act of 1965, Congress enlisted the resources of our private banking community to make low-interest student loans. By this means, greatly increased financial assistance can be provided at minimal cost.

I recommend legislation to convert the Health Professions Student Loan program to privately financed and federally subsidized loans for students in the health professions.

V. TO ADVANCE RESEARCH

Over the past ten years, Congress has increased the budget for health research thirteen-fold. The dividends from this investment are incalculable. Miraculous progress in medical discovery is making possible:
—development of support devices for the failing heart—and even replacement of a human heart by an artificial organ.
—advances toward the cure of cancers such as childhood leukemia and Hodgkin's disease.
—development of a less expensive and more efficient treatment for kidney failure.
—isolation of viruses causing respiratory infections and production of vaccines to immunize against them.

241

My fiscal 1967 budget provides increased funds for health research. If research makes major new breakthroughs in life-saving discoveries, I will submit requests for necessary additional funds. My overall budget provides for this contingency.

VI. TO MEET SPECIAL HEALTH PROBLEMS

1. *Mental Retardation*

We have begun to ease the tragic burden of the mentally retarded and their families. By construction of research and service facilities, and by support of state programs, the federal government helps combat this dread handicap.

We shall continue our increasing attack on this problem. It deserves the concern and attention of our most able specialists. Therefore, I intend to appoint a Committee on Mental Retardation to assess our progress, to seek out new and better ways to cope with this terrible disability, and to recommend a long-range and comprehensive plan of action.

2. *Nutrition for the Needy*

It is hard to teach a hungry child. This fact, known to parents and teachers alike, underlies the school lunch program throughout the nation.

This year 18 million school children will enjoy lunches prepared and served in their schools under this program. Yet too many children still fail to get a good lunch even though the cost is low. Some cannot afford the 25 to 35 cent lunch charge. Others in low income districts go to schools which lack lunch facilities.

Demonstration programs conducted in poverty areas in Colorado and North Carolina provided lunches this year at sharply reduced rates. The results were amazing.

Virtually all the children purchased the school lunch—less than one-third had done so before. The children were more alert and interested in learning. The absentee rate fell by as much as 37%. School drop-outs were reduced.

Too little of the federal assistance in the school lunch program has been directed toward children who need it most. Too much of our subsidy, particularly in the Special Milk program, goes to children who already get a federally supported school lunch, including milk, and whose parents can afford to pay for additional milk.

I am submitting to the Congress the *Child Nutrition Act of 1966* to redirect our efforts to provide food to those who need it most. The Act will:

—Extend the school lunch program to more needy children and give greater flexibility in providing low cost or no cost meals.

—Assist schools serving low-income districts to acquire kitchen and lunchroom facilities.

—Provide pilot school breakfast programs for those children who start the day hungry.

—Direct the Special Milk Program to those schools without food service, to schools serving children from low-income families, and to needy school children at whatever school they attend.

—Start demonstration summer programs to provide food service for needy children at child-care centers and playgrounds.

—Help state educational agencies strengthen their staffs to improve child nutrition programs.

I am requesting $50 million from the Congress for programs designed to provide adequate nutrition for disadvantaged children. This money is an addition to the $329 million in cash and commodities already included in the budget for school nutrition programs. The total federal program of $379 million is a major redirection of our child nutrition efforts to children who otherwise would grow up hungry, suffer the diseases that come from being ill-nourished, and lack the energy so essential to learning.

No child in an affluent America should be without an adequate diet. The new program will move us far toward that goal. But it will not do the job alone.

I am directing the Secretary of Health, Education, and Welfare, in cooperation with the Secretary of Agriculture and the Director of the Office of Economic Opportunity, to examine means by which the benefits of sound nutrition can be extended to every child who needs our help.

We now know that among elderly Americans, a poor diet is a root cause of poor health. It adds to the burden of our hospitals and health manpower. It contributes unnecessary misery to the burdens of old age.

I have directed the Secretary of Health, Education, and Welfare to initiate a special food service program at multi-purpose centers authorized by the Older Americans Act of 1965. Local organizations will be able to offer balanced, nutritous meals to the elderly—without charge or at reduced prices to those who are in need.

3. *Alcoholism*

The alcoholic suffers from a disease which will yield eventually to scientific research and adequate treatment. Even with the present limited state of our knowledge, much can be done to reduce the untold suffering and uncounted waste caused by this affliction.

I have instructed the Secretary of Health, Education, and Welfare to:

—appoint an Advisory Committee on Alcoholism;

—establish in the Public Health Service a center for research on the cause, prevention, control and treatment of alcoholism;

—develop an education program in order to foster public understanding based on scientific fact;

—work with public and private agencies on the state and local level include this disease in comprehensive health programs.

4. *Family Planning*

We have a growing concern to foster the integrity of the family, and the opportunity for each child. It is essential that all families have access to information and services that will allow freedom to choose the number and spacing of their children within the dictates of individual conscience.

In the fiscal 1967 budget, I have requested a sizable increase in funds available for research, training and services in this field. The National Institute of Child Health and Human Development will expand its own research and its grant program to study human reproduction. The Children's Bureau and the Office of Economic Opportunity will support family planning to the maternal and infant care programs in local communities when requested. State agencies will be aided by federal welfare funds to provide family planning services to mothers.

EDUCATION

I have proposed a total Federal investment in education and training during the coming year in excess of $10 billion—a threefold increase since 1961.

Our education programs must be administered wisely and well. Shortly after passage of the Elementary and Secondary Education Act of 1965, I directed that the Office of Education be reorganized to carry out its expanded responsibilities more effectively and efficiently. This reorganization has now been completed.

In addition, we established the new post of Assistant Secretary for Education in the Department of Health, Education, and Welfare to strengthen program coordination throughout the government.

The Congress has already put this nation on the path toward the achievement of goals to:

1. Extend special educational help to 12 million disadvantaged and handicapped children;

2. Eliminate illiteracy within a decade;

3. Bring public library services to 15 million more Americans;

4. Reduce by half the rate of high school dropouts over the next five years;

5. Guarantee the opportunity for education beyond high school on the basis of ability to learn, rather than ability to pay;

6. Provide college building and facilities to meet the needs of 9 million students expected by 1975.

Full educational opportunity for every citizen requires that we build on the beginnings we have already made. I recommend measures:

—to expand the Head Start program for preschool children

—to strengthen the Elementary and Secondary Education Act of 1965

—to expand federal assistance to higher education

—to improve the nation's libraries.

I. TO EXPAND THE HEAD START PROGRAM FOR
PRE-SCHOOL CHILDREN

Few programs have had the visible success of Operation Head Start. The dis-

advantaged children who have benefited from this program are already entering first grade—with new confidence in themselves and greater eagerness to learn.

I have requested funds almost to double the Head Start Program during the coming year to ensure:

—full year programs for 210,000 children

—summer programs for 500,000 children.

This marks a significant step in providing greatly expanded pre-school assistance for five year olds from disadvantaged homes, and summer nusery programs for 3 and 4 year olds.

II. TO STRENGTHEN THE ELEMENTARY AND
SECONDARY EDUCATION ACT OF 1965

Though funded only four months ago, the Elementary and Secondary Education Act of 1965 has already begun to bring its benefits to the Nation.

—Special help is being provided the disadvantaged—remedial teaching, health and food services, augmented teaching and counseling staffs.

—More books—interesting and up-to-date—have begun to appear on school library shelves.

—New approaches to old problems are being tried; instruction for the student extends beyond the classroom—to museums, hospitals, factories.

—Regional education laboratories are being developed to stimulate new techniques of teaching and learning in our schools.

—State educational agencies are strengthening their staffs and assuming greater responsibilities.

Educational deprivation cannot be overcome in a year. And quality cannot be achieved overnight.

I propose that the Elementary and Second-

ary Education Act be extended for four years.

My budget includes increased funds for each title of the Act.

In addition, I propose that coverage of the Act be enlarged—

—to raise from $2000 to $3000 the family income formula for allocating aid for education of the disadvantaged commencing in fiscal 1968.

—to earmark additional funds for children of American Indians and migrant workers.

Careful study of the "incentive grant" provision of Title I shows that payments would be made to many districts unrelated to need.

I therefore recommend repeal of the "incentive grant" provision of Title I in order to focus federal aid on basic grants to more than 20,000 local school districts.

Too many schools in urban and rural slums are ancient and in disrepair. Obsolete schools aggravate the problem of eliminating de facto segregation in our northern communities, thus depriving children of full educational opportunities.

There is a pressing need for long-range, community-wide planning to bring innovation and imagination in school construction.

I propose that $5 million be added to Title III to help communities in planning school construction to encourage innovation and to deal with obsolescence, overcrowding and special problems such as de facto segregation.

A recently completed study of the federally impacted area program, requested by Congress, has concluded that certain provisions should be revised.

I recommend revision of the existing law—

—to require school districts to absorb a uniform and fair share of the burden of educating children in federally-affected districts;

—to base payments on school expenditures in local districts rather than on national or state average per-pupil cost;

—to eliminate eligibility for federal impacted area assistance in those cases where government property is leased to private enterprises that pay local taxes.

III. HIGHER EDUCATION

Today, young people are seeking advanced learning in greater numbers than ever before. 1,430,000 new students will enter our colleges next September—more than the total enrollment only twenty years ago.

Our colleges and universities must keep pace with this growing influx of young Americans. And the Federal Government must be prepared to continue its assistance.

I recommend extension of the Higher Education Facilities Act for three more years, with authorization of $458 million for construction grants for fiscal 1967.

In a society that is growing more complex, advanced training is essential. 640,000 students will enroll in universities and institutions across the nation at the post graduate level next fall. This number will grow by another quarter million in the next five years.

I recommend that the grant program for graduate facilities be continued, and I propose that $200 million be made available for loans to build both undergraduate and graduate facilities.

In addition, I will soon send to Congress legislation to permit more effective use of federal resources in certain loan programs by applying credit from private financial institutions. This will make possible an additional $100 million for academic facility loans in fiscal 1967.

One out of every four of our institutions of higher learning is not good enough to get accreditation. Congress recognized this need last year by providing assistance to developing colleges.

I recommend that Title III of the Higher Education Act of 1965 be continued for two years, with its authorization increased from $5 million to $30 million next year.

By June, 890,000 students at 1,700 institutions will have borrowed $800 million to invest in college education under the student loan program of the National Defense Education Act. Last year, Congress expanded the opportunity for student loans by establishing a subsidized program through the nation's private banking system. Together with opportunity grants and the work-study programs, there now exists a wide range of student-assistance programs to help finance higher education.

To increase loan funds available to students who want college educations, I recommend the conversion of the direct loan program to a program in which loans will be made from funds provided by the private capital market, with the Government subsidizing these loans. The teacher "forgiveness" features for students eligible under the National Defense Education program will be retained.

I am proposing an orderly transition to the new student loan program so that no eligible student will be deprived of the needed financial assistance, and I will ask for the necessary funds to accomplish this purpose.

I also recommend that the "forgiveness" provision be extended to medical personnel who will settle in rural areas where the doctor shortage is most critical.

There are more than 12,000 unfilled vacancies for qualified social workers, at a time when we need their skills more than ever before. These workers are important to the success of our poverty, health, and education programs.

A Task Force on Social Work Manpower

and Education has just completed an extensive study of the problem. I have asked the Secretary of Health, Education, and Welfare to consult with educational leaders and other specialists and to submit recommendations to me to overcome this shortage in the ranks of our social workers.

IV. TO IMPROVE THE NATION'S LIBRARIES

Those who do not read are not much better off than those who cannot read. More than 100 million Americans have inadequate public library services. More than 15 million have none at all.

A library must be a living institution with trained staff and funds to obtain new books, periodicals, films, records and other material.

As the boundaries of learning are pushed back, our need for storehouses of knowledge grows greater. They offer man his link with the past and his vision of the future.

Most public libraries in the United States are poorly equipped to perform this vital role.

I recommend that Congress extend the Library Services and Construction Act for five more years, authorizing $57.5 million for Fiscal 1967.

DEPARTMENT OF THE PEOPLE

Through the programs entrusted to its care, the Department of Health, Education, and Welfare exercises continuing concern for the social well-being of all our people. Already, as I have indicated in this message, it has become possible to set ambitious goals for the future.

To improve our ability to chart our progress, I have asked the Secretary to establish within his office the resources to develop the necessary social statistics and indicators to supplement those prepared by the Bureau of

Labor Statistics and the Council of Economic Advisers. With these yardsticks, we can better measure the distance we have come and plan for the way ahead.

In health and education, we build with a double purpose: to meet today's needs, and to match tomorrow's hopes.

We look toward the time when every disease which need not happen will not happen.

—when every citizen can confidently expect care—competent, convenient care—if he is ill or injured.

—when every American receives the education and training he wants to enrich his life and fulfill his hopes.

With pain and ignorance no longer such fearsome enemies, our people will find a new freedom. Our society will be great as never before.

It is too early for self-congratulations. We must continue to plan and act. We march in a campaign which can have no retreats, no truce, no end: only new victories.

LYNDON B. JOHNSON

The White House
March 1, 1966

NOTE: For statements or remarks upon signing related legislation, see Items 337, 508, 573.

96   Remarks to Principal Field Officers of the Internal Revenue Service. *March 1, 1966*

Commissioner, gentlemen:

It is a pleasure to welcome you again here to the East Room of the White House. I am one man who is always glad to see the tax collectors; at least, I am today in my official capacity.

Taxes are never popular. No one ever enjoys paying them. But as your President, I see everyday what those taxes accomplish for this country. If it were not for the American taxpayer, the forces of aggression would have a free hand today not only in Vietnam, but elsewhere in the world; we would be slaves instead of free men.

The taxes that you collect and that we pay have resulted in our building the greatest highways in all the world. The taxes that you collect give us the greatest park system to be found anywhere in the world. The taxes you collect are going to be used to rebuild the cities of America in a manner in which we can take great pride. They are rapidly making us the best educated and healthiest people in all the world.

There was a time not many years ago when a man seriously injured had very little chance of survival. There was a time not many years ago when 2½ to 3 percent of the men wounded in the Korean war died. But because of the taxes you collect and the medical services they provide, less than 1 percent of the men wounded in Vietnam die.

When I talked to you last year I asked you to do three things: first, give the taxpayers better service; second, to attract more good people into the Internal Revenue Service; and third, to make sure that your doors are always open only to honest men and women.

I suggested that you adopt a broader recruitment program. I am pleased to learn from Sheldon Cohen that you have made important beginnings in enlisting qualified Negroes and qualified women for some of the top jobs in the Internal Revenue Service. I hope this is just a beginning.

You have had a good year since I spoke to you last March. Your gross revenue collections reached $118 billion. That is a rise of 5½ percent while we were cutting taxes. You collected all of this money while making savings of $13 million through improved management practices.

I was also impressed by one other statistic. Last year, by carefully checking, you refunded $239 million to taxpayers who had made mistakes on their own. You haven't forgotten that a good tax collector is not only efficient, but a good collector also ought to be fair and just—and he should treat the other fellow as he would like to be treated if he were on the other side of the desk.

As a taxpayer, I recently received one of your new form 1040's in the mail. You have made things a little easier for our taxpayers, and that is something that we must always try to do. We must also remember that a little courtesy and a little understanding can go a long way in making the job of tax collection less painful and make people more willing to enjoy what they are doing.

I have not asked any of you whether you are Republicans or Democrats, men or women, black, brown, or white. Sometimes I don't know what you are.

There are two criteria that I want you to never overlook: First, I want you to do what is right. That is the difficult one. Nearly every decision that gets to me is like this. It can go either way. I try to always resolve the doubt with understanding, and with understanding of my fellow man. So you do what is right according to your own training, your own teachings, your own environment, your own judgment, your own experiences—and the law.

Do what is right according to your own judgment and according to your own conscience. That is what I try to do—it is the best I can do.

Then always be sure that you do it within the Bill of Rights and the Constitution. I

was talking to a friend of mine the other day discussing a case involving the constitutionality of the poll tax. In presenting the case to Congress, it was argued that no one could prove this State discriminated against the Negro because a higher percentage of Negroes had poll taxes than the white people did. So it was difficult to establish discrimination, he claimed. They said it doesn't exist because more Negro people have it than white people.

But we can establish this: that we have free speech in this country and we are entitled to speak our minds. Who would ever think of charging a man so much per word for what he had to say?

We do have a free press in our country, but who would ever say to an editorial writer, "I am going to put a tax on each word that you put in that piece"?

We have the right to worship God in accordance with the dictates of our conscience, but who would ever say, "I am going to charge you so much to sit in a certain pew in a certain church on a certain Sunday"?

The court ruled: "It is just as ridiculous to charge a man to vote, and therefore, on that basis, it is in violation of the Constitution. Not because we discriminate against the Negro, but because we do not have a law that charges a man to vote or speak or write or go to church." They ruled the poll tax unconstitutional. And we must always ask: "Is what we are doing constitutional?"

Second, be compassionate in your understanding. Say, "Except for the grace of God, I might be in that man's position." Obey the law of the land, the Bill of Rights, the Constitution of the United States, and act with compassion in the administration of that law.

Our people, I think, have come to expect something close to perfection from your Service. So it is very difficult for you to live up to their expectations.

I want you to know that the reason I asked you to come here this morning is because I want you to know that you have my strong support. You have my pledge that the Internal Revenue Service, as long as I am President, is going to be a blue-ribbon organization. It will be protected from the unconstitutional, improper, political, religious, and bigoted views of those who seek to exploit it.

So I want to say you are serving your country well, and with distinction. You are serving it patriotically, and you have the gratitude of your President for what you are doing. I am grateful for what you have accomplished.

You estimate that you are going to bring in untold sums in the next budget. I hope that is right. I am confident that you are going to keep up your good work. Just remember that you are responsible to your own God, your own conscience, and to your own Constitution.

Thank you very much.

NOTE: The President spoke at 12:10 p.m. in the East Room at the White House. In his opening words he referred to Sheldon S. Cohen, Commissioner, Internal Revenue Service.

As printed above, this item follows the text released by the White House.

97   Remarks at the Swearing In of Lee C. White as Chairman, Federal Power Commission.   *March 2, 1966*

Mr. White, Mr. Swidler, members of the Cabinet, Members of Congress, members of the White family, my friends:

We have come here today to swear in the chairman of one of the most important Federal agencies in our Federal Government. While there is much in the statute books that tell us what the job is, there is little to tell of the kind of man that ought to hold that job.

I have certain beliefs about the dimensions of the man that I would choose to place at the head of a great governmental agency. First, he must be a public servant. The phrase is precise. "Public" means that he is of the people and "servant" means that he toils in their behalf. There can be no soft spots in this demand, for a sense of duty is foremost in the specifications of this agency's leader.

Second, this man must have courage. The need to be and to do right is never filled, until the act of justice is committed. He must have enough steel in his spine so that the noisy dissent of the crowd doesn't sway him from what he truly believes to be the correct course to follow.

Third, he must have a sense of fair play. Each day he must disprove Lord Acton's theory about the corruption of power. He must at all times be insulated against arrogance, for the corrosion of power is both noticeable and noxious.

The chairman and the members of a commission must always remember that they are the judges for the public interest and not the advocates of a special interest. They should listen to both sides of a question, weigh all the facts and all the evidence available, then come to a decision—a decision that is objective and a decision that is fair.

If you will pardon my allusion to the history of the ancients, one of the best summations of duty, courage, and fair play was uttered by the mother of a great king of Athens a long, long time ago. She said: "Look to the things of God. Know that you are bound to help all who are wronged,

249

bound to constrain all who destroy the law. What else holds state to state, save this alone: that each one honors the great laws of right."

I take you on this little excursion this morning into the philosophy of government, because today we have come here to this historic East Room in the White House to swear in a man whose acceptance of duty, whose courage, whose appreciation of the rule of right behavior reside comfortably within his daily life.

He succeeds a great Chairman, a friend who has served his Government with ability and devotion for many years. But Lee White also leaves the White House after 5 years of service to two Presidents, as well as many years of service to devoted Members of the Senate of both parties.

Whenever there was a knotty problem here at the White House to be examined and to be solved, Lee, with a quiet and luminous skill, set about to do just what needed to be done. I have always found him a man of good spirit with a tolerance for the nagging details of every problem, as well as very sound judgment about where the facts could be found and where the solution would take us.

The management of the Federal Power Commission is one of the great jobs and one of the key jobs in the Government of the United States. I received a lot of advice, I did a lot of consulting, I pondered long and hard about the man that I would select to succeed Chairman Swidler, who had rendered outstanding and distinguished service.

I have told you this morning some of the qualities in mind and heart that I was looking for, and that I found such a man on the White House staff that I inherited from President Kennedy was a source of mingled emotion, because the White House lost an able and devoted Special Counsel, but the country gained a judicious, highly trained lawyer, with a degree in electrical engineering thrown in, and now the FPC has a good Chairman.

Lee White has served his country and two Presidents with fidelity both to conscience and to pride. Moreover, he goes to the FPC with his sense of humor undiminished. Any man who can survive 5 years in the White House, never stumble over an assigned task, and leave with his ability to laugh unimpaired, is a man that I would warn all of you is to be reckoned with.

I believe the future of the Federal Power Commission to be in sure and skillful and, above all, fair and just hands.

Thank you very much.

NOTE: The President spoke at 11:55 a.m. in the East Room at the White House. In his opening words he referred to Lee C. White, new Chairman of the Federal Power Commission, and Joseph C. Swidler, outgoing Chairman. The oath of office was administered by Judge E. Barrett Prettyman, Senior Circuit Judge of the U.S. Court of Appeals for the District of Columbia.

98 Special Message to the Congress on Transportation. March 2, 1966

To the Congress of the United States:

Two centuries ago the American nation came into being. Thirteen sparsely populated colonies, strung out along the Atlantic seaboard for 1300 miles, joined their separate wills in a common endeavor.

Three bonds united them.

There was the cultural bond of a single language.

There was the moral bond of a thirst for

liberty and democratic government.

There was the physical bond of a few roads and rivers, by which the citizens of the colonies engaged in peaceful commerce.

Two centuries later the language is the same. The thirst for liberty and democracy endures.

The physical bond—that tenuous skein of rough trails and primitive roads—has become a powerful network on which the prosperity and convenience of our society depend.

In a nation that spans a continent, transportation is the web of union.

THE GROWTH OF OUR TRANSPORTATION SYSTEM

It is not necessary to look back to the 1760's to chronicle the astonishing growth of American transportation.

Twenty years ago there were 31 million motor vehicles in the United States. Today there are 90 million. By 1975 there will be nearly 120 million.

Twenty years ago there were 1.5 million miles of paved roads and streets in the United States. Today this figure has almost doubled.

Twenty years ago there were 38,000 private and commercial aircraft. Today there are more than 97,000.

Twenty years ago commercial airlines flew 209 million miles. Last year they flew one billion miles.

Twenty-five years ago American transportation moved 619 billion ton miles of cargo. In 1964, 1.5 trillion ton miles were moved.

The manufacturing of transportation equipment has kept pace. It has tripled since 1947. Last year $4.5 billion was spent for new transportation plant and equipment.

Transportation is one of America's largest employers. There are:

—737,000 railroad employees,

—270,000 local and inter-urban workers,

—230,000 in air transport,

—almost a million men and women in motor transport and storage.

Together with pipeline and water transportation employees, the total number of men and women who earn their livelihoods by moving people and goods is well over two and one-half million.

The Federal Government supports or regulates almost every means of transportation. Last year alone more than $5 billion in Federal funds were invested in transportation—in highway construction, in river and harbor development, in airway operation and airport construction, in maritime subsidies. The government owns 1500 of the nation's 2500 ocean-going cargo vessels.

Our transportation system—the descendant of the horse-drawn coaches and sailing ships of colonial times—accounts for one in every six dollars in the American economy. In 1965, that amounted to $120 billion—a sum greater than the gross national product of this Nation in 1940.

SHORTCOMINGS OF OUR SYSTEM

Vital as it is, mammoth and complex as it has become, the American transportation system is not good enough.

It is not good enough when it offers nearly a mile of street or road for every square mile of land—and yet provides no relief from time-consuming, frustrating, and wasteful congestion.

It is not good enough when it produces sleek and efficient jet aircraft—and yet cannot move passengers to and from airports in the time it takes those aircraft to fly hundreds of miles.

It is not good enough when it builds super-highways for super-charged automobiles—and yet cannot find a way to prevent 50,000 highway deaths this year.

It is not good enough when public and private investors pour $15 million into a large, high-speed ship—only to watch it remain idle in port for days before it is loaded.

It is not good enough when it lays out new freeways to serve new cities and suburbs—and carelessly scars the irreplaceable countryside.

It is not good enough when it adheres to custom for its own sake—and ignores opportunities to serve our people more economically and efficiently.

It is not good enough if it responds to the needs of an earlier America—and does not help us expand our trade and distribute the fruits of our land throughout the world.

Why We Have Fallen Short

Our transportation system has not emerged from a single drawing board, on which the needs and capacities of our economy were all charted. It could not have done so, for it grew along with the country itself—now restlessly expanding, now consolidating, as opportunity grew bright or dim.

Thus investment and service innovations responded to special needs. Research and development were sporadic, sometimes inconsistent, and largely oriented towards the promotion of a particular means of transportation.

As a result, America today lacks a coordinated transportation system that permits travellers and goods to move conveniently and efficiently from one means of transportation to another, using the best characteristics of each.

Both people and goods are compelled to conform to the system as it is, despite the inconvenience and expense of:

— aging and often obsolete transportation plant and equipment.

— networks chiefly designed to serve a rural society.

— services long outstripped by our growing economy and population, by changes in land use, by new concepts in industrial plant location, warehousing and distribution.

— the failure to take full advantage of new technologies developed elsewhere in the economy.

— programs and policies which impede private initiative and dull incentives for innovation.

The result is waste—of human and economic resources—and of the taxpayers' dollar.

We have abided this waste too long.

We must not permit it to continue.

We have too much at stake in the quality and economy of our transportation system. If the growth of our transport industries merely keeps pace with our current national economic growth, the demand for transportation will more than double in the next twenty years.

But even that is too conservative an estimate. Passenger transportation is growing much faster than our Gross National Product—reflecting the desires of an affluent people with ever-increasing incomes.

Private and Public Responsibility

The United States is the only major nation in the world that relies primarily upon privately owned and operated transportation. That national policy has served us well. It must be continued.

But private ownership has been made feasible only by the use of publicly granted authority and the investment of public resources—

— by the construction of locks, dams, and channels on our rivers and inland waterways.

— by the development of a vast highway network.

— by the construction and operation of airports and airways.

— by the development of ports and harbors.

— by direct financial support to the Merchant Marine.

— by grants of eminent domain authority.

— by capital equipment grants and demonstration projects for mass transit.

— in years past, by grants of public land to assist the railroads.

Enlightened government has served as a full partner with private enterprise in meeting America's urgent need for mobility.

That partnership must now be strengthened with all the means that creative federalism can provide. The costs of a transportation paralysis in the years ahead are too severe. The rewards of an efficient system are too great. We cannot afford the luxury of drift—or proceed with "business as usual."

We must secure for all our travellers and shippers the full advantages of modern science and technology.

We must acquire the reliable information we need for intelligent decisions.

We must clear away the institutional and political barriers which impede adaptation and change.

We must promote the efforts of private industry to give the American consumer more and better service for his transportation dollar.

We must coordinate the executive functions of our transportation agencies in a sin- gle coherent instrument of government. Thus policy guidance and support for each means of transportation will strengthen the national economy as a whole.

A DEPARTMENT OF TRANSPORTATION

I urge the Congress to establish a Cabinet level Department of Transportation.

I recommend that this Department bring together almost 100,000 employees and almost $6 billion of Federal funds now devoted to transportation.

I urge the creation of such a Department to serve the growing demands of this great Nation, to satisfy the needs of our expanding industry and to fulfill the right of our taxpayers to maximum efficiency and frugality in Government operations.

In so doing, I follow the recommendations of many outstanding Americans.

In 1936, a Select Committee of the United States Senate recommended a Department of Transportation, or, in the alternative, the consolidation of all transportation programs in the Department of Commerce.

In 1949, the Hoover Commission Task Force on Transportation recommended a Department of Transportation.

In 1961 President Eisenhower recommended such a Department in his Budget Message.

In 1961 a Special Study Group of the Senate Committee on Commerce recommended that all promotional and safety programs of the Federal Government be concentrated in a Department of Transportation.

Many distinguished Members of Congress have offered bills to create the Department. Private citizens, the nation's leading experts in the field, have made the same recommendation to me.

It is time to act on these recommendations.

SCOPE OF THE DEPARTMENT

I propose that the following agencies and functions be consolidated in the Department of Transportation:

1. *The Office of the Under Secretary of Commerce for Transportation,* and its Policy, Program, Emergency Transportation and Research staffs.

2. *The Bureau of Public Roads and the Federal-aid Highway Program it administers.*

3. *The Federal Aviation Agency.* This key agency, with its functions in aviation safety, promotion and investment, will be transferred in its entirety to the new Department. It will continue to carry out these functions in the new department.

4. *The Coast Guard,* whose principal peacetime activities relate to transportation and marine safety. The Coast Guard will be transferred as a unit from the Treasury Department. As in the past, the Coast Guard will operate as part of the Navy in time of war.

5. *The Maritime Administration,* with its construction and operating subsidy programs.

6. *The safety functions of the Civil Aeronautics Board,* the responsibility for investigating and determining the probable cause of aircraft accidents and its appellate functions related to safety.

7. *The safety functions and car service functions of the Interstate Commerce Commission,* principally the inspection and enforcement of safety regulations for railroads, motor carriers, and pipelines, and the distribution of rail car supply in times of shortage.

8. *The Great Lakes Pilotage Administration, the St. Lawrence Seaway Development Corporation, the Alaska Railroad,* and certain minor transportation-related activities

of other agencies.

As this list indicates, I am recommending the consolidation into the Department of those Federal agencies whose primary functions are transportation promotion and safety.

NATIONAL TRANSPORTATION SAFETY BOARD

No function of the new Department—no responsibility of its Secretary—will be more important than safety. We must insure the safety of our citizens as they travel on our land, in our skies, and over our waters.

I recommend that there be created under the Secretary of Transportation a National Transportation Safety Board independent of the operating units of the Department.

The sole function of this Board will be the safety of our travellers. It will review investigations of accidents to seek their causes. It will determine compliance with safety standards. It will examine the adequacy of the safety standards themselves. It will assume safety functions transferred from the ICC and the CAB.

I consider the functions of this Board so important that I am requesting authority from the Congress to name five Presidential appointees as its members.

RELATION TO OTHER GOVERNMENT ACTIVITIES

The activities of several departments and agencies affect transportation promotion and safety. Sound management requires that an appropriate and intimate relationship be established between those activities and the new Department of Transportation.

1. *The subsidy functions of the Civil Aeronautics Board.* Aviation subsidies—now provided only for local airline service—clearly promote our domestic transportation system. But subsidy awards are an integral

part of the process of authorizing air carrier service. This is a regulatory function.

Therefore the airline subsidy program should remain in the Civil Aeronautics Board. The Secretary of Transportation, however, will develop principles and criteria which the Board will take into consideration in its proceedings. In this way the subsidy program will be coordinated with overall national transportation policy.

2. *The navigation program of the Corps of Engineers.* The Corps of Engineers— through its construction of locks and harbor facilities and its channel deepening and river bank protection work—makes a major contribution to water transportation. The Department of Transportation should not assume the responsibility for that construction, but its Secretary should be involved in the planning of water transportation projects.

With the approval of the President, the Secretary of Transportation should also issue standards and criteria for the economic evaluation of Federal transportation investments generally. In the case of transportation features of multi-purpose water projects, he should do so after consulting with the Water Resources Council.

3. *International Aviation.* The Secretary of Transportation should provide leadership within the Executive Branch in formulating long-range policy for international aviation. While foreign policy aspects of international aviation are the responsibility of the Secretary of State, the Secretary of Transportation should insure that our international aviation policies are consistent with overall national transportation policy.

Subject to policy determinations by the President, the Civil Aeronautics Board regulates international aviation routes and fares as they affect the United States. This function has far-reaching effects on our foreign policy, our balance of payments, and the vi-

tality of American aviation. The Secretary of Transportation should participate in Civil Aeronautics Board proceedings that involve international aviation policy.

4. *Urban Transportation.* The Departments of Transportation and Housing and Urban Development must cooperate in decisions affecting urban transportation.

The future of urban transportation—the safety, convenience, and indeed the livelihood of its users—depends upon wide-scale, rational planning. If the Federal Government is to contribute to that planning, it must speak with a coherent voice.

The Department of Housing and Urban Development bears the principal responsibility for a unified Federal approach to urban problems. Yet it cannot perform this task without the counsel, support, and cooperation of the Department of Transportation.

I shall ask the two Secretaries to recommend to me, within a year after the creation of the new department, the means and procedures by which this cooperation can best be achieved—not only in principle, but in practical effect.

ROLE OF THE DEPARTMENT

The Department of Transportation will:
—coordinate the principal existing programs that promote transportation in America.
—bring new technology to a total transportation system, by promoting research and development in cooperation with private industry.
—improve safety in every means of transportation.
—encourage private enterprise to take full and prompt advantage of new technological opportunities.
—encourage high quality, low cost service to the public.

—conduct systems analyses and planning, to strengthen the weakest parts of today's system.

—develop investment criteria and standards, and analytical techniques to assist all levels of government and industry in their transportation investments.

THE INTERSTATE COMMERCE COMMISSION

The Cabinet level Department I recommend will not alter the economic regulatory functions of the Interstate Commerce Commission, the Civil Aeronautics Board, or the Federal Maritime Commission.

I do recommend, however, a change in the manner of selecting the Chairman of the Interstate Commerce Commission.

Today, the Chairman of this vital commission—alone among the Federal regulatory agencies—is selected, not by the President, but by annual rotation among the eleven commissioners.

This is not sound management practice in an agency whose influence on our rail, highway, waterway and pipeline industries is so far-reaching.

The ICC bears the demanding and challenging responsibility to keep federal regulation attuned to the needs and opportunities of a dynamic industry. Its jurisdiction extends to 18,000 transport companies. It handles 7,000 cases each year. No private corporation of such size and importance would change its chief executive officer once each year.

I shall shortly submit to the Congress a reorganization plan to give the President authority to designate the Chairman of the Interstate Commerce Commission from among its members, and to strengthen his executive functions.

SAFETY

105,000 Americans died in accidents last year.

More than half were killed in transportation, or in recreation accidents related to transportation.

49,000 deaths involved motor vehicles.

1,300 involved aircraft.

1,500 involved ships and boats.

2,300 involved railroads.

Millions of Americans were injured in transportation accidents—the overwhelming majority involving automobiles.

Each means of transportation has developed safety programs of varying effectiveness. Yet we lack a comprehensive program keyed to a total transportation system.

Proven safety techniques in one means have not always been adapted in others.

Last year the highway death toll set a new record. The prediction for this year is that more than 50,000 persons will die on our streets and highways—more than 50,000 useful and promising lives will be lost, and as many families stung by grief.

The toll of Americans killed in this way since the introduction of the automobile is truly unbelievable. It is 1.5 million—more than all the combat deaths suffered in all our wars.

No other necessity of modern life has brought more convenience to the American people—or more tragedy—than the automobile.

WHY WE ARE FAILING

The carnage on the highways must be arrested.

As I said some weeks ago, we must replace suicide with sanity and anarchy with safety.

256

The weaknesses of our present highway safety program must be corrected:

—Our knowledge of causes is grossly inadequate. Expert opinion is frequently contradictory and confusing.

—Existing safety programs are widely dispersed. Government and private efforts proceed separately, without effective coordination.

—There is no clear assignment of responsibility at the Federal level.

—The allocation of our resources to highway safety is inadequate.

—Neither private industry nor government officials concerned with automotive transportation have made safety first among their priorities. Yet we know that expensive freeways, powerful engines, and smooth exteriors will not stop the massacre on our roads.

WHAT CAN BE DONE

State and local resources are insufficient to bring about swift reductions in the highway death rate. The Federal government must provide additional resources. Existing programs must be expanded. Pioneer work must begin in neglected areas.

Federal highway safety responsibilities should be incorporated into the Department of Transportation, in a total transportation safety program.

I have already set in motion a number of steps under existing law:

1. *To strengthen the Federal role,* I am assigning responsibility for coordinating Federal highway safety programs to the Secretary of Commerce. I am directing the Secretary to establish a major highway safety unit within his Department. This unit will ultimately be transferred to the Department of Transportation. The President's Committee on Traffic Safety will be reorganized, strengthened and supported entirely by federal funds. The Interdepartmental Highway Safety Board will be reconstituted and the Secretary's role strengthened.

2. *To give greater support to our safety programs,* I am requesting increased funds for research, accident data collection, improved emergency medical service, driver education and testing and traffic control technology.

I have also asked the Secretary of Commerce to evaluate systematically the resources allocated to traffic safety, to insure that we are receiving the maximum benefits from our present efforts.

3. *To improve driving conditions,* I have ordered that high priority be given to our efforts to build safety features into the Federal-aid highway network.

4. *To save those who are injured,* I have directed the Secretary of Health, Education, and Welfare, in cooperation with the Secretary of Commerce, immediately to initiate projects to demonstrate techniques for more effective emergency care and transportation. He will work in full cooperation with state, local and private officials.

5. *To help us better understand the causes of highway accidents,* I have asked the Secretary of Commerce to establish accident investigation teams, who will bring us new understanding of highway accidents and their causes.

6. *To make government vehicles safer,* I have asked the Administrator of General Services, in cooperation with the Secretary of Commerce, to begin a detailed study of the additional vehicle safety features that should be added to the Federal fleet.

The Traffic Safety Act of 1966

More—much more—remains to be done. The people of America deserve an aggressive highway safety program.

I believe that the Congress—the same Congress which last year gave the Secretary of Commerce broad authority to set uniform standards for State highway safety programs—will join in our efforts to bring that program into being.

I urge the Congress to enact the Traffic Safety Act of 1966.

I urge greater support for state highway safety programs.

I urge the creation of a National Highway Research and Test Facility.

To begin, I recommend a $700 million, six year program.

The three components of this program are as critically important as the problems they address.

First, federal grants to the States for highway safety will be increased. With these funds, a comprehensive highway safety program can be developed by each State under standards approved by the Secretary of Commerce. Included will be measures such as driver education and licensing—advanced traffic control techniques—regular vehicle safety inspections—police and emergency medical services.

Second, automobile safety performance will be improved. Proper design and engineering can make our cars safer. Vehicles sold in interstate commerce must be designed and equipped for maximum safety. Safe performance design standards must be met in tomorrow's cars.

I recommend that the Secretary of Commerce be given authority to determine the necessary safety performance criteria for all vehicles and their components.

If, after a two year period, the Secretary finds that adequate voluntary standards are not satisfactory, he would be authorized to prescribe nation-wide mandatory safety standards. He would be also authorized to prohibit the sale in interstate commerce of new vehicles and their components which failed to meet those standards.

Third, the Federal government's highway safety research efforts will be expanded.

I recommend construction of a national highway safety research and test center.

Funds are needed to support research and testing in many disciplines related to highway safety. The public interest demands a better understanding of the human, highway and vehicle factors which cause death and injury. We must develop more effective counter-measures and objective standards to guide our national programs. Special accident teams should be organized—accurate data collection should be enlarged on a national basis—fellowship grants and research support should be made available to attract the best minds and talents of our Nation to this urgent work.

This new highway safety program would be transferred to the Secretary of Transportation upon the creation of the new Department.

Congress has not hesitated to establish rigorous safety standards for other means of transportation when circumstances demanded them.

Today's highway death toll calls for an equally vigorous and effective expression of concern for our millions of car-owning families. For unless we avert this slaughter, one out of every two Americans will one day be killed or seriously injured on our highways.

Safety Standards for Motor Vehicle Tires

I urge the Congress to act speedily and favorably on S. 2669, a bill establishing safety standards for motor vehicle tires sold or shipped in interstate commerce.

Most tires sold to American drivers are produced and properly tested by reputable companies. Nevertheless, evidence has shown that increasing numbers of inferior tires are being sold to unwitting customers throughout the country. The dangers such tires hold for high-speed automobiles and their occupants is obvious.

S. 2669 provides that the Secretary of Commerce shall establish, and publish in the Federal Register, interim minimum safety standards for tires. The Secretary would be required to review these standards two years from the enactment of the bill, and to revise them where necessary. A research and development program under his direction would improve the minimum standards for new tires, and develop such standards for retreaded tires.

Our driving public deserves the prompt passage of S. 2669, and the protection it will afford them from accidents caused by tire failures.

Safety at Sea

Last year 90 men and women lost their lives when the cruise ship Yarmouth Castle burned and sank in the calm waters of the Caribbean.

The Yarmouth Castle was exempt from United States safety standards—partially because of its "grandfather rights" under law. It was built before 1937.

We cannot allow the lives of our citizens to depend upon the year in which a ship was built.

The Coast Guard is presently completing its investigation of the Yarmouth Castle disaster. The Maritime Administration has already finished its investigation of financial responsibility.

Later in this session—when our inquiries are accomplished and our findings reported—*we will submit to the Congress legislation to improve safety measures and guarantees of financial responsibility on the part of owners and operators of passenger-carrying vessels sailing from our ports.*

Air Accident Compensation

The United States has declared its intention to withdraw from the Warsaw Convention. Under this pact, the financial liability of a member nation's airline is limited to $8300 for a passenger's death.

Discussions are underway in the International Civil Aviation Organization to increase this liability for passengers flying anywhere in the world. We have expressed our opinion that the limit of liability should be raised to $100,000.

RESEARCH AND DEVELOPMENT

Today the United States ranks as the world's leader in technology.

Despite this—and despite the importance of transportation in the competition for international trade—exclusive of national security and space, the Federal government spends less than one percent of its total research and development budget for transportation.

Under our system of government, private enterprise bears the primary responsibility for research and development in the transportation field.

But the government can help. It can plan and fashion research and development for a total transportation system which is beyond the responsibility or capability of private industry.

Through government-sponsored research and development we can—

—Fully understand the complex relationships among the components of a total transportation system.

—Provide comprehensive and reliable data

for both private and public decisions.

—Identify areas of transportation which can be exploited by private industry to provide safer and more efficient services to the public.

—Build the basis for a more efficient use of public resources.

—Provide the technological base needed to assure adequate domestic and international transportation in times of emergency.

—Help make significant advances in every phase of transport—in aircraft, in ocean-going ships, in swifter rail service, in safer vehicles.

The Department of Transportation—working with private industry and other government agencies—will provide a coordinated program of research and development to move the Nation toward our transportation goals. The Department can help translate scientific discovery into industrial practice.

SUPERSONIC TRANSPORT AIRCRAFT

The United States is pre-eminent in the field of aircraft design and manufacture.

We intend to maintain that leadership.

As I said in my State of the Union Message, I am proposing a program to construct and flight test a new 2000-mile-per-hour supersonic aircraft.

Our supersonic transport must be reliable and safe for the passenger.

It must be profitable for both the airlines and the manufacturers.

Its operating performance must be superior to any comparable aircraft.

It must be introduced into the market in a timely manner.

We have underway an intensive research and design program on the supersonic transport, supported by appropriations of $231

million.

The design competition for this aircraft and its engines is intense and resourceful.

I am requesting $200 million in Fiscal Year 1967 appropriations to initiate the prototype phase of the supersonic transport. My request includes funds for the completion of design competition, expanded economic and sonic boom studies, and the start of prototype construction.

We hope to conduct first flight tests of the supersonic transport by 1970, and to introduce it into commercial service by 1974.

AIRCRAFT NOISE

The jet age has brought progress and prosperity to our air transportation system. Modern jets can carry passengers and freight across a continent at speeds close to that of sound.

Yet this progress has created special problems of its own. Aircraft noise is a growing source of annoyance and concern to the thousands of citizens who live near many of our large airports. As more of our airports begin to accommodate jets and as the volume of air travel expands, the problem will take on added dimension.

There are no simple or swift solutions. But it is clear that we must embark now on a concerted effort to alleviate the problems of aircraft noise. To this end, I am today directing the President's Science Advisor to work with the Administrators of the Federal Aviation Agency and National Aeronautics and Space Administration, and the Secretaries of Commerce, and of Housing and Urban Development, to frame an action program to attack this problem.

I am asking this group to:

—study the development of noise standards and the compatible uses of land near airports,

—consult with local communities and industry,

—recommend legislative or administrative actions needed to move ahead in this area.[1]

ADVANCED OCEAN VESSEL CONCEPTS

After years of United States leadership, maritime technology in other countries has caught up with and, in some instances, surpassed our own.

The U.S. Merchant Marine suffers in

---

[1] On March 18, 1966, the White House made public a memorandum to the President, dated March 17, from Donald F. Hornig, Special Assistant to the President for Science and Technology. Mr. Hornig referred to the section on aircraft noise in the message on transportation. He stated that he had convened an ad hoc Jet Aircraft Noise Panel in October 1965 to examine the technical, sociological, governmental, economic, and legal aspects of the issue. The memorandum announced the completion of a report by the Panel, dated March 1966 and entitled "Alleviation of Jet Aircraft Noise Near Airports" (Government Printing Office, 1966, 9 pp.).

The principal recommendations of the Panel were:

—Initiation of Federally supported studies of the expected scope of the noise problem through 1975 and of the public and private programs which will be needed to combat the problem.

—Creation of a high level Federal Task Force to undertake, on an urgent basis, a "systems" type analysis of the problem in the vicinity of the Kennedy, O'Hare and Los Angeles airports, the analysis to be extended to other affected areas as soon as practicable.

—Development of valid, broadly applicable standards of noise measurement.

—Pursuit of a definitive technical study pointed toward a reduction in noise levels produced by jet engines and by aircraft, together with a determination of the costs associated with the various levels of improvement which may be technologically possible.

—Establishment of a Task Force to investigate methods for Federal participation in a coordinated program for compatible land utilization in the vicinity of airports.

—Starting an effort to identify and place into effect any modifications to operating procedures and take-off or landing techniques that would reduce noise without compromising safety (2 Weekly Comp. Pres. Docs., p. 404).

world competition because it bears much higher costs than its competitors. This can be offset in some measure by technological improvements.

The Department of Defense recently launched the Fast Deployment Logistics Ship program. This concept introduces to the maritime field the same systems approach that has proven so successful in other Defense and Aerospace programs.

To achieve comparable improvements throughout the maritime industry, I am directing the Secretary of Commerce, with the Secretary of Defense, the President's Scientific Advisor, and the Atomic Energy Commission, to conduct a study of advanced vessel concepts.

The work of this team will include:

—Research, development and planning of high speed, large capacity ships, devoted primarily to transporting preloaded containers of varying types between the major ports in the world.

—Research on an ocean-going Surface Effects Vessel capable of skimming over the water at speeds more than 100 knots.

—Continued exploration of the application of nuclear propulsion to merchant marine ships.

Our private shipyards should continue to serve the needs of the Country. They can become more productive and competitive through research and development and through standardization of ship construction. With a new Department of Transportation, we will increase our efforts to bring a modern, efficient merchant marine fleet to this Nation.

ADVANCED LAND TRANSPORT

Last year Congress took a long step towards advanced land transportation by enacting the High-Speed Ground Transportation Research and Development program. This program will be continued at the most rapid pace consistent with sound management of the research effort.

Similar vision and imagination can be applied to highway transport.

Segments of the Interstate Highway network already in operation are the most efficient, productive roads ever built anywhere in the world. Motor vehicles move at higher rates of speed, more safely and in greater number per lane than on conventional roads. Transportation costs are reduced, and less land area is needed for this volume of traffic.

With the network about half completed after 10 years, it is apparent that Interstate Highways, as well as other roads and streets, can become even more productive and safe.

Accordingly, I am directing the Secretary of Commerce to:

—Investigate means for providing guidance and control mechanisms to increase the capacity and improve the safety of our highway network.

—Conduct research into the means of improving traffic flow—particularly in our cities—so we can make better use of our existing roads and streets.

—Investigate the potential of separate roadways for various classes of vehicles, with emphasis on improving mass transportation service.

SYSTEMS RESEARCH

Some of our brightest opportunities in research and development lie in the less obvious and often neglected parts of our transportation system.

We spend billions for constructing new highways, but comparatively little for traffic control devices.

We spend millions for fast jet aircraft—but little on the traveler's problem of getting to and from the airport.

We have mounted a sizable government-industry program to expand exports, yet we allow a mountain of red tape paperwork negate our efforts. Worldwide, a total of 810 forms are required to cover all types of cargo imported and exported. In this country alone, as many as 43 separate forms are used in one export shipment. Eighty separate forms may be needed to process some imports. This is paperwork run wild.

I am directing the Secretaries of Treasury and Commerce and the Attorney General to attack these problems, through the use of effective systems research programs. And I have directed them to eliminate immediately every unnecessary element of red tape that inhibits our import and export programs.

TRANSPORTATION FOR AMERICA

The Founding Fathers rode by stage to Philadelphia to take part in the Constitutional Convention. They could not have anticipated the immense complexity—or the problems—of transportation in our day.

Yet they, too, recognized the vital national interest in commerce between the States. The early Congresses expressed that interest even more directly, by supporting the development of road and waterway systems.

Most important, the Founding Fathers gave us a flexible system of Government. Cities, states and the federal government can join together—and in many cases work with private enterprise—in partnerships of creative Federalism to solve our most complex problems.

For the very size of our transportation requirements—rising step-by-step with the growth of our population and industry—

demands that we respond with new institutions, new programs of research, new efforts to make our vehicles safe as well as swift.

Modern transportation can be the rapid conduit of economic growth—or a bottleneck.

It can bring jobs and loved ones and recreation closer to every family—or it can bring instead sudden and purposeless death.

It can improve every man's standard of living—or multiply the cost of all he buys.

It can be a convenience, a pleasure, the passport to new horizons of the mind and spirit—or it can frustrate and impede and delay.

The choice is ours to make.

We build the cars, the trains, the planes, the ships, the roads and the airports. We can, if we will, plan their safe and efficient use in the decades ahead to improve the quality of life for all Americans.

The program I have outlined in this message is the first step toward that goal.

I urge its prompt enactment by the Congress.

LYNDON B. JOHNSON

The White House
March 2, 1966

NOTE: For the President's remarks upon signing related legislation, see Items 442, 449, 523.

99   Citation Accompanying the National Security Medal Presented to Frank Byron Rowlett. *March 2, 1966*

CITATION

As Special Assistant to the Director of the National Security Agency, and as a leading force for more than three decades in the Nation's cryptologic efforts, Mr. Rowlett has made a profound contribution to the security of the United States.

A pioneer in modern cryptology, he has advanced the frontiers of this crucial field by applying his remarkable inventive skill and creative energy to a wide range of the most complex technical and technological problems. By providing the spark of insight, the initiative, and the leadership for new approaches, new techniques, and new technology, he has rendered service of incalculable value to the national intelligence effort and to the Nation's security.

NOTE: The President presented the National Security Medal to Mr. Rowlett at 12:20 p.m. in the President's Office at the White House.

100   Remarks Upon Signing the "Cold War GI Bill" (Veterans' Readjustment Benefits Act of 1966). *March 3, 1966*

Members of the Cabinet, distinguished Members of the Congress, invited guests, ladies and gentlemen:

During World War II when President Franklin D. Roosevelt signed the first Veterans' Readjustment Act, he stated on the occasion of that signing, "This law gives emphatic notice to the men and women of our Armed Forces that the American people never intend to let them down."

That first GI bill, and later the Korean GI bill, brought, out of the hardship of war, hope for all of our American service people. They returned home to find not just gratitude, but concrete help in getting a fresh start: with educational assistance, with medical care, with guarantees that permitted them to buy homes to live in.

263

They found opportunity which they used to enrich themselves and to enrich the Nation.

As we meet here today in this historic East Room and look around and see our friends gathered, we see the results of that first legislation.

One hundred and sixteen Members of the House of Representatives, in our Congress, received training under the GI bills, as did 11 United States Senators, 12 of the Governors of our States, 3 members of the President's Cabinet, 1 Justice of the Supreme Court, 6 of our astronauts, and 5 of the President's Special Assistants here in the White House.

The first two GI bills cost $21 billion. Our economists now estimate that they resulted in a return of some $60 billion in Federal taxes for that $21 billion invested.

The educational level of World War II and Korean war veterans averages about 2 years above the level of nonveterans. This difference exists primarily because of what the GI bills were able to do.

We made the most promising investment that a nation can make, an investment in the talent and the ambition of our citizens. The return on that investment has doubled and has redoubled ever since.

Today we come here in a time of new testing. Today, by signing a new Veterans' Readjustment Act—that was authored in the Senate by my colleague and friend of many years, Senator Yarborough, and reported in the House by Chairman Teague, with the unanimous support of his committee—we are reaffirming President Roosevelt's pledge of 22 years ago. We are saying to the brave Americans who serve us in uniform, in camps and bases, in villages and jungles, that your country is behind you; that we support you; that you serve us in time of danger.

To say this does not mean that all Americans agree on everything that is done or on every policy or on every commitment. But it does mean that once that policy is established, once that commitment is made, once that pledge is given, we support fully the young men who are the spearhead of that policy.

The Congress has passed this legislation. It passed it without a single dissenting vote. In doing so, it said: We will support these men who are defending our freedom to debate, who are joining in a most historic protest for their country—a protest against tyranny, a protest against aggression, and a protest against misery.

The budget I sent to Congress this year resulted from a very careful study of the Nation's resources. My Cabinet officers brought to my home in Texas, where I was recuperating from an operation, budget requests that they had gone over very carefully that amounted to $130 billion. They felt that they could not reduce beyond this amount. It was my sad duty to bring those requests in line with what I thought our resources were and what I thought the Congress would approve. And we got them down to a little under $113 billion.

Of that $113 billion, over $10 billion—$10.2 billion to be exact—will go this year to education and training. When I became President in fiscal year 1964, we were spending $4,750 million. Although I have been in the Presidency but a little over 2 years, we have more than doubled the amount that we are spending for education and training—from $4.75 billion to $10.2 billion—from fiscal 1964 to fiscal 1967.

Education gets more money in this budget than any other items except interest on the public debt, some $12 billion, and the Defense Department, which, as you know, exceeds $50 billion.

Well, I must be frank. I had felt that we

could start the new GI program, and that we should, by providing special funds for soldiers who served in combat areas. Others could be provided opportunity grants through the Higher Education Act. In that way, I was hopeful that we would not ask for more than we could get, or bite off more than we could chew in educational costs.

The Congress considered these measures, and in their judgment, as I say, passed this by a unanimous vote. They felt that we should go far in excess of what I asked for this year. The bill before me this morning exceeds my budget request by more than $245 million for fiscal year 1967, and by more than $1,800 million over the next 5 years.

Because it is for education, I am going to sign this bill, even though it provides hundreds of millions of dollars more than I thought it advisable to recommend or to ask for this year.

This is the first major measure enacted in this session of Congress, and a President just must not ignore the unanimous vote of both Houses of the Congress, the two Texas chairmen, Yarborough and Teague, and some 5 million men who will be the beneficiaries who have worn the uniform.

I want to call attention, however, and make a most solemn warning about future legislation. Unless we can balance our requests with prudence, and our concern with caution, then we are likely to get our figures back to that $130 billion that came over from the departments.

I am going to sign this measure this morning notwithstanding the fact that it goes further than I was willing to ask for this year, because, paraphrasing what Secretary Rusk said the other day in response to a question from Congress, he said, "Well, Senator, could it be that they could perhaps be wrong?" And it just could be that the President was wrong when he made his original request.

I supported this legislation when I was a Member of the Senate, and sometimes you look at things a little differently from one end of the Avenue than you do from the other.

I have tried to take into consideration all of the factors that should be weighed. I have heard the Vice President, the Secretary of Defense, and every commander—General Walt this week, General Westmoreland a couple of weeks ago—tell me about the dedication of our fighting men. I am convinced that these brave Americans who serve us on many fronts today, particularly in Vietnam and the Dominican Republic, and others, are the very best men that our country has ever produced. They are great soldiers.

I am going to resolve this doubt in behalf of the Congress, which has spent more hours considering this than I have, and sign this legislation in the hope that when the peace is won, we can provide the means of making great civilians in time of peace out of these great soldiers who served us in time of need.

Thank you very much.

NOTE: The President spoke at 11:10 a.m. in the East Room at the White House. During his remarks he referred to Senator Ralph Yarborough of Texas, Representative Olin E. Teague of Texas, Chairman of the House Committee on Veterans Affairs, Dean Rusk, Secretary of State, Vice President Hubert H. Humphrey, Robert S. McNamara, Secretary of Defense, Lt. Gen. Lewis W. Walt, Commanding General of the III Marine Amphibious Force in Vietnam, and Gen. William C. Westmoreland, Commander, United States Military Assistance Command, Vietnam.

As enacted, the Veterans' Readjustment Benefits Act of 1966 is Public Law 89-358 (80 Stat. 12).

101   Remarks at the Swearing In of the Chairman and Members of the
National Council on the Humanities.   *March 3, 1966*

Mr. Vice President, Members of Congress, Dr. Moe, distinguished members of the National Council on the Humanities, ladies and gentlemen:

In 1837, Ralph Waldo Emerson spoke to the Phi Beta Kappa Society at Harvard University and handed this challenge to America's learned men: "The office of the scholar," he said, "is to cheer and to raise and to guide men by showing them facts amidst appearances. He is the world's eye, and he is the world's heart."

Today, as we meet here in this historic East Room, 129 years later, we are very much in need of clear eyes and stout hearts. We need them now more than ever, and we need men of learning, too, more than we have ever needed them before.

We have proven our scientific and our technical genius. Science, as someone has said, has taught us to fly through the air higher and faster than the birds, to swim through the sea deeper and farther than the fish, but we have yet to learn how to walk the earth like men.

Science can give us goods, goods we need, but the humanities—art and literature, poetry and history, law and philosophy—must give us the goals that we have.

I believe that the National Council on the Humanities has a most crucial role to play in American life today, not only in enriching scholarship, but in enriching life for all people.

We believe in America that men of thought and men of action must not be isolated. They must be bound closely together. Congress was acting on that belief when it accepted our recommendations and established this Council in a rather adventuresome spirit and a rather far-reaching piece of legislation. As you have come here to do your work, I hope that you will also bear that in mind and act on that belief.

I hope you will use your freedom and your funds to call forth a new American scholar, one who can meet Emerson's challenge "to raise and to guide men." The American scholar will look for facts, and beyond facts he will look for value. He will aspire not only to knowledge, but to wisdom. He will know that learning exists not for its own sake, but, rather, for man's sake.

He will find his destiny in solving man's problems and not just in cataloging them. We spend too much time stating them and too little time finding the solution. He will remember Emerson's admonition that there can be no scholar without the heroic mind.

That, I know, is a rather large order. You are only a few men and women, with very limited time and resources. But every great enterprise starts with one man or, at the most, a few. And every great endeavor depends more on the daring than on the dollar, more on brainpower than on budgets.

I just had my budget busted wide open this morning by my colleagues from Texas, but it was on behalf of soldiers who need education. If it is going to be busted, it couldn't be busted for a better purpose.

I say that to you also. I have great confidence in this endeavor. Almost two centuries ago John Adams had this to say about the advance of learning: "I must study politics and war," he said, "that my sons may have the liberty to study mathematics and philosophy.

"My sons ought to study mathematics and

philosophy, geography and natural history, naval architecture and navigation, commerce and agriculture, in order to give their children a right to study painting and poetry, music and literature, architecture, tapestry, and porcelain."

So today, in a world that is very thirsty for genius, we must study all of these things at once if we are to produce a culture which comes anywhere near matching our wealth. We are not just going to talk about producing it, either; we are going to do something about it. And that's a change for America.

We do have the material power to conquer economic want. Now we need the will to attack the poverty of man's spirit. We have looked throughout America and selected you—you members of this Council— to lead the attack on the poverty of man's spirit.

From the moment that you take your oath, your job will be to cup your hands about the flame of our Nation's genius, to protect and to nourish that flame, to make a torch which will light the path of a people who are seeking greatness. I cannot forgo

the opportunity of saying to this somewhat adventuresome and courageous group of men in the Congress who provided legislative leadership in this field, "You have not only your President's gratitude, but the gratitude of the American people for your leadership."

To those of you who have come here this morning to embark on this new adventure and to take your oath, I say welcome—and on behalf of a grateful people express not only my admiration for your endeavors in this field and your leadership and your willingness to work with us, but my gratitude for your coming here to sign up today.

Thank you very much.

NOTE: The President spoke at 12:10 p.m. in the East Room at the White House. In his opening words he referred to Vice President Hubert H. Humphrey and Dr. Henry A. Moe, Chairman of the National Council on the Humanities.

The Council was established by the National Foundation on the Arts and the Humanities Act of 1965 (79 Stat. 845) to initiate and support individual programs and group projects designed to strengthen education and scholarship in humanistic subjects. The names of the 26 members of the Council are printed in the Weekly Compilation of Presidential Documents (vol. 2, p. 120).

---

102   Memorandum on the Processing of Federal Employees' Claims for Workmen's Compensation Benefits. *March 3*, 1966

[Released March 3, 1966. Dated March 2, 1966]

Memorandum for the Heads of Executive Departments and Agencies:

SUBJECT: Delay in Processing Workmen's Compensation Benefits for Federal Employees

While we strive to reduce the number of injuries and accidental deaths occurring in Federal employment, we must be mindful of the hardship and suffering where our efforts have failed. Fortunately, the Federal

Employees' Compensation Act provides one of the finest workmen's compensation programs in the country.

For this protection to be fully effective, the flow of family income should not be unduly interrupted. When the breadwinner's wages stop, delays in commencing benefit payments can create severe financial hardships. It has come to my attention that the average delay is now 71 days.

I believe that this excessive delay can be

shortened if Federal agencies strive to speed up their reporting procedures and increase the accuracy of their accident reports. Therefore, I am asking the members of my Cabinet and the heads of other Federal agencies to provide a top-level internal review of accident reporting in order to eliminate bottlenecks and develop streamlined procedures. Further, I am asking the Secretary of Labor to make available to other Federal agencies technical advice on this problem.

I believe that with increased diligence, this source of hardship can be diminished.

LYNDON B. JOHNSON

103   Message to the Congress Transmitting Annual Report on the Communications Satellite Program.   *March 3, 1966*

To the Congress of the United States:

A new communications era has begun.

The first commercial satellite is in orbit over the Atlantic Ocean, in an unchanging location linking millions of people, thousands of miles apart, in reliable telecommunications between North America and Europe.

The flights of our astronauts, the Olympic Games, international policy discussions, and other occasions of broad interest and major importance have been transmitted throughout the world by way of communications satellites. Today information is made available for improving health, warning against major storms, and increasing agricultural output.

This historic space bridge will be enlarged. Satellites scheduled to be launched later this year are to span the Pacific and expand coverage over the Atlantic.

The commercial satellite service will advance to provide this new and unique telecommunications capability to other areas of the world.

In the foreseeable future, entire newspapers and service from the world's greatest libraries will be able to enter the homes of all those eager for knowledge.

This dramatic effort follows from the Communications Satellite Act of 1962, which called for the establishment of a worldwide commercial communications system as soon as practicable.

With the Communications Satellite Corporation as the United States representative designated by the Act, an international consortium of participants in this global venture continues to grow. Forty-eight countries are now engaged in this joint venture, with the Corporation acting as manager on behalf of all participants under the international agreements.

In the forward movement of the communications satellite program, all agencies of the Government and the committees of the Congress have assisted in carrying out the objectives and purposes of the Act.

Under Section 404(a) of the Act, I am transmitting to the Congress a report on this national program, which is successfully advancing communications satellite technology to the benefit of the people of the United States and the world.

LYNDON B. JOHNSON

The White House
March 3, 1966

NOTE: The Annual Report on Activities and Accomplishments Under the Communications Satellite Act of 1962, January 1–December 31, 1965 (17 pp., Executive Office of the President) is also printed in House Document 400 (89th Cong., 2d sess.). A summary was released by the White House on March 3, 1966 (2 Weekly Comp. Pres. Docs., p. 315).

On the same day the White House also made public the annual report of the Communications Satellite Corporation for the year 1965 (February 1966, 25 pp.).

104   Memorandum Announcing Revised Guidelines Governing Development by the Government of Products or Services for Its Own Use. *March 3, 1966*

Memorandum to the Heads of Departments and Agencies:

Each of you is aware of my determination that this Administration achieve maximum effectiveness in the conduct of day-to-day operations of the Government.

We must seek in every feasible way to reduce the cost of carrying out governmental programs. But we must remember that our budgetary costs—our current out-of-pocket expenditures—do not always provide a true measure of the cost of Government activities. This is often true when the Government undertakes to provide for itself a product or a service which is obtainable from commercial sources.

At the same time, it is desirable, or even necessary, in some instances for the Government to produce directly certain products or services for its own use. This action may be dictated by program requirements, or by lack of an acceptable commercial source, or because significant dollar savings may result.

Decisions which involve the question of whether the Government provides directly products or services for its own use must be exercised under uniform guidelines and principles. This is necessary in order—

—to conduct the affairs of the Government on an orderly basis;

—to limit budgetary costs; and

—to maintain the Government's policy of reliance upon private enterprise.

At my direction the Director of the Bureau of the Budget is issuing detailed guidelines to determine when the Government should provide products and services for its own use. These guidelines are the result of long study, based on experience over the past six years since the current guidelines were issued.

Each of you is requested to designate an assistant secretary or other official of comparable rank to—

—review new proposals for the agency to provide its own supplies or services before they are included in the agency's budget;

—review experience under the new guidelines; and

—suggest any significant changes to the guidelines which experience may indicate to be desirable.

I do not wish to impose rigid or burdensome reporting requirements on each agency with respect to the new guidelines. However these guidelines will require that appropriate records be maintained relative to agency commercial or industrial activities. I am also requesting the Budget Director to report to me from time to time on how the new directives are being carried out, and whether experience suggests changes in the guidelines or in agency reporting requirements.

LYNDON B. JOHNSON

NOTE: The guidelines are printed in Bureau of the Budget Circular A-76, dated March 3, 1966.

105   Memorandum Establishing a Task Force on Summer Domestic Programs.   *March* 5, 1966

[Released March 5, 1966.   Dated March 2, 1966]

Memorandum for the Vice President

SUBJECT: Task Force on Summer Domestic Programs

Each year a number of serious problems, amenable to public action, arise or are exaggerated during the summer months. For instance:

—Youths on school vacation are searching for employment and could therefore profit greatly by additional job opportunities. While rising economic activity will open up many jobs for these young people, we cannot assume that it will take care of the entire problem.

—Children and youths on summer vacation place greater demands upon existing recreational and community facilities to occupy their time.

—Working mothers with school-age children have greater difficulty in maintaining their jobs.

—Unrest is typically greatest during the summer months.

At the same time, many resources which could be utilized to cope with social problems are freed up during the summer:

—School teachers, counselors, and university students seeking summer employment could be better utilized.

—Physical facilities of schools, such as classrooms and gymnasiums can be made more generally available.

—Certain jobs, such as park beautification, conservation work, and in tourist industries, are expanded in the summer and should be identified.

I believe that, with adequate prior planning, the Federal Government can make a significant contribution toward assuring that available resources are used in the most efficient manner to cope with those problems which emerge. This memorandum establishes a special task force to carry out the desired planning. Members of the task force, to be chaired by you, will be the Attorney General, the Secretary of Commerce, Secretary of HEW, Secretary of HUD, Secretary of Labor, Chairman of the CSC, and the Director of OEO.

I would expect this task force to: (a) identify and describe problems that are likely to arise next summer, (b) indicate appropriate action which should be taken to alleviate such problems, and (c) indicate how such action might best be implemented. In this connection, I would expect the task force to consider not only the most efficient use of Federal resources in combating such problems, but also how best to enlist the support of other public and private organizations. The potential problems to be considered by the task force should embrace the full range of domestic social concern, including employment, education, recreation, health, community relations, etc.

I request that this task force submit to me its recommendations by April 1, 1966.

LYNDON B. JOHNSON

NOTE: The recommendations of the task force were made public on April 11, together with a statement by the President in response thereto (see Item 171).

The memorandum was released at San Antonio, Texas.

106   Statement by the President Upon Announcing the Selection of a Task Force on the Health and Education Needs of the People of South Vietnam.   *March 6, 1966*

THE United States has a twofold objective in Vietnam—not only to help the Republic of Vietnam win its war against aggression but also to lay the groundwork for meaningful and durable peace.

The members of this mission will bring professional competence to the work of the health and education task force. This can only be the beginning of what must be a continuing effort on the part of both governments to give new promise and new purpose to the lives of the Vietnamese people.

NOTE: The President's statement was made public as part of a White House release announcing the selection of a task force, headed by Secretary Gardner, to study the health and education needs of the people of South Vietnam. The release stated that the task force would depart for Saigon on March 12 to help plan an intensified attack on hunger, ignorance, and disease in Vietnam in accordance with a joint pledge made by President Johnson and the leaders of the Republic of Vietnam (see Items 54–56).

The release noted that the task force would be composed of 15 leading experts in health and education, among them Mrs. Oveta Culp Hobby, former Secretary of Health, Education, and Welfare, Francis Keppel, Assistant Secretary for Education, HEW, and S. Douglass Cater, Jr., Special Assistant to the President. The release pointed out that the task force would be the second to visit Vietnam since the Honolulu Conference on February 7 and 8, a team of agricultural experts headed by Secretary of Agriculture Orville L. Freeman having arrived in Saigon on February 11.

The full text of the White House release (with names of the other task force members) is published in the Weekly Compilation of Presidential Documents (vol. 2, p. 331).

See also Item 85.

107   Text of Distinguished Unit Citation Awarded to the 121st Aviation Company (Air Mobile Light).   *March 7, 1966*

BY VIRTUE of the authority vested in me as President of the United States and as Commander-in-Chief of the Armed Forces of the United States I have today awarded

THE DISTINGUISHED UNIT CITATION

TO

THE 121ST AVIATION COMPANY

(AIR MOBILE LIGHT)

UNITED STATES ARMED FORCES

AND

ATTACHED UNITS

2D MEDICAL DISPENSARY (GENERAL)

80TH TRANSPORTATION DETACHMENT

(CARGO HELICOPTER FIELD MAINTENANCE)

82D MEDICAL DETACHMENT

(HELICOPTER AMBULANCE)

134TH MEDICAL DETACHMENT

257TH SIGNAL DETACHMENT

DETACHMENT 7, 30TH WEATHER SQUADRON,

UNITED STATES AIR FORCE

6TH AIRLIFT PLATOON

5TH GUNNER DETACHMENT

FOR

EXTRAORDINARY HEROISM

The 121st Aviation Company (Air Mobile Light) and attached units distinguished themselves by extraordinary heroism while engaged in military operations in the Republic of Vietnam on 5 December 1964. The members of this Company and the foregoing units demonstrated indomitable courage and professional skill while providing direct support for a Republic of Vietnam military ground operation in territory

known to be dominated by insurgents.
Their outstanding effectiveness resulted in
the success of aerial troop lifts despite exposure to intensive hostile gunfire, in the timely
modification of techniques which kept pace
with the rapidly changing tactical situations,
and in the on-the-spot field maintenance for
aircraft. Prompt medical assistance was
given to the combat soldier and a countless
number of friendly casualties were quickly
evacuated from the battlefield. Through
their fortitude, perseverance, and gallant efforts, these brave officers and men contributed in great measure to the progress of the
counterinsurgency effort conducted in the

Republic of Vietnam. The devotion to duty,
outstanding achievements, and extraordinary
heroism displayed by the members of the
121st Aviation Company (Air Mobile Light)
and the participating units reflect great credit
upon themselves and the Armed Forces of
the United States.

LYNDON B. JOHNSON

NOTE: The citation was made public as part of a
White House release announcing the award by the
President of the Distinguished Unit Citation to the
121st Aviation Company (Air Mobile Light),
United States Armed Forces. The release noted
that the 121st Aviation Company was in direct support of the Republic of Vietnam 21st Infantry
Division during operations against the Vietcong in
the vicinity of Ca Mau.

108   Special Message to the Congress Proposing Increased Pay, Retirement, and Health Benefits for Federal Employees. *March 7, 1966*

To the Congress of the United States:

Among the many blessings which Americans can count is a corps of Federal civil
servants that is unequaled anywhere in the
world. Honest, intelligent, efficient, and—
above all—dedicated, these men and women
represent a national resource and a national
asset.

America expects much of these public servants. We have made vigorous demands
on their time and energy. We have exacted
from them high standards of work and
conduct.

In recent years, we have moved steadily to
compensate these men and women equitably
and competitively for their quality performance in the public interest. To that end, the
Administration prepared and the Congress
enacted, the Federal Salary Reform Act of
1962. We established the principle that
Government workers are entitled to a pay
scale which compares favorably with pay in
private industry.

Such a pay scale is as much in the national
interest as it is in the interest of Government employees. I said when signing the
Government Employees Salary Reform Act
of 1964:

"America's challenges cannot be met in
this modern world by mediocrity, at any
level, public or private. All through our society we must search for brilliance, welcome
genius, strive for excellence."

We have been true to the principle of
comparability. Since 1961, the pay of Federal employees has increased by over 16 percent.

In the brief period since I have been President, employees of the Federal Government
have enjoyed pay increases amounting to
nearly 12 percent. These increases have
done much to close the gap between compensation for Government employees and
those in private enterprise.

The increases in basic pay, however, were
not accompanied by any significant benefits

in forms other than salary. Yet pay, retirement, and other fringe benefits are all parts of an employee's total compensation. Recognition of this basic fact is crucial in developing a rational and equitable system of compensation. Neither pay, nor retirement, nor other fringe benefits can be considered in isolation. For all of them together represent the worker's real reward.

The proposals which I am making today reflect this consideration.

I propose increases in Federal compensation of $485 million per year.

I am asking the Congress to enact legislation which will provide an average increase for Federal civilian employees amounting to 3.2 percent of total compensation.

On the average, direct salary increases will amount to 2.85 percent. The other increases are for fringe benefits to assist the Government employee in providing for his own economic security.

In considering these proposals, I urge careful study of the supporting data and background information contained in the two reports transmitted with this message:

1. The report of the Cabinet Committee on Federal Staff Retirement Systems, prepared in response to my request of February 1, 1965, for a review of Federal retirement policies and benefits.

2. The annual report to the President of the Director of the Bureau of the Budget and the Chairman of the Civil Service Commission on the comparison between Federal civilian pay levels and those in private enterprise—as required by law.

I also urge the Congress to take into account two other considerations of utmost importance to the Federal employee—and all wage earners—and the Nation as a whole:

—The wage-price guideposts which are key weapons in our defense against inflation, and

—Sound and responsible Federal fiscal policy.

Both of these considerations weighed heavily in my mind as I studied various possible recommendations to make to the Congress this year. For nothing will destroy the progress of the Federal employee in his efforts to achieve comparability more effectively than the erosion of inflation.

PAY

I recommend to the Congress the enactment of a pay raise for Federal employees—effective January 1, 1967—ranging from 1 percent to 4½ percent.

With these increases, nearly one million of the 1.8 million employees affected will achieve pay comparability with private enterprise. These employees include about 88 percent of all postal workers and the more than 470,000 Classification Act employees in grades GS–1 through GS–5.

The smallest increase of approximately 1 percent will go to the lowest of the two grades of the Classification system which are already above comparability. The modestly higher increases will go to the relatively few upper grades where the current comparability difference is larger and where, accordingly, our recruiting difficulties are greatest.

RETIREMENT

I shall not detail in this message all of the changes recommended by the Cabinet Committee on Federal Staff Retirement Systems. The report speaks for itself clearly and succinctly. I endorse it.

I call particular attention to three proposals which I believe to be most urgent. These are:

1. Those who reach age 55 with 30 years of service, should be allowed to retire with-

out reduction in annuity. The Government should also have the option to retire involuntarily, at age 55, employees in grades GS–13 and above who have 30 or more years of service.

2. We should guarantee that retirement, disability, and survivor benefits are at least equal to benefits payable under the Old-Age and Survivors Disability Insurance program of the Social Security system.

3. We should provide for the transfer to the Social Security system of service credits of employees who die, become disabled, or leave Federal employment before becoming eligible for Federal retirement systems benefits.

I recommend that these three proposals, like the basic pay increases, be made effective January 1, 1967.

I also recommend:

—The enactment into law of a clear statement of retirement policy, as set forth in detail on pages 10 and 11 of the Cabinet Committee's report.

—Adjustments between the Civil Service and the Foreign Service retirement systems.

The ultimate costs of all of the proposed changes in the retirement systems are set forth in tabular form on pages 21 and 22 of the Committee's report. This report also contains a sound financing plan. It is essential that we place our retirement system on a sound basis of financing as soon as possible.

I recommend that financing provisions be enacted as a part of the retirement legislation, including a .5 percent increase in contributions of both agencies and employees, effective January 1, 1967.

The report of the Cabinet Committee does not deal with changes in the military retirement system. Although the committee reviewed important aspects of military retirement, it agreed with the Secretary of Defense that recommendations for fundamental changes should wait completion of a broad management study now underway in the Department of Defense.

The retirement report and the recommendations for legislation presented by it are major steps forward in our continuing efforts to improve the compensation system for Federal employees. In my judgment, they are equal in importance to the 1962 Federal Salary Reform Act.

OTHER BENEFITS

I recommend a phased two-year increase in the Government's contribution to our civilian health benefits program.

The first increase should be effective on January 1, 1967; the second on January 1, 1968. These increases would restore the ratio of costs to the Government and costs to the employee established by the original Health Benefits Act of 1959.

The effective date of other important adjustments in our retirement system should be deferred for at least another year. The most important of these are to:

1. Extend Medicare to Federal civilian employees.

2. Continue benefits until age 22 for those surviving children of deceased Federal employees who are continuing their education.

3. Compute benefits on the basis of a guaranteed disability minimum to widows of employees who die after retirement for disability.

4. Continue benefits for a surviving widow if she remarries after age 60.

NEED FOR NEW KNOWLEDGE

If we are to continue to modernize our policy of total compensation, we need better information than is now available. We must examine all of the *fringe benefits* in our compensation system. These include leave, holiday pay, special pay differentials, unemployment insurance, Federal Employees Compensation Act benefits for duty-related accidents and illness, health benefits, life insurance, and counterpart benefits prevailing elsewhere in our economy.

I am recommending that the Congress appropriate funds for collection and evaluation of information on non-Federal fringe benefits in the budget of the Department of Labor for 1967.

CONCLUSION

The measures I am proposing meet the test of fairness to our employees. They also meet the test of economic responsibility.

For the past many months, the Government has appealed to labor and industry alike to hold price and wage increases within the guideposts established by the Council of Economic Advisers.

If our Government is to exercise continued leadership in the fight for price stability, then we must continue to practice what we preach. The Government has the added responsibility of not contributing to inflation by its own actions.

With five years of unprecedented economic expansion, our industry is now operating near the peak of its capacity. Added to this, we now have the obligation to support our fighting men in Vietnam and our commitment to freedom there.

This Administration has already proved that our nation does not have to live with depression or recession. Now we must prove that we can remain both strong and prosperous without endangering our economic stability.

Government employees have a direct stake in this effort. For none is more harmed by inflation—and harmed more quickly—than the wage earner and the salaried employee. It is of small value to him if the extra dollar he earns buys less and less with every passing week.

We are the wealthiest nation in history. We can afford whatever is necessary for both our welfare at home and our common defense abroad. But we can do this only by the exercise of fiscal prudence and economic responsibility during times when special demands are being made on our economy by the military needs of Vietnam.

I am certain that both Government employees and the leaders of their organizations will recognize that restraint serves both their cause and the national interest. They will recognize that these proposals meet three essential requirements:

—First, that taken together, pay, retirement, and health benefits amount to an increase of the maximum total compensation increase within the wage-price guidelines.

—Second, that the major increases will go to those Federal workers whose compensation is least comparable with private enterprise.

—And third, that these proposals move the entire pay scale toward full comparability in an orderly manner.

The annual cost of these proposals will amount to $485 million. If they are made effective on January 1, 1967—which I urgently recommend—the cost for the next fiscal year will be $240 million. These costs are fully provided for in the budget which I submitted to the Congress in January.

The Federal government is the largest employer in the nation. The largest employer has an undeniable responsibility to lead, and not merely to follow, in instituting and adhering to model employment practices.

A model employer can demand excellence in performance. A model employer can demand continuing awareness of the need for greater productivity, more imaginative conduct of Government programs, and substantial cost reduction. We have made those demands.

Federal officers and employees at all levels have responded with enthusiasm and skill. If they had not been determined to improve the efficiency and economy of Government operations, budget costs in both 1966 and 1967 would be some $3 billion higher than they are.

By the close of this fiscal year, the total compensation for our two and one-half million Federal civilian employees will be $20.4 billion a year. With expenditures of such magnitude, the President, the Congress, and Federal employees themselves, cannot fail to give the most careful consideration to every adjustment in pay, retirement, and health benefits. Each proposed adjustment must not only be merited, it should also be consistent with the principles of sound government.

LYNDON B. JOHNSON

The White House
March 7, 1966

NOTE: The report of the Cabinet Committee on Federal Staff Retirement Systems (80 pp., processed) was made public with the President's message. It is printed in House Document 402 (89th Cong., 2d sess.), together with the Joint Annual Report of the Director of the Bureau of the Budget and the Chairman of the Civil Service Commission.

The Federal Salary and Fringe Benefits Act of 1966 was approved by the President on July 18, 1966 (see Item 333).

See also Item 109.

109 Statement by the President on the Message on Pay, Retirement, and Health Benefits of Federal Employees. *March 7, 1966*

TODAY, I have sent to the Congress a Federal pay bill which provides increases in salary and fringe benefits averaging 3.2 percent.

This increase, exactly within the wage and price guideposts recommended by the President's Council of Economic Advisers, is designed to be just—and to fight inflation.

Every action we take should be advanced in the light of what effect it will have on our men in Vietnam—men who are fighting and dying for us now.

We here at home ought to set an example for them.

If we increase wages and show no restraint on prices, we will lose the war on inflation. We will severely handicap our men in Vietnam.

I have asked Government employees to set an example. I have asked them to live within the guideposts which we believe are a key bulwark against inflation.

For 5 years, our economy has been moving toward full use of its capacity. But as we near this long-sought condition, we must work together to preserve the value of the dollar from the threat of inflation.

Nothing will destroy the progress of Federal employees—and all wage earners—more swiftly than inflation.

We must sustain our 5-year long prosperity. We can do it.

As I have asked Government employees to stand firm in the fight against inflation, so have I asked, and continue to ask, all employers and employees in the Nation to exercise voluntary restraint. This great Nation can retain its economic strength and health, if we stand together to preserve our prosperity. That is why I am proud of the Federal pay increase bill.

NOTE: The President recorded the statement for radio and television broadcast. It was not made public in the form of a White House release. As printed above it follows the reading text made available by the White House press office.

For the President's message to Congress, see Item 108.

110   Letter to the Chairman, House Committee on Banking and Currency, on Receiving a Forecast of Business Investment Plans. *March 7*, 1966

Dear Mr. Chairman:

I have received your letter of March 5 referring to the Lionel D. Edie survey of business investment plans. The Council of Economic Advisers received a copy of their report sometime ago and has been studying it.

The Edie Survey has often in the past given a fairly reliable indication of business investment intentions. The regular investment survey conducted by the Department of Commerce and the Securities and Exchange Commission has substantially broader coverage. It has proven remarkably accurate in the past. The Department of Commerce and the SEC have a new survey that is now virtually complete, with final results to be available shortly.

The Council of Economic Advisers believes the Edie Survey substantially overstates the situation. The present expectation is that the Commerce-SEC Survey will show an investment gain for 1966 up only slightly over the 1965 gain—in the 15.5% to 16.5% range. You recall that total plant and equipment expenditures increased by 15.5% in 1965. The machinery and construction industries were able to accommodate it without excessive strain. In manufacturing in particular, the Commerce-SEC likely survey figures are far from the 32% predicted by Edie. Of course, as your letter noted, the economy is closer to full use of its resources this year.

If the final figures show an increase in 1966 comparable to the 1965 increase, we must continue to keep an extremely close watch on economic developments. We must be prepared to act quickly in the field of taxation if such action appears necessary. In this connection, I am pleased to learn that a Subcommittee of your distinguished Committee will be holding hearings later this month.

As I said in my Economic Report:

"We must always be prepared to meet quickly any problems that arise in the path of continued, stable economic growth, whether the problems call for fiscal stimulus or fiscal restraint. Background tax studies by both the Congress and Executive Branch should therefore be adequate to permit quick decisions and prompt action to accommodate short-run cyclical changes. If quick action is ever needed, we should not have to begin a long debate on what the changes in taxes should be."

I shall watch your hearings with great interest.

       Sincerely yours,

         LYNDON B. JOHNSON

[Honorable Wright Patman, Chairman, Banking and Currency Committee, House of Representatives, Washington, D.C.]

NOTE: Representative Patman's letter of March 5 called the President's attention to the 32 percent increase in business investments forecast for 1966 by the survey made by the Lionel D. Edie Company. "I am sure that you agree that a good rise in private investment is a healthy thing for our economy," the letter continued. "But an increase of this size appears to me as possibly too much of a good thing, at a time when our unemployment rate is already down to 4 percent, and we are also mounting a sizeable military effort in Southeast Asia."

Representative Patman's letter is printed in the Weekly Compilation of Presidential Documents (vol. 2, p. 338).

111   Annual Message to the Congress: The Manpower Report of the President.   *March 8, 1966*

To the Congress of the United States:

I report on a year of progress and fulfillment.

I report on a year of challenge and change.

February 1966 marked the twentieth anniversary of this Nation's 1946 commitment to provide job opportunities for every person, able, willing, and seeking to work.

February 1966 also brought the fifth anniversary of our longest and soundest period of peacetime prosperity. It marked the 60th consecutive month of visible proof that the 1946 commitment can be met.

A RECORD OF ACCOMPLISHMENT

Five years of sustained economic growth have effectively demonstrated that this Nation can:

1. Pursue an economic policy which creates millions of new jobs and reduces the burdens of unemployment and poverty.
2. Provide the necessary job opportunities to convert a flood of teenagers into a valuable national resource instead of an urgent social problem.
3. Set in motion manpower programs to transform the deprived, the disadvantaged, and the despairing into effective and self-respecting members of the Great Society.

Last year was one of harvest—and of new planting.

The fruits of sustained economic growth were realized in terms of increased employment and earnings for the American worker.

In 1965:

—The advance of 2.4 million jobs exceeded by one-third the increase of the labor force.

—Private nonfarm payrolls swelled by 42,000 added jobs each week.

—More than a million young Americans entered the work force, but there was work for them to do.

—Unemployment was reduced to its lowest rate in almost nine years.

—The American factory worker's weekly earnings reached $110.92. Although the cost of the things he bought went up 2%, *there was 4.5% more money in his pocket to buy them after paying his Federal taxes.*

Last year also saw the first combined effects of the new manpower, education, and poverty programs.

In 1965:

—More than 100,000 persons completed training under the Manpower Development and Training Act. Three out of every four were placed in jobs within ninety days after their course ended.

—More than 500,000 young men and women were approved for participation in the Neighborhood Youth Corps. The Corps helps those in school to stay there, and helps dropouts to return to school or begin work.

—About 200 area vocational-technical schools were approved for construction. 85,000 full-time students are receiving financial assistance to begin or continue vocational training.

—About 115,000 full-time college students in more than 1,100 colleges participated in work-study programs, which helped them to meet the costs of a college education.

—Work experience programs provided jobs, basic education, training—and hope and dignity—for 65,000 public welfare recipients with almost 200,000 dependents.

—Almost 30,000 young men and women were enrolled in the Job Corps. For many of them, it was their first opportunity for realistic training to help them find and keep jobs.

Across the land, more and more men and women became productive members of a great and productive society. More and more boys and girls, in and out of school, received the work experience and training which helped to fit them for responsible places in society and to save them from lifetimes of chronic unemployment and degrading poverty.

A year ago 5.0% of our workers were unemployed.

Now only 3.7% are out of work.

A year ago many of our programs to provide better training and wider educational opportunities were only beginning.

Today they are supplying thousands of trained workers for our expanding economy.

But our very success in banishing the spectre of mass unemployment from our land has brought new problems.

To sustain high employment, and continue our record of price stability, we must work harder than ever to match jobs and men.

Our success in reducing unemployment brings out more clearly than ever the fact that there is poverty in the midst of plenty. We cannot rest content:

—when employers seek skilled and experienced workers while thousands cannot find work because they lack proper training and education.

—when factories in some areas are unable to fill orders because they lack workers, while chronic unemployment endures in other areas.

This year we must make a special effort to see that our human resources are not wasted.

We must accelerate the growth of public and private training programs and make them available to all.

We must bring jobs to workers and workers to jobs.

We must eliminate the discrimination which wastes our manpower resources.

Our goal is not just a job for every worker. Our goal is to place every worker in a job where he utilizes his full productive potential, for his own and for society's benefit.

To achieve this goal, I have outlined below a new program to make full use of all our human resources.

Making the transition to an economy of sustained high employment is our immediate task. But we must not lose sight of the longer run.

We take pride in the growth of our economy, in the achievements of our scientists and engineers, and in the ability of our dynamic private-enterprise economy to put new technology to practical use. But the requirements of new technology demand continuing adjustments in our work force. To make those adjustments as smoothly as possible, every worker needs a first-rate education and opportunities for continuing education and training.

A MANPOWER PROGRAM FOR FULL EMPLOY-
MENT OPPORTUNITY

Earlier Manpower Reports proceeded from a central concern with excessive unemployment: 6% at the time of the first report, and still 5% two years later.

Now, with unemployment below 4% and falling, the attention of the Congress and the Nation must focus on the manpower prospects and problems which emerge as the products of unprecedented prosperity.

An unemployment rate of 3.7% in February marks another milestone along the country's course toward full realization of its economic potential.

It was in November 1953—more than 12 years ago—that the unemployment rate was last that low. A year ago it was still 5%.

Attaining an unemployment rate of 3.7% is a triumph for our Nation's economy. It is a tribute to the public and private policies that led to this achievement.

Because it does reflect an economy operating closer to the full use of its manpower resources, our celebration must be tempered with caution. We must be alert to assure that the pace of our advance does not become too rapid, endangering the healthy stability and sound balance of our expansion.

Yet to conclude that we must proceed cautiously does not mean that we should slam on the brakes or throw the economy into reverse.

We expect our labor force to expand by 1.6 million workers this year.

Thus, we must provide about 4,500 new jobs each day—31,000 new jobs each week—134,000 new jobs each month.

Moreover, we cannot rest on past accomplishments when the unemployment rate for Negroes was still 7% in February. It was down from 9.2% a year earlier, and from nearly 13% in February 1961. But we can-

not be satisfied when one out of every 14 Negro workers is without a job.

Nor can we be satisfied with a reduction of the unemployment rate for teenagers from 15½% in February 1961 and 14½% a year ago, to 10.9% last month. So high a rate for young workers still blocks far too many young men and women from beginning productive and rewarding careers.

Our achievement is worthy of celebration, but our task remains unfinished. We can and will move with appropriate caution to sustain our economic advance into even higher levels of manpower achievement.

The 3.7% rate is an average. It conceals the fact that some 3 million workers still lack jobs. It also conceals the fact that there are now more jobs in some areas and occupations than there are people to fill them.

—In the Great Lakes region, there is already a tight supply of both skilled and unskilled labor.

—There are shortages of machinists for the metal working industry throughout the country, and shortages of building trades craftsmen in many areas.

—The new education programs could be stunted for a lack of teachers, and the Medicare program thwarted for a lack of medical and nursing personnel.

Yet, while these shortages exist:

—There are pockets of chronic unemployment in many cities, in Appalachia, in the Mississippi Delta, and in other regions of economic distress.

—There are teenagers who need jobs to stay in school or to help support their families. They need to know that society has a place for them and a need for their services.

—There are millions employed in occupations and skills that do not fully utilize their capabilities.

There is no over-all labor shortage. But

the unemployed and underemployed are not fully matched with the jobs available.

Specific shortages of labor can slow up the expansion of the economy. They can put pressure on costs and prices.

We are determined to do whatever is necessary to keep the economy expanding and avoid inflationary bottlenecks.

PLANS TO HEAD OFF MANPOWER SHORTAGES

The time to deal with manpower shortages is before they develop.

Effective manpower policies can reduce unemployment and at the same time head off manpower shortages.

I am therefore:

1. Directing the Commissioner of Labor Statistics to include in the monthly employment reports, starting in March, the fullest possible information on existing or threatening labor shortage situations.

2. Establishing an office of Assistant Secretary of Labor for Manpower, to assist the Secretary of Labor in the discharge of his manpower responsibilities under existing legislation and as Chairman of the President's Committee on Manpower.

3. Instructing the Secretary of Labor to focus Manpower Development and Training Act programs to meet prospective manpower shortage situations, especially through on-the-job training.

4. Requesting the President's Committee on Manpower to submit to me by July 1, 1966 a report on the recently announced coordination plan for all manpower activities of the Federal Government.

5. Asking the President's Advisory Committee on Labor-Management Policy to make appropriate recommendations

to me on the manpower situation and related matters.

6. Referring the Report of the National Commission on Automation, Technology and Economic Progress to the President's Manpower and Labor-Management Policy Committees for advice regarding the Commission's recommendations.

At my request, the Secretary of Labor yesterday submitted to the Congress legislation to improve the administration of the Federal-State Employment Service. This legislation emerged from the unanimous recommendations of a task force of distinguished businessmen, labor leaders, educators and other manpower specialists.

I call at the same time on American management and American labor to take the affirmative action which is necessary to assure that inflation, resulting from the under-use of America's manpower potential, will not deprive us of the fruits of the most magnificent economic growth record in history.

A CALL FOR BOLD NEW APPROACHES

I am asking these agencies and groups to think boldly about new approaches.

What can we do to move the unemployed and the underemployed from places where jobs are scarce to places where workers are scarce? How do we move the jobs to the unemployed?

What can we do to encourage employers, who seek scarce skills, to redefine jobs in a way that employs more of the unskilled or semiskilled?

How can we enhance the mobility of workers in construction and similar occupations where demand shifts sharply among localities?

What can we do to mobilize the recently retired but still productive?

What can we do to make fuller use of our trained womanpower?

What can we do to break down artificial barriers against the entry of new workers into jobs that are hard to fill?

What can we do to insure that training and apprenticeship programs are open to all alike and are sufficiently extensive to meet our needs for skilled workers?

What can we do to help employers improve their own on-the-job training?

What can we do to encourage the employment of the physically and psychologically handicapped?

What can we do to facilitate the immigration of workers with scarce skills?

What more can we do to break down the barriers of discrimination that waste valuable manpower resources?

We already have many effective tools of an active manpower policy. In the year ahead we will expand and improve these programs.

Our most important new tool was provided by the Manpower Development and Training Act of 1962, strengthened by the Amendments of 1963 and 1965. Our manpower training programs must respond both to needs of people and the needs of the economy.

Our experience under the Act has proved that:
—people can be helped through education and training.
—the economy will benefit from the availability of additional workers.

Training will make useful and productive citizens of people previously considered beyond even the most elementary kinds of help.
—Mentally retarded individuals are being hired in increasing numbers by both Government and private employers, after successful training in various semi-skilled, office and service occupations.
—Vocational rehabilitation and manpower development programs are being applied more extensively to inmates of correctional institutions. During their period of confinement, they can prepare for jobs when they are released.

Federal manpower training programs are conducted in close cooperation with private industry. During the past year, we have significantly increased the number of on-the-job training programs approved under the Manpower Development and Training Act. In occupations ranging from tool and die makers to nurses aides and shipfitters, people are being trained *on the job*. The employment rate of over 85% testifies to the effectiveness of these programs.

In the next fiscal year, we will train and retrain 250,000 persons under these MDTA programs.

An expanding economy now presents both the opportunity and the necessity to upgrade the skills of the underemployed. This will meet the demand for workers. It will afford opportunity to people to move into higher skill and higher paying jobs—as high as their abilities permit.

The second major tool of our manpower policy is the Federal-State Employment Service. It must assume even greater responsibility not only in placing people, but in providing proper job and training information, guidance, and counseling to all who need it.

The administrative framework of the Service must be modernized.

The quality of those who provide its day-to-day services must be improved.

The methods of its operation need development.

More intensive research is needed to help guide our young people to occupations where they are most needed.

Vigorous manpower training and a re-vitalized job placement service are essential for a high-employment economy with price stability.

We will make the most of these tools in 1966.

THE SPECIAL PROBLEMS OF THE DISADVANTAGED

Certain groups in the nation have not shared fully in the benefits of our unprece-dented economic expansion. Much remains to be done to achieve full opportunity for these groups. As we expand *their* oppor-tunities, we expand *our* manpower resources.

—*Unskilled workers,* with almost double the national rate of unemployment, lack the training to develop their potential skills.

—*Nonwhite workers,* constitute 11% of our labor force, 20% of our unemployed, and nearly 25% of our long-term un-employed, they suffer the double dis-advantages of lower educational attain-ment and lingering discrimination.

—*Young Americans,* who will swell our work force for many years to come, still experience triple the national unemploy-ment rate.

—*Farm workers,* both operators and hired workers, remain the victims of high unemployment and underemployment.

—*Workers in surplus labor areas,* such as Appalachia, can benefit only from more vigorous economic development in their home areas or from migration to cen-ters of employment growth.

No society can be truly great—and no economy can be truly prosperous—if high, long-duration unemployment for some exists side by side with low, short-term unemploy-ment for others.

Special programs, suited to special groups, are needed to achieve full employment with price stability.

We must move again as we did last year to meet the impact of the more than 2 mil-lion young people—16 to 21 years of age—who will be looking for work next summer.

As we continue toward the Great Society, we will also bring increased employment opportunities to many groups.

—The rehabilitation and rebuilding of large blighted sections in our central cities will bring new vistas to those parts of Amer-ica where opportunities are needed most.

—The work of the Rural Community Development Service will open up new op-portunities for rural people, particularly in areas of greatest need. The new Commu-nity Development Districts, when pending legislation is passed, will bring greater plan-ning resources to rural areas. The result will be higher levels of social and economic development.

—Our efforts under the 1965 Public Works and Economic Development Act will be stepped up.

—Joint Federal-State efforts under the Appalachian Regional Commission are also being increased. I have recommended quadrupling the expenditures for special programs to reach the more than 17 million people residing in that area. Such an in-crease means increased resources for highway construction, development of natural re-sources, vocational education and health activities.

Our economy cannot be fully successful, or our society truly great, while differences in economic opportunity persist.

The programs and policies of this Admin-istration seek to reduce and ultimately to eliminate these differences. They are in-tolerable in a free and democratic society.

INVESTMENT IN HUMAN RESOURCES

In a prosperous economy, the root of most problems of unemployment and underemployment lies in deficiencies in education.

We must repair these deficiencies where we can.

We must prevent their recurrence in the next generation.

Fewer young people now drop out of school. But the number is still too high. If current trends continue, there will be over 8 million school dropouts between 1960 and 1970. The average American worker already has more than a high school education. The dropout will be at an ever-increasing disadvantage.

I am particularly concerned by the large numbers of young men who fail the Armed Forces qualification tests and must be rejected for military service. One-seventh of the young men examined cannot pass the equivalent of an elementary school examination.

Low educational attainment is a product, and in turn a producer, of poverty, unemployment, and discrimination.

This Administration is determined to bring increased education and training opportunities to all Americans in the coming year. We intend to:

—Improve vocational rehabilitation training for over 200,000 mentally retarded, severely disabled and handicapped individuals.

—Train or retrain 250,000 persons under manpower development programs.

—Have Community Action Programs in 900 areas, urban and rural, throughout the United States.

—Fund preschool classes for more than 200,000 children over the full academic year—and for another 500,000 youngsters during the summer. Almost 150,000 teachers, teacher aides, and neighborhood helpers will provide the needed service to these children.

—Operate 124 Job Corps urban and rural training centers, able to enroll approximately 45,000 men and women at any one time.

—Provide 125,000 part time jobs during the entire school year and another 165,000 summer jobs in the Neighborhood Youth Corps to help poor young people stay in school. Another 64,000 positions will be available for boys and girls out of school.

—Offer services, under the Work Experience Program, to over 100,000 public welfare recipients who support 300,000 dependents.

—Give basic education to 75,000 adults under grants to States for improving adult literacy.

—Conduct 350 different projects involving 4,500 VISTA volunteers to provide educational training and related services to the poor.

These specific programs are in addition to the enormous expansion in aid to our elementary, secondary and higher education systems. For next year, I have proposed a total federal investment in education of $10.2 billion—more than double the 4.75 billion dollar effort when I became President. This will move us forward toward our goal of providing full education for every citizen to the limits of his capacity to absorb it.

Teaching methods and materials, no matter how excellent, are not enough. They must be kindled by ingenious, flexible and responsive teachers and administrators. I have urged that Congress provide the funds for a new Teacher Corps—to be made up initially of 3,700 men and women. Combined into teams of experienced and intern teachers, they will be sharing their skills and understanding this Fall with the poor children who need them most.

I am also calling for increased activities which will provide this Nation with more high-quality teachers for the handicapped and to meet the impact of school desegregation.

Manpower demands for professional personnel are also increasing in many other fields. New research and teaching activities must be oriented to meet those demands. Grants, loans and other forms of aid are being made available to States, localities and educational institutions. They include:

—A significant increase in National Science Foundation support of basic research and science education, critically important for the advanced training of scientists and engineers.

—University grants for research and training of advanced degree students in the space sciences through the National Aeronautics and Space Administration.

—Help through the Health Professions Educational Assistance Act and other legislation to increase, by 1975, the number of medical school graduates by 50% and the number of dental school graduates by 100% over 1960.

—Training personnel to deal with the critical problems of water pollution under the Water Pollution Control Administration.

—Training programs for developing skills of persons who are needed in community development activities.

—Continued assistance in the development of high quality personnel for guidance and counseling—from elementary school to the university—under provisions of the National Defense Education Act.

We must provide full and free access to a first-rate education for all our youth, with later opportunities to develop their talents to the fullest measure of their ability.

The commitment of the Administration is to expand education and training opportunities for every citizen.

UNEMPLOYMENT INSURANCE AND MINIMUM WAGE

Sound fiscal and monetary policies, effective training programs, an efficient employment service, and expanding educational services can steadily provide new hope for the unemployed.

Yet, even in a high-employment economy, the protection of unemployment compensation remains essential. The present period of prosperity is the appropriate time to modernize and strengthen our system of Unemployment Insurance.

I have recommended that legislation be enacted to improve our system's financing and administration,

—to prevent abuses,

—to provide more realistic benefits for more workers, for longer periods.

Special protection is needed for those in our labor force who are still employed at substandard earnings. The minimum wage for American workers has been an essential part of national policy for almost thirty years. But both the level of the minimum and the number of workers covered have recently fallen behind the pace set by the rest of the economy.

I recommend that the minimum wage be increased and that the coverage of the Fair Labor Standards Act be extended to additional workers.

We must provide all possible assistance to those who seek work, and decent living conditions for those who do work.

The programs and policies of this Administration will be directed at these goals.

285

OUR OPPORTUNITY FOR THE FUTURE

This report has been of programs and policies, of legislation and appropriations. These are the means by which manpower policy is carried out.

The real basis of manpower policy is more fundamental.

It is the very essence of a free and democratic society.

It is our shared belief in the dignity of every human being.

This report has been of the gains of the past year.

To mark these gains is only to take new measure of the future. We are a people who draw confidence from the certainty of change. We are restless unless we can mold change to the highest human purpose.

With all that we have accomplished so far, with all that we are doing now, it is time to ask again: What of the future?

The future can be and ought to be a time of opportunity.

I see a future where the first two decades of people's lives are spent growing up, physically and mentally fit—training for citizenship and effective participation in their country's affairs—attaining the education for service, for a craft, for a profession—getting ready for their roles as workers, consumers, producers, and contributors to a free society.

I see a future in which education and training will be a permanent bridge between learning, employment and human development. Even as we develop new uses of technology, we recognize that people grow stale unless there is a continuous renewal of their knowledge, enrichment of their skills and development of their talents.

I see a future in which help to those seeking a station in life—whether it be the young dropout, the first offender, the older man with an outdated skill, the military rejectee—will have an opportunity to fulfill their hopes and expectations.

A manpower policy must be based on belief in the value of the individual and in the promise of welcome change.

A manpower policy should lead us to a society in which every person has full opportunity to develop his—or her—earning powers, where no willing worker lacks a job, and where no useful talent lacks an opportunity.

LYNDON B. JOHNSON

The White House
March 8, 1966

NOTE: The President's fourth report under the Manpower Development and Training Act of 1962 and the report of the Department of Labor are printed in "Manpower Report of the President and a Report on Manpower Requirements, Resources, Utilization, and Training" (Government Printing Office, 1966, 229 pp.).

The Fair Labor Standards Amendments of 1966, which provided for an increase in the minimum wage, was approved by the President on September 23, 1966 (see Item 479).

The Manpower Development and Training Amendments of 1966 was approved by the President on November 7, 1966 (see Item 588).

See also Item 112.

112   Statement by the President on the Manpower Message. *March 8, 1966*

MY ANNUAL Manpower Report demonstrates this nation's ability to build and sustain prosperity. February marked the 60th consecutive month of economic growth—the longest in our peacetime history. Unemployment fell to 3.7 percent—the lowest in more than 12 years.

In the past year we have created new jobs

for 2.4 million workers.

But there is still much to do. We must be bold and imaginative, and far-sighted. Too many Negroes, and too many teenagers, are still unemployed. Too many skilled jobs go begging while unskilled workers can't find a job.

When I became President we were spending $4.7 billion on education. My budget this year calls for $10.2 billion for education—more than double.

Few trained people are unemployed.

Few educated people are without work. Our job is to provide more education for more people—more training for the unskilled. This will mean more jobs, less welfare.

This report calls this nation to action.

NOTE: The President recorded the statement for radio and television broadcast. It was not made public in the form of a White House release. As printed above it follows the text made available by the White House Press Office.

For the President's message to Congress, see Item 111.

---

113   Remarks at the Swearing In of Elmer Staats as Comptroller General of the United States. *March 8, 1966*

Mr. Staats, Mr. Justice, Mr. Rich, Mrs. Staats, members of the Cabinet, Members of the Congress, my friends:

I was informed that Elmer Staats hoped that any complimentary remarks which might be made at his swearing-in ceremony this morning be directed to the staff of the Bureau of the Budget rather than to him personally.

Perhaps, when Mr. Staats hears some of the things that will be said about him in the next 15 years, it could just be that he may want to remember some of the nice things that I'm going to say about him today.

Of course, I am always delighted to compliment the staff of the Bureau of the Budget. The energy, the dedication, the imagination, and the uncomplaining hard work of these loyal American men and women who work in the Budget are a never-ending source of pride to me.

Because I remember in the first hours of my Presidency, the largest problem that I had to face was the construction of a budget during the month of December. Through long days (and seemed like much longer nights) the Budget people were my prime

allies in getting that job done. And in those beginning days, the man always by my side was Elmer Staats.

He has served this government faithfully and well for 26 years. He has been Deputy Director of the Bureau of the Budget under four different Presidents.

Whether they were Democrat or Republican, he served them all with equal fidelity and equal wisdom.

And that is why I chose him for this new assignment.

From the first, I was determined to put forward the best Comptroller General in America that I could find. Mr. Staats holds a unique and a very vital position in our government. While he has been appointed by the President, his ultimate responsibility is to the Congress and to the President, but most important of all, to the country.

There are 2½ million men and women in the Federal Government who work each day to advance the progress of this uncommon land. But in any group that large there are always a few who are doubters and who are faint-hearted. There are always some who lack the vision to anticipate our strength as a nation—or the courage to give that strength purpose. There are some who do not have the faith to lead, and who find fault with either our system of government or the men who try faithfully to serve it, or with some of their colleagues in the other branches such as the courts, the services, the legislative, the Executive, and so on.

We know that doubters or the fearful cannot build governments or create strength. It is easy to declare why failure is certain and success is dim.

But what really lasts and endures and prospers is the work of the builders. And this is the hard way, and this is the long journey, and this is sometimes the most difficult path. But nothing very valuable is very easily won.

Whenever there is a collision with fate, when history stops for a moment of crisis—it is the doubter who runs from the test of courage—and it is the builder who is firm in the face of fear.

And we who know him, know that Elmer Staats has always been a builder, a believer—not a doubter.

He believes in our system of government.

He has confidence in the wisdom of the Congress. He doesn't dwell on the minor imperfections that are always the part of any human system. He declares his faith in the hopes of this nation, and in the people who try to faithfully serve it.

So, General Staats, this morning in the presence of your wonderful family, and particularly your distinguished father-in-law, my old friend Bob Rich of Pennsylvania—whom I am so happy could be here with us—you launch a new career. We have full confidence that the entire Nation will reap the profits from your achievements—as you continue in the next 15 years of this term, as you have for the last 26, the work of the builder always serving faithfully and diligently all branches without fear, without favor, or without fuss.

NOTE: The President spoke shortly after noon in the East Room at the White House. In his opening words he referred to Elmer B. Staats, former Deputy Director of the Bureau of the Budget, Judge E. Barrett Prettyman, Senior Circuit Judge of the U.S. Court of Appeals for the District of Columbia, who administered the oath of office, Robert F. Rich, Representative from Pennsylvania 1930–1943 and 1945–1951, and Mrs. Elmer B. Staats.

---

114 Memorandum on Balance of Payments and Federal Expenditures Overseas. *March 8, 1966*

Memorandum for Cabinet Officers and Heads of Major Agencies:

Our balance of payments requires our continuing attention and concern. We achieved a substantial improvement in the overall deficit in 1965 and we look forward to further improvement this year.

Federal overseas transactions play an important role in our balance of payments, and for the past several years we have made a great effort to minimize the adverse impact that our Federal programs might have

on our balance of payments. But the requirements associated with Vietnam, both for military and for economic assistance, now demand ever greater vigilance in controlling our overseas Federal transactions.

Under the procedures which have been established to control the balance of payments impact of the Federal Government's overseas activities, you are scheduled to report by March 15 to the Bureau of the Budget on your agency's international transactions. I urge that you use this occasion to re-examine all of your overseas programs with the utmost care. Your objective should be to maximize receipts and to minimize expenditures abroad consistent with the achievement of U.S. objectives.

I have instructed the Director of the Bureau of the Budget to examine your reports carefully and to inform me promptly of the progress which is being made by each Federal agency in assisting the Nation to achieve equilibrium in its balance of payments.

LYNDON B. JOHNSON.

115   Remarks at the Swearing In of Andrew F. Brimmer as a Member, Federal Reserve Board.   *March* 9, 1966

Dr. Brimmer, Mr. Vice President, members of the Brimmer family, Chairman Martin, members of the Federal Reserve Board, most distinguished guests, Members of Congress, ladies and gentlemen:

Thirty-three years ago this week not a single bank in America was open for business. It was a time of depression and despair as Americans lost confidence not only in their dollar but in their system of government itself.

Today all of that seems to be behind us. Our banking system is sound and there is confidence in the American dollar. Instead of depression or recession, we are beginning our sixth year of uninterrupted prosperity, the longest in America's peacetime history.

No accident of history brought about this change. It has come because we have learned the economic facts of life and we now realize that recession and inflation are not inevitable. They can be avoided through sound economic fiscal policies. It has come because we have learned how we can work together, cooperating with each other for the benefit of all the people of our land.

The great abundance of America is the result of responsible cooperation between business and banking, between labor and Government. No member of that partnership, from Government's viewpoint, is more important or has greater responsibilities than

the Federal Reserve System of this country. The seven distinguished Governors of the Federal Reserve System share the task of deciding how much money and credit should be supplied to America's economy—and that, ladies and gentlemen, is no easy burden.

The entire Nation, every worker and every housewife, every businessman and every farmer, is affected by the progressive spirit and the wisdom and the prudence of the men who sit on that Board.

In the choice of those men who sit there, the President of the United States has no more far-reaching decision to to make. Today the Federal Reserve System of our Nation has a new Governor. I am proud of this choice. His qualifications, I think, are rare. For if it is true, as some have said, that not 1 man in 100,000 really understands the complexity of high finance and monetary policy, Dr. Andrew Brimmer is one that, I believe, does understand it.

He has been both student and teacher in major universities on both the east and west coasts of this land. He worked for several years in the Federal Reserve Bank of New York City. He is a doctor of economics from Harvard, a professor of economics on leave from the Wharton School of Finance at the University of Pennsylvania. We borrowed him from Pennsylvania to serve in the "little Cabinet" as Deputy Assistant Secretary for Economic Affairs in the important Department of Commerce.

He was the chief economist for that Department. He was also in charge of the voluntary program carried out by the businessmen of America which has done so much to correct our balance of payments problems by reducing our deficit from $2.8 billion last year to $1.3 billion this year.

Dr. Brimmer was born on a farm in the State of Louisiana. His achievements in life are his own. Through his own intelligence and by his own efforts he rose to the highest academic honors. In the process, he developed a deep feeling for Americans in every walk of life. He is still a young man at age 39.

Last month, in fact, he received the Arthur S. Flemming Award which is presented to the 10 outstanding young men in Government service. I don't know of a recommendation that I have received from any man in Government that was stronger than the recommendation Secretary Connor made of Dr. Brimmer and the work that he had done in the Commerce Department.

So, ladies and gentlemen, Dr. Brimmer brings energy and high professional standards, profound qualities of heart and mind to one of the most critical assignments in our public life today. He will recognize the challenges as they arise and I hope he will help us face them with intelligence, with knowledge, and with moderation.

I do not expect Dr. Brimmer to be an easy-money man or a tight-money man. He knows, as I think we all do, that the complexity of today's economy defies such a simple and such a rigid qualification. I expect Dr. Brimmer to be a right-money man, one who, I believe, will carefully and cautiously and intelligently evaluate the Nation's needs and the needs of all of its people, and recommend the policies which his conscience and his judgment tells him will best serve the national interest.

He takes office at a time when there is much to be done by all working together, cooperating. We must continue to sustain high employment without inflation. We must complete the adjustment of our balance of payments with other nations. We must meet the heavy demands of our military and economic effort in Vietnam without losing our momentum for social progress here at home.

To achieve all of this is not going to be easy. It is going to be difficult. It is going to try the best that is in all of us. The decisions are going to be many and they are going to be difficult, but I think that the people of America can all be glad that Dr. Andrew Brimmer will be helping us to make them.

So I welcome each of you to this historic East Room this morning to witness the swearing in of this most gifted American to this most responsible post.

NOTE: The President spoke at 10:40 a.m. in the East Room at the White House. In his opening words he referred to Dr. and Mrs. Andrew F. Brimmer and their daughter Esther, Vice President Hubert H. Humphrey, and William McC. Martin, Jr., Chairman, Board of Governors of the Federal Reserve System, who administered the oath of office. During his remarks the President referred to Secretary of Commerce John T. Connor under whom Dr. Brimmer served as Assistant Secretary of Commerce for Economic Affairs.

116   Special Message to the Congress on Crime and Law Enforcement.
March 9, 1966

To the Congress of the United States:

Crime—the fact of crime and the fear of crime—marks the life of every American.

We know its unrelenting pace:

—a forcible rape every 26 minutes,

—a robbery every five minutes,

—an aggravated assault every three minutes,

—a car theft every minute,

—a burglary every 28 seconds.

We know its cost in dollars—some $27 billion annually.

We know the cost it inflicts on thousands—in death, injury, suffering and anguish.

We know the still more widespread cost it exacts from millions in fear:

—Fear that can turn us into a nation of captives imprisoned nightly behind chained doors, double locks, barred windows.

—Fear that can make us afraid to walk city streets by night or public parks by day.

These are costs a truly free people cannot tolerate.

The war against crime may be slowing its increase for the moment. The most recent report of the Federal Bureau of Investigation show a 5% increase for 1965, compared to a 13% increase for 1964.

But we can take little comfort from such facts. We must not only slow, but stop—and ultimately reverse—the rate of crime increase.

The entire nation is united in concern over crime. The entire nation shares in the resolution to deal effectively with crime. But national concern is not enough. National resolution is not enough.

We must match our will with wisdom. We must match our determination with effective action.

The safety and security of its citizens is the first duty of government.

Today, therefore, I call on the Congress and the nation to join in a three-stage national strategy against crime, welding together the efforts of local, state, and federal governments.

WHAT WE HAVE DONE

This Administration—with the support of this Congress—is committed to assist local authorities. For the first time in our history, an Administration has pledged to the American people that the growth of crime—local, state, and national—will be checked.

We are working in a creative federal partnership to fulfill that pledge.

1. The Law Enforcement Assistance Act, passed last fall, provides a sound foundation upon which we can now build. Under its imaginative scope, we have already launched local and federal action—generations overdue—to modernize not only police work but all aspects of the system of criminal justice.

2. The Prisoner Rehabilitation Act, passed last fall, is the most significant legislative reform in modern American penology. Hundreds of prisoners already are working in daytime jobs as they finish their sentences at night. They are learning job skills that will bring dignity to themselves and support to their families.

3. The National Crime Commission and the District of Columbia Crime Commission, established last year, have launched

searching studies into the causes of crime and our present shortcomings in dealing with it.

4. The Federal Bureau of Investigation is expanding its National Academy six-fold. It will soon be able to train 1,200 rather than 200 law enforcement officials each year. It will provide special training for an additional 1,000 officers.

5. Federal efforts against organized crime have continued to increase. Racketeering indictments last year rose to a record 674, compared with 535 in 1964 and only 19 in 1960.

A Unified Attack

These programs are only initial steps on a long road. But they advance us far enough to see down that road more clearly.

And the plainest fact we can see is that piecemeal improvements will not be enough.

The need is not new. We have simply failed to meet it.

Despite the warnings of our law enforcement officials, years of public neglect have too often left the law enforcement system without necessary resources and public support.

Despite the devotion of our law enforcement officials, our law enforcement system does not deter enough of those who can be deterred. It does not detect and convict enough of those who cannot be deterred. It does not restore enough rehabilitated offenders into the law-abiding community.

Despite the dedication of our law enforcement officials, reforms too often defeat themselves because they do not go far enough.

There is a fundamental lesson we have too often ignored.

The problems of crime and law enforcement are closely interrelated.

One interlocking tie is within the very system of law enforcement.

Making police more effective is fruitless— if we continue to permit the overburdening of judges and the clogging of courts.

Increasing the number of judges is futile— if the number of competent prosecutors and defense attorneys remains inadequate.

An expanded judiciary cannot take advantage of modern thinking in sentencing— if new correctional facilities are not provided.

The best correctional programs will fail— if legitimate avenues of employment are forever closed to reformed offenders.

A second interlocking tie between all law enforcement problems is geographical.

Crime does not observe neat, jurisdictional lines between city, county, state, and federal governments.

Failure of a correctional system in one state may have a decided impact on the crime rate in another.

Shortcomings in federal or state law enforcement make more difficult the work of a city police department in its fight against racketeering.

Devoted police work in a city is of little consequence if it merely drives criminals to the adjacent county.

To improve in one field we must improve in all. To improve in one part of the country we must improve in all parts.

We must mobilize all of the resources of our creative federal system if we are to repel the threat of crime to our common well-being. The problems of crime bring us together. We must make a common response. There is no other way.

Our National Strategy

Even as we join in common action, we know there can be no instant victory. We face an immense journey. Ancient evils do not yield to easy conquest. Modern criminology has yet to light many corridors.

We cannot limit our efforts to enemies we can see. We must, with equal resolve, seek out new knowledge, new techniques, and new understanding.

In the battle against crime, unity can give us strength. But strength can give us victory only if it is joined with a bold and clear plan for the future as well as the present.

I propose a three-stage national strategy.

The first stage is an agenda for immediate action. These are the legislative steps we already know are needed—steps that should be taken without hesitation or delay.

The second stage is development of a comprehensive agenda of direct steps based on experiment and assessment for the future.

The third stage is a still broader agenda, an attack not only against crime directly, but against the roots from which it springs.

These three stages involve varying resources and commitments. But we must proceed on each of them with equal force—and we must do so now.

FIRST: THE IMMEDIATE ATTACK

Each of the four aspects of law enforcement calls for reform. There are steps we can now take.

A. To Improve Crime Prevention and Detection

We must improve the quality of local law enforcement throughout the country.

The front-line soldier in the war on crime is the local law enforcement officer. Federal aid to law enforcement at the state and local level was made possible by the Law Enforcement Assistance Act of 1965. Police, court, correctional, and university authorities have responded to the newly created Office of Law Enforcement Assistance with hundreds of imaginative ideas and proposals.

A number of projects are now under way:
—The management methods of modern industry will be adapted to law enforcement problems in a new management institute for police chiefs.
—Several New England states are combining their efforts in police training by establishing the first regional leadership school in the nation.
—The first intensive national training institute for state directors of corrections will bring the advice of experts to all states in their efforts to break the cycle of criminal repeaters.

In support of these programs and the many others to follow, I am asking Congress to increase appropriations for the Law Enforcement Assistance Act from $7.2 to $13.7 million.

Even seeking the most imaginative reforms, however, underscores a fundamental truth: how well a job is done depends on the training and ability of the men who do it.

I have directed the Attorney General to:
—Make grants to states, cities, and colleges and universities to elevate and intensify the training of law enforcement officers.
—Provide grants for a management exchange program, enabling police officials to travel to other departments for on-the-spot-studies of promising and effective approaches.
—Provide grants to establish closed-circuit television training programs to teach basic police subjects. The first such program, involving over 200 locations in a single state, is being launched now.
—Establish an award program, in consultation with state and local officials, giving annual public recognition to outstanding police officers and others who make notable contributions to the field of law enforcement.

I recommend legislation to establish a pro-

293

gram to send selected police officers to approved colleges and universities for a year of intensive professional study.

I recommend a loan forgiveness program under the National Defense Education Act for students who wish to enter the law enforcement profession.

If crime is to be controlled, we must control the weapons with which so many crimes are committed.

We must end the easy availability of deadly weapons to professional criminals, to delinquent youth, and to the disturbed and deranged.

We must stop the flow of firearms into dangerous hands.

It is not enough to say that gun control is a state responsibility. States with gun control laws now stand helplessly by while those laws are flouted daily by the unchecked sales of guns by mail.

Our Federal responsibility is clear. It is promptly to enact legislation, such as S. 1592, to regulate and control interstate traffic in dangerous firearms.

The front pages of our newspapers make us acutely aware of the human tragedies that flow daily from the unchecked purchase of firearms. Recent Congressional hearings added abundant evidence of the gravity of this problem.

There is no need to curtail the right of citizens to keep arms for such traditional pastimes as hunting and marksmanship. But there is a pressing need to halt blind, unquestioned mail-order sales of guns, and over-the-counter sales to buyers from out of state whose credentials cannot be known.

Only the federal government can give the several states and cities their first real chance to enforce their own gun laws. We must do so without further delay.

We must bring the latest and most effective

methods of law enforcement to the District of Columbia.

I have pledged to develop a program for the Nation's capital covering all aspects of crime and crime prevention.

In the longer run, we will look to the recommendations of the President's Commission on Crime in the District of Columbia. In the meantime, there are several measures which can be carried forward.

I recommend a substantial increase in police salaries to attract and retain the best qualified officers in the District of Columbia.

I recommend a pistol registration act prohibiting the sale of deadly weapons to those who have been convicted of violent crimes, to those with a history of mental instability, and to habitual alcoholics.

To strengthen the capability of District authorities, I have asked the Attorney General to provide experimental funds to:

—Revitalize the overburdened police communications system.

—Develop a computerized crime information system for the entire metropolitan area.

—Provide additional equipment to increase police mobility and patrol effectiveness.

B. To Facilitate the Prosecution of Criminals

We must intensify our campaign against organized crime.

The most flagrant manifestation of crime in America is organized crime. It erodes our very system of justice—in all spheres of government.

It is bad enough for individuals to turn to crime because they are misguided or desperate.

It is intolerable that corporations of corruption should systematically flaunt our laws.

This concern already is deeply shared by Congress. Statutes enacted in recent years have greatly strengthened federal authority to deal with racketeering. But another legislative tool is required.

Organized crime will stop at nothing to escape detection and prosecution. Torture and murder of witnesses, efforts to bribe prosecutors and jurors—these are not shocking exceptions. They are familiar racketeering techniques.

Such methods not only make it harder to prosecute racketeers—they poison the system of law enforcement itself. They require a strong antidote, and an important one is now pending in both Houses.

This legislation would expand the authority of the Department of Justice to immunize hostile but knowledgeable witnesses against prosecution and thereby enable them to testify without incriminating themselves.

Such immunity is already provided in laws covering a number of crimes. The pending legislation would extend it to such racketeering crimes as bribery, graft, bankruptcy fraud, jury-tampering and other schemes for the obstruction of justice.

We Must Modernize Our Criminal Laws.

I propose the appointment of a Commission to conduct a comprehensive review of all the Federal criminal laws and to recommend total revision by 1968.

A number of our criminal laws are obsolete. Many are inconsistent in their efforts to make the penalty fit the crime. Many—which treat essentially the same crimes—are scattered in a crazy-quilt patchwork throughout our criminal code.

The Commission will be composed of outstanding Americans, including members of the Congress, officials of the Executive branch, jurists and members of the bar. This Commission will bring to us the most modern and rational criminal code.

We are a nation dedicated to the precepts of justice, the rule of law and the dignity of man. Our criminal code should be worthy of those ideals.

C. To Enhance Justice in Our Courts

We must reform our bail system.

The administration of criminal justice must be fair as well as effective.

Whether a person, released after arrest, is likely to flee before trial or endanger society is not determined by the wealth he commands. Yet all too often we imprison men for weeks, months, and even years—before we give them their day in court—solely because they cannot afford bail.

Effective law enforcement does not require such imprisonment.

To correct this injustice, I urge the Congress to complete action on the pending Federal Bail Reform Act and to give favorable consideration to the District of Columbia Bail Agency bill.

These measures will insure fairness. They will provide an enlightened model for those states and communities which have not already undertaken bail reform.

D. To Reclaim and Rehabilitate Lives
in Our Prisons

We must establish a rational, coordinated correctional system.

No national strategy against crime can succeed if we do not restore more of our first offenders to productive society. The best law enforcement has little value if prison sentences are only temporary and embittering way stations for men whose release means a return to crime.

Today that situation is all too prevalent. In the Federal system, 30 percent of all parolees revert to crime. In most State systems the percentage is substantially higher. The task of breaking this cycle must be part of our program.

At present, we administer the prison, parole, and probation functions partly in the executive branch and partly in the judicial branch. I believe the effectiveness of our corrections programs depends on a rational, coordinated and unified approach.

Consolidating federal correctional efforts can reduce the number of repeaters.

It can strengthen the training and performance of correctional officials.

It can produce a career service of the highest professional order.

I recommend that the Federal prison, parole, and probation functions be unified within the Department of Justice to consolidate our presently fragmented correctional system.

We must capitalize on the beginning already made in rehabilitating prisoners.

The importance of up-to-date vocational training for inmates is clear. Chronic underemployment often goes hand-in-hand with crime. In our federal prisons, one of every three prisoners worked less than 6 months of the two years before confinement.

I am, therefore, directing the Secretary of Labor to develop effective ways to provide correctional institutions with job information for "good risk" parolees.

I am also directing the Chairman of the Civil Service Commission to re-examine the policies of all federal departments and agencies regarding the hiring of released "good risk" offenders. I am asking him to prepare progressive and effective policies to deal fairly and sensibly with them. I urge the

states, local governments, and private industry to do the same.

We must deal realistically with drug addiction.

Drug addiction is a double curse. It saps life from the afflicted.

It drives its victims to commit untold crimes to secure the means to support their addiction.

Drug addiction has been a matter of federal concern for more than a half century. The Bureau of Narcotics has pursued its enforcement duties energetically and effectively. Seizure of illegal narcotics and marijuana rose 62 percent from 1962 to 1965.

But our continued insistence on treating drug addicts, once apprehended, as criminals, is neither humane nor effective. It has neither curtailed addiction nor prevented crime.

Recognizing this, we have proposed legislation to authorize the civil commitment of certain addicts, while retaining full criminal sanctions against those who peddle and sell narcotics.

This measure can reclaim lives. It can begin to eliminate the driving hunger for drugs that leads so many into lives of crime and degradation.

I urge Congress to enact this legislation.

The federal government seeks to share its knowledge, its experience and its research in this area. I have already asked the Secretary of the Treasury to develop materials which will enable local law enforcement organizations to train in far less time a far greater number of specialists in narcotics control.

I am today directing the Secretary of the Treasury to establish clinics in those cities where narcotics addiction is most prevalent to help train local law enforcement officials.

By enacting the Drug Abuse Control

Amendments of 1965, Congress has demonstrated its concern over the illegal flow of non-narcotic drugs. Traffic in these drugs offers a new source of income to the underworld and threatens our young people.

By these amendments, Congress has provided new weapons in the control of this traffic, and this Administration will use them with determination. *In my 1967 Budget, I propose to double the funds for this program.*

SECOND: A COMPREHENSIVE AGENDA

These various proposals are only beginning steps. If we knew today of measures to deal more effectively with crime, we would seek to adopt them. But we do not yet have the answers.

We must press forward for greater knowledge, better tools, and deeper insights. This is the task on which the National Crime Commission has already embarked. The Commission is composed of nineteen distinguished citizens, judges, law enforcement officers and other experts.

It is engaged in some 40 projects with state and local authorities.

It is drawing on the services of more than 200 of the nation's leading police chiefs, judges, sociologists, and other specialists.

The Commission is:

—Surveying key American cities to learn where and when certain kinds of crime are committed, and which people are most likely to become victims. Such facts—now largely unknown—are essential to intelligent police work.

—Consulting 2,200 law enforcement agencies to identify successful police methods developed by local initiative and imagination. Communities everywhere should know about and benefit from these methods.

—Seeking new ways to break the logjams

in our criminal courts, where crowded calendars are a daily reminder that too often justice delayed is justice denied.

—Analyzing alternatives to traditional, costly—and unsuccessful—prison sentences, in the effort to reclaim young first offenders and break the spiral of repeated crime.

—Studying the sources of public respect and support for local police and police attitudes toward all segments of the community. Without mutual respect, effective law enforcement is not possible.

—Exploring, in conjunction with the Law Enforcement Assistance Office, how to bring the remarkable advances of modern science to effective application in law enforcement.

The computer has revolutionized record-keeping in modern industry. Surely it can do as much for criminal records.

Modern electronics has made it possible to summon a doctor from his seat at the opera. Surely it can do as much to make police instantly responsive to public needs.

And there may well be yet unimagined contributions which science can bring to the field of law enforcement.

The Commission's final report, due next year, can help provide specific blueprints for our national strategy. Its work will help replace the crutches of slogans, habits, and reflex with the firm support of knowledge and fact.

No matter how creative or detailed the blueprint we develop, we cannot succeed without parallel concentration by state and local authorities. They must undertake detailed planning of their own for reforms that take account of their own special strengths, needs, and traditions.

Some states and cities have already begun to do so. There is much for us to learn from them. But in many areas, there is no such broad planning, no recognition of the need for a unified attack on crime.

Therefore, I am asking the Attorney General to work with the governors of the 50 states to establish statewide committees on law enforcement and criminal justice.

Such state committees can assist—and be assisted by—the National Commission. They can stimulate the growth of public involvement and the development of a comprehensive anti-crime agenda in every part of the country.

THIRD: ATTACKING CRIME AT THE ROOTS

A century ago, Thoreau wrote that "There are a thousand hacking at the branches of evil to one who is striking at the root." So it remains today.

The efforts I have described—more effective police action, more efficient courts, improved corrections, comprehensive planning for major reform—all are urgently needed.

And yet all of them together can permit us only to strike more quickly and surely at the branches. The roots of crime will remain.

An effective strategy against crime must also rest on a base of prevention. And that base can come only from action against the wellsprings of crime in our society.

Our commitment to insuring social justice and personal dignity for all Americans does not flow from a desire to fight crime. We are committed to those goals because they are right.

But social conditions which foster a sense of injustice or exploitation also breed crime. More than thirty years ago, Clarence Darrow observed:

"It is very seldom that any one is in prison for an ordinary crime unless early in life he entered a path that almost invariably led to the prison gate. Most of the inmates are the children of the poor. In many instances they are either orphans or half-orphans; their homes were the streets and byways of big cities, and their paths naturally and inevitably took them to their final fate."

The programs now underway to eliminate the degradation of poverty, the decay of our cities, the disgrace of racial discrimination, the despair of illiteracy—are all vitally important to crime prevention.

At the same time, even as we seek to fight crime by fighting injustice, the ways we deal with crime should not foster further injustice:

—Bail requirements need not add families to the welfare rolls.

—Court procedures need not increase a sense of unfair and differential treatment.

—Sentencing practices need not require that the poor go to jail while others pay fines.

—Imprisonment need not result in loss of job skills.

Social injustice is not the sole reason for crime. Social justice is not the sole cure.

Even the broadest social programs cannot be panaceas. The lives and attitudes of persons long neglected do not change upon command. The effects of even the most energetic programs may be long in coming. The vast majority of our citizens who suffer poverty and discrimination do not turn to crime.

But where legitimate opportunities are closed, illegitimate opportunities are seized.

Whatever opens opportunity and hope will help to prevent crime and foster responsibility.

Effective law enforcement and social justice must be pursued together, as the foundation of our efforts against crime.

The proposals I am making today will not solve the problem of crime in this country. The war on crime will be waged by our children and our children's children. But the difficulty and complexity of the problem cannot be permitted to lead us to despair.

They must lead us rather to bring greater efforts, greater ingenuity and greater determination to do battle.

LYNDON B. JOHNSON

The White House
    March 9, 1966

NOTE: For statements or remarks upon signing related legislation, see Items 286, 598.

    See also Item 117.

---

117   Statement by the President in Connection With the Message on Crime and Law Enforcement.   *March 9, 1966*

UNTIL our streets are safe for every woman and every child, we cannot call ourselves a truly civilized nation.

Until we root out drug addiction, we cannot call ourselves a truly healthy nation.

Until we can sleep safely in our homes and work peacefully in our shops, we cannot call ourselves a truly law-abiding nation.

Until we can safeguard all our children from the perils of delinquency, we cannot call ourselves a truly progressive nation.

The cost of crime to our economy is nearly $30 billion a year—more than all of us together spend for medical care. This must and can be stopped.

I call upon every American, as I have today called upon the Congress, to join in a national, unified campaign to reverse the rising tide of crime in American life.

NOTE: The President also recorded the statement for radio and television broadcast.

For the President's message to the Congress, see Item 116.

---

118   Message to Queen Juliana on the Occasion of the Wedding of Princess Beatrix of The Netherlands.   *March 9, 1966*

[Released March 9, 1966.   Dated February 25, 1966]

Your Majesty:

On the happy occasion of the wedding of Princess Beatrix, Mrs. Johnson joins me in sending our very best wishes, and those of the American people. All my countrymen will share with our close friends of The Netherlands the pleasure of this important event in the life of your family and your great nation.

Mrs. Johnson and I recall with pleasure the hospitality you graciously extended to us when we last visited The Netherlands.

    Sincerely,

LYNDON B. JOHNSON

[Her Majesty, The Queen of The Netherlands, Soestdijk, The Netherlands]

NOTE: The text of the message was posted on the bulletin board in the Press Room at the White House. It was not made public in the form of a White House press release.

119 Remarks at the Signing of the Cape Lookout National Seashore Bill. *March* 10, 1966

Distinguished guests, Chairmen Jackson and Aspinall, Members of Congress, my friends:

A few months ago I stated that the clear water and the warm sandy beaches of our coastline are our Nation's real treasure, but I also observed that this kind of a treasure is not always secure. The question that many times faces us is: Will it be owned by a handful of the wealthy people, or will we preserve it for the pleasure of every American?

Will it be strewn with broken glass and rusting cans and commercialized beyond recognition, or will we leave a part of it as God created it and as man found it?

Today our generation meets here in the historic East Room of the White House to repeat its pledge to preserve some of our inheritance, unspoiled, for the generations that are to follow us. Today I repeat my pledge that in the time that may be allotted me as your President I will never slacken for a moment my efforts to make this a more beautiful nation.

This administration intends to be a conservation administration. I do not want my children, or my grandchildren, or those who may come after me that may bear my name, to ever be able to point to blight and trash as their inheritance from me.

We have come here this morning to sign a bill for the creation of the seventh national seashore in America. It is located at Cape Lookout, North Carolina. I am very happy to observe and pleased to compliment you Members of Congress who participated in this record that we have made, by saying that 3 of those 7 national seashores have been established in the little over 2 years of this administration.

Thanks to the generosity of the State of North Carolina and its vision, and the effectiveness and the vision of a truly great conservation Congress led by men who are conservation minded and who are knowledgeable in that field, we are today setting aside a 58-mile stretch of wild and beautiful shoreline for the use of future generations of all Americans.

This will be another important link in the great network of national parks that some of us have worked so long to establish. Today we have more than 26 million acres in 215 park areas from one end of this land to the other. There are really just a few park areas that are left and we are proceeding to meet that challenge with due dispatch.

But despite all the progress that we have already made, the real challenge of conservation is just beginning. Great national parks and great national seashores located in faraway, distant places do not satisfy the needs of the people who are a part of our urban civilization. The serenity of nature must be more than a once-a-year experience—that is, if we are to be a whole and happy people. This experience should touch our daily and weekly lives.

Unless we begin now to restore the environment in and around our cities, where more than 3 out of 4 people are going to be living in the year 2000, we will be condemning a large part of our population to an ugly, drab, and mechanical fate.

I believe that we can avoid that fate.

I see an America where city parks and plazas, as numerous as today's parking lots, bring rest and relaxation to shoppers and to office workers. If I were the mayor of any big city in America today, I would immediately put the best minds in my city to work to plan and program areas within reach of my population, and see if I could effect a coordination between the city, the State, and the Nation so that the people who make up the industrial genius of this empire will have a place to take their kids and to relax and to rejuvenate themselves for the mighty production that may be ahead in the following years.

I see an America where city streets are lined with trees and city courts are filled with flowers.

I live in a little community of 600. My daughter wrote an article last year and they paid her for it. She took the money and put four live oak trees down the plaza of that town. They were planted in memory of her grandmother, as I observed last week. And it made the town look like a different place. The bank planted some flowers in front of its doors. The merchants down the street got some shrubs and put them up there.

That can be and should be and is being done all over America. Because that is an assignment that doesn't have to come out of Washington. That is something that every lady who belongs to a garden club can make a contribution to. That is an assignment that every businessman can contribute to. That is a business getter. People will come to look at his lawn and his window and admire it and maybe make a purchase while they are there.

I see an America where our air is sweet to breathe and our rivers are clean to swim in.

I see an America where bicycle paths, running through the hearts of our great cities, provide wholesome, healthy recreation for an entire family. Instead of our having to appropriate hundreds of millions

to take care of juvenile delinquents, how much better it would be if we would just spend a part of it where they could enjoy themselves and have useful recreation.

I see an America where picnic areas are within an hour's drive of every city. I look back to the days of 1935 when President Roosevelt first started our highway parks and I built some 400 of the roadside parks in our State along our highways. And every day when I drive through that area I see family after family out there enjoying that vision that a great leader demonstrated 30 years ago.

I see an America where nearby lakes offer weekend camping and fishing and boating for all of our people.

This is the great conservation. This is the way that we must go.

This will be a large part of the Great Society, because the kind of lives that our children and our grandchildren will lead will depend on the plans that we make today and that you execute tomorrow. They, and history, are going to judge each of us accordingly.

I want to be judged—as we judge the great conservationists of yesterday—as benefactors of our people and as builders of a more beautiful America. We can't leave it as we found it, but we can improve on what we have.

Thank you very much.

NOTE: The President spoke at 11:10 a.m. in the East Room at the White House. In his opening words he referred to Senator Henry M. Jackson of Washington, Chairman of the Senate Committee on Interior and Insular Affairs, and Representative Wayne N. Aspinall of Colorado, Chairman of the House Committee on Interior and Insular Affairs. During his remarks the President referred to his daughter, Lynda Bird Johnson.

As enacted, the Cape Lookout National Seashore bill is Public Law 89–366 (80 Stat. 33).

120   Letter to the President of the Senate and to the Speaker of the House Proposing the Establishment of an American Revolution Bicentennial Commission.   *March* 10, 1966

Dear Mr. President: (Dear Mr. Speaker:)

I have the honor to transmit, for the consideration of Congress, a joint resolution establishing an American Revolution Bicentennial Commission.

Nothing in our proud heritage surpasses the significance of that great struggle for freedom nearly two hundred years ago. The Colonies at that time contained hardly more than three million people. Yet they also contained the greatest group of leaders ever assembled on the stage of history: men like Washington, Jefferson, Adams, Paine, Franklin, and Mason. These were men of vision. They were men of courage. They were men of ideas.

These great leaders, warmed by the love of liberty, gave to their fellow-Americans a driving force which inspired them to move from a colony of limited horizons to a powerful and mighty nation of free men and abundant opportunity.

The blood of men of many colors, many faiths, and many origins was spilled on the battlefield of this cause. Their names were American names: Attucks, Salvadore, L'Enfant, De Kalb, de Medici, Salomon.

But the American Revolution was more than a war. It was a political event. It was a social upheaval.

Above all, the American Revolution was a belief in the supreme worth and dignity of the individual—the idea that all men were created equal and entitled to life, liberty and the pursuit of happiness.

That idea was developing in the Thirteen Colonies long before the first guns sounded at Lexington and Concord. From 1766— and even before—a series of events showed,

as John Adams declared, that "the Revolution was effected before the war commenced. The Revolution was in the minds and hearts of the people."

It is fitting to plan now for the two-hundredth anniversary of these events. In the rich diversity that is America, each community will celebrate in its own way and will draw its own inspiration from the Revolution. But the Federal Government must be prepared to share its knowledge and resources with states, local communities, historical societies, and others across the Nation. The Bicentennial Celebration should be a truly national effort.

I propose that we establish an American Revolution Bicentennial Commission, composed of members of Congress and the Executive Branch and distinguished and outstanding Americans appointed by the President.

This Commission will:

—Provide a creative and helping hand to State, local, and private groups in their commemorations;

—Increase our knowledge and appreciation of the American Revolution through our schools and universities and our historians and scholars;

—Plan for celebrations at the national level;

—Recall to America and to the world the majestic significance of the Revolution.

In planning this Bicentennial Celebration, we must remember that we are celebrating not only the birth of American ideals, but the birth of ideals that today encircle the globe.

Ours was a true revolution of liberty. It

was not a revolution of tyranny. It was not a revolution of aggression. It was a revolution for the greatest cause in the affairs of man—freedom and human dignity.

The impact of the American Revolution on the rest of the world was electric. This small, struggling nation became the rallying point for friends of freedom throughout Western civilization.

To these shores came great men like Lafayette, Von Steuben, Kosciuszko, and Pulaski. It was Pulaski himself who said, "Wherever on the globe men are fighting for liberty, it is as if it were our own affair."

Those words have special significance for our own generation. Today, the Vietnamese people are fighting for their freedom in South Vietnam. We are carrying forward our great heritage by helping to sustain their efforts.

From 1776 on, wherever human beings have dreamed of a better society, wherever they have determined to bring reality to their dreams, they have been moved by the eloquence of the Declaration of Independence. They have found guidance and sustenance in the actions of the men who saw our nation through the crisis of its birth.

I send this recommendation to the Congress with special pleasure. The Bicentennial Commission will help us commemorate the American Revolution with all the dignity and spirit it deserves.

For we must never forget Thomas Jefferson's proud and confident declaration of the meaning of the American Revolution in the whole long sweep of human history:

"I shall not die without a hope that light and liberty are on steady advance. . . . The flames kindled on the 4th. of July 1776. have spread over too much of the globe to be extinguished by the feeble engines of despotism. On the contrary they will consume those engines, and all who work them."

Sincerely,

LYNDON B. JOHNSON

NOTE: This is the text of identical letters addressed to the Honorable Hubert H. Humphrey, President of the Senate, and to the Honorable John W. McCormack, Speaker of the House of Representatives.

For the President's statement announcing the signing of a resolution establishing the American Revolution Bicentennial Commission, see Item 323.

---

121 The President's News Conference Following a Meeting With the Executive Committee of the Governors' Conference.
March 12, 1966

OPENING REMARKS

THE PRESIDENT. [1.] If you will come in quickly—we are running late for the next meeting—I will review exactly what has happened. Governor Reed is to my right. Bill[1] has given you a list of those that attended the meeting: Governor Burns of Hawaii, Governor Hansen of Wyoming, Governor Johnson of Mississippi, Governor Volpe of Massachusetts, Governor Scranton of Pennsylvania.

Governor Hughes was in Japan and Governor Connally has another commitment and couldn't be here.

FEDERAL-STATE-LOCAL RELATIONSHIPS

[2.] The questions discussed were divided into three parts: What did we have in

---

[1] Bill D. Moyers, Special Assistant to the President.

mind in the establishment of the commission to study Federal, State, and local governments referred to in our State of the Union Message? We discussed that at some length and I explained to the Governors what I had in mind and told them we would go into more detail in our meeting later; that we wanted to know what new institutions and new partnerships were needed to attack these problems.

How could we best organize the Federal Government field structure? How could we go about getting the best and right information on how effective these programs were, our new programs for this year, such as river basin commissions, community health services, multi-State training schools, and so on and so forth? Bill will give you any fill-in on that that you may want.

TAXATION OF INTERSTATE BUSINESS

[3.] The next question was with regard to H.R. 11798. That is the bill introduced by Representative Willis. It sets up uniform formulas that States have to follow in imposing taxes on business engaged in interstate commerce.

My statement in response to their query and discussion of it was that the bill was controversial. Many States have opposed it because they didn't like the thought of being subjected to such formulas. Some businessmen were against it because they thought it would overburden them by increased taxes.

There is a need to simplify and reform the whole area of State taxation of interstate business. That is a tough area full of legal and constitutional complexities. The key question is: What is the best approach? We are trying to study and determine this now.

The Federal Government has a keen interest in insuring fair and just treatment for business and States. We don't have all the answers. There are other alternatives that we are looking at. For example, 11 States have already enacted model codes. The question is: Should those be extended and are they really model? Would they be good for the Nation?

In the meantime, we have our experts here studying H.R. 11798 which concerns the Governors. We are looking at it carefully and looking at the other alternatives as well. We are open to their suggestions. We will be glad to have any comments they have. We are designating Secretary Fowler [2] to act as the Federal Government's representative in reviewing the existing proposals and any the Governors might submit.

DISTRIBUTION OF FEDERAL REVENUES TO STATES

[4.] The third one was the question of the Federal Government acting as a partner in restoring fiscal balance and strengthening State and local governments by making available for their use some part of the great and growing Federal tax revenues over and above the existing aids. I told the Governors that we were redistributing Federal revenues; we were increasing our distribution to the States.

When I became President, a little over 2 years ago, we were spending $4.75 billion for education. This year we are spending $10.2 billion for education. That represents more than double the previous amount, an increase of $5 billion; although our budget was $6 billion more than last year exclusive of Vietnam, that we had cut out a lot of old programs in order that we can make new distributions to the States.

That meant research stations, that meant closing of military bases, that meant effecting economies in other routes so we could have

---

[2] Henry H. Fowler, Secretary of the Treasury.

what we popularly call Great Society programs—education, health, and conservation in these fields. I illustrated it by the fact that Federal expenditures for aid to State and local governments rose from $10.3 billion in fiscal 1964 to $14.6 billion in fiscal 1967, an increase of 40 percent in distribution in 3 years.

The share of Federal aid to State and local governments has risen from 6.4 percent in 1964 to 9.9 percent in 1967. The examples of major programs aimed at States and local governments that we spelled out were: $1.3 billion under the Elementary and Secondary Education Act; $600 million in medical care and social security amendments; new programs to clean up rivers, modernize hospitals, help law enforcement along the line of the crime message.

ECONOMIC OUTLOOK

[5.] That pretty well covered it. I discussed the problem we had with the economy, unemployment dropping to 3.7. I told them we couldn't tell this far ahead just what strains would be put on our economy. We had to watch it very carefully. We couldn't anticipate what would happen in Vietnam very far ahead as near as we could anticipate for—but we might have to ask for extra money. At least we were going to forgo every possible expenditure that we could that we felt could be eliminated that was archaic or obsolete, and I hoped they would do likewise.

Governor Reed can comment or say anything he wants to. We will go into the Appalachian meeting following this one. I am running a little late. We will go to the meeting this afternoon and have a general exchange of briefings on the state of the Nation—the state of the world, a briefing on the state of the Nation, and I hope a briefing

on the state of the States. We will hear from them about the State conditions.

We will tell them what we believe the national condition is and we will review in some detail the world condition. Our people will report to you as much as they can after those meetings, and Governor Reed, as the Chairman of this group, if you have any observations, you can make them now, too, so we can go on.

COMMENTS BY THE CONFERENCE CHAIRMAN

[6.] GOVERNOR REED. Thank you, Mr. President.

This marks the third time that the Executive Committee of the National Governors' Conference has had an opportunity to meet with the President. In my recollection, this is the most opportunities that have ever been afforded the Governors to have direct communication with the President. We are very grateful for it.

The President has outlined the areas that we had concern in and I know I speak for my fellow Governors when I say that we are relieved, we are encouraged for the prospects of closer liaison between Federal and State governments.

There are many new programs to be implemented, and we feel that meetings of this type will help better inform the Governors as to the President's view as to how these should be implemented.

We are also delighted with the prospects of continuing closer relationships with our Federal Government. In all these areas the President has outlined his thinking, and we are very pleased that a meeting of this kind has been possible and feel that this is going to result in greater and better Federal-State relationships.

THE PRESIDENT. Governor Reed and his group, the Executive Committee, called upon me at the ranch following my operation last fall. This meeting really grew out of that meeting. I have never participated in a more constructive one. Everything that we do in these respective fields that he enumerated will be done only after a full discussion with the Governors and in full cooperation with them.

The meeting was helpful to me. It was constructive. It was nonpartisan. It was in the very best traditions of the American political system.

Thank you.

GOVERNOR REED. Mr. President, we feel the prospects were never better for Federal-State relationships. We are very grateful to you.

ADDENDUM TO OPENING REMARKS

[7.] THE PRESIDENT. I might add, in addition to the names I gave you, Governor Farris Bryant is sitting in these meetings with me, along with two or three others who are not Governors, but Governor Bryant's experience as Governor, his participation in the Governors' Conference, and so forth—he was here and I asked him to participate in this meeting and be helpful to me and to the Governors today. He will be participating in the meeting later this afternoon.

As all of you know, he is the former chairman of the Governors' Conference.

Any questions you want to ask me, I don't want to dodge or delay them. I will be glad if you will try to be limited with them.

QUESTIONS

[8.] Q. I gather you are going to send up a message on State-Federal relations.

THE PRESIDENT. We have always referred to it in the State of the Union Message.[3]

---

[3] See Item 6.

They wanted me to add to it today. We have done that. As we get to it, we will spell it out in more detail.

[9.] Q. Mr. President, the Governors' Conference is on record for the so-called Heller plan.[4]

THE PRESIDENT. That is what we were talking about in the distribution of funds. We told them we were distributing a good deal of funds now.

POSSIBILITY OF TAX INCREASE; DEFICIT ESTIMATES

[10.] Q. Mr. President, when you told the Governors that we might have to ask for extra money, were you thinking in terms of an increase in personal taxes, sir?

THE PRESIDENT. I haven't reached any conclusions on that. I think that we have anticipated as accurately and as nearly as we can our appropriations and our revenues for this fiscal year and for the next one. We have no illusions, though, that they may have to be adjusted.

I did review with the Governors the record on our estimates to date. I don't know if the Herald-Tribune would be interested, but I will be glad to give it to you.

Q. Yes, sir.

THE PRESIDENT. In the 1964 budget estimate, the President's estimates were down $1.1 billion from the original estimate as submitted to the the Congress. In the fiscal 1965 budget they were down $1.4 billion from the estimate that he submitted to Congress. At the moment—the estimate he submitted to Congress—we are within about a billion dollars of that estimate, notwithstanding the increased, unanticipated Viet-

---

[4] A revenue-sharing plan proposed by Walter Heller, former Chairman of the Council of Economic Advisers, under which surplus Federal tax receipts would be distributed annually to the States for use as they determined.

nam expenditures, because our revenue has gone up also.

That is a 3-year period. We will know more about it June 30th, but we estimated, as you will recall, a deficit of $5.3 billion, and we think that deficit will be in the neighborhood of that figure, within roughly a billion dollars.

Contrast that with fiscal 1959's budget. They estimated $500 million surplus and had a deficit of $12.4 billion. In 1956 we had a $4.1 billion deficit; in 1957 a $4.4 billion deficit. So we cannot tell at this time, but we think that our estimates on budget revenues and expenditures show an excellent guess.

The Budget Director says it is perhaps the best estimating record in the memory of the Budget, and we did review that in some detail.

But we do want to make it clear that we cannot foresee how many planes we are going to lose, how many shells we are going to fire, how many losses we are going to suffer, but as near as we can anticipate them, we have provided for them in the budget.

I might say that as of March 10th, that our estimates for January and February are running a little under what we estimated we would spend in Vietnam for those periods. That is an unusual period, as you know, because of the weather and other things, but we are running a little under. We may well run over next month.

Q. That is the period January to date?

THE PRESIDENT. Yes.

Reporter: Thank you, Mr. President.

NOTE: President Johnson's fifty-seventh news conference was held in his office at the White House at 11:55 a.m. on Saturday, March 12, 1966. It was held as part of a day-long meeting with Governors from more than 40 States who came to the White House at the President's request.

See also Items 122–124.

---

122   The President's News Conference Following a Meeting With the Appalachian Governors.   *March 12, 1966*

THE PRESIDENT. [1.] Ladies and gentlemen, we are running a little bit late, about 15 minutes, for the other meeting. That is not uncommon for men in political life. But we want to give you a very brief résumé of what happened. Those in attendance at the meeting, as you will observe, are Governor Wallace of Alabama, Governor Tawes of Maryland, Governor Rockefeller of New York, Governor Moore of North Carolina, Governor Rhodes of Ohio, Governor Mc-Nair of South Carolina, Governor Smith of West Virginia, Governor Clement of Tennessee, and Governor Scranton from Pennsylvania, who was to be spokesman. We were unable to have Governors Godwin, Breathitt, and Sanders.

APPALACHIAN REGIONAL COMMISSION REPORT
FOR 1965

[2.] Governor Scranton and Cochairman Sweeney [1] have presented me with the 1965 Appalachia report,[2] which should be available to you. We had a general discussion of the program. I had a brief statement which Mr. Moyers [3] will make available to

[1] Governor William W. Scranton of Pennsylvania, State Cochairman of the Appalachian Regional Commission, and John L. Sweeney, Federal Cochairman.

[2] The annual report of the Appalachian Regional Commission, covering the period March 9–June 30, 1965, was transmitted to the President on December 31, 1965 (Government Printing Office, 1965, 27 pp.).

[3] Bill D. Moyers, Special Assistant to the President. For the statement see Item 123.

you. The meat of it was that 100 percent of the highway message, which Congress authorized in Appalachia, had been approved by the Commission. Twenty percent of it was already under the planning and construction stage. We approved 125 public facility projects. We have 105 more under consideration. We had put $400 million extra in development contracts in the Appalachian area in 1965 and 1966 over what we had done in 1964.

Under the educational aid, Appalachia will be a prime beneficiary of the $1.3 billion educational aid bill.

A disproportionate share of the less fortunate people in Appalachia are over age 65. I have been told today that Medicare will substantially ease the financial burden faced by these people and the private and public institutions which provide their hospital and medical services.

I expressed great personal satisfaction from today's meeting. I thanked each of the Governors for their nonpartisan and patriotic support and effective work. We observed that there has been no relationship in my experience in Government that had been more constructive or more cooperative. We are grateful for the leadership of Mr. Sweeney.

That was about it.

I would like for Governor Scranton to make any observations that he may care to make. He made a very fine, constructive statement, and he can repeat as much of it as he dares or cares to. Then each Governor will be glad to make any observations he wants, and will answer any of your questions. I hope you will understand though that we do have them all waiting for us at a 1:30 lunch.

MR. MOYERS. The Appalachia report will be available. The President's opening state-

ment is being mimeographed, and will be available in 15 or 20 minutes.

REMARKS OF THE GOVERNORS

GOVERNOR SCRANTON. I simply reported to the President that I personally know of no Federal program that has started off better than this one. As you know, this is a unique Federal-State relationship. There has never been anything like it before.

As a group, I believe that we feel strongly that it not only works extremely well, but we highly recommended to the President that a relationship of the same sort might be made in other programs of the Federal Government, or in other regional establishments which are now being contemplated under the EDA.

Likewise, we informed him that though our particular budget is forced to take a cut because of the problems in Vietnam, we understood this and were able to arrange it within ourselves, which is remarkable in view of the fact that New York has become a part of us this year, and other States seem to be interested in joining us, too.

We also suggested in the future if he could, by the time that world problems might be a vacant sum, that we might go up to what we have received in 1965 and 1966. But this has caused no problem in going ahead with the programs, which have been initiated more rapidly and with greater success than any Federal program with which I have been concerned.

THE PRESIDENT. Governor Clement.

GOVERNOR CLEMENT. We are very pleased in Tennessee with the program of the Appalachia plan.

THE PRESIDENT. Governor Smith.

GOVERNOR SMITH. We have been very pleased, and are very glad to be able to help

New York get the mileage.

THE PRESIDENT. Governor McNair.

GOVERNOR McNAIR. South Carolina has been very pleased. It has been very helpful.

THE PRESIDENT. Governor Moore.

GOVERNOR MOORE. We think this is the ideal Federal-State relationship. We hope that it can be used in other fields.

THE PRESIDENT. Governor Wallace.

GOVERNOR WALLACE. Alabama is very pleased with the program.

THE PRESIDENT. Governor Tawes.

GOVERNOR TAWES. We are, too.

THE PRESIDENT. Governor Rockefeller.

GOVERNOR ROCKEFELLER. We are pleased with the program, and West Virginia, in reference to the highway program. There was a discussion regarding the possibility of using the authority in the act to allow States to prefinance on programs in view of the cutback which I think was unanimously adopted by the Governors.

THE PRESIDENT. Governor Rhodes.

GOVERNOR RHODES. There has always been a raging question between the States and the Federal Government as to whether they can work together. I think your administration has given a prime example of how they can work together. We thank you.

THE PRESIDENT. Are there any questions? Ladies and gentlemen, thank you.

Reporter: Thank you, Mr. President.

NOTE: President Johnson's fifty-eighth news conference was held in the Cabinet Room at the White House at 12:45 p.m. on Saturday, March 12, 1966.

See also Items 121, 123, 124.

123 Statement by the President on the Progress of the Appalachian Program. *March 12, 1966*

A YEAR AGO last Wednesday I met with most of the Appalachian Governors in the Rose Garden to sign the Appalachian Regional Development Act of 1965.

At that time I said that the Appalachian program was "the truest example of creative federalism in our times."

The actions of the Appalachian Regional Commission, during the past year, have demonstrated the truth of that statement. Every action that has been taken by the Commission has been without dissent—from either the States or the Federal Government.

Almost 100 percent of the major highway mileage which the Congress has authorized under the Appalachian act—some 2,300 miles—has been approved by the Commission. Approximately 20 percent of that mileage is already either in the planning or construction stages.

Approximately 125 public facility projects designed to expand and improve the economic base of the region have been approved by the Commission. Among these are: vocational educational schools, hospitals, airports, sewage treatment plants, industrial access roads, libraries, educational TV stations, junior and senior colleges, and strip mine reclamation.

The States have forwarded for consideration an additional 125 projects.

In 11 of the Appalachian States, State and local development districts have been funded and staffed with Appalachian funds. These units will enable a coordinated development effort to move ahead at full speed within the Appalachian region.

All 12 of the Appalachian States have submitted their plans for land conservation activity under the Appalachian act. Funds will now be distributed to individual farmers to improve their land, conserve other public investments such as small watershed lakes and the Appalachian streams.

The funds that I have requested under the authority of the Appalachian act are designed to make up past deficiencies of Federal spending in the Appalachian region. They are, of course, only a portion of the total Federal effort that will be made to bring the Appalachian region into the mainstream of American economic life.

Because of the high incidence of poverty in Appalachia, the region will be greatly assisted by the $1.75 billion that has been budgeted for the Office of Economic Opportunity in the coming fiscal year. The projects already started have eased the day-to-day hardships faced by many Appalachians.

Because our national program of assistance to schools is based on a low-income formula, Appalachia will be a prime beneficiary of the $1.3 billion we have asked the Congress to appropriate in fiscal 1967.

A disproportionate share of the less fortunate people in Appalachia are over age 65. I have been told today that Medicare will substantially ease the financial burden faced by these people and the private and public institutions which provide their hospital and medical services.

My greatest personal satisfaction from today's meeting is the support which the Governors have given the Appalachian program. I have assured them of my continued commitment to the program and the goal most desired by the Governors and myself. Our goal is the achievement of Appalachia's full participation in our rapidly expanding and prosperous American economy.

I reaffirm that commitment this morning.

NOTE: For the President's remarks on March 9, 1965, upon signing the Appalachian Regional Development Act of 1965, see 1965 volume, this series, Book I, Item 103.

See also Item 122 above.

---

124 The President's News Conference Held at the Close of the Governors' Conference. *March 12, 1966*

THE PRESIDENT. [1.] Ladies and gentlemen of the press, I will give you a brief rundown. Bill Moyers [1] will supply you with any other information that I leave out.

I will ask Governor Reed of Maine, the chairman of the Governors' Conference and his executive committee that met with us this morning, to make a statement. Any Governor will respond to any question you may have to ask.

RÉSUMÉ OF EARLIER MEETINGS

[2.] In the program this afternoon, I presented Gen. Ellis Williamson,[2] who has

just returned from Vietnam. He went in with the first Army group to go into South Vietnam. He spoke and took questions.

Secretary McNamara spoke at some length and took questions. He left for a week's vacation, and I let him leave earlier. Then we asked General Taylor to address the group briefly.[3]

The Chairman of the Joint Chiefs of Staff, General Wheeler, spoke to the Governors. Secretary Rusk spoke at some length and took all the questions that were presented. The Vice President closed the meeting with a very eloquent statement.

---

[1] Bill D. Moyers, Special Assistant to the President.

[2] Brig. Gen. Ellis W. Williamson, outgoing Commander of the 173d Airborne Brigade.

[3] Gen. Maxwell D. Taylor, Special Consultant to the President and former U.S. Ambassador to the Republic of Vietnam.

Bill will review the substance of those.

I reviewed with them the treaty, the joint resolution, the historical background, the troops that we had there, the economic situation, and other matters of our relations with other nations—the state of the world as we see it. Secretary Rusk discussed it by continents. He went into some detail on Latin America, Africa, Asia, and Eastern and Western Europe, and this country.

Then we talked about the state of the Nation.

During lunch we talked about the state of the States and what conditions were in the States. Some Governors made observations about them. Governor Reed made a statement in conclusion and Governor Rhodes made a statement.

I will ask Governor Reed to speak to you now and say anything that he may desire. He will speak as long as he wants to—as long as you may want him to—and then we will be open for questions.

Governor Reed of Maine.

REMARKS BY THE CONFERENCE CHAIRMAN

[3.] GOVERNOR REED. Thank you very much, Mr. President. First, let me state that I am very confident that probably never in the history of the United States has a President ever been so generous of his time with the Governors of these United States.

President Johnson indicated early in his tenure that he wanted to work closely with the Governors and he has followed this up with a number of very important sessions with the chief executives of the United States.

I know I speak for every Governor of every State and every Territory when I express my deep gratitude to him for the amount of time he has devoted to keeping us informed, improving the relations between the State governments and the Federal Government.

Much has been said about the role of the States being submerged, that the Federal Government is more or less taking over and moving into these areas. The President today has very emphatically, by deed and word, indicated that he firmly believes in the sovereignty of the States and the important partnership we must play in order to develop our country to its greatest degree.

This, I feel, is without precedent, and it certainly is deserving of the highest commendation on the part of the Governors to the Chief Executive of the United States. In fact, we have had his time throughout the day. First with the executive committee of the National Governors' Conference to discuss problems that you were briefed on earlier. Then with a group of the Appalachian Governors, and finally with the reception, the luncheon, and with this complete afternoon devoted to a thorough, in-depth briefing on the situation in Vietnam.

We have been taken into the confidence of our President and his chief advisers, and we certainly are going to respect an obligation to treat with great circumspection the information that he has divulged to us.

I do want to say, and state it most emphatically, that every Governor of the National Governors' Conference stands foursquare behind the President of the United States.

RESOLUTION IN SUPPORT OF VIETNAM POLICY

[4.] I would like at this time to read to you a resolution that was adopted unanimously at the session this afternoon. It was presented by Governor Rhodes of Ohio.

"WHEREAS President Lyndon B. Johnson has asked the Governors of the 50 States to come to Washington for the purpose of discussing ways to improve the coordination between the Federal Government and the

States in the fulfillment of their mutual objectives; and

"WHEREAS the President included in the discussions a review of the circumstances surrounding the conflict in which this Nation is engaged in Vietnam; and

"WHEREAS the President has given the Governors a complete and candid review of the situation in Vietnam; and

"WHEREAS the Governors have been given the greatest freedom in the expression of their convictions and the exchange of their views on the Vietnam situation; and

"WHEREAS it is the unanimous opinion of the Governors here assembled that the policies being followed by the President in pursuit of our national objectives in Vietnam are sound and the only rational policies to be followed under the circumstances;

"Now, THEREFORE, BE IT RESOLVED, By the Governors of the States assembled in Washington, D.C. on this 12th day of March 1966, that they do wholeheartedly support and endorse the policies and programs in Vietnam being pursued by the United States of America under the leadership of President Lyndon B. Johnson."

I believe that resolution sums up the complete and utter support that the Governors have for the administration's position in this conflict.

I could go on and enumerate and take more time, but in essence, we are completely united behind the President, and we also feel that the vast majority of the American public subscribes wholeheartedly to our objectives, that the very small number who participate in demonstrations, draft card burnings, and so on, represent an infinitesimal, small portion of the people of these United States.

We think it very important whenever we speak to speak out forthrightly that this is

the position of the United States. In our trip to Vietnam last fall, in which I was chairman of the 10-member Governors' delegation going there, the first question we received from the foreign press was: How do the American people stand on Vietnam? Do these demonstrations represent a large portion of our population?

We were able to state without reservation this was not so. The American people are wholeheartedly behind the President. I don't believe I could state it any more emphatically than to say that every Governor here is wholeheartedly behind our President.

MEETINGS WITH THE GOVERNORS

[5.] THE PRESIDENT. I would say that the Secretary of State reiterated an announcement he had made on another occasion when he met with the Governors. I guess we have met with the Governors and their executive committee at least a half dozen times in the 2 years I have been President. We have met with all the group at least three or four times; the executive committee at other times.

We have invited the Democratic Governors and the Republican Governors—all the Governors—together.

The Secretary told them today that we would make available any diplomatic, political representative of the State Department and any military representative they desired to come to their legislatures for any briefing.

We also made it clear that any Governor who could arrange to go firsthand to Vietnam, we would be glad to see that that was arranged. A dozen or so of them have already done that and have contributed valuable suggestions to us.

NOMINATION OF GOVERNOR FARRIS BRYANT
AS OEP DIRECTOR

[6.] I have asked Governor Farris Bryant, from the State of Florida, to come here and meet with us today. I have asked Governor Bryant—I haven't even told all the Governors this yet, so I will just make this announcement now—I have asked Governor Bryant to join this administration. I will send his nomination to the Senate very shortly to succeed Governor Ellington as head of the Office of Emergency Planning. He will sit on the National Security Council. He will handle our stockpile matters. He will be the President's representative with all the Governors of all the States. He is, as you all know, a former Governor of Florida.

I had a biographical sketch here, but I have misplaced it. I will ask Bill Moyers to give it to you a little bit later.

The Governor has served in public life for years with distinction in the State of Florida. He is a graduate of Harvard University. He served in the legislative body of that State and served as Governor of that State and is now in private life. At great sacrifice, I have asked him to dispose of his law practice, give up his various business connections, come here and take over this job. He will take the oath just as soon as his nomination is consented to by the Senate.

I have talked to the chairman of the committee and he assured me they will have a prompt hearing on it. We look forward with great pleasure to having Governor Bryant with us. Bill will give you a biographical sketch.

We will be glad to take any questions you have, or if you have any individual questions of any Governor, or if any Governor cares to make any comment—get things out in the open here. This is a rather open society in this country. And if it is not, these reporters will make it open when they leave here!

QUESTIONS

VIETNAM POLICY

[7.] Q. Governor Reed, was any effort made to get other Governors to sign the declaration? The Governors who are not here? I think there are 12.

GOVERNOR REED. That question hasn't been brought up, but I do intend to write each Governor, and the ones who were not present, to give them an opportunity also to subscribe to the resolution. There is no question in my mind that they will all respond affirmatively in this respect.

Q. But, Governor, when you say the conference wholeheartedly supports the President in his stand, do you mean to include those Governors not present, among them Governor Hatfield of Oregon?

GOVERNOR REED. Well, it is impossible for me to commit the Governors who are not present. This proposal was passed unanimously. I have every reason to believe that the other Governors will subscribe to it, but I cannot, of course, say carte blanche until I've had a chance to contact them.

Q. Governor Reed, last December the Republican coordinating committee, which includes five Republican Governors, including some, I believe, who are present at this meeting, called for a naval blockade of the port of Haiphong and the bombing of military targets—particularly military targets—in North Vietnam. Does their statement today represent a change in position from last December?

GOVERNOR REED. Not being a member of that committee, it would be impossible for me to comment concerning their views on it.

Q. Was any question raised along these

lines during your meeting?

GOVERNOR REED. No, sir. The questions were raised, yes, but there was no question among the Governors when it came to supporting this resolution.

[8.] Q. Governor, is there any reason why the phrase "under the circumstances" was used at the tail end of that resolution?

GOVERNOR REED. Not to my knowledge, no. Governor Rhodes constructed the resolution, and I would say that to my knowledge there was no particular concern about it.

Q. Could we ask Governor Rhodes?

GOVERNOR REED. Governor Rhodes had to leave to return to Ohio. I am afraid we would not be able to contact him.

THE NATIONAL GUARD AND THE RESERVES

[9.] Q. Sir, can anybody tell us—Mr. McNamara is not here—why Mr. McNamara said he thought he would not still call the National Guard or Reserves?

THE PRESIDENT. I do not think that that is a matter we would want to go into in detail. It is not necessary at this time. He emphasized that it was not necessary at this time. When and if it is, we will call them. But I have made that clear at various press conferences.

The Reserves mean just what they say: They stand in reserve. When we need to call the Reserves, we will call them.

I will tell you a little story about a boy I asked one time to come stay all night with me. His mother said no, he couldn't go. He had a little brother about 12 years old that was overweight and we nicknamed him "Bones." Cecil was the one I wanted to spend the weekend with me and his mother said, "No, Cecil, you can't go." Cecil kind of whined a little bit and said, "Mama, I don't think that's fair. Bones

done been two wheres and I ain't been no wheres."

So there have been some people that have been called before and already served. There are some people that haven't served at all. So at the moment we are not asking those who have served before to come back and do duty again or those that were called up before to come back and be called up again. We are asking some to give their service for the first time. But when and if it is necessary to call the Reserves, we will do it.

The Secretary explained that he could not give any written guarantee that that would not be necessary, but at this time it isn't.

FURTHER QUESTION ON THE VIETNAM POLICY

[10.] Q. Mr. President, is there anything you can say about the unanimous support given you by the Governors on your Vietnam policy?

THE PRESIDENT. I welcome any support that I can get from anyone. I am gratified that the leaders of the States represented here, and the Governors who visited our troops in Vietnam, would feel as they do. No one gave me any advance notice that Governor Rhodes from Ohio would make his speech and offer his resolution. I did not anticipate that he would.

All we wanted to do was to do what we did 8 months ago—to bring them up to date on what we were doing, what our plans were, why we were doing certain things, and to permit them to ask any question they wanted to ask. They did that.

At the conclusion, the Governor of Maine, who was chairman and who had asked for a meeting, was gracious enough to express his appreciation for at least our hospitality and our lunch and the meeting.

Following the Governor's statement, Governor Rhodes arose and presented the resolution and read it. Governor Reed heard a second and a vote was taken on it. I hope it is not too displeasing to anyone. It is very pleasing to me and most Americans welcome the unity that it indicates.

NATO DEVELOPMENTS

[11.] Q. Mr. President, did any question come up on NATO or did you explain what is happening in NATO today?

THE PRESIDENT. Yes. Secretary Rusk pointed out the developments in the NATO countries, the action that had been taken in the last few days there, as he did in other parts of the world.

DISCUSSION OF FOREIGN POLICY

[12.] Q. Mr. President, although there was unanimous endorsement of your policy during the discussion, was there any criticism or questioning of specific aspects of the policy?

THE PRESIDENT. Yes, there were a good many questions about why we did this and why we didn't do that and what we were doing here, and what reason we were using. This is not a regimented society. I can assure you that the man who becomes the chief executive of any State in this Union speaks his mind freely when he chooses to, and some of them chose to today.

I would not say that there was any doubt or difference or any argument that took place, or that there was even any serious objection presented, you understand. General Wheeler gave them reasons for his observations. General Williamson gave them his. Secretary McNamara went into considerable detail and answered I don't know how many questions. Bill can go into the details on the number. But I would

guess there were 50, 75, maybe 100 questions asked this afternoon.

None of them showed any bitterness or any envy or any displeasure. They were searching for information and asking for facts, and they got them. I thought it was a very constructive meeting.

TAX ACTIONS

[13.] Q. What did you tell them, sir, about taxes? Any income tax raise?

THE PRESIDENT. We discussed in the meeting with the executive committee this morning what has been happening on the Hill. I believe that I observed that the President had asked for about $6 billion in additional revenue as a result of the acceleration of corporation taxes, acceleration of income taxes. That was a one-time thing, I emphasized. We don't expect Vietnam to be a permanent thing. We hope it is not. We felt that that was what we should do now.

The chairmen of the committees advised us, and Mr. Mills of the Finance Committee,[4] that they thought this was the proper course to take before Congress reassembled. We asked for $6 billion, and the House acted on it and the Senate offered some amendments to it. I am told now that the conference amendment will recommend that we get about $6 billion 10 million. I am hopeful that the conference report will be adopted.

The chairmen of the House committees met with me day before yesterday and the chairmen of the Senate committees met with me yesterday afternoon and they indicated that they believe the conference report will be adopted. If it is adopted we will be very

---

[4] Representative Wilbur D. Mills of Arkansas, Chairman of the House Committee on Ways and Means and of the Joint Committee on Internal Revenue Taxation.

grateful for the extra $10 million, as well as the $6 billion we asked for.[5]

I know all of you are pleased to know that the mutiny that was in the air may have been worked out and we may be getting along a little better.

GOVERNORS' VISITS TO VIETNAM

[14.] Q. Mr. President, have any of the Governors taken you up on the offer to go to Vietnam?

THE PRESIDENT. Yes, I think there have been probably 15 that have been out there and there will be others from time to time. I told them we would be glad to hear from them to suit their convenience. Each Governor explained to me, who couldn't be here today, that he was either sick or had a legislature in session, or some justifiable reason he couldn't come, and we will communicate with them also.

DEFICIT ESTIMATES

[15.] Q. Mr. President, can you clear up the matter of the deficit you were talking about to us this morning? You used the figure $5.3 billion. If you are referring to the current fiscal year, I was puzzled by the fact that the original estimate was $6.4 billion.

THE PRESIDENT. I was under the impression that the original estimate was $5.3 and the present is $6.4.

Q. The present estimate was $6.4. Is that what you are saying we will be within a billion dollars of?

THE PRESIDENT. No. The $5.3 billion was within a billion of—it is $1.1 billion to be exact. Between $5.3 billion and $6.4 bil-

lion there is $1.1 billion difference. We don't expect the $6.4 billion—we don't expect to reach that, although the estimate was made January 1st.

As I said this morning, our military expenditures in the months of January and February amount to approximately what we expected. The first 6 months of the year we ran in the neighborhood of about $50 billion. We are projecting that the last 6 months will go much faster, maybe $58 billion. But we are not up to that yet. Therefore, I would expect that in that area, and some of the other areas, perhaps some of the bigger areas, we will cut that $6.4 billion down to where it will be more nearly in line with the $5.3 billion.

I don't want to be positive about that. I was talking to these men, and I'm not giving you a guarantee—[*inaudible*]—McNamara promise to get out of Vietnam by a certain time. It does have a lot of "ifs" to it. If you are going to publish it at all, you are required to publish all the "ifs."

Mr. McNamara said, "if we have stable governments," and "if they didn't come in from the North," and if these other things. So I want to point out that if we go along according to our plan, we hope to be under a billion dollars of what I told Congress originally. The budget says $1 billion 400 million in 1965, and $1 billion 200 million in 1964, so those will be the two best predictable years in the history of the Government.

ECONOMY IN FEDERAL AND STATE GOVERNMENTS

[16.] Q. Mr. President, you said that the Federal Government would try to economize in every way possible, and you said you told the Governors you hoped the States

---

[5] The Tax Adjustment Act of 1966 was approved by the President on March 15, 1966 (see Item 132).

would do likewise. Is there any particular area where the States——

THE .PRESIDENT. No, no! I wouldn't want anything I said to indicate that I was trying to direct or influence or even persuade any Governor to handle his business in any particular way. I said what I have said to you several times, and what I frequently say to my own Cabinet: to please take a new look at everything you are doing to see if you can find any way to eliminate anything obsolete or archaic or anything that can be postponed.

I told the Governors that that was what I was doing, and some of them indicated that they were trying to do the same thing. I think we are all called upon during this emergency to exercise the greatest frugality and prudence in order that we may have sufficient resources to complete our assignment in Vietnam.

Reporter: Thank you, Mr. President.

NOTE: President Johnson's fifty-ninth news conference was held in the Blue Room at the White House at 4:45 p.m. on Saturday, March 12, 1966. See also Items 121–123.

125   Statement by the President on the Fifth Anniversary of the Alliance for Progress.   *March* 14, 1966

My fellow citizens of the hemisphere:

Since becoming President, I have often restated my own, and our country's, resolute commitment to the goal of a better life for all the people of the Western Hemisphere.

Many Presidents have worked to shape that goal.

We are proud of the good-neighbor policy of President Franklin D. Roosevelt.

President Eisenhower broke new and fertile ground with the Act of Bogotá in 1960—an act growing from the understanding compassion of one people for another.

President Kennedy built on these efforts and gave them increased emphasis with the announcement of the Alliance for Progress on March 13, 1961, 5 years ago.

Today, by word and deed, Americans are helping to fulfill the hopes of those who have little and pray that one day they can have more.

The Johnson administration seeks history's description as a time when, the dreaming and the planning having laid the foundations, the doing and building were underway.

The last 2 years of this vast cooperative effort between the United States and the nations of Latin America are solid evidence that deeds are matching our words.

During these 2 years Latin America has achieved a per capita growth rate of 2.5 percent. The average rate for the preceding 3 years was less than 1 percent. This recent increase of 150 percent is a fact which friends of the hemisphere must note with pride—and new hope for the future.

In fiscal years 1965 and 1966, those Latin American countries cooperating with U.S. programs of action are putting visible results before their people.

Together we are:
—improving 7,000 miles of road
—building 130,000 dwelling units
—irrigating 136,000 new acres of farmland
—adding 530,000 kilowatts to power generating capacity
—providing classrooms for 1 million students

—building 450 new health facilities

—spending $200 million to provide financing for expansion and construction of over 5,000 industrial firms

—spending $250 million in providing agricultural credit to 450,000 farmers.

Equally important, reforms are changing and modernizing these institutions in Latin America essential to the growth of a sense of community that stretches throughout the hemisphere.

Governments, business concerns, labor unions, and cooperatives are working with the people of our hemisphere to attain economic and social progress under free institutions.

   —We are building the machinery of cooperation through the Inter-American Committee on the Alliance for Progress.

   —We are enlisting the support of private groups and voluntary agencies in ever-increasing measure. The Peace Corps, Partners for the Alliance, Council on Latin America, AFL–CIO, private foundations, and universities are making vital contributions.

   —We are introducing the principle of mutual aid among the Latin American nations. We are giving new energy to economic integration within Latin America. The Economic and Social Act of Rio de Janeiro, approved last November, gives impetus to these concepts.

   —We recognize that fulfillment of all our goals will require continuation of our joint efforts beyond 1971. I said last November that the United States is prepared to extend mutual commitments beyond the period originally foreseen in the Charter of Punta del Este. Self-help and mutual aid will be yardsticks in determining the scope of our contribution.

In country after country, nations in the hemisphere are acting to mobilize resources for public and private investment—to reform and modernize the institutions—to expand trade and market opportunities within and outside the hemisphere—and to provide a solid base for the support and cooperation of imported capital and technical assistance.

External support is also coming in increasing measure from the Inter-American Development Bank, the World Bank and its affiliates, and the United Nations. This support has increased by about $200 million in the last 2 years.

For its part, the United States has already committed nearly $5 billion to the nations of Latin America to assist them in their struggle to modernize and achieve a better life for their people. In recent months significant steps have been taken to give Latin America greater access to our markets:

   —This administration has insisted that our participation in the International Coffee Agreement be more effective.

   —This administration recommended the Congress withdraw the special import fee on sugar.

   —This administration removed the quota restrictions on lead and zinc.

After a temporary period of setback, there are now most hopeful signs of a renewal of large-scale private foreign investment in Latin American development, often in joint ventures with Latin American associates. Business leaders interested in Latin American investment have been invited to the Cabinet Room frequently to discuss steps to help the people of the hemisphere.

Three years ago the 19 Latin American countries were deeply concerned over their trade position in the world.

During the past 2 years the trend has changed.

Our experts now predict that export

earnings for 1965 will show an increase of $1 billion over the 1963 level, providing additional resources for investment in development.

Yet we must do more than provide money and technical assistance and improve trade. Investments must be made directly in human beings. In every forum, I have advocated and directed that American resources be invested in education, health, and improved living and working conditions. Such efforts are not easy to organize. They require the mobilization of human resources in scarce supply. But they are among the most rewarding of all investments.

Today I want to issue a new call to our sister nations in the hemisphere to enlarge our truly revolutionary cause—the cause of enlarging the lives of all our people.

I am determined to contribute America's resources to this spirit of change—a spirit now slowly, surely, confidently growing in the Western Hemisphere.

All of us in the Organization of American States have seen and understand the lessons of history. Together we are strong. Divided we are weak. Together we must

shape the future to our hopes.

In every nation in the hemisphere the needs and the beliefs and the prayers are the same. We want peace and opportunity—the chance to live in dignity, to choose and plan and work and achieve the best for our families.

I believe that in the next 5 years we will see a continent constantly growing in prosperity and in unity—growing in its capacity to meet the desires and needs of its own people and in its contribution to peace and freedom in the world at large.

That is what Bogotá and Rio and Punta del Este were all about.

For my own part, I want to help make all this a reality and "to create out of the human spirit, something that did not exist before."

This is fulfillment. And this is our commitment.

NOTE: The President also read the statement in the Yellow Oval Room at the White House before a group of Ambassadors representing the Latin American countries.

The Alliance for Progress was first proposed by President Kennedy on March 13, 1961 (see "Public Papers of the Presidents, John F. Kennedy, 1961," Item 78). It was formally established by the Charter of Punta del Este on August 17, 1961.

126 Message to the Congress Transmitting Fourth Annual Report of the Peace Corps. *March 14, 1966*

To the Congress of the United States:

I transmit herewith from the Secretary of State the Fourth Annual Report of the Peace Corps.

This is a report of service to our neighbors throughout the world. It is the story of new opportunities for growth and learning among our own people.

The expansion of the Peace Corps has been as dramatic as its promise.

Five years ago today the Peace Corps was eleven days old. By mid-summer, 1961, 120 Volunteers were serving in 3 countries. At the close of fiscal year 1965 there were 8,624 Volunteers serving in 46 countries. Africa received 3,278 Volunteers —Latin America received 3,214—the Near East and South Asia, 1,285, and the Far East, 847.

There are many examples of Peace Corps

impact. One is Afghanistan. Nine Volunteers went there in 1962 to begin the Peace Corps' work. As of June 30, 1965, there were 136 Volunteers in Afghanistan, located in 19 different towns and villages. Peace Corps teachers reach nearly 40 per cent of all Afghan students at the secondary and university levels.

There are other measures of progress. I am pleased to note that as the number of Volunteers has risen, the cost per Volunteer has declined. During fiscal year 1963, for example, the annual cost per Volunteer was $9,074. For 1965 the cost was reduced to $8,028. The estimate for fiscal year 1966 is $7,832.

The Peace Corps is the largest producer and consumer of language materials in the world. Since 1961, 20,000 trainees have received instruction in one or more of about 60 languages in the Peace Corps training curricula. Twenty additional languages are under consideration for inclusion in future training programs.

Since its inception, 150,000 Americans have volunteered for Peace Corps service. Some 15,000 have served abroad in 49 nations.

As of June 30, 1965, 4,545 Volunteers had completed service and returned to the United States. Thirty-seven percent of all returned Volunteers are continuing their education. Government service is attracting 17.8 percent, while another 16.4 percent are teaching. The remaining 28.5 percent are engaged in private business, non-profit organizations and miscellaneous activities.

It is fair to say that the lives of virtually all Volunteers have been changed by their service in the Corps. They have become aware—in a unique and profound way—of the bond of suffering and hope that unites men and women on every continent. And they are returning home with a new understanding of their nation and the world.

No more valuable experience can be gained by any man.

LYNDON B. JOHNSON

The White House
March 14, 1966

NOTE: The 80-page report, entitled "Peace Corps, Fourth Annual Report" and dated June 30, 1965, was released with the President's message.

---

127 Letter to Secretary Gardner on the Achievements of the Federal-State Vocational Rehabilitation Program. *March 14, 1966*

Dear Mr. Secretary:

I am very proud of the achievements of the Federal-State vocational rehabilitation program in rehabilitating disabled citizens. By teaching new skills to the handicapped, this program has brought hope and independence to thousands of disabled individuals and their families.

My January budget forecasts that 215,000 handicapped individuals will be rehabilitated during fiscal year 1967, a 25% increase over the current fiscal year.

As we plan for the larger program, I believe we should do better than we have in rehabilitating persons who are now on our public welfare rolls. In the last several years, although the absolute numbers have increased, the proportion of welfare recipients receiving training has declined from 15% to 13%. I think this trend should be reversed. While human values are always our prime consideration, we should not ig nore the sound public investment that would result by reducing our public welfare rolls through vocational rehabilitation.

I would like you to review the possibilities in this area and report to me with recom-mendations for Federal and State action by June 1.

Sincerely,

LYNDON B. JOHNSON

[Honorable John W. Gardner, Secretary of Health, Education, and Welfare, Washington, D.C. 20201]

128   Remarks at the Signing of the Supplemental Military Authorization Bill.   *March* 15, 1966

Members of the House and Senate, Secretaries of the Services, members of the Joint Chiefs, ladies and gentlemen:

The bill that we have come here to approve this morning authorizes appropriations of more than $4 billion, 800 million for the support of the Defense Establishment of the United States of America. Later today the Congress will act upon the appropriation of some $13 billion. This is authorization for only a part of that appropriation, but this bill will help to meet the military needs that we have in Vietnam.

I also believe that it will do something else. By its overwhelming vote on this measure, I believe the Congress has repeated its declaration to the American people that they stand behind our fighting men in Vietnam.

Let me remind you that it was just 25 years ago that the Congress extended the Selective Service Act by only one vote. That was in August, as I recall it, before Pearl Harbor in December. On the eve of Pearl Harbor the House of Representatives, of which I was then a Member, by a vote of 203 to 202 turned this country from the brink of the cliff and saved the Army from being dismantled.

We had refused to fortify Guam a short time before that. We had sent several false impressions throughout the world by our action.

Now in contrast, this supplemental military authorization bill passed the House of Representatives, under the bipartisan leadership of the Armed Services Committee and its members, by a vote of 392 to 4; it passed the Senate by a vote of 95 to 2. This overwhelming vote is visible confidence in our modern Defense Department and the civilians and the military who direct the destinies of that department.

In all the history of military movement, there has never been the equal of the Defense Department's accomplishment of moving more than 100,000 men 10,000 miles in 150 days and moving them with equipment, doctors, housing, ammunition, vehicles, planes, and support materiel. In speed, quantities, and efficiency, history recalls no similar achievement of that kind and it deserves the recognition and the gratitude of every single American who lives securely in the United States today.

The overwhelming vote on this measure also testifies that we may have learned something from recent history. It is a lesson which we should have learned long ago for it was really one of our Founding Fathers, John Jay, who warned us: "It is too true, however disgraceful it may be to human nature, that nations in general will make war whenever they have a prospect of getting anything by it."

I believe that many of the world's nations

have since learned the final futility of war. Most of the world's leaders today, I believe, genuinely desire peace, but there are still a few who do not. So to those who ask what our present struggle in Vietnam really means, let me say: Our purpose is to demonstrate to the remaining advocates of violence that there is more human profit to be had from peace than there is from war.

That is the real purpose of the more than 200,000 brave Americans who are at this moment risking their lives 10,000 miles from home. That is the real purpose of the Congress in registering such dramatic support for legislation of this kind. That is the only purpose of the President and this administration in Vietnam.

How sad it is that such great sums must be spent for the bombs and the planes and the gunpowders of war. How joyous it would be if these great resources could be put, instead, to the service of peace. We have said this and we have repeated it time and time again, and we will never tire of saying it, and I repeat it now: The people of Vietnam, North and South, have the same basic human needs. The people of Asia and the people of China have the same basic human needs.

They need food, shelter, and education. They need an end to disease and to disaster. They need a future for their children. They need hope. They need peace. These are the very simple things, the basic things, the building blocks of life and of civilization.

They are the vital and fundamental things that all men have in common; that all men can together seek and together achieve.

In my Baltimore declaration of April of last year, I said to the people of the world how much we would welcome taking some of the funds that we are now spending in bombs and bullets and putting in efforts to rid that area of disease and disaster and provide education and training. At that time I recommended the study and the creation of a Southeast Asia Development Bank, which will soon come into being as a result of the efficiency of this Congress.

So, again, this morning I repeat that we look forward with hope and with prayer to the day when the leaders who provoked and the leaders who continue this aggression in Vietnam will finally abandon their hopeless attempts at conquest. It is my greatest wish to someday stand here and sign another bill, one that is designed to bring progress and fulfillment to a Southeast Asia which is at peace with itself and also at peace with the rest of the world.

Thank each of you for coming this morning to this little ceremony. We will now sign the bill.

NOTE: The President spoke at 9:05 a.m. in the East Room at the White House. As enacted, the supplemental military authorization bill is Public Law 89–367 (80 Stat. 36).

The Asian Development Bank Act was approved by the President on March 16, 1966 (see Item 133).

For the President's Baltimore address of April 7, 1965, see 1965 volume, this series, Book I, Item 172.

129 Memorandum on the Need for Training in Modern Management Methods. *March 15, 1966*

Memorandum for Heads of Departments and Agencies:

Managing the complex affairs of the Fed-

eral Government is an exacting task. The American people deserve, and demand, that the Government apply to its operations the most efficient management techniques available. Our programs must be both effective and economical. This requires intensive hard-headed analysis in every program of every agency.

The need for people in each department well trained in modern management methods is great. This need has been clear to me for some time and has been made even more evident with the introduction of the new Planning-Programming-Budgeting System.

One way you can meet this need is to recruit as many of the best, analytically trained people as you can find.

Another way is to train the most able and promising people now on your staff in modern techniques of program analysis and management.

Therefore, I have asked the Chairman of the Civil Service Commission and the Director of the Bureau of the Budget to or-

ganize an education program in these techniques at several universities. I want you to nominate some of your most able people for this intensive training in modern, analytic methods.

The Chairman and the Budget Director will be sending you details on this program.

LYNDON B. JOHNSON

NOTE: On July 13, 1966, the White House announced that 83 Federal employees had been selected to participate in the new training program during the 1966–67 academic year, and would devote a year to graduate study at one of seven universities conducting special management courses for them. The release stated that the 83 men and women had been selected by Charles L. Schultze, Director of the Bureau of the Budget, John W. Macy, Jr., Chairman of the Civil Service Commission, and the National Institute of Public Affairs, a private, non-profit organization which was assisting the Government in carrying out the program.

An announcement concerning the selection of the participants in the President's Mid-Career Educational Program is printed in the Weekly Compilation of Presidential Documents (vol. 2, p. 932).

130   Memorandums on U.S. Participation in International Organizations and Programs.   *March* 15, 1966

Memorandum for the Heads of Departments and Agencies:
SUBJECT: United States participation in international organizations and programs

I have today sent the attached memorandum directing the Secretary of State to take certain actions which I believe are essential to effective participation by the United States in international organizations.

I expect the heads of all departments and agencies that contribute to the Government's activities in this field to give their full cooperation to the Secretary of State in carrying out my instructions.

This work must receive high priority and the personal attention of the responsible offi-

cials in all agencies concerned if this Nation's interest in improving international organizations as instruments for peace and progress is to be fulfilled.

LYNDON B. JOHNSON

Memorandum for the Secretary of State:
SUBJECT: United States participation in international organizations and programs

The Federal Budget for 1967 contains this statement:

". . . we intend to play an increasingly active role in reviewing the program and budgetary proposals of the various international organizations."

The purpose of this memorandum is to

set forth what I believe that increasingly active role should be.

No nation has been a greater supporter of the United Nations, its specialized agencies and other international organizations than the United States. We are today a member of some 65 such agencies.

Our continued strong support is necessary and desirable.

—if the world community is to live in peace,

—if we are to cooperate internationally in extending the benefits of modern agriculture, health, and education to the less fortunate, and

—if international problems in such fields as meteorology, telecommunications, and aviation are to be given the joint attention required for their resolution.

The United States has by far been the largest financial contributor to the international organizations.

—Since 1946, we have provided a total of $3.6 billion in direct contributions.

—Since 1956, our annual contributions have grown from $100 million to an estimated $237 million for the next fiscal year, an overall increase of 137 percent.

Moreover, we can expect the programs and budgets of these international agencies to expand further in future years to meet the growing needs of the world community. The United States shall continue to meet its fair share of the financial requirements of these organizations.

If we are to be a constructive influence in helping to strengthen the international agencies so they can meet essential new needs, we must apply to them the same rigorous standards of program performance and budget review that we do to our own Federal programs. Our purpose in this undertaking must be to see that

—future expansion of the activities of the international organizations is governed by the tests of feasibility and reasonableness,

—the programs of the organizations are vigorously scrutinized so that funds are allocated only to high priority projects which we are convinced are in the interests of the international community and of our own country, and

—each international agency operates with a maximum of effectiveness and economy.

To achieve this purpose, we must

—decide what we can best accomplish through multilateral action, as compared to action through our own direct programs,

—clarify the objectives of our membership in each international agency,

—organize ourselves for more effective participation in each organization, and

—insist that the money we spend through international agencies is in our national interest and in the best interest of the world community.

I expect you to continue to direct and coordinate the activities of the U.S. departments and agencies involved in international organization affairs and to instruct our representatives to those organizations. I shall look to you to direct this Government's work in

—reviewing and establishing our long-term policy objectives in each major international organization,

—analyzing and determining the U.S. position on programs and budgetary needs of each organization on a timely and continuing basis, and

—recommending steps to improve the effectiveness of each organization in contributing to the objectives of the world community and the United States.

Ambassador Goldberg has unique responsibilities in a wide range of matters relating to the United Nations system. I shall continue to rely heavily on his advice and counsel.

The heads of other Federal departments and agencies have significant interest in activities of the various international organizations. I expect them to provide you with expert assistance in their specialized fields. In this work, the close cooperation of all agencies is needed to provide the essential unity of our effort.

I expect the Director of the Bureau of the Budget to work with you and other agency heads to help assure that the positions we take on the budgets of international organizations reflect a searching scrutiny of requirements and priorities for the expenditure of funds.

I am sending copies of this memorandum to all department and agency heads.

LYNDON B. JOHNSON

NOTE: On March 15 the White House also made public a statement by the President outlining the proposals made in the two memorandums (2 Weekly Comp. Pres. Docs., p. 393).

---

131   Memorandum on the Need for Controlling Expenditures by Federal Agencies. *March* 15, 1966

Memorandum for the Heads of Executive Departments and Agencies:

SUBJECT: 1966 Budget Expenditures

Last November, I wrote certain Departments and Agencies that it was imperative to hold 1966 expenditures to the absolute minimum required for carrying out essential responsibilities.

Today, the need is *doubly imperative.* As the rising costs of Vietnam are added to the private demands generated by a prosperous highly employed economy, the necessity to guard against inflation takes on added urgency.

In this period, your careful control over every dollar of Government spending will not only *avoid direct waste* of our resources, but will also help prevent the indirect and inequitable waste that results from the deterioration of the dollar's value.

Therefore, I am asking that you

—*Report to the Budget Director no later than April 1* your best and most up-to-date estimate of Fiscal 1966 expenditures for your agency—for the administrative budget and for the major trust funds (i.e., those shown separately in table B–4, page 390, of the 1967 budget) as well.

—*Identify the programs involved and explain the reasons for the differences* if your latest estimate for 1966 differs from the amount shown for your agency for 1966 in the 1967 budget document.

LYNDON B. JOHNSON

NOTE: For a statement by the President in response to a detailed report by the Director, Bureau of the Budget, on cost reduction efforts by Federal civilian agencies during fiscal year 1966, see Item 603. See also Items 181, 197, and related material in the Index under the heading "Cost reduction."

132 Statement by the President Upon Signing the Tax Adjustment Act of 1966. *March 15, 1966*

I SIGN into law today the Tax Adjustment Act of 1966—a measure providing some $6 billion in additional revenue over the next 15 months.

The new tax law has three objectives:

—It provides additional funds needed to support our troops in Vietnam.

—It provides a careful measure of fiscal restraint to balance our economic expansion with reasonable price stability.

—It carries out desirable and timely improvements in tax collection procedures.

The committees of Congress, headed by Representative Mills and Senator Long, assisted by Representative Byrnes and Senator John Williams, are to be complimented for their skill in framing and steering this vital measure through Congress in such a short period of time and delivering it on the day requested. By signing this bill tonight, rather than tomorrow, we are saving the Government a million dollars in revenues. That more than makes up for the lights we are using.

By acting swiftly—and responsibly—the Congress has demonstrated once again that we have the determination to meet our commitments abroad—and the capacity to rise to changing economic circumstances at home.

This act also provides for the payment of social security benefits to some 370,000 persons, age 72 and over, who are not now insured under the social security program.

This amendment and the 1965 amendments to the social security program are important steps toward bringing economic security to older citizens. But there is much yet to be done.

I have already asked the Secretary of Health, Education, and Welfare to complete a study of ways and means of making social security benefits more adequate, while keeping the program financially sound.

I want these proposals to be ready to present to the next Congress.

You'll be hearing more from me on this subject in the months ahead.

We are living in very hopeful and challenging times. Our economy—the real engine of our Nation—is now operating very close to full capacity. We are in the 61st month of the longest peacetime prosperity in the history of the Nation. Profits, wages, sales, incomes are all at alltime highs. Unemployment last month reached a 12-year low of 3.7 percent of the labor force. Not another nation on earth—regardless of its system of government—can match that total economic record.

But we are not satisfied with this achievement. An unemployment rate of 3.7 percent does not sound good to the more than 3 million Americans who are still out of work. We must continue to grow, continue to train, continue to educate, until all Americans have job opportunities.

We know we can achieve that goal. We know we have the will and the skill to make our economy an instrument of happiness and progress for every American.

But we must exert that will—and apply that skill. If, through carelessness, or selfishness, or shortsightedness, we allow our economy to run too far, too fast, we can expect demands for additional fiscal, price, wage, tax, and expenditure restraints.

The choice is before us. We can be prudent and restrained and continue to enjoy this great era of prosperity. Or we can be foolish and flee to mischief we know not of.

The tax bill which I will shortly sign is, I believe, a force for prudence and restraint. Based on the best thinking available in the Government, and the best information available in the Nation, it is the right measure at the right moment.

Every great nation must be disciplined so that its greatness endures. The Greeks admonished mankind with the simple rule: Nothing in excess. This is good advice today.

I can make no prediction here today on the need for additional taxes later this year. No one can make that prediction, because no one knows what the future holds. But you may be assured that this administration stands ready to act when action is needed—if it is needed. I am certain that the Congress stands ready to respond in the same manner.

In the meantime, there is work and duty ahead for all of us—to discipline ourselves and our actions, to be prudent, to be as wise as we can—so that what we have worked so hard to build will last and prosper.

NOTE: As enacted, the Tax Adjustment Act of 1966 is Public Law 89–368 (80 Stat. 38).

In his statement the President referred to Representative Wilbur D. Mills of Arkansas, Chairman of the House Ways and Means Committee, Senator Russell B. Long of Louisiana, Chairman of the Senate Finance Committee, Representative John W. Byrnes of Wisconsin and Senator John J. Williams of Delaware, ranking Republican members of the committees, and John W. Gardner, Secretary of Health, Education, and Welfare.

Secretary Gardner's proposals for increasing social security benefits are summarized in the President's remarks at Social Security Administration headquarters in Baltimore on October 12, 1966 (see Item 509).

133   Remarks at the Signing of the Asian Development Bank Act. *March 16, 1966*

Mr. Vice President, Secretary Rusk, Secretary Fowler, Mr. Black, distinguished Ambassadors, Members of the Congress, my fellow Americans:

This is a moment in which history and hope meet and move on from here as partners. Less than 1 year ago, on April 7, 1965, I asked for the creation of the Asian development plan to seek economic advance and social justice for all of Asia. I pledged the full support of the United States of America to that task.

Today we have begun to redeem that pledge. The act I sign this morning authorizes the United States of America to ratify the charter of the Asian Development Bank.

Seldom have nations joined together in a collective venture that is so endowed with promise. For that reason this moment is a very special one for so many people:

—First, for the Asian leaders, who conceived and organized the bank and who are so ably represented here today by the Ambassadors from their countries.
—For the people of those non-Asian nations which have signed the charter, and whose Ambassadors have come this morning to bespeak again their vision and their generosity.
—For my great friend, a true American, Eugene Black, whose energy and tact have been as indispensable as his experience and wisdom.
—And to the Congress of the United States and the members of both parties who have acted to invest in this enterprise not only the resources but the faith of the 190 million people whom they represent.

This act is an economic Magna Carta for

the diverse lands of Asia. Its charter links 31 countries in a union against the involuntary economic servitude imposed on the people of Asia by time and circumstance and by neighbor and nature. There is also a deeper meaning. This billion dollar bank is a symbol that the twain *have* met, not as Kipling predicted, "at God's great Judgment Seat," but at the place of man's shared needs.

It is no longer possible to be a mere observer at that place. It is not possible—and it is not right—to neglect a people's hopes because the ocean is vast, or their culture is alien, or their language may be strange, or their race different, or their skin another color.

Asia just must no longer sit at the second table of the 20th century's concern. The economic network of this shrinking globe is too intertwined. The political order of continents is too involved with one another. The threat of common disaster is too real for all human beings to say of Asia, or any other continent, "Yours . . . is another sphere."

I believe that those who make that case are no less patriotic and no less sincere than those who believe that we cannot shorten the length of our reach into the world.

But I believe equally as firmly that those people are wrong. And while I expect they will continue to make their argument of isolationism versus globalism—for we all are determined to preserve their right to speak up in this land—I hope they, too, expect me to try to keep on making my case for realism. That, I think, is the right of the President of this country, and the President feels that is his duty.

And what is that case? It is simply that there is no rest from the trials of freedom, there is no recalling what the pace of change has done to the map of this big world, there

is no reducing our responsibilities while the challenges of progress will not permit us to name the site for our duel or the weapons that we use.

It is that we cannot turn from the place of shared needs and expect either peace or progress to follow us.

So today we have come here to the historic East Room of the White House and gathered at this place to start a journey together.

The Asian Development Bank is the first step of what I conceive to be a very long journey.

We are taking another today by announcing that we have pledged a half of the $24 million that is needed to construct the large Mekong River project, the Nam Ngum tributary project in Laos. Seven other countries, Japan, the Netherlands, Canada, Thailand, Denmark, Australia, and New Zealand, are joining us in that effort.

For the United States it is our first major commitment under our promise to expand economic and social development in Southeast Asia. The Nam Ngum project is the Mekong Committee's highest priority undertaking and, like the Asian Development Bank, it represents a major accomplishment in joint cooperation in the world.

The first phase of the project will include a dam and power station with an installed capacity up to 30,000 kilowatts. Additional generators up to 120,000 kilowatts can be installed as they are needed. An international transmission line, with a link across the Mekong River, will connect the power station with the capital of Laos and northeast Thailand.

This is just one example of how the fruits of technology—and the ingenuity of cooperation—can bring new life to whole new regions of the world.

More, yes, much more, awaits our response. Schools and hospitals can be built. Rivers can be tamed. New crops and new breeds of livestock can be developed. There are no bounds to the possibilities, if there are no limits to our dreams.

It has been said that "no statue was ever erected to the memory of a man or woman who thought it was best to let well enough alone."

So it is with the nations that we represent here today. We seek no statues to our memory. We seek only one real monument, a monument with peace and progress for its base and justice for its pinnacle.

Together—your lands and mine—we will build it.

Thank you very much.

NOTE: The President spoke at 9:40 a.m. in the East Room at the White House. In his opening words he referred to Hubert H. Humphrey, Vice President of the United States, Dean Rusk, Secretary of State, Henry H. Fowler, Secretary of the Treasury, and Eugene R. Black, adviser to the President on Southeast Asian social and economic development and former President of the World Bank.

As enacted, the Asian Development Bank Act is Public Law 89–369 (80 Stat. 71).

For the President's address on April 7, 1965, asking for creation of an Asian development plan, see 1965 volume, this series, Book I, Item 172.

134 Remarks Upon Accepting the Robert H. Goddard Trophy. *March* 16, 1966

Mrs. Goddard, Dr. Pickering, Mr. Webb, Mr. Vice President, Congressman Miller, distinguished guests:

I have been visiting with our Ambassador from France, who has just returned. We were just watching the space shot and wondering how Jim Webb was making out. We didn't realize that we were going to detain you.

Mrs. Goddard, we know this is a very happy occasion for you. Back in 1926 your husband, with you at his side, launched the world's first liquid-fueled rocket on his Aunt Effie's farm in Auburn, Massachusetts.

I have always felt that we have at least some things in common. My wife has always been at my side in every endeavor of any moment that I have ever undertaken. And we had *our* Aunt Effie, and she had just come back from her farm in Alabama that week.

So today, exactly 40 years later, you and the billions of people of the world could see this morning, just a few moments ago,

another vindication of the great hopes and the great dreams of that great man to whom you were married.

I sat there with the Secretary of State, and the former Secretary of State, Mr. Acheson, and others, as we saw this rocket, based upon the principles that he discovered, launch men into a new space adventure.

I never see one of these shots without crossing my fingers and saying a prayer for Jim Webb and the men in his organization, because we never know what the outcome will be.

I think if I were writing my own epitaph this morning I perhaps would prefer to be remembered, for the period that I was Vice President, more by this one thing than any other. President Kennedy asked me to attempt to organize and give direction to the Space Agency. I interviewed about 19 men throughout the United States and finally selected Jim Webb, and I prevailed upon him to come and begin this undertaking.

I remember calling President Kennedy

from my office in the Capitol, and I said, "I think we have the man. His name is Jim Webb." He said, "Well, bring him on in and we will announce it in a few minutes."

Within 15 minutes from the time I called the President originally, Jim Webb was out here being announced as the new Space Administrator. I have been very proud of that announcement every moment since.

Your modesty and your humbleness, your great executive ability and your great courage, your Marine spirit and determination have made us the envy of all the world, Mr. Webb, and we salute you publicly.

Dr. Goddard was a great prophet, a true prophet. To some it seems almost incredible that a year before Lindbergh had even flown the Atlantic he was dreaming and working to take us up into the stars. Like so many prophets, he was long without honor in his own country, but he never lost faith because his faith was founded on fact. He could turn aside the rebuffs of the shortsighted; he could laugh at the jokes of his detractors.

I just wish this morning that he could be here with us to observe what we have just seen. I don't think he would be the least surprised by the progress we have made. I think that he would be very proud.

This is a very proud moment for me, too, Mrs. Goddard, and you have helped make it so. I never had the scientific vision that your great husband had. I did not foresee the space age nearly as early as he did. And I am rather glad I didn't, because I was the subject of enough rebuffs and talks about basketballs and things like that that I did many years later. But when it did become apparent that the space age was upon us, I did, with the help of Congressman Miller

and the Vice President and others, try to do something about getting this Nation interested.

I was looking at some of the columns the other day written by our leaders in Government commenting upon our meeting of the Democratic caucus where we devoted our entire caucus to the subject of space and its future. I remember how complimentary they were about that particular meeting. They still are being published, too. They appear in the papers every now and then, these same people.

We said to our Senators, then, that we had to make up for a lot of lost time—time that was lost, in part, because this Nation wouldn't listen to your husband. We haven't wiped out all the deficiencies in our program yet, but we have caught up and we are pulling ahead.

In accepting this award this morning, I want to declare once again that so long as I am in public office, I am going to do everything within my power and my capability to prevent us from falling behind. We intend to land the first man on the surface of the moon and we intend to do this in the decade of the sixties.

The whole Nation now understands the true significance of America's space efforts. The story of man's advancement down through the ages is, of course, the story of his victories over the forces of nature. The health and comfort he enjoys, the leisure he possesses, the abundance of the food he eats, all of these are the result of his unending determination to probe the secrets of the world around him.

In 1958 when we introduced the legislation to create the National Aeronautics and Space Administration, I said in the Senate at that time, "I believe that the development of the space age will bring the beginning of the longest and greatest boom of abundance and prosperity in the history of man."

Well time is bringing out that belief. The future belongs to those of faith and daring and vision. I am proud this morning to be in the presence of the men who represent that future and who have come here to be with us on this occasion: Vice President Humphrey, who has given great seriousness and vital leadership to our space program in the Nation; Congressman George Miller, who from the very beginning has been in on the first launch; Senator Anderson, who is not with us; Congressman Albert Thomas, who left us just a few days ago.

All of these men had the faith, the daring, the vision, and the spirit of adventure that has brought us where we are.

Dr. Pickering, I believe this is the real meaning of the space age which we are in. I thank you and Mrs. Goddard for making this event possible.

Now as we return to our schedule for the rest of the week, I know that each of us is saying a silent prayer for Scott and Armstrong. May God be with them and you.

NOTE: The President spoke at 12:10 p.m. in the Fish Room at the White House after receiving the Robert H. Goddard Trophy from the National Space Club. In his opening words he referred to Mrs. Robert H. Goddard, widow of the pioneer in rocket research, Dr. William H. Pickering, Director of the Jet Propulsion Laboratory, Pasadena, Calif., James E. Webb, Administrator of the National Aeronautics and Space Administration, Hubert H. Humphrey, Vice President of the United States, and Representative George P. Miller of California.

During his remarks the President referred to Charles E. Bohlen, U.S. Ambassador to France, Dean Rusk, Secretary of State, Dean Acheson, Secretary of State during the Truman administration, Senator Clinton P. Anderson of New Mexico, Representative Albert Thomas of Texas, who died on February 15 (see Item 71), and Maj. David Scott and Neil A. Armstrong, Gemini 8 astronauts (see Item 135).

In presenting the trophy, Dr. Pickering read the following citation: "To the Hon. Lyndon B. Johnson, who as a United States Senator shaped the nation's space program from its infancy; helped to assure its adequate organization, funding and execution; and who as Vice President and Chairman of the National Aeronautics and Space Council, and later as President, provided the leadership for United States pre-eminence in space."

135   Statement by the President Following the Safe Return of the Gemini 8 Astronauts. *March 16, 1966*

THE ADMINISTRATOR of NASA, Mr. James Webb, has informed me that Neil Armstrong and David Scott report they are "A–Okay." All of us are greatly relieved.

They—and those who are joining in their recovery—have shown remarkable courage and poise under stress. They are disappointed that their mission could not continue, but Gemini 8 accomplished the first docking in space—a major step on the course we have set. The information they have acquired will help us to perfect the spacecrafts that will carry us even further.

From their skill and strength we all take heart, knowing that the personal qualities of the astronauts and their colleagues will ultimately prevail in the conquest of space.

We are very proud of them.

NOTE: The statement was read to the press by Bill D. Moyers, Special Assistant to the President, at approximately 11:40 p.m., after Gemini 8 had splashed down safely in the Pacific following difficulties encountered in flight. The statement was not made public in the form of a White House press release.

136 Remarks on Equal Employment Opportunity in the Federal Government. *March 17, 1966*

Mr. Vice President, members of the Cabinet, Chairman Macy and members of the Commission, ladies and gentlemen:

I asked you to come here today for a very special purpose. I want to talk to you about a goal of this Government that is very close to my heart. I did not invent this goal. It was established by President Eisenhower by Executive order, first, in the Federal Government. But I want to see, and I intend to do everything I can to see, that the goal is finally reached.

With your help, I want this administration to be recognized as one in which we finally achieve full and equal opportunity for persons of every race, color, creed, and nationality in every part of the United States Government.

As long as any American is denied the chance to fully develop and to use his talents, to become all that he can be, then every American is less than he should be. If race, skin color, religious beliefs, sex, or national origin prevent anyone from reaching the heights, then we have all wasted a human being. We have failed that person and, finally, we have failed our country.

Too many of our fellow citizens are still restrained by a straitjacket that was strapped upon them by the mere accident of their birth.

Too many of our fellow citizens do not get the education or the training that they need to become productive members of our society.

Too many of our fellow citizens are prevented from fully using the education they do get.

Yet we expect, and we get, full participation from Americans of all races, creeds, colors, and nationalities in Vietnam. More

than 200,000 Americans of every description are fighting there now—some are dying—to protect our own freedom and to preserve the freedom of others.

If our magnificent young men can die for freedom in a foreign land, how can we refuse any of them a full measure of freedom and opportunity here at home?

Our Government has long been one avenue by which members of minorities have entered into full participation of our national life.

As of June 1965 the Government had about 375,000 members of minority groups on its rolls, of which 308,657 were Negroes. Negroes accounted for 13.5 percent of the Federal work force, while they actually made up approximately 10 percent of our overall population. Negro employment has increased during the 3 years ending June 1965 by 5.3 percent, while total Federal employment increased by only 1.6 percent during the same period.

During the same time frame, the number of Negroes in high paying jobs has increased significantly. But we must not rest on our laurels. We still have a long way to go before we can claim full and equal opportunity as a fact in our Government life.

The Civil Service Commission, acting under the authority of Executive Order 11246, has issued new regulations which will become effective on and after April 3d. These new regulations call upon you to undertake action programs. And let me underline that one word "action"—action to achieve the great objective of equal employment opportunity. Chairman Macy of the Civil Service Commission will be my eyes and ears to see that we get action.

These plans must tax the limits of our

imagination and our creativity. They must go beyond the limited objective of eliminating discrimination. If we are going to have equal employment opportunity in the Federal Government, we must attack that problem on many fronts.

If members of minority groups can't be employed because they can't find housing, then we must find housing.

If they can't be employed because school systems do not give them the necessary education, then we must work with the school systems to see to it that the right kind of training is provided.

If they can't be employed because there is no vocational training available in the community, then we must see to it that we have programs that provide specialized training to help them meet their needs.

These and a host of other actions are open to us. We must take them. Almost a year ago I spoke to the graduating class at Howard University. Last June, I said, "It is not enough just to open the gates of opportunity. All of our citizens must have the ability to walk through those gates."

When the historians catalog these times in which we now live, if it is written that we were fair men who tried to bring decency and equality into American life, then, I believe our great-grandchildren will be proud.

It is more than doing what is needed. It is doing what it right.

If there lives somewhere in this great Nation one man or one woman whose talents could advance the cause of our country, and those skills are buried because of discrimination, the tragedy is vast and the Nation is the loser.

In the last year, we have tried to do some things to break, for the first time, these barriers in leadership.

A Negro scholar and exceptional administrator for the first time sits in the President's Cabinet.

The brilliant Solicitor General of the United States is a Negro, the first to hold this high office. An exceptional Negro is now the first of his race to sit on the Federal Reserve Board of this Nation. A most charming and intelligent lady is our first woman to be both an Ambassador and a Negro. For the first time, an able Negro lady is a United States Federal judge.

These are a few of the breakthroughs in which reason and sanity triumphed.

So I challenge each of you here today, and each of you within the sound of my voice, to try to accept this as your own creed.

With your leadership and with your personal commitment to this objective, I have high confidence and great hope that we can build a government where talent and energy and integrity will prevail and where discrimination will not.

Thank you very much.

NOTE: The President spoke at 11:10 a.m. in the Civil Service Commission auditorium. In his opening words he referred to Hubert H. Humphrey, Vice President of the United States, and John W. Macy, Jr., Chairman of the Civil Service Commission. During his remarks he referred to Thurgood Marshall, Solicitor General, Andrew F. Brimmer, member of the Board of Governors of the Federal Reserve System, Mrs. Patricia R. Harris, U.S. Ambassador to Luxembourg, and Mrs. Constance Baker Motley, nominated January 26, 1966, to be United States District Judge for the Southern District of New York.

Executive orders of President Eisenhower affecting equal employment opportunity in the Federal Government include Executive Order 10577 of November 22, 1954, of which section 4.2 prohibits racial, political, or religious discrimination (3 CFR, 1954–1958 Comp., p. 218), and Executive Order 10590 of January 18, 1955, which established the President's Committee on Government Employment Policy (3 CFR, 1954–1958 Comp., p. 237).

For the text of Executive Order 11246 of September 24, 1965, "Equal Employment Opportunity," see the Weekly Compilation of Presidential Documents (vol. 1, p. 305), the Federal Register (30 F.R. 12319), or Title 3 of the Code of Federal Regulations (3 CFR, 1965 Supp., p. 167).

For the President's commencement address at Howard University on June 4, 1965, see 1965 volume, this series, Book II, Item 301.

137 Remarks on the Appointment of the Postmaster General as Chairman, Interdepartmental Committee for Savings Bonds. *March* 18, 1966

WE HAVE come here this morning to welcome Postmaster General Larry O'Brien into still another very important job. Larry is going to assume the chairmanship of the Interdepartmental Committee for Savings Bonds. There is no task being performed by any officer of this Government that is more important at the present time.

Every savings bond is a contribution to our national security. Not all of us can help directly to win the fight for freedom in Vietnam, but every one of us can do his share to support our men who are out there in Vietnam fighting for us.

Every one of us, by participating in the savings bond program, can help to bear the cost of conflict.

Every one of us can contribute to conserving the buying power of our American dollar.

During the 3½ years that John Macy has served as Chairman of this Committee, there has been a substantial growth in the rate of savings bond sales throughout the United States Government.

The President, the Vice President, all the members of the Cabinet have already enrolled in the savings bond program and buy their bonds regularly. I want to see every single employee of the Federal Government helping to set an example for the rest of the Nation to follow. With the higher interest rate that I recently announced, the bonds that we buy now will earn more money. Savings bonds are today competitive with most other forms of saving and there is no form of saving which does more direct good for this country of ours that we all love.

I would like us to eventually double the holdings of these bonds among Federal employees. I realize that all of us have many personal needs, obligations, responsibilities. Some will not be able to participate as fully in the payroll savings program as they would like to or as their neighbors may be able to. But I do believe that every Government employee can and should participate to some degree.

I do not hesitate to ask all of you to do that. For the program is not only patriotic, it is also prudent. Each bond that we set aside strengthens the financial security of our own families as well as the economy of our own country. So I again urge every Federal department and agency head to devote his very best efforts to expanding this vital program under the leadership of its new, popular, dynamic Chairman, the Postmaster General, Larry O'Brien.

I am grateful to all those Government employees who are already buying bonds through the payroll savings plan. And I urge them now to increase their purchases if that is at all possible. And I urge those who have not yet entered the program to enter it—enter it at the earliest possible opportunity.

There just is no better investment than the United States savings bond—for it is a direct stake in the future of your country.

NOTE: The President spoke at 11:45 a.m. in the Theater at the White House. During his remarks

he referred to John W. Macy, Jr., Chairman of the Civil Service Commission.

Following the President's remarks, Postmaster General Lawrence F. O'Brien and Secretary of the Treasury Henry H. Fowler spoke briefly. Their remarks are printed in the Weekly Compilation of Presidential Documents (vol. 2, p. 405).

---

138   Letter to the President of the Senate and to the Speaker of the House Transmitting Report "A Ten-Year Program of Federal Water Resources Research." *March 19, 1966*

[Released March 19, 1966. Dated March 18, 1966]

Dear Mr. President: (Dear Mr. Speaker:)

Last year, through my Special Assistant for Science and Technology, I asked the Committee on Water Resources Research of the Federal Council for Science and Technology to speed the development of a comprehensive, long-range water research program.

That task has now been completed.

This report—"A Ten-Year Program of Federal Water Resources Research"— is the result of our efforts.

The growth of our population and industry has placed new demands on our water supplies. We are confronted with water shortages in many sections of our country. Today, virtually every river system in America is touched by pollution. This menace grows more serious each day.

As I have said before, we must combine all of the means at our disposal—Federal, state, local and private—to meet the challenges posed by our water resource problems. The Water Resources Planning Act and the Water Pollution Control Act, passed at the last session, and the Clean Rivers Demonstration Act now pending in the Congress are important steps forward.

We must seek the knowledge and understanding essential to support our efforts.

We must apply the very best of science and technology to solve our mounting water resource problems.

We must continue our search for bold, new ideas.

A strong, well planned program of research has now become a national necessity. The growth of knowledge in this vital area is important to our future.

The ten-year research program outlined in the report—which will be refined and revised as the future state of our knowledge grows—establishes a guideline for action. The report pinpoints those areas of research in need of immediate attention and specifies research goals in over 40 important categories. It has been used as a basis for preparing our Fiscal Year 1967 Budget requests.

I recommend that the various committees of Congress concerned with our water resources carefully consider what this report has to say.

Sincerely,

LYNDON B. JOHNSON

NOTE: This is the text of identical letters addressed to the Honorable Hubert H. Humphrey, President of the Senate, and to the Honorable John W. McCormack, Speaker of the House of Representatives.

The report, entitled "A Ten-Year Program of Federal Water Resources Research" and dated February 1966 (Government Printing Office, 88 pp.), was issued by the Committee on Water Resources

Research of the Federal Council for Science and Technology.

139 Memorandum Approving Release of Copper From the National Stockpile. *March 21, 1966*

Memorandum for Honorable Franklin B. Dryden, Acting Director, Office of Emergency Planning:

I approve your recommendation and the recommendations of the Secretaries of State, Treasury, Commerce, the Acting Secretary of Defense and the Acting Chairman of the Council of Economic Advisers regarding the release of 200,000 tons of copper from the national stockpile.

In accordance with the provisions of Section 5 of the Strategic and Critical Materials Stockpiling Act, as amended (50 U.S.C. 98(d)) and based on the recommendations mentioned above and the opinion of the Attorney General, I herewith determine that such release is required for purposes of the common defense. Disposals should be made through regular producer channels on a periodic basis and in such a way as to facilitate the orderly distribution of copper supplies with priorities to defense and defense-supporting users, such as ammunition manufacturers, as necessary.

I also approve the other recommendations in your memorandum of March 17.

LYNDON B. JOHNSON

NOTE: The memorandum was read by Bill D. Moyers, Special Assistant to the President, in his office at the White House at 11:35 a.m. on Monday, March 21, 1966. It was not made public in the form of a White House press release.

See also Item 636 and note.

140 Special Message to the Congress on Consumer Interests. *March 21, 1966*

To the Congress of the United States:

The consumer's interest is the American interest.

In guarding it, in promoting it, we improve the lives of every man, woman, and child in our nation.

Consumers are all the people—the worker, the farmer, the businessman, and their families.

Every domestic program of the Federal Government in a very real sense is directed toward the consumer. When we work to stem pollution, improve transportation, or rebuild our cities, we promote the welfare of the American consumer.

The consumer has a right to a dollar of stable purchasing power.

I pledge to defend that right with all the ability and determination at my command.

All Americans can take pride in the economic record of recent years.

We are in the 61st month of unparalleled prosperity—the longest in our peacetime history.

A year ago 5.0% of our workers were unemployed. Now only 3.7% are out of work.

Today, our programs to provide better training and wider educational opportunities are supplying thousands of trained workers for our expanding economy.

Our standard of living has never been

higher. Real consumption per capita—the way the average standard of living is measured—has advanced nearly 10% in the past two years—as large a dollar gain as in the preceding 8 years combined. That record could not have been achieved if inflation had eroded the value of the dollar and undermined the foundation of our prosperity.

This Administration intends to maintain that record.

A new and progressive program is needed if we are to protect the American consumer's rights in the marketplace—his right to be informed, to choose, to be protected from unsafe products and to be heard in the councils of Government.

I recommend that the Congress enact comprehensive measures to secure these rights.

The American consumer has tremendous impact on the variety and quality of the goods and services available on the market.

The consumer buys what he wants. He cannot and should not be told what to buy. But he must be told what is available for purchase.

If the consumer is to be a wise sovereign in our progressive market economy, he must be fully informed. Free consumer choice—indeed, our free enterprise system—must rest on a firm foundation of reliable information on the costs and contents of the products we buy.

Today I renew my request that the Congress enact legislation to strengthen this foundation in two critical areas—lending and packaging.

I proposed legislation in these areas two years ago. President Kennedy made a similar recommendation four years ago. We have learned much from careful study of these proposals by the Congress and the public. Everything we have learned reaffirms my conviction that:

—We *can* have equitable and effective laws on lending and packaging,

—We *can* protect both the consumer and the overwhelming majority of honest businessmen from the minority of producers who would compete unfairly and infringe the rights of the consumer and their fellow businessmen,

—We *need* reform in the credit area and we should encourage States to enact legislation to correct abuses,

—We *need* such legislation urgently. We *can* now act wisely without further delay.

TRUTH IN LENDING

Every consumer and every business in America benefits from our system of consumer credit. Credit and the economy have grown together. Last year merchants, lending companies, and financial institutions extended about $75 billion in new installment credit to consumers.

Consumer credit:

—permits purchase of many of the goods and services which enrich the quality of American life—the homes, the automobiles, and household appliances we buy.

—finances the costs of higher education, travel, and other activities which broaden and develop the human spirit.

—relieves suffering and distress by spreading major medical expenses over a period of time.

—enables our young families to acquire and furnish homes early in life when good housing is most needed and best enjoyed.

Over the years, this system has worked well. Lenders charge reasonable rates. Borrowers repay their debts promptly. But a minority of unscrupulous operators charge all that the traffic will bear. They wring from the unwary purchaser a price far higher than the credit market requires.

The right of the consumer to know the actual cost of his credit has been ignored for too long. Credit is a commodity. The consumer has just as much right to know the cost of borrowing money as to know the price of any other article he buys.

Credit charges are a key item in the consumer budget. They totaled $24 billion last year. It is important that consumers be able to plan their budgets wisely—and prudently—in this important area.

Yet, many consumers had no information on how these credit costs relate to the cost of the article being financed.

They were confused by statements of credit rates described in unusual or even misleading terms.

They unknowingly paid higher prices for credit than reputable lenders were charging.

We must protect and inform the consumer in his use of the consumer credit system. Our credit structure will be sounder when the consumer has this information.

I therefore renew my recommendation for legislation requiring lenders to state the full cost of credit, simply and clearly, and to state it before any credit contract is signed.

This legislation will help consumers:

—budget their incomes more intelligently, because they will know the price of credit in the same clear terms as the price of milk or gasoline.

—compare credit costs so they shop for the best combination of quality and price—including *all* of the charges involved.

—avoid unscrupulous lenders who use excessive credit charges and other sharp practices.

This legislation will also help the legitimate lender by offering protection against any competitor who seeks to gain business by misrepresenting credit costs. It will insure the fair and effective competition that legitimate lenders desire.

It will *not* regulate the cost of credit itself, or interfere with existing laws.

It will *not* reduce the volume of credit.

It will *not* dampen the vigor of consumer buying.

This legislation will right the balance of legal protection between lenders and borrowers.

I urge the Congress to act to insure that the American consumer is given a clear price tag when he shops for credit.

FAIR PACKAGING AND LABELING

Americans can choose among an unprecedented assortment of products when they go shopping.

In the average supermarket today, the housewife finds 8,000 items—more than five times the 1,500 items she found just 20 years ago. She also does an increasing amount of shopping in the "self-service" store—a product of efficiency in distribution. But with more products to choose from and fewer sales people to answer her questions, the housewife relies heavily on the package itself as her source of information in making a choice.

American industry has made enormous strides in providing attractive and informative packaging. American manufacturers maintain one of the highest standards of quality in the world. They know that packages which accurately and fully describe their wares are the best salesmen.

Nevertheless there are instances of deception in labeling and packaging. Practices have arisen that cause confusion and conceal information even when there is no deliberate intention to deceive. The housewife often needs a scale, a yardstick, and a slide rule to make a rational choice. She has enough to do without performing complicated mathematics in the stores.

It is not enough to hope that such practices will disappear by themselves. The Government must do its share to insure the shopper against deception, to remedy confusion and to eliminate questionable practices.

I urge the Congress to enact fair packaging and labeling legislation to:

1. Require that each package provide simple, direct, accurate and visible information as to the nature and quantity of its contents, including ingredients where this is important.

2. Keep off the shelves packages with deceptively shaped boxes, misleading pictures, confusing or meaningless adjectives, inappropriate size or quantity markings, and promotional gimmicks that promise nonexistent savings.

3. Provide for the establishment of reasonable and appropriate weight standards to facilitate comparative shopping.

This legislation will not make packaging less attractive or less efficient. It will not prevent economies of scale in packaging, nor will it impose costly restrictions.

An accurate and informative package and label need not add to the producer's cost. It will add to the welfare of the American consumer.

PROTECTION FROM DANGEROUS SUBSTANCES

The consumer must not only be informed. He must also be protected from dangerous drugs, foods, and other substances.

Our ability to conquer pain and disease has increased dramatically. But we must not allow the development of new drugs and nutrients to outstrip our capacity to test and certify them for safety and effectiveness.

I recommend three related items of legislation to reinforce consumer protection.

THE CHILD SAFETY ACT

Children must be our first concern. They are our hope and our future.

Too many children now become seriously ill—too many die—because of accidents that could be avoided by adequate labeling and packaging of dangerous substances. This is senseless and needless tragedy.

Most drug manufacturers have taken responsible action in providing appropriate warnings on drug labels. The Food and Drug Administration has accomplished much in reducing the incidence of these private tragedies. But both have been greatly handicapped by gaps in the laws dealing with hazardous substances and materials.

It is still true, for example, that present law nowhere provides for inspection of unpackaged toys and novelties that may be poisonous to children.

To extend legal protection for the safety of all our citizens, especially our children, I recommend legislation to:

—bring all hazardous substances, regardless of their wrapping, under the safeguards of the Federal Hazardous Substances Labeling Act;

—ban from commerce those household substances that are so hazardous that warning labels are not adequate safeguards;

—ban the sale of toys and other children's articles containing hazardous substances, regardless of their packaging;

—require labels to warn consumers against

possible injury from drugs and cosmetics, and from food in pressurized containers;

—limit the amount of children's aspirin available in retail packages;

—require certain potent drugs attractive to children to have safety closure caps.

DRUG SAFETY ACT

Each year the Food and Drug Administration receives over 4,000 requests for study and approval of new drugs. Each new product is carefully analyzed and tested. This process is a basic consumer protection in which the United States leads the world.

But it is just as basic that the law require more accurate and detailed labeling of dangerous drugs—and that it deal specifically with drugs whose period of potency and purity is limited.

To make these improvements, and to protect the lives of all of our citizens, I recommend legislation to:

—authorize the Government to require records and reports of experience and to require labeling changes on any drug, whether old or new;

—require certification of all drugs whose potency and purity can mean life or death to a patient, thus extending the law which now applies to insulin and antibiotics; and

—control the unsolicited distribution of drug samples.

PROFESSIONAL TRAINING AND COOPERATION AMENDMENTS

The task of protecting the consumer cannot and should not be left solely to the Federal Government. The Government can and should provide creative Federal leadership to help States and local communities in their own constructive and determined efforts.

As a step forward, Federal assistance is needed to strengthen and enlarge State and local professional staffs in the food and drug areas.

To begin to meet our Federal responsibility, I recommend legislation authorizing expansion of the Food and Drug Administration's training programs for non-Federal officials. This will be the first in a series of measures to broaden Federal-State-local corporation in this vital field.

REVITALIZING THE FOOD AND DRUG ADMINISTRATION

In addition to these legislative proposals, *I pledge continued efforts to revitalize the Food and Drug Administration.* This process is already well underway.

This agency has performed notably in the past. Yet the scope of its responsibilty has been considerably broadened in recent years. The public interest demands that it receive the additional support it needs to perform its many new functions.

I recently appointed a new Commissioner of Food and Drugs to give the agency new leadership and new direction. I have directed him to conduct a thorough review of the agency's roles and missions and to move purposefully toward a new structure fitted to the demands of the times. I have also asked him to recruit personnel with the most outstanding backgrounds in science and public service.

The responsibilities of the Food and Drug Administration are heavy. But they will be met.

To strengthen the Food and Drug Administration, I have proposed, in the Fiscal Year 1967 Budget, the largest single in-

crease ever requested for this agency.

I believe that the interests of the Nation fully support this request. I urge the Congress to provide the necessary funds and enact the recommended legislation to enable this important agency to fulfill the needs of our people.

COSMETICS AND MEDICAL DEVICES

Assurance of the safety and effectiveness of the drugs we buy has the highest priority. But further action may be necessary to protect the consumer against harmful cosmetics and against medical devices that are neither safe nor effective.

I have asked the Secretary of Health, Education, and Welfare to begin a thorough analysis of the legislative authority now available and to recommend new steps that may be needed to close the gaps in the laws dealing with cosmetics and medical devices.

THE PROGRESS WE HAVE MADE

Since my Message on Consumer Interests in 1964, much has been accomplished.

—The Federal Trade Commission has launched an intensive program to protect consumers from unfair marketing practices. It has established a Consumer Complaints Bureau in the District of Columbia and is prepared to help the States develop such programs of their own.

—The Federal Power Commission's Natural Power Survey estimates that by 1980 as much as $11 billion per year can be saved in the cost of electricity for Americans. The Commission stemmed the rising cost of natural gas and retroactively reduced rates. As a result more than $650 million has been refunded and annual gas costs to

consumers have been reduced by $130 million.

—The Department of Defense has issued an important directive designed to protect servicemen as consumers, with special emphasis upon full disclosure of credit charges.

—The Department of Agriculture has established a Consumer and Marketing Service to coordinate the Department's many and varied consumer services.

—The Department of Commerce has taken steps to assure a greater consumer voice in the development of product standards, and has adopted improved procedures for product standardization.

These are but a few actions of the many Federal agencies which protect the interests and serve the needs of the consumer.

TO HELP THE POOR FAMILY

I have instructed the Director of the Office of Economic Opportunity to give particular attention to the consumer needs of our poverty-stricken families. Studies have shown that they suffer most cruelly from lack of consumer protection and lack of buyer "know how." I consider this the most urgent challenge in the field of consumer information and education.

We must deal with the fact that today 34 million Americans—7 million families—must try to stretch poverty-level incomes to meet living costs. Studies show that these people are plagued by consumer problems unknown to the affluent majority.

They are unable to shop effectively for bargains or to buy in economical quantities.

They are often victimized by excessive costs of credit and merchandise.

They are subjected to countless fradulent and deceptive marketing and financing practices.

341

Most of these problems are symptoms of the basic maladies which we are attacking in the War on Poverty. Programs of consumer information and protection cannot cure them—but such programs can lessen their impact.

The Office of Economic Opportunity has already made 56 grants, totaling almost $3,-000,000, to support consumer education and related programs throughout the country. In the future, this Office will become a clearing-house for distribution of educational materials to the poor. It will be a powerful source of incentive and support to the poor in their efforts to achieve fair play in the marketplace.

I pledge the all-out effort of the Federal Government to help our poorest citizens to spend their limited funds more efficiently as we work to enhance their incomes.

Credit is a particular problem for the poor. Often it is available only at high interest rates, and its overextension can lead to the garnishment of wages and the loss of jobs. The situation is particularly severe because the poor are susceptible to emergencies that eliminate any limited financial reserves they may have.

Cooperative sources of low-cost credit, such as credit unions, combined with sound and impartial debt and financial counseling, and with legal services, can be of great benefit to the poor.

I am directing the Director of the Office of Economic Opportunity and my Committee on Consumer Interests to intensify their efforts to encourage the development of such services in Community Action Programs.

THE OUTLOOK FOR THE FUTURE

The measures I have recommended—truth in packaging, truth in lending, and the others—will help protect the consumer

in the marketplace.

But beyond this there lies an even more important concern—that the consumer continue to have a dollar of stable purchasing power. Even the wisest consumer laws will not help the American public if their hard earned dollars and savings are eroded by inflation.

The rewards and challenges of prosperity are central to the consumer's interest today. For the past 5 years, the American consumer has participated in and contributed to an unparalleled and uninterrupted economic advance.

This has been the most inflation-free expansion in the history of our Nation. Apart from the improvements in quality and the benefits of new goods, the upward drift in prices has been only one-fourth as rapid as the growth in the real income of consumers. The healthy growth of consumer income has been built on

—rapid technical advances by business;
—productivity gains from the greater skill and diligence of labor;
—cooperation among labor, management, and Government;
—prudent fiscal policies;
—the careful efforts of consumers to get the most for their money.

The success of our efforts to bring full prosperity to the American economy has sharpened the challenge of maintaining price stability.

We are determined to have the benefits of both full employment and price stability—not one at the expense of the other.

That environment of stability is strengthened whenever responsible action is taken on prices and wages.

It is strengthened when we support a pay bill for Federal workers consistent with the Administration's wage-price guideposts.

It is strengthened when businessmen lower

prices to share the benefits of lower costs and rapid productivity gains.

It is strengthened when unions bargaining for wage increases stay within the bounds of productivity gains, as they did in many industries last year.

On many occasions, I have asked management and labor to make their price and wage decisions with full regard to the interest of the entire Nation in price and cost stability. I renew that request today.

The consumer's interest is broad in scope. So are the efforts required to promote and protect that interest. The recommendations I have made will require action on many fronts by many groups.

The Congress holds the key to historic achievements in areas of consumer information and safety. This Administration will marshal its forces to promote consumer welfare in close cooperation with the States and local governments.

Yet the basic job of furthering the consumer cause lies in the hands of private citizens—the consumers themselves. With the full cooperation of all, we can look ahead toward an ever-rising standard of living for American consumers.

Together, we can achieve a free marketplace where better goods can be bought, where real incomes continue to increase, and where the dollar's purchasing power remains firm and stable.

LYNDON B. JOHNSON

The White House
March 21, 1966

NOTE: For the President's remarks upon signing related legislation, see Items 508, 576, 594.

141   The President's News Conference of March 22, 1966

THE PRESIDENT. I am ready if you have any questions.

QUESTIONS

ADDRESS BEFORE FOREIGN SERVICE INSTITUTE

[1.] Q. Can you tell us anything about the nature of your speech tomorrow? [1]

THE PRESIDENT. No, it is going to be very brief. It is before a group Secretary Rusk wanted me to come over and visit with. I do not imagine it would be more than 15 minutes, 10 or 15 minutes. I am working on it now.

POLITICAL SITUATION IN SOUTH VIETNAM

[2.] Q. Mr. President, sir, can you give us an assessment of the political situation in South Vietnam?

THE PRESIDENT. I think you have about the same information I do. I don't think that there is much I have received which would shed any light on what has been reported.

TAXES AND THE STATE OF THE ECONOMY

[3.] Q. Mr. President, a lot of the economists would like you to raise taxes, and ask Congress to raise taxes soon. Have you any comment on that?

THE PRESIDENT. We get a lot of advice on economics from time to time. I think that is natural. We try to weigh it all and study it and draw our own conclusions. We conferred with the economists available to the President and the leaders in this field in the House and Senate last fall and concluded

---

[1] See Item 142.

that it would be desirable, in addition to the $6 billion we would begin taking out on Medicare in July, to have a tax adjustment act of roughly another $6 billion, a little over $4 billion, or which would be running at a rate of a little over $4 billion at the end of this year.

So we had $6 billion come out in January, and medical care that we provided again in January, and something over $4 billion that we provided in March. We are watching developments every day. I get reports on what is happening.

Retail sales for January and February have just been reported to me. They are slightly below November and December. New orders for durable manufactures declined in February. Housing starts have fallen to the lowest level in 3 years. I believe they are 17 percent under January—I would like to check this figure, Bill [2]—and some 11 percent under February of last year, the same month last year. It is about 11 percent under.

Some farm prices and foods are leveling off. The money supply declined in February and the growth of business loans slowed down. Numerous municipal bond issues and some corporate issues have been postponed.

The increase of inventories in January was a moderate increase. Unemployment exceeds 6 percent in about 19 or 20 of the major labor markets, so we still have some problems there.

We are running just a little under our estimated expenditures in Vietnam the first 3 months of this year. We hope to pick that up and accelerate it some in the next 3 months. We had planned to run at roughly $50 billion, or at the rate of $50 billion a year for the first 6 months, that is, June 30

to January 1, and $58 billion from January 1 to June 30, for an average of $54 billion compared to $49 billion last year.

That would add about $5 billion or $6 billion, or maybe $7 billion to the economic bloodstream for extra expenditures, so we have taken out $6 billion for Medicare and we will take out $4 billion or $5 billion more with $6 billion for taxes, and this will bring us about to $12 billion to be pulled out.

We have to see what effect that has. If more needs to be taken out, we will give consideration to it. Some of that will depend, I think, on appropriations.

We are asking all of the departments, as I have told you from time to time—I do this every few months—to take a new look at their expenditures to see if there is anything that appears to be obsolete, or that is unnecessary, and forgo anything that they can.

Congress is adding some expenditures that we did not ask for. They may add some more. I read the Record every morning and it looks like there are some things that we tried to make some reductions in that they might put back in. So we will have to watch our expenditures.

There are three things that the economy suggests for consideration in a period where you are having as full employment as we are having now, and the gross national product has reached the level this one has. One of them is control of prices and wages, but very few people want to go to controls as we had to in World War II, and as we had to in Korea. Of course I don't want to, and I hope we won't have to, but that is something we have to consider always.

The second thing is the tax bill [3] that would take some more money out or draw it off. That will depend on our appropria-

_____

[2] Bill D. Moyers, Special Assistant to the President.

[3] See Item 132.

tions and our expenditures, what reaction we get from this March action of taxes, and the January action of Medicare.

Third, is curtailing expenditures. Now they are being curtailed in some State governments and some city governments, and some of the bond issues are being held back. There has been some slowdown in our own operations, withholding construction in certain areas. We will watch it very closely and see what happens in these unemployment markets, in retail sales, in housing, and in the money market, and then take whatever action is indicated.

We don't want to act prematurely. We don't want to put on the brakes too fast, but it is something that requires study every day, and we are doing that.

THE OPERATING ENGINEERS UNION

[4.] Q. Mr. President, are you taking action against the Operating Engineers Union in New Jersey, which seems to have exceeded the wage-price guidelines in their contract demands?

THE PRESIDENT. No, I have not.

FURTHER QUESTIONS ON THE STATE OF THE ECONOMY

[5.] Q. Mr. President, frequently in the past when you reviewed the economy with us, you have emphasized largely the prosperity aspects with things improving. Today you cited a number of negative or down factors. I wonder, sir, is it fair to conclude that you are saying that the inflation or the threat of an inflation is probably not as bad as some of the economists or politicians have maintained?

THE PRESIDENT. My statement is made without reference to economists or politicians. This just happened to be the report that I received on the 20th. There are some good things in it, like increase of inventories in January. There was a moderate increase.

The decline in NASA's budget for 1967 will free many highly skilled workers that are now in tight supply. They estimate we will have between 50,000 and 100,000 people that will be freed unless we accelerate that budget.

The relationship between unfilled orders and shipments of durable goods today remains in sharp contrast with the situation a decade ago, when this sector got us into trouble. There are current backlogs of 3½ months of shipments. In 1956 they ran 4½ to 5 months. That would be on the negative side. The decline of $150 million in military family housing will help ease the tight supplies of building materials.

Widespread indication is that banks are rationing customers by tightening credit standards and rejecting loan requests of their less profitable customers, and in the municipal field notable was a cancellation of a $440 million New Jersey issue. Stock prices are down. They were up the last 2 days.

Throughout the next 15 months, the increases in Federal revenues which are drawn out of the economy will exceed the increases in Federal expenditure that add to private purchasing power.

That is a significant thing.

Even though defense expenditures continue to increase, the shift toward restraint emerges by any measure of the budget because of the austerity in nondefense expenditures.

We are up to $600 million over last year with new tax laws and increased revenues from the growth of the economy.

In fiscal 1967 the cash budget will move into surplus, thus swinging toward restraint by more than $7 billion from the current fiscal year. On the administrative budget the move toward restraint shows up in a decline of the deficit from $6.4 billion to $1.8 billion.

Durable shipments meanwhile inched up one-tenth of 1 percent. I think that durable manufacturers' new orders declined 1.3. The biggest element was a 20 percent drop in aircraft orders. Machinery showed a decline. Steel orders shot up 20 percent. It goes back and forth, both of them. I think some days the news is good and some days it is different.

NATO PROBLEMS

[6.] Q. Mr. President, sir, in the light of the developments of the past few weeks, could you give us your assessment of NATO's problems and future?

THE PRESIDENT. I may do that in the morning, and I don't want to take the bloom off the rose.

U.S. POLICY TOWARD COMMUNIST CHINA

[7.] Q. Mr. President, there has been quite a bit of discussion about China lately on Capitol Hill and elsewhere. I wonder if you could tell us how you view the China problem in the light of these discussions, and specifically whether you favor the admission of Communist China to the United Nations in the foreseeable future?

THE PRESIDENT. I think the Secretary of State covered the administration's position very thoroughly Sunday. If he didn't, the Press Secretary did. If not, I would call to your attention that we have watched with interest and complete understanding the testimony of various committees, those of Mr. Zablocki in the House, and Mr. Ful-

bright in the Senate,[4] and the testimony about that part of the world. We think that it is very good to have the opinion of these professors and experts, and Ambassadors and other people.

As far as I am aware, it is not the position of this country that creates the problems with China. It is China's own position. We are very anxious to try to have more contact with her and more exchanges with her, but as has been explained by all of these people, she hangs up the phone. Until there is some change on China's part, I doubt that these academic discussions will do much more than satisfy people's yearning for information.

APPOINTMENT OF SPECIAL ASSISTANT TO THE
PRESIDENT: ROBERT KOMER

[8.] THE PRESIDENT. I am naming Robert Komer, of Chicago, Illinois, as my Special Assistant, and he will primarily have the assignment of duties involving the peaceful reconstruction in Vietnam.

As you know, Mr. Komer is a dedicated man on the National Security Council staff. I am promoting him to be Special Assistant at $30,000 a year. He will be leaving for Vietnam on Tuesday morning with Secretary Vance[5] and Mr. Bill Moyers, my Press Secretary and Special Assistant, for a few days of visit in that area.

Q. Did you say Mr. Moyers was going?
THE PRESIDENT. Yes, sir.

INDEPENDENCE OF LABOR

[9.] Q. Sir, what do you think about labor going into independence? You have

---

[4] Representative Clement J. Zablocki of Wisconsin, member of the House Foreign Affairs Committee, and Senator J. W. Fulbright of Arkansas, Chairman of the Senate Foreign Relations Committee.
[5] Cyrus R. Vance, Deputy Secretary of Defense.

had your ups and downs with labor before. Are you worried about this or not?

THE PRESIDENT. Are you informing me or asking me?

Q. Both. I am reminding you and asking you.

THE PRESIDENT. Well, I would say that as far as I have been aware, labor has always been independent and should be. I am very pleased with the attitude of their leaders. You are probably more distressed than I am, and perhaps not as happy.

SURVEY WORK IN VIETNAM

[10.] Q. Could you give us a little more detail on the survey work that Mr. Moyers and Mr. Vance and Mr. Komer will be doing?

THE PRESIDENT. We have had Mr. Freeman [6] out there. He came back with about 50 recommendations. We have had Mr. Gardner out there and he has come back with a few which will be available to me. I sat up until 2 o'clock this morning talking to General Rudder, Dr. Cain, and others who were on the Gardner mission.[7]

We have the best experts available in this country involved in studying the peaceful reconstruction of Vietnam, their education problems and health problems, productivity problems and agricultural problems. We selected Ambassador Porter [8] the latter part of last year and called him here in January. We had meetings down here at Warrenton. We are trying to concentrate our energies and all of our expertise and knowledge to help these people help themselves and have a better way of life.

Mr. Komer will be the counterpart in Washington of Mr. Porter in the field. I want him to go there and meet with Ambassador Lodge and General Westmoreland [9] and try to get an on-the-ground picture and come back here and help me see that these people get what they need in that particular field.

Mr. Komer met yesterday with Secretary Rusk, with Secretary McNamara, with Mr. Gaud in Mr. Bell's department,[10] and spent a good deal of time with me and Mr. Moyers. Cy Vance is going out there. I asked him if they could ride along with him. Bob McNamara and I agreed that we would try to work it out. That is Tuesday morning after the Indian dinner here Monday night for the Prime Minister.[11] They will leave in the morning.

MILITARY SITUATION IN SOUTH VIETNAM

[11.] Q. Mr. President, could you bring us up to date on the military situation in Vietnam?

THE PRESIDENT. I do not have any information that you do not have. You see the reports. There is nothing to speculate about. You can see what is happening. Our men are doing a very fine job. Their

[6] Orville L. Freeman, Secretary of Agriculture.

[7] The task force, headed by Secretary of Health, Education, and Welfare John W. Gardner, which was established by the President on March 6, 1966, to study the health and education needs of the Vietnamese people (see Item 106). James E. Rudder, President of Texas A. & M. College, College Station, Texas, and Dr. James C. Cain of the Mayo Clinic, Rochester, Minn., were among the 15 experts who left for Saigon on March 12.

[8] William J. Porter, U.S. Deputy Ambassador to the Republic of Vietnam.

[9] Henry Cabot Lodge, U.S. Ambassador to the Republic of Vietnam, and Gen. William C. Westmoreland, Commander, United States Military Assistance Command, Vietnam.

[10] David E. Bell, Administrator, Agency for International Development, and William S. Gaud, Deputy Administrator.

[11] Prime Minister Indira Gandhi of India (see Item 149).

morale is high. Their competence is to be applauded.

This is Earl Rudder, this old friend of mine who is a rancher from Brady, Texas, of whom General Bradley [12] says, "No soldier in my command has ever been wished a more difficult task than which befell the 34-year-old commander . . . James E. Rudder (who) was to take a force of 200 men, land on a shingled shelf under the face of a 100-foot cliff, scale the cliff, and there destroy an enemy battery of coastal guns," while they were dropping hand grenades on their heads.

He commanded at Normandy. He has been out at the front with our boys in Vietnam. He said that he had never seen the morale of any troops as high and never seen an army any more effective. He never saw better coordination, that it was absolutely marvelous, unbelievable, that you could move 200,000-odd men that far, that fast, that effectively. We moved their housing and their medicine and their food and their ammunition and their equipment and everything with them.

He said they have had a wonderful effect on the Vietnamese, and that the boys felt they had a mission and they were fond of the Vietnamese people and they were working very well together. He said that they would protect themselves during the day and advance and take the valleys, and spend the evenings trying to fix up the schools and teach the children.

Dr. Cain said that they saw 30 men brought in, all of them wounded and in terrible shape. He said in less than an hour he went down the line to each one of them, and most of them were wanting to get back. Probably over half of them would be back in a short time. Dr. Cain said he didn't

believe there would be a single casualty in the group because of the prompt treatment they received.

So I would say that the reports from that front are good. We must not be too optimistic and we must not exaggerate what is taking place. But I get about 100 letters a week from them, and I would say they are my greatest source of strength. If I get real depressed when I read how everything has gone bad here, I just ask for the letters from Vietnam so I can cheer up.

THE NOVEMBER ELECTIONS

[12.] Q. Mr. President, a number of Congressmen, Democrats running from marginal districts in the House, are worried about what Vietnam is going to do to their chances in November. How do you think about it?

THE PRESIDENT. I don't believe the Congressmen are as worried as the Republican leaders are. I have watched that, and I discussed that yesterday some. We have had 18 polls made from New York to the west coast, and they compare to 1964. We found yesterday, I think, 12 of them showed that they were in better shape than they were in 1964, 3 were in the same shape, and 3 may drop.

But they had dropped in one case from 61 to 56. In another case they dropped from 63 to 61. In another one, they dropped two or three points.

The Congressmen don't feel that way. What you have been reading are the handouts. We interviewed 270 of the Congressmen. We asked a series of questions about Vietnam. They are all worried about the sacrifices our men are making there, but there are not many of them who have any doubt about the justice of our cause or the wisdom of our course.

---

[12] General of the Army Omar N. Bradley, former Chairman of the Joint Chiefs of Staff.

The vote today shows that. I have been reading where you called this a mutiny, with a vote of 87 to 2 in the Senate today. In the case of the economic aid bills, we had fewer votes cast against them than we have ever had before.

The achievements before Easter are surprising to anyone who has watched the developments in this town as long as I have. The Congressmen on both sides have done a good job, and I don't think that the Republican Congressmen, except in rare instances, have too much to be worried about. Most of them have a chance to be reelected. There are some of their Senators that are going to have some trouble, but it has been a productive year. I think we will probably have 15 or 20 measures signed before Easter, which is something unusual.

We have the Southeast Asia bank development, the economic aid, the military aid, the North Carolina seashore bill, the minimum wage here in the District, and the tax bill. I have seen tax bills take 2 years to get through.

This passed in 2 months, and we received it the day we asked for it. That is a $13 billion bill today. They did not take a dime from it. We asked for $6 billion, and you said we had "mutiny" running around here for 2 or 3 days. Then we received it, and it was $6 billion 10 million.

That is the kind of "mutiny" we like, where you give us all that we ask for, and then add a little supplement to it.

Congress has done a good job. They are doing a good job. Some folks play politics. They give out statements. I see them on the ticker—about three or four handouts a day. They are usually some new pressman who has been hired, or a fellow who thinks he is being paid by the column, like a stringer. He gives out these handouts and provokes fights. He puts a little twist on it. But the Congress is doing a good job, and the people know it. We are moving along with the program and they know it.

I had lunch today with Mr. McNamara. He spent almost 30 days testifying all morning and all afternoon. But he has cleared every single bill for which he is responsible, even next year's appropriations. That is for 1967.

He testified on economic aid and the military supplemental before the House Armed Services Committee, the Senate Armed Services Committee, the House Appropriations Committee, the Senate Appropriations Committee, then had a week's vacation.

Secretary Rusk is doing the same thing. The Congress is doing fine, and the elections are going to be fine. We are glad to have them, and they are a good thing. There is not any real indication of a serious problem for either group. There are these people who pick these figures out of the air. I heard someone the other night talking about 74 or 80 House seats. It was amusing. I wondered how much he knew about any House seat.

Q. Mr. President, do you have any plans to get out in the campaign, to explain your attitude on the Congress or to help any particular Congressman?

THE PRESIDENT. I am explaining my attitude now, and that is why I want you to help me. My attitude is good. I think the Congress has done a good job. I am not just talking about Democrats. I am talking about the Congress generally. I think that the people know it. I would not forgo a chance to give my advice if it was solicited in the right way, under the proper auspices, with appropriate sponsorship. But I have no dates set yet.

I want to try to complete this campaign to prevent aggression, to defeat social misery, and to find a way to the peace table in Vietnam. This is occupying our time now. We are trying to get our Alliance for Progress program in topflight shape. I have spent some time with former Ambassador and now Secretary Gordon.[13] We are very proud of what has happened in Latin America. The last 2 years we have raised their growth rate from 1 percent to 2½ percent. We think that is a real achievement.

We are very interested in the developments on the African Continent. We have just named a new Assistant Secretary to succeed Mr. Williams,[14] Assistant Secretary Joe Palmer, who was in to see me this morning. He is one of the distinguished heads of the Foreign Service Institute who headed the Congo task force for us.

We are talking about inviting Ambassador Gronouski[15] home for consultation in the next few weeks. He has done a very outstanding job in Poland for us. We want to talk to him and encourage him in his work.

We have a good many world problems. We have spent some time in the last few days conferring with our allies about General de Gaulle's views on the NATO alliance. We will be having more to say about that.

POSSIBILITY OF A EUROPEAN TRIP

[13.] Q. Mr. President, is there any chance of your taking a trip to Europe before the end of the summer?

THE PRESIDENT. I have no plans at all along that line. I think that is something for you and Bill Moyers to talk about from time to time, which you all enjoy.

---

[13] Lincoln Gordon, Assistant Secretary of State for Inter-American Affairs, and former U.S. Ambassador to Brazil.

[14] G. Mennen Williams, former Assistant Secretary of State for African Affairs.

[15] John A. Gronouski, U.S. Ambassador to Poland.

Q. Mr. President, have we overlooked anything? We are trying to get another news story.

THE PRESIDENT. I would say we all ought to be commended for our good spirits and jolly frame of mind. I appreciate the good humor you are all in. I don't know how to account for it.

HANOI

[14.] Q. Have you heard anything at all from Hanoi that has changed the picture in the last few months? Has there been any sign of an interest in going to the peace table, as you mentioned a moment ago?

THE PRESIDENT. No. We work at that every day, and we have discussions around the world in that field. We have some of our top men, and some that are not at the top level, always carrying on discussions. But there is nothing that would justify my responding in the affirmative to what you have said.

DISCUSSIONS WITH PRIME MINISTER GANDHI

[15.] Q. Mr. President, can you say anything at all about what you may be discussing with Prime Minister Gandhi?

THE PRESIDENT. Yes. I am looking forward with a great deal of pleasure to seeing the Prime Minister again. We have met on several occasions. Mrs. Johnson and I spent some time with her when we were in her country in 1961. I had lunch with her Ambassador today, and spent a good while visiting with him about the agenda.

We will be talking about our relations and what the American people can do, working with the people of India, to promote peace and prosperity. I want to hear about her ideas and any suggestions she may have as to what we can do that we are not doing in these fields.

We will, of course, talk about some of the things that were on the agenda last year when a visit was postponed, and again when I planned to see Prime Minister Shastri and was prevented from doing so by his death. We will take up where we left off there. We look forward to a very pleasant and very productive visit.

MR. KOMER'S NEW DUTIES

[16.] Q. Mr. President, would Mr. Komer continue to handle the same duties in addition to the new assignment, or is this a change?

THE PRESIDENT. No, this will be a new assignment and a very responsible one. He will be working very closely with Secre-tary Rusk, Secretary McNamara, Administrator Bell, and Mr. Marks of the USIA,[16] on my behalf, as my Special Assistant.

I think he will have his hands pretty full on that. We are going to call him, for our in-house purposes, "Special Assistant for Peaceful Reconstruction in Vietnam."

I have talked to each Secretary about what I expect him to do. I talked to Mr. Komer at some length. It has been a matter that has been evolving since the first of the year.

Reporter: Thank you, Mr. President.

NOTE: President Johnson's sixtieth news conference was held in his office at the White House at 4:15 p.m. on Tuesday, March 22, 1966.

---

[16] Leonard H. Marks, Director, United States Information Agency.

142   Remarks on the North Atlantic Treaty Organization to the Foreign Service Institute.   *March 23, 1966*

Mr. Secretary, ladies and gentlemen:

I am very pleased to address the Foreign Service Institute this morning and to come here to meet with so many Americans that are preparing to serve their country abroad. As one who believes that we cannot shorten our reach in the world, I am greatly encouraged by the number and the quality of those who are studying at this Institute. You have the gratitude of your countrymen and my own assurance of support.

We have come a long way from the day that someone observed that "some diplomat no doubt will launch a heedless word and lurking war leap out."

That was more than half a century ago when diplomacy was often war by another name. Today your task is different. Those of you about to go abroad represent a continuity of purpose in a generation of change. That purpose is to build from reason and moderation a world order in which the fires of conflict yield to the fulfillment of man's oldest yearnings for himself and his family.

Your job, wherever you serve, is peace. That is the task that faces all of us today.

The question, as always, is how? How do we, for example, maintain the security of the Atlantic community upon which so many of the world's hopes depend?

For the answer, we must begin with the gray dawn of the world of 1945, when Europe's cities lay in rubble, her farms devastated, her industries smashed, her people weary with war and death and defeat.

Now from that desolation has come abundance. From that weakness has come power. From those ashes of holocaust has come the rebirth of a strong and a vital community.

The Europe of today is a new Europe. In place of uncertainty there is confidence; in place of decay, progress; in place of isolation, partnership; in place of war, peace.

If there is no single explanation for the difference between Europe then and Europe now, there is a pattern. It is a luminous design that is woven through the history of the past 20 years. It is the design of common action, of interdependent institutions serving the good of the European nations as though they were all one. It is the design of collective security protecting the entire Atlantic community.

So I have come here this morning to speak to you of one important part of that design. I speak of a structure that some of you have helped to build: the North Atlantic Treaty Organization.

Let me make clear in the beginning that we do not believe there is any righteousness in standing pat. If an organization is alive and vital, if it is to have meaning for all time as well as for any particular time, it must grow and respond and yield to change. Like our Constitution, which makes the law of the land, the North Atlantic Treaty is more than just a legal document. It is the foundation of a living institution. That institution is NATO, the organization created to give meaning and reality to the alliance commitments.

The crowded months which immediately preceded and followed the conclusion of the North Atlantic Treaty 17 years ago had produced an atmosphere of crisis. It was a crisis that was born of deep fear: fear for Europe's economic and political vitality, fear of Communist aggression, fear of Communist subversion.

Some say that new circumstances in the world today call for the dismantling of this great organization. Of course NATO should adapt to the changing needs of the times, but we believe just as firmly that such change must be wrought by the member nations working with one another within the alliance. Consultation, not isolation, is the route to reform. We must not forget either in success or abundance the lessons that we have learned in danger and in isolation: that whatever the issue that we share, we have one common danger—division; and one common safety—unity.

What is our view of NATO today?

We see it not as an alliance to make war, but as an alliance to keep peace. Through an era as turbulent as man has ever known, and under the constant threat of ultimate destruction, NATO has insured the security of the North Atlantic community. It has reinforced stability elsewhere throughout the world.

While NATO rests on the reality that we must fight together if war should come to the Atlantic area, it rests also on the reality that war will not come if we act together during peace. It was the Foreign Minister of France who, in 1949, insisted that to be truly secure, Europe needed not only help in resisting attack, but help in preventing attack. "Liberation," he said, "is not enough."

The success of NATO has been measured by many yardsticks. The most significant, to me, is the most obvious: War has been deterred. Through the common organization, we have welded the military contributions of each of the 15 allies into a very effective instrument. So convincing was this instrument that potential aggressors took stock and counted as too high the price of satisfying their ambitions. It has been proved true that "one sword keeps another in the sheath."

War has been deterred not only because of our integrated military power, but because of the political unity of purpose to which that power has been directed and bent. It is difficult to overstate the importance of the bonds of culture, of political institutions, traditions, and values which form the bedrock of the Atlantic community. There is here a political integrity and an identity of interests that transcends personalities and issues of the moment.

If our collective effort should falter and our common determination be eroded, the foundation of the Atlantic's present stability would certainly be shaken. The mightiest arsenal in the world will deter no aggressor who knows that his victims are too divided to decide and too unready to respond. That was the lesson that we learned from two world wars. Yet a nation—not by the action of her friends, but by her own decision to prepare and plan alone—could still imperil her own security by creating a situation in which response would be too late and too diluted. Every advance in the technology of war makes more unacceptable the old and narrow concepts of sovereignty.

No one today can doubt the necessity of preventing war. It is our firm conviction that collective action through NATO is the best assurance that war will be deterred in the Atlantic world.

Look at the Atlantic community through the eyes of those who in years past have yearned for conquest. The sight is sobering. Integrated commands, common plans, forces in being in advance of an emergency for use in any emergency—all of these testify to a collective readiness and the integrity of collective purposes. To other eyes, NATO can only be a clear warning of the folly of aggression.

NATO today, therefore, must be shaped on the experience of the past. Reliance on independent action by separate forces—only loosely coordinated with joint forces and plans—twice led to world wars before 1945. But collective action has proved successful in deterring war since 1945—during 20 years of upheaval and grave danger.

We reject those experiences only at our own peril.

For our part, the United States of America is determined to join with 13 of her other allies to preserve and to strengthen the deterrent strength of NATO. We will urge that those principles of joint and common preparation be extended wherever they can be usefully applied in the Atlantic Alliance.

We are hopeful that no member of the treaty will long remain withdrawn from the mutual affairs and obligations of the Atlantic. A place of respect and responsibility will await any ally who decides to return to the common task.

For the world is still full of peril for those who prize and cherish liberty—peril and opportunity.

These bountiful lands that are washed by the Atlantic, this half-billion people that are unmatched in arms and industry, this cradle of common values and splendid visions, this measureless storehouse of wealth, can enrich the life of an entire planet.

It is this strength—of ideas as well as strength of arms, of peaceful purpose as well as power—that offers such hope for the reconciliation of Western Europe with the people of Eastern Europe. To surrender that strength now by isolation from one another would be to dim the promise of that day when the men and women of all Europe shall again move freely among each other.

It is not a question of wealth alone.

It is a question of heart and mind. It is a willingness to leave forever those national rivalries which so often led to the

353

useless squandering of lives and treasure in war.

It is a question of the deeper spirit of unity of which NATO is but a symbol. That unity was never better expressed than when, at the conclusion of the North Atlantic Treaty in 1949, a great French leader declared that "nations are more and more convinced that their fates are closely bound together—that their salvation and their welfare must rest upon the progressive application of human solidarity."

And it is to the preservation of human solidarity that all of our efforts today should be directed. So let all of you of the Foreign Service Institute make it your task, as well as mine.

Thank you and good morning.

NOTE: The President spoke at 9:33 a.m. in the Department of State auditorium. In his opening words he referred to Dean Rusk, Secretary of State. The address was broadcast.

During the course of his remarks the President referred to Robert Schuman, Foreign Minister of France when the North Atlantic Treaty Organization was established.

On May 18 the White House made public the following Joint Declaration which was simultaneously released in the capitals of Belgium, Canada, Denmark, the Federal Republic of Germany, Greece, Iceland, Italy, Luxembourg, the Netherlands, Norway, Portugal, Turkey, and the United Kingdom. The text of the declaration follows:

"The North Atlantic Treaty and the organization established under it are both alike essential to the security of our countries.

"The Atlantic Alliance has ensured its efficacy as an instrument of defense and deterrence by the maintenance in peacetime of an integrated and interdependent military organization in which, as in no previous alliance in history, the efforts and resources of each are combined for the common security of all. We are convinced that this organization is essential and will continue. No system of bilateral arrangements can be a substitute.

"The North Atlantic Treaty and the organization are not merely instruments of the common defense. They meet a common political need and reflect the readiness and determination of the member countries of the North Atlantic community to consult and act together wherever possible in the safeguard of their freedom and security and in the furtherance of international peace, progress and prosperity."

143 Statement by the President on the Occasion of World Meteorological Day. *March 23, 1966*

ON JUNE 10, 1964, at Holy Cross College, I pledged that this Nation would move ahead with plans for a worldwide weather system, in collaboration with other nations, toward a goal beneficial to all mankind.

On the occasion of World Meteorological Day, I now reaffirm that pledge.

Today, we recognize the efforts of scientists and technicians everywhere—working as individuals and working as a single scientific community—to improve our understanding and prediction of the weather.

This day symbolizes for us—and for all mankind—a new dawn of hope for a better, safer, and more meaningful life.

In a world grown tired of wars, it commits all nations to work together in joint programs of peace.

It looks to the time when all our science and technology, and all the wonders of the space age, will give us the power of which man has always dreamed—not the power of one nation over another, but the power of the human race over the forces of nature.

We know now that our environment is global and indivisible. Knowing this, it follows that the only way to achieve significant improvement of weather services and prediction is by vigorous international cooperation and by worldwide dissemination of weather data.

The instrument of this program is the

World Meteorological Organization—a specialized agency of the United Nations with a membership of 127 countries. Through the World Meteorological Organization, the concept of a World Weather Watch is now taking shape. On this occasion, I am proud to say that the United States strongly supports international cooperation in this vital field.

Much must be accomplished to transform hope into reality. Scientifically, we must move toward a better understanding of our environment. Technologically, we must move toward developing improved systems. But there are no insuperable obstacles—and the opportunities are too great for us to ignore.

Our own Nation's efforts in this worldwide project will continue to be coordinated by the Environmental Science Services Administration under the leadership of Secretary of Commerce John T. Connor.

An Interagency Committee for International Meteorological Programs has already developed a series of proposals to carry us well into the decade of the seventies. I have asked the Secretary of Commerce, Dr. Donald Hornig, my Science Adviser, and Charles Schultze, the Director of the Budget, to study these proposals and to recommend to me a plan of action for America's role in this important international program.

NOTE: For the President's commencement address on June 10, 1964, at Holy Cross College, see 1963–64 volume, this series, Book I, Item 396.

144 Statement by the President at an "E" Awards Ceremony Honoring Significant Contributions to the Export Expansion Program. *March* 23, 1966

OUR ECONOMY is now in the sixth year of unprecedented prosperity, the longest peacetime economic expansion we have ever enjoyed.

Despite the added strain on our resources created by the conflict in Vietnam, we continue to enjoy prosperity without the evils of inflation.

Despite the flow of dollars needed to support our more than 200,000 fighting men in Southeast Asia, as well as hundreds of thousands more who are helping to keep peace throughout the world, we have reduced the deficit in our balance of payments. Last year that deficit fell to its lowest level in 8 successive years, and we are on the way to correcting the remaining deficit.

We could not have done this without

the hard work and imagination of those American businessmen who went out and developed new world markets for the products of American enterprise.

Our exports have now climbed to the highest level of any nation in history—$26.6 billion. This is an increase of 32 percent in the past 4 years. And it has benefited all Americans, for every billion dollars in exports creates 134,000 jobs and some $75 million in profits.

Each of the 12 flags that were awarded here today is the visible symbol of some company's contribution to all that we have achieved. Today, the number of companies that have earned this distinction reaches 700.

As we redouble our efforts to raise our exports to even higher levels, I look forward to the time when we will also have doubled the number of organizations which will come to deserve this award.

NOTE: The President's "E" awards were established by Executive Order 10978 of December 5, 1961, entitled "Establishing Presidential Awards for Significant Contributions to the Export Expansion Program" (3 CFR, 1959–1963 Comp., p. 498). The order stated that the awards "may be made to persons, firms, and organizations engaged in the marketing of products who make significant contributions to the expansion of the export trade of the United States. It shall consist of a flag having a field of white upon which will appear a blue 'E.' "

The names of the companies receiving the awards follow: American Plywood Association, Takoma, Wash., Bandag, Inc., Muscatine, Iowa, Carpco Research and Engineering, Inc., Jacksonville, Fla., ColorTran Industries, Inc., Burbank, Calif., The Cornelius Co., Anoka, Minn., Digital Equipment Corp., Maynard, Mass., Douglas Aircraft Co., Inc., Santa Monica, Calif., Prentice-Hall International, Inc., Englewood, N.J., Rocky Mountain Dental Products Co., Denver, Colo., Sprout, Waldron, and Co., Inc., Muncy, Pa., Texas Instruments, Inc., Dallas, Texas, and Victor Comptometer Co., Chicago, Ill.

145 Remarks at the Swearing In of Farris Bryant as Director, Office of Emergency Planning. *March 23, 1966*

Governor Bryant, Mrs. Bryant, daughter, Congressman Sikes, ladies and gentlemen:

They tell a story down in Louisiana about the time Hurricane Betsy passed through there and picked up everything that was in its path. One farmer was wiped out. The wind took his house, his barn, his livestock, his car, and a great deal of his topsoil. Finally the farmer looked over at his wife and family and laughingly said, "Well, honey, we have lost everything, but we do still have the mortgage!"

Each year natural disasters hit thousands of American families and American businesses, destroying their property and leaving them with nothing but debts. It is the task of the Director of the Office of Emergency Planning to work with the States and the local communities to help these people back on their feet. This great responsibility alone would, in my opinion, make the Director of the Office of Emergency Planning one of the most important men in the entire Federal Government.

But his responsibilities go far beyond disaster relief.

—He sits with the President as a member of the National Security Council of this Nation.

—He coordinates all the civil defense activities of this country.

—In a national emergency he directs the use of this Nation's manpower, industry, transportation, and communications.

—He is responsible for our stockpiles of critical materials.

—He coordinates the telecommunications activities of the entire Federal Government.

This job calls for a very extraordinary man. He must be the President's ambassador to the Governors. He must enjoy the confidence of the American industrial community. He must be a man with the ability to foresee any eventuality and to plan for every eventuality.

Since I came back from New York today I have thrown four or five things out of my basket and said, "Send that over to Farris Bryant." But most of all he must understand the complexities of this great industrial society that we have in America.

We had such a Director in Buford Ellington.

We are fortunate now to have found a

worthy successor—Farris Bryant. As a former Governor, a distinguished lawyer, and an outstanding businessman, Governor Bryant is the ideal man for this most difficult assignment. We looked long and hard for such a man. We are delighted, once we found him, that he could be persuaded to come and accept this post and render this service for his country. He understands the problems of business. He understands the problems of State and local government. And he will be able to work effectively, I believe, with both.

Governor Bryant comes to Washington not to dictate, but to cooperate; not to force, but to assist. He will represent what I believe to be the very best of our system of creative federalism.

Our entire National Government is made up of men like Farris Bryant. They represent every State and they speak for every community in America.

They didn't come to Washington to be rulers. They came here to be servants and hopefully to be doers. Each of them believes in our system of local governments.

Each believes in our great free enterprise system.

I just left a meeting in the Fish Room where we presented the "E" awards to the outstanding firms in this Nation who have established an alltime record in exports shipped to foreign countries.

Each believes, of course, in the dignity and rights of every American citizen.

Together they are working for a better, richer, freer, and a stronger country.

Farris Bryant has come to Washington—at great personal sacrifice—to help us try to achieve those goals. As my ambassador to all 50 Governors he will serve as a vital link of communication between the States and the Federal Government. He will help us achieve a new era of respect and understanding so that we can work together for the Great Society in America.

Thank you very much.

NOTE: The President spoke at 6:10 p.m. in the Cabinet Room at the White House. In his opening words he referred to Farris Bryant, former Governor of Florida, his wife and daughter, and Representative Robert L. F. Sikes of Florida.

146   Statement by the President Upon President Gursel's Return to Turkey. *March 25, 1966*

OUR distinguished friend, President Cemal Gursel of Turkey, came to the United States on February 2 for medical treatment. There was hope that new therapeutic procedures only recently developed in this country would be useful in treating his illness of several years.

We were initially encouraged by his progress at Walter Reed Hospital, only to be shocked by the news on February 8 that his health had suffered a grave new blow. Our best talent, coupled with the skill of the eminent Turkish doctors who accom-

panied the President, was exerted to the utmost in the hope that the President might return to his home in fully restored health. We are saddened that this hope was not to be realized.

We have been deeply honored to have President Gursel come to our country to seek medical treatment. As he returns to his homeland, our prayers go with him.

NOTE: In addition to issuing the statement the President went by helicopter from the White House to Andrews Air Force Base, Md., near Washington, to pay his respects to President Gursel who was returning home after suffering a series of paralytic strokes. The Turkish leader died in September. President Johnson's messages of sympathy appear below as Item 460.

The statement was made available by the White House Press Office. It was not made public in the form of a White House press release.

147 Statement by the President Upon Signing Bill Providing for the Alaska Purchase Centennial, 1967. *March 26, 1966*

IN 1967 the United States will observe the 100th anniversary of its purchase of Alaska from Russia. The bill I have signed today provides for United States participation in the celebration and exhibitions which will take place throughout Alaska.

It is appropriate that all America should participate in this centennial celebration, because the acquisition of the territory which has become the largest State in our Union was a milestone event for our entire country.

The purchase of Alaska was the largest acquisition of land since the Louisiana Purchase. It was the last great land area that the United States was to acquire. When

the Stars and Stripes were unfurled over what is now Sitka, Alaska, on October 18, 1867, the destiny of the North American Continent was permanently altered.

The centennial celebration now being planned by the people of Alaska will, through restoration of historic relics, preserve for all time an important part of the American heritage. And the permanent projects which are planned as part of that celebration will contribute to the long-range development of this great and important State.

NOTE: As enacted, the bill (S. 2614) is Public Law 89–375 (80 Stat. 82).

148 Remarks of Welcome to Prime Minister Gandhi of India on the South Lawn at the White House. *March 28, 1966*

Madame Prime Minister:

We are very glad that you are here. I feel very privileged to welcome you as the leader of our sister democracy. I have even greater pleasure in welcoming you as a good and gracious friend.

Someone has said that all pleasure is edged with sadness. Only 2 months ago we looked forward to receiving your gallant predecessor here in our Capital in Washington. We share your grief in his sudden and untimely death.

We are reminded that three American Presidents—Abraham Lincoln, Woodrow Wilson, and Franklin D. Roosevelt—were similarly stricken while engaged in that most demanding of all public tasks, the task of

working the hard passage from conflict back to peace. It is good to know that this task which Prime Minister Shastri had so ably begun is now in your strong and sympathetic hands.

Our thoughts also go back to the visits of another great Indian leader, those in 1949, 1956, and 1961 of your late father. Few have ever held a larger place in the hearts of the American people, and few ever will. We like to think, Mrs. Gandhi, that he belonged to us, too.

My countrymen and yours will be asking what we shall talk about during these next few days. Perhaps, with your permission, I may say just a word about that now. I think they can be reasonably sure that we will not be wasting any of our time.

Our concern will be with very practical questions. I look forward to getting your thoughts, Madame Prime Minister, on how peace can be obtained or made more secure, in Asia and throughout the world. I shall seek your counsel on the problems of Southeast Asia, where India, under the Geneva Accords, has for so long played such a special role.

I will speak of my deep desire, which I know you share, for the continued improvement in relations between India and her great sister nation, Pakistan. The United States values deeply the friendship of both India and Pakistan. Nothing, we know, is more painful or more costly to all concerned than a falling out between one's friends.

I shall look forward, Mrs. Gandhi, to getting a better understanding of the urgent economic and social problems with which your Government is now concerned. I will welcome that frankness and candor and detail that always mark conversations between good friends.

Economic stability and political tranquility depend on how well we accomplish commonplace tasks: the production of food, its transportation, the supply of fertilizer, family planning, electricity for farm and village, the realization of economic growth and opportunity.

We shall be concerned with these essentials. The solution of these problems lies, we know, with the Indian Government, but the United States believes in backing the efforts of those who are determined to solve their own problems. We know, Madam Prime Minister, that India under your leadership will have such determination.

We want to learn how we can best help you and how our help can be used to the very best effect. Your people and ours share the conviction that however difficult the problems there are none that a strong and a vigorous democracy cannot solve.

You have long been aware, Madam Prime Minister, of the fascination that Indian culture holds for Americans. This extends from the Hindu epics to the modern Indian novelists, and from the painters of the Ajanta Cave and the Ak Bar Court to your brilliant film producers of the present day. I venture to think that there is much about the United States that your students find equally interesting. Before our conversations end, I hope to be able to announce an imaginative new step to encourage and to facilitate these common interests.

Well, so much for our work in the days ahead.

I hope there will be time for something more. For Mrs. Johnson and our daughters and I look forward to renewing an old friendship, to matching, if possible, in warmth and spirit your own hospitality in the years past.

Let me say once more how much we appreciate your making this long journey at this busy time to visit us here in the United States.

I think I speak for every American when I say that we are very proud and very honored to have you today as our guest in this country.

NOTE: The President spoke at 11:10 a.m. on the South Lawn at the White House, where Prime Minister Indira Gandhi was given a formal welcome with full military honors. During his remarks he referred to former Prime Ministers of India Lal Bahadur Shastri, who died in January 1966, and Jawaharlal Nehru, Mrs. Gandhi's father.

See also Items 149, 152–154.

Prime Minister Gandhi responded as follows:

Mr. President, Mrs. Johnson, Your Excellencies, ladies and gentlemen:

I thank you, Mr. President, for your warm words of welcome and for this gracious reception to me. I have had the privilege and the great pleasure of visiting America many times. Each visit has been an education, an enlarging of the circle of friends, and a deepening of understanding.

I come today as a friend, and I bring with me the greetings and good will of the Indian people.

Mr. President, you have visited India with Mrs. Johnson. We have very pleasant and happy memories of that occasion. You are known in India not only as a great President of a distant country, but as a man of high idealism and a warmhearted friend who has come to our help in a time of need.

You have mentioned your interest in peace, Mr. President. We in India are greatly interested and concerned about peace, for to us it is not only a question of an ideal, but one of very practical necessity to give us time and opportunity to deal with those other problems and questions which you have mentioned; that is, to be able to develop our country, to give opportunity to our own people to stand on their feet, to deal with the many obstacles and difficulties which a longstanding poverty has imposed on us.

I am grateful to you for your kind invitation. As I meet you again, I recall your moving words on the theme of poverty. Declaring unconditional war on the pockets of poverty in your own coun-

try, you have said, "We want to give people more opportunity. They want education and training. They want a job and a wage. They want their children to escape the poverty which has afflicted them."

May I say, Mr. President, that important as these words are for the American people, they cannot mean as much to them as they do to us in India who have so long been denied the very basic decencies of life. We know that in our own war on poverty we have a noble friend, one who believes that the distant sufferer is his own brother.

India and the United States cannot and should not take each other for granted or allow their relations to drift. As friends committed to common ideals, they can together make this world of ours a better place in which to live.

Mr. President, may I express my gratitude not only for the welcome you have given me, but for the kind words which you have said for my father and our late Prime Minister, Mr. Shastri. I know how greatly Mr. Shastri was looking forward to his visit here. I hope that I shall be able to fulfill what he had in mind and what he had hoped to do.

Mr. President, may I greet you and the American people on behalf of the people of India.

149   Toasts of the President and Prime Minister Gandhi of India. *March 28, 1966*

Madam Prime Minister:

I have heard—and I do in part believe—that Queen Victoria, speaking in a different age and under different circumstances, once gave the following estimate of two of her prime ministers.

"Mr. Gladstone," said she, "talks to me as if I were a public meeting—but Mr. Disraeli speaks to me as if I were a woman."

Tonight I am very pleased to tell our friends who have assembled here that we have spoken to our gracious visitor not only as a woman with an understanding heart— but also as a leader with a sense of vision— and a builder with a valued view of faith.

India is a vast and varied land. The roots of freedom and justice run deep in the Indian past. Its culture was full and

strong centuries before the dawn of the Christian era.

The world has listened to the wisdom of India spoken through the voice of an eloquent leader.

Once, many years ago, he said: "Democracy demands discipline, tolerance, and mutual regard. Freedom demands respect for the freedom of others. In a democracy changes are made by mutual discussion and persuasion and not by violent means."

These were the words of Prime Minister Nehru. This was the belief of Prime Minister Shastri. Their fidelity to freedom's cause created, with Mahatma Gandhi, a new nation—conceived in struggle, grown strong in sacrifice.

And now tonight Prime Minister Gandhi

comes to this house and to this table, the custodian of her nation's hope, and the steward of her nation's dreams.

Today we here in the White House talked about the work and the sacrifice that is needed to make those dreams a modern reality. Together we discussed the practical ways that India and the United States can help to build a world where life is hopeful and where life is happier for all our peoples, as well as the peoples of all lands.

Prime Minister Gandhi's goal is to weld the Indian nation into a land where the words of its founding fathers come true and their views of its future become real.

There is much that binds India and the United States together. Both our nations have the deep-felt obligation to the basic dignity of man—and the conviction that people can solve their problems by free choice far better than they can by any arrangement of force. There is in India and there is in this country the strong tradition of freedom that just will never die.

I remember very clearly tonight my visit to India in 1961.

I remember what I saw and what I felt and what I heard throughout that great land. The thousands of students along the roads and in the cities—each of them quite impatient to know and to learn. I saw the teachers and the scholars, the public servants, and the people, searching, yearning, discovering, hoping. And I think of our young people here and what we have done in the last year to achieve a new revolution in education—beyond the wildest dreams of just a decade ago.

Now, how can we bring into closer union the spirit and the courage of these people, and particularly of these two countries?

I have given a good deal of thought to that in the last few months, and tonight I would propose that we mark this historic visit of Prime Minister Gandhi with a lasting endowment for the benefit of inquiring young minds in the Indian nation.

So may we, Madam Prime Minister, with the permission of your Government and the American Congress, launch a new and imaginative venture. We shall call it an Indo-American Foundation. I would propose that this Foundation be established in India, and that it be endowed with $300 million in Indian currency owned by the United States. Other foundations all over the world will cooperate, I am sure, with an enterprise of this kind.

I would suggest that this Foundation be organized as an independent institution—with distinguished citizens of both our countries on its board of directors. I would propose that the new Foundation be given a broad charter to promote progress in all fields of learning—to advance science—to encourage research—to develop new teaching techniques on the farms and in the factories—to stimulate, if you please, new ways to meet old problems.

The journey to our future is over a very long and a very winding road. Every mile will be challenged by doubt. But together, Madam Prime Minister, we must avoid the detours that intrude on our safe journey toward a time when, as your father promised, life will be better for all of our people.

So, ladies and gentlemen, let us honor those who are so welcome here tonight. Let us ask you to join in honoring the Chief of State whose wise and gifted Prime Minister we have enjoyed so much today, and that we welcome so warmly this evening.

I should like to ask those of you who are assembled here to join me now in raising your glass in a toast to the great President of India.

NOTE: The President proposed the toast at 10:35 p.m. at a dinner in the State Dining Room at the

White House. Prime Minister Gandhi responded as follows:

Mr. President, Mrs. Johnson, Your Excellencies, ladies and gentlemen:

Your words, Mr. President, were exceedingly moving. You have spoken of India and her wide variety. We who live there are naturally deeply conscious of it, while at the same time we are fully aware of the underlying and the basic unity which binds together all our people.

You have quoted some words of my father. I should like to quote something which you yourself have said. You said, Mr. President, "Reality rarely matches dreams, but only dreams give nobility to purpose."

In the United States you have matched your dreams in many ways. Yet you still seek, and rightly, to offer the American people a better and a more purposeful life. You have called this idea "The Great Society." In India we also have our dreams, which may seem trite to you who sit here, because they appear so simple—food barely sufficient to keep one from hunger, shelter to keep out the wind and the rain, medicines and education by which to restore the faith and the hope of our nearly 500 million people.

But everything in life is relative. There is an old proverb in my country. A person says, "I complained that I had no shoes until I met a man who had no feet."

Mahatma Gandhi said once, and it is something which my father often repeated, that we in India had to work to wipe the tear from every eye. That, of course, is a big task and I doubt if it can be done in any country. And yet we have been trying to do that for 18 long years. Two centuries of subjugation cannot be washed away so easily. It takes time. It takes work. It takes courage.

India is changing, as no doubt your advisers who have been to India have told you, Mr. President. Nowhere in the world can the contrast be so striking. We have not only different levels of development between the different states, but even within each state. We have often several centuries existing side by side. We have some of the greatest irrigation works in the world, and yet in parts of our State of Rajasthan, desert families store precious water under lock and key.

During a tour of some of these border areas a couple of months or so ago, I myself experienced the great hardship of doing without water and measuring the miles from well to well. Some 12 million or more of bullock carts still churn the dust of our village roads. Yet in other parts of India we are building three nuclear powerplants.

Average agricultural yields are low, and at the same time there are areas where we obtain sugar cane yields that compare favorably with those in Hawaii or in Java.

A third of the illiterate people in the world are in India. Yet we are steadily conquering illiteracy.

In our State of Maharashtra, village after village vies to achieve total literacy. Parents learn from their children so that the honor of the village is upheld. In Madras people have banded together to improve their schools. They have given 100 million rupees beyond what the Government spends on their schools.

In the Punjab, little workshops make lathes and pumps that have revolutionized the countryside.

The seeming inconsistencies and conflicts of India are legion. The setbacks, and we have had many, are heartbreaking. Yet the signs of change are clear and constantly growing.

Sometimes critics point to an example of success and say, "This proves nothing. This is a mere drop in the ocean of Indian poverty." How wrong this is, for every success reinforces the prospect of further success. It shows that success is possible. The example and the confidence it generates radiates outward.

This, Mr. President, is really our major problem. Years ago when we visited the villages to persuade people to try for a better life, they turned to us and said, "There can be no better life; God wills it this way. This is our lot and we have to suffer it." Today not a single voice will be heard like this. There is only one demand, that we do want a better life. We want better schools and more schools. We want bigger hospitals and more hospitals, and all the other signs of progress and signs of raising the standards of living.

This I think is a very big achievement.

You talked, sir, of democracy. May I tell you one more story which I shared with the Vice President a short while ago. It happened during our first elections. I had gone to speak in a village where just the day before the leader of an opposition party had spoken. When my speech was ended, an elderly gentleman got up from the audience and said, "We have listened very carefully to what you have said, but just the day before somebody came"—so and so came—"and he said the exact opposite. Now, which of you was telling the truth?"

Now, this you can understand is an extremely tricky question to ask a public speaker. I said, "Well, I think that what I said was the truth, but I have no doubt that the gentleman thought that what he said was the truth.

"The whole point of democracy is that everybody should say whatever he thinks is the truth, and you, the people, have to really judge which is the correct version, and which is the right version or the right thing for you."

Well, this was a rather difficult explanation for them, and they said, "Now, you tell us, do you belong to the Congress Party?" I said, "I do."

"Is your party in power? Is it forming the Government?" I said, "Yes, it is." "Then what business have you to send somebody here who tells us incorrect things? It is your business to keep them away."

This was one of the stops where I was supposed to stay only 10 minutes, but I stayed for 2 hours trying to argue out the whole point about elections, freedom of expression, and so on. I can't say that I got any further at the end of 2 hours.

But now, years later, we find we have got further. Nobody today in India would put such a question. They know that the different parties have their points of view, and these points of view are put before the people, and the people judge, not always rightly, but I think they try to judge rightly. Certainly, from election to election they have shown a great maturity.

India very definitely is on the move. Mr. President, the United States has given India valuable assistance in our struggle against poverty, against hunger, against ignorance, and against disease. We are grateful for this act of friendship. But we also know that our own "Great Society" must and can only rest securely on the quality and the extent of our own effort.

This effort we are determined to make: we owe it to our friends, and even more so we owe it to ourselves.

Nevertheless, I believe that it is of the greatest importance, to use your own words, to bring into closer union the spirit and courage of both our countries. I welcome your intention to set up an Indo-American Foundation, which will give tangible shape and form to this union.

The present-day world offers the possibility of bringing together one people with another. The young men and women of your Peace Corps are well known and well loved in our country. Every endeavor to sustain and enlarge this people-to-people partnership is a good effort and is welcome.

Friendship with America is not a new thing for us.

Those of us in India who have been involved with the struggle for freedom have known from our earliest days your own struggle here. We have been taught the words of your leaders, of your past great Presidents, and above all we were linked in friendship because of the friendship which President Roosevelt showed us and the understanding which he showed during some of the most difficult days of our independence struggle. I have no doubt it was also this understanding and friendly advice given to the British Government which facilitated and accelerated our own freedom.

But there again the major effort had to be on our own, and this is what we want today: that we should bear our burden, as indeed we are doing, but that a little bit of help should come from friends who consider it worthwhile to lighten the burden.

Because, Mr. President, India's problems today are her own, but they are also the world's problems. India has a position in Asia which is an explosive position. India, if it is stable, united, democratic, I think can serve a great purpose. If India is not stable, or if there is chaos, if India fails, I think it is a failure of the whole democratic system. It is a failure of many of the values which you and we both hold dear.

That is why, Mr. President, I welcome your words and I welcome this meeting with you, which has been most valuable to me.

I invite you, ladies and gentlemen, to join with me in drinking a toast to the President and Mrs. Johnson, our friends, the American people, and the Great Society, not just for America, but for all who dream of it, for all who struggle to transform those dreams into reality.

---

150   Statement by the President Upon Signing Bill To Abolish the Postal Savings System. *March* 28, 1966

I AM pleased to sign into law today H.R. 8030—a bill to abolish the Postal Savings System.

I consider this more than just a passing event. In one respect, it represents the end of an era. In another respect, it represents our willingness—a n d determination—to meet the changing needs of our times.

I hope that other Government agencies will take note of this bill signing. I hope they will intensify their search for the most efficient and economical way to serve the American public. Our citizens are entitled to confidence in their Government, and they will be confident only when they are certain that their taxes are carefully and frugally spent.

I sign this bill with the assurance that no

postal worker will be adversely affected.

I also sign it with the assurance that no American saver will be inconvenienced. For those who would still like to deposit their savings with the United States Government, I can think of no better way to do so than through United States savings bonds. With the increase in interest that I

announced just last month, these bonds will be giving more than twice the interest of the Postal Savings System.

NOTE: The statement was not made public in the form of a White House press release. As printed above, it follows a text made available by the White House Press Office.

As enacted, the bill (H.R. 8030) is Public Law 89–377 (80 Stat. 92).

151 Statement by the President Upon Signing Bill Extending Mandatory Provisions of the Coal Mine Safety Act. *March 29, 1966*

I HAVE approved H.R. 3584 "To amend the Federal Coal Mine Safety Act so as to provide further for the prevention of accidents in coal mines."

The bill is designed to extend the mandatory safety provisions of that act to coal mines regularly employing less than 15 men underground, which are now exempt from the requirements.

Its primary purpose is to reduce casualties in coal mines.

During the early months of 1963 two major coal mine disasters occurred, with 59 lives lost. President Kennedy directed Secretary of the Interior Udall to review present mine safety regulations and to present his views on the need for further legislation to prevent accidents in the future. This bill stems from the recommendations made by Secretary Udall.

The efforts of many, many men made possible the enactment of this much needed legislation. Some of them are truly pioneers in the cause of mine safety legislation and their association with this legislation goes back a decade or more: Congressman Dent of Pennsylvania and his colleagues on the House Education and Labor Committee; Senator Morse of Oregon and his col-

leagues on the Senate Labor and Public Welfare Committee; Senator Clark of Pennsylvania, who has labored on this legislation for many years; Senator Jennings Randolph of West Virginia, whose association with the legislation dates back to his service in the House of Representatives. All miners—and their families—who are assured of greater protection as a result of this bill owe them a debt of gratitude.

While this bill has been under consideration in the House and Senate, during 1965 and 1966, underground disasters have occurred at coal mines killing a total of 24 men. One of the disasters occurred as recently as March 2, 1966, killing three men in a small mine that normally employed four persons.

This bill is not a cure-all and it will not prevent all disasters, but it will give greater protection by extending the safety provisions of the Federal Coal Mine Safety Act to all underground coal miners, by strengthening enforcement orders upon a finding of a serious violation of safety requirements, and by enlarging and intensifying coal mine safety educational programs in cooperation with the States.

In enacting this bill we have sought to

achieve the paramount purpose of reducing casualties in coal mines, but to achieve it with the minimum burden upon the coal mining industry. This, we believe, we have accomplished.

NOTE: As enacted, the bill (H.R. 3584), approved on March 26, is Public Law 89–376 (80 Stat. 84).

152 Joint Statement Following Discussions With Prime Minister Gandhi of India. *March* 29, 1966

AT THE INVITATION of President Johnson, Mrs. Indira Gandhi, Prime Minister of the Republic of India, has been on an official visit to the United States of America. During her visit, Prime Minister Gandhi met the President and members of the United States Government.

The President and the Prime Minister discussed India's efforts for the improved well-being of its people. Prime Minister Gandhi emphasized the high priority which India attaches to economic development. President Johnson assured Prime Minister Gandhi of the deep interest of the Government and the people of the United States in participating in international efforts, particularly those under the leadership of the International Bank for Reconstruction and Development, to assist India in its own massive efforts to raise the living standards of its people within the framework of a parliamentary democracy.

The President and the Prime Minister discussed India's emergency food grain requirements resulting from last year's unprecedented drought. They agreed that the problem should be viewed not in isolation but in the context of an incipient worldwide food deficit, a challenge to humanity as a whole that merits the sustained and serious attention of all nations.

The Prime Minister described measures which the Government of India is taking to achieve self-sufficiency in the nation's food production. The President assured her that, Congress willing, the United States will continue to participate generously in the international effort to alleviate India's immediate food deficit problem. The President told Mrs. Gandhi that he intended to send a special message to Congress shortly to seek its endorsement of such U.S. assistance. Both of them agreed that further participation of other countries in meeting India's emergency food needs is also highly desirable.

Prime Minister Gandhi welcomed the President's proposal for the establishment of an Indo-U.S. Foundation to promote progress in all fields of learning. The President and the Prime Minister look to this cooperative endeavour to develop new teaching techniques in farm and factory, to advance science and to increase research.

President Johnson and Prime Minister Gandhi agreed that following the Tashkent Declaration there had already been considerable progress toward reestablishing the conditions of peace in the subcontinent and that it is necessary that this process continue in order that the peoples of both countries may concentrate their energies once again on the urgent tasks of national development. They also agreed on the importance of continuing to give full support to the United Nations objectives of refraining from the use of force and of resolving conflicts between nations through peaceful means.

During their discussions, President Johnson and Prime Minister Gandhi reviewed recent developments in south and southeast Asia in the context of the universal desire of men and women everywhere to achieve peace that respects liberty, dignity, and the pursuit of a better way of life. In this connection the President explained the policies the United States is pursuing to help the people of the Republic of Vietnam to defend their freedom and to reconstruct their war-torn society. The Prime Minister explained the continuing interest and efforts of her country in bringing about a just and peaceful solution of this problem.

Prime Minister Gandhi affirmed the determination of her nation to defend the freedom and territorial integrity of India and explained the challenge presented to it by the aggressive policies of the People's Republic of China. The Prime Minister

and the President agreed that such aggressive policies pose a threat to peace, particularly in Asia.

The President and the Prime Minister consider that the visit has reaffirmed the strong bonds of friendship between the United States and India, based upon a shared commitment to constitutional democracy and a common revolutionary heritage. Their highly informative, frank, and friendly discussions have contributed to a valuable personal understanding between their two countries and their two peoples.

Prime Minister Gandhi extended a warm invitation to President Johnson to visit India. The President expressed his gratitude for the invitation and his hope that he could visit India again.

See also Items 148, 149, 153, 154.

153 Special Message to the Congress Proposing an Emergency Food Aid Program for India. *March 30, 1966*

To the Congress of the United States:

In recent months I have been watching with deep concern the emerging problem of world food supply. And I have been especially concerned with the prospect for India. During this past week I have discussed the Indian food problem with the Prime Minister of India, who has been our welcome and distinguished guest here in Washington. I am persuaded that we may stand, at this moment, on the threshold of a great tragedy. The facts are simple; their implications are grave. India faces an unprecedented drought. Unless the world responds, India faces famine.

Strong efforts by the Indian government, and our help, have so far averted famine. But in the absence of cooperative and energetic action by the United States, by other nations and by India herself, some millions

of people will suffer needlessly before the next crop is harvested. This, in our day and age, must not happen. Can we let it be said that man, who can travel into space and explore the stars, cannot feed his own?

Because widespread famine must not and cannot be allowed to happen, I am today placing the facts fully before the Congress. I am asking the endorsement of the Congress for a program that is small neither in magnitude nor concept. I am asking the Congress, and the American people, to join with me in an appeal to the conscience of all nations that can render help.

I invite any information that the Congress can supply. Our people will welcome any judgments the Congress can provide. The executive branch, this nation and the world will take appropriate note and give proper attention to any contributions in counsel and advice that Congressional debate may produce.

If we all rally to this task, the suffering can be limited. A sister democracy will not suffer the terrible strains which famine imposes on free government.

Nor is this all. The Indians are a proud and self-respecting people. So are their leaders. The natural disaster which they now face is not of their making. They have not asked our help needlessly; they deeply prefer to help themselves. The Indian government has sound plans for strengthening its agricultural economy and its economic system. These steps will help India help herself. They will prevent a recurrence of this disaster. I also propose action through the World Bank and the Agency for International Development to support this strong initiative by the Government of India.

THE CRISIS

Since independence India has done much to increase her output of agricultural products. Her agriculture has not been neglected. From 1950 to 1965 she increased food production 75 percent. This is a creditable achievement. But India has had to contend with a continuing and relentless increase in population. Her people have also consumed more from a higher income. Accordingly, she has remained heavily dependent on our help. Last year we provided, under Public Law 480, more than 6 million tons of wheat, equal to more than two-fifths of our own consumption. To keep this supply moving, the equivalent of two fully loaded liberty ships had to put in at an Indian port every day of the year.

Now India has been the victim of merciless natural disaster. Nothing is so important for the Indian farmer as the annual season of heavy rain—the monsoon. Last year, over large parts of India, the rains did not come. Crops could not be planted, or the young plants withered and died in the fields. Agricultural output, which needed to increase, was drastically reduced. Not since our own dustbowl years of the nineteen-thirties has there been a greater agricultural disaster.

Indian leaders have rightly turned to the world for help. Pope Paul VI has endorsed their plea. So has the World Council of Churches. So has the Secretary General of the United Nations. So has the Director General of the Food and Agriculture Organization. And so, in this message, does the President of the United States.

I have said that effective action will not be cheap. India's need is for at least 11 to 12 million tons of imported grain from January to December 1966.

Food in this world is no longer easy to find.

But find it we must.

Here is what I propose.

THE PROGRAM

Last fiscal year we supplied six million tons of food grain to India. So far in this fiscal year, I have allotted 6.5 million tons of grain for shipment to India—more than the total of six million tons which we had planned to provide as a continuation of past arrangements. It is even more necessary in this emergency to keep the pipelines full and flowing and to insure that there is no congestion of rail or sea transport. India, furthermore, estimates an additional six to seven million tons of food grain will be necessary through next December beyond what has already been committed or expected.

I propose that the United States provide

three and one-half million tons of that requirement, with the remaining three and a half million tons coming from those nations which have either the food to offer or the means to buy food. I invite those nations to match the amount which we will supply. For example, I am delighted to be informed that Canada is prepared to provide a million tons of wheat and flour to India.

Every agriculturally advanced country can, by close scrutiny of its available supplies, make a substantial contribution. I ask that every government seek to supply the maximum it can spare—and then a little more. I ask those industrial countries which cannot send food to supply a generous equivalent in fertilizer, or in shipping, or in funds for the purchase of these requisites. All know the Indian balance of payments is badly overburdened. Food and other materials should be supplied against payment in rupees, which is our practice, or as a gift.

It is not our nature to drive a hard mathematical bargain where hunger is involved. Children will not know that they suffered hunger because American assistance was not matched. We will expect and press for the most energetic and compassionate action by all countries of all political faiths. But if their response is insufficient, and if we must provide more, before we stand by and watch children starve, we will do so. I therefore, ask your endorsement for this emergency action.

I have spoken mostly of bread-grains. The Prime Minister of India spoke also of other commodities which can meet part of the requirements or replace part of the need. In response to her needs, I propose that we allot up to 200,000 tons of corn, up to 150 million pounds of vegetable oils, and up to 125 million pounds of milk powder to India. The vegetable oil and milk powder are especially needed for supplementing the diets of Indian children.

In addition, India's own exchange resources can be released for food and fertilizer purchases if we make substantial shipments of cotton and tobacco. I am suggesting the allotment for this purpose of 325-700,000 bales of cotton and 2-4 million pounds of tobacco. Both of these commodities we have in relative abundance.

I request prompt Congressional endorsement of this action.

I urge, also, the strong and warmhearted and generous support of this program by the American people.

And I urge the strong and generous response of governments and people the world around.

India is a good and deserving friend. Let it never be said that "bread should be so dear, and flesh and blood so cheap" that we turned in indifference from her bitter need.

FURTHER ACTION

The Indian people want to be self-supporting in their food supply.

Their government has adopted a far-reaching program to increase fertilizer production, improve water and soil management, provide rural credit, improve plant protection and control food loss. These essentials must be accompanied by a strong training and education program.

I have directed the Secretary of Agriculture, in cooperation with AID, to consult with the Indian government to ascertain if there are ways and means by which we can strengthen this effort. We have long experience with short courses, extension training and similar programs. If they can be used, I feel certain that American agricultural experts would respond to an appeal to serve in India as a part of an Agricultural Training Corps or through an expanded

Peace Corps. Many of our younger men and women would especially welcome the opportunity.

I am determined that in our assistance to the Indian government we not be narrowly limited by what has been done in the past. Let us not be afraid of our own enthusiasm. Let us be willing to experiment.

The Indian government believes that there can be no effective solution of the Indian food problem that does not include population control. The choice is now between a comprehensive and humane program for limiting births and the brutal curb that is imposed by famine. As Mrs. Gandhi told me, the Indian government is making vigorous efforts on this front.

Following long and careful planning and after discussions in recent days with Prime Minister Gandhi, I have proposed the establishment of the Indo-U.S. Foundation. This Foundation will be financed by rupees, surplus to our need, now on deposit in India. It will be governed by distinguished citizens of both countries. It will be a vigorous and imaginative enterprise designed to give new stimulus to education and scientific research in India. There is no field where, I hope, this stimulus will be greater than in the field of agriculture and agricultural development.

Finally, in these last days, the Prime Minister and I have talked about the prospects for the Indian economy. The threat of war with China and the unhappy conflict with Pakistan seriously interrupted India's economic progress. Steps had to be taken to protect dwindling exchange resources. These also had a strangling effect on the economy. Indian leaders are determined now to put their economy again on the upward path. Extensive discussions have been held with the World Bank, which heads the consortium of aid-giving countries.

The United States interferes neither in the internal politics nor the internal economic structure of other countries. The record of the last fifteen years is a sufficient proof that we ask only for results. We are naturally concerned with results—with insuring that our aid be used in the context of strong and energetic policies calculated to produce the most rapid possible economic development.

We believe Indian plans now under discussion show high promise. We are impressed by the vigor and determination of the Indian economic leadership. As their plans are implemented, we look forward to providing economic assistance on a scale that is related to the great needs of our sister democracy.

An India free from want and deprivation, will, as Mahatma Gandhi himself once predicted, "be a mighty force for the good of mankind."

LYNDON B. JOHNSON

The White House
March 30, 1966

NOTE: A joint resolution supporting U.S. participation in food relief for India was approved by the President on April 19, 1966 (see Item 180). See also Item 154.

---

154   Remarks at a News Briefing Held in Connection With the Message on Food for India. *March* 30, 1966

[*A news briefing on the Indian food program was held at 10:30 a.m. on Wednesday, March 30, 1966, in the Fish Room at the* White House. The President entered the room in the course of the briefing and joined in the question-and-answer session. Other officials present were Orville Freeman, Secretary of Agriculture; William B. Macomber, Assistant Administrator, Office of Near East-South Asia, Agency for International Development; and Bill Moyers and Robert Komer, Special Assistants to the President. During the briefing it was stated that the United States would spend $1 billion over an 18-month period in food aid for India and that assistance from Canada and other countries was expected. The President was asked how soon he hoped Congress would act on the resolution he had requested (see Item 153). His response and the remainder of the briefing follow:]

THE PRESIDENT. In a matter like this, we don't put a time on it. I put a special paragraph in the message this morning inviting anything they could contribute to this discussion, asking them to debate it, approve it, and make any recommendations they want to.

The Easter holidays are coming on. There is no deadline. It is not like a tax bill or expiration of the draft or something of that kind. We want them to take ample time to have hearings, debate the question, modify, amend, or improve.

We have the authority to do it without asking them, but we know that the size of the contribution is such that they will be in on the landing, so it seems to me more desirable that they also be in on the take-off.

Q. Mr. Secretary, did your $1 billion figure include the cotton?

SECRETARY FREEMAN. Yes.

Q. On tobacco and cotton, Mr. Secretary, do the usual end-use conditions apply, consumption in India? Could they be used to acquire foreign exchange?

SECRETARY FREEMAN. I am not sure I understand your question.

Q. Normally our stuff has to be consumed or used in India.

SECRETARY FREEMAN. The answer is yes.

Q. Mr. Secretary, on this self-help program that they have launched, do we have any projection as to when the Indians may become self-sufficient in agriculture?

SECRETARY FREEMAN. The Indians themselves have said that with the plan they have launched, they are shooting for a target of being self-sufficient in agriculture by 1971. We have not made an estimate yet and I really couldn't make one at this point. Give me another year and I think I could make one. At this point I wouldn't want to pass judgment on that prediction.

Q. Mr. Secretary, does this Indo-United States Foundation, which the President proposed the other night, require congressional authorization?

SECRETARY FREEMAN. That is referred to the Congress and is going to the respective committees under a special provision in the Food and Agriculture Act of 1965. If the committees do not act negatively in connection with it, it automatically goes into effect.

Q. Mr. Secretary, the last report we have had on the controversy over getting the fertilizer plants going in India was that the program was still lagging because of difficulties between the private companies and the Indian Government. Can you tell us how this is coming along?

SECRETARY FREEMAN. The regulations and restrictions that the private sector felt to be such as to be unworkable have been removed. Now these matters are being expedited. There has been established a special Cabinet level committee, chaired by the Indian Minister of Agriculture, to expedite the processing within their government and overcome any bureaucratic hurdles.

I think that the complaints of the private fertilizer companies have been answered and that from here on out, particularly in light of the generally satisfactory discussions and the fine relationship that the President and the Prime Minister exhibited during this visit, that they will be encouraged and I feel confident that we will have more activity from the private sector of the economy in India.

THE PRESIDENT. I think it fair to observe some people were watching developments in the last few days and were awaiting this visit to see what came out of it.

Q. You mean the fertilizer industry in this country, Mr. President?

THE PRESIDENT. Yes.

Q. Mr. Secretary, is there any shortage of shipping to handle this volume?

SECRETARY FREEMAN. No, it will move expeditiously.

Q. Mr. Secretary, in addition to our appeal to all nations, is India making its own basic appeal to these countries?

SECRETARY FREEMAN. Indeed, yes. They have made a strong appeal and they have a traveling team, some of the prominent people in their government, that has actually called on different countries around the world. They have had their Ambassadors make an official request. They have been taking strong measures to try to get other countries to assist.

Q. You say the shortage is 17 million and they could get by with 11 million? How can they do that?

SECRETARY FREEMAN. They will just eat less. The amount of intake is going to drop a bit. Also, they are going to scrape the barrel dry. They had a good crop last year. Some has been tucked away and that is going to come out. They have very, very modest reserves. They feel they will have to spend that. Mother Hubbard's

cupboard is going to be bare. Some people will be hungry, but they feel there won't be starvation and they can get by with this small help.

Q. How much money in foreign exchange do the Indians need to get their new agriculture program underway? What is the status of that?

SECRETARY FREEMAN. They need an awful lot more, of course, than they have. If you were living in an ideal world and they could go and buy everything they need, it would be a lot more than they have. I don't have the immediate, current foreign exchange position which is very hard to surface, but let's say that they have doubled their own foreign exchange allotments for agricultural purchases outside and will continue to invest more.

Q. Excuse me, sir. I am not talking about purchasing wheat. I am talking about purchasing raw materials for fertilizer plants, and so on.

SECRETARY FREEMAN. This is what I was talking about. Do you have a dollar figure on that?

MR. KOMER. The Indians are finalizing their fourth plan frame, which is due to go into effect in April, but will be postponed primarily because of the Pak-Indian war. Until we see their plan we will not know precisely how much they are allocating to various sectors of the economy. But in this area alone they have allocated 30 percent more of the central government budget to agriculture and that proportion should go up because, as the Secretary said, they are giving top priority to agriculture in the new fourth plan.

SECRETARY FREEMAN. I think $100 million, since we have been conferring with them, to buy fertilizer around the world, is a safe figure.

Q. Mr. Secretary, this reallocation of priorities giving emphasis to agriculture—over what time period is this taking place?

SECRETARY FREEMAN. For the foreseeable future. It is built into the current 4-year plan.

Q. When did it start?

SECRETARY FREEMAN. It starts now. It started within the last 6 months. But it is built now into the budget which is their 4-year plan and a part of that is in their foreign exchange allocation.

Q. Reference is made in the message, Mr. Secretary, to AID. Is there any special program that we don't already know about?

SECRETARY FREEMAN. In this connection, if you read it closely, the President has suggested the possibility of an agriculture training corps or unit, or the word hasn't come out, seeking to use our agriculturists more effectively, perhaps something like the short courses that have been so successful in our land-grant colleges, to take those Indians who have had some agriculture training and update their training and get them out to do a more effective job of training and education in the agriculture sphere. We are working on getting some of the details of how this can be done right now.

THE PRESIDENT. I might elaborate on that. Dave Lilienthal [1] and others who are very familiar with the problems there have said to me that you don't really help agricultural production a lot in a minister's office. Where you get the job done is out on the farm with know-how itself. We do a very exceptional job with TVA, the Agricultural Department, and various national and regional organizations, the Farm Bu-

reau and others calling folks together and planning, talking, educating, and training, and so forth.

If we could just have some farm know-how right at that acre level, it would do more to increase production than anything else. How do we get that farm know-how at that level? We just didn't have time to work out that detail before my message went up. But I said to the Prime Minister that I would be very glad to send through the Peace Corps, or some appropriate agency, competent agricultural people. We could take some of our rupees and hire some of her people to receive this training and give them a short course in the hope that we could meet that deficiency that Mr. Lilienthal and others pointed up, namely, know-how at the acre level.

Q. Would a county agent plan be advisable in this situation?

THE PRESIDENT. We haven't gone into the details. We didn't have that in mind. That is a little more all-enveloping than we had given attention to now. Eventually it might come to that. But we thought more of bringing in people by the hundreds and giving them brief, expert training that they could communicate back to their neighbors.

Q. Mr. President, how do you appraise Mrs. Gandhi's visit [2] now that she has left town?

THE PRESIDENT. I thought it was very good, very fruitful, very productive, very satisfactory from our standpoint. We had very lengthy and detailed exchanges. We will, of course, have to see what the Congress' reaction to this message is, and to the aid message, and then there will be all the big hurdles and the details of the World Bank and the negotiations that will take

---

[1] David E. Lilienthal, former Chairman of the Tennessee Valley Authority, who was appointed in December 1966 to head a nongovernmental planning group to study the long-range development of the Vietnam economy.

[2] See Items 148, 149, 152.

place there. Things went very well at our level. I cannot speak for her, but I think she feels the same way.

Q. Is there any chance that you may be able to accept her invitation?

THE PRESIDENT. I would like very much to.

SECRETARY FREEMAN. Mr. President, Carroll Kilpatrick [3] has a son in the Peace Corps working on poultry in India right now.

Q. I was going to ask the Secretary: This $1 billion of our cost, what is the cost in rupees? How do you figure that? What does it cost the Indians?

SECRETARY FREEMAN. I don't know what the exchange rate is now.

Q. Mr. President, wouldn't the new foundation you propose have something to do with the know-how at the acre level also?

THE PRESIDENT. Yes. We will have to wait for the Congress to take some action and go through the steps of selecting the members and setting it up. This is just the beginning.

MR. MOYERS. This is all on the record, ladies and gentlemen, and there will not be an 11 o'clock briefing in order to give you time to file.

THE PRESIDENT. I think I might make an announcement. I do not know whether I ought to do this or not, but I do not want any of you to take seriously someone's statement over at the State Department that we have named a new Ambassador to Japan because I have just read about it.

Q. Mr. Reischauer [4] is going to stay there?

THE PRESIDENT. I don't know. I guess in the good old days that was the way they named Ambassadors. Those days are gone and forgotten.

> "The bridge of the railroad
> Now crosses the spot,
> And the old diving logs
> Lay sunk and forgot."

If any of you are interested in knowing, we have reached absolutely no decision on wage and price control, taxes, or cutting expenditures. The only man I know who has his mind made up on it is not in the White House executive department.

Reporter: Thank you.

NOTE: The text of the complete news briefing is printed in the Weekly Compilation of Presidential Documents (vol. 2, p. 467).

---

[3] Reporter from the Washington Post.

[4] Edwin O. Reischauer, U.S. Ambassador to Japan.

---

155 Remarks Before the National Legislative Conference of the National League of Cities. *March* 31, 1966

Mayor Cavanagh and his colleagues, Congressman Ashley and Mr. Healy, delegates of the National League of Cities conference:

I want to thank you, Mr. Mayor, for asking me to come here this morning.

When the burdens of the Presidency seem unusually heavy, I always remind myself that it could be worse—I could be a mayor of a city instead.

So I welcome this opportunity to come here this morning.

I went to the East Room in the White House last night, where I talked to some of the Nation's leading businessmen, many of whom are your partners in municipal growth.

All of our progress and all of our hopes rest on the American economy, an economy that is bursting, really, with riches and with rewards.

—73½ million of our citizens are now working in civilian jobs. That is up more than 7 million in the last 5 years.

—The lowest unemployment rate in more than 12 years.

—Industrial production up 9 percent in the last 12 months.

—Retail sales up 9 percent over last year in the past month.

—The average manufacturing worker bringing home over $110 a week.

—Corporate profits providing the highest sustained rate of after-tax return on owners' capital—higher now than in the entire period for which we have any data in the Federal Government. It is up from $26 billion 700 million after taxes in 1961 to $44 billion 500 million after taxes in 1965; that is, from 1961 to 1965, up $17 billion-plus, or a 66 percent increase.

This is the American economy that will bring us victory against discrimination, against despair, against poverty. This is the economy which will give us the jobs for more than 1½ million people (net) who are entering our labor force this year alone. This is the economy that could defuse social dynamite, recharge our social purpose so as to make it possible for us to avoid dramatic explosions like we had at Watts just a few months ago.

This is the economy which can produce the goods that our men need to win the battle that they are fighting at this moment, 10,000 miles from home in Vietnam.

But it is an economy that we want to keep healthy. We can allow the last 5 years of unprecedented prosperity to be endangered and to be swallowed by inflation unless we take care. We cannot allow continued prosperity to founder on rising costs and shrunken dollars, skyrocketing ad-

vances and threats to the consumers' pocketbooks, and threats to the mayors' programs also.

So this is really a testing period for our leadership, mine and yours. This is a testing period for our economic maturity and our commonsense. We do not want to check our economic expansion unless that is absolutely necessary, but one thing is clear and one thing is imperative: Our expansion must continue to be orderly. The American economy must be marshaled with reason and managed with restraint.

You and I are some of the managers. We must balance our efforts against some plain and some telling truths. What are they?

Our effort in Vietnam is budgeted in fiscal 1967—June 30 to June 30 next year—to cost $6 billion more than it did in 1966. But during this same period, over this same year, our gross national product is estimated to grow by $45 billion to $55 billion or more.

What does that mean? That means we have some $40 billion to $50 billion of extra output that is available for our civilian economy.

If there is a problem of overheating the economy, it is going to be because consumers and businessmen, State and local governments, will want to spend substantially more than the $40 billion or $45 billion over and above what they spent last year. If further restraint on the economy is needed, it will primarily be because civilian demand is too large.

Last December the Federal Reserve Board began building a new restraint into the economy through tight money and through high interest rates. I did not agree with Bill Martin and the other three members of the seven-man Federal Reserve Board that it was either the time or the means to take that action; but they did take it. It was estraint and it is beginning to bite—as you may have observed, in some of your proposed bond issues.

This was December. Then on January 1 we took that $6 billion out of the economy in the form of higher payroll taxes for social security and Medicare. You will remember we had the columnists and commentators writing in the fall that we would have a big dip in January, because there was "speculation"—that is a word they use—"speculation" or "informed sources believe" or "high sources whisper."

But one of the buck sheep went through the fence and said, "We are going to have a big dip because of the $6 billion." Then the little typewriters ran for 2 weeks on that subject.

There was reason to believe that if you reached in and took $6 billion out, that would have its effect. I think it is bound to have its effect, whether we see it or not. But instead of the dip, it went the other way, so we proposed a tax bill that would take about $6 billion more. We had $6 billion in January. We signed a tax bill March 15th to take $6 billion more over a period of time.

We put excise taxes back on the automobiles and the telephones. In a period when we wanted to stimulate the economy and give it a shot in the arm, we had repealed them the year before, and the year before that, and it had a very desirable effect. It did what we wanted.

Now when we want to restrain it and keep it from overflowing the pitcher, we took $6 billion out in Medicare and $6 billion out in auto and excise and accelerated corporation and accelerated personal payments. We speeded up these personal and corporation payments.

But I warn you—and my prediction in

this regard will be almost up to Drew Pearson's 85 percent—it will bite. How much it will bite is a question for the speculative financial writers. We just honestly don't know whether we have done enough. I would hate to do too much, because if I just threw one man out of a job and he had to go and live off unemployment compensation for a while, I would feel bad about it.

But I do have a responsibility, and if we haven't done enough, we want to do enough. Contrary to the general tone of the financial press, I don't believe the American economy is shooting off into outer space.

The housing sector can only be described as weak. It was down 17 percent last month over the month before. Down 11 percent under that month a year ago.

The recent inventory accumulations have been moderate. The order backlogs are lengthened in only a very few fields, and even there they are not long in comparison to 1955 and 1957.

We still, this morning, have 3 million unemployed. Seventy-eight percent of those are adults; 47 percent of those 3 million are male; 81 percent of them previously held full-time jobs.

The average rate of capacity utilization is now about equal to the average rate that is preferred by management, and more capacity is coming into our economic stream every day.

Unit labor costs in manufacturing in February were only four-tenths of one percent higher than a year earlier. The expansion of business loans in February was very moderate. That bite began to be felt.

But now let's look at the other side of the coin. Some strains on the economy are already becoming very apparent. Labor shortages are being felt in several States in a good many industries. Investment plans for 1966 are already $2 billion higher than we had estimated in January. I want to talk to you about some of those investments a little later this morning.

Our balance of payments position is being weakened because of the demand for things here, and because of the rapid expansion of imports to meet that demand. This suggests that the domestic producers are not meeting the demands that are required of them.

But most serious for all of us is this: Prices are moving up too fast to be comfortable. Day before yesterday we had a one-half of one percent increase in consumer prices announced. That one-half of one percent was between January and February. One month, one-half of one percent up.

Over the last 5 months, wholesale prices have been rising at the rate 5½ percent a year. Increases at these rates cannot long be tolerated.

I asked Mrs. Johnson this morning, even as she has changed cooks, is she exercising all the care in her buying that she did in times that weren't so prosperous. I remember a lot of times when I had a different kind of meat. Sometimes it was meat of a kind I didn't like. It was a cheaper cut. I remember a lot of times we didn't have the fresh vegetables. That was when they had gone up because of a freeze we had in Florida which affected the cucumbers or green peppers, or one we had in Texas that affected lettuce or some of the other items.

I just wonder if the women of this country couldn't get out their lead pencils and put on their glasses and look at some of these price lists and see where these shortages are occurring and see where these prices are advancing, and say goodby to those products that insist on going up and up. Just say,

"I don't have to have that. I will ju substitute."

That would have a good effect, I think I hope they will do it. I will tell you why inflation, inflation, inflation.

I remember during the McCarthy perio in this town, when Senator McCarthy wa running his investigation, you couldn't wa in any hostess' home without them saying "What do you think about McCarthy?" A month ago it was, "What do you thin about the pause?" Now it is, "What d you think about inflation?"

I want to tell you about inflation. Eight percent of all of these price increases com from two items: farm prices for foods, relatively limited group—butter and por and meat and fresh vegetables that went u because of freezes in parts of the countr (now they tell me those prices will level of particularly if we watch some selective buy ing)—plus three metals. Three metals an food prices are responsible for 80 percent o this increase.

So now we can do something about tha I hope that we do, because the amber ligh is on. In 5 months wholesale prices up a a rate of 5½ percent. So we must procee with caution and we must use some com monsense. We must see that some r straint is applied by our judgments, by ou selections, and by our plans.

We are touching the brakes in Januar again in March, but we don't want to pu both feet on the brakes and turn us int a skid that is a recession or a depressio We have learned that lesson from just lool ing back down the road just a few year We want no more economic accidents o collisions or sudden wrecks. We haven had one for 60 months. We have bee stable. We have the most stable prices o any nation in the world.

Now, if more restraint is needed, I have said that so far as the Federal Government is concerned, we will exert it. When? When the fiscal advisers and the men in the administration and the Congress whose prudent judgment I respect consider we need it.

It is already clear that our ability to meet demands in some fields, such as construction and capital goods, is at this moment under a strain. But we have not decided in the executive branch of the Federal Government that the situation is such as to require either price or wage controls or, either, to require a tax bill. When we do, we will try to let all of you know it at the same time and let all of you participate equally in it.

So beware of the impressionists and the alarmists. When and if this comes, we will do it deliberately, carefully, thoroughly, and make the appropriate announcement.

Last night I asked a group of 200 of the leading businessmen in this country: "How many of you would recommend tomorrow a tax increase to the Congress for the purpose of restraining our economy? Those of you that would, I wish you would raise your right hand."

Not a hand went up. That doesn't mean we won't recommend a tax increase. That doesn't mean we will. That just meant of those 200 present, there wasn't one that thought it was wise.

I talk to the mayors and get their judgments. I talked to the Governors last week and got their judgment. I will talk to the leaders of labor. I have already talked to a good many of them, but I will have them to dinner and get their judgment. I am seeing some Congressmen and Senators today to get their recommendations and judgment.

But last night I made this specific request

of your investment partners in the Nation, the outstanding business leaders, to go back home and review their plans for their investment projects to see what plans they had involving construction that could be stretched out, deferred, curtailed, or abandoned.

It may be that when those 800,000 men that Mr. McNamara takes in the service this year come back out of their uniform they would like to have a job. It is not absolutely essential that every businessman always get in the market at its high. It is not absolutely essential that every mayor wait until the cost of money goes up higher than it has been in years and then dash in and want a lot of it.

It is not absolutely essential that a project that has been years in developing has to get out and compete with the Defense Department or defense industry at the moment when all of you need a little copper. We can pass laws that can adjudicate these matters. It is better if we just regulate ourselves, if we can. We have been doing a pretty good job of that the last several months.

Our balance of payments reduced the deficit from $3 billion to $1.2 billion just through voluntary action. Our labor leaders have maintained a very reasonable wage increase policy. Most of our prices over the country have remained relatively stable, but considering all the other things, the chances we had to make mistakes, we have made relatively few of them.

Now I am going to meet with the leaders of the workingmen of this country. I am going to talk to them about the desirable cautionary moves that I think we should take. We will ask them to practice restraint. I am going to ask our Cabinet tomorrow again what I have already asked them to do:

377

to practice what I preach; that is, for each department of this Government, each agency, to review and carefully examine how we can defer any of the expenditures in this budget.

They are coming in to see me tomorrow morning to answer a request I made several weeks ago, to see if there is anything for which the money has been appropriated that they can postpone. I want them to examine particularly these Federal and federally-supported construction expenditures, so we can reduce our total construction obligation in the last quarter of this year as much as possible.

I am hoping that I can cut down my planned expenditures in April and May and June and cut up my planned revenue. I can tell you now our revenue is going to make a material jump. If I can get our expenditures down and revenue up, as you mayors know, that is a desirable situation.

I am going to ask the Cabinet to apply this request and this study to every possible form of construction because that is where the bind is, that is where the bite is deep, except that construction that is vitally necessary to immediate military needs.

We have plans for $60 billion in plant investment next year, according to our estimate. But Bob McNamara, at the Defense Department, cut out $640 million of military construction and said we will postpone it. It was already authorized and appropriated for, but we will postpone it. We will get by with what we have.

I see the Governor of New Jersey postponed the turnpike up there because it cost $440 million. There is $1 billion there.

We are going to look at all of these things we have been doing to see what we can hold back so we won't give the unnecessary competition the next quarter and the next few quarters to come.

I believe this group of mayors can best serve the interests of your community and certainly I know it will serve your country if you, when you get home, would order a review of your plans for the next months ahead with a particular view to deferring or postponing any capital plant investment that you think is possible.

The Federal Government is doing it. I have asked the Governors to do it. I have asked the businessmen, the private managers, to do it, and this morning I am asking the mayors to do it. The investments that you are making in your cities are vital to the future of this country. I know that every one of us would like to complete them all at once, but there are a good many mayors and Governors and even presidents in the country that have made building plans when the costs were high, when money was high, and when labor was high, only to have some opponent criticize them down the road and point out that they got in at the high and would regret it.

I wanted to add two little rooms to a house that we have down home that we will occupy some of these days, but I asked Mrs. Johnson last night to defer those two rooms because the construction people who would be working on them would be very much in demand. We have had our plans for several months, and spent a lot of hours and dollars talking about them, but we are just going to defer.

That is a little thing, but if everybody does that, it won't get too tight, it won't heat up too much, the economy won't get out of our hands, and the prices won't go up 5 percent in the next 5 months. You can be your own judge. Nobody is dictating to you or forcing you. There is no law requiring it. Yet, let's see if we can use our own good judgment.

If we attempt to do too much and do it

too soon, we will end up by accomplishing less by borrowing our money and issuing our bonds when the cost of money is the highest. So I would hope that you would take that good, hard look. Look at your equipment purchases. See if there are any of them where you can substitute or get by a little longer or repair them. Look at your construction projects and see which one of those could be slipped just a little bit so you won't put any more demand than you have to on this elevator that is already overloaded.

I hardly need to remind you men of experience and sophistication that your own interests are widely and deeply involved. I don't think money will always be as tight as it is today. I don't believe that loans are always going to be as hard to get as they are today. I don't believe that bonds are always going to be as costly as they are today or going to be as difficult to sell. Construction costs now are high and you know and I know that the effect of more construction is just going to make it higher.

I am not asking you to refuse the essential needs of your people, but in January my budget cut almost $17 billion of expenditures from the departmental requests to my Cabinet. We are continuing tomorrow to try to cut some more in addition to that $17 billion. But we can't make much progress if the Federal Government cuts out more than $16 billion—between $16 billion and $17 billion—if the private plant investment goes up more than 16 percent, as they are predicting; and particularly if the States and counties and the cities do not take needed actions.

So I am asking you this morning to please put first things first, to be selective, to excel in management. None of you can object to that way of putting it: to be great mayors by being better leaders who set the national

interests beside the local interest and take a broad view of both, and balance them.

So I have come here to ask for your wisdom and to ask for your help in this time of trial. Together, I think, we have proved over the past 5 years that we need not accept a depression or a recession or a boom or a bust as a fact of American life. Now I think it is up to us to prove that we do not have to pay the price of inflation in order to have employment and to have men working at reasonable pay.

I think if we work together we can make some headway. With continued restraint from your Government on your level and mine, with the help of the business leaders, with the cooperation of the labor leaders and the laboringmen of this country, we can all together keep this economy booming—but also keep it balanced.

Our wealth and our strength is continuing to grow. With that growing wealth we can push on to better days. We face these problems together, but still, we here in this room are the most fortunate generation of leaders in all of our history. I am firmly and passionately convinced that it is within our power to make the city a shining tower of a mighty new civilization and to make the slum, the ghetto, and the hovel, all of these, a memory of an outmoded past.

Now, we can't do all this transformation overnight, and it is regrettable that we have to move in our transition as slowly as we are. But I believe that many now living will see the day when every one of our citizens in this Nation lives in a decent home and enjoys the dignity and security that is the mark of a free society. I believe that we are going to see in this country, as a result of your leadership and what cooperation we can give, not only cleaner cities but healthier cities, more beautiful cities, more challenging cities, cities built not simply to satisfy man's appetite, but cities that will stir men's souls.

I believe the future generations will look back on our era as the dawn of the Golden Age of urban living. I am not asking you to stop. I am not asking you to spurt. I am asking you to apply a prudent judgment and excel in management in a critical period when more than 100 men died last week so that we could enjoy the freedoms that are ours now.

I believe our grandchildren and their grandchildren that come after them will look back at all of us in gratitude some day for having been the first of the leaders to start up that long road which will place the great American city at the summit of a new stage in the life of civilized man.

So I leave you with gratitude for the leadership that you are giving your communities. I don't confine that gratitude, Mayor McKeldin, just to Democratic mayors. All mayors are included.

I came here not only to thank you, but to ask for your help to the extent that you feel that it is in the best interests of your people and the best interests of your country. I don't think that we ever ought to have anything compulsory that we can do better voluntarily. I think by reasoning together, as I have been doing the last few months, that we may perhaps avoid some of the harassing details that come in an over-generated economy.

I lived through the OPA, the War Labor Board, and the WPB in two periods of my life, World War II and the Korean war. I remember going home one time and going out to see a farmer neighbor. I told him I wanted to bring back a ham. Lady Bird wanted to serve Sunday night buffet and hams were hard to get. I bought the ham and I said, "How much?" He said "$3."

I pulled out my wallet and gave him $3. Then I said, "How many stamps?" He said, "How many which?" I said, "How many stamps are required for this?"

"Oh," he said, "you are talking about the OP&A." (I was a Congressman and I wanted to be very careful to do what I should do, because some of these columnists were kind of looking over my shoulder and I knew some who came to dinner would want to know where I got the ham. There had already been some discussion about a 12-pound ham, whether that is big enough or not too big to be considered unethical.)

So I paid the $3 and said, "What about the tickets and the stamps?" He said, "Oh, you are talking about the OP&A."

"Well," he said, "we just never did put that in down here!"

Now, we don't want to go through that period again. We don't want to put them in down here. So unless you just feel a compelling need—some men do; I saw some grown men, friends of mine, I thought they wanted to wear nylon stockings themselves during the shortage of nylon stockings—but unless you just feel the higher call from up yonder or a compelling need to get in at the high—the fellows that got in at the high of the market yesterday were sorry after they read the stories last night. Some of you may be sorry.

I don't tell you what to do. I don't urge you what to do for your own community. You, yourselves, are better judges than I. I do point out what I think any leader ought to point out that is worthy of leading you, and that is that we do have some thermometers there and we have looked at the temperature charts and we have cautioned taking it easy and a little rest for the immediate period until we can see things a little further down the road. If you can, and if you will find a way to help us, we will be much obliged.

NOTE: The President spoke at 10:50 a.m. in the International Ballroom at the Washington Hilton Hotel before the Second National Legislative Conference of the National League of Cities. In his opening words he referred to Mayor Jerome P. Cavanagh of Detroit, President of the National League of Cities, Representative Thomas L. Ashley of Ohio, and Patrick Healy, Executive Director, National League of Cities. During his remarks the President referred to William McC. Martin, Jr., Chairman of the Board of Governors, Federal Reserve System, Drew Pearson, syndicated columnist, Joseph R. McCarthy, Senator from Wisconsin 1947–1957, Robert S. McNamara, Secretary of Defense, Richard J. Hughes, Governor of New Jersey, and Theodore R. McKeldin, Mayor of Baltimore and former Governor of Maryland.

As printed, this item follows the text of the White House release.

156 Remarks at the Launching of the 1966 Cancer Crusade. *March 31, 1966*

Mr. and Mrs. Peck, Miss Dillard, Mrs. Dillard, ladies and gentlemen:

I appreciate very much all of you coming here this morning and allowing me to join with this sweet little girl and Gregory Peck to really launch the kickoff for the 1966 Cancer Crusade.

I know that you come here as busy Americans, but very dedicated people. You symbolize the more than 2 million volunteers in this country who serve each year in the fight against cancer.

Your theme is one of hope and of promise. Although cancer still remains one of the dread enemies, there are more people being cured today of cancer than ever before in our national life. The Federal Government, through its National Cancer Institute, is conducting now and is supporting research that we think offers great hope.

Hodgkins disease, if discovered early, can now be fully controlled in 40 percent of the cases for periods up to 15 years by the X-ray treatment. Drugs are proving very effective against certain forms of cancer. One type of malignancy in women can now be cured with chemicals. Leukemia, which takes the lives of so many of our children, is yielding itself to research. More than 100 children with this disease have survived 5 years or longer and they are free of symptoms following drug treatment. Our scientists believe that leukemia may be caused by a virus. If this should be proved, perhaps a vaccine could give us some added protection against it.

So these are the things that the American Cancer Society is trying so hard to bring to the attention of all of the American people through their pamphlets, through meetings like this, through programs that they have planned. Those of you engaged in that work are breaking through the fear of superstition that has surrounded this terrible disease all of my life. You are telling Americans that early detection and early treatment may save the lives of innumerable Americans.

So working hand in hand with our scientists and our researchers and our surgeons, your Federal Government and your President is very proud of the role that we are playing in cancer research, in publicizing the efforts that we are making, in trying to lead and educate our people.

Two new programs now are getting underway which will do much to assure early detection and early treatment. On the one hand, Medicare, which we struggled and fought for for so many years, will provide the financial resources to bring treatment to a larger number of our older citizens who are, of course, the most susceptible to cancer. On the other hand, the regional medical programs that I proposed last year for the treatment of heart disease, cancer, and stroke, in which the Congress cooperated, will assure that the greatest number of all of our people can now have access to the latest results of all of our medical information and medical treatment.

Some day I hope and am going to pray that we will find a cure for cancer. I want it done in my time. I want to play my part in it. I want to do something about it.

The loneliest moment I ever had in my life was when I learned that my mother was gone from me, because of this terrible disease.

The foundation for this breakthrough is being laid by the men and women who are here today. And a great unified national effort is underway and I am so proud to salute the leaders and the doers in this field. This gives me a chance, again, to especially express the appreciation of the President and the people of this Nation to the distinguished artist, Mr. Gregory Peck, for the innumerable voluntary hours of work that he has given to the good causes which have led to a better life for Americans: our poverty program, our beautification program, our peace program, our health program, our education program, the things that give us a richer and fuller and more useful life.

It is a pleasure to have him here this morning with this attractive little lady who is a doer and shows it can be done. I want to welcome you and thank you at the same time.

NOTE: The President spoke at 12:15 p.m. in the Cabinet Room at the White House. His opening words referred to actor Gregory Peck, Crusade Chairman for the American Cancer Society, and his wife, and to Julie Alice Dillard of Santa Rosa, Calif., and her mother, Mrs. James Dillard.

Mr. Peck introduced 9-year old Julie Alice, the 1966 Society poster girl who was cured of cancer. She presented to the President the first copy of the educational folder which was distributed during the Crusade.

157 Remarks at a Meeting Marking the Inauguration of the State-Federal (Title 19) Medical Assistance Program. *March 31, 1966*

Secretary Gardner, Senator Long, Congressman Mink, ladies and gentlemen:

We are delighted to have you come here to visit with us this morning. This is a very special occasion because adequate health protection and medical care once were considered great privileges in America, privileges that were limited to just those who could afford it.

But today this Nation has greater wealth, and I think it also has a greater heart. We are learning to think of good health not as a privilege for the few, but as a basic right for all. In spite of our growing concern and our great progress in health, we still produce a set of health statistics each year which are shocking for the world's wealthiest nation.

—Sixty percent of America's poor children have never been to a dentist.

—In Detroit more than a thousand preschool children lose the sight of an eye each year for lack of medical attention.

—In Boston an examination of 1,400 preschool children showed that half had serious health problems.

—Children of low-income families in America, for lack of medical care, grow up with twice as many serious eye defects, twice as many hearing losses, twice as many speech impediments, as the children of more fortunate families.

—Half again as many poor children as wealthy ones grow up crippled in America.

Now we can and we are going to change all of that. So today we launch a program that is aimed at erasing those heartbreaking figures, a program that is authorized by title 19 of the Social Security Amendments of 1965. This new partnership will operate as a State-Federal partnership. As the States launch and operate their own tax-supported medical assistance program, the Federal Government will share 50 to 80 percent of the cost.

By 1975 we hope to see this program cover all people in all age groups in every State who cannot afford the medical care they need.

North Dakota, Oklahoma, Illinois, Minnesota, Hawaii, Pennsylvania, and Puerto Rico are the first to launch programs under title 19. Nine million children and adults in these States, and nearly two-thirds of the children in Puerto Rico, are eligible for the help that this program offers.

So I have, with great pleasure, invited representatives today of these six States and Puerto Rico to come here to the White House Cabinet Room to visit with us to conclude their partnership agreements to receive the Federal grant award entitling them to draw on Federal contributions which could exceed $60 million for the quarter which began January 1.

Dr. Ellen Winston, the Commissioner of Welfare, tells me that another 24 States are at work on their plans and are hoping to be in operation by the year's end. This is good news.

I am very delighted that we have the vitality and the reactivation and the sense of mission and the deep purpose that Dr. Gardner and Secretary Cohen have brought

to the Department of Health, Education, and Welfare. I am very grateful for the cooperation that has been given me by the leaders in the House, Chairman Mills and Congressman Byrnes; and in the Senate by Senator Russell Long, who is here this morning, and other Members of the Senate Finance Committee in this field.

If we are intense—and the slang expression is "hipped"—on any subjects around here, it is food for our bodies, for our children, and education for their minds and health for their physiques. Health, education, and food—we won't call it HEW; we will call it HEF, Dr. Gardner.

I spent a good part of this week talking to a very gracious lady who is the leader of almost 500 million people who die at almost half the life expectancy that we have. The trucks of Bombay run up and down their streets every morning picking up people who died the night before because of malnutrition and lack of food.

We have witnessed in our experiences in Vietnam the health conditions of their people. And all over the world we have a problem of health and of food and of education. This morning I pointed out we have 7 million more people working than we had 5 years ago. I got a new budget estimate this morning. Now our income is way up because people have jobs and are working, earning, and paying. We can say, really, we have 7 million taxpayers today that were probably taxeaters in some form or other only 5 years ago.

So if we will give some attention to our education, some attention to the health of our children, and some attention to correcting these deficiencies that we can spot at this early age in life, it will not only be self-satisfying to those of us who have a part in it, but it will be financially responsible and productive.

383

I think that we should point out that for a long time in our country we have considered public support for education a basic investment, but today we are declaring that the health of our people is just equally worthy of that support, equally important to the Nation's future, and at this particular time we declare, so that all who have ears can hear and all who have eyes can see that the world's wealthiest nation can never be satisfied until we are the world's healthiest.

This program, I think, will help us reach that goal. We hope by what we do here as a result of this innovation, as a result of this wise legislation that was passed in 1965, that we can set an example that the other nations of the world will want to emulate.

Thank you, Doctor, for coming here. We welcome those representatives of the States that are launching this program, this kickoff, and we welcome aboard all the other States that may learn about it and want to participate.

NOTE: The President spoke at 12:45 p.m. in the Cabinet Room at the White House. His opening words referred to John W. Gardner, Secretary of Health, Education, and Welfare, Senator Russell B. Long of Louisiana, Chairman of the Senate Finance Committee, and Representative Patsy T. Mink of Hawaii. During his remarks he referred to Wilbur J. Cohen, Under Secretary of Health, Education, and Welfare, Representative Wilbur D. Mills of Arkansas, Chairman of the House Ways and Means Committee, and Representative John W. Byrnes of Wisconsin, member of the committee.

For the President's remarks at the signing of the Social Security Amendments of 1965, see 1965 volume, this series, Book II, Item 394.

158 The President's News Conference of March 31, 1966

THE PRESIDENT. I have an announcement or two I would like to make while I am here, if you want to use them, and then I will be glad to answer any questions, if you have any, that may occur to you. We will call this, I guess, a White House impromptu press conference.

ADDITIONS TO THE WHITE HOUSE STAFF

[1.] I want to announce today two new additions to the White House staff.

ROBERT KINTNER

As a Special Assistant to the President and as Secretary to the Cabinet, I am naming a man who is an old White House reporter and known to most of you, Mr. Robert Kintner, the former executive with the National Broadcasting Company.

When I came to Washington sometime in the early thirties, I remember coming back on the train with President Roosevelt, and I first met Bob Kintner and his wife Jean. They have been friends ever since, and I have asked him to come and work with me. He will work at the highest level with the Cabinet, and as a liaison not only with each Cabinet department, but with the other agencies that report to the President.

He will take a substantial part of the work that Jack Valenti is doing with the Cabinet at present, and Joe Califano.[1] They are dividing it, and Mr. Kintner will assume that responsibility and relieve them for other work.

He will advise me on a broad range of matters, including organizational and administrative problems, coordination of the

[1] Jack Valenti and Joseph A. Califano, Jr., Special Assistants to the President.

Great Society programs, as well as topflight Presidential personnel.

Mr. Macy [2] does not replace him or change his duties in any way, but frequently I am unable to interview and evaluate all of the people. He will originate suggestions from here on top quality personnel. Any of you that don't want to get on the public payroll had better dodge Bob when he is walking down the hall.

Bob Kintner is a man of wide experience in public affairs, journalism, and executive management. He is an innovator, administrator, and a genuine doer. I think the Government is fortunate to secure his services.

WALT WHITMAN ROSTOW

[2.] I am also naming as Special Assistant to the President Mr. Walt Whitman Rostow. Mr. Rostow is presently Assistant Secretary of State for Policy Planning and Counselor of the Department of State. He is one of the most original thinkers that I know. He is a man of long experience in academic and governmental circles.

He will come to the White House to work principally, but not necessarily exclusively, in the field of foreign policy. I will especially look to him for the development of long-range plans in that field, as well as special coordination of Latin American development, in which we are intensely interested, and in which he has played a very special part in CIAP (Inter-American Committee on the Alliance for Progress).

It is one of his fields of particular interest, and I shall look to him as a catalyst for ideas and programs on the various continents of the world.

As Special Assistants to the President, Mr. Kintner and Mr. Rostow will earn $30,000 annually. The Press Office will have biographical material on each man available when we have finished here.

QUESTIONS

I will be glad to answer any questions on this subject or any other that you may have, and if Smitty will keep time on us, so that I can count this as a regular, impromptu, unannounced, hurried-up press conference, I will appreciate it.

PURPOSE OF MEETINGS WITH MAYORS AND
BUSINESSMEN

[3.] Q. Mr. President, in your speech today over at the mayors,[3] you seemed to indicate a new sense of urgency and concern about the inflationary threat. Is there any single event or group of events that you can identify that have caused this concern and led you into this series of meetings, such as last night and today?

THE PRESIDENT. No. When I came into the Presidency, that led me into them. I regard the institution of the Presidency as requiring responsible leadership, and I think the country expects the President to provide that leadership. Shortly after the tragedy that took President Kennedy away from us, I asked the labor leaders of this country to come meet with me and counsel with me and discuss the problems of the Nation. They have done that at frequent intervals since then. I have done the same thing with the business leaders. I think I met with them the night before I went to the hospital last October. I met with them, I

---

[2] John W. Macy, Jr., Chairman, Civil Service Commission, and personnel adviser to the President.

[3] See Item 155.

believe, again in July. I met with them last February or March again.

I have had innumerable meetings of this kind. They are not anything new, not anything panicky, not anything frantic, not anything different. We have a review of the general problems that may be facing the Government at the time that we have the meetings. It happened that Mr. Murphy, the president of Campbell Soup,[4] who happens to be head of the Business Council, asked me to address the Business Council last year, and I was unable to do so. I talked to them by telephone, if you will remember.[5] He asked for an appointment the other day to come and see me on other matters, including a trip that he was taking. In the course of the discussion, we talked about when we could get back together again. Wednesday night seemed to be a desirable night.

Secretary Rusk took them on a trip around the world. He discussed the African Continent, the Western Hemisphere, the Middle East, Southeast Asia, India, Pakistan, the Tashkent Agreement, the Soviet Union, the Chinese situation, Vietnam.

The Vice President discussed his trip and a variety of matters involving economics, military, political.

The Secretary of Defense talked about the number of men in the Department, the operation of that Department, the problems facing that Department, our military strength, our equipment, various matters.

Each of them took questions on any subject—not the British system of appearing before the House of Commons and answering questions, but we extend it a little further. We have had all the Congress

in this year. We have had a number of the labor leaders in this year—Mr. Meany and Mr. Reuther.[6] We plan to have a dinner of this kind for them just as soon as we can arrange it. We are trying to be in touch with Mr. Meany to see what his pleasure is in the matter.

We will have educators, lawyers, doctors, dentists, and newspaper people in. And when we have these meetings, they will have the privilege of doing what you do twice a day here, ask questions about matters that concern you.

One of the matters that I think indicates a need for information and pointing up of problems just at this moment is our cost of living. Every poll shows that our people are concerned with the cost of living. Every day the President is concerned with the cost of living. Every day every housewife is concerned with it.

So when I called in the Governors the other day,[7] I pointed up to them that we are approaching full employment. We had 3 million unemployed, 73 million employed. I gave them my view as I did the mayors this morning, as I did the businessmen last night, as I did Mr. Meany and Mr. Reuther when I met with them earlier this year, as I did all the Congress—every Member of the House and every Member of the Senate, as I did all the House chairmen and all the Senate chairmen, and as I did you last week.

There is not much difference. New facts come in. We get a new picture on revenues one day, and a price rise one day, a price decline another day, and they change the story some—but the general problem that you have is an economy where you have most of your people working at reasonably good

---

[4] W. Beverley Murphy, President of Campbell Soup Company and Chairman of the Business Council.

[5] See 1965 volume, this series, Book II, Item 632.

[6] George Meany, President of the AFL–CIO, and Walter Reuther, President of the United Automobile Workers of America.

[7] See Items 121–124.

wages and shortages developing, things of that kind. So we discussed that last night. We discussed it this morning. We will be discussing it with the Congressmen, with the Senators, with the country, with the Governors, with business and labor, et cetera.

BUSINESS REACTION TO DISCUSSIONS

[4.] Q. Mr. President, how sympathetic did you find the businessmen to your suggestions that they cut back on capital investments?

THE PRESIDENT. I outlined to them the situation as I saw it. I made no demand of them and just pointed up to them what we could accomplish together if we all had the same information and understood the same problem. I thought the reaction both from the standpoint of the questions asked and the exchanges that occurred were very constructive and very helpful.

I don't want to be recommending myself for the approval they gave us, but they all applauded the statements made by the various Cabinet officers, by the Vice President, and by myself. They all had a good understanding of them. They asked questions. Several of them got up and pointed out how they appreciated this, that there had never been the flow of information between any President and the industrial leadership in this country that we had now, meeting every few months and discussing them, that our door had always been open to them and they appreciated this.

I asked them about how many of them would recommend a tax increase if they were President. I answered some of the questions they asked me. We had a good constructive meeting. A good many of them were kind enough to say they thought

this was the best meeting we had ever had together.

We had the Secretary of State who had to go to another meeting, and the Vice President who had to go to another meeting. The Secretary of Defense appeared before the dinner. We ate dinner in about 45 minutes. We went in to dinner about 8, I guess, and came out about 9.

I had a reception line and shook hands with each one of them. Then we went in and had the Secretary of State, the Secretary of Defense, and the Vice President, in that order. We went in and ate at 8 o'clock; we came back at 9 o'clock. Then I spoke to them for 15 or 20 minutes, answered questions, and had each member of the Cabinet there, plus the Chairman of the Council of Economic Advisers, plus the Chairman of the Federal Reserve Board, Mr. Martin, and plus the Director of the Budget, Mr. Schultze. I told them that each man would be ready to answer any question any businessman had to ask, and we would be glad to have their complaints, their suggestions, their criticism.

POLITICAL SITUATION IN VIETNAM

[5.] Q. I wonder, sir, if you can give us your views and comments on the current domestic political trouble in South Vietnam, and specifically, should there be a change in government, what effect this might have on the war?

THE PRESIDENT. I would answer all your questions in one sentence, that there is not any information that I could give you that would add to what you have read in the papers. I think that there is a very adequate free flow of information out there, and everything that is reported to this Government in that field is pretty well known to you either simultaneously, by the time I get it, or maybe sometimes a little ahead of me.

DUTIES OF THE SPECIAL ASSISTANTS

[6.] Q. Mr. President, could it be said that as your new Special Assistant, Mr. Rostow will take over all or many of the duties and assignments handled by McGeorge Bundy? [8]

THE PRESIDENT. It could be, but that would be inaccurate. It would not be true. Most of the men play any position here. We hope—I hope Mr. Rostow can. Part of the work Mr. Bundy did we will say will now be done by Mr. Komer. Some of the work Mr. Bundy did is now being done by Jack Valenti and Bill Moyers.[9] There will be some of the things Mr. Valenti and Mr. Moyers formerly did that Mr. Kintner will do. He will be Special Assistant. He will be paid $30,000 a year.

He will be at the service of the President, and if he needs to play first base or second base or third base, I hope that he can do it. He is equipped to do it. I don't want him to play any position too long, because he gets too familiar with you all—and familiarity breeds contempt.

CONSUMER PURCHASES

[7.] Q. Mr. President, in your speech this morning you seemed to be advocating in some sense a buyers' strike. I hate to use that word, but you suggested that housewives and consumers might not——

THE PRESIDENT. No, I would not use that word, and I did not advocate that. You were very accurate on my statement yester-

day on the tax situation. But I did not advocate any buyers' strike. I won't advocate any kind of strike, ever.

Q. I just wondered if you would give us your thinking on this matter?

THE PRESIDENT. I did this morning. I can't add anything to that. I think it would be wise for all of us to be selective in our purchases, and when we see that a commodity is scarce or that it has suffered from the weather or from some other unusual situation that has resulted in the price skyrocketing, that we can just turn the other cheek, go the other way, and that will have a very good effect and balance things out.

I think it would be good if our wives chose to do so. I am not requiring them to do it or forcing them to do it, or trying to make them do it. Don't get that in there. But I think it would have a good effect if we would really put on our glasses and look at these prices and see who it was that had a commodity or product that was in short supply, and whether we could make any substitute or exchange for it.

My mother used to say, "The one eats the most cornbread gets the most cake." I assume that was because we had more cornbread than cake. That is a thing we might all practice now when our fellow man is working and buying.

MEXICAN AMERICANS

[8.] Q. Mr. President, have you heard anything to the effect that Mexican Americans feel they should have more attention?

THE PRESIDENT. Yes, I have heard that all my life. And I agree with them. I think they should have more attention. I am going to give them all the attention I can. I haven't given them enough. I want to give them more. I think that they are entitled to more consideration in Government

---

[8] McGeorge Bundy, former Special Assistant to the President.

[9] Bill D. Moyers, Special Assistant to the President.

employment than they have received. I think they have been discriminated against in housing, in education, in jobs. I don't think we can be very proud of our record in that field.

I want to see it improved. I feel a very high regard and great respect for their people and a deep affection for them. I want to do everything I can to improve their lot. I think some of their complaints and their protests have been well founded, and they have pointed up some things that we needed to hear. I hope that the appropriate people, including the President, can take prompt action on it.

Q. Mr. President, do you think they might be included in the coming up Conference on Equal Opportunity?

THE PRESIDENT. I have not explored that. I don't know the thinking behind it. But they can be included in any conference any time they would have one. My door is open to them always. I am very anxious to exchange views with them. If they are ready for a conference, I will be ready for one.

BUSINESS OPINION ON TAX INCREASE

[9.] Q. Mr. President, when you asked the businessmen last night if any of them would call for a tax increase now if he were President, can you say what their response to that was?

THE PRESIDENT. I asked anyone who felt that they would recommend to the American people that the Congress increase taxes now to raise their right hands, and there were no hands raised.

CONGRESSIONAL ACTION AND THE BUDGET

[10.] Q. Mr. President, in relation to the talk about inflation currently——

THE PRESIDENT. Whose talk? General?

Q. Yes, general talk. Would you comment on various actions that the Congress has taken with your budget, both in cutting and adding to?

THE PRESIDENT. We have a great problem in housing in this country, particularly in the cities. If you will go into the center of our cities and see how some of our people live—the fact that there are not many people building or renovating or improving, or who have been providing in the past desirable housing for our poor people—you can see the problem we have.

We are trying to find a new approach to that through the experimental rent supplement. We don't know that that is the answer. But the National Association of Real Estate Boards, and the home builders' industry, and the experts in housing in private and Government circles feel that it is worth testing.

So we asked, as you know, for a modicum of money for that experiment. It was authorized last year. I went to the hospital and the appropriation was held over until this year, until the Appropriations Committee could consider it further. Due to the fact that a good part of the fiscal year is gone, the money we asked for last October—October, November, December, January, February, and March have passed—the Committee reduced that request for a Teacher Corps and for a rent supplement to a figure around $21 million, the two of them, I believe, $21 or $22 million.

Now that was a great issue, and you all had your backgrounders that the future "fall" of the Johnson administration was just around the corner.

That was the test, and I read about it for about 3 days here and sat trembling, waiting for the announcement of that roll call, because everything depended on that $22 million vote. They had it and it was adopted.

Then in the same bill they added one that was not so important, $41 million to school districts in the impacted areas, some of which are rather wealthy districts—some adjoining here that are in rather good shape. That was over and above the budget. So they attempted for 2 days to reduce the $21 million, and then in 2 minutes put in $41 million. That is a sample of the reaction on that appropriation bill.

The Coast Guard bill I signed this morning,[10] and you have a statement on that— the total authorization is $126 million. The Committee and the Congress in their wisdom saw fit to add $23,079,000 in excess of what we desire or request or think is desirable this year.

The GI education bill was the first bill we got this year.

Is Senator Long[11] still here? He is gone, but that came out of the Congress, and a good many were here who signed it. That added almost $300 million to our budget this year, and will add almost $2 billion over the total period. Now we have cut, as I said this morning, $16 or $17 billion from the departmental requests, and there are certainly more that may be able to be reduced. Any place we can find something that we think it is wise to forgo, we are going to do it.

We have Cabinet officers coming in here tomorrow to meet. I hope Mr. Kintner can be here to meet with them the first time. We are going to look at anything under their jurisdiction that could be forgone or eliminated or postponed or stretched

out in the hope of saving money, particularly in the tight places where labor is tight and commodities are tight, lumber and construction and those fields. But the whole field we will review. Now we do that nearly every month, but we will do it again tomorrow.

If we can impound anything that we don't have to spend, we will do it. In my judgment—I talked to the Chairman of the Appropriations Committee again this morning; I am in consultation with the men in the House and Senate Appropriations Committees nearly every week—I believe it is fair to assume that the committees and the Congress will not substantially, I am speaking in terms of billions now, reduce that $112 billion-plus budget.

I don't think they will reduce it. Now we are going to have a lot of speeches on it and we are going to have a lot of talking and there are going to be a good many handouts. They are going to say we ought to cut expenditures, but you cut one of these veterans hospitals and see what a buzzsaw you run into—or you eliminate some post office and you cut out some water project or you defer some of these things.

My judgment is that the money we have in the impacted areas, milk for children who can afford to pay for it, land-grant college aid, defense loans, some of those items we have cut, from the Record that I read every morning, they are going to be put back in.

I thought we could reduce them and have a new formula, because we would be putting more back in, in education, this year. I would like to have a million and a half children who have no school lunch at all to have a school lunch before a rich man's child gets milk at a subsidy. But I am not going to be unreasonable about it. Congress has their viewpoint and I have mine. I will

---

[10] See Item 159.

[11] Senator Russell B. Long of Louisiana, majority whip of the Senate.

try to reconcile them and try to keep it to a minimum of friction.

I don't think that we can reduce the present budget by billions. We will have to let time see. So you look at these men who tell you about how much they ought to reduce the budget. You say, "Okay, give me your bill of particulars." Then look at their roll call on the $41 million. Well, they did not have a roll call on that—excuse me, that was the $41 million addition—but look at the roll call on the GI bill, $300 million.

We have a bill up there for a wage increase. We have agreed to move the Government workers and the military along each year for wage increases within the 3.2 increased productivity. Last year, as you know, we increased both of those, the Congress did. I had to come back for several hundred million dollars more this year in a supplemental to pay for that over-riding. I hope they won't do that this year.

I have had a general understanding that we would try to stay to the guidelines, but there will be efforts to increase it. If I had to just make a prediction, and I was really anxious to keep as good a record as Drew Pearson [12] says he has, I would predict that the budget that finally comes to me in the form of an appropriation bill is increased over what we submitted.

Does that summarize what you want?

FBI CHARGES AGAINST DRAFT EVADERS

[11.] Q. Mr. President, yesterday the FBI filed some charges against some people who were involved in trying to evade the draft. Do you have some thoughts on a problem of this kind in the country today?

THE PRESIDENT. I don't understand that word—soughts? Oh, thoughts. No. I

saw that report. That is about the extent of my information on it, Sid.[13]

INFILTRATION BY NORTH VIETNAMESE

[12.] Q. Mr. President, there are reports that the North Vietnamese are infiltrating into the South in greater numbers. Can you comment on that?

THE PRESIDENT. Well, they are infiltrating into the South, and they are infiltrating in substantial numbers. They have been for some time. I think that is very evident. They are suffering very heavy casualties. They are attempting to find an answer to their problem there. They are bringing in a good many more people than they did in the early days of the conflict out there and for that reason, it has been necessary for us to do likewise.

But I believe last week they had the second largest week of casualties that the enemy has ever suffered out there. I think that the count of those actually killed by body count, plus those who die, according to our estimate from those wounded, will be in the neighborhood of 50,000 since the first of the year. I get that report each morning. Their dead by body count is in excess of 10,000. Their wounded is something we estimate at more than three times that much. They lose most of their wounded, and we lose less than 1 percent of ours.

NATO

[13.] Q. Mr. President, President de Gaulle has now set a specific timetable for withdrawal of NATO, of the NATO Command from France, and of French officers from the NATO Command. Do you have

---

[12] Author of the syndicated column "Washington Merry-Go-Round."

[13] Sid Davis of Westinghouse Broadcasting Co., Inc.

any comment on this?

THE PRESIDENT. No, I have no comment. We are keeping in constant touch with that situation. I have communicated my views to the General, and as he spells out his to us and to the other nations involved, we will receive them, consider them, and act appropriately. When we do, we will keep you fully informed.

U.S. FORCES IN VIETNAM

[14.] Q. Mr. President, does the increased infiltration by the North Vietnamese

indicate we may have to increase substantially our forces over there?

THE PRESIDENT. We will, as I told you last July, from time to time add to our forces in such numbers as our Joint Chiefs and General Westmoreland [14] may feel is desirable, and as the President may approve.

Merriman Smith, United Press International: Thank you, Mr. President.

NOTE: President Johnson's sixty-first news conference was held in the Cabinet Room at the White House at 12:50 p.m. on Thursday, March 31, 1966.

[14] Gen. William C. Westmoreland, Commander, United States Military Assistance Command, Vietnam.

---

159 Statement by the President Upon Signing Bill Authorizing Appropriations for the Coast Guard. *March 31, 1966*

I HAVE today approved H.R. 12762 which authorizes appropriations of $126,079,000 for the fiscal year 1967 for the procurement of vessels and aircraft and construction of shore and offshore establishments for the Coast Guard.

This authorization is $23,079,000 in excess of my request. These additional authorizations added by Congress are intended to accelerate the Coast Guard's vessel, aviation, shore units and housing replacement and augmentation programs.

The funds I requested for these programs in the 1967 budget are commensurate with the authorization originally requested, rather than the amounts included in H.R. 12762.

The funds the administration requested in the 1967 budget take into account the several long-range programs of the Coast Guard. The aviation program is being funded at an *increase* of $4 million over the 1966 level. In all respects except the establishment of

additional new helicopter air stations, accomplishment of the aviation program is on schedule. All necessary actions for safety and effectiveness of on-going aviation operations are being taken. The 1967 budget, moreover, provides for the sixth of a total of fifteen new air stations called for by the aviation program.

The program for shore units is in its initial year in 1966 with funding of $10.2 million. This is increased in the 1967 budget to $13.8 million.

Three hundred and ninety-nine sets of public family quarters are being budgeted in 1967 at a cost of $6.7 million. This substantial budget request follows closely the 1966 acquisition of 548 sets of quarters at Fort Jay on Governors Island, New York. Although the Coast Guard has been deficient in provision of housing for its families, very substantial progress will be continued at the budget level which was requested.

For the vessel replacement and augmentation program, three of the largest cutters are budgeted in 1967 just as three were budgeted in 1966.

The 1967 budget for vessels differs from that for 1966 primarily in that it makes no request for 210 foot length medium endurance vessels, five of which were included in 1966 funding. Sixteen of the new medium vessels have been funded thus far of a total program requirement of 30. It has become apparent that perhaps a smaller vessel can be employed effectively at lower cost in many of the situations for which 210 foot length vessels were originally planned. A 1-year pause in construction of these vessels is desirable in order to develop new plans.

Funds are provided in the 1967 budget for this planning and also for design of a ship for oceanographic work and for studies leading to the design of a class of replacement icebreakers.

In all areas other than new vessel construction the 1967 budget equals or exceeds that of 1966.

Thus, while I have approved this measure, I consider the funds requested for the Coast Guard in the 1967 budget adequate for Coast Guard operations. Therefore I do not intend to revise my budget request to fund this unnecessary increase.

NOTE: As enacted, the bill (H.R. 12762), approved by the President on March 30, is Public Law 89–381 (80 Stat. 96).

160   Remarks Upon Signing Bill Authorizing Medals Commemorating the 250th Anniversary of the Founding of San Antonio. *March 31, 1966*

Senator Yarborough, Representative Gonzalez:

I am most pleased that you could be here today for this very satisfying occasion.

This bill authorizes the striking of medals in commemoration of the 250th anniversary of the founding of San Antonio. The occasion is a proud one.

San Antonio is a great American city—rich in culture, traditions, and memories. It is a city founded on bravery and nurtured by determination.

It is a city that occupies a special place in the heart of every Texan—and really in the heart of every American. For me, it holds an even added significance. It was there that Mrs. Johnson and I were married 31 years ago.

But San Antonio is much more than just

a city of memories. It is a growing, vibrant, and exciting city, very much a part of 20th-century America. And that is the real meaning of this authorization. I am confident that it is a barometer that foretells the success of Hemisfair 1968 as an international exposition.

Hemisfair 1968 is San Antonio's way of telling the world that progress is the wave of its future. And this bill is the Nation's way of seconding the motion.

And so I sign this bill with best wishes for the future success of a great city and its splendid citizens.

NOTE: The President spoke at 1:40 p.m. in the President's office at the White House. His opening words referred to Senator Ralph Yarborough and Representative Henry B. Gonzalez, both of Texas. As enacted, the bill (H.R. 7526) is Public Law 89–382 (80 Stat. 98).

As printed above, this item follows the advance text released by the White House.

161 Letter to the President of the Senate and to the Speaker of the House Requesting Extension of the Medicare Enrollment Deadline. *March 31, 1966*

Dear Mr. President: (Dear Mr. Speaker:)

I would like to commend, for your early consideration, an amendment to the Social Security Act which would extend from March 31 to May 31 the deadline for enrollment in the medical insurance portion of the Social Security health insurance program for the aged.

As you know, the Social Security Administration has conducted an energetic campaign to inform all citizens who are already 65 that they must enroll by March 31 to be eligible for medical insurance coverage, which becomes effective July 1.

The results of this effort have been remarkable. More than 86% of the 19.1 million older people have already signed up; an additional 5% have responded by declining to enroll.

Despite this enormous response, there will be some older citizens who will want to enroll after March 31—because they did not act quickly enough, or because somehow they were not reached with news of this opportunity.

The present law permits enrollment after March 31—if there is good cause for the failure to enroll before the deadline. But under this provision, late enrollees cannot have protection for six months after enrollment.

I believe it would be unfortunate to delay protection to these late enrollees—some of whom are those with the greatest need for medical insurance.

Under my proposal, therefore, those enrolling in April and May would be eligible for protection on July 1 when the program goes into effect.

Enrollment of the remaining eligible citizens between March 31 and June 1 would present no administrative problems; there would still be one month between the deadline and the first payment of benefits.

I have asked the Secretary of Health, Education and Welfare to transmit to you the appropriate draft language for the amendment. I hope you will give it prompt and sympathetic consideration.

Sincerely,

LYNDON B. JOHNSON

NOTE: This is the text of identical letters addressed to the Honorable Hubert H. Humphrey, President of the Senate, and to the Honorable John W. McCormack, Speaker of the House of Representatives.

A bill extending the Medicare enrollment deadline was approved by the President on April 8, 1966 (see Item 168).

On March 6, 1966, the President signed Proclamation 3707 designating March as National Medicare Enrollment Month (2 Weekly Comp. Pres. Docs., p. 331; 31 F.R. 4191; 3 CFR, 1966 Comp., p. 30).

162 Letter Concerning Construction of Freeways in the District of Columbia. *April 1, 1966*

Dear Commissioner Tobriner:

Thank you for your letter of March 31, 1966, transmitting the statement of the Policy Advisory Committee on the plans for interstate freeways within the District of Columbia, and advising me that the Board of Commissioners has endorsed the statement of the Committee.

The Committee's decision to seek the aid of a consultant, and its unanimous statement following the consultant's report, are reassuring to me and will be reassuring to the Congress and the citizens of the District of Columbia. This review demonstrates that freeways, which the District must have, can and will be located and constructed in ways that reflect all significant community needs and values. I hope that the necessary funds will speedily be made available.

Sincerely,

LYNDON B. JOHNSON

[Hon. Walter N. Tobriner, President, Board of Commissioners, District of Columbia, Washington, D.C.]

NOTE: Commissioner Tobriner's letter was made public by the White House along with the President's reply.

The Policy Advisory Committee, which had undertaken the study on January 19 at the President's request, recommended "that certain freeway projects, for which construction is either underway or imminent, should proceed without delay, and that future project plans be reviewed with increased emphasis on the reduction of the impact of such construction on our communities."

Mr. Tobriner's letter stated that the Commissioners "strongly support actions to reduce such community impact in the District of Columbia, even though the obvious measures that are contemplated by the Committee will undoubtedly result in increased construction costs."

The complete text of the letter is printed in the Weekly Compilation of Presidential Documents (vol. 2, p. 487).

The 3-page "Statement of the Policy Advisory Committee on Current Freeway Plans for the District of Columbia," dated March 31, 1966, was made available with the text of the letters.

163 Statement by the President on the 17th Anniversary of the North Atlantic Treaty Organization. *April 4, 1966*

SEVENTEEN YEARS AGO today, with the signing of the North Atlantic Treaty, the Western nations drew together in a historic undertaking to safeguard the freedom, common heritage, and civilization of our peoples.

For the United States this meant rounding the last corner on the long road from self-imposed isolation to full acceptance of our responsibilities in the world. For our allies the North Atlantic Treaty signified a departure, no less historic, from traditional pursuit of national interests narrowly construed. In the treaty we together acknowledged a common destiny and the duty to pursue it together.

We decided that if we didn't hang together, we would hang separately. Nearly two decades of time have demonstrated the wisdom of those who read the lesson for the future in two world catastrophes out of the past.

The Atlantic alliance deterred the threatened aggression which brought it into being.

Behind the military bulwark it raised from the Black Sea to the North Cape, an era of unprecedented growth and well-being began.

Within the framework of security it provided, the vision of a united Europe became a practical undertaking, now far advanced.

The Atlantic alliance has succeeded perhaps better than its founders dared hope. Yet we must never forget why it has prospered.

The unique quality of the alliance for peace lies in the joining of sovereign nations in an integrated system of collective defense. We and our partners, in painstaking effort, created the peacetime planning agencies and integrated military commands called the North Atlantic Treaty Organization. These institutions afford practical assurance that aggression would be met by allies acting at once and as one. They have insured the peoples of the Atlantic community 17 years of peace.

NATO was created as an instrument of peace. Its objectives are to remove temptation to aggression and to provide the foundation for seeking a settlement in Central Europe, based on the principle of self-determination, providing increased security for East and West alike. Every lesson of our common experience argues that these objectives should be pursued in closest concert.

Together with 13 other allied nations, we have declared our resolve to carry on, to strengthen and perfect our NATO system

in this constructive spirit. We shall not abandon an institution which has proved itself in the hour of peril.

We look forward to the day when unity of action in the Western family is fully reestablished and our common interests and aspirations are again expressed through institutions which command universal support among us.

NOTE: For President Truman's address on April 4, 1949, at the signing of the North Atlantic Treaty, see "Public Papers of the Presidents, Harry S. Truman, 1949," Item 68. See also President Johnson's address on the North Atlantic Treaty Organization delivered before the Foreign Service Institute on March 23, 1966, Item 142 above.

164   Remarks at a Program in Recognition of Cost Reduction Achievements by the Department of Agriculture. *April 5, 1966*

Secretary Freeman, Chairman Cooley, Congressman Michel, distinguished award winners, and my friends in the Department of Agriculture:

First of all, I want to thank the Secretary for asking me to come here and share this pleasure with you this morning. And I want to thank each of you for the high honor that you have achieved, the success that has attended your efforts, the results that have come your way, and those that are still in the offing.

I want to personally and publicly express my deep satisfaction and pleasure to the House of Representatives. As I said to the distinguished Speaker and majority leader yesterday, I am very proud of Chairman Cooley and Congressman Michel and the other Members of the great Committee on Agriculture for their constructive and prompt action in connection with our food for India resolution which we submitted, it just seems, a few hours ago.

They have already considered it, had their hearings, reported it, and passed it without a roll call. That is the way I like to see them handle legislation in the House of Representatives, Harold.

The farmers of America, because of their ingenuity, because of their diligence, their hard work, their stick-to-it-iveness, their desire to give a value received, have given us an abundance that we can now, as good friends of all the peoples of the world, help to supply our neighbors in need.

There is no greater satisfaction that can come to any human being than the one that came to us the other day, when we learned of the possibility of some millions of people dying of famine in India this year, when we could open our warehouses to them and take the fruits of our bounty and the products of our labor over the years that we had stored, and share part of it with them and still have sufficient reserves on hand to take care of our own people.

I am very proud of the way Secretary Freeman has administered the Department of Agriculture. He has shown imagination and he has shown diligence. He has shown a prudence and a thrift that makes him one of the greatest administrators that this Government has ever known. He has always looked after the interests of the farmer, but he has not been unaware of the interests of all Americans.

I just asked him a few minutes ago, when they were talking to me about saving $15 million in storage rates, "How much do you spend in the Department of Agriculture just storing surpluses?" The man that answered me said, "When Mr. Freeman came in, the taxpayers were spending $400 million a year on storage costs. We are spending $200 million a year now."

That means that we have disposed of some of the stuff we had in storage. That means we have improved on the storage, we have improved on the rates. And the net result is that the taxpayer is spending just half as much now as he did when the Secretary took office.

In all of these economies and all of these good management practices, each employee of the Department of Agriculture can justly take pride. As public servants we know, or at least we ought to know, that the habits that we are most in need of reforming are our own, although Mark Twain used to say that nothing so needs reforming as the other people's habits.

Our Government is very complex and times change. It keeps us busy trying to keep up with the needs of the moment and of the hour. Old ways quickly become inefficient ways, and inefficiency leads to waste. We have a war on waste and we are trying to prove to the people who work in Government that we just cannot afford the waste that we have been enjoying in the years past.

I believe that waste is a crime. I believe that waste is against our freedom. I believe that waste is against our progress. Thus, I believe that waste is against the American people. So I have said that controlling waste is like bailing a boat; you have to keep at it. There is no time to rest. All of our great dreams, all of our visions, and all of our plans will come to nothing if we do not press forward with our reforms.

We are a rich and expanding nation. We are the wealthiest nation in the world, the healthiest nation in the world, the best educated nation, and the one that I think has the most to really be thankful for. We are educating our young, we are caring for our sick, we are providing opportunities for our poor, we are rebuilding our cities, we are beautifying our country, we are exploring the heavens—and Mrs. Johnson is exploring the Rio Grande, I see from the morning paper.

But nevertheless, in doing all these things we have to sometimes drag some of our most respected and our best intentioned colleagues and get them by the neck and drag them every step of the way. These efforts I think are vital to our future and the future of this world, but they have a price tag attached because progress never comes cheaply. Our citizens should be willing to pay that price because they have shown their willingness time and time again to do that.

Some of our people feared the socialism of social security. Well, that's when I came to town. And I remember the horror that some Congressmen expressed before we passed the first social security bill, although there were really less than a dozen of them voted against it when we called the roll back in 1935. But some feared the socialism of social security. And a good many, I remember, spoke for a number of years about the Fair Deal of Medicare. But they are here, both of them. Thank God the status quo did not prevail.

Now I see here this morning that the status quo is not prevailing. You are reforming, you are improving. A year ago last November, at the first Cabinet meeting following my election to the Presidency, I said that "as a nation, we cannot afford to waste a single dollar out of our resources on old programs which once may have been essential, but which time and events have overtaken."

So I have come here this morning because a great Cabinet officer and his entire Department have taken that directive to heart. Under Orville Freeman's leadership, with the help of Jane, this Department became one of the great leaders of all the civilian agencies—and she made more than her 50 percent contribution, too, Orville.

I am glad to honor these Special Award Merit winners today because you show that you have a determination to build a great record here. I have noted, for example, that your new packaging methods for dried milk will save $120,000 a year. Now, none of these cost-cutting ideas was in practice when we first declared the war on waste. These ideas came from Federal employees. They came from people who work for their Government who have ingenuity and imagination.

The record of the Department of Agriculture shows that effective and efficient Government is responsive and warm and concerned with our people. That is why I wanted to come by this morning, to say thanks to each of you for what you have done, and to tell you that I will be watching in the days ahead for any improvements that you can make. I wanted to let you know that all the people in this land are grateful to you for not being satisfied

with that old, worn-out phrase, "Well, we have always done it this way." You are looking up, not down. You are moving ahead, not backward. And that truly is the real strength of our Government.

I think every person in this room, and every person in this country, should be grateful for the great production record that the farmers of this Nation have made. They have given us food when we needed it, quality that has never been excelled; they have given us an abundance that not only will take care of all of our needs, but will make it possible for us to help the other starving millions of people of the world.

I was talking to the Prime Minister of India. And when I left her and returned to the Mansion I realized that except for the great work that the farmers of America had done, and the great work that the Department of Agriculture had done in counseling, in guiding, and in helping them, that more people would starve in India this year than live in both North Vietnam and South Vietnam. So that's a record that you can be proud of.

I see that your committee in the House, as I just observed, is equally as efficient. It believes in cost consciousness. It believes in saving money. Otherwise, it could have taken 2 or 3 weeks around here, hearing my India bill the other day. They reported it out promptly. I hope the Senate committee will follow your example, Mr. Cooley, and save money by acting on this measure before the Easter holidays.

Now one little thought I want to leave with you before I get away: One of my assistants just reminded me that this morning the last employee in the White House signed up to buy a savings bond. That gave us a 100 percent record. Just a few days ago we were under the Department of Agriculture. You had 42 percent of your people that bought bonds and we had 41. And we started doing something about it.

Of course, we don't have as many people over at the White House as you have in the Department of Agriculture, and maybe I was a little more persuasive with them than I can be with you.

I know the problems that all of us have in this day of rising costs, when we are trying to meet all the needs of our families, but we have men out in Vietnam who have made great sacrifices and are making great sacrifices for us. At this particular time we have launched a savings bond program. We want it to go well in the country, and I just hope the Government can set a good example.

I have raised the interest rates so that you can get a fair return on your investment. I think that if you can possibly spare the money, it would be a good thing for you to do for yourself and for your family. I know it will be a good thing to do for your country. So I hope that I may be able to come back here in the not too distant future and

have the Secretary tell me that that 42 percent record of yours may not have been improved as much as our few employees improved mine over at the White House, but at least improved it enough to justify my coming back and thanking you.

Goodby.

NOTE: The President spoke at 10:15 a.m. on the patio at the Department of Agriculture after presenting awards to 37 employees of the Department who were credited with ideas that saved more than $26 million in Federal funds. In his opening words he referred to Orville L. Freeman, Secretary of Agriculture, Representative Harold D. Cooley of North Carolina, Chairman of the House Committee on Agriculture, and Representative Robert H. Michel of Illinois, member of the agriculture subcommittee of the House Committee on Appropriations.

During his remarks the President referred to Representative John W. McCormack of Massachusetts, Speaker of the House of Representatives, Senator Mike Mansfield of Montana, majority leader of the Senate, Mrs. Orville L. (Jane) Freeman, wife of the Secretary of Agriculture, and Mrs. Indira Gandhi, Prime Minister of India, who had recently completed a visit to the United States (see Items 148, 149, 152).

For a statement by the President upon signing the resolution supporting U.S. participation in food relief for India, see Item 180.

165 Remarks at a Ceremony Honoring Mrs. Mona M. Dayton as "Teacher of the Year." *April 5, 1966*

Mrs. Dayton, Secretary Gardner, Mr. Dubinsky, my friends:

I am delighted to be here with you this morning to pay this very just tribute to this very dedicated lady.

My thoughts, like those of many Americans these days, are very much on battles and soldiers and the bitter necessities of war. But I am very delighted this morning to take a moment away from these concerns, although not completely away.

I thought this morning of something that General Omar Bradley said many years ago. I was just reading his book the other

day describing the landing on Normandy.[1] General Bradley said, "The teacher is the real soldier of democracy. Others can defend it, but only he can make it work."

So we are here today to honor a woman who makes democracy work. She is a soldier in the greatest and the most glorious battle that man has ever fought—the battle for the truth and the understanding that alone has set man free, and that will, alone and ultimately, keep men free.

This is the third time that I have honored

[1] "A Soldier's Story" (New York: Henry Holt & Co., Inc., 1951).

such a soldier as Teacher of the Year, but never, I think, have Look magazine and the Council of Chief State School Officers made a more deserving or a better choice. We have certainly never honored a more unusual teacher than the remarkable and renowned lady we have come here this morning to congratulate, Mrs. Mona Dayton of Tucson, Arizona.

She has done more than just teach her first graders how to read and write. She has taken the great outdoors of Tucson as her classroom, and the great desert as her desk. She has taken the animals as her teaching assistants, and she has taken nature and beauty by one hand, and boys and girls by the other, and she has made them dance together in a happy circle of understanding and respect.

In Mrs. Dayton's class, I am told that there are a number of 6-year-old scientists who know how to build a sun dial and know how to construct a model volcano. That is very impressive. When I was 6 years old I knew little about model volcanoes, but I have learned a lot since then from sitting on top of the real thing.

Mrs. Dayton, your remarkable class also contains, I am informed, some young naturalists. Their classmates, I hear, include an owl and a 6-foot boa constrictor. I had better not let Mrs. Johnson and Liz Carpenter hear about that or they will take another tour to Arizona from Big Bend. And I am happy that that boa constrictor is not here with you today.

But Mrs. Dayton has opened the eyes and the ears of her first graders so much that there are poets among them. A little girl named Karen described a night in the desert, and this is the way she described it:

"Stardust on the cactus,
Owls in their nest,
Birds listening to your words in the wind."

This child and her teacher help explain why Government has increased its commitment to education and to training, since I became President, from a little less than $5 billion to a little over $10 billion in less than 3 years.

Today Mrs. Dayton receives a pin and a plaque which symbolize her honor. I know that she shares my view that in this day and age we can get no more value from every dollar we spend than that we spend on education and on health.

I was looking at the figures with my Budget Director this morning. The last 3 years we have taken our health expenditures in the Nation from a little under $5 billion to a little over $10 billion, and it is paying such rich dividends in the solutions and the answers we are finding to disease.

So, Mrs. Dayton, you receive my congratulations. I also want to appoint you this morning to serve on the commission which will select next year's Presidential Scholars here at the White House. America's teachers are not only making democracy work, they are helping it to flourish and to triumph, and they deserve our gratitude, for as it has been said, "Through the teacher's hands pass all members of every profession."

I am so glad that you could be here with us, and you could be hearing some of these things that you deserve during your lifetime. I have with me this morning a teacher that I started out teaching with in the first school I taught in many years ago, Mrs. Opal Way Brooks.

Come over, Mrs. Brooks. I want you to meet Mrs. Dayton. She and I both taught in the same school a few years ago.

And Mrs. Brooks, I want you to know another teacher. He is a retired man. He is here with me this morning and I want him to come over and meet you—Mr. Dubinsky. He has been teaching me for about 30 years, too. Now he is going away. They said he retired while he could still read his obituaries. He is going to be away for about 7 weeks and then he is going to come back to us.

NOTE: The President spoke at 12:05 p.m. in the Cabinet Room at the White House. In his opening words he referred to Mrs. Mona M. Dayton, a first grade teacher from Tucson, Ariz., John W. Gardner, Secretary of Health, Education, and Welfare, and David Dubinsky, outgoing President of the Inter-

national Ladies Garment Workers Union. During his remarks he referred to, among others, Mrs. Elizabeth S. Carpenter, Press Secretary and Staff Director for the First Lady, and Mrs. Opal Way Brooks, of Pearsall, Texas.

Mrs. Dayton was chosen "Teacher of the Year" from a group of finalists selected by a screening committee of national educational leaders. The National Teacher of the Year Award is sponsored annually by Look magazine in cooperation with the Council of Chief State School Officers, an organization of State superintendents and commissioners of education.

166 Remarks Upon Accepting the Special Albert Lasker Award for Leadership in Health. *April* 7, 1966

Mrs. Lasker, Dr. DeBakey, Dr. Rusk, members of the awards committee, members of the Lasker Foundation, and distinguished guests:

I come here this morning to accept gratefully the 1965 Albert Lasker Award for Leadership in Health, but I want to make it clear to all of those who participate in this ceremony, and to all of those who may read of it, that I share this honor with the Members of the 88th and 89th Congresses who played such an important part in translating our recommendations and our proposals into reality.

They have declared that not only life but a healthy life must be among man's inalienable rights. Since I became your President a little over 2 years ago, we have increased our Federal investment in education from a little less than $5 billion to a little more than $10 billion per year. Since I became your President a little over 2 years ago, we have increased your investment in health from a little less than $5 billion to a little over $10 billion this year.

Now this is not just a box score figure. It means that this coming year we will spend $10 billion more on education and health than we were spending when I became Pres-

ident. It means we will have reduced death and disability. It will mean a longer lifespan for our people. It means that we will triumph over the preventable or controllable diseases which still afflict our citizens.

We have the lowest loss rate per wounded soldiers that any army ever had on a battlefield. In Vietnam we are losing less than 1 out of every 100 men who are wounded. The enemy is losing a much, much higher percentage. And that one we are losing is less than half of what we lost in Korea. That speaks for the great advances that the science of medicine and the great skill that the doctors and surgeons have displayed in that area of the world.

Where income and productivity are lowest in America, disease, disability, and death are highest in America. As family incomes decline, infant mortality ruthlessly goes up. And when medical care is dispensed, the 15 million children of the poor always await at the end of the line. But we mean to change that. We cannot stop there, because every single minute in the underprivileged two-thirds of the world 20 people die of malaria and smallpox and cholera and other infectious diseases.

During the few minutes that I am speaking to you this morning, 100 persons, 100 of our fellow human beings, will die of ailments that we have learned to control in the first 50 years of this century. In the underdeveloped two-thirds of the world, the average life span is only 35 years, 35 years that is very often plagued with a great deal of what is, today, unnecessary suffering.

That is why, when we were making our studies last year of our aid programs, when some of you were attending me at Bethesda, we decided then that instead of participating, as we had been, to the extent of trying to industrialize some nations, trying to improve their communications, trying to build them concrete highways, and so forth, that we would direct our efforts to those who would help themselves and help themselves particularly in the field of improving the body and health, improving the mind with schools, and improving the human being with food.

So we are concentrating our energies and our aid program and our investment in the world today on education, on health, and on food.

We had a great demonstration of the Congress' ability to act, and act wisely, thoroughly, and somewhat promptly in the measure that they completed yesterday—the Indian food resolution whereby the people of America will send to India something in the neighborhood of $1 billion worth of food to help feed some 35 or 40 million people who might not pull through at all without this food.

The thing that gave me such great pride was that there in the Congress, made up of 535 Members—members of both parties, members of both sexes, members of several races—there was not a single vote cast against that bill in either House. That

speaks not only for the intelligence of the Congress and the foresight of the Congress, but the compassion of the American people.

So I submitted to Congress the International Health Act of 1966, an act which will create an international career service to health, an act which will help our health professionals strengthen medical training and gain valuable experience in the developing countries. It will combat malnutrition, it will help conquer disease which disables millions of people. It aims at eradicating smallpox by 1975, at freeing 800 million people from malaria in the next 10 years, of sharply curtailing measles and cholera.

The magnitude of this task will make the work of the last 50 years, great as it has been, seem very small. Our work in health is tragically incomplete.

Now, I know some of you are going to remind me that we didn't get a rule on that health bill the other day. We didn't expect to get a rule that day. That never did get in our report. Two of our Members left early because they didn't anticipate a vote. And when they did vote, because they were not there the rule was not reported.

But somehow or other I kind of have a feeling that the reporters will get two stories for the price of one—we may get that bill reported some of these days and I know that all of you will join with me in expressing the hope that we do.

So this morning I accept this award with a pledge that every dollar of it will go to charitable causes in the field of health and education. I accept this award with the hope that we can do more at home and then—with all the power of my mind and my voice and my hand—try to turn the vision of the American people beyond the borders of the United States and turn it to the lands where suffering people await answers that only the leadership of America can give.

Years ago Louis Pasteur said, "I hold the unconquerable belief that science and peace will triumph over ignorance and war; that nations will come together not to destroy, but to construct; and that the future belongs to those who accomplish most for humanity."

What will we accomplish for humanity? Well, I am so proud that Mrs. Lasker and her distinguished and beloved and generous husband, who came from my State of Texas, have already accomplished much for humanity with their leadership and with their generosity. And as long as there are lives to be saved, as long as there are bodies to be healed, as long as there are mouths to be fed, I cannot for a moment ever forget that history will judge us, and she is looking over our shoulder now.

I know, too, that Mary Lasker and the members of this distinguished jury will never let the people of this land forget it. I could observe that they are going to want me to spend more money than I can spend this year, but I guess if I have to get overridden

on anything I hope that the generosities will be displayed in the fields of food for our children, education for their minds, and health, medicine, doctor and dental care for their bodies, because there is so much in this world to do and there is such a little time that we have to do it.

Thank you all.

NOTE: The President spoke at 11:15 a.m. in the Cabinet Room at the White House. In his opening words he referred to Mrs. Albert D. (Mary) Lasker, cofounder of the Albert and Mary Lasker Foundation for medical research, Dr. Michael E. DeBakey of Houston, Texas, former Chairman of the President's Commission on Heart Disease, Cancer and Stroke, who presented the award to the President, and Dr. Howard Rusk, Director of the Institute of Physical Medicine and Rehabilitation, New York University, and former member of the Commission.

The award consisted of a gold statue of Winged Victory on a marble base which bore the following inscription: "The 1965 Special Albert Lasker Award presented by the Albert and Mary Lasker Foundation to Lyndon Baines Johnson, President of the United States, for outstanding contributions to Health Legislation for all Americans through Medicare, Medical Education and Research."

The Indian food resolution referred to was approved by the President on April 19 (see Item 180).

The proposed International Health Act of 1966 was not adopted by the 89th Congress.

---

167 Letter to Archbishop Lucey Presenting Him With a Memory Book Recording the Occasion of His 50th Anniversary Luncheon. *April 8, 1966*

Your Excellency:

Four weeks ago, business and civic leaders of San Antonio honored you at a luncheon observing your fiftieth year as a priest, and your twenty-fifth year as Archbishop of San Antonio.

It was with great regret that I was unable to attend and participate in so memorable an occasion.

However, I am pleased to find that I will

have a part in this event, after all.

On behalf of the Luncheon Committee, it is my great pleasure to present to you this bound volume . . . a memory book of the luncheon. It is signed by all who attended.

Sincerely,

LYNDON B. JOHNSON

[The Most Reverend Robert E. Lucey, Archbishop of San Antonio, 2826 Old Moss Street, San Antonio, Texas]

168 Remarks in San Antonio at the Signing of the Medicare Extension Bill. *April 8, 1966*

Congressman Gonzalez, Your Excellency Archbishop Lucey, Mr. Mayor, Judge, other public officials, ladies and gentlemen:

First, I want to explain that the reason Henry took so much time was because I asked him to. Henry said that he had a little statement of about 2½ minutes, and I told Henry this was my day off, this was Good Friday, that I had come to San Antonio at my own invitation. Nobody had asked me to come here. I came because I wanted to. I wanted to because I get a great deal of pleasure out of returning to the scenes of my childhood—as you can observe by my frequent visits back to the Pedernales.

And then there are other reasons, too. I wanted to see Archbishop Lucey, and I wanted to be with him today as he has been with me for almost 30 years now.

I remember what my father said to me about public service when I was a little boy walking around, following him barefooted and standing there in the hot sand of Blanco County, and squeezing the dirt up between my toes. He used to say to me, "Son, if you are to speak for people, you must know them, and if you are to represent people, you must love them."

Now sometimes among our more sophisticated, self-styled intellectuals—I say self-styled advisedly; the real intellectual I am not sure would ever feel this way—some of them are more concerned with appearance than they are with achievement. They are more concerned with style than they are with mortar, brick, and concrete. They are more concerned with the trivia and the superficial than they are with the things that have really built America.

I received a good deal of my political philosophy right here in San Antonio. Before I was born, my father was writing the bill—my grandfather wrote it because my father asked him to, as he wasn't a lawyer—my father was introducing a bill and speaking for the bill that saved the Alamo. It was being torn down and a hotel would have replaced the Alamo. And he got a good lady to put up enough money long enough to hold the structure until the legislature could pass a bill to preserve the Alamo. That was in 1905. I was born in 1908, I believe.

Thirty-five years ago I took my first train trip out of Texas and it originated here in San Antonio. I went to Washington from San Antonio as an employee of the people of San Antonio, in this district—the first time I had ever crossed the boundary of this State in a train.

It took me 3 days to get there, and I had a chance to do some heavy thinking en route. Hitler was on the march. We were in the depths of the depression. We knew nothing about old age assistance or Medicare or social security. People were starving. Farms were being foreclosed. The hungry and the unemployed lined our streets. And most of our political leaders seemed to be oblivious to what was happening.

I remember the first slum clearance housing bill that President Roosevelt signed. I was one of two Congressmen at that signing ceremony. I guess that is the reason I have always liked these signing ceremonies since.

I remember the first project under that bill came to Texas, where people could have public housing, cheap housing, clean housing, decent housing, for their children to sleep in.

We had a three-bedroom home with a

living room-dining room combination, a kitchen, and a bath, for $14 a month. It was the cheapest constructed project in the United States and the cheapest rent.

Today I have great pride in it. And that is why I am working so hard to get some more housing under our supplemental rent subsidy.

I remember Archbishop Lucey, and he wasn't nearly as respectable then as he is now—he was kind of a Bolshevik in the minds of a lot of people when he came down here—but I remember his writing me and quarreling and fussing and just doing everything that he could do to try to help do something for these women that were picking pecans in San Antonio for 8 cents an hour, poor women working all day for 60 cents—picking pecans for 8 cents an hour.

That is why I was one of three Congressmen from Texas that signed the petition back in the thirties to force a vote to discharge a committee, to bring the wage and hour bill out—a bill that would guarantee not 8 cents an hour but the magnificent sum of 25 cents an hour! And there were only three Texans signed that petition and two of them got defeated at the next election. I just point that up, that was a 25-cent minimum wage bill, to show you how far we have come.

I have a recommendation before the Congress now for $1.60.

But Maury Maverick voted for that 25 cents and W. D. McFarlane voted for it, and both of them got beaten in the next election.

I remember the Social Security Act that we are talking about today. When they called the roll on it, I believe it was in 1935, I remember a good friend of mine was worrying about whether he should vote for it or not. He said, "It is socialism. They are going to destroy our system of government."

I pled with him not for minutes but for hours in the Speaker's office, trying to convince him that it was a constructive and far-reaching measure.

I remember up here by the Maverick Cafeteria, in the building in downtown San Antonio, standing out there in 1935 and seeing little Mexican children go up to the garbage can outside that cafeteria and take the grapefruit hulls out of that garbage can, and try to get enough food in their body to sustain them by hulling the hulls. I saw that with my own eyes and I have not forgotten it.

I came back here again today to see how the people of San Antonio live, because I can't forget that you can't speak for them if you don't know them, and you can't represent them if you don't love them.

So I told Henry I wanted him to take whatever time he needed. If any of you want to leave you can leave. If any of you are in a hurry you can go on. I stay in a hurry all the time. I am back home now and I am not going to hurry. I am going to do what I like to do.

This great city has meant a lot to me, not only in my political philosophy, but a good deal of other philosophy. Here is where I was married, and here is where I have been elected. I would never have been in the United States Senate except for the people of San Antonio. In the first primary I lost this county by 12,000 votes, and that is before they really realized how tough the election was on the West Side. In the second primary I carried it by 99, instead of losing it by 12,000. That gave me the great victory of 87 in the entire State of Texas. I remember that. And I see a lot of the veterans of that campaign here.

I am so proud of San Antonio because of your interest in human beings, in humanity, and in good, constructive causes that

405

advance the best interest of the people—
p-e-e-p-u-l—the poor people of this country.

There is not one single Congressman in
the House of Representatives of 435, including the Speaker, the Leader, and the
Whip, that has a better record than Henry
Gonzalez, and I am so proud of him. I
am proud that I had enough courage to
come here before he was a Congressman,
when he was a defeated candidate a time or
two, and speak for him after President
Eisenhower had come in ahead of me to
speak on the other side, and to do what little
I could to express my faith in Henry. He
has justified it every moment since.

For your own personal information, I
will say he is one Congressman that has
never had his arm twisted even the slightest. I have never called him on the telephone and asked for his vote or told him how
I would like for him to vote, and I have
never allowed anybody else to do it, because it is a pure waste of time. Henry was
born and grew up and learned how to vote
before he ever came to Washington. And
when you get men like that, you don't have
to counsel them.

So we come here now to sign this bill
today, and I come with both a pledge and
a plea. My plea is to 1⅓ million Americans
that are over 65 years of age and that are
not yet covered by Medicare. The pledge
is to those citizens who missed the March
31st deadline, just past, and did not enroll
in Medicare, and now, under this legislation,
they will have until May 31st to sign up
because of what Henry, Senator Yarborough, and Members of the House and Senate did in passing this bill we will sign this
morning.

I want to ask each of you to make it your
personal job not to come to me or to Henry
a few years from now and say they just for-
got to sign up, or they didn't hear about it,
but for you to go out and get them to sign
up now while they have the time and while
they can qualify.

The plea is that these citizens contact
their local Social Security offices and consider signing up for the valuable protection
that the Medicare law will give them.

So I plead with every American to go and
talk to your neighbors, because there are
1,300,000 of them that are going to miss the
boat; there are 1,300,000 of them who should
get their rights under the law now. And
in order to do that, they must sign up. So
each good American should accept this personal challenge to ask every person they
know over 65, "Have you registered? If
not, register at once."

There was a wise old Frenchman one
time who said that growing older is no more
than a bad habit which a busy man has no
time to form. So this morning I urge every
American to exercise his right and to acquire
this protection.

My friends here in this beautiful Victoria
Plaza, you are a model for the rest of the
citizens of this Nation. I think that those
guests this morning should know that every
single man and woman who lives here is
already registered for Medicare.

Since I signed the Medicare and Social
Security Amendments last July in Independence, Missouri, in the presence of that great
Democratic President, and his wife, Harry
S. Truman—you will remember that President Truman was the first President who
actively urged this particular program—
since that time, almost 17 million Americans,
almost 9 out of every 10 of our older citizens,
have already enrolled for medical insurance
coverage.

Getting 17 million to do something from
July to now is a man-sized job, itself. But

we still have 1,300,000 to go. And I am not going to let you forget it until we get every one of them signed up.

Our work is not going to be completed until we are sure that everyone who can use the protection of this program has joined it. Every older American must have the opportunity to live out his life in security without the fear that serious illness will be accompanied by a financial ruin.

That is what Medicare is all about. What to do? How to live? Who will pay the doctor? Who will pay the hospital? Who will pay for the medicine? Who will pay the rent? Well, these are questions that older Americans that I have known all of my life have dreaded to answer. Now Medicare is changing a lot of that.

There is hope because we respect the dignity of the individual. I thought that some of our sophisticated folks might say this morning that Henry was introducing too many people. That is why I told him to take all the time he wanted. But that just shows how he feels about human beings. He didn't want one single person to be neglected. He wanted to recognize the dignity of every person here, because they might be pretty unimportant to a stranger but they are not unimportant to Henry or to me. They lead our people and they provide for them.

So I think that we must have hope and we must recognize that there is in the place of charity now dignity, and where the children, the kinfolks, and the public agencies were the sole reliance just a few months ago, you now can have self-respect and realize that the machinery of government and the methods that we have evolved, the contributions of the individuals and the Government altogether—you can now have self-respect and still provide for your medical bills and

your medicine, your nursing care, and things of that kind.

We have taken the bitter years that I talked about in the early thirties and I think we have made them better years. In the doing, we have reclaimed, I think, a lot of lost pride and we have given a lot of new meaning to tomorrow.

As I sign this bill today, I am determined to do more. I don't think that we must ever be satisfied in this growing, adventuresome country of America with the status quo. We must be determined to do more, because there is always going to be more that needs to be done.

Since I became President a little over 2 years ago, I have already signed and approved laws increasing social security benefits by more than $1½ billion—increases of more than $1½ billion, an increase of in the neighborhood of 7 percent. Yet too many of our older citizens are still trying to get along on income that is too small now to meet their needs, even though we have increased it 7 percent in 2 years.

So social security benefits which are the main source of their income still need to be increased, and they will be increased in the years ahead. Only by recognizing the facts of life can we really make it better for people that are over 65.

Social security protection must be improved for our disabled workers and for their families. Several weeks ago I asked the Secretary of Health, Education, and Welfare, Mr. John W. Gardner, to complete his study as soon as possible on improving the benefits and the financial structure of the social security program.

I asked Secretary Gardner to develop sound and workable plans for these changes at as early a date as possible. Because—I will let you in on a secret—I intend to make these recommendations to the next session of Congress, and I expect you folks to have Henry back up there to help me get them passed.

Now I can't tell you about all the recommendations because we are now studying them. I want you to study them and let us hear from you. But this is what I would like to do: I would like to increase insurance benefits across the board for 21 million beneficiaries—the aged, the disabled, the widows, and the orphans, including an increase in the monthly minimum, the monthly maximum, and the total family benefits. That is what I would like to do.

We don't have a dictatorship, so no man can mash a button and get it done, but that is what I would like to do, what I hope to do, what I want to do, and with your help and with God's help, that is what we will do.

I would like to improve insurance protection for the widows and the orphans. I would like to keep our social security and public welfare programs up to date in relation to increased earnings.

I would like for our individuals now on welfare rolls to be provided additional incentives for them to find work.

And Medicare need not just be for people over 65. That is where we started.

Archbishop, you know, I have been wondering for some time now why we shouldn't bring our compassion and our concern to bear not just on people over 65 but upon our young children under 6.

The President of an African country told me the other day—I had lunch with a bunch of their Ambassadors yesterday and we discussed it again—in their country that one out of three babies born died with measles, and the United States of America had come in with one of our most modern 20th century machines and had vaccinated 750,000 little children.

The President of this African country said to me, "We men may not always like some of the things you in America do, but our women would never let us criticize them because since you vaccinated those 750,000 children we have not lost one from measles."

The satisfaction that I get from believing that we in America saved the lives of 250,000 little children is a satisfaction that never comes from a paycheck or a greenback.

And I want to let you in on another secret: That is one of the reasons I asked John Gardner, because of my concern for these young folks—the Secretary of Health, Education, and Welfare—to create new plans for a new program that you haven't ever had before, to assist in financing dental services for children.

Luci spent all the way down here this morning fussing at me because I didn't say eye services for children. Because Luci was almost ready to get married before she found out she couldn't read very well, that she had had something wrong with her eyes since she was a child. When she corrected it, and found it out, why, it was reflected the next month in her grades, and I think in her looks. She not only couldn't see how to read well, but she couldn't see how to look well.

So we are going to have these new plans and we are going to have these new programs. And we are going to someday point out that we started them right here at this scene this morning. We are never going to stop trying to find new ways to make Medicare sensitive to what our people need, and make it sensitive to what we ought to do to lift the quality of life in this land and in this world.

I have 3 minutes to get to church and I want to conclude by saying this, because this is one of the things that the church does, and does so well: I am not interested in building skyscrapers or moving mountains or pouring concrete. Those are all necessary in the modern world of communication and industrialization, and so forth. But since I have become President we have increased our expenditure for educating the mind from a little less than $5 billion to over $10 billion in 2½ years. We have more than doubled it.

We have increased our expenditures on health from a little under $5 billion—we were spending $1 billion when President Kennedy came into office—to a little over $10 billion this year. This is part of it here—more than double. So $10 billion extra this year goes into the mind and the body. Considering our loans, our grants, our aid, and our Public Law 480, and other things, we are spending additional billions on food.

So when everything else is gone and forgotten, I hope the people will remember that in this year of our Lord 1966, on Good Friday, we met here as neighbors and friends, and we concerned ourselves about human beings, and we dedicated whatever time is left for us, we dedicated our efforts and our talents to freeing the ignorant from the chains of ignorance and illiteracy, and teaching them to read and write, and to learn.

Whatever time is allotted us, we have tried to remove disease from the skins and the bodies of our people, and we have tried to find food to give them nourishment and to give them strength.

And if I am ever to be remembered by any of you here, I want to be remembered as one who spent his whole life trying to get more people more to eat and more to wear, to live longer, to have medicine and have attention, nursing, hospital and doctors' care when they need it, and to have their children have a chance to go to school and carry

out really what the Declaration of Independence says, "All men are created equal."

But they are not equal if they don't have a chance to read and write, and they don't have a chance for a doctor to take care of their teeth or their eyes when they are little and their parents don't know about it.

So that is the purpose of our being here this morning. Sometime we are going to come back here and take stock, as the country merchant says, and see what progress we have made. There has been a revolution in this country and in this world in the last few years. I hope that the years of 1964, 1965, 1966, 1967, and 1968 will show that we moved ahead, that we made progress, that we weren't just concerned with what was in our platform, but we were concerned with what we did about it; that we just weren't concerned with style and appearance, we were concerned with achievement; that we weren't just concerned with talking about medical care for 20 years, we wanted to sign it and to put it into effect; that we weren't interested in talking about people that didn't have homes and didn't have roofs over their heads, and all these eloquent phrases that get you elected to office, but what we are concerned about is what did you do about it after you were elected.

Well, here is what we did about it, just one little place; here is what we are doing about it, just another little place.

We are going to continue to do it every day as long as we have the authority and this mission.

Thank you very much.

NOTE: The President spoke at 11:45 a.m. at Victoria Plaza in San Antonio, Texas, at a ceremony marking the signing of the bill (Public Law 89–384, 80 Stat. 99). In his opening words he referred to Representative Henry B. Gonzalez of Texas, the Most Reverend Robert E. Lucey, Archbishop of San Antonio, W. W. McAllister, Mayor of San Antonio, and Charles Grace, Judge of Bexar County, Texas.
During his remarks the President referred to F.

Maury Maverick, Representative from Texas 1935–1939, William D. McFarlane, Representative from Texas 1933–1939, Senator Ralph Yarborough of Texas, President Maurice Yameogo of Upper Volta in Africa, who visited the United States in 1965 (see 1965 volume, this series, Book I, Items 141, 142, 144), and Luci Baines Johnson, the President's daughter.

For the President's remarks with President Truman in Independence at the signing of the Medicare bill and the social security amendments, see 1965 volume, this series, Book II, Item 394.

Secretary Gardner's recommendations on improving social security benefits are included in the President's message to Congress of January 23, 1967.

169 Letter to Secretary Gardner Requesting a Progress Report on Preparations for Launching Medicare. *April* 8, 1966

[Released April 8, 1966.   Dated April 7, 1966]

Dear Mr. Secretary:

I expect shortly to sign the bill to extend until May 31 the deadline for initial enrollment of persons 65 years and over in Medicare's supplementary health insurance program.[1] According to your report, more than 16.8 million people or about 88 percent of the estimated 19 million eligible have already signed up. I want you to spare no effort to raise that percentage as high as possible. I realize the magnitude of the task, but we should not be satisfied so long as anyone who is qualified for this program fails to enroll because he did not learn in time.

The launching of Medicare is a historic undertaking. Under your leadership the Department of Health, Education, and Welfare has been making a great effort to insure a successful launch. I want to be sure that we leave nothing undone to prepare the Federal Government, the States, the providers of hospitals and health services, and the American people for the massive job ahead. Will you, therefore, provide me with a progress report on tooling up for Medicare and on what remains to be done between now and July 1. I would like your report, particularly to cover the following:

1. Are persons covered by Medicare fully informed of their benefits?

2. Are hospitals, nursing homes, and other institutions in compliance with necessary conditions of participation? What assistance are we giving to be sure that they meet requisite quality standards?

3. Are all the administrative agents, e.g., Blue Cross, Blue Shield, and private insurance companies fully prepared to carry out their appropriate functions?

4. Have the various professional organizations been fully consulted and are their views reflected in implementing regulations?

5. Have cooperative arrangements with the states been worked out to cover their functions? What progress have they made?

6. Have methods of reimbursement been established for hospitals, nursing homes, and physicians that are equitable and efficient?

7. What is the status of hospital committees to ensure effective use of beds?

8. What alternative arrangements are being developed to provide facilities, services, and personnel to meet the increased demand for medical care?

9. Are the Social Security Administration, the Public Health Service, the Welfare Administration, and all other elements of your Department administratively staffed with people trained and in position to handle

---

[1] See Item 168.

410

public inquiries and the administrative tasks ahead?

I am concerned not only that we be ready to launch Medicare on July 1. We must take steps to provide the quality and quantity of medical care of which this nation is capable. This requires better health facilities, more doctors and other health personnel, and better utilization of health personnel. It is imperative that we secure the new legislation which I have requested of the Congress—to modernize our hospitals and nursing homes, to train new types of health personnel, and to develop a partnership in health with the states and communities. I hope you will keep me advised of the progress of this legislation.

I am convinced that we must reexamine on a broad scale our nation's use of health manpower. I shall shortly appoint a National Advisory Commission on Health Manpower. It will consider ways in which the health care provided to all our citizens can be improved by more effective use of doctors and supporting health personnel.

Sincerely,

LYNDON B. JOHNSON

[Honorable John W. Gardner, Secretary of Health, Education, and Welfare, Washington, D.C.]

NOTE: On May 24, 1966, the White House made public a progress report to the President from Secretary Gardner on steps taken to put the Medi-

care program into effect on July 1, 1966. The report, dated May 23, noted these developments:

(1) Ninety percent of Americans 65 or over had signed up for the voluntary part of Medicare covering doctors' bills;

(2) Over 90 percent of the Nation's hospitals had asked to participate in providing services under the basic program;

(3) State health departments, the Blue Cross-Blue Shield plan, private insurance companies chosen to help administer the program, and professional organizations such as the American Hospital Association and American Medical Association were helping hospitals to meet the conditions of participation.

The report is printed in the Weekly Compilation of Presidential Documents (vol. 2, p. 687).

On May 21, 1966, the White House announced that Operation Medicare Alert, a community action program under the Office of Economic Opportunity, had contacted 4½ million senior citizens in its program to enroll the elderly poor for health benefits under the new Medicare legislation. Throughout the country 13,000 paid workers from among the elderly poor, assisted by 67,000 volunteers, contacted those who had not enrolled to encourage them to sign up for benefits under the new program. There were 467 Medicare Alert projects in 47 States, Puerto Rico, and Guam, the release stated. In Maine, Medicare Alert workers rode horses to visit those living in areas where there was no access by road. In other States the problem was to reach those who could not read or did not speak English (2 Weekly Comp. Pres. Docs., p. 681).

The National Advisory Commission on Health Manpower was established, along with the President's Committee on Health Manpower, by Executive Order 11279 of May 7, 1966 (2 Weekly Comp. Pres. Docs., p. 621; 31 F.R. 6947; 3 CFR, 1966 Comp., p. 110).

The letter was released at San Antonio, Texas.

---

170   Statement by the President Upon Signing Bill Authorizing an Official Residence for the Vice President. *April* 10, 1966

I AM SIGNING S. 2394, authorizing the Administrator of General Services to plan, design, construct, furnish, and maintain an official residence for the Vice President on approximately 10 acres at the Naval Observatory in Washington.

The bill I sign today is an authorization

measure. Funds for the construction of the residence can be obtained only after Congress again approves whatever appropriations it deems wise and necessary.

In this connection, the Vice President has informed me that he wrote to the Director of the Budget Bureau, Mr. Schultze, on April

7, 1966, requesting that no funds for construction be sought at this time. In the words of the Vice President's letter, "This is the time, instead, in which our government is setting an example of prudent budget practices, delaying those construction projects which are not of the highest priority. This is a project which is desirable but deferrable."

The Congress within the past 9 days acted upon this measure and sent it to me. And while I shall sign this legislation into law, I shall repeat the Vice President's request

that funds for construction of the residence not be appropriated by the Congress during this period. Congress has been considerate, and at a more opportune time funding this authorization might be justified. I agree with the Vice President's statement in his letter to the Director of the Budget that he "would not feel it necessary nor appropriate for the Congress to provide funds for construction at this time."

NOTE: As enacted, S. 2394 is Public Law 89–386 (80 Stat. 106).

The statement was released at San Antonio, Texas.

---

171   Statement by the President in Response to a Report of the Vice President's Task Force on Summer Domestic Programs. *April 11, 1966*

IT IS MY HOPE that the Vice President, with the cooperation of relevant departments and agencies, will continue to develop practical, imaginative programs for our young people. Special intensive efforts must be made on their behalf as the young are our greatest natural resources.

These programs should take into consideration the particular problems facing young people during summer school recess. Jobs and recreation needs intensify; working mothers now have small children at home who need constant attention; and it is essential that more community facilities be made available throughout the day and into the early evening. It is my hope that under the direction of the Vice President specific answers will be found to the problems faced by our youth today, particularly those living in deprived areas.

NOTE: The President's statement was made public as part of a White House release summarizing a report to the President from the task force on summer domestic programs, established by the President's memorandum of March 2, 1966 (see Item 105).

The release stated that the task force had considered a broad range of problems which arise during the summer months, but recognized that such problems are related to basic concerns present throughout the year. It noted that the Vice President placed special emphasis on the importance of relating activities undertaken in the coming summer to the country's long-range involvement and concern for the fundamental problems of education and training, employment, health and welfare, community relations, recreation, and housing.

The release continued as follows:

"The task force determined that a large number of skilled and unskilled persons, particularly young people, will be seeking employment this summer. Despite the decline in unemployment that has taken place over the past year, almost 1.8 million American boys and girls—16 to 21 years old—will be looking for work and will not be able to find it unless steps are taken to assist them.

"More than 2.7 million children under the age of 14 who should participate in some form of day care or supervised recreation program during the summer months will not have access to such programs unless additional resources are made available by Federal, State, and local governments and the private sector.

"The task force reported to the President that an encouraging number of activities are now planned or are already under way to meet these special summer needs.

"In particular, the task force recommended to the President that the youth opportunity campaign, which last year produced more than 1 million additional summer jobs from the private and public sectors, be repeated this year. The task force noted that preliminary planning for a youth opportunity campaign is already under way.

"The task force noted the importance of the Elementary and Secondary Education Act and title II of the Economic Opportunity Act in helping meet the needs of youth below working age. Approximately 5 million young Americans below age 14 will be involved in special summer programs, including a variety of special summer educational projects funded under title I of the Elementary and Secondary Education Act and Project Head Start, funded under the Economic Opportunity Act.

"The task force recommended that special concern be given to meeting the employment, recreation, education, and related needs of young people residing in deprived areas. The task force emphasized that the vigorous cooperation of State and local governments is essential to this enterprise. Without their cooperation, in partnership with private organizations and private business leaders, Federal efforts will fall far short of meeting the summer as well as the year-round needs of our youth."

See also Items 172, 385.

The statement was released at San Antonio, Texas.

172   Statement by the President on the 1966 Youth Opportunity Campaign.   *April* 11, 1966

IN 1965, faced with the alarming prospect of hundreds of thousands of young Americans—16 through 21—looking for work in the summer and not finding it, this administration launched a Youth Opportunity Campaign.

In 1966, we are faced with that prospect again.

In 1966, 1,800,000 of our youth will look for work in the summer without finding it.

Some of these youngsters will be looking for temporary summer jobs. But getting those jobs may be the difference between being able to go back to school or not going back.

Almost a million of them will be trying to find their places in life, trying to become independent, self-sufficient.

If we fail them, it will mean that we are failing our future.

—It will mean that one out of every six white 16- through 21-year-olds looking for work won't find it.

—It will mean that one out of every five nonwhite youths looking for work will not find it.

—Finally, it will mean that we have allowed our youth who will represent 14.3 percent of our country's summer work force to become 50 percent of our summer unemployed.

Last month, I asked the Vice President to chair a task force on summer domestic programs. Their recommendations included one that there be a 1966 Youth Opportunity Campaign.

I accept that recommendation.

In 1965, a concerted effort, particularly by private employers large and small, produced a million jobs for our young people. Our country again proved its ability to respond to a serious situation.

In 1966, we can, in my judgment, increase by at least a million the work and training opportunities this summer for our boys and girls—in a way that is good for them and good business for all of us.

The private employer's role

I hope and believe that private employers who were largely responsible for our 1965 success, will exceed that success in 1966.

—There are 620,000 firms in this country which employ from 10 to 100 workers. I hope that at least half of these firms will agree to take on one extra summer trainee.

—There are 60,000 larger plants, employing over 25 million people. If each of them will add 1 extra summer trainee for each 100 employees, this will mean another 250,000 trainees.

I hope other large organizations—labor unions, trade associations, churches, colleges—will make a similar effort. This could mean another 25,000 to 50,000 trainees.

So this program can get started immediately, I am asking that these things be done:

—That all private employers who are disposed to do so make their own arrangements immediately for taking on one or more extra trainees this summer.

—If advice of this action, including the name of the trainee, is given by mail to the Secretary of Commerce, Youth Opportunity Campaign Unit, Washington, D.C., it will be appropriately acknowledged.

—That all other private employers and organizations who are willing to cooperate in this program so advise the nearest State employment office.

—That all State employment offices be advised, through the U.S. Employment Service, to establish special Youth Opportunity registers for this special summer program.

—That all boys and girls 16 through 21 who want to work this summer and who don't have jobs get in touch immediately with the nearest employment service office. If this is difficult, write to the Department of Labor, Youth Opportunity Campaign Unit, Washington, D.C.

The Federal Government's role

I expect the Federal Government to do its share:

I am again directing the Government departments and agencies to make every effort to find meaningful work or training opportunities this summer for 1 extra trainee for every 100 employees on their present payrolls.

—This is to be done, for the most part, in the field offices and installations around the country.

—These opportunities will be given, so far as this is practicable, to boys and girls 16 through 21 who need them the most because of economic or educational disadvantages.

—There is a potential employment here of 25,000 trainees.

—Programs under the Vocational Education Act will be expanded from last year's 7,500 students to 26,000 students this summer.

—The work-study program, originally planned to provide opportunity for 76,000 students in over 1,400 communities, will be expanded to assist 100,000 more.

—I am asking that activity under the Manpower Development and Training Act be immediately intensified to provide training opportunities for at least 80,000 youths.

—I have directed a reallocation of Economic Opportunity Act funds to permit an extension of the Neighborhood Youth Corps program to an additional 25,000 boys and girls.

I ask again that the Governor of each of the 50 States, and the mayor of each city with a population of over 10,000, consider whether a trainee employment program like the one we are working out for the Federal Government will be possible and practicable. One percent of the number of their employees would be 30,000.

Task force appointment

I am asking the Vice President, as Chairman of the Youth Opportunity Task Force, to appoint an advisory committee to implement and work out the details of the program. This advisory committee will include representatives of the U.S. Department of Commerce, the U.S. Department of Labor, the Small Business Administration, State and local governments, and business and labor organizations.

It must be clear that this program will be worthwhile only if it means extra work-training opportunities over and above those which would normally be offered. It would be worthless or worse if this program only replaced regular employment opportunities.

It must also be clear that we cannot and do not assure all boys and girls work this summer. We all will do the best we can.

A boy or girl who wants a chance to work and who is denied that chance costs this country more than it can afford. This is a special problem demanding special attention.

NOTE: For a memorandum to the Vice President in response to a progress report on the campaign, see Item 385. See also Items 105, 171.

The statement was released at San Antonio, Texas.

173 Statement by the President Upon Signing Bills Authorizing Disposals From the Stockpiles of Platinum and Bauxite. *April 14, 1966*

I HAVE SIGNED two measures which enable the Nation to once again reap new benefits from previous prudence.

Our national stockpile of strategic and critical materials now contains supplies of platinum and refractory bauxite in excess of our defense needs. Yet American industry, which has an urgent need for these materials, finds them increasingly hard to obtain. The bills I have just signed will permit us to make an orderly transfer to industry of the Government's excess holdings.

S. 1488 authorizes the disposal of 126,300 long tons of refractory grade bauxite, which are in excess of our strategic objectives for the stockpile. This bauxite is needed now by the manufacturers of furnace linings essential for the production of steel and other metals.

S. 2642 authorizes the disposal of 316,300 troy ounces of platinum which are also in excess of our strategic objectives. Platinum is in increasingly short supply in the chemical and electrical industries, and in the petroleum industry where the use of platinum is rising rapidly.

These disposals will be made at no loss to the taxpayers and in a manner which will protect producers, processors, and consumers against disruption of their usual markets.

As I observed last fall when taking similar action in regard to nickel and zinc, surplus materials in our stockpiles win no battles while they lie in storage bins. Nor do they play their proper role in helping our economy.

These valuable materials were originally acquired to prevent shortages in strategic materials in time of war or national emergency. When our supplies of these materials rise beyond any such foreseeable need, and when there is need for them in our current economy, they should be removed from the stockpiles and put to work for our Nation.

During the present session, we have sent to the Congress 24 bills authorizing disposal of such excess materials from our national stockpiles. The disposal plans were drawn up in close consultation with the affected industries.

I am pleased with the speed shown by the Congress in responding favorably to the platinum and refractory bauxite proposals. Eleven additional bills have already passed the House, and four more have been carefully examined by the House Armed Services Committee.

It is my hope and belief that the Congress will continue to act promptly and affirmatively on these disposal measures.

Each orderly disposal of surplus materials has an immediate effect on the national welfare. It helps to:

—maintain our defense production,

—sustain a healthy, growing economy without inflation,

—put the taxpayer's investment to work in the economy, and reduce the cost of maintaining unnecessary stockpiles.

The prompt action which the Congress has already taken toward accomplishing these objectives is a further demonstration of what can be accomplished through the close partnership of the Congress, the executive branch, and American industry. This partnership safeguards and furthers our national interest and protects the rights of the American consumer.

NOTE: As enacted, S. 1488 is Public Law 89-394 (80 Stat. 119), and S. 2642 is Public Law 89-390 (80 Stat. 116).

The statement was released at San Antonio, Texas.

174 Remarks Upon Arrival at the International Airport in Mexico City. *April 14, 1966*

Mr. President, Mrs. Diaz Ordaz, members of the First Family, my friends of Mexico:

This is almost a homecoming for the Johnson family. Thirty-one years ago we came to Mexico on our honeymoon. Since then, on every occasion possible, we have crossed the border into your country, visited in your cities and your countryside, and we have enjoyed, on many occasions, visits from your leaders and your Presidents.

I first met President Adolfo López Mateos in the late fifties when he came to the United States. Later, as President, I visited with him in the United States at Chamizal at El Paso, and in 1964 your own distinguished President honored us with a visit that he and his wife made in our home in Texas.

So when I come to Mexico, I feel that I come to the home of my friends. We are here today to present to your country a statue of one of our most beloved and most re-

spected Presidents, Abraham Lincoln. We present that statue to people that we consider our most treasured friends.

Mr. President, we are grateful to you for this beautiful reception, for your gracious remarks. We will look forward to exchanging views with you in the hours that we are permitted together.

I said to your distinguished and able Ambassador, Ambassador Margain, on the way down on the plane today, that while we faced many trying problems in the world today, I did not believe there had ever been a period in the history of the United States and Mexico when we faced fewer problems, when we had better understanding, and when there was a stronger friendship that exist between the people than exists today.

That is because, Mr. President, you and your distinguished predecessors have understood our people and have provided a fore sighted leadership for your people that has brought us together in understanding and friendship.

Although in other parts of the world neighbors fight neighbors, neighbors are in dispute with neighbors, there are no armies that patrol our borders, there are no guns that protect the frontiers of Mexico and the United States. Our people cross the boundary freely and work and play together.

And if I could have my one wish granted today, it would be that we could live in a world where we had the same peaceful relations with our neighbors as we have with the people of Mexico. But if we are to have peace in the world, we must try to solve the problems that cause the wars: the problems of illiteracy, the problems of ignorance, the problems of disease, the problems of poverty, the problems of misunderstanding.

Mr. President, we salute you for the leadership that you are providing your own great nation and the contribution you are making to other nations in the world in a program that will bring peace to all human-

kind. While war clouds hover over certain parts of the world as we meet here this afternoon, we truly and genuinely and sincerely hope that the day may soon come when all the world can live together in peace as do the people of the United States and Mexico.

Mr. President, our distinguished Secretary of State, the majority leader of the United States Senate, the minority leader of the United States Senate, leaders of our House of Representatives, join me on this occasion in thanking you for this very cordial welcome and in saying to you: *Muchas gracias, Señor Presidente; muchas gracias a todo México!*

NOTE: The President spoke at 6 p.m. at the International Airport in Mexico City, following a 21-gun salute and remarks of welcome by President Gustavo Diaz Ordaz that began his 2-day visit to Mexico.

During his remarks the President referred to Adolfo López Mateos, former President of Mexico, Hugo B. Margain, Mexican Ambassador to the United States, and to Dean Rusk, Secretary of State, Senator Mike Mansfield of Montana, majority leader of the Senate, and Senator Everett McKinley Dirksen of Illinois, minority leader of the Senate, who were members of the United States delegation which accompanied the President to Mexico.

See also Items 175–177.

175 Remarks in Mexico City at the Dedication of the Abraham Lincoln Statue. *April* 15, 1966

Mr. President, my friends:

It is impossible for me to tell you how proud I am to be here with you today, in company with the leadership of the United States Senate, prominent Members of the House of Representatives, and the Senators and Congressmen from the States of Illinois and Kentucky that gave us Abraham Lincoln.

The President of the United States could ask for no greater honor than to be invited to stand on the soil of our good friend, Mex-

ico, beside a leader as beloved and respected as your great President, Diaz Ordaz.

For me this occasion has a very special meaning. All my life I have known, and lived with, and worked alongside the sons and the daughters of Mexico. I have been here on many different occasions; my wife and I spent the first days of our marriage here in this beautiful city, Mexico City.

To come back now to the people and the scenes of so many pleasant memories, to come as the leader of your sister Republic to the north, where your country is held in such high esteem, is for me a moment never to be forgotten.

The tribute that your great Foreign Secretary Carrillo Flores has just paid to Abraham Lincoln will touch the hearts of all of my countrymen.

All nations rightly praise their own famous men.

But only a truly great people pause to pay tribute to the great of other lands.

And that is what Mexico is doing today.

What Abraham Lincoln stood for is what binds our two nations—and, indeed, this entire hemisphere—together.

More than geography and common economic interests and a regional system of mutual assistance, we are held together by common values and by shared beliefs.

That is why we share equally Bolívar and Washington, San Martín and Jefferson, Juárez and Martí and Lincoln. They were sons of a common heritage.

In his time and place, Abraham Lincoln brought the best in our common civilization to bear on the cruelest problems that ever confronted a leader: civil war and the enslavement of a minority of his people.

In these trials he clung to the belief that every human being was unique and precious—equal in the eyes of God and before the law.

He believed that the pillars of a great society were equality of opportunity, individual freedom to excel, and justice—political and social justice—for every citizen.

And so he walked among us—bearing on his shoulders the burdens of a nation's greatest test—proving that true greatness lies in loyalty to those universal principles which span every age.

Now in this age, we in this hemisphere are today engaged in another great test—we are engaged in a vast social revolution touching the lives of millions of peoples on two continents.

And like Lincoln's, this is a test of whether freedom can work.

It is a test of whether men through liberty can overcome the weight of the past and lift from their brothers the blight of hunger, the blindness of ignorance, and the burden of disease.

We are in the midst of that test.

We must demonstrate to our peoples that their destiny is not class struggle but common struggle to achieve that proud and that modern Latin America which is at once the dream of a generation and the interest of the world community.

This is a battle which only the people of Latin America can win.

But it is the desire of my people, our commitment, and our privilege to work side by side in this great human adventure.

History will judge us not only by the nobility of our sentiments or the poetry of our words, but history will judge us by the action that we take to bring these sentiments to life.

For my country's part, we are guided by certain basic convictions upon which our faith in the future rests.

First, every member of the American community of nations has a natural right to its independence and sovereignty. No country may abridge those rights. For as your own Benito Juárez said, "Respect for the rights of others is peace."

Second, the United States maintains its commitment to government by consent of the governed—a consent to be granted in free and honest elections. It does not seek to impose on others any form of government. But let us stand determined on this principle: Despots are not welcome in this hemisphere.

Third, my administration believes that both stable democracy and effective economic development depend ultimately on social justice. There has never been stable democracy where economic power and privilege were concentrated in the hands of the few. Where the many work, let the many earn.

Fourth, we believe the struggle for social justice and more efficient and equitable use of natural resources must be led by each country in its own behalf. My administration will not be deterred by those who tenaciously or selfishly cling to special privileges from the past. And we will not be deterred by those who say that to risk change is to risk communism.

Fifth, we do not wish to see communism spread in this hemisphere, but we believe that the threat to the liberty and independence of the Latin American peoples from communism cannot be met merely by force. We will continue to concentrate our assistance mainly in economic and social fields and to encourage our Latin American neighbors, where possible, to limit their outlays for military purposes. We are encouraged that democracy flourishes in countries such as Mexico where expenditures for education and development are high.

Sixth, we are convinced that the future of Latin American industrialization—as well as the basic welfare of the peoples themselves—urgently requires the parallel modernization of rural life. This must combine more equitable forms of landholding and all the measures that are needed to raise production and productivity. And your two Presidents this morning discussed at length steps that we are going to take to do both.

Seventh, we shall continue to work with your own able President Diaz Ordaz and work with our Latin American friends throughout the hemisphere to augment and to stabilize earnings from traditional exports, while assisting efforts to expand those new exports on which Latin American trade will increasingly depend in the future.

Eighth, we believe that the drawing together of the economies of Latin America is critical to this hemisphere's future. Only in this way can the hemisphere develop

—truly efficient industries;
—expanded foreign exchange earnings; and
—a sound foundation for a full Latin American partnership in building a peaceful world community.

One of the challenges of hemispheric integration is the linking of North and South America through the Pan American Highway.

It is one ambition of my Presidency to work with the other nations of this hemisphere toward closing the several hundred miles of the gap that now exists. We must await the studies that are now nearing completion, but together we should look to the day when the old precolonial links across the Isthmus are fully restored, the good lands of Panama are open for agriculture, and families and commerce can move anywhere between Laredo and the southernmost tip of Argentina.

Señor Presidente Diaz Ordaz, my country takes great heart in what you, in Mexico, are doing. We see today a people who are forging ahead. We see today a nation that is proud and a people that are confident.

You are confident of the future because you are confident that you can secure for your people a constant increase in material well-being and social justice.

You are confident that you can deal with all other neighbors in independence, friendship, and dignity.

You are confident that you can help your less advanced neighbors also to move ahead with you.

And you are confident that you can maintain in the modern world your own personality—loyal to your own traditions and aspirations.

Mexico's progress is witness that the goals of the alliance are realistic and its methods are valid.

I have served with four American Presidents who showed their concern and their friendship for Mexico and Latin America. Franklin Roosevelt lifted our eyes to the promise and the problems of Latin America with the good-neighbor policy. Harry Truman's boldness brought forth point 4 and its compassion to the Western Hemisphere and to the entire world. Dwight Eisenhower plowed new and fertile and productive fields with the Act of Bogotá. And John F. Kennedy, building on and expanding and refining that act, gave fresh impulse to all our ideals in the alliance.

Twenty-nine months ago, the first week of my Presidency, my first act as President of the United States was to pledge my country again to the faith and the direction of these four Presidents and their relations with the nations in this hemisphere.

I am proud today to report to the Mexican people and to all of our Latin American friends that our common effort is proving itself with specific results. Our dreams are becoming realities.

As I speak to you here today, I have been involved in the executive branch of my Government for 6 years. The first 3 years, the average growth rate in Latin America was 1 percent. In the last 3 years of my Presidency, that growth rate is now 2½ percent. This achievement, in which Mexico, the United States, and all the other countries of Latin America can take great pride, will continue strong, I predict, in the year 1966. We believe that the growth rate in that year will exceed the 2½ percent of this year.

Ahead, of course, lie many problems that

are still yet to be overcome. Hard work and perseverance, not hope alone, will bend them to solution.

At the recent meeting of the Economic Ministers in Buenos Aires, we were right to take stock of what we have learned since 1961 and to plan and to chart the course ahead.

Now we must give necessary impulse to, as I said to your President this morning, new and additional initiatives; we must open new paths; we must breathe new energy into our efforts.

And to that end, I will in the months ahead join with Latin American leaders in exploring the proposal of the President of Argentina for a new meeting at the very highest level to examine our common problems and to give the Alliance for Progress increased momentum.

Such a conference should be prepared with the utmost care. We should examine every idea which might advance our common interest, be it old or new. Careful preparation need not be the enemy, however, of imaginative action and new adventures.

It will take time and faith and stubborn effort to achieve together the goals that we set ourselves in the Charter of Punta del Este 5 years ago.

But this we must do. This we will do. There is no other way, in our time and in this hemisphere, to show what free men and what free nations can do working together.

And so let all of us, let all of the world know that we know our challenge. I saw it, riding through the streets of your beautiful city with your great President last evening; I saw it in the hopeful face of young Mexico, in the hundreds of thousands of little children who are the future of this great land; I saw young people, with minds to be educated, with bodies to be protected from disease; I saw young boys and girls who one day will be able to find a job and who will raise their families in peace, and some will lead this great nation tomorrow.

And this is the challenge that faces the people of America and faces the people of Latin America, and this is a challenge that we will—shoulder to shoulder—accept.

Once again, I want to say how very proud and very happy I am to be here with you today, *Señor Presidente,* you, my good and warm friend, and to be among your gracious people of Mexico.

Very shortly I will return to the other side of the river, but I will leave, to enjoy the hospitality of your great people, Mrs. Johnson

and my Secretary of State and the distinguished delegation from the Congress. And before I leave, I should like to say this: May we all always seek justice and peace together.

Come what may, may we always be good neighbors—and may we always be good *amigos.*

NOTE: The President spoke at 12:02 p.m. in Mexico City before a group of some 5,000 persons gathered at the Parque Polanco for the dedication of the Abraham Lincoln statue. During his remarks he referred to, among others, Gustavo Diaz Ordaz, President of Mexico, Antonio Carrillo Flores, Foreign Secretary of Mexico, and Arturo Illia, President of Argentina.

See also Items 174, 176, 177.

---

176 Remarks to the Staff at the American Embassy in Mexico City. *April* 15, 1966

Secretary and Mrs. Rusk, Ambassador and Mrs. Freeman, my friends, ladies and gentlemen:

I drove down the street with great pride as my eyes looked upon this beautiful building put here by the talented hands of architects from my State. And as I walked into this building, I looked back over my memories in government and thought that never in my 35 years in public service in Washington had our country been more fortunate in its selection of a Secretary of State than it is now with Dean Rusk.

He is guiding our relations with other nations with a skill and an understanding and a compassion that is unequaled, in my judgment, in my lifetime. He has built around him one hundred or more of the ablest Ambassadors that any administration has ever assembled to serve the interests of our Nation. It gives me great pride to pay just tribute to the work being done by Ambassador and Mrs. Freeman here in Mexico.

But what really gives me the greatest pride

and the greatest pleasure is to come here and look into the smiling faces that stand around me in this beautiful building, and see the folks that take care of the daily chores and that reflect such great credit on the country they serve. No nation ever had more competent or more loyal or more dedicated public employees than the United States of America, and no department ever had more of those kinds of employees than the Department of State.

So I want to say to each of you at your desk, at the tasks that engage you, that your President is proud of the work you do, is grateful to you for the loyalty that you give and the sacrifices that you make, and the credit that you reflect upon your country.

I observed the other day a statement my father made to me when I was a little boy and he was talking about public service. He said, "To understand people, you must know them and to properly speak for them and represent them, you must love them." For that reason he always leaned over backward to be democratic. There was no little farmer from the humblest village in the land that he didn't want to know, because he got more from the farmer than he gave.

I think that each of you who carry on with your work, serving our national interest each day, could profit by remembering that statement: To know the people of Mexico you must understand them, and to represent and carry out our program and our purpose with them you must love them.

I have been coming across this border all my life. I have been working with the people of Mexico ever since I was a child. My first playmate was a little Mexican boy. We raced our horses together, when we were both just learning to ride. I remember he told me he didn't want to run a race with me, because his horse wasn't as fat as mine and therefore couldn't run as fast.

I said, "Well, I will just solve that problem. We will make him as fat." So we got a big bucket and got in the oat bin and we fed that horse nearly all afternoon. Then we filled him full of water and then we took him out and ran the race. Then the horse died.

But all my life the Mexican people have been my friends and my playmates, my closest associates and my most trusted allies, and my most loyal supporters. They have been intimidated, they have been criticized, they have been browbeaten, sometimes they have been hauled into court for voting for me, but they have always been there.

I brought my bride to Mexico City on our honeymoon. I have come back here at every opportunity. So, we are very thankful we were given the chance to come here again and show the people of this nation the great respect and friendship we have for them, and to say to those of you who serve my administration and your country so well that I am mighty grateful and proud of you.

NOTE: The President spoke at 1:05 p.m. at the American Embassy in Mexico City. In his opening words he referred to Dean Rusk, Secretary of State, Fulton Freeman, U.S. Ambassador to Mexico, and their wives.

See also Items 174, 175, 177.

177   Joint Statement Following Informal Discussions With President Diaz Ordaz of Mexico. *April 15, 1966*

PRESIDENT Gustavo Diaz Ordaz and President Lyndon B. Johnson were greatly pleased that the occasion of the unveiling of a statue of Abraham Lincoln provided an opportunity to renew their cordial personal relationship and to resume their informal conversations begun during their meeting in November 1964.

The two Chiefs of State, conscious of the significance of the principles for which Benito Juárez and Abraham Lincoln both fought, have reiterated in their respective nations their adherence to freedom, human dignity, and a mutual respect among peoples. These principles are the basis of democratic

life. The Presidents expressed their conviction that these also constitute the foundation of the firm friendship between Mexico and the United States. The two Presidents recognized with pleasure the high level of understanding reached in the relations between their two countries in recent years.

President Diaz Ordaz reaffirmed to President Johnson the principles of the foreign policy of Mexico, in relation with the other American Republics, which, in addition to the fundamental principles of self-determination, non-intervention, and peaceful solution of controversies, include the need for maintaining constantly open the doors to dialogue. President Johnson reviewed with President Diaz Ordaz a number of problems of world-wide importance, and reaffirmed the commitment of the United States to the same fundamental principles, as well as its commitment to a continuing search for peace throughout the world.

The two Heads of State reiterated the general opinion expressed in previous meetings of the Presidents of Mexico and the United States that it is in the interest of both countries to seek to maintain the access which each has to the markets of the other and to broaden these wherever possible. The Joint Trade Committee established in 1965 was discussed by both Presidents as a major step forward in expanding the already large area of mutual interests which exist between the two countries in matters of commercial interchange.

Specific problems involving border trade between the two countries were mentioned by President Diaz Ordaz. The two Presidents agreed that their two Governments should study these problems with the aim of determining what measures could be taken to expand legitimate border trade in goods produced in both countries to the benefit of the border region.

The two Presidents discussed their deep concern regarding the international market for cotton, which is the leading Mexican export product and is also of great interest to the United States and to other Western hemisphere countries. The Presidents agreed that their two Governments should consult with each other and with other interested governments on the problems of production and marketing of cotton. Regarding the International Cotton Institute, created for the purpose of promoting the increase in cotton consumption, both Heads of State expressed their determination to continue the support of their Governments

for the greater success of its mission.

President Diaz Ordaz reaffirmed his intention to continue the policy of promoting the economic development of Mexico at a rate substantially greater than the population increase, within a framework of monetary stability, which is so important in protecting the real income of the majority of the people. The two Presidents noted with satisfaction the increasing rate of economic and social progress in the hemisphere as a whole during the past two years and expressed their determination to continue their mutual cooperation to achieve the objectives of the Act of Bogotá of 1960, the Charter of Punta del Este of 1961, and the Economic and Social Act of Rio de Janeiro of 1965.

The two Presidents were in agreement that the Supervised Agricultural Credit Program under the Alliance for Progress has proved an excellent example of the cooperation between the public and private banking institutions of both countries in carrying out the objectives of the Act of Bogotá and the Charter of Punta del Este, as already mentioned, contributing effectively to the expansion of agricultural productivity and the modernization of rural life.

The two Presidents expressed their determination to improve the relations between the frontier cities of both countries, and to elevate the life of those who live in the border region. They agreed to create a commission which would study the manner in which these objectives could be realized by cooperative action to raise the standard of living of the respective communities, from a social and cultural as well as a material point of view.

The two Presidents expressed their determination to create an Abraham Lincoln Fund in Mexico and a Benito Juárez Fund in the United States in order to grant scholarships to the youth of the hemisphere who might be selected by a Joint Commission in order to continue their studies in institutions of higher learning of both countries.

The two Presidents agreed on the need to support the efforts for Latin American economic integration. President Diaz Ordaz expressed his satisfaction with the recent initiative of President Johnson in suggesting the creation of a special fund for the financing of pre-investment studies of multinational projects in support of regional integration. Both Presidents expressed their satisfaction that this work is moving forward under the leadership of the Inter-American Committee on the Alliance for Progress (CIAP) with the active participation of the Inter-American Development Bank. They also noted with satisfaction the progress being made toward integration through the work of the Latin American Free Trade Association and the Central American Common Market.

The two Presidents were pleased to note the progress achieved in the acquisition of lands, the transfer of residents and the construction of installations provided for in the convention for the solution of the Chamizal problem. They agreed to instruct the members of the International Boundary and Water Commission to intensify their efforts to bring about the change in the boundary as soon as possible.

The two Presidents expressed their satisfaction at the manner in which the agreement reached on March 22, 1965, regarding the problem of the salinity of the waters of the Colorado River, is operating. They were in agreement regarding the need for mutual consultation before proceeding to carrying out works which in the future might create problems of a nature similar to that mentioned previously.

The two Presidents agreed on the importance for their countries of the study which, under the auspices of the International Atomic Energy Agency, is being carried out to determine the technical and economic possibilities of installing, at some point in Mexico near the United States border, a plant to desalinate sea water through the use of nuclear energy.

Finally, the two Presidents requested their respective Foreign Secretaries to continue their discussion of matters of common interest. President Diaz Ordaz expressed to President Johnson the deep gratitude of the Mexican people to the American people for the gift of the statue of Abraham Lincoln and reaffirmed that he considered it a most friendly act that the Chief of State of the United States should have desired to come in person to associate himself with the homage rendered to the Great Emancipator. President Johnson expressed his appreciation for the extraordinarily generous and friendly reception by the Mexican Government and people.

NOTE: The joint statement was released at Mexico City.

178 Statement by the President Upon Signing Bill Relieving Certain Explorer Scouts From Duties on Imported Band Uniforms. *April 18, 1966*

I HAVE TODAY signed H.R. 8647, for the relief of the Troubadors Drum and Bugle Corps of Bridgeport, Conn.

The bill relieves a group of underprivileged Explorer Scouts from customs duties on band uniforms imported from Mexico.

The duties imposed were substantially beyond their means or expectations.

I recognize the worthy motives that inspired the passage of H.R. 8647, and I shall not deny relief to these young men after Congress has unanimously approved a measure in their behalf.

Nevertheless, in fairness to others who import goods from abroad, relief of this kind should be sparingly accorded. I do not regard approval of the measure as establishing a favorable precedent for Presidential action on similar bills in the future.

NOTE: As enacted, H.R. 8647 is Private Law 89–241 (80 Stat. 1625).

The statement was released at San Antonio, Texas.

179   Statement by the President on the First Privately Owned Facility for Reprocessing Fuel From Nuclear Powerplants.   *April* 19, 1966

CHAIRMAN SEABORG of the Atomic Energy Commission has advised me that the Nation's first privately owned plant for reprocessing of fuel from nuclear powerplants soon will be in operation in Cattaraugus County, New York.

This plant, owned by the Nuclear Fuel Services, Inc., is a noteworthy step in the development of a strong, self-supporting nuclear industry in the United States. It will provide facilities to process spent radioactive fuels discharged from nuclear powerplants to recover the unburned fuel and other valuable material. The construction of this plant with private capital has reduced Government capital expenditures which might have been otherwise necessary. This represents a major step toward placing this important atomic energy operation in the private sector of our economy. It is a splendid example of Government-industry cooperation to bring the benefits of the peaceful atom to our country. It is another instance where the U.S. Government is following the sound policy of turning over to private industry a service for which industry has shown a competence and willingness to perform.

180   Statement by the President Upon Signing Resolution Supporting U.S. Participation in Food Relief for India.   *April* 19, 1966

I HAVE approved H.J. Res. 997, "To support United States participation in relieving victims of hunger in India and to enhance India's capacity to meet the nutritional needs of its people."

Through this joint resolution the Congress has acted with dispatch, statesmanship, and humanity.

It supports and endorses my recent offer to enlarge our food shipments to the people of India to help them avoid the suffering that would otherwise result from the worst drought in a century.

India simply cannot sustain its 500 million people from its drought-stricken resources until the next major harvest in November.

When others were in need and we could help, our people have always responded with responsibility and compassion.

However distant other lands may be, in the end our people understand that we are a part of a human family.

I am confident that the prompt reaction of the Congress will encourage the govern-

425

ments of other nations to help bridge the gap left in India by this great natural disaster.

Some nations, among them Canada, have already responded on a substantial scale. Others, with limited resources of their own, have, nevertheless, reached out generously to help.

We hope that all nations will pause now and ask themselves: What more can we do?

At stake is the salvation of countless families and, in particular, millions of children— a great nation's future citizens.

None of us can rest easy until we know in our hearts that we have done everything that is possible to protect them from malnutrition, hunger, and even from starvation itself.

I am confident from my talks with Prime Minister Gandhi that the Indian Government will use the time gained by our assistance—and that of others—to mount a determined and effective policy to raise India's own agricultural production. In the end, only by its own efforts can the people of India be fed.

Our assistance has already looked beyond the present drought to enlarging the next harvest. We granted some time ago a $50 million loan for chemical fertilizers and are helping Indian agriculture in many other ways. The assistance of many governments, international organizations, and private industry will all be required in this essential, longrun effort.

In other times, famine in one nation was regarded as a fact to be passively accepted.

Now, however imperfect our organization, we must learn to behave like a world community; for modern communications have brought nations closer than our own States were, not so long ago.

The joint resolution I approve today recognizes and contributes to this vision of where we are and where we must go.

NOTE: As enacted, H.J. Res. 997 is Public Law 89-406 (80 Stat. 131).

For the text of a joint statement following the President's talks with Prime Minister Gandhi see Item 152. See also Items 153, 154.

181 Memorandum on Cost Reduction in the Federal Government. *April 20, 1966*

Memorandum for the Heads of Departments and Agencies:

If Federal agencies were still operating at their 1964 level of efficiency, my 1966 and 1967 budgets would have to be $3 billion higher. These savings mean that we are getting more value for our tax dollars. It means the American people are $3 billion better off.

This makes clear why I consider cost reduction so important. It explains why I want every Government employee to think hard about opportunities for cost reduction, and why I want the best ideas publicized for all to use. A good idea from one agency

should not stop there, but must be made known throughout the Government.

Some time ago I asked the Budget Director to develop a system of exchanging information about cost reduction among Federal agencies. He has prepared the pamphlet which is attached—the first issue of a series of "Cost Reduction Notes."

"Cost Reduction Notes" describes imaginative actions which have produced savings in one agency and which carry promise of applicability throughout the Government. The ideas vary widely, but they were chosen as ones likely to be useful to agencies with differing responsibilities. By bringing the ideas together in a pamphlet which will be circulated throughout the Federal Government, we are seeking to multiply the savings already achieved.

I want "Cost Reduction Notes" to be read widely in every agency, both in Washington and in the field. I want each idea to be considered carefully. I hope that many of them can be put to use.

LYNDON B. JOHNSON

NOTE: The pamphlet "Cost Reduction Notes," No. 1, April 1966 (Government Printing Office, 10 pp.) was made available with the release.

182 Letter to the President of the Senate and to the Speaker of the House Transmitting Bill Encouraging the Substitution of Private for Public Credit. *April 20, 1966*

Dear Mr. President: (Dear Mr. Speaker:)

I have the honor to transmit "The Participation Sales Act of 1966." This important legislation is designed to forward our objective of substituting private for public credit.

For many years the Federal Government has carried on lending programs to finance essential activities which would not otherwise receive adequate financial support. Under these programs direct loans are made to help the farmer, the businessman, the home buyer, the veteran, the student, our colleges, and our schools. As of June 30, 1965, the volume of these Federal loans exceeded $33 billion.

Desirable as these activities are, Federal lending neither can, nor should, shoulder the entire job.

Under our system of free enterprise it is far better for the Government to mobilize private capital to these ends.

And it is far better for the Government to stimulate and supplement private lending rather than to substitute for it.

To do this, we sell Federal loans directly, or in some cases, sell "participations" in pools of loans, to private investors. The Government acts as both middleman and underwriter for the loans, assuring adequate and economical financing for desirable proj-

ects while at the same time attracting the maximum participation of private investors.

This substitution of private for public credit provides sound financing for worthwhile projects with a minimum of Federal participation.

In encouraging private participation in Federal credit programs, I am building on the outstanding work begun and carried forward by:

—President Eisenhower's Administration;

—The 1958 Commission on Money and Credit, chaired by Frazar B. Wilde and of which Secretary of the Treasury Fowler and many other distinguished citizens were members;

—President Kennedy's 1962 Committee on Federal Credit Programs, under the Chairmanship of former Secretary of the Treasury Dillon.

The substitution of private for public credit has many advantages:

—It makes more effective use of the taxpayer's dollar.

—It offers the private investor an opportunity for sound investment and a fair return.

—It benefits business and those of our citizens who are helped by the vital programs made possible both by Federal and private investment.

In this fiscal year we expect to replace a total of $3.3 billion in public credit with private credit. In fiscal 1967, with the help of legislation such as the proposal I am submitting today, we believe that private credit can be substituted for public credit, advantageously to all concerned, in the amount of approximately $4.7 billion.

As private credit is introduced on an increasing scale, the need to coordinate the sales of Federal loans also increases. It would defeat the purpose of improving the operation of the credit market if loans offered under particular programs interfered with each other or with the orderly financing of the public debt through the sale of Treasury securities.

The Participation Sales Act of 1966 will help solve this problem in two important respects.

First, instead of the Government making a number of relatively small and uncoordinated offerings of loans in the market, the Act provides for pooling many loans together and selling participations in the pool.

The pooling of mortgages and loans and the sale of participations in the income and repayments from loans in the pool is not new. It has been used to advantage over the past several years by the Export-Import Bank, the Veterans Administration, and the Federal National Mortgage Association.

Second, this legislation would extend the pool participation technique to other lending programs, including:

—Farmers Home Administration;
—Office of Education;
—College Housing;
—Public Facilities Loans;
—Small Business Administration.

The pool technique adopted by this legislation has a number of advantages:

—It assures the Government the best

possible return on the sales of financial assets;
—It provides the investor with a widely accepted and highly desired asset;
—It provides a means for attracting private participation in loans made with relatively low interest rates for special purposes;
—It reaches sources of capital which would not be available for loans or mortgages offered individually, thus widening the reservoir of credit for vital projects.

The proposed legislation has two other major provisions.

1. Rather than have each of the Agencies concerned conduct their own separate sales programs, the sale of participations would be centralized in a single agency—the Federal National Mortgage Association. This agency has already built up extensive experience with this technique in its mortgage pooling operations.

Individual agencies would continue to administer their credit programs, but the pooling of credits and sales of participations in the pools would be handled by the Federal National Mortgage Association. This centralization will greatly increase the efficiency of the sales operation and help coordinate this program with the Treasury's debt management operations.

2. In many cases the Congress has established Federal credit programs in which the interest rate charged to the borrower is below the market rate. The difference represents a net charge to the taxpayer. The Act provides that, in all such cases, the Appropriations Committees of both Houses must authorize in advance the amounts of participations which could be sold against these assets. In this way, the safeguards of the annual appropriations process can be applied to this aspect of the program.

The Participation Sales Act of 1966 will permit us to conserve our budget resources by substituting private for public credit while still meeting urgent credit needs in the most efficient and economical manner possible.

It will enable us to make the credit market stronger, more competitive, and better able to serve the needs of our growing economy.

But above all, the legislation will benefit millions of taxpayers and the many vital programs supported by Federal credit. The Act will help us move this Nation forward and bring a better life to all the people.

I am enclosing a joint memorandum from the Secretary of the Treasury and the Director of the Bureau of the Budget which discusses in detail the major features of this legislation.

I urge speedy enactment of this legislation.

Sincerely,

LYNDON B. JOHNSON

NOTE: This is the text of identical letters addressed to the Honorable Hubert H. Humphrey, President of the Senate, and to the Honorable John W. McCormack, Speaker of the House of Representatives.

The text of the draft bill and the joint memorandum from the Secretary of the Treasury and the Director of the Bureau of the Budget is printed in House Document 426 (89th Cong., 2d sess.). The memorandum is also printed in the Weekly Compilation of Presidential Documents (vol. 2, p. 552).

The Participation Sales Act of 1966 was approved by the President on May 24, 1966 (Public Law 89–429, 80 Stat. 164).

---

183   Remarks Upon Presenting the Medal of Honor (Posthumous) to the Father of Milton L. Olive III.   *April 21, 1966*

Mr. and Mrs. Olive, members of the Olive family, distinguished Mayor Daley, Secretary Resor, General Wheeler, Members of the Senate, Members of the House, ladies and gentlemen:

There are occasions on which we take great pride, but little pleasure. This is one such occasion. Words can never enlarge upon acts of heroism and duty, but this Nation will never forget Milton Lee Olive III.

President Harry Truman once said that he would far rather have won the Medal of Honor than to have been the President of the United States. I know what he meant. Those who have earned this decoration are very few in number. But true courage is very rare. This honor we reserve for the most courageous of all of our sons.

The Medal of Honor is awarded for acts of heroism above and beyond the call of duty. It is bestowed for courage demonstrated not in blindly overlooking danger, but in meeting it with eyes clearly open.

That is what Private Olive did. When the enemy's grenade landed on that jungle trail, it was not merely duty which drove this young man to throw himself upon it, sacrificing his own life that his comrades might continue to live. He was compelled by something that is more than duty, by something greater than a blind reaction to forces that are beyond his control.

He was compelled, instead, by an instinct of loyalty which the brave always carry into conflict. In that incredibly brief moment of decision in which he decided to die, he put others first and himself last. I have always believed that to be the hardest, but the highest, decision that any man is ever called upon to make.

In dying, Private Milton Olive taught those of us who remain how we ought to live.

I have never understood how men can ever glorify war. "The rockets' red glare, the bombs bursting in air," has always been for me better poetry than philosophy. When

429

war is foisted upon us as a cruel recourse by men who choose force to advance policy, and must, therefore, be resisted, only the irrational or the callous, and only those untouched by the suffering that accompanies war, can revel.

Let us never exult over war. Let us not for one moment disguise in the grandest justifications of policy the inescapable fact that war feeds on the lives of young men, good young men like Milton Olive. I can never forget it. I am reminded of it every moment of every day. In a moment such as this, I am reminded all over again how brave the young are, and how great is our debt to them, and how endless is the sacrifice that we call upon them to make for us.

I realize, too, how highly we prize freedom—when we send our young to die for it.

There are times when Vietnam must seem to many a thousand contradictions, and the pursuit of freedom there an almost unrealizable dream.

But there are also times—and for me this is one of them—when the mist of confusion lifts and the basic principles emerge:

—that South Vietnam, however young and frail, has the right to develop as a nation, free from the interference of any other power, no matter how mighty or strong;

—that the normal processes of political action, if given time and patience and freedom to work, will some day, some way create in South Vietnam a society that is responsive to the people and consistent with their traditions;

—that aggression by invading armies or ruthless insurgency must be denied the precedent of success in Vietnam, if the many other little nations in the world, and if, as a matter of fact, all Southeast Asia is to ever know genuine order

and unexploited change;

—that the United States of America is in South Vietnam to resist that aggression and to permit that peaceful change to work its way, because we desire only to be a good and honorable ally, a dependable, trustworthy friend, and always a sincere and genuine servant of peace.

Men like Milton Olive die for honor. Nations that are without honor die, too, but without purpose and without cause. It must never be said that when the freedom and the independence of a new and a struggling people were at stake this mighty, powerful Nation of which we are so proud to be citizens would ever turn aside because we had the harassments that always go with conflict, and because some thought the outcome was uncertain, or the course too steep, or the cost too high.

In all of this there is irony, as there is when any young man dies. Who can say what words Private Olive might have chosen to explain what he did? Jimmy Stanford and John Foster, two of the men whose lives he saved that day on that lonely trail in that hostile jungle 10,000 miles from here are standing on the White House steps today because this man chose to die. I doubt that even they know what was on his mind as he jumped and fell across that grenade.

But I think I do know this: On the sacrifices of men who died for their country and their comrades, our freedom has been built. Whatever it is that we call civilization rests upon the merciless and seemingly irrational fact of history that some have died for others to live, and every one of us who enjoys freedom at this moment should be a witness to that fact.

So Milton Olive died in the service of a country that he loved, and he died that the men who fought at his side might continue to live. For that sacrifice his Nation honors him today with its highest possible award.

He is the eighth Negro American to receive this Nation's highest award. Fortunately, it will be more difficult for future Presidents to say how many Negroes have received the Medal of Honor. For unlike the other seven, Private Olive's military records have never carried the color of his skin or his racial origin, only the testimony that he was a good and loyal citizen of the United States of America.

So I can think of no more fitting tribute to him than to read from a letter that was written to me by this patriot's father, dated March 10.

"It is our dream and prayer that some day the Asiatics, the Europeans, the Israelites, the Africans, the Australians, the Latins, and the Americans can all live in One-World. It is our hope that in our own country the Klansmen, the Negroes, the Hebrews, and the Catholics will sit down together in the common purpose of good will and dedication; that the moral and creative intelligence of our united people will pick up the chalice of wisdom and place it upon the mountain top of human integrity; that all mankind, from all the earth, shall resolve, 'to study war no more.' That, Mr. President, is how I feel and that is my eternal hope for our Great American Society."

Ladies and gentlemen, I have no words to add to that.

[*Secretary of the Army Stanley R. Resor read the citation, the text of which follows.*]

CITATION

THE PRESIDENT of the United States of America, authorized by Act of Congress, March 3, 1863, has awarded in the name of The Congress the Medal of Honor, posthumously, to

PRIVATE FIRST CLASS MILTON L. OLIVE, III
UNITED STATES ARMY

for conspicuous gallantry and intrepidity in action at the risk of his life above and beyond the call of duty:

Private First Class Milton L. Olive, III, distinguished himself by conspicuous gallantry and intrepidity at the risk of his own life above and beyond the call of duty while participating in a search and destroy operation in the vicinity of Phu Cuong, Republic of Vietnam, on 22 October 1965. Private Olive was a member of the 3d Platoon of Company B, 2d Battalion (Airborne), 503d Infantry, as it moved through the jungle to find the Viet Cong operating in the area. Although the Platoon was subjected to a heavy volume of enemy gun fire and pinned down temporarily, it retaliated by assaulting the Viet Cong positions, causing the enemy to flee. As the Platoon pursued the insurgents, Private Olive and four other soldiers were moving through the jungle together when a grenade was thrown into their midst. Private Olive saw the grenade, and then saved the lives of his fellow soldiers at the sacrifice of his own by grabbing the grenade in his hand and falling on it to absorb the blast with his body. Through his bravery, unhesitating actions, and complete disregard for his own safety, he prevented additional loss of life or injury to the members of his platoon. Private Olive's conspicuous gallantry, extraordinary heroism, and intrepidity at the risk of his own life above and beyond the call of duty are in the highest traditions of the United States Army and reflect great credit upon himself and the Armed Forces of his country.

LYNDON B. JOHNSON

NOTE: The President spoke at 12:15 p.m. in the Rose Garden at the White House. In his opening words he referred to Mr. and Mrs. Milton B. Olive,

431

Jr., of Chicago, Ill., father and stepmother of Private Olive, Richard J. Daley, Mayor of Chicago, Stanley R. Resor, Secretary of the Army, and Gen. Earle G. Wheeler, Chairman of the Joint Chiefs of Staff. During his remarks he referred to Lt. James B. Stanford, Private Olive's company commander, and Specialist 4 John W. Foster, two of the four men whose lives were saved.

The text of the letter to the President from Milton B. Olive, Jr., made public by the White House on April 21, follows:

Honorable Sir:

Chicago's Fifth Army Headquarters has informed us that the Congressional Medal of Honor is to be awarded posthumously to our son, P.F.C. Milton Lee Olive.

This welcome news brought renewed encouragement to heavy hearts and somber spirits. It also overwhelmed us with the greatest pride and the deepest humility.

Many people and news reporters have asked why he did it. How do you feel? Across six thousand years of recorded history, man has pondered the inevitable. The conclusion is, it is too profound for mortal understanding. Perhaps, you too, Mr. President, and the American people would like to know how I feel. I have had to use strength, taken from the courage of a brave soldier to be able to bear a heavy cross. I suppose that Divine Providence

willed it and that nothing could be more glorious than laying down your life for your fellowman in the defense of your country.

Our only child and only grandchild gave his last full measure of devotion on an international battle field 10,000 miles from home. It is our dream and prayer that some day the Asiatics, the Europeans, the Israelites, the Africans, the Australians, the Latins, and the Americans can all live in One-World. It is our hope that in our own country the Klansmen, the Negroes, the Hebrews, and the Catholics will sit down together in the common purpose of good will and dedication; that the moral and creative intelligence of our united people will pick up the chalice of wisdom and place it upon the mountain top of human integrity; that all mankind, from all the earth, shall resolve, "to study war no more." That, Mr. President, is how I feel and that is my eternal hope for our Great American Society.

Your life of dedicated service is a reflection of Humanity at its best. May we wish for you longevity and civilization's greatest blessing.

Most respectfully,

MILTON B. OLIVE, JR.

The text of the President's telegram to Milton B. Olive, Jr., inviting him and other members of his family to the ceremony, is printed in the Weekly Compilation of Presidential Documents (vol. 2, p. 554).

184 Letter to New Members of the President's Advisory Committee on Labor–Management Policy. *April 22, 1966*

Dear Mr. ———:

I am delighted that you have agreed to serve on the President's Advisory Committee on Labor-Management Policy.

This Committee has been of great help to the nation. It has focused the wisdom and experience of some of our leading citizens on the vital issues of wage and price policies, productivity, collective bargaining, and industrial relations. Through its work over the past six years, your government, the labor movement, management and the general public have benefitted from a greater understanding of the problems of a growing and dynamic free enterprise society.

Today, we are facing the basic question of how to continue our unparalleled prosperity and maintain a stable and healthy economy. The first task of the Committee will be to address itself to this most important question. With this in mind, I have asked the Committee Chairman, Secretary of Labor W. Willard Wirtz and the Committee Vice Chairman, Secretary of Commerce John T. Connor to call the Committee together in the very near future.

I greatly appreciate your willingness to participate in the work of the Committee. Through public spirited citizens such as yourself we will find the new and creative solutions and that will move this country closer to the goal of a better life for all our people.

Sincerely,

LYNDON B. JOHNSON

NOTE: This is the text of identical letters, dated April 21, 1966, and addressed to 9 newly appointed members of the President's Advisory Committee on Labor-Management Policy. An excerpt was read by Joseph Laitin, an assistant press secretary, at his news conference at the White House at 11:30 a.m. on Friday, April 22, 1966. The complete text was later made available by the White House.

On April 22, 1966, the White House announced that the Committee would meet in Washington on May 4 and 5, 1966. The Committee was established by Executive Order 10918 of February 16, 1961 (3 CFR, 1959–1963 Comp., p. 445) to study and make recommendations to the President with respect to policies that may be followed by labor, management, and the public to promote sound wage and price policies, increased productivity, industrial peace, and a higher standard of living. The Committee is composed of the Secretary of Labor and the Secretary of Commerce, who alternate as Chairman, and 19 other members designated by the President, 5 of whom are drawn from the public at large, 7 from labor, and 7 from management.

The 9 newly appointed members to whom the President's letter was sent were: Donald C. Burnham, president of Westinghouse Electric Corp., Edgar F. Kaiser, chairman of Kaiser Steel Corp., J. Ward Keener, president of B. F. Goodrich Co., W. B. Murphy, president of Campbell Soup Co., I. W. Abel, president of United Steelworkers of America, Arthur S. Flemming, president of the University of Oregon, Howard W. Johnson, president of Massachusetts Institute of Technology, Page Keeton, dean of the University of Texas Law School, and Owen M. Wilson, president of the University of Minnesota.

The names of the other members, and of the 9 outgoing members, are printed in the Weekly Compilation of Presidential Documents (vol. 2, p. 558). See also Item 201.

185   Remarks in Response to the Report of the National Commission on Community Health Services.   *April* 22, 1966

Mr. Folsom, Secretary Gardner and distinguished members of the Committee, ladies and gentlemen:

I welcome you—and I welcome your report, whose purpose is the same as mine: that is, to make good health for every citizen not only our Nation's promise but its possession.

I am particularly indebted to you, Secretary Folsom, for your fine contributions to public service in this country. You have always been available, you have always been willing, and you have always been constructive in your work for the people of this Nation.

I would like to say to you, and through you to the members of your commission, that you have performed a vital and a needed service in serving on this National Commission on Community Health Services.

While I can assure you we will not embrace all your recommendations and we will not fund them all immediately, they are exciting, they do face up to the problems that we must in time face up to, and, as a matter of fact, as you spoke you were discussing some that I had been going over this morning with some of my counselors here in the Federal Government.

Yesterday our Consumer Price Index was up, and one reason it was up was because of the increase in services. One of the increases in services was in our medical costs, and one of our medical costs was in our hospital costs. One of our hospital costs is that, traditionally, people who serve us in our hospitals get pretty low wages, and when the labor market tightens up, employment gets scarce. Why, they either leave the hospital and go to something else—and it is very difficult to replace them. You have to replace them with higher wages—so that gets into extra costs.

Now, there's not anything you can really do about reducing expenditures that will change that situation much. A tax bill won't even change that situation much. A control bill won't change that situation much. So any of the alternatives we have, really doesn't get at that.

What it actually means is that we are going to have to have more people trained in this field and we are going to have to have more facilities in this field, and there are just more people using these fields.

We have more medicine and better medicine; we have more hospitals and better hospitals; we have more health care and better health care—but we don't have enough.

And our goal is up there—it's got to be. We've got to keep our eyes on the stars and our feet on the ground, and it's pretty hard to do that and still keep your equilibrium around here.

Some people want us to go further faster.

Our budget this year is $113 billion; our budget last year was $99 billion—that's a rather substantial increase. Some of it is Vietnam, but in the 2½ years since I became President, our appropriations for education have gone from 4.75 billion—and you have been greatly interested in this field— from 4 and 3 quarters billion to 10 billion 200 million. Now that is more than double in 2 years.

It took us a long time to ever get $4 billion—when President Kennedy took over it was about $1 billion. And then we got up to 4 billion plus, and now we've got it from 4 to 10. That's a pretty big jump.

Now, some people think that jumped pretty fast, that we don't have the trained personnel, we don't have the proper organization. We don't have the—Secretary Gardner has had to do a lot of reshuffling, reworking, reorganizing, to get people that can handle that much money and handle it wisely and plan it wisely and get a dollar's worth of value out of a dollar spent.

In the field of health we were spending about $5 billion a year when I became President 2½ years ago. This year we will have over 10, so we've doubled it in a little over 2 years.

In education we've doubled it; in health we've doubled it. We'll spend over $10 billion more this year in health and education—just two items—than we did when I became President 2½ years ago.

So—and poverty—we were spending none, classified as such. Now this year our appropriation will be almost $2 billion in those fields. So when you add that on to education, health, and so forth, you get in excess of a $10 billion figure.

Now all of those things are going to have to be added to, are going to have to be improved, are going to have to be enlarged, as the years go on. And we have the resources to do it. We must be sure that we do it in the right way, with the proper personnel, with the proper planning, with the proper management, with the proper standards, with the proper relationship between the Federal and the State and the local units.

Now we're trying to do that. I spent a long time yesterday trying to work on a commission of scholars and elected officials and others to get this relationship thing straightened out. I spent a good deal of my day working with Secretary Gardner and others on trying to get the personnel of these things straightened out.

And the very things that you talk about in your report must become a part of our goal for the years to come.

But I don't want to suffer any illusions that we are going to realize them all immediately, because it's going to take time and we're going to have to prepare the way. We must learn to walk before we run.

Now, we have entered an age in which these miracles are commonplace. Already our doctors are doing unthinkable things. You're reading about it on the ticker—I just went to check before I walked in here—about the very unusual thing that happened down in Houston yesterday. Our doctors are probing the interior of arteries with tiny lights and cameras.

Through electronic sensors in an astronaut's couch, scientists can monitor the physical condition of space explorers. And a waiting-room chair may soon report a patient's pulse and blood pressure before he enters a doctor's office. (My fellow gets mine before I get out of bed every morning, but I'm sure that he will welcome the day when he can get it in the reception room instead of having to come in there.)

But as I said, less than 24 hours ago in an operating room in Houston, Dr. DeBakey and others had a dramatic breakthrough— a surgeon implanted an electrically-powered artificial heart in a human patient.

All this knowledge would profit us little, though, unless we use it for the good of every citizen in every community. Our age, rich as it is with miracles, is still an age where too many families must travel too far and pay too much to receive treatment. Our health services are not organized to get the full benefit of our health manpower. We are trying to do that, as I told you, with our Commission—and under the dynamic leadership of one of the ablest Cabinet officers to ever serve in this town, Dr. Gardner.

The responsibility for providing the best services in every community can't be met just here in Washington, though. It is going to take time and talent; it is going to take State leaders; it is going to take com-munity leaders; it is going to take neighborhood leaders. And how we can coordinate all this leadership and keep them working together in a consensus, so to speak, is a problem we still have.

Now, you have taken the leadership of this Committee and you have produced a report, and you have agreed. And I welcome it and I thank you.

You have concentrated not so much on just Federal efforts but on the whole broad range—State and community planning.

You have underscored an important national goal, and that is to make health available to all the people. I am sufficiently progressive that I want to see it made available to all the people of the world—not just here. I want to set an example here that they can emulate elsewhere. I think that we have made great progress. In HEW alone, our health expenditures have grown from less than $1 billion in 1961 to a billion 4 in 1963; up to 6.9 for 1967. Now, that's 8 times as much in only 6 years. And when we bring our Medicare in there, and so forth, you can see we run over the 10 billion figure.

Your report makes an important contribution to our efforts and I can assure you that we will study it carefully. We won't agree with you on all the 98 major recommendations, we won't get them implemented, even in our time allotted us. We can make a drastic mistake by going too far too fast without proper preparation.

I am trying to pull all these things together, and I can guarantee you, and through you, your Committee, that these recommendations are going to receive the "carefullest study," as Secretary Hull used to say—the most serious consideration. And I trust that a great many of them will be implemented and funded and that the citizens for whom they were prepared will reap the rich result for which they were intended.

I don't think you men know—and I want this ceremony to emphasize it again—just how very much your contribution of your time and your prestige and your effort to studies of this kind means to your President and to your country.

We have made revolutionary advances in this country in many fields in a matter of months—30 months: in conservation, in food production and distribution, in medicine, in health, in hospitals, in education— in all these things. And almost without exception they have been the results of task forces, they have been the results of studies, they have been the results of commissions, where men and women who made up this effort have outlined a long-range plan in a democratic way for their fellow citizens. And it has relieved my burden immeasurably.

And I am so happy that the President of this country can still call on any citizen in this country, Republican or Democrat—particularly Republicans, because Democrats may want to be postmasters (we have a leverage over them)—but call on men to come in here and serve not their party but serve their country. And whatever is good for their country is really good for their party and for themselves in the final analysis.

So one of the greatest rewards that comes to me, and one of the most satisfying

things that comes to a President, is the knowledge that men like you and those associated with you in this endeavor would spend the midnight oil that you spent trying to find better health for all the people of this land.

Thank you.

NOTE: The President spoke at 12:15 p.m. in the Cabinet Room at the White House. In his opening words he referred to Marion B. Folsom, Chairman of the National Commission on Community Health Services and former Secretary of Health, Education, and Welfare, and John W. Gardner, Secretary of Health, Education, and Welfare. During his remarks he referred to Dr. Michael E. DeBakey of Houston, Texas, heart surgeon, and to Cordell Hull, Secretary of State during the administration of Franklin D. Roosevelt.

The Commission's 309-page report is entitled "Health is a Community Affair." It was the work of six task forces on community health problems and was based on 21 community action studies drawn from towns and cities ranging in population from 30,000 to 3.5 million.

The Commission was established in 1962 as a private corporation under the sponsorship of the American Public Health Association and the National Health Council. Supported by private and public funds, it conducted a nationwide study of community health needs, resources, and practices.

Other members of the Commission include Dr. Milton Eisenhower, President of Johns Hopkins University, LeRoy Collins, Under Secretary of Commerce, Boisfeuillet Jones, President of the Woodruff Foundation, Edwin L. Crosby, Director of the American Hospital Association, and 28 other businessmen, educators, public officials, and citizens representing a national cross section.

186 Remarks at a Retirement Ceremony for Toinette M. Bachelder of the White House Staff. *April 22, 1966*

Ladies and gentlemen, and fellow occupants of the White House:

I think this is a very great privilege for me, although it is not particularly a pleasure.

I think Toi really ought to be ashamed of herself. This is the first time that I have

left the country since I have been President, and she tried to sneak out of the White House in my absence!

I appreciate the personal reasons which are causing Toi to leave us, but I have no intention of letting anyone who is as much a part of the history of this White House as you are go without devoting some attention to your departure.

I will always be grateful to this gracious lady, as will all the Presidents who have served with her, for the work that she has done for them and for the country. I remember Toi from my boyhood days when I was just a young, green Congressman—and she was even younger. (How do you like that for recovery?)

MISS BACHELDER. Wonderful!

THE PRESIDENT. Some day the Navy is going to use my services in connection with the recovery of space people if I come back that quickly!

But as I said in my letter to Miss Bachelder, the best I could do while I was out of the country: "You have been witness to what most people who live in this country can only read in the history books. You have seen this from first hand and no history book can ever capture all the truth or all the spirit of all the Presidents you have known."

If you decide to do what some other fellows have done—start writing about your impressions around this table or around these various rooms—I hope that you will let me see the galley proofs.

MISS BACHELDER. I don't think you have anything to worry about.

THE PRESIDENT. Give me a chance. The fact that you have stayed in this house as long as you have is a great tribute to you. It also is a great tribute to the man that I loved so much and that you loved so much, whose picture is on that wall there, who had the vision to bring you here originally. You and he together were an inspiration to thousands and thousands of young people who suffered from the affliction of polio.

By your very life you gave hope to thousands when they were in the midst of despair.

I don't think you even know it, but we have some people who have looked at you with such admiration that they have really conquered polio themselves. They work here in the White House—have even worked for me, and worked for me a long time and I didn't even know they had had polio. So I think that you should realize by your courage and your grit, your never-failing good humor and your inspiration, your devotion to duty and your ability to transact business efficiently, you have replaced many tears with smiles and with laughter.

I am not going to say goodby to you because I refuse to believe that you are going very far away.

MISS BACHELDER. I am not.

THE PRESIDENT. I want you to always think of the White House as part of your home. I want you to know that as long as I am here you not only have a very special place in our memories, but there will always be a place for you at our table.

Someone once said that home is the place where, when you go there, they always let you in. Toi, I know that I speak for all your friends in the White House staff when I say that your home here will always welcome you. The White House gates will always swing wide for you. We will be better off if you use them, and we hope you will.

MISS BACHELDER. Thank you so much. You are awfully kind to take time from your busy schedule for me, and I appreciate it.

NOTE: The President spoke at 12:30 p.m. in the Cabinet Room at the White House. Miss Bachelder worked at the White House for 33 years, having been brought from Warm Springs, Ga., by President Franklin D. Roosevelt.

187 Remarks Upon Proclaiming National Defense Transportation Day and National Transportation Week. *April 22, 1966*

Secretary Connor, distinguished Members of the Congress, distinguished leaders of labor and business communities, and my very dear friends:

I have asked you to come here today because I am proclaiming the week of May 15th as the National Transportation Week.

I am also today proclaiming Friday, May 20th, as National Defense Transportation Day.

I have invited these leaders of our great transportation industry here because I believe this occasion is doubly significant. At this very moment, two bold and vital items of transportation legislation are pending in our Congress. They will give the green light to the revolutionary era that our entire transportation system must now launch upon.

The first of these measures calls for the creation of a Cabinet-level Department of Transportation.

And let us be clear about this proposal. It is much more than just a desirable Government reorganization plan. I believe that it is very critical to the future of transportation in the United States.

It would be difficult for me to overemphasize what I really believe is at stake, because transportation is more than a major force in the 20th century, modern America.

—First, it is a source of employment to more than 2½ million of our citizens.
—It is the source of one in every five dollars of our economy.
—It is the lifeline of travel and commerce.

And our system of transportation, the greatest in history, was built by the genius of free enterprise. And as long as I am your President it is going to be sustained by free enterprise.

But we must face facts. And a system that just "grow'd like Topsy" is no longer adequate in times as complex and as changing as those we're going through today.

In the next two decades the demand for transportation in this country is going to double. But we are already falling behind—our transportation lifeline is tangled—our gears are worn and they're dangerously strained.

—Too many of our highways today are congested and are unsafe.
—Too many of our airways are reaching the saturation point.

We read about this every day when we pick up the paper or when we tune in our radio or television commentator, yet we just seem to accept it and do nothing about it:

—Highways that are congested and unsafe.
—Airways that have reached the saturation point.
—Equipment that is old and obsolete—and what is modern and good is often in very short supply.
—Our new technologies are being ignored.
—Our research and development, all admit, are inadequate.
—Our governmental policies need better coordination and the Government needs better leadership.

We spend here in the Federal Government $6 billion annually of your money on transportation. But we must spend it wisely—and I would like to spend it effectively, if you would give me the instruments to do so.

The Federal Government has more than 100,000 employees involved in transportation programs, and we must employ their talents in a purposeful effort and coordinated—if you will give us permission to do so.

We have a variety of agencies and bureaus scattered all over the place, administering what we refer to as transportation policy. But instead of aiding and encouraging and providing constructive leadership for our transportation industry, we too often find them harassing and hindering and confusing it.

Now we can change all of that. Out of this partnership between the Government and industry and labor can grow a well-planned and thoroughly coordinated national transportation system, and we think we can make it fast, and efficient, and safe, and dependable, and completely up to date.

And we think if we do that, that all Americans will benefit.

So we have proposed that a National Transportation Safety Board be created under the Secretary of Transportation. The sole function of this board will be safety—safety of people who travel. This board will:

—Investigate the accidents to seek their causes, and do it in a judicial and, I trust, non-emotional way;

—It will determine compliance and whether we're getting it with our safety standards;

—It will carefully examine the adequacy of such standards;

—It will assume the safety functions that are transferred from the ICC and the CAB.

A second bill now before Congress commits the Government for the first time in history to try to do something about the slaughter—the senseless slaughter on our highways.

Each year 50,000 Americans die on American highways. Each year 100,000 Americans are permanently disabled on American highways. Each year nearly 4 million Americans are injured on our highways. Now this has a frightening familiarity—and familiarity has bred, if not contempt, I'm afraid an inexcusable indifference.

Another statistic that's equally grim but not so familiar—and one that I hope you'll remember—is, since 1961 we have lost four times as many American servicemen in motor vehicle accidents as our enemies have been able to kill in the fighting in Vietnam.

Now we must no longer tolerate such anarchy on wheels.

We can no longer tolerate unsafe automobiles.

We can no longer tolerate poorly planned and badly lighted highways that all of us are responsible for, and perhaps I am more responsible than anyone in this room.

We can no longer tolerate ineffective safety programs that result from the complete lack of basic research into what is truly and actually causing our accidents.

The Highway Safety Act of 1966 will move us out of the stone age of ignorance and reaction.

It will support the State programs of driver education and of licensing procedures.

It will establish a Federal research and testing center to probe the why's and the how's of traffic accidents—in the context of the total environment: the driver, the automobile, the road.

It will establish a program of strict safety standards for our automobiles. And I just cannot overemphasize the need for such standards.

The alternative to Federal standards is unthinkable.

What do we have? What is the alternative? Fifty different sets of standards for 50 different States. And that is going to be the result, the inevitable result, of our do-nothing action here.

The American people, I think, could become aroused. I believe the American people want constructive action in this area. I believe they want to move forward in this field.

But I want to be, and I think you want to be, fair and intelligent. And the American driver and the great industry that provides his car—I want them all to get a fair shake. And judge not lest ye be judged, and we all can be judged in this instance, from the President of the United States down to the youngest boy with a driver's license. And it is just silly for us to continue slaughtering 50,000 people.

I'm not here to blame any one or any individual or any group, except myself, and I would blame myself this morning if I didn't say that I think the time has passed and it is here, for us to start doing something about it.

Now I have taken my stand; I have submitted my recommendations. They're going to step on some people's toes; some are going to become martyrs; some are going to harass and delay and obstruct and be selfish, as they always are when you present recommendations to the Congress. But I want to appeal to you in the name of 50,000 people who are dying today to please come and cooperate and coordinate, and let's try—let's try with everything we've got to reduce this slaughter.

Now these programs, I believe, are the beginning. I think they'll provide solid steps for making material reductions of the deaths that are now taking place on our roads.

And so, today, I sign this proclamation on a note of excitement and hope. Because of the actions we take this year, our children, I think, will come of age in a modern society—where transportation is not only fast and economical but where it's safe.

And if we can bring that about I think each of you will be proud to say to your grandchildren that you sat in this room today

when we launched this effort, when we signed this transportation proclamation, when we appealed to the Congress to give us a decision and some guidelines and some rules—and when we moved ahead.

I said to a man last night how much I felt we had to be thankful for in our Government. I had innumerable problems that I couldn't find the answer to. But I looked back over and saw where I'd been in the last few weeks, and the cooperation that had existed with this system that was set up almost 200 years ago by our forefathers, and how the Supreme Court and the courts, and how the Congress, and how the Executive, and how the people of both parties, of different religions, of different races, of different sections—how they were coordinating and working together. And I don't think I have ever been prouder of our whole system than now.

I had a report from Governor Bryant on the Governors he had talked to. And you couldn't tell who was a Democrat or a Republican from the report he had. He just gave the Governor by name and said: "Here's what he said and how he wants to help."

I had a report from our mayors, and it gave me great satisfaction that we don't engage in name calling and smearing and exposing and humiliating our coworkers and our colleagues in other branches of Government. We're all concerned with one thing. We're so busy moving ahead that we, trying to get ahead, don't spend any time trying to get even.

And that's what I want to say to the transportation industry this morning: whether you run a big railroad line with a choo-choo, or whether you have a diesel truck, or whether you have an inland waterway, or whether you come under the Army Engineers or the Reclamation Service, or whether you're afraid of getting a little tax on diesel fuel or an airline ticket, or how or who makes an automobile or how dangerous it is, or how many the manufacturer personally killed himself, or he didn't kill last year—let's submerge all these personal feelings in the matter and just keep our eye on the big ball.

There are 50,000 people that are dying. Now there are 1,400 that have died in Vietnam since January the 1st. We lost 50,000—50 times as many people dying right here under your nose as you're talking about dying out there. Now, we don't want a single one of them to die. And I'm going to try to do something about keeping their deaths to a minimum out there. And I'm also going to try to do something about keeping them at a minimum here.

But we need the help of every person in this room. And, you may have to back up a little bit, you may have to moderate your views a little bit, you may have to quench your thirst for a little blood a little bit and not run over the President or the Congress with your pressure. But come on and let us help with these two things:

—A transportation leader in the Cabinet that can sit there and can speak for every element and know what he's talk-

ing about.

—An act that will give us the ways and means and *modus operandi* to do something about these 50,000 people that are dying, these 100,000 that are permanently disabled, this mass slaughter.

Now, we don't have long to do it between now and election. And I hope those of you that have been a little picayunish and got out your glasses and tried to find something wrong with this suggestion or that one will kind of give and take a little bit, and next time we meet here in the room Senator Mansfield will be bringing me a bill and saying "Right here's where you sign—on the dotted line."

NOTE: The President spoke at 1 p.m. in the East Room at the White House prior to signing Proclamation 3718 "National Defense Transportation Day and National Transportation Week, 1966" (2 Weekly Comp. Pres. Docs., p. 559; 31 F.R. 6567; 3 CFR, 1966 Comp., p. 45).

In his opening words he referred to Secretary of Commerce John T. Connor. During his remarks he referred to Farris Bryant, Director of the Office of Emergency Planning and former Governor of Florida, and to Senator Mike Mansfield of Montana, majority leader of the Senate.

The bill creating a Cabinet-level Department of Transportation was approved by the President on October 15, 1966 (see Item 523).

The National Traffic and Motor Vehicle Safety Act and the Highway Safety Act were approved by the President on September 9 (see Item 449).

188   The President's News Conference of *April* 22, 1966

QUESTIONS

THE PRESIDENT [*in response to a question before the arrival of the official stenographer*]. [1.] I haven't received that note. I saw Reuters [1] carried a dispatch that it would be delivered to us today. I think that you know that we have exchanged corre-

spondence with General de Gaulle.[2] He has given his viewpoints and we have given ours. We have all the decisions related to them constantly reviewed and I believe they will be discussed with the Secretary as soon as he gets back.

I don't have anything to add to what we

---

[1] British news agency.

[2] President Charles de Gaulle of France.

have said at this stage. I haven't seen the letter.

UNREST IN VIETNAM

[2.] Q. Mr. President, it has been about a month now, since the unrest has broken out in Vietnam. I wonder what comments or observations you might have to make about that.

THE PRESIDENT. We think that the Vietnamese people are going through a trying period. They are trying to build toward and develop a constitutional government. We realize that the Vietnamese military and our military also have a problem, along with our allies—Australian, New Zealand, Korean, and all the others associated with us there—in maintaining a unit capable of directing a successful resistance effort.

We agreed in Honolulu to do everything we could, not only to continue the resistance and defeat aggression but to try to defeat social misery and establish a stable, democratic society and to seek peace.

I doubt that the Vietnamese people have ever seen such efforts made in this direction as have been made following the Honolulu conference.[3]

There are regional, religious, and tribal differences there. The country is split by those differences. In some ways they accentuate these differences.

I think the Prime Minister indicated in his January 15 speech, as he confirmed in our meeting in Honolulu, that there was a widespread feeling that, despite the war, they should move toward a constitutional and democratic government. It affects all of us. I believe we are moving in that direction.

I think it is also clear that the Communists hoped the Vietnamese people will not be able to carry it out, or that the military will not remain united, or that our people here will

get tired and want to change.

But I do believe that in due time that the constitutional government will be formed.

RESULTS OF THE HONOLULU CONFERENCE

[3.] Q. Mr. President, some have said this Honolulu meeting may have caused some of the problems we have seen in the past weeks in Vietnam.

THE PRESIDENT. I don't think there is any basis for that at all. I think that the leaders of the Government in Vietnam have indicated their desire to have constitutional government, and many people believed to be opposed to the military effort in Vietnam were very anxious to get ahead with the pacification effort.

Prior to Honolulu, we had Ambassador Porter[4] come in and we had organized that. A good many of the Senators and others had urged us to increase our economic assistance, speed up our educational development and our health program.

So we met with the representatives of the Vietnamese Government for that purpose. We outlined our plans rather successfully. We are very proud of what happened.

I don't think that there is any connection with the Honolulu conference and the statements that it brought about a crisis. I had a report here this morning from Ambassador Lodge.[5] I don't have his full report, but here is a quotation from the weekly report which I think gives us reason to be pleased with our discussions in Honolulu.

He says, "For the first time in the history of this country, some competitive spirit is in evidence on who cares the most for the underdog. This would not have happened

---

[3] See Items 53–56.

[4] William J. Porter, Deputy U.S. Ambassador to the Republic of Vietnam.

[5] Henry Cabot Lodge, U.S. Ambassador to the Republic of Vietnam.

without Honolulu."

I think from all of the people who know what happened there, they are very glad that the meeting took place. They are very satisfied with its accomplishments.

THE PACIFICATION PROGRAM IN VIETNAM

[4.] Q. Mr. President, Senator McGee [6] has said more South Vietnamese troops will have to be used in the pacification program and that would mean more American troops would have to be used in combat. Do you have any comment?

THE PRESIDENT. I haven't seen the Senator's statement. We have secured the interest and deep concern and cooperation of the Vietnamese Government which is essential. General Westmoreland [7] and those under his command will cooperate in this effort as outlined in Honolulu and as followed by the Vice President, Secretary of Agriculture, and Secretary Gardner.

Whatever cooperation is necessary for General Westmoreland to help the Government of Vietnam accelerate education, production, health efforts, I am sure it will be done.

One of our primary objectives at Honolulu was to get General Ky [8] and General Westmoreland to understand how important we felt it was to carry along this two-pronged approach to matters there, not only military but economic.

MANAGEMENT OF VIETNAMESE WAR

[5.] Q. Mr. President, some of the Republicans have been a little more vocal in their criticism of the administration in Vietnam. Congressman Ford [9] used the word "mismanagement" and former Senator Goldwater [10] said they are not prosecuting the war to the fullest. Do you have any comment or reaction to these statements?

THE PRESIDENT. No, I think we can expect some people to be critical of what we do and the way we do it. I am sure that you find that in all periods of strain like the one we are now going through. This is not anything new.

I picked up a note this morning I had Mr. Jacobsen [11] write General Westmoreland in February about a need for some spark plugs at a certain place. A Member of Congress was rather critical of General Westmoreland and Secretary McNamara.

I inquired about the situation and General Westmoreland wrote Mr. Jacobsen back and said, "My response to the President in Honolulu was that there are no shortages in supplies for the troops in Vietnam which adversely affect combat operations or the health and welfare of the command. This is a valid appraisal of the supply situation." That was February 19th.

We recognize that every day you do not have all you want, where you want it, when you want it, in an operation as big as the United States Government conducts. I ran out of lead pencils last night in my night reading about 2 o'clock. I wondered why they didn't sharpen some that were there. They had all broken off. But there was nobody around to criticize so I had to get up and go to my coat pocket and get a new pencil.

---

[6] Senator Gale W. McGee of Wyoming.

[7] Gen. William C. Westmoreland, Commander, United States Military Assistance Command, Vietnam.

[8] Prime Minister Nguyen Cao Ky of South Vietnam.

[9] Representative Gerald R. Ford of Michigan, minority leader of the House of Representatives.

[10] Barry Goldwater, Senator from Arizona 1953–1965 and Republican candidate for President in 1964.

[11] Jake Jacobsen, Legislative Counsel to the President.

We have those problems. There is no mistaking it. It is going to be increasingly difficult as we carry on this effort so far from home. It requires so much in the way of health facilities, material supplies, ammunition, guns, and planes.

I don't want to play down the fact that we do make mistakes and that we do have criticisms at times. But I would say that I am very grateful for the general support and the general reaction of the Republicans, as I am of all Americans.

I think they have tried to be generally, with a few possible exceptions, very helpful to us in this whole effort.

THE NOVEMBER ELECTIONS

[6.] Q. Mr. President, what do you see shaping up as the major issue or issues in the November election?

THE PRESIDENT. I think that we probably emphasize the election a little bit too much too early. We don't have any national election in the terms of an administration, selection of a President or Vice President, this year.

There will be congressional elections, some senatorial elections. But I reviewed them for the purposes of answering questions of some of the Democratic leaders and committeemen about the Democratic seats that are up. This time it looks like in the Senate most of the Senate seats are reasonably safe.

I think even the most optimistic opponent won't assume there is more than one or two in doubt of the Democrats. It just happens it is a good year for us. The Republicans have, I think our boys feel, about six in the Senate that have serious problems. I don't look for any great sweep with that number—two on one side and six on the other.

In the House the men will be campaigning, of course, on their record. I don't believe any Congressman on the Democratic ticket ever had a more comprehensive record or a better record to campaign on.

The sentiment everywhere seems to support that record. Most of the polls show that 90 percent of the people think that we have gotten along well with Congress. The polls run from 85 to 95 percent, the President working with the Congress. I think I have reviewed now about 30 polls. I think Kentucky was off from 64 to 63, and a Southwestern State was off one or two points although we still have a 56 margin.

Except for that, there were rather substantial increases in the other areas. Our men don't know where some get this information that there is going to be any great difficulty this year. I guess it must be the wish is father to the thought, or maybe you people promote some of this doubt.

When you get out and see the folks, I think they approve of the education program. Our problem is to keep the Congress from appropriating far in excess of the budget. Someone told me the other day they are considering appropriating several hundred million dollars more in the health-education bill than we recommended. I know this year they have already appropriated almost $300 million more in the GI bill, they authorized that; $20-odd million more in the Coast Guard; $41 million more in the deficiency for impacted areas.

The agriculture bill today is $128 million more. So it seems like the Congress is not only for the programs, but for spending more on them than we have recommended.

I would think that we are going to have a rather peaceful and constructive preelection period, unless some of you fellows provoke some disputes up there.

EFFECT OF WAR ON THE ELECTION

[7.] Q. Mr. President, do you think the Vietnamese war will hurt the Democrats in the fall election?

THE PRESIDENT. I don't really believe that any of you want to make this a Democratic or a Republican Army or Air Force or Navy or war. I never use the party term in connection with the servicemen and what they are doing. I don't see many people that do.

I try to talk to the leaders of both parties in this country about the national interest and I have never seen many of them put their party ahead of their country. I doubt that they will.

SPENDING FOR DOMESTIC PROGRAMS

[8.] Q. Mr. President, Senator Bobby Kennedy [12] said he thinks that the domestic program this year has been cut where it will especially hurt the poor—in health, education, and housing. Do you have any comment?

THE PRESIDENT. Our budget was $99 billion last year, and it is $113 billion this year. I think about $5 billion of it is in the Great Society programs generally for the poor. I have repeated to you many, many times that since I succeeded President Kennedy we have increased the spending appropriations for education and health and poverty from $10 billion to $12 billion more in the last 2 years than was being spent before.

We want to continue to spend as much for education and health as we think the budget will permit. I never object to anyone being interested in education or health, or any of those things. I am glad to have the help of all I can in that field. We are going to need it. I may not be able to go as fast and as furiously as some think is possible, but we

are making great progress and we are going to be making more.

MILITARY OPERATIONS IN VIETNAM

[9.] Q. Mr. President, you have spoken of the political situation in Vietnam. Could you report to us on the military operations?

THE PRESIDENT. I don't have anything that I could tell you that you haven't seen in the papers. I get the intelligence briefings every night and the operation reports every morning, but I hear out of my left ear on the radio just about what I am reading. Sometimes I believe you fellows get these things—they court you—before they get to me with some of them.

There is a sizable operation going on there now. I have been very proud of the way our men have conducted themselves. I think we have the very best in military leadership under General Westmoreland.

DIPLOMATIC DEVELOPMENTS

[10.] Q. Mr. President, is there any hope of changes in the diplomatic front?

THE PRESIDENT. No, I don't have anything that I could announce that is new there. We expressed ourselves on Senator Mansfield's [13] suggestion. We had made that type of suggestion in somewhat similar form several times before. I think that nearly everybody in this country has heard from us several times.

If you have any information from them through any of your sources that will encourage me, we would surely welcome it. I think you know how we feel about it. We must continue to hope and try. We will do that through every avenue, but to say to you that there has been any indication from the

---

[12] Senator Robert F. Kennedy of New York.

[13] Senator Mike Mansfield of Montana, majority leader of the Senate.

Vietcong or from North Vietnam that they are ready to cease their aggression, I have to say no.

They are still determined to swallow up the people of South Vietnam and by force bring them to their knees. I presume they still think they can do it.

SERVICEMEN'S TOUR OF DUTY

[11.] Q. Mr. President, in the event that this continues for some time in Vietnam, is there any plan now for consideration that may extend the servicemen's tour of duty beyond the 12 months they are currently serving now?

THE PRESIDENT. No.

Q. Mr. President, it looks like they will be able to handle the 12 months.

THE PRESIDENT. The answer to your question is no.

TESTIMONIAL DINNERS FOR MEMBERS OF CONGRESS

[12.] Q. Sir, in light of your years in the House and Senate as a Member of the legislative branch, have you any thoughts about the desirability or need of testimonial dinners for legislators to help meet expenses?

THE PRESIDENT. I have spoken at many testimonial and appreciation dinners at various times for various Members and others

who have received awards from time to time. I have expressed my appreciation to distinguished Members of Congress.

Q. Mr. President, do you think it is appropriate for these dinners to be used to raise money for a Congressman's personal use?

THE PRESIDENT. I have had no information about any dinners held for anyone to obtain funds for personal use, none that I have ever attended that I knew were being held for that purpose.

I always understood that they were having an appreciation dinner or testimonial dinner but I didn't know that it was for personal, or political, or local campaign, or national.

I have been asked to appear, and have. I see from your papers what is reported and I see that Senator Stennis and Senator Bennett [14] are considering the facts in the case. I would think the appropriate thing to do would be to have the body set up by the Senate to receive all the information that is available and make its judgment, and I would be willing to have confidence in their judgment.

Merriman Smith, United Press International: Thank you, Mr. President.

NOTE: President Johnson's sixty-second news conference was held in his office at the White House at 5 p.m. on Friday, April 22, 1966.

[14] Senator John Stennis of Mississippi, Chairman of the Senate Select Committee on Standards and Conduct, and Senator Wallace F. Bennett of Utah, member of the committee.

---

189 Remarks in Baltimore at the Celebration of the Bicentennial of American Methodism. *April 22, 1966*

Bishop Lord, my beloved friend Mayor McKeldin, my colleagues and associates in Washington, your very able Senators Brewster and Tydings, distinguished delegates to the Methodist Convocation, ladies and gentlemen:

I am moved by your introduction, Bishop Lord, especially by your reading of the letter from Bishop Coke and Bishop Asbury to our first President, George Washington.

I pray that I may so conduct myself in office that I too may inspire, among the

Methodist people of America, a "warm feeling" in their hearts.

The Lord is my witness that I shall try.

I have lived and I have worked with Methodists all of my life. Methodist men and women—including circuit riders much like those brave and hardy souls who stopped by the White House last Tuesday on their way over here—were a part of the early history of my State.

They devoted themselves to making my part of America a much better place to live in, although some people in modern magazines still think it is a horrible place. But they built our schools and our hospitals and they built our homes for our orphans. And somehow or another they had enough energy, and perhaps some cash, left over in the late 1920's to build a football team at Southern Methodist University. And they sent it north, and they gave Army and Notre Dame and Pittsburgh and all the big ones the greatest scare they ever had.

Now nobody has underestimated Texas Methodists since that time.

And looking out in this Methodist audience tonight, I sense in the air the same spirit of good will, the same commitment to good works, that was typical of all of those early Methodists that I knew in the Southwest.

For yours is really a church that was founded on social conscience—that was founded on the dream of social justice for all human beings.

From John Wesley to your leaders of today, Methodists have always believed that works of compassion among men were part of God's will in action.

The Social Creed of the Methodist Church—written in 1940—is a most eloquent statement of that belief.

I want to read aloud some parts of that creed for each of you tonight:

"We stand for equal rights and complete justice for all men in all stations of life . . .

". . . for adequate provision for the protection, the education, the spiritual nurture, and the wholesome recreation for every child . . .

". . . for the abatement of poverty and the right of all men to live . . .

"We believe that it is our Christian duty to do our utmost to provide for all men the opportunity to earn an adequate livelihood . . .

"We believe that society has a right to expect that every person, not physically or mentally incapacitated, shall be constantly engaged, so far as possible, in some vocation productive of common good . . .

"We oppose all forms of social, economic, and moral waste."

Bishop Lord, it would be very hard for me to write a more perfect description of the American ideal—or of the American commitments in the 1960's. What you have said in the Social Creed of the Methodist Church is what I along with Senator Brewster and Senator Tydings and others in both Houses of Congress are trying to write into the laws of our country today—and in the hearts of all of our people.

For our people—of every faith—have come to believe that the works of compassion are the legitimate and are the necessary concern of the entire Nation and particularly of the National Government, and of the States and of the cities, and of the churches and the schools, and of industry and labor and the private citizen.

It was not always so. It was not so when I came to Washington 35 years ago. Then the question was always, "Should we do this? Where are we going to get the money? Should we commit ourselves to great programs in education, or in employment, or in health care, or in relieving poverty?"

Today the question is—ask yourself, "Are

we doing enough for human beings?"

Well, I want you to know that from the depth of my soul I welcome the change of heart that has changed the question.

The answer—because we are Americans—must always be no. No, we're not doing enough, we're not satisfied with the status quo, we're not going to sit still, we're going to keep moving. And so long as millions of little children are poorly taught and poorly fed—Lady Bird has a favorite story of the lady that walked up to a little child and said, "Why aren't you eating today?" And he said, "It's not my day to eat." A member of a very large family, but it was true.

So long as many men live out their lives without useful work, and without any skills, and without any training, and without hope; so long as disease wastes thousands of young lives, and so long as poverty haunts the aged, the answer is no.

But let me tell you this evening something of what we are doing. For even the most astute mind may miss the meaning of what has been happening these last few months. Even the most deeply concerned observer may not sense how powerful are the forces of compassion in America today.

And there is no more dramatic place to begin, than with education.

When the Methodist Church in America was founded two centuries ago, education was—as it had been in Europe—chiefly the province of the well-to-do. Yet our wise men knew that democracy could not endure unless the people were schooled in the arts of citizenship—unless they could read and figure and form their own opinions.

A great President of the Republic of Texas said, "Education is the guardian genius of democracy"—the guardian genius of democracy! "It is the only dictator that free men will recognize. And it is the only ruler that free men will accept."

John Adams said, in 1765, "The preservation of the means of knowledge among the lowest ranks is of more importance to the public than all the property of all the rich in this entire country."

Exactly two hundred years later the Congress adopted and I signed the Elementary and Secondary School Act at the one-room school that I first attended as a child of 4 years old.

Now—in the coming year—almost $2 billion of Federal funds will go into our elementary and secondary schools all over this land.

—almost a billion dollars specifically to help 7½ million disadvantaged children.

—hundreds of millions will go for school libraries, for school textbooks, for educational laboratories where men and women learn new and better ways of teaching.

In higher education—where Methodists have contributed mightily to American learning—more than $300 million will be spent by your Government this year to build classrooms and libraries and laboratories.

Two and a half years ago we did not have such a program.

Sixty million dollars will go to bright students whose needs are great.

Another $100 million will go to needy students on work-study grants.

Loans guaranteed by the Government will aid more than three quarters of a million students.

I am told that any boy or girl that graduates from school today and does not have the financial means—and his family does not have the financial means—can go to college, if they have a transcript from high school of having done good work in that high school, by one of three means—money is not the test: they can get a job that we help provide, they can get a scholarship where we will give them the schooling if their grades are high enough, or they can get a loan that the Government guarantees. But they just cannot stay home, if they want to go to college, because they don't have the money. Every boy and girl in this country that wants to go to high school, that is capable of going to high school, that parents cannot send to high school—in the last 2½ years we have provided the ways and means for them to go to college.

Altogether in the 3 years, almost 3 years, since I became President, we have moved from a Federal appropriation of 4.8 billion to 10 billion 200 million this year, from a little under 5 to a little over 10—more than doubled our expenditures for education—increased them this year $5 billion.

Now this is the fruit of compassion. But it is also the dictate of necessity. For we, the strongest, the most powerful, the richest nation on earth, have learned from the Book of Proverbs that:

"By wisdom a house is built,

By understanding it is established;

By knowledge the rooms are filled with all precious and pleasant riches.

A wise man is mightier than a strong man,

And a man of knowledge than he who has strength."

Your Methodist creed opposed every form of social, economic, and moral waste.

And there is no more tragic and meaningless waste than that of prolonged illness. And in accordance with your creed and my feelings in the matter we are going to do something about that in this country. In the 3 years that I have been President our expenditures for health are moving from 5 billion 100 million to 10 billion 300 million which is more than double. For health, from 5 billion 3 years ago to 10 billion this year.

Two years ago, millions of Americans looked upon their retirement years with grim foreboding. They lacked the means to face the illnesses that come with age.

For most of them, the answer came last year—with the enactment of Medicare. In the year that will begin this June, $3 billion will be paid out under this program to cover the major costs of hospital and medical care for older Americans. And medical care will be supplemented by a grant program to the States for 7 million poor who will receive assistance.

Now there is so much more to tell you about what we are doing about better health in America.

Three years ago we were helping to provide comprehensive health care to 12,000 poor mothers—12,000 poor mothers were receiving care 3 years ago. This year 140,000 poor mothers are receiving care.

Three years ago we were helping to rehabilitate 120,000 disabled persons—so that they might become productive members of society after their rehabilitation. This year we will aid more than 200,000, and we will spend three times as much as we did in the year 1964, shortly after I came to the Presidency.

Three years ago we were beginning a new program of assistance to community mental health centers—just beginning to treat the mentally ill in the communities where they belong. And now we are supporting the staffs in those centers, and by June of 1967 we will have aided projects affording comprehensive mental health services for 28 million Americans!

By next year we hope to begin a great new hospital program—using direct Federal and guaranteed private loans—that will modernize 260,000 hospital beds over a 10-year period. And I am going to announce tonight, we are going to start right at Johnson City, Texas.

Our expenditures for health research have

grown by more than a third in 3 years' time. Almost $1½ billion will go this year to the fight against heart disease and cancer and stroke and communicable and other diseases.

And weren't you thrilled and aren't you praying for that poor man down in Houston, Texas, where they had that miraculous breakthrough, and made that installation? And that Dr. DeBakey, who is head of that skilled team of surgeons, has headed up my committee on heart and cancer and stroke—and we are going to do something about these killers in America.

And I want to remind all you good Methodists that had enough money to get to Baltimore that it is on the poor that the burden of ill health falls most heavily.

You stand in your creed "for the abatement and prevention of poverty"—the abatement and the prevention of poverty!—"and the right of all men to live."

So does America on this April evening in 1966.

We are not concerned just with the appearance. We are concerned with the achievement. We are not just concerned with a promise in a platform. We are concerned with the performance when you get in office—and that is what we are going to do.

So we shall continue to try to uproot and destroy the causes of poverty—the lack of skills, the lack of jobs, the lack of basic education, the lack of decent housing—that challenge the conscience of an affluent America.

We are fashioning our tools as we go. We will make mistakes. We are making them now—many of them. You will read about most of them. Few ever escape the poison pens. Our yearly budgets will never seem sufficient. We will arouse hopes that cannot be quickly fulfilled. But the alternative is to put your hands in your chair and sit

and fold your arms and say, "Let the rest of the world go by," and "I'm not going to do anything about it." Well, we are going to do something about it!

We are moving—we are moving with a program that was only a dream 3 years ago. We will invest this year $1 billion 750 million, in the following:

—in Head Start, for little children,
—in Job Corps, for unemployed youth,
—in community action programs,
—in the Neighborhood Youth Corps,
—in adult basic education,
—in work-experience programs,
—in VISTA volunteers.

We can, we will, and we must do more. We are learning much from the experiences of these years—how to make our commitments more effective, how to call out the best efforts of the poor themselves. We shall not be stampeded into unwise programs—neither shall we swerve aside in our determination to strike the bonds of wretched circumstance from 9 million American families.

One of the great problems I have—I have some that don't want to go at all and I have others that want to go all tonight. And in these programs you have to have plans, and you have to have personnel, and you have to have substance, and you have to have direction, and you have to be sure that you are trying to get a dollar's worth of value out of a dollar received.

You just cannot mash a button and set up a big organization and have them trained. And I am not funding all the programs that I got authorized last year. And the reason I am not, it would take $3 billion more extra this year. But more than that, it would take trained personnel that have not had the experience that I want, to come and learn and think before they talk sometimes.

We *are* going to do something about these

9 million American families, though, at the bottom of the heap, for we have heard the call of Isaiah, to

"Seek justice
Correct oppression,
Defend the fatherless,
Plead for the widow."

Of all that we do, as a people, for social justice in America, nothing is so powerful a force for good as a strong economy.

Tonight, the unemployment rate is a third lower than it was 3 years ago.

Tonight, the number of nonfarm payroll jobs is up 10 percent above that of 3 years ago.

Tonight, the gross national product is 18 percent higher than 3 years ago—at current prices.

Tonight, personal income after taxes in America is 18 percent higher than 3 years ago. Tonight the farmers' income for the first quarter is a substantial increase over the first quarter last year. And we expect a very fine year for the farmer.

These are not the product of one man's wisdom, or of a thousand. They are the visible signs of a new national will in America:

—A will to forge a more bountiful America for all of our people;
—A will to offer each man and woman and child the opportunity to share in that bounty;
—A will to break the grip of disease and ignorance and discrimination and poverty from this land—in our time—now!

And I ask you, is this too much to ask of ourselves? Is the task so great that we are foolish to attempt it?

Do you want to have it said of you? And have your grandchildren point at you and say, "You were the one that looked forward and said, 'Let's move and let's do some of

these things,'" or do you want them to say that you were satisfied to just let matters go as they are?

I do not believe that John Wesley would have thought that we were foolish to attempt this. I do not believe that the founders of American Methodism would have thought so. At least those preachers that I listened to as a boy down in Johnson City did not think so. I do not believe that their descendants gathered to celebrate two triumphant centuries of service to America. I do not believe you think so tonight.

A great French writer wrote about John Wesley:

"Such was the preponderance of this man, who had not so much ruled, as weighed down on his people and stamped them with his massive imprint, that when we lowered him into the grave we seemed not to be burying our head, but laying a foundation stone."

On that foundation stone and on that ideal of compassion for our brothers on this earth, let us—you and I and all the children of God in this land—let us build a temple that is worthy of the blessings He has given us.

The thing that we want in this world more than anything else is peace with our fellow man. But no doctor can cure a disease unless he finds the cause, and you must deal with the cause. And what are the causes of misunderstandings, what are the causes of differences, what are the causes of war, what are the causes of all this bloodshed? Ancient feuds dictated by illiteracy and by ignorance and by disease, and diseased minds and diseased bodies dictated by hungry children crying for food that they do not get—hunger and disease and illiteracy and ignorance—these ancient enemies of mankind.

Now we cannot do it all in a night, but

we can have our goal. And we can keep our eyes in the stars. And we must keep our feet on the ground. But in this country, in the time allotted me, I'm going to, from every pulpit that I am permitted to speak from, try to appeal to my fellow man and remind him of the Golden Rule of do unto others as he would have them do unto him.

I do not want to confiscate business, and I do not want to expropriate property, and I do not want to weaken our free enterprise system. It is the greatest in all the world and it has brought us all the power and all the wealth and all the advantages, taught us how to explore the stars. But I am going to say to all of us who are beneficiaries of it, that we have an obligation to our brother and we have an obligation to every American child that he shall have an equal opportunity to learn to read and write, to have food in his stomach, to have his body free from disease.

And while we are doing that I am not going to confine our efforts just to my own children or just to my own town or my own State or my own Nation. I am concerned with all the 3 billion human beings that live in this world. I was concerned with the people of Europe when a dictator was marching through, gobbling up selfless countries and helpless countries. And we came late. We were tardy. Churchill's voice held things until we finally waked up, and got there.

But just as I was concerned then—the human beings that were in concentration camps—I am concerned now with the little brown men in Southeast Asia whose freedom they are trying to preserve—and others who want to engulf them and overrun them, and dominate them, and by power and by force subjugate them, too. And those peo-

ple die at 35—and earn the magnificent sum of $65 per year.

When a man said to me the other day, "Now this is not our sphere of influence and these are not our kind of people," I thought I had heard those strange words in some of the racist doctrines that I had heard as a child. My kind of people are human beings wherever they are—all 3 billion of them. And with your help and with God's help, we are going to strike body blows and make advances on doing something about the causes of war, as well as winning those wars after they come.

We do not want war. We want peace. We have gone to every capital seeking it. I have sent Ambassadors to more than 40 nations in person to plead for it. We have said: We will talk to any government anytime, anywhere. We will stop our fighting if you stop yours, but do not ask us to stop doing everything we are doing while you pound us. And do not ask us to stop everything we are doing while you march and advance and conquer helpless men, women, and children.

We think that in due time the policies and the programs that are good for America will be good for other people in the world. And when they relieve themselves of their illiteracy and ignorance, when they conquer the disease to the extent that we have—and we are making great progress. One country in Africa, the head of state was in to see me not long ago, and he said, "I do not know how long our men will have a high regard for the United States and like them, but our women will always love your country." And I said, "Why, that's interesting—I'm interested in women that feel that way about us." He said, "Because one out of every three of our children dies every year with measles—out of every three children born in our country one of them dies with measles." He said, "You sent the Navy machine over there and you vaccinated them for measles—and you vaccinated 750,000 last year and we haven't lost a child." And he said, "our mothers appreciate your saving our children."

And when I wandered home about 11 o'clock that night—for dinner—I kind of appreciated myself for having been the instrument of yours in saving, instead of destroying, saving 250,000 lives.

Mayor McKeldin, I want to thank you for being here. You are a source of inspiration to me. I don't know whether you understand this or not—you're a Republican and I'm a Democrat—but I have always observed that you don't know how to spell either word when the interests of your country are at stake, and you put your country ahead of your party.

I couldn't come to Baltimore, though, without saying to the people of Baltimore I am so grateful for the help and the comfort and the encouragement they give me in the burdens that I try to carry as best I can. And I am especially grateful for the two fine United States Senators that are there helping me do it. And—I am grateful, too, for the mayor!

NOTE: The President spoke at 8:30 p.m. at the Lyric Theater in Baltimore before a group of 2,500 Methodist ministers and laymen. In his opening words he referred to the Reverend John Wesley Lord, Methodist Bishop of Washington, Theodore R. McKeldin, mayor of Baltimore and former Governor of Maryland, and to Senator Daniel B. Brewster and Senator Joseph D. Tydings, both of Maryland.

During his remarks the President referred, among others, to Dr. Michael E. DeBakey of Houston, Texas, former Chairman of the President's Commission on Heart Disease, Cancer and Stroke and one of a group of surgeons who had implanted an electrically-powered artificial heart in a human patient, and to Maurice Yameogo, President of Upper Volta, who visited the United States in 1965 (see 1965 volume, this series, Book I, Items 141, 142, 144).

For the President's remarks on signing the Elementary and Secondary Education Act of 1965, see 1965 volume, this series, Book I, Item 181.

190 Special Message to the Congress Transmitting Reorganization Plan 3 of 1966: Public Health Service. *April 25, 1966*

To the Congress of the United States:

I transmit herewith Reorganization Plan No. 3 of 1966, prepared in accordance with the Reorganization Act of 1949, as amended, and providing for reorganization of health functions of the Department of Health, Education, and Welfare.

I

Today we face new challenges and unparalleled opportunities in the field of health. Building on the progress of the past several years, we have truly begun to match the achievements of our medicine to the needs of our people.

The task ahead is immense. As a nation, we will unceasingly pursue our research and learning, our training and building, our testing and treatment. But now our concern must also turn to the organization of our Federal health programs.

As citizens we are entitled to the very best health services our resources can provide.

As taxpayers, we demand the most efficient and economic health organizations that can be devised.

I ask the Congress to approve a reorganization plan to bring new strength to the administration of Federal health programs.

I propose a series of changes in the organization of the Public Health Service that

453

will bring to all Americans a structure modern in design, more efficient in operation and better prepared to meet the great and growing needs of the future. Through such improvements we can achieve the full promise of the landmark health legislation enacted by the 89th Congress.

I do not propose these changes lightly. They follow a period of careful deliberation. For many months the Secretary of Health, Education, and Welfare and the Surgeon General have consulted leading experts in the Nation—physicians, administrators, scientists, and public health specialists. They have confirmed my belief that modernization and reorganization of the Public Health Service are urgently required and long overdue.

II

The Public Health Service is an operating agency of the Department of Health, Education, and Welfare. It is the principal arm of the Federal Government in the field of health. Its programs are among those most vital to our well-being.

Since 1953 more than 50 new programs have been placed in the Public Health Service. Its budget over the past 12 years has increased tenfold—from $250 million to $2.4 billion.

Today the organization of the Public Health Service is clearly obsolete. The requirement that new and expanding programs be administered through an organizational structure established by law more than two decades ago stands as a major obstacle to the fulfillment of our nation's health goals.

As presently constituted, the Public Health Service is composed of four major components

—National Institutes of Health
—Bureau of State Services

—Bureau of Medical Services
—Office of the Surgeon General

Under present law, Public Health Service functions must be assigned only to these four components.

This structure was designed to provide separate administrative arrangements for health research, programs of state and local aid, health services, and executive staff resources. At a time when these functions could be neatly compartmentalized, the structure was adequate. But today the situation is different.

Under recent legislation many new programs provide for an integrated attack on specific disease problems or health hazards in the environment by combining health services, state and local aid, and research. Each new program of this type necessarily is assigned to one of the three operating components of the Public Health Service. Yet none of these components is intended to administer programs involving such a variety of approaches.

Our health problems are difficult enough without having them complicated by outmoded organizational arrangements.

But if we merely take the step of integrating the four agencies within the Public Health Service we will not go far enough. More is required.

III

The Department of Health, Education, and Welfare performs major health or health-related functions which are not carried out through the Public Health Service, although they are closely related to its functions. Among these are:

—health insurance for the aged, administered through the Social Security Administration;

—medical assistance for the needy, administered through the Welfare Administration;

—regulation of the manufacture, labelling, and distribution of drugs, carried out through the Food and Drug Administration; and

—grants-in-aid to States for vocational rehabilitation of the handicapped, administered by the Vocational Rehabilitation Administration.

Expenditures for health and health-related programs of the Department administered outside the Public Health Service have increased from $44 million in 1953 to an estimated $5.4 billion in 1967.

As the head of the Department, the Secretary of Health, Education, and Welfare is responsible for the administration and coordination of all the Department's health functions. He has clear authority over the programs I have just mentioned.

But today he lacks this essential authority over the Public Health Service. The functions of that agency are vested in the Surgeon General and not in the Secretary.

This diffusion of responsibility is unsound and unwise.

To secure the highest possible level of health services for the American people the Secretary of Health, Education, and Welfare must be given the authority to establish—and modify as necessary—the organizational structure for Public Health Service programs.

He must also have the authority to coordinate health functions throughout the Department. The reorganization plan I propose will accomplish these purposes. It will provide the Secretary with the flexibility to create new and responsive organizational arrangements to keep pace with the changing and dynamic nature of our health programs.

My views in this respect follow a basic principle of good Government set by the Hoover Commission in 1949 when it recommended: "that the department head should be given authority to determine the organization within his department."

IV

In summary, the Reorganization Plan would:

—transfer to the Secretary of Health, Education, and Welfare the functions now vested in the Surgeon General of the Public Health Service and in its various subordinate units (this transfer will not affect certain statutory advisory bodies such as the National Advisory Cancer and Heart Councils);

—abolish the four principal statutory components of the Public Health Service, including the offices held by their heads (the Bureau of Medical Services, the Bureau of State Services, the National Institutes of Health exclusive of its several research institutes such as The National Cancer and Heart Institutes, and the Office of the Surgeon General);

—authorize the Secretary to assign the functions transferred to him by the plan to officials and entities of the Public Health Service and to other agencies of the Department as he deems appropriate;

Thus, the Secretary would be

—enabled to assure that all health functions of the Department are carried out as effectively and economically as possible;

—given authority commensurate with his responsibility; and

—made responsible in fact for matters for which he is now, in any case, held accountable by the President, the Congress, and the people.

v

I have found, after investigation, that each reorganization included in the accompanying reorganization plan is necessary to accomplish one or more of the purposes set forth in section 2(a) of the Reorganization Act of 1949, as amended.

Should the reorganizations in the accompanying reorganization plan take effect, they will make possible more effective and efficient administration of the affected health programs. It is, however, not practicable at this time to itemize the reductions in expenditures which may result.

I strongly recommend that the Congress allow the reorganization plan to become effective.

LYNDON B. JOHNSON

The White House
April 25, 1966

NOTE: Reorganization Plan 3 of 1966 is printed in the Weekly Compilation of Presidential Documents (vol. 2, p. 573), the Federal Register (31 F.R. 8855), and in Title 3 of the Code of Federal Regulations (3 CFR, 1966 Comp., p. 191). It became effective on June 25, 1966.

191 Telegram on the Death of Louis A. Johnson. *April 25, 1966*

I JOIN in sorrow as Americans everywhere mourn the death of your husband.

Dedicated to America and dynamic in his service to her interests, Louis Johnson brought the distinction of accomplishment to his public trust.

His energy and ability were reflected throughout both his government and his private career. The awesome responsibility which was his both in the office of Secretary of Defense and in his other official duties testifies to the respect and confidence of his associates.

His loyalty and devotion to our Democratic Party will always be a source of inspiration to all who espouse its high ideals and labor toward their fulfillment.

Lady Bird and I want to express our deepest sympathy to you and to your family. Our thoughts are with you, and we pray that you may find comfort in God's abundant blessings throughout this sad and difficult time.

LYNDON B. JOHNSON

[Mrs. Louis A. Johnson, 317 Buckhannon Avenue, Clarksburg, West Virginia]

NOTE: Louis A. Johnson served as Assistant Secretary of War during the Roosevelt administration and as Secretary of Defense March 1949–September 1950.

192 Statement by the President Upon Announcing the Appointment of the National Commission on Architectural Barriers to Rehabilitation of the Handicapped. *April 26, 1966*

MORE THAN a quarter of a million Americans are in wheelchairs, and many persons have some other disability which makes entering and leaving the average building a major problem. Research ha provided us with some of the standards t make buildings and facilities more accessibl to the handicapped. We now must put thi information to practical use by eliminating architectural barriers from existing buildings, and preventing them in the vast amount of public and private construction which lies ahead.

NOTE: The statement was made public as part of a White House release announcing the appointment of the National Commission on Architectural Barriers to Rehabilitation of the Handicapped by Secretary of Health, Education, and Welfare John W. Gardner. The Commission was established by section 3 of the Vocational Rehabilitation Act Amendments of 1965 (Public Law 89–333, 79 Stat. 1282).

The release stated that the Commission would be chaired by Leon Chatelain, Jr., past president of the American Institute of Architects, a member of the executive committee of the President's Committee on the Employment of the Handicapped, and a trustee of the National Society for Crippled Children and Adults, and would present its recommendations through Mary E. Switzer, Commissioner of Vocational Rehabilitation.

The names of the 14 other members of the Commission are printed in the Weekly Compilation of Presidential Documents (vol. 2, p. 578).

193   Remarks at the Swearing In of Robert L. Bennett as Commissioner of Indian Affairs.   *April 27, 1966*

Mr. and Mrs. Bennett and family, distinguished Secretary of the Interior, Members of the Senate and the House of Representatives, ladies and gentlemen:

One of the hardest tasks that a President has is to find the right man for the right job at the right time, but when he succeeds, it is a source of great pride and satisfaction to him. And I feel that pride and that satisfaction as we meet here in the historic East Room this morning.

My pleasure is redoubled by the fact that we have found this man from the ranks of our own Federal career civil servants. I may be a little partial to those who have served their country with diligence and dedication through the years, but I am in the process every day of ferreting out from the millions of people who serve their Government faithfully those who merit promotion and who deserve advancement.

I started out back in the early thirties. I have been with the Government now 35 years. And I may not have deserved all the promotions I've got, but you can't say that I haven't been promoted from time to time. I recognize it, I appreciate it, and I am grateful for the system that would permit it.

As I look back here and see a good many of my colleagues of yesteryears, I am grateful for what the people have done to them, too. Clint Anderson over there will not admit it, but he and I were NYA Administrators in the early thirties together, a long time before he ever dreamed he would be a United States Senator from New Mexico.

And speaking of United States Senators, one of the greatest was Robert La Follette.

This morning Mr. Robert La Follette Bennett—who bears this great name of an American who fought all of his life for the rights of his fellow citizens, named for a man who is revered from one end of the country to the other, and now his namesake—comes here to assume a position in which he will be able to carry on that proud tradition. He will be doing it for those problems that he is familiar with and that he thoroughly understands.

I want to make this prediction this morning: that Bob Bennett is going to be one of the greatest Indian Commissioners that the United States of America has ever known. I predict this not because he, himself, is of Indian descent, but because he has already distinguished himself in a lifetime of service to the Federal Government. He first joined the Indian Bureau in 1933 as a clerk in the great State of Utah. And except for his service with the Marine Corps during the Second World War, and his 2 years with the Veterans Administration thereafter, he has been concerned with Indian affairs ever since.

I have noticed that most of the people who come from the great State of Utah have a rare dedication to their Government and an unusual competence. Well, Mr. Bennett is going to need all the experience and all the ability that he can muster. For 161 years have passed since that great President Thomas Jefferson charged his countrymen to treat the original inhabitants of our country "with the commiseration that history requires."

President Jefferson pointed out that our European ancestors found the American Indian "occupying a country which left them no desire but to be undisturbed." That desire was thrust aside by history and Thomas Jefferson's pleas were ignored.

We cannot turn back the hands of time today, but we can, after 161 years of neglect, honor Jefferson's plea. Others have tried. They have known some success, yet far too many of our Indians live under conditions which made a mockery of our claims to social justice. In 1966, the year that is known as the most prosperous year that the United States of America ever enjoyed, Indians on reservations this year have the lowest standard of living in the entire United States.

I was observing some figures upstairs. I am going to deviate just a moment because it may be interesting to some of those who hear this argument about spending all the time. It looks like Congress is going to spend more than we recommend they spend. But I was worried about that. It looks like they may up the budget $3 billion this year

already from what they reported from the committees. We could stand some of the upping in Indian housing, because I observed that a certain type of worker in this country, the industry he is in, gets a subsidy, and the amount of total subsidy amounts to $6,500 per year per worker.

I observed the subsidies that we grant on loans—some of them 2 percent, some of them 3 percent, some of them 3½, below the prime rate of 5½ percent—and how many millions that amounts to in a year!

I noticed some of our irrigation-reclamation amounts to as high as $6,000 or $7,000 per family, a hundred-odd thousand dollars sometimes on one farm.

I noticed the payments we had made over a period of years that were in the form of supplements. And then we are debating a very serious matter in the Senate today involving $11 million, or $600 for a poor family. We can send a man a farm check in certain areas of the country for $180,000 for one farm, yet we really get worked up about a $600 subsidy for a poor man who has already paid a fourth of his income for housing in one of our substandard housing areas.

Well now, on most of the reservations in this country, 90 percent of our Indians do not today have decent housing in the year of our greatest prosperity. If we can't do it now, when can we do it? On some reservations, large Indian families have annual incomes of less than $2,000 per year. Indian family income today is less than one-quarter of the national average for the whole country. Now that is something that we ought to be concerned about.

The reason we have this little swearing-in ceremony this morning is not only to honor Mr. Bennett, but to let the country know some of these facts. Because if the President won't tell the country, and you won't tell the country and the Congress, well, we can't do anything about this 90 percent substandard housing and about incomes of under $2,000 a year.

Commissioner Bennett, your President thinks the time has come to put the first Americans first on our agenda. And we are going to give you that job this morning as soon as you are sworn in. From this hour forward, we are going to look to you to discharge that responsibility. I want you to put on your hat and go back over there to that Bureau and begin work today on the most comprehensive program for the advancement of the Indians that the Government of the United States has ever considered. And I want it to be sound, realistic, progressive, adventuresome, and farsighted.

I want the Secretary of the Interior to support you. I want Senator Anderson and Senator Jackson and the Members of the Congress here to pick up that thing and let's write it into the laws of this land so we can remove the blush of shame that comes to our cheeks when we look at what we have done to the first Americans in this country.

I want, during my administration, the time that I am allotted, to put an end to substandard housing and to substandard programs. I am going to depend on you to tell me what needs to be done not only by your Bureau, but by the other departments and agencies in this Government. I want to give you my pledge here this morning that if you fulfill this charge, you will have the full power of the institution of the Presidency of the United States behind you.

Do anything you have to do. If there are cobwebs in the Bureau, then clean them out. Let's set up some Civil Service boards to start hearing the cases, but let's clean them out. Let's get some "can-do" people at work. If you meet resistance, well, I think you know what to do about that. And if you need them, I am going to ask Dillon Ripley to admit you free—Clint Anderson is on the Board over at the Smithsonian—and you go over there and find some of those tomahawks that are still around the Smithsonian.

Thank you very much.

NOTE: The President spoke at 11:40 a.m. in the East Room at the White House. In his opening words he referred to Robert L. Bennett, his wife, and Stewart L. Udall, Secretary of the Interior. During his remarks he referred to Senator Clinton P. Anderson of New Mexico, Robert M. La Follette, Senator from Wisconsin 1906–1925, Senator Henry M. Jackson of Washington, and S. Dillon Ripley, Secretary of the Smithsonian Institution.

194 Remarks on Presenting the Fannie and John Hertz Foundation Award to Dr. Ali Javan and Dr. Theodore H. Maiman. *April 27, 1966*

Dr. Javan, Dr. Maiman, members of the Hertz Foundation, ladies and gentlemen, friends:

You have made a significant contribution to scientific knowledge and I welcome all of you to the White House Cabinet Room to recognize that this morning.

The man for whom this award is named has also made a very vital contribution. This man came to us as a boy and he made our land his land. America was his adopted land. He believed in America and he loved our way of life.

One of his last acts was to attempt to guarantee that that way of life would be preserved for future generations, for our

children and our children's children. So
he took the fruits of his success, and he
made them a foundation from which men
like yourselves could reach into the
unknown.

What you have achieved as brilliant,
imaginative members of a free society, and
what I know you are going to achieve in
the future, is really testimony to what free
men can do when they unite in purpose and
in patriotism. So I hope that you will permit me this morning to congratulate you,
to wish you well, to exchange greetings and
renew friendships with some of my old
friends who are here, and to thank you for
coming and giving me this opportunity, as
President of this country, to participate in
a small way in your moment of success.

NOTE: The President spoke at 1:45 p.m. in the
Cabinet Room at the White House. In his opening
words he referred to the recipients of the award,
Dr. Ali Javan and Dr. Theodore H. Maiman, developers of the laser beam.

Dr. Javan, professor of physics at Massachusetts
Institute of Technology and a native of Iran, was
honored for his pioneering work in the stimulated
emission of light, which resulted in the first reduction to practice of a high precision, continuous wave
gas laser. His work was done in 1959–1960 while
he was on the technical staff of the Bell Telephone
Laboratories.

Dr. Maiman, president of Korad Corp., a subsidiary of Union Carbide, was recognized for similar
work in the field of light emission, which resulted
in the reduction to practice of the first operating
laser, a pulsed high power solid state laser. His
work was also done in 1959–1960.

The Fannie and John Hertz Award in the field
of applied physical sciences consisted of $20,000
and a bronze medallion. The recipients were selected by a committee of prominent scientists headed
by Dr. Augustus B. Kinzel, president and executive
officer of the Salk Institute.

195 The President's Toast at a Dinner for Prime Minister Jens Otto Krag of Denmark. *April 27, 1966*

ONE of my countrymen has said that
although he never really expects to see
Heaven, it is all right—because he has seen
Denmark.

Mr. Prime Minister, I have not seen
Heaven either. But I, too, have seen Denmark. So I know what to look forward to.

Or, at least, what to hope for.

We have a saying in this country that good
things usually come in small packages. This
is not easy for a native of Texas to admit.
But when we look at your own country, it
just can't be denied.

What most of the human race still seeks
and prays for in the future is already part
of Denmark's history.

In so many ways, you in Denmark have
been a shining example for the rest of the
world to follow. We in America are proud
of our free public schools. But Denmark's

public schools were a reality while ours were
still only a noble ideal.

We are proud of our recent achievements
in caring for our sick and providing for our
aged. Yet, we are really only acquiring today what you have had for nearly a century.

We are today engaged in a great national
effort to improve our American cities. We
want to make all of them places of health
and beauty, as well as convenience. And
when the doubters and the critics tell me
that it can't be done, I say to them: Go look
at Copenhagen.

Above all, your countrymen—the descendants of the Viking warriors—are now leaders
in the world's desperate search for lasting
peace.

One of your Danish authors has rightly
written:

"Look at us, follow our example; learn

from our peaceful civilization . . . See how we, who not so many centuries ago were at war with each other, have reached the point where we consider war an absolutely ridiculous and antiquated method of settling disputes. But as a rule no citizens of the great nations . . . listen to these shouts because practically speaking nobody there understands our language."

Mr. Prime Minister, let me assure you that we Americans do understand your language.

For it is also ours. It is the language of peace. And it calls for a world where men can say of every nation what they now say of yours—

"And her ways are ways of pleasantness,
And all her paths are peace."

Ladies and gentlemen, I give you King Frederik and Queen Ingrid.

NOTE: The President spoke in the State Dining Room at the White House.

As printed above, this item follows the advance text released by the White House.

196 Special Message to the Congress Proposing Further Legislation To Strengthen Civil Rights. *April 28, 1966*

To the Congress of the United States:

Last year I came before the Congress in an hour of crisis to recommend new and powerful guarantees of the right to vote.

Americans faced again the ancient questions:

Who shall take part in the process of democracy?

Shall it be only those born with white skins?

If a man's color should *not* be the sole criterion for determining his right to vote, how shall we make sure that Negroes are not denied the ballot?

I asked the Congress, on that March night in 1965, to strike down all restrictions to voting in all elections—Federal, State and local—which have been used to deny Negroes the right to vote.

Less than five months after I spoke, the Congress perfected and passed our Voting Rights Act of 1965.

I said then that the challenge of voting discrimination had been nothing less than a test of our faith in democracy. Congress met that test. The Voting Rights Act of 1965 reaffirmed the equality of man and government by all the people.

The fruits of the Voting Rights Act and of the Civil Rights Act of 1964 are already impressively apparent.

Discrimination in places of public accommodation—perhaps the most unbearable insult to Negro citizens—has been made unlawful. The mandate of that law has spread faster and more effectively than its most optimistic supporters believed possible.

Discrimination in employment is now illegal. Opportunities closed to Negroes in the past have begun to open.

The discriminatory use of federal funds has been prohibited. The effect of that prohibition—strengthened by new federal procedures—is now being felt in schools, hospitals, welfare programs and in many other areas once blighted by racial bias.

The Community Relations Service has helped to bring new understanding to areas where community tensions have threatened to disrupt peaceful progress. Now that the Service has been integrated with other civil rights facilities in the Department of Justice and is being enlarged, we expect it to be even more effective.

In the five states where voter discrimination was once most severe, Negro registration has increased by 50%. Voter registration by local officials and federal examiners appointed under the Act has exceeded 330,000.

At the time of the 1964 national election, less than 25% of the Negro citizens of voting age in those five states were registered to vote. We expect that by the time of the next elections in these states the figure will reach 50%. It is already over 40%.

This achievement serves to renew our faith in the ultimate triumph of a Government in which all free men can participate. It strengthens our resolve to extend the franchise to all who are eligible.

For a democracy cannot be fully realized, when in these five states more than a million eligible Negroes remain unregistered. The challenge to them—and to those in government and private life who labor with them for their just share in the electoral process—is as critically important as the legislative need to enact today's civil rights laws. The statutes now on the books have given Negro Americans the key to freedom. Now it must be used.

I

Once more this year I am asking the Congress to join in an attack on the discrimination that still afflicts our land.

Four times in nine years the representatives of the people have labored through days and nights—through weeks and months—toward the passage of civil rights legislation.

I was part of each of those efforts. I know the fatigue and the triumph that accompanied them. Thus I do not ask for new laws lightly.

Yet discriminatory racial practices still exist in many American communities. They deny the Negro his rights as a citizen. They must be ended.

I ask the Congress:

First, to reform our federal criminal statutes to provide Negroes and all who labor or speak for racial justice the protection of stronger and more effective criminal laws against interference with the exercise of long established rights.

Second, to establish detailed procedures of jury selection in federal courts so that discrimination may be banished—and to create forceful guarantees that state court juries also will be selected without discrimination of any kind.

Third, to broaden the Attorney General's authority to bring suit for the desegregation of schools and public facilities—enabling him to commit the government's legal resources where they are most critically needed.

Fourth, to declare a national policy against racial discrimination in the sale or rental of housing, and to create effective remedies against that discrimination in every part of America.

II

Perhaps the most evident threat to civil rights in 1966 is the danger that recently secured rights may be violently denied by a relatively few racial fanatics.

Citizens who honor the law and who tolerate orderly change—a majority in every part of the country—have been shocked by attacks on innocent men and women who sought no more than justice for all Americans.

The effect of that violence extends far beyond individual victims. Every assault or murder that goes unpunished reinforces the legacy of violence—the knowledge that it is dangerous for a Negro to assert his rights, or even for others to stand up for those rights.

Our federal system assumes that local law enforcement will extend protection to all. Yet the speed with which the fanatics strike has made the work of prevention extremely difficult—even for zealous local police authorities. In some areas, local authorities have been slow or even unwilling to act against the most brazen violence.

So it is that new measures are essential if rights guaranteed by the United States Constitution to every citizen are to be protected.

Laws enacted a century ago to contain racial terror and Klan violence are now clearly inadequate. One of the most important of these statutes requires proof not simply of an act violating a person's civil rights. It also requires the often-difficult showing of specific intent to do so and proof of a conspiracy.

Further, no matter how brutal the crime and no matter what the motive of the criminal, it is possible that the courts will conclude that some degree of involvement by local officials may well be required by these ancient statutes.

And, finally, though offenses may range from threats to murders, only a single set of penalties is provided, and those may be inadequate to suit the gravity of the crime.

Law enforcement authority so restricted cannot be effective. And if that authority is lacking, so is justice. What gain is there for either conscience or country if we proudly affirm human rights and then permit those rights to be swept aside by lawless fanatics?

Accordingly, today I propose the enactment of legislation to make our authority against civil rights violence clear and sure. The legislation I offer is designed to prohibit any interference with the exercise of fundamental rights by threats or force, by any person—whether as an individual or in a group and whether privately or officially.

The measure enumerates these rights, including voting, education, housing, employment, jury service, and travel. And it provides for graduated penalties, permitting our

courts to make appropriate responses to differing degrees of interference or intimidation.

Further, we shall ask for an expansion of the Federal Bureau of Investigation, specifically to permit it to increase its effective role in the enforcement of civil rights laws.

At times in the recent past, as many as one-third of the Bureau's agents have been assigned to the investigation of civil rights matters. The number of civil rights complaints the Bureau investigated in the last ficsal year was 143 percent more than the figure for 1961. These responsibilities place a heavy burden on the Bureau's field staff.

On the advice of Attorney General Katzenbach and FBI Director Hoover, I recommend that Congress authorize an appropriation providing for another 100 FBI agents and additional supporting personnel—to strengthen our capacity to deal with civil rights crimes.

In every city and town and rural community, law-abiding men and women must look for protection primarily to improved local law enforcement. But the federal government has its responsibilities to see that federal rights are secured and their transgressors brought to justice.

We shall meet these responsibilities.

III

The fabric of law enforcement extends from the police patrol to trial and correction. Racial discrimination in any part of this fabric can spoil the rest.

It is necessary that we improve our investigative resources. It is necessary that we strengthen federal authority against interference with basic rights and impose meaningful sanctions on those who violate them.

Yet if we go only this far—and permit racial discrimination to corrupt the selection

463

on juries—we shall leave at the center of our legal system a potential for injustice that mocks our hopes for a great and just society.

Trial by a freely selected jury of one's peers is not a new right. It has its roots in the Magna Carta. Blackstone described it as the "grand bulwark" of man's liberties.

Yet we have been reminded in recent months that in many areas the exclusion of minority groups from jury service remains systematic and complete.

Denying jury service to any group deprives it of one of the oldest and most precious privileges and duties of free men. It is not only the excluded group which suffers. Courts are denied the justice that flows from impartial juries selected from a cross section of the community. The people's confidence in justice is eroded.

Jury discrimination takes many forms, open and subtle, intentional and inadvertent:

—Many jury officials may compile their basic list of potential jurors from membership lists, clubs and civic organizations that tend to exclude minority groups.

—Some state laws require jury officials to make highly subjective judgments of a juror's "integrity, good character and sound judgment."

—Even when the list of qualified jurors has been fairly compiled, officials in many areas are still free to exclude a particular class of citizens arbitrarily when they make assignments to particular juries.

None of today's civil rights laws give sufficient protection against these practices.

An 1875 statute makes it a Federal crime for officials in either Federal or State courts to exclude jurors because of their race. But criminal sanctions operate only upon individuals—not upon an entire system.

What is required is not the punishment of individuals. It is the restoration of integrity in the system itself.

The time has come for new legislation redeeming the promise made to every American: a fair trial by a jury of his peers.

I recommend legislation stating explicitly for all our courts that the right to serve on grand or petit juries shall not be denied on the basis of race or color, religion, sex, national origin, or economic status.

For Federal courts, the legislation will carefully prescribe each step of the jury selection process.

In state courts, the Attorney General and private citizens will be empowered to sue wherever discrimination in jury selection exists. Federal courts will have broad authority to grant relief.

IV

Ten years after the Supreme Court of the United States declared racial segregation in public schools to be unconstitutional, the Congress found it necessary to give new force to the Court's decision.

The Civil Rights Act of 1964 provided that all programs receiving Federal financial assistance—including public education—must be administered on a non-discriminatory basis. The Act called for withdrawal of funds where discrimination remained. It also gave the Attorney General authority to file and intervene in suits to desegregate schools.

Enforcement of the 1964 Act has brought more progress in real integration in one year than in all the preceding nine years.

While there are still far too few Negro children in desegregated classrooms, the number has multiplied several times. It must and will grow substantially again in the fall.

In providing financial assistance, this Administration has insisted on an end to discrimination. But whether or not our assistance is accepted, the requirements of the Constitution must still be met. Segregated schools are still illegal. The law of the land must be and will be upheld.

Thus the Department of Justice has insisted, in more than 40 school suits under the 1964 Act, that whether or not school boards receive financial assistance, desegregation must proceed.

Despite marked gains of the last two years, the fact remains that today—twelve years after the Supreme Court's decision on segregation in schools—only one in thirteen Negro school children in the South attends classes with white children.

Two amendments to the 1964 Act are needed to strengthen the campaign against racial discrimination in the schools.

One would enlarge the Attorney General's initiative under the Civil Rights Act of 1964.

That Act authorized the Attorney General to file suits to help communities where severe local pressure and the poverty of aggrieved citizens made private suits impossible. Yet this authorization was qualified by the requirement that the Attorney General first receive a complaint from a parent unable to sue on his own before the government's legal resources could be brought to bear.

Although the Attorney General can move directly against discrimination in voting, in employment or in public accommodations, with respect to school discrimination he must first receive a complaint before acting. In communities where the atmosphere of intimidation and ignorance of the law's protection is most severe, the filing of a complaint is most unlikely.

Thus where the need of the Attorney General's intervention is the greatest, his help is least likely to become available.

Accordingly, I propose that the Act be amended to allow the Attorney General to file suit directly, without waiting for a complaint, against discrimination in public schools or public facilities.

The second amendment would give the Attorney General the tools to deal with interference against voluntary school desegregation—the same tools that he now has when school desegregation comes under a court order.

The Civil Rights Act of 1960 included provisions to protect court-ordered desegregation from interference. These provisions were reasonably adequate when the desegregation of difficult areas was begun under court order.

But today, principally because of wide acceptance of the Office of Education's desegregation standards, many school districts are desegregating for the first time without the direct compulsion of court orders.

This is a hopeful sign—and one that imposes a new obligation on the government. We must provide adequate assurances against interference to parents and children eager to desegregate schools, and to people siding with and encouraging them in the exercise of their rights.

The criminal legislation I have already described dealing with intimidation would apply to any violent obstruction of school desegregation. *But I also recommend civil injunctive procedures against violence, threats of violence or any other interference with school desegregation.*

v

The day has long since passed when problems of race in America could be identified with only one section of the country. The social and economic toll exacted by discrimination in employment, for example, is felt in all sections.

The Federal government has worked strenuously to bring leadership to a national effort against such discrimination through the President's Committee on Equal Employment Opportunity, Plans for Progress with industry, and establishment of the Equal Employment Opportunity Commission under the Civil Rights Act of 1964.

Other specific legislative steps can now be taken to bolster this effort. The first year's experience of the Equal Employment Opportunity Commission suggests that it should be endowed with enforcement power and that its coverage should be broadened.

Proposals focussing on these purposes are already before the Congress. *I urge that these needs be given the fullest legislative consideration, and that the Senate complete action on the Bill passed by the House of Representatives yesterday.*

Freedom from discrimination is not enough. There must be freedom from the disadvantage that 200 years of discrimination helped create. There must be freedom of opportunity, freedom to work.

We look to those at the White House Civil Rights Conference this June and to private employers across America to help us find new ways to match the Nation's promise of Civil Rights by the fact of civil results—in *full* and equal employment opportunity.

VI

We undertake to expand and reform the civil rights laws this year with the clear understanding that legal reforms can be counted only a small part of a national program for the Negro American.

We know that the more important challenges of racial inequality today are emphatically national.

Negro ghettos indict our cities North and South, from coast to coast. Hope of cutting back the severe unemployment rate among Negroes is tied directly to the expansion of our national economy. And the ultimate need in human terms—of a more generous idea of brotherhood and a more responsible conception of equality—are part of the unfinished business in every state.

The time has passed when we could realistically deal effectively with racial problems by the passage of what could be strictly defined as civil rights laws.

In fact the most disturbing current measures of the impact of discrimination are economic facts that cover the entire nation:

—Non-white Americans constitute only 11 percent of the national labor force, but they make up 20 percent of the unemployed. They take home less than 7 percent of the total personal income of all Americans.

—One-fifth of the entire population lives in poverty. One-half of non-white Americans live in poverty.

—In junior high schools across the country, 12 percent of white children are in school grades below their age level—compared to 30 percent of Negro children.

Poor housing, unemployment and poverty, while they affect racial minorities particularly, will not be defeated by new civil rights laws. Thus, the programs that Congress has adopted go far beyond the vindication of civil rights.

The Elementary and Secondary Education Act of 1965 will enrich the quality of our public schools.

The Housing Act of 1965 will provide part of the decent low and middle-income housing our cities desperately need. Beyond this, adoption of the Demonstration Cities Act this year will launch a major attack on the blight of urban ghettos.

Amendments to the Manpower Development and Training Act adopted in 1965 will help unskilled Negroes, as well as whites, prepare for a role in the economies of today and tomorrow.

The Economic Opportunity Act of 1965—the Anti-Poverty Act—is reaching out with new hope for the disadvantaged—for those pre-school children, teenagers, and older men and women who have never before had cause to hope.

We do not call any of these "civil rights programs." Nevertheless, they are crucial, and perhaps decisive elements in the Negro American's long struggle for a fair chance in life.

It is self-evident that the problems we are struggling with form a complicated chain of discrimination and lost opportunities. Employment is often dependent on education, education on neighborhood schools and housing, housing on income, and income on employment. We have learned by now the folly of looking for any single crucial link in the chain that binds the ghetto.

All the links—poverty, lack of education, underemployment and now discrimination in housing—must be attacked together. If we are to include the Negro in our society, we must do more than give him the education he needs to obtain a job and a fair chance for useful work.

We must give the Negro the right to live in freedom among his fellow Americans.

I ask the Congress to enact the first effective federal law against discrimination in the sale and rental of housing.

The time has come for the Congress to declare resoundingly that discrimination in housing and all the evils it breeds are a denial of justice and a threat to the development of our growing urban areas.

The time has come to combat unreasoning restrictions on any family's freedom to live in the home and the neighborhood of its choice.

This year marks the hundredth anniversary of the first statute enacted by the Congress in an attempt to deal with discrimination in housing. It reads:

"All citizens of the United States shall have the same right, in every State and territory, as is enjoyed by white citizens thereof to inherit, purchase, lease, sell, hold and convey real and personal property."

For 100 years this law has reflected an ideal favoring equality of housing opportunity. Acting under this statute and the Fourteenth Amendment, the Supreme Court has invalidated state and local laws prohibiting the sale of houses to Negroes. It has prohibited the enforcement of racially restrictive covenants. It has struck down state legislation imposing undue burdens upon minority groups with respect to real estate transactions.

There is nothing novel about the Congressional concern with housing that I now ask you to expand. Programs enacted by Congress have, for more than three decades, stimulated the development of private housing, and directly financed hundreds of thousands of public housing units.

The historic Housing Act of 1949 proclaimed a national goal for the first time: "a decent home and suitable living environment for every American family."

The great boom in housing construction since the Second World War is, in large part, attributable to Congressional action to carry out this objective.

Yet not enough has been done to guarantee that *all* Americans shall benefit from the expanding housing market Congress has made possible.

Executive Order No. 11063, signed by President Kennedy on November 20, 1962, prohibited housing discrimination where Federal Housing Administration and Veterans Administration insurance programs are involved. That Executive Order clearly expressed the commitment of the executive branch to the battle against housing discrimination.

But that Order, and all the amendments that could validly be added to it, are inevitably restricted to those elements of the housing problem which are under direct executive authority.

Our responsibility is to deal with discrimination directly at the point of sale or refusal, as well as indirectly through financing. Our need is to reach discrimination practiced by financial institutions operating outside the FHA and VA insurance programs, and not otherwise regulated by the government.

Our task is to end discrimination in all housing, old and new—not simply in the new housing covered by the Executive Order.

I propose legislation that is constitutional in design, comprehensive in scope and firm in enforcement. It will cover the sale, rental and financing of all dwelling units. It will prohibit discrimination, on either racial or religious grounds, by owners, brokers and lending corporations in their housing commitments.

Under this legislation, private individuals could sue in either state or federal courts to block discrimination.

The Attorney General would be empowered to sue directly for appropriate relief, wherever he has reasonable cause to believe that a pattern of discrimination exists.

The legislation would direct the Secretary of Housing and Urban Development to make factual studies, and to give technical assistance to the Community Relations Service and all other public and private organizations working to eliminate discriminatory housing patterns.

The bill I am submitting to the Congress this year would leave in effect the many state laws that have preceded the Federal government in the field of fair housing. We would hope to enact a law that will not only open the fight against discrimination where there are no state laws against it, but also strengthen the enforcement efforts of states which have fair housing programs now.

The ghettos of our major cities—North and South, from coast to coast—represent fully as severe a denial of freedom and the fruits of American citizenship as more obvious injustices. As long as the color of a man's skin determines his choice of housing, no investment in the physical rebuilding of our cities will free the men and women living there.

The fair housing law I propose this year is an essential part of our attempt to rejuvenate and liberate America's growing urban areas—and more importantly, to expand the liberty of all the people living in them.

A nation that aspires to greatness cannot be a divided nation—with whites and Negroes entrenched behind barriers of mutual suspicion and fear.

It cannot tolerate:

—overcrowded ghetto schools, producing new thousands of ill-trained citizens for whom the whole community must be responsible.

—rising health hazards and crime rates in the ghettos' ugly streets and homes.

—the failure of expensive social programs, such as urban renewal, where there is no way out and up for Negro residents.

The truly insufferable cost of imprisoning the Negro in the slums is borne by our national conscience.

When we restrict the Negro's freedom, inescapably we restrict a part of our own.

Negro Americans comprise 22% of the enlisted men in our Army combat units in Vietnam—and 22% of those who have lost their lives in battle there. We fall victim to a profound hypocrisy when we say that they cannot buy or rent dwellings among citizens they fight to save.

VII

No civil rights act, however historic, will be final. We would look in vain for one definitive solution to an injustice as old as the nation itself—an injustice that leaves no section of the country and no level of American life unstained. This Administration has pledged that as long as racial discrimination denies opportunity and equal rights in America, we will honor our Constitutional and moral responsibility to restore the balance of justice.

Yet no amount of legislation, no degree of commitment on the part of the national government, can by itself bring equal opportunity and achievement to Negro Americans. It must be joined by a massive effort on the part of the States and local governments, of industry, and of all citizens, white and Negro.

Hundreds of thousands of Negro Americans in every part of the country are making that effort now. They know that the responsibilities of citizenship follow inevitably from the achievement of civil rights and economic opportunity.

They know that an obligation lies before them, to take full advantage of the improved education and training that is now becoming available to them—in the public schools, in vocational training, in the universities.

They know that it is their task to lead others in the quest for achievement and social justice—to inspire them with confidence, with perseverance, with the mutual forbearance on which our democracy depends.

VIII

We are engaged in a great adventure—as great as that of the last century, when our fathers marched to the western frontier. Our frontier today is of human beings, not of land.

If we are able to open that frontier, to free each child to become the best that is in him to become, our reward—both spiritual and material—will exceed any that we gained a century ago through territorial expansion.

Whether we shall succeed is an issue that rests in the heart of every American. It rests in the determination of Negro Americans to use the opportunities for orderly progress that are now becoming—at last—a reality in their lives. It rests in our common willingness to expand those opportunities in the years ahead.

That issue can and will be decided in only one way. For we have not come this far to fail within sight of our goal.

LYNDON B. JOHNSON

The White House
April 28, 1966

NOTE: For statements or remarks upon signing related legislation, see Items 286, 573, 574, 598.

---

197   Memorandum on Cost Reduction in the Federal Government. *April 29, 1966*

Memorandum to Heads of Departments and Agencies:

One year ago I asked each of you to establish a formal, systematic program to reduce the cost of Government. Your cost reduction goals for both this and the next fiscal year were to be the maximum which imaginative, prudent management could achieve. You were requested every 6 months to reassess your progress, reevaluate your goals, and look hard once again for new opportunities for savings.

You know what progress your own agency is making. I also want you to know how the Government as a whole is doing.

First goals established for fiscal year 1966 totaled $871 million for all civilian departments and agencies.

This was good. I am now pleased to learn that your latest estimates are even better.

—By December 31—the mid-point of the fiscal year—the civilian departments and agencies had already taken actions to save over $700 million.

—As a result of your latest reviews, the total goal for fiscal year 1966 has been raised by $161 million. It is now slightly over $1 billion—$1,032 million.

In the latest review, you also established goals for fiscal year 1967 which begins on July 1. For that fiscal year, which is still 2 months away, the present goals of the civilian agencies total $946 million.

The Department of Defense measures its cost reduction program somewhat differently. Its goal is to save $6 billion by the end of fiscal year 1968 from savings actions taken by the end of fiscal year 1966. Defense is making good progress. So far it has achieved $3,075 million of its goal.

A good record to date is not a signal to relax. Our savings goals must continue to be ambitious and imaginative, and we must be fully successful in meeting them. What I said in my 1967 budget message still holds: "I believe we are making good progress in reducing costs and improving efficiency, but I will never be satisfied that we have done all we should." It is vital that you continue to give this cost reduction program your full attention.

LYNDON B. JOHNSON

198 Remarks to the Recipients of the 1966 National Civil Service Awards. *April 30, 1966*

Chairman Macy, Secretary Sisco, distinguished Federal civil servants:

I had thought that I would just receive you privately in the office and have a little personal visit with you, but when I reviewed your record, I came to the conclusion that I would much prefer that the country know about you than for me just to have that information confined to my own room.

In my special message to Congress last month on Federal pay, I had this to say: "Among the many blessings which Americans can count is a corps of Federal civil servants that is unequaled anywhere in the world." I am pleased this morning to welcome you to the White House and to express my appreciation for the 10 men and women who have accepted this invitation, who have proved themselves to be unexcelled even among the civil servants.

These are the 1966 winners of the National Civil Service League Awards. This award is given for efficiency, quality, and economy in Government management. I hope that as they added women this year to the recipients that they will add imagination to the criteria next year. Because in the 35 years that I have spent in the Government, I haven't seen many people, if any, that I did not believe were people that wanted economy, people that tried to be efficient, folks that were generally loyal to our system of government, and most of the time were people of quality.

I am afraid that after we stay here and get adjusted to our environment and our travels are limited and our associations become set, that we may not always wake up in the middle of the night with a bright new idea and submit it the next morning. So I hope that we will stress imagination and creativeness, initiative, new ideas, how we can do something quicker, how we can do it better, why we ought to do something we are not doing, why we ought to discard the status quo, and proceed to things we know not of, sometimes, in the hope that out of that will come something revolutionary and something worthwhile.

So Mr. Macy—if you are listening and can "read me"—I hope that when we get ready to have this meeting next year that we will put into the things that we want to see in our Federal civil servants efficiency, quality, economy, dedication, and imagination.

There is no question in my mind that every person in this room today could be earning a great deal more money in private enterprise.

Your achievements have singled you out as being men and women of excellence, and excellence is not easy to come by, either in or out of the Government. Because we are not all excellent, I would say that perhaps 50 percent of the staff of the White House spends 50 percent of their time trying to explain, deny, correct, justify, or make clearer someone's action that may not have been efficient, or may not have been accurate, or may not have been excellent.

I often think of the great waste that one little inefficient statement or inefficient step, or one action that was misunderstood or misinterpreted, just how much it may cost the Government and cost our whole enterprise system. So I do want to bear down pretty heavy on excellence.

Yet for all the monetary awards that you have sacrificed, I believe that you have gained something more precious. You have gained the opportunity to work for human welfare, to work for progress, to work for efficiency, and in many cases to work for peace.

I think probably the most satisfying thing that came to me last year was the statement, and I believe the fact, but certainly the statement that this Government had saved the lives of 250,000 children in one of the small countries of the world. That gave me a reward and a satisfaction that I didn't get out of that paycheck that I endorsed this morning and sent on down to the bank, because I don't know whatever happens to it after it gets there. It is just routine.

But if you can feel that that came from some little part of your effort, it is worth a lot more than these fancy titles, these big salaries, and these fancy country clubs that you can belong to, if you are getting all the monetary reward that the traffic will bear. The fact that you may contribute just one little bit to peace in the world could give you more satisfaction than being the recipient of a great estate as a result of someone's will.

You have assisted me in the development of my budget, you have organized and directed new programs, you have led the way in new discoveries for the welfare and security of the people, you have contributed new ideas which have led to economy and improvement in Government. Because you have done these things, I want to especially commend you, thank you, and say to you that I don't believe there is a higher calling than Government service.

I don't think I have to sell you on that or you wouldn't be here, if you thought there was a higher one. But I do want you to know that your achievements should serve as a shining example to all the young people throughout our land that are trying

471

to decide today what they ought to do.

I am glad that I don't hear the complaining today about the Government worker that I heard as a young man. I think we have matured some. When I first came into public life, I heard a lot of people talking about professional politicians and they had a kind of a stigma attached to a person in public life. Then I heard a lot of professional politicians talk about bureaucrats and they didn't always pronounce it right. Those things distressed me through the years I have served. And I am glad I don't hear them now.

We always have our complainers and we have people who like to point up what is wrong, but by and large I think the Government servant today is more respected, better recognized, and probably more rewarded than he has been before. One of the reasons for that is that you have observed some of the mistakes that your predecessors have made and you have improved.

Also I think another reason is Mr. Macy, and the leadership that he has given as Chairman of the Civil Service Commission, the leadership he has given the President and the leadership he has given the country in trying to develop a body of meritorious civil servants from the Cabinet level on down. He has had something to do with selecting every person that I have selected in the Government. The only person that he didn't really have much to do with selecting is talking to you and maybe he is glad of that.

NOTE: The President spoke at 12:55 p.m. in the Cabinet Room at the White House. In his opening words he referred to John W. Macy, Jr., Chairman, Civil Service Commission, and Joseph J. Sisco, Assistant Secretary of State for International Organization Affairs.

The recipients of the 12th annual awards of the National Civil Service League, a nongovernmental citizens organization, were Mr. Sisco; Oscar Bakke, Director, Eastern Region, Federal Aviation Agency; William O. Hall, Assistant Administrator for Administration, Agency for International Development; F. Stewart Brown, Chief, Bureau of Power (and Chief Engineer), Federal Power Commission; Bernard Strassburg, Chief, Common Carrier Bureau, Federal Communications Commission; Mary E. Switzer, Commissioner of Vocational Rehabilitation, Department of Health, Education, and Welfare; Mrs. Charlotte Moore Sitterly, physicist in charge of "Atomic Energy Levels" program, National Bureau of Standards; Dwight A. Ink, Assistant Secretary for Administration, Department of Housing and Urban Development; Ellis H. Veatch, Chief, Military Division, Bureau of the Budget; and Paul H. Riley, Deputy Assistant Secretary of Defense (Materiel Requirements).

199 Remarks at the Signing of the Small Business Act Amendments of 1966. *May 2, 1966*

Distinguished guests and friends:

I welcome you here, Members of Congress, small business leaders, those in and out of Government, who have worked so long and so hard to increase small business' share of this Nation's national prosperity.

I have invited you here this morning to this historic East Room in the White House to ask you to witness the signing of a bill that will make the Small Business Administration a more effective friend of small business in America and to outline to you a progressive and reasonable method of financing the programs of the Small Business Administration and the other agencies of our Government.

There is an important relationship between these two. They are part of this administration's effort to make sure that our Government assistance programs are wisely planned and organized—that they are supported by private efforts wherever that is possible—that they are managed by the most competent men available for public service.

The bill I will sign today allows the Small Business Administration to set up two separate revolving funds, one for business loans, another for disaster loans.

In this way the disruptions in the business loan program, which have sometimes occurred when disasters have struck various communities, we think in the future can be avoided.

The bill that the Congress has sent me increases by $125 million the amount of loans that the Small Business Administration may have on its books at any one time. And we may expect the Small Business Administration to use this authority to serve more firms than it has ever served before.

These are necessary changes if the agency is to carry out its small business program I have proposed for the coming fiscal year.

Our budget for the fiscal year 1967 proposes that SBA make available about $725 million in loans, in guarantees, and in other commitments to the small businesses of this country. That $725 million is the largest amount of financing that the Small Business Administration has undertaken in its entire history. It is more than four times what the agency accomplished in 1960.

This is an impressive goal and an impressive program, as it must be if it is to keep pace with the growth of small business in the United States in the last 4 years.

There are now about 300,000 more small business firms operating in America than there were just 4 years ago.

There were 20 percent fewer failures among all businesses last year than there were in 1961. You know only too well that the great part of those failures came among the small businesses of this country.

Profits after taxes in small manufacturing corporations were nearly three times greater in 1965 than they were in 1961.

Small business has taken a much greater share of military prime contract awards. In 1961 the small firms obtained $3.6 billion of those awards. In 1965 that $3.6 billion had jumped to $4.9 billion, an increase of 36 percent in the last 4 years.

So we are planning and we are working for a growth industry—for almost 5 million businesses from the corner store to the small manufacturer—for those millions of men and women who, by their initiative, their determination, and their hope, keep the wheels moving in our economy.

The reason we have asked so many Members of Congress to come here this morning is because this is basically and essentially an idea of theirs. This is a congressional program. Its interest is there, it was nurtured there, it was born there, and they watch over it zealously.

We feel this bill is essential for the growth and development of small business. But we believe it is only half the answer to what small business needs in this country.

This bill that the Congress has sent me gives the Small Business Administration the authority to carry out our program for the coming year. But it just gives us the authority, it doesn't give us the money. And authority without money doesn't amount to much.

So we proposed to the Congress last year a way of providing the funds—the money—that is necessary to carry out the small business program.

Today the Small Business Administration has only a limited amount of money for its lending operations. That does not mean the agency doesn't have assets. Far from it. It has in its revolving fund, in its loan portfolio today, loan paper that is worth more than a billion and a half dollars.

These tremendous assets, owed to the

Small Business Administration by those small business borrowers who have taken their loans in the last few years, represent the taxpayer's money.

Their representatives in Congress have appropriated it to the Small Business Administration over the past several years to be used for a specific purpose; that is, investment in small business concerns.

But there is no reason for the Small Business Administration to clutch on and hold on to this large inventory. We think it can, and we think it should be able to sell its loans to private investors.

We believe that is the kind of cooperation we should have in our free enterprise system. In that way it would be able to generate new funds for its expanded lending program.

The Small Business Administration has long had the authority to sell its seasoned loans as well as to make them. It has used this authority over the years, to provide new capital to assist more small businesses.

But what we are asking for is an efficient and a practical way of achieving this goal. We believe that we should authorize the Small Business Administration to sell participations in its loan portfolio—they would be more attractive—to sell shares in this great billion and a half pool of outstanding loans.

Those shares would be guaranteed by the Small Business Administration. They would be sold to the private investors throughout America, large and small.

The Federal National Mortgage Association, the "Fannie Mae," would act as the trustee.

And once the certificates are sold, the proceeds would come back to the Small Business Administration. They would be available for lending to other dynamic small firms that today are hungry for capital that

is tight and the desire to produce and to expand.

The legislation that we have asked for to achieve this was passed by the Senate by an overwhelming vote. It is under active consideration in the House of Representatives.

We believe that it is necessary for small business and we believe that it is sound for the Government and the people of this country.

The Small Business Administration is not the only Federal agency that is in need of financing authority. If selling certificates of participation makes sense, as all of our economists and most of our lenders believe, it makes sense as well for other Government programs and that is why we have urged the Congress to authorize these sound fiscal procedures for agencies throughout the Government.

We make no claim that this is a policy that is original with this administration. In 1954, in 1955, in 1956, in 1958, President Eisenhower and his administration affirmed his belief that private capital should be substituted for the Government's investment in housing mortgages. In 1954, President Eisenhower said, "The policy of this administration is to sell the mortgages now held by the 'Fannie Mae' as rapidly as the mortgage market permits."

In 1955, he made clear his position that "private capital will be gradually substituted for the Government investment until the Government funds are fully repaid and the private owners take over responsibility for the program."

President Eisenhower very wisely appointed a Commission on Money and Credit. In 1961 the Eisenhower Commission, made up of his Budget Director and others, called once again for the maximum substitution of private for Federal credit.

In 1962, President Kennedy's Committee on Federal Credit reported that "unless the urgency of other goals makes private participation infeasible, the methods used should facilitate private financing, should encourage long-run achievement of program objectives with a minimum aid from the Government."

As recently as 1963, the Republican members of the House Ways and Means Committee, led by Congressmen Byrnes, Curtis, and others argued, "The administration also can reduce its borrowing requirements by additional sales of marketable Government assets."

That is what we are trying to do through legislation that we have submitted. We are trying to further the substitution of as much private credit for public credit as possible and to ask their participation with us in this joint venture wherever and whenever we can under our sound, free enterprise system.

We want to extend the principle of private participation to SBA and to its sister agencies throughout the Government. We realize that we have come a long way.

This morning it will be my great pleasure to sign my name to the first part of this program, the program that gives us the authority. We call it the Small Business Act amendments of 1966.

We do treasure the hope that in the days to come that we will have another opportunity for all of you to come here and witness another signing which will do more than give authority, it will give the "do re mi" to carry out that authority.

NOTE: The President spoke at 11:35 a.m. in the East Room at the White House.

As enacted, the Small Business Act amendments of 1966 (S. 2729) is Public Law 89–409 (80 Stat. 132).

On May 24, 1966, the President approved the Participation Sales Act of 1966 (Public Law 89–429, 80 Stat. 164).

---

200 Remarks at a Ceremony Commemorating Poland's National and Christian Millennium.   *May 3, 1966*

Senator Muskie, Members of the Cabinet, Members of the Congress, distinguished guests and friends:

Senator Muskie, I enjoyed hearing so much what you had to say, and I am deeply honored by this gesture of the Polish-American Committee.

I am well aware of the historical significance of this beautiful work of art. For hundreds of years the Black Madonna has brought strength to the brave citizens of Poland. It has been a symbol both of greatness and of hope.

As much as I treasure the gift, I feel that others will treasure it with me. So I am asking Archbishop Krol to put it on permanent display at the Catholic Church in Panna

Maria, Texas, the first Polish church in the United States.

I accept it with great gratitude and with much pleasure because—I might add incidentally, and it hasn't always been incidentally—those who attend that church and I have always had something in common every election year.

So I accept it with this pledge: that as long as I am allowed to serve as your President I will never cease to work for closer ties, for closer friendship, and for closer cooperation between the United States of America and Poland.

Today as we meet here at the 1,000th anniversary of Polish Christianity and nationhood, it is also the 175th anniversary of a document that holds a place of honor among the noble statements of human rights, the Polish Constitution of 1791.

All men who revere liberty acknowledge their indebtedness to those landmarks in the struggle for individual freedom.

And that is why I have asked you to come here to the Rose Garden today.

Life has never been easy for the people of Poland. Time and again she has endured the unwelcome intrusion of her larger and her more powerful neighbors.

Time and again she has endured suffering and sacrifice, only to recover and to rebuild.

In all of this, her proud and resourceful people left an indelible mark on Western civilization.

We, in America, owe a very special debt to Poland. For almost two centuries ago her sons joined our own Revolution and Polish patriots fought under the American flag.

Nor can we forget the millions of Polish immigrants whose personal faith and whose tenacious labor helped to tame this continent. Our national heritage is rich with the gifts of Polish people.

Our debt and our long ties with the people of Poland give us a very special interest in their problems and in their future.

Twice in this century Poland has been devastated by war, yet her people have remained loyal to the ancient faith and to the human values that it represents. Even as we meet here today, they are meeting by the hundreds of thousands at the historic monastery of Jasna Gora. Led by a great Polish cardinal, they are offering prayers of hope and thanksgiving which reflect their enduring belief in God and in their national destiny.

In Poland, and in other countries in Eastern Europe, new ideas are winning friends. Windows are opening to the world—only slightly in many places, but they are opening.

And despite the severe limitations on its national freedom, limitations that prevent many Polish-Americans from celebrating this day on Polish soil, the ancient spirit of Poland is not dead. Her people still yearn for a lively future in Europe and among the community of nations.

We see this, for one thing, in economic policy.

Poland, and some of her neighbors in Eastern Europe, are sensing the vigor of individual enterprise. Men are coming to understand that decentralized decision-making is proving more efficient than highly centralized state control.

Profits are coming to be understood as a better measure of productivity and personal incentive as a better spur to effective action on behalf of the national economy.

How hopeful these signs are, we cannot yet say.

I will be meeting with our distinguished Ambassador very shortly and we will be reviewing all the problems and concerns in that part of the world. There is no greater American today, no one performing a more valuable service than our own distinguished Ambassador John Gronouski, who is returning home.

We can only trust that they foreshadow a new reliance upon, if not a new understanding of, the individual as the most important element of society.

If they reflect a willingness to respond to reality, if they signal a readiness to sift ideas for their own worth rather than to dismiss them as politically impure, if they reflect a gradual rebirth of reason and open discourse among men, then seeds exist for genuine confidence that things, indeed, may yet change.

For this reason, it is not vain, on this day of great memories, for us to also think of great dreams and to speak of great hopes.

Chief among them is the future of Europe.

So vast are the resources of that continent, so important its policies to the rest of the world, so vital its prosperity to the entire world economy that Americans ignore the future of Europe only at the expense of peace and progress on both continents.

Men and nations must labor long to bring to reality a Europe free of artificial political barriers that block the free movement of people, of ideas, and of commerce; a Europe that is secured by international inspected arms control arrangements that remove the age-old fears of East and West alike; a Europe of interdependent friends in which the strength of each adds to the strength of all; a Europe in which the people of every nation know again the responsibilities and the rewards of free political choices.

Not because we have treasure to gain or territory that we desire to acquire, but because we have common roots and common interests, the United States of America today seeks to help build that kind of Europe.

It was in that spirit that the Marshall plan was offered 19 years ago and it is still the spirit of American policy.

Our guiding principles are these:

First, our alliance with Western Europe, we believe, is in the common interest of all who seek peace. It is a charter for changing needs and not a relic of past requirements.

It was and it continues to be a basis for security, solidarity, and advance in Europe. It remains our conviction that an integrated Atlantic defense is the first necessity and not the last result of the building of unity in Western Europe, for expanding partnership across the Atlantic, and for reconciling differences with the East.

As we revise the structure of NATO to meet today's realities, we must make sure that these forward-looking purposes are served and are served well.

Second, we believe that the drive for unity in Western Europe is not only desirable but we believe it is necessary. Every lesson of the past and every prospect for the future argue that the nations of Western Europe can only fulfill their proper role in the world community if increasingly they act together. From this base of collaboration, fruitful ties to the East can best be built.

Third, we will encourage every constructive enrichment of the human, cultural, and commercial ties between Eastern Europe and the West.

Fourth, we will continue to seek ways to improve relations between the people of Germany and their fellow Europeans to the east, and to move towards a peaceful settlement of the division of Germany on the principle of self-determination.

Fifth, we welcome growing participation by the nations of Eastern Europe in common efforts to accelerate economic growth in the developing areas of the world and to share in the worldwide war on poverty, hunger, and disease among the peoples of the world.

It was almost 2 years ago at the George Marshall Memorial Library in nearby Lexington, Virginia, when I said that we must continue to build bridges across the gulf which has separated us from Eastern Europe. Since that time, we have taken limited steps forward along what will no doubt be a very long road.

In Poland alone, we have dedicated an American-financed children's research hospital in Krakow, increased support for CARE, Church World Services, and American Relief for Poland in their food and medical programs for hospitals and needy individuals. We have reached an understanding between our National Academy of Science and the Polish Academy of Science on an important exchange program similar to the one that we have reached with Rumania, Yugoslavia, and the Soviet Union.

We have invited Poland to cooperate in our satellite program.

We have increased by 44 percent in the second half of 1965 the number of Polish visitors who come to the United States for academic, scientific, and technical purposes. We have increased by more than $200,000 the sale in Poland of American books, newspapers, plays, motion pictures, and television programs. Our International Media Guarantee program with Poland is the largest in the world.

These have all been taken under the direction of one of our greatest Americans, as I mentioned a few moments ago, who will report back to the President and the Cabinet in the next few days—John Gronouski.

These are small steps. But, as Cicero once said, "The beginnings of all things are small." From these, we will take other steps to help revive the intellectual, the commercial, and the cultural currents which once crisscrossed Europe, from London to Budapest, from Warsaw to Paris, from Frankfurt to Krakow, from Prague to Brussels.

As one additional step, and as I pledged in my State of the Union Message, I am today instructing the Secretary of State, Mr. Dean Rusk, to send to the Congress legislation making it possible to expand trade between the United States of America and Eastern Europe. The intimate engagement of peaceful trade, over a period of time, can influence Eastern European societies to develop along paths that are favorable to world peace.

After years of careful study, the time has now come, I think, for us to act, and act we should and act we must.

With these steps, we can help gradually to create a community of interest, a community of trust, and a community of effort. Thus will the tide of human hope rise again.

It is a good occasion that has brought us together here today.

In issuing this proclamation, I am asking all of the American people to join in the observance of historic events which have inspired man's long walk on this earth.

May we draw new resolve, even now, from the Polish Millennium and Constitution Day.

Thank you, my friends, for coming here.

NOTE: The President spoke at 11:15 a.m. in the Rose Garden at the White House. In his opening words he referred to Senator Edmund S. Muskie of Maine who, on behalf of Americans of Polish descent, had presented him with a replica of the Black Madonna, Our Lady of Czestochowa, symbol of Polish independence and patriotism. Senator Muskie's remarks are printed in the Congressional Record of May 3, 1966 (p. 9083).

During his remarks the President referred to, among others, Archbishop John Joseph Krol of Philadelphia and Stefan Cardinal Wyszynski of Poland. A delegation from Panna Maria, Texas, was present at the ceremony.

The President spoke following the signing of Proclamation 3720 "Commemoration of Poland's National and Christian Millennium" (2 Weekly Comp. Pres. Docs., p. 604; 31 F.R. 6679; 3 CFR, 1966 Comp., p. 48). The anniversary was further marked on July 30 by the issuance of a commemorative stamp, and on October 16 by the dedication at Doylestown, Pa., of the National Shrine of Our Lady of Czestochowa. For the President's remarks on that occasion, see Item 528.

The legislation making it possible to expand trade between the United States and Eastern Europe, to which the President referred near the close of his remarks, was not adopted by the 89th Congress.

201   Remarks at a Meeting of the President's Advisory Committee on Labor-Management Policy.   *May 4, 1966*

I HAVE ASKED you here this morning to seek your counsel.

This Committee has written a proud record from the start. Many of you have been members since its creation in 1961, serving your Nation and two Presidents. To you and to the new members, I say: At this time we need the benefit of all your wisdom and skill.

We stand together in a truly remarkable effort. It is indeed a hallmark of our democracy that men representing industry, labor, Government, and the public have gathered here today. You are joined in a common cause—economic prosperity for all Americans.

I ask you to consider the crucial domestic issue of the day—the maintenance of our unparalleled prosperity with economic stability.

I ask you to look at this problem not from the standpoint of labor or business. I want you to ask yourselves:

—If you were President, what would you do?

The economy grows stronger every day. We are now approaching solutions to old problems—full employment, plants operating at capacity, sustained and uninterrupted growth. But as we near these historic achievements, we face new problems in the challenge of prosperity. Disquieting signs are beginning to appear.

Consumer prices have risen 2.8 percent in the past 12 months. Wholesale prices are up 4 percent.

There are indications of wage increases substantially above those in prior years.

Skilled labor is short in some industries and in some areas.

The consuming public—of which we are all a part—is concerned about keeping the cost of living down.

Some seek an answer in higher taxes. Others urge wage and price controls. A few look to even higher interest rates.

These are some of the facts and some of the solutions we hear today.

But I want you to consider all of the facts and all of the alternatives.

I have asked Secretary Wirtz, Secretary Connor, Chairman Ackley, and their colleagues to give you any information you need or want to help in your deliberations.

This prosperity of the past 5 years has benefited all Americans—the workingman, the businessman, the farmer, and the professional. So long as I am President, I will do everything in my power to maintain that prosperity with stability, to maintain healthy profits and fair wages. This is our common goal.

To help achieve this goal, I seek your advice.

I particularly seek your views and constructive suggestions on the more critical problems we face:

—How effective is the program of voluntary restraint?

—What is the role of business and labor in such a program?

—What is the role of governments—Federal, State, and local—executive and legislative branches—in these times?

—What are your views on tax and monetary policy?

—What is the role of the wage-price guideposts?

—How do we maintain stable costs for essential services, such as medical care, that are now pushing the cost of living up?

These are not simple questions.

They cannot be fully answered at the end of 2 days of meetings. For they present uncharted terrain even for our best economists—because free peoples have never known such prosperity.

NOTE: The President spoke in the Fish Room at the White House at the opening session of the Com-

mittee's 2-day meeting in Washington. In the course of his remarks he referred to W. Willard Wirtz, Secretary of Labor, John T. Connor, Secretary of Commerce, and Gardner Ackley, Chairman of the Council of Economic Advisers.

As printed above, this item follows the advance text released by the White House.

A letter from the President to 9 new members of the Committee appears above (see Item 184 and note).

202 Remarks Upon Signing Order Establishing the President's Council and the Citizens' Advisory Committee on Recreation and Natural Beauty. *May 4, 1966*

Members of the Cabinet, distinguished friends in the Congress, and invited guests:

I thank you for indulging me while I addressed the first meeting in several months of the President's labor-management advisers in the Fish Room. I had to answer some questions then, so I am a little tardy.

I never think of America's beautification program without a deep feeling of pride— pride in our vision of what our country can be, and pride in what we have already done.

I will say, though, that for all my personal interest in beautification, some people, including some very close to me and on the platform this morning, seem to think that I am not quite interested enough. Sometimes she has to prod me a little bit. Sometimes I would actually swear she is shoving.

But as many of you know, Mrs. Johnson does have a slight, detectable interest in beautification.

It was the poet Wordsworth who said that "Nature never did betray the heart that loved her"—and I think that Lady Bird has ample reason to believe that. There are flowers and trees and beautiful things all through this Capital City this year that seem to nod when she goes by.

So I know this is a happy occasion for her today when I could carry out her suggestion

and ask you to come here and redouble our efforts to try to beautify our land.

The Executive order I am about to sign adds two new members to the Government's Recreation Advisory Council: the Federal Power Commission, headed by the White House former General Counsel, Mr. Lee C. White, present Chairman of the Commission; and the General Services Administration, headed by Mr. Lawson B. Knott. In addition to that, it greatly broadens the functions of the Council to cover natural beauty as well as recreation.

To assist and to advise this Council—to give it added direction and to give it increased purpose—I have established a 12-man Citizens' Advisory Committee on Recreation and Natural Beauty. I have asked the distinguished American, Mr. Laurance Rockefeller, to assume the chairmanship of this Committee, and he has graciously accepted and indicated his willingness to serve his country again. Mr. Rockefeller and most of the members are present with us today.

So I want to say to all of the Committee members that just because they are serving without pay does not mean that they will be serving in an honorary capacity. Any time I get volunteers, I put them to work. That may be one of the reasons that Jack Valenti has made some of the decisions he has made lately.

We have just begun to scratch the surface of ugliness and neglect and decay throughout our countryside and within our cities. The task of this Committee will be to tell us where we go from here.

How can we provide nearby recreation areas that will bring relief from the noise and congestion of our cities?

What can Government departments and agencies do to bring a touch of beauty into the daily lives of all of our citizens?

What can we do to help our State and local governments improve the beauty of locally-owned property?

What can we do to encourage business firms and factories to beautify their surroundings?

What can we do, what can every American do, to become a better conservationist?

What can we do to employ the talents and the energies of our retired citizens in local beautification projects?

Well, these are a few of the questions that could be answered, should be answered soon, if we really plan to pass on to our children a nation that is rich in promise as well as in the past.

Last year, in signing the Assateague Seashore bill, I quoted some words of a great American naturalist. It was Henry David Thoreau who said: "It is a noble country where we dwell, fit for a stalwart race to summer in."

I said then that it remains for us to preserve both that vision and the beauty which gave it rise.

I am asking this morning the members of this new Committee to roll up their sleeves and get to work and begin to provide leadership and inspiration in this effort. From this moment forth, the opportunity for rec-

reation and the daily experience of beauty just must be made a part of our gross national product. For a nation that calls itself great must have spirit as well as have strength, must have poetry as well as have prosperity.

So I ask all of you Americans to join in such greatness.

I just suggested to Senator Jackson in the corridor coming in that I wish he would take every surplus area we have in the United States, as a member of the Armed Services Committee. We have declared hundreds of them surplus, and I know because I get petitions from back home talking about Mr. McNamara's actions. But I wish he would take those areas and sit down with the Secretary of the Interior and see if we could not turn some of those old Army installations, or some of those old Air Force areas, or some of those old Navy yards into recreational areas that are adjacent to where people live.

We have a wonderful Big Bend Park that Lady Bird has been visiting, but it is a long way for me to go to get to stroll in the woods. It is a long way for people to go who live in Washington and Baltimore and Philadelphia and New York and Los Angeles. We need some of these areas right where the people live.

There is not a front yard in the country, there is not an apartment house in the land, there is not a public building anywhere, there is not a street, there is not a sidewalk, and there is not a road that cannot be improved and be made more beautiful.

How to make them more beautiful—when and how and where—is a part of your undertaking.

Thank you very much.

NOTE: The President spoke at 10:22 a.m. in the Rose Garden at the White House before signing Executive Order 11278 "Establishing a President's Council and a Committee on Recreation and Natural Beauty" (2 Weekly Comp. Pres. Docs., p. 607; 31

F.R. 6681; 3 CFR, 1966 Comp., p. 107). In the course of his remarks he referred to Jack Valenti, Special Assistant to the President, whose decision to resign had recently been announced, Senator Henry M. Jackson of Washington, and Secretary of Defense Robert S. McNamara.

On the same day the White House made public a list of members of the Citizens' Advisory Committee and announced that Secretary of Commerce John T. Connor would serve as the chairman of the President's Council (2 Weekly Comp. Pres. Docs., p. 608).

The Recreation Advisory Council was established by Executive Order 11017 of April 27, 1962 (3 CFR, 1959–1963 Comp., p. 597). The Recreation Advisory Council was expanded and renamed the President's Council on Recreation and Natural Beauty by Executive Order 11278 (cited above).

203 Statement by the President on the Increase in the 1967 Wheat Acreage Allotment. *May 5, 1966*

SECRETARY FREEMAN informs me that this increase is certain to result in a substantial rise in farm income, continuing a favorable upward trend that is steadily moving our agricultural community into full-fledged partnership in the overall prosperity of the country.

The enhanced income represents improved use of a great American resource. I am proud of the contribution that agriculture is making to the overall economy. American wheat, furthermore, is saving millions of people around the world from starvation.

The combination of expanding exports and voluntary domestic farm programs has brought us a long way in recent years. Not so long ago, we were fighting costly surpluses; now we are increasing wheat acreage in order to maintain necessary reserves.

Secretary Freeman has announced that net farm income will rise by $1 billion this year to more than $15 billion. This is an aggregate level surpassed only in the postwar years of 1947 and 1948.

On a per farm and per capita basis, net farm income will set new records this year as it did in 1965. The increase in wheat acreage announced today means that farmers can look forward with confidence to continued higher levels of income in 1967.

The strengthening of farm income will continue to be a major objective of my administration. Increased production and marketing efficiency, intelligent and cooperative operation of the Food and Agriculture Act will, I am confident, make it possible for us to reach our goal of parity of income for the adequate-sized family farm, while at the same time decreasing the real cost of an improved diet to the consumer.

NOTE: The statement was read by Bill D. Moyers, Special Assistant to the President, at his news conference at 11:20 a.m. on Thursday, May 5, 1966, at the White House. Mr. Moyers announced that the President had directed Secretary of Agriculture Orville L. Freeman to increase the wheat allotment for 1967 by 7.7 million acres, bringing the total allotment from the 1966 figure of 51.6 million acres to 59.3 million acres in 1967. See also Item 281.

The statement was not made public in the form of a White House press release.

204   Remarks at a Meeting With Federal Enforcement Officials To Deal With the Problem of Organized Crime.   *May 5, 1966*

General Katzenbach, Director Hoover, Mr. Cohen, General Vinson, Mr. Acheson:

I know how deeply all of you share my concern over the scope and the power of organized crime in this country. It constitutes nothing less than a guerrilla war against our society.

This is a war that takes scores of lives each year in gangland violence.

It is a war that terrorizes thousands of our citizens. It is a war in which billions of dollars are drained off by illegal gambling, narcotics, prostitution, loan-sharking, arson, and other forms of racketeering.

Most damaging of all are the efforts of racketeers to seek protection against honest law enforcement by corrupting our public officials. Such evil strikes at the heart of our democracy. It corrupts individual officials. It breeds a general contempt; it saps public respect for law and for law enforcement.

We have sought to fight this war with every Federal resource. The intense and vigorous efforts of the Justice Department and the Treasury Department have given the Nation great cause for encouragement. Federal prosecutions in organized crime have risen from 17 in 1960 to 491 last year.

During the same period, the Federal Bureau of Investigation, the Intelligence Division of the Internal Revenue Service, the Bureau of Narcotics and other agencies of the Government have been gathering more and more information on organized crime throughout the country. As a result of this work, we have been able:

—to identify the membership of criminal syndicates

—to anticipate many of their activities

—to prosecute their members.

So this morning I salute and I congratulate all of the dedicated Federal officials who are joined in this concerted campaign.

Still, if we are to be realistic about the nature of organized crime, we must recognize that it cannot be uprooted by any short campaign. Criminal syndicates continue to bore into the structure of our society. As we apply pressure in one area, such as gambling, racketeers shift to another, such as infiltrating legitimate business.

This makes our job very much more difficult—and it makes it much more important. The campaign against racketeering must not only be continued but it must be accelerated.

So I am today calling on each Federal department and agency of this Government that has been engaged in the war against organized crime to redouble its efforts.

I am today directing the distinguished Attorney General, our chief law enforcement officer, to act as the focal point of the Government's renewed drive against these corporations of corruption.

A society can be neither great nor just as long as organized crime exists.

Of course we know that there will be no instant victory.

But today we do want to serve notice on all syndicates of crime that victory will come.

It will come through the joint efforts and the cooperation of all concerned Americans.

It will come through a new partnership between Federal, State, and local governments.

Together, we will match our determination with effective action, fairly taken, to rid our land of the menace of organized crime.

And to those of you who are leading principals in this attack, I salute you and I extend my congratulations and I pledge you my full support.

NOTE: The President spoke at 1:40 p.m. in the Cabinet Room at the White House. His opening words referred to Nicholas deB. Katzenbach, the Attorney General, J. Edgar Hoover, Director of the Federal Bureau of Investigation, Sheldon S. Cohen, Commissioner of Internal Revenue, Fred M. Vinson,

Jr., Assistant Attorney General (Criminal Division), and David C. Acheson, Special Assistant for Enforcement to the Secretary of the Treasury.

Also present at the meeting were William G. Hundley, Chief, Organized Crime and Racketeering Section, Department of Justice, and Donald W. Bacon, Assistant Commissioner (Compliance), Internal Revenue Service.

For the President's memorandum to the heads of Federal departments and agencies engaged in the war against crime, see Item 205.

205 Memorandum on the Federal Government's Drive Against Organized Crime. *May 5*, 1966

Memorandum for Heads of Departments and Agencies Participating in the Federal Organized Crime Drive:

Organized crime constitutes one of the most serious threats to a peaceful and prosperous society. It drains untold millions of dollars yearly from our national wealth. It carries corruption and violence in its wake. It erodes respect for the law.

The Federal investigative agencies can be proud of their accomplishments during the past several years in identifying and amassing evidence against the leaders of organized crime in this country. The success of the Department of Justice in securing indictments and convictions in organized crime cases is due to the ability of your many separate investigative units to work closely together towards a common goal. You have demonstrated that this unified coordinated program of action can be effective in combating organized crime.

I have today stated my determination to continue and accelerate this priority program.

To add further strength to our efforts, I have asked the Attorney General, as the Nation's chief law enforcement officer, to act as a focal point of the Federal Government's attack on organized crime.

I want each of you to give him your help and support.

To accomplish our purpose, each investigative unit in your department or agency participating in the drive against organized crime should:

—*Carefully review* its current organized crime programs and present detailed status reports to the Attorney General, with emphasis upon allocation of personnel and upon suggested areas of new and additional investigation.

—*Report periodically in detail* to the Attorney General on the progress of its organized crime investigations showing for each current or proposed investigation the planned area of inquiry, the number and type of personnel assigned, and the expected prosecutive potential.

—*Establish direct lines of liaison* with the Department of Justice to enable the Attorney General to carry out his responsibility for directing this program.

To uproot the menace of organized crime from our society, we must work closely together, attain new levels of cooperation and match our will with effective action.

LYNDON B. JOHNSON

NOTE: For the President's remarks of the same date stating his determination to "continue and accelerate this priority program," see Item 204.

206   Statement by the President Upon Signing Bill Authorizing
Disposal From the Molybdenum Stockpile.   *May 6, 1966*

THREE WEEKS AGO I signed two bills authorizing the sale of platinum and refractory bauxite from our national stockpiles. I expressed the hope that Congress would work toward swift passage of the other stockpiles disposal measures.

The Congress has continued to justify that expectation by its prompt action on H.R. 13369—a bill that authorizes the release of 14 million pounds of stockpiled molybdenum, now excess to our strategic stockpile requirements. I have signed H.R. 13369 into law today. This measure has enabled us to meet the urgent needs of industry. It will return to the Treasury nearly $24 million of the taxpayer's money and it will leave in the stockpile an ample supply of molybdenum to meet future strategic requirements.

The continuing unparalleled expansion of our economy—which is now in its sixth consecutive year—and our military requirements in Vietnam have resulted in an increasingly short supply of molybdenum. Without the prompt action of the Congress in authorizing the orderly movement of molybdenum from our stockpile into the hands of industry, the production of high-strength, high-grade steel would be seriously disrupted.

Molybdenum imparts to steel a toughness which is of particular importance in the manufacture of armorplate and other military products. It is also needed in space research and in the missile industry.

In April, when Congress authorized the disposal of platinum and refractory bauxite, those critical materials were on their way to industry within a matter of days.

We are ready to take similar steps in the case of molybdenum.

I have today directed the Administrator of the General Services Administration to begin moving into the hands of industry and users throughout the Nation without delay, the 14 million pounds of critically needed molybdenum covered by this new legislation.

Congress still has before it 22 similar measures for the disposal of excess strategic materials. Ten of these have already passed the House. I urge that the Congress take prompt and final action on all of the stockpile bills.

In this way, working together in a close partnership of Congress, the executive branch, and industry, we can safeguard our national welfare, sustain a healthy economy, protect the interests of the American consumer, and give our boys in Vietnam the tools they need.

NOTE: The statement was released at San Antonio, Texas, on May 6. As enacted, the bill (H.R. 13369), approved by the President on May 5, is Public Law 89–413 (80 Stat. 135).

The bills authorizing the sale of platinum and refractory bauxite were approved by the President on April 14 (see Item 173).

207   Statement by the President on the Demonstration Cities Program on the Occasion of the Nomination of Two Assistant Secretaries of Housing and Urban Development.   *May 6, 1966*

I AM particularly hopeful about contributions that both of these fine administrators will bring to the demonstration cities program. This important legislation is now before the Congress and I urge its prompt passage.

The cities program is our first national attempt to apply a bold, forward-looking concept to our urban problems. I believe that the demonstration cities program is going to do more than any other Federal program to help make our cities, small and large, exciting and safe, healthy and inspiring, and places where people can come to live the good life. It is an important and vital addition to our other programs.

I do not expect miracles from this program tomorrow but we must begin to plan intelligently now; we must begin to program the

costs now. Our cities are growing far faster than our population as a whole. The challenge of this new urban America is already upon us.

NOTE: The statement was read by Deputy Press Secretary Robert Fleming at his news conference at 3:45 p.m., on Friday, May 6, 1966, at San Antonio, Texas. Mr. Fleming announced the President's intention to nominate Don Hummel, former mayor of Tucson, Ariz., and former president of the League of Mayors, as Assistant Secretary for Renewal and Housing Assistance, and H. Ralph Taylor of New Haven, Conn., president of Taylor-Hurley Associates, a private consulting organization specializing in urban renewal and development, as Assistant Secretary for Demonstrations and Intergovernmental Relations.

The Demonstration Cities and Metropolitan Development Act of 1966 was approved by the President on November 3. For his remarks at the signing ceremony, see Item 574.

The statement was not made public in the form of a White House press release.

208   Statement by the President Upon Establishing the National Advisory Commission on Health Manpower.   *May 7, 1966*

THE UNITED STATES is facing a critical shortage of manpower in carrying out its commitment to improve health care for our citizens.

On July 1, more than 19 million Americans will be eligible for health services under Medicare. We expect a heavy drain on our limited resources for those services.

Additional manpower will be needed for expanded programs of maternal and child health care, service to crippled or retarded children, and for mental patients.

New health services for migratory workers, new attacks on heart disease, cancer, and stroke, and additional new hospitals and

health facilities will require trained staffs.

Therefore, I am appointing today a National Advisory Commission on Health Manpower, to be headed by J. Irwin Miller, chairman, Cummins Engine Co., Inc., Columbus, Ind. Its members include distinguished leaders from the health professions, the universities, and other sectors of public and private life.

I have asked the Commission to recommend bold, imaginative ways to:

—improve the utilization of health manpower in Government agencies and in private life; and

—speed up the education of doctors and

other highly trained health personnel without sacrificing the highest quality of learning.

I hope to receive periodic advice from the Commission before it submits its final report next year.

In the meanwhile, I have directed the Federal Government to act vigorously to deal with problems in this area. I have requested Secretary McNamara and Secretary Gardner, together with Chairman Macy of the Civil Service Commission, and Administrator Driver of the Veterans Administration to conduct a joint effort to improve the utilization of health manpower by Federal agencies. I have also requested Secretary Wirtz, in consultation with others, to explore the feasibility of establishing a national roster of draft-eligible doctors. Such a study should be helpful to the Commission in making recommendations to me.

I strongly believe that these efforts by this new Commission and by the Government will bring real advances in our progress toward our national goal: adequate and economical health care for every citizen.

NOTE: On the same day the President signed Executive Order 11279 "Establishing the President's Committee on Health Manpower and the National Advisory Commission on Health Manpower" (2 Weekly Comp. Pres. Docs., p. 621; 31 F.R. 6947; 3 CFR, 1966 Comp., p. 110).

The members of the President's Committee, all of them Government officials, are listed in section 1 of the order. The members of the National Advisory Commission as announced by the White House Press Office follow: J. Irwin Miller, chairman of the board, Cummins Engine Co., Inc., Columbus, Ind., chairman; Dr. Russell Nelson, president, Johns Hopkins Medical Center, Baltimore, Md.; Dr. Robert Ebert, dean, Harvard Medical School, Cambridge, Mass.; Dr. Alonzo Yerby, commissioner of hospitals, New York, N.Y.; Dr. James Cain, physician and consultant, Internal Medicine Section, Mayo Clinic, Rochester, Minn.; Dr. Dwight Wilbur, specialist in internal medicine, San Francisco, Calif.; Quigg Newton, president, Commonwealth Fund, New York, N.Y.; Dr. Joseph Volker, vice president for health affairs, University of Alabama, University, Ala.; Albert Dent, president, Dillard University, New Orleans, La.; Kermit Gordon, vice president, Brookings Institution, Washington, D.C.; Joseph Wilson, president, Xerox Corp., New York, N.Y.; Thomas Vail, publisher, Cleveland Plain Dealer, Cleveland, Ohio; Mrs. Mary Bunting, president, Radcliffe College, Cambridge, Mass.; Joseph Beirne, president, Communications Workers of America and vice president, AFL–CIO, Chevy Chase, Md.; Charles Odegaard, president, University of Washington, Seattle, Wash.

The statement was released at San Antonio, Texas.

---

209   Statement by the President on the Need for a Treaty Governing Exploration of Celestial Bodies.   *May 7, 1966*

JUST AS the United States is striving to help achieve peace on earth, we want to do what we can to insure that explorations of the moon and other celestial bodies will be for peaceful purposes only. We want to be sure that our astronauts and those of other nations can freely conduct scientific investigations of the moon. We want the results of these activities to be available for all mankind.

We want to take action now to attain these goals. In my view, we need a treaty laying down rules and procedures for the explora-

tion of celestial bodies. The essential elements of such a treaty would be as follows:

The moon and other celestial bodies should be free for exploration and use by all countries. No country should be permitted to advance a claim of sovereignty.

There should be freedom of scientific investigation, and all countries should cooperate in scientific activities relating to celestial bodies.

Studies should be made to avoid harmful contamination.

Astronauts of one country should give any

necessary help to astronauts of another country.

No country should be permitted to station weapons of mass destruction on a celestial body. Weapons tests and military maneuvers should be forbidden.

I am convinced that we should do what we can—not only for our generation, but for future generations—to see to it that serious political conflicts do not arise as a result of space activities. I believe that the time is ripe for action. We should not lose time.

I am asking Ambassador Goldberg, in New York, to seek early discussions of such a treaty in the appropriate United Nations body.

NOTE: The statement was read by Deputy Press Secretary Robert Fleming at his news conference at 11 a.m. on Saturday, May 7, 1966, at San Antonio, Texas, for release at 5:30 p.m. It was not made public in the form of a White House press release.

Agreement by the United States with other nation members of the U.N. Outer Space Committee on a draft treaty to govern space exploration was announced by the President on December 8, 1966. See Item 643.

---

210 Message to the Congress Transmitting First Report of the National Advisory Council on the Education of Disadvantaged Children. *May 9, 1966*

To the Congress of the United States:

Seven months ago, Public Law 89–10, providing massive aid to improve elementary and secondary education, went into effect. At that time we called upon leaders of education in States and local school districts to translate this financial assistance into educational services for the millions of disadvantaged children in our schools: the children who desperately need additional attention if they are to overcome the handicaps of poverty.

I am happy to transmit to you the first report of the National Advisory Council on the Education of Disadvantaged Children. Their comments on the progress which has been achieved by States and local schools reveal that educators from all levels of Government are working together to provide equal educational opportunities for all.

I am particularly encouraged by the major focus of activities identified in the report: to improve language skills in the early years. Nothing could be more fundamental than this work in assisting children who have been denied normal educational opportu-

nities through poverty or neglect.

The commission members have not failed to point out areas in the program that need additional attention. I have pledged that every effort will be made to meet these problems—and I am confident that the Congress will join in these efforts.

We have begun a major campaign to solve a long-standing problem. The first year of this work has proved that we are on the right road, but we still have far to go.

LYNDON B. JOHNSON

The White House
May 9, 1966

NOTE: The 33-page report (processed) was dated March 31, 1966.

The National Advisory Council on the Education of Disadvantaged Children was established by title I of the Elementary and Secondary Education Act of 1965 (79 Stat. 831). For the President's statement upon signing the act, see 1965 volume, this series, Book I, Item 181.

Dr. O. Meredith Wilson, president of the University of Minnesota, served as chairman of the Council, and the staff director was Thomas W. Carr. The other members of the Council follow: Louis Bruno, superintendent of public instruction, State of Washington; John H. Fischer, president of Teachers College, Columbia University; Edward B. Hanify,

Ropes, Gray, Best, Coolidge & Rugg, Boston, Mass.; Frank E. Karelsen, Karelsen, Karelsen, Lawrence & Nathan, New York, N.Y.; Elizabeth D. Koontz, president, Department of Classroom Teachers, National Education Association; Mildred L. Lillie, Justice, District Court of Appeals, Los Angeles, Calif.; Sidney P. Marland, Jr., superintendent of schools, Pittsburgh, Pa.; Victor G. Reuther, director

of education programs, United Automobile Workers; Joseph Rosen, principal, George Howland Elementary School, Chicago, Ill.; Terry Sanford, Raleigh, N.C.; and Ralph W. Tyler, director, Center for Advanced Study in Behavioral Sciences, Stanford, Calif.

The message was released at San Antonio, Texas.

211   The President's Telephone Greetings on the 82d Birthday of Harry S. Truman.   *May* 9, 1966

MR. PRESIDENT, I understand that you think I have more important things to do than wishing you a happy birthday. Well, for the first time in your life, you're wrong.

Mrs. Truman may know of some other times, but I certainly don't.

I want you to know that I'll never be too busy to pay my respects to a great American.

I am well aware that you get a little impatient with these annual birthday celebrations. I've often thought you'd rather have your friends cussing you than praising you. That may be why you became a Democrat.

But the trouble is, Mr. President, that nobody has anything left to fight with you about. We've had 13 years to see the wisdom of your policies. There's not a right-thinking person in the free world today who would want to go back and change one of them.

And so, Mr. President, I'm afraid that you're going to have to go right on, paying the price for greatness.

There's nothing I could do about it even if I wanted to. The Senate passed a resolution the other day demanding that I make your birthday greetings official, on behalf of the whole country and I've already signed the proclamation.

I'll tell you something else: You're not only going to have to put up with your admirers on this birthday, but on many birthdays to come. Like George Washington, you are first in the hearts of your countrymen, and there's no getting out of it.

Happy birthday, Mr. President, and God bless you.

NOTE: The President spoke by telephone from the LBJ Ranch. Mr. Truman was attending a birthday luncheon at the Muehlebach Hotel at Kansas City, Mo.

As printed, the remarks follow the text read by Deputy Press Secretary Robert H. Fleming at his news conference at 12:55 p.m. on Monday, May 9, 1966, at San Antonio, Texas. They were not made public in the form of a White House press release. See also Item 212 below.

212   Proclamation 3724 "Eighty-Second Birthday of Harry S Truman."   *May* 9, 1966

By the President of the United States of America a Proclamation

Harry S Truman, the thirty-third President of the United States, was born eighty-two years ago on the 8th day of May, 1884.

Throughout his life, Harry S Truman has devoted himself unceasingly to the cause of freedom, peace, and the betterment of his fellow man. His historic decisions during his service as President of the United States, from 1945 through 1952, have made the world a better and safer place not only for his fellow citizens but for the entire human race.

Harry S Truman's deep concern for the well-being of each individual American will never be surpassed by any President. His wise and passionate pursuit of justice, opportunity, and security for every citizen set an example which every President of the United States will strive to emulate so long as the Nation and the Presidency shall endure. And it has won him a permanent place in the hearts of his countrymen.

Among the legacy Harry S Truman gave to history are included the United Nations Charter which, under his guidance, the United States became the first major power to ratify; the formulation and successful operation of the Truman Doctrine, which played a major role in preserving free institutions in Greece and Turkey; the Marshall Plan, which played a major role in rebuilding the war-depleted economies of Western Europe; and such outstanding legislative accomplishments for the welfare of the American people, as the National School Lunch Act, the National Mental Health Act, the Atomic Energy Act of 1946, the National Heart Act, the Minimum Wage and Hour Act amendments of October 26, 1949, the Act of September 23, 1950, providing Federal assistance for school construction in federally impacted areas, and the Federal Coal Mine Safety Act amendments of July 16, 1952.

His accomplishments have been recog-

nized by friendly nations throughout the world. His contributions to peace have been especially honored by the creation of the Harry S Truman Center for the Advancement of Peace, to be located at the Holy City of Jerusalem.

The Senate of the United States, in which he served faithfully and well before ascending to the Presidency, has further recognized this Nation's indebtedness to Harry S Truman by calling upon the President of the United States to extend upon the occasion of his eighty-second birthday, May 8, 1966, the admiration and gratitude of all our people.

I am proud to honor this request and do hereby extend to the Honorable Harry S Truman this expression of our profound and lasting gratitude and appreciation for his long years of devoted service to his country.

IN WITNESS WHEREOF, I have hereunto set my hand and caused the Seal of the United States of America to be affixed.

DONE at the City of Washington this ninth day of May in the year of our Lord nineteen hundred and sixty-six, and of the [SEAL] Independence of the United States of America the one hundred and ninetieth.

LYNDON B. JOHNSON

By the President:
DEAN RUSK
Secretary of State

NOTE: Proclamation 3724 was signed on Monday, May 9, 1966, because of the birthday luncheon honoring President Truman in Kansas City, Mo., on that date. The text of the proclamation was released at San Antonio, Texas.

See also Item 211.

213   Remarks Upon Presenting the Big Brother of the Year Award to the Reverend William F. Graham.   *May 10, 1966*

DR. GRAHAM, when they told me you were going to receive the Big Brother of the Year Award, I recalled some lines from a hymn that I used to sing as a boy. I believe they are appropriate for the occasion today:

"Throw out the life-line across the dark wave,

There is a brother whom someone should save ..."

I'm not going to ask you to sing it, but I'm sure you remember the rest of the words.

Few men have thrown out as many lifelines as Billy Graham. They are lifelines of hope, of faith, of guidance, and of spiritual strength. Today, one of those lifelines is coming back—with a word of thanks from a group of very dedicated Americans.

The Good Book tells us that, "Whatsoever a man soweth, that shall he also reap." In your case, Dr. Graham, it is a rich harvest of satisfaction—and gratitude.

Big Brothers of America are honoring you today for your leadership and influence among the youth of our Nation. I know something about that leadership—and I have seen some of the results of that influence. It is no small thing.

A man's character is molded in his youth. Or, as Wordsworth once wrote: "The child is father of the man."

I do not despair of our youth. I think our young men and women in the Peace Corps, in Vietnam, and in our community action poverty programs, have established themselves as the finest generation in the history of this Nation. But it's reassuring to know there are great men like you who have helped so many of them along the early part of their journey.

NOTE: As printed above, this item follows an advance text released by the White House.

214   Remarks to Reporters at the Conclusion of a Security Council Meeting on Vietnam.   *May 10, 1966*

Ladies and gentlemen:

We are delighted to welcome back one of our most dedicated public servants and one of our most valuable counselors, Ambassador Lodge.

Earlier this afternoon he reported to me privately in some detail about the events in his area of the world and his evaluation of the situation there.

He brought back information that we do not always get from the written cable. I had a very profitable visit with him. We had a thorough exchange of viewpoints.

I asked him to join me in the Cabinet Room and make available to my other counselors here his impressions and judgments and conclusions, as well as a general review.

This is the first time that he has been back in almost 9 months. He will be here through the week. He will spend some time with Mr. Komer and Mr. Rostow, and some time with the various people at the table. They will divide into various groups.

This afternoon we had an agenda that included a rather full report from General Wheeler on the military situation in Vietnam. We had a discussion of the political and economic situation, the issues as he sees them—a general report from Ambassador Lodge.

He was followed by a discussion led by Secretary Rusk on the key political issues, at the conclusion of which Secretary McNamara supplemented some of General Wheeler's statements on the military situation there and the issues involved on his part.

I reviewed with them some of my views on Vietnam from the day I took over the Presidency: on education, health, agriculture, the economy of South Vietnam, my Baltimore speech, the Honolulu Conference, our desire to get the Government of South Vietnam, General Westmoreland, and others to cooperate with Ambassador Lodge and Ambassador Porter in the efforts that we were making in this field.

We not only have military problems here, as everyone knows, but we have political problems and economic problems.

I have asked one of my most trusted and able advisers, Mr. Komer, to take command of this operation and head the post here, with Secretary Rusk, Secretary McNamara, and others, in an attempt to make this economic and political program effective.

Mr. Komer discussed, at some length, the key economic issues there. We reviewed generally the effects of the Honolulu Conference; Secretary Freeman's visit with 15 of

the outstanding people from our universities and our colleges, who made a thorough study; and Secretary Gardner's report.

Mr. Komer will arrange to have certain task forces meeting throughout the week while Ambassador Lodge is here.

That is the essence of what took place this afternoon. I have explained to these wise men, all of whom I rely on for advice, to supply me with all the information and knowledge they had.

I have it now and I have passed as much of it on to you as I could.

NOTE: The President spoke at 7:20 p.m. in the Cabinet Room at the White House. In the course of his remarks he referred to Henry Cabot Lodge, U.S. Ambassador to the Republic of Vietnam, Robert W. Komer, Special Assistant to the President, Walt W. Rostow, Special Assistant to the President, Gen. Earle G. Wheeler, Chairman of the Joint Chiefs of Staff, Dean Rusk, Secretary of State, Robert S. McNamara, Secretary of Defense, Gen. William C. Westmoreland, Commander, United States Military Assistance Command, Vietnam, William J. Porter, Deputy U.S. Ambassador to the Republic of Vietnam, Orville L. Freeman, Secretary of Agriculture, and John W. Gardner, Secretary of Health, Education, and Welfare.

For the President's Baltimore speech of April 7, 1965, see 1965 volume, this series, Book I, Item 172.

Material relating to the Honolulu Conference of February 6–8, 1966, appears above as Items 53–55.

For the missions to Vietnam by Secretaries Freeman and Gardner to which the President referred at the close of his remarks, see Items 56 and 106. See also Item 85.

215 Statement by the President Following the Transfer of the Water Pollution Control Administration to the Department of the Interior. *May 10, 1966*

THE REORGANIZATION plan transferring the Water Pollution Control Administration from the Department of HEW to the Department of the Interior became effective today.

The Congress has acted wisely in permit-

ting this reorganization plan to become effective.

Under the leadership of Secretary Udall, the Government is now better organized to carry out concerted action against the pollution that blights America's waters.

I deeply appreciate the support of Congress in this vital matter of streamlining the Government organization to fight pollution effectively.

NOTE: For the President's message to the Congress transmitting Reorganization Plan 2 of 1966, see Item 91.

216   Remarks at the Woodrow Wilson School for Public and International Affairs, Princeton University. *May 11, 1966*

Governor H u g h e s, President Goheen, trustees, faculty and students, Secretary Gardner, distinguished guests of Princeton:

I am happy that I could come here today to help celebrate Princeton's continued growth. It is good that one of the Nation's oldest universities is still young enough to grow.

This commitment to the increase of higher learning has deep roots in this country. Our forefathers had founded more than 50 colleges before the Republic was half a century old.

With a sure sense that the pursuit of knowledge must be part and parcel of the pursuit of life, liberty, and happiness, they set in motion two forces which have helped to shape this land.

The first was that learning must erect no barriers of class or creed. The university was to nourish an elite to which all could aspire. Soon after our first colleges came the first scholarships for worthy students who could not pay their own way.

The second idea was that the university would not stand as a lonely citadel isolated from the rest of the community. Its mission would be to search for truth and to serve mankind. As Woodrow Wilson later said: "It is the object of learning not only to satisfy the curiosity and perfect the spirits of individual men, but also to advance civilization."

THE VITAL FLOW

We who work in Washington very much know the need for the vital flow of men and ideas between the halls of learning and the places of power. Each time my Cabinet meets, I can call the roll of former professors—Humphrey and Rusk, McNamara and Wirtz, Katzenbach (another distinguished Princetonian), Gardner, and Weaver. The 371 major appointments I have made as President in the 2½ years that I have occupied that Office, collectively hold 758 advanced degrees. Two of my own White House counselors I borrowed from Princeton, and they are here with me today—Dr. Donald Hornig and Dr. Eric Goldman. And so many are the consultants called from behind the ivy that a university friend of mine recently said to me: "At any given moment a third of the faculties of the United States are on a plane going somewhere to advise—even if not always to consent."

While learning has long been the ally of democracy, the intellectual has not always been the partner of government. As recently as the early years of this century the scholar stood outside the pale of policy, with government usually indifferent to him.

That, I am glad to say, has changed.

The intellectual today is very much an inside man. Since the 1930's our Government has put into effect major policies which men of learning have helped to fashion.

More recently, the 89th Congress passed bill after bill, measure after measure, suggested by scholars from all over the country whom I had placed on task forces that were appointed in 1964.

In almost every field of governmental concern, from economics to national security, the academic community has become a central instrument of public policy in these United States.

THE AFFLUENCE OF POWER

This affluence of power for an intellectual community that once walked on the barren fringes of authority has not been won without some pain. An uneasy conscience is the price any concerned man pays, whether politician or professor, for a share of power in this nuclear age.

More than one scholar, thus, has learned how deeply frustrating it is to try to bring purist approaches to a highly impure problem.

They have come to recognize how imperfect are the realities which must be wrestled with in this most complicated world.

They have learned that criticism is one thing and that diplomacy is another.

They have learned to fear dogmatism in the classroom as well as in the Capital—and to reject the notion that expertise acquired in a lifetime of study in one discipline brings expertise in all other subjects as well.

They have learned, too, that strident emotionalism in the pursuit of truth, no matter how disguised in the language of wisdom, is harmful to public policy—just as harmful as self-righteousness in the application of power. For as Macaulay said: "The proof of virtue"—and, we might add, of wisdom—

"is to possess boundless power without abusing it."

The responsible intellectual who moves between his campus and Washington knows, above all, that his task is, in the language of the current generation, to "cool it"—to bring what my generation called "not heat but light" to public affairs.

The man for whom this school is named always believed that to be the scope of real scholarship. He never doubted the interdependence of the intellectual community and the community of public service. "The school," he said, "must be of the Nation."

A WORTHY CALLING

So today we dedicate this building not only to the man, but to his faith that knowledge must be the underpinning of power—and that the public life is a calling that is worthy of the scholar as well as the politician.

There was once a time when knowledge seemed less essential to the process of government. Andrew Jackson held the opinion that the duties of all public offices were "so plain and simple" that any man of average intelligence could perform them.

We are no longer so optimistic about our public service. The public servant today moves along the paths of adventure where he is helpless without the tools of advanced learning.

He seeks to chart the exploration of space, combining a thousand disciplines in an effort whose slightest miscalculation could have fatal consequences.

He has embarked on this planet on missions that are no less filled with risk and no less dependent on knowledge.

He seeks to rebuild our cities and to reclaim the beauty of our countryside. He seeks to promote justice beyond our court-

494

rooms, making education and health and opportunity the common birthright for every citizen. And he seeks to build peace based on man's hopes rather than man's fears.

These goals will be the work of many men and of many years. We are still wrestling to provide a world safe for democracy just as Wilson did more than 50 years ago. We are still fighting to gain the freedoms that Roosevelt talked about more than 30 years ago. All of these will call for enormous new drafts of trained manpower that will be available for public service.

Over the next 4 years, the Federal Government will need 30,000 more scientists and engineers and 6,000 more specialists in health, technology, and education.

By 1970, our State governments, Governor Hughes, must grow by more than 600,000 to keep pace with the times. Employment for State and local government will exceed 10 million persons. Each year over the next decade, our Nation will need 200,000 new public school teachers to keep up just with our growing population.

THE CITIZEN-SOLDIERS

The call for public service, therefore, cannot be met by professionals alone. We must revive the ancient ideal of citizen-soldiers who answer their nation's call in time of peril. We need them on battlefronts where no guns are heard but where freedom is no less tested.

Here at the Woodrow Wilson School, you have done much to raise the sights of public service. I urge you to continue to promote its excellence at all levels. We intend to do the same in Washington, sparing no effort to assist those who select this as their life work.

I have asked Chairman John Macy of the Civil Service Commission to head a task force that will survey Federal programs for career advancement. I have asked him to study an expanded program of graduate training which, with the help of the universities, can enlarge our efforts to develop the talents and broaden the horizons of our public service career officers.

I also intend next year to recommend to our Congress a program of expanding opportunities for those exceptionally talented who wish to go into training for the public service. We will assist:

—students that are planning careers in Federal, State, or local governments,

—colleges and universities that are seeking to enrich their own programs in this field, and

—local and state governments that are seeking to develop more effective career services for all of their employees.

Our concept of public service is changing to meet the demands of the hour. A new public servant has emerged. He may be the scholar who leaves his study for the crucible of power in his State or national capital. Or he may be the young man or woman who chooses public service but does not abandon at its doorstep the techniques of scholarship and the search for knowledge.

These men and women will help us to answer the question that Franklin Roosevelt, our great American leader, asked more than 30 years ago: Will it be said that "Democracy was a great dream, but it could not do the job"?

President Roosevelt did not doubt the answer. Even as troubles mounted, he took the starting steps to strengthen a Federal structure capable of carrying this Nation safely through its crisis. With his detractors and his defacers, with his dissenters and his doubters, just as Wilson had had to carry them a few decades before, he began to organize the modern Office of the President and to bring American Government into the mid-twentieth century.

THE ESSENTIAL QUESTION

And now, as we enter the final third of this century, we are engaged again today—yes, once again—with the question of whether democracy can do the job.

Many fears of former years no longer seem so relevant. Neither Congress nor our Supreme Court indicates to me any signs of becoming rubber stamps to the Executive. Moreover the Executive shows no symptoms of callous indifference to the ills that we must cure if we are to preserve our vitality. State and local governments are more alive and more involved than they were 30 years ago. And our Nation's private enterprise has grown many times over in both size and vitality.

Some men, I remember vividly, said it was socialistic to consider enacting the social security measure. Some men said it was high-handed to favor the minimum wage when I first voted for it—25 cents an hour. Some said it was the sign of an overbearing police state when I proposed the voting rights bill only a short time ago. Those who would change the status quo have been called many names, not only by the demagogue on the stump, but on occasions by the intellectual on the platform.

Forgotten now are the charges of socialism that were hurled at social security by the defenders of the status quo. Silent are the voices which cried "high-handed" at the minimum wage. Irrelevant today is the denunciation of the voting rights law as an overbearing act of a central authority, an act of a police state.

The issue for this generation is a different kind. It has to do with the obligations of power in the world for a society that strives, despite its worst flaws, always to be just and fair and human. Like almost every issue we face, this is one in which scholars and public officials alike have a crucial stake.

Abroad we can best measure American involvement, whatever our successes and failures, by one simple proposition: Not one single country where America has helped mount a major effort to resist aggression—from France to Greece to Korea to Vietnam—not one single country where we have helped today has a government servile to outside interests.

There is a reason for this which I believe goes to the very heart of our society: The exercise of power in this century has meant for all of us in the United States not arrogance but agony. We have used our power not willingly and recklessly ever, but always reluctantly and with restraint.

Unlike nations in the past with vast power at their disposal, your United States of America has never sought to crush the autonomy of her neighbors. We have not been driven by blind militarism down courses of devastating aggression. Nor have we followed the ancient and conceited philosophy of the "noble lie" that some men are by nature meant to be slaves to others.

THE RECENT LESSONS

As I look upon America this morning from the platform of one of her greatest universities, I see, instead, a nation whose might is not her master but her servant.

I see a nation conscious of lessons so recently learned:

—that security and aggression, as well as peace and war, must be the concerns of her foreign policy;

—that a great power influences the world just as surely when it withdraws its strength, as when it exercises its strength;

—that aggression must be deterred where possible and met early when undertaken;

—that the application of military force, when it becomes necessary, must be for limited purposes and must be tightly controlled.

Surely it is not a paranoid vision of America's place in the world to recognize that freedom is still indivisible—still has adversaries whose challenge must be answered.

THE STERNEST CHALLENGE

Today, of course, as we meet here, that challenge is sternest—at the moment—in Southeast Asia. Yet there, as elsewhere, our great power is also tempered by great restraint. What nation has announced such limited objectives or such willingness to remove its military presence once those objectives are secured and achieved? What nation has spent the lives of its sons and vast sums of its fortune to provide the people of a small, striving country the chance to elect a course that we might not ourselves choose?

The aims for which we struggle are aims which, in the ordinary course of affairs, men of the intellectual world applaud and serve: the principle of choice over coercion, the defense of the weak against the strong and the aggressive, the right of a young and frail nation to develop free from the interference of her neighbors, the ability of a people— however inexperienced, however different, however diverse—to fashion a society consistent with their own traditions and values and aspirations.

THE SCHOLAR'S OBLIGATION

These are all at stake in that conflict. It is the consequences of the cost of their abandonment that men of learning must examine dispassionately. For, I would remind you, to wear the scholar's gown is to assume an obligation to seek truth without prejudice and without cliché, even when the results of the search sometimes are at variance with one's own predilections and own opinions.

That is all we expect of those who are troubled—even as we are—by the obligations of power the United States did not seek but from which the United States cannot escape.

It was twenty-six years ago that Archibald MacLeish asked of all scholars and writers and students of his generation what history would say of those who failed to oppose the forces of disorder then at loose in Europe.

We must ask of this generation the same question concerning Asia.

MacLeish reminded that generation of the answer that was given by Leonardo when Michelangelo indicted him for indifference to the misfortunes of the Florentines. "Indeed," said Leonardo, "indeed, the study of beauty has occupied my whole heart."

Other studies, no matter how important, must not now detract the man of learning from the misfortunes of freedom in Southeast Asia.

While men may talk of the "search for peace" and the "pursuit of peace," we really know that peace is not something to be discovered suddenly—it is not a thing to be caught and contained. Because peace must be built—step by painful, patient step. And the building will take the best work of the world's best men and women.

It will take men whose cause is not the

497

cause of one nation but whose cause is the cause of all nations—men whose enemies are not other men but the historic foes of mankind. I hope that many of you will serve in this public service for the world.

Woodrow Wilson knew that learning is essential to the leadership that our world so desperately yearns for and needs today. Before he came to Princeton, he attended a small college in North Carolina and went to classes every day beneath a portal which bore the Latin inscription: "Let learning be cherished where liberty has arisen."

Today, this motto which served a President must also serve all mankind. Where liberty has arisen, learning must be cherished—or liberty itself becomes a very fragile thing.

So we dedicate this building today—not only to the man; not only to the Nation's service—but to learning in the service of all mankind.

There can be no higher mission.

NOTE: The President spoke at 11:15 a.m. in Princeton, N.J., at the dedication of Woodrow Wilson Hall at the university's Woodrow Wilson School of Public and International Affairs where he was awarded an honorary degree of Doctor of Laws. In his opening words he referred to Richard J. Hughes, Governor of New Jersey, Robert F. Goheen, President of Princeton, and John W. Gardner, Secretary of Health, Education, and Welfare. Speaking of the academic figures among his Cabinet and advisers, the President named Vice President Hubert H. Humphrey, Secretary of State Dean Rusk, Secretary of Defense Robert S. McNamara, Secretary of Labor W. Willard Wirtz, Attorney General Nicholas deB. Katzenbach, Secretary of Housing and Urban Development Robert C. Weaver, Special Assistant for Science and Technology Dr. Donald F. Hornig, and Special Consultant Dr. Eric F. Goldman.

217 Letter to the U.S. National Chairman for United Nations Day. *May 11, 1966*

[Released May 11, 1966. Dated April 30, 1966]

Dear Mr. Kaiser:

I appreciate greatly your consenting to serve this year as U.S. National Chairman for United Nations Day.

UN Day should have special significance for Americans. The United States has provided both birthplace and homeplace for the United Nations; the UN has enjoyed warm bipartisan support from five U.S. Presidents, from the Congress and from an overwhelming majority of the American people. Support for the United Nations has been a major element of U.S. foreign policy since 1945.

As UN Day Chairman, I know that you, with the cooperation of the various State Governors, Mayors and other local officials, will encourage appropriate observances of this commemorative event throughout the country. This year the United Nations is twenty-one years old, and Americans should join other peoples of the world in welcoming it to majority.

I am happy that I can count on your outstanding talents and ability for this important job.

Sincerely,

LYNDON B. JOHNSON

[Mr. Edgar F. Kaiser, 300 Lakeside Drive, Oakland, Calif.]

NOTE: The President on the same day issued Proclamation 3725, "United Nations Day, 1966" (2 Weekly Comp. Pres. Docs., p. 633; 31 F.R. 7107; 3 CFR 1966 Comp., p. 53).

218   Statement by the President Upon Signing Bills Providing for the Disposal of Excess Stockpiled Commodities.   *May 11, 1966*

THE 10 stockpile disposal bills I have signed into law today will once again enable us to reap the benefits of past prudence and apply them to our present needs.

I applaud the prompt and wise action of the Congress.

And I commend the truly American effort that helped make this legislation a reality—the close partnership of the executive branch, industry, and the Congress.

These 10 bills authorize the disposal from our stockpiles of vanadium, chromite, fluorspar, bismuth, thorium, asbestos, rhodium, ruthenium, and mica.

All of these commodities are needed to help turn the wheels of commerce, but among them, vanadium ranks as the most important. This metal is in critically short supply. It is vitally needed for the manufacture of high-strength steels used for construction and for tools, and as a special alloy in our aircraft and missile programs.

I have asked the Administrator of the General Services Administration to begin moving immediately into the hands of industry the vanadium and other materials covered by the legislation.

As I have said before, our stocks of excess metals will win no battles while they lie idle in storage bins. Instead, they are needed—and needed now:

—To give our fighting men in Vietnam the arms and equipment they must have to do the job.
—To maintain orderly markets essential to the continued prosperity of our great American industries and the continued high employment of American workers.
—To help improve our balance of payments position.

—To reduce the costs of maintaining unnecessary inventories of strategic materials.

In short, by moving excess commodities from stockpile to smelter and factory, we benefit the taxpayer and the economy as a whole.

The 10 measures I have signed today bring to 13 the number of stockpile bills approved by Congress at this session.

Twelve remaining bills are now before the House Armed Services Committee and are awaiting action. I urge swift passage of these remaining bills to enable us to safeguard the national interest, sustain a healthy economy, and support our troops in Vietnam.

Congress has the opportunity to write a strong record on stockpile legislation. Under the leadership of our distinguished Senators Russell and Symington and Representatives Rivers and Philbin, I am confident that Congress will achieve this goal.

NOTE: As enacted, the bills signed by the President are as follows:

H.R. 13365 (chromite) . . . . Public Law 89–415
(80 Stat. 136)
H.R. 13367 (fluorspar) . . . . Public Law 89–416
(80 Stat. 136)
H.R. 13368 (bismuth) . . . . Public Law 89–417
(80 Stat. 136)
H.R. 13371 (phlogopite mica) . . Public Law 89–418
(80 Stat. 137)
H.R. 13373 (muscovite mica) . . Public Law 89–419
(80 Stat. 137)
H.R. 13578 (rhodium) . . . . Public Law 89–420
(80 Stat. 138)
H.R. 13579 (thorium) . . . . Public Law 89–421
(80 Stat. 138)
H.R. 13580 (asbestos) . . . . Public Law 89–422
(80 Stat. 138)
H.R. 13663 (ruthenium) . . . . . . Public Law 89–423
(80 Stat. 139)
H.R. 13774 (vanadium) . . . . Public Law 89–424
(80 Stat. 139)

Before adjournment on October 22, Congress enacted 9 of the 12 additional stockpile disposal bills recommended by the President. For his statements upon signing these measures, see Items 283 and 572.

Details as to the status of the 3 remaining bills are printed in the Weekly Compilation of Presidential Documents (vol. 2, p. 1547). Statements by the President on signing bills for the disposal of stockpiled platinum, bauxite, and molybdenum are printed above as Items 173 and 206.

219 Statement by the President Upon Receiving a Report on Crime in the District of Columbia. *May* 12, 1966

I AM ENCOURAGED by the report on crime in the District of Columbia in April which I have today received from Chief John B. Layton of the Metropolitan Police Department. The added efforts and added resources which have been thrown into the war against crime in the District during the past 9 months have begun to show results.

In April, for the first time since June 1962, the number of Part I offenses* reported in the District decreased—by 7.3 percent—from the number reported during the same month of the previous year.

For 6 consecutive months crime index offenses (which include all Part I offenses except negligent homicide, nonforcible rape and larceny under $50) have decreased from the prior year. The decrease in April was an encouraging 12.8 percent.

For 6 consecutive months reports of housebreaking have been fewer than in the previous year.

For 6 consecutive months reports of auto thefts have been fewer than in the previous year.

In 7 of the past 9 months, and for the last 2 months, reports of robberies have been fewer than in the previous year.

I am likewise encouraged by the fact that there has also been a decrease in juvenile delinquency in the District. Notwithstanding an increase in the total number of young people in the District, the number of complaints recorded by the Juvenile Court during the first quarter of 1966 was 23 percent below those recorded during the first quarter of 1965. There has been a downward trend in juvenile delinquency for over a year.

There is no reason for complacency in these figures, but there is reason for hope, and for confidence that we can do better.

I have urged Chief Layton to continue the fine efforts of the Police Department. I am grateful to all those other parts of the Washington community who have helped—the news media, the parents, the schools, the many dedicated people who are bringing hope and opportunity to those who never dared to hope.

There is nothing more to be desired than a National Capital free of crime. I will continue to work toward that goal, and I am looking forward to the report of the District of Columbia Crime Commission to suggest additional steps that can be taken.

---

*Part I offenses are: criminal homicide, rape, robbery, aggravated assault, housebreaking, grand larceny, petit larceny, and auto theft.

NOTE: The 10-page report (processed) is entitled "Current Status and Effectiveness Report, Special Anti-Crime Programs" and is dated May 10, 1966.

The footnote in this item, marked with an asterisk, is part of the statement as released.

220 Remarks on Presenting Scholastic Achievement Awards to Three
Blind College Students. *May 12, 1966*

Miss Bowman, Mr. Dennis, Miss Gearreald,
Secretary Gilpatric, Mr. Merrill:

When my friend Ros Gilpatric, who has
served his country and his generation so long
and so well, suggested to me that I would
have the opportunity to be here with you
folks this morning, I thought this was one
invitation that I could not pass up.

I am really very grateful to not only my
friend Mr. Gilpatric, but to Miss Bowman,
Mr. Dennis, and Miss Gearreald for letting
me be a part of this ceremony.

You don't know how much pride and
pleasure I feel in having you here in the
Cabinet Room. I am sure that this will give
hope to thousands of others throughout this
great land of ours.

The great poet Milton, speaking of the
frustrations of his own blindness, once said,
"They also serve who only stand and wait."

You brilliant young people that are here
this morning did not choose to just stand
and wait. Instead, you chose to meet life
and meet it on its own terms—and you are
conquering it. I believe that this achievement which we honor here is only a
beginning.

Just a few months ago, if I may look backwards, I appointed to one of the highest
legal offices in this country, the Tax Court
of the United States of America, a person
who is blind. He sits there in authority and
in judgment on the most powerful corporations in the land, the moneyed interests, and
everyone, for that matter, who is concerned
with taxes—and everyone who lives here is.

He is only one of many who are so handicapped, who are now serving in positions of
very high authority and responsibility, not
only in the Government of the United States,
but in the industrial might of this country.

So I would like for you to feel that you
have helped yourselves and by your example
you have done a good deal more than that.
You have helped thousands of others. You
have provided them stimulation and inspiration. You have proved beyond any doubt
that no one is really condemned to a life of
frustration and failure because of some
accident of nature.

You have helped to bring the light of
inspiration into what we might call the darkness of despair. I am pleased to observe
that you are symbols of determination, and
it is a great honor for me to give you these
awards this morning which really reflect the
admiration, the applause, and I might say
the affection of not only your President, but
of your countrymen.

Thank you very much.

NOTE: The President spoke at 12:15 p.m. in the
Cabinet Room at the White House. In his opening
words he referred to the three award winners, Bar-
bara Ann Bowman of Oberlin College, Ronald A.
Dennis of Williams College, and Karen L. Gearreald
of Agnes Scott College. He also referred to Roswell
L. Gilpatric, former Deputy Secretary of Defense,
and Allen H. Merrill, President of Recording for the
Blind, Inc., which sponsors the annual scholastic
achievement awards to blind students. The 1966
award winners were assisted, as are some 1,500 blind
college students yearly, by recorded instructional
material provided by the national nonprofit
organization.

221 Remarks at a Congressional Dinner Held in the National Guard Armory. *May 12, 1966*

Thank you Senator Magnuson, Mr. Vice President, Mr. Speaker, Majority Leader Mansfield, Majority Leader Albert, Senator Smathers, Congressman Boggs, my dear friend Jess Larson, who has been chairman for this great occasion, my fellow Democrats:

I am delighted to be here tonight with so many of my very old friends as well as some members of the Foreign Relations Committee. [*Applause*]

You can say one thing about those hearings, although I don't think this is the place to say it.

Will Rogers once said, "I am not a member of any organized political party. I am a Democrat." I ran across that quotation last night in a magazine article, and I jotted down what it said:

"This week, any Democrat in the United States could borrow Will Rogers' words and describe his own status with as much accuracy as humor. The Democratic Party is disorganized, in debt, and leaderless. Democrats are wondering where their next candidates are coming from."

That article appeared shortly before the congressional campaign of 1954, and I must confess it had a very personal meaning for me. It said the Democrats might do all right in the House, but we were in such great trouble in the Senate "that Lyndon Johnson has very little chance of ever becoming majority leader."

Well, the voters thought otherwise. They gave President Eisenhower a Congress that could get things done. I bring this up tonight because we are in an election year and I want to remind you of how much trouble the Democrats always seem to have in an election year before the votes are counted.

I know that when election time rolls around this year, the American people are not going to disown the most productive Congress ever assembled under the greatest leadership that ever led a Congress in the city of Washington. I know I am not going to, and I don't think Senator Long, the Democratic whip and the Chairman of the Finance Committee, and Wilbur Mills, the Chairman of the Ways and Means Committee, and Senator Anderson and others who made such a contribution are ever going to let our people forget that we worked together to pass the Health Insurance Act for the Aged, which means Medicare, and the Older Americans Act, which means new security and hope for all the older people of this country.

Our young people will not forget that we passed the first Elementary and Secondary Education and the Higher Education Acts for all the young people of this country.

Our poor will not forget that this Congress passed the Economic Opportunity Act of 1965, the Appalachian Regional Development Act, the Public Works and Economic Development Act. They will not forget Project Head Start, or the Job Corps, or the Neighborhood Youth Corps, or VISTA, or the Urban and Rural Community Action Program.

Our servicemen will never forget that it was this Congress that passed the Veterans Readjustment Benefits Act and the GI bill.

Our immigrants and their families are not going to forget that it was this Congress that passed the Immigration and Nationality Act.

Our farmers will not forget that when the Democratic administration came into power, our farm income was a little over $11 billion, and it has increased now to over $15 billion.

Our workers will not forget the fact that we passed the Manpower Act, the Job Development Act, and the Vocational Rehabilitation Act.

I don't think that our minorities will ever forget that this Congress passed the historic Voting Rights Act. That is the first effective voting rights act that has been passed in 100 years.

Our city dwellers will not forget the Housing and Urban Development Act, or the pioneering program of rent supplements for low-income people, or the new grant program for the urban growth and renewal projects. Nor will they forget the Department of Housing and Urban Development, which will turn the legislative promises into live realities all down through the years to come.

Our travelers and our conservationists will not forget the Highway Beautification Act, or the Water Pollution Act, or the air control pollution bill.

Our sick and our suffering citizens will not forget the heart and stroke measure.

Our businessmen will not forget that together we have tonight created and sustained the longest and the brightest season of prosperity in all American history.

Nor will labor, or the consumer, or the wage earner, or the housewife forget the place that all of them have enjoyed under the Democratic sun.

All this was only a promise when this Congress, that meets here tonight, met for the first time. It was in our platform. I am proud tonight that the promises in that platform have been redeemed. Between 80 and 90 percent of the pledges in that platform are now the laws of the United States of America!

I defy any Congress or any administration to ever equal that percentage record. And I thank the Speaker and the leadership and every Member of the Congress here for it.

I said 2 years ago that our society will never be great until every young man and woman is set free to scan the farthest reaches of the human mind. So this Congress heard, and this Congress acted. We lifted the sights and we stretched the horizons of every child by education. We made every classroom a treasure house, and every teacher the guardian of the riches by which a great nation is built.

I said 2 years ago that our cities are decayed and our housing is inadequate and our transportation is inefficient. This Congress heard, and this Congress acted. We have created a landmark Department of Housing and Urban Development, and we will soon create another Department of Transportation.

I said 2 years ago that the beauty of our countryside was in danger; that our air and our water were polluted; that our parks and our seashores were overcrowded. And again this great Congress, led by great leaders, heard and acted. We added 186,000 acres to our parks, and 100 miles to our national seashores. We acted to beautify our highways. We passed the first comprehensive antipollution measure in the history of the Federal Government.

This Congress that is here tonight did it, and you can be proud of it. Your people can be proud of you.

But the task is not yet finished. We still have work to do. The Great Society is not a safe harbor. It is not a resting place, a final objective, a finished work. It is a challenge constantly to be renewed. That is our goal—and the country needs every one of you back here next January, not to get the country moving again—some think it is moving too much now—but to build a foundation, and to move our Nation forward.

I want to say one other thing to you tonight. I spent the afternoon walking among the armless and legless men—our fighting men who yesterday were in Vietnam carrying our burdens for us. I hear every day from those who are troubled and frustrated about Vietnam. Some doubt the wisdom of any action there, but I receive thousands of letters from people all over this land, from our men in Vietnam—and I talked to 40 of them this afternoon.

They tell me that the people of our country have not lost the spirit, and have not lost the courage, and have not lost the wisdom which has kept America a free people all these years.

I came to this town 35 years ago. Fresh in my memory then were the problems that confronted another Democratic President in World War I, and I saw men here and there, in both bodies of the Congress, and in various sections of the country, who had opposing views about the wisdom of the leadership of Woodrow Wilson.

I ran for the Senate in 1941, and was defeated in July by 1,311 votes. I have always wondered if it wasn't intended that I should have been, because the next month, as a Member of the House, I cast my vote to support the President to keep from sending the Army home. That vote prevailed by only one vote—203 to 202. I am glad that my district was represented on that vote—that I hadn't moved over to the Senate.

But when you think what those Democratic Presidents went through, when freedom and liberty were threatened, and the load and the burden that they and their Congresses carried, and the division that then existed, you can be thankful tonight for this Congress, for these leaders, for the American people who have learned at painful cost that freedom is not indivisible.

Our people have learned that aggression, I think, in any part of the world, carries the seeds of destruction to American freedom. I believe, I think I know, that the majority of our countrymen still agree with the words that a great American hero spoke a long time ago. It was Sergeant Alvin York who once said, "Liberty and freedom and democracy are so very precious that you do not fight to win them once and then stop. You do not do that. Liberty and freedom and democracy are prizes that are awarded only to those people who fight to win them and then keep on fighting eternally to hold them."

Sergeant York was not a man of war, but of peace. His message has meaning, great meaning, for every American, and every generation of Americans. We are and always will be men of peace. We have always hated the horror of war. We will have our differences and our disputes and we will do it without questioning the integrity or the honor of our fellow man.

But we as a nation have never abandoned and we will never surrender this world to those who want to dominate it and to those who want to destroy it.

If we were to turn our backs on freedom in South Vietnam, if Vietnam were to fall to an aggressor's force, what an empty thing America's commitment to liberty would really turn out to be.

So I say tonight to my party and to my countrymen: We shall stand there with honor. We shall stand there with courage. We shall stand there with patience. That is the stand that this Congress has taken, and that is the stand that we will continue to take. It is the stand, I believe, that the vast majority of the free people of the world will respect. It is the stand that the vast majority of Americans will demand.

So I say to you, my great leaders in the Congress, to our committee chairmen in the House and the Senate, to the members of every one of those committees, go out there in the countryside and tell them this fall that America will persevere until peace comes to Vietnam. That is our dream. That is our hope. That is our prayer. And when that day comes there will be rejoicing in our land and in the world.

And once again we will not only have a peace-loving people that seek no territory, that seek no domination, but we will have a peaceful 50 States that are prosperous as they have never been before. We will have the highest per capita income of any people anywhere. We will have the best housing and the best health and the best education and the best food and the best clothes and the best recreation. But most of all, we will have a liberty and a freedom that was dreamed of by our forefathers and that is preserved by you.

Good night.

NOTE: The President spoke at 9:42 p.m. at the National Guard Armory in Washington before a group of 6,000 Democrats present at the fundraising dinner. In his opening words he referred to Senator Warren G. Magnuson of Washington, Vice President Hubert H. Humphrey, Representative John W. McCormack of Massachusetts, Speaker of the House of Representatives, Senate Majority Leader Mike Mansfield of Montana, House Majority Leader Carl Albert of Oklahoma, Senator George A. Smathers of Florida, Representative Hale Boggs of Louisiana, and Jess Larson, former Administrator of General Services, who served as chairman for the occasion.

During his remarks the President referred to, among others, Senator Russell B. Long of Louisiana, Representative Wilbur D. Mills of Arkansas, and Senator Clinton P. Anderson of New Mexico.

---

222   Letter to the President of the Senate and to the Speaker of the House Transmitting a Summary of the National Atmospheric Sciences Program, Fiscal Year 1967. *May 13, 1966*

Dear Mr. President: (Dear Mr. Speaker:)

I have the honor to transmit to the Congress a summary of the Federal Government's "National Atmospheric Sciences Program" for Fiscal Year 1967, prepared by the Federal Council for Science and Technology.

The summary covers the coordinated activities of 10 Federal agencies engaged in 25 important lines of scientific research and service. These efforts are directed at:

—better understanding the atmosphere in which we live;

—finding new ways to predict the weather;

—providing greater insights into the challenge of controlled weather modification.

The potential economic benefits of this research are enormous and important not only to Americans, but to men everywhere.

To move successfully from the hopes of research to the reality of results means that we must first increase our knowledge of the atmosphere. Much of the progress in this field will come from the Government's atmospheric science program which supports research and experimentation in creative partnerships across the nation with the scientific community and industry.

Taken alone, however, our own studies and research will not be enough, for the environment is global and indivisible. We know, for example, that a storm along the Florida coast may well begin off the shores of another continent.

We can reach our goals sooner if we work

closely with other nations in mutually beneficial endeavors. Together, we can share our knowledge and take new strides to cope with the ancient enemies of storm and drought and flood. That is why I have recently pledged that the United States will participate in the World Weather Watch, the most extensive international effort yet devised to enhance our knowledge of the world's atmosphere.

The world has already begun to reap the benefits of advanced space technology. Two weather satellites, the ESSA 1 and 2, are now in orbit. Through these scientific marvels, intense storms on both sides of the Indian Ocean were detected in time to help minimize danger and damage. This is only the beginning of the vast promise modern

science holds, in peaceful pursuits, to unlock the mysteries of our atmosphere and to make our lives and the lives of our children easier and happier.

I urge the committees of Congress interested in the atmospheric sciences program to consider the attached summary report.

Sincerely,

LYNDON B. JOHNSON

NOTE: This is the text of identical letters addressed to the Honorable Hubert H. Humphrey, President of the Senate, and to the Honorable John W. McCormack, Speaker of the House of Representatives.

The President transmitted ICAS Report No. 10, entitled "National Atmospheric Sciences Program, Fiscal Year 1967" (48 pp.). The report, dated January 1966, was prepared by the Interdepartmental Committee for Atmospheric Sciences and made available "for official use only" by the Federal Council for Science and Technology.

223   Remarks on Signing Supplemental Appropriations Bills Providing Funds for the National Teacher Corps and the Rent Supplement Program. *May 13, 1966*

Mr. Vice President, Secretary Gardner and Secretary Weaver, Senator Mansfield, and Members of the Senate and the House, my friends:

On January 20, 1937, Franklin D. Roosevelt mounted the steps of the Capitol for his Second Inaugural. That day, he reaffirmed for his people one true measurement of our advancement as a nation:

"The test of our progress," he said, "is not whether we add to the abundance of those who have much; it is whether we provide enough for those who have little."

Franklin Roosevelt—and the men of Congress—won enduring honor because they made this century a century of hope: Hope for the dispossessed people of the earth, hope for all the poor and the forgotten.

Today as we meet here with the signing of this act, we mark a new beginning, a

beginning of two bold programs—the National Teacher Corps and the Rent Supplement Program.

It has been many months since Congress authorized both of these programs. But the appropriations needed to translate idea into reality were slow in coming.

Today, however, we mark the end of hope and struggle for these legislative programs. And today we can be proud that this is still the century of hope; that a great nation is still meeting the challenge to "provide enough for those who have little."

For the first time, Congress is enabling private enterprise to take a direct hand in meeting the housing needs of poor families. At an average cost of $600 per housing unit, we will help low-income families have decent housing. Thus we are being not only compassionate, but cost-conscious. Because our present cost-per-unit for public housing averages in excess of $1,000.

This program is very modest, but it is flexible and imaginative, and it is experimental. It puts a new tool in the hands of those who are helping to build better housing for all Americans. While every man's house cannot be a castle, it need not be a hovel.

Among those who have little, there are also those who have little learning, and they have little opportunity for it.

For these, the schoolchildren of our city slums and our rural pockets, the National Teacher Corps will mean a great deal.

There are those who would have us wait before launching the Teacher Corps—wait until there are more funds, wait until things are settled in Vietnam, wait until education programs are on a firmer footing. Wait until we—oh, just wait, wait, wait!

To them I must this morning reply: This is no time to wait. The men and women who have volunteered for service in the Teacher Corps have already waited long enough. The slum schools which urgently need our attention and need our assistance have waited long enough. And the poor children of this Nation who desperately require attention now must not wait any longer for this help.

That is why I have instructed Secretary Gardner and Commissioner Howe to take steps immediately to launch the Teacher Corps, to recruit and to train the maximum number that this very small appropriation will allow. By next fall, those teachers will be on duty.

We will seek high quality and deep commitment among all those who serve. They must be like the young volunteer from Macon, Georgia, who wrote, "I don't particularly get pleasure out of being in the slums, but I want to do something about them. The Teacher Corps will prepare me to work

in any area at any time, and it is the opportunity of a lifetime."

They must be like JoAnn Navorr and Frances Nichols and Alberto Huerta—three of the first Teacher Corps volunteers whom you see here on the platform with me today. JoAnn, who comes from Los Angeles, is a returned Peace Corps volunteer and a qualified language instructor. Frances, a student at Berea College in Kentucky, helped organize the Appalachia volunteers and worked with the poor children in Kentucky for more than 2½ years. Alberto, who comes from Laredo, Texas, and is fluent in Spanish, wants to be a teacher of Mexican-American children.

There was a period when I was a teacher of Mexican-American children. It gave me the greatest satisfaction of my life.

We need more volunteers like these three. I don't know, Alberto, where you will go. You may not follow the route I did after I left that Mexican-American school. But you can't ever tell. They will do a lot for you while you are trying to help them.

The other night after Ray Scherer's television broadcast, one of Mike Mansfield's colleagues and one of my Senate friends, said to me, "Well, all my life I heard that any boy born in America had a chance to grow up and be President, and now I believe it."

So the hour is already late. Many June graduates who were considering the Teacher Corps have begun already, because it is late, to look elsewhere for the year ahead.

I appeal to them all over this Nation this morning to reconsider that decision. I call on them to think again about coming and helping us and helping those more unfortunate. No service at this time could be more valuable to your country.

I also call on the Congress to reconsider— to make available the funds that we need, and we desperately need, for a Teacher Corps in fiscal 1967. I hope that Congress, which has already done so much for so many, will do just a little more, and give the Teacher Corps a chance to help others.

I know from personal experience how bitter is the want and how great the need of poverty's prisoners. I know, too, what a decent house and what a decent education can really do to end that want and to help fill that need.

It was years ago that Justice Holmes told a reunion of his Harvard classmates that they were fortunate because, as he said, and I quote, "In our youth our hearts were touched with fire."

Today it is not enough to touch with fire the hearts of just a few in this country. We must take the light to all the dark places in this Nation, and here this morning, in your presence, with God as our witness, we make that start.

NOTE: The President spoke shortly after 11 a.m. in the Rose Garden at the White House. In his opening words he referred to Vice President Hubert H. Humphrey, Secretary of Health, Education, and Welfare John W. Gardner, Secretary of Housing and Urban Development Robert C. Weaver, and Senate Majority Leader Mike Mansfield of Montana.

As enacted, the Second Supplemental Appropriation Act, 1966, is Public Law 89-426 (80 Stat. 141).

224   Memorandum on June Buying by Federal Agencies. *May 13, 1966*

Memorandum for the Heads of Executive Departments and Agencies
SUBJECT: Prevention of June Buying

I want you to take steps immediately to see that there is *no* so-called "June buying" in your department or agency this year. Wasteful purchasing and inventory practices are an affront to the taxpayer and cannot be tolerated.

The ordering of goods and services at the end of the fiscal year to prevent the lapse of available appropriation balances is indefensible at any time. It is absolutely unthinkable this year—with men fighting and dying in Vietnam and inflationary pressures worrying us at home.

I am asking each of you personally to do whatever is necessary to insure that in your department or agency:

—orders for supplies, materials, and equip-

ment are kept to the minimum needed to carry on essential, approved programs.

—inventories are held to normal levels.

—new contracts for future services and advance payments to contractors and vendors are made only in accordance with established plans.

By May 18, will you please report to me, through the Director of the Bureau of the Budget, the specific steps you have taken to provide top level control of your department's purchases during the remainder of the fiscal year, in the context of preventing June buying.

LYNDON B. JOHNSON

NOTE: In response to the President's memorandum, Budget Director Charles L. Schultze submitted on June 14 a memorandum report on steps taken throughout the executive branch to prevent "June buying." The text of the report, issued as a White House press release, is printed in the Weekly Compilation of Presidential Documents (vol. 2, p. 773).

225   Memorandum on the Charging of Fees for Government Services.
      May 17, 1966

Memorandum for the Heads of Departments and Agencies

SUBJECT: User charges

When the Federal Government provides *special services* for *special groups,* it is both *good economics* and *good government* to charge fees for these services

—*good economics,* because user charges make possible an efficient allocation of resources among alternative programs

—*good government,* because user charges ensure equitable treatment of the general taxpayer.

At a Cabinet meeting on February 11, 1965, I emphasized the importance of user charges and called on each of you to

—develop and actively support legislative proposals to establish or revise user charges

—review and keep up-to-date user charges which are established administratively.

The Bureau of the Budget has just released a report on the results of the user charge program during fiscal year 1965. Progress was made. These are the highlights:

—collections from user charges were $1,408 million, up $137 million over the year before

—Congress enacted three significant user charge measures which

..made permanent the 5% ticket tax on air passenger travel

..increased Patent Office fees—for the first time since 1932

..increased security registration fees.

—Executive departments and agencies, through administrative action, increased 171 fees, decreased 28 fees, and established 56 new fees. For example

..the Atomic Energy Commission established a new fee for the conversion of U–233 uranyl nitrate to oxide and metal

..the Food and Drug Administration increased fees for establishing tolerances for pesticide chemicals

..the Agricultural Stabilization and Conservation Service substantially decreased fees charged to producers applying for price-support loans, reflecting a simplified loan operations procedure.

All of these accomplishments represent progress, but there is still much to do.

First, important user charge measures requested in my budget are now pending before the Congress. These proposals involve diverse activities of the Federal Government. Their passage would add $326 million in user charge receipts. Transportation user charges alone—for air, highway, and waterway transportation—would add $245 million.

I again call on each of you to give user charge legislative proposals your continuing active support.

Second, the responsibility for reviewing and revising administrative user charges is a continuing one. These charges should reflect the costs of providing service: if costs rise, user charges should be increased; if costs fall, user charges should be reduced.

I again ask you to keep administrative user charges current.

User charges are an essential element in responsible Federal fiscal management. I am determined that user charges in this

administration will be as comprehensive and current as our efforts can make them.

LYNDON B. JOHNSON

NOTE: The Bureau of the Budget report to which the President referred is entitled "User Charges; Annual Progress Report" (May 1966, 25 pp.).

226 Remarks Upon Accepting on Behalf of the Nation the Joseph H. Hirshhorn Fine Arts Collection. *May 17, 1966*

Mr. Vice President, Justice Fortas, Secretary Udall, Mr. and Mrs. Hirshhorn, Mr. Ripley, Mr. Stevens, ladies and gentlemen:

This is a magnificent day for the Nation's Capital and for the millions of Americans who will visit our Capital in the years to come.

It is also a very inspiring climax to a career that has been devoted to art. From the days of his youth in Brooklyn when he first began collecting reproductions of art work, until this very hour, this distinguished American, Joseph Hirshhorn, has been driven by a passion for painting and sculpture. Throughout the world he has sought the great art of our time, those expressions of man's will to make sense of his experience on earth, to find order and meaning in the physical world about him, and to render what is familiar in a very new way.

I know that Joseph Hirshhorn will go on seeking out the best in modern painting and sculpture for many years to come, but he will never have a finer hour than this, for today he offers the fruits of a lifetime in the full service of art to all the citizens of a grateful Nation. Few men have been privileged to make such a gift to their generation and to all of those that will come after them.

Several months ago Mrs. Johnson journeyed to Joseph Hirshhorn's home in Connecticut. I wasn't sure she would ever come back. But she is here today and she did

come back filled with awe and admiration for the great works that were collected there. She came back, too, with a great sense of affection and respect for the owners of that work. She has told me many times since then of her hope that Mr. Hirshhorn would see his way clear to make his collection available to all the people of this country.

Many suggestions were made to Mr. Hirshhorn about the disposition of his collection, as well there might be, and I think every proffer that was made to him I heard about the next morning by rumor from people who were frightened by it. These offers came from among private collectors and they realized that his collection was virtually without parallel in its field. That he has now chosen the Nation's Capital is a cause for real celebration, great pride of all of us, and, Mr. Hirshhorn, the deepest gratitude of the American people.

Now we must go forward. We must begin to build a museum that is worthy of the collection, and worthy of our highest aspirations for this beautiful city, the Capital of our country. Washington is a city of powerful institutions, the seat of government for the strongest nation on earth, the place where democratic ideals are translated into reality, where we are not just concerned with appearance, but with achievement.

Washington also must be a place of beauty and a place of learning. Its buildings and its thoroughfares, its schools and its concert halls, its museums, should reflect a people whose commitment is to the best that is within them ever to dream.

So in the National Gallery collection, in the Freer and the Corcoran Galleries, in the museums of the Smithsonian, in the Kennedy Center that is to come, in the Pennsylvania Avenue plan—and now, in the Hirshhorn Museum and Sculpture Garden—we have the elements of a capital of beauty and a capital of learning that is no less impressive than its power.

So, Mr. Hirshhorn, here this morning, in the beautiful Rose Garden of the White House, on the steps of the White House itself, we accept on behalf of all of the American people your splendid gift to all of your fellow citizens. We shall treasure it. We shall use it well in giving pleasure and enlightenment to men and women of every age, to men and women from every walk of life.

And now to the 10 million who visit this Capital each year we say to them that we have a very special inducement in store for you, one that we think that every visitor will want to partake of and participate in and enjoy as the result of the patriotism and the generosity of one of America's most distinguished philanthropists—Joseph Hirshhorn.

NOTE: The President spoke at noon in the Rose Garden at the White House. In his opening words he referred to Vice President Hubert H. Humphrey, Associate Justice of the Supreme Court Abe Fortas, Secretary of the Interior Stewart L. Udall, Joseph H. Hirshhorn and his wife Olga, S. Dillon Ripley, Secretary of the Smithsonian Institution, and Roger L. Stevens, Chairman of the National Council on the Arts. The collection of 6,300 paintings, drawings, and sculptures, valued at $25 million—$50 million, constitutes one of the largest private art collections in the world.

In a letter to the President of the Senate and to the Speaker of the House, the President on the same day transmitted a draft bill providing for the construction and administration by the Smithsonian of the proposed Hirshhorn Museum and Sculpture Garden (see Item 227).

---

227   Letter to the President of the Senate and to the Speaker of the House Proposing Establishment of the Joseph H. Hirshhorn Museum and Sculpture Garden.   *May 17, 1966*

Dear Mr. President: (Dear Mr. Speaker:)

One of the greatest privately-owned collections of contemporary sculpture and paintings in the world has been offered to the people of the United States by Mr. Joseph H. Hirshhorn of New York City, and the Hirshhorn Foundation.

I commend to the consideration of the Congress legislation enabling the Smithsonian Institution to accept this gift on behalf of all our people.

GIFTS OF THE PAST

The Nation has been fortunate in the great tradition of private contributions which have

enriched the cultural life of its Capital City. James Smithson's bequest, for the increase and diffusion of knowledge, led to the establishment of the Smithsonian Institution in 1846, and thus to the foundation of a national center of learning and the arts. William Corcoran made an enduring contribution to the life of the Capital by founding, in 1859, the gallery that bears his name. Early in this century Charles Freer donated to the Institution the splendid collection of Oriental art that since 1922 has been housed in the Freer Gallery.

In 1937 Congress accepted the magnificent gift of Andrew Mellon that led to the erection of the National Gallery of Art. Then in 1938, farsighted legislation laid out the program of the National Collection of Fine Arts, which is joining the National Portrait Gallery in the Smithsonian's restored Patent Office Building.

Washington is emerging as a major cultural center, befitting the capital of a great nation. During recent years, the tempo of this development has quickened, and our citizens have caught the vision of a Washington equal in beauty and learning to the power of its institutions. Encouraging evidence of this is the outpouring of gifts for the John F. Kennedy Center for the Performing Arts.

THE HIRSHHORN GIFT

Now a superlative collection of works of contemporary art, enough to furnish an entire museum, has been offered to the Smithsonian Institution. It affords Washington a brilliant opportunity to broaden and strengthen its cultural offerings.

That we may seize this opportunity I am transmitting, for the consideration of the Congress, the attached bill to provide for the establishment of the Joseph H. Hirshhorn Museum and Sculpture Garden. This legislation would provide an appropriate Mall site on which the Board of Regents of the Smithsonian Institution would be authorized to construct a gallery of art and a garden of sculpture, to be known as the Joseph H. Hirshhorn Museum and Sculpture Garden.

The Hirshhorn Collection is the fruit of a lifetime of dedicated effort and discerning judgment, and its presentation to America is a testament to the generosity and public spirit of its donor. More than fifteen hundred pieces of sculpture and over four thousand eight hundred paintings and drawings, with a total value in excess of twenty-five million dollars, have been offered, together with a million dollars for the purchase of additional works.

The enjoyment of our people, and the contributions to knowledge that will result from the acceptance of this grand offer, are truly beyond price. Millions of Americans will soon be able to see, within walking distance of the National Gallery and its masterpieces of painting from earlier centuries, the work of those who have shaped the art of our time.

Thus Joseph Hirshhorn's gift will enrich, not only the city of Washington, but the citizens of every State who visit their nation's Capital.

I urge the Congress to respond to this magnificent offer by adopting the measure I am forwarding today.

Sincerely,

LYNDON B. JOHNSON

NOTE: This is the text of identical letters addressed to the Honorable Hubert H. Humphrey, President of the Senate, and to the Honorable John W. McCormack, Speaker of the House of Representatives.

The text of the draft bill forwarded with the President's letter was included in the White House release. For the President's remarks on November 7 upon signing the measure, see Item 587.

On May 21 the White House announced the conclusion of an agreement between Paul Mellon, President of the National Gallery of Art, and Stewart L. Udall, Secretary of the Interior, concerning the site of the proposed Sculpture Garden. The release stated that the Garden would be located in L'Enfant Square, a four-acre park area between the Natural History Museum and the National Gallery of Art on the north side of the Mall.

See also Item 226.

228   Remarks at a Democratic Party Dinner in Chicago.   *May 17, 1966*

Mayor Daley, Governor Kerner, my delightful friends, Governor Branigin of Indiana and Governor Breathitt of Kentucky and Governor Bryant of Florida, my very able Secretary of Labor, Secretary Wirtz, my beloved colleague for many years and my friend, Senator Douglas, distinguished Comptroller of the Currency, Mr. Saxon, Mr. Siragusa, Mr. Krim, Members of the great Illinois congressional delegation, reverend clergy, Archbishop Cody, Bishop Ford, Rabbi Cohen, my fellow Democrats:

When I arrived in your city tonight, I was reminded of a remark I made several weeks ago to the mayors' convention in Washington. I told them that whenever the burdens of the Presidency seemed unusually heavy, I always remind myself that it could be worse. I just might have been a mayor of a city instead of President of the United States!

There is no more important job in public life. We in Washington can pass laws. We can develop forward-looking programs for all the people. But those laws and those programs have to be carried out by far-sighted and talented and capable leaders back in the local communities.

The people of this great city of Chicago are unusually fortunate. For more than a decade now you have enjoyed the steadfast leadership of a man who is recognized the world over as a great and talented municipal executive—your courageous and intelligent and hardworking mayor, Richard J. Daley—the number one mayor in all the United States of America.

Every time I visit Chicago, the progress that you have made impresses me. Your lakefront grows more beautiful, year by year. Your office buildings, your houses, your schools, and your thoroughfares are now

being imitated by the city planners in the other cities throughout the land.

We are living tonight in what I have called the century of change—and in Chicago you are making certain that it is a change for the better. And that is the same goal that we are striving for in your National Capital in Washington.

And I want to remind you people of Illinois that you are equally fortunate in having an able, aggressive, and attractive Governor, my old friend, Otto Kerner. I know that none of the Governors will take any offense when I tell you that I believe him to be one of the best 50. And I am, too, so happy to have with me tonight another son of Illinois and Chicago, a brilliant scholar from this delightful city, the great Secretary of Labor, Willard Wirtz.

And when each of you votes for Adlai Stevenson III for State Treasurer, you will have your funds well-managed and well-secured. And I hope that you won't forget him when the election comes around.

And I don't want you to forget that a vote for Don Prince for State superintendent of public instruction will be a vote for better schools for every schoolchild in the State of Illinois.

You people are fortunate, you have much to be thankful for: You have one of the best and the most effective congressional delegations in all the House of Representatives—one which gives wholehearted support to the President of the United States and to the Democratic Party. And I just could not come to the city of Chicago and to Cook County without thanking you for each one of these men: first, Bill Dawson; Congressman Kluczynski; Congressman O'Hara; Congressman Murphy; Congressman Yates; Congressman Pucinski; Congressman Danny

Rostenkowski; Congressman Annunzio; Congressman Ronan.

And that's a test for a fellow from Texas!

We have one man with us tonight who can testify to that from personal experience—my old friend, and one of the great Senators of our time, Paul Douglas. I was thinking about Senator Douglas as I was preparing these remarks on my way out here today—about his vision, about his capabilities, about his deep love and his deep devotion to this country for which he fought in World War II and for which he has fought every day of his public life.

Senator Douglas has spent his life in the service of humanity. For 28 years he was a great, outstanding teacher at your University of Chicago. And when the call of public service came, he went to Washington to help remake our country, remake it with the same enthusiasm and with the same wisdom with which he used to mold the minds of the young people of the Midwest.

I know how Senator Douglas must have felt while taking his seat in the Congress. I remember very well my own emotions when I caught a train to leave my State for the first time to go to Washington as a young man back in November 1931—some 35 years ago.

I took along on that train more than a suitcase. I took some dreams and some hopes and some ideas. All of them were based on my belief that we could do much to improve the lot of the average American. I have never forgotten those dreams or those hopes. And tonight, with the help of a wonderful Congress that the people have given us, I seem to see some of those dreams come true.

I remembered then—and I remember now—Edmund Burke's statement that was made more than 175 years ago, that "Government is a contrivance of human wisdom to provide for human wants. Men have a right that these wants should be provided for by this wisdom."

And that is what this administration and this Congress have been trying to do—provide for human wants.

I was working to provide for human wants back in the days of the National Youth Administration. And tonight one of the great pleasures that I get from coming to Chicago is to see that great Federal judge, Bill Campbell, who in those days was NYA Administrator of Illinois and I was NYA Administrator.

And I don't think it was Bill that said this, but I didn't really believe then that he would grace the bench as he has all these years, when I saw him as NYA Administrator, and I know he must not have ever envisioned me where I am tonight. As a matter of fact, after my television show the other night down at the ranch that some of you may have seen, one of my neighbors came up to me and he said, "Lyndon, you know I've heard all my life that a boy, any boy, born in America had a chance to someday grow up and be President. And now I believe it!"

Even in this day of prosperity, even in this day of great affluence, the needs of our people are deep and they are broad and they are wide.

I have seen a lot of changes in the 35 years that I have been in Washington. And that is exactly how it should have been. When we do not change we remain static and we do not go forward.

We have made progress in these 35 years. In three decades we have seen more progress in this great country than all of the civilizations in history could even imagine.

I saw the other day that one critic was complaining about how the 1958 dollar was worth more than the one that we've got today.

I wondered why he stopped at 1958. Look at what has happened since I went to Washington in 1931 and brought my hopes and my suitcase to the Nation's Capital.

The real question is not how much the dollar was worth then but how much the workingman could buy with his pay envelope.

I asked my economists when I heard of that statement—and I didn't have any when I got on the train to leave home from Texas—to take all the 1932 statistics and to convert them for me to 1965 prices.

And here is the story that those figures tell:

In 1932, the average factory worker made $17 a week when Roosevelt became President. Now, you're going to say that $17 bought more—and it did. But you convert that $17 into today's dollars, 1966 dollars, and it will buy only $39 worth of today's goods.

But today's factory worker does not get $39, today's factory worker buys $111 worth of goods. His true purchasing power has increased by 300 percent. Now that's what's been done for the average worker.

Now let's take the case of the farmer. In 1932, the average farmer cleared $304 a year. When you convert that in today's dollar, it will buy $869 worth of goods.

But the average farmer today can actually buy not $869 worth of goods but $4,280 worth of goods. He has a purchasing power 400 percent greater than he had in 1932. And that may be why the Democratic Party with the workers and the farmers carried 44 States in 1964 and are going to carry that many more in 1966.

Now what about the people that are not workers or not farmers. Well, I'll tell you what's happened to them.

Their dividends have multiplied threefold. They rose from 6.4 billion in 1932 to nearly 19 billion last year. And remember that these are dollars with the same purchasing power—from 6 to 19.

When I came to Washington, nearly 5 percent of all Americans were illiterate. We have cut that figure in half today.

The average American had only an eighth grade education. Today he gets almost four years of high school—and before the end of my lifetime I want to see him—the average American—get a college education. And that's what we are working for.

Back when I went to the Capital a newborn child could expect to live to be 62 years of age.

A child born today can expect to be around until the year 2036—a life expectancy of more than 70 years. And I hope that with the progress we're making with our cancer and our heart research—the law we passed last year—he just may be around a lot longer than 70.

In 1932 half of our retired people were living on less than $60 a month—and we're still now talking in terms of today's dollar.

If they got sick, the bills for the doctor and the hospital had to come out of that $60 a month. Tonight we have doubled their income and they have Medicare to help with their medical bills. I might add that a lot of people thought Medicare would never get on the books, but $3 billion will be paid out in it this year.

In 1932, 90 percent of our farm homes were lighted by kerosene lamps. Tonight 98 percent of our farm homes are lighted with electricity.

Not one of these changes came about without a long and bitter struggle.

Many of them were delayed far too long. Every time the President or a Congressman or a Senator presented a major piece of legislation to improve the welfare of the public, there was always somebody around to warn that we were spending ourselves into bankruptcy.

Some bankruptcy!

I say that because right now we are in the sixth year of our longest uninterrupted era of prosperity in the history of our Nation. Profits, sales, wages, incomes are higher than they have ever been before.

When the Democratic administration took office in 1961 the gross national product—that is the total value of all goods and all services we enjoy—was $504 billion. In the first quarter of 1966 it was not 504, it was $714 billion. This is an increase of more than $210 billion—or more than 41 percent. And tonight, May the 17th, it is even larger—and it is still going up and up.

In January, the Council of Economic Advisers estimated the gross national product of 1966 would not be $504 billion, but would fall within a range of $717 billion to $727 billion. And we might even exceed the top of this range. Some experts tonight believe that it will even go to $735 billion or higher.

In fiscal 1961 we took in Federal taxes of some $78 billion. This year we are taking in more than $100 billion, or 29 percent more.

From the time I became President until tonight we have increased our expenditures for health and education and training by $10 billion. And that is just a little over 2 years.

Since I came to Washington, this country has learned something important. We have learned that the right thing to do is usually the smart thing to do.

We have learned that the money we spend on health and education is not a gift but it is an investment. These investments come back in the form of higher earnings, they come back in more personal expenditures, they come back in additional taxes. In education, for example, we know that a college

graduate will earn nearly $140,000 more than the high school graduate during his lifetime.

We know that the money we spend on health is just as much an investment. If we can reduce sick leave in this country by only one day per worker every year, we can add $3 billion to our gross national product.

We know that every child born in this country is entitled to have the fullest measure of freedom that we can provide and he should have every equality of opportunity.

And finally, we know that every citizen, according to his conscience, has a duty to work for the advancement of the greatest system of government ever known—the system that we call democracy—the system that we call our own free enterprise system.

We have worked for that advancement through both of our political parties and in spite of any temporary differences that we have had.

I remember very well some of the remarks I made the day before the election when I closed my campaign in my home State.

I said then—and I want to repeat them tonight—"I have tried as best I could to lead this country to peace and to lead this country to prosperity.

"I have tried all the time to be President of all the people. I have tried to treat every man equally. I have tried to protect and make secure every man's constitutional rights."

Tonight I repeat that pledge. I was elected to my office as a Democrat.

As much as I love my dear Democratic Party, I love my America much more. The decisions I made last night and those that I made tonight transcend party considerations, because they involve the destiny of all of the people of America. The marines, the army, the airmen, and the sailors who man the carriers off the coast of Vietnam tonight— they know no parties. They wear no Republican jackets or no Democratic caps.

So I have tried to base my decisions and my thinking and all of my actions on what I think is really best for this country. I believe that is what my country expects me to do.

So tonight I ask each of you present here to give me a matching pledge. I ask you and I ask every American to put our country first if we want to keep it first. Put it above parties, if you want to seize the larger victories—the victories of freedom, and the victories of peace, and the victories of prosperity.

Put away all the childish divisive things, if you want the maturity and the unity that is the mortar of a nation's greatness.

I do not believe that those men who are out there fighting for us tonight think that we should enjoy the luxury of fighting each other back home.

So I ask you to carefully read the statements of every public official and of every candidate for every office and read them carefully, and then judge for yourself. Ask yourselves, "Is he helping the cause of his country or is he advancing the cause of himself?" Ask him, "Is he trying to draw us together and unite our land, or is he trying to pull us apart to promote himself?"

This is the measuring stick that I ask the people of America to judge us by.

I ask you, my friends, to put your faith in reason. I ask you to come together as a people and as a nation. I ask you to join hands and trust ourselves to God's hands, so that we can, together, bring peace to this world and a richer, better life to all who so earnestly desire it, and so urgently seek it.

A quarter of a century ago, a power-mad leader started marching through Poland engulfing free people. The courageous voice of Winston Churchill held that dictator until we could rally our forces, until we could unite our people, until we could bring relief to freedom's forces.

Following World War II, when our men returned and we had a chance to judge what we had been through, our Nation decided and our Congress decided that we should, as a matter of our Nation's highest policy, declare that all would-be adventurous conquerors who sought to engulf free people with power and with might and with force, and to conquer them with arms, these conquerors would have to meet and resist the forces of the United States of America in the various alliances of the world.

Our people and their representatives in the Congress decided that it was wiser to warn the dictators in advance that they would have to meet the United States if they took the road of aggression. And we did warn them. We did it in NATO, in collective security. We did it in SEATO, in the Southeast Asia Treaty Organization. We said that if any nation that is a part of this treaty—and there were 8 of them signed it—finds itself under attack and asks for our help, they will get it. And they are getting it tonight in Vietnam.

I do not genuinely believe that there is any single person anywhere in the world that wants peace as much as I want it.

I want the killing to stop.

I want us to join hands with others to do more in the fight against hunger and disease and ignorance.

But we all know from hard-won experience that the road to peace is not the road of concession and retreat.

A lot of our friends tell us how troubled they are and how frustrated they are. And we are troubled and we are frustrated, and we are seeking a way out. And we are trying to find a solution.

As Commander in Chief, I am neither a Democrat or Republican. The men fighting in Vietnam are simply Americans. Our policy in Vietnam is a national policy. It springs from every lesson that we have learned in this century. We fought in the First World War and then we failed to build a system of collective security which could have prevented the Second World War.

Standing in this great city of Chicago on October 5, 1937, one of the greatest leaders ever to be produced in America, Franklin D. Roosevelt said:

"When an epidemic of physical disease starts to spread, the community approves and joins in a quarantine of the patients in order to protect the health of the community against the spread of the disease. . . .

"War is a contagion, whether it be declared or undeclared. It can engulf states and peoples remote from the original scene of hostilities."

The country heard him, but did not listen.

The country failed to back him in that trying hour. And then we saw what happened when the aggressors felt confident that they could win while we sat by.

That was what President Truman remembered in 1947 in Greece and Turkey.

That is what he remembered during the blockade of Berlin and when the attack came in Korea.

That is what President Eisenhower remembered in 1954 when he laid before the Senate the SEATO Treaty, and during the crisis over Quemoy and Matsu.

That is what President John F. Kennedy remembered when, in the face of Communist aggression in Laos and Vietnam, he began to send American forces there as early as 1962.

Yes, we have learned over the past half century that failure to meet aggression means war, not peace.

In carrying out that policy we have taken casualties in Berlin and Korea, and now in Vietnam.

We have had 160,000 American casualties from World War II up until Vietnam. Now every morning I look at those casualty figures. I measure them not as statistics, but man by man.

As of this morning, we lost 1,705 Americans in Vietnam in the year 1966—1,705. But we lost 49,000 last year on our highways.

But I tell you that if we fail in frustrating this aggression, the war that would surely come in Asia would produce casualties not in the hundreds or seventeen hundreds, but in the hundreds of thousands and perhaps in millions.

Your Government therefore, under your President, is determined to resist this aggression at the minimum cost to our people, and to our allies, and to the world.

I do not know what—who men may be trying to influence, and I do not seek to influence any tonight. But I do tell you here and now that we do not seek to enlarge this war, but we shall not run out of it.

America is determined to meet her commitments tonight, because those commitments are right.

As I said after a meeting yesterday with Ambassador Lodge just as he was returning to his post of duty:

—We shall continue to struggle against aggression and social misery in South Vietnam;

—We shall use our influence to help this young nation come together and move toward constitutional government;

—We shall seek an honorable peace.

Let those though who speak and write about Vietnam say clearly what other policy they would pursue.

And let them weigh their words carefully. Let them remember that tonight there are 300,000 young Americans, our own boys, out there somewhere in Southeast Asia, on the land and on the sea and in the air. They are there fighting to quarantine another aggressor. They are there fighting for the peace of the world.

And let them remember that there are men on the other side who know well that their only hope for success in this aggression lies in a weakening of the fiber and the determination of the people of America. And so long as I am President, the policy of opposing aggression at minimum cost shall be continued.

I sent our ambassadors to more than 40 countries. I wrote letters to nearly 120 in the world asking for assistance, asking for peace. My plea was well received in all the nations of the world except the two most concerned, Red China and North Vietnam.

After 37 long days, while our men in uniform waited and while our planes were grounded on my orders, while our ambassadors went from nation to nation, we finally were forced to the conclusion that the time had not yet arrived when the Government of North Vietnam was willing or could even be persuaded to sit down at a peace table and try to reason these problems out. Therefore, our arguments need to be more persuasive and our determinations need to be more convincing and more compelling than they have been.

All I can say to you tonight is that the road ahead is going to be difficult. There will be some "Nervous Nellies" and some who will become frustrated and bothered and break ranks under the strain, and some will turn on their leaders, and on their country, and on our own fighting men. There will be times of trial and tension in the days ahead that will exact the best that is in all of us. But I have not the slightest doubt that the courage and the dedication and the good

sense of the wise American people will ultimately prevail. They will stand united until every boy is brought home safely, until the gallant people of South Vietnam have their own choice of their own Government.

More than that, not just that one little country of 14 million people, but more than a hundred other little countries stand tonight and watch and wait. If America's commitment is dishonored in South Vietnam, it is dishonored in 40 other alliances or more that we have made.

So I leave you with the assurance that we love peace and we seek it every hour of every day. Any person who wishes to test us can give us the time and the date and the place, and he will find us occupying our peace chair at the negotiating table with any government who genuinely and who sincerely wants to talk instead of fight.

Perhaps my sentiments and my feelings are best expressed by the words of President Roosevelt when he prepared, only a day or so before he died in 1945, this speech and never had an opportunity to deliver it: "We seek peace—enduring peace. More than an end to war, we want an end to the beginnings of all wars—yes, an end to this brutal, inhuman and thoroughly impractical method of settling the differences between governments."

Somewhere tonight a great son of Wisconsin, Ambassador Gronouski, is winging his way across the waters to report to me in the Capital his conversations and his efforts to find a way to bring peace to this world.

The men who fight for us out there tonight in Vietnam—they are trying to find a way to peace. But they know—and I don't understand why we don't all recognize—that we can't get peace just for wishing for it. We must get on with the job until these men can come marching home, someday, when peace is secure not only for the people of America, but peace is secure for peace-loving people everywhere in this world.

NOTE: The President spoke at 8 p.m. following the dinner at McCormick Place. In his opening words he referred to Mayor Richard J. Daley of Chicago, Governor Otto Kerner of Illinois, Governor Roger D. Branigin of Indiana, Governor Edward T. Breathitt of Kentucky, Farris Bryant, Director of the Office of Emergency Planning and former Governor of Florida, Secretary of Labor W. Willard Wirtz, Senator Paul H. Douglas of Illinois, Comptroller of the Currency James J. Saxon, Arthur B. Krim, Chairman of the President's Club which had sponsored a reception prior to the fundraising din-

ner, Ross David Siragusa, Chairman of the Board of the Admiral Corp., the Most Reverend John P. Cody, Catholic Archbishop of Chicago, Bishop Louis H. Ford, pastor of St. Paul Church of God and Christ of Chicago, and Rabbi Seymour J. Cohen of the Anshe Emet Synagogue of Chicago.

Later in his remarks the President referred, among others, to William J. Campbell, Chief Judge of the United States District Court for the Northern District of Illinois, Henry Cabot Lodge, U.S. Ambassador to the Republic of Vietnam, and John A. Gronouski, U.S. Ambassador to Poland, who was returning to report on the results of a special mission undertaken in an effort to end the Vietnam conflict.

229 Letter to the President of the Senate and to the Speaker of the House Transmitting the National Oceanographic Program for Fiscal Year 1967. *May 18, 1966*

Dear Mr. President: (Dear Mr. Speaker:)

I am pleased to forward for consideration by interested committees of Congress the National Oceanographic Program for Fiscal Year 1967. This report describes the activities of all Federal Agencies currently engaged in oceanography.

Although we are daily learning more about the stars and skies above us, the sea around us remains largely a mystery. This "hydrospace" covers seven out of every ten miles of the earth's surface, yet we have glimpsed only faintly the vast promise which the world's oceans hold for the benefit of mankind.

That promise is as boundless as the sea itself. One day, the sea may yield fertile harvests to nourish the hungry. Ultimately, we may be able to tap the abundant store of minerals, chemicals, and energy locked in the sea so that no nation—large or small, young or old—will lack the resources essential for the prosperity and well-being of its people.

Our National Oceanographic Program will help us drive back the frontiers of the

unknown through marine research, surveys, and ocean engineering. From this work, we will gain knowledge which will help sustain our prosperity, enhance our national defense, and:

—develop faster and more comfortable means of transportation.

—step-up our attack against water pollution.

—permit more accurate forecasts of the storms and tides that endanger life and property.

—exploit marine and mineral resources to their fullest potential.

Over the past years, we have moved closer to the fulfillment of some important objectives. Recent significant and exciting advances include:

1. *The Sea Lab II*—This is the Navy's "Man-in-Sea" project. Conducted off the coast of California late last year, it showed that man can live and work for long intervals, and at great depths, in an undersea habitat.

2. *Project Mohole*—Design of the world's largest stable deep-ocean drilling platform

has been completed by the National Science Foundation. I urge that Congress appropriate the funds so that construction of this vital instrument can begin promptly. The Mohole Project will provide the answer to many basic questions about the earth's crust and the origin of ocean basins. It will teach us how to drill in the ocean depths—the prelude to the future exploitation of resources at the bottom of the sea.

3. *Nuclear Research Submarines*—A nuclear-powered long-endurance, deep-water research vessel is under construction by the Navy and the Atomic Energy Commission. When completed, this vessel will help us map the ocean bottom, give us new information on the control and use of marine life and minerals—and how to find and retrieve from the ocean objects of commercial, scientific, and national security value. This revolutionary vessel will perform a variety of tasks thought impossible only a few short years ago.

The Government-wide character of the National Oceanographic Program bears special mention. Through the planning of the Inter-Agency Committee on Oceanography of the Federal Council for Science and Technology, the many separate elements of the program are coordinated into an effective and efficient effort. Working together with industry, the universities, and state and local governments, the Federal Government must continue to keep this Nation in the forefront of oceanographic science and engineering.

As Longfellow well observed, the sea divides—but yet unites—mankind. Through our exploration of the sea, we can move toward a new era in which science can fulfill its creative promise to bring a better and happier life to all the peoples of the world.

Sincerely,

LYNDON B. JOHNSON

NOTE: This is the text of identical letters addressed to the Honorable Hubert H. Humphrey, President of the Senate, and to the Honorable John W. McCormack, Speaker of the House of Representatives.

The 107-page report, entitled "National Oceanographic Program, Fiscal Year 1967" (ICO Pamphlet 24, March 1966), was published by the Interagency Committee on Oceanography of the Federal Council for Science and Technology.

230　Statement by the President Upon the Death of Theodore Francis Green. *May 19, 1966*

THEODORE GREEN was one of the first men I met when I came to Congress. Through all my years of public life he remained a friend and inspiration. I was not alone in those whose lives were strongly influenced by him and who felt deeply honored to work beside him. He championed integrity. He was a gentleman. His service to his Nation is the legacy he sought to leave.

It will be an enduring memorial to a wise and honorable man.

NOTE: Senator Green served as U.S. Senator from Rhode Island from January 1937 until his retirement in January 1961.

The statement was read by Bill D. Moyers, Special Assistant to the President, at his news conference at 11:15 a.m. on Thursday, May 19, 1966, at the White House. It was not made public in the form of a White House press release.

231 Remarks at the Swearing In of Bernard L. Boutin as Administrator, Small Business Administration.   *May 19, 1966*

Mr. and Mrs. Boutin and family, General Clark, Members of the Cabinet, distinguished Members of the House of Representatives and the Senate, ladies and gentlemen:

I am delighted to welcome you here this morning to this ceremony in the East Room. Small business is part of the American way of life.   A man's desire to become his own boss has always been a part of our national dream.   If we lose that, we will lose something that is very precious to all of us.

Even big business depends upon the 5 million small businesses, because they provide most of our services and they are a very vital source of new products and new ideas.

Small business is also very essential to this Nation's national defense.   I am happy to note that small business' share of our defense contracts in this country continues to rise. It was $4.9 billion in 1965—an increase of 36 percent in only 4 years.

So you see, Mr. Boutin, this is a very important area.   You go into this new assignment knowing that this administration is deeply interested in and concerned about all of the activities of the Small Business Administration.   In operating your agency, I want you to keep in mind that there is really no such thing as a small businessman.

They are all outstanding Americans who are operating small businesses. But the owner of a corner grocery store has just as much right to the help of his Government as the president of a big supermarket.

I believe that you are the type of leader and administrator who will see that he gets it.

Mr. Boutin has served his Government with ability and distinction in two very important posts.   He first served as Administrator of the General Services Administra-

tion and most recently as Deputy Director of the Office of Economic Opportunity.   Before that he was mayor of a small New Hampshire town where he acquired firsthand experience with so many problems for which he is now going to be responsible for providing the leadership.

And we are going to work hard to help you.   On May 2d I signed a bill which increased the ceiling for outstanding Small Business Administration loans and separated the business loan funds from the disaster loan funds.   In this way, we ended the disruptions in the business loan program which have sometimes occurred when a major disaster would strike a community.

I said then that this was only step one. We are now trying to take step number two. We asked the Congress to allow the Small Business Administration, along with certain other Government agencies, to pool outstanding loans and sell participation shares to private business.

This will put private capital into effective partnership with Government programs to make more capital available to small business which badly needs it.   Since October we have not had that money to lend to them.

Yesterday the House passed the Participation Sales Act which approves the method of financing that we had requested.   A similar bill had already passed the Senate.   As soon as the two houses resolve the differences in the bill, we will be ready to move.

I am very grateful to Senator Sparkman and Senator Robertson in the Senate, and Congressman Patman and all of those associated in the House, for helping on this small business legislation, as well as making it possible for us to provide the funds to finance these endeavors.

In anticipation of this, Mr. Boutin, I am today issuing my first directive to you. I want you, not later than the 26th of this month, to start accepting new small business loan applications in all your regional offices throughout the country.

Let's tell the Nation that the Small Business Administration has reopened its doors that were closed too long. In giving you the keys to those doors, Mr. Boutin, I ask you to remember the real value of the people who are going to come through them.

The father of the free enterprise system, Mr. Adam Smith, described the value of the small businessman in these words:

"A small proprietor . . . who knows every part of his little territory, who views it with all the affection which . . . small property naturally inspires . . . is generally of all improvers, the most industrious, the most intelligent, and the most successful."

Mr. Boutin, this administration and its leadership in the Congress, most of those men of both parties are here this morning, are interested in helping the improvers. We want them to succeed. We are concerned with the man who operates a small business.

Let's make small business one of the biggest growth industries in the country. We expect you to provide the leadership in the executive department that will bring unity in the executive branch of the Government, that we hope can bring support of both parties in the Congress, and that will bring the respect of all the people of America.

I believe that you are the type of man who can do that and we will be standing by to applaud you and to support you.

NOTE: The President spoke at 12:11 p.m. in the East Room at the White House. In his opening words he referred to Bernard L. Boutin and his wife and to Deputy Attorney General Ramsey Clark who administered the oath of office to Mr. Boutin. Later the President referred to Senator John J. Sparkman of Alabama, Senator A. Willis Robertson of Virginia, and Representative Wright Patman of Texas.

For the President's remarks on May 2 upon signing the Small Business Act Amendments of 1966, see Item 199.

The Participation Sales Act of 1966 was approved by the President on May 24 (Public Law 89-429, 80 Stat. 164).

On May 24 the White House made public three releases relating to small business: the text of Proclamation 3726 designating the week beginning May 22 as Small Business Week; the announcement of a report from Secretary McNamara on the share of prime contracts awarded by the Department of Defense to small business firms between July 1965 and March 1966; and the announcement of the presentation by the President of the Small Businessman of the Year award to Elfrain D. Vassallo of Ponce, Puerto Rico, a manufacturer of metal jalousies.

The three releases appear in the Weekly Compilation of Presidential Documents (vol. 2, pp. 685-686). Proclamation 3726 is also printed in the Federal Register and the Code of Federal Regulations (31 F.R. 7551; 3 CFR 1966 Comp., p. 55).

232   Remarks at a Ceremony Marking the Transfer of the Water Pollution Control Administration to the Department of the Interior.   *May 20, 1966*

Secretary Udall, my old friends on the platform from the Department of Interior, ladies and gentlemen:

I am very proud to be here today with a Department whose mission I applaud and whose Secretary I so greatly admire.

Stewart Udall and I share a love for the land and the outdoor life. We are both conservationists, though he outdoes me at times in that. He even manages to conserve his strength by letting Mrs. Johnson paddle his raft down the Rio Grande.

So, that brings me into the real purpose of my visit to the Interior Department today—water.

It is a simple word for most men, but it has never been very simple for me. As Mike Straus and Oscar Chapman will remember, I grew up in a very dusty corner of our country where water, and not bread, was the staff of life. The land was harsh and life was hard.

Generations of my people, my neighbors, my friends, and my kin, had fought for water, prayed for water, and on occasions had died for water. When water did come, the Pedernales River would rise in the spring, flooding the valley.

The first few years I spent in Washington, I spent most of the time in the Public Works offices under the leadership of the Secretary of this Department, or in the Secretary's office, itself. And I might say a good many of my nights were spent here.

I remember many, many times staying here until 1 or 2 o'clock in the morning during the days when we were building the dams on the Colorado, when we were electrifying the countryside, and when we were bringing the transmission lines connecting with our urban centers in that area that were using the water from the dams to generate the power.

So I resolved to do something about these hardships brought about by water and I gave a large part of my public life to better management of our natural resources, to larger visions of a more bountiful and, thus, a more beautiful America. I gave a part of myself to that great task and I am still giving.

That is why I came over here this morning. I want to give you my personal thanks. I want to give each of you my personal encouragement and I want to give all of you a personal challenge.

We have come a long way since men fought and died for water, and Nature held whole regions hostage to her whims. Men of faith and foresight have come with every generation to love the land and to nourish it. They have acted to halt decay and bar exploitation, to magnify our splendor and to multiply our resources. And they have reaped the harvest promised in the Bible passage that says, "Speak to the earth and it shall teach thee."

You have been among such men. Your vision and dedication have earned the gratitude of this Nation. But because you are such men, I believe you would be the first to say that the work has just begun and the greater harvest awaits.

The work is now your work, more than it has ever been before, because the transfer of water pollution control to this great Department of Interior gives you a new opportunity and a much greater responsibility.

I hope you are excited by that prospect, because your President is, your Congress is, and your Secretary is. And I believe that he will give every ounce of his great energy and imagination to helping you meet this challenge.

But it is you who must meet it and it is you who will surmount it. It is your energy, your imagination, and your minute-by-minute enthusiasm that will really decide whether we master change or whether we are mastered by it.

The tides of change are running deep and swift this morning. There are questions which you must help to answer. Must our progress engulf us? Shall we choke on our own success? Does our society need to tolerate filthy rivers, poisoned air, strangled cities, and tangled roads? Too few parks? Too few beaches? Too little wildlife? Too much ugliness and too little beauty?

Well, I think there is only one answer. No. No, we must not. No. No, we will not.

That answer has already been affirmed by this administration and by our leadership in the Congress. It has been given life by bold new legislation and by new dynamic programs. The answer is on the record and here is just a part of it.

More than 40 important conservation bills passed. The water pollution control bill, the air control bill, the open space program, the Wilderness Act. All landmarks. All real. A new Land and Water Conservation Fund for our States and our cities. The new Bureau of Outdoor Recreation to run it.

Then, the first new national park in our country in 17 years and a parade of 23 new national park areas. Four new national seashores. All crowned by a bright new concept in parks—the Ozarks National Riverway.

And now the Congress has approved our suggestions on the reorganization plan transferring water pollution control to you. Congress is this very minute considering the clean rivers bill and I hope, and I feel sure, that they will approve that, too.

So, we are on the move. We are harnessing progress to our purpose. We are overtaking our problems and we are closing on our dream of a Great Society. How fast we move, how much we achieve, depends once more on you, on your imagination, on your dreams, on your creativeness, your re-sourcefulness, your determination to push on from past success to future triumphs.

As I said in my Conservation Message to the Congress, "The work will not be easy. It cannot be completed in a year or even in five years, but there will never be a better time to begin."

I didn't think it would take long this morning and I am grateful for your indulging me, because I wanted to come back to the scenes of earlier years here to say to those of you who are carrying on that you have my gratitude and this Department has my confidence.

You shall always have this administration's full support. Together we can attain the vision that we share—America the strong, America the free, America the beautiful—one shining Nation and people.

Thank you very much.

NOTE: The President spoke at 11:08 a.m. in the auditorium of the Department of the Interior. In his opening words he referred to Stewart L. Udall, Secretary of the Interior.

Early in his remarks the President referred to former Secretary of the Interior Oscar L. Chapman and to Michael W. Straus, formerly Director of Information in the Office of the Secretary and later Commissioner of Reclamation. Both were in the Department during the years when the President, then in Congress, was an active proponent of public power and rural electrification.

The Federal Water Pollution Control Administration was transferred from the Department of Health, Education, and Welfare to the Department of the Interior by Reorganization Plan 2 of 1966. For the President's special message of February 28 transmitting the plan to the Congress, see Item 91. See also Item 215.

---

233 Letter to the President of the Senate and to the Speaker of the House Requesting Increased Borrowing Authority for TVA. *May 20, 1966*

Dear Mr. President: (*Dear Mr. Speaker:*)

I am pleased to transmit to the Congress proposed legislation to amend the Tennessee Valley Authority Act by raising to $1,750 million the ceiling on TVA's authority to issue revenue bonds.

Thirty-three years ago the Congress created the Tennessee Valley Authority. The success of this venture is a tribute to the vision of those in both political parties who worked to make a reality of this experiment in regional cooperation.

Today large industrial firms nourish the economy of this once poor region, encouraged by plentiful transportation and low-cost electric power.

Today green pastures and leafy woodlands have replaced the desolate brown craters of eroded acres.

Today almost every farm in the Tennessee Valley has electric power, while only three out of every hundred were served in 1933.

Today the per capita income of this region is 69 percent of the national average, compared to 45 percent at the time of TVA's creation.

Congress has shown its wisdom in allowing TVA flexibility to do its job well. In 1959, the Congress gave TVA authority to issue revenue bonds—up to $750 million—to finance capital improvements in its power program. Congress also acted wisely by placing a specific limitation on the borrowing authority so it could periodically review the TVA power operations to determine future needs.

TVA has used its authority well. Funds are no longer appropriated to TVA to finance power operations. On the contrary, TVA is paying back the original U.S. investment in power facilities, with interest, and is making payments to State and local governments in lieu of taxes.

The power demands in the Tennessee Valley should about double in the next ten years, which is consistent with the rate of growth for private utilities. TVA must have the authority to issue bonds to finance its operations, just as other utilities do to meet future demands.

TVA will need new borrowing authority before the end of fiscal year 1967. I recommend, therefore, an increase of $1 billion—from $750 million to $1,750 million—which should provide borrowing authority for at least seven more years.

Without an increase in borrowing authority, TVA cannot continue to carry out its responsibility to meet the growing demand for electric power in the Tennessee Valley. This is essential to the well being of the people and the economy of this region. For this reason, I respectfully urge the Congress to give early and favorable consideration to this proposed legislation.

Sincerely,

LYNDON B. JOHNSON

NOTE: This is the text of identical letters addressed to the Honorable Hubert H. Humphrey, President of the Senate, and to the Honorable John W. McCormack, Speaker of the House of Representatives.

The proposed amendment to the Tennessee Valley Authority Act was approved by the President on August 12. For his remarks at the signing ceremony, see Item 382.

---

234 Memorandum Further Restricting Employment in Federal Agencies and Travel by Federal Personnel. *May 20, 1966*

Memorandum for Heads of Executive Departments and Agencies
SUBJECT: Further restrictions on employment and travel

In view of the high costs of the conflict in Vietnam and in the interest of avoiding inflationary pressures at home, I asked all major agencies last March to defer projects and expenditures wherever this could be done without harm to the national interest.

To further this effort, I would like each department and agency to adopt formal programs of

(1) deferring the filling of vacant positions, and

(2) foregoing some previously planned travel.

It should not be too great a hardship to stretch out the filling of vacancies and, in some cases, even to forgo replacing a portion of those who leave their positions in your agency. To help accomplish this, you might require that decisions to fill vacancies be approved at a higher level than now prevails.

Similarly, some travel, which seemed important at the time your 1967 budget request was formulated, should be reconsidered in light of the substantial increase in demands on the economy since that time. I believe this is possible even though I realize that the 1967 budget allowances were made on a very restrictive basis.

It is *not* my intention to defer or eliminate the *essential;* for example, travel for law enforcement, or for necessary supervision of field establishments, are costs which—if the activities are to be carried on efficiently—must be borne. On the other hand, it should be possible to reduce travel that might be *desirable* rather than *essential,* such as for attendance at professional conferences or meetings.

Will you please send me a report through the Budget Director by June 3 of the steps you are taking in your agency to carry out the suggestions in this memorandum?

LYNDON B. JOHNSON

NOTE: The President referred to his memorandum of March 15 on the need for controlling Federal expenditures (see Item 131).

The requested report was transmitted to the President on June 18 in the form of a memorandum from the Director of the Bureau of the Budget. It was not made public by the White House.

---

235   Remarks by Telephone to the Convention of the United Automobile Workers. *May 20, 1966*

Mr. Reuther, Secretary Wirtz, my fellow Americans:

Thank you very much, Walter. I heard the nice things you had to say and although I don't deserve them, I appreciate them very much.

I am honored to receive this award. I accept it from you and I accept it for you. No group in America has done more for the cause of social justice than the UAW and no leader has shown more competence or courage in that cause than has Walter Reuther.

I know that you are enlisted in the struggle for human freedom and social justice here and abroad. And it is for those goals that we struggle tonight in South Vietnam, to give the people of that country a chance to make their own choices, under a constitutional process they are now preparing, free from the tyranny and the terror which others would impose upon them by brutal force.

Despite the tests that we have in the world tonight, and despite the burdens which each morning brings to the President of the United States, I want to talk to you tonight, at your invitation, and I want to talk as an optimist.

At any given moment over the past two centuries, observers of American life were convinced that the United States was about to come apart at the seams. Yet, we have survived crisis after crisis—even the appalling impact of a civil war in which the death toll matched in population terms that of Britain in World War I. Not only have we survived, but we have managed to transform ourselves from a rural, agrarian society to an urban, industrial nation while expanding the meaning of our ancient heritage of freedom.

At every stage along the way there were those who said the tasks were impossible.

They said that the immigrant could never be assimilated into American life. They said he would always remain a stranger in our midst. But they were wrong!

They said the Catholic and the Jew would perpetually stand outside the door. But they were wrong!

They said the workingman would never be given full economic citizenship. And again they were wrong!

Time and time again we have been told that the American people were incapable of making compassionate adjustments, that they were prisoners of past prejudices and past grievances. History has proven those claims were wrong, too.

So this week we celebrate the 12th anniversary of the Supreme Court's epic decision that our schools should be colorblind.[1] That decision triggered a debate which has been running ever since, and it continues tonight.

Can the American people overcome the burdens of old divisions and old hatreds? Can they welcome the Negro as a full member, a sharing partner of our society?

The answer to that question just must be yes; and I believe it will be yes.

Twelve years have passed since that historic decision of 1954. What has happened

is the chronicle of a people beginning to realize that what is written in the books of their laws should also be written in the daily chapters of their lives.

What has happened is the testimony of a people who are learning, however slowly, that to be born equal is God's doing; to live equal is up to us.

I do not believe that we will turn from the pursuit of social justice. I say that knowing that even at this moment we have very bitter evidence of how far we are from its full attainment. But the lesson of 12 years is that compassion, when it ceases to be a cliché of the platform and the pulpit, can become the binding cement of a new fraternity.

This is the time for bridges to be built, not for antagonisms to be aroused. This is the time for those to act who have the power to change what just must be changed. For privilege is power, and its misuse, especially to uphold an unjust status quo grown obsolete, is a dangerous wrong.

It is the time, too, for passion to bow to reason. The gains since 1954 must be steppingstones to greater fulfillment, not future reminders of what might have been.

I am not an optimist tonight because I see no more anguish, no more heartache, and no more reverses. As surely as the stream flows to the ocean will the search for social justice in America always continue to be a painful quest. But more than 30 years of public life have convinced me that social justice for all Americans, even if slow, is certain, and you—you who make up the men and women of the UAW—can help to hasten the day when that social justice comes.

The days of uproarious industrial conflicts are behind us—the days of flamboyant heroes and identifiable villains, of the rhetoric of "scabs" and "sitdowns" and "shutouts" and "yellow-dog contracts"—those were days of

[1] On May 17, 1954, the Court, in *Brown* v. *Board of Education of Topeka, Kans.,* and related cases, declared racial segregation in the public schools unconstitutional. The text of the decision is printed in United States Supreme Court Reports, 1954 (349 U.S. 294, 99 L. Ed. 1083).

528

drama and combat, and I know some men who lament their passing.

But what labor has lost in drama, it has gained in solid achievement. What were dreams during the New Deal, job security and social security, unemployment compensation, Medicare, good wages, have come true today.

The income of our workers is up 33 percent in the last 5 years alone. The true purchasing power of today's factory worker is just 300 percent of its 1932 level.

The children of labor no longer have to take second- or third-best in educational opportunities, and the resources that we have poured into education have created jobs in construction and allied industries and produced better trained citizens who can command higher salaries, and who demand more goods and services, including automobiles.

All of our programs to improve the life of the American people, from the rebuilding of our cities to the preservation of our beauty, have been national fringe benefits for the laboring man.

Well, what now?

I hope this country, and I hope the UAW, is never content. We must go on now to a new agenda. We must administer the programs that we have passed. We must just do that job well, and it is going to be more difficult administering them by the executive branch than it was legislating them by the congressional branch.

This does not mean that we must ease up on work that is started but is far from finished. I have already said that civil rights and social justice are never achieved by just passing a law. Poverty is never wiped out just because we declare war on it.

One test of American liberalism is whether we stick with these jobs when the opposition is broken and when the headlines move to the back page. But there must be new business to tackle, too, and the time to start that business is tonight.

So let's all of us start thinking in a big way, as UAW does things in a big way. Let's start thinking about education without the binding assumption that education is only for children. There should be large-scale educational opportunities on a continuing basis, especially for those who did not get their share of education when they were young.

Let's start thinking as hard about underemployment as we have been thinking and working to reduce unemployment. Our goal ought to be not just any job for everybody, but a job that uses all that every man and woman has to offer. So let's start thinking about full potential as we have thought about full employment.

The way we measure it, unemployment is almost down to 3½ percent, and we are very proud of cutting it about in half in the past 5 years since John Kennedy took the oath as President. But the rest of the truth is that we are probably using no more than half of the human potential in this country.

Yes, we talk about manpower shortages. They are only the result of our failure to train people to use more than just a small part of their talent. We waste manpower all over this country. We let seasonal unemployment happen as though nothing could be done about it. We watch shortages of labor develop in some areas when there is unemployment in others not far away.

As I speak to you there in California tonight, only a few miles from you thousands of untrained youngsters roam the streets without work, while factories in their area have jobs going begging because they do not have manpower.

So let's ask some hard questions, questions about the adequacy for the next decade of

529

a true national labor policy that is built almost entirely on a program that was developed to meet the depression of the thirties.

Do you know that three out of every four Government employees tonight, State and local, who are now administering labor programs, are working in unemployment insurance and employment service offices? Only one in four is working on all the other labor programs put together.

Now, let's face it squarely, that a serious default of social policy and social justice is the inadequacy of the attention that we give to the potential of our older people. We just haven't started to think honestly about how to give meaning to that part of life which lies beyond the age of 60 or 65, or 70. So let's all of us begin to work to build a whole new ideal of what ought to be the meaning of growing old. Our concept tonight is still cushioned by the problems of the thirties.

So let's all of us start paying as much attention as you have in the UAW to the uses of our free time, to the building of parks and recreation areas, to the saving of our rivers, to cleaning our air, to the beautifying of our land.

Let's start paying as much attention to these things as we have to the uses of labor. Let's start thinking more soberly and realistically about the fact that ours isn't a roller coaster economy any more. It doesn't depend on the stock market and it doesn't and it must not depend on war.

This is just not labor's agenda. It is all America's agenda. As Samuel Gompers used to say, "We do not value the labor movement only for its ability to give higher wages and better clothes and better homes. We value the labor movement because your purposes are human purposes, your scope is the limitless potential of human beings."

This is the face of social justice.

As we tackle these problems, and as we strive with all our might to realize for every citizen real membership in American society, we will learn what was learned 100 years ago by a very small group of Philadelphia citizens who set out to secure for Negroes the right to ride street cars. The report of their committee said:

"Thus now, as always, the evils which men fear they shall be called upon to encounter as a result of doing what is just and humane are discovered, when they are really encountered, not to be evils at all, but to be blessings pure and simple."

There are many blessings awaiting us. Under the leadership of the UAW we have brought many of those blessings to the people of this Nation.

Tonight we have in our budget $10 billion more for health and education than we had in our budget when I became President only 2½ years ago. Your leadership and your locals helped to make that drive successful, but we are just beginning.

We have realized the things that the liberals have talked about and dreamed about for many years. Most of their programs tonight are on the statute books. So some of us seem to be a little bit frustrated. We don't need to stop, though.

What we really need to do is to roll up out sleeves, command the best among us to come and take charge of sound and solid administration of all these new programs from Medicare to elementary education, to see that they are applied equally to all Americans—and then to lay out a new agenda that will command the attention and the support of all good Americans.

That agenda awaits work from all of us. It will beautify our countryside. It will develop our highways. It will bring seashores and parks and playgrounds close to our cities where most of our people are going to live.

There is much left for all of us to do and I hope as you meet there in California with Walter Reuther and Secretary Wirtz and the other great leaders who counsel with me, that you will evolve a program that we can consider and put on the agenda and start to work on.

The Vice President and I met tonight for more than 2 hours with Secretary Rusk and Secretary Acheson and Secretary McNamara and others talking about the future of America. We have a bright future before us. We wish we could be there with you to see you in person to talk about it, but under the circumstances we did not think that was advisable, so I hope you will forgive me and forget that I had planned to come.

I look forward to seeing you, and those of you at the convention that can come with Mr. Walter Reuther to the White House to visit with me at some time convenient in the next few weeks. I am proud of the contribution that you have made to good government in this country and I thank you for the support that you have given this administration.

NOTE: The President spoke by telephone at 11:12 p.m. from the Cabinet Room at the White House to the Convention in Long Beach, Calif. His opening words referred to Walter Reuther, President of the United Automobile Workers of America, and to W. Willard Wirtz, Secretary of Labor, who represented the President at the 30th Anniversary Rally

of the trade union. During his remarks the President referred to Vice President Hubert H. Humphrey, Dean Rusk, Secretary of State, and Dean Acheson, former Secretary of State (1949–53) and Special Adviser to the Secretary of State on France and NATO March 15—June 17, 1966.

The award to which the President referred was the union's Social Justice Award conferred every 2 years at its national convention. Mr. Reuther, speaking prior to the President's remarks, noted that it is given to "great Americans for their contribution in extending the frontiers of social justice and human betterment." He then read the inscription on the plaque awarded to the President:

"UAW Social Justice Award. To President Lyndon B. Johnson, Architect of the Great Society, with Admiration, Affection and Deep Appreciation for Your Contribution in Extending the Frontiers of Social Justice and Human Betterment. You have demonstrated the courage to oppose what is wrong and the compassion to do what is right. You have worked with dedication and determination to lift the burden of fear and insecurity from the aged and the sick, to broaden educational opportunities for the young, to remove the ugly barriers of discrimination and to abolish poverty so that all may share in the blessings of abundance. Under your inspired leadership America can build a better tomorrow in which men are more concerned about the quality of their goals than the quality of their goods, in which the rising star of science and technology can serve man's peaceful purposes and in which man's ancient dream of a world with peace, freedom, justice and human brotherhood can be brought to practical fulfillment.

"Presented on behalf of the Officers, Executive Board Members and UAW Members on the occasion of the 20th Constitutional Convention of the UAW, Long Beach, California, May 20, 1966."

The plaque was presented to the President at the White House by Mr. Reuther on the evening of February 20, 1967.

236   The President's News Conference of May 21, 1966

THE PRESIDENT. I have a brief statement I thought you would be interested in.

STATEMENT ON VIETNAM

[1.] We are watching the situation in Vietnam very closely. We believe everything possible should be done to bring the various factions to an understanding of the

need for unity while the constitutional process is moving forward. That is what our people are trying to do.

General Westmoreland and Ambassador Lodge [1] are both in Vietnam now. We are

---

[1] Gen. William C. Westmoreland, Commander, United States Military Assistance Command, Vietnam, and Henry Cabot Lodge, U.S. Ambassador to the Republic of Vietnam.

in very close contact with them by cable, and our lower level people have other communication.

The South Vietnamese are trying to build a nation. They have to do this in the teeth of Communist efforts to take the country over by force. It is a hard and a frustrating job, and there is no easy answer, no instant solution to any of the problems they face.

We are not in Vietnam to dictate what form of government they should have. We have made it abundantly clear that it is our wish to see them increasingly able to manage their own affairs with the participation of an ever broader share of the population. We regret any diversion from that task and from efforts to defeat the Communist attempt to take over South Vietnam.

I will, of course, during the day and the week, and all the time that I am in this office, until we have a satisfactory solution of our problems in that area of the world, be in close touch with the Secretary of State, the Secretary of Defense, Mr. Rostow,[2] and other experts, both here and out there.

I know of nothing that I could add that would contribute to improving the situation. Therefore, I think I have said about all that I can on that general subject today.

I will answer any questions you may have on any other matters that may interest you.

QUESTIONS

[2.] Q. There is a technical matter, Mr. President. Has this statement been duplicated or mimeographed?

THE PRESIDENT. It will be given to all of you, and it will be in the transcript, too.

---

[2] Dean Rusk, Secretary of State, Robert S. McNamara, Secretary of Defense, and Walt W. Rostow, Special Assistant to the President.

CLARIFICATION OF REMARKS AT DEMOCRATIC PARTY DINNER IN CHICAGO

[3.] Q. Mr. President, can you clarify your Chicago speech?[3] The New York Times and other people have thought that you were indicating that some people were less patriotic than others and that you might be interested in purging some members of your own party. Can you give any indication as to what you meant in Chicago?

THE PRESIDENT. No, I had no such feeling of that kind. I didn't think the speech was susceptible to that interpretation. I do think it is very important that the President of this country have the right, and I think he does have the duty and the obligation when the Nation is involved in the serious difficulties that we have in the world, to make it clear to all would-be opponents, and certainly those who challenge our system in Vietnam and other places, that the President is supported by the people of this country—that the President is determined to carry out the duties of his office.

In doing that he will find people who differ with him, who disagree with him, who dissent from the policies of the Government or the Congress or of his Cabinet officials. We all understand that. We accept that.

We just want to be sure that others understand that. Because we have dissent does not mean that we have been dissected, and because we do have differences does not mean that we are torn to pieces, as we sometimes think other countries are when we read about what is happening.

Q. Have you seen any signs, Mr. President, that that is what other countries think of us now?

THE PRESIDENT. No.

---

[3] See Item 228.

THE SITUATION IN VIETNAM

[4.] Q. Mr. President, so we are clear, did I understand you at the beginning when you read your statement to say that you would take questions on other subjects but not on the present situation in Vietnam?

THE PRESIDENT. I don't want to be charged with barring you from asking anything you want to. I made clear what I had to say on the subject, sir.

Q. Mr. President, I wonder if you could give us any impression as to what your attitude toward Premier Ky [4] now is, in light of the present situation?

THE PRESIDENT. I think what I have said on that subject is what I should say today and I don't believe I would go further. I don't believe a direct response to your question would do anything to contribute to solving the serious problem that your country has out there.

Q. Mr. President, have you possibly had any communication with Thich Tri Quang in response to his letter to you? [5]

THE PRESIDENT. I think I have said all I want to say on that. I think that question has been answered by others, if you will check the record.

COMMENTS ON MEETINGS CONCERNING NATO

[5.] Q. Mr. President, can you tell us something about your talks yesterday about NATO, the meeting last night?

THE PRESIDENT. Yes. Ambassador Bruce has been here for several days. Secretary Acheson, Secretary Ball and Ambassador Bruce, Mr. Rostow, Mr. Moyers,[6] and others have, over the period of several weeks, been exchanging ideas and views preparatory to the ministerial meeting in Brussels in early June.

The Belgian Foreign Minister [7] has been here carrying on consultations, as have other foreign ministers. Before Ambassador Bruce returned we decided that we would spend the last 3 or 4 days reviewing the problems of NATO.

As a matter of fact, someone said it looks like we are going to call this NATO Week because we were spending a good deal of our appointment calendar on that subject.

We did finish up our meetings for the week last night, and Ambassador Bruce, I believe, left this morning. We are exchanging views with the 14 members of NATO, and we have given Ambassador Bruce our views to carry back to London with him.

Secretary Rusk is making preparation for the Brussels meeting. Things have gone orderly and I think thoroughly and satisfactorily.

GENERAL EISENHOWER'S LETTER ON NATO

[6.] Q. Mr. President, have you seen General Eisenhower's letter to Mr. Zablocki [7a] on the NATO situation?

THE PRESIDENT. No.

Q. Did you discuss it with anyone?

THE PRESIDENT. No.

---

[4] Nguyen Cao Ky, Prime Minister of the Republic of Vietnam.

[5] On May 16 Thich Tri Quang, a leader of the Buddhist opposition, appealed to the President and Ambassador Lodge for American intervention against Premier Ky. The appeal was made in a message delivered to the U.S. Consulate in Hue.

[6] David K. E. Bruce, U.S. Ambassador to the United Kingdom, Dean Acheson, former Secretary of State (1949–53) and Special Adviser to the Secretary of State on France and NATO March 15–June 17, 1966, George W. Ball, Under Secretary of State, and Walt W. Rostow and Bill D. Moyers, Special Assistants to the President.

[7] Pierre Harmel.

[7a] Representative Clement J. Zablocki of Wisconsin.

[7.] Q. Mr. President, could you tell us how you regard some of the very recent polls that show considerable public dissatisfaction over both Vietnam and the economic situation as to inflation?

1. The Economic Situation

[8.] THE PRESIDENT. I think that the public very generally always feels that we should get a better price for the things we sell and have a lower price for the things we buy.

I have observed that in polls all my life. I think there is somewhat more concern now than you would have in a normal period because we are coming close to reaching our objective of full employment. As we do, as labor gets scarce, as commodities get scarce, there are increases.

But comparatively speaking—I will get this chart for you on prices—comparatively speaking, our price situation is so much better than any other of the major nations of the world.

We have much to be thankful for.

Here is a chart I had made last night— that I asked for in connection with price statistics.[8] You will see the consumer price here as 100, for 1960, and here it is in 1966. In Japan it is 140. In Italy it is 130. In France it is 120-plus. In the United Kingdom it is 120-plus. In Germany it is 115, in that neighborhood. In the United States it is under 110. It looks like about 108.

Our average price increase has been less than 1½ percent a year. Rates in other countries have been at least double that.

Germany has the next best record with an annual rate of 3 percent.

For France and the United Kingdom the average yearly rise has been 3½ to 4. Italy's annual rate of inflation is 5 percent. Japan leads the parade with a rate of about 6½ percent.

So the cost of living record of the United States is far superior to the performance of any other major industrial country.

We are reaching a point that we have worked for so long, trying to get employment for most of our people. When you reach that situation, you run into other problems. I would rather face the problems I face now for this reason: increases in wages have come faster than the prices. The fact that people have work, and the fact that we have income coming into our Treasury to permit us to increase our educational efforts, our health efforts, our beautification efforts, our conservation efforts—I would rather have these problems than problems that come when unemployment is high and incomes low.

I spent some time this morning with the Secretary of the Treasury and the Director of the Budget[9] on the debt limit. We have expenditures planned for this year of $106 billion 400 million. We believe that they will be under that.

It is difficult to predict. I don't want to have our credibility questioned if we are off a half percent out of 100. But we are hoping that that expenditure could be under what we predicted, which would be unusual. It is unusual for the President to spend less than he says he is going to spend 18 months later.

Our revenue, we believe, will be up some. We rather believe our deficit will be less

---

[8] The chart "Consumer Prices in U.S. and Other Major Countries" was prepared by the Council of Economic Advisers and dated May 20, 1966.

[9] Henry H. Fowler, Secretary of the Treasury, and Charles L. Schultze, Director of the Bureau of the Budget.

than we predicted in January. I think even less than we predicted 18 months ago.

So on that problem, we recognize it. We are aware of it. We give a good deal of attention to it. The best minds in the Nation are dealing with it. It is one that we prefer to have than ones we have had.

2. Discontent With War

[9.] Now I will answer your Vietnam question. The longer we are there, the more sacrifices we make. The more we spend, the more discontent there will be. The more dissatisfaction there will be, the more wish and desire there will be to get out. Leading that parade is the President.

If you want to feel that it troubles you 100 percent, just double that and make it 200 percent for the President. Say his concern doubles yours. I am glad to say that a substantial majority of those that you refer to do approve of the course of action that we have taken. They do support their Government.

There are others who have different plans. Some would pull out, run out. Some would run in further. Some would just stand still and do nothing. You are aware of our plan.

We think that under the circumstances we are doing the best that we can. We would like to have peace. We have had two pauses. We have had economic proposals. We have had diplomatic invitations extended to all 115 or 120 countries. We sent Ambassadors to some 40 of them.

We have asked the United Nations to help. We have supported the Secretary General U Thant when he proposed that he take a trip. They would not receive him. We sent Mr. Harriman, Mr. Gold-

berg,[10] and the Secretary of State to other capitals.

We had 200 conferences privately. We had visits to 40 countries publicly. We have been unable to get the other people to sit down and talk instead of fight. We are trying to provide the maximum deterrents that we can to Communist aggression with a minimum cost. That is our policy.

We think we are doing the best we can, given these facts. There are some, I think— a very small percentage of the dissatisfied— who would run out. There is a somewhat larger percentage who would run farther in. When you add the two together and put them with the group that would just sit and try to hold—you don't hold when you sit, that is the trouble, you get into deeper trouble—if you put those together, you will have collectively a certain percentage of opposition.

But those who approve of what we are doing are almost twice as many as all these various factions combined. I don't think this detailed explanation will change anyone's mind, but I hope it does give you my view of it. That same view will apply down the road. That has been it all along.

THE DEFICIT FOR FISCAL YEAR 1966

[10.] Q. Mr. President, are you talking of this fiscal year?

THE PRESIDENT. I am talking about fiscal 1966, which will end June 30, a month from now. We predicted that our deficit would be $6.4 billion. This January we predicted that. That was with several billion addi-

---

[10] W. Averell Harriman, Ambassador at Large, and Arthur J. Goldberg, U.S. Representative to the United Nations.

tional for Vietnam we had not anticipated. But we are getting several billion additional revenue we had not estimated. Seventeen months ago we predicted the deficit would be $5.3 billion. I believe that our deficit will be lower than the $6.4 billion and lower than the $5.3 billion.

I would say our expenditures would be $106.4 billion, as we predicted, minus a few hundred million, or plus a few hundred million. I must have that flexibility there. But that means that even with all the extra Vietnam expenses, our expenditures are not going to be greatly over what we anticipated.

Our revenues, the last estimate we made, I believe were $100 billion. I believe our revenues now will be $102.5 billion, and I would like to make it clear that it could be more.

That would leave you about $4 billion, or a little less than a $4 billion deficit compared to the $6.4 billion we predicted. You must give us several hundred million either way on those. But it appears that we will not spend a great deal more than we anticipated, and we may even spend less. I think we will. That depends on our June buying.

We will take in a good deal more than we anticipated, at least $2½ billion more, and it could be more.

I would think the problem that you are concerned with on revenues would be covered by these figures that we have.

THE DEBT LIMIT

[11.] Q. What is the debt limit figure you will ask for?

THE PRESIDENT. That will be given by the Secretary. I am not sure that a deficit situation has been made. It will be between $330 billion and $335 billion. It is $328 billion now. I would have to have a little range because, again, it is not decided.

OUTLOOK FOR A TAX INCREASE

[12.] Q. Mr. President, on this economic thing, it sounds like you are a good distance away from a tax boost.

THE PRESIDENT. I don't want to comment on your hearing or about the way it sounds to you. I have a problem with these lights and sounds on the telephone. I frequently don't hear them ring. But I have given you the facts and the speculations.

Q. Is there any change in the outlook for a tax increase?

THE PRESIDENT. We are considering all these things now. When we have any recommendations to make, you will be among the first to know them.

I see the chart go up and down based on predictions and speculations. I don't see that it really serves any good purpose. Until we reach the conclusion that we should make a recommendation, I don't want to create any false impressions one way or the other.

EFFORTS TO DEAL WITH CAUSES OF RACIAL TENSION

[13.] Q. Mr. President, have you any thoughts on what seems to be indications of mounting racial tension in this country, such as Watts and in some other areas? [11]

THE PRESIDENT. Yes, we are very concerned with the problems in Watts. We have been in close touch with the local officials who are dealing with that problem in the State and in the area. I commented on that last night.[12] I would refer you to some of the statements I made about the desir-

---

[11] The Watts district of Los Angeles, a predominantly Negro area, was the scene of extensive riots in the second week of August 1965. See 1965 volume, this series, Book II, Items 426 and 453.

[12] See Item 235.

ability of trying to avoid provoking antagonisms and trying to pull people together.

I was talking to Mr. Ramsey Clark [13] just a few days ago. He spent a good deal of time on that situation. A lot of problems come into play when in areas people are urging skilled workers to come to work for high wages. We have unemployed men who cannot qualify for those jobs because they don't have training. Even if they could qualify, sometimes they can't get to work because of transportation.

There are those things, and we are concerned with them. We are working with the local officials. We are proceeding as rapidly as we can to contribute what we can to their solution.

Last night I said: [13a]

"But the lesson of 12 years is that compassion, when it ceases to be a cliché of the platform and pulpit, can become the binding cement of a new fraternity.

"This is the time for bridges to be built, not for antagonisms to be aroused. This is the time for those to act who have the power to change what just must be changed. For privilege is power, and its misuse, especially to uphold an unjust status quo grown obsolete, is a dangerous wrong.

"It is the time, too, for passion to bow to reason. The gains since 1954 must be steppingstones to greater fulfillment, not future reminders of what might have been."

That is why Secretary Wirtz,[14] with whom I spent a good deal of time yesterday, is working so hard on his manpower training and development and on his Neighborhood Youth Corps.

That is why we are working so hard on our poverty and educational problems. That is why we are trying to conduct experiments in transportation. That is why we are urging and pleading with our people to help us meet this desperate housing problem.

People are living with their families and their children, in a good many of our cities, while rats are running through the room where their children eat and sleep. We have had the very minimum amount of housing built for people with low incomes in the large cities, too little.

That is why we are striving so earnestly to have some of our experiments put into practice, like the rent supplement, and to get private business to take on some of this development. We have a limited number that can be built under public housing—about 35,000.

We have housing, transportation, and training problems we are dealing with.

I had a memorandum this morning from the Vice President on meetings he has had with mayors. I have reports of meetings he has had with Governors. We are trying to do what we can to find training and employment for people this summer.

He met with the Council of State Governors, the Conference of Mayors, the National League of Cities, the International City Managers, the National Association of Council Officials.

In addition, we have had Secretary Weaver and Mr. Shriver, Gardner Ackley,[15] Secretary Wirtz, and others working on this problem to try to find answers.

We have made great progress in this field in the last 2½ years. We are appropriating

---

[13] Deputy Attorney General Ramsey Clark, who as the President's personal representative led the team of Federal officials who developed, with Governor Edmund G. (Pat) Brown of California and Mayor Samuel Yorty, the 1965 program of assistance to Los Angeles.

[13a] See Item 235.

[14] W. Willard Wirtz, Secretary of Labor.

[15] Robert C. Weaver, Secretary of Housing and Urban Development, R. Sargent Shriver, Director of the Office of Economic Opportunity and former Peace Corps Director, and Gardner Ackley, Chairman of the Council of Economic Advisers.

almost $10 billion more for education and health since I became President than we were the day before.

We are spending about $2 billion more on poverty each year, not to mention what the States, counties, and cities are doing.

I will have a copy of this chart made for any of you who want it.

PROBLEMS OF MEXICAN-AMERICANS

[14.] Mr. President, in this same vein, I asked you a couple of months ago about the Mexican-Americans and their unrest. Can you tell me what the situation is today?

THE PRESIDENT. I went to California on a conference in that field when I was Vice President. I have done everything I could to contribute to a better understanding. I had Members of the House who were of Mexican-American ancestry go on a visit with me to Mexico.

During that time we talked about the desirability of a meeting with the Latin American leaders in the United States, that is, the Mexican-Americans. Since then, some of my people in the White House have had conferences with Members of the House and Senate, and other leaders of various organizations, the G.I. Forum, the LULACS,[16] the veterans organizations, and others.

We have been concerned about the special problems of the Mexican-Americans and other Spanish-speaking peoples in our country. I am very familiar with those in the Southwest.

We hope that we can arrange a meeting to invite the Mexican-American leaders and others to the White House to meet with members of the staff and probe more deeply

into their problems and the actions that can be taken.

I have tried to find qualified employees for the Government from this group. I now have a good many requests out for recommendations.

Q. What about the White House conference coming up? Will that include members of that group?

THE PRESIDENT. No, the White House conference flowed from my Howard speech,[17] but we will be glad to have one of the same type for their problems.

DIPLOMATIC EFFORTS IN VIETNAM WAR

[15.] Q. Mr. President, a few minutes ago, a bit earlier, you alluded to the intensive diplomatic efforts that this Nation has conducted in order to try to get a settlement in Vietnam.

Would you now say that those efforts are stagnant? Is there anything in the diplomatic area——

THE PRESIDENT. Not at all. We are working every day at it. We will as long as I am President. I think that answers the only way I can now. I assume your next one will be to please tell you what is going on.

I had two nice long visits with Ambassador Gronouski,[18] who is returning to engage in conversations next week that will have a bearing on this general field.

Every day we get reports from other countries and their reactions to suggestions that

---

[16] The American G.I. Forum of the United States, an organization of Mexican-American veterans of the U.S. Armed Forces, and the League of United Latin American Citizens.

[17] The President's commencement address at Howard University in Washington on June 4, 1965. See 1965 volume, this series, Book II, Item 301. For remarks by the President on June 1 to the delegates to the White House Conference "To Fulfill These Rights," and for his statement on August 25 upon receiving the report of the Conference, see Items 248 and 408.

[18] John A. Gronouski, U.S. Ambassador to Poland.

have been made. I would say that we religiously and determinedly are pursuing every lead we can get to take advantage of every possibility that might lead to a negotiating table.

That is why I said it again the other night: If you will name the day and the place, you will find this Government ready to sit down with any other government to discuss these things.

I have with some of our most experienced and some of our new and fresh men. Ambassador Gronouski is very new to this field. He is a very creative person and an imaginative person.

I have been interested in some of his reports he has been making about some of his recent conversations and what he proposes to say in the days ahead. This week I saw a number of Ambassadors. These appointments—Congressmen, Senators, Ambassadors, Deputy Secretaries, Assistant Secretaries—do not always appear on this appointment list for obvious reasons.

I will meet with some today, including a Supreme Court Justice; you can't list them always because that creates more problems than the meeting solves.

No one wants peace in the world more than the United States of America. There is no one willing to go further to obtain it than this President.

Merriman Smith, United Press International: Thank you, Mr. President.

NOTE: President Johnson's sixty-third news conference was held in his office at the White House at 12 noon on May 21, 1966. The President also read a portion of his statement on Vietnam for radio and television.

237   Remarks to Members of the International Labor Press Association. *May 23, 1966*

Secretary Wirtz, Secretary Connor, distinguished editors, visitors:

It is a pleasure to welcome you here to the White House. The 350 publications that you represent reach, I am told, almost 20 million Americans. Most of your readers can be counted on to support the programs and the legislation that the distinguished Speaker and the leader of the Senate just spoke about, legislation that I think will keep our country marching ahead if they are kept informed. It is your job and also part of mine to help keep them informed.

I think it is a tribute to you that in some ways the copy in your publications has been getting less dramatic these days.

As I said last Friday to your friends at the United Auto Workers Convention at Long Beach, California:

"The days of the uproarious industrial conflict are behind us—the days of flamboyant heroes and identifiable villains, of the rhetoric of 'scab' and 'sitdown' and 'shutout' and 'yellow-dog contract.'"

The days of open warfare between labor and management with "winner take all" seem to have passed. Of course, there are still inequities, and where we find inequities we must correct them. I have urged the Congress to enact a new unemployment compensation bill. And Senator Long, the leader of the Senate, told me this afternoon as soon as the House passed that bill—it has already been reported—he will take it up in the Senate, and he will, he hopes, add some of the provisions that were modified in the House bill back in the Senate.

We believe that bill should include benefit standards. The present law we think is inadequate. We think it does not cover enough workers. We think it does not meet the economic demands of this period in the 20th century.

I am also urging Congress, as Speaker McCormack told you, to act this week to modernize the minimum wage by raising standards to $1.40 in 1967 and $1.60 in 1968.

I was one of three Members of Congress from my State in 1938 who signed a petition to bring up the minimum wage in the House of Representatives. The other two were defeated that year because they signed that petition.

To show you how far we have come since 1938 when I was a young man in the Congress, that bill provided a 25 cent minimum wage and two out of three men from my State that supported it were defeated. So we have made at least some progress, and I predict before the week is over we will pass a bill that will include 7 million extra people, that will raise the minimum wage not to 25 cents but to $1.60.

But the battle for job security and the battle for social security, pensions, medical care, and decent wages for most workers has already largely been won. Now we must go back to some new business.

What should that new business be?

I would like to think with you this afternoon and ask ourselves some questions.

What can we do to extend education beyond childhood and bring new opportunity to adults who were left behind?

What can we do to give the worker not merely a job but a job that uses all of his abilities?

What can we do to stop the wasteful squander of our human potential?

With unemployment at a 12-year low of 3.5 percent, our economy demands full and not partial use of our human resources. So what can we do about the unequal distribution of our labor force and about seasonal unemployment?

These are all questions that have important meaning, I think, to the men and women who labor in this country, as well as very important meaning to all the Nation.

But there are other challenges that also face us. Labor cannot content itself with what some call the bread and butter issues. So you must join us in the effort to improve our total environment.

For it is the worker who has the biggest stake in the quality of our public education. He does not have the choice of turning to a private school for his children.

It is the worker who has the biggest stake in mass transportation. The highway, the bus, and the train are his links to his livelihood.

It is the worker who has the biggest stake in conservation and natural beauty, and playgrounds that are close to his home for his children, because he does not own a hunting lodge or a home on the seashore.

It is the worker who has the biggest stake in rebuilding our decaying cities because he cannot escape to an expensive suburb.

There is scarcely a measure we have proposed to this Congress and to its leaders that we reviewed this afternoon which does not directly affect the workingman. He has been taken into our calculations in all of our recommendations to the Congress.

It is the workingman, the man who reads your publications, who has the power to turn such ideas as we have recommended into legislative programs that we can execute. Most of you realize this, I think, and your leaders realize it.

Labor leaders were prime movers behind our demonstration cities program. But some have called this program too small to bother with. What they don't understand is that it represents a whole new departure and it is a chance to renew entire urban communities at one time, instead of trying to do it piece by piece. If I were a mayor, I would embrace this program and the rent supplement program with it. I would work for them and I would strengthen them.

There has been far too little modern housing built in our big cities in this country. There is tragically little public housing available to the needy. We build less than 35,000 units in the entire United States per year. So we need to get our foot in the door, and fast, to open that door to the day when private housing provides a decent home for every family in this land.

I think that is what your readers would want, and I think that is what they would work for, too, if they could understand the real need and the real urgency that prevails.

These are two of the most important programs on the agenda of the Congress, and with your help we want to give them life, and we want to make them work.

The time has also come to do something about the effects of a workingman's job on his health. This problem has been neglected far too long, it has been overlooked, but it must be neglected no longer.

Since World War II, dozens of new materials and hundreds of new manufacturing processes have been introduced into our factories, and when they have been introduced new hazards have been introduced, too. We do not know the full long-range impact of these hazards on the health of all the men who work in these factories. We do not know enough about what really happens to men and women who handle chemicals, plastics, asbestos, petroleum products, and glass.

We do not know enough about the effects on a worker that is subject to extremes of heat and cold, noise or humidity. Despite all the research that we have done for these men who have been subjected to the extremes of heat, cold, noise, and humidity, we do not know the effects these have on their lives.

We do not even know the full effects of radioactivity, even though we have researched it for years.

But we do know that these hazards are real. We do know that work-related diseases and other physical and mental disorders are on the rise, and that trend must be reversed. We are moving to reverse it.

Last March we amended the Federal Coal Mine Safety Act to extend Federal safety precautions to all the Nation's coal miners. They had urged this step for years, and I was proud to be able to sign it into law, making it a reality.

Now we are going to extend Federal health standards to cover not only coal miners but to all miners as well.

The Metallic and Nonmetallic Mine Act, which has passed the House and is now in the Senate committee being studied, will protect our men mining copper and uranium, or working in sand and gravel quarries— practically everyone who labors under the earth to earn his livelihood.

I am also directing the Secretary of Health, Education, and Welfare to make an intensified study of all occupational health. He will report to me at the earliest possible moment on what your Government can do:

—First, to isolate and eliminate the hazards to occupational health that now exist; and

—Second, to test new products and processes so that precautions can be taken to prevent health hazards before they occur.

We are no longer content in America with achieving only the greatest good for the greatest number. Today the measure we apply to our national progress is how much we improve the lot of all, and especially of those who have the least.

541

What we have done in the past in the service of our conscience is only a prolog to what should now be done in the service of our vision. I urge you, as influential members of a great segment of American society to turn your hearts and your minds and your pens to the enlargement of that vision.

In the last 2½ years we have passed many measures in Congress: some 24 in the education and health field alone, many in the conservation field, many in the recreation field, many in the beautification field.

All of these measures, I think, that constitute what we call the Great Society, have been and will be of great benefit to the working people of this country, your audience—those who read your newspapers.

I think the medical care bill that goes into effect July 1 will be a measure with revolutionary possibilities. Now our big problem is to find competent administration for all those measures.

There are many cobwebs. There are many difficulties. They present many problems: How to bring the elementary school bill into practice; how to bring the medical care to reality and do it justly, do it fairly, and do it without discrimination.

I don't know whether you realize it or not, but in the last 2½ years, since I became President, we have increased the appropriations for health and education alone by almost $10 billion—$10 billion. And someone has to watch each of those dollars from the time it leaves the Treasury until it is spent in the various 50 States in this land.

So we not only have a job of legislating, we have a job of administering. We are trying to do that.

We started a poverty program in this country and we are now spending almost $2 billion—the Federal Government alone, to say nothing of the cities, counties, and States. That is a new program, a difficult

program. It has many heartaches and backaches in it. But it is better to have started it and failed in some instances than to have never thought of it at all.

I ask you to carefully review the things we have considered. Some of our recommendations have not been followed. The House Ways and Means Committee this week eliminated some provisions from the unemployment compensation bill that I wanted very much to pass. But that is what you call the check and balance system.

Senator Dirksen eliminated 14(b) [1] in the Senate, but I never committed myself to deliver Senator Dirksen.

I did my best to pass that bill in the House. We passed it by a few votes. I talked to 61 Senators that I thought we could influence in the Senate, and most of them were ready to support the measure. But there was a group that did not favor it. We will have to try again, and try again we will.

But I think we must realize that this Nation has made great progress, that we have moved forward. I doubt that there has ever been a period in our history—speaking of the last 5 years—when the worker got a fairer share of the total income, when the employer had better profits, and when the Nation benefited more.

Last week I visited the city where I taught before coming to Washington. I had left there 35 years ago. I looked up the statistical data to compare conditions then and conditions now.

It was rather startling. The average worker in manufacturing enterprises when I came to Washington in the year 1931–32 was making $17 a week. But, you say, they

[1] Section 14(b) of the Taft-Hartley Act (Labor-Management Relations Act of 1947, 61 Stat. 151). In his special message to the Congress on labor of May 18, 1965, the President recommended repeal of the section. See 1965 volume, this series, Book I, Item 258.

were 1932 dollars. And they were.

I had my economist convert that into present day dollars, and it ran about $30 a week. And I didn't have an economist when I came here, I might add.

The average farmer during that period made $300 a year, but converting that into present day dollars he made $800 a year. This year he makes $4,500. This year the worker who made $32 in 1932 makes $111— three times as much.

I believe in the last 5 years wages have gone up some 30-odd percent. Profits have gone up 46 percent in the 5 years since the Democratic administration came here— President Kennedy, Secretary Wirtz, and the rest.

So we have much to be thankful for.

That doesn't mean that there are not many improvements yet to be made. We cannot be satisfied with the status quo. We cannot stand still. We are not going to, notwithstanding the fact that the polls sometimes indicate that we are moving ahead too fast, that we need to be checked. I have found that people are able to do that when they think we need to be.

But we are going to have vision. We are going to dream dreams. We are going to look ahead. We are going to continue to try to deserve the right to say that we are

the best read, the best fed, the best clothed, and the most prosperous nation in all the world.

If we can only hold ourselves together and continue to believe in our system and our country, to the end that we can have not only prosperity but can lead in the effort to bring peace to all the world, it will be a great day for America.

That occupies my every waking moment. Thank you very much.

NOTE: The President spoke at 5:58 p.m. in the East Room at the White House to approximately 150 editors of union publications who were meeting in Washington. In his opening words he referred to W. Willard Wirtz, Secretary of Labor, and John T. Connor, Secretary of Commerce. Later he referred to Senator Russell B. Long of Louisiana, Senate majority whip, Representative John W. McCormack of Massachusetts, Speaker of the House of Representatives, John W. Gardner, Secretary of Health, Education, and Welfare, and Senator Everett McKinley Dirksen of Illinois, Senate minority leader.

The unemployment compensation legislation to which the President referred was not adopted by the 89th Congress.

For his statements and remarks upon signing the minimum wage bill (Fair Labor Standards Amendments of 1966), the Demonstration Cities and Metropolitan Development Act of 1966, the Federal Coal Mine Safety Act Amendments, and the Federal Metal and Nonmetallic Mine Safety Act, see Items 479, 574, 151, and 462, respectively.

For a statement by the President on the inauguration of the Medicare program, see Item 309. See also Item 314.

---

238   Statement by the President Announcing a National Planning Conference on the Education of Disadvantaged Children. *May 24, 1966*

I HAVE asked the U.S. Commissioner of Education, Harold Howe II, to call a national planning conference in Washington, July 18–20, on education for disadvantaged children.

The program provided by title I of the Elementary and Secondary Education Act

of 1965 has been started and the funds for this fiscal year dispersed in an unusually brief span of time. Its value has been clearly demonstrated. There are 7 million children who are receiving a better education this year because our State and local school systems moved swiftly and with ingenuity to use these funds. We must now assure ourselves that progress is universal. The gains made in some schools can be duplicated throughout the Nation if we exchange information and ideas quickly.

To this end I have suggested to Commissioner Howe that he invite the chief education officer of each State to name a four-man delegation to the conference. This delegation would be comprised of the State's title I coordinator, a representative from a State college or university, and a representative each from an urban and a rural area.

The conference will provide a working environment for exchanging ideas and exploring new methods of educating the children of poverty. It can concern itself with problems discussed in the report of the National Advisory Council on Education of

Disadvantaged Children.

I have asked Commissioner Howe to make the results of the conference known to all State educational agencies, and I hope this meeting will be the forerunner of a series of similar conferences in each State before the fall school opening. We cannot rest until every boy and girl who needs special help in school receives it in the most effective, imaginative form that American ingenuity can devise.

NOTE: The National Conference on Education of the Disadvantaged was held at the Mayflower Hotel in Washington July 18–20, 1966. The report of the Conference (OE–37004; 86 pp.) was published by the Government Printing Office.

For the President's message of May 9 transmitting to the Congress the first annual report of the National Advisory Council on the Education of Disadvantaged Children, see Item 210.

239   Memorandum on the Government's Joint Financial Management Improvement Program.   *May 24, 1966*

Memorandum for the Heads of Departments and Agencies:

Secretary Fowler, Budget Director Schultze and Comptroller General Staats have just informed me about their plans to accelerate the pace of the Joint Financial Management Improvement Program. They have asked Civil Service Chairman Macy to assist in this worthy undertaking.

I have a strong and continuing interest in the development of business-like financial systems throughout the Federal Government. Such systems are essential to assist in carrying out a basic pledge of this Administration—to get a dollar's value for a dollar spent. We must have financial systems which:

—provide the information our managers need for effective cost control—for wag-

ing the war on waste,

—develop cost consciousness in men and women at every level of responsibility in every agency,

—assure financial integrity in everything the Government does,

—provide the types of financial data needed to support the planning-programing-budgeting system initiated last August, and

—enable the Government to apply the best and most efficient management and operating techniques.

I am particularly pleased that the central agencies—representing both the legislative and the executive branches—will spearhead, with your active participation, a renewed joint program in this vital area of direct interest to both the Congress and the President.

The legislative groundwork for this program was laid sixteen years ago. While much progress has been made, much more is necessary if we are to discharge the responsibility placed upon us by the Budget and Accounting Procedures Act of 1950. Accordingly, I request the head of each executive department and agency to take immediate action to:

—Insure that the system of accounting and internal control in his agency meets management needs and conforms to the principles, standards, and related requirements prescribed by the Comptroller General.

—Work with the Civil Service Commission in developing a more vigorous program for recruiting and developing the professional personnel to design and operate effective financial management systems.

—Assure that financial reports and cost data provide adequate support for the planning-programing-budgeting system.

—See that the agency's managers are given the basic tools they need—responsibility centered cost-based operating budgets and financial reports—for setting and achieving maximum cost reduction goals.

The Budget Director will issue more detailed instructions with respect to this program. Your full support is needed. I want every manager—the general manager and the financial manager alike—to feel and respond to your personal demands for the use of highest quality, business-type financial information systems.

I want every manager to think of his part of the total Government in terms of everything he owns, everything he owes and the full cost of doing every job in relation to the products resulting from these costs. I want him to think of minimal costs and cost reduction as profit. And I want him to think in terms of his profit as a result of how he uses all the resources entrusted to him. These goals cannot be fully achieved without sound financial management practices.

With increased assistance by the central agencies, and a positive action program on your part, we can readily achieve what is contemplated in the Budget and Accounting Procedures Act—the utilization of the best business practices in the day-to-day management of our Government.

LYNDON B. JOHNSON

NOTE: On the same day Charles L. Schultze, Director, Bureau of the Budget, issued instructions on the program in the form of a memorandum to the heads of executive departments and establishments (Bureau of the Budget Bulletin No. 66–6, 3 pp.).

240 Remarks Upon Signing a Bill To Reduce Freight Car Shortages. *May 26, 1966*

Mr. Vice President, Senator Magnuson, Congressman Staggers, my longtime friends of the House and the Senate, distinguished guests:

I want to thank you very much for coming over here this early this morning. This is really a tribute to the House of Representatives. We give them special recognition for this.

I understand they are going in at 10 o'clock and we never want to be followers, we want to be leaders, so we had to go in at 9 o'clock, although I am a man of an evening nature, myself. I don't like these early dates. But

I do thank you for coming here.

We are here to take an important step, we think, in trying to eliminate a serious bottleneck that has affected most of our States and our economy. We face a freight car shortage that has gone from bad to worse in recent years. It has hurt our consumer and farmer, business and labor, and has in some respects curtailed our defense effort.

Since World War II our railroads have scrapped almost 300,000 more cars than they have purchased. By 1965 we had over a million less cars than we had just 40 years ago.

In the past, these cars have fallen into short supply primarily during our harvest season. We have let that situation slide now until what was once a chronic yearly problem now seems to be a problem chronically the year around. We don't want to tolerate that—

—not as long as a single farmer lacks a boxcar to ship the grain that he has worked so hard to grow against the weather and the insects;

—not as long as lumber mills must close because their products cannot be moved from their mill to their manufacturer and the shortages drive up their prices;

—not as long as businessmen have goods that are ready to ship, but must wait for freight cars and lose money during that waiting period.

This is a challenge that confronts all of us in Government, and industry as well. I am very proud of the transportation industry generally. The men in the railroad business, I think, have taken on a new look and a new approach. They are very concerned with their country and national interests and how they can improve the image of their business and the operation of it.

I think the same thing is true of the other elements of our transportation picture—the trucks, the waterways, and the others.

I really, genuinely, believe that our Nation has much to be thankful for when we recognize the competency and the efficiency of the men in the transportation industry, all of whom we hit over the head on occasions when problems develop. But all you have to do is just have a few hours or a few days of what we have in some of our ports overseas sometimes—Vietnam and other places—to really appreciate what you have at home.

Chairman Bush and the very fine members of the Interstate Commerce Commission have gone on the attack. They have been using their emergency powers. They are doing everything they can, but they, too, recognize that stopgap measures are not enough.

Our railroads have been forced to operate under some outmoded regulations because it is cheaper to rent a freight car, often for as little as $2 a day, than it is to build a freight car for $15,000 capital investment. So no wonder a railroad witness testifying before the Commerce Committee said, "It takes guts to spend money on freight cars, even if you've got the money."

Now this bill will improve that. It will benefit every farmer, consumer, and worker whose job depends on full production and the movement of his goods to market. It will benefit the railroads by increasing freight capacity—that is the most profitable part of their business, as we all know.

The freight car shortage is only a symptom of our larger transportation challenges, so the measure that we will shortly sign is not a cure-all, certainly not a final answer. We make no pretensions about its overall, comprehensive, long-enduring effect on transportation, but it is a part of the total effort that we are carrying out on many fronts to use transportation—to use it in better and more effective ways, to give it nore recognition and more respect, to serve he needs of our growing population, our xpanding economy, and the great industries hat have made America the leading nation n all the world.

In my transportation message to the Congress, I said, "America lacks a coordinated ransportation system that permits travelers nd goods to move conveniently and effi-iently" across the country. I am very en-ouraged by the reception that the Members of the House and the Senate have given to hese recommendations and to this message, nd I have reason to believe there will be ome adjustments and certainly some im-provements on what I have recommended.

I hope before we go home this year that we will have a transportation system and a ransportation department that will coordi-nate and make much more efficient all of hese operations. The new Cabinet-level Department of Transportation before the Congress, I think, will enable us to do that. Our transportation system will neither speed nor strangle our progress. It will improve our living standard, and I think it is a matter hat deserves first attention.

So I am confident that we will have action on the Department of Transportation for the same good reasons that we got action on the freight car bill. That is a tribute to the Congress because this Congress believes in aking action where there is clear and urgent need for action. So it gives me great pleas-ure this morning to sign this bill—and to particularly thank Senator Magnuson and Congressman Staggers and all of their hard-working colleagues for delivering this bill here.

I might add that it would give me even greater pleasure—I'll enjoy it a lot more, Maggie, if you will bring that transportation department bill down here before this great and this productive 89th Congress adjourns.

I know that some of you are wondering how many bills we are going to have this year, and of what nature. I was delayed a little bit because a fellow was talking to me about taxes. I said, "How much more in taxes do you want to pay this year?" Well, he wasn't quite sure, and didn't know. But we have a great deal to be thankful for. We don't spend much time acknowledging it. We are all somewhat cynical and we really don't like to admit that things are good for us, but if we were citizens of an-other land for a very short time we would want to come back where we are.

I came to this town 35 years ago. And when I came here, the average factory worker got $17 a week. They are getting $111 now. But you say, "Well, there is a difference in dollars." Well, there is. The $17 then would buy about $39 worth of goods. So $39 and $111, that is the progress that the man who works with his hands has made.

When I came here 35 years ago, in Mr. Hoover's administration, just before Novem-ber 1931, the average farmer had an annual income of a little over $300 a year. Now in today's dollars that is a little over $800. The net income per farm this last year was $4,400. That represents some progress for the man on the farm—$4,280 to be exact.

The dividend people have risen from $6.4 billion in 1932 to $19 billion last year.

Our population has increased, our country is bigger, but so are our dividends, $6 billion to $19 billion.

When I came here, 5 percent of all Amer-icans were illiterate and during that period we have cut that in half.

Now we do have a prosperous economy. We do have our prices increasing. We are concerned that all of the advances we made are not eaten up with the cheapness of the dollar, the whittling away, increased prices, and inflation coming on. So some people said, "Well, why don't you put on controls?" We know the problem we had with wage and price controls during the war. We know that they were just absolutely not satisfactory to anyone.

Some of them said, "Why don't you cut the total expenditures that the Government is making?" All of us say that, all of us want to do that, and we all look over our budget just like our family budget. But the thing that I want to cut most, Mrs. Johnson wants to cut least. And the things both of us think we can get by without, Luci and Lynda just must have.

That is true in Government as well as it is in business. There is hardly any businessman who has reduced his budget through the years. Our Federal budget has increased less than the industrial budget in this country, the labor budget in this country, the State and local government budgets in this country.

Our capital investment is way down, Federally speaking, compared to theirs over the period of years. But this year, in an attempt to curtail and cool off and take from the economy, we have passed some tax bills. Some of you have forgotten them. We have pulled some things out of the economy.

We had a corporate speedup that took $1.1 billion out of the economy right at the first of the year. We signed it March 15th. We had an excise tax that was due to go off. We put it back on. That brought us in about $800 million. You haven't forgotten that. That's March 15th.

We had a graduated withholding increase, and that was almost another $1 billion— $840 million, to be exact. Last year you remember they said, when we put in Medicare, "We are going to have a recession because we are taking so much out." So we are taking out this year for those over 65,

$6.1 billion for increased social security and Medicare.

We have had a collection speedup so the companies that withhold the money from their employees just don't keep it. They send it right on in within 3 days, and that brings in $900 million.

We have had an increase in revenue with the same tax rate. So while Congressmen don't make any more, a good many people who made $30,000 last year will make $44,000 this year, and the tax on that extra $14,000 puts them in a different bracket. So that brings us an additional $1.7 billion.

And the savings bonds. The employees— there are not many of them at the White House—but they are 100 percent signed up on a payroll savings plan. The Chrysler Company looked at it and Mr. Townsend is performing a great service for us. He got all of the Chrysler people to sign up 100 percent. Larry O'Brien has done an unbelievable job on the payroll savings. He has gone out and said, "Give your Government one-half percent. There are a lot of men giving their lives for their country; you give them one-half percent. Let them buy a little bond every payday." As a result, they have gone up to 60 and 70 and 80 percent in nearly every department of the Government. So from savings bonds we will pull out an extra $1½ billion.

That is $13 billion we have taken out of this economy this year. They tell me that if you add about $11 billion a quarter, that is a reasonable addition to the economy— an increase in our gross national product. In four quarters that would be $44 billion. They predict now it could be $55 billion to $60 billion that is being added, things are so prosperous. We are taking $13 billion of that out. So you add $44 billion and the $13 billion we are taking out from your $55 billion, and you see where we are.

Now it may be we ought to take out more. I wish I knew. If it were black and white, I would give you a recommendation this moment, but I don't know. I don't know how much more you all are going to take out in the Congress. The present record shows you are going to put about $3 billion in. But I have confidence in the Senate. While traditionally it hasn't cut appropriations bills deeply, during my period there— I am gone and they may have changed. I hope they have. We will have to see how much they take out of it.

But we are concerned that we don't go too far too fast. Now I had rather be concerned about that than concerned that my party is not going to have employment, and my party is not going to have good prices for their products, and my party is not going to have these things, or my Government.

A fellow said to me the other day that he was real distressed, that things were just going to pot right quick, because of these prosperous conditions. I said, "Well, one thing is sure, I believe I'll never be afraid of inflation if you are running things.

"My experience with you gives me some reason to believe that the farmer doesn't need to worry about having too big prices and too much income if you take over. He doesn't have to worry about all the people being employed and buying too much during that period."

So what we have to worry about this morning is what an even balance is. And by and large, we have nothing to really go home and cry about. This country is doing very well. That is not because of me. That is not because of you, or the Vice President, or the distinguished deputy Republican leader, my friend Les Arends.

That is because of this system we have that our forefathers figured out. When we run into these little obstacles like freight car shortages and others, we just all get together and put our shoulders to the wheel and try to solve it, and at least improve it with this measure.

In the days ahead, we are going to have a lot of problems to solve. But we are big enough to meet them and we are going to meet them and we are going to try to meet them in a spirit of understanding, in a spirit of faith in what our Founding Fathers did, and with a tolerance and an understanding of each other.

I went out to the hospital the other day to see a good many veterans, but one was a veteran of many wars, General Eisenhower. Another one was a veteran of a good many political and military struggles, the minority leader, Senator Dirksen. And then a good many from Vietnam.

I told General Eisenhower when I left there, "General, I tried to express a little understanding of your problems as President when I was leader, and some of my more vociferous Senators made criticisms at times about why didn't I go join your party that I voted for it so many times." I said, "I want you to know that I have been rewarded 100 percent in the 3 years I have been here for everything I did during that period. You have shown a little understanding and you have shown a little desire to cooperate."

So we don't get anywhere, really, when we divide up, slice up, and cut up our fellow man in the eyes of the world. The fact that you would come here this morning and participate in a little ceremony of this kind, members of both parties, all of you unite in this action, and I hope unite in other actions that are pending, correct what needs to be corrected, improve what needs to be improved, recommend to me what ought to be done.

If you don't think things are going right, put on your hat and come on down here.

You have to wait 15 or 20 minutes sometimes, but come on down and tell me about it. I would even rather have you do that than write me, because somehow or other there is always somebody in your office when you write me a letter that lets it leak out and I read about it in the paper. Sometimes I read about my mail on the ticker, and I don't get the letter for a week. I just go looking for it. I have had to call one or two fellows and say, "Put it in the mail. Come on, let me have it so I can get to it."

But I think this is a wonderful Congress and you good people of both parties that make it up deserve a lot of credit. As long as I can—I might have to withdraw a little of it in late October or early November out

there if some of you get after me too hot—but as long as I can, I am going to give you recognition for the job that you have done.

Thank you.

NOTE: The President spoke at 9 a.m. in the East Room at the White House. In his opening words he referred to Vice President Hubert H. Humphrey, Senator Warren G. Magnuson of Washington, and Representative Harley O. Staggers of West Virginia. Later he referred to John W. Bush, Chairman of the Interstate Commerce Commission, Luci Baines and Lynda Bird, his daughters, Lynn Alfred Townsend, President of the Chrysler Corporation, Lawrence F. O'Brien, Postmaster General, and to Representative Leslie C. Arends and Senator Everett McKinley Dirksen, both of Illinois.

As enacted, the freight car bill (S. 1098) is Public Law 89–430 (80 Stat. 168).

For the President's Special Message to the Congress on Transportation and for his remarks upon signing the bill authorizing the Department of Transportation, see Items 98 and 523.

241 Letter to the President of the Senate and to the Speaker of the House Transmitting Proposed Election Reform Act of 1966. *May 26, 1966*

Dear Mr. President: (*Dear Mr. Speaker:*)

Public confidence in the elective process is the foundation of public confidence in government. There is no higher duty of a democratic government than to insure that confidence.

Public participation in the political process is the foundation of that process. There is no clearer responsibility of a democratic government than to advance that participation.

Yet for decades we have tolerated the growth of seeds of cynicism from the underbrush surrounding our present method of financing political campaigns.

Despite regular rhetoric about citizen involvement, we have done nothing in fact to encourage public support for the nomination and election of public officials.

And despite the soaring expense of polit-

ical campaigns, we have done nothing to insure that able men of modest means can undertake elective service unencumbered by debts of loyalty to wealthy supporters.

We have laws dealing with campaign financing. But they have failed. Too narrow in their scope when passed, now they are obsolete. Too narrow in their purpose then, now they are inadequate. They are more loophole than law. They invite evasion and circumvention. They must be revised.

In my State of the Union Message I said:

"As the process of election becomes more complex and costly, we must make it possible for those without personal wealth to enter public life without being obligated to a few large contributors.

"Therefore, I will submit legislation to revise the present unrealistic restrictions on contributions—to prohibit the endless proliferation of committees bringing local and state committees under the act—to attach strong teeth and severe penalties to the requirement of full disclosure of contributions—and to broaden the participation of the people, through added tax incentives, to stimulate small contributions to the party and to the candidate of their choice."

I enclose for your consideration the proposed Election Reform Act of 1966. This measure is designed to achieve four broad purposes:

First, it would for the first time make effective past efforts to achieve complete public disclosure of campaign funds. The bill would require all candidates and all committees supporting them for federal office to report, clearly and promptly, the sources of all their funds and how these funds are spent.

Second, it would also require disclosure by members of Congress of gifts and income.

Third, it would revise existing law and for the first time make effective the ceilings on the size of contributions.

Fourth, this proposal seeks a goal not even contemplated by earlier laws—the active encouragement of widespread public participation in the financing of political campaigns through tax deductions.

I.

Campaigns are not merely a periodic political pageant. They are an unparalleled instrument of public education in the issues of the nation and of the community.

The need for such campaigns, and the need to finance them, are hardly evils. The more people reached by a campaign, the closer we approach the democratic ideal of full participation in the decisions of government.

Yet the more people reached, the more

funds required. It is here that there is a potential for danger—the possibility that great wealth can be used to achieve undue political influence.

It is that danger to which Congress responded with the Federal Corrupt Practices Act 41 years ago and with the Hatch Act 26 years ago. These measures sought to insure that a tide of funds from the few did not engulf the interests of the many:

—By limiting the total amount a candidate or political committee could spend;

—By limiting the total amount an individual could contribute to a campaign;

—By requiring public disclosure of campaign funds.

These are surely valid aims. But they have not been achieved. Under present law, for example, national political committees can raise and spend no more than $3,000,000 in any year. But the law does not limit the number of national political committees, nor does it apply at all to committees active in only one state.

Similarly, while present law limits Senatorial candidates to expenditures of $25,000 and House candidates to $5,000, it does not limit the number of committees that can raise and spend money on behalf of those candidates.

In the light of the accelerating cost of political campaigns, it is hardly surprising that such supporting committees have proliferated. Legal ceilings on expenditures enacted when the possibilities of radio were only faintly glimpsed—and when there was no television—can have small relevance today.

The loophole through which committees have streamed, is matched by the loophole in the limitation on individual contributions.

The Hatch Act limits contributions to $5,000 to a single federal candidate or to any single political committee supporting that candidate. But it does not limit the number of $5,000 contributions an individual or single interest can make—to each national committee established for a candidate or party—and there is no limit to the number of such committees.

Neither does present law limit spending by state committees for federal candidates. And it does not require these committees to submit any reports, thwarting the aim of full disclosure at the outset.

Even in the case of national committees and candidates who do report, the disclosure may not be sufficient to identify the giver or the particular candidate benefitting from a contribution.

A further, major defect in present law is that it specifically excepts primaries. In many cases primary contests are decisive. In most cases, they are financially burdensome. They remain, however, entirely outside the law.

II.

The proposed Election Reform Act of 1966 seeks, completely and systematically, to correct these omissions, loopholes and shortcomings. It would do so through eight provisions, both corrective and positive.

COMPLETE PUBLIC DISCLOSURE

1. Not only every candidate, but also every committee—state, interstate, or national—that supports a candidate for federal office would be required to report in detail on every contribution and expense item over $100.

The treasurer of every political committee would be required to submit complete reports, on standardized forms, four times during the year and on the fifteenth, tenth, and fifth days before an election.

For the first time, candidates for President and Vice President would be included under this disclosure provision.

2. The present unrealistic exclusion of primaries from the coverage of the law would be ended. This Act would bring primary campaigns and convention nomination contests under the disclosure law.

There is a similar omission concerning primaries in connection with criminal laws against vote-buying and vote-selling. These offenses are adequately dealt with when they occur in general or special federal elections. But they are not covered in federal primaries. There is no reason for this distinction and the Election Reform Act would make these laws fully applicable to primaries as well.

3. The Election Reform Act would require all gifts of over $100 received by members of the legislative branch of the Government for themselves, their wives and minor children, and all income from personal services received by such member or on his behalf to be reported annually. Appropriate criminal sanctions would be provided for failure to comply.

In the executive branch, the acceptance of gifts of more than nominal value is already strictly forbidden by Executive Order 11222 of May 8, 1965.

For such reports to be made by members of the legislative branch can do much to demonstrate that wealthy interests are not permitted to affect—or even appear to affect—the conduct of government through their largesse.

EFFECTIVE AND REALISTIC LIMITATIONS ON CAMPAIGN FINANCING

1. Beyond making political financing public lies the equally demanding task of making it democratic. The Act thus would

limit to $5,000 the total amount that could come from any single source to the campaign of any candidate. The present $5,000 limit could no longer be evaded by putting the maximum amount into different pockets in the same suit.

2. At the same time, the Act would repeal present ceilings on total expenditures by candidates for federal offices. As we have learned from experience, artificial limits breed artificial disclosures. And as we have learned, the present limits on total campaign expenses are decidedly artificial.

The cost of campaigning varies from year to year and from state to state, depending on the size of the district and the heat of the campaign. More important, spending limitations defeat the essential purpose of disclosure: to allow public opinion to exert the controlling influence on how much a candidate spends.

3. The Act also would extend the present prohibition against political contributions by government contractors to fully cover corporate contractors.

Under present law, all government contractors other than corporations are barred from making political contributions at any level of government. But corporations with government contracts are barred only from contributing to federal candidates.

Consistency and good sense require that corporations also should be forbidden to make contributions at the state and local level—where finances are, inevitably, related by party to national political campaign finances.

ENCOURAGING WIDESPREAD CITIZEN PARTICIPATION

These first six steps are essentially corrective, altering or refining present inade-

quacies. The parallel goal never before established by federal law is to enlarge the base of widespread financial support for political campaigns.

This is a necessary goal for a practical reason—to meet the financial burdens of modern political campaigning without inviting the undue influence of large contributors.

But widespread support is a worthy goal for a still more important reason—the infusion and involvement of large numbers of citizens into the election process. We propose two steps to expand participation by the great majority of American citizens.

1. We recommend a special tax deduction, in an amount up to $100, for contributions to any candidate or to any organizations supporting a candidate, in any election campaign or primary, federal, state or local.

This deduction would be allowed in addition to the standard deduction and would not be limited to those who itemize their deductions.

There would be a separate line on every tax return for this deduction.

2. As another means of expanding participation, the Act would permit the sale of campaign souvenirs at prices not exceeding $5. These would become the only items of any kind—including advertising—that any candidate or committee would be allowed to sell.

Broadened financial support is sound for all candidates. For candidates who are not themselves wealthy, it can mean the difference between running and not running.

Finally, one area not covered by the legislation I forward today is the solicitation of political contributions from federal employees by other federal employees.

This is not a matter for which legislation is needed. Congress has already passed the laws. I am asking the Attorney General, in consultation with the Chairman of the Civil Service Commission, to conduct a thorough review of all the regulations and memoranda issued pursuant to those laws to make certain that those regulations are sufficiently comprehensive to carry out not only the letter, but the spirit of the laws passed by Congress.

III.

There is far more at stake in the proposals I submit today than who wins and who loses a particular campaign. The essence of our democratic system is the clash of ideas between differing men and differing parties.

If lack of funds results in an abridged campaign, the public is deprived of the opportunity to hear all viewpoints fully expounded.

If lack of freedom from ties to wealthy interests discourages able men from seeking elective service, both they and the public are deprived of necessary leadership.

If lack of clear disclosure results in skepticism about the entire political process, the public loses the benefit of its own involvement in and respect for that process.

This Election Reform Act of 1966 seeks to avert those dangers.

It seeks honest, straightforward disclosure.

It seeks fair restriction on the exercise of mighty influence by the rich.

It seeks to promote the exercise of widespread influence by the many.

It seeks, in short, to enlarge democracy, and I urge its prompt enactment.

Sincerely,

LYNDON B. JOHNSON

NOTE: This is the text of identical letters addressed to the Honorable Hubert H. Humphrey, President of the Senate, and to the Honorable John W. McCormack, Speaker of the House of Representatives.

The text of the draft bill was also made public by the White House.

The Election Reform Act was not adopted by the 89th Congress (see Statement by the President upon signing the Foreign Investors Tax Act and Presidential Election Campaign Fund Act of 1966, Item 612 below).

Executive Order 11222 of May 8, 1965, is entitled "Prescribing Standards of Ethical Conduct for Government Officers and Employees" (30 F.R. 6469; 3 CFR, 1965 Supp., p. 130).

---

242   Proclamation 3727, Prayer for Peace, Memorial Day, 1966. *May 26, 1966*

By the President of the United States of America a Proclamation

Americans will be fighting and dying in Vietnam this Memorial Day, 1966, in fulfillment of our commitment to freedom. Their sacrifice is part of an ancient legacy that begins with man's first act of transcendent courage, and that contains all that is noble and selfless in human character.

Our own liberty was won in struggle against tyranny. In two world wars and in Korea, brave Americans and their allies gave their lives that men might live and prosper in freedom.

We shall not forsake their sacrifice. We shall—because we must—persevere.

We are totally committed to defeat this aggression.

This nation has never left the field of battle in abject surrender of a cause for which it has fought.

We shall not do so now.

We shall see this through.

Yet as we protect freedom by courage in arms, we shall every day continue the search for an honorable peace.

It is tragic that young lives must be sacrificed, that great sums must be spent for the instruments of war, when the work of peace awaits man's accomplishment in every land. America today—as in past years—is prepared to join in that work with any nation whose devotion is to peace with its neighbors, and a better life for its people. Let the guns of aggression be silent, we say, that the sounds of the builders, of the planters, of the teachers, may be heard.

On this Memorial Day, as we honor the memory of brave men who have borne our colors in war, we pray to God for His mercy. We pray for the wisdom to find a way to end this struggle of nation against nation, of brother against brother. We pray that soon we may begin to build the only true memorial to man's valor in war—a sane and hopeful environment for the generations to come.

The Congress, in a joint resolution approved May 11, 1950 (64 Stat. 158), has requested the President to issue a proclamation calling upon the people of the United States to observe each Memorial Day as a day of prayer for permanent peace and designating a period during each such day when the people of the United States might unite in such supplication:

Now, THEREFORE, I, LYNDON B. JOHNSON, President of the United States of America, do hereby designate Memorial Day, Monday, May 30, 1966, as a day of prayer for permanent peace, and I designate the hour beginning in each locality at eleven o'clock in the morning of that day as a time to unite in such prayer.

I urge the press, radio, television, and all other information media to cooperate in this observance.

I also urge all of the people of this Nation to join me in prayer to the Almighty for the safety of our Nation's sons and daughters in Vietnam, for His blessing on those who have sacrificed their lives for this Nation in this and all other struggles, and for His aid in building a world where freedom and justice prevail, and where all men live in friendship, understanding, and peace.

By House Concurrent Resolution 587, the Eighty-ninth Congress has officially recognized that the patriotic tradition of observing Memorial Day began one hundred years ago in Waterloo, New York. In conformity with the request contained in that concurrent resolution, it is my privilege to call attention to the centennial observance of Memorial Day in Waterloo, New York, on May 30, 1966.

IN WITNESS WHEREOF, I have hereunto set my hand and caused the Seal of the United States of America to be affixed.

DONE at the City of Washington this twenty-sixth day of May in the year of our
        Lord nineteen hundred and sixty-
[SEAL] six, and of the Independence of the
        United States of America the one
hundred and ninetieth.

                    LYNDON B. JOHNSON
By the President:
  DEAN RUSK
    Secretary of State

243 Remarks at a Reception Marking the Third Anniversary of the Organization of African Unity. *May 26, 1966*

Mr. Vice President, Secretary Rusk, Ambassador Diop, Your Excellencies, distinguished guests:

Three years ago yesterday the heads of your governments signed the Charter of the Organization of African Unity. It was a memorable day for your continent and for all the modern world into which Africa has emerged as an indispensable partner.

The charter signed on that day declares that "It is the inalienable right of all people to control their destiny," that "freedom, equality, justice and dignity are essential objectives . . . of the African peoples." It pledges to harness the natural and human resources of Africa for the total advancement of your peoples.

My country knows what those words mean. To us, as to you, they are not mere abstractions.

They are a living part of our experience as men and as nations.

They sum up the basic aspirations which your people and mine share in common: to secure the right of self-government, to build strong democratic institutions, and to improve the level of every citizen's well-being.

We have learned that these aspirations are indivisible. If it takes self-determination to become a free nation, it also takes a climate of regular growth to remain one. And that means the wise development of human and natural resources.

Whether nations are 5 years old or 190 years old, the striving for these goals never really ends. No nation ever completes the task of combining freedom with responsibility, liberty with order—and applying these principles, day after day, to our new problems.

Because these principles are imbedded in the hearts of Africans and Americans alike, I have asked you to come here today to join me in commemorating the founding of the Organization of African Unity.

It is a good occasion to reaffirm a unity of purpose that transcends two continents.

I.

As your charter and as our Declaration of Independence set forth, we believe that governments must derive their just powers from the consent of the governed.

This is the core of political freedom and the first principle of nation-building.

In the past 15 years, belief in self-determination has fired the swift momentum of Africa toward full participation in the community of nations. It has been a truly remarkable era in which more than 30 nations have emerged from colonialism to independence.

The road has not been traveled without difficulty. Its end is not even yet in sight. There have been ups and downs—and of course there will be more. But as one of your distinguished ambassadors has pointed out, "What matters most about new nations is not that they have growing pains but that they are in fact growing."

There is in Africa today an increasing awareness that government must represent the true will of its citizens. Across the continent the majority of people prefer self-government with peril to subservience with serenity.

This makes all the more repugnant the narrow-minded, outmoded policy which in some parts of Africa permits the few to rule at the expense of the many.

The United States has learned from lamentable personal experience that domination of one race by another leads to waste and to injustice. Just as we are determined to remove the remnants of inequality from our midst, we are also with you—heart and soul—as you try to do the same.

We believe, as you do, that denial of a whole people's rights to shape their national future is morally wrong. We also know that it is politically and socially costly. A nation in the 20th century cannot expect to achieve order and sustain growth unless it moves—not just steadily but rapidly—in the direction of full political rights for all of its peoples.

It has taken us time to learn this lesson. But having learned it, we must not forget it.

The Government of the United States cannot, therefore, condone the perpetuation of racial or political injustice anywhere in the world. We shall continue to provide our full share of assistance to refugees from social and political oppression.

As a basic part of our national tradition we support self-determination and an orderly transition to majority rule in every quarter of the globe. These principles have guided our American policy from India to the Philippines, from Vietnam to Pakistan. They guide our policy today toward Rhodesia.

We are giving every encouragement and support to the efforts of the United Kingdom and the United Nations to restore legitimate government in Rhodesia. Only when this is accomplished can steps be taken to open the full power and responsibility of nationhood to all the people of Rhodesia—not just 6 percent of them.

The disruptive effects of current sanctions fall heavily upon Zambia, adding a difficult burden to that young republic's efforts to strengthen its national life. I have informed President Kenneth Kaunda that we will work with him in trying to meet the economic pressures to which his country is being subjected.

The foreign policy of the United States is rooted in its life at home. We will not permit human rights to be restricted in our own country. And we will not support policies abroad which are based on the rule of minorities or the discredited notion that men are unequal before the law.

We will not live by a double standard—professing abroad what we do not practice at home, or venerating at home what we ignore abroad.

II.

Our dreams and our vision are of a time when men of all races will collaborate as members of the same community, working with one another because their security is inseparable, and also because it is right and because it is just.

This vision requires ever-increasing economic and social opportunity.

I know the enormous tasks that Africa faces in fulfilling its aspirations. I know how compelling is her need to apply modern science and technology to enrich the life of her people.

Much has been accomplished in the years since independence came to many members of your organization. You are proving what can be done when freedom and determination are joined with self-help and external assistance.

We have been particularly heartened by the impetus toward regional cooperation in Africa.

The world has now reached a stage where some of the most effective means of economic growth can best be achieved in large units commanding large resources and large markets. Most nation-states are too small, when

557

acting alone, to assure the welfare of all of their people.

This does not mean the loss of hard-earned national independence. But it does mean that the accidents of national boundaries do not have to lead to hostility and conflict or serve as impossible obstacles to progress.

You have built new institutions to express a new sense of unity. Even as you grapple with the problems of early nationhood, you have sought out new possibilities of joint action—the OAU itself, the Economic Commission for Africa, the African Development Bank, and sub-regional groupings such as the Economic Community of Eastern Africa.

Growth in Africa must then follow the inspiration of African peoples. It must stem from the leadership of African governments. Assistance from others can provide the extra resources to help speed this growth.

Such assistance is already underway. In the last 5 years aid from all external sources has amounted to over $8 billion. The United States of America has extended approximately 2 billion of that 8 billion.

But none of us can be content when we measure what is being done against what could be done.

We are anxious to work with you to fulfill your ambitions.

Working with others, we are prepared to help build with you a modern Africa.

I can think of many missions on which America and Africa can work together.

First, to strengthen the regional economic activities that you have already begun.

My country has offered the African Development Bank technical assistance funds to finance surveys of project possibilities, and loan funds for capital projects. We are ready to assist regional economic communities through technical assistance and through the financing of capital projects. These will help to integrate the various economic regions of Africa.

Second, to increase the number of trained Africans.

We have been devoting a large part of our aid funds for Africa to education. This proportion will increase.

This year we are assisting in the development and the staffing of 24 colleges and universities. We are financing graduate and undergraduate training for over 2,000 African students in the United States. Altogether, almost 7,000 African students are studying with us now. We are helping some 40 secondary and vocational training institutions in Africa. We are aiding 21 teacher training institutions while also providing thousands of teachers, mostly through our Peace Corps.

But these efforts are not enough. One of the greatest needs is to overcome the frustration of many qualified students who are unable to obtain a higher education.

To help meet that problem, we propose:

—to assist your effort to make certain African universities regional centers of training and professional excellence;

—to explore with your governments an African student program for deserving students to attend African universities.

Third, to develop effective communications systems for Africa.

Africa is an immense continent embracing 37 states with still more to emerge. Their communication links were formed in colonial times and tie them more to the outside world than to each other.

Africa's continental development needs a modern communications system to meet regional requirements.

The United States has already financed several capital projects for communication facilities. We have provided technical assistance to communication services in a number of countries. I have authorized new surveys looking to the widening of existing telecommunications.

Communication satellites offer a striking opportunity to make even greater advances. To use these satellites effectively, ground stations must be built to bridge the continent. They would provide the essential links between the satellite and the conventional networks.

The United States is prepared to assist in the building of these stations. We will examine the need for additional ground links to enable Africa to secure greater benefits from these satellites.

These immediate actions illustrate some of the opportunities for cooperative effort. Other possibilities deserve early study.

Africa's great distances require more modern road, rail, and air links. The continent's great lakes and rivers could provide an enormous internal transport network.

The development of regional power grids offers an exciting possibility for regional cooperation and for national growth.

Opportunities for investment are still largely untapped despite the fact that African countries have welcomed private enterprise.

Africa's farm production does not meet the nutritional needs of its fast-growing population.

African territories may need special help in training their people and in strengthening their institutions as they move toward self-government.

So we want to explore these and other ways to respond to African needs. I have instructed the Secretary of State and other American officials to review our own development policies and programs in Africa. We shall be seeking new ideas and advice from American scholars, businessmen, and experts concerned with Africa's problems.

Our Ambassador to Ethiopia, Ed Korry, will be working full-time in the weeks ahead to follow through these initiatives. We wish to discuss these new cooperative approaches and ideas with African governments, as well as with other governments and international groups.

The United States wants to respond in any way that will be genuinely helpful—from the private American citizen to a combination of many nations, from a bilateral effort with a single African country to regional programs.

Above all, we wish to respond in ways that will be guided by the vision of Africa herself, so that the principles we share—the principles which underlie the OAU Charter—come to life in conformity with the culture and the aspirations of the African peoples.

III.

It was once said of Americans that "With nothing are we so generous as advice. . . . We prefer being with people we do things for to being with people who do things for us." But it is no longer a case of what we can do for or even with the people of Africa. We have come to recognize how much we have to learn from you.

As one of the great Africans—Dr. James Aggrey—wrote: "If you go to Africa expecting something from us, and give us a chance to do something for you, we will give you a surprise."

As we have deepened our relations with you, we have learned that Africa has never been as dark as our ignorance of it; that Africa is not one place and one people but a mosaic of places and peoples with different values and with different traditions; that the people of Africa want to decide for themselves the kind of nations they wish to build.

We have learned not only about you but

we have learned about ourselves. We have learned more about our debt to Africa and about the roots of so many of our American cultural values and traditions.

The human enterprise of which we are all a part has grown through contacts between men of different tribes, different states, and different nations. Through those contacts we have learned new ideas, new insights into ourselves, new ways of looking at the universe of nature and—most importantly—new understanding of man's relation to his brothers.

It is this knowledge that endures.

It is this deepening appreciation and respect for the diversity of the world—each man and nation in it—that increases the possibilities for peace and order.

Your Excellencies, I hope that during your stay in our country you will look in on the African programs at our universities, foundations, and institutes. These programs are contributing to the mutual understanding we both seek.

In this connection, American publishers have produced hundreds of books about Africa in recent years. One of the most recent is this handsome volume on African art in American museums and in private collections.

This book was prepared for the U.S. In-

formation Service in Africa and it will help increase the understanding and the appreciation of your rich cultural heritage.

I would like you to accept a personal copy of this book as a memento of our meeting here in the East Room at the White House today.

The Organization of African Unity has become an important organ for building that peace and order. On this third anniversary my countrymen join me in asking you to come here this afternoon, and join me in saluting you and the people that you so ably represent.

Thank you very much.

NOTE: The President spoke at 6:55 p.m. in the East Room at the White House to the ambassadors of the 36 member states of the Organization of African Unity and some 300 guests. In his opening words he referred to Hubert H. Humphrey, Vice President of the United States, Dean Rusk, Secretary of State, and Ousmane Socé Diop, Ambassador of Senegal. Later he referred to Edward M. Korry, U.S. Ambassador to Ethiopia, and to Dr. James Aggrey (1875–1927), a native of Accra who after training in the United States served many years as a missionary and teacher in Africa.

At the close of his remarks the President presented to each African ambassador a gift copy of the book "African Art in American Collections" by Warren Robbins and R. H. Simmons (New York: Frederick H. Praeger, 1966).

The Charter of the Organization of African Unity was signed by 26 nations on May 25, 1963, in Addis Ababa, Ethiopia. The text of the Charter is printed in the United Nations Treaty Series (vol. 479, p. 39).

---

244   Letter to the Governor of Alaska on the Completion of the Last Major Step in the Transition to Statehood.   *May 27, 1966*

Dear Bill:

It gives me great pleasure to announce the completion of the last major step in Alaska's unique program of transition from territorial status to statehood.

The Director of the Bureau of the Budget informs me that he has signed deeds conveying the airports at Nome, Northway, Umiat, Summit, Gulkana, Cold Bay, Bettles and Cordova to your State. That action completes the transfer to Alaskan ownership of twenty-one small airports previously owned by the United States and operated by the Federal Aviation Agency.

When Alaska became a State in 1958, the Federal Government was still performing there many of the functions normally carried out by State and local governments, such as construction and maintenance of roads, law enforcement, the administration of justice, fish and wildlife management, provision of certain recreation and health services and the operation of a number of small community airports.

You, the citizens of Alaska, and the Federal Government—all working together—began to take actions immediately to make Alaska a State in fact as well as in name.

A major step in reaching that goal was the Alaska Omnibus Act (P.L. 86-70) which, along with provisions designed to give Alaska equal treatment with the other States, authorized a unique five-year program of transitional grants totalling $28.5 million to help the State take over the functions still being performed by the Federal Government. The Act also authorized the transfer to Alaska of Federal property used in connection with functions assumed by the State.

The transition has now been completed. The transfer of the last group of airports is the final step.

I am gratified that the transition has gone so well. I commend the employees of your State and the Federal Government, particularly the Federal Aviation Agency, who worked so cooperatively during this period. And I congratulate you and all Alaskans on assuming your new responsibilities so successfully.

Sincerely,

LYNDON B. JOHNSON

[Honorable William A. Egan, Governor of Alaska, Juneau, Alaska]

NOTE: This is the complete text of the letter, portions of which were read by Bill D. Moyers, Special Assistant to the President, at his news conference at 11:45 a.m. on Friday, May 27, 1966. It was not made public in the form of a White House press release.

The Alaska Omnibus Act (Public Law 86-70) is printed in the United States Statutes at Large (73 Stat. 141).

---

245   Statement by the President on the Fifth Anniversary of the Food Stamp Program.   *May 28, 1966*

WHEN the food stamp program took its first experimental step in McDowell County, the Nation watched to see if this Federal-State-local effort could effectively help low-income families share America's food abundance.

Today, with the enthusiasm and cooperation of State officials, welfare people, business interests, and the entire community of McDowell County, the food stamp program is helping well over 1 million people in some 300 areas throughout the country.

NOTE: The President's statement was made public as part of a White House release commemorating the inauguration of the Department of Agriculture's food stamp program on May 29, 1961, in McDowell County, W. Va.

Citing a report to the President from Secretary Freeman, the release pointed out that average gains of 8 percent in retail food sales follow introduction of the program into typical areas. This results in increased demand for the produce of local farmers, since "livestock products and fresh fruit and vegetables account for more than 80 percent of the increase in food used."

These figures reflect an improvement in the diet of participating families, the release added. "Needy households . . . buy food coupons with the money they would normally spend for food. They then receive additional coupons free of charge. These additional coupons, the Federal Government's contribution to the program, give the low-income households the added food-buying power they need to meet their nutritional requirements and to participate more fully in our agricultural abundance. The coupons are spent like money in retail food outlets authorized by USDA's Consumer and Marketing Service to accept them. Total coupons issued in March were valued at $17.3 million and bonus coupons issued amounted to $6.4 million" (2 Weekly Comp. Pres. Docs., p. 717).

The release concluded with a list of additional areas in 15 States scheduled to participate in the program by June 15.

Later releases concerning the expansion of the food stamp program appear in the Weekly Compilation of Presidential Documents (vol. 2, pp. 1193, 1273, and 1685).

246   Remarks at a Memorial Day Service in Arlington National Cemetery. *May 30, 1966*

Mr. Sutphin, Colonel Connett, General Wheeler, General Herrick, ladies and gentlemen:

There is a special roll of honor that I would like to call today:

—Lt. Colonel Seldon R. Edner of San Jose, California
—1st Lt. George B. Smith of Los Angeles, California
—1st Lt. Leland Williams of Taylor County, Texas
—1st Lt. Revier Harding of Fort Worth, Texas
—Staff Sergeant William Goodwin of Tacoma, Washington
—Lt. Colonel Alfred Medendorp of Grand Rapids, Michigan
—Lt. Colonel Frank Lynn of Chicago, Illinois
—Major Rudolf Anderson of Del Rio, Texas
—Specialist Fourth Class James T. Davis of Livingston, Tennessee.

Who were these men?

Edner was the first American killed in Greece where, in 1947, we decided to help the people of that country resist aggression.

Smith and Williams were killed in the airlift which prevailed over the blockade of Berlin in the winter of 1948 and 1949.

Harding and Goodwin were the first American soldiers killed in the struggle against aggression in Korea.

Medendorp and Lynn were killed on Kin-

man Island when in 1958 aggression was attempted in the Taiwan Straits.

Anderson was the airman that was shot down over Cuba during the crisis of 1962 when an effort was made to place offensive weapons on that island.

Davis was the first American killed in the resistance to aggression in Vietnam.

These men represent all those Americans who have risked their lives—and lost them—in the peace-building efforts that America has made since 1945.

They were sent on their missions because this Nation believes that peace is not something that just happens.

Peace does not come just because we wish for it.

Peace must be fought for. It must be built stone by stone.

In the first half of this century we learned that there can be no peace if might makes right—if force used by one nation against a weaker nation is ever permitted to succeed. We have learned that the time to stop aggression is when it first begins. And that is one reason we are in South Vietnam today.

Modern weapons and means of communications, even more than common aspirations, have created a single world community.

There is no going back. This is the way it will be as far ahead as any of us can see.

We can only go forward to help make that community one in which nations respect the rights of other nations and live at peace with one another.

For the American interest will be well served if our children grow up in a world of independent nations capable of assuming collective responsibility for the peace. Our interest—and the interest of world peace—will not be served if nations continue to violate the independence of other nations.

So, as our men and our allies today fight in Southeast Asia, we are working on many fronts to build a mosaic of peace and human progress.

We are working to strengthen the Atlantic world and, from that firm base, to build bridges of cooperation to the East.

We are trying to assist the governments and peoples of Latin America, Asia, and Africa to work together to lift the burdens of poverty and ignorance and disease.

We ache to turn all our energies—more of our resources—and all our talents to building that kind of world community.

But there will be no community to build if aggression achieves in Vietnam what it has been denied from Greece to Korea to Berlin.

The conflict in South Vietnam is confusing for many of our people.

The aggression there does not take the form of organized divisions marching brazenly and openly across frontiers.

It takes the form of men and equipment coming down from the North on foot or in trucks, through jungle roads and trails, or on small craft moving silently through the water at night.

It takes the form of well-organized assassination, kidnaping, intimidation of innocent citizens in remote villages. Last year, more than 12,000 South Vietnamese civilians were murdered or kidnaped by terrorists.

That kind of aggression is just as real and just as dangerous for the safety and independence of the people of South Vietnam as was the attack on South Korea in June of 1950.

Without the flow of men and equipment from the North, the war would soon end. But what our people see looks on the surface to some of them more like a civil war than external aggression.

Peace will never come to the world if the outcome of this kind of aggression—insurgency mounted from outside a nation—is accepted as a substitute or tantamount to free elections.

There is a second source of confusion. The people of South Vietnam are now in the midst of a historic transition. They are trying to form, for the first time, a constitutional government that represents their own traditions and values.

Their country has deep in its history strong regional feelings—and equally strong religious groupings—which have sometimes been in conflict.

As they try now to forge a constitutional system these differences seem to emerge sharply. Various groups clash as they seek to influence the shape of things to come. Turmoil results.

It is tragic, in the present turmoil, that some choose acts of desperation to express their political beliefs. This quite unnecessary loss of life only obscures the progress that is being made toward a constitutional government. It only clouds the sacrifices of thousands of lives that have already been made for the cause of independence and political hope in South Vietnam.

Seldom has a people been called upon to build a nation and to wage war against externally supported aggression at the same time. But I believe that South Vietnam is moving toward a government that will increasingly reflect the true will of its people.

That day will come sooner if the South

Vietnamese keep their internal quarrels and differences within bounds and concentrate on taking together their first steps toward constitutional government.

But there will be no transition to the politics of compromise and to the secret ballot if the external aggression against South Vietnam is not now defeated.

Our policy is devoted to that end.

As President Kennedy said just 2 months before his life was taken, "We want the war to be won, the Communists to be contained, and the Americans to go home. . . ."

We have sought to bring the conflict in Vietnam from the battlefield to the conference table. Twice we have stopped the bombings of military targets in North Vietnam as a sign of our desire to negotiate. And we waited and listened for 37 days—to get no satisfactory reply.

We have sought the help of the United Nations in arranging international peace talks.

We have sent emissaries to more than 40 nations asking them to urge our adversaries to reason with us.

We have sent word privately to Hanoi and to Peking of our willingness to talk without conditions.

We have told them that there are ways to end the bloodshed.

Nothing has happened.

Infiltration from the North has continued at an even higher pace. The fighting, as we speak, goes on. The infiltration is stepped up. The hordes come marching in.

So, until peace comes, or the Communists are willing to talk about peace, we must persevere.

I know of no time in our history when our brave men in arms have performed with greater skill or courage than they have performed in Vietnam.

They went into combat in a difficult climate, against a thoroughly professional enemy, in an unfamiliar kind of war. From the first day of combat they have not failed us once.

In Vietnam the United States is committed to a decent and a limited purpose: to defeat aggression and to let the people of Vietnam decide in peace their own political future.

So I pledge to those who have died there, and to those who have been wounded there—to those who are now fighting there, and to those who may yet fight there, that we shall help the people of South Vietnam see this through.

On this Memorial Day, it is right for us to remember the living and the dead for whom the call of their country has meant much pain and sacrifice.

And so today I remind all of my fellow countrymen that a grateful Nation is deeply in their debt.

NOTE: The President spoke at 11:18 a.m. in the Amphitheater at Arlington National Cemetery. His opening remarks referred to Robert F. Sutphin, President of the Memorial Day Corporation of the Grand Army of the Republic, Lt. Col. James A. Connett, Post Chaplain at Fort Myer, Va., Gen. Earle G. Wheeler, Chairman of the Joint Chiefs of Staff, and Maj. Gen. C. J. Herrick, Commanding General, Military District of Washington.

247   The President's News Conference of *June* 1, 1966

REVIEW OF CABINET MEETING

THE PRESIDENT. [1.]   Bill [1] thought that an efficient and effective way for handling your problem of coverage would be for me to review what transpired in our Cabinet meeting and to ask those who made the presentations to stay here and make a brief report to you, or at least to be available for any questions that you might have.

First, Secretary Gardner [2] presented the medical care picture, 15 or 20 minutes for the presentation of the number of signups, the progress that had been made in that field, the hospital and medical needs and problems, and so forth.   Secretary Gardner is here and will be available to you.

We reviewed the foreign aid program— what has been done in various parts of the world, our development loans, technical assistance, the Alliance for Progress, our international education and health proposals. Mr. Bell [3] reviewed the status of the legislation in the House committee and the Senate committee.   He is here and will take any questions.

We had a legislative forecast of various measures the administration has sent up. We had the chart over there.   Larry O'Brien and Joe Califano [4] will review that with you.

We went over the economic situation. Mr. Ackley [5] spent about 15 minutes reporting on the economic situation.

The civil rights conference was reviewed by the Vice President and Mr. Katzenbach,[6] both of whom were in attendance this morning.

We went into our savings bonds report from the departments and Mr. O'Brien talked on that for about 5 minutes.

I reviewed the meetings I have had with some 20 to 30 staff members of Mr. Rostow's [7] office, and the meetings I have had with the Under Secretaries of various departments, I went over with the Secretaries our exchange of ideas.

I also reviewed with them the meeting I had yesterday with the Assistant Secretaries.

We discussed earlier in my office with Mr. Ball [8] and others the agenda in Brussels this week.   We reviewed our policies in Africa and Latin America.   I am encouraged because the growth rate there for the last 3 years has been 2½ percent as compared to 1 percent in the preceding years.

We also mentioned the Southeast Asia situation, with particular reference to India and Pakistan and developments there following our meetings with the President of Pakistan and the Prime Minister of India.

PERSONNEL VACANCIES

[2.]   We talked with the Cabinet about certain personnel vacancies in certain departments.   We have very few vacancies. Mr. Macy [9] is here.   He can give you a report on it if you wish.

We have some six or eight ambassadorial

---

[1] Bill D. Moyers, Special Assistant to the President.

[2] John W. Gardner, Secretary of Health, Education, and Welfare.

[3] David E. Bell, Administrator, Agency for International Development.

[4] Lawrence F. O'Brien, Postmaster General, and Joseph A. Califano, Jr., Special Assistant to the President.

[5] Gardner Ackley, Chairman, Council of Economic Advisers.

[6] Nicholas deB. Katzenbach, Attorney General.

[7] Walt W. Rostow, Special Assistant to the President.

[8] George W. Ball, Under Secretary of State.

[9] John W. Macy, Jr., Chairman, Civil Service Commission.

vacancies, fewer than we have had any time in 5 years. We will have a vacancy in the Under Secretary of State for Economic Affairs, Mr. Mann's [10] place.

We have a couple of General Counsel vacancies, one in Defense and one in HUD. We have an Assistant Secretary vacancy over at Health, Education, and Welfare, and a Republican vacancy on one of the boards. The number of vacancies is very low, but we did review those.

SAVINGS BOND SALES

[3.] Mr. O'Brien reported that the first 3 weeks of the current bond campaign showed an increase from 60 percent to 64 percent.

Bond sales are up from $206 million to $330 million. The outstanding increases were in the Executive Offices, 59 percent to 67 percent; Department of State, 60 percent to 69 percent; Department of Labor, 46 percent to 55 percent; Civil Aeronautics Board, 70 percent to 77 percent; and General Accounting Office, 66 percent to 80 percent.

The May drive will be extended through June in order to achieve our goal of 75 percent participation. I am hopeful that the results obtained during our Federal Government campaign will set an example for the rest of the Nation.

If any of you have any specific questions on any of these subjects—Medicare, foreign aid legislation, personnel, civil rights, foreign policy—we will be glad to try to answer them.

---

[10] Thomas C. Mann, Under Secretary of State for Economic Affairs.

QUESTIONS

APPRAISAL OF THE ECONOMY

[4.] Q. Mr. President, on the economy, about 6 weeks ago you were trying to slow down. Now there seems to be a feeling that you have been, perhaps, too successful and you have slowed it down more than you would like. What would your current appraisal be?

THE PRESIDENT. No, we haven't reached that conclusion. We are studying all the indicators. The gross national product is exceeding our expectations, and we are trying to give careful attention to that and every other indicator.

We will have a rather detailed meeting on that this afternoon, and look at our revenues and our expenditures, among other things.

There is some indication that the estimates for this year will show that so far as our cash budget is concerned—and that includes all of our trust funds—we will probably take in more than we will spend.

It appears that we will actually have a cash surplus this year. But there is many a slip 'twixt the cup and the lip between now and January.

DISCUSSION ON VIETNAM

[5.] Q. Mr. President, did the Cabinet meeting include any kind of a general discussion or a report from Secretary McNamara [11] on the political situation in Vietnam?

THE PRESIDENT. No.

---

[11] Robert F. McNamara, Secretary of Defense.

[6.]   Q. Mr. President, were you talking about this fiscal year when you said——

THE PRESIDENT. This calendar year.

INDIA AND PAKISTAN

[7.]   Q. Mr. President, can you be any more specific about your discussion about India and Pakistan?

THE PRESIDENT. No. We reviewed the legislation on the billion dollar food program area, and the conferences we had with the Prime Minister when she was here.[12]

We were pleased with the progress that had been made at Tashkent[13] and the subsequent conferences with the President of Pakistan and the Prime Minister of India. We have a new American Ambassador going to Pakistan shortly,[14] and we have had new reports from India.

Our programs are proceeding according to plan, and we think that we have had very fruitful results from our meetings with the leaders of those two countries.

NATO POLICIES

[8.]   Q. Mr. President, did you develop any new policy lines on NATO at your meeting today?

THE PRESIDENT. We had an extended meeting earlier this morning. The full Cabinet did not participate in that. We will be having those meetings from time to time.

Secretary Rusk[15] will return in a few days from the Brussels meeting and will participate in further discussions with us. In his absence, Secretary Acheson,[16] Secretary Ball, Mr. Rostow, and Mr. Moyers will be working with their staffs in the NATO area.

Our policies are moving forward according to schedule. It is consuming a good deal of our time, but it is worthy of it. We have a deep interest in that area of the world—in Europe. We are appropriately devoting a good deal of our energies to them.

EAST-WEST TRADE BILL

[9.]   Q. Mr. President, did you discuss your East-West trade bill at all this morning, and what might be done to get it through Congress?

THE PRESIDENT. Yes, we did at our earlier meeting. That is an important part of our program for that area of the world. We are very hopeful that the Congress will agree with us on the wisdom of our proposals and in due time will act upon them.[17]

OPEN HOUSING PROVISION

[10.]   Q. Mr. President, did the open housing provision come up at the Cabinet meeting, particularly Senator Dirksen's stand on it?[18]

THE PRESIDENT. Yes. The Attorney Gen-

---

[12] See Items 148, 149, 152–154, 180, 311.
[13] Capital of the Soviet Republic of Uzbek in Central Asia and site of a conference between India and Pakistan in January 1966 which resulted in partial withdrawal of troops from the disputed Kashmir territory.
[14] Eugene M. Locke of Dallas, Texas.
[15] Secretary of State Dean Rusk, U.S. representative at the Brussels meeting of NATO foreign ministers.
[16] Dean Acheson, former Secretary of State (1949–1953) and Special Adviser to the Secretary of State on France and NATO March 15—June 17, 1966.
[17] The East-West trade bill was not adopted by the 89th Congress.
[18] See message on civil rights, Item 196. Senator Everett McKinley Dirksen, minority leader of the Senate, was opposed to open housing legislation.

eral discussed the hearings that have been held in the House. He felt that the hearings brought out some very excellent testimony. He is hopeful in due time action would be taken in the subcommittee and in the full committee, and we could get action in the House in a reasonable time.

WHITE HOUSE CONFERENCE ON CIVIL RIGHTS

[11.] Q. Mr. President, there seems to be some dissension among the civil rights leaders at the White House conference on civil rights.[19] Are you optimistic that they will come out with something productive from the conference?

THE PRESIDENT. We always have differences. I think maybe you are inclined not to overlook any of them. Of these differences, we hammer out a course that will result in making progress in this field—a field that we think desperately needs continuing attention.

We are very hopeful that under the leadership of this council, the 2,500 delegates can discuss the pros and cons of various proposals and give their judgments about the wisdom of undertaking them. All of them will be fully and thoroughly considered. We will do everything we can to continue to make rapid advances in the field of civil rights and justice.

I believe there are many more areas of agreement for us than there are disagreement. There are many more constructive things likely to come out of this conference than the little dissension and different viewpoints suggest.

Most of the delegates, I think, realize that there are many problems that must be faced; they have views on how to deal with them. They won't all be in agreement, but I wouldn't get upset about that, or excited.

---

[19] See Item 248.

BRIEFING OF REPUBLICANS ON VIETNAM

[12.] Q. Mr. President, Senator Dirksen seems to feel that the Republicans ought to be briefed on Vietnam. Do you agree with him?

THE PRESIDENT. I think I am pretty well aware of Senator Dirksen's feelings. He and I are pretty much in agreement. They are being fully informed.

Q. Does that mean you have had a briefing for them, or are planning one?

THE PRESIDENT. That means I had a rather extended talk with him in the hospital. As he told them up there the other day, I have had another since then with him. We spend a good deal—I would say a substantial portion of our time—either briefing them or you.

Q. Mr. President, in view of the situation now in Vietnam, is it your feeling——

THE PRESIDENT. We didn't really go into Vietnam here today in the Cabinet. But if you want to spend a little time on Vietnam, if you have a particular interest in it, I will answer your questions.

I am keeping the Cabinet here to answer your questions on the subjects they discussed. If you want to spend time on Vietnam, I will go into it.

VIETNAM ELECTIONS

[13.] Q. I just wondered, in view of the internal turmoil now, do you foresee that elections can go ahead on September 11?

THE PRESIDENT. We are concerned about the problems they are having out there, but, as I have said in the last two or three statements I have made, we realize the difficulties a nation has in proceeding to constitutional government. We are working with them to bring that kind of government about.

We are hopeful that it can be done as early

as possible. We solicit the support, the counsel, and assistance of everybody concerned in helping us attain it.

That kind of representative government is a much desired objective, and we believe that in time it is attainable. We are working very much to that end.

PROGRESS OF LEGISLATIVE PROGRAM IN U.S. AND OF ELECTORAL COMMITTEE IN VIETNAM

[14.] Q. Mr. President, regarding the legislative forecast here, because Congress may want to go home a little earlier this year than last, are you submitting any priority list to them on administration programs you have?

THE PRESIDENT. No. We try to avoid that old trap. When you list priority bills, a fellow's bill that is not included might cause him to get upset.

We make our recommendations and express the hope that all of them will be duly considered and acted upon. Of course, a good many of them will be modified and amended, and some of them will be postponed and delayed.

But I think we are making very good progress. We are very pleased with what the Congress is doing.

The last 3 weeks—I was reviewing this with some of them last night—we passed the assets participation bill, which was very important to us.

We passed the minimum wage bill in the House.

We have some other major pieces of legislation during that period—a substantial step in each direction.

We have our truth-in-packaging in the Senate now. It's very important.

We have our military construction up in the House today, and our narcotics bill.

So we are making solid progress right on down the road.

We are very concerned about our foreign aid in both the House and the Senate. We have completed our hearings.

I have asked each Cabinet officer to review all of their measures: Agriculture—the food for freedom bill and the REA financing; Interior—the various conservation bills; HUD—the rent supplement and the cities legislation; HEW—the Teacher Corps.

We are doing all of that. Most of these hearings are out of the way now. In a good many instances, one House or the other has already acted upon them. Now we will try to move as many of them as we can down the stretch. There is not anything that is a critical emergency, or anything that is in great difficulty that should cause us to panic.

I feel about our legislative program very much like I feel about the question on Vietnam. I don't think we should panic because we have some problems.

Politics is never easy in our country—even with all of our experience—and it certainly isn't easy in the midst of aggression like that being waged against South Vietnam. But with reasonable unity and proper diligence—and by constantly keeping in mind our national interest—we will achieve our objectives here and there.

I am encouraged by the progress we are making in Congress, and I am encouraged by the progress the electoral committee is making out there—although I don't get to follow its progress in the press as fully and in depth as I would like to. I have to go back and dig up some of the cables from day to day, because the progress that the committee is making in the electoral developments is not as headline-grabbing as some of the other distressing incidents.

Nevertheless, they are moving forward

step by step. While there will be missteps, the direction is sound.

That is about the same way here at home. There will be some missteps, but we are going in the right direction. I think that you will find that the historians will record that you lived in a period when we made greater progress in health, education, conservation, and development throughout the world than in any similar period in history.

It is a very exciting time to live in. There are many constructive things that we can all do. I know we all want to.

Q. I assume from what you say that Mr. O'Brien delivered a fairly optimistic report.

THE PRESIDENT. I don't believe in these "optimistic" or "pessimistic" terms. I would say it is a constructive report, one that shows progress. Probably 35 or 40 percent of our bills are already signed, and that many or more are already out of the committee and passed in one House.

If you had that kind of batting average when the session was over with, you wouldn't consider it a disaster. We want to make as much progress as we can, and we are doing that. You have to make allowance for certain criticisms.

I picked up the ticker the other day and read, I believe over a period of an hour, where there had been seven real denunciations. When it was added up, it didn't amount to much. At the end of the day, they passed the bill they were denouncing by a rather substantial vote.

There is nothing as dead as yesterday's newspaper, and the criticism. What we want to do is get that legislation passed.

What we want to do out in Vietnam is to have this electoral committee make progress. It may not make many headlines, but if it can bring about constitutional government, we will be very pleased.

REVIEW OF AID PROGRAMS

[15.] In our developments in NATO, Africa, Latin America, in this hemisphere, and India and Pakistan, the Philippines and Korea, and all of those areas of the world, we are encouraged and are proud of the progress that has been made. Mr. Bell reviewed that in some depth today. He pointed out that in a number of countries we have been able to reduce our assistance. He talked of what the future held for us in a rather comprehensive and successful program. It is working.

As I pointed out, in Latin America the growth rate is $2\frac{1}{2}$ percent, up considerably in the last 3 years.

We just returned from a visit to Mexico.[20] I had a chance a few weekends ago to spend an entire weekend with the Foreign Minister.[21] He told me never in the history of the two countries did we have a better relationship. All of the things that divided us, our differences, most of them had been solved—the water salinity, the Chamizal, the various things we had controversy about.

We didn't go into great depth country by country today. We discussed these general areas.

The answers are good. The economy is good. The employment is good. The wages are good. The profits are good. The farm income is good. So, as a people, we are doing well. We all have ambitions. We have higher goals and we want to do

---

[20] See Items 174–177.
[21] Antonio Carrillo Flores, Mexican Foreign Secretary.

better, but the reports today were constructive and encouraging.

POSSIBILITY OF TAX INCREASE

[16.] Q. Sir, can you say from your review of the economy whether you feel we are moving any further away or closer to a tax increase?

THE PRESIDENT. I think we just have to study this thing from day to day and take into account everything that is happening. We have to see how much Congress appropriates. We have to see what our revenue is. We have to discuss our expenditures and get good readings on that.

I don't want to make any prediction or do any speculating. You can see the inadvisability of doing that. If I even give the alternatives available to me, someone not really experienced is likely to predict that I intimated something that might affect the market 10 points, up or down. I know you don't want to be a party to anything like that.

Frank Cormier, Associated Press: Thank you, Mr. President.

NOTE: President Johnson's sixty-fourth news conference was held in the Cabinet Room at the White House at 12:55 p.m. on June 1, 1966, following his meeting with the Cabinet. Members of the Cabinet were present at the news conference.

248   Remarks to the Delegates to the White House Conference "To Fulfill These Rights." *June 1, 1966*

Mr. Randolph, Mr. Heineman, all the delegates to this Conference:

It was one year ago at Howard University that I called for a conference whose theme and title would be "To Fulfill These Rights." I said that its object would be to help the Negro American move beyond opportunity to achievement.

And now you have come tonight from every region of this great land, from every walk of life, to play your part in this momentous undertaking and in this great adventure.

You are here because you represent the humane and the progressive spirit of our people. Through two centuries of trial and triumph that spirit has moved the American democracy from an ideal to a powerful reality.

You are here tonight because your country needs your collective judgment. The dilemma that you deal with is too deeply rooted in pride and prejudice, too profound and complex, and too critical to our future for any one man or any one administration to ever resolve.

No matter how committed to its resolution, this issue is beyond the mastery of one man or one group of men.

So you are here, finally, because in your variety of background and circumstance you symbolize those who have a stake in including the Negro American in our society. And that is everybody—Negro and white, rich and poor, manager and worker, city dweller and suburbanite.

I do not mean to say that every American feels that he has such a stake, because if he did there would be no need for this Conference. Some believe that they can put enough miles or enough dollars between them and the Negro's problems to escape the consequences of those problems altogether.

Yet we know that the country is not large enough, nor any man wealthy enough, to offer or to gain a sanctuary from the effects of widespread poverty and widespread discrimination.

571

Some believe that the Federal Government can assume their personal responsibilities for justice to the Negro American. They contend, even when they refuse to admit it, that the mere existence of Federal funds and programs and civil rights laws makes private action unnecessary.

Yet we know that no national government, however enlightened, can by itself change the conditions of Negro life in America.

There are some who think that the Negro should be denied inclusion in our society. There are some, too, who counsel the Negro to refuse a share in the society, even where it is offered—to "go it alone," to seek and acquire power independently, so he may owe nothing to others.

Yet, I genuinely believe that our whole experience as a people is otherwise. Those who have tried to divide us have always ultimately failed. Those who have built castles of prejudice have seen them come crumbling down. Those who have whispered the counsel of despair and the counsel of separatism have been ignored.

For our beautiful America is not a planetary system with many atmospheres, and many calendars, and many temperatures. It is one large island of earth inhabited by mortal men of many races, and many faiths, and many colors of skin.

They all cry the same way. They all laugh the same way. If they are to build just and fruitful lives for themselves and their children, then they must do it here— and I earnestly believe we must do it together.

This does not require that righteous anger ever be silenced. This does not require that harmony be purchased at the price of individuals' freedom.

What it does require is a recognition that beneath the tumult of events that separate men from one another runs the thread of a common destiny. For we shall either move this Nation towards civil peace and towards social justice for all of its citizens, or for none.

We shall either find the means to open employment to all of our workers—to find decent housing for all of our families—to provide a good education for all of our American children—or we shall see the American promise spoiled for each of them.

So then let us pursue that promise not in dreary conformity, not in mutual suspicion and fear—but in the knowledge that freedom and justice cannot be the province of one race or nation alone.

In our quest of that promise, let each man give whatever he has to give.

If it be the courage to endure the scorn of bigots, let him give that.

If it be the wisdom and the patience to teach children that are born into blight and suffering, then let him give that.

If it be the chance of a job and the training it requires, then let him give that.

If it be the willingness to change old ways and to hear the cry of those in need, let him give that.

If it be the power to pass new laws, or to enforce and execute old laws with conviction and fairness and justice, then let him give that.

But men of reason who are honest with each other know that there is so much to be done that really we should have done a long, long time ago. If only then we had acted— if only then we had sought justice—we might have been spared the ordeal of conscience that has brought us in this room, together at this hour tonight.

But we did not act. For reasons of ignorance, or prejudice, or hate, or greed, or fear, or indifference, or blindness, or whatever, we waited—long—too long we have waited.

And now the awakening has come.

In the last 12 years it has increased in both strength and in will. Reason has insisted that it come. Courage—of the Negro, first, and then of the white who joined the cause of justice—has swelled its ranks. And we are acting.

More has been done than men thought possible just a short time ago: in stripping away legal barriers—in opening political opportunity—in attacking the lack of skills and jobs, and education and housing that are really the taproots of poverty.

In all of these efforts we have made mistakes. And we will make others, for we know too well our own weaknesses. We will arouse hopes, as we have already done, that cannot be quickly fulfilled.

But I came here tonight—at the end of a long day—to tell you that we are moving and that we shall not turn back.

There is evidence of hope, even beyond the legislation enacted and the programs started.

Not long ago a businessman from the Middle West wrote us a letter at the White House.

He had attended our planning conference last November that many had counseled me against. They had some recommendations on this one, too.

But he had returned home filled with a new awareness of the Negro's condition in America. And he seemed to be fired with a determination—a determination to improve those conditions and to improve them in his own backyard, in his home community.

He listed 17 steps that his city had taken since last November to open up new channels of communication between the races. This man had inspired many of those steps and he had taken a part in bringing all of them about.

He did not claim that he had single-handedly changed the terms of Negro life in his city for the better, because he knows that real change—visible, lasting change—will take time and money and the work of many hands.

But he had made a start. He had planted a seed—indeed, a whole row of seeds. And years from now there will be a harvest in this city in the Middle West, a harvest of hope where there might have been a howling desert of despair and bitterness.

Not every one of us can plant as many seeds as this man did, but each of us holds one of them in his hands. And together we can make a harvest for the generations to come.

So do not expect from me, or from any man, a miracle.

I see some of the distinguished persons here tonight from whom the hopeless people throughout this country do sometimes expect a miracle. But do not expect us, even working shoulder-to-shoulder together, to put right in 1 year or 4 all that it took centuries to make wrong.

I came here to tell you tonight that I am prepared to give my days—and such talents as I may have—to the pursuit of justice and opportunity for those so long denied them.

I will sleep tonight in the house where Lincoln slept. It was 100 years ago that a civil war was fought in this country to free the Negro from slavery. The Negro won that war, but he lost the battle still to come.

Emancipation was a proclamation, but it was not a fact. I came here tonight to tell you that in the time allotted me, with whatever energy and ability I have, I do not intend for history to repeat itself.

True, more legislation has been signed in the last few months, few years; true, Negro opportunity has been proclaimed. But we still must go on to make it a fact.

I came here to say to my friend Philip

Randolph and to my friend Ben Heineman, to every man and woman at this head table, to every member of the Council, and especially to every one of the 2,500 people whose children will remember that they came and they saw and they conquered here at this Conference in Washington: that your President may not agree with everything that you do, but he will consider everything you say, and that he believes that we are approaching this in the right way.

As Jefferson said, "I prefer the recommendations of the many to the judgment of the few."

A very perceptive and unusually alert reporter—and we do have some of them—in the Cabinet Room at the White House this afternoon was quick to point out to me some developments at the Conference and to ask me what comment I had on the "great dissension" that exists.

I said, "First, I want to observe that that is something that you people never overlook." But along with that dissension are a lot of people that are plowing the furrows that are going to come up with constructive ideas, with vision, and with a platform that will bring a lot of people into agreement on goals that we have yet to achieve.

I read in a newspaper coming out tonight a very fine column by a good friend of mine of many years. He went around the world with me and I called him back from a distinguished ambassadorial post to make my first appointment to the USIA to succeed Ed Murrow.

He was relating a conversation that he had had with a Philadelphia banker. We usually think of Philadelphia lawyers. But this banker was pointing out to him that they had employed a few Negro secretaries and clerks at the bank, but they had not yet gone much further.

Carl Rowan was discussing that question.

And I read on in the column, because I hoped he was going to say, before he ended, that he could give the Philadelphia banker an example. Well, we have a Negro, for the first time, on the Export-Import Bank that is dealing with all the nations of the world. We have a Negro on the Federal Reserve Board that is lending money instead of borrowing it.

Eleven percent of our population are Negroes and the Federal Government has 15 percent of its employees who are Negroes. We are proud of the work that they render.

We are not satisfied that we have attained equal and exact justice and equal employment, but I have been working at it very diligently for 5 years. And I am now going to give a good example of it, because I have a very unusual pleasure and pride to introduce to you a great soldier. I might say that the President of the United States does not often have the opportunity to introduce another speaker.

But I am glad that tonight I do have that opportunity. I am going to introduce to you one who 12 years ago established in the field of civil rights a beachhead from which we shall never retreat.

Since that day, he has already occupied two great offices—distinguished Justice of the Court of Appeals, and tonight a great Solicitor General of the United States of America. When he accepted this call and left his lifetime job to take a temporary one in this administration—not knowing how long it would be but realizing that it offered an opportunity to serve his country—I recall that he had argued already 33 major cases before the Supreme Court.

But he was really just in the kindergarten class then, because before he finishes his term he will probably have argued more cases before the Supreme Court than any other American. And let no man ever say that he is not a qualified lawyer and judge.

I am very proud that he serves my administration. I am very proud that his is the voice of the people of all the United States before the highest and greatest court of this land.

And nothing, I think, could be really more appropriate than that this man should speak to the first great national conference that has ever been called to really consider the rights and the opportunities of Negro Americans.

Now I consider it my high honor and my very great privilege to present to you the man who has been in the forefront and will continue to be in the forefront of all the battles for all the things that are good for our country—Thurgood Marshall, the Solicitor General.

NOTE: The President spoke at 10 p.m. at the Sheraton-Park Hotel in Washington to a dinner meeting of the Conference delegates. In his opening words he referred to A. Philip Randolph, President of the Brotherhood of Sleeping Car Porters, honorary chairman of the Conference, and to Ben W. Heineman, chairman of the board of the Chicago & Northwestern Railway Co., chairman of the Conference. Later he referred to Carl T. Rowan, who returned to journalism after serving as Ambassador to Finland and—following Edward R. Murrow—as Director of the United States Information Agency, Andrew F. Brimmer, member of the Board of Governors of the Federal Reserve System, Hobart Taylor, Jr., a Director of the Export-Import Bank of Washington who had served as Associate Counsel to the President and as Executive Vice Chairman of the Committee on Equal Employment Opportunity, and Thurgood Marshall, Solicitor General.

For the text of the President's commencement address at Howard University in Washington on June 4, 1965, his October 5 announcement of the planning session for the 1966 Conference, and his remarks at the November 16 reception for the participants, see 1965 volume, this series, Book II, Items 301, 548, and 613.

For the President's statement on August 25, 1966, upon receiving the final report of the Conference, see Item 408.

249   Statement by the President Following the Landing of Surveyor I on the Moon. *June 2, 1966*

OVERNIGHT the eyes of Surveyor I have become the eyes of the world on the moon. Another exciting chapter in the peaceful exploration of the universe is open for men to read and share.

Millions of Americans who stayed up late or got up early have already seen the remarkable pictures taken by Surveyor I on the moon this morning. Even now they are being displayed and printed around the world.

We have conducted our space program openly since the basic law creating the National Aeronautics and Space Administration was passed by the Congress in 1958. I am asking Mr. Webb and his colleagues to offer the best possible prints of these remarkable photographs to the world scientific community as soon as possible, as we did with the Ranger pictures from the moon and the Mariner IV pictures from Mars last summer.

We can be as proud of the openness of our space program as we are of its successes.

And I assure you that we are particularly proud today that Surveyor performed so well on its very first test flight.

The odds against achieving full success in such a difficult mission on the first flight were understandably great. This moment of triumph for all who have participated in the Surveyor project has been well earned, for back of Surveyor's perfect performance on this first flight are years of hard work, painstaking care, and brilliant engineering.

Today our Nation salutes the highly deserving team of scientists, engineers, technicians, and managers—in Government, industry, and the universities—who had a vision and the skills to pursue it successfully.

As the day approaches when men may land on the moon, it is of the greatest importance that we agree to exchange openly all information that could affect their safety and welfare. It is equally important that we preserve these regions for peaceful, scientific activities. I welcome the constructive approach of the Soviet statement of May 31

on a treaty I have proposed to cover these matters and hope that progress can be made rapidly.

NOTE: The Soviet statement to which the President referred is in the form of a letter dated May 30 from Foreign Minister Andrei Gromyko to United Nations Secretary General U Thant (U.N. Doc. A/6341).

For the President's statement of May 7 on the need for a space treaty and for his announcement on December 8 of agreement on a draft treaty, see Items 209 and 643.

250 Statement by the President Upon Transmitting to the Senate the International Labor Organization's Convention 122 Relating to Employment Policy. *June 2, 1966*

I HAVE today transmitted to the Senate, with the request for the advice and consent of that body for its ratification, Convention 122 of the International Labor Organization concerning employment policy. This convention, adopted at the International Labor Conference in 1964, is thoroughly in accord with this Nation's economic and legislative goals.

ILO Convention 122 provides that each member state shall declare and pursue, as a major national goal, an active policy designed to promote full and productive and freely chosen employment.

A major aim of this policy, as enunciated in the convention, is the fullest possible opportunity for suitable employment irrespective of race, color, sex, religion, political opinion, national abstraction, or social origin.

The Government of the United States can and does wholeheartedly associate itself with the philosophy and intent of Convention 122.

The convention parallels our own Employment Act of 1946. That act declared the continuing policy and responsibility of the Federal Government to be the use of all practical means to foster and promote conditions under which there will be afforded useful employment opportunities—including self-employment—for all those able, willing, and seeking to work, and to promote maximum employment.

This policy has been strengthened by a number of our country's statutory and administrative actions. The 1964 Manpower Report declared the aim of the Government to insure all men the self-respect and economic security that flows from full use of their talents.

This aim, reiterated in the 1965 Manpower Report, has been given much impetus in recent legislation. The Manpower Development and Training Act of 1962, the Economic Opportunity Act of 1964, the Civil Rights Act of 1964 with its equal employment provisions, and the Public Works and Economic Development Act of 1965—all directed toward the goal of affording all our workers the opportunity of participating in our economic life on a full and nondiscriminatory basis.

It is in the spirit of this philosophic and legislative history that I express the hope that the Senate of the United States will, in its wisdom, give favorable consideration to ratification by our Government of Convention 122 of the International Labor Organization.

NOTE: The proposed convention was still pending in the Senate at the end of 1966.

251   Message to Provisional President García-Godoy Following the Election in the Dominican Republic. *June 2, 1966*

FEW PRESIDENTS have had a more complicated task than the one you successfully accomplished yesterday.

You led the Dominican people from the turbulence of civil strife to the tranquility of free elections. There can be no greater tribute.

On behalf of the United States Government and people I express sincere admiration for your wisdom, courage and tenacity.

LYNDON B. JOHNSON

[Honorable Hector García-Godoy, Provisional President, Dominican Republic]

252   Remarks to Members of the Governors' Conference Subcommittee on Traffic Safety. *June 3, 1966*

Governors and ladies and gentlemen:

I am very grateful for your taking time out to come here to discuss the highway safety problem with us.

I have given thought to your replies to my letter of last March. There is no doubt in my mind that the real key to solving the problem will finally lie in your hands.

The Federal Government can and will be of such help as is possible. We think we can help with national safety standards. We think we can help with some money that may be available. We will try to contribute to research and provide such leadership as we have, but the ultimate responsibility must, should, and will finally rest back home.

We know the statistics on this subject are national statistics. People are getting killed every day on the roads in Texas, Kansas, California, Nebraska, and the other States. So you have a legal responsibility.

The Federal Government does not wish to issue the drivers' licenses. You, not the Federal Government, should inspect the vehicles or see that they are inspected. Your able and effective State troopers enforce the traffic laws. What you do not always have are the essential resources. That is what we in Washington are trying to help you obtain.

We believe that our people throughout the Nation in every State are concerned. We believe that they are aroused. We have been building up to this point for a long time. We realize that the time has come now to try to move forward—to take new and necessary steps.

Since the automobile was first invented, we have had 1,500,000 deaths from automobile accidents. That is three times as many as our enemies have ever been able to kill in all of our wars.

Between 1961 and the end of last year, motor vehicles killed many more times as many of our servicemen as the Vietcong were able to kill in Vietnam.

Automobile accidents kill or injure more

of our children and teenagers than any single disease that we have in this country. We must think of the untold grief and suffering brought to the homes throughout this land by these accidents. We must think of the lost lives and the lost opportunities.

Over the last Memorial Day weekend, 540 Americans died. That is the highest toll for any holiday in the history of the United States.

These statistics have become all too commonplace. But complacency must never stand in the way of progress, in the way of safety, or in the way of doing something about this very difficult problem. Indifference must no longer be excused.

Anything which touches the lives of so many citizens asks for Government action. The people ask for it. I believe with your help, with your leadership, we are going to get that action.

For the first time in our history we are going to face this traffic safety problem squarely. I believe we will conquer it.

The traffic safety legislation that I have sent the Congress will move us out of the age of ignorance. I believe it will establish a program of strict national standards for automobiles. I cannot stress too strongly the need for these standards.

The only alternative is unthinkable—50 standards for 50 different States. I believe

that this would be chaotic.

The legislation that we have proposed will give us the resources to try to find out what causes the accidents. We are going to take a good, hard look—unemotionally and unsentimentally—at all the factors: the car, the road, the driver.

This legislation will let us apply that knowledge to the manufacture of safer automobiles and the construction of safer highways, and it will give us the necessary tools to develop and implement your own State safety programs.

The time for action has come. The need for standards is here. Every day that we postpone, more lives will be wasted. Every day lost puts us that much further behind.

So I would like to ask you to keep in touch with us through Governor Farris Bryant, as we move this program forward. I believe it will benefit every man, woman, and child in all of your States.

NOTE: The President spoke at 11:29 a.m. in the Cabinet Room at the White House.

The President's letter of March 24 to the Governors, to which he referred early in his remarks, was not made public.

For remarks by the President on September 9 upon signing the National Traffic and Motor Vehicle Safety Act and the Highway Safety Act, see Item 449.

Farris Bryant, Director of the Office of Emergency Planning and former Governor of Florida, was also serving as the President's liaison officer to the Governors.

253   Remarks to Members of the National Council of Senior Citizens. *June 3, 1966*

President Edelman, Under Secretary Cohen, Commissioner Ball, the officers and members of the National Council of Senior Citizens:

It is fitting that we should come together once more on the eve of a great new era for older Americans. Next month the medical

care program that you and I labored so long and so hard for will become a cherished reality.

We hope that never again will an older American need to go without basic medical care simply because he can't afford it.

We hope that never again will children

and grandchildren have to sacrifice their future to pay the medical bills of the older members of their family.

We hope that never again will our aged be threatened with economic ruin whenever illness strikes them.

Medical care will free millions from their miseries. It will signal a deep and lasting change in the American way of life. It will take its place beside social security, and together they will form the twin pillars of protection upon which all our people can safely build their lives and their hopes.

There will be problems at first while we make up the ground that we have lost through years of neglect. Doctors and nurses, hospital beds and personnel, will be in short supply in some communities. To make up the most ground in the shortest time, we will need all the help that we can get.

I have asked you this morning—you and every one of your local organizations—to get in there and help all that you can.

Please tell your members and your friends to cooperate with their physicians in scheduling their hospitalization. Alert your hospitals to the requirements of the law, particularly the nondiscrimination requirements of title VI. Encourage them to meet those requirements.

Above all, help your health officials to evaluate the impact that medical care will have on local facilities. Be the leaders and the doers in modernizing and expanding those health facilities.

Together we must—and we can—make this program work. Together we will guarantee older Americans the care that they need and the care that they deserve. Together we can quicken the race and add to the number of successes already achieved.

In the past 2½ years we have increased appropriations for health and education by

almost $10 billion. Some of it has trained more doctors, dentists, and nurses. Some of it has built more hospitals and nursing homes. All of it has been well spent. But it is just the beginning of the greater returns and rewards that we really have a right to expect.

So I do not see Medicare as a problem. I do not believe the few of little faith who have said that it would fail. I see it as a blessing. I say it will succeed. I see it as a beginning and not an end. I say it is another battle in the large struggle to ennoble man's life. And I ask—and I expect—every man's hand to join with mine in that.

Several weeks ago, I told the United Auto Workers convention that was then meeting in California that we just have not started to think honestly about how to give meaning to that part of life which lies beyond the age of 60 or 70.

So let us begin today.

Let us start here and now to build a new ideal of what ought to be the meaning of growing old. Let us here proclaim a bill of rights for older Americans. And let us make it our guide in the years ahead.

What will we have in that bill of rights?

The first right is the right to an adequate income. In 1936, with the passage of the Social Security Act, we built an income floor in America for millions of retired workers. Since then we have raised that floor and broadened it for the benefit of nearly every American over 65.

But that floor is still too low. Nearly 5½ million of our senior citizens still live in poverty and many, many more on incomes that cover only the barest essentials of life. And we intend to improve and to try to help correct this.

The second right is the right to a decent home. Since the beginning of 1964, our commitments for senior citizens' housing have already increased from 110,000 to nearly 175,000 units—an increase of nearly 60 percent. And while these 175,000 units will house more than a quarter of a million older people, it is obvious that we have just begun to scratch the surface.

The 1960 census shows us that nearly 3 million elderly families were living in totally inadequate housing. We would like to correct this. We intend to correct this. We want to give every senior American a dwelling that is not only adequate, but also designed for his particular comfort and safety. One of the most promising answers to this special problem is the new rent supplement program that is now before Congress that will permit private building to help us solve this great problem.

The third right is the right to a meaningful retirement. A great nation cannot just put its older citizens on the shelf. It must provide a life for them where leisure has purpose and purposes give fulfillment. Some of our senior citizens want to work, and they should be given that right. Some of them want to go back to school, and they should be given that right. Some of them want to develop new skills and hobbies, and they should be given that right. And some want to volunteer their services in community programs, and they should be given that right.

I see all of these as major and attainable rights—not just distant dreams, but practical goals to reach for today if there is to be a truly great society tomorrow.

But essential to them and underlying each is the basic right of every older American to a decent income. It is a major objective of this administration to improve the level of benefits provided by our social security system. As your President, I have already signed into law provisions increasing social security benefits for more than $1½ billion a year, an increase already of some 7 percent.

Yet, notwithstanding that, too many of our older citizens are still struggling along on shoestring incomes, suffering real hardships and suffering real need. Social security benefits are the major source of retirement income for just about all older Americans. For half of them they are the only source. Now average benefits of $80 a month for a retired worker and $142 a month for a couple are just not good enough—and not nearly fair or not nearly decent enough.

I propose, therefore, that we increase social security benefits across the board for the entire 21 million beneficiaries now on the rolls: retired older people, disabled people, the widows and the orphans—and for those who will come on the rolls in the future. I think it will make for a better future not just for older Americans, but for just about every family today and tomorrow.

I have already asked the Secretary of Health, Education, and Welfare to develop for me proposals for the improvement of social security benefits in time for the next session of Congress. This will be a very high and a very major priority on my agenda.

Now I want to close by thanking you and your organization for the contribution that you have already made to the Medicare program. You have helped to inform millions of its purpose by your role in Medicare Alert. You deserve much of the credit for the gratifying results. Ninety percent of all the people 65 or over in this country—17,200,000 persons—are now signed up to pay $3 a month for the voluntary part of the program covering physicians' fees. I doubt if ever before in history that many people in so short a period ever agreed to any single thing.

We are not just hoping for success in this

580

program, we mean to try to guarantee success. Last night we sent telegrams to 200 of the Nation's top medical and hospital leaders. On June 15 they will meet with me here at the White House for a final examination of the future of medical care—to review every plan, to discuss every problem, to take every necessary step that we can anticipate in advance to make sure that the reality of Medicare matches the hopes that we have had for the last 20 years.

I think that you agree with me that we are not concerned with appearance; we are concerned with achievements. We are concerned with accomplishments.

I thank you from the bottom of my heart for standing by us over the years. I count on your support in the exciting and challenging days ahead.

I think it was Thomas Jefferson who said of the Presidency: "It is a splendid misery." With all the miseries that the President has every day, the strength that comes to him that permits him to overcome them and to endure them, without succumbing to them, comes in the knowledge and satisfaction he gets from knowing that in efforts like yours

and ours together your country has made substantial progress toward helping 17,200,-000 to lift this yoke and this burden that has been around their necks and on their backs all these years, and to give them a feeling of dignity, independence, and confidence that will permit them to go on and live out their remaining 10, 15, 20, or 30 years in confidence—and with a minimum of discomfort and with a maximum amount of proper treatment and proper care.

That is a satisfaction that means a lot to me. And it ought to mean a lot to you, because you have had so much to do with bringing it about.

Thank you.

NOTE: The President spoke at 12:17 p.m. in the Rose Garden at the White House after receiving the Award of Merit of the National Council of Senior Citizens. In his opening words he referred to John Edelman, President of the Council, who presented the award, Wilbur J. Cohen, Under Secretary of Health, Education, and Welfare, and Robert M. Ball, Commissioner of Social Security. Later he referred to John W. Gardner, Secretary of Health, Education, and Welfare.

For the President's remarks by telephone on May 20 to the convention of the United Automobile Workers of America in Long Beach, Calif., see Item 235.

254 Statement by the President on the Fifth Anniversary of the Central American Common Market. *June 4, 1966*

ON THIS fifth anniversary of the Central American Common Market, we salute our Central American friends for what they have accomplished by placing the common good of the region above more narrow interests.

The facts speak for themselves: Trade between the five partner-nations has more than quadrupled since the Common Market came into being 5 years ago. In 1960 intraregional trade amounted to $32 million;

in 1965 it amounted to $130 million.

This is a triumph for idealism plus good business sense.

It is no coincidence that in 1965 the Central American region as a whole achieved an increase of 2½ percent in gross national product per capita, which is the yearly minimum target of the Alliance for Progress. This achievement stems from the same spirit of enlightened statesmanship and imaginative self-help which have made the Central

American Common Market one of the brightest success stories in Latin American development.

We hail the Central American Common Market as a giant stride toward the eventual goal of Latin American regional economic integration. What it has accomplished in so short a time should serve as a stimulus for the achievement of the larger goal. We pledge our continuing support for this

young, progressive Central American institution—and for the Latin American regional movement—which are so fully in keeping with the Charter of Punta del Este.

NOTE: The Central American Common Market was established by the Charter of the General Treaty on Central American Economic Integration, signed on December 13, 1960, at Managua, Nicaragua, by Guatemala, El Salvador, Honduras, Nicaragua, and Costa Rica. It went into effect on June 3, 1961. The text of the Charter is printed in the United Nations Treaty Series (vol. 455, p. 3).

255 Statement by the President Upon Signing Bill Authorizing Conveyance to Utah of Lands Bordering the Great Salt Lake. *June 4, 1966*

I HAVE signed S. 265, a bill "To authorize the conveyance of certain lands to the State of Utah based upon fair market value."

This bill authorizes the immediate conveyance to Utah of 250,000 acres of Federal land, which border the Great Salt Lake. It allows Utah up to 6 years to determine whether it wishes to pay the fair market value of the land as determined by the Secretary of the Interior. It provides for the reversion of the land to the United States if Utah decides not to pay for all of it. It authorizes Utah to make leases with private parties for use of the land on any terms and conditions it chooses, which leases will be binding on the United States, even if the land reverts to the United States.

I have been assured by Governor Calvin L. Rampton of Utah that the Utah State Land Board will issue leases only on terms and conditions acceptable to the Secretary of the Interior. Inasmuch as this land may

revert to the United States, I consider this assurance to be essential to approval of the bill and to the future administration of these potentially valuable lands. In addition I have the assurance of Governor Rampton and the sponsor of the bill, Senator Frank E. Moss, that the State of Utah will purchase the Federal interest in the land at fair market value.

In order that the national interest be fully protected I shall submit to Congress next week an amendment to this law requiring the approval of the Secretary of the Interior of all State leases on this land. I am advised that the appropriate committees will act expeditiously.

NOTE: The statement was read to the press on Saturday morning, June 4, 1966, at San Antonio, Texas. It was not made public in the form of a White House press release.

As enacted, S. 265, approved on June 3, is Public Law 89-441 (80 Stat. 192). An amendment to the bill was approved by the President on August 23, 1966 (Public Law 89-542, 80 Stat. 349).

256 Remarks in Response to Emergency Board Report on the Airlines Labor Dispute. *June 7, 1966*

FIVE WEEKS ago I appointed an emergency board to investigate the dispute between five major domestic airlines and the union. That board has now submitted its report to me.

The dispute between the airline companies and the union threatens to cripple the vital flow of people and products across America. These airlines fly 6 out of every 10 domestic passenger miles. Over 35,000 airline employees are involved—from mechanics to flight deck personnel.

The issues are complex and important. Eight national issues involved all of the companies; 40 local issues involved four of the companies. The recommendations of the board reflect the highest order of judgment, imagination, and wisdom.

I appreciate the work that this board has done. Its three members—Senator Wayne Morse of Oregon, Professor Richard Neustadt of Harvard University, and David Ginsburg, a Washington attorney—have unselfishly taken time from their busy lives to devote to this case.

Together, these men worked many long days patiently gathering and analyzing the evidence. They heard testimony from all of the parties—presented with great conviction and skill. A record of almost 2,000 pages has been compiled. On this record, this independent and able board arrived at its recommendations.

Those recommendations form the framework for a just and prompt settlement, which is in the national interest.

Without such a settlement, there would be a disruption of the movement of men and materials needed to support our commitments to freedom's cause throughout the world. Hundreds of thousands of citizens who depend on rapid, convenient airline service will have to go without it.

I do not believe that either labor or management wants this.

Ever since the day I became President, I have asked labor and management to work together with me to improve the lives of every American. They have responded to this call. Today, they have another opportunity—and obligation—to show the Nation the progress that can come from mutual trust and cooperation.

NOTE: The President spoke at 5:40 p.m. in the Cabinet Room at the White House.

The 67-page report presented the board's findings in its investigation of disputes between Eastern Airlines, Inc., National Airlines, Inc., Northwest Airlines, Inc., Trans World Airlines, Inc., and United Air Lines, Inc., and their employees represented by the International Association of Machinists (NMB Case No. A-7655).

The board was established by Executive Order 11276 of April 21, 1966 (2 Weekly Comp. Pres. Docs. p. 557; 31 F.R. 6233; 3 CFR, 1966 Comp., p. 106).

See also Items 322, 360.

257 Remarks at the Ceremony Honoring the Presidential Scholars of 1966. *June 7, 1966*

Secretary Gardner, distinguished scholars, your parents, your teachers:

Every week I welcome dozens of visitors to this historic White House. I greet distinguished men and women from every walk of life and from every corner of our land. But the most honored guests are always those who are set apart by high achievement.

So I welcome you here today as members of very distinguished company. Of course, I am very happy that you are younger members, because ever since my early days as a teacher I have been interested in and attracted to the young. I have tried to keep young by meeting with the young and learning from them.

Last week I met with the graduating class from the high school where I taught in Texas, almost 30 years ago. Today I meet with you. Tomorrow I will meet out here with more than 1,000 students from the rural electric cooperatives from every State in the Union.

And by the end of the week I should feel, and I hope I do feel, as young as you do.

I have asked you to come here so that I could thank you and compliment you and your teachers and your parents. But I also want to challenge you. So this afternoon I bring you more than a medallion to mark your honor. I bring you the pride and the hope of a Nation that cherishes excellence and commitment, and that has never needed your kind of excellence and commitment more than it needs it right now.

You have been born into an age which will give you no rest. You will find that there is no security on this earth, except the security of opportunity. You will discover that democracy has never been more a voyage of adventure, and never less a safe harbor, than it is in the time in which you live. And as long as you live, you will make that voyage in a world awash with waves of turbulence and change.

Our dizzying ability to discard the old and to create the new; our giant leaps in travel and quantum jumps in communication; our marvelous capacity to shrink the world and our terrifying ability to destroy it—all these and more are the challenges that surround you. They make standing still impossible and retreat unthinkable for the young scholar, the young businessman, the young farmer—every member of your generation.

The world that your elders have created is full of promise, but it is far from perfect. We stand now, your generation and mine, where Robert Frost had his mounted rider pause and say: "But I have promises to keep, and miles to go before I sleep."

As young people you probably feel like the horse in that famous poem. You shake your harness and you are eager to get on. I hope you are, because tomorrow is coming up very fast behind you.

Today, almost half our population is already under 30 years of age. In 5 years almost half our people will be under 26 years of age. But it is not your numbers alone that make you so important. Your Government does not count you as faceless digits. Your country does not count you as punched holes in a manpower computer card. We do not count you. What we really do is count upon you.

We count upon you as individuals. We prize your individuality. We work here in Washington to encourage and to enlarge it—to give your individualism new room and new reason to grow.

We are moved by a first principle that should be familiar to you as scholars—Plato's timeless insight that "States are as the men are, they grow out of the characters of men."

So we look to you for the qualities of national greatness. Your country looks to your character, your convictions, your individual commitment to the ideals of democracy—and to the works of democracy without which the ideals are just so many dime-store decorations.

I do not believe that you want it said of your generation that you committed social suicide. I do not believe you want it said of any American boy or girl that they squandered their lives in small and petty pursuits. I do not want the finger to point at a single one of you and say: "There is the spoiled fruit of affluence—soft at the core." And neither do we want the judgment on this Nation to read: Its children were pampered and without purpose.

You will have to earn your tomorrow. Many of your grandfathers and grandmothers—and some of your parents—built this Nation by hand and will, by day and by night and against the elements, the circumstances, and great odds. They succeeded because they looked not to themselves but to those who followed—to their children and their children's children—to the birthright of a better life their sweat and sacrifice would buy for you.

Yes, that was yesterday. But today the questions that hold the answer to the future are not very different. I ask them now of you—and I ask them now of every member of your generation: Who are you thinking of? What will you build? How much will you leave behind?

Not long ago they called you "The Silent Generation." But you proved them wrong and you didn't need the electric guitar to do it. Then it was "The Shook-Up Generation." And now it is "The Beat Generation." Well, I do not believe the labels, but I do believe in young people and I do believe in you. I believe in you for what you are—individuals and individualists. I believe in your spirit and your spunk. And I think you have shown plenty of both.

The Presidential Scholars program has been running 3 years. In the first year the commission picked a girl named Lucille Toly. In the third year, this year, they picked her sister, Caroline Toly. The odds against this are huge in such stiff competition. No wonder the commission was so surprised when told that it had picked two girls from one family out of the 200 million people who live in this country. The girls are the daughters of Michael T. Toly, a sheetmetal worker in Seattle, Washington, and a member of Local 99 of the Sheetmetal Workers Union.

A sheetmetal worker's daughters achieving intellectual distinction is an "only-in-America" story. And every American is so proud that that could happen here in our country.

Now it shows that in your generation that you have zest and you have zeal and you have love of life. And it shows in your concern for life—your willingness to fight poverty and to win social justice at home and throughout the world. It shows in the courage and independence of your ideas. And it shows your impatience with the old prescriptions.

It shows in your search for a new and more meaningful identity, your conviction that morality and responsibility must always guide your quest. It shows in your appraisal of modern society and giant organizations—in your recognition that both must still serve and not master the individual.

So your opportunity today lies in working for your country and for your fellow citizens—on voter education, in civil rights programs, in city planning and in management, in countless problem areas.

It lies in the Peace Corps and in the Teacher Corps and in VISTA—and as my daughter, Luci, reminded me a few moments ago, in the Volunteers for Vision.

Yes, opportunity and challenge meet also in the obligations of military service when that kind of duty is necessary. We wish that it were never necessary, but unfortunately we do not live in a world where the wish is father of reality.

We live in a world where men still pursue their ambitions with force. And there is no escape hatch from this kind of reality—not yet, anyway.

There will always be some, of course, who share the view of the young man who last week excused himself by saying that "Patriotism just doesn't turn me on." Well, nobody wants to turn him off, either. No American, young or old, must ever be denied the right to dissent. No minority must be muzzled. Opinion and protest are the life breath of democracy—even when it blows heavy.

But I urge you never to dissent merely because someone asked you to or because someone else does. Please know why you protest. Know what it is that you dissent from. And always try, when you do disagree, to offer a choice to the course that you disapprove. For dissent and protest must be the recourse of men who, in challenging the existing order, reason their way to a better order.

I was delayed seeing you a little bit today, because three distinguished Americans—Senator Morse, Professor Richard Neustadt, and a distinguished young lawyer, Mr. David Ginsburg—who make up an emergency labor board, have been reasoning together between employer and employee to avoid a crippling nationwide airline strike that would ground the planes that haul 6 out of 10 people in this country.

There has been protest and there has been dissent. There has been a demand for a change from existing order. They want to go to a better order. But these three men, appointed by the President, have been hearing the pros and cons and the improvements and the problems. They have collected 2,000 pages of testimony. This is the way it should be.

Yes, we can always be a young country. We can always be a people of the future. We can be that nation that was foreseen by Senator Cass of Michigan more than a century ago when a French visitor asked him: "If this be the youth of the Republic, what will be its old age?"

"Sir," the Senator replied, "it will have no old age."

Thank you very much.

NOTE: The President spoke at 5:50 p.m. on the South Lawn at the White House. In his opening words he referred to John W. Gardner, Secretary of Health, Education, and Welfare. During his remarks he referred to, among others, Senator Wayne Morse of Oregon, Richard Neustadt, and David Ginsburg, members of an emergency board on the airlines labor dispute (see Item 256), and Lewis Cass, Senator from Michigan, 1845–1857.

The 121 Presidential Scholars of 1966, announced by the President on May 28, were chosen for their superior intellectual attainment and potential from among the Nation's outstanding secondary school graduates. The Scholars were selected by an independent commission appointed by the President and headed by Dr. J. E. Wallace Sterling, president of Stanford University. The group included at least one boy and one girl from each State, the District of Columbia, and Puerto Rico. Two were selected from among Americans living abroad.

In announcing the selection of the 1966 Scholars, the White House release stated that there were 63 boys and 58 girls. "They will study at 61 colleges. Fourteen are going to Harvard, 12 to Radcliffe, 7 to Yale, 6 to Stanford, 5 each to Cornell and the Massachusetts Institute of Technology, and 3 each to Oberlin College and the University of Michigan. No other college will be receiving more than two. Nineteen of the Scholars intend to major in mathematics, 8 in English, 6 each in chemistry, physics, and engineering, and 20 are undecided. Five Scholars plan to study medicine. The other 41 Scholars are divided among 24 fields of study."

The names of the 1966 Presidential Scholars and of the members of the commission which selected them are printed in the Weekly Compilation of Presidential Documents (vol. 2, p. 714).

258   Remarks to Student Winners of a Contest Sponsored by the National Rural Electric Cooperative Association. *June 8, 1966*

My good friend, Clyde Ellis, members of the Association, students:

Clyde Ellis has just told you that your annual Washington visit is the result of a suggestion that was made several years ago. I am very proud of that. I wish all my suggestions were carried out so faithfully for so long.

I am delighted, with Mrs. Johnson, to greet and welcome you to the White House today. I believe deeply in your effort to learn more about your Government. I have strong feelings about the program which is responsible for your being here—the rural electrification program.

You are a bit young, perhaps, to remember the days when rural America lived in darkness; when farm families gathered in the kitchen in winter because it was the only warm room; when a mother did her sewing and her children did their homework by the flicker of a kerosene lamp.

You are perhaps too young to remember the first days of the REA—that exciting time when lights went on across the land and families went into their front yards at night to see their windows glowing. The farmer and his wife learned then the happiness of being freed from the backbreaking work that had been their heritage.

There are many of us here, though, today who do remember—and for us the greatest proof that all the effort, all the political combat, all the struggle was worth it, is to see the young people who have benefited from our efforts—young people who will never have to remember the darkness.

Rural electrification wasn't an isolated event in our history. It was part of a con-

tinuing revolution in America which has brought the marvels of science and technology within the reach of all.

Today we are still in the midst of that revolution. And today, more than ever before, progress brings problems as well as promise.

The pace of change is getting faster. In earlier ages, man had trouble learning to change fast enough, but today we are faced with the difficulty of keeping up with our own progress. We have thrust ourselves headlong into the world of the satellite and the computer—and we have learned again that power to create also means power to destroy, that power to produce means also the power to pollute, that power to change destroys old values.

So you will inherit this technical revolution—and you will face the same question that it poses for your elders: Will man be the master or the servant of his inventions? Will our future be one of growing happiness—or growing confusion?

Before long, you will be able to span this continent—or the Atlantic Ocean—in 2 hours or less. This new mobility will bring its problems—for the old certainties of time and place will never be the same again.

You may someday learn your lessons by engaging in long conversations with a computer. Your diseases will be diagnosed with the help of a computer, and you may gain added life from an artificial heart or transplanted organs. Every one of these developments raises serious questions for you—some of them as deep and mystifying as life itself.

In your future, jobs requiring little imagination can easily be performed by machines; clerical and maintenance work will grow more scarce. Your generation will be required to think seriously about the proper function of human beings—when our old ideas of work are no longer useful to us any more.

In your lifetime, space will become more crowded and less quiet. You will be faced not only with the problem of achieving peace on earth but perhaps on the moon as well.

It will be commonplace for you to see live television programs relayed by satellite from the other side of the world; you will dial telephone calls to Europe and Africa. And this progress, too, will present a problem: What good is it to know more about the world, unless we really understand more?

A while ago I received a report from the National Commission on Technology and the Economy—a study which lays down some very stern challenges for the next 10 years.

By 1975, just a few years away, the experts tell me more than 18 million more Americans will need jobs than in 1964. So we must provide about 1.7 million additional jobs each year for the next 10 years.

More than a million people—perhaps you among them—will leave our rural areas in the next 10 years to live in cities. Will our cities then be able to provide a decent life for this increased population?

By 1975 the demand for unskilled workers will decrease even more—and, as that happens, our obligation to educate and train our citizens will be even greater.

Even as we struggle with the demands of fast change, our Nation must tackle an urgent backlog of unfinished jobs—in education, in health, transportation, pollution control, resource development, recreation.

Who will work to improve our inadequate schools and our libraries?

Who will build the parks and clear the slums?

Who will clean up the countryside and restore our natural resources?

Who will patrol the streets, and operate the hospitals and the rest homes?

Who will staff social welfare agencies, teach in the colleges, and plan the new towns?

Who will lead the way in beautifying the cities and the countryside?

Well, I hope that you will provide the answer—by considering a career in public service.

I made a suggestion several years ago that all of our young people consider offering some of their time to public service. I am glad that you responded to that by coming here today, taking this training, and engaging in this work, even though temporary, in your Nation's Capital.

Our changing future is going to require the talents of more and better public servants than ever before. There can be no higher or more urgent calling for you as you face the future.

But the new age will also require much of those who do not enter public service—the housewives, the businessmen. If we are to solve our problems, our citizens must develop a new sense of citizenship—a new concern for the public good. I pointed this out in our colleges and universities throughout the land. I spoke of it at the University of Nebraska a few years ago. I spoke of it at the University of Kentucky. And I remind you of it again here today.

We simply can't afford any longer the luxury of indifference—the indifference of the manufacturer who pollutes our streams, or the indifference of voters who deny their responsibility to support education.

The future will require more cooperation. To paraphrase Ben Franklin: We must all pull together—or our society could pull apart altogether.

We have come a long way since the days when the farms were lighted for the first time. The journey has brought us problems, but it has also created new possibilities for you—new chances for education, new economic security, new freedom.

Your most stirring possibility is the chance that you have—unequaled, I think, in any other land at any other time—the chance for useful service to your fellow man.

I hope that you will return your gifts of education and wealth and freedom—return them in service, for never was your help more desperately needed in this world.

My generation was blessed with the opportunity to turn on the lights of rural America. As we came along, less than 10 percent of our homes were electrified. Now almost 100 percent of our rural homes are electrified.

But your generation has a far more exciting challenge, and that is to bring the light of education, the light of abundance, the light of good will to all the dark places in this land and this world.

So be sure that by your visit to Washington, by your concern for your Nation's future, you are making a good start toward spreading that light.

Thank you for coming here. I hope you enjoy your stay. I know you will profit by it. And I should like to see each and every one of you spend some time in service to your country.

Thank you and goodby.

NOTE: The President spoke at 12:30 p.m. on the South Lawn at the White House. In his opening words he referred to Clyde T. Ellis, executive manager, National Rural Electric Cooperative Association.

The group was composed of about 800 high school students, winners of the 10th annual Rural Electric Youth Day essay contest sponsored by the Association. The weeklong tour of Washington for youths from areas served by rural electric systems was first proposed by President Johnson in 1957 while he was serving as majority leader of the Senate.

The report of the National Commission on Technology, Automation, and Economic Progress (210 pp., processed) was transmitted to the President on January 29, 1966.

259 Statement by the President on the Death of Test Pilots Joseph A. Walker and Carl S. Cross. *June 8*, 1966

JOE WALKER and Major Cross gave their lives in advancing science and technology. Their deaths remind us how dependent we are on men of exceptional ability in the development of new vehicles in flight.

They died while training for demanding assignments in a new field of major national interest—research on supersonic transport flight. They added immeasurably to the progress this Nation is making in that effort.

I extend my deepest sympathies to their families.

NOTE: Mr. Walker, chief research pilot for the National Aeronautics and Space Administration, and Air Force Major Cross were killed in an in-flight collision during testing of the experimental XB–70A bomber near Edwards Air Force Base, Calif., on June 8.

The statement was read by Bill D. Moyers, Special Assistant to the President, at his news conference at 5 p.m. on Wednesday, June 8, 1966, at the White House. It was not made public in the form of a White House press release.

260 Statement by the President Upon Sending to Foreign Nations Prints of Lunar Photographs Made by Surveyor I.
June 8, 1966

THIS EFFORT is made in order that careful study of the photographs will be possible around the world. We intend that the knowledge we derive from space will be available for the enrichment of our common experience and the advancement of peaceful undertakings in the exploration of outer space.

NOTE: The statement was read by Bill D. Moyers, Special Assistant to the President, at his news conference at 5 p.m. on Wednesday, June 8, 1966, at the White House. Mr. Moyers announced that the President had sent the photographs to the Chiefs of State of more than 100 foreign nations, including the Soviet Union, and to the world's scientific community.

The statement was not made public in the form of a White House press release.

261 Remarks to Graduates of the Senior Seminar in Foreign Policy. *June 9, 1966*

Mr. Vice President, Secretary Ball, Members of the Senate and Congress, graduates, honored guests, members of the press corps:

It gives me a great deal of pleasure this morning to greet the graduates of the Senior Seminar in Foreign Policy. This year of study has prepared you for the highest posts of responsibility in your Service. I have been able personally to judge the high standards set by some of your alumni who are now our ambassadors and senior officials with whom I frequently come in contact.

I am encouraged that among you are representatives of the four armed services and five other Government departments. This, I think, reflects the revolution in foreign affairs of the past generation. Because foreign policy is no longer just two-way communications between foreign offices. Almost every major branch of Government is involved in some way in foreign policy. The need for teamwork between all of us has never been greater.

The unique relationship of Secretaries Rusk and McNamara and Mr. Bell symbolizes the kind of cooperation that I think

we need at every level of this Government. It is more than encouraging—I think it is quite essential to a strong foreign policy.

The very close and special ties between the President and the Foreign Service should always be close, for the Constitution places on the President the direct responsibility for the conduct of foreign relations. The Foreign Service, like the Office of the President, belongs to no one single department. It serves the whole of this Government.

So the Senior Seminar provides a year of thought, reflection, and study to some of the most talented in our Government. This chance to look backwards and forwards—and all around—in my judgment, has never been more essential.

This present moment of history stands balanced between high danger and great and rare opportunity.

The danger is clear enough—in Southeast Asia and other areas where human misery and vaulting ambitions continue to threaten peace and security in the world. Much of our effort must be devoted to preventing the forces of aggression from asserting themselves or dealing with them when they do.

But there is—I deeply believe—a very rising tide of good sense in the world and a growing determination to get on with the constructive tasks that are ahead of us.

And that is why, with our Latin American friends, we are constantly seeking ways to accelerate the Alliance for Progress.

That is why, with our friends in Africa, we are constantly searching for ways to accelerate that continent's economic and social development.

That is why, in the whole arc from Teheran to Tokyo and Seoul, we are working with the governments and with the peoples of free Asia as they seek increased development and increased regional cohesion.

And that is why, as we face the reorganization of NATO, we are concerned not merely with the relocation of troops and of headquarters, but with bettering relations among Atlantic nations and between the East and the West.

This has a special meaning for those of you who are graduating here today.

Those who bear an operating responsibility in foreign policy can never be content merely to handle today's problems with efficiency and discipline. They must every day ask each in his own field: What can we do—that we are not doing—to tip the balance a little bit in favor of order, in favor of progress, and in favor of peace in the world?

What can we start doing now which will enlarge the prospects of life for the people of a generation from now?

I ask those questions to myself every morning and every night.

And I look to you and your colleagues to help me find the answers to those questions.

The work we do will consume not only today, and this month, and this year, but the work we do will consume many lifetimes to come. So I urge you to remember

that Americans often grow impatient when they cannot see light at the end of the tunnel—when policies do not overnight usher in a new order.

But politics is not magic. And when some of our fellow citizens despair of the tedium and the time necessary to bring change (and I mean no criticism to anyone; I hope the sensitive will not take notice) as for example in Vietnam today, I believe they really forget our history.

It was on July 4, 1776, that the Continental Congress adopted the Declaration of Independence in Philadelphia. Not for many years did the shape of true order and security finally emerge.

The seat of Government in those days moved from Philadelphia to Baltimore and then to Philadelphia again; to Lancaster and to York and back to Philadelphia; to Princeton to Annapolis to Trenton; then to New York City and finally here to Washington.

The Articles of Confederation were adopted in 1777, but they were not ratified by all of the States until 1781—the year that the war ended.

A small elite group—55 men from 12 States—met in our Constitutional Convention. One State would not participate. The meeting was called for May 14, 1787, but it did not have a quorum until some 11 days later. The Convention labored until September 17, before the Constitution was finished. Nine more months passed before that document was ratified by our people.

And after George Washington was elected President, down in 1789, Congress needed almost 4 months to get a quorum to come to organize. Washington was not inaugurated, finally, until April 30. Thirteen years had passed since the colonies, our colonies, had set out to become a nation.

So we ought never to be complacent when change is so painfully slow in coming. We must constantly work to accelerate its pace. And don't think we don't! But let me counsel you who are going on now to important posts in the far corners of the world, those of you who are taking up very difficult tasks in the field of foreign policy: Be restless and discontented with things as they are; always strive and constantly work to change them, but never despair because the task is greater than you are and the time to finish it is really longer than you have.

It gives me great pleasure this morning to present to this class, here in this beautiful Rose Garden of the first house of the land, your diplomas—and to congratulate each of you on the completion of your studies in the Senior Seminar. To you and to your families I extend the gratitude of all of us who benefit from your service.

There has never been a time in my judgment in the Federal Government when better equipped and better trained, more dedicated and more experienced and merited personnel, diligently and with dedication,

try to serve the best interests of their country.

There is no one really, that ever campaigns on doing what is wrong. We all think we want to do what is right. But finding out what is right is our problem. We find—in attempting to get that answer—that experience and dedication to country, and belief in the ideals and principles of our Founding Fathers, better equips each of us to ultimately find the answer that will preserve the liberty and the freedom not only of those few of us who are fortunate enough to occupy this hemisphere, but, we hope, ultimately to all people who desire freedom and liberty in this world.

Thank you very much.

NOTE: The President spoke at 11:20 a.m. in the Rose Garden at the White House before a class of 25 Senior Seminar graduates, Foreign Service School, Department of State. In his opening words he referred to Vice President Hubert H. Humphrey and Under Secretary of State George W. Ball. During his remarks the President referred to Dean Rusk, Secretary of State, Robert F. McNamara, Secretary of Defense, and David E. Bell, Administrator, Agency for International Development.

262 Letter to the President of the Senate and to the Speaker of the House on the Need for a Washington Metropolitan Area Transit Authority. *June 9, 1966*

Dear Mr. President: (Dear Mr. Speaker:)

This is the Congress which promised the citizens of the Nation's capital a new system of mass transportation. I hope it will also be the Congress which extends that promise to the citizens of the entire Washington metropolitan area.

The economic well-being of this region—and the efficient functioning of the Government itself—depend more and more each year on adequate mass transportation facilities. No system of freeways, no matter

how extensive or well planned, can suffice much longer.

The Congress, of course, has recognized this. The first session of the 89th Congress:

—Authorized a 25-mile, $431 million rapid transit system, largely within the District of Columbia;

—Authorized the appropriation of $150 million in Federal and District funds toward the system's construction;

—Appropriated $6.2 million to begin final engineering of the system.

But that system, even when completed, will only begin to solve our transportation problems.

In 1950, nearly three-quarters of the area residents lived within the boundaries of the District of Columbia. By 1970, however, that situation will be almost totally reversed. At that time, there will be an estimated 1,688,000 citizens living in our Maryland and Virginia suburbs—67 percent of the area's swelling population.

Even today, this shifting population is creating massive traffic problems, with more than a million automobiles entering and leaving our city every 24 hours. Even with a full mass transit system—on a regional basis—that figure is expected to double by 1985. Without such a system, a complete breakdown in area transportation would be only a matter of time.

We simply cannot allow that to happen. Our goal—the goal of both the Congress and the Administration—must continue to be a regional system of rapid rail transit.

As a major first step toward achieving that goal, I am transmitting herewith legislation to authorize and approve an interstate agency with the power to plan and finance a region-wide system. When approved by the Congress, this legislation will:

—ratify for the District of Columbia the compact—already ratified by Maryland and Virginia—creating the Washington Metropolitan Area Transit Authority;

—grant the consent to the compact which is required both by the Constitution and by Section 301(a) of the 1960 Transportation Act;

—transfer, on September 30, 1967, the re-

sponsibility for the mass transit system from the National Capital Transportation Agency to the Transit Authority.

This legislation will not create a regional system. It will not build a mile of rail rapid transit. It does not impose on the United States, or on the District of Columbia, any financial obligation. But it is essential if we are to move ahead, for the Transit Authority will become the administrative framework within which further progress can be charted.

I believe such progress will be forthcoming. The legislatures of both Maryland and Virginia, by prompt ratification of the proposed compact, and by enactment of appropriate enabling legislation, have shown their determination to help meet the mass transit needs of the National Capital region. I urge the Congress, and at this session, to echo that determination.

A memorandum explaining the nature and background of the proposed legislation in more detail accompanies this letter.

Sincerely,

Lyndon B. Johnson

NOTE: This is the text of identical letters addressed to the Honorable Carl Hayden, President pro tempore of the Senate, and to the Honorable John W. McCormack, Speaker of the House of Representatives.

The text of the draft bill and the memorandum, also made public by the White House, is printed in House Document 452 (89th Cong., 2d sess.). The memorandum is also printed in the Weekly Compilation of Presidential Documents (vol. 2, p. 751).

On November 6, 1966, the President approved a bill "to grant the consent of Congress for the States of Virginia and Maryland and the District of Columbia to amend the Washington Metropolitan Area Transit Regulation Compact to establish an organization empowered to provide transit facilities in the National Capital Region" (Public Law 89–774, 80 Stat. 1324).

263   Remarks of Welcome to President Schick of Nicaragua on the South Lawn at the White House. *June 9, 1966*

Mr. President, distinguished honored guests, ladies and gentlemen:

Mr. President, I want to welcome you to Washington this morning on behalf of the United States Government and of the American people.

Our two countries share many ties and many interests. One of the strongest stands before us: your Ambassador and the Dean of our Diplomatic Corps, Dr. Sevilla-Sacasa, who has been untiring in his efforts, constant in his purpose, and always has attempted to serve not only the interests of the people of your country but the people of this entire hemisphere.

It is always good, Mr. President, when the heads of governments can come together. Each of us, each day, constantly faces new challenges. We here in the United States, for example, are now engaged in a great battle to eliminate the last elements of racial discrimination in this society of ours.

Mr. President, we are trying so hard to improve our entire educational system in this country. Because in every society education is the ultimate basis for responsible citizenship, for economic growth, for social progress.

We are determined, Mr. President, to improve the health of our young and of our old. And in the days ahead—this month— we will take some of the most revolutionary steps ever taken since the founding of our Republic in advancing health measures for the benefit of all the people of this country.

We are very much determined to keep our land beautiful in the face of an industrial civilization which threatens the landscape, the air, and the water.

I know that in your country, you too, Mr. President, face similar problems as your people strive to create a modern Nicaragua and as they desire to play their part as citizens of the hemisphere.

I am particularly proud that we could pay respect and honor—not just to you as President, although we are pleased that you could stop here on your visit to this country, but to pay respect and honor to every Nicaraguan citizen. We are especially pleased to observe Nicaragua's loyal collaboration in the Central American Common Market effort.

We know that in the field of education, in the field of health, and in the field of social betterment, no geographical lines divide human beings. Wherever the human heart beats, wherever the head thinks, people everywhere want the same things: better education for their children, better health for their families, better homes to live in.

I congratulate you, Mr. President, along with your Central American neighbors, for the progress that has been made toward a better and a fuller economic integration. We feel this is essential to improve the economic lot of the good people who inhabit this continent with us. Your visit coincides closely with the fifth anniversary of the Common Market endeavor which was so happily marked last week.

Our two countries share common objectives on the world scene as well as in this hemisphere.

And as the leaders of the world scene have come and gone from Washington, there has always been one person who joined with the officials of the United States to pay them respect and understanding—regardless of their political philosophy or from which continent they came. That person was the distinguished Dean of the Diplomatic Corps, our friend Sevilla-Sacasa. So this, too, acknowledges and pays to him a tribute that we think is long overdue.

Mr. President, we look forward to a continuation of the strong effort that is carrying us forward in this hemisphere toward the most desirable objectives and toward goals that we believe are attainable.

Today, I have asked some of the leaders of all groups, factions, and parties of this Government to come here and exchange suggestions and ideas with you as to how we can make a better life for our people.

We are happy that you could come to see us.

NOTE: The President spoke at 1:05 p.m. on the South Lawn at the White House, where President René Schick Gutiérrez was given a formal welcome with full military honors. President Schick responded as follows:

Your Excellency, President of the United States Lyndon Johnson, Mrs. Johnson, honorable representatives of the United States Government, honorable members of my own party, Your Excellency, the Dean of the Diplomatic Corps accredited to the United States of America, ladies and gentlemen:

In reality, I have been deeply moved and touched by the welcome that you have given me so generously and nobly this morning, President Johnson. I think this is perhaps a witness and a tribute to the friendship that happily has existed for so long between Nicaragua and the great American people. I have been deeply moved. I accept this on behalf of my own country because I know this is a tribute that is being rendered, not to me personally, but to my own country.

And on behalf of the people of Nicaragua I would like to express my deep appreciation for this welcome—it represents the open and frank and sincere friendship that has always bound us with the United States—and to thank you, President Johnson, for your very generous words.

I appreciate these all the more considering the source and person of your high virtues, your strong execution of policies, and your great struggle to fight for freedom, for justice, and for democracy throughout the world. All of these characteristics are well known not only to the people in my own country, but to people all over the world.

I would like to thank you especially, Mr. President, for this generous act of receiving the members of my party and receiving me in this extraordinary welcome which really has been very pleasing to my people and to my country.

I want to also express my deep appreciation to you because at your side, as you have greeted me, you have your wife, Mrs. Johnson. She is well known for the great assistance she has given you, not only in matters of the heart but also in matters of politics and for her work for social benefit, for education, for culture, and for health of your citizens of this great country.

So on behalf of the people of Nicaragua I would like to express my appreciation and present respectful greetings to the First Lady of the United States of America, whose heart is imbued we know with sentiments of love for all of mankind.

I want to thank you also, Mr. President, for your kind references to Dr. Guillermo Sevilla-Sacasa, the Ambassador of Nicaragua to the United States, as he has been for quite a long time. He has been my teacher. I worked with him in the Embassy during the course of several years. What little I was able to learn, what little I know, I learned from him.

I have learned from him some of the qualities he displays so well, the frankness of openness, of sincerity, of nobility of spirit, of generosity and especially the deep-rooted sentiments that he has of friendship for the United States of America which has been our policy for so many years. I want to express to him and render tribute to him on this date as Chief Executive of Nicaragua to him who yesteryear was my teacher and who now is my subordinate for the wonderful things that he has been able to do for me.

In the world today that is so convulsed with so many struggles, in this world in which there is so much restlessness and so much source for preoccupation, in this world in which there exist ideologies different from our own that threaten the very roots of our common Western civilization, I understand, Mr. President, that on your shoulders there rests a great many burdens and you have a great many sources of concern and a great deal of responsibility for the many problems that you have to deal with.

But I would like to tell you on this day and like to tell you publicly and like to tell you categorically that my country, which is a small one as far as territory is concerned, but which is a large one as far as our aspirations of our people and as far as the love that we have for the principles of justice and of liberty, shares your aspirations and shares your ideals and will be today, as we have been yesterday and will be tomorrow, completely with you in following the enlightened policies that you are setting forward and pursuing for the good, not only of the people of the United States but for all mankind.

I was especially pleased to hear your references to education. I heard your words with a great deal of pleasure because I myself am an educator and have believed for all my life that education should be the basic principle sought after for the happiness

595

of the life of our people. For many years I have struggled first as a grade school teacher, then as a high school teacher, a university professor, and a minister of education, struggled to obtain for education first place, preferential place, in our national budget.

I am delighted to be able to see that I finally achieved that goal, because in the budget for 1966 education occupies the first place in our budget followed closely by the fight against problems affecting the health of our people to which you have also made reference and to which I think a great deal of effort should be devoted.

And, Mr. President, I would like to make reference here, since I am speaking from this position that we have achieved of giving education such a primary boost in our budget, that we have been able to do this with the very, very generous help that we have received from the United States, not only in the field of technical assistance but also economically through grants and through loans that we characterize as soft loans because of their long-term and because of the low interest rates that they bear.

President Johnson, I don't want to abuse any more of your kindness in receiving me here and in the kindness of the people that are together at this ceremony and especially of your lovely wife, because of the hot sun that is burning down on all of us, that is burning our faces and making people uncomfortable, but I must, as a good Nicaraguan and a son of the land of Ruben Dario, make use of this literary reference here to the sun and say as Chief Executive of Nicaragua that the sun that is now burning on our faces is also the sun that can be compared with the way your actions are illuminating the world, with the sun that is inspiring you to greater efforts to solve problems and encouraging people in all latitudes of this globe to uphold the principles of the dignity of man, the principles of freedom, and the principles of justice, the principles that you as a leader of the Government of the United States have always defended so well and are developing them also as a great leader of our own Western Hemisphere.

Because we all recognize the work that you have done in the development of these ideals and principles of our hemisphere and also developing ideals shared by other like-minded people throughout the world, because of your work in the struggle that you are engaged in in South Vietnam, I pay tribute to you because I consider that this is where the borders of the United States really are. Ideological borders of a country go far beyond any geographical borders. They go as far as the aspiration of a people will take them.

And before concluding, and again I ask your indulgence for having abused the generosity of the people who are standing here today, I would like to pay a special thanks to you for the tribute that you have rendered to my country in this military review and I want to express my great appreciation because the highest symbol of your nationhood, your flag, greeted me and the members of my party as representatives of the people and the Government of Nicaragua in whose name I again express my thanks.

I would like to tell you that we will be solidly with you because we are a peace-loving people and lovers of justice and of freedom. We will express and maintain solidarity with you now and throughout the years to come. You can count on us. You can count on the solidarity of the countries of Latin America and especially of our own neighbors in Central America and, of course, of our own Nicaragua, because we share your aspirations, we share your efforts, we share your desire for finding peace in this world.

Finally, Mr. President, you said that some representatives of your Government were going to come and exchange ideas with me. I expect to learn a great deal from them. I don't think they will learn that much from me, because I have little experience, but I do have a heart that is full of love for freedom, for justice, and for the reign of law.

Finally, I would like to express my thanks to the generous tribute that has been rendered to us by this great country, a tribute rendered for our own very small country which, however, spiritually feels on a par with this country of yours.

Thank you very much.

264   The President's Toast to President Schick. *June 9, 1966*

Mr. President:

You and the distinguished members of your party come to Washington as friends and collaborators.

We have been impressed by your achievements in bringing new levels of stability and

prosperity to your nation.

We share the pride of Nicaragua and your sister republics in the great strides made within the Central American Common Market. Together you are blazing important trails in the quest of Latin American economic integration.

We are mindful of the support which you have given to the common cause of the free world in Vietnam and the Dominican Republic.

You have done your country great honor by your important visits to mutual friends in Europe and the Near East.

It is a genuine pleasure to have you again in our midst—in this house. As you say in

Spanish, *Esta en su casa.*

I ask you to raise your glasses with me in honor of President Schick of the Republic of Nicaragua, whose country and whose people are represented here today by our friend, President Schick.

NOTE: The President proposed the toast at a luncheon in the State Dining Room at the White House. As printed above, this item follows the advance text released by the White House.

---

265   Remarks After a Meeting With Representatives of the American Bankers Association in Connection With the Student Loan Program.   *June* 10, 1966

Mr. Davis, Mr. Walker, Commissioner Howe, Mr. Muirhead, my friends, ladies and gentlemen:

I have just come from a very high level meeting behind closed doors with some of the country's leading bankers. But before the stock market begins to flutter, I want to reassure you that I am meeting with these bankers not because we have any grave problems, but because we do have a very great program.

These gentlemen here with me this morning represent financial institutions throughout this Nation. They have given very strong support to the guaranteed student loan program which is a vital feature of the Higher Education Act of 1965.

Today, they have told me of the plans that they have made and what they are doing to make this program an outstanding success.

Under this new loan program, families will finance college education for their children in the same way that they finance the purchase of a home: through long-term, federally guaranteed private loans.

For millions of families, the financial burden of college education will now be

lifted; new opportunities will open for American students.

This program, I think, is one more example of creative federalism. Its success depends not so much on the guarantee by the Federal Government as it does on the imagination and the public spirit of the private lending institutions throughout this country.

The American Bankers Association has been working for months to guarantee the complete success of this program.

I have been delighted to meet with its leaders today—to discuss with them some of the details and some of their experiences, to review some of the material that they have assembled, some of the literature that they have produced, and some of the recommendations that they are making to their member banks in all the States of the Union.

I have received their report. It is encouraging. Their attitude is a fine one. And I think that as a result of this meeting and the work that they have already done, the legislation we have already passed, that not only will many thousands of young people be attending college who otherwise would not have been able to attend, but we will further strengthen our free enterprise system.

I pay tribute to the bankers of America who have given their Government a lending hand and have extended it also to those coming young men and women who need an education and who, when they get it, will reward us all with their increased knowledge and with their support of the finest governmental system in all the world.

I will leave these men with you now. I ask you to have mercy upon them.

Thank you.

NOTE: The President spoke at 12:44 p.m. in the Cabinet Room at the White House to members of the press. In his opening words he referred to Archie K. Davis, President of the American Bankers Association, Charls E. Walker, Executive Vice President of the Association, and to Harold Howe II, Commissioner of Education, and Peter P. Muirhead, Associate Commissioner for Higher Education, Department of Health, Education, and Welfare. Prior to the President's remarks, Association representatives had presented him with a copy of a brochure "Banking's New Opportunity" being distributed to banks throughout the country to encourage participation in the student loan program.

For the President's remarks on signing the Higher Education Act of 1965, see 1965 volume, this series, Book II, Item 603.

266 Remarks Upon Presenting the President's Award for Distinguished Federal Civilian Service. *June 13, 1966*

Secretary Ball, Mr. Macy, distinguished award recipients, members of the Cabinet, my friends in the Congress, ladies and gentlemen:

We have come here this morning to honor five distinguished career employees of the Federal Government for their most unusual and outstanding service to this country. They are all men who are rich in experience. They are also innovators. In their separate fields each of them has displayed that initiative and imagination which mark the creative man in every profession. So it is our very good fortune as a Nation that they do not stand alone even when they stand out. They have been helped and supported along their separate paths by what I believe to be a first-rate civil service in this country.

Many young nations in the world are reaching for a fairer share of the 20th century's progress. Their demands are just; their needs are many. These young struggling nations—all of them—need more food, more industry, more capital, more goods, and more technology. But no nation has a need that is more important than their

need for trained, dependable, competent manpower.

We know from our own history how very important is the fair administration of laws by men who place the country's welfare always above their own. That is one definition of a truly good and great public servant.

In our day, tired answers to old problems will just not do. The problems we have are so complex that often even the most inspired solution will prove barely adequate. So this places a very special and great responsibility on the civil servant in this country. Today I look to the Federal career service to produce for this Government men and women of broad vision, with new answers, with good ideas. And we ask them to consider not merely their own department, not only the Federal Government, but the future of this land. When we find such men, I take a peculiar pleasure and delight in honoring them. That is what we are doing here today with the gentlemen who are the recipients of this award.

First, Dr. Elson B. Helwig, who has made

the Armed Forces Institute of Pathology an institute of world renown.

Second, Mr. Robert E. Hollingsworth, who has used imaginative methods within the Atomic Energy Commission to liberate and to encourage the fullest expression of the creative energies of his staff.

Third, Mr. H. Rex Lee, who as Governor of American Samoa helped that tropical island to become, in 5 years, a place of progress and vitality.

Fourth, Mr. Thomas C. Mann, who has represented this great Nation at home and abroad with diligence, with intelligence, with great foresight and good judgment for almost a quarter of a century in some of the most important, the most difficult, the most harassing posts which any public servant could occupy.

And, finally, Dr. James A. Shannon, who is one of our chiefs of staff in the war on disease. His deployment of men and resources in that war have led, if not yet to victory, have led to the continuing retreat of heart disease and cancer and many other medical enemies of man that we feel today we have on the run.

So I have asked you, their families, some of their special friends, and some of the elite in our Federal civil service to come here and join me today in honoring these men—in honoring the career of the civil service, of which they are excellent symbols. The gentlemen here, by their past accomplishments can give all of us renewed confidence in the future of this land and our dedicated civil service to which we already owe so much.

I appreciate your presence here this morning and I have attempted, in my own way, to express the debt to these individuals that I feel a grateful nation owes them.

Thank you very much.

NOTE: The President spoke at 11:35 a.m. in the East Room at the White House. In his opening words he referred to George W. Ball, Under Secretary of State and Chairman of the Distinguished Civilian Service Awards Board, and to John W. Macy, Jr., Chairman, Civil Service Commission.

The recipients of the award served in the following positions in the Federal Government: Dr. Elson B. Helwig, Chief, Department of Pathology, Armed Forces Institute of Pathology, Department of the Army; Robert E. Hollingsworth, General Manager, Atomic Energy Commission; H. Rex Lee, Governor of American Samoa, Department of the Interior; Thomas C. Mann, Under Secretary of State for Economic Affairs, Department of State; and Dr. James A. Shannon, Director, National Institutes of Health, Department of Health, Education, and Welfare.

267 Special Message to the Congress Transmitting Reorganization Plan 4 of 1966 Relating to the National Zoological Park. *June 13, 1966*

To the Congress of the United States:

I transmit herewith Reorganization Plan No. 4 of 1966, prepared in accordance with the Reorganization Act of 1949, as amended, and providing for a reorganization relating to the National Zoological Park located in the District of Columbia.

Today, all responsibilities for the administration of the Park are vested in the Smith- sonian Institution with one exception—the function of preparing plans and specifications for the construction of buildings and bridges at the Zoo. That statutory responsibility is now conducted by the Board of Commissioners of the District of Columbia.

Under the accompanying reorganization plan, the responsibility for the preparation of these plans and specifications would be transferred from the D.C. Board of Commissioners to the Smithsonian. The complete administration of the Park would then be vested in one agency—the Smithsonian Institution. This will allow the more efficient and effective development and management of the Park.

In 1912, the functions to be transferred were vested in the Municipal Architect of the District of Columbia and in the Engineers of the Bridges of the District of Columbia. In 1952, they were transferred to the Board of Commissioners.

When the 1912 Act was passed, the District of Columbia shared the costs of capital improvements in the National Zoological Park. In 1961, it ceased sharing these costs, and the Federal Government assumed complete responsibility for financing the improvements. Accordingly, the District Government retains no capital improvement responsibilities for the National Zoological Park except those functions relating to construction plans and specifications for build-

ings and bridges, as specified in the 1912 statute. Upon the transfer of these remaining functions to the Smithsonian Institution, the administration of the National Zoological Park will, at last, be fully centered in one agency. It is not practicable at this time, however, to itemize the resulting reduction in expenditures.

I have found, after investigation, that each reorganization included in the accompanying reorganization plan is necessary to accomplish one or more of the purposes set forth in Section 2(a) of the Reorganization Act of 1949, as amended.

I recommend that the Congress allow the reorganization plan to become effective.

LYNDON B. JOHNSON

The White House
June 13, 1966

NOTE: Reorganization Plan 4 of 1966 is printed in the Weekly Compilation of Presidential Documents (vol. 2, p. 769), in the Federal Register (31 F.R. 11137), and in Title 3 of the Code of Federal Regulations (3 CFR, 1966 Comp., p. 192). It became effective on August 23, 1966.

268 Statement by the President on Announcing His Intention To Renominate Lawrence J. O'Connor, Jr., to the Federal Power Commission. *June 13, 1966*

I HAVE thoroughly reviewed and evaluated Commissioner O'Connor's service on the Federal Power Commission since his appointment by President Kennedy. I have been impressed by his integrity, conscientiousness, and the substantial contribution he has made to the Commission's deliberations. As the only member of the Commission who is an accountant, he is of special value in many of the highly technical and involved accounting questions that come to the Commission for decision. His decisions

on the critical issues coming before the Commission have reflected a strong commitment to the public interest.

NOTE: The President's statement was made public as part of a White House release announcing the nomination for reappointment of Mr. O'Connor to a second 5-year term with the Federal Power Commission. The release stated that Mr. O'Connor, a native of Tulsa, Okla., had been educated at the Rice Institute and the Harvard Business School and had been employed in private industry for some 20 years before joining the Department of the Interior in 1959. He was appointed to the Federal Power Commission by President Kennedy on August 13, 1961.

269   Remarks Upon Signing Bill Authorizing a Powerplant at the Grand Coulee Dam. *June 14, 1966*

Mr. Vice President, Secretary Udall, Senator Magnuson, Senator Jackson, Congressman Foley, distinguished Members of the Congress, ladies and gentlemen:

I am happy to see so many of the distinguished leaders of the electric power industry here this morning. I am very happy to welcome our friends from Canada to the Rose Garden. My first trip outside the United States, after I became President, was to meet with my good friend, Prime Minister Pearson, in order to sign the Columbia River Treaty.

Without that treaty, providing for the construction of three storage dams on the upper Columbia River, this great expansion of Grand Coulee would not have been possible.

This morning I am signing not one but two very important measures. The first is a bill authorizing a third powerhouse for Grand Coulee Dam. The second is an appropriation request for $3 million, so we can begin construction of that powerhouse immediately.

Our Canadian friends will finish their projects by 1973. We want to be ready to use the benefits that are going to flow from those dams.

This authorization builds on a project which was begun more than 30 years ago. And not a year has passed which did not bring new benefits and greater prosperity to the people of the region that it serves. The whole Nation, I think, has benefited greatly, for the development of the resources of any region always adds to the strength and prosperity of all the regions.

New industries have been created. New towns have been established. Thousands of homes and farms have been modernized with modern electricity. Tens of thousands of new jobs have been created, and close to half a million acres of farmland have been irrigated.

All this came as a surprise to some people who originally opposed the whole concept of Grand Coulee Dam. There is a famous quotation from one of those early skeptics. "Up in the Grand Coulee country," he said, "there is no one to sell power to except coyotes and jackrabbits, and there never will be."

Well, today, the two powerplants of the Grand Coulee are straining to full capacity. This third powerplant, so desperately needed, will make Grand Coulee Dam larger than any hydroelectric project now in operation anywhere in the world. The 3.6 million kilowatts, added to the 2 million already there, will bring Grand Coulee's capacity to 5.6 million kilowatts. The Grand Coulee Dam is an excellent example, for this new powerhouse, like the two already existing, will benefit both private utilities and consumer-owned co-ops alike. They will enjoy those benefits, because they have decided to share them as equal partners.

We have a right to be proud of the accomplishments of the American electric institute. We have only 6 percent of the world's population. Yet we produce 40 percent of the world's electricity.

During the past 30 years our population has increased by 50 percent. But our capacity to produce electricity has increased not by 50 percent, but by 10 times that amount, 500 percent. The lives of our people are enriched in a thousand ways by this abundance of energy. And it is brought to them at rates that they can afford. In fact, average electric rates in the United States have fallen from 2.46 cents in 1935 to 1.59 cents today.

We have accomplished this miracle within the diversity of our free enterprise system. Some 80 percent of our people are now served by private systems. The other 20 percent have chosen to get their service from public systems and cooperatives. And as the years pass, we see mounting evidence that the jealousies and the antagonisms which once stood between public and private power in this Nation are disappearing.

This is especially true in the Pacific Northwest—not only in connection with the Grand Coulee Dam, but in the mutual use of such facilities as the Hanford atomic energy plant and the non-Federal Columbia River dams.

By 1980—only 14 years from now—the demand for electric energy will be nearly three times as large as it is today. If we are going to meet that demand, we are going to have to continue to strengthen that partnership.

And so to you leaders of the electric industry who have come here with us this morning—to you leaders in the Congress—I want to say: Thanks for what we have accomplished together. It is tremendous. But the job which lies ahead is equally monumental. It will take the best efforts of all of us. So let us now take a step forward by signing these two measures and getting on our way.

Thank you very much.

NOTE: The President spoke at 9:35 a.m. in the Rose Garden at the White House. In his opening words he referred to Vice President Hubert H. Humphrey, Secretary of the Interior Stewart L. Udall, and to Senator Warren G. Magnuson, Senator Henry M. Jackson, and Representative Thomas S. Foley, all of Washington.

As enacted, the bill (S. 1761) authorizing construction of the powerplant and the appropriation of funds, is Public Law 89–448 (80 Stat. 200).

For the President's remarks with Prime Minister Lester B. Pearson of Canada on January 22, 1964, at the signing of the Columbia River Agreement, see 1963–64 volume, this series, Book I, Item 134.

270   Remarks at the Graduation Ceremony of the Capitol Page School. *June 14, 1966*

Mr. Vice President, graduates of the Capitol Page School, your parents, Members of Congress:

I want to welcome you here this morning to the Rose Garden at the White House because I am very proud to speak to you as a fellow alumnus of Capitol Hill.

You have reason to be proud too, I think, for you have been a part of what we think is the most productive session of Congress in the history of the Republic. You have seen men rise to great challenges, master them, and move on to greater ones.

You have helped to create the fruits of that leadership—the laws that will make it

possible for our people to achieve a better way of life.

The landmark legislation that's passed by this Congress will in time, in my judgment, change the face of this entire Nation.

So I want, this morning, to thank you for your part in that effort, and I also want to congratulate you as a graduate.

This is a very good time, I think, to be a young man. More roads are opening every day to more opportunities for more young Americans than at any time in the history of this country. What counts is how you choose those opportunities.

For you, identity is measured by what you

choose to do—by the worth of what you achieve.

Even before I came to Washington as a young man, I noticed how many men said what had to be done could not be done. But, as I learned in the Congress, every step that needs to be taken can be taken by men who are determined to join hands and journey forward together.

There is another lesson I learned in Congress—the need for leaders in every branch of public and private life to work together, for parties to seek common objectives.

We have had an excellent example of that here in the White House just in the last few days. I asked the leaders of Congress of both parties to come and talk to Secretary Rusk after his return from the NATO Conference in Brussels, to talk about Vietnam, to talk about the Dominican Republic, and to talk about other important foreign policy matters.

I did not ask them as Democrats or as Republicans. They came here as Americans and as my partners in this Government of the United States of America. I wanted them to have the latest and the fullest and the most complete information that we had in the executive department, because I needed their frank and their informed and their helpful judgments. I received it. I am grateful for it.

I have no doubt that the congressional leadership took away as much confidence and understanding and hope as they left behind. And that is really what leadership means—but it is not all of it.

The White House and the Congress can give only a part of the leadership this Nation requires and demands. The rest is up to its citizens, to the people who make up the 200 million Americans that inhabit our shores. The rest is up to the young and to the old among us.

So this morning I congratulate you and I challenge you and I ask each of you for a commitment to leadership. You could be the leaders, for instance, in education.

Today most of our children are untouched by education until they are at least 6 years old. But we know that the child's mind is wide open as early as 4. In the formative years we now largely ignore it. You can take the lead in remedying that.

You could commit yourself to finding new ways to teach the very young, to train them earlier so that they would be better prepared to enter high school and college, and to enter it earlier—to equip them earlier with the discipline and the purpose that would bring them fulfillment in life sooner.

You could be the leaders in answering other educational questions. If 16 years of elementary and secondary and college education were good enough for present generations, are they going to be good enough for your generation? Should we not keep pace with the knowledge explosion and aim perhaps to give every child an extra 2 years of schooling?

Well, that is an answer we need. That is a challenge we present. And there are countless others your generation must meet and solve. I would welcome discussing them this morning, if you had the time and I had the time.

You are young now, but what will your old age be? Now is the time to think about that, to lead in doing something about it. It takes time, you know—we spent 20 years getting medical care. And from the time you start a program, until you get it inaugurated, a good deal of time elapses.

How could we add 10 more meaningful years to our life? Living longer is not the answer. Greater leisure is not the answer. How to live more completely, or more purposefully, or more productively, how to lengthen real happiness and real fulfillment?

Well, these are the answers we seek. Our older people need new training, and they need new opportunities for not just a longer, but a longer and a much larger life.

We in Government are working on these problems of the very old. And we are certainly concerned with the problems of the very young—much more so now, I think, than we were a few years ago. We are now using the best brains outside of Government to help us master them, and I ask you to join us.

In a few days I am going to write a letter to the Secretary of HEW asking him to set up a very special group to make a very special study about what we can do in the twilight period of peoples' lives in this country—and to come in with strong recommendations that we can evaluate and consider.[1]

And I want to ask you to join the best brains in helping us formulate some of these programs. I want each of you to walk out in the world determined—determined to move it, to contribute to it, and to shape it— to be leaders and not followers.

Now that is the commitment that carried me into public life as a very young man. I did not announce when I came here 35 years ago that I was going to roll up my sleeves and remake America, because I had read Rex Tugwell's announcement, and I saw that he telegraphed his shots. He didn't quite succeed all at the same time, although I had the same ideas and the same ambitions.

So you may not telegraph all you plan to do. You may not announce all you plan to do. But I do hope that you have the

hope and the idea and the plan to roll up your sleeves and do something about improving conditions in this country and leaving this land a better place than you found it.

I feel that is the commitment that is responsible for me standing here as your President today. And I think one of you could, and very likely will, stand in this same place some day. Someone said to me the other night after seeing the television show I appeared in, "The President's Country"—and my part of this land: "You know, I had always heard all my life that any boy born in America had a chance to grow up and be President and now I believe it."

So I would remind each of you that any boy born in America has a chance to grow up and be President. It may happen to you. I hope if it should happen to you that you will be prepared for it.

Count it a day lost when the people of America can't go to sleep at night without knowing the world is a better place at bedtime than it was at breakfast.

The opportunity is here. Your parents have provided you with tools, ammunition, and implements that are given to no other people of your age in the world. You have more food, more clothes, better per capita income, better housing, more luxury, more recreation, better trained teachers, better schools than your young folks of any other area in the world.

I know that you have taken advantage of it or you would not be here graduating this morning. But I hope in the days ahead you will feel that you have a personal challenge and a personal responsibility to pick up where you are this morning and develop this land—not just by enduring the status quo that you have found, but by improving it, by remaking it, by developing it into a fuller and richer life, not only for all of our

---

[1] The proposals of Secretary of Health, Education, and Welfare John W. Gardner on increasing social security benefits are summarized in the President's remarks at the Social Security Administration headquarters in Baltimore on October 12, 1966 (see Item 509).

older people, but for all of our younger ones that may follow you.

Thank you very much.

NOTE: The President spoke at 11:32 a.m. in the Rose Garden at the White House prior to presenting diplomas to the 26 members of the graduating class and greeting members of their families. In his opening words he referred to Vice President Hubert H. Humphrey. During his remarks he referred to Dean Rusk, Secretary of State, and Rexford G. Tugwell, author and political scientist who served as Under Secretary of Agriculture 1934–1937 and as Governor of Puerto Rico 1941–1946.

271   Remarks at a Meeting With Medical and Hospital Leaders To Prepare for the Launching of Medicare. *June 15, 1966*

Mr. Vice President, Secretary Gardner, my good friend Senator Anderson, ladies and gentlemen:

Not many weeks ago Secretary Gardner briefed me and subsequently I asked him to bring to the Cabinet meeting a briefing on what preparations we had made in connection with the very significant event in the lives of all of us—namely, the launching of a new program called Medicare in this country.

I was so deeply impressed with that briefing that I decided to call together at the White House America's most respected and most responsible health and hospital leaders to continue the discussion we began that day. Now, all of you may not be respected and all of you may not be responsible—we will have to see, after you have left town!—but that was our judgment. And we do not claim that all of the respected and responsible are here either, but we do feel that you are a very good cross section and rather representative. That is why you have been asked to come here.

We have started the countdown for medical care in this country. In 15 days from now, we will begin the greatest contribution to the well-being of older citizens since social security was launched 30 years ago. We so much want this program to be a success.

I believe that every good American wants it to be a success. I believe that each of you share that hope.

So I want to welcome you to this meeting that we have called, for what I believe to be a very noble purpose, and that noble purpose is to improve the life of our people.

A little later on I will elaborate on some of my thinking in the last few weeks about calling together the Director of the National Institutes of Health and the directors of the nine individual institutes, as well as the Surgeon General, and asking them to commune with the leaders in respective fields in this country, so that in the days ahead we can put as much effort into prolonging the prime of man's life as we are in extending our knowledge of outer space. They both have good purposes. I am not sure they have equal effort and equal funds.

Now never before, except in mobilizing for war, I think, has any government made such extensive preparations for any undertaking as we have made in connection with medical care.

I have one stenographer just assigned to me to write letters to Gardner and ask him if he has thought of this or that. Because I know that out of 200 million people in this country there are still left a few "I told you so's"—even in my own party.

And these people take peculiar delight in saying, "Why didn't they do so-and-so?"

And these cynics say, "If they had only done so-and-so," and "Why couldn't they have anticipated this?" The fellow that does not have the responsibility always has the suggestions as to how it could have been done better.

So we are trying to anticipate those things and trying to plan for them—trying to get everyone cooperating and working together, to see if we can't do as efficient a job as a voluntary society and a democratic society can do.

In the past year, through a massive program, we have tried to reach virtually every American over 65 years of age with the news about medical care. Now we may not have reached every one of them—we have tried to, I said. But more than 90 percent of them—between 17 and 18 million—have signed up for elective medical benefits.

Now, to do this we have sent thousands of workers out in the country, into the field, to consult and exchange views with hospital authorities. We have held more than 2,000 meetings with members of the health profession—to say nothing about the hours that we spent testifying before Senator Anderson and Congressman King and the other committees.

We have opened around-the-clock medical care information posts to handle questions about this new venture. We have earnestly, genuinely, sought the advice and the cooperation of the people who could be constructive and who could be helpful—the American Medical Association, the American Hospital Association, and the various high professional groups in this country.

And this morning I want to publicly pay them tribute for their response and for their patriotism and for their public spirit.

Now in these last 15 days we are coming around the bend and we do not want to let up. We are going to try to be in contact with every hospital. We will be available to every doctor and to every hospital officer in this Nation to deal with any problem that may arise.

I have asked that the Governors be specially briefed. I have asked that the Congressmen and the States be specially briefed. I have asked that we send field people to the areas where they need further information and where there is still work to do. And that is being done this week.

But the work on today's agenda is for you to decide. What we asked you to come here for is to help us by giving us advice on how we can best help *you* to prepare, at the community level, for as smooth and as successful an operation as can be had in this kind of a venture.

Then it will be your job to get action—action at the community level—to solve the problems which could hamper this program.

Now we know there are going to be problems.

One of them arises from compliance with the laws of the land, specifically the Civil Rights Act. In some communities older people may be deprived of medical care because their hospitals fail to give equal treatment to all citizens and they have discrimination practices.

Well, we believe the answer to that problem is a simple one and that Congress has given it in the law itself. We ask every citizen to obey the law.

A majority of hospitals—we think more now than 80 percent—have already assured us that they will. And I am hopeful that most of the others—when it is understood and when it is explained—will make an attempt to come into compliance. But we cannot rest easy as long as any of our older citizens lose their rights because of hospital defiance or because of delay.

Now we are going to hear about these

cases. Mr. Rayburn, who served here 50 years, used to say that it is typical of the American people to give more recognition to a donkey that will kick a barn down than to a carpenter who will build one.

That applies to all of our people. And to those who still stand outside the gates I want to say this: Please comply. If you discriminate against some older citizens in your community, then you make it very difficult for the whole program.

The Federal Government is not going to retreat from its clear responsibility and what the Members of Congress have written into the law. And I hope that you will not retreat either.

So you are here today to help us make this reality clear to your communities. Because there is always a last minute hope that we can "fudge it" a little bit and we can prolong it and "it won't be necessary." Now that is one problem and it is a serious problem for the 20 percent group, as you can see.

Another problem will face some communities, and that is, their hospitals are always crowded and Medicare is going to add to the patient load. And if the hospital is already crowded, why, we just make present bad matters worse. Now, we do not think this is a national problem—in every State in the Union and in every community. It arises only in certain localities. We have identified those particular localities where we think the problem is most severe.

Eighty-eight counties have serious overcrowding now and we think that is where our problems are going to be. This affects about 3 percent of the Nation's population. And you are going to have ample coverage of that, ample pictures of it, and ample articles about it. I want to prepare you in advance. They are going to broadcast it good. It is going to affect, we think, about

3 percent, and we want to minimize it as much as we can.

In each of these communities your leadership can be helpful and, we think, will be necessary to try to insure the efficient use of hospital beds and efficient use of medical manpower, and to work out wise programs for handling the patient load.

We all know from our experiences in other programs—it may be a local box supper or a local football game on Thanksgiving—we know there are those who abuse their privileges.

And there will be some abuse from all these millions of people under Medicare— because we are all human beings. There will be some who will demand unnecessary treatment. There will be some who want to "fix it under the table," who want a special privilege. There will be some who make unusual requests for hospital care.

Now when these demands arise we want to appeal to you, and through you as leaders down to the very bottom of the grassroots, to try to help us stand firm against these abuses.

Washington is no place to patrol matters in 50 States. The farther you get away from the community, the less efficient you are and the more expensive you are. So we hope that at the local level this can be done. Now we think that these abuses—that you can watch after them better than anyone else; and we want to help you in any way that you think we can help.

There is another problem which deserves attention, and one that we are watching closely. With the start of medical care there may be growing pressure toward higher prices for hospital and medical services.

There is something about full employment: We work for years to try to get jobs for all of us; we work for years to try to get to where we can buy certain things; and as soon as we do, although we sell a lot more of them, people like to raise their price a little bit so they can raise their profits a little bit. That is human nature.

We must try to be concerned with these higher prices for hospital medical service or we can undo a lot of the good that we have done. So we ask the responsible medical societies and professional leaders to take the lead in trying to help us prevent unreasonable costs for health services. And the best prevention is intelligent self-restraint by doctors and hospital officials.

Now I hope your discussion of these and other problems today in your own meetings will be bold and frank and thorough. I hope, too, that you will enter into these discussions knowing that you are a very select group in which great trust is placed and which bears great responsibility, and that in my judgment the little program that you will have at your meeting and your participation here in this meeting will make history that your descendants will be proud of.

We still talk about Abigail Adams hanging out her washing here in the East Room. Now you are not going to hang out any washing here today, but you are doing something much more significant and much more enduring—and something that your descendants are going to take great pride in.

In a little more than a fortnight, for the first time in the history of America, every senior American will be able to receive hospital care—not as a ward of the State, not as a charity case, but as an insured patient.

I am not 65 yet, but I have known a good many people in my lifetime that were 65; and they have been mighty close to me. And I have seen the skim over their eyes when they looked at me, wondering whether they were going to be welcome in their sister-in-law's home, or whether their brother-in-law would be happy when they

are all there using the one bath, or how they were going to pay the doctors or for the medical services—and how grateful they were for the consideration that the preacher and the women of their church had extended to them in times of illness, and how they loved the doctor that could come anytime in the night, who gave his whole life, even away from his own family, and waited to have his bills paid year after year after year, in drought or insects or too much rain or too little!

And I know that those people over 65 know that this is really heaven itself that they no longer have to wonder how their son-in-law or their brother-in-law or their sister-in-law is going to feel, that they have some little hope that they can get into a nursing home, or if the pain gets in the right place they can go to a hospital where they can get some care—not with a tin cup in their hand saying, "Please, ma'am," but because their Government has provided for it as it has social security.

One of the most memorable events in my life was standing in the Speaker's office in this Capitol, and hearing a man talk about the socialism of social security—how dangerous it was. He was close to me, he was such a good man—and so genuinely believed that it would destroy this country. And I pled with him: Please, please, please go and support that measure; and he finally did. And as I recall, less than a dozen voted against it on final passage.

I look back 30 years now and see how far we have come. No longer would an enlightened, constructive man feel that way about social security. There is not 1 out of 100 who would think of repealing it.

And I think in due time you will feel this way.

I heard Mrs. Johnson say to Secretary Gardner the other day: "Your life must be an interesting and exciting one. Tell me about some of the things that you are doing that excite you the most."

And he said, "I think the thing that gives me the greatest sense of achievement and the greatest satisfaction is reading the letters, and hearing the stories, and participating in the work, and doing the planning, and staying up around the clock to see that this burden, this yoke, this 'sack of cement' that these old people have been carrying on their shoulders, is removed—and they now can see the sight of the Promised Land when finally with their card they can go in and have some medical treatment as a result of their Government's planning, and their own planning, and the hospital planning, and the medical planning."

So this is a great accomplishment, a great achievement. It is not just an image or an appearance. It is not something we are just talking about. We are right in sight of the Promised Land—and we do want it to be successful.

Now there are going to be doubters and there are going to be detractors. There always will be. They complain about the consequences. I want to—for their benefit, although I do not want to give them over-recognition, but I want to anticipate it and I want you to anticipate it because you will see it serialized—I want to recall the words of Bernard Shaw and he said, "Nothing is worth doing—unless the consequences may be serious."

I remember a very controversial man in our community. One time when I went to him and asked what he thought about a doubter and detractor who appeared on my horizon very often, he said, "Very little harm; very little good." And there're people that—that really leave little behind them. Very little harm, very little good. You don't have to doubt them, you don't have to detract them, you don't have to pay much attention to them, because what they do is not very controversial. Now we believe—in this country, in the Congress, in the Nation, in the White House—that this job is worth doing. And with your help we think we can do it.

And I am calling, very shortly, a meeting (I want to serve notice on Secretary Gardner publicly because I don't want to give him a chance to object privately) of the Director of the National Institutes of Health and the directors of the nine individual institutes, as well as the Surgeon General of the Public Health Service. I am asking them to come here to meet with me for the purpose of hearing what plans, if any, they have for reducing deaths and for reducing disabilities and for extending research in that direction.

I firmly believe that if we can pull together these men and if we can hold such a meeting and follow it up with having them have meetings with other experts in the 50 States in these particular fields, and then come back and meet with me 3 months later—when I take that checksheet and see just what they have, like when you take a car in to get it filled with—the tires filled and the radiator checked and all those things—we will go down their checklist and we will see what specific efforts they are going to make to reduce deaths among the leading killers, especially arteriosclerosis of the heart and the brain, and various forms of cancer, and to reduce disabilities such as arthritis and severe mental and neurological diseases or illness.

You know it is only since 1945 that death from tuberculosis has ceased to be considered the will of God. And it is only since the early fifties and the development of the Salk vaccine that polio is no longer striking terror in the heart of every mother, every parent, in this country.

Now actually a great deal of basic research has been done. I have been participating in the appropriations for years in this field. But I think the time has now come to zero in on the targets by trying to get this knowledge fully applied. There are hundreds of millions of dollars that have been spent on laboratory research that may be made useful to human beings here if large-scale trials on patients are initiated in promising areas. Now Presidents, in my judgment, need to show more interest in what the specific results of medical research are during their lifetime, during their administration. I am going to show an interest in the results. Whether we get any or not I am going to show an interest in them.

And I hope that meeting with the head of the NIH and the individual institute directors might energize—or make a contribution, I guess, is a better way to put it, to plans for specific results. And that is, specific results in the decline in deaths and disabilities.

At present, a very small percentage of research money is spent on clinical research to test new drugs and treatments on human beings. And until we do this, we won't have any major new ways of reducing deaths and disabilities. But after I have heard plans which may not be specific today, I will then ask these men to return to me to give me more concrete proposals and recommendations that they have received from you and from their own knowledge, say, in 3 months. And then I would hope that for whatever time is allotted me in the White House, that about every 6 months we could come back and see what progress we are making. Because these men are now responsible for over a billion dollars of research and training money. And I want them to be sure that they have the best defined programs and goals that can be originated in this country.

To do what? To prolong the prime of life for all of our people. Now, if I can hold two or three such meetings, I feel that with the deep sympathy and interest and leadership of the President, we will be able to get more results for the survival of our people than anyone else has ever done in the history of mankind. Think about what a laudable objective that is!

I would like to start children to school earlier. I would like to keep them there longer. I would like for them to be prepared better. And I would like to lose fewer of them when they discover America, and keep all those that discover America living as long as possible—and living in a wholesome and constructive and happy atmosphere as long as possible.

It gives me great satisfaction to walk into a home where a person that is 93 years old can go into his shower in his wheelchair and turn it on by himself, or where a crippled lady who is 84 does not have to bend over to open the refrigerator because it is on a platform especially designed for her.

So I want to see us use all the knowledge we can—to better prepare our children so they are better prepared as our adults, and their eyes are tested, and their teeth tested, and that their mental retardation problems are detected early, so that we can save at least a part of this great waste.

Do you know we are taking in in the neighborhood of $10 billion more this year than I thought we would take in a few months ago? (I said in the neighborhood; that gives me flexibility, I hope, because we really don't know until we get the income tax payments calculated. But we are going to take in several billion more.)

That is a wonderful feeling—to have that much more coming in. Now why is it coming in? Because more people are working. They are being paid more money.

And as this unemployment is reduced, as their skills are developed, as they are up-graded, as they are promoted, as they earn more—then we get more. And that gives you more to do this research to prolong life and to better educate people.

And what we are doing in this country is contagious. It is spreading to other areas of the world. I can't imagine any field of endeavor, unless it is preaching or teaching or public life, that can be as satisfying as healing the sick and ministering to their needs—and seeing that in this country.

Look at the problem we have in Vietnam. They earn $65 a year and they die at 35. That is their average life expectancy. But because of the leadership of you and your profession and your group, our life expectancy, because we're Americans, is more than doubled.

We can't be satisfied with that. We are going on and do a better job. And the first job we are going to get on with is medical care, July 1. And then there are going to be other and equally important developments down the road.

Thank you so much for coming.

NOTE: The President spoke at 11:10 a.m. in the East Room at the White House before a meeting attended by approximately 300 representatives of the American Medical Association, the American Hos-pital Association, and State medical and hospital associations. In his opening words he referred to Vice President Hubert H. Humphrey, Secretary of Health, Education, and Welfare John W. Gardner, and Senator Clinton P. Anderson of New Mexico.

During his remarks the President referred to Rep-resentative Cecil R. King of California, who along with Senator Anderson sponsored the Medicare bill in Congress, Sam Rayburn, Representative from Texas 1913–1961, who served as Speaker of the House of Representatives 1940–1947, 1949–1953, 1955–1961, and Dr. Jonas Salk of New York City who developed the first effective vaccine against poliomyelitis.

The meeting of medical leaders was announced by the White House on June 3, 1966. The release stated that the June 15 meeting would be the last of a series of consultations with the health community held over the past year. During the past year, the White House added, Government officials had par-ticipated in conferences with more than 2,000 local medical organizations and had held hundreds of working sessions with medical, hospital, and other groups to develop guidelines for the program.

The release noted that the 1-day working session would include panel discussions of problems which might arise in certain communities with high pro-portions of older persons. The release also an-nounced that the President had asked the Department of Health, Education, and Welfare to establish a special around-the-clock Medicare information serv-ice at Social Security headquarters in Baltimore to deal with any problems arising under the Medicare program, and that Social Security district offices would be prepared to respond to inquiries from any beneficiary, physician, hospital administrator, or other individual (2 Weekly Comp. Pres. Docs., p. 730).

For the President's statement following a meeting with health officials, see Item 293.

272 Remarks to Members of a Goodwill Delegation From Austria. *June 15, 1966*

Mr. Flajnik, Ambassador Riddleberger, Am-bassador Lemberger, Senator Fulbright, Members of the Congress, distinguished Members of the Austrian delegation, ladies and gentlemen:

As an American I was very proud as I listened to Mr. Flajnik's remarks a moment ago. I think it is a very great thing for the United States of America to have partici-pated in the economic miracle of Austria.

It is a very great thing for the Western community that Austrian politics have evolved in a peaceful and constructive direc-tion. I think it is a very great thing for our world that the major powers were able to work out a fair and a reasonable treaty which guarantees Austrian independence.

These are milestones in the quest for peace.

611

But we in this country feel humble in the face of that history. We are well aware who are the real heroes in this story. While the Marshall plan did help provide some of the financial resources that were needed during that time, we know that the real heart of this effort—the backbone of it all—was the strength, the fortitude, and the endurance of the Austrian people.

We stood here and watched with great admiration as they transformed the ruins of war into a modern and prosperous nation. We did try to help where we could and when we could. But the spirit and the energy which rebuilt your cities and factories and roads and schools were yours. That is something we need to recognize.

That is the only way that nations are really built—through their own efforts. It is a long and sometimes difficult way. But today's Austria is ample proof that it can be done—that it is worth the effort.

Most of all, the postwar history of Austria is a source of great encouragement. For the Austria of 1945 the confrontation of the great powers presented a danger and a challenge to peace in Europe. For years Austria hung in that balance called the cold war. For years there was doubt that settlement was even possible. It seemed neither side could afford to trust the other to permit a guarantee of independence and neutrality. Negotiations at first produced only failure and deadlock. Time and again success slipped through our fingers.

Finally, after years of negotiation—after nearly 400 meetings with Soviet representatives, reason prevailed. On May 15, 1955, the treaty was signed.

We learned that reconciliation does not always come quickly. But we also learned that if we are patient and sustain our commitments, if we maintain our efforts, and if we are certain of our principles—but willing always to negotiate as reasonable men—then fair and just solutions can usually be found.

So today, 11 years later, we meet here to observe and to comment on the benefits of this settlement. Despite limited natural resources and a very long history of economic hardship, Austria has today almost eliminated poverty. It has created a system of social security that is unparalleled in the world. It has raised per capita income from $417 in 1948 to $1,262 in 1965, an increase of 300 percent. It has been a force for good in the international organizations and in the other less developed parts of our world. It has exercised always a moderating influence on East-West relations.

Austria, I think, is an example of how unfinished business of peace in Europe can be attained through reason, patience, understanding, and determination, all based on strength and unity.

Austria is proof that intractable problems between the East and the West can be resolved at the expense of no nations or peoples.

The wounds of recent European history, it is true, are deep. And they will not heal overnight—nor do we expect them to.

But change is the one certitude in a changing world. The logic of history and economics—yes, indeed, of survival—should in due time move us all toward an increasing sense of mutual interests and inter-dependence. As this awareness increases, nations, hopefully, will abandon the idea that ideologies and parochial advantages can ever really be imposed by force.

Our own posture toward the East, I hope, is clear. As I told a group of our Polish friends who met here just a very few weeks ago, "We will encourage every constructive enrichment of the human, cultural, and commercial ties between Eastern Europe and the West." We have worked along these lines for some time. We have made some progress. And we will continue.

In the past year, for example, a few of the less known efforts:

—Educational and cultural exchanges with Czechoslovakia have almost doubled. Exchanges with Rumania are up about a third.

—Our universities have signed new and expanded exchange programs with Bulgaria, Czechoslovakia, and Hungary.

—An American airline has opened the first direct American service to Czechoslovakia in almost 20 years.

—Rumania has allowed several hundred dual nationals and relatives of U.S. citizens to join their loved ones here in our country.

—For the past 2 years the United States has participated in the annual Budapest Industrial Fair.

—Our trade with Czechoslovakia rose from $24 million in 1964 to $44 million the next year, 1965.

—Peaceful trade with the Soviet Union is now up to $87 million in 1965 as against $54 million the year before—a hopeful sign; an encouraging sign.

—American exports to Rumania rose from $1 million in 1963 to $6½ million last year.

—The Commodity Credit Corporation will now accept East European bank guarantees for credit up to 3 years on exports of our farm products.

—The Yugoslavs have been making a root-and-branch economic reform—helped by the sale of American surplus farm products, export-import guarantees, and loan repayment extensions. Now their factories are competing with each other in the marketplace and increasingly with producers from abroad.

—Early last month I called for a treaty to keep the moon free for exploration and use by us all, and to prohibit the use of celestial bodies for weapons, for weapons tests, and for military maneuvers. I acknowledge the leadership of Ambassador Waldheim, the Austrian Ambassador to the United Nations, the distinguished Chairman of the Outer Space Committee.

I reviewed this only last evening in the White House with Ambassador Goldberg and others at the reception for members of the United Nations. At the end of the month the Soviet Union proposed a treaty very much along the same lines. So I am glad to tell you and proud to tell you and happy to tell you that we are encouraged that—we hope that negotiations looking toward agreements can be started at an early date and without great delay.

I do not want to overemphasize or to exaggerate. No one of these steps by itself will heal the wounds of the years gone by. But we are on a journey which will not end today or even in this decade. And I do believe that this journey is the right course for us to take. I do think each of these steps that I have enumerated, each of these exchanges, will produce better understanding, and will finally lead us to a solution that is much to be preferred to the ones that have been practiced in times gone by.

We are going to take new steps to consult with our allies in the days ahead. We are determined not to cease our efforts just because we have problems and because difficulties arise or because frustrations abound. In the course of things these are expected. They will diminish as the hope of unity in Europe increases.

We of the West must maintain our fundamental unity of purpose while we constantly search for areas of common understanding with the East. I hope to provide some leadership in that direction.

We must remain strong so that weakness never tempts the ambitious.

The division that has plagued Europe over the past two decades is slowly giving way, I believe, to new possibilities for understanding and to new possibilities for cooperation. I think your visit here is another evidence of that. So let us reach for those possibilities that are at hand. And let us work to create new opportunities along the way.

We are very pleased that you could come our way. We know that you will leave more than you will take with you, but we hope that in what you leave and what you take will be a promise for humanity and will be certainly worth the effort and the expense that has gone into it.

We are delighted that you could spend this time in our Rose Garden here. I am sorry that the clouds didn't cover up the sun a little bit. I am afraid the heat may be a little unbearable at the noon hour. We have so enjoyed your coming and I look forward to a little brief visit with each of you.

Thank you.

NOTE: The President spoke at 12:35 p.m. in the Rose Garden at the White House to a group of 30 Austrian business and professional men who were visiting the United States on a goodwill tour. In his opening words he referred to Bruno Flajnik, spokesman for the group, James W. Riddleberger, U.S. Ambassador to Austria, Ernst Lemberger, Austrian Ambassador to the United States, and Senator J. W. Fulbright of Arkansas, Chairman of the Senate Foreign Relations Committee. Later he referred to Kurt Waldheim, Austrian Ambassador to the United Nations.

On behalf of the delegation, Mr. Flajnik presented the President with a "ceremonial sword of peace" which, he said, would serve as a symbol of Austria's role at the Congress of Vienna and of the role of the United States in world affairs today.

For the President's remarks at the ceremony commemorating Poland's national and Christian millennium, see Item 200.

273 Remarks to the Delegates to a Conference of State Legislative Leaders. *June 16, 1966*

Governor Bryant and distinguished legislators:

I hope all of you have seated yourselves; I think it is asking enough of you to sit out in this sun without asking you to stand and listen to a speech. We would have you in the East Room except for the fact that some of our million-odd visitors happen to be going through there at this time of day and we do not want to cut them off because we might get a resolution in that connection if we did!

I am very grateful to you for coming here to Washington to participate in this conference in the Nation's Capital. The role of a legislator is one that is very familiar to me. I grew up in that tradition. My father was elected to the Texas Legislature 4 years before I discovered America. And he completed his service there in the early twenties.

So I had some understanding of the problems of a legislator during my formative years.

Automobiles, at that time, were a novelty in our country. And I remember how my father traveled back and forth to Austin in a horse and buggy. And I think that we could truly say that during that period it was really horse and buggy government.

But we had our problems and our challenges. They were anti-prohibition and anti-Klan and anti-women suffrage and all those things in those days. They have changed some now, and the 20th century and the problems of 1966 are somewhat different.

But having been in the legislative atmosphere in Washington for 35 years, with the background that I have, I think you can understand why I am anxious to have you come here. Because I think we are entering a new era of relations between the State and the Federal Government. I think we are going to prove that federalism, America's unique contribution to political science, will be equal to the challenges that face us in the 20th century.

There are some who say that the State governments have become obsolete, that they have failed to meet their challenge. But if we admit such failure we admit that the American system has failed. And I think that you know and I know that that is not true.

So, if we come here together and reason together, and exchange viewpoints and accept facts, and draw conclusions and make recommendations, we can prove, I think, that Federal, State, and local governments can join together shoulder to shoulder to insure all the social and economic development which our age demands.

Now that is not an easy task. And I realize that the domestic approaches are not always at that moment as enthusiastically received by the States, by the counties, by the cities, by the homefolks, as they are when they are presented.

Yesterday I talked to a group about medical care. And if I had made the observations 20 years ago about medical care that I made yesterday, I would have been driven out of the Capitol. It has taken a good long period of time for our people, all of them, to see and accept that development. So has it taken them a good long time to really see and accept and embrace the Bill of Rights. It took us a good period of time to see them formulated, and to see them guaranteed, and to see them preserved.

As a matter of fact, the court works on them every day to see that they are not chipped away. I do not have time to go into it with you in detail this morning, but I would hope that this Government in this time, in our time, would be remembered for its own particular Bill of Rights. I think that a citizen of America—black or white or brown, Catholic or Jew or Baptist or Protestant, any kind, north or south, east or west, farmer or cab driver—I think that he ought to have the right to be free, and to break it down in some detail, I would say that is the right to vote—unchallenged, unintimidated, unblackmailed, unhandcuffed.

He ought to have that right. He ought to have the right to eat in any public cafe. He ought to have the right to sleep where the public is welcome. He shouldn't have to drive night after night to try to find a bed, because his religion is such or his color is such that he cannot be accepted because of the peculiarities of someone who holds him out—themselves out to serve the public. So I think he ought to have a right to be free.

I think every child born in this country ought to have a right to all the education he can take. Now we are debating whether it should start at 4 years old or 6 years old, or whatever age. That is a detail we can work out. But I do believe that we, in our time, can and have and must do something about the right of every child to get all the education he can take.

I am not interested in the image or the appearance of it. I am interested in the accomplishment and the achievement. I am interested in the results we obtain.

Now, what are we doing in that field? We passed the Elementary School Act. It was pretty difficult getting it passed. I have been around here for 30 years hearing people talk about Federal aid to schools. And it has been generally opposed by very vociferous people.

The Jewish organizations—I went out and made a speech to B'nai B'rith, and the next morning they resolved against my elementary school bill. I was like the lawyer who said he made the greatest speech that he ever made in his lifetime before the jury. He was asked, "What did they do to your client?" And he said, "They hung him."

I thought at one time that I had the Catholics where they would go along with the school bill, only to find that the subcommittee didn't think so at all. And just about the time I had it all put together, one of my Baptist friends called up and said that he wanted me to know that he thought the Pope had taken over Washington and they couldn't go along with that bill, either.

One of my secretaries told him that I couldn't talk then. He said, "Why?" She said, "He is out talking to Dr. Graham—he is swimming with Dr. Graham." He said, "You don't mean he is swimming in the middle of the day—the President?" She said, "Yes, he is out swimming before lunch." He said, "Who did you say he was swimming with?" She said, "Dr. Graham." He said, "Our Billy?" And I think the fact that Dr. Graham was here—"our Billy" was here at that time—kind of helped us to put those factions together.

But, the fact that the B'nai B'rith and the Catholic organizations on welfare and Dr. Graham and the Baptists and others finally agreed on the elementary school bill—it had never been done before—we have over a billion dollars this year going down on the basis of needs to children.

We have a vocational education bill. We have a higher education bill. For the first time in the history of America, a poor child that has the qualifications, who has completed the prescribed course of study—that child can either get a job to go to college, can get a loan to go to college, or can get a scholarship to go to college. Now that has never existed before, so I think we ought to have a right to all the education we can take.

The right to good health in this country, I think is another right that this Government—Democrats and Republicans, independents and progressives, reactionaries and conservatives, and liberals and radicals—all of them ought to join together in the right to good health. And we are trying to do everything we can about it.

We have roughly 18 million people who are going to have hospital treatment available to them, medical treatment available to them, nursing home treatment available to them, medicines available to them. Most of you are not 65. But I imagine most of you have an uncle or an aunt or a grandma who is 65. And you must know what a relief it is for them to have the feeling that without bothering their son-in-law or brother-in-law they can go in, not as a charity patient, or not because some mayor has called up and said, "We will let them occupy a bed down here that the city will pay for." But they can go in with their card and have hospital care and nursing care and medical care.

Now, we have a billion dollars that we are spending on medical research so that the time will come when our life expectancy will not be 70 years, but will be materially increased. I have spent the morning talking to some very exciting people: Ambassador Porter, who is just here from Vietnam (he is the principal deputy to Ambassador Lodge—he is in charge of our civil program out there) and Mr. Robert Komer, who is a top man on my Security Council staff in charge of Vietnam matters.

We have two phases of the war out there. I am going to let you in on a secret. You have heard just about the military phase; this other has been kept under wraps. We do not know much about it, because Captain Carpenter giving an order to come in to bomb his position is much more dramatic than some fellow that is washing up the kids, and treating their wounds, and teaching them to read and write—a Marine who has fought all day, that is working all night to help in these things.

But we are doing a great job there on health. And what we are doing on education, and on health, and on conservation, and on beautification, and on housing, and on slums in this country is contagious. And it is moving to other countries. It is setting an example for other countries.

In Vietnam today the average citizen dies at 35—at the age of 35! Now because of what we have done—all these domestic programs that a lot of people don't approve of when they start, and they got a lot of holes, you can run a wagon through them sometimes, until you get them perfected. So did the veteran's pension. So did the bonus. So did social security. So did agriculture conservation. So did REA. I remember the great weaknesses we had in that program the first year. But who would repeal REA and social security and school lunch and those things now?

So we are trying to put some of those things in—not just in this country but in other countries. We have distributed 11 million schoolbooks to the children of Vietnam, in this nation of 14 million, already. We have doubled their rice production. We are going to materially increase their life expectancy. And when Uncle Sam leaves that country—and it can't be too soon to suit us—we hope that we can provide all the help they need until they are able to take over themselves. Then that we can come back home just as we have on every other effort that we have made in that direction, and let them carry on and develop. But one thing you can be sure of: We are going to make a material contribution to their education, to their production, to their way

of life, to their health, to increasing their life expectancy.

So these rights—the right to be free, the right to receive all the education you can take, the right to good health, the right to enjoy the fruits of conservation and scenic beauty, as you are seeing here in the first house of the land, but I would like to see in every city and county and courtyard and city hall and State yard in this Capital—all of those things are making progress in this country and I think are spilling over into other nations.

Why? Because an essential, basic part of our defense of this country is to serve notice on all the people who live in this world with us that gangsterism and aggression and force are not to be rewarded.

Now we were hesitant to do that in World War II when Hitler went through Poland. We thought we could sit that one out. We had a lot of the fathers of that time who said it was not our concern. They carried umbrellas around saying that we had been to Europe to save democracy in World War I, and that we shouldn't get involved in World War II.

But we find that when an aggressor is on the march, when a conqueror is out to subjugate, that he doesn't just eliminate the most desirable. We have what other people want. And if they develop the strength and the power to take it, don't you think they won't! So, in due time, almost too late—when I think of some of the problems I have now, I am rather thankful they are not any more than they are because I remember in August before Pearl Harbor in December, that President Roosevelt had a Congress that voted 203 to 202 to extend the draft—by only one vote. And I think what the consequences would have been if we had sent the Army home!

But we had men in the Senate at that

time, that were on the Foreign Relations Committee, who said they had better information than the President. Thank goodness the President had that one-vote margin! And I am not sure that some higher force didn't contribute to it. Because I thought I had been elected to the Senate in July of that year, but they counted down there about a week and I was finally defeated for the Senate 1,311 votes. I had to return to my House seat. And I was there to cast 1 of those 203 votes that did not send the Army home.

So when you come in here today in this period of time when we are trying to guarantee not only our Bill of Rights but our rights to good health, our rights to education, our rights to be free, our rights to enjoy ourselves and raise our families in good environments, and our rights to liberty and freedom—it means we cannot have those rights unless we try to help other people preserve them, too.

So we say to any other would-be conqueror: When and if you attempt by force to subjugate people, you will meet the United States of America.

President Eisenhower and Secretary Dulles presented to the Congress a commitment of that kind and the Congress entered into it 82 to 1.

And we were called upon to perform on that commitment when aggression started. We are now doing our best to provide the maximum amount of deterrence with the minimum amount of loss.

We have lost over 2,000 men who have died in battle in Vietnam this year—2,000. We lost 50,000 on our highways last year. But would that we had not lost any!

But we cannot tell what the days ahead hold for us. We know they are going to be difficult. We know they are going to require sacrifice. Everything we have ever done in our history to preserve freedom has required it. But we are going to continue on, to carry out our military effort to prevent that deterrent—and our civil effort to educate and to improve the health and to give the training and to increase the production on the civil side of the people in that country.

And I am very grateful—I didn't know you had a resolution considered. I get a good many resolutions and it is always heartening when I get one like this. I hear a lot about petitions these days. That is a right that we all enjoy and that we freely exercise.

But I am delighted that as a result of your judgments and your deliberations and your experiences, that you would feel that you would want to pass a resolution such as I had read to me.

Secretary Rusk has just returned from a NATO conference in Brussels. We regret very much that General de Gaulle has felt it necessary to express himself as he has. We have accepted what he has said more in sorrow than in anger. And we, and our other allies in NATO—the 14—have met and have reached judgments which are in the process of being executed.

We hope in due time that events will prove that those judgments are wise. We believe in collective security and we are going to make whatever contribution to it we can. We are doing the same thing in Southeast Asia.

We have met with the Prime Minister of India and with the President of Pakistan. And we think we have made a contribution to trying to bring about better understanding in that part of the world.

We have just completed a year of trial in the Dominican Republic. Under a provisional government, we have said to all the would-be conquerors that you cannot, by force, come in and set up governments and enslave people. We will provide the assistance that is necessary through the Organization of American States in cooperation with our neighbors in this hemisphere to make this hemisphere safe from would-be conquerors, and allow the people, themselves, to select their own type of government. And in a free election, with numerous observers from all factions, by a majority in excess of over 200,000, a President has been chosen, and will be installed.

So the hemisphere is making progress. Two and a half years ago our per capita growth was 1 percent in this hemisphere. It is now in excess of 2½.

I had a group of African diplomats in last week. We are very concerned with their problems. We are doing what we can to help those newly born nations achieve not only the independence that they have so long sought and desired, but during this growing period to help them by more material means establish stability. So when you look at Europe, when you look at Africa, when you look at Asia, we have a great deal to be thankful for.

We are moving ahead. We are making progress. Our Nation can be proud of what it is doing there as well as what it is doing here. In no period of our national history have we made more progress in the field of education and health and conservation than we have made in the sixties. And in all of that effort we welcome your cooperation and we welcome your support—and we think as a result of your meeting here that good things will flow from it.

I propose to submit to the Congress this next session—I have 90 measures I have submitted this time, I have only had 60 of them acted upon by the House committee. I met with their chairman yesterday. So I do not think I will submit much more this session—may have one or two extra things. But, next year I am going to submit to Con-

gress legislation for a management exchange program that will allow Federal officials to work out arrangements with State and local governments and to give State and local officials a chance to work at the Federal level.

We have done some of this by mutual exchange. But I hope to have legislation that will underwrite a program where we can bring all phases of our Government closer together.

I think the States will have to adopt appropriate arrangements, and I hope they will want to. We are considering, and I solicit your suggestion, ways in which the Government can help States and cities in their training programs of junior officials.

I have already asked the Director of the Budget to report to me before the start of the next Congress on how we can lend Federal support to programs for training State and local executives. I find that one of the best sources of the employees for the Federal Government are men who have been trained at the State level. And I thank you for producing those men and for making them available to us in our military and in our civilian effort.

Governor Bryant has a specific injunction and responsibility to not only maintain contact with each of the Governors of the 50 States and the Territories, but also to maintain contact with the legislative leaders of both parties in those States.

We make mistakes, and we know it and we regret them. We wish we could avoid making them. Perhaps if we can hear from you soon enough you can correct them before they develop into very serious matters. So, in the spirit of give and take I want you to know that we are grateful for your coming here.

I need all the help I can get. I am doing my deadlevel best to provide this country and our people with as good a government as I am capable of. I am doing the best I can. But I can do better—if the Governors of the States, if the responsible legislative leaders of that State, will come in and tell me of things that we can do, and emphasize those things more than if they just tell others about things that we should not have done.

No man in public life—and certainly not one who has reached the stage that I am in now—ever ran on a platform of doing what was wrong. We all think that we are doing right. But our problem is not to do what is right. Our problem is to know what is right.

And when you have to look at this problem of 120 nations with their diverse populations and their backgrounds, and their environments and their geography, and their views and their ancient hatreds and their traditions, when you have 50 States—and I can assure you that the people of Maine and the people of Mississippi don't always see everything alike—then you must make the decision (as President Truman said, "The buck stops here") on what is in the national interest, what is the greatest good for the greatest number.

Now Mr. Rayburn used to have a favorite saying that any donkey could kick a barn down, but it took a good carpenter to build one.

Yesterday I met with the doctors. The day before I met with the bankers. Today I am meeting with the legislators. Tomorrow I will meet with the labor people. The next day I will meet with the committee chairmen.

Over the weekend I met with the legislative leaders of both parties who felt the need of more meetings and who commented on our candor. And I told them everything that I knew—all in the hope that we can not only do what is right but we can do what is right by knowing what is right. So

please feel that you are honored by your people—to help your country have the best government that it can possibly have at every level. And I am trying to do that without regard to party, without regard to prejudice, and without regard to the passions of the moment.

Men in this Government are selected on the basis of merit. They are given responsibility and they are supported. If they make mistakes, I try to correct them. And we make plenty. But I think that we can do a better job if all of you will come in here and help us "build this barn."

I am trying, with everything I have got, to build the best barn I can—to put in this goldfish bowl that is called America the best example that we can of what is good, and what is fair, and what is just, and what is right, and something that every other nation would like to emulate.

And we are charged with many motivations. I said to a friend of mine the other night in New York—he'd asked me this question why we would be out 10,000 miles fighting for 14 million people so they could be free and have liberty.

And I said: "We are not just fighting for 14 million. We are fighting for almost 3 billion people who also want freedom and liberty. I know another nation that you are interested in has a few hundred thousand population, and they are not going to be able to stand up to conquerors with their little limited forces if we throw in the towel, and move out of the way of the advancing tide, and come running home, or surrender, or pull in our horns, or send up the white flag. We are fighting for a hundred nations' freedom and liberty, and we are going to continue to fight until men are convinced that it is better to talk than to fight."

We have been convinced of that a long time. We are ready to do that any time, anywhere, with any government. And all they have to do to test us is to name the place and the date, and they will find us there. But until the other side sees the same thing you cannot have a unilateral contract.

The strength that you have given your President and your country by your resolution is appreciated. And I would like to tell each of you that personally. If you will get out of that sun and come in the shade, and walk through the office, I will show you where I spend a good many hours every day.

Again thank you personally.

NOTE: The President spoke at 11:45 a.m. in the Rose Garden at the White House to the delegates to the National Legislative Leaders Conference. His opening words referred to Farris Bryant, Director of the Office of Emergency Planning, former Governor of Florida, and coordinator of the conference.

During his remarks the President referred, among others, to his father, Sam Ealy Johnson, Jr., who served in the Texas State Legislature 1905–1909 and 1917–1925, evangelist William F. (Billy) Graham, William J. Porter, Deputy U.S. Ambassador to the Republic of Vietnam, Henry Cabot Lodge, U.S. Ambassador to the Republic of Vietnam, Robert W. Komer, Special Assistant to the President for Peaceful Reconstruction in Vietnam, and to Capt. William S. Carpenter, Jr., commander of C Company, Second Battalion, 502d Infantry Regiment in Viet-

nam, who on June 9 called for U.S. air strikes on his own position to save his men from annihilation by North Vietnamese troops. The President also referred to John Foster Dulles, Secretary of State during the Eisenhower administration, Dean Rusk, Secretary of State, Charles de Gaulle, President of France, Mrs. Indira Gandhi, Prime Minister of India, Mohammed Ayub Khan, President of Pakistan, and Sam Rayburn, Representative from Texas 1913–1961, who served as Speaker of the House of Representatives 1940–1947, 1949–1953, 1955–1961.

The resolution which the President mentioned in the closing paragraph was read by Mr. Bryant. In it the legislative leaders expressed their gratitude for the United States military forces in Vietnam and their endorsement of the President's effort "to preserve the independence and security of the people of South Vietnam, to defeat the efforts of Communist aggression, and to achieve as speedily as possible a peaceful and honorable settlement."

The National Legislative Leaders Conference met in the Indian Treaty Room, Executive Office Building, June 15–16, 1966. During the conference the legislative leaders met with Cabinet members and other Federal officials. Discussions were held on such topics as "New Health, Education and Welfare Programs," "The States Part in Poverty Programs," "Law Enforcement and the States," "Metropolitan Problems and the States," "The President's Traffic Safety Program," "Resources and Water Pollution," "Financing Public Services Today," and "Federal-State Cooperation in Telecommunications." The final session was entitled "Creative Federalism—Establishing Better Communications Between the Federal Government and the States."

274 Statement by the President on the Pacification and Development Programs in Vietnam. *June 16, 1966*

MANY AMERICANS who watch the political turmoil and our military progress in the battle against aggression in Vietnam are not always conscious of our effort to win the "other war" in this devastated country. This is a war against misery and want, against insecurity and terrorism, and for better education, health, and welfare for the people of Vietnam.

I regard these programs of pacification

and development, to which our own military establishment also contributes heavily, as equal in importance to the magnificent effort of our military men.

The progress reported to me by Ambassador Porter is impressive, even though I will be the first to say that we and our Vietnamese allies still have a long way to go. We will continue to collaborate fully with Vietnam in those social, economic, and health-education-welfare programs designed to provide an embattled people with security and the essentials to which they are entitled.

NOTE: The statement was read by Bill D. Moyers, Special Assistant to the President, at his news con-

ference at 4:30 p.m. on Thursday, June 16, 1966, at the White House. It was not made public in the form of a White House press release.

In the statement the President referred to William J. Porter, Deputy U.S. Ambassador to the Republic of Vietnam.

275 Remarks at the Swearing In of Stanley Ruttenberg as Assistant Secretary of Labor for Manpower. *June 17, 1966*

Mr. and Mrs. Ruttenberg and family, Secretary Wirtz, members of the Cabinet, my friends in the Congress, ladies and gentlemen:

One of the special joys of the Presidency is the occasional opportunity to improve the future by rewarding past achievements.

This is such an occasion.

Stanley Ruttenberg has been an architect of America's manpower policy. Now, as the Assistant Secretary of Labor for Manpower, he will be one of its master builders. And, therefore, he has his work cut out.

We have been thinking small, instead of thinking big, about the use of our human resources. And we think that this has been one of the most serious of our failures at social policy.

Today we hear from many quarters that the advance of our economy ought to be slowed down in part because increasing manpower shortages threaten us with serious inflation.

Businessmen that I talk to frequently tell me that they can't get the workers they need.

Housewives write the President to say that they can't get help in the house or in the yard and that they have given up trying to get things repaired that need to be fixed.

But, last month's report shows that unemployment is up again—it is now 4 percent—and 3 million people are now looking for work and can't find it.

The recent door-to-door survey of three counties in the Mississippi Delta shows an unemployment rate there of over 50 percent.

We are going to line up almost a million extra jobs for young people in America this summer. But there will be another million that will still be unemployed.

More and more of our older Americans are retiring earlier and earlier—many of them want to work. And they are able to work.

Somehow this just doesn't seem to make sense.

I don't believe that there is really a manpower shortage in this country today. There is a very—in my judgment—serious waste of manpower. One of the ways, I think, to stop inflation is to stop the waste of the human potential.

If this is good economic policy, certainly it is even better human policy.

At least three things should be done to try to make this policy work:

First, we need to improve our research to show the reasons why people are out of work, not just how many are unemployed.

Our unemployment reports should show not only unemployment, but underemployment and the extent of involuntary "nonparticipation in the work force."

They have got to be expanded to show where the remaining unemployment is—so that we can move in on it. They may have to be expanded to show who the unemployed are—so that we can get to work on each situation.

So that is why I am asking the very distinguished Secretary of Labor and you to make these necessary changes in our unemployment reports.

I am also asking you to work with other interested agencies to extend immediately the manpower inventory that has already been undertaken in Chicago, St. Louis, Houston, and the Mississippi Delta area.

I should also like to have the fastest possible collection of complete manpower resources information in those 5,000 census tract areas with the greatest unemployment.

I am asking the Secretary of Labor and the Secretary of Commerce to submit soon a report on manpower in our construction industry.

It is time to do something about the fact that this industry continually reports the most serious manpower shortages—yet it appears that it has the second highest reported annual unemployment rate.

Now, second, we think there should be fuller coordination between public and private manpower programs; between those of Federal, State, and local agencies; and between those being developed within our own Federal Government. I want the steps outlined in the manpower report of March 1966—steps which will achieve this coordination—to be greatly speeded up.

Third, and finally, management and labor must each recognize that the public interest in manpower policy is as important now as price policy and wage policy. I cannot direct this, but I am going to try to encourage it. I am very hopeful that business and labor will respond.

Secretary Ruttenberg, you will have quite a lot to do in this new job. I hope these measures will help you. You assume your duties with an outstanding, distinguished record—a proven record—and your country's confidence that at least your President and the Secretary of Labor believe that you are the best possible man in this country to do this very important job.

Thank you very much.

NOTE: The President spoke at 11:15 a.m. in the East Room at the White House. In his opening words he referred to Stanley Ruttenberg, former Special Assistant to the Secretary of Labor for Economic Affairs, his wife, and Secretary of Labor W. Willard Wirtz, who administered the oath of office.

For the President's manpower report to Congress of March 8, 1966, see Item 111.

276 Memorandum on Ethical Conduct on the Part of Government Officers and Employees. *June 17, 1966*

Memorandum for the Heads of Executive Departments and Agencies:

I am pleased to share with you the enclosed report from John Macy concerning ethical conduct of Government officers and employees. Your thoughtful and diligent implementation of the new standards of Executive Order 11222 is commendable.

The traditions of honesty and integrity in the military and civil service of the United States are properly a source of pride for all Americans. We intend in this Administration to ensure that their pride and confidence are maintained and strengthened. We hold a public trust, and we shall hold it high.

I expect you to see to it that officers and employees throughout your agency adhere firmly and without compromise to their responsibility for fair and impartial dealings with all who have business with the Government.

LYNDON B. JOHNSON

NOTE: Executive Order 11222 of May 8, 1965, is entitled "Prescribing Standards of Ethical Conduct for Government Officers and Employees" (30 F.R. 6469; 3 CFR, 1965 Supp., p. 130; see also 1965 volume, this series, Item 241).

The report from John W. Macy, Jr., Chairman of the Civil Service Commission, dated June 9, 1966, was made public by the White House on June 17. The report, in the form of a memorandum to the President, follows:

MEMORANDUM FOR THE PRESIDENT

Subject: *Ethical Conduct of Government Officers and Employees*

Significant benefits are resulting from the new standards of ethical conduct which you established a year ago, May 8, 1965, by Executive Order 11222. Indeed, the clarity and emphasis of your intentions on this matter have produced an entirely new climate of concern among executive branch personnel—a healthy, everyday concern—for impeccable conduct and meticulous avoidance of conflict of interest. And this heightened awareness is becoming well known to the business community, to political scientists and to the press.

True, the new standards are high and their strict limitations on acceptance of gifts, entertainment or favors have brought minor grumblings, from within and outside the Government, since they require substantial change from past practices in some cases. However, the amount of such complaint is not large and, in my judgment, is far outweighed by an increased confidence among employees and the public generally that agencies of the executive branch have joined in common cause to achieve both the appearance and the reality of honest, fair and impartial conduct of the public's business.

Question also has been raised whether the proclamation of strict ethical requirements, such as those concerning gifts and favors and the disclosure of outside business and financial interests, does not in itself impugn the integrity of public officials and thereby make public service less attractive. I find this question is largely academic. There is no evidence whatever during this first year that uncompromising ethical standards, publicly known, adversely affect the recruitment or retention of persons of high quality and integrity in the Government service.

Top Presidential Appointees

One innovation of the new program was the requirement that the heads of executive departments and agencies, full-time members of boards and commissions, and certain appointees in the Executive Office of the President furnish me a confidential statement of outside employment and financial interests. About 165 top officials were covered by this provision.

My review of their statements has revealed that, by and large, your appointees are persons of relatively modest means and have carefully restricted their outside interests. The disclosure requirement has not been onerous, even though it involves quarterly reports of changes.

In a few cases, I have had to go back to the individual concerned to discuss stock holdings or business connections which indicated a possible conflict with official responsibilities. So far all questions have been resolved through clarification of the facts or adjustment in the arrangements that gave rise to the question. As of this time, there are about four such cases on which I have discussions pending in order to insure that your standards are fully met.

The disclosure requirement for top Presidential appointees has had this good effect of eliminating some potential individual problems. It also has been beneficial as leadership example to other key agency officials who must report outside employment and financial interests under the requirements of CSC and agency regulations.

Commission and Agency Regulations

The Commission's regulations under the order established a uniform pattern and minimum requirements for agency regulations throughout the executive branch. They carry forward the ethical standards of the order and incorporate general standards of employee conduct on related matters such as gambling, lobbying, misuse of privileges, and other conduct prejudicial to the Government. Agency heads may supplement these minimum standards with requirements suited to their particular needs.

Additionally, the CSC regulations provide for counseling and advisory service to employees and establish procedures for remedial or disciplinary action as needed to enforce the standards. Each agency head has designated a top-ranking employee as counselor and as his representative to the Commission for program coordination.

Each agency's regulations are being published in the Federal Register. This is an extremely useful innovation. It has ensured a thoughtful review and careful drafting of ethical policies and practices related to the agency's mission, while taking into account the proper rights and privileges of employees. It directs the attention of the press and those who do business with the Government to your firm intention that the affairs of Government are to be conducted openly, honorably, honestly and impartially. And it constitutes legal notice to the business community of the bounds of propriety in relationships with Federal officers and employees.

The review and coordination of agency regulations—62 executive departments and agencies—has been time consuming but a rewarding task. Central assistance by the Commission has achieved a common interpretation of the order and its intentions, a force and clarity in drafting, and a pooling of useful approaches to the delineation of propriety in difficult or awkward situations that face Federal officials—for example, in agencies which have at once both the responsibility for promoting the interests of a segment of private business and for regulating some aspects of its affairs. The new regulations reflect a number of changes in agency practices which have been brought about by their heightened awareness of ethical considerations.

Conclusion

I am gratified by the attitude of serious purpose which has characterized agency implementation of the new ethical standards. Experience may reveal ways in which further improvement can be made, but during this first year there has been no indication that any revision of Executive Order 11222 is needed or desirable. All indications are that the innovations of the order are a major step forward in ensuring the maintenance of high ethical standards and the confidence of the public in the integrity of officers and employees in the executive branch.

JOHN W. MACY, JR.
Chairman

277 The President's News Conference of June 18, 1966

THE PRESIDENT. I have some announcements and appointments, and some statements that I will review with you. The Press Office will have copies of these announcements available as soon after the meeting as possible. When I conclude, I will be glad to attempt to answer any questions that you may have.

HOUSING FOR THE POOR

[1.] Fifteen months ago, I urged the Congress to adopt a new concept in housing for our poor.[1] I urged a program to make it economically possible for private enterprise for the first time to take a direct hand in meeting the housing needs of 7 million American families that are living now in substandard dwellings.

Last year the Congress enacted the rent supplement program into law. Last month

it appropriated the money to put that program into action.[2]

Today we are ready to begin assigning the funds to the first projects. Secretary Weaver has set aside over $600,000 to provide for more than 1,000 units of modest but decent housing.

These projects are located in Boston, in Cleveland, in the Delta area of Mississippi, in New Orleans, in New York, in Omaha, in Pasco, Washington, in Philadelphia, in Providence, in Saginaw, Michigan, in San Antonio, and in the Watts area of Los Angeles.

The project in Providence climaxes a dream begun nearly a century ago. In 1883 a Dr. Chase Wiggins set up a trust to found the Building, Sanitary and Educational As-

---

[1] See 1965 volume, this series, Book I, Item 90 (p. 237).

[2] The rent supplement program was enacted as part of the Housing and Urban Development Act of 1965 (Public Law 89–117, 79 Stat. 451). Legislation appropriating funds for the program was approved by the President on May 13, 1966, and September 6, 1966 (see Items 223, 439).

sociation to build housing for the laboring classes. He stipulated, however, that the money could not be used until the trust reached $500,000.

That event has coincided with the inauguration of the rent supplement program—and the association will now sponsor its first housing.

In Omaha, Nebraska, an association for the blind was formed in 1946. Through contributions made to its White Cane Drive, it accumulated enough money to buy some land. Now, with the rent supplements, it can build on that land low cost housing for blind people with low incomes.

These examples are just a beginning. They should be a spur to further action.

All that remains is for the Senate to approve the regular appropriation bill to carry this program forward. Today I urge them once again to do so. This promise to our poor must be fulfilled and I believe it will be.

The Dominican Republic

NOMINATION OF JOHN HUGH CRIMMINS AS AMBASSADOR

[2.] I want to announce that I intend to nominate John Hugh Crimmins of Maryland as United States Ambassador to the Dominican Republic. He will succeed W. Tapley Bennett, who has been assigned as Ambassador to Portugal.

Secretary Rusk, Assistant Secretary Gordon—he's Assistant Secretary for Latin America—and Ambassador Ellsworth Bunker [3] each recommend Mr. Crimmins for this important post.

---

[3] Dean Rusk, Secretary of State, Lincoln Gordon, Assistant Secretary for Inter-American Affairs and U.S. Coordinator, Alliance for Progress, and Ellsworth Bunker, U.S. Representative to the Council of the Organization of American States.

Mr. Crimmins is one of our outstanding career Foreign Service officers. He has had wide experience in Latin American affairs, particularly in the Caribbean area and in the economic field.

His recent assignments include duty in our Embassy in Rio de Janeiro. From late 1961 to February 1963 he served as Director of the Office of Caribbean and Mexican Affairs and then as Coordinator of Cuban Affairs until 1965.

Since January, Mr. Crimmins has served with distinction as Deputy Chief of Mission and Chargé d'Affaires in Santo Domingo. He is proficient in Spanish and Portuguese. His demonstrated competence, experience, and language ability make him very well qualified for this special assignment.

This appointment continues our policy of rewarding those in our career service who have demonstrated their merit and their capacity to handle posts of the highest responsibility.

U.S. REPRESENTATION AT INAUGURATION

[3.] We have received a note from the Provisional Government of the Dominican Republic inviting the United States to send a special mission to the inauguration of President-elect Joaquin Balaguer on July 1. I have asked Vice President Humphrey to represent the United States on this important occasion—as it was my privilege to do at the inauguration of President Bosch [4] in 1963.

He will carry the best wishes of this country to the President-elect and the Dominican nation as they resume constitutional government and launch a new effort to seek economic prosperity and social justice under the Alliance for Progress.

---

[4] Juan Bosch, former President of the Dominican Republic.

The Dominican Republic deserves the salute of us all for the free and fair elections and the massive participation of the Dominican people in them.

The victory belongs to the Dominican people for making the electoral process an effective instrument for expressing their will. But it belongs also to the leaders of the Dominican Republic—to Provisional President García-Godoy, Dr. Balaguer, Professor Bosch, Dr. Bonnelly [5]—for their leadership and their high sense of responsibility.

The Organization of American States can take great satisfaction over its helpful contribution. For the victory of the Dominican people is shared by all the peoples of this hemisphere.

The Dominican Government and the people know that they can count on the continued support of the Organization of American States. The United States, for its part, stands ready to cooperate in mutual efforts under the Alliance for Progress to advance the economic and social well-being of the Dominican people.

TRIBUTE TO AMBASSADOR ELLSWORTH BUNKER

[4.] Finally, I wish to say a few words about Ambassador Ellsworth Bunker. He belongs not only to the United States but to the hemisphere. He has rendered great service to both.

Wise in the ways of statecraft, unvacillating in his faith in the democratic process, tenacious in the pursuit of fair solutions, firm and patient in the face of adversity, respected by all for his integrity and impartiality—he has brought high honor to himself and his country and the Organization of American States which he represented.

OTHER PRESIDENTIAL APPOINTMENTS AND NOMINATIONS

[5.] I have spent some time yesterday and today and preceding days on appointments. I am delighted to announce today that I expect to nominate for reappointment Gerald F. Tape of New York to be a member of the Atomic Energy Commission for a term of 5 years, expiring June 30, 1971.

I expect to nominate Dr. Samuel M. Nabrit, president of Texas Southern University, as a member of the Atomic Energy Commission, to succeed Mrs. Mary I. Bunting, for a term expiring June 30, 1970.

I expect to reappoint Rosel H. Hyde as a member of the Federal Communications Commission and to designate him as Commission Chairman. He is now a Republican appointee to that Commission.

I also intend to nominate Nicholas Johnson, present Federal Maritime Administrator, to fill the existing vacancy on the Federal Communications Commission created by the resignation of E. William Henry.

I intend to nominate Winthrop Knowlton to be Assistant Secretary of the Treasury for International Affairs to replace Merlyn Trued, who has recently resigned.

I have today accepted with regret the resignation of Adm. William F. Raborn as Director of the Central Intelligence Agency.

To replace Admiral Raborn, I am naming Richard McGarrah Helms, who is currently serving as Deputy Director of the Central Intelligence Agency.

I also intend to appoint Mr. Henry D. Owen as the new Chairman of the Policy

_____
[5] Rafael Bonnelly, former President of the Dominican Republic.

Planning Council replacing Mr. Rostow. Mr. Owen is currently Acting Chairman of the Policy Planning Council at the State Department.

U.S. REPRESENTATION AT GUATEMALAN INAUGURATION

[6.] I have asked Governor John Connally [6] to head our delegation to the inauguration of President-elect Mendez Montenegro June 28 to July 2.

President-elect Montenegro has been the distinguished dean of the law school at San Carlos University. He leaves the classroom to assume the highest office of his country. The Guatemalan people, in reaffirming their faith in constitutional government through free and peaceful elections, have picked one of their most distinguished educators to guide their destiny for the next 4 years. I have asked Governor Connally and the delegation accompanying him to carry the best wishes of the United States Government and people to the Guatemalan nation for this historic occasion.

STATEMENT ON VIETNAM

[7.] In the past few weeks the battle in Vietnam has become more intense. The large forces infiltrated from the North into South Vietnam in recent months are now being engaged—sometimes at their initiative, sometime at ours. The forces of South Vietnam, the United States, and our allies have responded with skill, courage, and effectiveness.

During this period my advisers and I have—almost on a daily basis—continued closely to examine and to scrutinize what the aggressor has been doing and our own course of action.

[6] Of Texas.

We have examined the alternatives open to us—including all suggestions from those who have not shared our views.

In the light of the full information available to the President of the United States, we sincerely feel that the national interest requires that we persist in our present policy. That policy is to bring to bear the ground, naval, and air strength required to achieve our objective.

I must observe that this does not mean that we shall not increase our forces or our operations. It is not good national policy publicly to declare to those conducting aggression that there are particular limits on how we shall act to defeat that aggression.

But our objectives remain what they have been:

—to guarantee that infiltration, subversion, and terror mounted and infiltrated from North Vietnam cannot swallow or conquer South Vietnam;

—to permit the people of South Vietnam to select their own government and to build a way of life which conforms to their own traditions and desires.

In meeting this objective, we must also reassure the world that America's agreements, once they are made, are not broken.

We are not fighting to remain in South Vietnam, not to hold bases there, not to control the affairs of that people.

We are there to defeat aggression, to permit a young nation to develop its own destiny, to help its people rebuild and create a modern nation even before the guns go silent.

But to these limited objectives we are fully committed.

What are our prospects?

I must frankly tell you that our intelligence indicates that the aggressor presently bases his hopes, we think, more on political differences in Saigon and Washington than on his military capacity in South Vietnam. While we have differences and divisions, I want our men in the field and our people at home to know that our course is resolute, that our conviction is firm, and we shall not be diverted from doing what is necessary in the Nation's interest and the cause of freedom.

By every evidence available to us, the majority of the people of South Vietnam seem determined to fight for the right to work out their own affairs. They want to go forward with economic reform, with greater social justice, and a constitutional government.

They must do this in the midst of a bitter and ugly war. Since January 1, 1966, we have lost 2,200 of our men; the South Vietnamese have lost 4,300 of their men; our allies have lost 250 of their men.

But the Vietcong and the North Vietnamese have lost three times our combined losses. They have lost 22,500 of their men.

Our attacks on military targets in North Vietnam have imposed a growing burden on those who support the insurgency in the South. We must continue to raise the cost of aggression at its source. And that is the sole purpose of our use of air strength against selected military targets.

In the South, I am encouraged that the Vietnamese are carrying forward the first steps in building a constitutional process. I discussed that at some length this week with Ambassador Porter, who was here in company with Mr. Komer.[7]

The rules for electing a constituent assembly on September 11 have now been formulated. We can expect continued ferment even after the elections are held. Rival political forces are contending for power. This is natural and this is inevitable at this point in the political life of a developing nation.

We shall continue to back the Vietnamese effort to achieve government by the consent of the people, even as they fight the war.

Economically, important steps are underway to control inflation. You will see announcements about them on the tickers today—to expand the flow of supplies to the people, to carry forward the Vietnamese program of revolutionary development.

Here in the United States I believe our people are determined to see this through. In recent primaries, not one candidate for Congress was able to make opposition to the resistance of aggression in South Vietnam a successful position. And more than 125 have now been passed upon by their constituencies. A minority of our people are willing to pull out. Another minority are prepared to see us use our total power. The rest of us, while we may debate this or that dimension of policy, are determined that this Nation honor its responsibility, and its commitment, to help Vietnam turn back aggression from the North.

We must go forward as nations and men have always gone forward in dark moments, confident that when they are right they will prevail. I am confident that we shall gain an honorable peace in South Vietnam.

There are, I believe, very few governments among the more than 120 in the world who do not wish to see an honorable peace at the earliest possible moment. To those few I would say this:

There is honor for all in making peace.

Let the killing stop.

As the Government of Vietnam said in the Declaration of Honolulu,[8] "stop killing your brothers, sisters, their elders and their chil-

---

[7] William J. Porter, Deputy U.S. Ambassador to the Republic of Vietnam, and Robert W. Komer, Special Assistant to the President for Peaceful Reconstruction in Vietnam.

[8] See Item 55.

dren—come and work through constitutional democracy to build together . . . a life of dignity, freedom and peace . . . ."

Look about us in Asia.

Look at the vitality, the economic and social progress of the nine Asian and Pacific nations meeting in Korea.

Look at the new resolve in Indonesia to come to grips with their problems of economic and social development.

Look at the new determination of India and Pakistan to work for their people and to live in peace. Look at the new efforts of the people of Asia to come together and work together in peace.

Ask yourselves: What is the wave of the future?

Is it aggression?

Is it for one nation to conquer another?

Or is it for us all to work together as brothers in growing more food, building more schools, providing better health to all of our people?

I genuinely and sincerely believe it is the latter.

I will be glad now to take questions from you for whatever period of time you feel desirable.

QUESTIONS

POSSIBILITY OF TAX INCREASE

[8.] Q. Mr. President, there have been some varying forecasts from members of the Cabinet, Secretary Fowler and Secretary Connor,[9] as to the prospects of a tax increase. I am wondering if you could clear the situation up as of now?

THE PRESIDENT. Twenty-five years ago I would have been concerned about what I have seen about the quotations from the

---

[9] Henry H. Fowler, Secretary of the Treasury, and John T. Connor, Secretary of Commerce.

Secretary of Commerce and the Secretary of the Treasury. But when I read their statements, I seem to detect that they are expressing in response to inquiries made of them their views about what may develop in this particular field.

I don't think any of us are in a position to state at this time, nor do I desire to speculate on what a decision might be. We are watching all the factors that must be considered, primarily the appropriations measures that are being guided through the Congress, the Government budget itself, and our expenditures in Vietnam, as well as the private factors in the economy.

When we have gone further along with our appropriation bills, and when we have seen evidences that we think justify a decision, I will announce one.

I have not interpreted what the Secretary of Commerce or the Secretary of the Treasury has said as being a positive statement of policy of this administration, but rather as their personal feelings, and perhaps a speculation.

As for me, I do not care to speculate and am not in a position to do so now, because the interpretation that would be placed on it might bring about some misunderstandings and misapprehensions. I think it is best to just wait until a decision is made— then announce it.

ON BOMBING HANOI

[9.] Q. Mr. President, would you please explain for us why it is wrong for us to bomb the capital in North Vietnam, and who has ordered this theory into the policy?

THE PRESIDENT. I don't think I would want to comment on the tactics or strategy at this point.

Q. Don't you think the people would understand better if you did?

THE PRESIDENT. Well, I have to be guided by my best judgment in the matter. I will have to do that.

STATEMENTS OF CIVIL RIGHTS LEADERS

[10.] Q. Mr. President, on the march from Memphis to Jackson,[10] some of the present leaders of that march have made statements that are considered quite inflammatory and alarming by a lot of people—such as seizing power and burning down courthouses. I wonder what your reaction is to that march?

THE PRESIDENT. I have not seen the statements that you refer to. I will take a look at them.

WILLINGNESS OF HANOI TO NEGOTIATE

[11.] Q. Mr. President, there is a Canadian envoy now in Hanoi, and a French envoy is going there presumably to probe the North Vietnamese position on negotiations. Do you see anything in the situation now which would lend any credence to any disposition on the part of North Vietnam to negotiate?

THE PRESIDENT. I have no information that I could make available that would give you any encouragement.

POSSIBILITY OF A MEETING WITH GENERAL DE GAULLE

[12.] Q. Mr. President, Senator Mansfield,[11] among others, proposes that a meet-

ing between you and President de Gaulle[12] might now be useful. Do you think such a meeting would be useful at this time?

THE PRESIDENT. I would of course be very happy to see General de Gaulle if he felt a visit would be useful. I am not familiar with any suggestion Senator Mansfield has made in that regard.

General de Gaulle would always be welcome. Our representatives are in constant touch with his government. And we feel no lack of communication.

RUSSIAN INTEREST IN A SPACE TREATY

[13.] Q. Mr. President, would you give us your reaction, sir, to renewed Russian interest in a space treaty, and whether you think that this might lead to other agreements with the Soviet Union?

THE PRESIDENT. I did not hear you.

Q. Could you give us your reaction to this renewed Russian interest in a treaty on space and the moon, and whether you think that might lead to other agreements?

THE PRESIDENT. We welcome any indication from them at any time in matters of this nature. We have made our proposal. We are very hopeful that our proposal and theirs can be carefully considered—and will prove fruitful.[13]

ADMIRAL RABORN'S RESIGNATION

[14.] Q. Mr. President, would you care to amplify on your brief announcement of Admiral Raborn's resignation? Is it health or other affairs?

THE PRESIDENT. No. Admiral Raborn

---

[10] Civil rights march through the State of Mississippi, conducted by Dr. Martin Luther King, Jr., president of the Southern Christian Leadership Conference, for the purpose of encouraging Negroes to register to vote. The marchers reached Jackson, Miss., on June 26 and held a rally of 15,000 persons before the State Capitol.

[11] Senator Mike Mansfield of Montana, majority leader of the Senate.

[12] Gen. Charles de Gaulle, President of France.

[13] On December 8, 1966, the President announced that an agreement had been reached between the United States and other member nations of the United Nations Outer Space Committee on a draft treaty to govern space exploration (see Item 643).

had retired. I asked him upon the resignation of Mr. McCone to come here to serve for a period that would be agreeable to him, for such time as he might feel that he could do it. I told him at that time that Mr. Helms would be his Deputy Director and I would hope that Mr. Helms could succeed him at the end of his tour of duty.

He considered my request and although he had no desire to return to Washington, he agreed to come and serve for an indefinite period. He has done that; now he desires to return to California.

Mr. Helms is agreeable to accepting responsibilities heretofore administered by Admiral Raborn.

PROBLEMS OF THE PRESIDENCY

[15.] Q. Mr. President, what is the order of priority of your worries these days? Given the urgent demands of Vietnam, how do you fit in the concerns of NATO, civil rights, the congressional elections, and so forth?

THE PRESIDENT. I think they are all problems in the life of a President. He must try to give whatever time is necessary to each problem and to apply the best judgment that he can to it. That I try to do.

I have a great deal of assistance and a great many helpmates. I am very thankful for the quality of my advisers. I have never worked up any priority of worries.

We do have problems and concerns from day to day. But we have so much more to be grateful for and thankful for, and be encouraged about, than we do to worry about.

When I look about the world, I sometimes feel that conditions may be somewhat depressing to us here in the United States. I look at the problems of other leaders—I

don't know of a single one whose situation I would trade for ours. I know of none that is not confronted with somewhat the same types of problems and the same types of worries and sometimes much more aggravating and much more serious than mine have been up to now.

PUBLIC OPINION POLLS

[16.] Q. Do the polls worry you?

THE PRESIDENT. No. We always would like to see what we do and what we say approved by our associates and by our constituency—but that is not always the case. When it is not, we regret it and take due notice of it and engage in proper introspection.

But polls vary from week to week and month to month. Those are things that we do not ignore, but they are not one of my burdens.

ON A POSSIBLE MEETING WITH COMMUNIST
CHINA

[17.] Q. Mr. President, Senator Mansfield also suggested—urged a meeting between Secretary Rusk and the Foreign Minister of Communist China. Can you give us your reaction as to whether you think this would be useful?

THE PRESIDENT. I read Senator Mansfield's speech with a great deal of interest and pleasure. I asked Secretary Rusk to give the majority leader's observations very careful consideration. He is doing that.

I have not discussed in detail with Senator Mansfield any information he may have about the willingness of the Chinese Foreign Minister to meet with Secretary Rusk. But I think we have made it very clear that we will be delighted to review the Senator's views, any information he has, and give careful consideration to them.

VIETNAM WAR COSTS

[18.] Q. Mr. President, in January the administration's estimate for the cost of the war in Vietnam in fiscal 1967 was $10.5 billion. I wondered as the beginning of the fiscal year approaches if there has been any revision of that figure up or down?

THE PRESIDENT. Yes, the expenditures vary from month to month. You have high months and low months. The first several months they ran about as estimated. We had a month or two where they were high, and we had a month or two where they were less than expected.

We do not have any recent figures. We are trying to get as much information as we can as fast as we can this month. We would like to see the expenditure figure go up some because it would mean that we would get earlier deliveries and increase our effort.

But I am not in a position today to give you with any degree of accuracy what it will be. We have ample funds to take care of our needs. The Congress has provided generously for us, even more than I have asked in certain fields.

Perhaps early in July, the first 10 days, I can give you a little better figure on the fiscal year. It is not a great deal different, in my judgment, from what I have said before. We expect the deficit to be considerably less than we anticipated in January. That will be largely due to an increase in revenues. I would hope that some small part of it, a few hundred millions, could be the result of reduction in domestic expenditures or stretch-out in them.

My Budget Director constantly admonishes me not to give any hard and fast figure. In a budget of over $100 billion, with a 1 percent variance, it is very easy to be off a billion dollars. But I would say within that range that our deficit would probably be, instead of $6.4 billion as we predicted last January—it will be somewhere in the neighborhood of $3 billion to $4 billion deficit.

That estimate could be off a few hundred million. But the deficit will be much less than we predicted in January, and we think, much less than we predicted 18 months ago. We are very pleased with the administrators of this administration for having always had less deficit than they predicted—which is quite unusual they tell me in budget history. In our 3 Johnson administration years we have had less deficit each year than we promised.

We could have some unusual emergency come up, but I don't think we will miss it much in the next 12 days of this month.

COMMENTS OF U.S. SENATORS ABROAD

[19.] Q. Mr. President, can you give us your thinking, sir, on the propriety of a United States Senator going abroad and making critical comments about the internal policy of another nation?

THE PRESIDENT. I think that it would be a better policy to let the Senators judge the propriety of their own actions. It is not for the executive branch to be passing upon statements of Senators.

There are a great many statements made by the Senate that an Executive will approve of, and some maybe that he will disapprove of. But I don't think, as a general policy, it is wise for us to set up any censorship down here. I just have to leave it up to their judgment.

633

QUESTIONS ON THE VIETNAM STATEMENT

[20.] Q. Mr. President, you have today restated your determination to see the Vietnam war through. How can this point be made more clearly to Hanoi and the Vietcong? Isn't that the central problem?

THE PRESIDENT. I would hope that they take notice of our actions from time to time and I believe they do—of which the statement today is a part.

Q. Mr. President, in that connection, does the statement imply or mean that there may be a stepup in air strikes in North Vietnam?

THE PRESIDENT. I think you just have to take the statement and read it. We will stand on it. I would not want to get boxed in by a commitment to the New York Times that I would do this or that. I would want to feel at liberty to do whatever the national policy required, as I said in the statement.

And I think it is very clear on that, when you have a chance to read it. I know you would want your country to have some flexibility in case our national interests required it. If it does, I assure you we will exercise it.

FUTURE MEETINGS WITH SOUTH
VIETNAMESE LEADERS

[21.] Q. Mr. President, do you still hope to meet Premier Ky[14] in Honolulu this summer?

THE PRESIDENT. We would like to have further meetings between representatives of this Government and the South Vietnamese Government as the civil program develops, as we step up our education and health and election methods—the general things we discussed at Honolulu.

---

[14] Nguyen Cao Ky, Prime Minister of South Vietnam.

Just when that will be, and just who will be there will have to be determined by the events. But we do expect periodically to check on what advancements have been made and try to improve our efforts and expedite them as much as possible.

Mr. Komer will be going out there Sunday to meet with the leaders of the South Vietnamese Government and our own staff in this general field. As a result of his meetings with Mr. Porter, we have made a number of decisions and approved some of the suggestions of the Government of Vietnam. We will be cooperating in them.

A little later there will be other Cabinet members going out. I would hope that sometime during the year, after sufficient time elapses for our agricultural, education and health, and electoral programs to make headway that we can take a good look at them and see how they can be improved and expedited.

THE NEED FOR MAINTAINING A FLEXIBLE
POSITION ON VIETNAM

[22.] Q. Mr. President, on your Vietnamese announcement, sir, would you care to give us your view, as you have at sometimes in the past, as to whether the expanded military activities will increase the risk of widening the war?

THE PRESIDENT. No, I think I will stand on my statement because I don't want to be speculative. I do not see that there is much to be gained by telegraphing your shots to the aggressor.

I tried to anticipate the yearning for particular moves of this kind, and to cover it in my statement. I don't want to get fenced in by a commitment to the Washington Post or any other person, so that I feel we can be flexible when we need to.

THE PRESIDENT'S CAMPAIGN PLANS

[23.] Q. Mr. President, can you tell us how you feel about a President campaigning in off-year elections and whether you intend to do so this fall?

THE PRESIDENT. Well, I think that the President certainly ought to and has the right to make his views known to his people. That is what I am doing this morning and expect to do so as long as I have these responsibilities.

I have no specific plans at this time. I have no doubt but what I will be expressing my views from time to time. There will be various interpretations placed upon them.

If I plan to go out in the hinterlands, I will be glad to try to give you as much notice as I have myself. I haven't made any decisions on any place at this time.

Q. Mr. President, Congressman Ford[15] is quoted this morning as now calling the Vietnam war "President Johnson's War." Do you feel that this or other things that have been said lately are harming the bipartisan approach to the effort?

THE PRESIDENT. No, I don't—I wouldn't want to comment on that. Let's not provoke any difficulties within the Government.

THE CIVIL RIGHTS BILL

[24.] Q. Mr. President, I wonder if you would give us your views on the chances of passing the open housing section of the civil rights bill?

THE PRESIDENT. We have made our recommendations. We see the developments and the problems. I talked to the Attorney General last night about the situation. I talked to some of the Members of Congress today. We do have difficulties. We are

---

[15] Representative Gerald R. Ford of Michigan, minority leader of the House of Representatives.

trying to resolve them and get a bill that can be approved by a majority of the Congress. We hope we will be successful.

I am not sure at this moment what will be the result of the Attorney General's conferences and his efforts with various individuals. The Members seem to be willing to give consideration to various approaches. They are making some. We are making some. I just have to see how successful we are.

Generally speaking, we are hopeful we will get a good civil rights bill as near our recommendations as possible. We don't always get all we ask for.

We have asked for about 91 bills this session and we expect the House to act on almost 70 of them before they leave on July 4. In the Senate, of the 91 there are about 33 that remain to be acted upon. We expect some of them to be acted on between now and the holidays. We think that the Congress will act very sympathetically on our recommendations as a general matter.

THE DOMINICAN REPUBLIC

[25.] Q. Mr. President, when the Dominican crisis began last year, there were a lot of predictions of gloom and doom with our policies and those of the OAS with regard to the eventual outcome of events of the situation there. I wonder how you feel now that the thing has worked out pretty well. I wonder if you could give us your thoughts on that?

THE PRESIDENT. Yes, I did that in my statement. There is very little I can add to that, except that we went through a very difficult and trying period there, as we frequently do with problems in various parts of the world. But under the skilled leadership of the Provisional President, García-Godoy, and Ambassador Bunker and the members of the OAS group, the people—more than a million of them—went to the polls and had a free choice. They selected a government of their own choosing. And very shortly that President will be inaugurated.

The decision was a decisive one. I have paid due recognition to the efforts of all parties involved, Mr. Bonnelly, Professor Bosch, Mr. Balaguer, and Ambassador Bunker. I would say that we are rather glad that the Dominican people had an election and they have made the decision. We look forward to working with them and helping in any way we can in their new efforts with their constitutional government.

Al Spivak, United Press International: Thank you, Mr. President.

NOTE: President Johnson's sixty-fifth news conference was held in his office at the White House at 11:40 a.m. on Saturday, June 18, 1966. The President later repeated portions of the conference before cameras in the White House Theater.

---

278 Statement by the President Upon Announcing His Intention To Designate Rosel H. Hyde as Chairman, Federal Communications Commission, and To Appoint Nicholas Johnson as a Member. *June 18, 1966*

THE COMBINATION of Rosel Hyde's long FCC experience and Nicholas Johnson's demonstrated and creative abilities demonstrated throughout his teaching career and his public life will advance the public interest in the critically important work of this agency. The vital decisions relating to our rapidly changing communications industry call for the high talents possessed by these fine public servants.

NOTE: The statement was made public as part of a White House release announcing the appointments. The release stated that Mr. Hyde, a career employee who entered the Federal service in 1924, had been a member of the Federal Communications Commission since 1946 and had served as Chairman in 1953 and 1954. The release pointed out that he was one of the Nation's leading experts in the communications field, and had conducted the first general frequency allocation proceedings of the Federal Radio Commission in 1928 and the general television proceedings of 1949–1952 which contributed to the extension of television service.

Nicholas Johnson, the release noted, had been appointed Federal Maritime Administrator in February 1964 and had previously served as a law clerk to Justice Hugo L. Black, as a member of the law faculty of the University of California, and as an associate member of a law firm in Washington, D.C.

---

279 The President's Foreword to the Science Advisory Committee Report "Handling of Toxicological Information." *June 20, 1966*

[Released June 20, 1966. Dated June 8, 1966]

THE NUMBER of chemical compounds to which people become exposed is already vast and increasing daily. This is a result of our steadily advancing industrialization, changes in agricultural practices and advances in the biomedical sciences. All segments of our population are exposed either deliberately or in the course of daily living

636

to many such compounds. Of particular importance are the effects of chemicals to which people may be exposed at low concentrations over prolonged periods, because in these cases the toxic effects may be subtle and difficult to discern.

The Panel on the Handling of Toxicological Information has examined the ramifications of this complicated problem of industrialized societies and has made a number of recommendations. Among these is the recommendation that there be established, by the Department of Health, Education, and Welfare, a computer-based facility to cope with the flood of toxicological information and to make it quickly available to people with a legitimate need for it.

Because of the widespread interest in the subject matter of this report, I have directed that it be published and made generally available.

LYNDON B. JOHNSON

NOTE: The report, dated June 1966, is entitled "Handling of Toxicological Information, a Report of the President's Science Advisory Committee" (Government Printing Office, 1966, 21 pp.). See also Item 280.

280   Letter Assigning to HEW Responsibility for Developing a Computer-Based File on Toxic Chemicals. *June* 20, 1966

[Released June 20, 1966. Dated June 16, 1966]

Dear Mr. Secretary:

The Department of Health, Education, and Welfare, under your direction, has taken giant strides in the last year to improve the health of this Nation's people. That struggle is never-ending, and further measures are needed.

My Science Advisory Committee has recently studied the availability of information concerning the toxic effects of the ever-growing number of chemicals which are introduced into our environment. The Committee has recommended that responsibility be assigned to a single Federal department for the development of a computer-based file of toxicological information. I hereby assign that responsibility to the Department of Health, Education, and Welfare.

The need to productively use the many chemical substances now available without endangering the environment in which we live is a critical national problem of massive dimensions. The cooperation of industry, the academic community, and all interested individuals and institutions will be essential to an effective national effort. Accordingly, the toxicological information file to be developed by your Department must be open to all people with a legitimate need to know its contents.

I am transmitting to you a copy of the full report of my Science Advisory Committee. It is a most timely comment on an important national problem.

I will be greatly interested in the progress of your Department in the establishment of the recommended system and in your plans for providing broad access to it.

Sincerely yours,

LYNDON B. JOHNSON

[The Honorable John W. Gardner, Secretary of Health, Education, and Welfare, Washington, D.C.]

NOTE: On the same day the White House issued a release announcing the President's letter to Secretary Gardner and the report of the President's Science Advisory Committee entitled "Handling of Toxicological Information" (see Item 279).

The release pointed out that with progressive industrialization "all segments of the population are exposed to an ever-increasing number of chemical compounds in the environment. This occurs as a result of the use of chemicals to promote health, industry, and agriculture. It also results from frequent exposure to chemicals and from pollution of water and air. Because the number of compounds is so vast and exposure so common, it is important that we pay particular attention to actual or potential toxic effects caused by them."

281 Statement by the President on Savings Through Reduction of Surplus Stocks of Wheat and Feed Grains. *June* 20, 1966

BECAUSE we have been successful, through our voluntary agriculture programs, in eliminating the burdensome grain surplus that existed in 1961, I was able recently (May 5) to announce a 15 percent increase in the national wheat acreage allotment for the 1967 crop.

Secretary Freeman has noted that this was a historically significant event which signaled the beginning of a new flexibility and adaptiveness in our great agricultural production plan. It demonstrated our ability, under the Food and Agriculture Act of 1965, to adjust supply to global and domestic demand. I have instructed Secretary Freeman to look further at this time into the likely supply and demand situation for next year.

NOTE: The statement was made public as part of a White House release announcing that Orville L. Freeman, Secretary of Agriculture, had advised the President that a substantial reduction in U.S. wheat and feed grain stocks between 1961 and 1966 had resulted in savings of about half a million dollars per day in storage and handling charges, and had predicted that storage costs would continue to decline in fiscal year 1967.

"Secretary Freeman told the President," the release added, "that Commodity Credit Corporation's storage and handling costs for all agricultural commodities in fiscal year 1966 are estimated at $238 million—or about $665,000 per day on the average. This compares with a daily average cost of about $1,162,000 in fiscal year 1961, when the total cost for storing and handling commodities reached $427 million.

"Thus annual storage-handling costs for all commodities declined about $189 million between 1961 and 1966. Storage costs of wheat and feed grains declined even more than that, to nearly $200 million. They dropped from $390 million in F.Y. 1961 to an estimated $193 million for the year ending June 30, 1966.

"The Secretary predicted that storage costs will continue to decline in fiscal year 1967 as the full effect of a large surplus draw-down, in recent months, is reflected in the carrying charges on inventory."

The release noted also that the adjustment of wheat and feed grain supplies had had the effect of increasing both current farm prices and the income of grain producers.

For the President's May 5 announcement of an increase in wheat acreage allotments, see Item 203.

282   Distinguished Unit Citation Awarded to the 1st Battalion (Airborne), 503d Infantry, 173d Airborne Brigade (Separate), USA. *June 20, 1966*

BY VIRTUE of the authority vested in me as President of the United States and as Commander-in-Chief of the Armed Forces of the United States I have today awarded

THE DISTINGUISHED UNIT CITATION

(FIRST OAK LEAF CLUSTER)

FOR EXTRAORDINARY HEROISM

TO

THE 1ST BATTALION (AIRBORNE),

503D INFANTRY,

173D AIRBORNE BRIGADE (SEPARATE)

UNITED STATES ARMY

AND THE ATTACHED UNITS

HEADQUARTERS AND HEADQUARTERS COMPANY,

COMPANY A, COMPANY B, AND COMPANY C

OF THE 1ST BATTALION (AIRBORNE),

503D INFANTRY, 173D AIRBORNE BRIGADE

(SEPARATE)

THE 1ST TEAM OF THE 3D RADIO RELAY UNIT

THE COMPOSITE SQUAD OF THE 173D ENGINEER

COMPANY

The foregoing companies of and units attached to the 1st Battalion (Airborne), 503d Infantry, 173d Airborne Brigade (Separate) distinguished themselves by extraordinary heroism in action against hostile forces in the vicinity of Bien Hoa, Republic of Vietnam, on 8 November 1965. The morning after the Battalion had conducted a search operation and learned from patrols that a strong hostile element was in the general area, Company C, the lead Company, encountered a well-entrenched and camouflaged Viet Cong force. When the insurgents opened fire with a volume of automatic weapons fire, the United States forces retaliated.

As the battle grew in intensity and it became evident that Company C had engaged a battalion-size Viet Cong element which attempted to surround the flanks of this American unit, Company B was committed to secure the right flank of Company C. Simultaneously, elements of Company A attacked the left flank of the insurgent force. Although Company B met strong resistance and fought at close range in a dense jungle area, it succeeded in penetrating the hostile circle around Company C. Then, as Company B's open flank was being enveloped, the brave men of this Company broke a hostile encirclement for the second time.

Despite the constant Viet Cong assaults, their continual attacks in human waves, and the many casualties sustained by the American units, the gallant and determined troops of the 1st Battalion (Airborne), 503d Infantry repulsed the Viet Cong and inflicted severe losses upon them. After a battle which raged throughout the afternoon, elements of the 1st Battalion (Airborne), 503d Infantry defeated a numerically superior hostile force and, on the following morning, counted four hundred and three Viet Cong dead in the immediate area.

The devotion to duty, perseverance, and extraordinary heroism displayed by these members of the 1st Battalion (Airborne), 503d Infantry and the attached units are in the highest traditions of the United States Army and reflect great credit upon themselves and the armed forces of their country.

LYNDON B. JOHNSON

283 Statement by the President Upon Signing Five Stockpile Disposal Bills. *June 21, 1966*

THE FIVE stockpile bills I signed today once again mark the achievement that comes from unity of purpose.

American industry, the Congress, and the executive branch have joined together in a creative partnership to make this legislation a reality.

Approximately $500 million worth of metals and materials—from aluminum to sisal—no longer required in our stockpiles will be freed to meet the urgent needs of mills, factories, and laboratories across the Nation.

As a result, the taxpayer, the economy, and our defense effort will benefit.

I particularly want to call attention to the action of the aluminum industry. Through its cooperation with the Government a long-range disposal program has been worked out to the mutual advantage of all concerned.

Congress has already passed 18 stockpile bills at this session. Under the able leadership of Senators Russell and Symington and Congressmen Rivers and Philbin I believe that prompt action can be taken on the remaining 7 bills before the session ends.

NOTE: As enacted, the bills signed by the President are as follows:

H.R. 13366 (aluminum)...... Public Law 89–460
(80 Stat. 212)
H.R. 13768 (celestite)........ Public Law 89–461
(80 Stat. 212)
H.R. 13769 (cordage fiber Public Law 89–462
(sisal)). (80 Stat. 212)
H.R. 13770 (crocidolite asbes- Public Law 89–463
tos (harsh)). (80 Stat. 213)
H.R. 13773 (opium).......... Public Law 89–464
(80 Stat. 213)

See also Items 173, 206, 218.

284 Remarks of Welcome to King Faisal of Saudi Arabia on the South Lawn at the White House. *June 21, 1966*

Your Majesty, Ahlan wa Sahlan:

Though the pronunciation of that traditional Arabic greeting may not be fully correct, the warmth of the welcome it conveys is very real and sincere. We have long looked forward to Your Majesty's visit. We are greatly honored and very pleased to have you here today at the White House as our guest.

I know that you are no stranger to our country. You first came to the United States in 1943 as the guest, then, of President Franklin D. Roosevelt at a time when we were deep in a global war to turn back aggression. I am sure that you sensed even in those dark days the dedication of this country and its people to the defense of human rights, to the dignity of the individual, and to the freedom and independence of all countries.

Your Majesty yourself contributed significantly to these principles by your participation in the 1945 San Francisco conference which established the United Nations. Among the many links which our two countries share, we have worked together in that great international organization in the cause of peace and progress in the world.

Since those stirring days, you have visited our country many times and in various capacities. These visits have, I am sure, given you a deep insight into our problems as well as our efforts to surmount those problems. They have also given us the opportunity to draw upon your wisdom and to learn from you.

Your country, under Your Majesty's wise rule, has made great strides forward. Roads, public works, health services, new schools—and new educational opportunities for the young men and women of Saudi Arabia—all these stand as eloquent testimony to your active development efforts.

We have watched these with keen interest and real admiration. We Americans are proud to have played a part in Saudi Arabia's development. From this cooperation, the respect and understanding between our two governments and our two peoples have grown.

Our relations with Saudi Arabia have long been close and cordial. They have been characterized by friendship, frankness, and a mutual consideration for each other's problems. We are living in a world of change, but we, like you, favor change by peaceful methods. Only thus can the God-given talents of all of our citizens be constructively devoted to the arresting challenges which today face mankind.

Your Majesty, we are very delighted to have you here again as the distinguished and much respected and admired leader of a great and friendly country. The American Government and the American people, for whom I speak, extend their hospitality to you. I am confident that you will find it as warm as proverbial Arab hospitality. We look forward, too, to very fruitful exchanges of views these next few days.

As the venerable Arabic saying has it, "Our house is your house." Once again, I extend to you on behalf of all the American people a hearty welcome to our land.

NOTE: The President spoke at 11:40 a.m. on the South Lawn at the White House, where King Faisal ibn Abd al-Aziz al-Saud was given a formal welcome with full military honors. King Faisal responded as follows:

Your Excellency:

It gives me great pleasure to extend to Your Excellency my profound thanks and gratitude for the good words which you were kind enough to express and which, if they denote anything, they denote Your Excellency's high prestige and what you enjoy in this connection.

While you have said that you have been waiting and looking forward to my visit to your country, I, too, on my behalf, have been looking forward to coming and getting acquainted with Your Excellency for the high prestige which Your Excellency enjoys not only in this country, but in the world as a whole.

We meet with you in what Your Excellency has mentioned about the hopes of creating a world which would be preserved by justice and peace and prosperity.

In a speech Your Excellency delivered last May, you mentioned something that you were looking forward to, a kind of society in which every country respects every other country, and which is covered by justice and peace. I wish to assure Your Excellency that we are quite agreed with Your Excellency in this connection.

At this time, which is swayed by too many currents and too many problems, we are looking forward to a world which will be prevailed upon by liberty, by prosperity, and by amity. Those currents of doctrines have obliged us to defend ourselves for the sake of peace and for the sake of independence and freedom and well-being of the world.

This defense of protection imposes upon us first and foremost the faith in Almighty God. After that, we have to try to follow the best ways to reach with these peoples the way of peace, amity, and cooperation to prosperity.

As Your Excellency has been good enough to mention, I am not a stranger to this country. I have sensed in these people, the American people and their Government, their love and their faith for independence and well-being of the whole world.

Since that very first time of my visit, I have tried and done my very best to make rapprochement between the American people and the other Arab countries. Thanks to God, I have succeeded to a certain extent in this connection. If there is still some strain or tension in some quarters in the Arab-American relations, I am hoping that we will be able eventually to bring together the two in the field of cooperation.

If we follow the way which makes it possible to insure a world of peace which is based on justice and prosperity and the cooperation for all, by the God of grace we will attain our goal.

Your Excellency, you have been good enough to refer to our efforts in connection with developing

641

our country for the welfare of its people. All that we have done we consider not to be sufficient enough for what our people are aspiring to in the field of prosperity, development, and welfare.

But we are going on our way according to our potentialities and possibilities. We faithfully hope that we may reach the goal which is aspired to by ourselves and our people in the shortest of time.

I am pleased, Your Excellency, that myself and my colleagues are to be the guests of Your Excellency and of the friendly people of America.

I reciprocate the wishes expressed on the part of Your Excellency that our coming talks will reach something which will be in the interest of our own two countries and to the world as a whole.

I wish to reiterate my thanks to Your Excellency for what we have found—a good reception and a kind welcome.

Thank you very much.

285 Toasts of the President and King Faisal.
June 21, 1966

Your Majesty:

Your presence here this evening is an occasion we have long anticipated. It is a very welcome and a very vivid reminder of the bonds of friendship which exist between our two countries. These ties were initiated by two of the most illustrious leaders that your country and mine have known—your late, distinguished father King Abdul Aziz ibn Saud, and our President Franklin Delano Roosevelt.

Their meeting in 1945 marked a milestone in history. They laid the basis of understanding and cooperation between our two countries. These have endured to this day. They will continue to do so. They are predicated on improving the lot of both of our peoples and securing for them and for all peoples the blessings of peace and prosperity. Though circumstances have changed, I know that both our countries and peoples pursue these same goals today.

Our meeting today gave me a deeper realization that we face many common and similar problems. One, in particular, is very near to my heart.

I come from a part of the United States which bears a great deal of similarity to parts of Your Majesty's country. Water is a problem of overriding concern to parts of the United States just as it is to Saudi Arabia.

We know it is written that, "Everything living was created from water." Fortunately, modern technology has come to our aid. It holds out the promise of large supplies of water through desalting.

To make this promise a reality, your country is planning a desalting installation larger than any that now exists anywhere. We, too, are seeking ways to purify water at a price that men can afford. We are very pleased to be cooperating with Your Majesty's Government in this very highly important field to both of our countries.

We, like you, are seeking to improve our education and provide better opportunities for all our young people. The wise use of the great wealth of our subsoil demands our best efforts. We have watched with respect and admiration the progress that Saudi Arabia has made, under Your Majesty's wise guidance, in all of these endeavors.

The roster of those who have joined us in extending our welcome to you this evening, Your Majesty, symbolizes the variety of our common interests as well as the depth and the warmth of our friendship.

I recognize, Your Majesty, that the solutions we find for our problems will not always be the same. Differences in history, customs, traditions, and geography inevitably produce different outlooks. But where such differences are, we can both learn from them and, I trust, benefit from them.

In the past, our common respect for human dignity and abiding faith in spiritual values have been the cornerstone of our relations. They will chart the course of our future relations as well. As a long recognized champion of these basic principles of constructive human conduct, we are very proud and quite privileged to welcome Your Majesty here to the White House tonight.

We hope your stay with us will be a pleasant and profitable one. We know from our discussions today that you will leave with us more than you take away.

So my good friends who have come here this evening from all parts of this Nation, may I ask you now to join me in a standing tribute to His Majesty, King Faisal ibn Abd al-Aziz al-Saud—a great ruler, a wise statesman, and a warm friend of our country.

NOTE: The President spoke at 9:40 p.m. in the State Dining Room at the White House. King Faisal responded as follows:

"Your Excellency, Mr. President:

"Permit me to take this occasion to assure you of my great pleasure and gratitude for having met with you. I sensed in the meetings with you today your good intentions, that you are a man of mature thinking. This undoubtedly will have a great effect on me.

"I have sensed that you are a man of great personality, a man of integrity, a man of decision. This will certainly have great results not only as far as the citizens of this country are concerned, but, indeed, as far as the rest of the world is concerned, also.

"Mr. President, your reference to the fact that the good relations which have existed for a long time between your country and mine, relations the basis of which were laid down by the late President Roosevelt and the late King Abdul Aziz ibn Saud, reminds me of the stages through which these relations have gone for more than 21 years.

"I am very pleased that these relations have improved and they have grown better as time has gone by.

"Mr. President, at times differences of opinion have arisen between us. But such differences have had absolutely no effect on the basis on which our relations stand. These were built on the principles of sincerity, of loyalty, for the good of all.

"And no matter what differences may arise, from time to time, this will have absolutely no effect on the relations between your country and mine.

"I do appreciate your assurance, Mr. President, the assurance given to me, for continued cooperation between your country and mine in the interest of the peoples of both countries. That, of course, includes the efforts which we intend to make, jointly, to find means whereby water can be made available in our country where it is very much needed.

"As you pointed out in your remarks, Mr. President, I would like to quote a saying from the holy Koran which is, in effect, in conformity with what you pointed out, "God says that he made everything living out of water."

"Without water there can be no life. Water, therefore, is very essential to us.

"We realize that we face a great many difficulties in trying to carry out our constructive programs. The most serious of these difficulties is to find ways to make water available.

"Unavailability of water is the greatest source of difficulty, as far as we are concerned. Water is a source of life and in our country it is scarce. I am hopeful that through the joint efforts between you and us we can find ways and means whereby water will be made more available for the good of our people and, also, for the good of your people here.

"Mr. President, having understood your intentions, your aspirations, your ambitions for your people and for the future of your people, I am inspired to look to you as a leader with a great deal of admiration, because you are working not for your own good, but for the good of your own people, the entire people.

"Mr. President, your reference to the achievements which have been realized in my country reminds me of the principles that you discussed with me this evening. And it is my prayer, it is my hope, that I will be able to realize greater things for my people in service to all of them for the good of all, for the welfare of humanity, for the dignity of man, and for the peace of mankind.

"And I would like to thank you, in closing, Mr. President, for making it possible for me, on this occasion, to meet persons, people of this country, who represent different walks of life, people who have their value, have made great contributions, and who are working hard for the good of all the people of this country.

"I would like to reiterate, Mr. President, my

appreciation for all the kindness that you have shown to me, my admiration for you as a person, the wonderful reception accorded to me, and the good care that has been shown to me. All of this indicates or proves to me that you are a man with

a very large heart, a very wise mind, a man who is striving hard to work for the good of all.

"Thank you very much."

As printed above, this item follows the text released by the White House.

286   Remarks at the Signing of the Bail Reform Act of 1966. *June 22, 1966*

Senator Ervin, Chairman Celler, Mr. Attorney General, distinguished members of the House and Senate Judiciary Committees, and all of the other good citizens who have worked so hard to finally make it possible for us to have this ceremony this morning:

Our Nation stands today at the threshold of a new era in our system of criminal justice. Those of you who have come here this morning—and scores of others like you throughout this great land of ours—are the mind and the force of this new era.

So today we join to recognize a major development in our entire system of criminal justice—the reform of the bail system.

This system has endured—archaic, unjust, and virtually unexamined—ever since the Judiciary Act of 1789.

Because of the bail system, the scales of justice have been weighted for almost two centuries not with fact, nor law, nor mercy. They have been weighted with money.

But now, because of the Bail Reform Act of 1966, which an understanding and just Congress has enacted and which I will shortly sign, we can begin to insure that defendants are considered as individuals— and not as dollar signs.

The principal purpose of bail is to insure that an accused person will return for trial, if he is released after arrest.

How is that purpose met under the present system? The defendant with means can afford to pay bail. He can afford to buy his freedom. But the poorer defendant

cannot pay the price. He languishes in jail weeks, months, and perhaps even years before trial.

He does not stay in jail because he is guilty.

He does not stay in jail because any sentence has been passed.

He does not stay in jail because he is any more likely to flee before trial.

He stays in jail for one reason only—he stays in jail because he is poor.

There are hundreds, perhaps thousands, of illustrations of how the bail system has inflicted arbitrary cruelty:

—A man was jailed on a serious charge brought last Christmas Eve. He could not afford bail, so he spent 101 days in jail until he could get a hearing. Then the complainant admitted that the charge that he had made was false.

—A man could not raise $300 for bail. He spent 54 days in jail waiting trial for a traffic offense for which he could have been sentenced to no more than 5 days.

—A man spent 2 months in jail before being acquitted. In that period, he lost his job, he lost his car, he lost his family—it was split up. He did not find another job, following that, for 4 months.

In addition to such injustices as I have pointed out, the present bail system has meant very high public costs that the taxpayer must bear for detaining prisoners prior to their trial.

What is most shocking about these costs—to both individuals and to the public—is that they are totally unnecessary.

First proof of that fact came because of really one man's outrage against injustice. I am talking now of Mr. Louis Schweitzer, who pioneered the development of a substitute for the money bail system by establishing the Vera Foundation and the Manhattan bail project.

The lesson of that project was simple. If a judge is given adequate information, he, the judge, can determine that many defendants can be released without any need for money bail. They will return faithfully for trial.

So this legislation, for the first time, requires that the decision to release a man prior to the trial be based on facts—like community and family ties and past record, and not on his bank account. In the words of the act, "A man, regardless of his financial status—shall not needlessly be detained . . . when detention serves neither the ends of justice nor the public interest."

And it specifies that he be released without money bond whenever that is justified by the facts. Under this act, judges would—for the first time—be required to use a flexible set of conditions, matching different types of releases to different risks.

These are steps that can be taken, we think, without harming law enforcement in any manner.

This measure does not require that every arrested person be released.

This measure does not restrict the power of the courts to detain dangerous persons in capital cases or after conviction.

What this measure does do is to eliminate needless, arbitrary cruelty.

What it does do, in my judgment, is to greatly enlarge justice in this land of ours.

So our task is to rise above the debate between rights of the individual and rights of the society, by securing and really protecting the rights of both.

I want to personally thank Senator Ervin, Congressman Celler, the Attorney General, the members of the Justice Department, and his predecessors who worked on this legislation. I also want to thank the able and distinguished leadership of all members of the Senate and the House Judiciary Committees, and the other Members of those two bodies, for what I consider very fine work in making this legislation a reality.

I am proud now, as a major step forward, to sign the Bail Reform Act of 1966 into the law of the land.

NOTE: The President spoke at 9:40 a.m. in the East Room at the White House. In his opening words he referred to Senator Sam J. Ervin, Jr., of North Carolina, Representative Emanuel Celler of New York, Chairman of the House Judiciary Committee, and Attorney General Nicholas deB. Katzenbach.

As enacted, the Bail Reform Act of 1966 is Public Law 89–465 (80 Stat. 214).

287   Joint Statement Following Discussions With King Faisal of Saudi Arabia. *June 22, 1966*

AT THE INVITATION of President Johnson, His Majesty King Faisal ibn Abdul Aziz al-Saud is paying an official visit to the United States of America. His Majesty and the distinguished members of the Saudi Arabian Government who accompanied him were warmly welcomed by the President and members of the United States Government. They subsequently met with the President and with senior members of the

United States Government for a comprehensive review of problems of mutual concern to their countries and their peoples.

In these talks they noted with approval the close and cordial relations which have long existed between Saudi Arabia and the United States of America. These relations are based on mutual respect, a common belief in the basic principles of freedom, justice and human dignity and the independence and territorial integrity of all states. They reaffirmed their opposition to aggression, in any form, and their determination to continue the efforts of their two governments to promote the cause of peace with honor and dignity for all. They asserted the importance of solving international problems by peaceful means on the basis of right and justice. They supported the right of peoples to self-determination.

They reviewed the great strides that have already been made in the improvement of material and social conditions of their countries and pledged themselves anew to cooperate by all appropriate means to further the welfare of their peoples. They noted the threat posed by international Communism to the free nations of the world and their determination to guard against this threat.

His Majesty and the President particularly welcomed this opportunity to become personally acquainted. They are confident that the genuine personal esteem that marked their frank and comprehensive exchange of views will lead to heightened mutual understanding between the United States and Saudi Arabia and to a further strengthening of the bonds of cooperation between their countries and peoples.

His Majesty leaves on June 23 for New York City where he will continue his official visit to the United States.

288 Remarks and Citation at the Medal of Honor Ceremony for Lt. Charles Q. Williams, USA. *June 23, 1966*

Lieutenant Williams, Secretary Resor, Members of the Cabinet, distinguished Members of the Congress, ladies and gentlemen:

We have come here this morning to honor a very brave American soldier.

The acts of extraordinary courage to which we pay tribute were not performed with any hope of reward. They began with a soldier doing his duty—but they went so far beyond the call of duty that they became a patriot's gift to his country.

Lieutenant Williams and a very small band of Americans and Vietnamese fought for 14 long hours against an enemy that outnumbered them more than five to one.

During those long hours, Lieutenant Williams was wounded five times. Any single one of those wounds might have caused another man to completely abandon the fight. Yet Lieutenant Williams continued to rally his men, to protect his wounded, to hold off the enemy until help could come.

Few men understand what it really means to draw deep from the wellsprings of such bravery. Few have ever made that kind of journey—and far fewer have ever returned.

We have another such man with us here this morning. He is Brigadier General John T. Kennedy, one of the oldest living holders of the Medal of Honor.

General Kennedy, would you please stand? General Kennedy and Lieutenant Williams have a great deal in common.

Both are natives of the great State of South Carolina.

Both displayed unique valor in distant lands fighting for their country.

Both bear the scars of their heroism.

The presence of General Kennedy here in the White House this morning reminds us all that in the course of human history the optimists are sometimes right.

It was in the year 1909, when I was only 1 year old, when young Lieutenant Kennedy was serving in the Philippines. There were some who could not believe that the Filipinos had any future as a free and independent country. Some of them thought that the only choice was internal anarchy or colonial rule.

Years later—in the 1940's—the Philippines passed through a long night of foreign occupation, and then of Communist guerrilla war. Some thought that a free and confident nation could never emerge from those years of long struggle.

But they were wrong.

The people of the Philippines, under imaginative and dedicated leadership, proved that democracy and social reform are stronger than the forces of terror and oppression.

Today, as we meet here, the Philippines is a vital and growing nation true to its own traditions and ambitions—a creative force in the emerging community of Asia.

As we meet here this morning, we are reminded that all over the world many young nations are today struggling to achieve the same kind of results. They seek to be free from outside coercion, to achieve real social and economic progress, to determine their own futures, and to work constructively with their own neighbors.

South Vietnam is such a nation. We are supporting her in her brave struggle to achieve these goals, with the help of men like Lieutenant Williams.

History will note that neither of these two heroes who are here with us today, neither General Kennedy nor Lieutenant Williams, ever fought to promote narrow American interests.

Neither fought to build an American empire.

Neither fought to enslave a single human soul.

They fought, instead, to help make possible a better life for people newly emerged from colonial rule.

They fought, at great personal risk, for a world of peace—a world that might become, however slowly, worthy of the human spirit.

And in the process, each of these men added a new dimension to the Medal of Honor.

Lieutenant Williams, it is hard for your President to find words to tell you of the deep gratitude and admiration that your fellow Americans have for you.

But I do rejoice that I may present to you, in the name of the Congress of the United States and of the grateful people of America, the Medal of Honor—for the bravery and the gallantry that you displayed at the risk of your life, far above and beyond the call of duty.

You don't know how much satisfaction I get out of seeing this lovely lady who has been by your side—this wonderful, typically American family here in the first house of the land to see you receive the award and the recognition that only a courageous, dedicated, devoted American could receive in this house.

Secretary Resor will now read the citation.

[The text of the citation, read by Stanley R. Resor, Secretary of the Army, follows]

THE PRESIDENT of the United States of America, authorized by Act of Congress, March 3, 1863, has awarded in the name of The Congress the Medal of Honor to:

FIRST LIEUTENANT CHARLES Q. WILLIAMS,
UNITED STATES ARMY

for conspicuous gallantry and intrepidity in action at the risk of his life above and beyond the call of duty:

First Lieutenant Charles Q. Williams (then Second Lieutenant), Infantry, distinguished himself by conspicuous gallantry and intrepidity at the risk of his own life above and beyond the call of duty while defending the Special Forces Camp at Dong Xoai, Republic of Vietnam, against a violent attack by hostile forces that lasted for fourteen hours, June 9 to 10, 1965.

Lieutenant Williams was serving as Executive Officer of a Special Forces Detachment when an estimated Vietcong reinforced regiment struck the Camp and threatened to overrun it and the adjacent District Headquarters. He awoke personnel, organized them, determined the sources of the insurgents' main effort, and led the troops to their defensive positions on the south and west walls. Then, after running to the District Headquarters to establish communications, he found that there was no radio operational with which to communicate with his commanding officer in another compound. To reach the other compound, he traveled through darkness but was halted in this effort by a combination of shrapnel in his right leg and the increase of the Vietcong gun fire. Ignoring his wound, he returned to the District Head-

quarters and directed the defense against the first assault.

As the insurgents attempted to scale the walls and as some of the Vietnamese defenders began to retreat, he dashed through a barrage of gun fire, succeeded in rallying these defenders, and led them back to their positions. Although wounded in the thigh and left leg during this gallant action, he returned to his position and, upon being told that communications were re-established and that his commanding officer was seriously wounded, Lieutenant Williams took charge of actions in both compounds. Then in an attempt to reach the communications bunker, he sustained wounds in the stomach and right arm from grenade fragments.

As the defensive positions on the walls had been held for hours and casualties were mounting, he ordered the consolidation of the American personnel from both compounds to establish a defense in the District building. After radio contact was made with a friendly air controller, he disregarded his wounds and directed the defense from the District building, using descending flares as reference points to adjust air strikes. By his courage, he inspired his team to hold out against the insurgent force that was closing in on them and throwing grenades into the windows of the building.

As daylight arrived and the Vietcong continued to besiege the stronghold, firing a machine gun directly south of the District building, he was determined to eliminate this menace that threatened the lives of his men. Taking a 3.5 rocket launcher and a volunteer to load it, he worked his way across open terrain, reached the berm south of the District Headquarters, and took aim at the Vietcong machine gun one hundred and fifty meters away. Although the sight was faulty, he succeeded in hitting the machine gun. While he and the loader were trying to return to the District Headquarters, they were both wounded. With a fourth wound, this time in the right arm and leg, and realizing he was unable to carry his wounded comrade back to the District building, Lieutenant Williams pulled him to a covered position and then made his way back to the District building where he sought the help of others who went out and evacuated the injured soldier.

Although seriously wounded and tired, he continued to direct the air strikes closer to the defensive position. As morning turned to afternoon and the Vietcong pressed their effort with direct recoilless rifle fire into the building, he ordered the evacuation of the seriously wounded to the safety of the communications bunker. When informed that helicopters would attempt to land as the hostile gun fire had abated, he led his team from the building to the artillery position, making certain of the timely evacuation of the wounded from the communications area, and then on to the pickup point. Despite resurgent Vietcong gun fire, he directed the rapid evacuation of all personnel.

Throughout the long battle, he was undaunted by the vicious Vietcong assault and inspired the defenders in decimating the determined insurgents. Lieutenant Williams' conspicuous gallantry, extraordinary heroism, and intrepidity at the risk of his own life above and beyond the call of duty are in the highest traditions of the United States Army and reflect great credit upon himself and the Armed Forces of his country.

NOTE: The President spoke at 11 a.m. in the East Room at the White House. In his opening words he referred to Lt. Charles Q. Williams, recipient of the Congressional Medal of Honor, and Stanley R. Resor, Secretary of the Army. Lieutenant Williams' wife and four children from Fayetteville, N.C., were also present for the ceremony.

Following the reading of the citation Lieutenant Williams spoke briefly. The text of his remarks is printed in the Weekly Compilation of Presidential Documents (vol. 2, p. 822).

289   Remarks at the Presentation of the Young American Medals. *June 24, 1966*

Mr. Attorney General, Director Hoover, distinguished medal winners, my friends from the Senate and the House, ladies and gentlemen:

We have come here this morning to honor three young men who are tender in years but mature in action, who by their devotion, their intelligence, and their courage have demonstrated what is best about the coming generation of young Americans.

Jon Hanshus is honored for his meaningful contributions to other young people. While others worried about the employment problems of the young, Jon Hanshus was translating his concern into an effective program of service.

David Crowe and Jeffrey Gallagher served in another way—by sudden and heroic actions, in utter disregard for their own safety.

Each of these three young men has, in Shakespeare's words, "borne himself beyond the promise of his age, doing in the figure of a lamb, the feats of a lion."

In times such as these, to talk of bravery often means to talk also of sorrow.

But today, though tragedy or near tragedy underlie two of these awards, we honor courage and service with both pride and pleasure.

Our honorees were chosen from 59 nominations, a record number, from all parts of our Nation.

Among these other nominations was that of Everett D. Boston of Grafton, West Virginia, who dived into an icy river to rescue two youths from a submerged automobile. Now 19, Everett Boston serves anew, as a soldier fighting for his country in Vietnam.

In San Diego, California, 14-year-old Linda Lowe twice entered the burning home of a neighbor to bring two children to safety.

In Oxford, Alabama, another 14-year-old, James William Bennett, used the first-aid training that he had received as a Boy Scout to administer artificial respiration and thus save the life of a youth who had been kicked by a horse.

In Dearborn, Michigan, Heather Lynn Clark, 17, nearly blind since birth, has rendered impressive service as a volunteer worker at a veterans hospital and in working with handicapped children.

So it is with a great deal of pride and real pleasure to me that I welcome you here today not only so that we can pay honor to you, but through you to honor the other nominees and the thousands of young Americans who daily perform acts of valor and service for their communities and for their country.

So to them and to you I offer the congratulations, the admiration, and the gratitude of all the American people. You are welcome here. We are honored that you have come.

NOTE: The President spoke at 11:15 a.m. in the Cabinet Room at the White House. In his opening words he referred to Attorney General Nicholas deB. Katzenbach and J. Edgar Hoover, Director, Federal Bureau of Investigation.

The President presented the gold Young American Medals to the following: David Eugene Crowe, aged 7, of Cherokee, Kans., who at the age of 5 and blind in one eye singlehandedly rescued his three younger sisters from their burning home; Jeffrey James Gallagher, aged 17, of Haskell, N.J., who waded through a wall of fire and led two men out of the burning wreckage of their airplane; and Jon Arthur Hanshus, aged 19, of Eau Claire, Wis., who organized a youth employment service for the young people of that city and found more than 700 previously nonexistent jobs for them.

Winners were selected by the Young American Medals Committee, composed of Mr. Hoover, Solicitor General Thurgood Marshall, and Jacob Rosenthal, Director of Public Information, Department of Justice.

290 Statement by the President Following Senate Approval of the Traffic Safety Bill. *June 24, 1966*

I APPLAUD the action of the Senate today in its overwhelming approval of the traffic safety bill which I urged the Congress to enact.

I particularly want to applaud the efforts of Senators Magnuson and Ribicoff.

This is landmark legislation. It will move us out of the Stone Age of ignorance and inaction.

For the first time in our history, we can mount a truly comprehensive attack on the rising toll of death and destruction on the Nation's highways that last year alone claimed 50,000 American lives.

We can no longer tolerate such anarchy on wheels. This measure with its stringent and mandatory Federal auto safety standards is going to reverse the trend.

I urge the House to speed passage of this vital legislation that will benefit every man, woman, and child in our land.

NOTE: The National Traffic and Motor Vehicle Safety Act and the Highway Safety Act were approved by the President on September 9, 1966 (see Item 449).

291 Statement by the President on the Government's "Mission SAFETY-70" Program. *June 27, 1966*

I AM PLEASED to learn from Secretary of Labor Wirtz that more than 50 departments and agencies have inaugurated programs in the past year to meet the objective of Mission SAFETY-70. That objective is to reduce Federal employee injuries and costs 30 percent by 1970.

I have never believed that the Government can afford the attitude that, "Accidents will happen." Our philosophy must be, "Accidents should not happen."

We have now begun to put that philosophy into effect. Secretary Wirtz' report shows:

—A 4.3 percent decline in the overall Federal injury frequency rate.
—A reduction from 2 to 26 percent in the injury rates among the 14 largest agencies, employing over three-fourths of the 2½ million Federal workers.
—One thousand fewer disabling injuries to Federal employees during the first year of the program.

We are pleased with these results. But we must press on to meet our long-range goals. Accidents still cost the Government about $200 million each year, plus untold human suffering. Agency heads must now translate their declarations of intent—and their written programs—into tangible results.

The major cause of death in the Federal service is motor vehicle accidents. Government vehicles cover nearly 2¾ billion miles annually. We must look more carefully at both the drivers and the vehicles they operate. Our drivers must be carefully selected, thoroughly tested, and properly trained. Our vehicles must comply with the highest safety standards and must be maintained in top condition.

But auto and other accidents away from work cause just as much suffering and just as much production loss as those accidents which occur on-the-job. Off-the-job safety programs are becoming increasingly important, and I expect administrators to encourage their employees to live safely as well as work safely.

Finally, I expect to see the establishment and improvement of internal operating procedures to provide uniform accident data for Government-wide summary and analysis.

The Federal Government has rightly taken the lead in national accident prevention programs—particularly those which occur on our highways. We intend to do everything we can to help the States reduce this wholesale slaughter of American citizens.

In the process, however, we must be certain that our own house is in order. That is the meaning—and the challenge—of Mission SAFETY-70.

NOTE: Secretary Wirtz' report, dated June 1966, is entitled "Mission SAFETY-70—One Year of Progress, Report to the President by the Secretary of Labor" (6 pp., processed).

292 Statement by the President on the Reorganization of the Public Health Service. *June 27, 1966*

TWO MONTHS AGO I submitted to Congress a reorganization plan to modernize the Public Health Service. Over this past weekend that plan has become a reality.

I want to express my deep appreciation to the Congress for this important measure.

Together we have taken another forward step in our unremitting efforts to improve Government, to bring it up to date, and to make it a modern instrument of service for our citizens.

This is a particularly significant reorganization.

For the first time in over two decades, the Public Health Service can be reshaped to perform its vital role of matching the miracles of modern medicine to the needs of all Americans. It will help us achieve the full promise of the landmark health measures enacted by the 89th Congress.

Since 1953 more than 50 new medical programs have been placed in the Public Health Service. Its budget over the past 12 years has increased tenfold—from $250 million to $2.4 billion.

Before this reorganization plan became effective the Public Health Service was obsolete in its organization, a major obstacle to the fulfillment of the Nation's health goals.

Now, under the new reorganization plan, the Public Health Service can be strengthened and streamlined.

I have asked Secretary of Health, Education, and Welfare John Gardner and Surgeon General William Stewart to move ahead as rapidly as possible to carry out the new plan. Under their leadership the Public Health Service will operate more efficiently and effectively as it conducts the medical research and develops the resources we need to build a better, healthier tomorrow for all our people.

NOTE: For the President's message to Congress transmitting Reorganization Plan 3 of 1966, see Item 190.

293 Statement by the President Following a Meeting To Review Goals for Medical Research and Health Services. *June 27, 1966*

TODAY, I have met with Secretary Gardner, the Surgeon General, and the top Government team connected with medical research and health services. These men constitute my strategy council in the war against disease. We began a review of the targets and the timetable they have set for winning victories in this war.

The National Institutes of Health are spending more than $800 million a year on biomedical research. I am keenly interested to learn not only what knowledge this buys but what are the payoffs in terms of healthy lives for our citizens.

We know what has been achieved in the past. The widespread application of polio vaccines reduced that dread disease from 34,000 cases in 1954 to almost zero last year.

Medical research helped cut the tuberculosis death rate by 87 percent since the end of World War II. The number of hospital beds occupied by tuberculosis victims has been cut in half.

Ten years ago experts predicted there would be an increase of more than 200,000 patients in State mental hospitals within a decade. Yet today, largely as a result of psychiatric research and new drugs, there has been *not* an increase but a reduction of 83,000 patients.

These examples provide dramatic proof of what can be achieved if we apply the lessons of research to detect, to deter, and to cure disease. The Nation faces a heavy demand on its hospitals and health manpower. Medical research, effectively applied, can help reduce the load by preventing disease before it occurs, and by curing disease when it does strike.

But the greater reward is in the well-being of our citizens. We must make sure that no life-giving discovery is locked up in the laboratory.

I plan to meet again in a few months with my health strategy council to review their plans and to establish our goals.

NOTE: A list of the members of the President's "health strategy council" was furnished to members of the press along with the text of the President's statement. Listed as members were Secretary of Health, Education, and Welfare John W. Gardner, Under Secretary Wilbur J. Cohen, Assistant Secretary for Health and Scientific Affairs Dr. Philip R. Lee, the Surgeon General, Dr. William Stewart, 17 officials of the Public Health Service, and the Chief Medical Director of the Veterans Administration, Dr. H. Martin Engle, and his assistant.

294 Statement by the President in Response to Report of the National Commission on Food Marketing. *June 27, 1966*

I RECEIVED today the report of the National Commission on Food Marketing.

This report deals with a most vital subject—the structure and performance of the Nation's food marketing system.

That system is America's largest industry. Last year consumers bought $85 billion worth of food, nearly one out of every $5 they spent.

I appreciate the effort and dedication of the 15 men and women of the Commission, chaired by Judge Phil Gibson. Together, they have increased our fund of knowledge about the food industry.

As Senator Hart has stated, the Commission's report is a good beginning. No one study can contain all the answers and solutions. No one study can really be considered final—but rather part of a continual process of exploration and examination in our search for solutions.

The diversity of opinions and views in the Commission's report are healthy reflections of the complexity and importance of the issues.

I have referred the Commission's report, together with the individual dissenting views, to the Director of the Bureau of the Budget for the review and study of all interested agencies of the Government.

I know that we will also benefit by the review of the report by the Congress to which it has also been submitted.

The work of the Commission will receive careful attention and discussion in the months ahead. And it will help us in our efforts to achieve greater abundance for our society.

NOTE: The report, entitled "Food From Farmer to Consumer," is dated June 27, 1966 (Government Printing Office, 113 pp.).

The National Commission on Food Marketing was established in 1964 by Public Law 88–354 (78 Stat. 269).

295 Remarks to Delegates to the National Youth Conference on Natural Beauty and Conservation. *June 27, 1966*

Miss Sharp, Mr. Fox, members of the Conference, ladies and gentlemen:

I am so happy that you could come here this morning; I wish it was more comfortable for you out there on the lawn. But it is a pretty lawn even if we don't have a cover and it's not air conditioned. And it's pretty because a lot of people work on it every day.

One of the brightest parts of every day for me is to read and to hear about the work that's being done in this country in the field of conservation and beautification. And I'm so pleased that you young leaders, from all parts of this land, would be interested enough to come here, make your contribution, and take home all that you can see and hear during this Conference.

This morning I started my day by hearing Miss Sharp and Mr. Fox on the "Today" show. And I don't think that I have ever been prouder of the young people of my country than I was of them when they were speaking their thoughts.

I'm so glad that in this day and age when we have so many critical problems that we have people like Secretary Udall and Mrs. Johnson and Mrs. Weaver and Mrs. Freeman and others who are excited about conserving this Nation, and who are dedicated to making it a more beautiful country. And I am particularly grateful to some of the industrial leaders of this country that they would give of their profits to make this a more beautiful land as well as a prosperous land.

But the ones that really have charge of the kind of a country that we're going to live in in the years to come are you delegates to this Conference. As Mrs. Johnson said to you, if you dream dreams, you are going to determine whether this is a beautiful land or not. You're going to determine what kind of conservation measures we take. You're going to translate the dreams and the talk of today into action of tomorrow.

And I'm so proud that when there are many things to divert you, when there are many roads that lead into other directions, that you are willing to come here and apply your knowledge to making this a more beautiful land.

We're so happy you're here; we wish for you the best. We thank you in advance for all that we know you're going to do for your land.

Thank you.

NOTE: The President spoke on the South Lawn of the White House shortly after Mrs. Johnson had completed her remarks officially opening the Conference at 10 a.m. The 500 delegates were members of leading youth organizations representing 20 million young people throughout the country. Participating in the Conference were representatives of the Boy Scouts of America, Boys' Clubs of America, Camp Fire Girls, the 4–H Clubs, Future Farmers of America, Future Homemakers of America, Girl Scouts of the U.S.A., Girls Clubs of America, and the Young Men's and Young Women's Christian Associations.

The President's opening words referred to the Conference cochairmen, Jacquelene Sharp of Jackson, Miss., a student at Knoxville College, and George Fox of Michigantown, Ind., a student at Purdue University. Later he referred to Secretary of the Interior Stewart L. Udall, Mrs. Robert C. Weaver, wife of the Secretary of Housing and Urban Development, and Mrs. Orville L. Freeman, wife of the Secretary of Agriculture.

The President's remarks were not made public in the form of a White House press release. As printed above, they follow the text made available for use in the Weekly Compilation of Presidential Documents.

296 Memorandum on the Use and Management of Computers by Federal Agencies. *June 28, 1966*

Memorandum for Heads of Departments and Agencies:

I want the head of every Federal agency to explore and apply all possible means to

—use the electronic computer to do a better job

—manage computer activity at the lowest possible cost.

I want my administration to give priority emphasis to both of these objectives—nothing less will suffice.

The electronic computer is having a greater impact on what the Government does and how it does it than any other product of modern technology.

The computer is making it possible to

—send men and satellites into space

—make significant strides in medical research

—add several billions of dollars to our revenue through improved tax administration

—administer the huge and complex social security and medicare programs

—manage a multi-billion dollar defense logistics system

—speed the issuance of G.I. insurance dividends, at much less cost

—save lives through better search and rescue operations

—harness atomic energy for peaceful uses

—design better but less costly highways and structures.

In short, computers are enabling us to achieve progress and benefits which a decade ago were beyond our grasp.

The technology is available. Its potential for good has been amply demonstrated, but it remains to be tapped in fuller measure.

I am determined that we take advantage of this technology by using it imaginatively to accomplish worthwhile purposes.

I therefore want every agency head to give thorough study to new ways in which the electronic computer might be used to

—provide better service to the public

—improve agency performance

—reduce costs.

But, as we use computers to achieve these benefits, I want these activities managed at the lowest possible cost.

At the present time, the Federal Government

—uses 2,600 computers

—employs 71,000 people in this activity

—spends over $2 billion annually to acquire and operate this equipment, including special military type computers.

Clearly, we must devote our best efforts to managing this large investment wisely and with the least cost.

I approved a blueprint for action when I approved the Bureau of the Budget "Report on Management of ADP in the Government."

The Congress recognized this need when it enacted Public Law 89–306 (the Brooks Bill) last October. This legislation provided specific authorities to

—the General Services Administration, for the procurement, utilization and disposition of automatic data processing equipment

—the Department of Commerce, for the development of data processing standards and the provision of assistance to agencies in designing computer-based systems

—the Bureau of the Budget, for exercising policy and fiscal control over the implementation of these authorities

These agencies are seeking actively to put into effect ways for improving and reducing the cost of this huge and complex operation.

In my Budget Message for 1967 I told the Congress of my intent to make sure that this huge investment is managed efficiently.

The Federal Government must give priority attention to

—establishing better and more effective procurement methods

—making fuller use of existing facilities through sharing and joint-use arrangements before acquiring additional equipment

—re-utilizing excess equipment whenever feasible

—achieving, with industry cooperation, greater compatibility of equipment.

I expect all agencies to cooperate fully

with the Bureau of the Budget, the General Services Administration, and the Department of Commerce in accomplishing these objectives.

I want the Director of the Bureau of the Budget to report to me on December 31, 1966, and every six months thereafter, on the progress that is being made throughout the Federal Government in improving the management of this very important technology.

LYNDON B. JOHNSON

NOTE: The "Report to the President on the Management of Automatic Data Processing in the Federal Government," prepared by the Bureau of the Budget, is printed in Senate Document 15 (89th Cong., 1st sess.).

For the President's 1967 Budget Message to Congress, see Item 26.

The first of the semiannual progress reports on use and management of electronic computers in the Federal Government was issued by the Bureau of the Budget on February 23, 1967 (OD–196, 5 pp., processed).

---

297   Statement by the President Following House Committee Approval of the Demonstration Cities Bill.
June 28, 1966

I APPLAUD the action taken by the House Banking and Currency Committee this morning in its overwhelming approval of the administration's Demonstration Cities Act. This is vital legislation—important to the future of American cities, large and small.

It will help rebuild where there is blight and renew where there is decay. This is good news for the future of every city in America and the citizens that live in our cities.

It will allow the cities, the Federal Government, and private enterprise to join together in a common effort to achieve the goal of the better life for all our people.

NOTE: The Demonstration Cities and Metropolitan Development Act of 1966 was approved by the President on November 3, 1966 (see Item 574).

The statement was posted on the bulletin board in the Press Room at the White House. It was not made public in the form of a White House press release.

298 Remarks to the Press Following a Meeting To Review Plans for the Inauguration of Medicare. *June 28, 1966*

Ladies and gentlemen:

We had a review—one of a series of reviews—with the Secretary of Health, Education, and Welfare, the Surgeon General, and others concerning the inauguration of the Medicare program to be effective July 1.

They have reported to me the progress that has been made. It has been substantial progress in getting hospitals that are eligible within compliance.

We reviewed it State by State. We tried to anticipate some of the problems that will come into being when the act takes effect.

The Secretary will discuss with you the general outline of our meeting this morning. The Secretary will also take any questions that you may have specifically on the subject of our meeting or upon Medicare, or upon individual problems or individual States.

I think things are moving along very well in these last few days. All the States are not in 100 percent, but substantial progress has been made and is being made.

Secretary Gardner, Secretary Cohen, and the Surgeon General have made a rather good report. I hope we use every hour that is left to make available to our aged people all the facilities that are in existence.

I observe that there are a few States that still have problems. The Surgeon General, the Social Security offices, and others are working very closely with them.

We hope that every hospital, every doctor, and every eligible older citizen will be understanding and cooperative, to try to work together in this worthwhile objective that we are undertaking for the first time in this country.

I want to commend Secretary Gardner, Mr. Cohen, and the Surgeon General for what they have done. I will be receiving further reports from them from time to time.

NOTE: The President spoke at 12:32 p.m. in the Fish Room at the White House. Following his remarks a press briefing was held in which the following officials participated: John W. Gardner, Secretary of Health, Education, and Welfare, Dr. William H. Stewart, Surgeon General, Public Health Service, Wilbur J. Cohen, Under Secretary of Health, Education, and Welfare, and S. Douglass Cater, Jr., Special Assistant to the President. The complete text of the briefing is printed in the Weekly Compilation of Presidential Documents (vol. 2, p. 843).

299 Remarks to Delegates to the Conference of State Commissions on the Status of Women. *June 28, 1966*

Secretary Wirtz, very distinguished and attractive delegates:

We are very disappointed that you couldn't enjoy the heat and the beauty of the Rose Garden, but we ranchers do pray for rain. Occasionally, our prayers are answered.

Mrs. Johnson has gotten in the habit here lately—trying to get this grass to grow on the White House lawn—of asking for rain more often than she gets it. I hope you will understand and indulge us. If none of you have ever had to move in from the backyard on short notice, then you are entitled to criticize us.

I am quite pleased and delighted this afternoon to be able to come here to join you in celebrating the first long steps toward

657

full and equal rights that we have taken in this country on behalf of the women of America.

Four and a half years ago, I believe it was in December 1961, Esther Peterson first came to my office in the Capitol in quest of money from the Congress. A good many people do that these days—but she came for a very unique and very unusual and very fine purpose. She was trying to finance the President's commission to study the status of women.

In the following February, many of you will remember that you met at my home with Mrs. Johnson at The Elms to pay our honor and our respect and tribute to the Commission's Chairman, that very great lady, Mrs. Eleanor Roosevelt.

So it seems to me that I have been close to your program for a good, long time now. I share all of your pride in the accomplishments and the achievements of this group.

Many of the recommendations of your first report to the President have already been implemented. Some of the old inequities and the barriers have already been swept away. We do now have an excellent Federal equal pay law.

Similar action has already been taken in 33 States of the Union and the District of Columbia. I know that you are intent on finishing that job.

Last winter, a Federal court made real the principle that women are "persons" under the Constitution. You may have heard about the longtime leader in the suffrage movement who used to say that when she died, she hoped her epitaph would be: "Born a woman, died a person." Well, that is what the court decision did.

Now, under an Executive order, women in Government enjoy equality in appointments and advancements. My problem—it seems I have always had that problem, too—

is finding these women. I hope you will continue to help me in the talent search that we are conducting for women scientists, women judges, women ambassadors, women administrators, and for women to occupy leadership posts in our Federal Government.

Now, with the creation of 48 State Commissions on the Status of Women during the past 2 years, much of our future activity is going to be out in the States and in the communities. You are helping erase inequities before the law.

Two hundred and eighty-four State statutes passed last year were passed to improve the civil and political status of women. That is adequate testimony to your efforts and to the results that you have obtained.

State commissions have done much to stimulate continued education for women. Child care centers have been improved. Centers have been set up by many States to find outlets for talented volunteers.

All around this country mayors are now appointing civic beautification committees. In practically every instance they are looking to the women, as I do here in Washington, for leadership in that field.

Believe me—if you could overhear some bedroom conversations—I get leadership in that field.

Last year in the Head Start project, 200,000 women volunteered their services to help us with the Head Start centers. That is one of our most successful programs. One of the reasons it is successful is because women provide leadership to make it successful. There will be even more this summer.

I doubt that there are many causes in this country that are more rewarding than the Head Start cause.

Recently, some underprivileged children in a Head Start project in Massachusetts were given a vocabulary test. The teacher held up flash cards of various objects to see if they could identify them. One of these cards was the picture of a teddy bear. More than 60 percent of the children identified it as a rat. Their world, evidently, had more rats in it than teddy bears.

That is the kind of a world this administration is determined to change—and is changing. Now, it is everyone's job to do something about it, but I know who is going to do something about it first. I will let you in on that secret: It is going to be the women of this country.

For nearly two centuries now, the Bill of Rights—that we all will be talking about July 4—has been the foundation of all the freedom that we enjoy and that we hope other people can obtain throughout the world. Now, let's take the Bill of Rights and magnify these freedoms for all of our people in this Great Society in which we live.

Americans must have the right to live their lives without discrimination because of race, color, religion, or sex.

They must have the right to vote in every place in this land.

They must have the right to a decent job in every place in this land.

They must have the right to a fair wage in every State in this Union.

They must have the right to sufficient food.

They must have the right to a decent home.

They must have the right to good medical care.

I have had three conferences already this week on medical care and I have another one coming up tomorrow. It is a real big job to get 18 million people signed up. It is going to be a bigger job getting the administration smoothed out. But anything that is as important as this is worth doing. We are not a bunch of "can't do" people.

Our people must have a right to expect what I have this afternoon—beauty in their surroundings.

They must have the right to proper recreation for their children. That is why we are adding so much to our public domain and trying to get parks that are close to where our people live.

As beautiful as Wyoming is, I am still paying for Mrs. Johnson's last trip out there. I just wish that she could have gone down on the Potomac and enjoyed the same beauties.

The people who live in New York, Philadelphia and Washington cannot all go across the country with all their children. So we are trying to arrange for places like Assateague, which is close to the population centers.

They must have the right to an education. And this is the provision that Secretary Wirtz put in here.

I first heard him advocate on my ranch porch shortly after I became President that the most important thing we could do was to see in this country that every boy and girl born in this land had the right to get all the education they could take. As a result, we passed 24 education bills—the elementary education bill, the kindergarten (Head Start) bill, the secondary education bills, the vocational education bill, the higher education bill.

Any person that graduates from high school in this land today, that is unable to take care of his own expenses in college, can either go to college by getting a work project job, by getting a scholarship, or by getting a loan.

Now, I haven't been out of college too long, but none of those things existed when I was in college.

We are quickly coming to the promise that Secretary Wirtz first made—that every child born in this country has a right to get all the education he can take.

Women have been in the forefront of nearly every great social reform that we have had in America. I want to remind you women leaders here this afternoon that not all of these battles have yet been won. The timing is right—and it is right now—to win these battles.

So your work will be as effective, I think, as you want to make it.

I know that you have tremendous energy. I know that you are dedicated people. After all, those who have created life are most likely to breathe fresh life into the next generation. That is what I hope you will dedicate your efforts to—to that end.

I have delayed until now an announcement that is important and, I think, that will interest you. I thought it appropriate that you know it first—although these people out here who constantly recite the First Amendment to me think that I should not keep these things secret very long.

Today it is with real and genuine regret that I have accepted the resignation of Margaret Hickey as Chairman of the Citizens' Advisory Council on the Status of Women. She has given us her outstanding talents and has given great leadership to the Council since its creation.

All America is in her debt. Her President is particularly appreciative of what she has done. The Council's success is hers as much as it is anyone's in this country. We will miss Margaret Hickey in her old role, but I know that she will be active in public affairs, as she has always been.

I am glad to be able to announce, before we have any speculation on that subject, that my very dear friend, Senator Maurine Neuberger, has accepted the chairmanship. There are few women in this land who have provided better leadership than Senator Neuberger for a longer period of time.

Senator Neuberger has been active in the work of the Council for many years now. When she voluntarily retires from a distinguished career in the Congress at the end of this session, Maurine will bring to all women of this country and to the leaders of her Government the benefit of her compassion and her wisdom, her experience and her energy.

We are very sorry to have one remarkable woman leave your leadership, but we are very happy that another remarkable woman is willing to step up and take her place as your leader, to continue your objectives, to aid in achieving your goals, and to make the American woman the envy of all the world.

Thank you very much.

NOTE: The President spoke at 5:48 p.m. in the East Room at the White House. In his opening words he referred to Secretary of Labor W. Willard Wirtz. Later he referred to Mrs. Esther Peterson, Assistant Secretary of Labor for Labor Standards and Vice Chairman of the Interdepartmental Committee on the Status of Women, Margaret Hickey, outgoing Chairman of the Citizens' Advisory Council on the Status of Women, and Mrs. Maurine B. Neuberger, incoming Council Chairman who served as Senator from Oregon from November 9, 1960, to January 3, 1967.

The third annual Conference of State Commissions on the Status of Women met in Washington June 28–30.

300 Message Commemorating President and Mrs. Eisenhower's Golden Wedding Anniversary. *June 29, 1966*

DWIGHT D. EISENHOWER has given a lifetime of service and sacrifice to this Nation and to the cause of freedom throughout the world. Through it all he has had his beloved Mamie Eisenhower at his side. She has been an abiding source of strength and understanding for her husband from the days when he served his country as a young lieutenant to the years of his service as a great President, and that is why the entire Nation rejoices as the Eisenhowers approach their 50th wedding anniversary on Friday, July the first.

It is a historic occasion as well as a cause for private celebration. For not since the time of John Quincy Adams have a President and his First Lady achieved this golden milestone in their lives. All of us owe the Eisen-

howers a debt that can only be repaid now with our affection and our deepest gratitude. In the years of peace that they have richly earned as they labor to build the new Eisenhower College, they can truly be sustained by the admiration of their fellow Americans.

I know that Mrs. Johnson and I can speak for all Americans in extending to President and Mrs. Eisenhower our very warm and heartfelt congratulations and our good wishes for many more years of life together. We want them to know that they will celebrate 50 years of marriage in the glow not only of their union but of the Nation's unshakeable esteem.

NOTE: The President recorded the message on film in the Theater at the White House. It was not made public in the form of a White House press release.

301 Summary of the President's Remarks at a Meeting With the National Advisory Commission on Health Manpower. *June 29, 1966*

THIS is health week for me. On Monday I met with my health strategy council—Secretary Gardner, the Surgeon General, the Directors of the National Institutes of Health—to discuss how we can better apply research knowledge to the prevention and cure of disease. Yesterday, I held a meeting with Secretary Gardner and other officials to review the status of hospital facilities for Medicare patients. Today, I'm pleased to meet with you as you begin your work.

All the health issues we discussed earlier in the week are of urgent concern. But none of them is more important than the one with which you will be dealing in the next

few months: health manpower.

The national demand for health manpower today exceeds the supply—and this may be the case for several years. This fact gives your job a special importance.

As you begin your work, I hope you will concentrate on making practical recommendations about how the Nation can deal with this problem.

First, I need your advice about the Federal Government's use of its health manpower:

—Are we setting an example for the Nation in the efficient use of health manpower?

—Should we establish new forms of health

661

manpower utilization?

Second, we need answers to these same questions as they apply to non-Federal health manpower.

Third, we need your advice on how to develop additional health manpower—not only high-level specialists, but technicians and allied health professionals.

We have important commitments today in the health field, not only at home but around the world. The conflict in Vietnam places additional burdens on our health manpower resources. And in 2 days we launch Medicare—the most significant health venture enacted by Congress in this era.

All of these activities mean one thing: We must do more with the resources we have.

As you begin your work, I offer you my support—and I wish you well. Millions of Americans depend on your deliberations and your accomplishments.

NOTE: The President met with members of the Commission shortly before 11 a.m. in the Cabinet Room at the White House following which the Press Office made public this summary of his remarks.

For the President's statement following his meeting with the health strategy council on Monday, June 27, 1966, see Item 293.

302   Special Message to the Congress Transmitting Reorganization Plan 5 of 1966: National Capital Regional Planning Council. *June 29, 1966*

To the Congress of the United States:

I am transmitting Reorganization Plan No. 5 of 1966, prepared in accordance with the Reorganization Act of 1949, as amended.

The time has come to recognize the readiness of local governments in the Washington Area to undertake a role which is properly and rightfully theirs. To that end, I am submitting a reorganization plan to abolish the National Capital Regional Planning Council.

Comprehensive regional planning is vital to the orderly development of our metropolitan areas. Nowhere is it more important than in the National Capital Region.

To be most effective, regional planning must be a responsibility of the area's State and local governments acting together to solve mutual problems of growth and change. It should not be a Federal function, although the Federal Government should support and advance it.

The need for cooperative planning was recognized years ago in the National Capital Region. The establishment of the National Capital Regional Planning Council in 1952 to prepare a comprehensive development plan was a major step in meeting that need.

However, the Council was designed for conditions which no longer exist. It was established by Federal law as a Federal agency financed by Federal funds because the various local jurisdictions then felt they were not in a position to provide the financing necessary for area-wide comprehensive planning.

The situation that existed in 1952 has been changed by two major developments

—the founding of the Metropolitan Washington Council of Governments, and

—the inauguration of a nationwide urban planning assistance program, commonly referred to as the "701 Program."

The Metropolitan Washington Council

of Governments, established in 1957, is a voluntary association of elected officials of local governments in the area. It has a competent professional staff and has done constructive work on area-wide development matters.

It had a budget of nearly a quarter of a million dollars for fiscal year 1965, mostly derived from local government contributions, and has developed to the point where it can fully carry out the State and local aspects of regional planning.

The urban planning assistance program provides for Federal financing of two-thirds of the cost of metropolitan planning. The National Capital Regional Planning Council, as a Federal agency, is not eligible for assistance under this program. The Metropolitan Washington Council of Governments, however, became eligible for that assistance under the terms of the Housing and Urban Development Act of 1965. Accordingly, the elected local governments of the National Capital Region have declared their intention of undertaking the responsibility for area-wide comprehensive planning through the Council of Governments.

The reorganization plan will not alter the basic responsibilities of the National Capital Planning Commission. That Commission will continue to represent the Federal interest in the planning and development of the Region. Indeed, its work should increase as comprehensive regional planning by the Council of Governments is accelerated. In accord with the reorganization plan, the Commission will work closely with the Council of Governments in regional planning. The Commission will also deal directly with the suburban jurisdictions and assume the liaison functions now exercised by the National Capital Regional Planning Council.

The reorganization plan will improve existing organizational arrangements of and promote more effective and efficient planning for the National Capital Region.

It will also result in long-range savings to the Federal Government. The regional planning effort of the Council of Governments is supported in part by local contributions. The same work done by the National Capital Regional Planning Council has been supported totally with Federal funds. The plan will eliminate this overlapping effort.

Annual savings of at least $25,000 should result from the reorganization plan.

The functions to be abolished by the reorganization plan are provided for in sections 2(e), 3, 4, 5(d) and 6(b) of the Act approved June 6, 1924, entitled "An Act providing for a comprehensive development of the park and playground system of the National Capital" (43 Stat. 463), as amended (66 Stat. 783, 40 U.S.C. 71a(e), 71b, 71c, 71d(d), and 71E(b)).

I have found, after investigation, that each reorganization included in the accompanying reorganization plan is necessary to accomplish one or more of the purposes set forth in Section 2(a) of the Reorganization Act of 1949, as amended.

I recommend that the Congress allow the reorganization plan to become effective.

LYNDON B. JOHNSON

The White House
June 29, 1966

NOTE: Reorganization Plan 5 of 1966 is printed in the Weekly Compilation of Presidential Documents (vol. 2, p. 848), in the Federal Register (31 F.R. 11857), and in Title 3 of the Code of Federal Regulations (3 CFR, 1966 Comp., p. 192). It became effective on September 8, 1966.

303 Message to the Congress Transmitting Final Report of the Office of Alien Property. *June 29, 1966*

To the Congress of the United States:

I am pleased to transmit the Annual Report of the Office of Alien Property for Fiscal Year 1965 as required by Section 6 of the Trading with the Enemy Act. It is the 23rd report of proceedings under that Act.

As this report indicates, we have reached the end of a very long road. After June 30, 1966, for the first time in 49 years, there will be no Government unit whose sole task will be the processing of alien property matters arising from the wartime seizure of property. Some alien property work remains which cannot be completed by June 30, 1966, principally because it is affected by litigation or proposed legislation. These remaining matters will be completed in the future by the part-time work of personnel of the Civil Division of the Department of Justice. But this does not detract from the fact that as of April 30, 1966, the staff which has completed the processing of about $900,000,000 in vested property will have closed all but about 50 of the more than 67,500 claims which were filed, all but about 450 of approximately 62,000 accounts, and it will have pending only about 30 of the more than 7,000 cases which it has litigated.

The imminent closing of the Office of Alien Property is another step in our determination to find the most efficient way to serve the American public. In the War Claims Act of 1948, as amended, Congress has authorized thousands of American citizens to file claims against the net proceeds of vested property which are maintained in the War Claims Fund. Since the costs of the Office of Alien Property are deducted from the proceeds of vested property, closing the Office will soon mean the end of deductions of its administrative costs, thereby leaving more funds for the claimants to share. And the public generally will benefit by the absorption into other necessary work of the mere handful of knowledgeable and dedicated employees who have brought this fruitful work virtually to its close.

LYNDON B. JOHNSON

The White House
June 29, 1966

NOTE: A memorandum for the President from the Attorney General, dated June 28, 1966, concerning the closing of the Office of Alien Property, with a summary of the highlights of the Department's activities in the field of alien property, was also released.

The report was entitled "Annual Report, Office of Alien Property, Department of Justice, Fiscal Year Ended June 30, 1965" (22 pp., processed).

304 Remarks of Welcome to Prime Minister Holt of Australia on the South Lawn at the White House. *June 29, 1966*

Mr. Prime Minister and Mrs. Holt:

We greet you this morning as friend and partner. It is a very genuine pleasure to welcome you and Mrs. Holt, and the distinguished members of your party, to our country.

My personal ties to your country are as deep as a man's can be. During the war I found among you open-hearted friendship when I was far from home. Now, once again, our two nations are fighting side by side in the defense of freedom.

The first thing that I read every morning are the battle reports from Vietnam. I want you to know that I follow the exploits of 4,500 Australians fighting there with the same interest and concern as those of our own men. Mr. Prime Minister, I take great pride in their courage and their dedication. I derive great strength from the sacrifices they are making.

You in Australia know that in Vietnam we are meeting a challenge which just must be met. It must be met because it is always dangerous to let aggression succeed. It must be met because our SEATO commitments require us to defend the people of South Vietnam from external attack.

It must be met because the security of Australia and the United States of America is directly at stake in preserving the independence and the freedom of the nations of Southeast Asia.

We also know that behind the struggle against aggression in Vietnam a vital, free Asia is rapidly emerging. Shielded by the courage of the Vietnamese and their allies, many Asian countries are driving forward with real success in their economic and social development.

We all know of the remarkable growth of Australia and Japan in recent years. But last year the growth rate in South Korea was 8 percent; in Taiwan it was 7 percent; in Malaysia it was 5½ percent; in Thailand it was 6 percent. Growth in Iran has been averaging better than 6 percent a year.

Pakistan is rapidly recovering from the setback caused by the conflict last year.

Last week I received word from India which moved me greatly. The monsoons have begun. It looks as though the rainfall this year will be ample and the harvest will be good. With adequate rainfall, the courageous measures of the Indian Government, and the support of the world community, I hope and I expect that India will surge forward in the year ahead.

Indonesia is turning the corner into the most promising phase of its postwar history.

Meanwhile, there is rising in Asia a new spirit of regional association and regional self-confidence. It was that spirit to which I responded and which I tried to encourage in the talk I gave in Baltimore in April 1965.

Now the dream of an Asian Development Bank is a reality, binding up the peoples from Teheran to Seoul in a great common enterprise. Work goes forward to develop the Mekong Valley, despite the conflict close by.

I know that Australia has, for many years, assumed a major responsibility for the security and the development of its region, through the Colombo Plan, the Mekong Committee, SEATO, and bilateral contributions to developing regions of the area. Our own security is heightened because we are joined with you in ANZUS.

But we feel a new sense of fellowship and common destiny is emerging in Asia. We followed with great interest the recent meeting in Seoul of the Asian and Pacific Council, in which your Government participated.

Nations that were long isolated from each other are now beginning to know each other and to find new common ground. Old antagonisms are giving way to a new awareness that there are great possibilities in working together, great challenges to be met, and great jobs to be done.

Above all, Asia is proving once again that stability and power are not to be found in tyranny and aggressive wars against a neighbor.

Stability and power come from free men and free nations working together on behalf of the people. We both know that should we fail in Vietnam these new possibilities in free Asia would be endangered or destroyed.

Mr. Prime Minister, as you come this morning to this house on your long-awaited visit, I wish to tell you—and, through you, to tell your wonderful people—that we shall not fail. We shall persist. We shall succeed.

The good, brave people of South Vietnam shall be given their chance to forge their own destiny in peace.

The free peoples of Asia shall be given their chance to shape the destiny of their own region.

These are your goals in Asia, Mr. Prime Minister, and they are also the goals of the United States of America.

Welcome.

NOTE: The President spoke at 12:25 p.m. on the South Lawn at the White House, where Prime Minister Harold E. Holt was welcomed with full military honors. The Prime Minister, whose visit was described as a working visit, responded as follows:

Mr. President and Mrs. Johnson:

Thank you for your warm welcome, Mr. President. You have said warm and generous things about Australia and its people.

What a memorable morning for the Australian people and for an Australian Prime Minister. I thank you for the honor which, by this ceremonial, you have accorded to my country and you have accorded to me. What has been done will be appreciated deeply by my people as it is by myself as head of my Government.

We meet, Mr. President, as heads of government while our two nations are again comrades in arms. This is at least the fourth time in this century that Americans and Australians have combined together with other friendly forces to resist aggression.

We fought alongside each other in two World Wars, and then Australia was the first country, I believe, to announce itself beside you when America made the historic decision to bring its strength to the aid of South Korea.

I say historic decision advisedly, because I believe that to have been, Mr. President, one of the turning points in human history. I believe at that critical point of time was decided the issue of whether we handed Asia over to penetrating, aggressive communism, or whether we kept intact a large part of Asia as member countries of the company of free people throughout the world.

Australia was with you when you decided on the decision, critical also to you and to us, in South Vietnam, another battleground against Communist aggression.

You have spoken of the task force of Australians which is now assembled in Saigon. You will be aware, Mr. President, that in other parts of Southeast Asia Australia is making a military contribution, small by the standards of your own great country, but useful in the company in which we find ourselves there.

I know that this task force in South Vietnam will acquit itself with distinction. The men that are serving there are men of quality. They are well-trained. The 1st Battalion was accorded the highest commendation by your own leaders and by the leaders of South Vietnam. The task force which follows them will acquit themselves with no less courage and distinction.

The outcome of this struggle is critical for the hopes that you and we share for a better and more secure way of life for the free people of Asia.

You have spoken of the vital free Asia that is emerging. I can speak of this from some personal experience, because not merely do we have a view from "Down Under" which is perhaps a different perspective from that of others in different parts of the world, but it has been my own good fortune in recent times to have traveled over several of these countries of Southeast Asia.

What has occurred over recent years is a transformation. To go through Thailand, Malaysia, and even South Vietnam itself, and see the massive support being rendered there, see the security, the progress which has been found possible by these other countries where communism has successfully been held in check—to see these things is to give heartening encouragement to go on with the job of resisting aggression where we find it.

But it does not take a war to bring Americans and Australians close together. We like each other. Friendships form quickly between us. We have many mutually beneficial links: our trade with each other; the investment that you make with us with your capital. We cooperate in many constructive international interests and causes.

You mentioned, Mr. President, your time in Australia 25 years ago. A new Australia has arisen since then. When can we see you there again? And this time we hope with Mrs. Johnson, and perhaps the whole family.

You will be encouraged to see the national growth in which many American skills and resources have assisted.

Mr. President, we recognize all too clearly in my own country that on you, personally, falls the heavy and at times lonely responsibility of free world leadership. On your country these burdens have been assumed in comparatively recent times in terms of modern history. But America has shouldered those burdens firmly, and you have inspired and encouraged us all by the strength of your own resolution.

You know that in Australia you have an understanding friend. I am here, sir, not asking for anything—an experience which I am sure you value at times when it is not so frequent as it might be.

You have in us not merely an understanding friend, but one staunch in the belief of the need for our presence with you in Vietnam. We are not there because of our friendship; we are there because, like you, we believe it is right to be there, and, like you, we shall stay there as long as seems necessary in order to achieve the purposes of the South Vietnamese Government and the purposes that we join in formulating and progressing together.

And so, sir, in the lonelier and perhaps even more disheartening moments which come to any national leader, I hope there will be a corner of your mind and heart which takes cheer from the fact that you have an admiring friend, a staunch friend, that will be "all the way with LBJ."

305   Toasts of the President and Prime Minister Holt. *June 29, 1966*

Mr. Prime Minister, Mr. Vice President, gentlemen:

It has been said that a poem is like a picture—worth a thousand words of prose. So today I want to welcome you, Mr. Prime Minister, with just a few lines from a grand poem. It begins like this:

"I love a sunburnt country,
A land of sweeping plains;
Of ragged mountain ranges;
Of droughts and flooding rains.

"I love her far horizons,
I love her jeweled sea,
Her beauty and her terror,
The wide brown land for me."

The poem ends:

"Though earth holds many splendors,
Wherever I may die,
I know to that brown country
My homing thoughts will fly."

Any American who read those words would think of our own broad land, the United States. No man from Texas could help think of the sunburnt country, the wide, brown land that we call home.

An Australian, Mr. Prime Minister, what would he think of? Surely of his own homeland. For these words were written by an Australian about Australia. But it speaks from the heart to Americans also about America.

Our countries could hardly be farther apart physically, yet we could hardly be closer in spirit, in tradition, in outlook, in friendship. As our able Ambassador, Edward Clark, has said, we are natural partners. We are, both of us, an immigrant people, men and women who crossed wide oceans to form a new world.

We found rugged and largely empty continents. But we poured ourselves into the land. We emerged as great nations.

Our nature is to work hard and to build high. Our nature is to prize the individual as our foremost national treasure. Both of us believe in government as the servant of the people. Ours is a heritage of human rights and of responsibility. Our highest hope is peace in the world.

But when duty summons us, we are there. We have become accustomed, when duty calls, to be there together—as we were in North Africa together, in New Guinea together, at Cebu Island, in Korea, and as we stand today shoulder to shoulder in Vietnam.

Every American is grateful for the truth that so many men of peace have spoken: When a fight comes looking for you, it is good to have Australians standing and fighting by your side.

So today in your capital of Canberra, our ministers are meeting as partners in SEATO. Tomorrow they will be meeting as partners in the ANZUS Treaty. In these, as in most other enterprises that occupy us, we are closely working together. So, pray God, shall it always be.

Mr. Prime Minister, it gives us a great deal of pleasure and happiness to welcome you back to the United States. It is a pleasure to have you come here in the first house of the land to meet with some of our most distinguished leaders in Government, business, and agriculture as the leader of the Australian people and the Australian Government, as a staunch partner in the common cause of peace with justice, and always as our very good, warm, and cherished friend.

We ask you to remember us to one of the great friends of the United States, one of the world's leading statesmen, your predecessor, Prime Minister Menzies. He has thrilled us in this room on many occasions with his eloquence.

A very wise man once said, "A faithful friend is the medicine of life." So, Mr. Prime Minister, we fear no illness.

Gentlemen, I should like for you, my friends, to join me in a toast to the distinguished Prime Minister of the Commonwealth of Australia—Mr. Holt.

NOTE: The President spoke at 2:18 p.m. in the State Dining Room at the White House. In his opening words he referred to Prime Minister Harold E. Holt of Australia and Vice President Hubert H. Humphrey. Later he referred to Edward Clark, U.S. Ambassador to Australia.

Prime Minister Holt responded as follows:
Mr. President and your many distinguished guests:
This is a memorable moment that no man who is not completely insensitive to human affairs could either forget or erase as a recollection moving to himself, and an occasion which will be received with pride by my own country.

This company around us contains people whose names are international words, words of distinction, meaningful names contributing to the American democracy which, in these difficult times, has been called upon to give leadership to the free people throughout the world.

It is a difficult world. There are many complex and difficult situations. In the democratic society which we share as inheritors of a great democratic tradition, it is good that people should express themselves articulately. But finally there is a point of responsibility in which experience, judgment, and, we hope, wisdom can come together to accept the responsibility of leadership which a democratic people have entrusted to the head of the nation.

You, sir, carry that responsibility in this, the greatest power, economic and military power, that the world has ever known. I carry it in respect of a small community of people, but occupying an area of land about the same as the United States of America—if we leave Alaska out of the picture. I don't know why we should leave Alaska out of the picture, but it spoils my illustration if I can't. But at least there is still a lot of country left to the two of us.

I want to say a word or two about that, if I may. Before doing so, Mr. President, I have mentioned that I have looked around this room and have seen many friends and many notabilities. One of the closest friends is seated at your table.

You did great service to Australia when you selected Ed Clark to be your representative. He has endeared himself to all with whom he has come in contact there. I felt that I should start paying the Department of State a monthly amount for the meals that I have been consuming there. At one stage they were so frequent I suggested he might install me in one of the back rooms to save the running time going backwards and forwards.

In addition, I see those great astronauts that you sent out as ambassadors for your country. I have one of them here at the table with me. In my office in Canberra at this time there is a picture of the two of them fitting a space helmet onto my grandson. It is one of my most treasured possessions.

Sir, you mentioned a little earlier today your visit of 25 years ago. The Australia of that time compared with the Australia of today is an entirely different country.

I think you ought to have some understanding of the problems of growth that we have faced, because I know at times we have our friendly discussions as to whether we ought to be doing more, or this, or that.

We, for our part, want to carry our own share of the responsibility which exists amongst us in the Southeast Asian region.

Next week you will be celebrating your July 4th, your Declaration of Independence Day. I think it is about this week that a great British occasion is celebrated, the Magna Carta signing at Runnymede.

On your Independence Day you celebrate this notable occasion which is part of the heritage of freedom of people who study these matters around the world. In the long struggle for freedom, the American Declaration of Independence is an important chapter.

At the time you signed that Declaration, you were less than 2½ million people. When the first foundation of Australia occurred, 12 years later, you were less than 4 million people. In those intervening years, you have grown to—what?—190-odd millions at the present time.

We, at the end of the two World Wars, having sustained about half a million casualties in those two World Wars, were still about 7 million people. We set about as vigorously as we could to the business of building our population and developing a nation. We were a long way behind you in the race. It is not an aspiration of ours to catch up, but it is an aspiration of ours to build a strong Australia, a country which can make a contribution to the affairs of the world in order to preserve, as you wish to preserve, the things we stand for.

We believe we can make a significant contribution, and the stronger we grow, the more populous we become, the more we develop our resources, then the better we think that will be for all like-minded people. We are busily about that task.

Although we have, and you mentioned it in that poem, I recall, our problems of drought, of flood, economic recession in the 1930's, and the problems of a country of small population with great transportation costs, with great tasks of development, and inadequate capital resources for that development, we are still managing to make pretty good progress.

Today our 11.5 million people have one of the highest standards of living in the world. I think we rank about third per capita in the use of motor cars, if that is a test of a standard of living. Unfortunately, we haven't the good roads that you have on which to drive them.

We have, I think I can claim, the highest standard occupancy of houses to be found anywhere in the world. It is a good community and a community of fine people.

We are not lacking, by any means, in resources. We have, for many years, established a high export income which brings this small country, in terms of population, amongst the 12 top trading nations in the world. We shall improve that rating considerably over the years ahead because we seem to have uncovered a Pandora's box of mineral wealth.

Almost every week that passes turns up some amazing new discovery. We, with American, British, and European capital, are now launched on the business of getting that mineral production underway.

Could I just give you a couple of illustrations? It is not so long ago that we felt that we should place an embargo on the export of iron ore, and we maintained that for some years because we felt we needed the iron ore for our own domestic steel industry. Then they started discovering high-grade iron ore by the mountainful. In Western Australia currently it is estimated that there is somewhere between 15,000 and 18,000 million tons of iron ore above 60 grade.

Already the Japanese have placed orders with us for about $2,300 million of this iron ore, and inquiries, in fact orders, have actually been taken from the United Kingdom, and inquiries from Europe as well.

We have the largest bauxite deposits in the world. Broken Hill has recently been exploiting very large manganese deposits. There has been a recent new discovery of nickel. And so it goes. Our production of copper, lead, and zinc are too well known for me to mention here.

But I do just mention these things, Mr. President, because you are not going to find our country a liability. We have managed to stand on our own feet in terms of what we have provided for ourselves without turning to you for aid at any time, and we intend to go on that way.

Increasingly you will find us capable of taking part in the exciting new developments that are occurring in Southeast Asia and which, in turn, will have a quite critical bearing on what happens in Asia as a whole.

I say exciting new developments because you mentioned some of them in what you said to us earlier today. I live in the area. I have what I call the "View From Down Under." But I travel a good deal on my own official business through the countries to the north of us.

I believe that while attention is being concentrated on the episodic reporting, the day-to-day reporting, of what has been going on in South Vietnam, that this country, and, indeed, the rest of the world, has lost sight of the fact that there are other countries in the region for whom you have been buying time, whom you have enabled to build themselves in strength, whom you have enabled to strengthen their defenses or strengthen their economies.

Perhaps measured by the achievement of a tremendous economic power such as this, what occurs amongst these populations with relatively primitive industrializations or economies is of little consequence, measured statistically. But it means a lot to the people in that area and eventually it will mean a lot to Asia as a whole.

I hope you carry this in mind, because for anybody who has lived in that region there is a new era of hope, of expectation, opening up before us. The gathering at Seoul just a few weeks ago, the atmosphere at the SEATO Conference, which I formally opened on Monday of this week in Canberra—all these things and many others, that time permitting could be mentioned, promise a more exciting, positive, and constructive future for that area of the world.

Do you believe, does anyone believe, that we would have had this hopeful emergency of favorable development in Indonesia if it had not been for the fact that you were sticking on in South Vietnam, that it had become clear to the whole of Asia that the resolution was there, and that eventually this situation, complex and difficult though we all know it to be, will be brought under a degree of control which will enable the rest of Asia to breathe and go on with its business?

We will all be making a contribution to those positive, constructive measures which you have emphasized repeatedly as the need which exists for the world of the future.

We don't live in a world where victory can be won and sustained by military means alone. In Asia, of all countries, there has to be a feeling that there will be a better life, that life is to have some meaning for them, that the people will be fed, that they will be educated, that their health will be attended to, that there will be this positive and constructive side to the efforts which are now being made.

In every military force with which I have come in contact in the course of this year, of whatever country I have visited, and of the friendly forces which are assisting in South Vietnam, I don't know one in which there is not included in the military program an active program of civic action and rural development.

The cynics and the critics can point to inadequacies, failures of achievement, but the spirit is there, the sentiment is there, the excitement, the dynamism, the movement is there. It is something which I have never felt in this way in Asia before.

So, Mr. President, I think you can feel, you can claim, that American policies have gained much, even at this stage, in Asia, and there are people there who are today living more hopefully, looking more expectantly to a brighter future because of what they believe to be the intentions of your Government.

I said earlier I am not going to weary you by repetition of it now, but our own country is there not because we just go along with everything that America wants to do. There are some people who say that.

I think Australia has a record as an independent-minded, quite spirited people. But we are there not just because you are there. My greatest worry, frankly, Mr. President, not knowing you as I know you now, when you assumed the Presidency, was that perhaps there might be some weakening in the American effort in Vietnam. We were deeply relieved when we found that in the new American President there was the firmness of resolution, the clarity of recognition which assured continued, uninterrupted effort; indeed, an accelerated and augmented effort in this field.

We are involved far more directly than you are. If this area were to go, where, then, do you attempt to hold the line? Perhaps an attempt is made in Thailand, perhaps down the neck of the Malay Peninsula. I don't think anyone would attach greater confidence to our capacity to hold the line in these places than where we are trying to hold it today.

In the meantime, there would have been more people overrun, more disaster, more destruction. You are right to be where you are, and we are right to be there with you. That, at least, Mr. President, is our conviction.

Thank you for what you mean to the people whose hopes rest with you.

May I finally say I don't know whether I can draw, with your facility, upon poetry, but there is the old poem that will come readily to your mind:

> "Say not the struggle naught availeth,
> The labour and the wounds are vain,
> The enemy faints not, nor faileth,
> And as things have been they remain.

> "And not by eastern windows only,
> When daylight comes, comes in the light;
> In front the sun climbs slow, how slowly,
> But westward, look, the land is bright."

We feel that there are brighter developments, Mr. President, and we look confidently with you, combining together in order to secure the kind of outcome from these terrible difficulties in which we have found ourselves immersed in order to produce for Southeast Asia and finally for Asia, and, indeed, I believe, for the well-being of the world as a whole, that better world order to which we all aspire.

This, at least, is the vision. It is your vision; it is a vision that we are happy and proud to share with you.

Thank you for the warmth of your hospitality to me today and for the message of friendship that I will be able to carry back from this room to the staunchest ally you ever had.

[As printed above, this item follows the text released by the White House.]

306 Remarks to the YMCA Youth Governors.
June 29, 1966

Distinguished Governors, and friends:

This is the second year that I welcome the YMCA Youth Governors to the White House. Speaker Sam Rayburn told me a long time ago that the way to stay young is to associate with young people. So my motives for meeting with you here on this late afternoon are not entirely unselfish.

The bond which unites you and which brings you here today is your deep interest in the process of the government of your country.

I hope that this interest will expand into service for your country, for government today needs your vitality and intelligence if it is to meet its growing responsibilities in this troubled world.

You may not be aware that half of the people in the United States are now under 30 years of age. The proportion is increasing. So if we are to achieve all of our many national goals, it is youth who will have to do it.

Your generation is perhaps the first in history for whom change is a normal way of life. You are inheriting a world that is filled with crisis and danger, but it is also a world that is filled with unlimited promise.

Since you were in elementary school, man has found the means to explore outer space. One barrier after another is falling to this surge of scientific progress.

Nine out of ten drugs and medicines that are used against disease today have been developed since you were in the first grade.

Mankind has doubled its store of scientific knowledge—doubled it just since you were born.

More new nations have emerged in 20 years than in the previous 200 years.

These are just a few of the indicators of the rapid change that is taking place in the world in which you live.

Every person is shaped not only by his family and his schooling, but is shaped as well by the time in which he lives.

So today's age of change has produced in you a hunger for change, too.

Your generation all over the world demands more freedom than mine ever asked for.

There has never been a more restless desire for liberty, for self-government, for education, for good health, and for personal attainment.

Our Government has placed itself firmly behind all of these hopes and aspirations for human progress. This is our natural role in history. But I must remind you although it is our natural role, it is not an easy role.

So as you move toward adult leadership, no one can promise you that you will not face the same problems and perils that we have always faced. Your future is by no means guaranteed. You will have to reach out for it. You will have to work every day for it. I ask each of you to work with me on your problems of today, and to solve them for the sake of your tomorrow.

The opportunities are all around you. For example, every 10 years in this country we hold a White House conference to discuss the needs and the opportunities of the young people in the United States of America. The last one was held in 1960. And so today I am asking Secretary Gardner of the Department of Health, Education, and Welfare to begin planning for the next conference in 1970. It is not too early to plan ahead. We are looking 4 years down the road because tomorrow is coming up very fast behind us.

I have asked Secretary Gardner to pump some young blood into that conference. I don't think we should just bring teachers, parents, and other older citizens to Washington to discuss young people's problems and tell young people what they ought to do while they are young. I want some of you here. Your President and your Government want young America here, not just to listen but to be listened to.

When this conference convenes, it could take its theme from something that Emerson wrote a long time ago. It seems to fit your era even better than his. He wrote:

"If there is any period one would desire to be born in, is it not the age of revolution . . . when the energies of all men are searched by fear and hope . . . when the historic glories of the old can be compensated by the rich possibilities of the new era? This time, like all times, is a very good one—if we but know what to do with it."

I think this, too, is a very good time. I hope that you know what to do with it. It is the destiny of your generation to take this new world of limitless opportunity and to make it far better than it is.

You have come here today to the White House, the first house of your land. You can come saying that you are proud, through your leadership and achievement, that you have already begun this task. You have much to be thankful for, much to be proud of. And we, too—those of us who look to you for leadership—know that we are going to be proud of you in the years ahead.

Thank you very much.

NOTE: The President spoke at 5:30 p.m. in the Cabinet Room at the White House. During his remarks he referred to Sam Rayburn, Representative from Texas 1913–1961, who served as Speaker of the House of Representatives 1940–1947, 1949–1953, 1955–1961, and John W. Gardner, Secretary of Health, Education, and Welfare.

The fourth annual YMCA Youth Governors' Conference was attended by 42 young people from throughout the United States, chosen in Statewide elections by the members of YMCA's Hi-Y programs. The Conference was sponsored by the Reader's Digest Foundation of Pleasantville, N.Y.

307 Letters on the Occasion of the 60th Anniversary of the Federal Food and Drug Act of 1906. *June 30, 1966*

Dear Mr. Secretary:

I am pleased that we can join today in observing the 60th anniversary of the Federal Food and Drugs Act.

Congress, through the years, has built upon the foundations of the Federal Food and Drugs Act. The Food and Drug Administration has been given even larger responsibilities through these decades of revolutionary scientific and technological change.

The 89th Congress, as part of its record of accomplishment, enacted legislation last year to combat the illegal traffic in dangerous drugs. This year, I proposed to the Congress the Child Safety Act, the Drug Safety Act, and the Professional Training and Cooperation Amendments—all major steps to the work that Congress began in 1906.

We must and will protect our children from the potential hazards posed by drugs, household products, and toys that contain dangerous substances. We must and will insure the integrity of drugs vital to the health of all our citizens. And we must and will forge new links of cooperation between the Federal Government and the State and local governments—in not only professional training and cooperation, but in many other areas so vital to consumer health and well being.

I am confident that the Congress will respond to today's needs just as it did in 1906. In turn, we in the Executive Branch are moving ahead to protect and improve the health of this Nation's people. As one more step in this continuing effort, last week I assigned the Department of Health, Education, and Welfare the responsibility for developing a computer-based file of toxicological information. This is a critical tool in maintaining productive use of many chemical substances now available without endangering the environment in which we live.

I am confident that the program you have initiated to strengthen the organization and capabilities of the Food and Drug Administration will continue—thus assuring that the vision of Dr. Wiley and others who shared in his work will not be dimmed by time.

    Sincerely,

        LYNDON B. JOHNSON

[Honorable John W. Gardner, Secretary of Health, Education, and Welfare, Washington, D.C.]

Dear Dr. Goddard:

The greatness of our Nation is in large measure the sum of individual contributions by strong and selfless men and women. For this reason, I believe there can be no more appropriate commemoration of the 60th anniversary of the passage of the Federal Food and Drugs Act than the recognition you are according Dr. Harvey W. Wiley today. No one man did more to achieve this landmark legislation than Dr. Harvey W. Wiley.

The 1906 Act was an important first step in the effort to assure American families that the food they bought and the medicines they used were wholesome and safe. Time and

again, Congress has strengthened the original Act of 1906 as new hazards were exposed in the wake of scientific and technological progress. This year, I have asked Congress to enact additional legislation to protect our children from the tragedy of accidental poisoning from drugs and hazardous substances and assure the quality of our medicines.

The Food and Drug Administration has changed as its responsibilities have grown. Today, few agencies of Government have as vital a concern with the welfare of every American family as does the FDA. Just a little more than five months ago, I asked you to assume the challenge of strengthening the Food and Drug Administration to carry out fully and fairly the enlarged responsibilities which Congress has given the agency in recent years. Your progress, and that of the agency, in this brief period has been truly impressive. I know that the capabilities of the Food and Drug Administration will continue to grow, as they must to meet the challenges that we face today and those that will come tomorrow.

    Sincerely,

        LYNDON B. JOHNSON

[Honorable James L. Goddard, Commissioner, Food and Drug Administration, Department of Health, Education, and Welfare, Washington, D.C.]

NOTE: On the same day the White House issued an announcement in honor of the occasion. "Thursday, June 30," the release noted, "is the 60th anniversary of the passage of the Federal Food and Drug Act of 1906, frequently referred to as the Wiley Act. Dr. Harvey Wiley, the Chief Chemist of the United States Department of Agriculture, led the national movement for better consumer protection in the areas of foods and drugs. Upon signing the first Food and Drug Act into law, President Theodore Roosevelt appointed Dr. Wiley to be the first administrator of the program.

"In celebration of the anniversary, the Food and Drug Administration will dedicate a portrait of Dr. Wiley to be placed in the lobby of the new Food and Drug Administration building."

The letters to Secretary John W. Gardner and Commissioner James L. Goddard were posted on the bulletin board in the press room. They were not made public in the form of a White House press release.

For the President's assignment of responsibility for developing a computer-based file of toxicological information to the Department of Health, Education, and Welfare (referred to in the letter to Secretary Gardner) see Item 280.

308 Message to the Congress Transmitting the President's Annual Report on Food for Peace. *June 30, 1966*

To the Congress of the United States:

The United States in 1965 shipped $1.4 billion of food and fiber overseas under our Food For Peace program. This brings to $14.6 billion our food aid effort since the enactment of Public Law 480, the Agricultural Trade Development and Assistance Act of 1954.

Food For Peace moved into its second decade continuing food aid programs that had proved so beneficial in the past, initiating imaginative new approaches to spur self-help, and facing an array of difficult challenges. The increasing pressure of world population growth was the most disturbing indicator in a year otherwise highlighted with promise in the war against hunger and malnutrition. Population growth of 2 percent a year—increasing to 3 percent in some of the underdeveloped countries—made it difficult to increase per capita food consumption. There was more food grown in 1965 than in 1964. But there were 64 million more mouths to feed.

In simplest terms, the task of bringing food and population into balance—while maintaining progress in health, education, and economic growth—is the most critical challenge many countries are facing today. It will probably remain their most urgent challenge in the immediate years ahead. The world's capacity to respond will dramatically affect the course which individuals and nations choose in confronting their problems and their neighbors in coming generations.

This is a world problem. The stakes are too large, the issues too complicated and too interbound with custom and commerce, to leave the entire solution to those countries that have supplied, or received, the most food assistance during the postwar era. The experience, the ideas, the skills, and the resources of every nation that would avoid calamity must be significantly brought to bear on the problem.

The United States Congress recognizes the moral and practical implications of hunger and malnutrition. Over the years its members have taken the lead in developing programs to prevent famine and to improve diets. The basic instrument Congress has used for this effort has been Public Law 480—the authorizing legislation for the Food For Peace program.

It is not easy to measure the achievements of a program with such multiple objectives as Food For Peace—aiding the needy, assisting economic development, supporting U.S. foreign policy, increasing trade, bolstering American agriculture. Yet as we look back on more than a decade of effort, the accomplishments are remarkable by any test.

Hundreds of millions of people have directly benefited from American foods. The lives which otherwise might have been lost—the grief which otherwise might have occurred—could have dwarfed the total casualties of all the wars during the period. I tend to think historians of future generations may well look back on this expression of

America's compassion as a milestone in man's concern for his fellow man.

Food For Peace, however, is aimed at more than individual survival—and individual growth. It is directed toward national survival—and national growth. P.L. 480 has been an important resource in the growth process. With the day-to-day difficulties which countries face, we sometimes fail to recognize how far many of the nations we have aided have come in their development effort. An analysis of Food For Peace programing—which constitutes more than a third of our total economic assistance effort—is a good yardstick to measure such achievement. Frequently a country's development is directly reflected in its graduation from being a recipient of heavily subsidized food aid.

Consider, for example, the countries receiving our food and fiber for local currency in the first full year of operation a decade ago. There were 27 of them in mid-1956. Today, more than half have reached a point of economic development where they no longer require such aid. This group which had graduated from Title I programs, last year purchased more than $2 billion in agricultural commodities through commercial channels. This is more than triple their combined dollar purchase of a decade ago. Even excluding Britain, France and West Germany—today's big dollar customers who purchased only small amounts under P.L. 480 and left the program early—the gains are still impressive. Dollar sales of U.S. farm products to the other Title I graduates were well over a billion dollars last year— more than four times the amount in 1956.

Growing economic strength is also evident in that group of 13 countries receiving Title I food a decade ago which continued to buy U.S. farm commodities for local currency in FY 1965. They still face economic difficulties, but together these nations have more than doubled their dollar agricultural purchases from the United States over the ten-year period.

Global generalizations are difficult. But the broad pattern clearly shows substantial progress.

Indeed, the problems today are in many ways more serious than those facing the Congress when it enacted this law. The critical food shortage in India, though aggravated by drought, should be read as a warning that a crisis in food and population trends is already at the world's doorstep. The Food for Freedom legislation which I have proposed to Congress faces up to these problems. It takes into account the experience and lessons of P.L. 480, along with the changing conditions in food needs and supplies. It recognizes that the program will be judged in the long run by its success in encouraging self-help programs and attitudes in the recipient countries.

We have progressed a great deal during the past decade. We now know that food assistance can:

—make an important contribution to economic development
—serve the highest objectives of U.S. foreign policy
—help American agriculture
—strengthen the habit of international cooperation
—help to dispel Malthusian fears which have historically haunted mankind.

By any standards, this nation can be proud of its Food For Peace program. It gives me pleasure to submit to the Congress the annual report on the 1965 activities carried on under Public Law 480, 83rd Congress, as amended.

LYNDON B. JOHNSON

The White House
June 30, 1966

NOTE: The report is entitled "The Annual Report of the President on Activities Carried Out Under Public Law 480, 83rd Congress, as Amended, During the Period January 1 Through December 31, 1965" (173 pp., 36 tables).

On the same day the White House made public a summary of additional facts drawn from the annual report, as follows:

"—Shipments: Nearly 18 million tons of Food for Peace commodities worth $1.4 billion were shipped overseas during 1965. This brings total shipments since P.L. 480 began in 1954 to 155 million metric tons of farm products worth $14.6 billion.

"—New commercial record: Total U.S. agricultural exports in 1965—both P.L. 480 and commercial—reached $6.2 billion. The $4.8 billion in normal commercial exports of farm products was a record high.

"—Increased dollar savings: Foreign currencies received for title I sales were increasingly used to pay U.S. overseas expenses. During the year this saved a dollar outflow of $311 million. Of currencies to be generated by new title I agreements signed in 1965, over 20 percent will be set aside for U.S. uses, while 62 percent will be set aside for economic development loans to foreign governments.

"—Food-for-work gains: Over 12 million people in 49 countries received P.L. 480 commodities in 1965 as part payment of wages on food-for-work and other self-help economic and community development projects.

"—Donations for the needy: Direct donations of U.S. food and fiber, through private agencies and government-to-government arrangements, reached 93 million people in 116 countries, including 40 million school children and 10 million disaster victims.

"—Stress on nutrition: In view of findings that the quality of diet is as important as the quantity, the Agency for International Development spent $2.5 million to fortify milk and grain donations with additional vitamins and min-erals to combat the debilitating physical and mental effects of malnutrition.

"—Cooley loan activity: 38 Cooley loans worth $35 million were made last year to private enterprise overseas from local currencies generated by title I sales. This brings the total to 356 loans in 25 countries.

"—Market development programs: Since P.L. 480 began, more than half of the $109 million spent under USDA's Foreign Agricultural Service program to create and develop markets overseas for U.S. farm products has come from title I sales proceeds. Dollar exports of U.S. agricultural commodities increased from $2 billion in 1955 to $4.8 billion in 1965.

"—Financing research: Some 800 research projects in such fields as medicine, agriculture, and education were financed from title I sales proceeds. These scientific inquiries abroad were directed by the Department of Health, Education, and Welfare, the Department of Agriculture, and other U.S. Government agencies.

"—Benefits to education: 16 percent of total local currency disbursements—the equivalent of over $200 million—were directed toward the advancement of knowledge and education in 1965.

"—Books for U.S. libraries: Over 300 American libraries received 1.5 million publications from Library of Congress offices overseas supported by P.L. 480 local currencies.

"—Stepped-up dollar credit sales: In the past 4½ years, since title IV was enacted, 65 agreements for long-term dollar credit have been entered into with 23 countries. The 1.7 million metric tons of commodities shipped under title IV last year nearly equaled the combined tonnage shipped under this title in its first 3½ years of operation. Dollar repayments have totaled $35 million."

For the President's remarks on signing the proposed Food for Freedom legislation see Item 608.

309 Statement by the President on the Inauguration of the Medicare Program. *June* 30, 1966

MEDICARE begins tomorrow.

Tomorrow, for the first time, nearly every older American will receive hospital care—not as an act of charity, but as the insured right of a senior citizen.

Since I signed the historic Medicare act last summer, we have made more extensive preparation to launch this program than for any other peaceful undertaking in our Nation's history.

Now we need your help to make Medicare succeed.

Medicare will succeed—if hospitals accept their responsibility under the law not to discriminate against any patient because of race. More than 92 percent of the beds in our Nation's general hospitals are already in compliance with the law.

Medicare will succeed—if doctors treat their patients with fairness and compassion as they have in the past. I feel sure that most doctors do not plan to drive hard bargains with needy patients.

Medicare will succeed—if older patients cooperate in scheduling treatment and do not demand unnecessary hospital and medical services. I have confidence in the com-

monsense of our older Americans.

This program is not just a blessing for older Americans. It is a test for all Americans—a test of our willingness to work together.

In the past, we have always passed that test. I have no doubt about the future. I believe that July 1, 1966, marks a new day of freedom for our people.

NOTE: The President also read the statement before television cameras in the Theater at the White House.

The Medicare act was approved by the President on July 30, 1965 (Public Law 89–97, 79 Stat. 286). For the President's remarks on that occasion, see 1965 volume, this series, Book II, Item 394.

310 Remarks at the Swearing In of Richard Helms as Director of the Central Intelligence Agency. *June 30, 1966*

Mr. Helms, Members of the Cabinet, distinguished Members of the Congress, my friends:

It was a little more than a year ago that I asked Admiral Raborn to come out of a hard-earned retirement in California to take on one of the most critical tasks in Government and to succeed a great Director, John McCone, as head of the Central Intelligence Agency.

I knew that I was asking a great deal of this good man. He had already served his country—and he had served it long and well. He had capped his career by playing a vital role in the development of the Polaris missile system. But once again I felt that his country needed him and the President needed him, and he complied, though reluctantly, with my request. He agreed to make still one more contribution to the security of his country and he attached only one condition, that he could leave as soon as we decided upon a permanent successor.

We have come to the White House this

morning because both Admiral Raborn and I are satisfied that we have found the best man available as that successor. Both of us have worked closely during the past 14 months with the very able public servant whom we are swearing in today as the Director of the Central Intelligence Agency and who became a partner of Admiral Raborn as his Deputy by appointment at the same time the Admiral was selected.

I am extremely proud of both of these men and their colleagues. The nature of their work does not often allow public acknowledgment. Praised or damned (and we are living in an era where men who spend all their time concerned with the protection of the security of their country are frequently damned more than they are praised, I regret to say) these men must go about their work without standing up for bows and sometimes are not even permitted to speak out in their own defense. Their role is misunderstood by some of their supporters, and I never read a morning paper without seeing it being distorted by their critics.

In 2½ years of working with these men I have yet to meet a "007." I have met dozens of men who are moved and motivated by the highest and most patriotic and dedicated purposes—men who are specialists in economics, and political science, and history, and geography, and physics, and many other fields where logic and analysis are crucial to the decisions that the President of their country is called upon to make. Through my experience with these men I have learned that their most significant triumphs come not in the secrets passed in the dark but in patient reading, hour after hour, of highly technical periodicals.

In a real sense they are America's professional students; they are unsung, just as they are invaluable.

I do not want this opportunity to pass without at least this President paying great tribute, high respect, absolute complete confidence, and all the recognition that I am capable of giving to patriots like Allen Dulles and John McCone and Admiral Raborn.

In naming Richard Helms to the post of the Director of the Central Intelligence Agency on the eve of this hopeful event and wishing Godspeed to Admiral Raborn, we pause to give them the Nation's thanks for a job well done. A little later at his convenience Admiral Raborn will return to the White House to receive a very high recognition and award from the President in the company of the Cabinet and others for the outstanding job he has done.

It is a very special pleasure to me, to one who has spent 35 years in the Federal Government (not always under the protective arm of the Secret Service or the Civil Service) to see one of the high positions in this Government filled by a man who has devoted his entire career to the public service of his country. Dick Helms, the man we are naming to this post, is such a man.

Although he has spent more than 20 years in public life attempting to avoid publicity, he has never been able to conceal the fact that he is one of the most trusted and most able and most dedicated professional career men in this Capital. No man has ever come to this high and critical office with better qualifications.

I think it was Patrick Henry who said, "The battle is not to the strong alone, it is to the vigilant and to the active and to the brave," and it is to Dick Helms and to the Agency that he will now head that we must look for this vigilance. His own record and the past achievements of his Agency give us full confidence in the future operation of the Central Intelligence Agency with judgment, with intelligence, and above all with great public integrity.

Thank you.

NOTE: The President spoke at 10 a.m. in the East Room at the White House. In the course of his remarks he referred to former Directors of the Central Intelligence Agency John A. McCone and Allen W. Dulles.

On August 17, 1966, the President presented the National Security Medal to Vice Adm. William F. Raborn, Jr. For his remarks on that occasion see Item 387.

311   "Two Threats to World Peace"—Remarks in Omaha on the
      Occasion of the Sending of the Five-Millionth Ton of
      Grain to India. *June 30, 1966*

Governor and Mrs. Morrison, Mayor Al Sorensen, Governor Phil Sorensen, my dear and good friend Congressman Callan, ladies and gentlemen of the great State of Nebraska:

I want you to know, Governor Morrison, that I haven't been able to hear much about anything, since you and Mayor Sorensen and Governor Sorensen and Mrs. Morrison kept Lady Bird out here beautifying for an entire day, except about the glories of Nebraska. I am delighted to come back to Omaha and to this great State to confirm all the good things that she has said to me about you.

I have come to Omaha today because I want to speak to you about the most important business in our time—the business of peace in the world.

Two years ago this week, when I was also speaking out here in the Midwest, I said that the peace we seek "is a world where no nation fears another, or no nation can force another to follow its command. It is a world where differences are solved without destruction and common effort is directed at common problems."

This is still true as we meet here this afternoon. I am convinced that after decades of wars and threats of wars, peace is more within our reach than at any time in this century.

I believe this because we have made up our minds to deal with the two most common threats to peace in the world. We are determined to match our resolution with action.

But what are these threats?

First is the desire of most people to win a better way of life. That is true of you here in Omaha, and that is true of most people who want to win a better way of life everywhere in the world.

Second is the design of a few people, the design of some people, to force their particular way of life on other people.

Now if we ignore these threats, or if we attempt to meet them only by the rhetoric of visionary intentions instead of good works of determination, I am certain that tyranny and not peace will be our ultimate fate.

If the strong and the wealthy turn from the needs of the weak and the poor, frustration is sure to be followed by force. No peace and no power is strong enough to stand for long against the restless discontent of millions of human beings who are without any hope.

That is why we stand here this afternoon in Omaha, at the end of a very important lifeline. At the other end of that lifeline, 8,000 long miles out yonder, is India—India, a nation of 500 million human beings. The wheat here this afternoon is part of their shield against the catastrophe of drought and famine.

This single load of grain will provide the margin of life for more than 2,500 families throughout the entire balance of this year. But it is only a very tiny fraction of what America's response to India's need has been.

I would remind you that since January 1, 5 million tons of American wheat have already been shipped to India. That is more than 2½ times the annual wheat production of the State of Nebraska.

And this is only about half the grain that we and other nations are providing India this year in order to help her overcome the worst drought that her people have ever suffered in the history of her nation.

And America's job is not yet over.

Here, today, in the center of the greatest food-producing area anywhere on this globe, we Americans must face a sobering fact: Most of the world's population is losing the battle to feed itself. If present trends continue, we can now see the point at which even our own vast productive resources, including the millions of acres of farmlands that we now hold in reserve, will not be sufficient to meet the requirements of human beings for food.

In my Food for Freedom message that the President sent to the Congress, I requested the authority and the funds to provide food on very special terms to those countries that are willing to increase their own production.

We will lend America's technical knowledge. We will lend America's practical experience to those people who need it most and who are willing to prove to us that they are willing to try to help themselves. In addition to that, we will support programs of capital investment, water development, farm machinery, pesticides, seed research, and fertilizer.

We will introduce all the American know-how in their country to try to help them learn to produce the food that is necessary to satisfy the human bodies that live in their land.

Now these are only beginnings. We must work for a global effort. Hunger knows no ideology. Hunger knows no single race or no single nationality, no party—Democratic or Republican.

We recognize the contributions of the Soviet Union. We recognize the contributions of Yugoslavia in contributing food to India. We are glad that they saw fit to try to do their part. We welcome the support of

every nation in the world when that support is given to feeding hungry human beings. In this kind of cooperation we find the seeds of unity against the common enemies of all mankind.

I long for the day when we and others—whatever their political creed—will turn our joint resources to the battle against poverty, ignorance, and disease. Because I honestly believe that these enemies—poverty and ignorance and disease—are the enemies of peace in the world.

But that day is not here because some men, in some places, still insist on trying to force their way of life on other people.

That is the second threat that I want to talk about out here in Omaha today.

That is the second threat to peace—trying to force their way of life on other people. That is the threat that we are standing up to with our proud sailors, soldiers, airmen, and Marines in South Vietnam at this hour.

Now I want to point out to you that the conflict there is important for many reasons, but I have time to mention only a few. I am going to mention three specifically.

The first reason: We believe that the rights of other people are just as important as our own. We believe that we are obligated to help those whose rights are being threatened by brute force.

Individuals can never escape a sense of decency and respect for others; neither can democratic nations. If one man here in Omaha unlawfully forces another to do what he commands, then you rebel against the injustice, because you know it is wrong for one man here in Omaha to force another one to do what he wants him to do. Unless human concern has disappeared from all of our values, you also know that it is necessary—I emphasize "necessary"—to help that man that is being forced to defend himself.

This same principle is true for nations—

nations which live by respect of the rights of others. If one government uses force to violate another people's rights, we cannot ignore the injustice, the threat to our own rights, the danger to peace in the entire world.

That is what is happening at this hour in South Vietnam. The North Vietnamese are trying to deny the people of South Vietnam the right to build their own nation, the right to choose their own system of government, the right to live and to work in peace.

To those people in America who say they have never had this thing explained to them, I want to repeat that again.

The North Vietnamese at this hour are trying to deny the people of South Vietnam the right to build their own nation, the right to choose their own system of government, the right to go and vote in a free election and select their own people, the right to live and work in peace.

South Vietnam has asked us for help. Only if we abandon our respect for the rights of other people could we turn down their plea.

Second, South Vietnam is important to the security of the rest of all of Asia.

A few years ago the nations of free Asia lay under the shadow of Communist China. They faced a common threat, but not in unity. They were still caught up in their old disputes and dangerous confrontations. They were ripe for aggression.

Now that picture is changing.

Shielded by the courage of the South Vietnamese, the peoples of free Asia today are driving toward economic and social development in a new spirit of regional cooperation.

All you have to do is look at that map and you will see independence growing, thriving, blossoming, and blooming.

They are convinced that the Vietnamese people and their allies are going to stand firm against the conqueror, or against aggression.

Our fighting in Vietnam, therefore, is buying time not only for South Vietnam, but it is buying time for a new and a vital, growing Asia to emerge and develop additional strength.

If South Vietnam were to collapse under Communist pressure from the North, the progress in the rest of Asia would be greatly endangered. And don't you forget that!

The third reason is, what happens in South Vietnam will determine—yes, it will determine—whether ambitious and aggressive nations can use guerrilla warfare to conquer their weaker neighbors.

It will determine whether might makes right.

Now I do not know of a single more important reason for our presence than this.

We are fighting in South Vietnam a different kind of war than we have ever known in the past.

Sixteen years ago this month, North Korea attacked South Korea. By armed invasion across a national border, a Communist country attempted to conquer and overrun its neighbor.

The United States of America recognized this kind of aggression immediately and we acted. North Korean aggression failed. Why? Because President Harry S. Truman and the American people, working with the forces of the United Nations, supporting that great leader, had the courage to help the people of South Korea protect their homes and protect their country.

Those people are helping us in Vietnam now.

Today South Korea is still free and thousands of its young men are again fighting side by side with the Americans to defend another small country from being swallowed up by a more powerful Communist neighbor.

Today in South Vietnam we are witness to another kind of armed aggression.

It is a war that is waged by men who believe that subversion and guerrilla warfare, transported across international boundaries, can achieve what conventional armies could not.

They believe that in the long run a modern scientific and industrial nation such as ours is helpless to defend a smaller and weaker country against the imported terror of guerrilla warfare.

That is what is going on there. The Communist guerrillas, the Vietcong, choose their targets carefully. They aim at the heart of a struggling nation by murdering the schoolteachers, by murdering the agricultural extension workers, by killing the health workers, by assassinating the mayors and their families.

In 1965 alone the Communists killed or kidnaped 12,000 South Vietnamese civilians. That is equivalent to wiping out the entire population of Columbus, Nebraska, or Alliance County, or one out of every 25 citizens that live in this great city of Omaha.

If, by such methods, the agents of one nation can go out and hold and seize power where turbulent change is occurring in another nation, our hope for peace and order will suffer a crushing blow all over the world. It will be an invitation to the would-be conqueror to keep on marching. That is why the problem of guerrilla warfare—the problem of Vietnam—is a very critical threat to peace not just in South Vietnam, but in all of this world in which we live.

Let there be no doubt about it: Those who say this is merely a South Vietnamese "civil war" could not be more wrong. The warfare in South Vietnam was started by the Government of North Vietnam in 1959.

It is financed, it is supported, by an in-creasing flow of men and arms from the North into the South.

It is directed and it is led by a skilled professional staff of North Vietnamese, and it is supported by a very small minority of the population of South Vietnam.

The military tactics are different. The nature of the fighting is different. But the objective is the same as we found it in Korea. The objective is what? The objective is to conquer an independent nation by the force and power of arms. Might makes right, so think these Communist invaders.

Well, the war took a new turn in 1964. The North Vietnamese decided to step up the conflict in the hope of an early victory. They recruited and drafted more young men from the Communist areas in the South.

They slipped across the borders of South Vietnam more than three divisions of the North Vietnamese Regular Army. Today there are more than three North Vietnamese divisions fighting in South Vietnam.

They built all-weather roads. The trails turned into boulevards to replace the jungle trails that they had once used.

They began sending troops in by trucks rather than on foot.

They shifted over to heavy weapons, using imported ammunition, most of it coming from Communist China.

By any definition you want to use—any definition—any lawyer can tell you this: This is armed aggression, the philosophy that might makes right.

Well, America's purpose is to convince North Vietnam that this kind of aggression is too costly, that this kind of power cannot succeed.

We have learned from their prisoners, their defectors, and their captured documents that the Hanoi government really thought a few months ago that conquest was in its grasp. But the free men have rallied to prevent this conquest from succeeding.

In the past 15 months our actions and those of our fighting allies of Korea, Australia, New Zealand, and the Philippines, and the courage of the people of South Vietnam, have already begun to turn the tide.

The casualties of the Vietcong and the North Vietnamese forces are three times larger than those of the South Vietnamese and their allies.

Battle after battle is being won by the South Vietnamese and by the troops under that gallant leader from the United States of America, General "Westy" Westmoreland. He is getting some military advice on the side from some of our armchair generals in the United States, but it looks to me like he is doing pretty good using his own judgment.

The air attacks on military targets in North Vietnam have imposed, and will continue to impose, a growing burden and a high price on those who wage war against the freedom of their neighbors.

In the South the Vietnamese are determined that their own economic development, their own social reform and political progress cannot wait until the war ends, so they are now moving toward constitutional government.

For the past 2 months the political struggles in South Vietnam have been dramatized in our newspapers. They have been published on our television screen every day.

But all during this time, the Vietnamese citizens, representing every important group in the society, have been quietly meeting in orderly assembly. They have formulated rules for their elections. The rules have been accepted with only minor modifications by the government in Saigon.

And in the provinces and villages, the Vietnamese have gone on building schools for their children, improving health facili-ties and agricultural methods, and taking the first steps toward land reform.

So we can take heart from all of this. We are backing the Vietnamese not only in their determination to save their country; we are supporting their determination to build, to construct, a modern society in which the government will be their government, reflecting the will of the people of South Vietnam.

Our objective in Vietnam is not war. Our objective is peace.

There is nothing that we want in North Vietnam. There is nothing we want from North Vietnam.

There is nothing that we want in Communist China. There is nothing the American people want from Communist China.

We have made it very clear by every means at our disposal that we wish the killing to stop.

We have made it very clear that we wish negotiations to begin on the basis of international agreements made in 1954 and 1962.

For 37 long days we halted bombing in the North in the hope that the government in Hanoi would signal its willingness to talk instead of fight. But I regret to tell you that no signal came during those 37 days.

In many more ways than I can now tell you here in Omaha, we have explored and we are continuing to explore avenues to peace with North Vietnam.

But as of this moment, their only reply has been to send more troops and to send more guns into the South.

Until the day they decide to end this aggression and to make an honorable peace, I can assure you that we, speaking for the United States of America, intend to carry on.

No one knows how long it will take. Only Hanoi can be the judge of that. No one can tell you how much effort it will take. None can tell you how much sacrifice it will take. No one can tell you how costly it will be.

But I can, and I do here and now, tell you this: The aggression that they are conducting will not succeed. The people of South Vietnam will be given the chance to work out their own destiny in their own way, and not at the point of a bayonet or with a gun at their temple.

I hear my friends say, "I am troubled," "I am confused," "I am frustrated," and all of us can understand those people. Sometimes I almost develop a stomach ulcer myself, just listening to them.

We all wish the war would end. We all wish the troops would come home. But I want to see the alternatives and the calculations that they have to present that give them a better chance to get the troops home than the very thing we are doing.

There is no human being in all this world who wishes these things to happen—for peace to come to the world—more than your President of the United States.

If you are too busy, or not inclined to help, please count 10 before you hurt. Because we must have no doubt today about the determination of the American men wearing American uniforms, the Marines who are out there fighting in the wet jungles, wading through the rice paddies up to their belts, the sailors who are searching the shores and patrolling the seas, the airmen who are out there facing the missiles and the antiaircraft guns, carrying out their mission, trying to protect your liberty. The least they are entitled to is for you to be as brave as they are and to stand up and give them the support they need here at home.

These men are not going to fail us.

Now the real question is: Are we going to fail them? Our staying power is what counts in the long and dangerous months ahead.

The Communists expect us to lose heart.

The Communists expect to wear us down.

The Communists expect to divide this Nation.

The Communists are not happy about the military defeat they are taking in South Vietnam.

But sometimes they do get encouraged, as they said this week, about the dissension in the United States of America. They believe that the political disagreements in Washington, the confusion and doubt in the United States, will hand them a victory on a silver platter in Southeast Asia.

Well, if they think that, they are wrong. To those who would try to pressure us or influence us, mislead us or deceive us, I say this afternoon, there can be only one decision in Vietnam, and that is this: We will see this through. We shall persist. We shall succeed.

Other Presidents have made the commitment. I have reaffirmed it. The Congress has confirmed it. I plan to do all that I can in my own limited way to see that we not permit 14 million innocent men, women, and children to fall victims to a savage aggression.

There are many nations, large and small, whose security depends on the reliability of the word and the reliability of the power of the United States. The word of the United States must remain a trust that men can live by, can live with, and can depend upon.

Some day we will all work as friends and neighbors to grow more food, to build more schools, to heal the sick, to care for the old, to encourage the young.

We have programs in that direction in the United States going on now, and we are not going to junk them. But we are not going to tuck our tail and run out of South Vietnam either.

History is not made by nameless forces.

History is made by men and women, by their governments and their nations.

This Nation, working with others, must demonstrate in Vietnam that our commitment to freedom and peace is not a fragile thing. It can—and it will—sustain the major test and any test that may confront it.

With your support—with your faith—we will fulfill America's duty.

We have a proud and a glorious heritage. We are going to be true to it.

It was only 20 months ago that the people of America held a great national election. The people of 44 States of this Union, including the great State of Nebraska, gave me a direction and voted me a majority for the Presidency of this country. I believe that their vote was a trust, that as long as I held this high and most responsible office and gift of the American people, that I would do my best as President of the country, as Commander in Chief of the Army.

Now, there are many, many who can recommend, advise, and sometimes a few of them consent. But there is only one that has been chosen by the American people to decide.

With your support, with your prayers, with your faith, I intend to honor the responsibility and to be true to the trust of the office to which you elected me, and to preserve freedom in this country; to keep our commitments; to honor our treaties; and let the rest of the world know that when America gives its word, America keeps its word.

Thank you.

NOTE: The President spoke at 12:35 p.m. at the Omaha City Dock in Omaha, Nebr. In his opening words he referred to Governor and Mrs. Frank B. Morrison, Mayor A. V. Sorensen of Omaha, Lt. Governor Philip C. Sorensen, and Representative Clair A. Callan, all of Nebraska.

For the President's remarks in Minneapolis on June 28, 1964, defining the administration's peace goals, see 1963-64 volume, this series, Book I, Item 435.

For the President's special message to Congress on Food for Freedom, see Item 62.

312   Remarks in Des Moines at a Democratic Party Dinner. *June 30, 1966*

Governor Hughes, Governor Guy, Governor Morrison, Congressman Schmidhauser, Congressman Smith, Congressman Callan, Congressman Culver, Congressman Bandstra, Congressman Greigg, Congressman Hansen, my dear First Lady of the great State of Iowa, fellow Democrats:

[I]

I think I ought to make it clear at the outset tonight that this is a very selfish visit. In the grade school history books, most Presidents are pictured as forever smiling and always self-sufficient, altogether content to be desk-bound in Washington.

They never seem to need anything. Besieged by problems on every hand, with the winds of crisis always howling all around them, they seem to rest like some Gibraltar on a sea of self-assurance.

Some day I may rewrite a few chapters of those books. If I do, I will have something to say about the needs of a President, the needs of a President to get away from the big desk in the Oval Room, away from the telephone and the briefing papers that are brought in every minute of every hour; the needs of a President to go out again among the men and the women and the children whose servant he is; the needs of a President to experience, again, the strength that comes from the power for good that lies out there in the fertile lands and the great cities of America; to be refreshed once more by America's deep confidence in itself, by its conviction that we don't have any problem that we are not big enough to solve ourselves—and always remembering that all of our successes are always subject to improvement.

I confess tonight that I did not come out here just to talk to you. But I did come out here to draw strength from you. For no matter how steadfast in his determination a President may be, he is not, I can assure you, a Rock of Gibraltar.

As you may have heard on the grapevine, he is just a plain, simple, human being.

Two generations ago a President might have come to Iowa prepared to talk only about the farm program, more specifically and particularly about corn and hogs, as he might have talked only of cotton and trade in the South, or as he might have talked only of manufacturing and tariffs in New England.

Well, tonight I want to talk of other things. I want to tell you about some of the things that we have to be thankful for, some of the things that we have a right to appreciate.

The first thing that I want to mention from that high priority list of mine that I am thankful for is the Governor of the great State of Iowa, Harold Hughes.

And the Governor of your neighboring State, the great State of Nebraska, Frank Morrison.

And the Governor who has honored us with his presence tonight by coming here to Des Moines, the great Governor of the State of North Dakota, Governor Guy.

I want to thank each and every citizen of the great State of Iowa, their uncles, their cousins, and their aunts, for sending to the House of Representatives one of the greatest Democratic delegations that any State in the Union ever sent to Washington.

I don't think you are going to change horses in the middle of the stream. Polls notwithstanding, I have not the slightest doubt that every man, woman, and child in this room is ready to go out of here tonight and tomorrow, and the next week, and every day until November, to see that Schmidhauser, Smith, Culver, Bandstra, Greigg, and Hansen—and if you get over the line in Nebraska, Callan—are all sent back to Washington with a resounding vote.

Last year we passed 85 percent of our platform. This year we submitted 90 major measures for the benefit of all the people of America. With the help of this delegation in the House, we have already passed through the House of Representatives 60 of those 90 measures.

While I don't speculate, I anticipate that we are going to pass some more of the 90 before I let them come back to campaign for re-election.

But it is hot here tonight and I have had a long day, and I am going home. So I am not going to speak as long as I would like to, or as I am accustomed to. But I do want to speak to you of a whole nation, your Nation, that is remaking itself year by year, that is multiplying the abundance of all of its people.

Since January 1961, annual per capita income in America after taxes—since the Democrats came into office following a Republican administration—annual per capita income, the income of every individual in this country, after taxes, has been increased by 28 percent. And don't you let them forget it!

Now I don't want to give you a lot of statistics. I didn't ask you to bring your yellow tablet and take notes all evening as if you were in college history class. But I want to give you enough statistics to permit you to defend yourself between now and November.

You hear a lot of talk about people who want to leave politics at the water's edge and support us in Vietnam.

Well, the best way to support us in Vietnam is to *support* us—not to hamstring us, not to harass us, not to humiliate us, not to send word that broadcasts throughout the world that this is a divided Nation.

I am in contact with a lot of these folks who give me advice every day. I get a reasonable amount of it. If I don't have a chance to read my mail, I do have a chance to get the papers. And I get a good deal of it through the newspapers.

I want to say to all those people that I appreciate their advice. A man's judgment is no better than his information. I particularly appreciate the advice that contains information. I particularly appreciate judgments that are based on facts, on information, on knowledge, on evaluation.

The United States Government has the Joint Chiefs of Staff, the greatest intelligence services in the country, and has a network of ambassadors in every capital of the world, 120 capitals. It has a flow of information from every capital, even the few that it doesn't have representation in.

I use that information—and I need it. I am glad to have it supplemented by any volunteers who feel they have a little bit better approach or they have a little inside information.

But I do want you to know that in the final analysis, when the decision is made and you have to mash the button and the bell rings, it is like Mr. Truman said: "You can get all the advice from all the world, but you have to act on your own head, your own heart, and your own conscience."

Under our constitutional system, one man has the horrifying, terrifying duty to finally make the decision.

So this year I am told that we are going to talk about two things—about the war in Vietnam and about inflation.

The war in Vietnam is something we must talk about, spend a lot of time on, think about, and work at. We have a terrific responsibility there to provide the maximum deterrent possible to keep an aggressor from conquering 14 million innocent men, women, and children, with the minimum cost to the United States of America.

We have lost 2,000 lives, a little over, in Vietnam this year. We lost 50,000 lives on the highways. We could lose 200,000 in Vietnam. So every move we make must be deliberate, careful, prudent, and cautious, and must be based on the very best comprehensive information available anywhere.

I come here to pledge you tonight that without regard to party, race, religion, or any other element except what is right, the decisions affecting our men in Vietnam and affecting the foreign policy of the United States are going to be based on only one thing: that is, what is good for the United States of America and the free world.

Now on the inflation front, if you are distraught, if you are worried about high prices, if you have a stomach ulcer because of high wages, if you are concerned about hogs bringing too much, or calves bringing too much, or wages getting too high, and you are really worked up about inflation, it may be that you ought to vote Republican, because there is one guarantee I can give you from my 35 years' experience: If you vote Republican and by chance you should win, you won't have to worry very long about high prices—or high wages.

When I went to Washington we were worrying about some of these things. We were worrying about those 3-cent calves that we were raising down in Texas that I sold under contract last week for 28 cents. We were worrying about those $2.40 hogs that are bringing $22.40 today.

We were worrying about corn at 12 cents a bushel; that is, the corn you were not burning out here, that today sells for $1.13.

We were worrying about that $65-an-acre land that the insurance companies were foreclosing.

That is when I went to Washington following a Republican administration of 35 years ago.

After the last administration, your net farm income was $11 billion when you elected a Democratic President. In 1965 that $11 billion had gone to $14 billion.

Your net income per farm was $2,900. That has gone from $2,900 to $4,200.

Your calves that brought 21 cents brought an average of 23 cents.

Your hogs that brought 15 cents under the last administration bring 22 cents.

Your corn that brought $1.07 brings $1.19.

Your grain sorghum that brought $1.54 brings $1.79.

Your soybeans that brought $2 brought $2.09.

Your milk that brought $3.09 brings $3.65.

Those are the latest official figures of the average prices of the Department of Agriculture.

I want to ask someone to take enough of the proceeds of this dinner this evening— at least that which the Congressmen haven't already gotten off with—and get this little card mimeographed and put it on everybody's plate in lieu of that $100 ticket they bought. Because this is $100 worth of information to you. It may be worth thousands of dollars to you when you go to the ballot box.

When these folks start talking to you about inflation, you tell them that is something that you only have to worry about in Democratic administrations.

The unfinished economic business in America is for us to make a place at the table of our abundance for our brothers and for our countrymen. Who is it that can look out here into the Iowa countryside that I saw today and say that we cannot make such a place?

Surely not the Iowan whose personal income has risen faster than the national average in the last 5 years.

Surely not the Iowan whose hybrid seed corn is one of the 20th century's greatest blessings to mankind.

Surely not the men and women who exported almost a half-billion dollars of farm commodities to the world last year and who led all the States in livestock receipts with $2 billion in sales.

Harold Hughes is traveling throughout the Far East trying to find a market for more exports, for more Iowa products, all the time. And with your support, he is going to find them.

Now as I said, there are a few voices in the air tonight that tell us—and there will certainly be more as we get along between now and November—who tell the Midwest farmer that he has to beware. They are saying that someone over there in Washington is out to deprive him of his fair share of the Nation's prosperity.

They try to divide farmers from consumers; but they never remind you that farmers are consumers, too. No industry has more consumers of goods and services than the great basic industry of agriculture.

I want to let you in on a secret: Your Government in Washington is interested in consumers, too, just as the farmers are. Nothing can sap the prosperity that our people enjoy tonight faster than runaway price increases. No one is going to be hurt more than the farmers if inflation does run away and destroy our prices.

We have acted boldly, but we have not acted rashly, to keep price increases within tolerable limits. With management and labor, with manufacturers and farmers, we have sought to protect the interests of all of our people in price stability.

But there is another story about farm incomes in the 1960's. It is the story of a successful farm policy.

I want to acknowledge and pay tribute to that great leader of the farmers of America, Orville Freeman, the Secretary of Agriculture, who is here tonight.

That record shows that net income on individual farms right here in the great State of Iowa climbed 47 percent since Orville Freeman became Secretary of Agriculture.

That record shows that farm exports were up from $4.8 billion to $6.2 billion since Orville Freeman became Secretary of Agriculture.

I came out here to Iowa tonight to look you straight in the eye and to say to you something that you don't have to read in the New York Times: We in Washington are proud of that record.

We have promised plentiful food at fair prices for the consumer. We have promised full parity of income for the American farmer in the 1960's. And we stand tonight on that pledge and that promise.

I want to close this evening on another little note: The productivity of American agriculture is unequaled in this world. No other farmers are so skilled or are so prosperous as are Iowa farmers and American farmers.

In great areas throughout this world men tonight plow the ground with primitive plows, and some with just hoes in their hands. They sow and they reap with their own hands. They have no fertilizer and little or none of the science and the equipment that is familiar to American farming.

Yet their populations continue to grow. The result is as inevitable as it is tragic: malnourishment, starvation, the weakness that breeds disease, slows production, and destroys hope.

Today I engaged in a ceremony shipping wheat to India. Because of the great productivity, resources and generosity of America, 35 million people will not have to die from starvation in India this year because of what we have done.

We are bursting with plenty and we are helping. We will help more. Yet if we were to cultivate every available acre of our rich soil, we could never match the food needs of all the human beings in the world.

It is going to be only through a tremendous reform in the agriculture of these desperate countries, only a profound commitment to agricultural development, only an intelligent approach to the problem of diminishing resources and increased population that can give them the food that they must have if they are not to starve.

We have urged them to make that commitment. Our help will go in generous measure to those countries who are willing to help themselves. Our technology will be open to those countries who want to help themselves.

In our universities and in our colleges in America tonight there are 3,500 students of agriculture from other lands learning the techniques of the American farm. We hope that more students will come, for nothing is more critical to the future of this earth than the wise harvest of its bounty.

I know that Iowans who, for generations, have offered their skills and their human concern to less fortunate peoples will not hesitate to do so again.

689

So this evening in Iowa, hot as it is, has been good for your President. This may be just a warm-up of things to come between now and fall. But it is good for me to come here and see firsthand the statistics of prosperity and see them take on flesh and bones before my own eyes.

[II]

I know tonight that a world of challenges awaits everyone whose heart beats in this room. The dilemmas of world politics in a nuclear age, the struggle for freedom in Vietnam, the search for social justice in our own country—these will not be resolved just because we are prosperous and doing well, and everybody is working and getting a good price for his products.

These call for a policy of patience and daring, of commonsense and vision, of the wise use of power and its wise restraint when needs be.

This has been America's policy ever since we emerged as a modern world power following World War II. We applied this policy in Berlin. We applied it against raw Communist pressure. We applied it in Greece to resist the Communist efforts to take that little country over by guerrilla warfare. We applied it in Korea when the Communists marched armies across international boundaries in a flagrant invasion of a very weak and struggling little country. Yes, we applied it in Cuba—finally—to meet the threat of nuclear blackmail. And we applied it without any hesitancy in the Dominican Republic to protect the lives of innocent people and to permit the democratic processes to work again among those people.

So as your leader tonight, I want to say to you as candidly and frankly as I know how, for 21 years we have been willing to fight if we must, and always ready to negotiate if we can.

I believe that this policy has made possible a rebirth of moderation and commonsense, not just in the United States but throughout all the continents of the world. In the last few years, in country after country, on continent after continent, extremist leaders have suffered one defeat after another. They have been replaced by men of moderation who have assumed power as their successors.

That is why I am here to tell you tonight that the only wise policy to follow in Vietnam is the policy that has worked so successfully for two decades. We just must be patient, but we must be firm.

For as long as the Communist leaders in North Vietnam insist on waging war by crossing the boundaries of South Vietnam and assassinating human beings, as long as they spurn any interest in negotiations, we must use our power to resist their aggression, and use our power to try to change their minds.

I have never seen a Communist government come to power as a result of a free election. And I have never seen Communist aggression bow before its little neighbor's weakness.

Communist power respects only its neighbor's strength. Communist leaders turn from their ambitious designs only when they become thoroughly convinced of one thing, and that is that Communist power cannot and will not succeed.

As we meet here on the prairies, in the fertile black land of the great, freedom-loving State of Iowa tonight, I want to remind you that yonder in Hanoi, men who believe that they have more patience in the bank than we do, are watching and listening. They read our polls, even Iowa polls. They listen to our debates, even my speeches. They watch the results of our elections in every congressional district in the land. They see how perplexed some of our people are by the shadowy nature of guerrilla war. And they try to prey upon the compassion and the love of mothers and wives.

They say to themselves, as they said to a prominent leader just a few hours ago, "If we only wait long enough. . . ."

I am confident as I speak to you tonight that they in their hearts know that General Westmoreland is succeeding in Vietnam and they cannot defeat him there. But they do look to Washington and to America to create enough dissidence in this country to defeat him here.

Oh, how I do wish that I could talk to those men tonight. I would like to say to them that it is easy to misread the polls. It is easy to misunderstand the meaning of a debate in a democratic society where we encourage difference of opinion and dissidence, discussion. It is easy to misjudge the true nature of a diverse nation. It is easy to mistake our differences for weaknesses.

The Kaiser was mistaken in World War I, in 1917.

Hitler was mistaken when he marched through Poland in the late 1930's.

The Japanese were mistaken when we debated and refused to fortify Guam and spend $5 million when I was a young Congressman. They thought we couldn't or we wouldn't fight. We loved peace so much that we would not pay any price and they could march on with their armies and gobble up free and innocent people.

Well, the time came when we had to answer the call, and we did.

I want to say to those leaders in Hanoi tonight: "Don't make the same mistake that the Kaiser made, or that Hitler made, or that the Japanese made."

I haven't cleared this with every person in Washington, but I have cleared it with myself, and I believe with a majority of the people in 44 States of the Union. I would like to say this to those people yonder who seek to conquer by aggression:

"The American people, when they understand what is at stake, have never in their long and proud history run from their duty. And the American people will not run tonight."

I would say to them, if they are listening, that the American people have never left an ally in a fight. And we do not intend to abandon South Vietnam now.

I would say that the American people have elected as their President a man who is determined to honor our commitments, a man who is determined to stand with the people of Vietnam, stand with them until aggression has been ended and until the American soldiers can proudly come marching home.

So I say to my friends here in Iowa tonight, we could walk away; we could run out of Vietnam tonight. But I ask you what would happen to the millions of men, women, and little children who have fought all these years in order not to have to live under Communist domination? What would happen to these 14 million?

While we are on that subject, I would like you to take this down and put it in your notebook: What would happen to the other 42 alliances and agreements that we have with other nations? What would happen to ANZUS, to SEATO, to NATO, and to all these other countries that we have given our solemn word and our sacred honor that we would stand by them, if they saw us defaulting on one note, running out on one commitment, and tearing up one contract?

If we will not be true to our word in Vietnam with a nation of 14 million, how can a nation of a million and a half across the seas expect us to keep our contract there?

I think it is time for every nation to engage in a little introspection and ask themselves what would happen in their country where they depend on American strength and American support if we followed some of their advice and broke our contract, failed to keep our word, and came home with dishonor from Vietnam.

I ask you what would happen to the rising tide of hope in Asia tonight? What would happen to those little free nations which met in Korea last week to try to anvil and fashion a method of building a new future for their people behind a shield of American firmness in Southeast Asia?

Every independent nation in Asia—and they are not confined to Asia, either—every independent nation in Asia has a stake in what happens in Vietnam:

—Japan and Korea;
—The Republic of China and the Philippines;
—Australia and New Zealand—they may be up next;
—Thailand and Malaysia—and they are not going to stop in South Vietnam; Thailand is just next door;
—Burma and Cambodia and Laos;
—India and Pakistan;
—Singapore and Ceylon; and
—Indonesia, who has had some turns, we hope, for the better.

You cannot tell me that those who love freedom in Indonesia have not been encouraged by our commitment and our determination in Vietnam.

Now some of these nations are our allies, and others have no special ties to any major power. But I think they all have a big stake in one thing, and that one thing is being left alone. They know their independence is more secure, they know their future is more promising, if America stands firm in South Vietnam.

If we run, or if we quit the fight, if we abandon our efforts to keep stability in Asia,

every single nation there will once again be an easy prey for these hungry, yearning Communist appetites.

So to those who seek candor and frankness, I would say tonight: Firmness is a must; and as long as I am President of the United States we shall stand firm.

But there is another side, too, of American policy. That is that we would much rather reason than fight. In the words of the Prophet Isaiah, we have said time and time again, "Come now,"—to all men—"let us reason together."

We are using our power in Vietnam because the Communists have given us no other choice, no other alternative, no other substitute. We have repeated, and repeated, and repeated, time and time again, in 100 nations or more, that we desire to discuss peace at the conference table.

I want to again emphatically repeat that desire tonight in words that anyone can understand. I want to say that the Communist leaders in North Vietnam do not have to doubt what we mean by that statement. They do not have to be in the dark about our position or our intentions. They do not even have to read our speeches, or talk to our ambassadors, or to see the diplomats from other countries. If they will only let me know when and where they would like to ask us directly what can be done to bring peace to South Vietnam, I will have my closest and my most trusted associates at that time and at that place in a matter of hours.

There need be no long, legal-sized agenda. There need be no previous understanding of what will or what will not be discussed. There need be no commitments on either side. There need only be a room and a table, and people who are willing to talk to each other respectfully.

And that is just about as simple as a farm

boy knows how to make it.

I say to you tonight, and I say to them tonight, that this is one little way to stop this fighting. It is one way to move toward peace. It is one way to end the killing in the South and to stop the bombing in the North. This is, of course, our fervent desire.

But let me make this absolutely clear. I want the leaders of North Vietnam to know exactly where we stand. As long as they persist in their aggression against South Vietnam, America will resist that aggression.

As long as they carry the battle to South Vietnam and try to conquer by conquest, as long as they carry on this war which they have started, America will persevere.

And don't let them think because some Senator says on a television program he is going to put the heat on the President that we will not persevere, because they would be mistaking America as other leaders have to their sorrow in years past. They just cannot wear us down. They cannot escape paying a very high price for their own aggression if they continue with their evil acts.

But we do not want to be bellicose or belligerent. The minute they change their minds, the minute they should decide the price is too high for a policy that they now know cannot succeed, then America will be waiting.

As I said today in the great city of Omaha, with that enlightened, progressive Governor presiding, America will be waiting. Our purpose is not war. Our purpose, our hope, our desire, our prayer is peace in the world, good will toward men. If they just give us one single little chance, we will prove the good faith of the American people.

None of this, my friends, is going to be easy. But a world of small and new nations, a world where our word and our power can mean the difference between war and peace,

is looking to us tonight. It is counting on us tonight. It is expecting us to produce initiatives and to somehow, in some way, find a way.

I saw a young friend standing there tonight as we drove along who said, "Let's get out of Vietnam." I thought for that dear person how much I wish I could get out of Vietnam. I want to get out of Vietnam more than any single boy standing there in a rice paddy wants to get out tonight.

They all want to get out, but not a single one of them has written their President saying we ought to get out except with honor.

I don't know how much the people in Hanoi reading that sign and listening to these strident voices are encouraged to hold out just a little longer. But the thought did occur to me that the thing that you genuinely want most—getting out of Vietnam—is being postponed a little longer by you and your signs.

I am not angry; I am not even sorrowful. I sometimes think of the words, "God forgive them, for they know not what they do."

But we do know this: We are an honorable Nation; we protect the security of our people; we honor our commitments; we care about human beings, whether they are 14 million or 1 million; we do not bow and salute at any conqueror's aggression.

Once this Nation makes a pact, a treaty, or a commitment, it lives up to it in word as well as in deed.

I want to bring those boys home from Vietnam more than anyone in this room, just as I wanted to see them come marching home in World War II, just as I wanted to see them come marching home from the Pacific where they had spent many months. I spent a few months with them in the early days of that war. But I never saw a man that proudly wore the uniform who wanted

693

to come home defeated, who wanted to come home with his tail between his legs, who wanted to come home because he had been conquered.

There is not one of them out there—and I hope there is not one in here—who is willing to do that tonight.

Politics stops at the water's edge. I have received great comfort and strength from all the men that I have known who have preceded me in the most responsible job in the world. Mr. Hoover called me to his Waldorf Towers before he passed away and counseled with me on my problems as President. He knew what the problems of the Presidency were. He had experienced them.

No man ever reached that high office that didn't want to do, with all of the sincerity that he had in him, what was right. But the problem of the President is not doing what is right; the problem is knowing what is right.

President Eisenhower has communicated with me more than 30 times in 26 months, and has given me the wisdom that has come to him through the years as a student at West Point, as a young captain, as our European commander, as the Chief of Staff of the Army, as the President of Columbia, and finally as the Supreme Commander, Allied Powers in Europe, and President of the United States.

There is not a man I have on my Joint Chiefs of Staff in the prime of his life whose judgment I value more tonight than the judgment of Dwight David Eisenhower.

I called him and talked to him. I sent a general to see him. Then I put on my hat and went to his hospital room and talked to him for more than an hour before I issued the order that sent our men in to destroy the petroleum dumps near Hanoi and Haiphong.

I am very proud to say that that great patriot was one of the first to issue a statement approving of that action so everybody in the world would know that the former President and the present President were united and this Nation was not divided.

President Truman, from his home in Independence, Missouri, has come, has read, has seen, and has counseled, and he has agreed with the course we have taken.

I utter no words of criticism. I want to suppress no discussion. But I do hope that those who may not understand all the reasons for the judgments we have made will be a little tolerant, a little patient, and will ask themselves—as they start out always by saying, "I am confused," "I am worried," "I am troubled," "I am frustrated"—I would remind every one of them when they say that, they have no mortgage on stomach ulcers. I get them, too. I am troubled, too.

But I ask them when they get through with all of that palaver—for goodness' sake give me their program and give me their plan.

When you think of the burdens that we carry, the responsibilities of this high office, the headaches and the heartaches that it brings, you could get sorry for yourself if you had time. But then you ought to take a trip around the world. You ought to look at the leader of any other nation. There is not a single one of them that I would trade places with. They all have more problems than I have.

I do have one hidden asset, one great strength. I saw it on the faces of Omaha today. I saw it on the cheeks in Des Moines tonight.

Prosperous, yes. Healthy, yes. Happy, yes. Happy, God-fearing, freedom-loving people.

Fight if they must, ready to negotiate if they can, but let no would-be conqueror ever doubt us. We shall persist, and America shall succeed.

NOTE: The President spoke at 8:48 p.m. at the Veterans Auditorium in Des Moines, Iowa. In his opening words he referred to Governor Harold E. Hughes of Iowa, Governor William L. Guy of North Dakota, Governor Frank B. Morrison of Nebraska, Representative Clair E. Callan of Nebraska, Representatives John R. Schmidhauser, Neal Smith, John C. Culver, Bert Bandstra, Stanley L. Greigg, and John R. Hansen, all of Iowa, and Mrs. Harold Hughes, wife of the Governor of Iowa.

For the President's speech on the same day in Omaha, Nebr., see Item 311.

INDEX

[Main references are to items except as otherwise indicated]

Index

Index

Index

Index

Index

Index

Index

Index

[Main references are to items except as otherwise indicated]

Index

Index

Index

[Main references are to items except as otherwise indicated]

Index

Index

[Main references are to items except as otherwise indicated]

Index

[Main references are to items except as otherwise indicated]

Index

Index

Index

Index

[Main references are to items except as otherwise indicated]

Index

Index

Index

Index

Index

Index

A-31

[Main references are to items except as otherwise indicated]

Index

[Main references are to items except as otherwise indicated]

[Main references are to items except as otherwise indicated]

Index

Index

[Main references are to items except as otherwise indicated]

Index

A–38

[Main references are to items except as otherwise indicated]

Index

Index

[Main references are to items except as otherwise indicated]

Index

Index

[Main references are to items except as otherwise indicated]

[Main references are to items except as otherwise indicated]

Index

[Main references are to items except as otherwise indicated]

Index

Index

Index

Index

Index

[Main references are to items except as otherwise indicated]

Index

Index

[Main references are to items except as otherwise indicated]

Index

Index

Index

Index

Index

Index

Index

Index

[**Main** references are to items except as otherwise indicated]

Index

[Main references are to items except as otherwise indicated]

Index

Index

Schumacher, William E., 331 n.
Schuman, Robert, 142
Schweitzer, Dr. Albert, 82, 402
Schweitzer, Louis, 286
Science, 101, 418
  Atmospheric programs, 222
  Crime prevention role, 491
  Education, 95, 111, 586
  Exchange programs, 200, 503
  Instrument import tariffs, 601
  Lyndon B. Johnson Australian scholars, 545–546
  Research, 38, 79, 111, 222, 326, 402
  Teachers, Washington, D.C., 27
Science, National Medal of, 61, 652
Science, Polish Academy of, 200
Science, President's Committee on the National Medal of, 61 n.
Science Adviser to the President. See Science and Technology, Office of, Director
Science Advisory Committee, President's, 62, 82, 279–280, 326
Science Foundation, National, 38, 79, 111, 229, 319
Science and Technology, Federal Council for, 138, 222
Science and Technology, Office of, Director (Donald F. Hornig), 61, 98 ftn. (p. 261), 138, 143, 216, 326, 424 n., 635 [3], 637
Sciences, National Academy of, 79, 200, 461
Scientific, and Cultural Materials, Agreement on the Importation of Educational (Florence Agreement), 45, 529, 601
Scientists, 89, 95, 200
Scott, Lt. Col. David, 134–135
Scott, Sir Walter, 368
Scranton, Gov. William W., 121 [1], 122 [1, 2], 407, 428, 501 [20]
Scranton, Mrs. William W., 428
Screwworm eradication, U.S.-Mexico, 357
Seabees (Naval Construction Battalions), 456
Seaborg, Glenn T. (Chairman, Atomic Energy Commission), 48, 179, 361, 410–411
Seal of the President of the United States, 609

Seal of the United States, Great, 609
Seamans, Robert C., Jr., 625
Seashores, national, 119
SEATO. See Southeast Asia Treaty Organization
Second Supplemental Appropriation Act, 1966, 67 n., 223
Securities, Government, 431, 444, 445 [2], 451, 477 [2, 4], 492 [1], 494 [1], 578 [3]
Securities and Exchange Commission, 110, 445 [5], 470, 635 [18]
Security, national. See National security
Security Council, National, 124 [6], 145, 214
Security Council, U.N. See United Nations
Security Medal, National, 99, 387
Sedita, Frank A., 392, 511–512
Seidenberg, Jacob, 535 n.
Seitz, Collins J., 88 [11]
Selective Service, National Advisory Commission on, 315 n., 388, 536
Selective Service System, 67, 315, 320 [10], 388
  Draft evaders, prosecution, 158 [11]
  Draft requirements, 208, 521, 578 [2, 10]
Sellers, Dennis K., 331 n.
Semer, Milton P., 88 [7], 399
Senate luncheon remarks, 520
Senate Youth Program, 35
Senators, Inc., baseball club, 509
Senegal, 489
  Ambassador Ousmane Socé Diop, 243
  President Leopold S. Senghor, 488–489
Senghor, Leopold S. (President of Senegal), 488–489
Senior citizens. See Older persons
Senior Citizens, National Council of, 253
Senior Seminar in Foreign Policy, Foreign Service Institute, 261
Sensenbrenner, M. E., 436
Seoul, Korea
  Mayor Hyon-ok Kim, 561
  Release, 564
  Visit, 561–562, 565, 566a
Servicemen's Readjustment Act of 1944 (GI bill of rights), 100, 158 [10], 188 [6], 353
Sevareid, Eric, 52 [5]
Sevilla-Sacasa, Guillermo, 263, 478

Index

Index

Index

[Main references are to items except as otherwise indicated]

Index

Index

[Main references are to items except as otherwise indicated]

[Main references are to items except as otherwise indicated]

[Main references are to items except as otherwise indicated]

Index

Index

[Main references are to items except as otherwise indicated]

Index

Index

Index

Index

Index

Index

Index

Index